C000180736

STREET ATLAS Buckinghamshire and Milton Keynes

Amersham, Aylesbury, High Wycombe

Contents

II Mobile safety cameras

III **Key to map symbols**

IV **Key to map pages**

VI **Route planning**

VIII Major administrative and Postcode boundaries

1 **Street maps** at 3½ inches to 1 mile

214 **Index** of towns, villages, streets, hospitals, industrial estates, railway stations, schools, shopping centres, universities and places of interest

www.philips-maps.co.uk
First published in 1990 by
Philip's, a division of
Octopus Publishing Group Ltd
www.octopusbooks.co.uk
Endeavour House, 189 Shaftesbury Avenue
London WC2H 8JY
An Hachette UK Company
www.hachette.co.uk

Fourth edition 2010
First impression 2010
BUCDA

ISBN 978-0-540-09298-7 (spiral)

While every reasonable effort has been made to ensure that the information compiled in this atlas is accurate, complete and up-to-date at the time of publication, some of this information is subject to change and the Publisher cannot guarantee its correctness or completeness.

The information in this atlas is provided without any representation or warranty, express or implied and the Publisher cannot be held liable for any loss or damage due to any use or reliance on the information in this atlas, nor for any errors, omissions or subsequent changes in such information.

The representation in this atlas of a road, track or path is no evidence of the existence of a right of way.

Ordnance Survey and the OS Symbol are registered trademarks of Ordnance Survey, the national mapping agency of Great Britain.

Speed camera data provided by **PocketGPSWorld.com Ltd**

Post Office is a trade mark of Post Office Ltd in the UK and other countries.

Printed in China

Digital Data

The exceptionally high-quality mapping found in this atlas is available as digital data in TIFF format, which is easily convertible to other bitmapped (raster) image formats.

The index is also available in digital form as a standard database table. It contains all the details found in the printed index together with the National Grid reference for the map square in which each entry is named.

For further information and to discuss your requirements, please contact philips@mapsinternational.co.uk

Mobile safety cameras

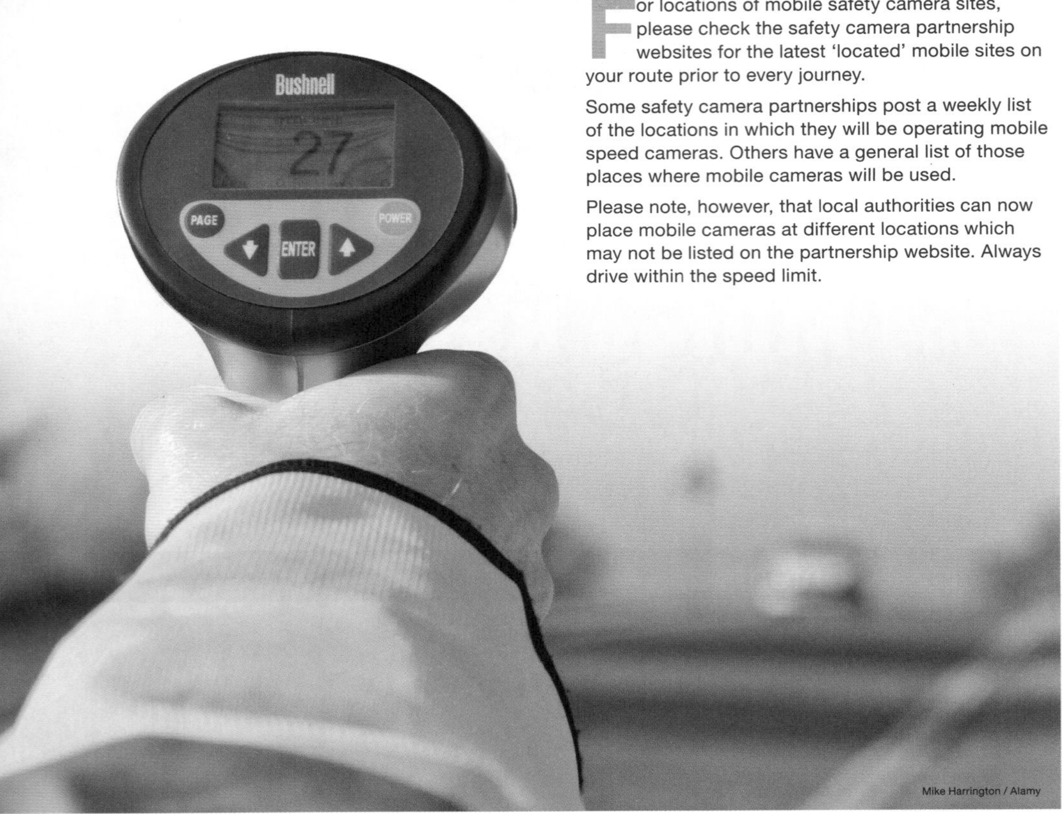

Mike Harrington / Alamy

For locations of mobile safety camera sites, please check the safety camera partnership websites for the latest 'located' mobile sites on your route prior to every journey.

Some safety camera partnerships post a weekly list of the locations in which they will be operating mobile speed cameras. Others have a general list of those places where mobile cameras will be used.

Please note, however, that local authorities can now place mobile cameras at different locations which may not be listed on the partnership website. Always drive within the speed limit.

Useful websites

Thames Valley Safer Roads Partnership
www.saferroads.org

Northamptonshire Casualty Reducton Partnership
reducingroadcasualties.com
www.northants.police.uk/default.aspx?id=275

Bedfordshire and Luton Casualty Reduction Partnership
www.drivesafely.org

Hertfordshire Safety Camera Partnership
www.hertsdirect.org/envroads/roadstrans/rsu/driving/safetycameras/hscpdetails/

London Safety Camera Partnership
www.lscp.org.uk

Surrey Safety Camera Partnership
www.surrey-safecam.org

Further information
www.dvla.gov.uk
www.thinkroadsafety.gov.uk
www.dft.gov.uk
www.road-safe.org

Key to map symbols

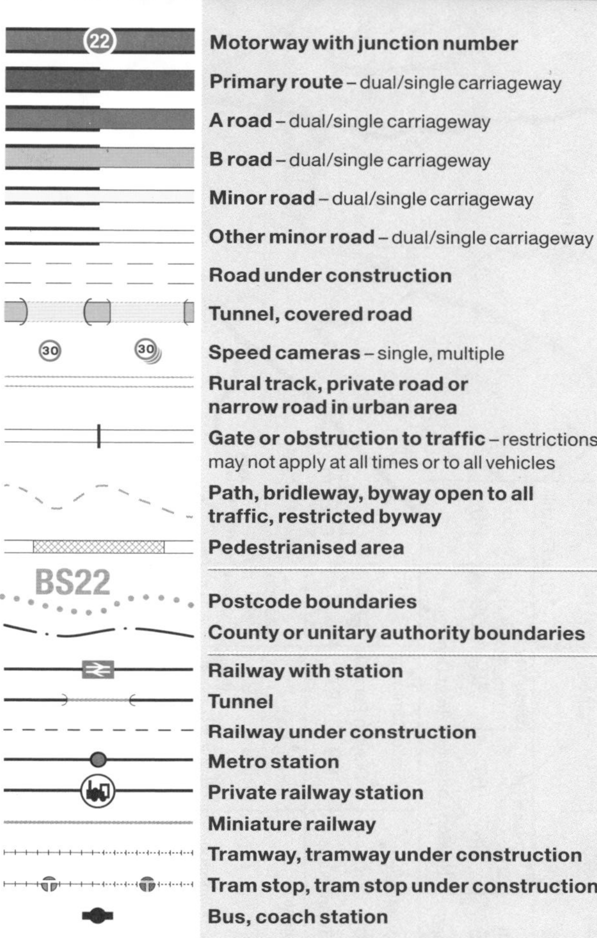

Motorway with junction number

Primary route – dual/single carriageway

A road – dual/single carriageway

B road – dual/single carriageway

Minor road – dual/single carriageway

Other minor road – dual/single carriageway

Road under construction

Tunnel, covered road

Speed cameras – single, multiple

Rural track, private road or narrow road in urban area

Gate or obstruction to traffic – restrictions may not apply at all times or to all vehicles

Path, bridleway, byway open to all traffic, restricted byway

Pedestrianised area

Postcode boundaries

County or unitary authority boundaries

Railway with station

Tunnel

Railway under construction

Metro station

Private railway station

Miniature railway

Tramway, tramway under construction

Tram stop, tram stop under construction

Bus, coach station

Ambulance station

Coastguard station

Fire station

Police station

Accident and Emergency entrance to hospital

Hospital

Place of worship

Information centre – open all year

Shopping centre, parking

Park and Ride, Post Office

Camping site, caravan site

Golf course, picnic site

Non-Roman antiquity, Roman antiquity

Important buildings, schools, colleges, universities and hospitals

Woods, built-up area

Water name

River, weir

Stream

Canal, lock, tunnel

Water

Tidal water

Adjoining page indicators and overlap bands – the colour of the arrow and band indicates the scale of the adjoining or overlapping page (see scale below)

The dark grey border on the inside edge of some pages indicates that the mapping does not continue onto the adjacent page

The small numbers around the edges of the maps identify the 1-kilometre National Grid lines

Abbreviations

Acad	Academy	Meml	Memorial
Allot Gdns	Allotments	Mon	Monument
Cemy	Cemetery	Mus	Museum
C Ctr	Civic centre	Obsy	Observatory
CH	Club house	Pal	Royal palace
Coll	College	PH	Public house
Crem	Crematorium	Recn Gd	Recreation ground
Ent	Enterprise		
Ex H	Exhibition hall	Resr	Reservoir
Ind Est	Industrial Estate	Ret Pk	Retail park
IRB Sta	Inshore rescue boat station	Sch	School
		Sh Ctr	Shopping centre
Inst	Institute	TH	Town hall / house
Ct	Law court	Trad Est	Trading estate
L Ctr	Leisure centre	Univ	University
LC	Level crossing	W Twr	Water tower
Liby	Library	Wks	Works
Mkt	Market	YH	Youth hostel

The map scale on the pages numbered in blue is 3½ inches to 1 mile

5.52 cm to 1 km • 1:18 103

0	¼ mile	½ mile	¾ mile	1 mile

| 0 | 250m | 500m | 750m | 1km |

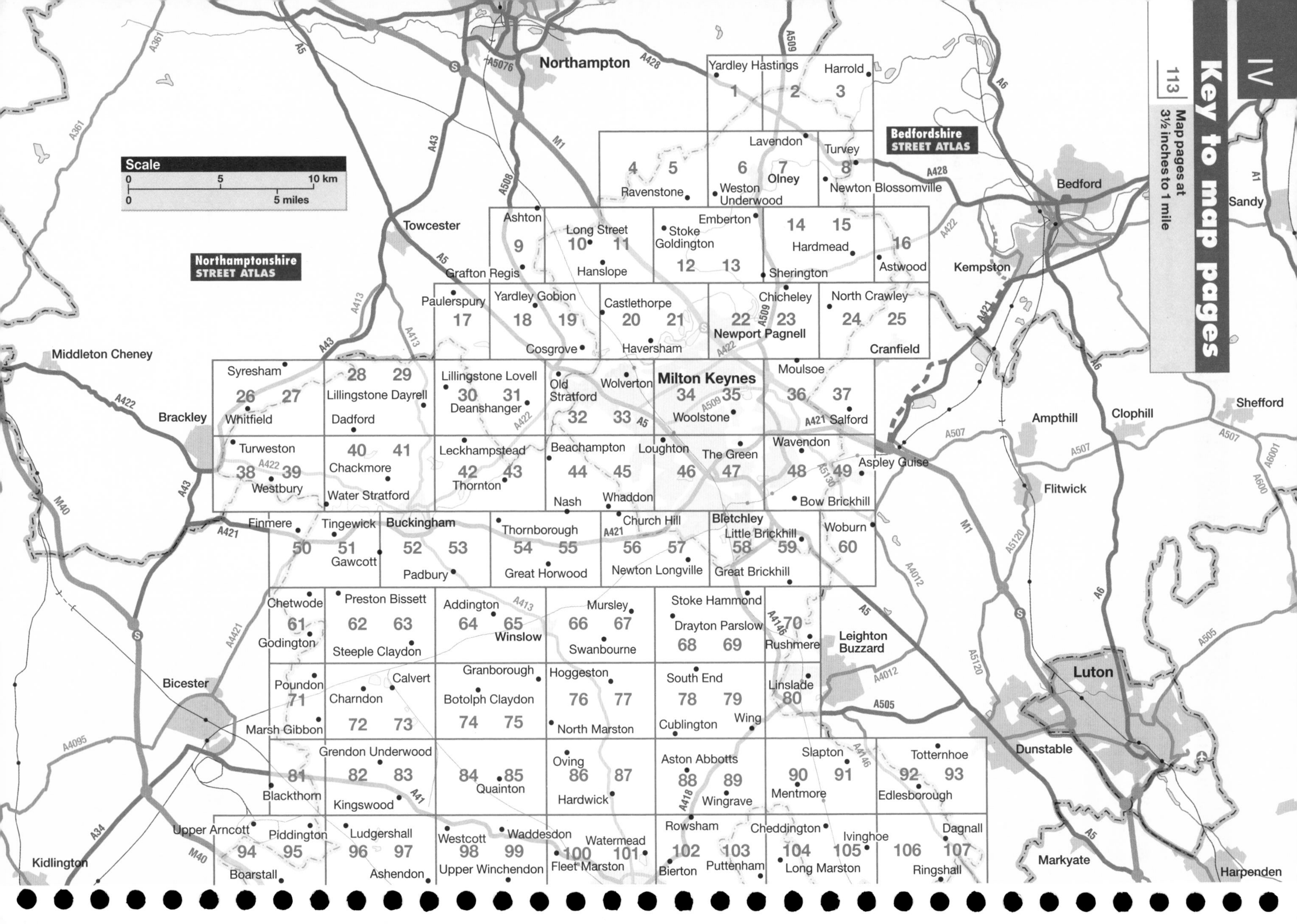

IV

Key to map pages

113 Map pages at 3½ inches to 1 mile

Bedfordshire STREET ATLAS

Northamptonshire STREET ATLAS

Scale
10 km
5 miles
0   5
0

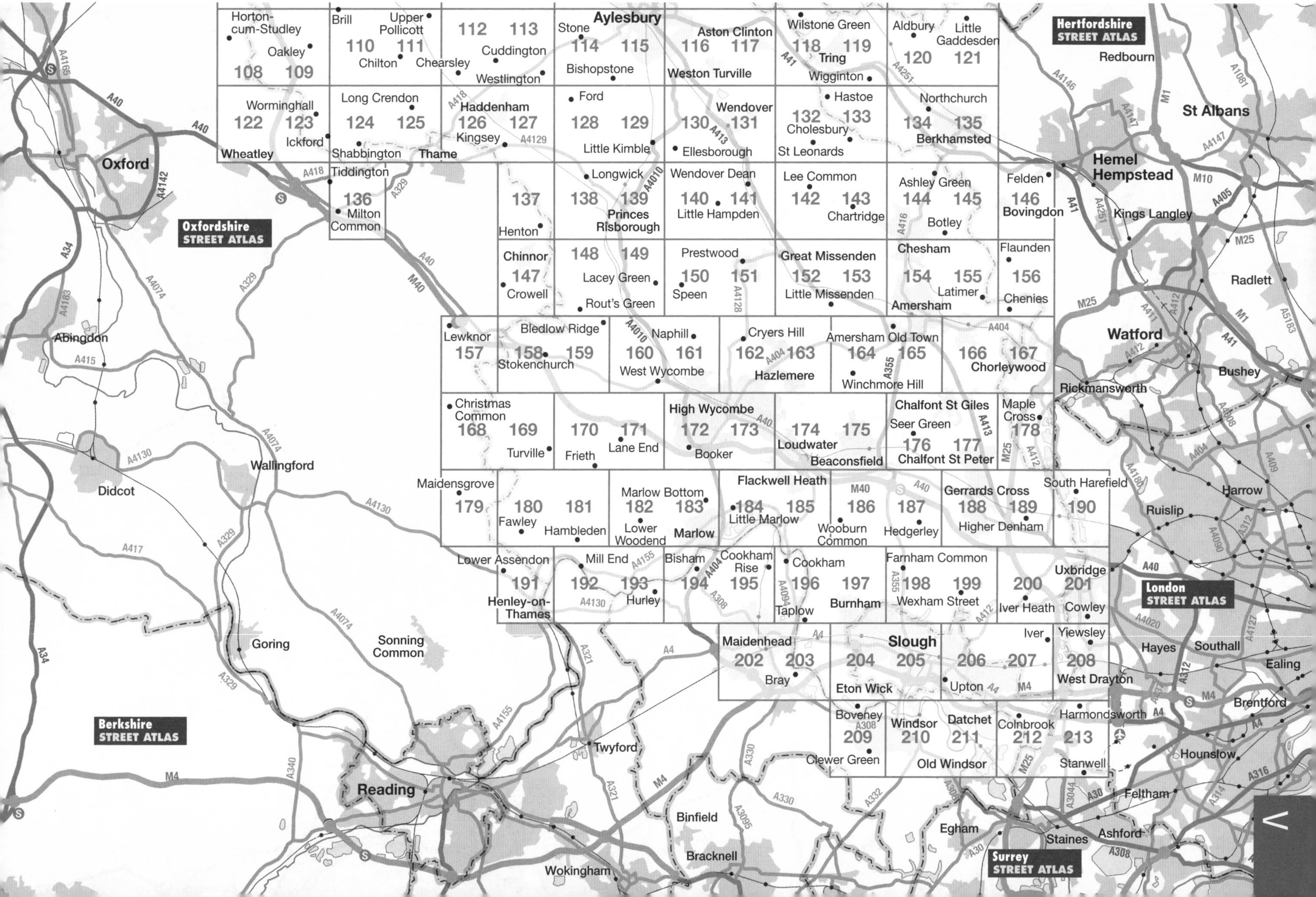
Hertfordshire STREET ATLAS
Oxfordshire STREET ATLAS
London STREET ATLAS
Berkshire STREET ATLAS
Surrey STREET ATLAS
Aylesbury
Oxford
Hemel Hempstead
St Albans
Watford
High Wycombe
Slough
Reading
Maidenhead
Marlow
Wallingford
Didcot
Abingdon
Henley-on-Thames
Beaconsfield
Amersham
Chesham
Berkhamsted
Tring
Thame
Princes Risborough
Uxbridge
Harrow
Windsor
108 109 110 111 112 113 114 115 116 117 118 119 120 121
122 123 124 125 126 127 128 129 130 131 132 133 134 135
136 137 138 139 140 141 142 143 144 145 146
147 148 149 150 151 152 153 154 155 156
157 158 159 160 161 162 163 164 165 166 167
168 169 170 171 172 173 174 175 176 177 178
179 180 181 182 183 184 185 186 187 188 189 190
191 192 193 194 195 196 197 198 199 200 201
202 203 204 205 206 207 208
209 210 211 212 213
V

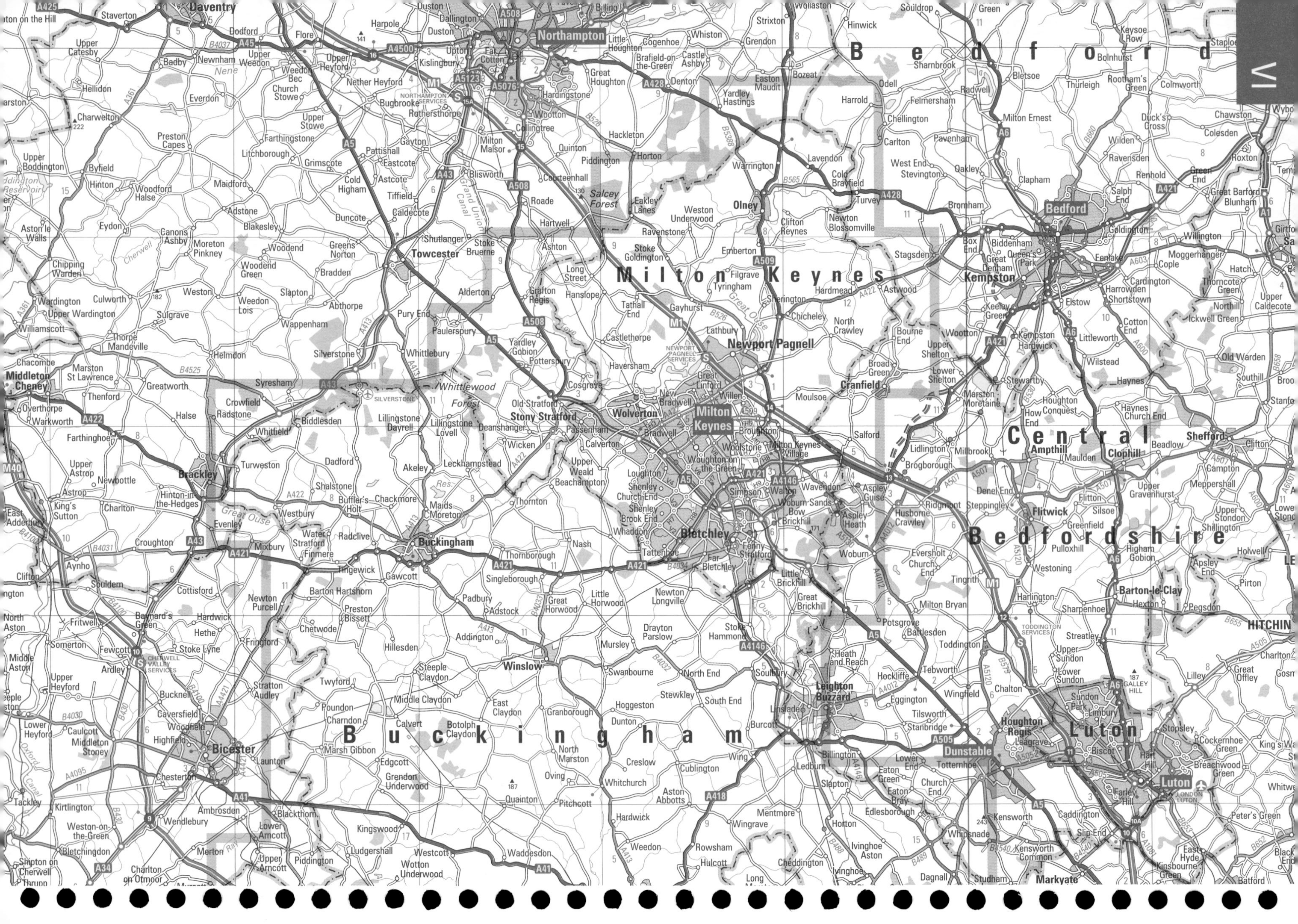
Bedford
Central Bedfordshire
Milton Keynes
Buckingham
Luton
Northampton
Daventry
Bedford
Kempston
Olney
Newport Pagnell
Cranfield
Towcester
Stony Stratford
Wolverton
Milton Keynes
Bletchley
Brackley
Buckingham
Winslow
Bicester
Leighton Buzzard
Dunstable
Houghton Regis
Luton
Ampthill
Flitwick
Clophill
Shefford
Barton-le-Clay
HITCHIN
Markyate
Middleton Cheney

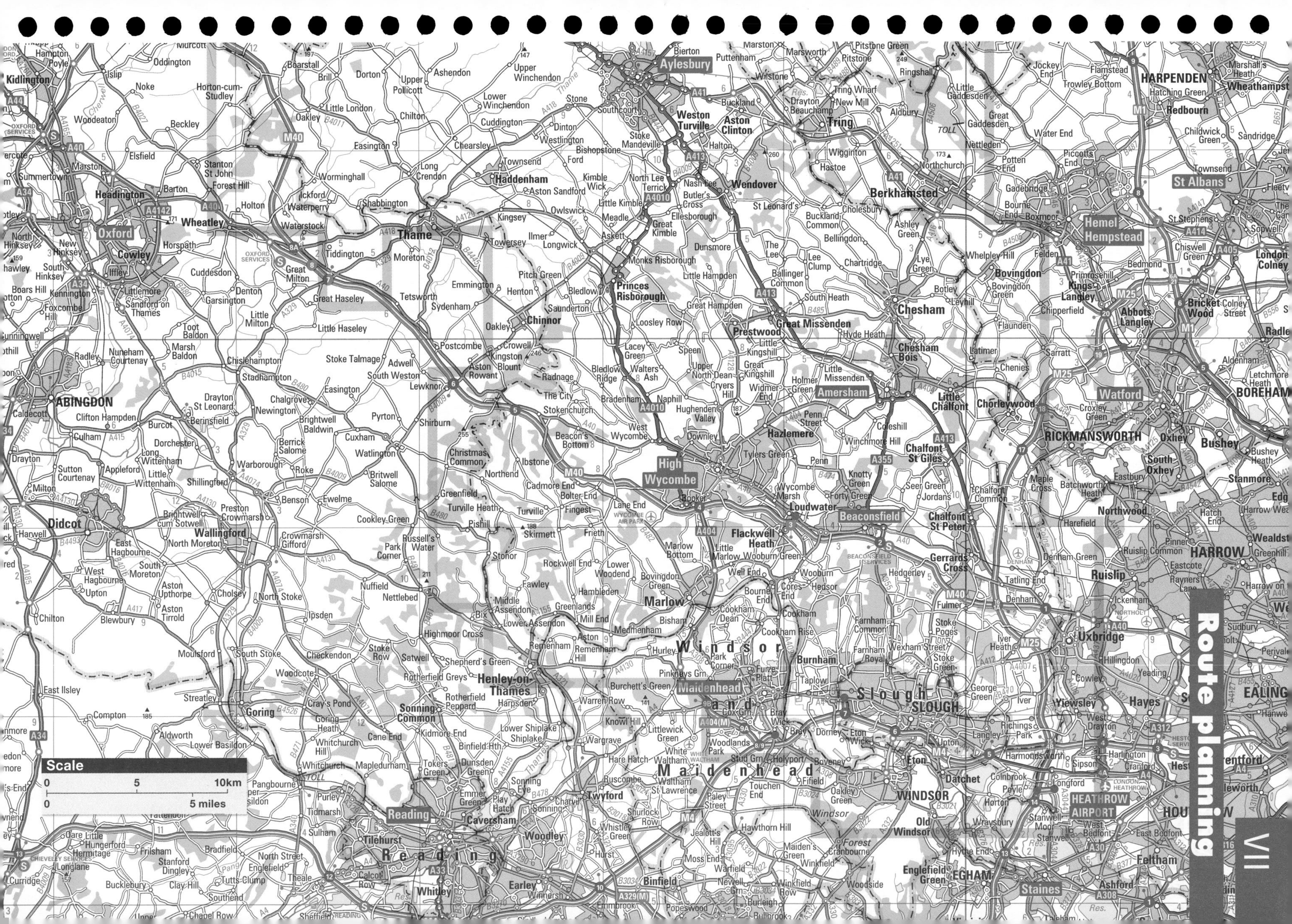
Scale
0
5
10km
0
5 miles
Kidlington
Oxford
Cowley
Headington
Wheatley
ABINGDON
Didcot
Wallingford
Thame
Aylesbury
Princes Risborough
Chinnor
High Wycombe
Marlow
Henley-on-Thames
Reading
Maidenhead
Slough
WINDSOR
Beaconsfield
Amersham
Chesham
Berkhamsted
Tring
Wendover
Hemel Hempstead
St Albans
HARPENDEN
Watford
RICKMANSWORTH
BOREHAMWOOD
HARROW
Uxbridge
HEATHROW AIRPORT
Staines
EGHAM

Major administrative and Postcode boundaries

County and unitary authority boundaries

District boundaries

Postcode boundaries

Area covered by this atlas

Scale

0 5 10 15 km

0 5 10 miles

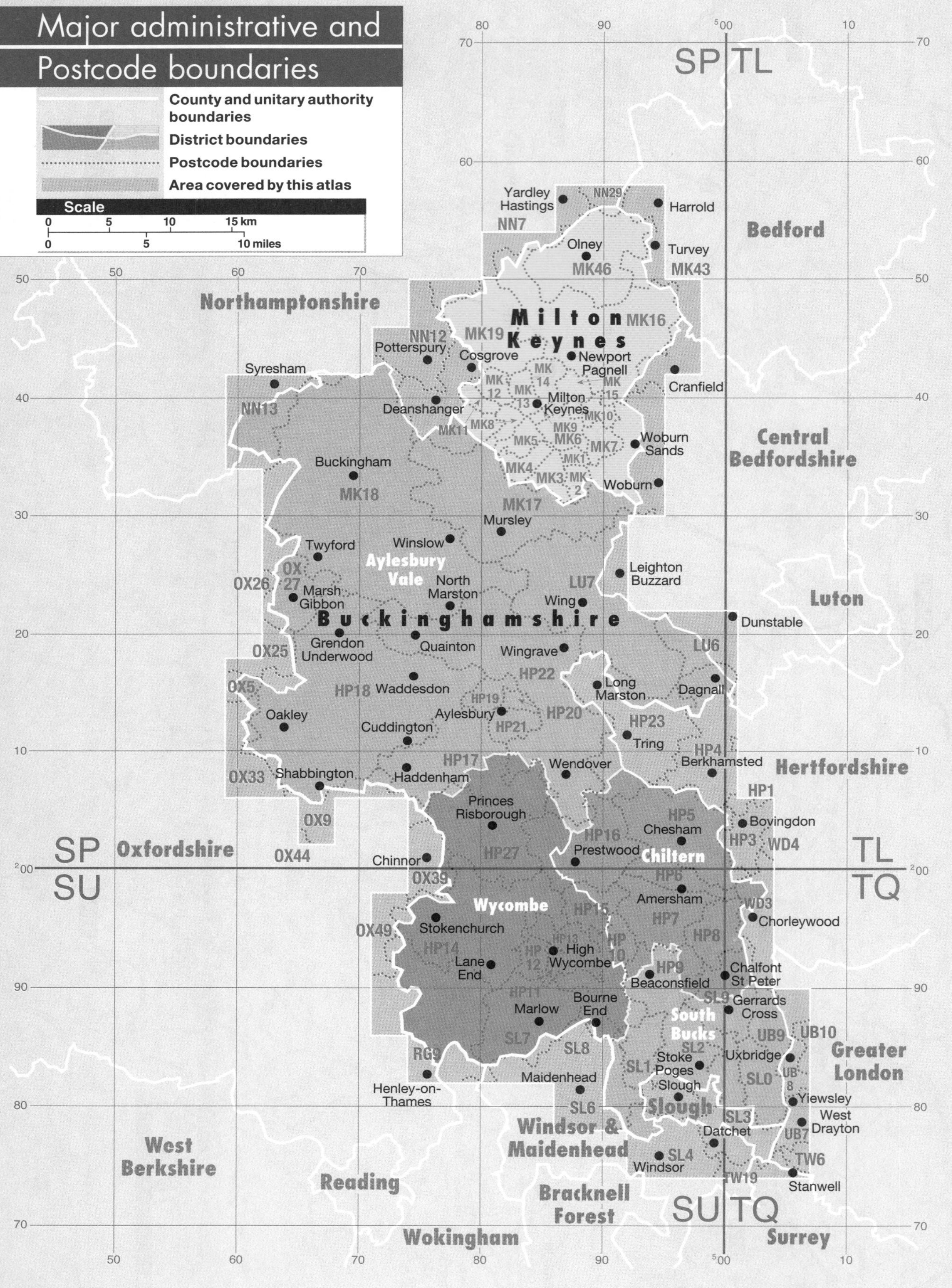

SP TL

Northamptonshire

Bedford

Yardley Hastings

NN29

Harrold

NN7

Olney

Turvey

MK46

MK43

Syresham

NN13

NN12

MK19

Milton Keynes

MK16

Central Bedfordshire

Potterspury

Cosgrove

Newport Pagnell

Deanshanger

MK 12

MK 14

MK 13

Milton Keynes

MK 15

Cranfield

MK11

MK8

MK9

MK10

Buckingham

MK18

MK4

MK5

MK6

MK7

Woburn Sands

MK1

MK3

MK 2

Woburn

MK17

Mursley

Winslow

Twyford

OX 27

Aylesbury Vale

North Marston

Leighton Buzzard

Luton

OX26

Marsh Gibbon

LU7

Wing

Dunstable

Buckinghamshire

OX25

Grendon Underwood

Quainton

Wingrave

LU6

OX5

HP18

Waddesdon

HP22

Long Marston

Dagnall

Oakley

HP19

HP20

HP23

Hertfordshire

Cuddington

Aylesbury

HP21

Tring

HP4

Berkhamsted

OX33

Shabbington

HP17

Haddenham

Wendover

HP1

OX9

Princes Risborough

HP5

Chesham

Bovingdon

SP

Oxfordshire

OX44

HP16

Prestwood

Chiltern

HP3

WD4

SU

Chinnor

HP27

HP6

TL TQ

OX39

Amersham

WD3

Wycombe

HP15

HP7

Chorleywood

OX49

Stokenchurch

HP13

HP 10

HP8

HP14

Lane End

HP 12

High Wycombe

HP9

Beaconsfield

Chalfont St Peter

HP11

SL9

Gerrards Cross

RG9

SL7

Bourne End

SL8

South Bucks

UB9

UB10

Marlow

SL2

Stoke Poges

Uxbridge

SL0

Greater London

Henley-on-Thames

Maidenhead

SL1

Slough

UB 8

Yiewsley

SL6

Slough

SL3

Datchet

UB7

West Drayton

West Berkshire

Windsor & Maidenhead

Windsor

SL4

TW6

Reading

Bracknell Forest

TW19

Stanwell

SU TQ

Wokingham

Surrey

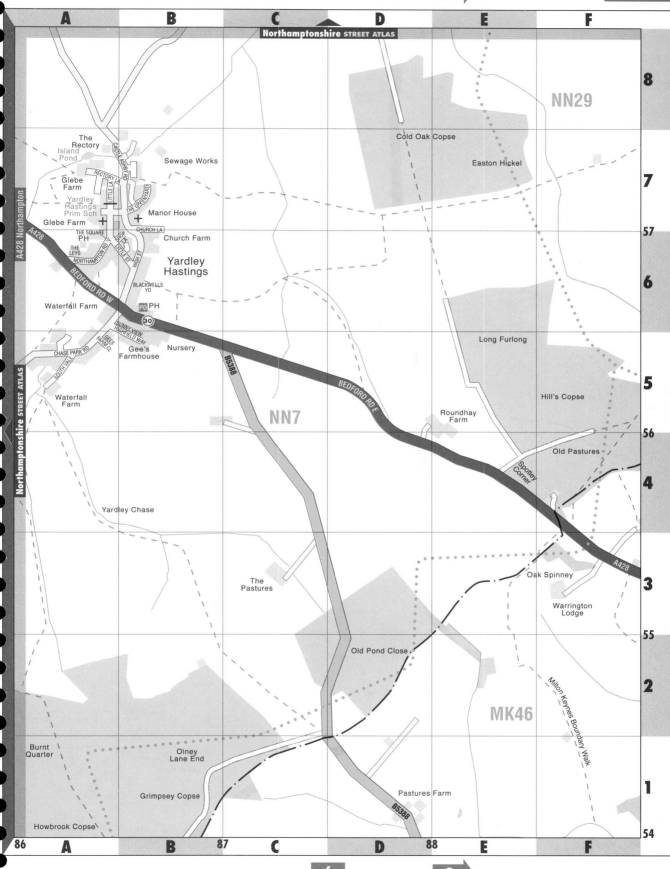

2

A B C D E F
Northamptonshire STREET ATLAS
8
NN29
Cold Oak Copse
Easton Hickel
The Rectory
Island Pond
CASTLE ASHBY RD
Sewage Works
7
RECTORY LA
Glebe Farm
LITTLE LA
THE GREENYARD
Yardley Hastings Prim Sch
Manor House
A428 Northampton
Glebe Farm
CHURCH LA
THE SQUARE
PH
Church Farm
57
A428
SHOP LA
THE LEYS
NORTHAMPTON RD
LITTLE ST
HIGH ST
Yardley Hastings
BEDFORD RD W
BLACKWELLS YD
6
Waterfall Farm
PO PH
30
SUNNY VIEW
HIGHFIELD WAY
GEES FARM CL
Long Furlong
CHASE PARK RD
Gee's Farmhouse
Nursery
B5388
SOUTH VALE
Northamptonshire STREET ATLAS
5
Waterfall Farm
BEDFORD RD E
Hill's Copse
Roundhay Farm
NN7
56
Old Pastures
Spotley Corner
4
Yardley Chase
A428
Oak Spinney
The Pastures
3
Warrington Lodge
55
Old Pond Close
Milton Keynes Boundary Walk
2
MK46
Burnt Quarter
Olney Lane End
1
Grimpsey Copse
Pastures Farm
B5388
Howbrook Copse
54
86 A B 87 C D 88 E F

6
2

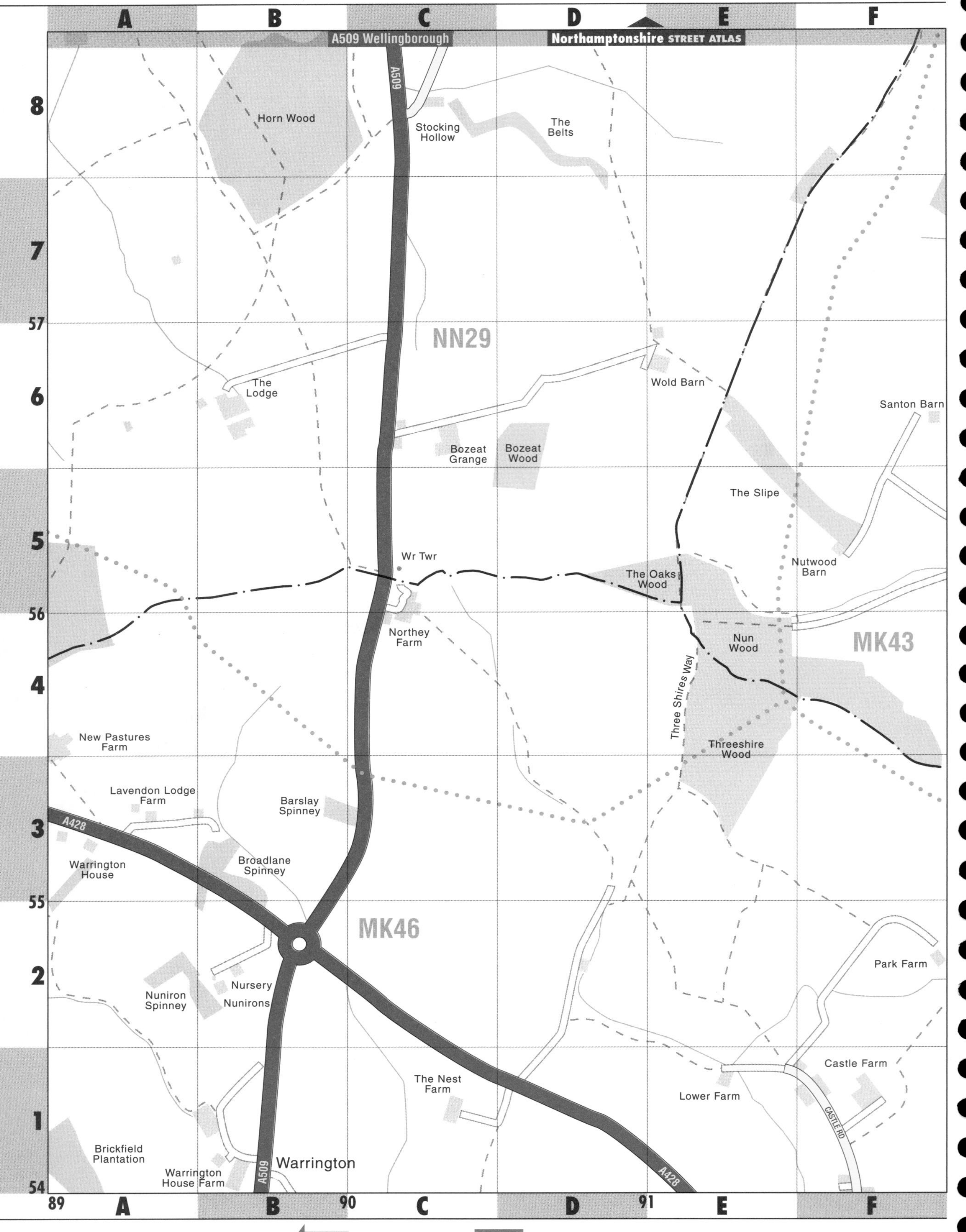

A	B	C	D	E	F

A509 Wellingborough

Northamptonshire STREET ATLAS

A509

8

Horn Wood

Stocking Hollow

The Belts

7

57

NN29

Wold Barn

6

Santon Barn

The Lodge

Bozeat Grange

Bozeat Wood

The Slip

5

Wr Twr

The Oaks Wood

Nutwood Barn

56

Northey Farm

Nun Wood

MK43

4

Three Shires Way

New Pastures Farm

Threeshire Wood

3

A428

Lavendon Lodge Farm

Barslay Spinney

Warrington House

Broadlane Spinney

55

MK46

2

Park Farm

Nuniron Spinney

Nursery Nunirons

Castle Farm

Lower Farm

1

CASTLE RD

Brickfield Plantation

The Nest Farm

A509

Warrington

A428

54

89	A	B	90	C	D	91	E	F

Warrington House Farm

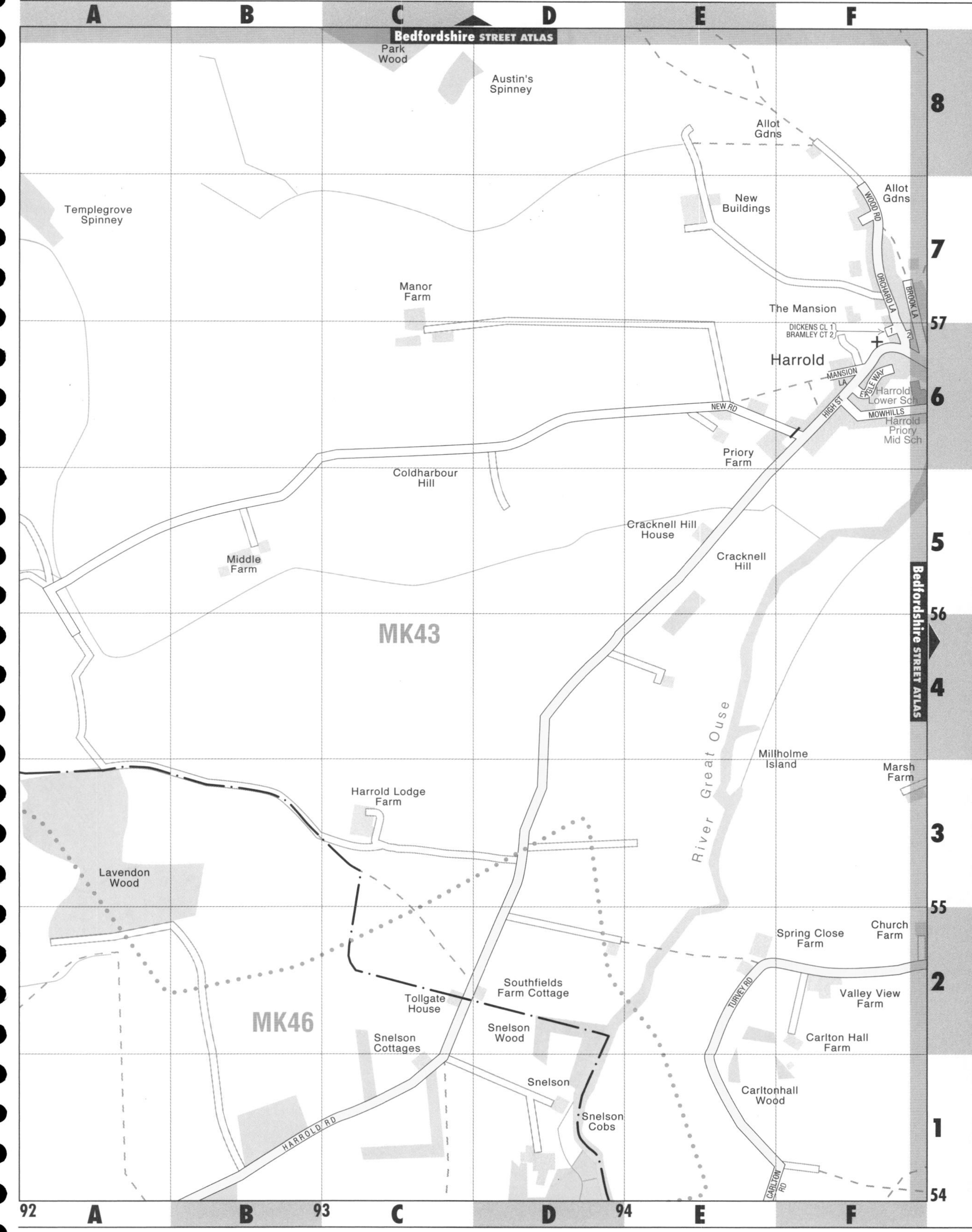

Park Wood

Austin's Spinney

Allot Gdns

Templegrove Spinney

New Buildings

Allot Gdns

8

WOOD RD

ORCHARD LA

BROOK LA

Manor Farm

The Mansion

7

DICKENS CL 1
BRAMLEY CT 2

57

Harrold

MANSION LA

NEW RD

HIGH ST

ISLE WAY

Harrold Lower Sch

MOWHILLS

Harrold Priory Mid Sch

6

Coldharbour Hill

Priory Farm

Cracknell Hill House

Cracknell Hill

5

Middle Farm

56

MK43

River Great Ouse

4

Millholme Island

Marsh Farm

Harrold Lodge Farm

3

Lavendon Wood

55

Spring Close Farm

Church Farm

Southfields Farm Cottage

TURKEY RD

Valley View Farm

2

MK46

Tollgate House

Snelson Wood

Carlton Hall Farm

Snelson Cottages

Snelson

Carltonhall Wood

1

HARROLD RD

Snelson Cobs

CARLTON RD

54

92

93

94

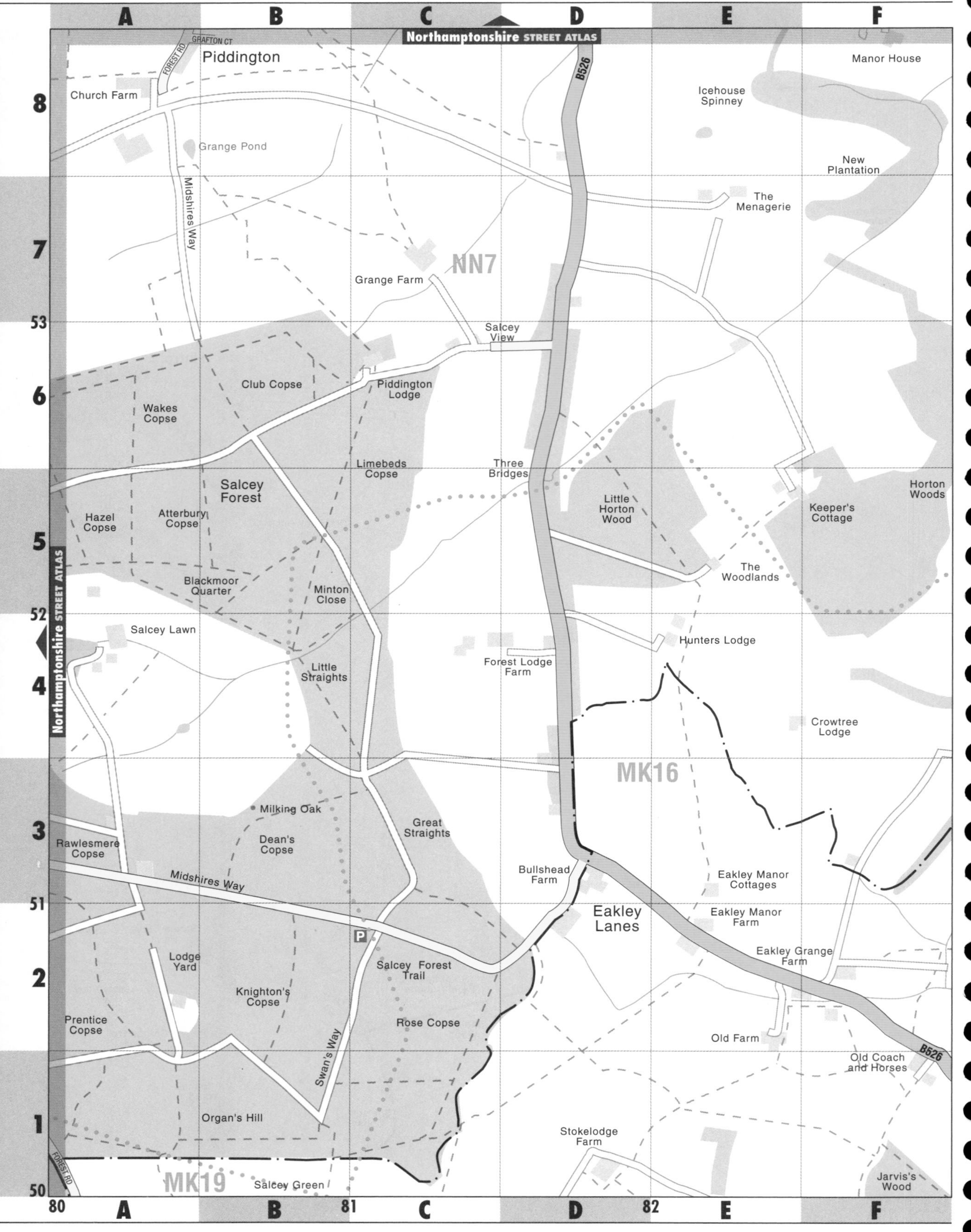

Piddington

Church Farm

Grange Pond

Midshires Way

NN7

Grange Farm

Salcey View

Club Copse

Piddington Lodge

Wakes Copse

Limebeds Copse

Three Bridges

Salcey Forest

Hazel Copse

Atterbury Copse

Blackmoor Quarter

Minton Close

Little Horton Wood

Keeper's Cottage

Horton Woods

The Woodlands

Salcey Lawn

Little Straights

Forest Lodge Farm

Hunters Lodge

Crowtree Lodge

MK16

Milking Oak

Dean's Copse

Great Straights

Bullshead Farm

Eakley Manor Cottages

Rawlesmere Copse

Midshires Way

Eakley Lanes

Eakley Manor Farm

Eakley Grange Farm

Lodge Yard

Knighton's Copse

P

Salcey Forest Trail

Rose Copse

Old Farm

Prentice Copse

Swan's Way

Old Coach and Horses

Organ's Hill

Stokelodge Farm

MK19

Salcey Green

Jarvis's Wood

Icehouse Spinney

Manor House

New Plantation

The Menagerie

B526

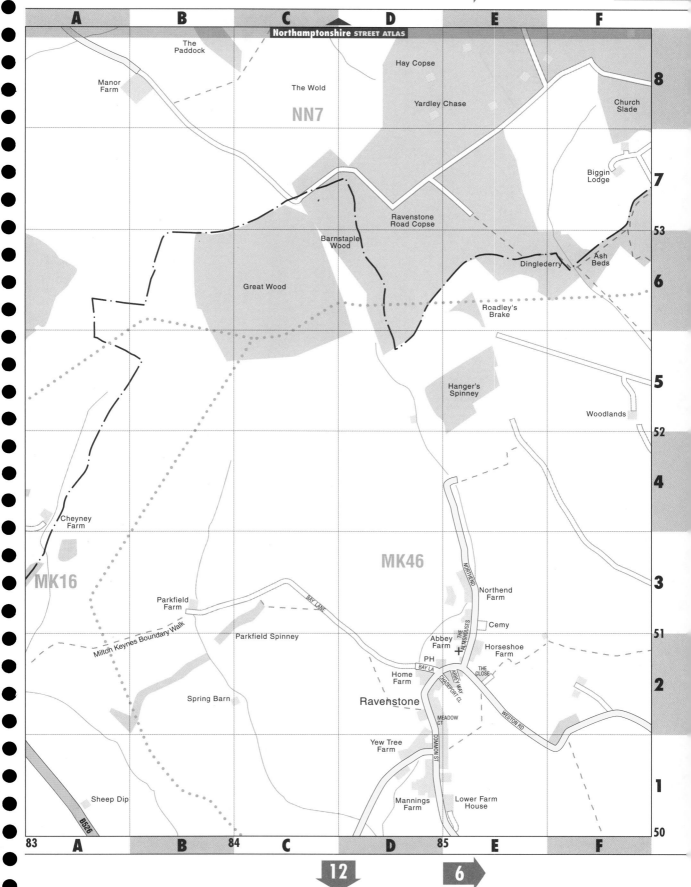

A B C D E F

Northamptonshire STREET ATLAS

The Paddock
Manor Farm
The Wold
Hay Copse
Yardley Chase
NN7
Church Slade
Biggin Lodge
Ravenstone Road Copse
Barnstaple Wood
Dinglederry
Ash Beds
Great Wood
Roadley's Brake
Hanger's Spinney
Woodlands
Cheyney Farm
MK46
MK16
Northend Farm
NORTHEND
Parkfield Farm
BAY LANE
Cemy
THE ALMSHOUSES
Abbey Farm
Horseshoe Farm
Parkfield Spinney
Milton Keynes Boundary Walk
PH
BAY LA
THE CLOSE
ABBEY WAY
CHASEPORT CL
Home Farm
Spring Barn
Ravenstone
MEADOW CT
WESTON RD
Yew Tree Farm
COMMON ST
Sheep Dip
Mannings Farm
Lower Farm House
B526
8
7
53
6
5
52
4
3
51
2
1
50
83
84
85

A B C D E F

8 Howbrook Copse
Grimpsey Copse
Yardley Chase
Olney Park Farm
Olney Park Cottages
Olney Hyde
Church Slade

NN7

7
Smith's Farm
Kilwick Wood
Court Farm

53

Sewage Works

6
Olney Ind Est
Warrington Road Farm

STILEBROOK RD
RABANS CL
ASPREYS

YARDLEY RD
B5388

5
SHORT MASSEY 1
CRAB TREE CL 2
SLATEPITS CFT 3
WOODPITS LA 4
Dickens Spinney
DRIFT WAY
LILLY HILL
FERNE
MIDLAND RD
Olney Mid Sch
WHITEHILL
LONG MASSEY
HAWKSWOOD
HOPPERS HL
MAYBUSH WLK
KENSINGTON PL

MK46

52
Olney
GUINEA ORCH
FISHERMANS CL
RIVETTS
CLICKER YD
DINGLEDERRY
Liby
Ousedale Sch Resr
OVERHILLS
FLAGGS MDW
STOCKEN CL
OLLEYS
WEST ST
ST JOSEPHS
COBBS GDN
THE OLD MEWS
B5388

4
CHERRY ORCH
LONG LA
WEST SIDE RISE
SPRINGFIELD RD
DELLS

WHITMEES CL
ANDING CL
DIDICKENS SPINNEY
Olney Inf Sch
JOHNSONS FIELD
ASHLEA
ELMLEA
THORNLEA
ORCHARD RISE
The Cowper & Newton Mus

HIGH ST

3
The Alcove
Pheasants Nest
Overbrook Spinney
BACON HILL
COURT CRESS
HOLLOW
STONE PIT CL
BEECH AVE
SPINNEY HILL RD
DAGNALL RD
THE PYGHTLE
PATTONS
SPRING LA
WELL CT
OAKDOWN CRES
STANLEY CT
TYNE ST
Weston Park

WESTON RD

51
Goosey Bridge
Sluice

2
The Wilderness
WOOD LA
Laundry Cottage
CROSS LA
Manor House
PH
Otter Pool
Heron Water

BRIDGE ST
A509

Church Farm
PO
HIGH ST
COWPERS
ORCH
FEVERS LA

1
THE CLOSE
Weston Underwood
River Great Ouse
Emberton Country Park

HARVEY DR

50
Grebe Lake
Visitor Ctr
Snipe Pool
The Willows

86 **A** 87 **B** **C** 88 **D** **E** **F**

F3
1 FOUNTAIN CT
2 BERRELL'S CT
3 ROSE CT
4 MARKET PL
5 OSBORN'S CT
6 CHURCH ST
7 PEMBROKE HO
8 CHANTRY RI
9 CLAY PIT LA
10 PEBODY PL
11 STONEMASONS CL
12 WAGSTAFF WY

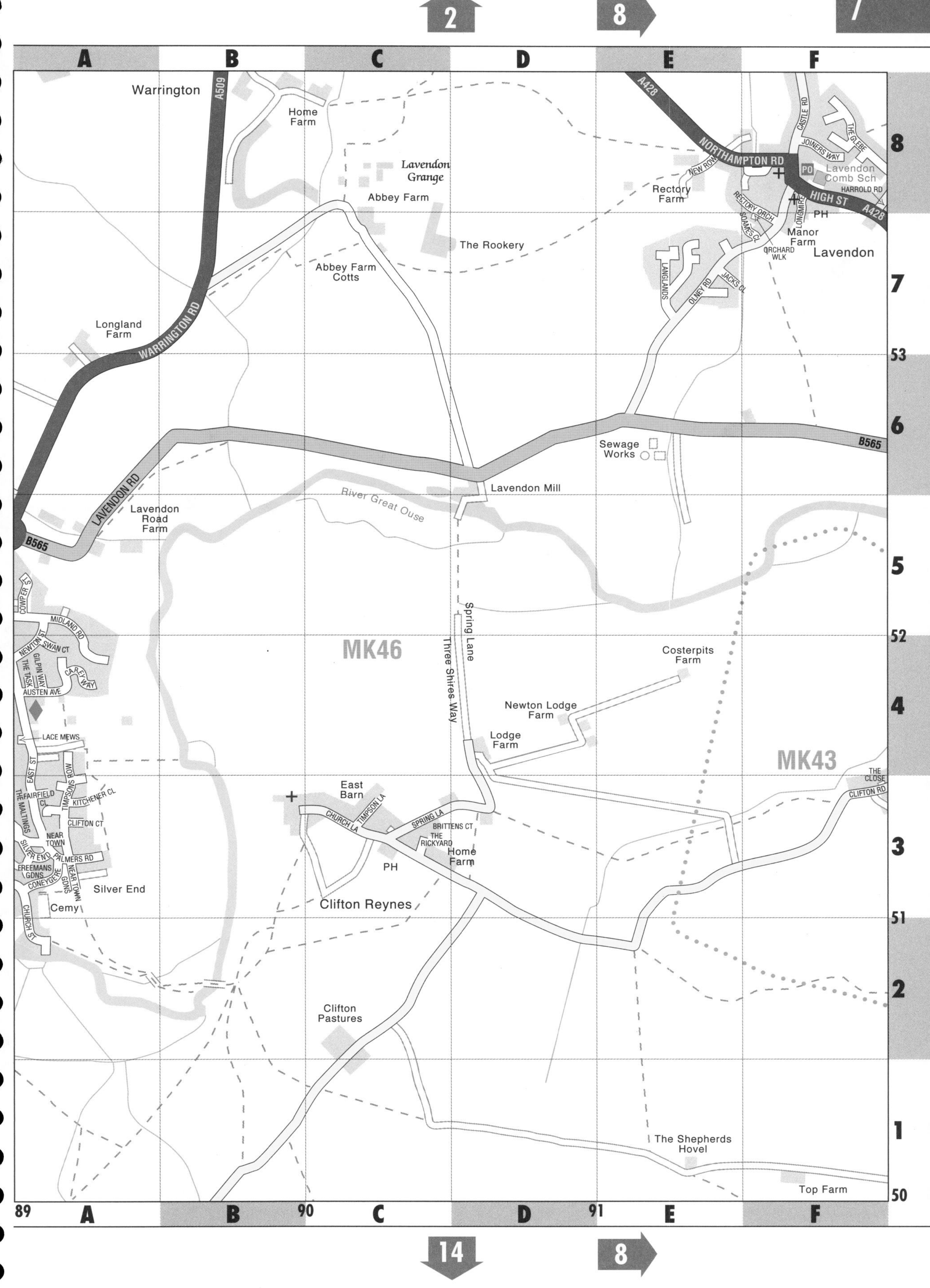
2
8
A
B
C
D
E
F
Warrington
A509
Home Farm
Lavendon Grange
Abbey Farm
A428
NORTHAMPTON RD
Rectory Farm
Lavendon Comb Sch
HIGH ST
PH
Manor Farm
Lavendon
The Rookery
Abbey Farm Cotts
Longland Farm
WARRINGTON RD
B565
Sewage Works
Lavendon Mill
River Great Ouse
LAVENDON RD
Lavendon Road Farm
MK46
Spring Lane
Three Shires Way
Costerpits Farm
Newton Lodge Farm
Lodge Farm
MK43
East Barn
CLIFTON RD
Home Farm
PH
Clifton Reynes
Silver End
Cemy
Clifton Pastures
The Shepherds Hovel
Top Farm
8
7
53
6
5
52
4
3
51
2
1
50
89
90
91
14
8

A **B** **C** **D** **E** **F**

8

HARROLD RD

Snip Wood

THE GLEBE

Uphoe Manor Farm

New Barn

Copymoor

CARLTON RD

7

A428

Cemy

New Park

Cricket Ground

Cemy

53

MK46

Turvey House

Turvey Lower Sch

New Gains Farm

6

B565

Chantry Farm

HAWTHORN CL

VINE ROW

MAY RD

GROVE CT

PORTL4

NORFOLK RD

Turvey

THE ROW

CHURCH TERR

PO

LAWS CL

THE PURTLE

BAMFORDS LA

CROFTENDS

MORDAUNT CL

ELMWD

BEDFORD RD

CRANES CL

HIGH ST

ABBEY SQ

30

A428

5

Cold Brayfield

Waterfield Farm

Brayfield Farm

Turvey Bridge

30

BRIDGE ST

THE GREEN

BAMFORDS YD

JACK S LA

Turvey Abbey

A428 Bedford

TURVEY MILL

LADYBRIDGE TERR

Ford

BRAYFIELD HO

TANDY'S CL

MILL GN

NEWTON RD

52

BAKERS CL

Long Belt

Abbey Farm

Bedfordshire STREET ATLAS

4

Newton Blossomville

Lodge

Top Lodge

Mossy Bank Wood

PH

Newton Blossomville CE Sch

Turvey Cottage

Woodside Cottage

CLIFTON RD

THE ROW

BROOK LA

River Great Ouse

New Wood

HARDMEAD RD

MK43

Home Farm

Westfields Barn

Keepers Cottage

3

51

Turvey Hall

2

Newton Park

Clifton Spinney

Gullet Wood

Newton Wood

Two Chimneys

Sheepwalks Spinney

1

Mast

Turvey Lodge Farm

50

92 **A** **B** 93 **C** **D** 94 **E** **F**

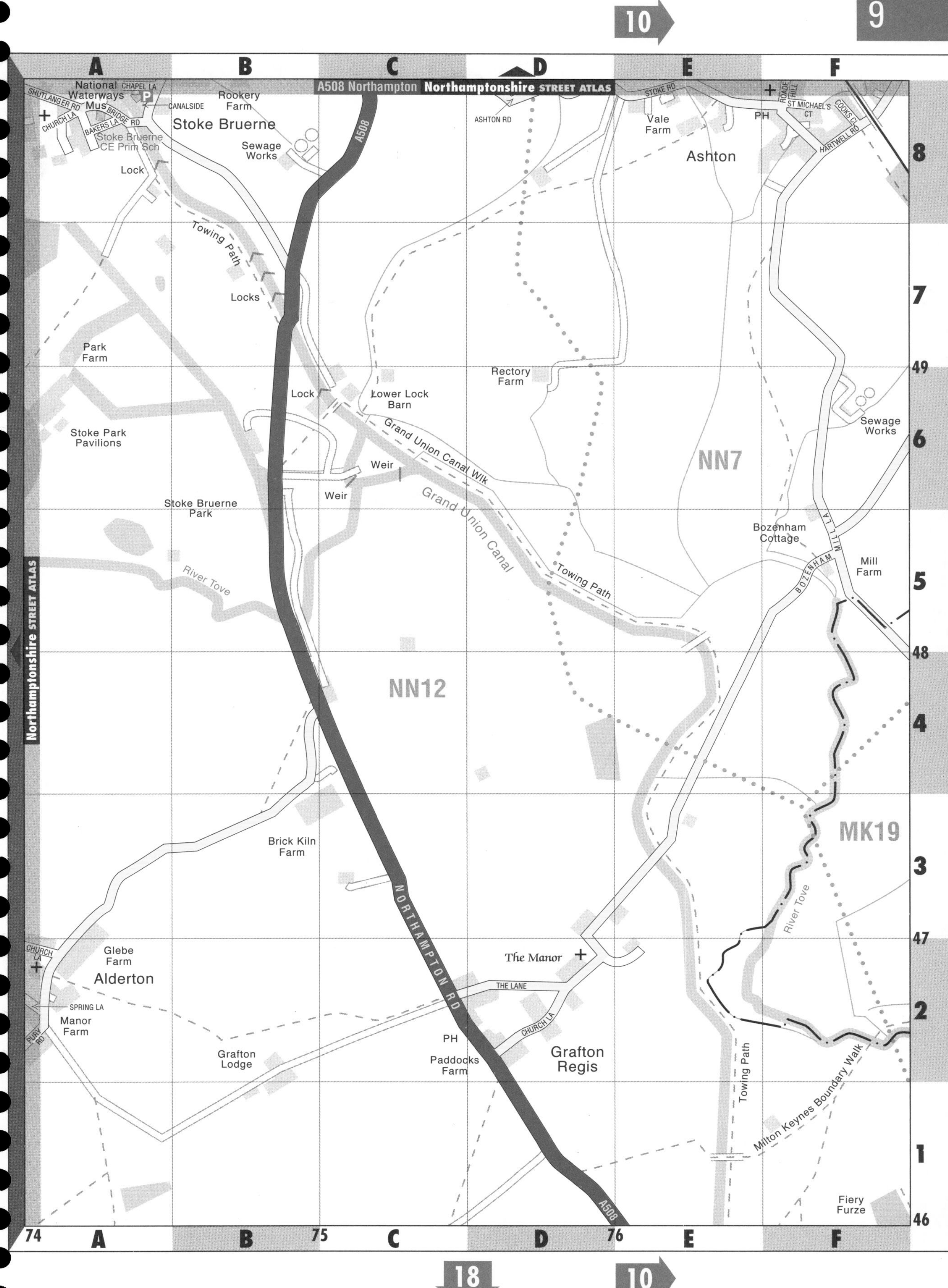

Northamptonshire STREET ATLAS

A B C D E F

8

National
Waterways
Mus
CHAPEL LA
P
Stoke Bruerne
CE Prim Sch
SHUTLANGER RD
BRIDGE RD
CHURCH LA
BAKERS LA
CANALSIDE
Rookery
Farm
Sewage
Works
Stoke Bruerne
Lock
STOKE RD
Vale
Farm
ROADE HILL
PH
ST MICHAEL'S
CT
HARTWELL RD
COOKS CL
Ashton
ASHTON RD

7

Towing Path
Locks
Park
Farm
Rectory
Farm

49

Lock
Lower Lock
Barn
Grand Union Canal Wlk
Sewage
Works

6

Stoke Park
Pavilions
Weir
Weir
Grand Union Canal
NN7
Bozenham
Cottage
MILL LA
BOZENHAM
Mill
Farm

5

Stoke Bruerne
Park
River Tove
Towing Path

48

NN12

4

Brick Kiln
Farm
MK19
River Tove

3

NORTHAMPTON RD

47

Glebe
Farm
CHURCH LA
Alderton
The Manor
THE LANE
CHURCH LA

2

SPRING LA
Manor
Farm
PURY RD
Grafton
Lodge
PH
Paddocks
Farm
Grafton
Regis
Towing Path
Milton Keynes Boundary Walk

1

A508
Fiery
Furze

46

Northamptonshire STREET ATLAS

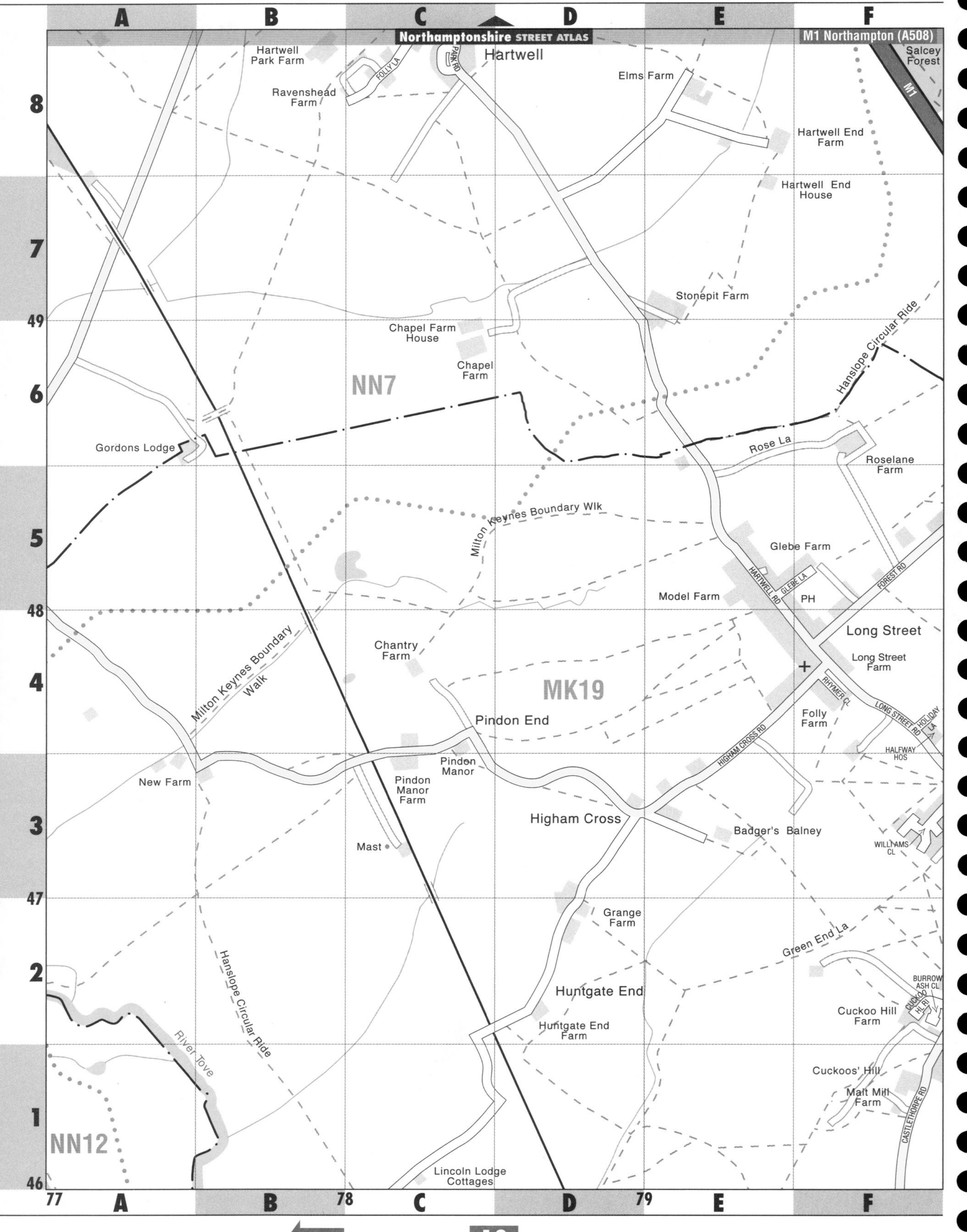

Salcey Forest

M1

Hartwell Park Farm

Ravenshead Farm

FOLLY LA

PARK RD

Hartwell

Elms Farm

Hartwell End Farm

Hartwell End House

8

Stonepit Farm

Hanslope Circular Ride

7

49

Chapel Farm House

Chapel Farm

NN7

Rose La

Roselane Farm

6

Gordons Lodge

Milton Keynes Boundary Wlk

Glebe Farm

HARTWELL RD

GLEBE LA

Model Farm

PH

FOREST RD

5

48

Long Street

Long Street Farm

Chantry Farm

Milton Keynes Boundary Walk

MK19

Pindon End

Pindon Manor

RHYMER CT

Folly Farm

LONG STREET RD

HOLIDAY LA

HALFWAY HOS

4

New Farm

Pindon Manor Farm

Higham Cross

HIGHAM CROSS RD

Badger's Balney

WILLIAMS CL

3

Mast

47

Grange Farm

Green End La

Hanslope Circular Ride

Huntgate End

BURROW ASH CL

DUCKLO HL

2

River Tove

Huntgate End Farm

Cuckoo Hill Farm

Cuckoos' Hill

Malt Mill Farm

CASTLETHORPE RD

1

NN12

Lincoln Lodge Cottages

46

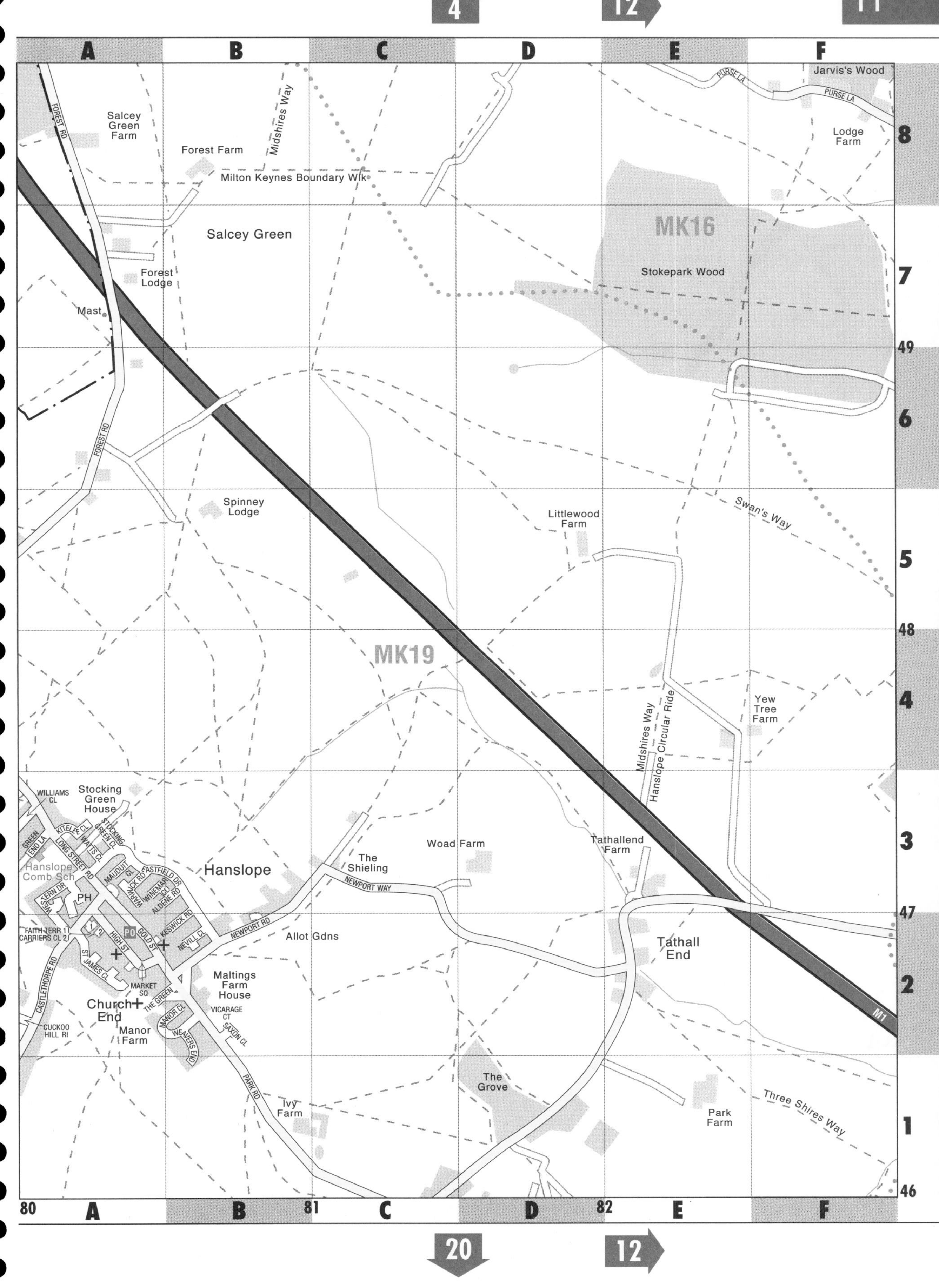
4
12
A
B
C
D
E
F
Jarvis's Wood
PURSE LA
PURSE LA
Lodge Farm
FOREST RD
Salcey Green Farm
Forest Farm
Midshires Way
Milton Keynes Boundary Wlk
8
MK16
Salcey Green
Stokepark Wood
Forest Lodge
7
Mast
49
6
FOREST RD
Spinney Lodge
Littlewood Farm
Swan's Way
5
48
MK19
4
Yew Tree Farm
Midshires Way
Hanslope Circular Ride
WILLIAMS CL
Stocking Green House
3
Woad Farm
Tathallend Farm
Hanslope
The Shieling
Hanslope Comb Sch
NEWPORT WAY
PH
PO
NEWPORT RD
47
FAITH TERR 1
CARRIERS CL 2
Allot Gdns
Tathall End
Maltings Farm House
MARKET SQ
2
Church End
VICARAGE CT
Manor Farm
CUCKOO HILL RI
M1
PARK RD
The Grove
Ivy Farm
Three Shires Way
Park Farm
1
46
80
81
82
20
12

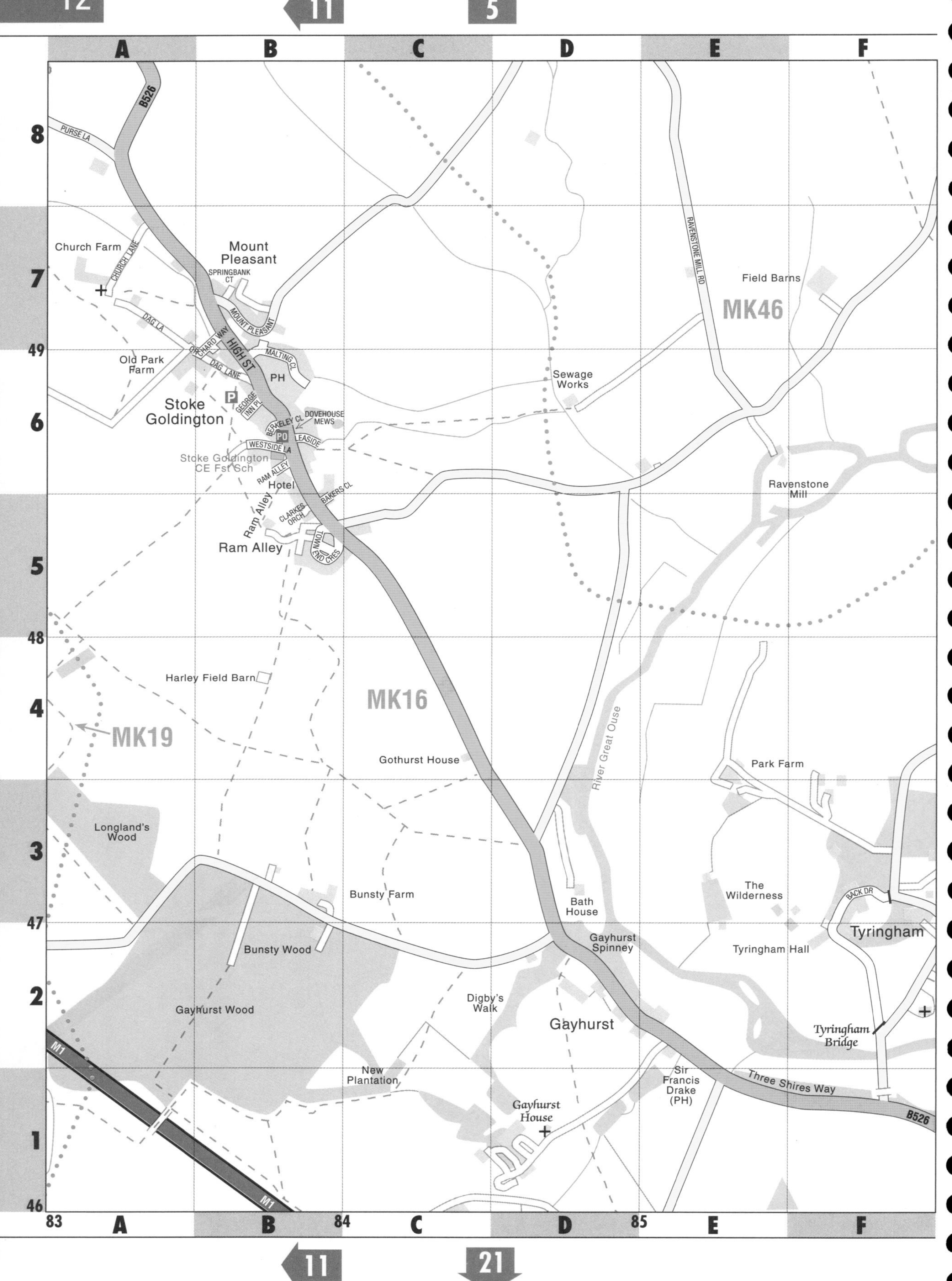
A
B
C
D
E
F
8
7
49
6
5
48
4
3
47
2
1
46
83
84
85
B526
PURSE LA
Church Farm
CHURCH LANE
Mount
Pleasant
SPRINGBANK
CT
MOUNT PLEASANT
DAG LA
CHARD WAY
HIGH ST
MALTING CL
Old Park
Farm
DAG LANE
PH
P
Stoke
Goldington
GEORGE INN PL
BERKELEY CL
DOVEHOUSE
MEWS
PO
LEASIDE
WESTSIDE LA
Stoke Goldington
CE Fst Sch
RAM ALLEY
Hotel
BAKERS CL
CLARKES ORCH
Ram Alley
TOWN END CRES
Ram Alley
RAVENSTONE MILL RD
Field Barns
MK46
Sewage
Works
Ravenstone
Mill
Harley Field Barn
MK16
MK19
River Great Ouse
Gothurst House
Park Farm
Longland's
Wood
Bunsty Farm
The
Wilderness
Bath
House
BACK DR
Tyringham
Bunsty Wood
Gayhurst
Spinney
Tyringham Hall
Gayhurst Wood
Digby's
Walk
Gayhurst
Tyringham
Bridge
M1
New
Plantation
Sir
Francis
Drake
(PH)
Three Shires Way
Gayhurst
House
B526
M1

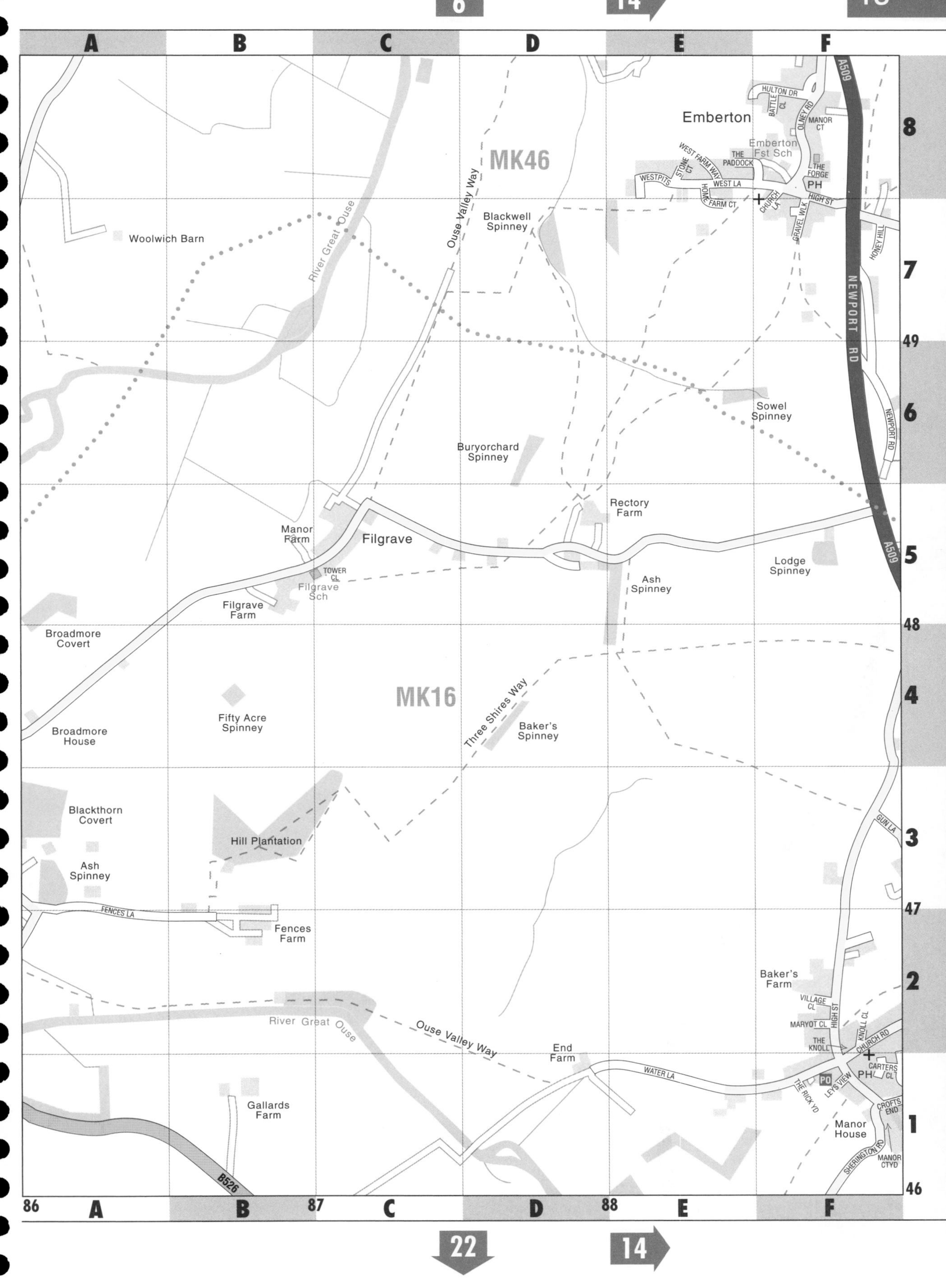
6
14
A
B
C
D
E
F
Emberton
HULTON DR
BATTLE CL
OLNEY RD
MANOR CT
Emberton Fst Sch
WEST FARM WAY
STONE CT
THE PADDOCK
THE FORGE
PH
WESTPITS
WEST LA
HOME FARM CT
CHURCH LA
HIGH ST
GRAVEL WLK
HONEY HILL
A509
MK46
Ouse Valley Way
Blackwell Spinney
Woolwich Barn
River Great Ouse
NEWPORT RD
Sowel Spinney
Buryorchard Spinney
Rectory Farm
Manor Farm
Filgrave
TOWER CL
Filgrave Sch
Filgrave Farm
Ash Spinney
Lodge Spinney
Broadmore Covert
MK16
Three Shires Way
Fifty Acre Spinney
Baker's Spinney
Broadmore House
Blackthorn Covert
Hill Plantation
GUN LA
Ash Spinney
FENCES LA
Fences Farm
Baker's Farm
VILLAGE CL
MARYOT CL
HIGH ST
KNOLL CL
THE KNOLL
CHURCH RD
River Great Ouse
Ouse Valley Way
End Farm
WATER LA
CARTERS CL
PO
PH
THE RICK YD
LEYS VIEW
CROFTS END
Gallards Farm
Manor House
SHERINGTON RD
MANOR CTYD
B526
8
7
49
6
5
48
4
3
47
2
1
46
86
87
88
22
14

13
7

A
B
C
D
E
F
8
7
49
6
5
48
4
3
47
2
1
46
Three Shires Way
Rectory Farm
Petsoe Manor Farm
Petsoe Manor
Petsoe End
Hill Farm
Clay Farm
Grange Farm
MK46
Hollington Wood
Wood Farm
Mulducks
Parrages Wood
Seven Acre Covert
Short Wood
A509
MK16
Gowle's Farm
Thickthorn Wood
GUN LA
FIELD CL
CHURCH END
PH
PARK RD
Sherington
CHURCH RD
GRIGGS ORCH
SCHOOL LA
Sherington CE Fst Sch
PERRY LA
PERRY LANE
HILLVIEW
CARTERS CL
CROFTS END
Crofts End
BEDFORD RD
Grange Farm
Brickyard Cottage
A422
NEWPORT RD
Chicheley Brook
Brandon's Wood
Bedlam
BEDLAM WLK
BEDLAM LA
Bedlam Spinney
A422
89
90
91

13
23

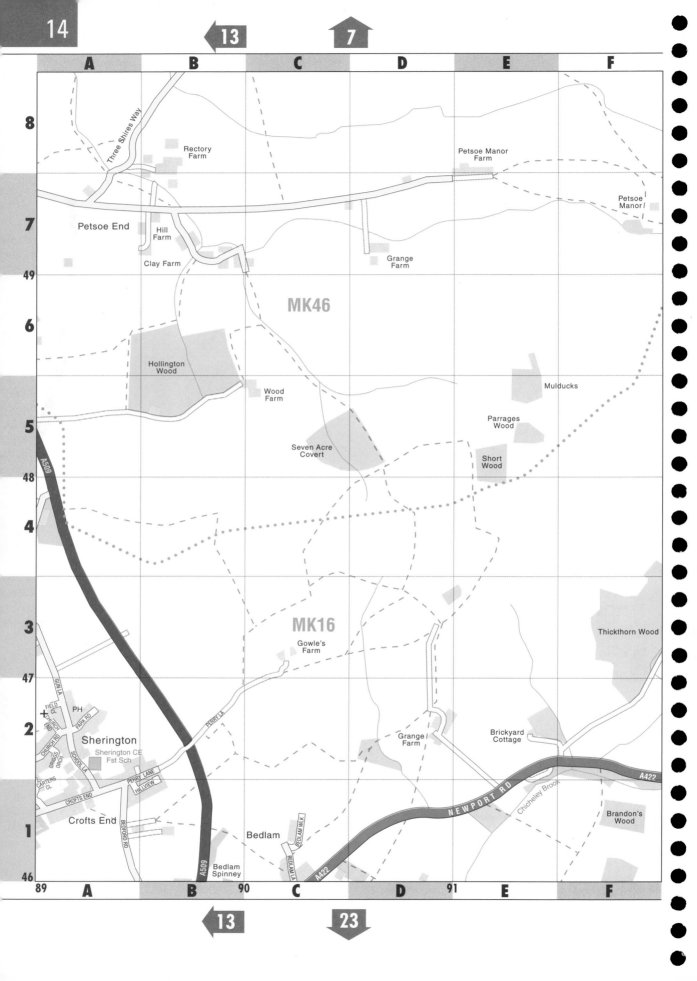

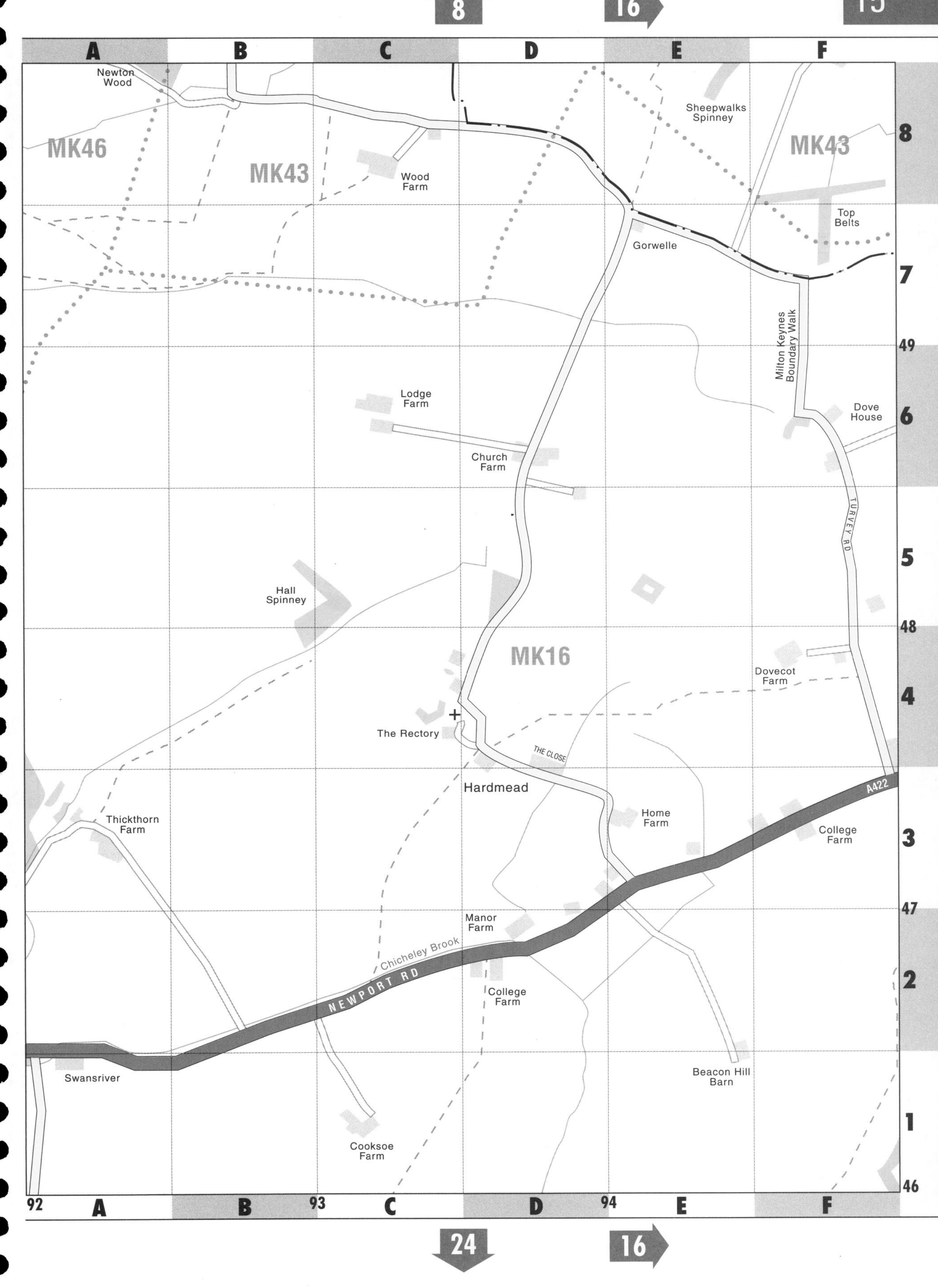
8
16
A
B
C
D
E
F
Newton Wood
MK46
MK43
Wood Farm
Sheepwalks Spinney
MK43
Top Belts
Gorwelle
Milton Keynes Boundary Walk
Lodge Farm
Dove House
Church Farm
TURVEY RD
Hall Spinney
MK16
Dovecot Farm
The Rectory
THE CLOSE
Hardmead
A422
Home Farm
Thickthorn Farm
College Farm
Manor Farm
Chicheley Brook
NEWPORT RD
College Farm
Swansriver
Beacon Hill Barn
Cooksoe Farm
8
7
49
6
5
48
4
3
47
2
1
46
92
93
94
24
16

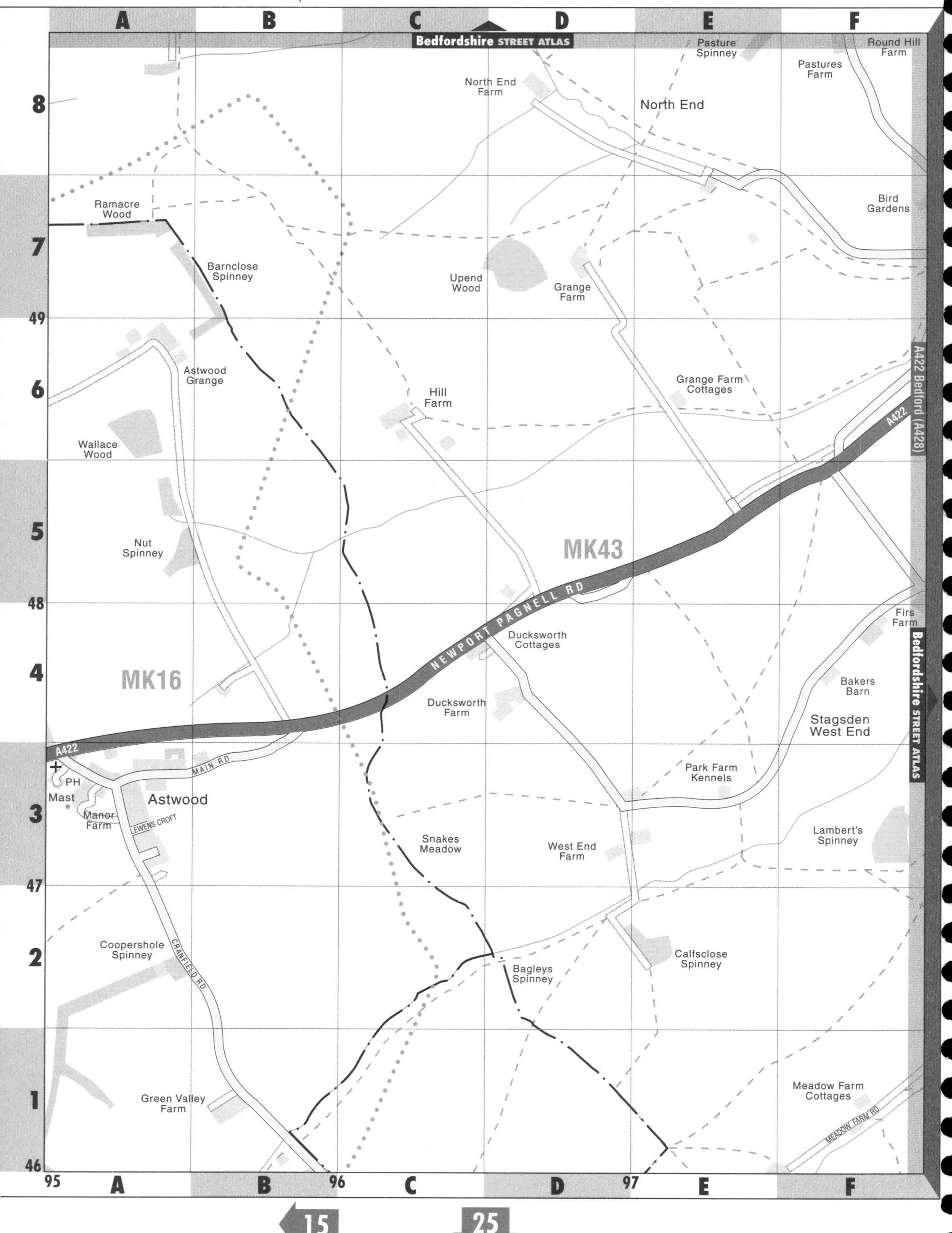

15

A B C D E F

Bedfordshire STREET ATLAS

8

Ramacre
Wood

7

Barnclose
Spinney

49

Astwood
Grange

6

Wallace
Wood

5

Nut
Spinney

48

MK16

4

A422

MAIN RD

PH
Mast

3

Manor
Farm

Astwood

LEWENS CROFT

47

2

Coopershole
Spinney

CRANFIELD RD

1

Green Valley
Farm

46

95 A 96 B C 97 D E F

15 25

North End
Farm

North End

Pasture
Spinney

Round Hill
Farm

Pastures
Farm

Bird
Gardens

Upend
Wood

Grange
Farm

Grange Farm
Cottages

A422 Bedford (A428)

A422

Hill
Farm

MK43

NEWPORT PAGNELL RD

Ducksworth
Cottages

Firs
Farm

Ducksworth
Farm

Bakers
Barn

Stagsden
West End

Park Farm
Kennels

Snakes
Meadow

West End
Farm

Lambert's
Spinney

Calfsclose
Spinney

Bagleys
Spinney

Meadow Farm
Cottages

MEADOW FARM RD

Bedfordshire STREET ATLAS

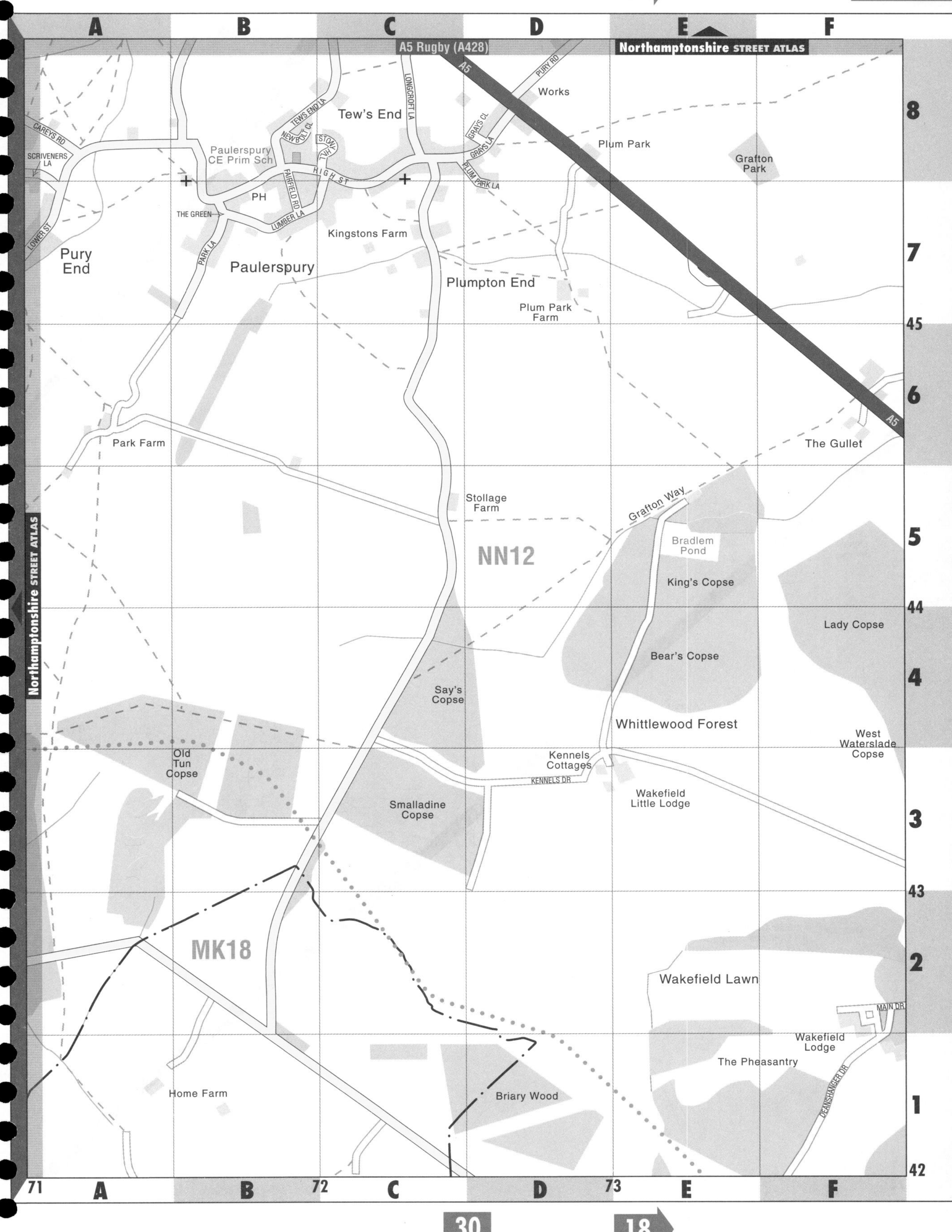

A   B   C   D   E   F

A5 Rugby (A428)

A5

PURY RD

Works

GRAYS CL

LONGCROFT LA

Tew's End

GRAYS LA

Plum Park

8

CAREYS RD

Paulerspury
CE Prim Sch

NEW CL CL

TEWS END LA

STOKE WK

Grafton
Park

SCRIVENERS
LA

PH

RIGHT ST

+

+

PLUM PARK LA

LOWER ST

THE GREEN

FAIRFIELD RD

LUMBER LA

Kingstons Farm

Pury
End

PARK LA

Paulerspury

Plumpton End

7

45

Plum Park
Farm

Park Farm

The Gullet

A5

6

Grafton Way

Stollage
Farm

Bradlem
Pond

NN12

King's Copse

5

Lady Copse

44

Bear's Copse

Say's
Copse

Whittlewood Forest

West
Waterslade
Copse

4

Old
Tun
Copse

Kennels
Cottages

KENNELS DR

Wakefield
Little Lodge

Smalladine
Copse

3

43

MK18

2

Wakefield Lawn

MAIN DR

Wakefield
Lodge

The Pheasantry

Home Farm

Briary Wood

DEANSHANGER DR

1

71   A   B   72   C   D   73   E   F   42

Northamptonshire STREET ATLAS

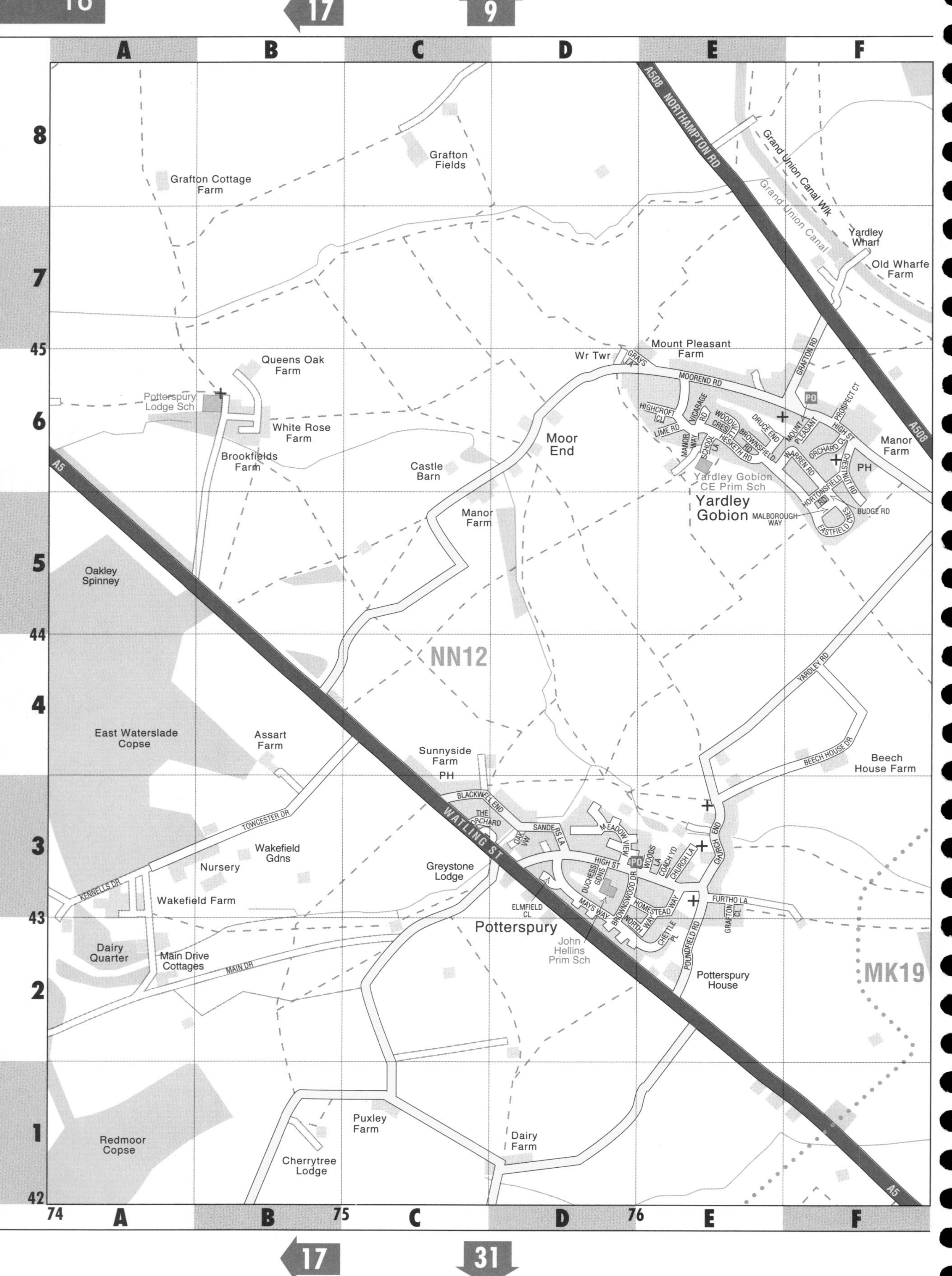

17
9

A   B   C   D   E   F

8

Grafton Cottage Farm

Grafton Fields

A508 NORTHAMPTON RD

Grand Union Canal Wlk

Grand Union Canal

Yardley Wharf

Old Wharfe Farm

7

45

Queens Oak Farm

Wr Twr

Gray's La

Mount Pleasant Farm

MOOREND RD

Grafton Rd

PO

PROSPECT CT

A508

6

Potterspury Lodge Sch

White Rose Farm

Brookfields Farm

Castle Barn

Moor End

HIGHCROFT CL

VICARAGE RD

WOODV CRESS

BROWNSFIELD RD

DRUCE END

MANOR WY

LIME RD

HESKETH RD

SCHOOL LA

ORCHARD CL

MARKET RD

MOUNT PLEASANT

HIGH ST

Manor Farm

PH

A5

Manor Farm

Yardley Gobion CE Prim Sch

HORTONSFIELD RD

CHESTNUT RD

BUDGE RD

EASTFIELD

Yardley Gobion

MALBOROUGH WAY

5

Oakley Spinney

44

NN12

Yardley Rd

4

East Waterslade Copse

Assart Farm

BEECH HOUSE DR

Beech House Farm

3

TOWCESTER DR

Wakefield Gdns

Nursery

Sunnyside Farm PH

BLACKWELL END

THE ORCHARD

SANDE RS LA

OAK VW

MEADOW VIEW

WOODS

COACH YD

CHURCH END

CARGH END

Greystone Lodge

KENNELLS DR

Wakefield Farm

WATLING ST

DUCHESS GDNS

HIGH ST

BROWNSWOOD DR

HOMESTEAD

COACH LA

CHURCH LA

FURTHO LA

GRAFTON CL

43

Dairy Quarter

Main Drive Cottages

MAIN DR

ELMFIELD CL

MEN'S WAY

CHETTLE PL

WORTH

POUNDFIELD RD

CHURCH WAY

Potterspury

John Hellins Prim Sch

PO

Potterspury House

MK19

2

Puxley Farm

Dairy Farm

1

Redmoor Copse

Cherrytree Lodge

A5

42

74 A B 75 C D 76 E F

17
31

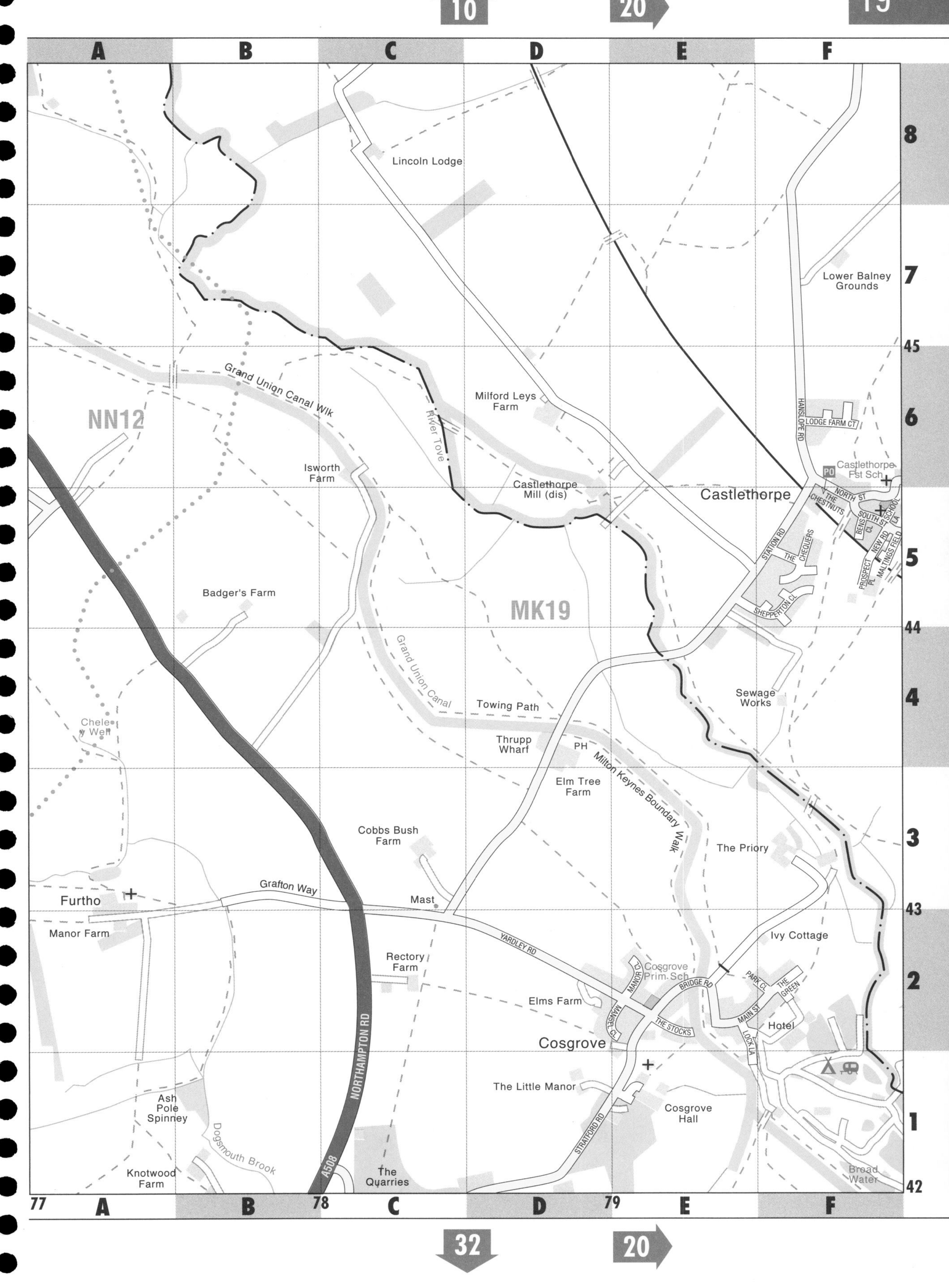

A B C D E F

8

7

45

6

Lincoln Lodge

Lower Balney
Grounds

NN12

Grand Union Canal Wlk

River Tove

Milford Leys
Farm

Isworth
Farm

Castlethorpe
Mill (dis)

Castlethorpe

HANSLOPE RD

LODGE FARM CT

PO
Castlethorpe
Fst Sch

THE CHESTNUTS

NORTH ST

SOUTH ST

NEW RD

SCHOOL LA

MALTINGS FIELD

PROSPECT PL

BROIS RD

STATION RD

THE CHEQUERS

SHEPPERTON CL

MK19

Badger's Farm

44

Sewage
Works

5

4

Grand Union Canal

Towing Path

Chele
y Well

Thrupp
Wharf

PH

Milton Keynes Boundary Walk

The Priory

3

Cobbs Bush
Farm

Elm Tree
Farm

43

Furtho

Grafton Way

Mast

Ivy Cottage

Manor Farm

YARDLEY RD

NORTHAMPTON RD

Rectory
Farm

Cosgrove
Prim. Sch

MANOR RD

Cosgrove

Elms Farm

BRIDGE RD

PARK CL

THE GREEN

Hotel

MAIN ST

LOCK LA

THE STOCKS

2

Ash
Pole
Spinney

The Little Manor

STRATFORD RD

Cosgrove
Hall

Broad
Water

1

Dogsmouth Brook

A508

Knotwood
Farm

The
Quarries

77 A B 78 C D 79 E F 42

19
11

| A | B | C | D | E | F |

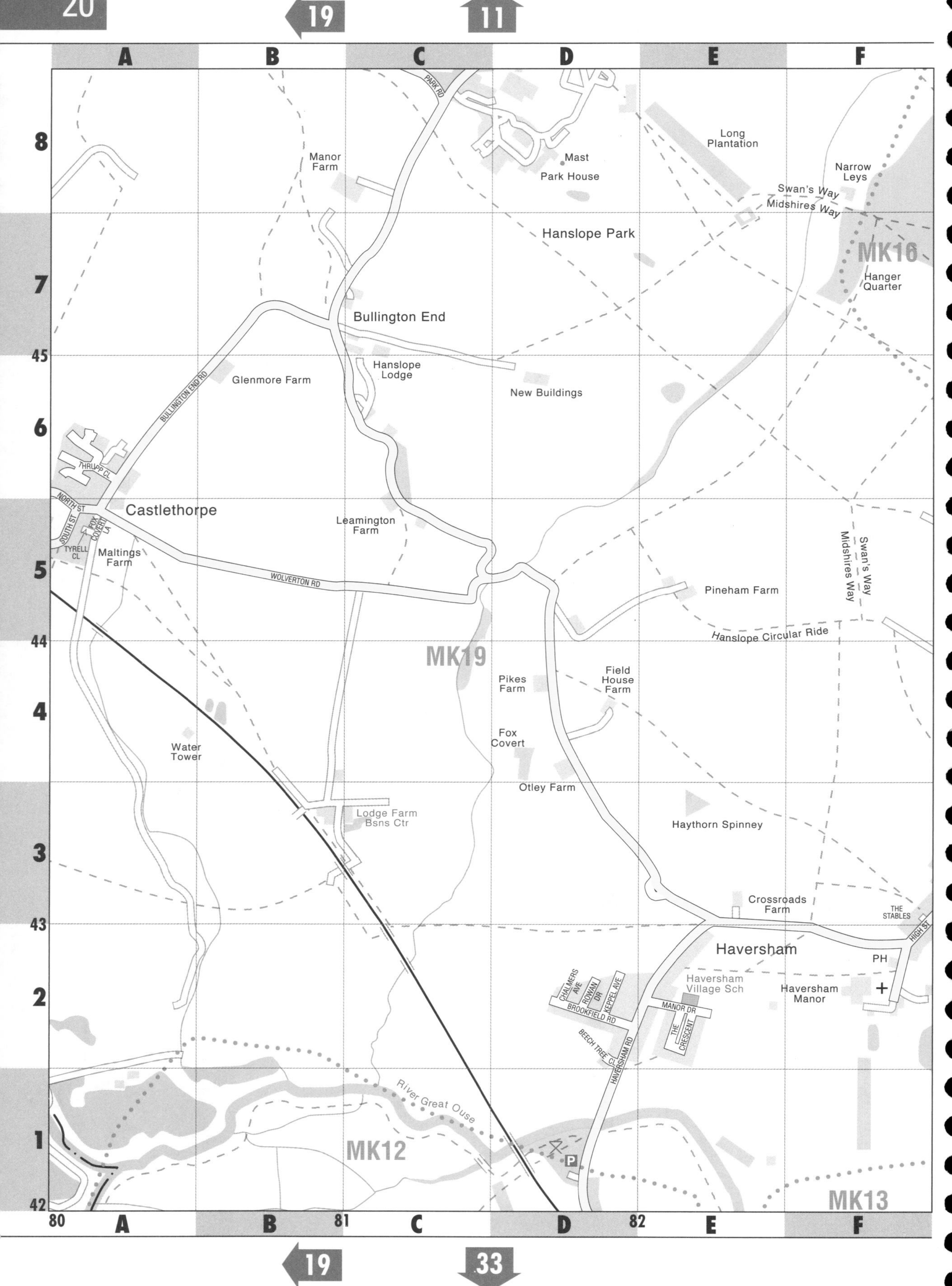

8

Manor Farm

Long Plantation

Mast
Park House

Narrow Leys

Swan's Way
Midshires Way

Hanslope Park

MK16

7

Hanger Quarter

Bullington End

45

Glenmore Farm

Hanslope Lodge

New Buildings

6

BULLINGTON END RD

THRUPP CL

NORTH ST

HIGH ST

Castlethorpe

FOX
COVERT
LA

Leamington Farm

TYRELL CL

Maltings Farm

5

WOLVERTON RD

Pineham Farm

Swan's Way
Midshires Way

44

MK19

Hanslope Circular Ride

Pikes Farm

Field House Farm

4

Water Tower

Fox Covert

Otley Farm

Lodge Farm
Bsns Ctr

Haythorn Spinney

3

Crossroads Farm

THE STABLES

43

Haversham

HIGH ST

PH

2

CHALMERS AVE

ROMAN DR

KEPPEL AVE

Haversham Village Sch

Haversham Manor

+

BROOKFIELD RD

MANOR DR

THE CRESCENT

BEECH TREE CL

HAVERSHAM RD

River Great Ouse

1

P

MK12

MK13

42

| 80 | A | | B | 81 | C | | D | 82 | E | | F |

19
33

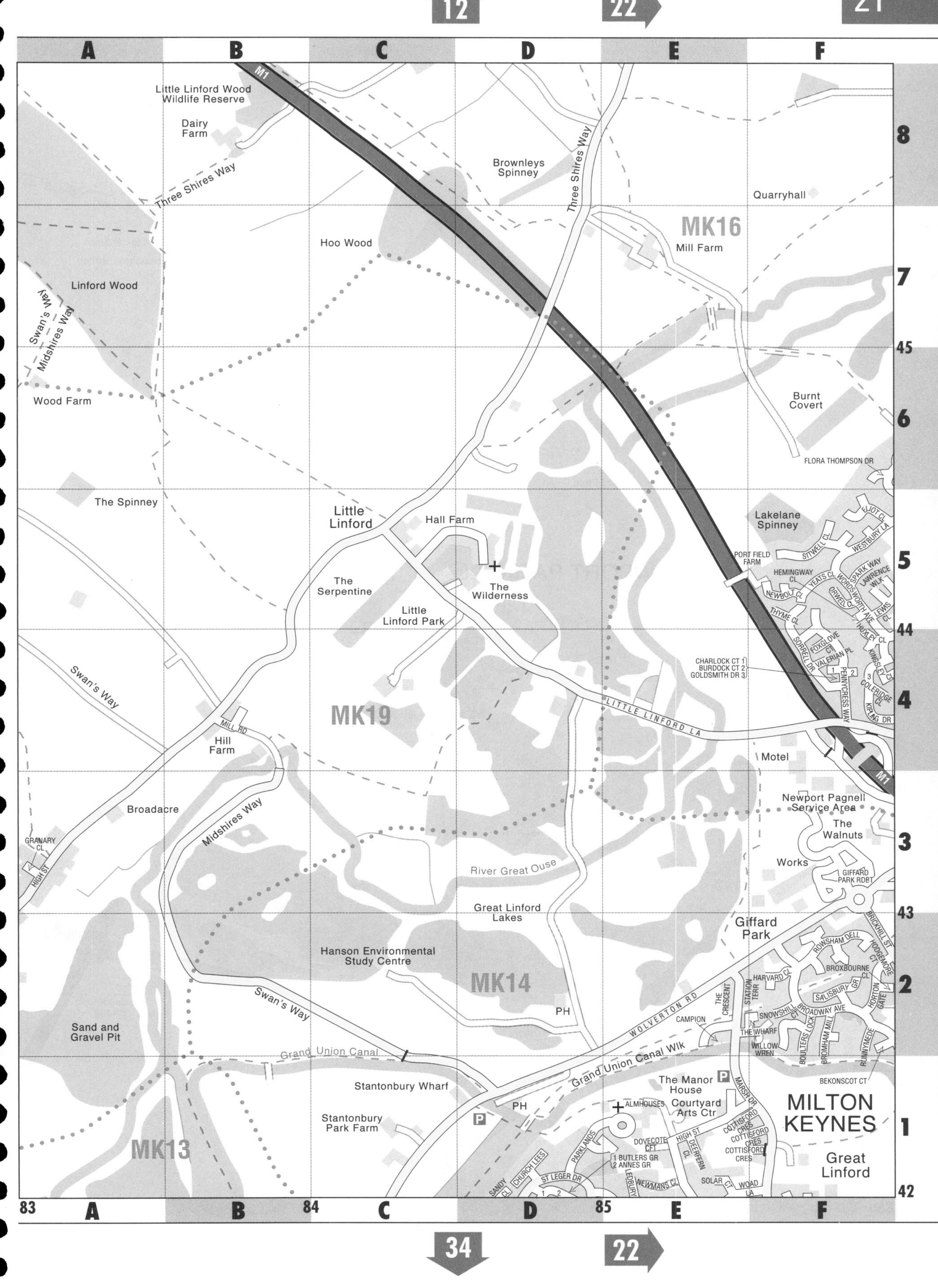
12
22
A
B
C
D
E
F
8
7
45
6
5
44
4
3
43
2
1
42
83
84
85
M1
Little Linford Wood
Wildlife Reserve
Dairy
Farm
Three Shires Way
Brownleys
Spinney
Quarryhall
MK16
Mill Farm
Hoo Wood
Linford Wood
Swan's Way
Midshires Way
Wood Farm
Burnt
Covert
FLORA THOMPSON DR
The Spinney
Little
Linford
Hall Farm
Lakelane
Spinney
The
Serpentine
The
Wilderness
Little
Linford Park
PORT FIELD
FARM
MK19
LITTLE LINFORD LA
MILL RD
Hill
Farm
Motel
Broadacre
Newport Pagnell
Service Area
The
Walnuts
GRANARY
CL
HIGH ST
Works
GIFFARD
PARK RDBT
River Great Ouse
Great Linford
Lakes
Giffard
Park
Hanson Environmental
Study Centre
MK14
PH
Sand and
Gravel Pit
WOLVERTON RD
CAMPION
THE CRESCENT
STATION TERR
THE WHARF
WILLOW WREN
Grand Union Canal
Grand Union Canal Wlk
Stantonbury Wharf
The Manor
House
Courtyard
Arts Ctr
ALMHOUSES
BEKONSCOT CT
MILTON
KEYNES
Stantonbury
Park Farm
MK13
Great
Linford
CHARLOCK CT 1
BURDOCK CT 2
GOLDSMITH DR 3
34
22

21
13

A B C D E F

8
7
45
6
5
44
4
3
43
2
1
42

Quarryhall Farm
Ash Spinney
B526
CHICHELEY HILL
Bridge House
Sherington Bridge
SHERINGTON RD
Inn Farm
Lathbury
CHURCH LA
INN FARM CT
THE CLOSE
Lathbury Park
New Woad Farm
Works
Kickle's Farm
NORTHAMPTON RD
River Great Ouse
FLORA THOMPSON DR
THOMAS DR
Bury Field
LARKIN CL
AUDEN CL
HEANEY CL
HOUSMAN CL
WODEHOUSE WLK
SHAKESPEARE CL
Lakes Lane Farm
CARROLL CL
Woad Farm
CHRISTIE CL
HERRIOT CL
SWIFT CL
LEWIS CL
Portfields Comb Sch
SHAW CL
WESTBURY LA
SCOTT DR
NEWPORT PAGNELL
LAKES LA
MK16
LAWNSMEAD GDNS
NORTH SQ
MILL ST
1 POLLYS YD
2 OUSEBANK ST
Cemy
Tickford Abbey
CHARLES WAY
QUEENS AVE
WINDSOR AVE
UNION ST
PO
COOPERS CT
HIGH ST
ST JOHN'S TERR
RIVER SIDE
CHURCH PAS
Liby
PRIORY CL
PRIORY ST
CASTLE MEADOW
ABBEY TERR
PARK VIEW
MILTON RD
KEYNES CL
CARLTON CL
LAGONDA CL
1 MORRIS WLK
2 COLLINS WLK
KINGSLEY CL
MARLOW DR
LAMB CL
WORDSWORTH AVE
BROWNING CL
BURNS CL
COWPER CL
LONGFELLOW DR
STILEY CL
WESTBURY CL
DOVECOTE
COURTHOUSE MEWS
BURY CL
TH
PAGG'S CT
CEDARS WAY
BURY ST
TICKFORD ARC
ST JOHN ST
CHURCH VIEW
Works
TICKFORD ST
CHICHELEY ST
Tickford End
CARLYLE CL
KEATS CL
BYRON DR
TENNYSON DR
ASH HILL RD
FOXGATE
PARK AVE
THE LODGE PK
BASSETT CT
BURY AVE
CROSS CT
SPRING GDNS
LOVAT ST
SILVER ST
RIVER CL
WATERHOUSE
DOVE CL
RIBBLE CL
ST MARGARETS CL
HIGHFIELD CL
IVY CL
LEARY CRES
THE CAMPINS
KIPLING DR
CHAUCER CL
MASEFIELD CL
DRYDEN CL
LINFORD AVE
GREENFIELD RD
PORTFIELDS RD
MANOR RD
SHIPLEY RD
WOLVERTON RD
30
SHEPPARDS CL
THE GREEN
Cedars Comb Sch
CALDECOTE ST
1 STATION RD
2 BEACONSFIELD PL
3 TANKARD CL
4 ST PAULS YD
DERWENT CL
TEIGN CL
TRENT DR
DART CL
AVON CL
SEVERN DR
BLYTHE CL
MEDWAY CL
CHARTWELL RD
WORCESTER CL
LITTLE LINFORD LA
NASEBY CT
CROMWELL AVE
BUCKINGHAM CT
ALMOND CL
LIME CL
BROAD ST
GREEN FARM RD
FRADERICA COTTS
BROCKWELL
NENE CL
THAMES CL
WELLAND DR
STOUR CL
WAVENEY CL
Swim Pool
VANTAGE CT
NORTH CRAWLEY RD
HILL VIEW
BRAMLEY MDWS
PIPPIN CT
BEECH CL
CHERRY RD
BALDWIN CRES
BARNSBURY GDNS
WHITTON WAY
MARSH END RD
BOWES CL
RICHMOND WAY
Tickford Park Prim Sch
DEBEN CL
THURNE CL
Cemy
LOVAT MDW CL
PLOVER CL
HOWARD WAY
M1
GREENLANDS CL
WALNUT CL
CYPRESS
WHITETHORNS
ANNESLEY RD
THE GROVE
NORWOOD LA
The Green
GOODMAN
HOLLAND WAY
WILLEN RD
Ind Est
1 SAMUEL CL
2 ADDENBROOKES
3 PAPWORTH CL
B526 LONDON RD
PENNY PARK RD
HOPTON GR
DOWNS FIELD
River Ouzel or Lovat
WOLVERTON RD
MILES CL
HORNBEAM
CARRINGTON RD 1
SANDRINGHAM CT 2
BALMORAL CT 3
WHADDON RD
PURCELL DR
KENNINGTON CL
GREEN PARK DR
The Kingfisher Ctr
MOUNTSFIELD CL
OSTERLEY CL
GLADSTONE CL
Ousedale Sch
Green Park Sch
SUNRIDGE CL
PETERSHAM CL
Sewage Works
A509
TANNERS DR
ELTHORNE WAY
HYDE CL
WATERLOW CL
RUSKIN CT
STANMORE GDNS
GREENWICH GDNS
FRIARY GDNS
ALEXANDRA DR
RANELAGH GDNS
A422
Ind Est
BURGESS GDNS
SYON GDNS
AVERY CT
Newport Stables
CALDECOTE LA
MK14
MIDBROOK CT
HARGREAVES NOOK
METCALFE GR
DILWICH CL
TABARD GDNS
TONGWELL LA
Caldecotemill Bridge
Weirs
Caldecote Mill
Giffard Park Prim Sch
HUNTSMAN GR
Giffard Park
SMEATON CL
BRICKHILL ST
BROADWAY AVE
PO
WEDGWOOD AVE
Blakelands
TELFORD WAY
BESSEMER CT
MONKS WAY
A509
Grand Union Canal
HAINAULT AVE
MINTON CL
Tongwell Lake
GLENFIELD
Caldecote
Caldecote Farm
TA Ctr
KNEBWORTH GATE
Ind Est
VERMONT PL
Ind Est
HARLE STONE CT
OVERSLEY CT
WHICHFORD
YEOMANS DR
DELAWARE DR
MICHIGAN DR
A422
MK15
M1

86 87 88

A B C D E F

21
35

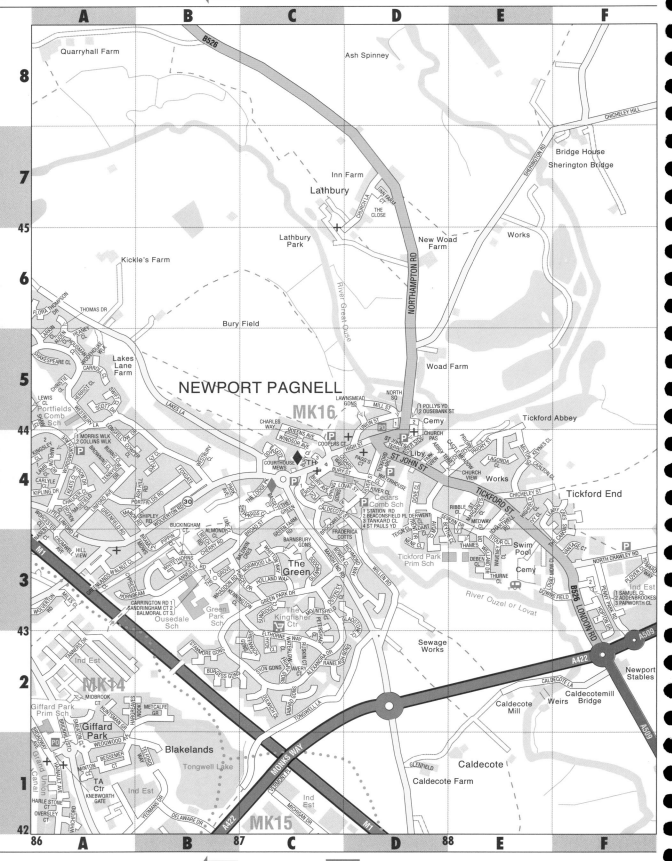

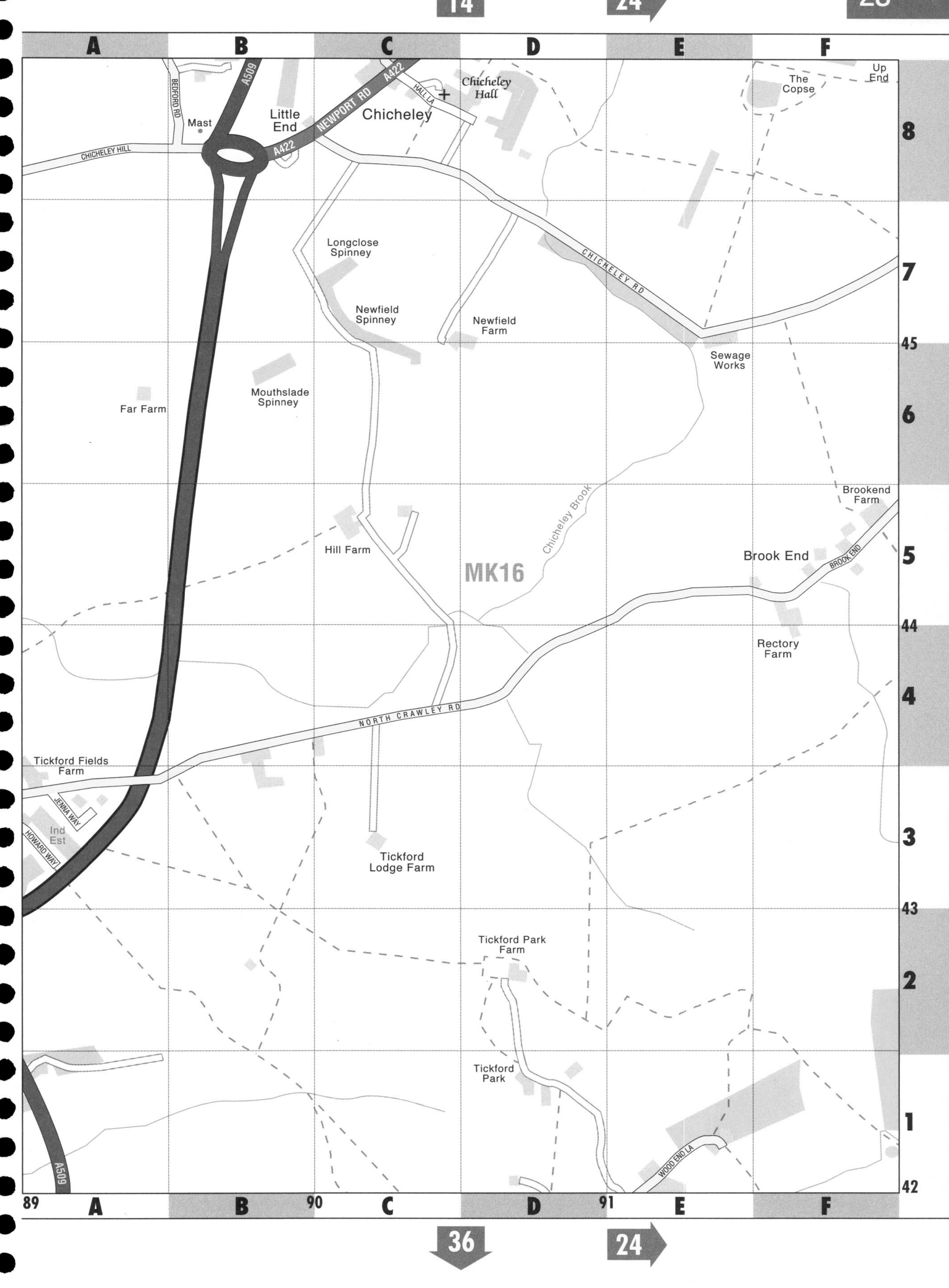
14
24
A
B
C
D
E
F
A509
BEDFORD RD
Mast
Little End
A422
NEWPORT RD
Chicheley
HALL LA
Chicheley Hall
The Copse
Up End
CHICHELEY HILL
Longclose Spinney
CHICHELEY RD
Newfield Spinney
Newfield Farm
Sewage Works
Mouthslade Spinney
Far Farm
Brookend Farm
Chicheley Brook
Hill Farm
MK16
Brook End
BROOK END
Rectory Farm
NORTH CRAWLEY RD
Tickford Fields Farm
JENNA WAY
Ind Est
HOWARD WAY
Tickford Lodge Farm
Tickford Park Farm
Tickford Park
WOOD END LA
A509
8
7
45
6
5
44
4
3
43
2
1
42
89
90
91
36
24

23
15

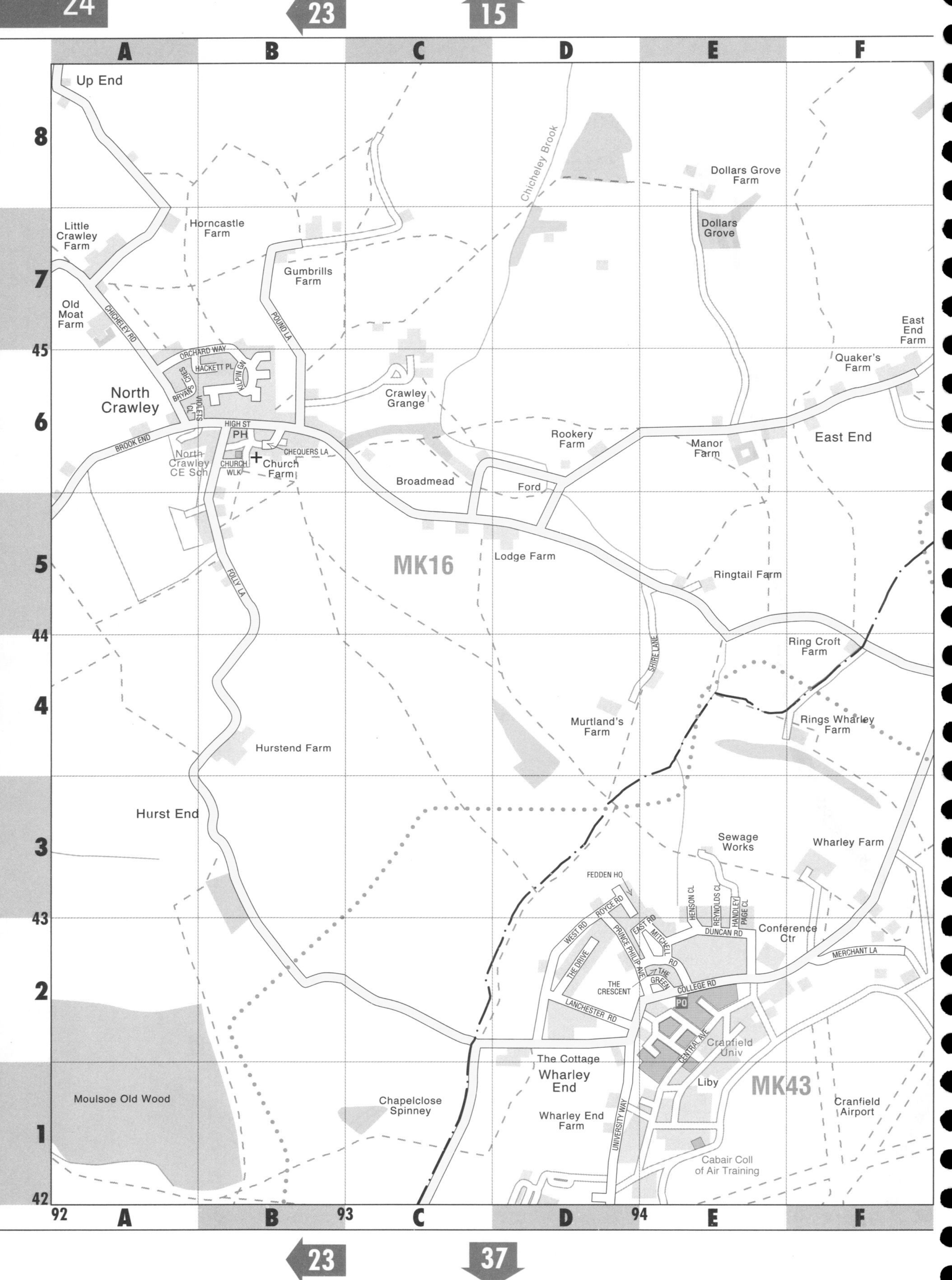
A
B
C
D
E
F
8
7
45
6
5
44
4
3
43
2
1
42
92
93
94
Up End
Little Crawley Farm
Horncastle Farm
Gumbrills Farm
Old Moat Farm
Chicheley Brook
Dollars Grove Farm
Dollars Grove
East End Farm
Quaker's Farm
CHICHELEY RD
POUND LA
ORCHARD WAY
HACKETT PL
KILPIN GN
BRYANS CRES
VIOLETS CL
North Crawley
HIGH ST
PH
BROOK END
North Crawley CE Sch
CHURCH WLK
Church Farm
CHEQUERS LA
Crawley Grange
Rookery Farm
Manor Farm
East End
Broadmead
Ford
MK16
Lodge Farm
Ringtail Farm
FOLLY LA
Ring Croft Farm
SHIRE LANE
Murtland's Farm
Rings Wharley Farm
Hurstend Farm
Hurst End
Sewage Works
Wharley Farm
FEDDEN HO
ROYCE RD
WEST RD
HENSON CL
REYNOLDS CL
HANDLEY PAGE CL
EAST RD
MITCHELL RD
DUNCAN RD
Conference Ctr
PRINCE PHILIP AVE
THE DRIVE
THE GREEN
MERCHANT LA
THE CRESCENT
COLLEGE RD
LANCHESTER RD
PO
CENTRAL AVE
Cranfield Univ
The Cottage
Wharley End
Liby
MK43
Moulsoe Old Wood
Chapelclose Spinney
Wharley End Farm
UNIVERSITY WAY
Cranfield Airport
Cabair Coll of Air Training

23
37

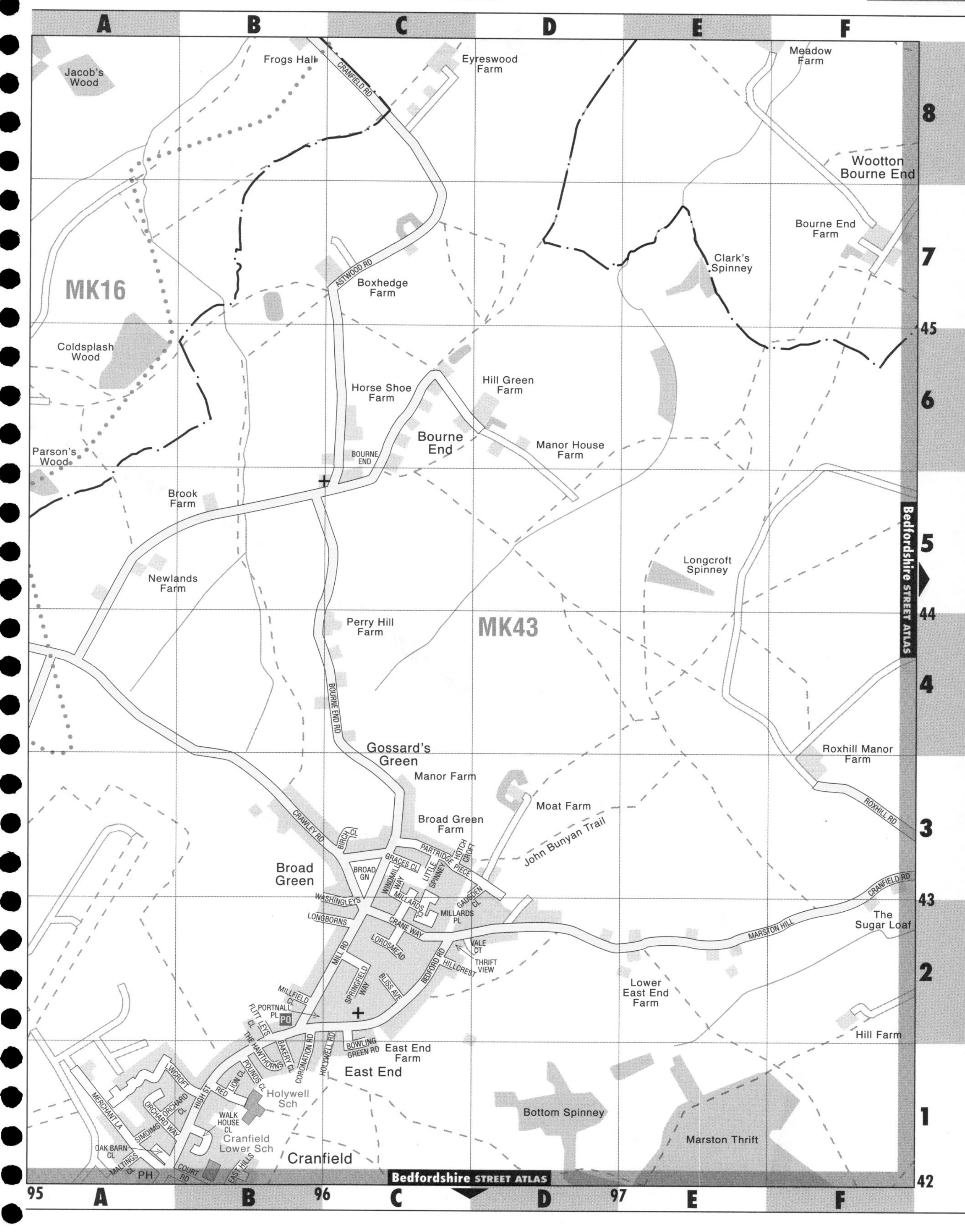

A   B   C   D   E   F

Jacob's Wood

Frogs Hall

CRANFIELD RD

Eyreswood Farm

Meadow Farm

8

Wootton Bourne End

MK16

ASTWOOD RD

Boxhedge Farm

Clark's Spinney

Bourne End Farm

7

45

Coldsplash Wood

Horse Shoe Farm

Hill Green Farm

6

BOURNE END

Bourne End

Manor House Farm

Parson's Wood

Brook Farm

Bedfordshire STREET ATLAS

Newlands Farm

Longcroft Spinney

5

44

Perry Hill Farm

MK43

BOURNE END RD

4

Gossard's Green

Manor Farm

Roxhill Manor Farm

CRAWLEY RD

Broad Green Farm

Moat Farm

ROXHILL RD

John Bunyan Trail

3

BIRCH CL

GRACES CLI

PARTRIDGE PIECE

LITTLE SPINNEY

HATCH CROFT

CRANFIELD RD

Broad Green

WINDMILL WAY

BROAD GN

MILLARDS CL

GADDEN CL

MARSTON HILL

The Sugar Loaf

43

WASHINGLEYS

MILLARDS PL

LONGBORNS

CRANE WAY

LORDSMEAD

VALE CT

2

MILL RD

BEXFORD HILL

HILLCREST

THRIFT VIEW

Lower East End Farm

Hill Farm

MILLFIELD CL

SPRINGFIELD WAY

BLISS AVE.

PORTNALL PL

PO

FLIT LEYS CL

ROWLING GREEN RD

East End Farm

BAKERY CL

HOLWELL RD

MERCHANT LA

LINCROFT

THE HAWTHORNS

CORONATION RD

POUNDS CL

HIGH ST

LUTON RD

East End

Bottom Spinney

1

OAK BARN CL

ORCHARD WAY

STMTHMS CL

ORCHARD CL

WALK HOUSE CL

Holywell Sch

Marston Thrift

MALTINGS

PH

COURT RD

Cranfield Lower Sch

EAST HILLS

Cranfield

42

95   A   B   96   C   D   97   E   F

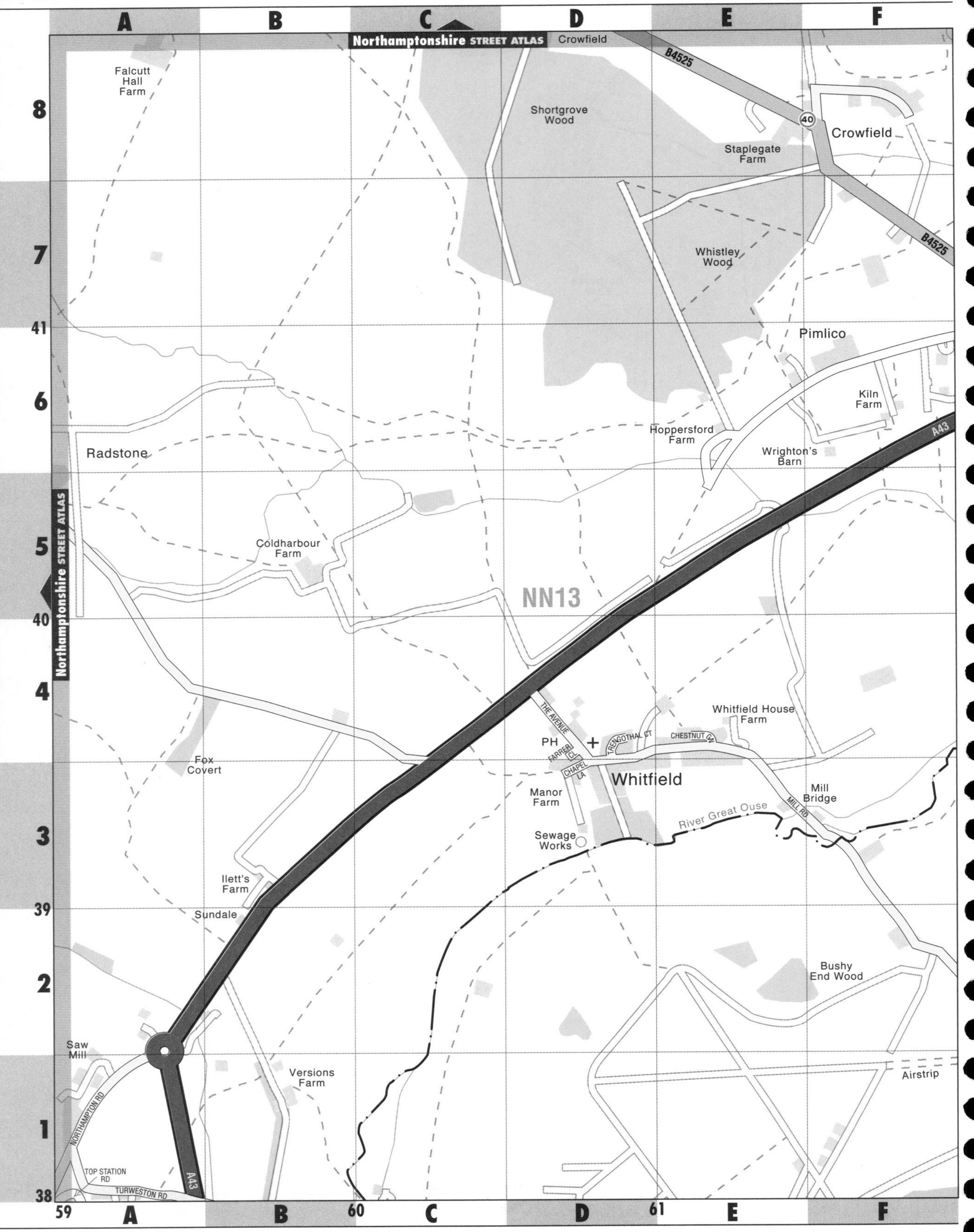

Crowfield

Falcutt Hall Farm

Shortgrove Wood

B4525

40

Crowfield

Staplegate Farm

B4525

Whistley Wood

Pimlico

Kiln Farm

Radstone

Hoppersford Farm

Wrighton's Barn

A43

Coldharbour Farm

NN13

Fox Covert

THE AVENUE

Whitfield House Farm

PH

FARRER CL

TRENGOTHAL CT

CHESTNUT CL

CHAPEL LA

Whitfield

Manor Farm

Mill Bridge

MILL RD

Sewage Works

River Great Ouse

Ilett's Farm

Sundale

Bushy End Wood

Saw Mill

Versions Farm

Airstrip

NORTHAMPTON RD

A43

TOP STATION RD

TURWESTON RD

A B C D E F

8 7 41 6 5 40 4 3 39 2 1 38

59 60 61

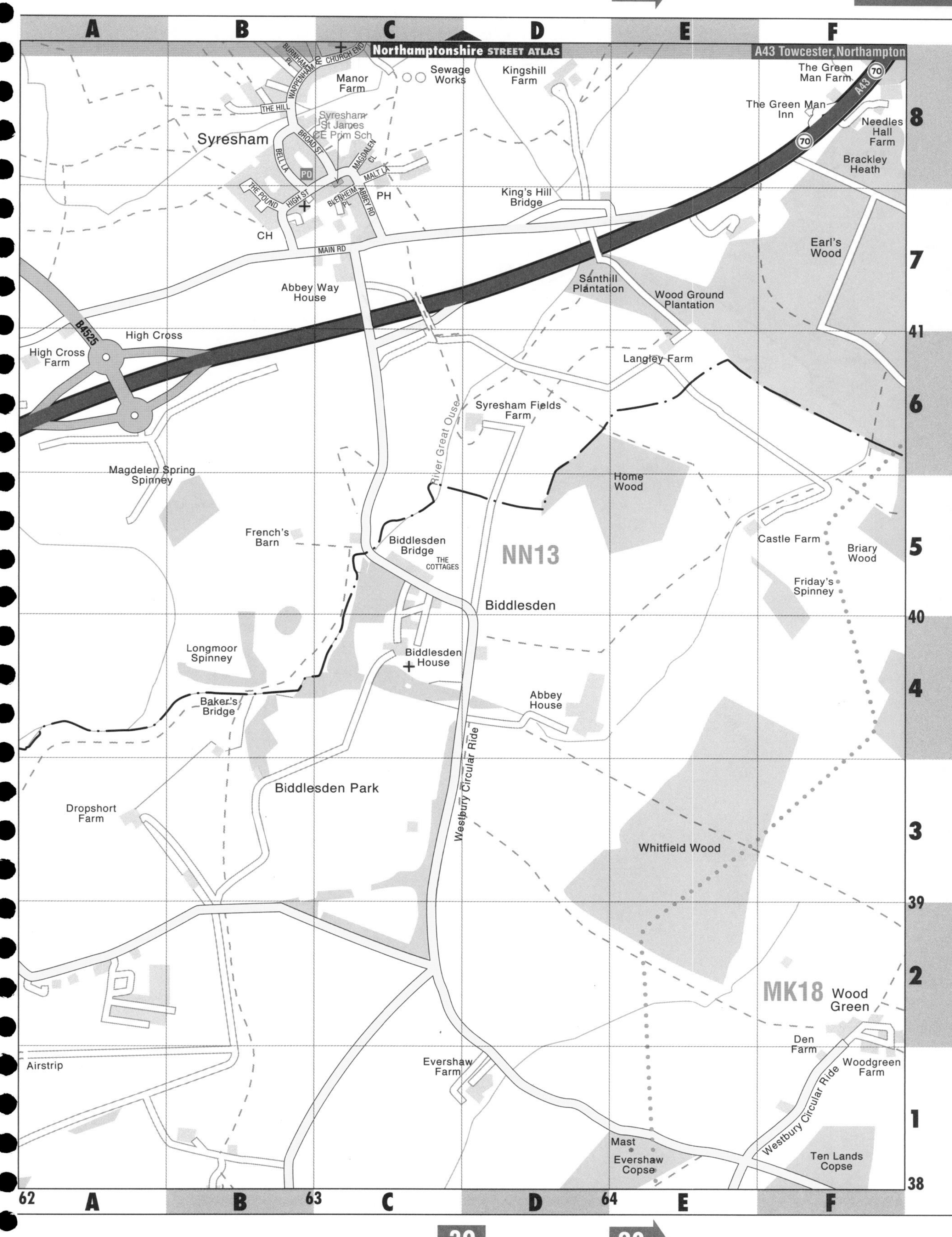

28

Northamptonshire STREET ATLAS

A43 Towcester, Northampton

Syresham

A · B · C · D · E · F

8 · 7 · 41 · 6 · 5 · 40 · 4 · 3 · 39 · 2 · 1 · 38

Manor Farm
Sewage Works
Kingshill Farm
The Green Man Farm
The Green Man Inn
Needles Hall Farm
Brackley Heath

Syresham St James CE Prim Sch
BURNHAM PL
WAPPENHAM RD
CHURCH END
THE HILL
BROAD ST
MAGDALEN CL
BELL LA
PO
THE POUND
HIGH ST
MALT LA
ABBEY RD
BLENHEIM PL
PH
CH
MAIN RD

King's Hill Bridge
Earl's Wood

Abbey Way House
Santhill Plantation
Wood Ground Plantation

B4525
High Cross
Langley Farm

High Cross Farm
River Great Ouse
Syresham Fields Farm
Home Wood

Magdelen Spring Spinney
Castle Farm
Briary Wood

French's Barn
Biddlesden Bridge
THE COTTAGES
NN13
Friday's Spinney

Biddlesden
Biddlesden House

Longmoor Spinney
Abbey House

Baker's Bridge

Dropshort Farm
Biddlesden Park
Whitfield Wood

Westbury Circular Ride

MK18 Wood Green
Den Farm
Woodgreen Farm

Airstrip
Evershaw Farm
Westbury Circular Ride
Ten Lands Copse

Mast
Evershaw Copse

62 · A · B · 63 · C · D · 64 · E · F

28

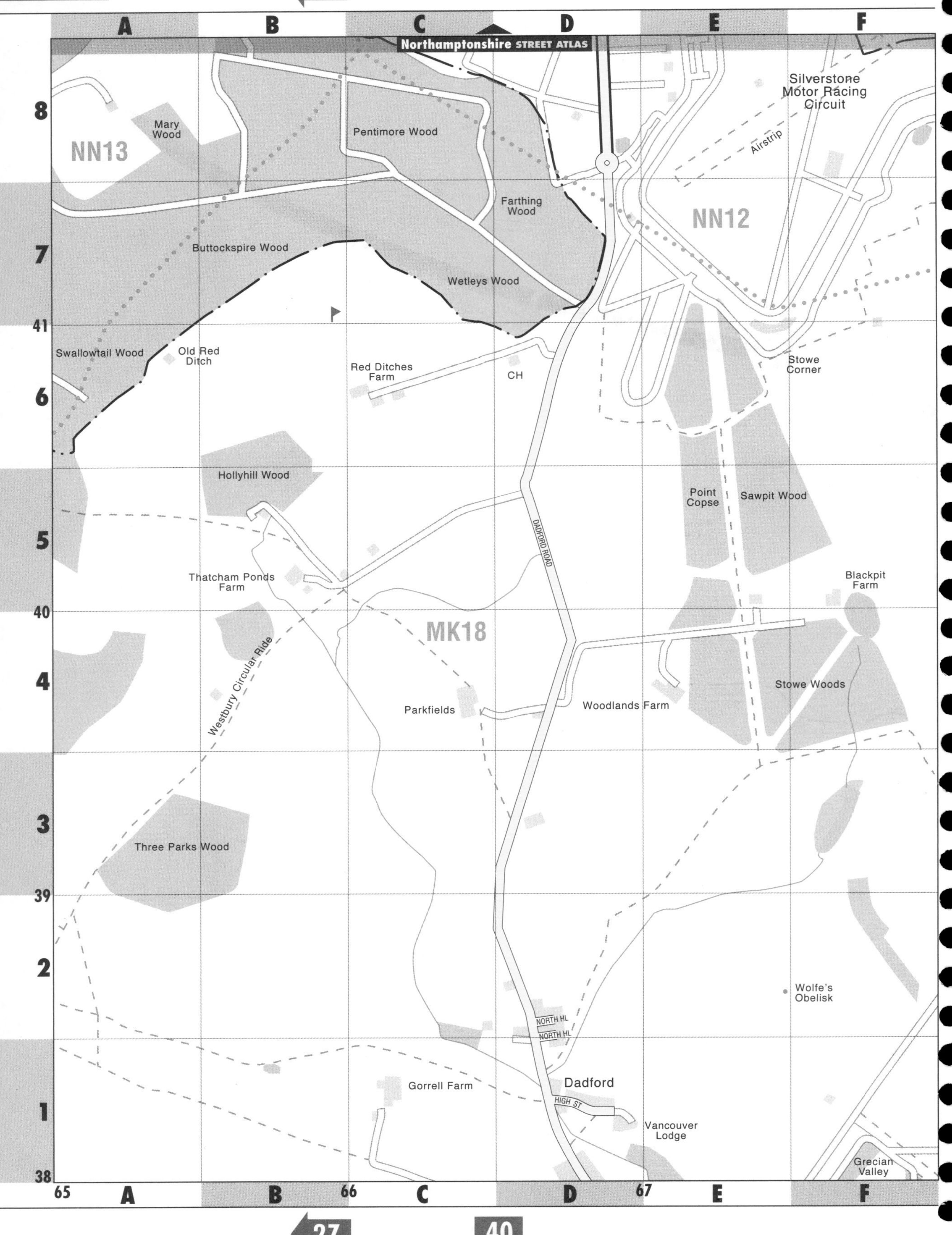

Northamptonshire STREET ATLAS

NN13

Mary Wood

Pentimore Wood

Farthing Wood

Buttockspire Wood

Wetleys Wood

NN12

Silverstone Motor Racing Circuit

Airstrip

Swallowtail Wood

Old Red Ditch

Stowe Corner

Red Ditches Farm

CH

Point Copse

Sawpit Wood

Hollyhill Wood

Blackpit Farm

Thatcham Ponds Farm

MK18

Westbury Circular Ride

DADFORD ROAD

Stowe Woods

Parkfields

Woodlands Farm

Three Parks Wood

Wolfe's Obelisk

NORTH HL

NORTH HL

Gorrell Farm

Dadford

HIGH ST

Vancouver Lodge

Grecian Valley

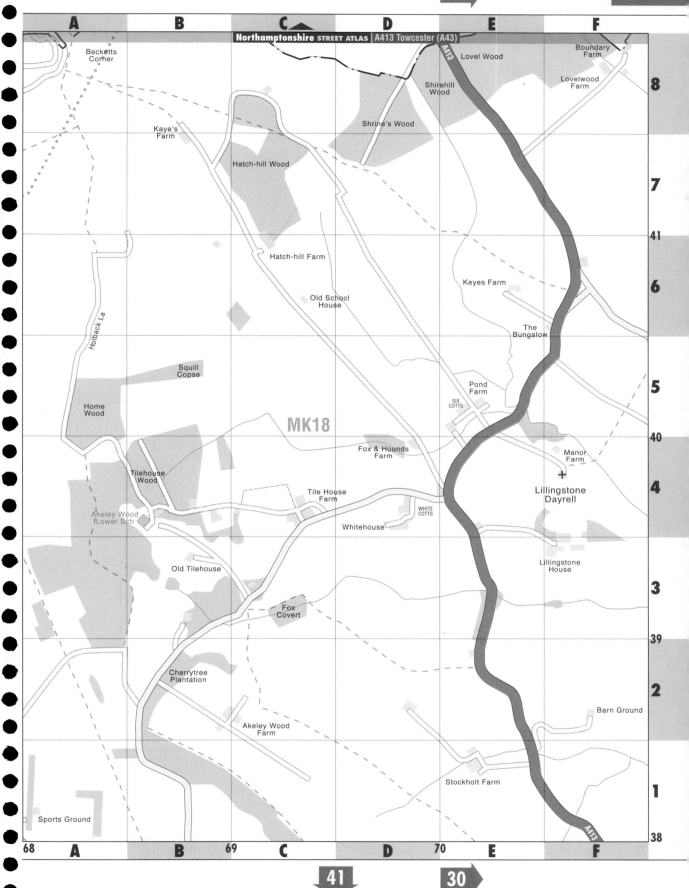

Beckett's Corner

Kaye's Farm

Hatch-hill Wood

Hatch-hill Farm

Old School House

Holback La

Squill Copse

Home Wood

MK18

Tilehouse Wood

Akeley Wood Lower Sch

Tile House Farm

Fox & Hounds Farm

Whitehouse

WHITE COTTS

Old Tilehouse

Fox Covert

Cherrytree Plantation

Akeley Wood Farm

Sports Ground

Lovel Wood

Shirehill Wood

Shrine's Wood

Lovelwood Farm

Boundary Farm

Keyes Farm

The Bungalow

Pond Farm

SIX COTTS

Manor Farm

Lillingstone Dayrell

Lillingstone House

Barn Ground

Stockholt Farm

A413

8

7

41

6

5

40

4

3

39

2

1

38

68   A   B   69   C   D   70   E   F

29
17

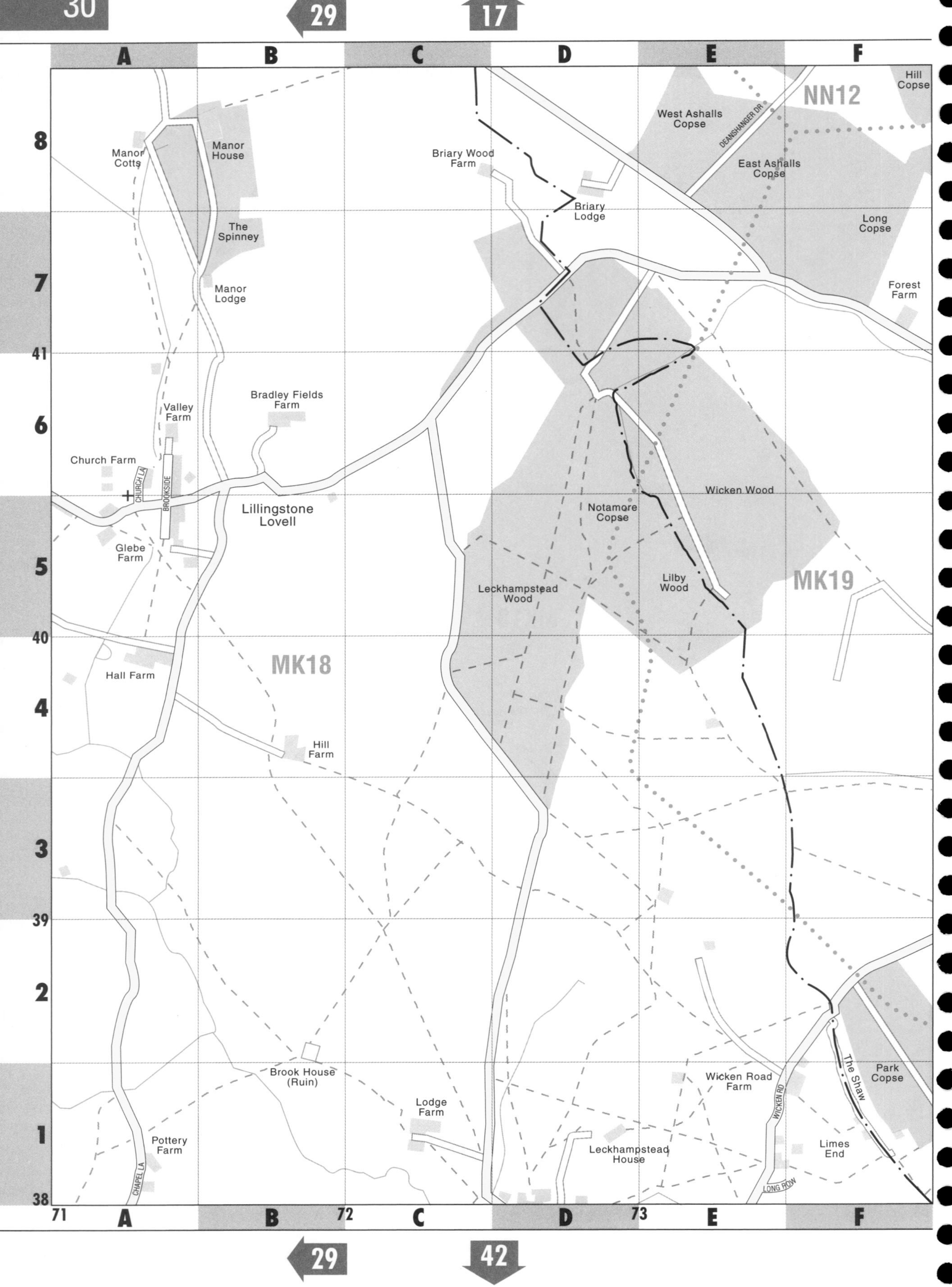
A B C D E F
8 7 41 6 5 40 4 3 39 2 1 38
71 72 73
Hill Copse
NN12
West Ashalls Copse
DEANSHANGER DR
East Ashalls Copse
Long Copse
Forest Farm
Manor Cotts
Manor House
The Spinney
Manor Lodge
Briary Wood Farm
Briary Lodge
Valley Farm
Bradley Fields Farm
Church Farm
CHURCH LA
BROOKSIDE
Lillingstone Lovell
Glebe Farm
Notamore Copse
Wicken Wood
Lilby Wood
Leckhampstead Wood
MK19
MK18
Hall Farm
Hill Farm
Brook House (Ruin)
Lodge Farm
Pottery Farm
CHAPEL LA
Wicken Road Farm
WICKEN RD
The Shaw
Park Copse
Leckhampstead House
Limes End
LONG ROW

29
42

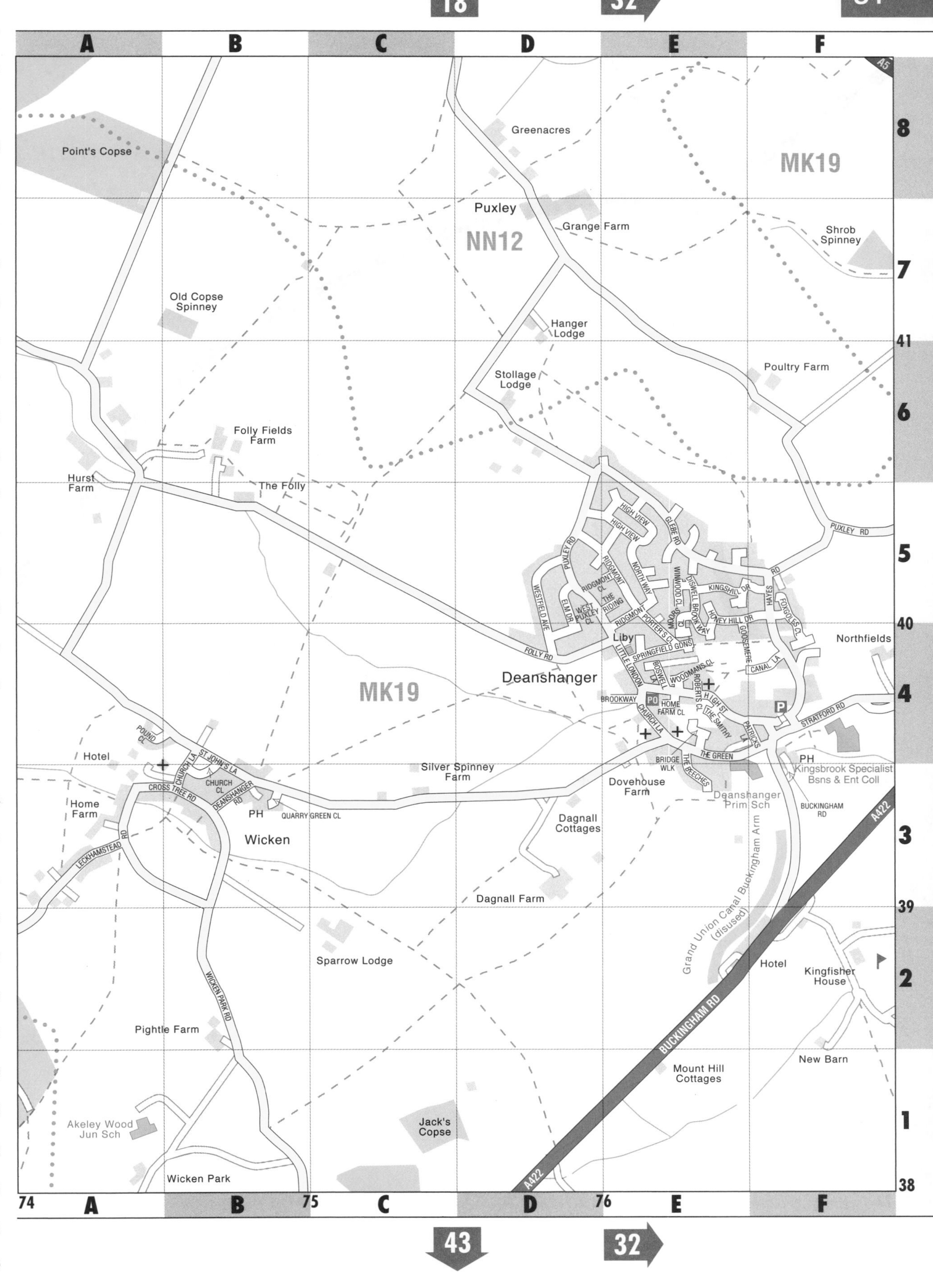

A   B   C   D   E   F

8

MK19

Greenacres

Point's Copse

Puxley

NN12

Grange Farm

Shrob
Spinney

7

Old Copse
Spinney

Hanger
Lodge

41

Poultry Farm

6

Stollage
Lodge

Folly Fields
Farm

Hurst
Farm

The Folly

PUXLEY RD

HIGH VIEW
HIGH VIEW
GLEBE RD
PULLEY RD

5

WESTFIELD AVE
ELM RD
RIDGMONT CL
NORTH WAY
RIDGMONT
WEST PUXLEY CL
THE RIDING
PORTER'S CL
WINWOOD CL
BOSWELL BROOK WAY
KINGSHILL
HAYES RD
FORGOLES CL

FOLLY RD

Liby

SPRINGFIELD GDNS

40

Northfields

MK19

Deanshanger

LITTLE LONDON
BOSWELL CL
WOODMANS CL
ROBERTS CL
HIGH ST
CANAL

4

Silver Spinney
Farm

BROOKWAY
PO
HOME FARM CL
THE SMITHY
PATRICKS
P
STRATFORD RD

Hotel

POUND CL
ST JOHN'S LA
CHURCH LA
CHURCH CL
DEANSHANGER RD
CROSS TREE RD
PH
QUARRY GREEN CL

Home
Farm

Dovehouse
Farm

BRIDGE WLK
THE BEECHES
THE GREEN
PH
Kingsbrook Specialist
Bsns & Ent Coll

LECKHAMSTEAD RD

Wicken

Dagnall
Cottages

Deanshanger
Prim Sch

BUCKINGHAM
RD

3

Dagnall Farm

39

Sparrow Lodge

Grand Union Canal Buckingham Arm
(disused)

Hotel

Kingfisher
House

2

WICKEN PARK RD

A422

Pightle Farm

BUCKINGHAM RD

Mount Hill
Cottages

New Barn

1

Akeley Wood
Jun Sch

Jack's
Copse

A422

Wicken Park

38

74   A   75   C   B   D   76   E   F

31
19

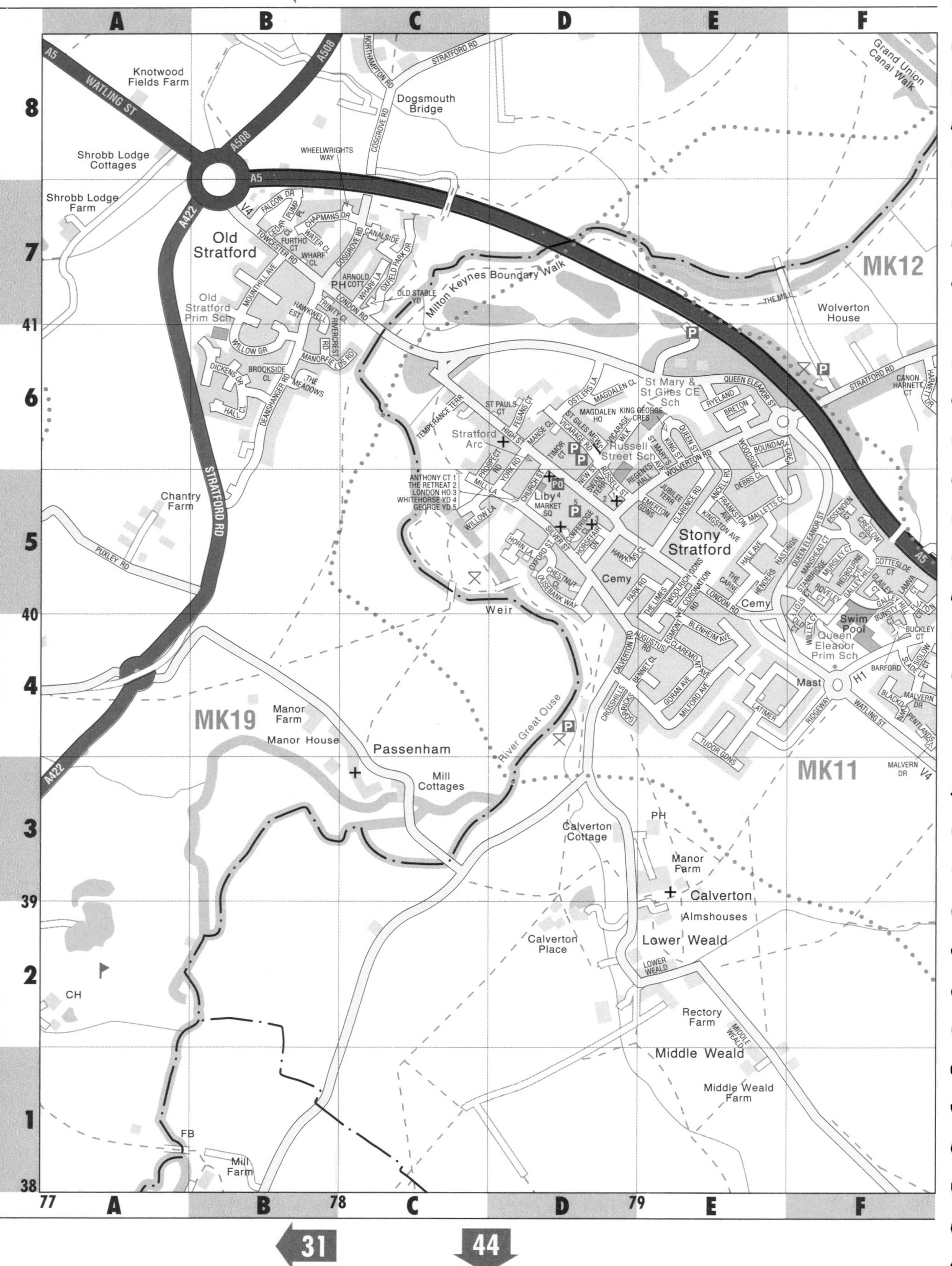
Knotwood Fields Farm
Shrobb Lodge Cottages
Shrobb Lodge Farm
Old Stratford
Old Stratford Prim Sch
Dogsmouth Bridge
Grand Union Canal Walk
Milton Keynes Boundary Walk
MK12
Wolverton House
Chantry Farm
Stratford Arc
St Mary & St Giles CE Sch
Russell Street Sch
Stony Stratford
Cemy
Weir
Swim Pool
Queen Eleanor Prim Sch
Mast
MK19
Manor Farm
Manor House
Passenham
Mill Cottages
River Great Ouse
MK11
Calverton Cottage
Manor Farm
Calverton
Almshouses
Calverton Place
Lower Weald
Rectory Farm
Middle Weald
Middle Weald Farm
CH
FB
Mill Farm
WATLING ST
STRATFORD RD
A5
A508
A422
V4
H1
PUXLEY RD
COSGROVE RD
NORTHAMPTON RD
LONDON RD
QUEEN ELEANOR ST
WOLVERTON RD
CALVERTON RD
RIDGEWAY
ANTHONY CT 1
THE RETREAT 2
LONDON HO 3
WHITEHORSE YD 4
GEORGE YD 5
Liby
PO
PH
Cemy

A B C D E F
8 7 41 6 5 40 4 3 39 2 1 38
77 78 79

31
44

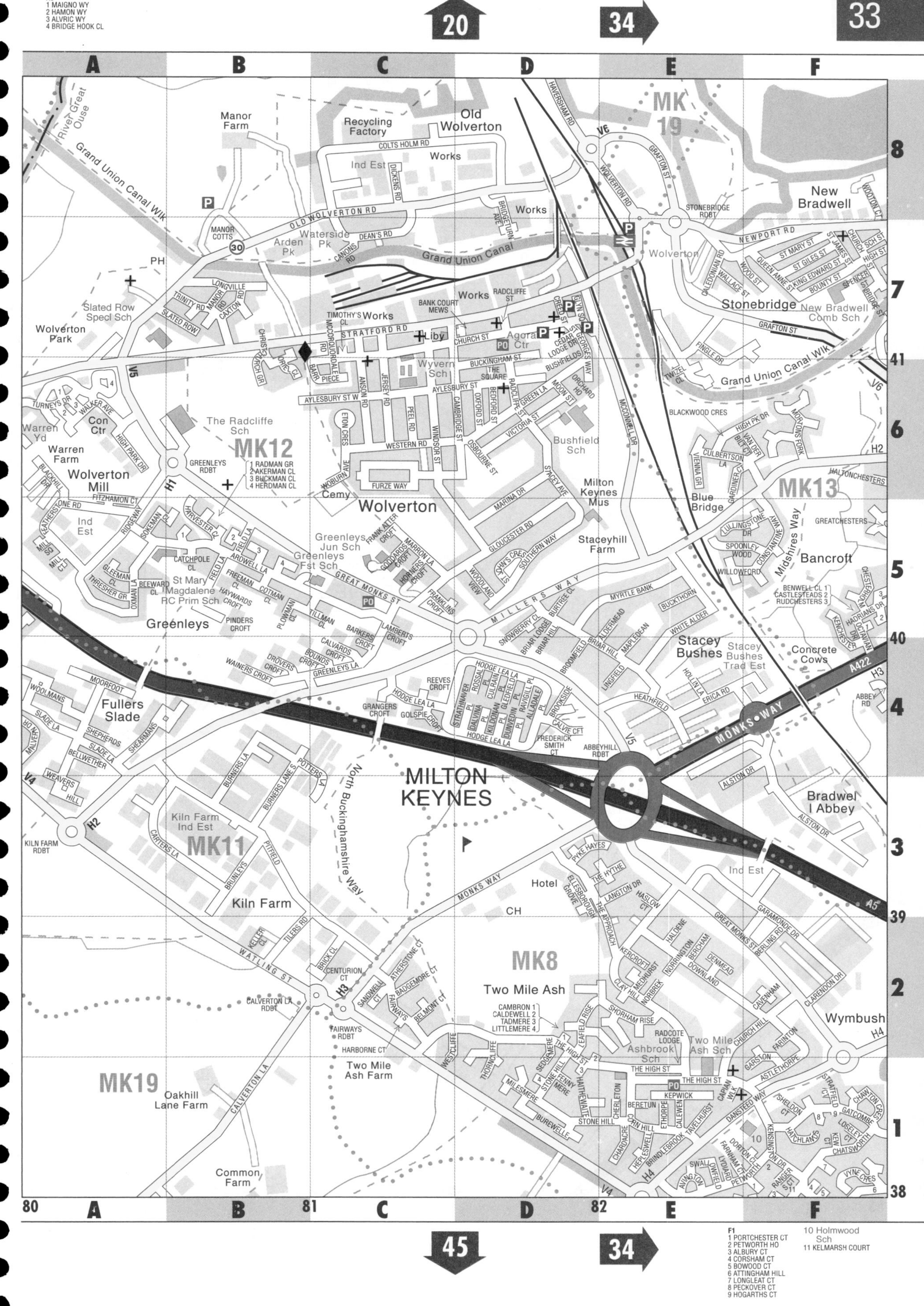

33
21

A B C D E F

8 7 41 6 5 40 4 3 39 2 1 38

River Great Ouse
Grand Union Canal
Grand Union Canal Wlk
Midshires Way
Cemy
Wolverton Rd
Stantonbury
Stantonbury Campus
L Ctr
Wood End Fst Sch
The Gatehouse Sch
Bury Lawn Sch
Great Linford
Great Linford Comb Sch
St Andrew's CE Inf Sch
Pepper Hill Fst Sch
Stanton Mid Sch
Windmill (dis)
Bradville
Monks Way
A422
H3
V8
B4034
Marlborough St
Research Centre
Thornton Chase
St Monica's RC Comb Sch
Brookswarde Comb Sch
Neath Hill
Trad Est
MK14
Linford Wood
Milton Keynes
MK13
Mast
Heelands
Stanton Wood
Priory Com Sch
Heelands Fst Sch
Bradwell
Bradwell Village Sch
YH
Southwood Sch
Downs Barn Sch
Conniburrow
Germander Park Fst Sch
Recn Gd
Stanton Wood Rdbt
Bancroft Rdbt
Bradwell Common
Summerfield Sch
Portway
H5
A509
V6
Rooksley
Trad Est
Racing Circuit
MK8
Midshires Way
Lodge Lake
National Badminton Ctr
Loughton Lodge
MK5
A5
H4
Portway Rdbt
North Grafton Rdbt
Law Cts
MK9
thecentre:mk
Co Off
Liby
Midsummer Pl
Theatre
Xscape
Central Milton Keynes
Milton Keynes Central
Superstore
MK6
Meadfurlong Sch
Penwith Sch
Exchange Ho
Acorn Ho
Witan Gate
Saxon Gate
Silbury Bvd
Midsummer Bvd
Avebury Bvd
South Saxon Rdbt
South Witan Rdbt
South Secklow Rdbt
Belvedere Rdbt
Campbell Park Rdbt
H6
V7

83 A B 84 C D 85 E F

A4
1 RICKYARD CL
2 PROVIDENCE PL
3 VICARGE GDNS
4 ALEXANDRA CT

C2
1 BUCKINGHAM SQ
2 CLARENCE HO

E1
1 APPLEYARD PL
2 RICHARDSON PL
3 LEYLAND PL
4 BARRINGTON MEWS
5 PETERSFIELD GN

F1
1 THE BOUNDARY
2 FISHERMEAD BVD
3 HELSTON PL

33
46

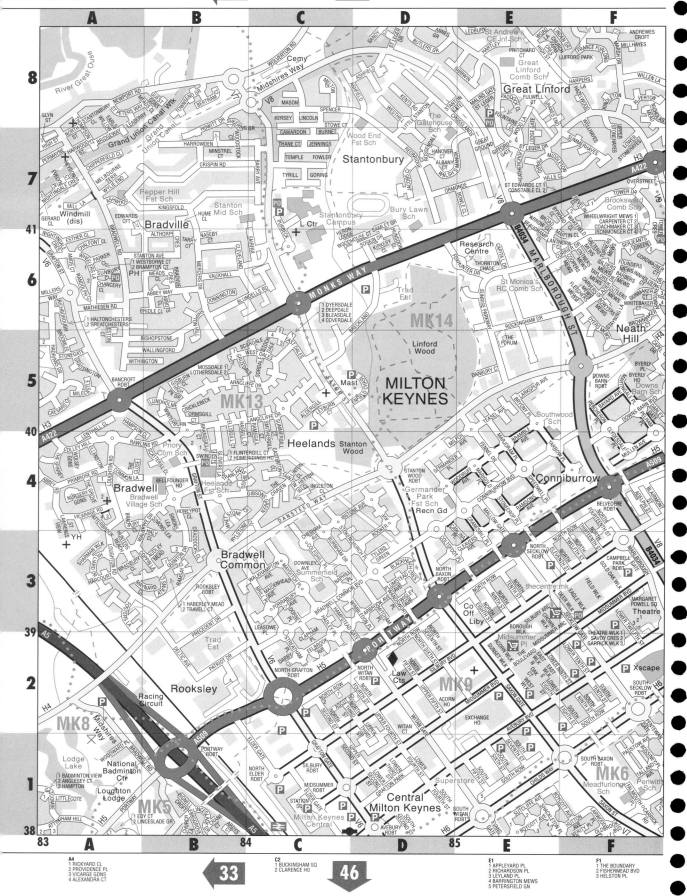

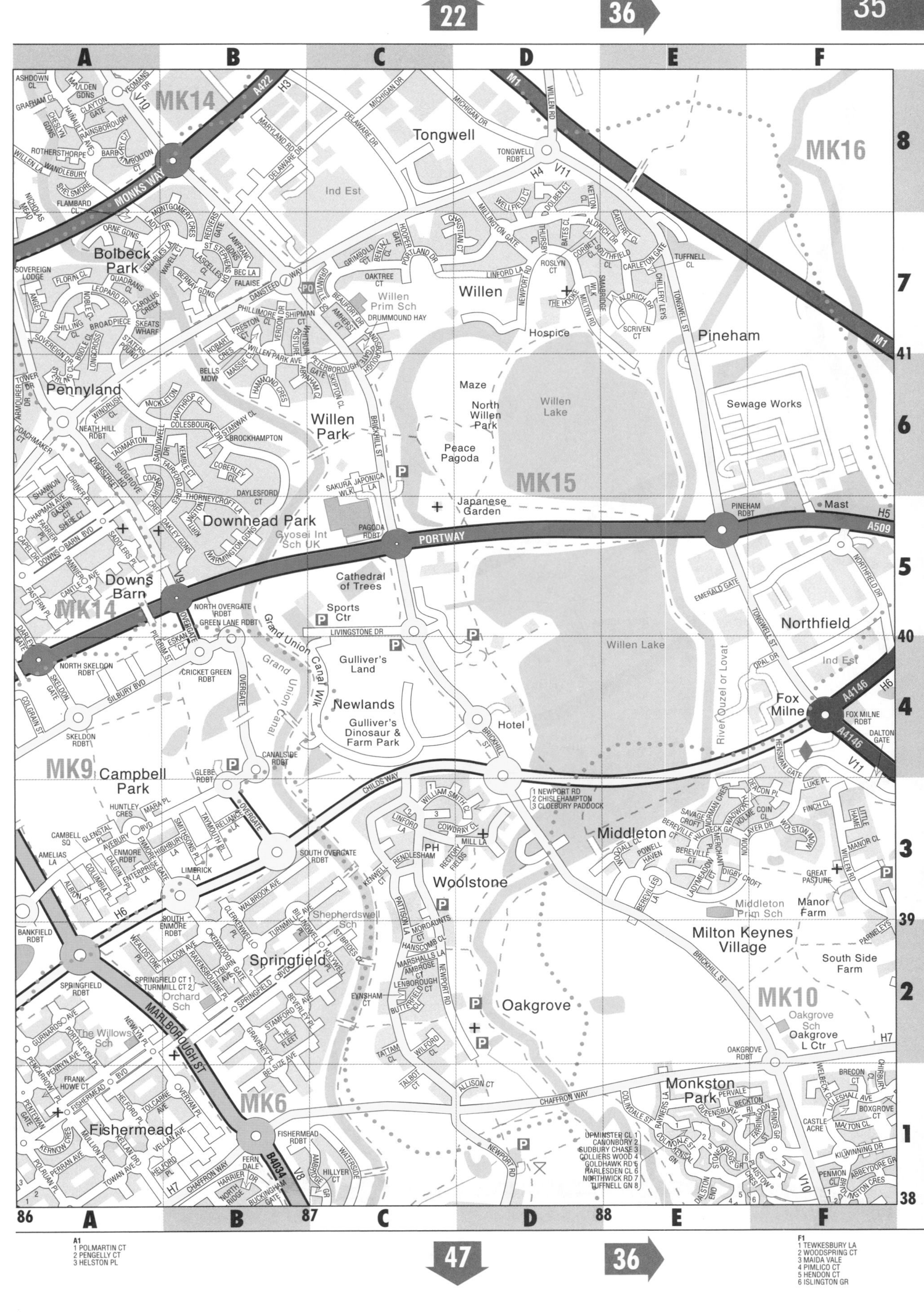

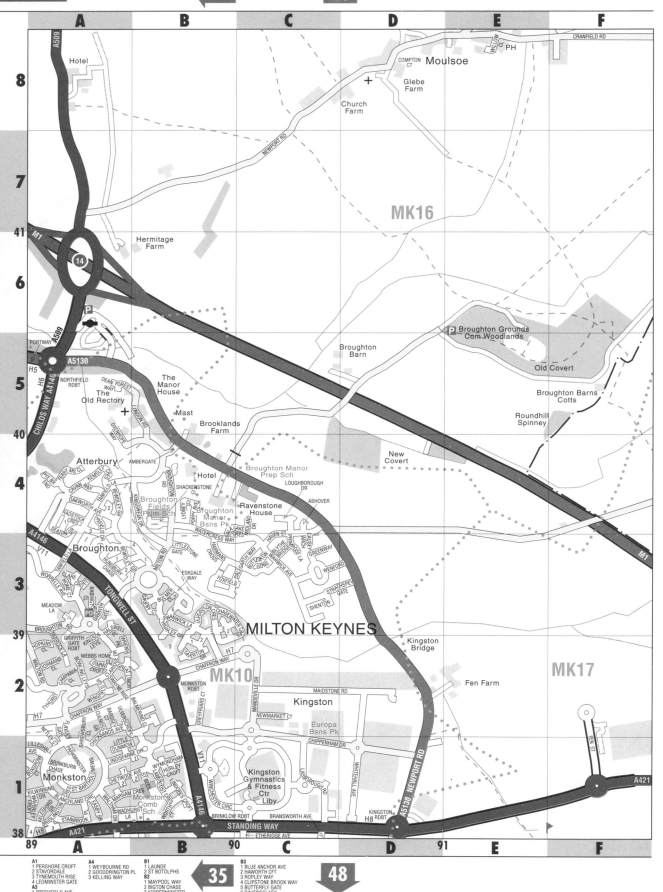

A1
1 PERSHORE CROFT
2 STAVORDALE
3 TYNEMOUTH RISE
4 LEOMINSTER GATE
A3
1 FRESHFIELD AVE
2 PAIGNTON WAY

A4
1 WEYBOURNE RD
2 GOODDRINGTON PL
3 KELLING WAY

B1
1 LAUNDE
2 ST BOTOLPHS
B2
1 MAYPOOL WAY
2 BIGTON CHASE
3 KIDDERMINSTER
WLK

B3
1 BLUE ANCHOR AVE
2 HAWORTH CFT
3 ROPLEY WAY
4 CLIPSTONE BROOK WAY
5 BUTTERFLY GATE
6 RAVENSGLASS
CROFT
7 ARDLEY MEWS

24

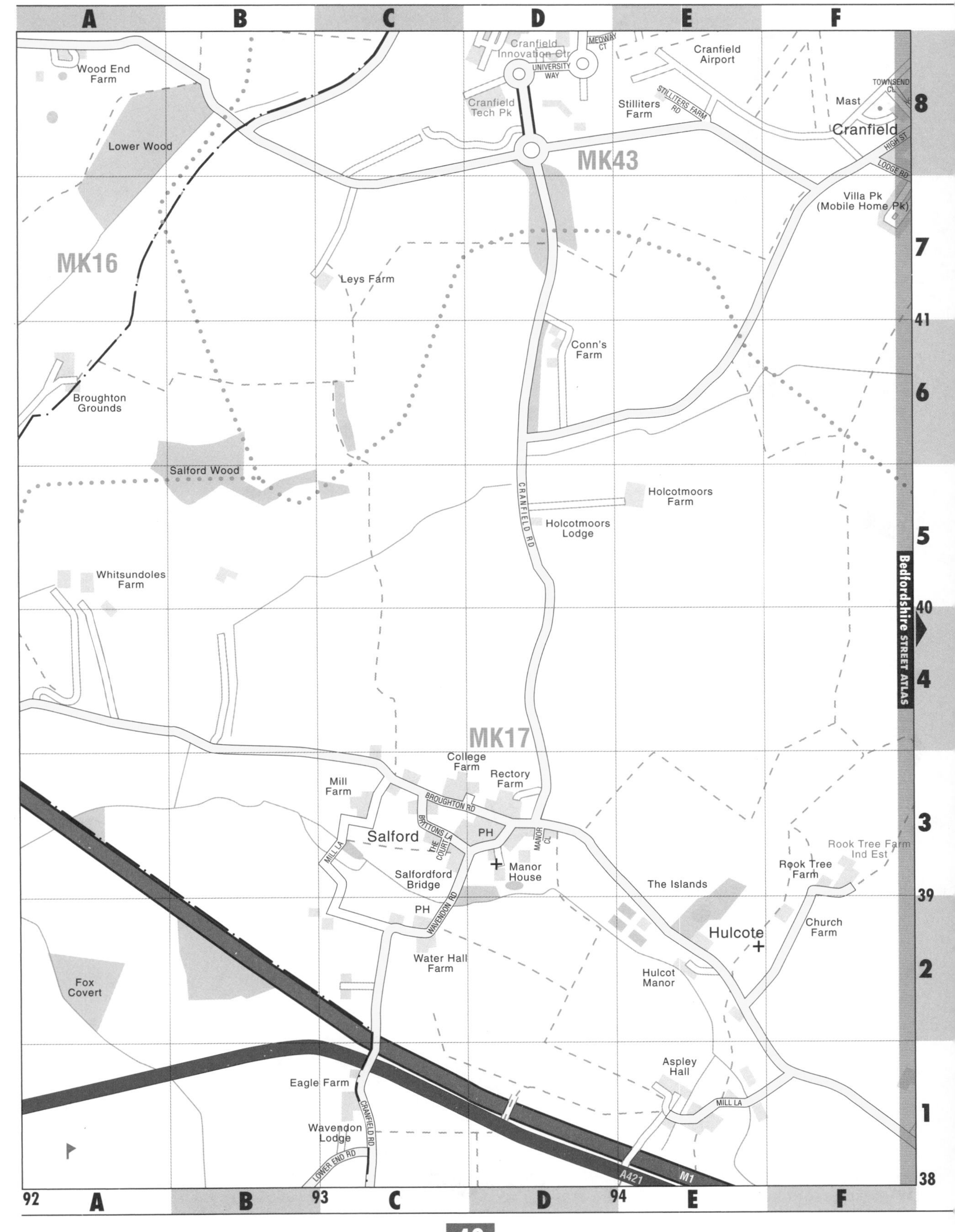
A
B
C
D
E
F
Wood End Farm
Cranfield Innovation Ctr
MEDWAY CT
UNIVERSITY WAY
Cranfield Airport
TOWNSEND CL
Cranfield Tech Pk
Stilliters Farm
STILLITERS FARM RD
Mast
Cranfield
HIGH ST
LODGE RD
Lower Wood
MK43
Villa Pk (Mobile Home Pk)
MK16
Leys Farm
Conn's Farm
Broughton Grounds
Salford Wood
CRANFIELD RD
Holcotmoors Farm
Holcotmoors Lodge
Whitsundoles Farm
Bedfordshire STREET ATLAS
MK17
College Farm
Mill Farm
Rectory Farm
BROUGHTON RD
BRITTONS LA
THE COURT
Salford
PH
MANOR CL
MILL LA
Manor House
Salfordford Bridge
Rook Tree Farm Ind Est
Rook Tree Farm
The Islands
PH
WAVENDON RD
Church Farm
Hulcote
Water Hall Farm
Hulcot Manor
Fox Covert
Aspley Hall
Eagle Farm
MILL LA
CRANFIELD RD
Wavendon Lodge
LOWER END RD
A421
M1
8
7
41
6
5
40
4
3
39
2
1
38
92
93
94
A
B
C
D
E
F

49

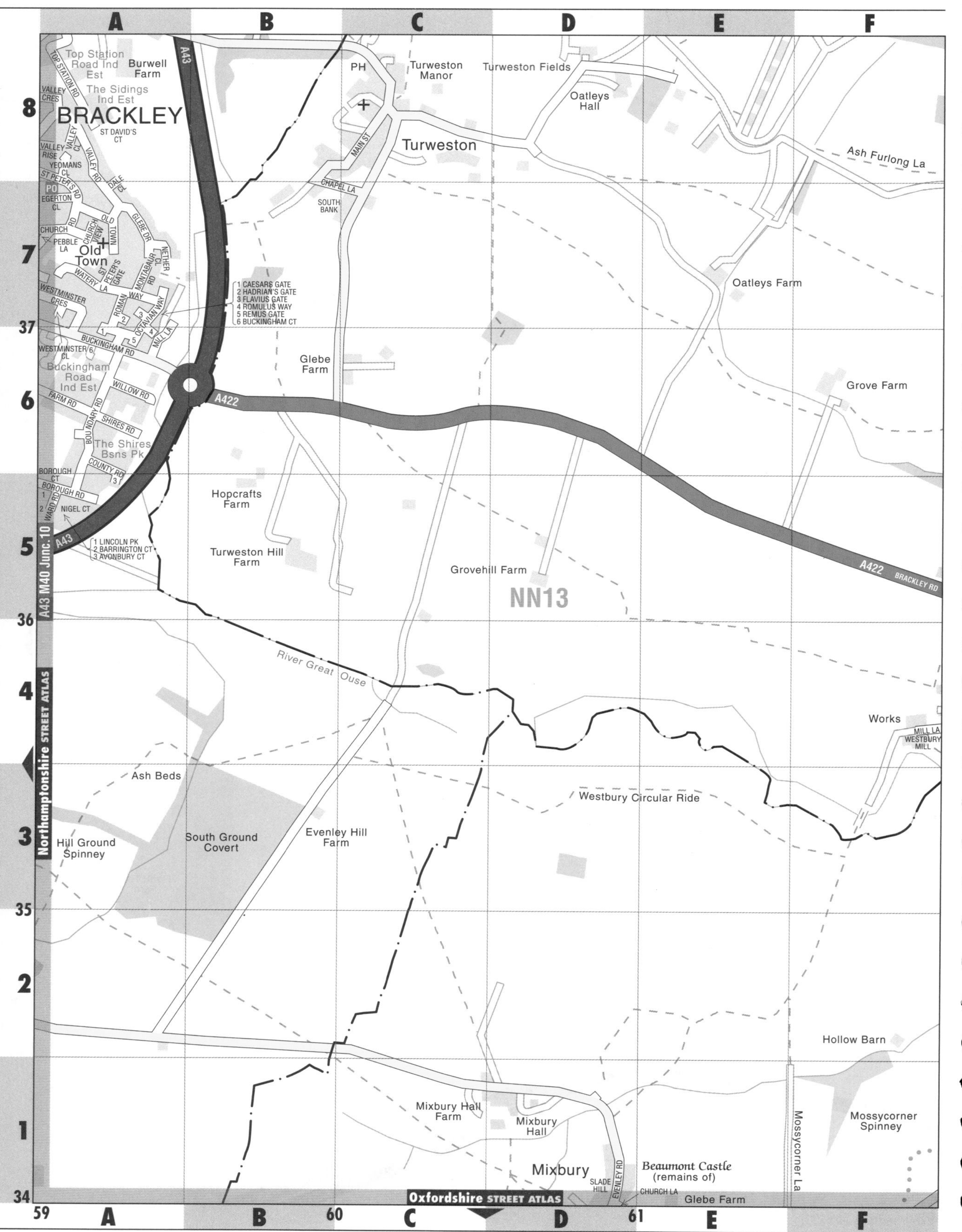

A B C D E F

8

BRACKLEY

Top Station
Road Ind
Est

Burwell
Farm

The Sidings
Ind Est

VALLEY
CRES

St David's
Ct

VALLEY
RISE

YEOMANS
CL

ST PETER'S RD

PO

EGERTON
CL

CHURCH
PEBBLE
LA

Old
Town

WATERY
LA

WESTMINSTER
CRES

7

ROMAN
WAY

OLD
TOWN

GLEBE DR

NETHER

CHURCH
VIEW

PETER'S
GATE

MONTABAUR
RD

OXFORD WAY

MCLA

1 CAESARS GATE
2 HADRIAN'S GATE
3 FLAVIUS GATE
4 ROMULUS WAY
5 REMUS GATE
6 BUCKINGHAM CT

37

WESTMINSTER
CL

Buckingham
Road
Ind Est

BUCKINGHAM RD

WILLOW RD

6

FARM RD

A422

Glebe
Farm

SHIRES RD

The Shires
Bsns Pk

BOUNDARY RD

COUNTY RD

Hopcrafts
Farm

BORLOUGH
CT

BOROUGH RD

NIGEL CT

5

A43 M40 Junc. 10

A43

1 LINCOLN PK
2 BARRINGTON CT
3 AVONBURY CT

Turweston Hill
Farm

36

River Great Ouse

Grovehill Farm

NN13

4

Ash Beds

Works

MILL LA
WESTBURY
MILL

Westbury Circular Ride

3

Hill Ground
Spinney

South Ground
Covert

Evenley Hill
Farm

35

2

Hollow Barn

1

Mixbury Hall
Farm

Mixbury
Hall

Mossycorner La

Mossycorner
Spinney

Mixbury

SLADE
HILL

EVENLEY RD

Beaumont Castle
(remains of)

CHURCH LA

Glebe Farm

34

PH

Turweston
Manor

Turweston Fields

Oatleys
Hall

MAIN ST

Turweston

CHAPEL LA

SOUTH
BANK

Ash Furlong La

Oatleys Farm

Grove Farm

A422

BRACKLEY RD

Northamptonshire STREET ATLAS

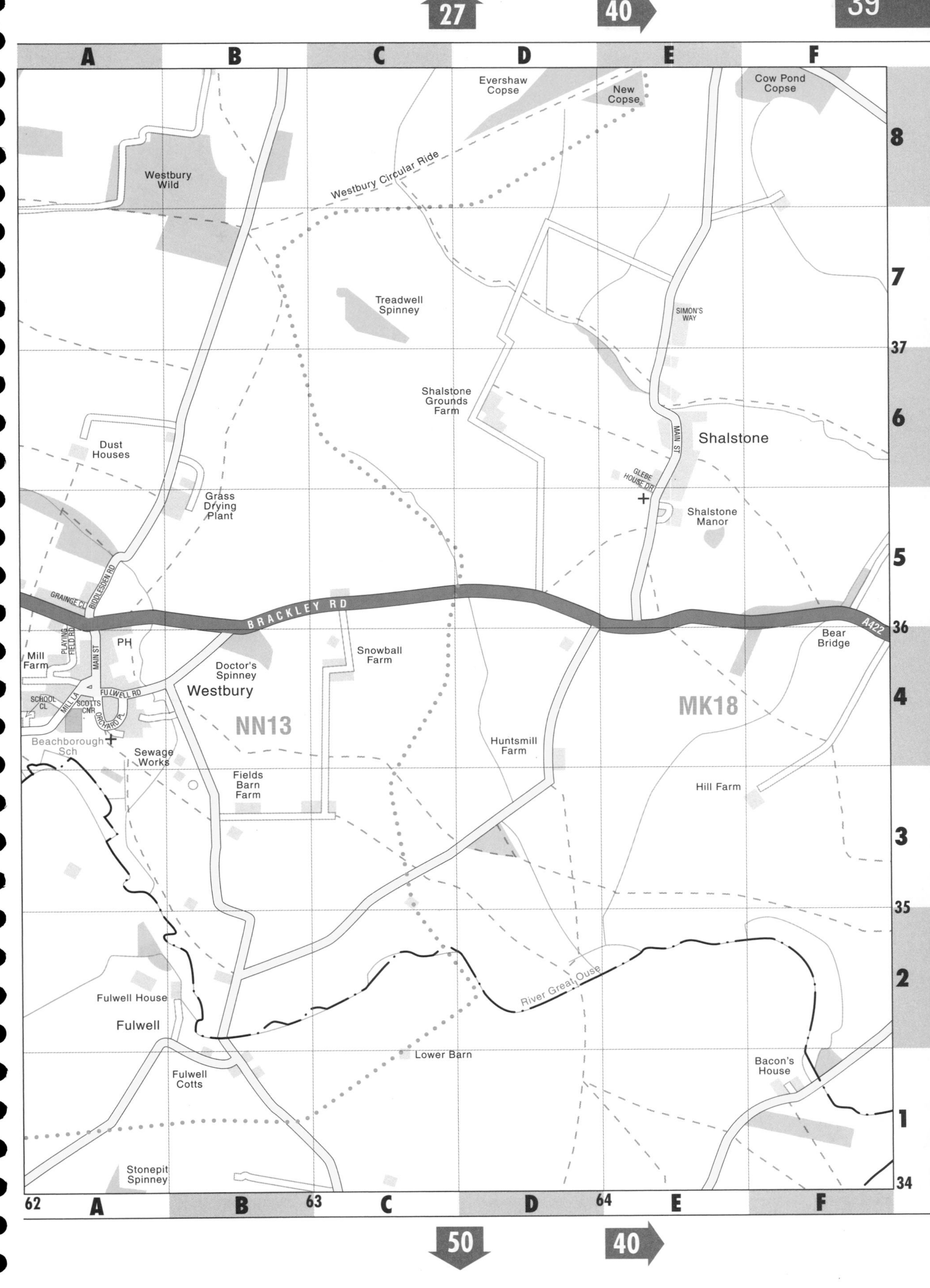
27
40
A
B
C
D
E
F
Evershaw Copse
New Copse
Cow Pond Copse
Westbury Wild
Westbury Circular Ride
Treadwell Spinney
SIMON'S WAY
Shalstone Grounds Farm
MAIN ST
Shalstone
Dust Houses
GLEBE HOUSE DR
Grass Drying Plant
Shalstone Manor
BIDDLESDEN RD
GRAINGE CL
BRACKLEY RD
A422
Bear Bridge
Mill Farm
PLAYING FIELD RD
MAIN ST
PH
Snowball Farm
Doctor's Spinney
Westbury
SCHOOL CL
MILL LA
FULWELL RD
SCOTTS CNR
ORCHARD PL
NN13
MK18
Beachborough Sch
Sewage Works
Huntsmill Farm
Fields Barn Farm
Hill Farm
River Great Ouse
Fulwell House
Fulwell
Lower Barn
Fulwell Cotts
Bacon's House
Stonepit Spinney
8
7
37
6
5
36
4
3
35
2
1
34
62
63
64
50
40

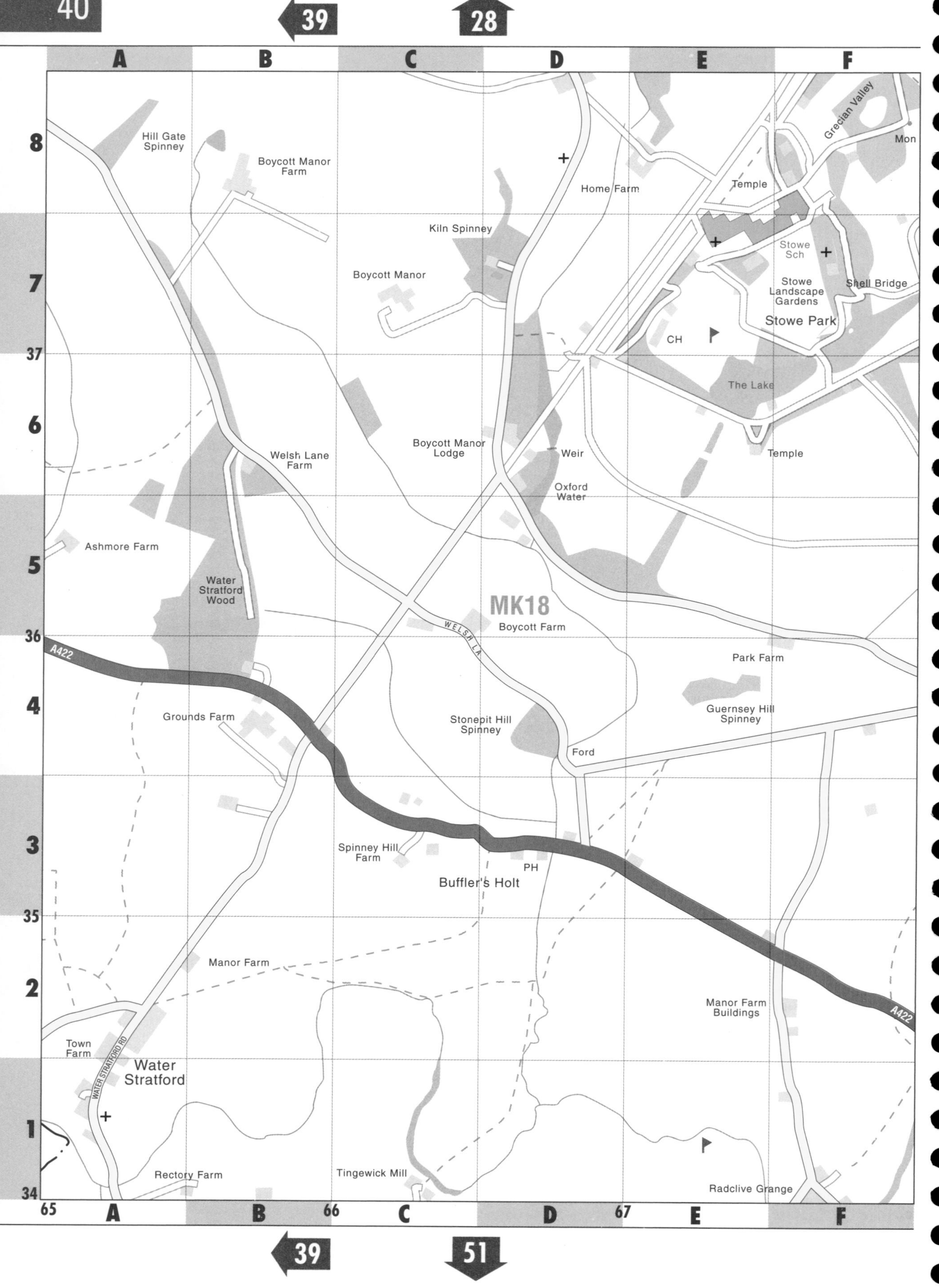

39
28

A B C D E F

8

Hill Gate
Spinney

Boycott Manor
Farm

Home Farm

Grecian Valley

Mon

Temple

Kiln Spinney

Stowe
Sch

7

Boycott Manor

Stowe
Landscape
Gardens

Shell Bridge

37

CH

Stowe Park

The Lake

6

Welsh Lane
Farm

Boycott Manor
Lodge

Weir

Temple

Oxford
Water

5

Ashmore Farm

Water
Stratford
Wood

MK18

Boycott Farm

Park Farm

36

A422

4

Grounds Farm

Stonepit Hill
Spinney

Ford

Guernsey Hill
Spinney

3

Spinney Hill
Farm

PH

Buffler's Holt

35

Manor Farm

2

Manor Farm
Buildings

A422

Town
Farm

WATER STRATFORD RD

Water
Stratford

1

Rectory Farm

Tingewick Mill

Radclive Grange

34

65 A B 66 C D 67 E F

39
51

WELSH LA

A B C D E F

8

7

37

6

Bourbon Tower

Home Farm

Akeley Wood Sch

Hillside Farm
St James & St John CE Prim Sch
THE SQUARE
PH
CHURCH HILL
CORONATION COTTS
Akeley
MAIN ST
LECKHAMPSTEAD RD
MANOR RD
CAPEL CL
CEDARS RD
CHAPEL LA
A413

Lodge
Lamport

Palladian Bridge

Stowe Castle Farm

New Inn Farm

Bycell Farm
BYCELL RD

Longs Wood

Foxcote Resr

5

36

4

35

3

STOWE AVE
THE MALTINGS
NEW COLLEGE CT
Dance Farm
PH
MAIN ST
St James & St John CE Prim Sch
Chackmore
Chackmore Farm Spinney
Chackmore Farm

MK18

Maids Moreton House
Vitalograph Bsns Pk
SCOTTS FARM CL
WALNUT DR
TOWCESTER RD
DUCK LAKE CL
PH
THE PIGHTLE
MANOR PK
MAIN ST
THE LEYS
Wellmore
MANOR RD
FOSCOTE RD

Maids Moreton

Maids Moreton CE Sch
SCOTTS LA
DUCK LAKE
AVENUE RD
SOUTH HALL
MALL CL
GLEBE TERR
CHURCH CL
GLEBE CL

Castle Fields

BUCKINGHAM

Manor Farm

PINE CL
GRANGE
TEMPLE CL
MORETON DR
VILLIERS CL
MANOR GDNS
The Manor
Buckingham Prim Sch
WATCHCROFT

2

MORETON RD
GLEBE AT SCOTT RD
ADAMS CL
HOLTON RD
BRADFIELD AVE
BEECH CL
HIGHLANDS RD
CARISBROOKE
NASEBY
PENN
KING CHARLES
KEYES
EDGE HILL
WATLOW
HILLTOP AVE
EDMONDS
HILLTOP CL
GIFFORD PL
Page Hill
CATHERINE
FOSSCOTT WAY

1 CHETWODE CL
2 NIGHTINGALE PL
3 CROPREDY CT
4 DE GLARE CT
5 BARTLETT PL

WOODLANDS
GRENVILLE RD
WESTERN AVE
OVERN AVE
OVERN CRES
Nat Res
ADDINGTON TERR
Buckingham
HILLESDEN WAY
LINDSEY RD
HILLESDEN WAY
PAGE HILL AVE
MIDDLE FIELD
WHARF VIEW
BUSBY CL
CHEYNE CL
HUBBARD
GREENWAY WLK

1

A422
BRACKLEY RD
River Great Ouse
Cemy
STOWE CL
STOWE RISE
COBHAM CL
THE PIGHTLE
PATEMAN CL
GLYNSWOOD RD
WEST ST
A422
Buckingham Chantry Chapel
PAYNES
MINSHULL CL
CANTELL
MARY MACMANUS DR
ADDINGTON RD
ORCHARD
Old Gaol Mus
H
Liby
HIGH ST
CORNWALL PL
MEADOW WLK
MEADOW ROW
SANDMARTIN CL
WHARF CL
LOWER WHARF
STRATFORD RD
WITTMILLS OAK
HAZLEY WLK
REDSHAW
MARCH
PITCHFORD WLK
OMILL CL
BURLEIGH PIECE
ROXWELL
A413

34

68 A B 69 C D 70 E F

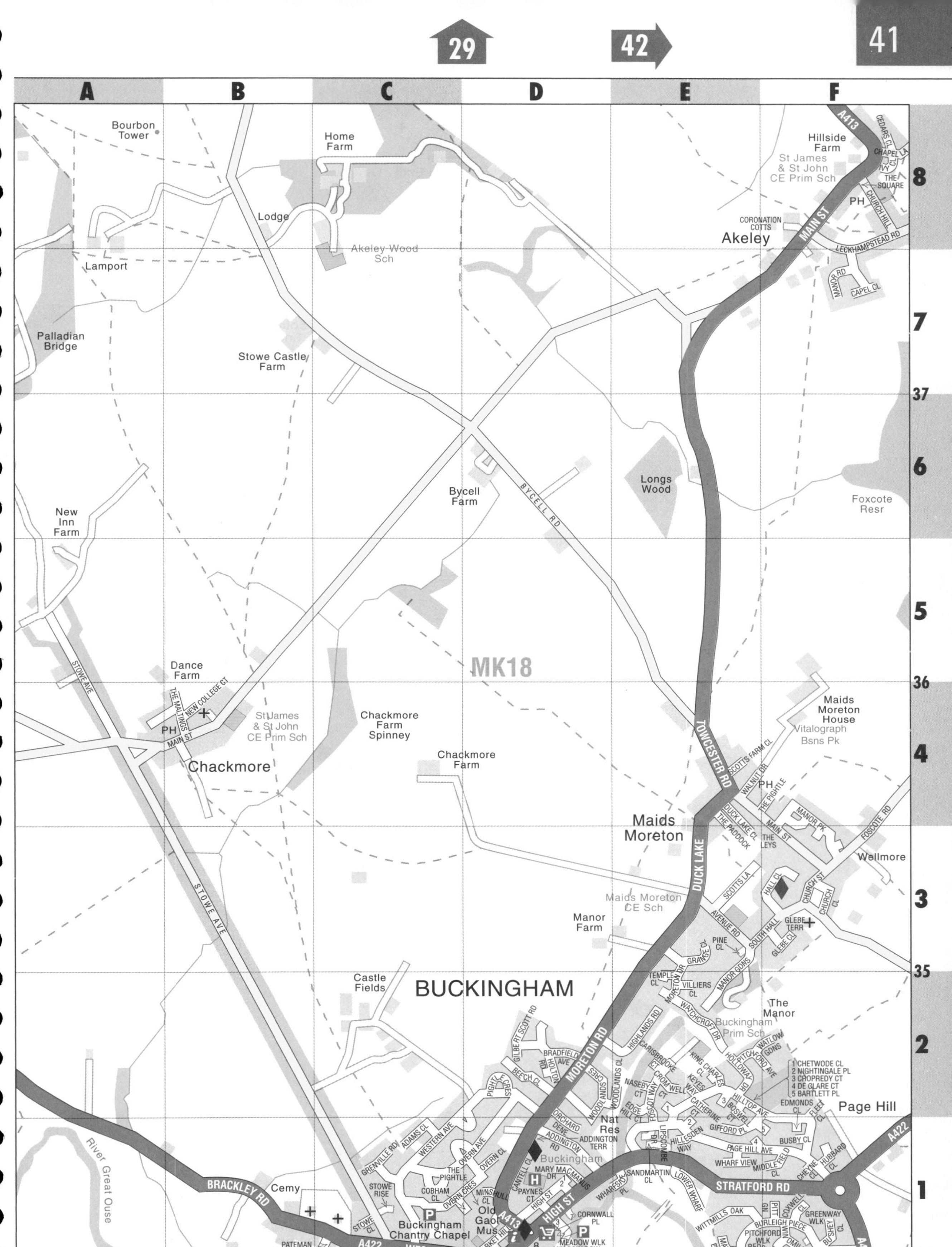

D1
1 NORTHEND CT
2 NORTHEND SQ
3 CORNWALLS MDW
4 Meadow Sh Ctr
5 MARKET SQ
6 VERNEY CL
7 CECILS YARD
8 Buckingham Ctr

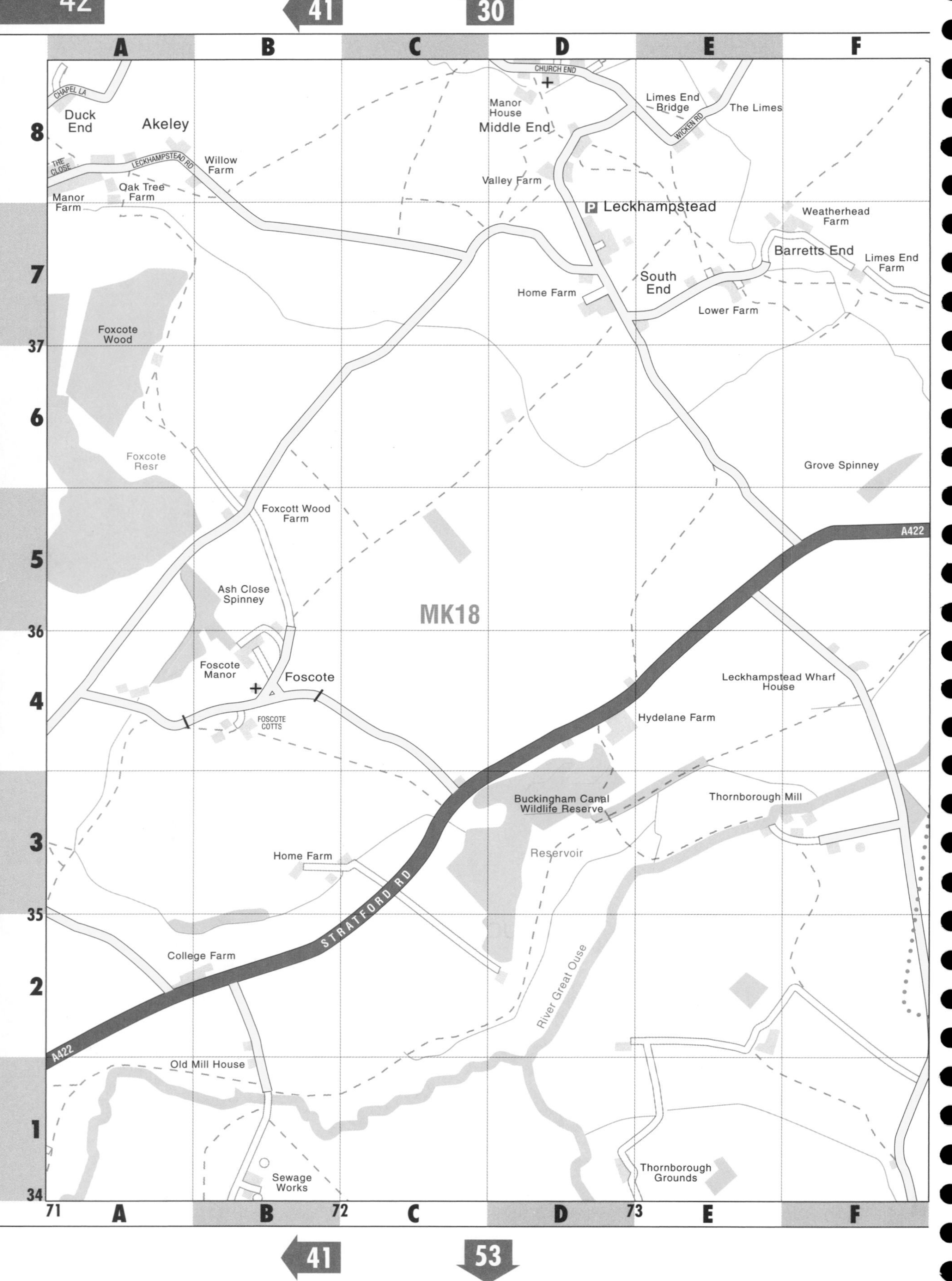
41
30
A
B
C
D
E
F
CHAPEL LA
Duck End
Akeley
THE CLOSE
LECKHAMPSTEAD RD
Willow Farm
Oak Tree Farm
Manor Farm
CHURCH END
Manor House
Middle End
Limes End Bridge
WICKEN RD
The Limes
Valley Farm
Leckhampstead
Weatherhead Farm
Barretts End
Limes End Farm
South End
Home Farm
Lower Farm
Foxcote Wood
Foxcote Resr
Grove Spinney
Foxcott Wood Farm
A422
Ash Close Spinney
MK18
Foscote Manor
Foscote
FOSCOTE COTTS
Leckhampstead Wharf House
Hydelane Farm
Buckingham Canal Wildlife Reserve
Thornborough Mill
Reservoir
Home Farm
STRATFORD RD
River Great Ouse
College Farm
A422
Old Mill House
Sewage Works
Thornborough Grounds
8
7
37
6
5
36
4
3
35
2
1
34
71
72
73
41
53

31
44

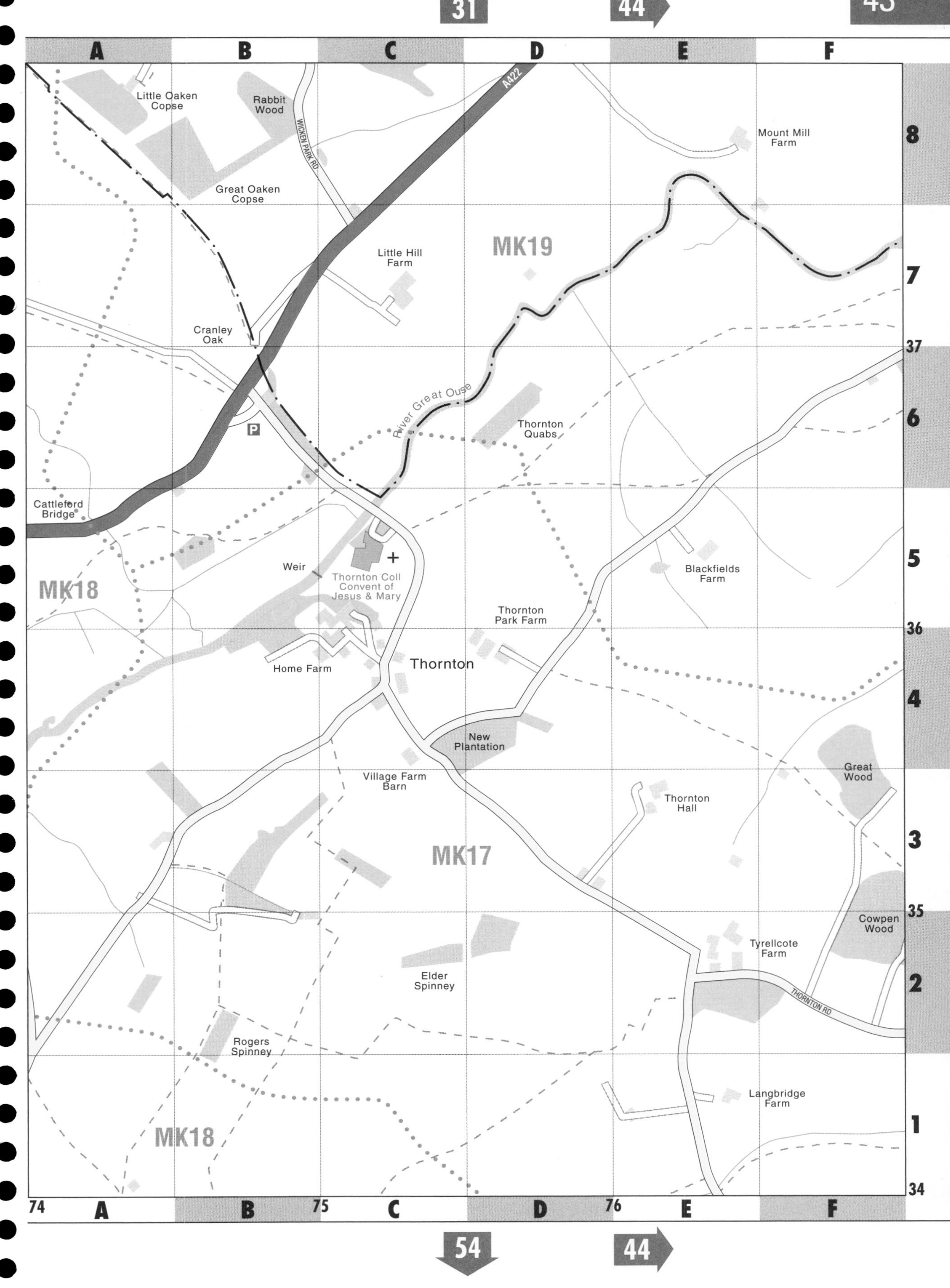
A
B
C
D
E
F
Little Oaken Copse
Rabbit Wood
WICKEN PARK RD
A422
Mount Mill Farm
Great Oaken Copse
MK19
Little Hill Farm
Cranley Oak
River Great Ouse
Thornton Quabs
P
Cattleford Bridge
Weir
Thornton Coll Convent of Jesus & Mary
Blackfields Farm
MK18
Thornton Park Farm
Home Farm
Thornton
New Plantation
Village Farm Barn
Great Wood
Thornton Hall
MK17
Cowpen Wood
Tyrellcote Farm
Elder Spinney
THORNTON RD
Rogers Spinney
Langbridge Farm
MK18
8
7
37
6
5
36
4
3
35
2
1
34
74
75
76

54
44

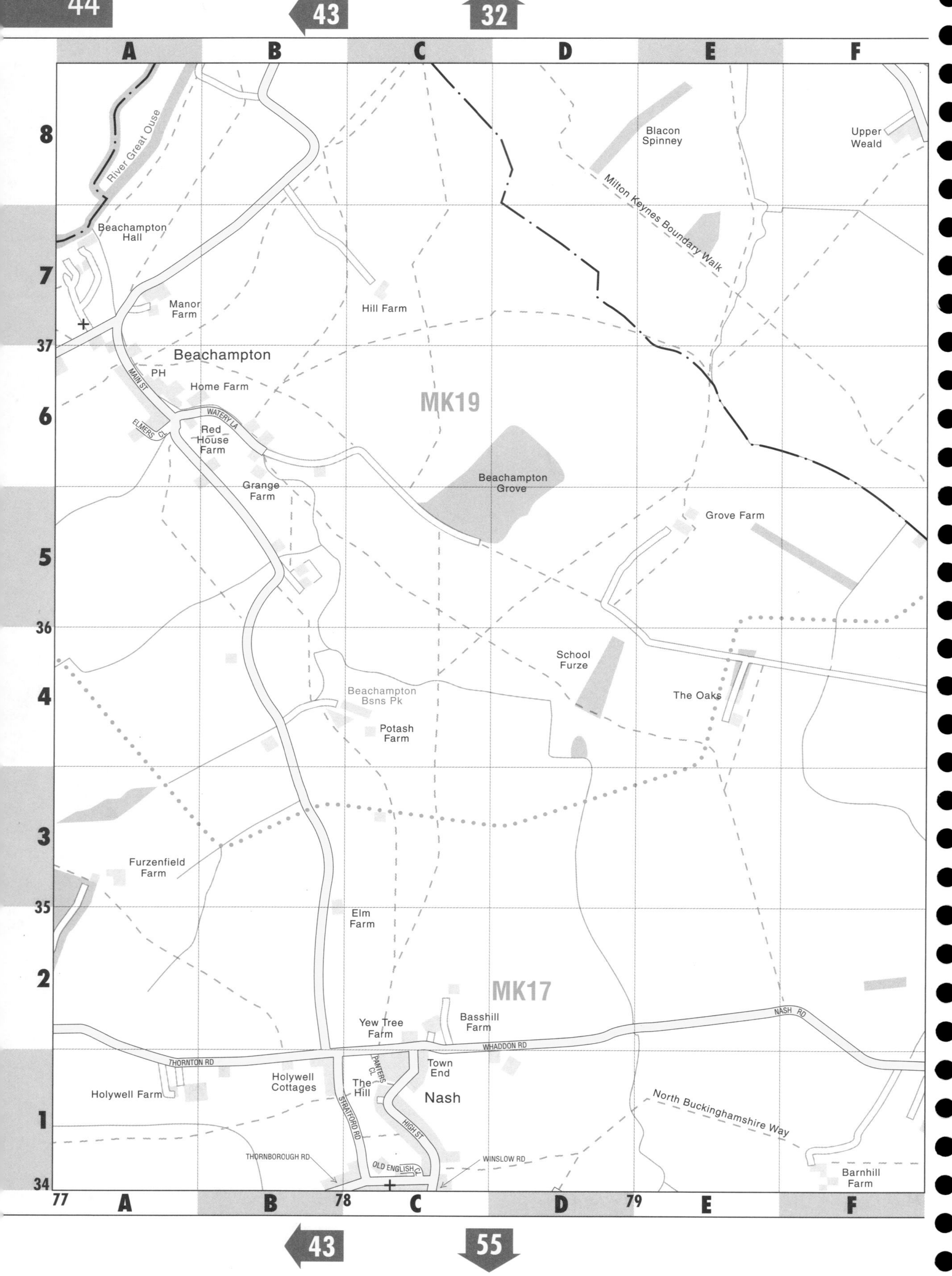
43
32
A
B
C
D
E
F
8
7
37
6
5
36
4
3
35
2
1
34
77
78
79
River Great Ouse
Beachampton Hall
Manor Farm
Beachampton
PH
Home Farm
MAIN ST
ELMERS CL
WATERY LA
Red House Farm
Grange Farm
Hill Farm
MK19
Blacon Spinney
Milton Keynes Boundary Walk
Upper Weald
Beachampton Grove
Grove Farm
School Furze
The Oaks
Beachampton Bsns Pk
Potash Farm
Furzenfield Farm
Elm Farm
MK17
Basshill Farm
Yew Tree Farm
NASH RD
WHADDON RD
THORNTON RD
Town End
PANTERS CL
Holywell Cottages
The Hill
Nash
Holywell Farm
STRATFORD RD
HIGH ST
North Buckinghamshire Way
THORNBOROUGH RD
OLD ENGLISH CL
WINSLOW RD
Barnhill Farm
43
55

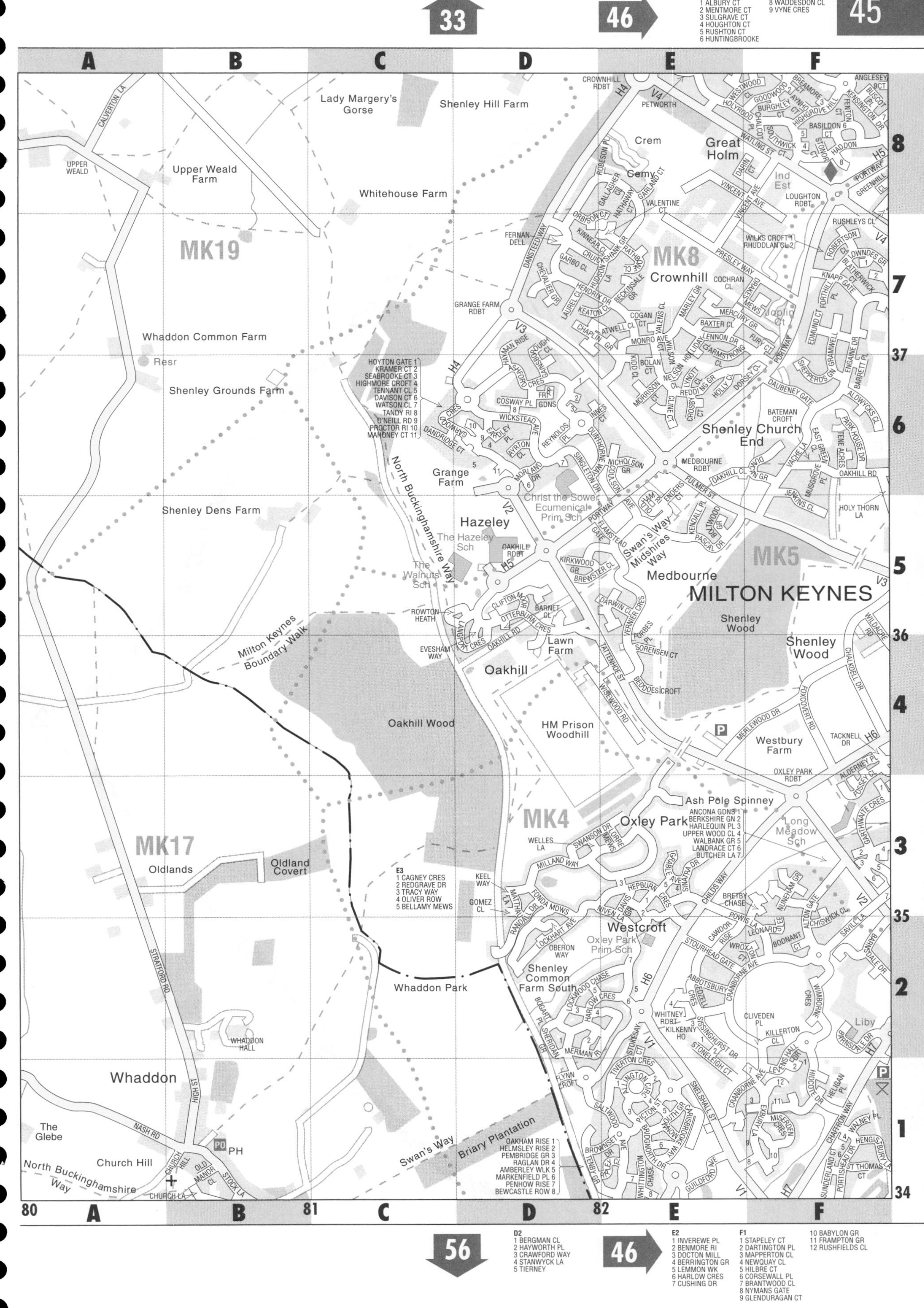

33

46

F8
1 ALBURY CT
2 MENTMORE CT
3 SULGRAVE CT
4 HOUGHTON CT
5 RUSHTON CT
6 HUNTINGBROOKE
7 HAMPTON
8 WADDESDON CT
9 VYNE CRES

Map labels

MK19

Upper Weald
Upper Weald Farm
Lady Margery's Gorse
Shenley Hill Farm
Whitehouse Farm
Whaddon Common Farm
Resr
Shenley Grounds Farm
Shenley Dens Farm

MK8
Crownhill
Crem
Gemy
Great Holm
Ind Est
Shenley Church End

HOYTON GATE 1
KRAMER CT 2
SEABROOKE CT 3
HIGHMORE CROFT 4
TENNANT CL 5
DAVISON CT 6
WATSON CL 7
TANDY RI 8
O'NEILL RD 9
PROCTOR RI 10
MAHONEY CT 11

North Buckinghamshire Way

Grange Farm
Grange Farm RDBT

Hazeley
The Hazeley Sch
The Walnuts Sch
Christ the Sower Ecumenical Prim Sch

MK5
Medbourne
Shenley Wood
Shenley Wood

MILTON KEYNES

Rowton Heath
Evesham Way
Oakhill
Oakhill Wood
Lawn Farm
HM Prison Woodhill

Milton Keynes Boundary Walk

MK17
Oldlands
Oldland Covert

E3
1 CAGNEY CRES
2 REDGRAVE DR
3 TRACY WAY
4 OLIVER ROW
5 BELLAMY MEWS

MK4
Ash Pole Spinney
Oxley Park
Long Meadow Sch

ANCONA GDNS 1
BERKSHIRE GN 2
HARLEQUIN PL 3
UPPER WOOD CL 4
WALBANK GR 5
LANDRACE CT 6
BUTCHER LA 7

Westbury Farm

Westcroft
Oxley Park Prim Sch
Shenley Common Farm South

Whaddon Park
Whaddon Hall
Whaddon

The Glebe
Church Hill
North Buckinghamshire Way

PO
PH

Swan's Way
Briary Plantation

OAKHAM RISE 1
HELMSLEY RISE 2
PEMBRIDGE GR 3
RAGLAN DR 4
AMBERLEY PL 5
MARKENFIELD PL 6
PENHOW RISE 7
BEWCASTLE ROW 8

Liby

D2
1 BERGMAN CL
2 HAYWORTH PL
3 CRAWFORD WAY
4 STANWYCK LA
5 TIERNEY

E2
1 INVEREWE PL
2 BENMORE RI
3 DOCTON MILL
4 BERRINGTON GR
5 LEMMON WK
6 HARLOW CRES
7 CUSHING DR

F1
1 STAPELEY CT
2 DARTINGTON PL
3 MAPPERTON CL
4 NEWQUAY CT
5 HILBRE CT
6 CORSEWALL PL
7 BRANTWOOD CL
8 NYMANS GATE
9 GLENDURAGAN CT
10 BABYLON GR
11 FRAMPTON GR
12 RUSHFIELDS CL

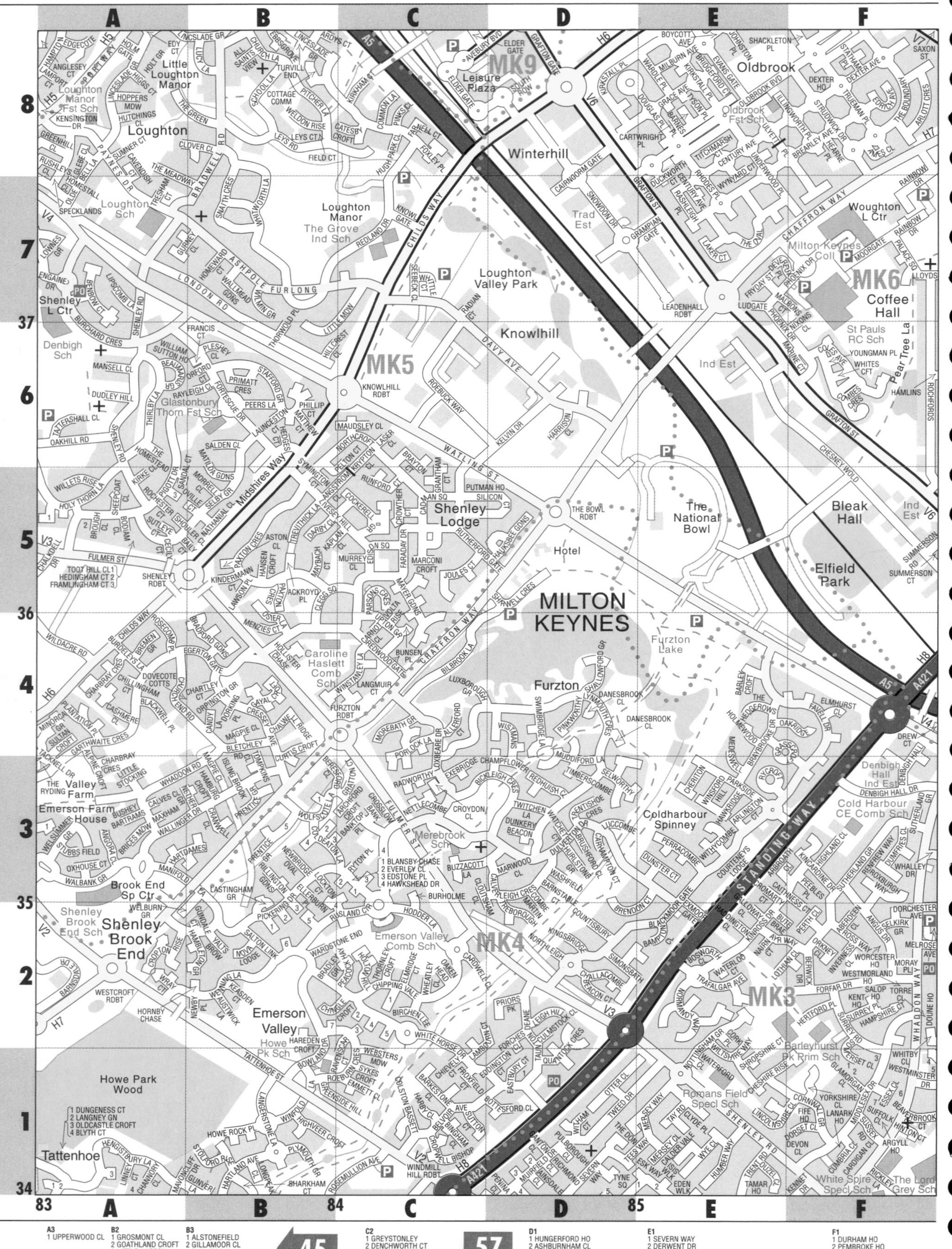

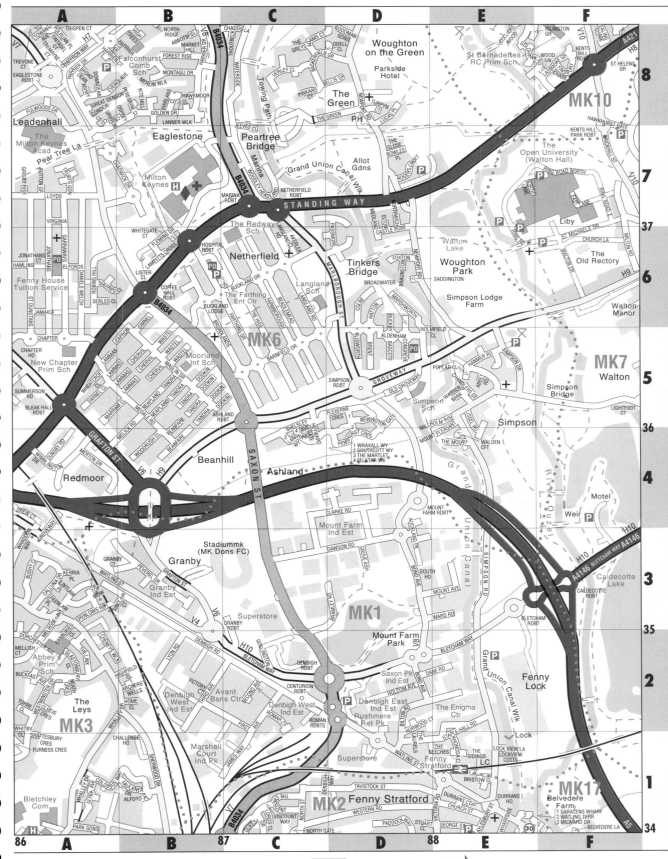
35
48

A B C D E F

Trispen Ct, Towan Ave, Polruan Pl, Tintagel Ct, Tremayne Ct, Chaffron Way, H7, Trevone Ct, Eaglestone Rdbt, Harrier Dr, Broad Dean, Ashby, Downdean, Everglade, Harrier Ct, High Trees, North Ridge, Abbotsfield, Market Hill, Forest Rise, Harrier Dr, V8, Falconhurst Comb Sch, Montagu Dr, Merlin Wlk, Kite Hill, Harlans Cl, Hawkmoor Cl, Great Denson, Condor Cl, Griffon Cl, Osprey Cl, Peregrine Cl, Golden Dr, Lanner Wlk, Fulwoods Dr, Leadenhall

B4034, Chadds La, Troutbeck, Waterside, Towing Path, Jeeves Cl, Peartree Bridge, Marina, Woodley Headland, Marina Rdbt, Netherfield Rdbt, The Greys, Adams Ct, Goodman Gdns, Odell Cl, Baskerfield Gr, Verley Cl, Bellis Gr, Pinkard Ct, The Green, The Green, Newport Rd, Turpyn Ct, Lucas Pl, PH, Woughton on the Green, Parkside Hotel, Colliers Wood, Islington Gr, V10, Ealing Chase, Golden Wood, Wood Gr, Ladbroke Gr, Finsbury Chase, Kents Hill Rdbt, St Helens Gr, H8, A421, St Bernadettes RC Prim Sch, MK10

The Milton Keynes Acad, Pear Tree La, Eaglestone, Chadwick Dr, Milton Keynes H, Grigby Rise, Button Gr, Trubys Gdn, Lloyds, Grand Union Canal Wlk, Allot Gdns, The Close, Bowles Pl, Rogers Croft, Hawkhurst Gate, Kents Hill Park Rdbt, The Open University (Walton Hall), Brickhill St, Ring Road North, North Lane, East Lane, Ring Road E, V10

Standing Way, Virginia, Whitegate Ct, Fleming Dr, Lampitts Cross, Hospital Rdbt, The Redway Sch, Langland Ho, Akerlea, Passmore, Northwich, Medland, Elton, Castle Rose, Liby, Church La, St Michaels Dr, Ring Rd W, Milton Rd, Walton Lake, Walton Dr, The Old Rectory, Jonathans Ct, Jonathans, Garraways, Hamlins, Elfords, Daniels Welch, Robins Hill, Fenny House Tuition Service, PO, Lister Cl, Squires Cl, Serles Cl, Coffee Hall Rdbt, Netherfield, Marlborough St, Tinkers Bridge, Foxton, Braunston, Newport Rd, Saddington, Woughton Park, H9, Langland Sch, Buckland Dr, The Farthing Ent Ctr, Broadwater, Marshworth, Simpson Lodge Farm, Walton Manor, St Dunstans, Jamaica, Chapter, Chapter Ho, Buckland Lodge, Broadlands, Farthing Gr, The Hide, Farmborough, Beadlemead, Langland Rd, Colne, Hatton, Buckby, Bascote, Aldenham, Congreve, Holmfield Cl, Blisworth, Brent, MK6, Barnfield Dr

New Chapter Prim Sch, Capron, Simnel, Lammas, Chervil, Wastel, Moorland Inf Sch, Maslin Dr, Dodkin, Tandra, Neapland, Medale Rd, Marram Cl, Melick Rd, Woodrush Cl, Beanfare, Ashland Rdbt, Wheatcroft Cl, Darnel Cl, Summerson Rd, Bleak Hall Rdbt, Simpson Rdbt, Groveway, Old Groveway, Poplar Cl, Hanmer Rd, Abbey Rd, Simpson Dr, Chandlers Ct, Warren Bank, Simpson Sch, MK7, Walton, Simpson Bridge, Lightfoot Ct, Flexerne Cres, Newington Gate, Shelsley Ave, Langley Wy, Heyward Gate, Penhurst Cres, Millholm Rise, Mount Pleasant, The Mount, Issel Rd, Walden Cft, Simpson, 1 Wraxall Wy, 2 Southcott Wy, 3 The Martlet, 4 Felstar Wk

Grafton St, Dunsby Rd, Wimblington Dr, Merton Dr, Redmoor, V6, H9, Beanhill, Saxon St, Ashland, Grand Union Canal, River Ouzel, Motel, Weir, Drew Ct, Groveway, Whaddon Way, Clarke Rd, Mount Farm Ind Est, Mount Farm Rdbt, Auckland Pk, Dawson Rd, Grove Ash, Stadiummk (MK Dons FC), Granby, Granby Ct, Peverel Dr, Grafton St, Watling St, Kerria Pl, Bushy Cl, Callina Dr, Lintlaw Pl, Greenlaw Pl, Top Mdw, Sinclair Ct, Granby Ind Est, Bond Ave, South Ho, Mount Ave, Simpson Rd, H10, Bletcham Way, A4146, Caldecotte Lake, Caldecotte Rdbt

Spenlows Rd, Mellish Ct, Dorchester Ave, Melrose Ave, Banburies Cl, Abbey's Prim Sch, Glastonbury Cl, The Linx, Cheneys Wlk, Highfield Cl, Archers Wells, Home Cl, Buckfast Ave, Westminster Dr, Neath Cres, Torre Cl, Cleeve Cres, The Leys, MK3, Whitby Cl, Shaftesbury Cres, Furness Cres, Whalley Dr, Challenge Ho, Sherwood Dr, V4, Superstore, Granby Rdbt, Lyon Rd, Denbigh Rd, H10, Bletcham Way, Gollington Way, Denbigh Rdbt, Bramley Rd, MK1, Mount Farm Park, Ward Rd, Bletcham Rdbt, V8, Bletcham Way, Grand Union Canal Wlk, Fenny Lock, Victory Ct, Third Ave, Avant Bsns Ctr, Second Ave, Denbigh West Ind Est, Centurion Rdbt, Saxon Pk Ind Est, Dane Rd, Holdom Ave, Bond Ave, Denbigh East Ind Est, Rushmere Ret Pk, The Enigma Ctr, First Ave, Romar Ct, Roman Rdbts, Marshall Court Ind Pk, James Way, Horwood Ct, Bilton Rd, The Laurels, Staple Hall Rd, Lock, Rhondda Cl, The Beeches, The Sidings, Lock View La, Lockview Cotts, Superstore, Watling St, Fenny Stratford, LC

Whalley Dr, Ultra Ave, Colossus Way, Faulkner Dr, Alford Pl, Bletchley Com, Park Gdns, V7, B4034, Denbigh Way, Tavistock St, The Crescent, North St, Lords Cl, Dukes Dr, Viscount Way, MK2, Fenny Stratford, Western Rd, North Gate, Paddock Way, Stuart Cl, Victoria Rd, George St, Durrans Ct, Church St, Bristow Cl, Aylesbury St, Wharfside, Durrans Ho, MK17, Belvedere Farm, 1 Saracens Wharf, 2 Watling Terr, 3 Milward Dr, Belvedere La, A5, 30

8 7 37 6 5 36 4 3 35 2 1 34

86 A B 87 C D 88 E F

58
48

47 36

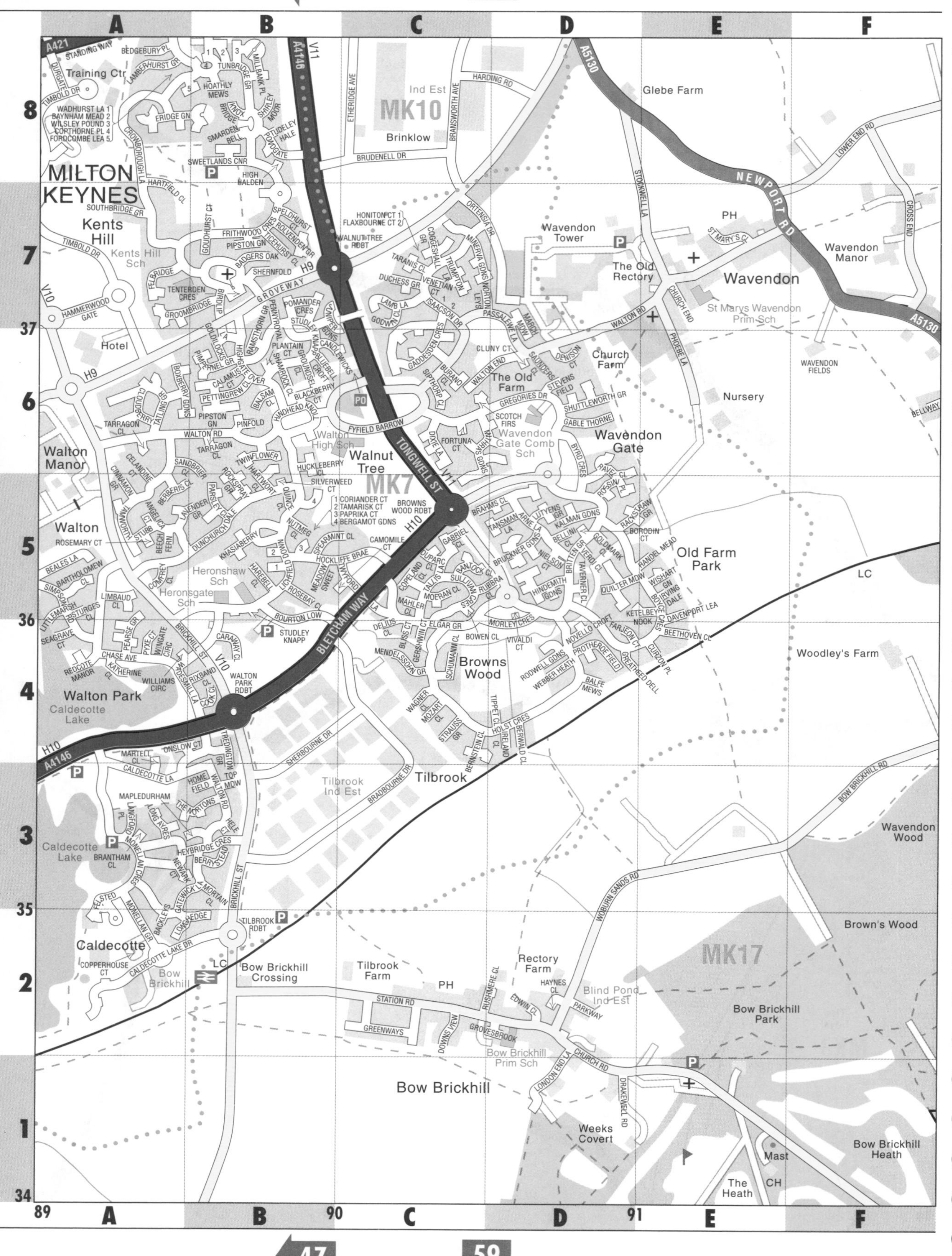
MILTON KEYNES
Kents Hill
Walton Manor
Walton
Walton Park
Caldecotte
Walnut Tree
MK7
MK10
MK17
Brinklow
Wavendon
Wavendon Gate
Old Farm Park
Browns Wood
Tilbrook
Bow Brickhill
Wavendon Wood
Brown's Wood
Bow Brickhill Park
Bow Brickhill Heath
Woodley's Farm
Glebe Farm
Wavendon Manor
Wavendon Tower
The Old Rectory
Church Farm
The Old Farm
Nursery
Weeks Covert
Rectory Farm
Tilbrook Farm
Caldecotte Lake
A421
A4146
A5130
NEWPORT RD
BLETCHAM WAY
TONGWELL ST
GROVEWAY
WOBURN SANDS RD
BOW BRICKHILL RD
STATION RD
CHURCH RD
WALTON RD
BRICKHILL ST

47 59

37

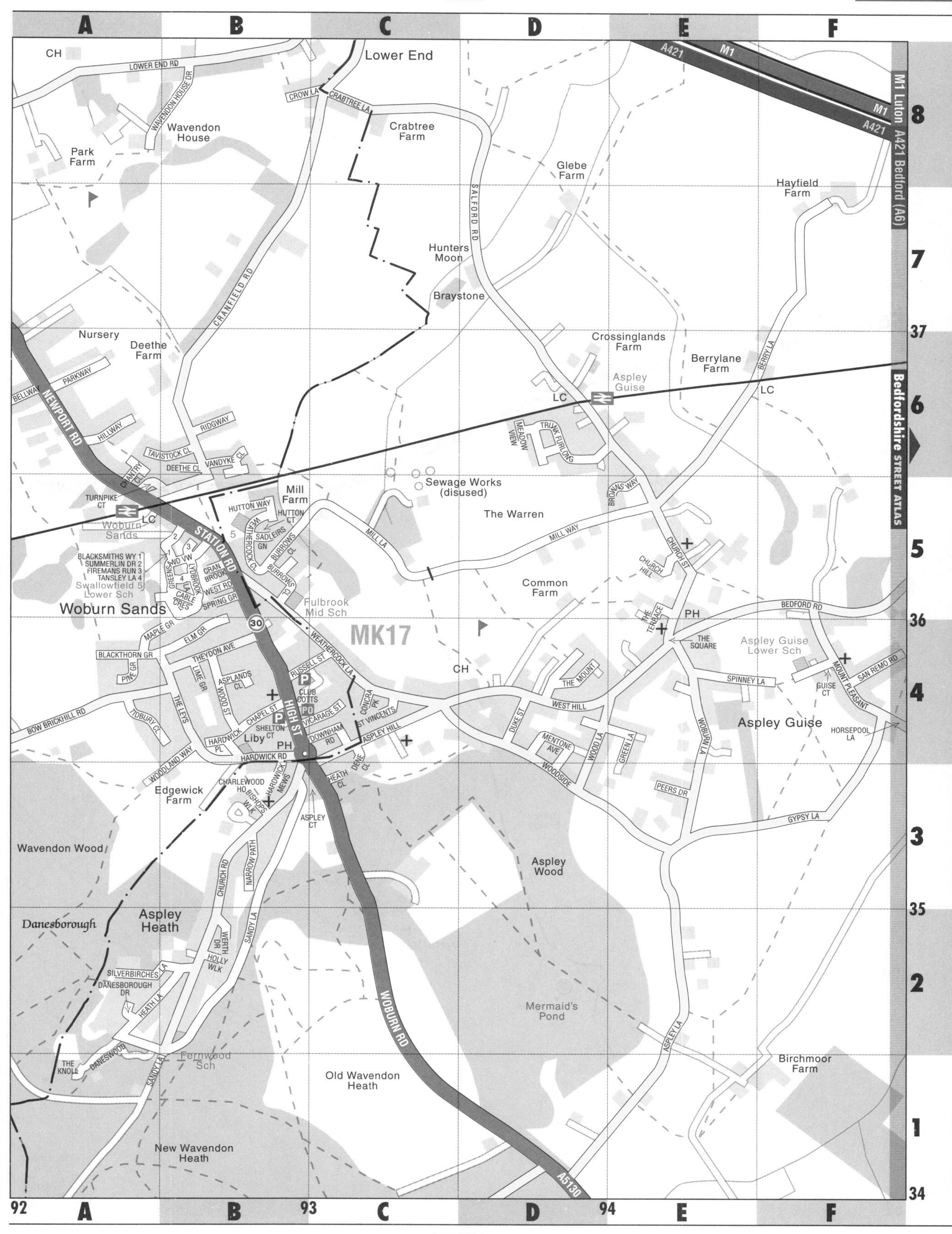

Lower End
Crabtree Farm
Wavendon House
Park Farm
Glebe Farm
Hayfield Farm
Hunters Moon
Braystone
Nursery
Deethe Farm
Crossinglands Farm
Berrylane Farm
Aspley Guise
Mill Farm
Sewage Works (disused)
The Warren
Woburn Sands
Common Farm
Fulbrook Mid Sch
MK17
Aspley Guise Lower Sch
Aspley Guise
Edgewick Farm
Wavendon Wood
Aspley Wood
Danesborough
Aspley Heath
Mermaid's Pond
Fernwood Sch
Old Wavendon Heath
Birchmoor Farm
New Wavendon Heath
NEWPORT RD
STATION RD
HIGH ST
WOBURN RD
SALFORD RD
CRANFIELD RD
BEDFORD RD
M1
A421
A5130
M1 Luton A421 Bedford (A6)
Bedfordshire STREET ATLAS

60

39

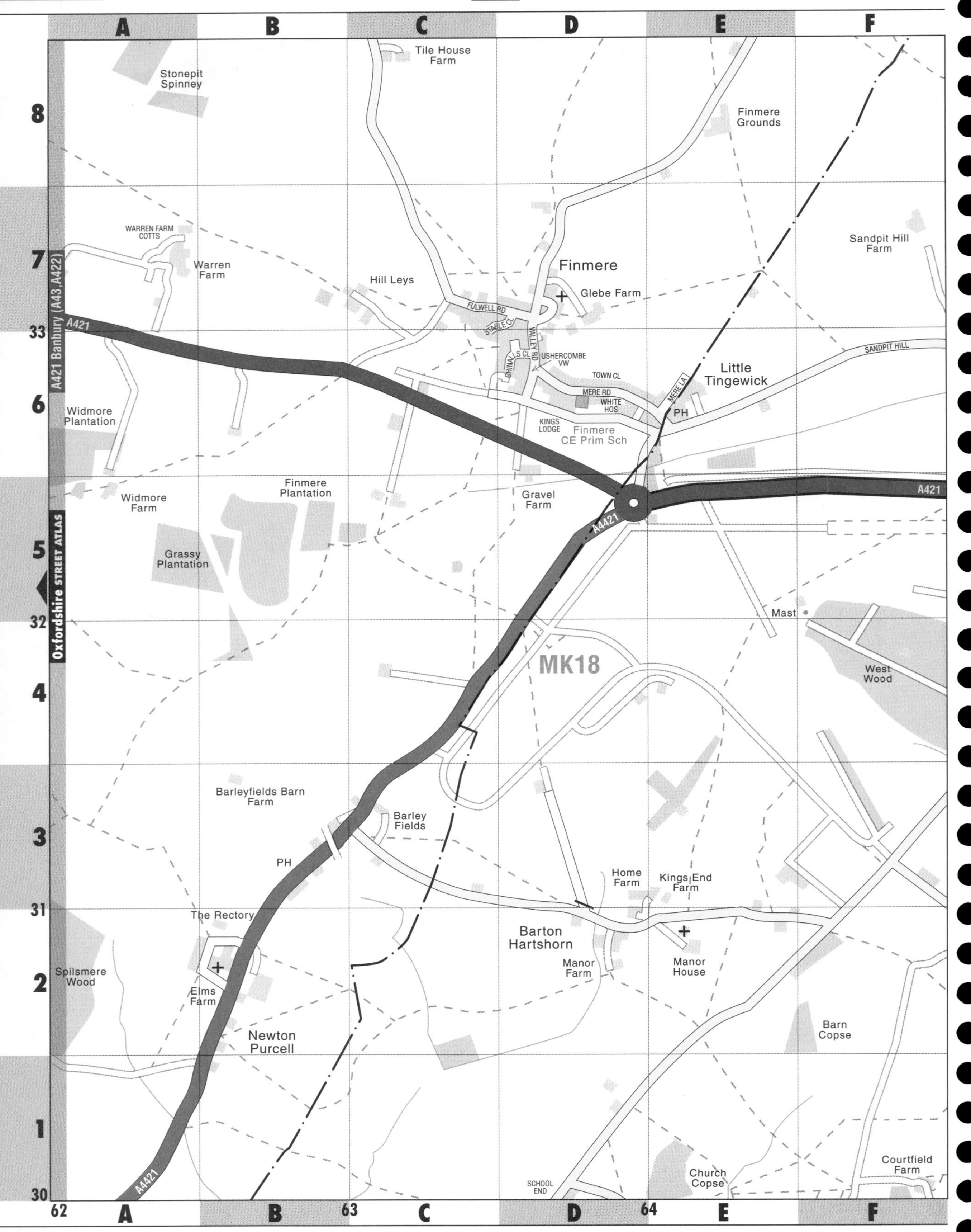

A
B
C
D
E
F
Tile House Farm
Stonepit Spinney
Finmere Grounds
WARREN FARM COTTS
Warren Farm
Hill Leys
Finmere
Glebe Farm
Sandpit Hill Farm
A421
FULWELL RD
STABLE CL
VALLEY RD
CHINALLS CL
USHERCOMBE VW
TOWN CL
MERE RD
WHITE HOS
MERE LA
SANDPIT HILL
Little Tingewick
PH
A421 Banbury (A43,A422)
Widmore Plantation
KINGS LODGE
Finmere CE Prim Sch
Finmere Plantation
Widmore Farm
Gravel Farm
A4421
Grassy Plantation
Oxfordshire STREET ATLAS
Mast
MK18
West Wood
Barleyfields Barn Farm
Barley Fields
PH
Home Farm
Kings End Farm
The Rectory
Barton Hartshorn
Spilsmere Wood
Elms Farm
Manor Farm
Manor House
Newton Purcell
Barn Copse
Courtfield Farm
Church Copse
SCHOOL END
8
7
33
6
5
32
4
3
31
2
1
30
62
63
64

61

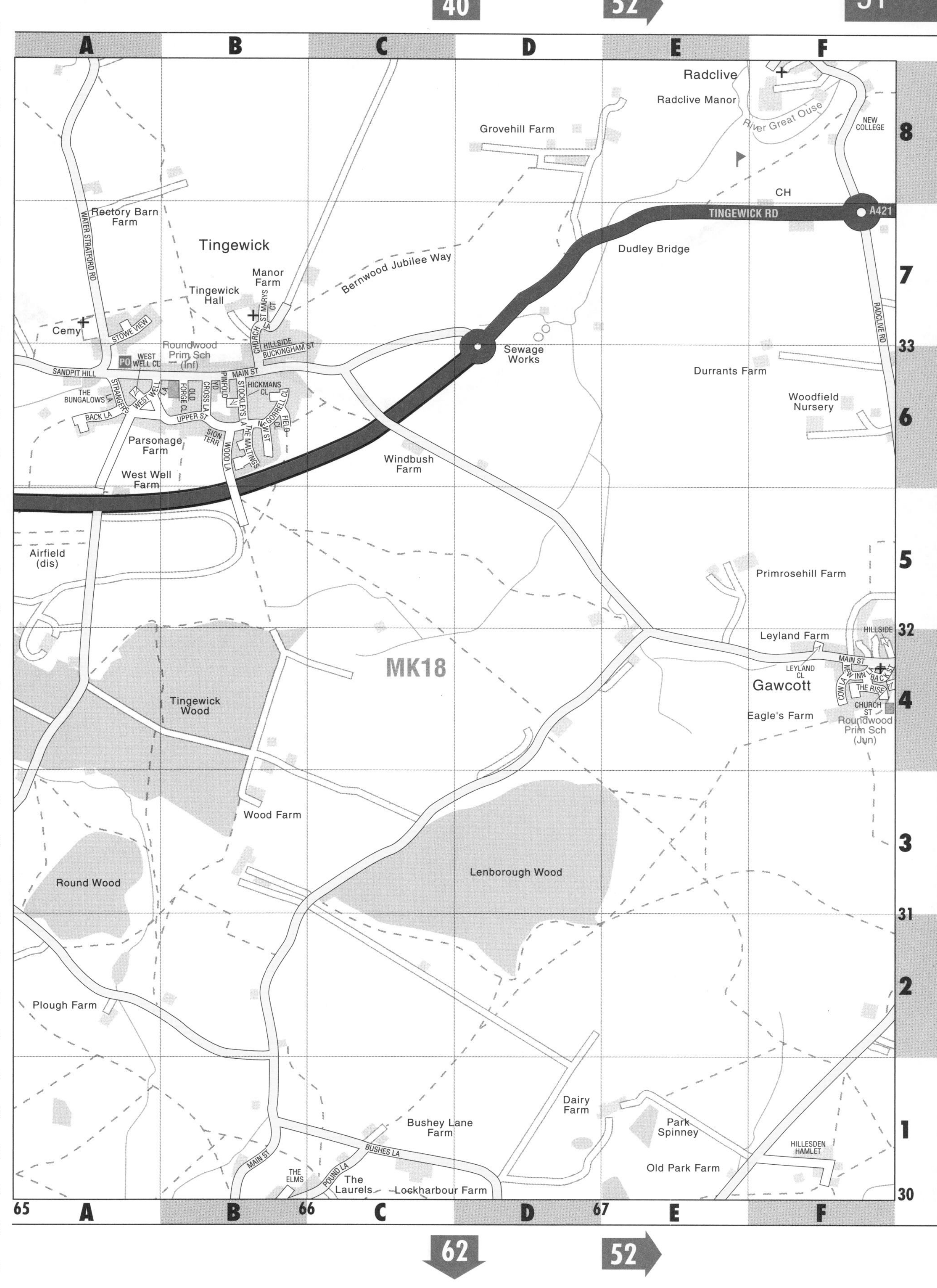

A | B | C | D | E | F

Radclive
Radclive Manor
River Great Ouse
NEW COLLEGE
8
Grovehill Farm
CH
Rectory Barn Farm
TINGEWICK RD
A421
WATER STRATFORD RD
Tingewick
7
Manor Farm
Bernwood Jubilee Way
Dudley Bridge
RADCLIVE RD
Tingewick Hall
CHURCH ST
ST MARYS CT
HILLSIDE
Cemy
STOWE VIEW
Roundwood Prim Sch (Inf)
BUCKINGHAM ST
33
WEST WELL CL
PO
Sewage Works
Durrants Farm
SANDPIT HILL
WEST WELL
MAIN ST
OLD FORGE CL
CROSS ST
PINFOLD
HICKMANS CL
STOCKLEYS LA
CORRELL CT FIELD
Woodfield Nursery
6
THE BUNGALOWS
STRANGERS
BACK LA
SION TERR
THE MALTINGS
CORRELL ST
WOOD LA
Parsonage Farm
Windbush Farm
West Well Farm

Airfield (dis)
Primrosehill Farm
5
Leyland Farm
HILLSIDE
32
MK18
LEYLAND CL
MAIN ST
Tingewick Wood
Gawcott
COW LA
INN
THE RISE
BACK
4
Eagle's Farm
CHURCH ST
Roundwood Prim Sch (Jun)
Wood Farm

Round Wood
Lenborough Wood
3
31

Plough Farm
2
Dairy Farm
Park Spinney
HILLESDEN HAMLET
1
Bushey Lane Farm
MAIN ST
BUSHES LA
POUND LA
THE ELMS
The Laurels
Lockharbour Farm
Old Park Farm
30

51
41

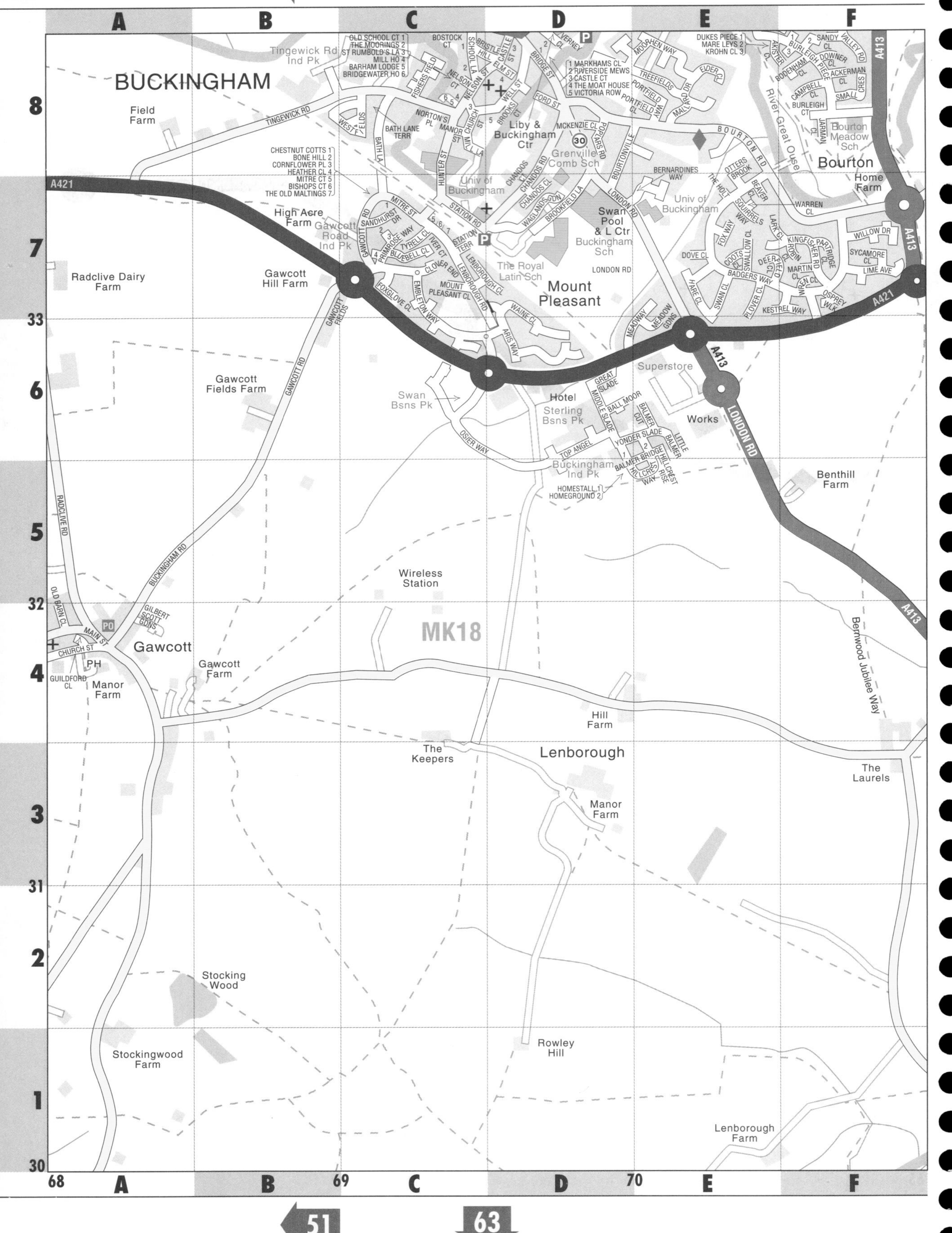
BUCKINGHAM
Field Farm
Tingewick Rd Ind Pk
Radclive Dairy Farm
High Acre Farm
Gawcott Road Ind Pk
Gawcott Hill Farm
Liby & Buckingham Ctr
Grenville Comb Sch
Univ of Buckingham
The Royal Latin Sch
Mount Pleasant
Swan Pool & L Ctr
Buckingham Sch
Bourton Meadow Sch
Bourton
Home Farm
River Great Ouse
Superstore
Hotel
Sterling Bsns Pk
Swan Bsns Pk
Works
Buckingham Ind Pk
Gawcott Fields Farm
Benthill Farm
Wireless Station
MK18
Gawcott
Gawcott Farm
Manor Farm
Hill Farm
Lenborough
The Keepers
The Laurels
Bernwood Jubilee Way
Stocking Wood
Stockingwood Farm
Rowley Hill
Lenborough Farm
A421
A413
LONDON RD
GAWCOTT RD
BUCKINGHAM RD
RADCLIVE RD
TINGEWICK RD
OSIER WAY
LENBOROUGH RD
BOURTON RD
OLD SCHOOL CT 1
THE MOORINGS 2
ST RUMBOLD'S LA 3
MILL HO 4
BARHAM LODGE 5
BRIDGEWATER HO 6
CHESTNUT COTTS 1
BONE HILL 2
CORNFLOWER PL 3
HEATHER CL 4
MITRE CT 5
BISHOPS CT 6
THE OLD MALTINGS 7
1 MARKHAMS CL
2 RIVERSIDE MEWS
3 CASTLE CT
4 THE MOAT HOUSE
5 VICTORIA ROW
DUKES PIECE 1
MARE LEYS 2
KROHN CL 3
HOMESTALL 1
HOMEGROUND 2
A B C D E F
8 7 6 5 4 3 2 1
33 32 31 30
68 69 70

51
63

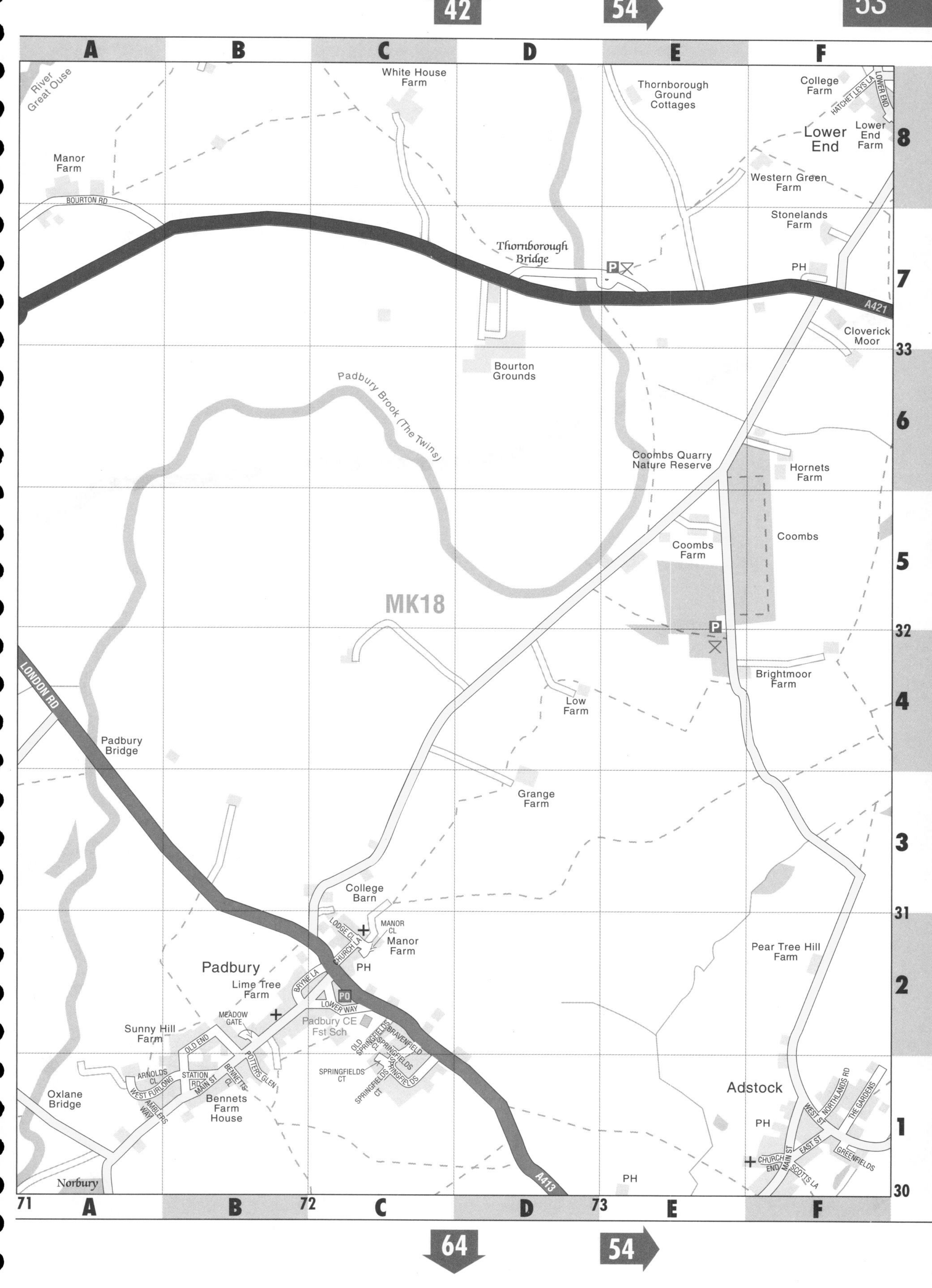
42
54
A
B
C
D
E
F
River Great Ouse
White House Farm
Thornborough Ground Cottages
College Farm
HATCHET LEYS LA
LOWER END
Lower End
Lower End Farm
8
Manor Farm
Western Green Farm
BOURTON RD
Stonelands Farm
Thornborough Bridge
P
PH
7
A421
Cloverick Moor
33
Bourton Grounds
Padbury Brook (The Twins)
6
Coombs Quarry Nature Reserve
Hornets Farm
Coombs
Coombs Farm
5
MK18
32
Brightmoor Farm
LONDON RD
Low Farm
4
Padbury Bridge
Grange Farm
3
College Barn
31
MANOR CL
LODGE CL
CHURCH LA
Manor Farm
Pear Tree Hill Farm
Padbury
PH
Lime Tree Farm
BRYNE LA
PO
2
LOWER WAY
MEADOW GATE
Padbury CE Fst Sch
Sunny Hill Farm
OLD END
BRAVENFIELD
OLD SPRINGFIELDS CL
SPRINGFIELDS
ARNOLDS CL
STATION RD
MAIN ST
BENNETTS CL
POTTERS GLEN
SPRINGFIELDS CT
WEST FURLONG
Adstock
Oxlane Bridge
Bennets Farm House
AMBLERS WAY
NORTHLANDS RD
THE GARDENS
WEST ST
1
PH
EAST ST
GREENFIELDS
CHURCH END
MAIN ST
SCOTTS LA
Norbury
A413
PH
30
71
72
73
64
54

53 43

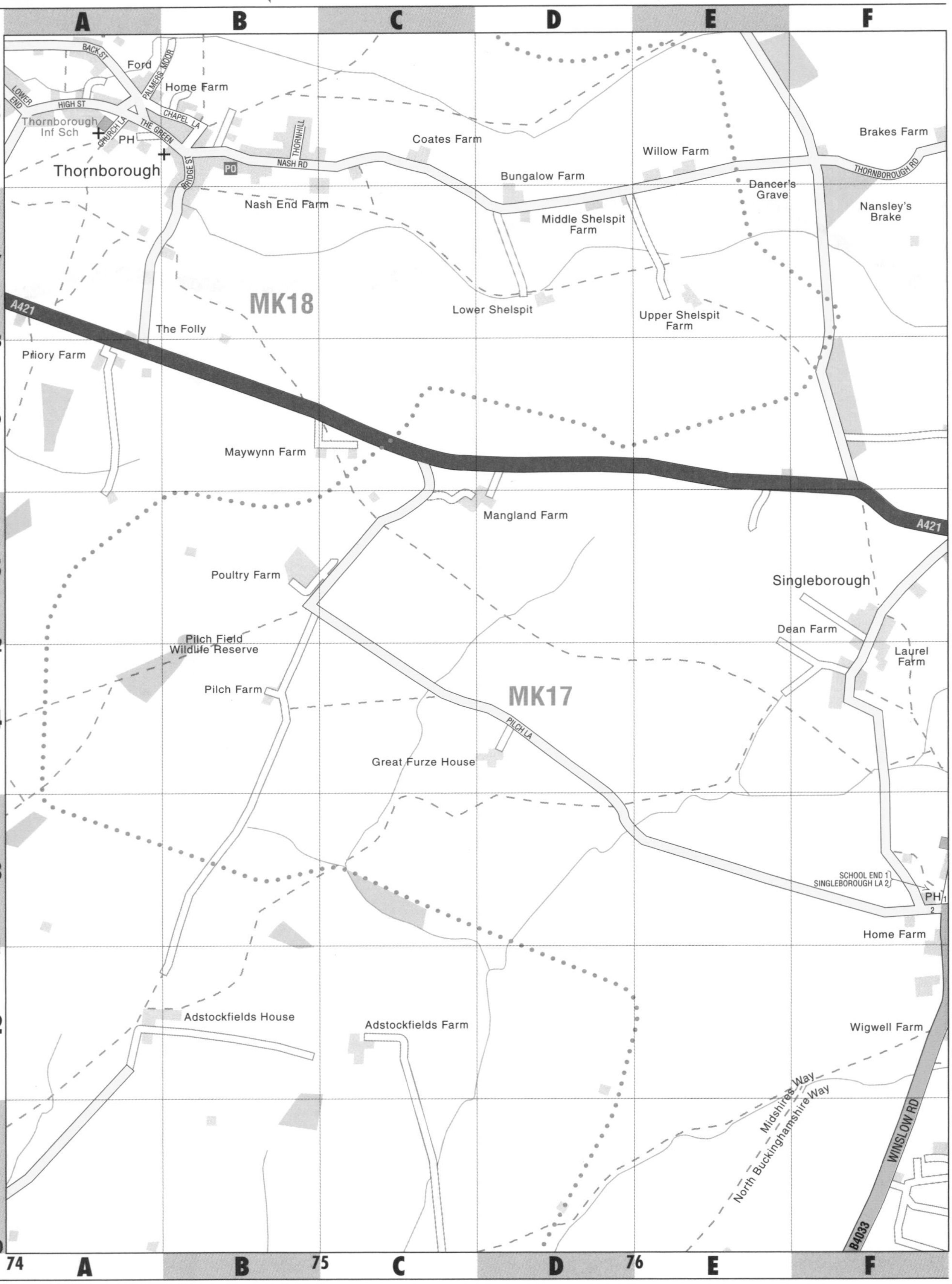

A B C D E F

8

Back St
Ford
Home Farm
Lower End
High St
Thornborough Inf Sch
PH
Palmers Moor
The Green
Chapel La
Thornhill
Coates Farm
Willow Farm
Brakes Farm
Thornborough
PO
Nash Rd
Bungalow Farm
Dancer's Grave
Thornborough Rd
Nash End Farm
Middle Shelspit Farm
Nansley's Brake

7

MK18
Lower Shelspit
Upper Shelspit Farm

A421
The Folly
33
Priory Farm

6
Maywynn Farm
Mangland Farm
A421

5
Poultry Farm
Singleborough
Dean Farm

32
Pilch Field Wildlife Reserve
Laurel Farm

Pilch Farm
MK17

4
Great Furze House
Pilch La

3
SCHOOL END 1
SINGLEBOROUGH LA 2
PH
2
Home Farm

31
Wigwell Farm

2
Adstockfields House
Adstockfields Farm

Midshires Way
North Buckinghamshire Way
Winslow Rd

1
B4033

30

74 A B 75 C D 76 E F

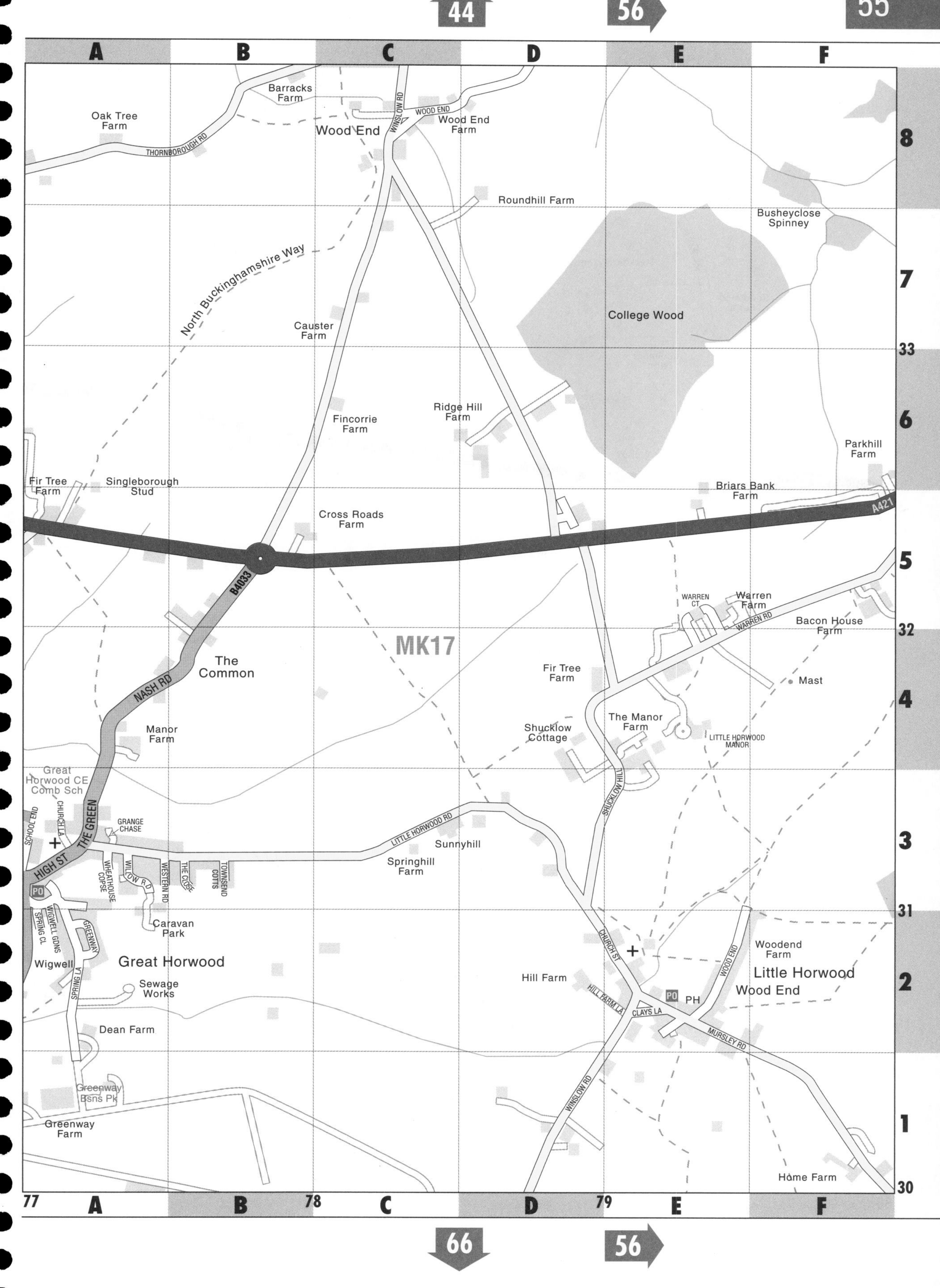
44
56
A
B
C
D
E
F
Barracks Farm
Oak Tree Farm
THORNBOROUGH RD
WINSLOW RD
WOOD END
Wood End
Wood End Farm
Roundhill Farm
Busheyclose Spinney
North Buckinghamshire Way
College Wood
Causter Farm
Fincorrie Farm
Ridge Hill Farm
Parkhill Farm
Fir Tree Farm
Singleborough Stud
Cross Roads Farm
Briars Bank Farm
A421
B4033
WARREN CT
Warren Farm
WARREN RD
Bacon House Farm
MK17
The Common
Fir Tree Farm
Mast
NASH RD
The Manor Farm
Shucklow Cottage
LITTLE HORWOOD MANOR
Manor Farm
Great Horwood CE Comb Sch
SCHOOL END
CHURCH LA
THE GREEN
GRANGE CHASE
LITTLE HORWOOD RD
SHUCKLOW HILL
HIGH ST
Sunnyhill
Springhill Farm
WHEATHOUSE COPSE
WILLOW RD
WESTERN RD
THE CLOSE
TOWNSEND COTTS
PO
SPRING CL
WIGWELL GDNS
GREENWAY
Caravan Park
CHURCH ST
Woodend Farm
Wigwell
Great Horwood
SPRING LA
WOOD END
Little Horwood
Hill Farm
Wood End
Sewage Works
HILL FARM LA
PO
PH
CLAYS LA
Dean Farm
MURSLEY RD
WINSLOW RD
Greenway Bsns Pk
Greenway Farm
Home Farm
8
7
33
6
5
32
4
3
31
2
1
30
77
78
79
66
56

55
45

A B C D E F

8
7
33
6
5
32
4
3
31
2
1
30

Church-hill Farm
Church Hill
Whaddon CE Sch
VICARAGE RD
LADYMEAD CL
STOCK LA
BRIARY VIEW
TENBY GR 1
CAISTER CT 2
SALTWOOD AVE 3
WHITTINGTON CHASE 4
GOODRICH GN 5
BYWELL CT 6
Bottlehouse Plantation
SHENLEY RD
KINGSMEAD RDBT
CHAFFRON WAY
V1
H7
ST ABBS CT
PORTISHEAD DR
GREAT ORMES
LANDS END GR
SNELSHALL ST
KELSEY CL
BALCARY GR 1
THORPENESS CROFT 2
SHENLEY RD
Bottlehouse Farm
Tattenhoe Bare Farm
Priory Rise Sch
MK4
Tattenhoe Park
CODDIMOOR LA
Thickbare Wood
Coddimoor Farm
Coddimoor Farm
Coddimoorhill Wood
STEINBECK CRES
Whaddon Chase
STANDING WAY
A421
BOTTLE DUMP RDBT
Woodpond Farm
BUCKINGHAM RD
Hogpound Wood
Bottledump
A421
Thrift Farm
Thrift Wood
Bletchley Leys Farm
WARREN RD
FERNFIELD
Broadway Wood
Fernfield Farm
MK17
Chase Farm
CHASE FARM BARNS
Stearthill Farm
Midshires Way
Swan's Way
Lower Salden Farm
Weasels'
WHADDON RD
Norbury Coppice
Salden Crabtree Farm
Salden Wood
Crabtree Farm
(dis)
Middle Salden Wood
Springfield Farm
Aqueduct

80 A B 81 C D 82 E F

55
67

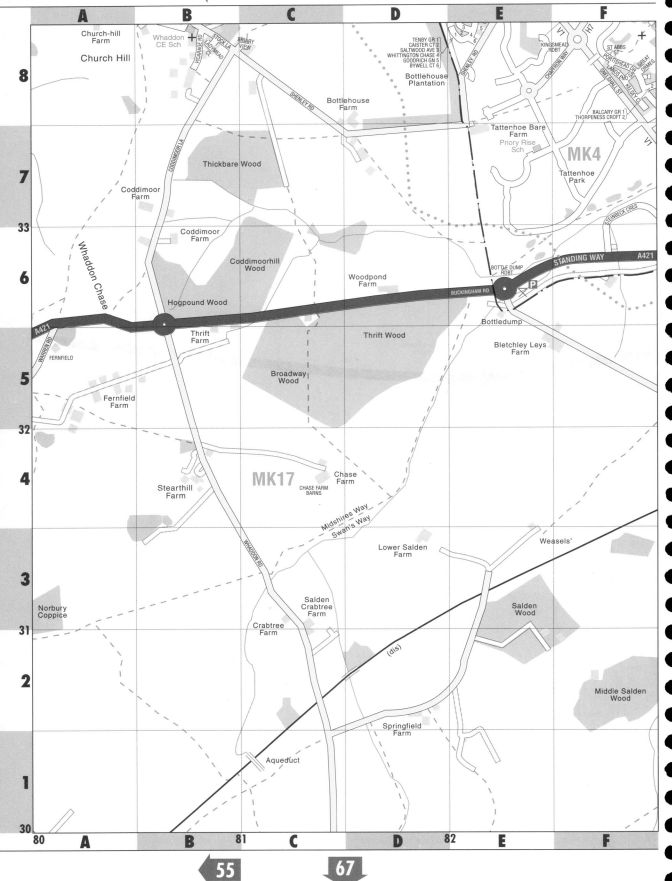

46
58

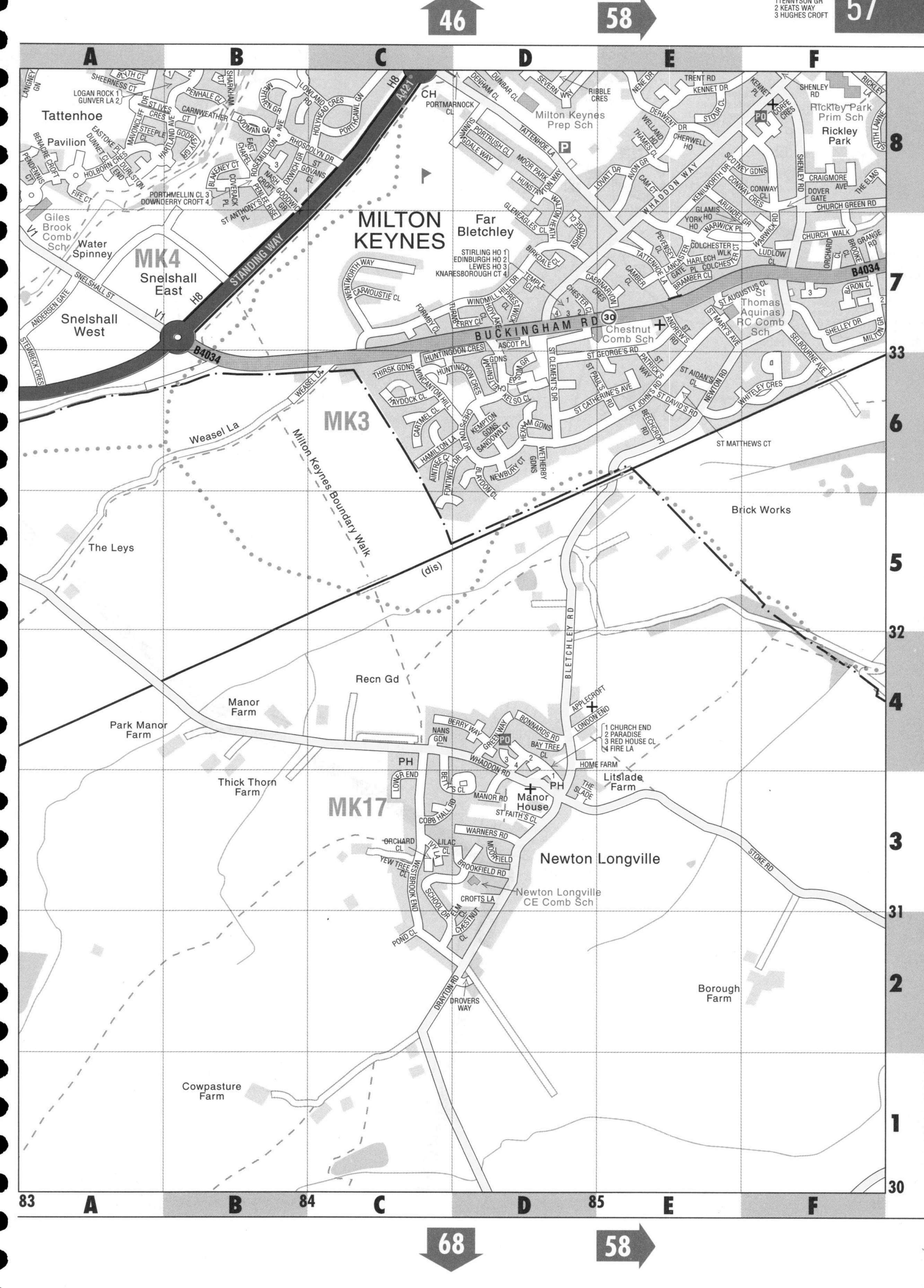
A
B
C
D
E
F
Tattenhoe
Pavilion
Giles Brook Comb Sch
Water Spinney
MK4
Snelshall East
Snelshall West
STANDING WAY
MILTON KEYNES
Far Bletchley
Milton Keynes Prep Sch
Rickley Park Prim Sch
Rickley Park
BUCKINGHAM RD
B4034
Chestnut Comb Sch
St Thomas Aquinas RC Comb Sch
MK3
Weasel La
Milton Keynes Boundary Walk
The Leys
(dis)
Brick Works
BLETCHLEY RD
Recn Gd
Manor Farm
Park Manor Farm
Thick Thorn Farm
MK17
Manor House
Litslade Farm
Newton Longville
Newton Longville CE Comb Sch
STOKE RD
DRAYTON RD
DROVERS WAY
Borough Farm
Cowpasture Farm
STIRLING HO 1
EDINBURGH HO 2
LEWES HO 3
KNARESBOROUGH CT 4
LOGAN ROCK 1
GUNVER LA 2
PORTHMELLIN CL 3
DOWNDERRY CROFT 4
1 CHURCH END
2 PARADISE
3 RED HOUSE CL
4 FIRE LA
ST MATTHEWS CT
8
7
33
6
5
32
4
3
31
2
1
30
83
84
85

68
58

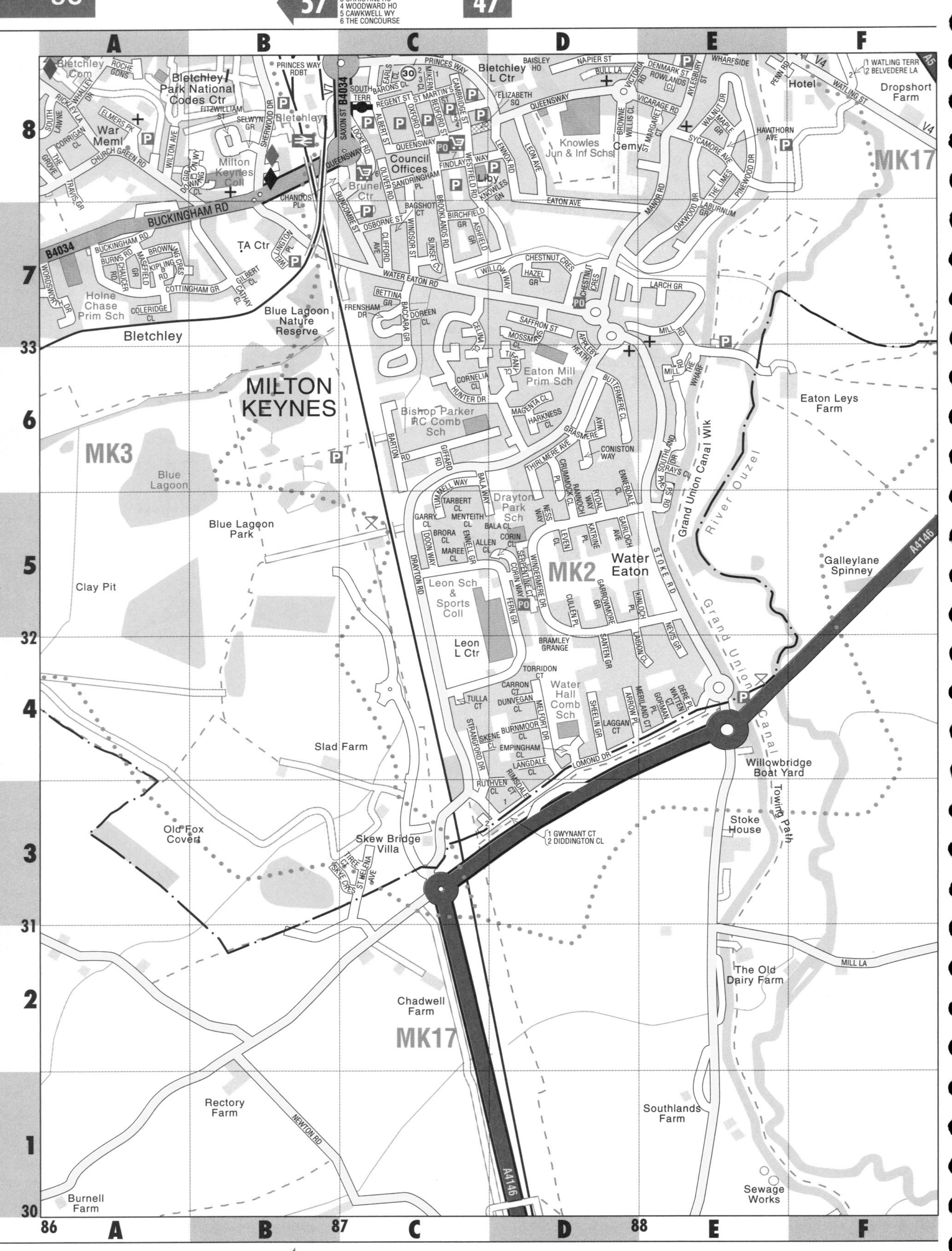

48
60

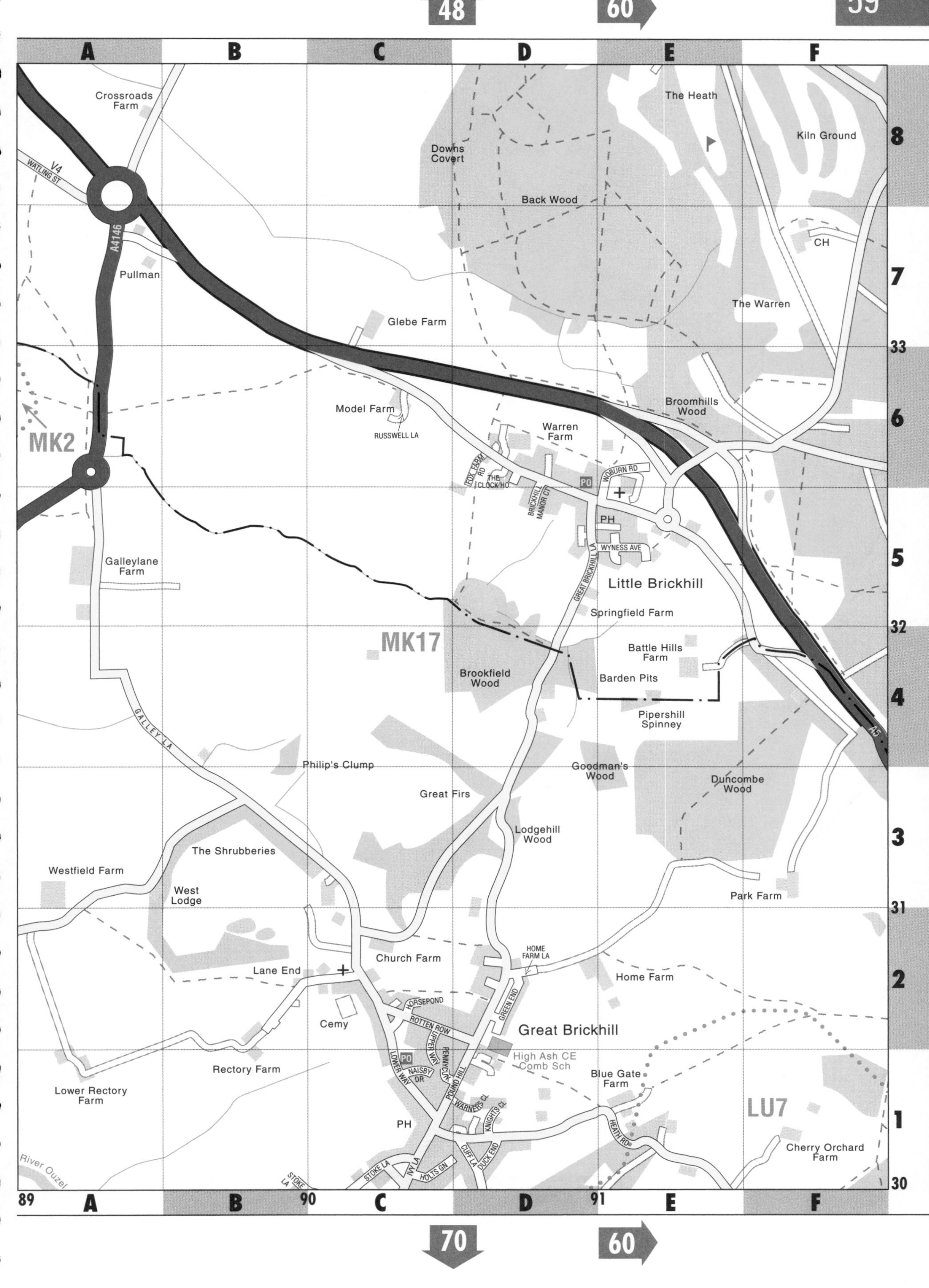
A
B
C
D
E
F
Crossroads Farm
The Heath
Kiln Ground
8
Downs Covert
V4
WATLING ST
Back Wood
A4146
CH
Pullman
7
The Warren
Glebe Farm
33
Model Farm
Broomhills Wood
RUSSWELL LA
Warren Farm
6
MK2
FOX FARM RD
THE CLOCK HO
PO
WOBURN RD
BRICKHILL MANOR CT
PH
WYNESS AVE
GREAT BRICKHILL LA
5
Galleylane Farm
Little Brickhill
Springfield Farm
MK17
32
Battle Hills Farm
Brookfield Wood
Barden Pits
4
GALLEY LA
Pipershill Spinney
A5
Philip's Clump
Goodman's Wood
Duncombe Wood
Great Firs
Lodgehill Wood
3
The Shrubberies
Westfield Farm
West Lodge
Park Farm
31
HOME FARM LA
Church Farm
Lane End
Home Farm
2
HORSEPOND
ROTTEN ROW
GREEN END
Cemy
Great Brickhill
UPPER WAY
PENNYCUIK
PO
High Ash CE Comb Sch
LOWER WAY
NAISBY DR
POUND HILL
Rectory Farm
Blue Gate Farm
Lower Rectory Farm
WARNERS CL
KNIGHTS CL
LU7
1
PH
HEATH RD
CUFF LA
DUCK END
Cherry Orchard Farm
River Ouzel
STOKE LA
IVY LA
HOLTS GN
STOKE LA
30
89
90
91

70
60

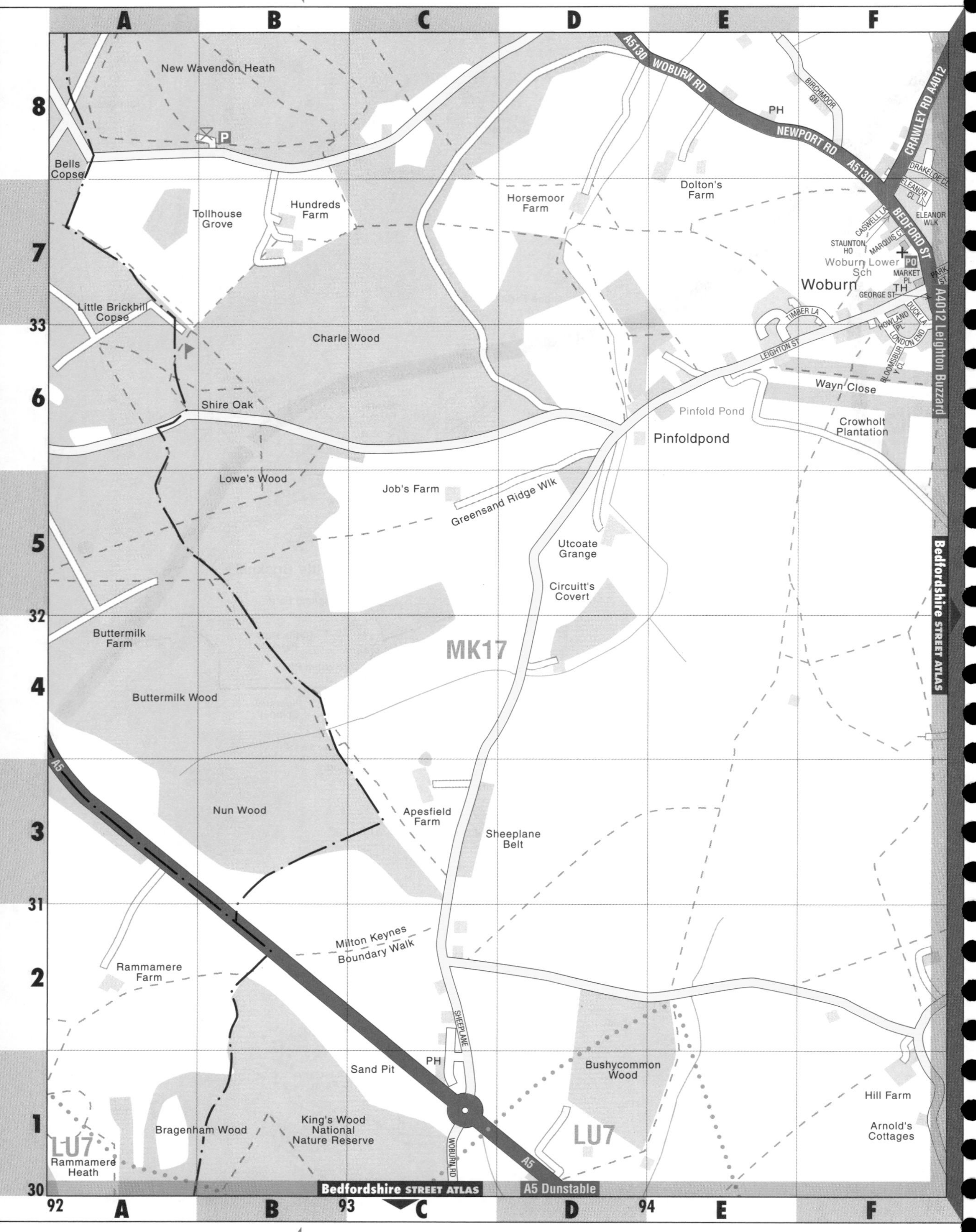

A B C D E F

8

New Wavendon Heath

P

Bells Copse

7

Tollhouse Grove

Hundreds Farm

Horsemoor Farm

Dolton's Farm

A5130 WOBURN RD

NEWPORT RD

PH

A5130

CRAWLEY RD A4012

BIRCHMOOR GN

DRAKELOE CL

ELEANOR CL

ELEANOR WLK

Little Brickhill Copse

CASWELL CL

STAUNTON HO

MARQUIS RD

Woburn Lower Sch

MARKET PL

TH

PO

BEDFORD ST

PARK ST

A4012 Leighton Buzzard

33

Charle Wood

Woburn

GEORGE ST

TIMBER LA

HOWLAND PL

DUCK LA

LONDON END

BLOOMSBURY V C L

6

Shire Oak

LEIGHTON ST

Wayn Close

Crowholt Plantation

Pinfold Pond

Pinfoldpond

Lowe's Wood

Job's Farm

Greensand Ridge Wlk

5

Utcoate Grange

Buttermilk Farm

32

Circuitt's Covert

4

Buttermilk Wood

MK17

A5

Nun Wood

Apesfield Farm

3

Sheeplane Belt

31

Milton Keynes Boundary Walk

Rammamere Farm

2

SHEEPLANE

Sand Pit

PH

Bushycommon Wood

Hill Farm

1

LU7

Bragenham Wood

King's Wood National Nature Reserve

WOBURN RD

LU7

Arnold's Cottages

Rammamere Heath

A5

A5 Dunstable

30

92 A B 93 C D 94 E F

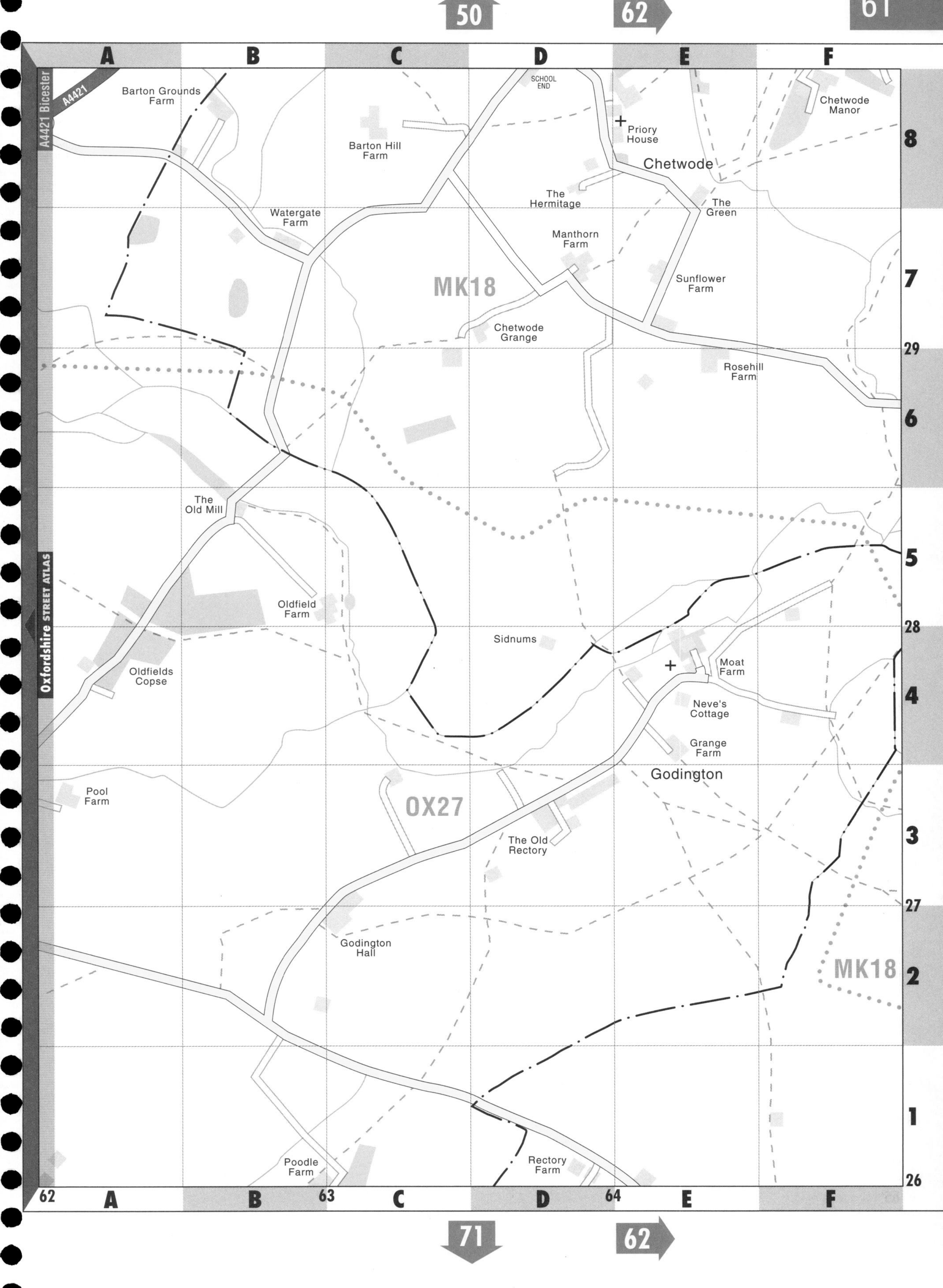

A4421 Bicester

Oxfordshire STREET ATLAS

A **B** **C** **D** **E** **F**

Barton Grounds Farm

Chetwode Manor

SCHOOL END

Priory House

Barton Hill Farm

Chetwode

8

Watergate Farm

The Hermitage

The Green

MK18

Manthorn Farm

7

Sunflower Farm

29

Chetwode Grange

Rosehill Farm

6

The Old Mill

5

Oldfield Farm

28

Sidnums

Moat Farm

Oldfields Copse

Neve's Cottage

4

Grange Farm

Pool Farm

OX27

Godington

The Old Rectory

3

27

Godington Hall

MK18

2

1

Poodle Farm

Rectory Farm

26

61
51

A B C D E F
Church Farm
PO
The Laurels
The Common
POUND LA
LEYS LA
SCHOOL LA
Preston Bissett
THE SQUARE
MAIN ST
Thorpes Farm
Poplars Farm
Jubilee Farm House
Jubilee Farm
College Farm
Fir Tree Cottage
Copperhouse Farm
Buryfield Spinney
Casemore Farm
Westfield Farm
Manor Farm
MK18
Cowley Farm
OX27
Cowley Old House
Cowley Lodge
Twyford Mill
Three Bridge Mill
Church View Farm
Twyford CE Fst Sch
CHURCH ST
GRANGE CL
SCHOOL LA
MILL LA
BROOK FARM CL
Home Farm
MAIN ST
Twyford
PO
Hall
PH
BICESTER RD
OX27
MANOR CT
ROSEHILL CRES
PORTWAY RD
Portway Cottages
8
7
29
6
5
28
4
3
27
2
1
26
65
66
67

61
72

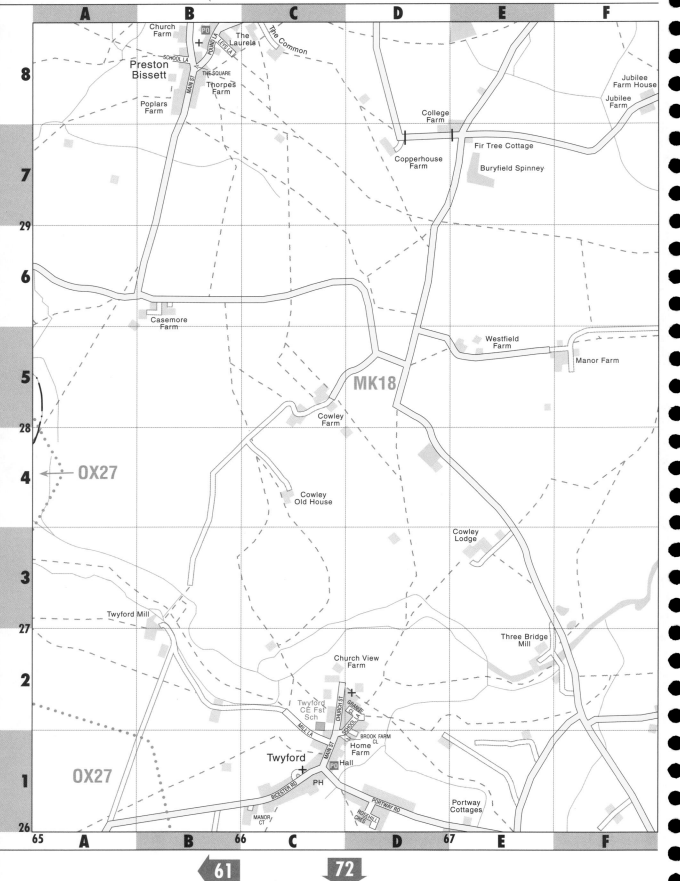

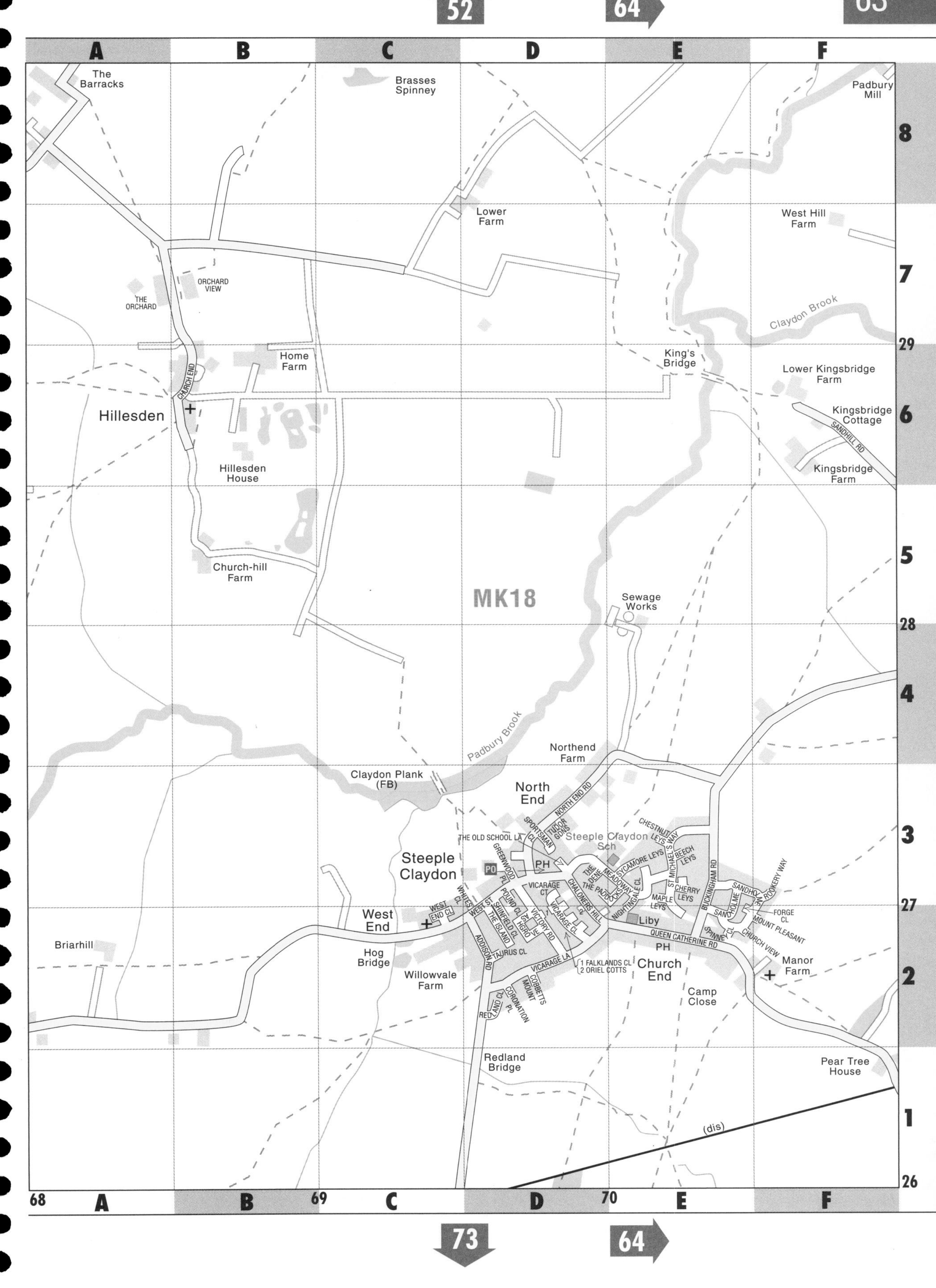

The Barracks

Brasses
Spinney

Padbury
Mill

8

Lower
Farm

West Hill
Farm

7

ORCHARD
VIEW

Claydon Brook

29

THE
ORCHARD

Home
Farm

King's
Bridge

Lower Kingsbridge
Farm

Hillesden

Kingsbridge
Cottage

6

SANDHILL RD

CHURCH END

Hillesden
House

Kingsbridge
Farm

Church-hill
Farm

MK18

5

Sewage
Works

28

Padbury Brook

4

Claydon Plank
(FB)

Northend
Farm

North
End

NORTH END RD

3

THE OLD SCHOOL LA

Steeple Claydon
Sch

CHESTNUT

SYCAMORE LEYS

ST MICHAEL'S WAY

Steeple
Claydon

SPORTSMAN CL

TUDOR GDNS

PH

PO

GREENWOOD

THE MEADOWAY

THE PADDOCK

BEECH LEYS

CHERRY LEYS

BUCKINGHAM RD

ROOKERY WAY

27

VICARAGE
CT

CHALONERS HILL

MAPLE LEYS

SANDHOLME

MOUNT PLEASANT

FORGE
CL

West
End

WEST END CL

THE ISLAND

WINTINGHAM CL

Liby

CHURCH VIEW

WEST
WHITES

POUND CL

SANDFIELD CL

VICTORY RD

VICARAGE CL

PH

Briarhill

Hog
Bridge

ADDISON RD

TAURUS CL

VICARAGE LA

QUEEN CATHERINE RD

SPINNEY

Manor
Farm

2

Willowvale
Farm

COBBETTS

1 FALKLANDS CL
2 ORIEL COTTS

Church
End

RED
LION CL

CORONATION
MOUNT

Camp
Close

Redland
Bridge

Pear Tree
House

1

(dis)

26

63
53

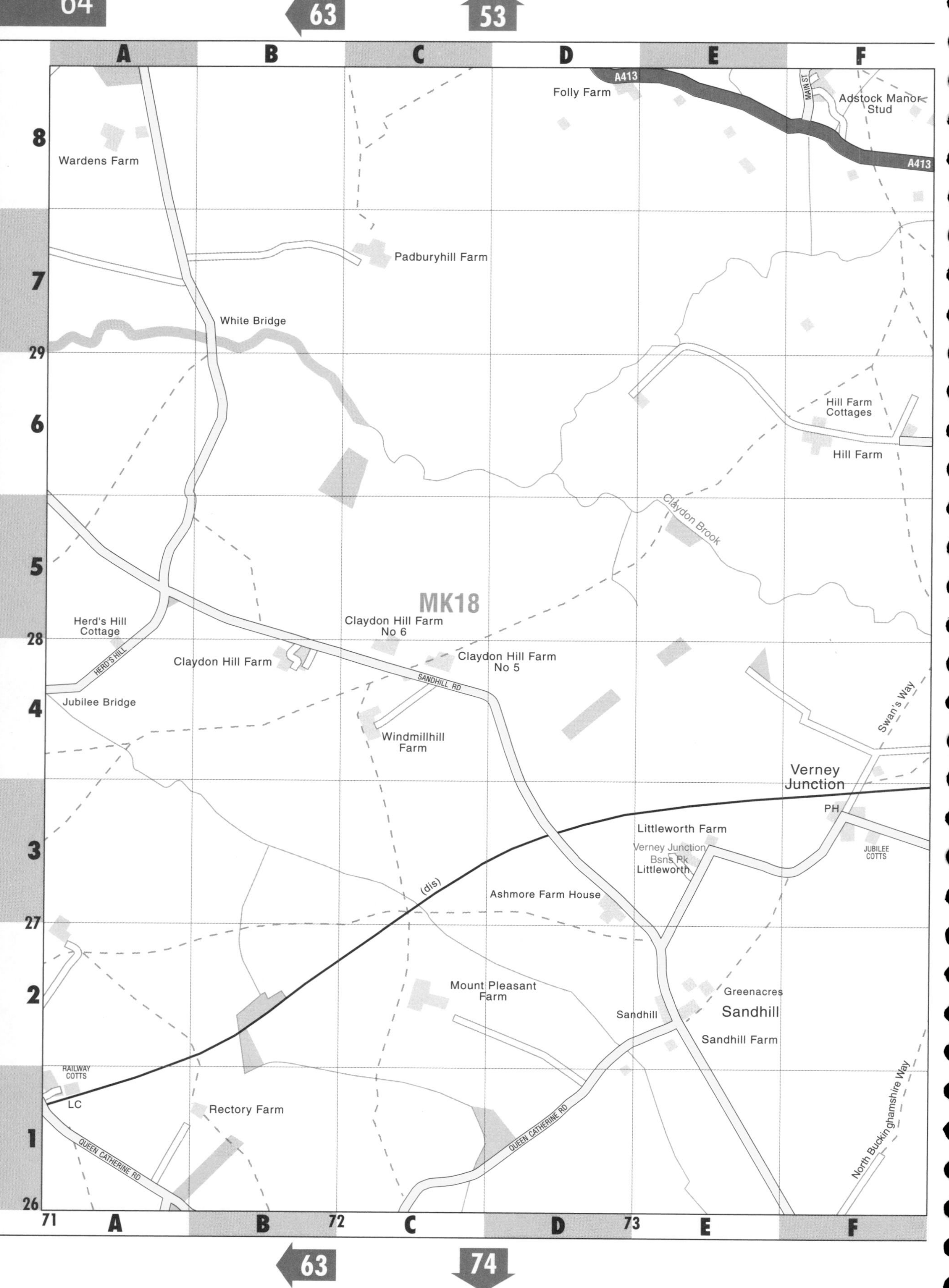

A B C D E F

8

Folly Farm

A413

Adstock Manor Stud

MAIN ST

A413

Wardens Farm

7

Padburyhill Farm

White Bridge

29

Hill Farm Cottages

6

Hill Farm

Claydon Brook

5

MK18

Herd's Hill Cottage

Claydon Hill Farm No 6

28

Claydon Hill Farm

Claydon Hill Farm No 5

SANDHILL RD

HERD'S HILL

Swan's Way

4

Jubilee Bridge

Windmillhill Farm

Verney Junction

PH

3

Littleworth Farm

JUBILEE COTTS

Verney Junction Bsns Pk

Littleworth

(dis)

Ashmore Farm House

27

Mount Pleasant Farm

Greenacres

2

Sandhill

Sandhill

Sandhill Farm

North Buckinghamshire Way

RAILWAY COTTS

LC

Rectory Farm

QUEEN CATHERINE RD

1

QUEEN CATHERINE RD

26

71 A B 72 C D 73 E F

63
74

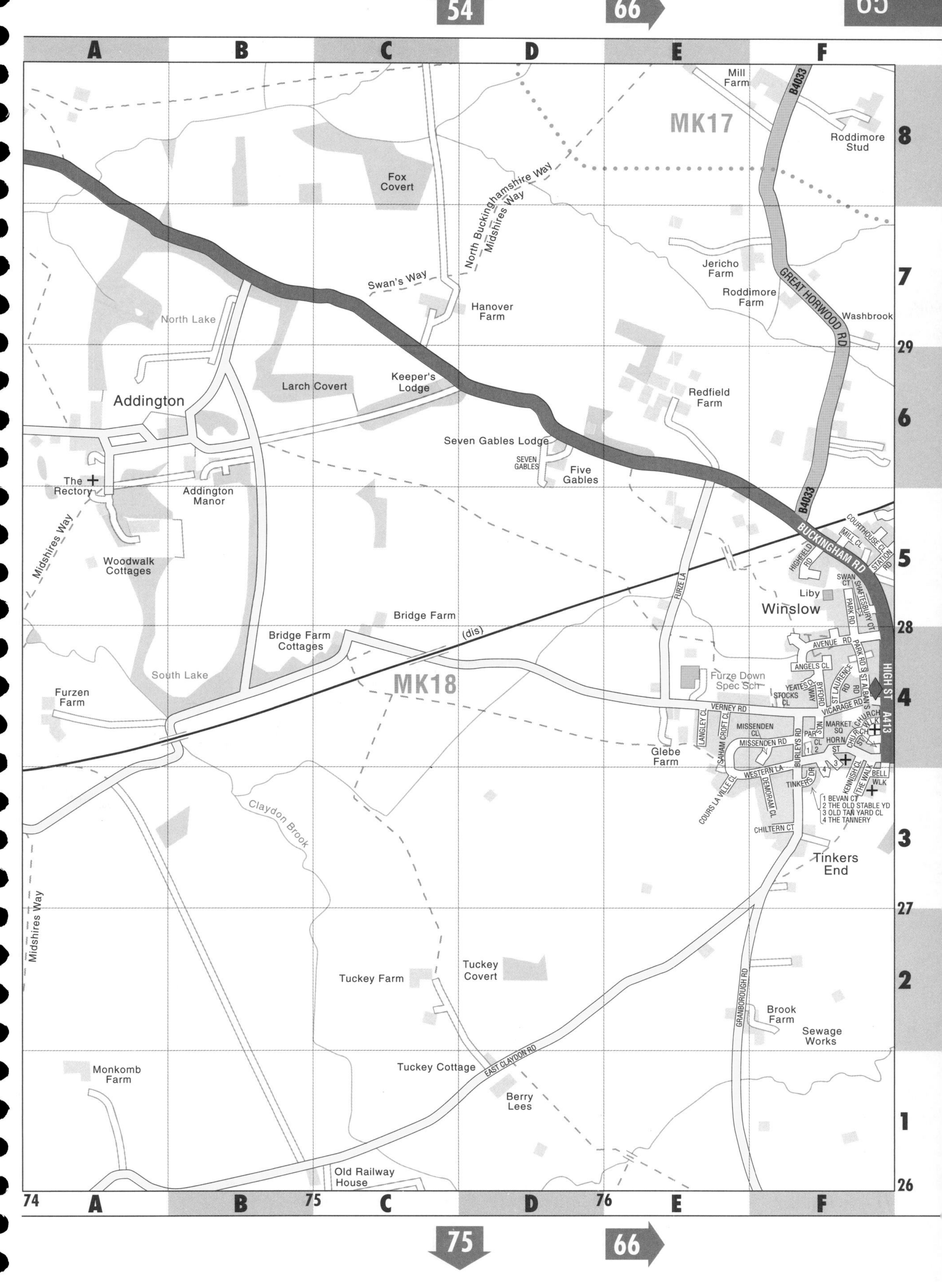

54
66
A
B
C
D
E
F
Mill Farm
B4033
MK17
Roddimore Stud
8
Fox Covert
North Buckinghamshire Way
Midshires Way
Swan's Way
7
Jericho Farm
GREAT HORWOOD RD
Roddimore Farm
Washbrook
Hanover Farm
North Lake
29
Keeper's Lodge
Larch Covert
Addington
Redfield Farm
6
Seven Gables Lodge
SEVEN GABLES
Five Gables
The Rectory
Addington Manor
Midshires Way
B4033
BUCKINGHAM RD
Woodwalk Cottages
5
Winslow
Liby
28
Bridge Farm
(dis)
Bridge Farm Cottages
MK18
South Lake
Furzen Farm
Furze Down Spec Sch
HIGH ST
A413
4
Glebe Farm
Claydon Brook
1 BEVAN CT
2 THE OLD STABLE YD
3 OLD TAN YARD CL
4 THE TANNERY
CHILTERN CT
3
Tinkers End
Midshires Way
27
Tuckey Covert
Tuckey Farm
GRANBOROUGH RD
2
Brook Farm
Sewage Works
Monkomb Farm
Tuckey Cottage
EAST CLAYDON RD
Berry Lees
1
Old Railway House
26
74
75
76
75
66

A B C D E F

8

Greenway Farm

Mount Pleasant

The Hollows

Horwood House

7

Fishpond Spinney

Osierbed Spinney

29

The White House

(dis)

Roddimore Covert

Moco Farm

6

Clare Farm

Canada

Foxhole Farm

1 STATION COTTS
2 OLD STATION CL

TANK HOUSE RD

THE SPINNEY

MCLERNON WAY

COMERFORD WAY

MAGPIE LAKE CL

TANGWELL LA

RUDDS CL

FLEDGELINGS WLK

Spring Corner

Dodley Hill Farm

MK17

Midshires Way

Station Rd Ind Est

OLD MILL FURLONG

STATION RD

SCOTT EVANS CT

DANDES WAY

LONGLANDS CT

KEACH CL

LONGLANDS WLK

TOTTS CL

LAMB CL

MEETING OAK LA

BEAMISH WAY

Redhall Farm

5

Winslow CE Comb Sch

Abovemead Farm

PICCADILLY MEWS

28

CROCKETTERS ROW

OAKWAY

ELMFIELDS GATE

NOBLE HOUSE

NORTH CROFT

Winslow Rd

MK18

P

GREYHOUND CT

GREYHOUND

PO

ELMSIDE

SHEPHERDS ROW

FAIR MDW

COPSE

GATE

THE CLOVERS

ROW END

4

Winslow

Ivy Farm

Duck End

FIELD END

CHARLTON CL

SN HILL

A413

SHEEP ST

Hotel

CLAYCUTTERS

TENNIS CL

LYNE CL

Shipton Mead Farm

Cross Bucks Way

B4032

Winslow Rd

B4032

Rands Farm

SHIPTON

Jubilee Cottages

3

Shipton Farm

Swanbourne House Sch

27

Shipton Bridge

2

Claydon Brook

Haybush Farm

BENNETT'S HILL A413

Midshires Way

Swan's Way

1

Bennett's Hill

North Hill Farm

26

56
68

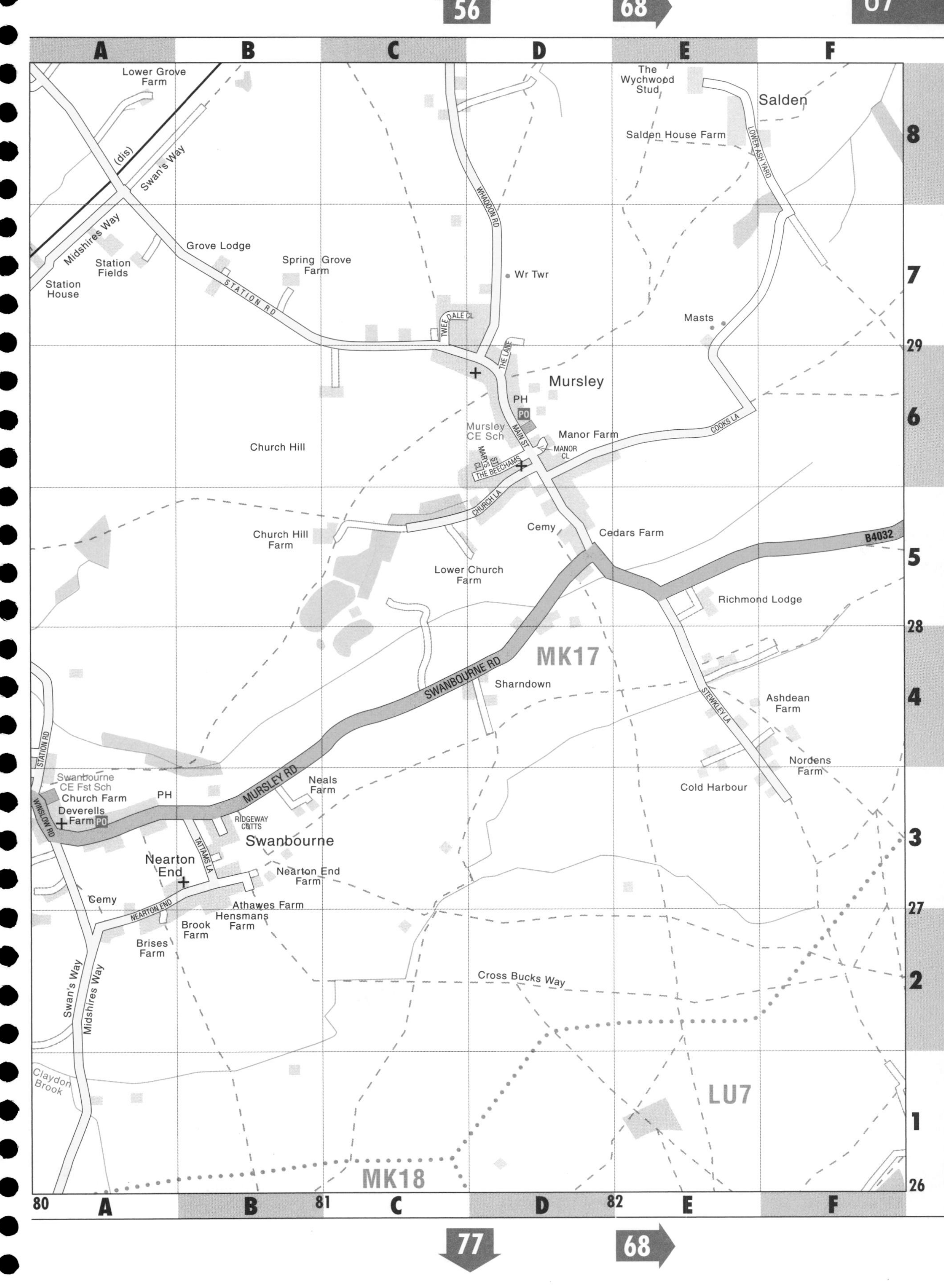
A
B
C
D
E
F
Lower Grove Farm
(dis)
Swan's Way
Midshires Way
Station Fields
Station House
Grove Lodge
STATION RD
Spring Grove Farm
WHADDON RD
Wr Twr
TWEEDALE CL
THE LANE
The Wychwood Stud
Salden
Salden House Farm
LOWER ASH YARD
Masts
Mursley
PH
PO
Mursley CE Sch
MAIN ST
Manor Farm
MANOR CL
COOKS LA
ST MARY'S CL
THE BEECHAMS
CHURCH LA
Church Hill
Church Hill Farm
Cemy
Cedars Farm
B4032
Lower Church Farm
Richmond Lodge
MK17
SWANBOURNE RD
Sharndown
STEWKLEY LA
Ashdean Farm
Nordens Farm
Cold Harbour
STATION RD
Swanbourne CE Fst Sch
Church Farm
PH
MURSLEY RD
Neals Farm
Deverells Farm
PO
WINSLOW RD
RIDGEWAY COTTS
Swanbourne
TATTAMS LA
Nearton End
Nearton End Farm
Cemy
NEARTON END
Athawes Farm
Hensmans Farm
Brook Farm
Brises Farm
Swan's Way
Midshires Way
Cross Bucks Way
Claydon Brook
LU7
MK18
8
7
29
6
5
28
4
3
27
2
1
26
80
81
82

77
68

67
57

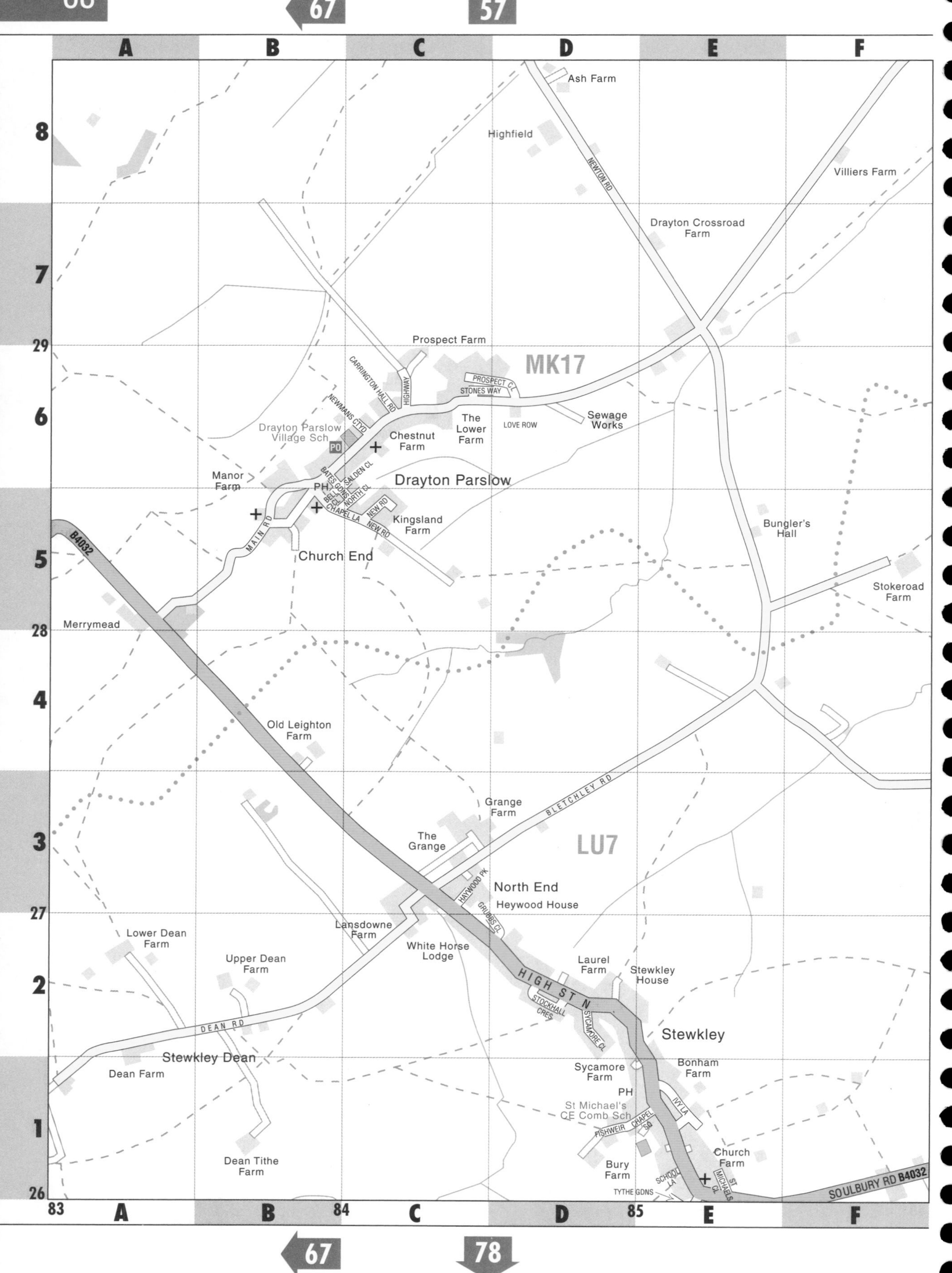
A
B
C
D
E
F
8
7
29
6
5
28
4
3
27
2
1
26
83
84
85
Ash Farm
Highfield
NEWTON RD
Villiers Farm
Drayton Crossroad Farm
Prospect Farm
MK17
CARRINGTON HALL RD
HIGHWAY
PROSPECT CL
STONES WAY
NEWMANS CTYD
Drayton Parslow Village Sch
PO
Chestnut Farm
The Lower Farm
LOVE ROW
Sewage Works
Manor Farm
PH
BATES GDNS
SALDEN CL
NORTH CL
BELL CL
CHAPEL LA
NEW RD
Drayton Parslow
Kingsland Farm
MAIN RD
B4032
Church End
Bungler's Hall
Stokeroad Farm
Merrymead
Old Leighton Farm
Grange Farm
BLETCHLEY RD
The Grange
LU7
HAYWOOD PK
North End
Heywood House
GRUBBS CL
Lower Dean Farm
Lansdowne Farm
White Horse Lodge
Upper Dean Farm
Laurel Farm
Stewkley House
HIGH ST N
STOCKHALL CRES
SYCAMORE CL
DEAN RD
Stewkley
Stewkley Dean
Dean Farm
Sycamore Farm
Bonham Farm
PH
St Michael's CE Comb Sch
IVY LA
FISHWEIR
CHAPEL SQ
Church Farm
Dean Tithe Farm
Bury Farm
SCHOOL LA
ST MICHAELS CL
TYTHE GDNS
SOULBURY RD B4032

67
78

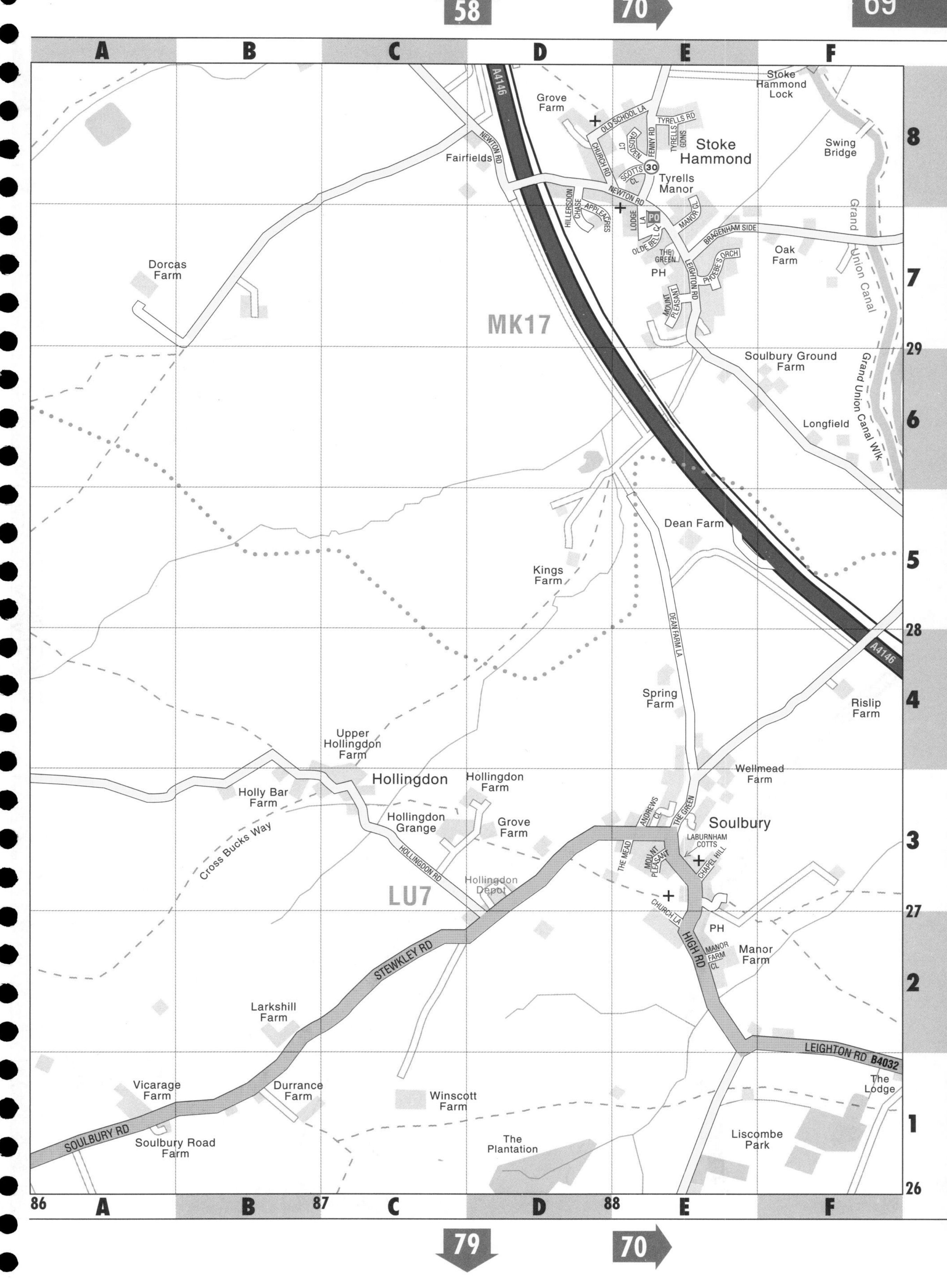
58
70
A
B
C
D
E
F
8
7
29
6
5
28
4
3
27
2
1
26
86
87
88
79
70
A4146
Grove Farm
OLD SCHOOL LA
TYRELLS RD
TYRELLS GDNS
Stoke Hammond Lock
Stoke Hammond
Swing Bridge
NEWTON RD
Fairfields
CHURCH RD
GADSDEN CT
FENNY RD
SCOTTS CL
30
Tyrells Manor
HILLERSDON CHASE
APPLEACRES
LODGE LA
PO
MANOR CL
BRAGENHAM SIDE
OLDE BELL CL
THE GREEN
PH
LEIGHTON RD
PHOEBE'S ORCH
Oak Farm
Grand Union Canal
Dorcas Farm
MOUNT PLEASANT
MK17
Soulbury Ground Farm
Grand Union Canal Wlk
Longfield
Dean Farm
Kings Farm
DEAN FARM LA
Spring Farm
Rislip Farm
Upper Hollingdon Farm
Hollingdon
Hollingdon Farm
Wellmead Farm
Holly Bar Farm
Hollingdon Grange
Grove Farm
ANDREWS CL
THE GREEN
Soulbury
LABURNHAM COTTS
CHAPEL HILL
THE MEAD
MOUNT PLEASANT
Cross Bucks Way
HOLLINGDON RD
Hollingdon Depot
LU7
CHURCH LA
PH
HIGH RD
MANOR FARM CL
Manor Farm
STEWKLEY RD
Larkshill Farm
LEIGHTON RD B4032
Vicarage Farm
Durrance Farm
Winscott Farm
The Lodge
SOULBURY RD
Soulbury Road Farm
The Plantation
Liscombe Park

A **B** **C** **D** **E** **F**

8

STOKE LA

Ivy Lane Farm

Sewage Works

Stockgrove Farm

Stockgrove Park Ho

River Ouzel

MK17

Greensand Ridge Wlk

7

Paper Mill

Partridge Hill

Oak Wood

Stockgrove Country Park

Visitor Ctr

P

29

Furze Hill

Alders Farm

Partridge House

CH

Upper Kiln Farm

Kiln Farm

Shire Oak

6

Rushmere Park

Bragenham Farm

Bragenham

Red Bridge

BRAGENHAM LA

PH

Stapleford Mill

5

P

Stapleford Farm

Ludley Cottage

28

Grand Union Canal

River Ouzel

LINSLADE RD

A4146

4

LU7

Nares Gadley Farm

Rushmere

Grand Union Canal Wlk

THE HEATH

CH

Chelmscote Manor Farm

Broad Oak

HEATH DUKES RIDE

SANDY LA REDWOOD GLADE

3

Cross Bucks Way

Grange Mill

PLANTATION RD

Greensand Ridge Wlk

REDWOOD GLADE

27

OLD LINSLADE RD

MANOR CT

P

TALL PINES

2

Old Linslade Manor

Old Linslade

Corbettshill Farm

OXENDON CT ROBINSWOOD CL

TAYLOR RIDE WOODLAND AVE DINGLE DELL

Dollar Farm

LEIGHTON RD

B4032

LEIGHTON BUZZARD

1

PH

STOKE RD

GLOBE LA

Sewage Works

BOSSINGTON LA THE MARTINS DR

A4146

Linslade Wood

26

Valley Farm

A **B** **C** **D** **E** **F**
89   90   91

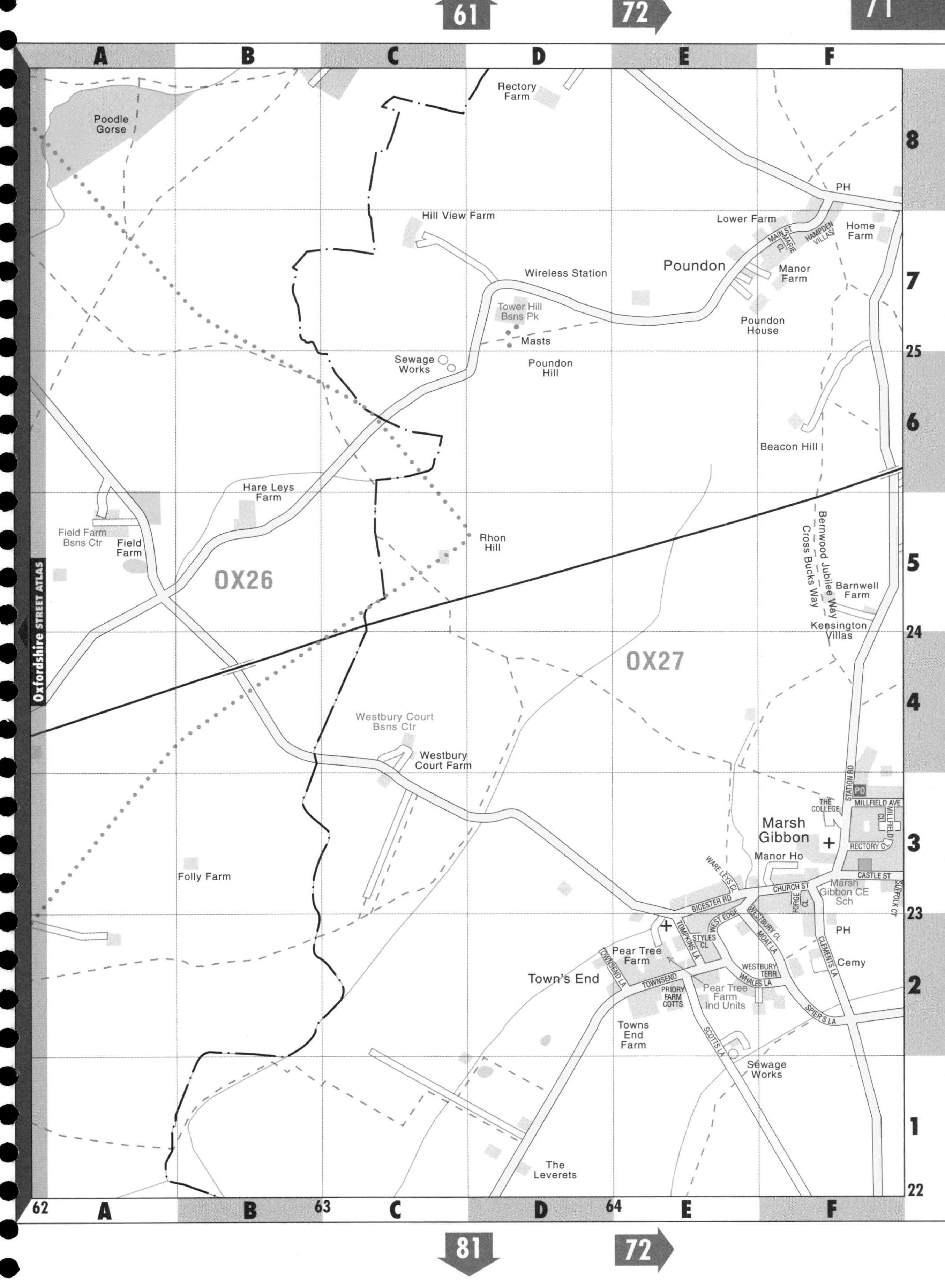

A B C D E F

Poodle Gorse

Rectory Farm

8

PH

Hill View Farm

Lower Farm

Home Farm

Poundon

Manor Farm

7

Wireless Station

Tower Hill Bsns Pk

Poundon House

25

Masts

Sewage Works

Poundon Hill

6

Beacon Hill

Hare Leys Farm

Bernwood Jubilee Way

Cross Bucks Way

Field Farm Bsns Ctr

Field Farm

OX26

Rhon Hill

Barnwell Farm

5

Kensington Villas

24

OX27

4

Westbury Court Bsns Ctr

Westbury Court Farm

STATION RD

PO

THE COLLEGE

MILLFIELD AVE

MILLFIELD

Marsh Gibbon

RECTORY CT

3

Manor Ho

CASTLE ST

Folly Farm

WARE LEYS CL

Marsh Gibbon CE Sch

SUFFOLK CT

CHURCH ST

FORGE

BICESTER RD

23

WEST EDGE

STYLES CL

TOMPKINS LA

WESTBURY CL

MOAT LA

PH

Cemy

CLEMENTS LA

Pear Tree Farm

TOWNSEND LA

WESTBURY TERR

WHALES LA

Town's End

TOWNSEND

PRIORY FARM COTTS

Pear Tree Farm Ind Units

2

SPIER'S LA

Towns End Farm

SCOTTS LA

Sewage Works

1

The Leverets

22

62 A B 63 C D 64 E F

Oxfordshire STREET ATLAS

71
62

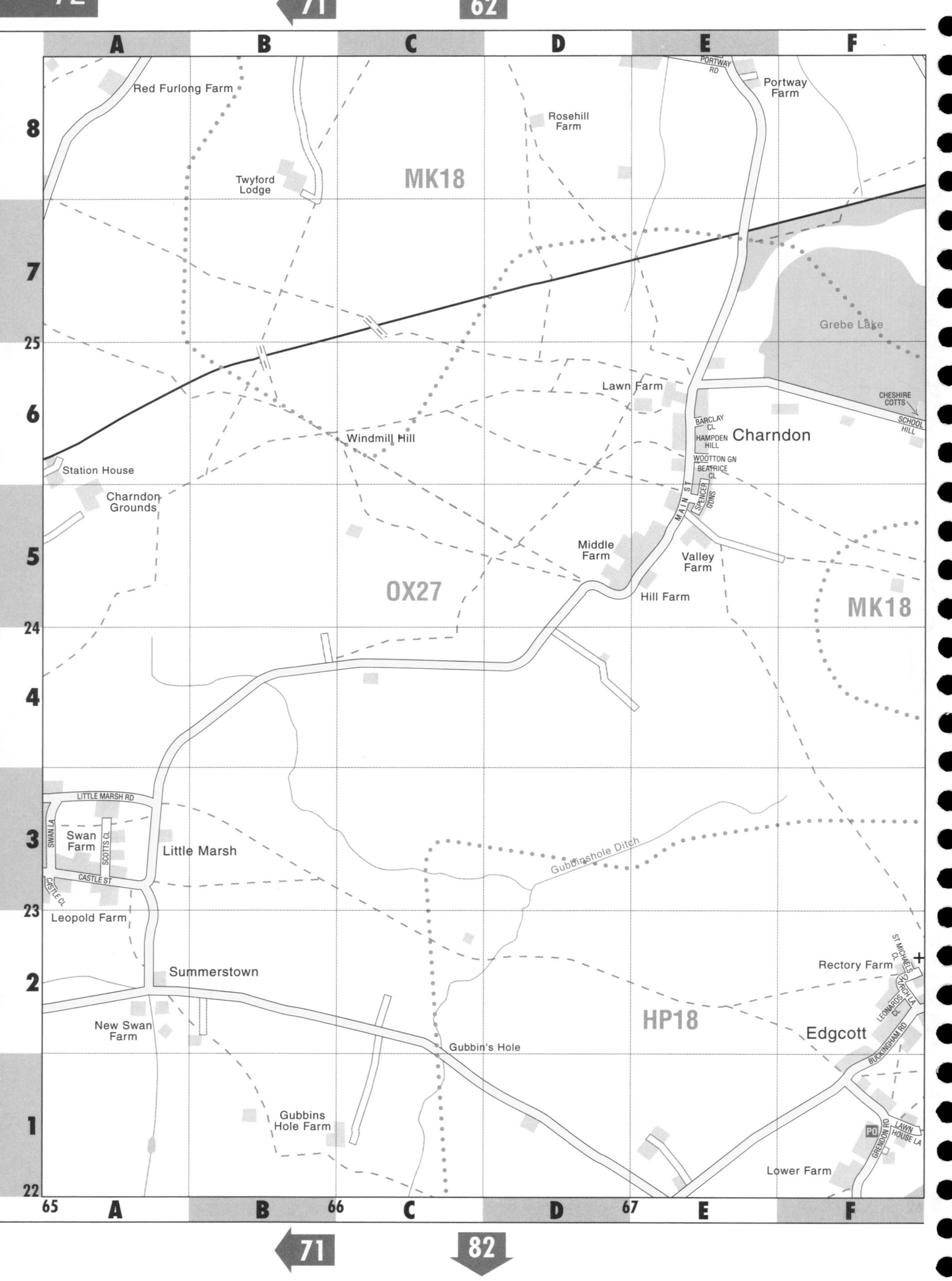
A
B
C
D
E
F
8
7
25
6
5
24
4
3
23
2
1
22
65
66
67
Red Furlong Farm
Twyford Lodge
MK18
Rosehill Farm
PORTWAY RD
Portway Farm
Grebe Lake
Lawn Farm
CHESHIRE COTTS
SCHOOL HILL
BARCLAY CL
HAMPDEN HILL
Charndon
WOOTTON GN
BEATRICE CL
MAIN ST
SPENCER GDNS
Windmill Hill
Station House
Charndon Grounds
Middle Farm
Valley Farm
Hill Farm
OX27
MK18
LITTLE MARSH RD
SWAN LA
Swan Farm
SCOTTS CL
Little Marsh
CASTLE ST
CASTLE CL
Leopold Farm
Gubbinshole Ditch
Summerstown
New Swan Farm
Gubbin's Hole
HP18
Edgcott
ST MICHAELS CL
CHURCH LA
Rectory Farm
LEONARDS CL
BUCKINGHAM RD
Gubbins Hole Farm
PO
GRENDON RD
LAWN HOUSE LA
Lower Farm

71
82

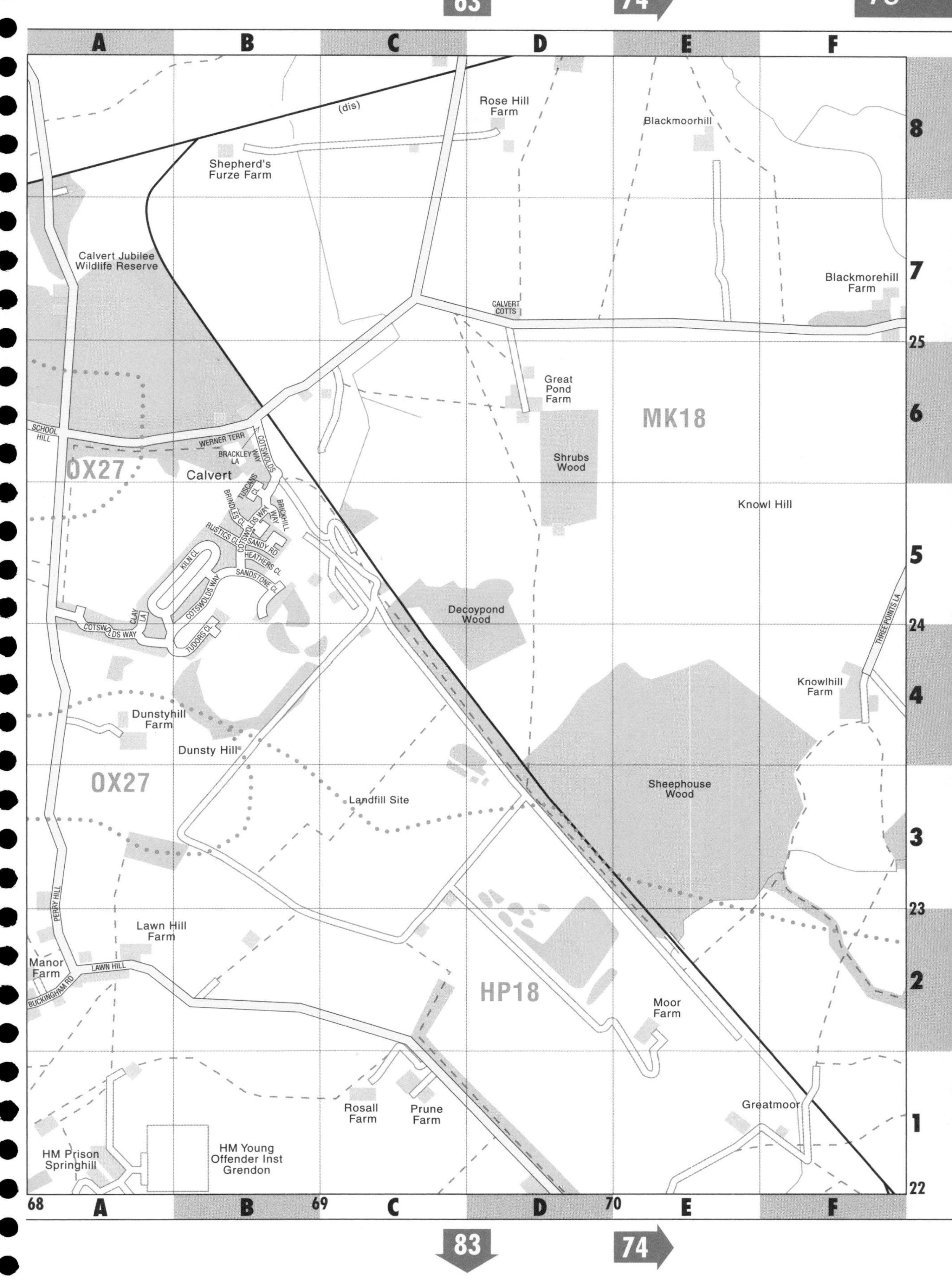

A B C D E F

(dis)

Rose Hill
Farm

Blackmoorhill

Shepherd's
Furze Farm

8

Calvert Jubilee
Wildlife Reserve

Blackmorehill
Farm

7

CALVERT
COTTS

25

SCHOOL
HILL

Great
Pond
Farm

MK18

6

OX27

WERNER TERR

BRACKLEY
LA

Calvert

COTSWOLDS WAY

Shrubs
Wood

Knowl Hill

TUSCANS
CL

BRINDLES CL

RUSTICS CL

SANDY RD

BRIDGHILL
WAY

TUSCANS
WAY

KILN CL

HEATHERS CL

SANDSTONE CL

COTSWOLDS WAY

TUDORS CL

CLAY LA

COTSWOLDS WAY

Decoypond
Wood

5

24

THREE POINTS LA

Dunstyhill
Farm

Knowlhill
Farm

4

Dunsty Hill

OX27

Landfill Site

Sheephouse
Wood

3

23

PERRY HILL

Lawn Hill
Farm

Manor
Farm

LAWN HILL

HP18

Moor
Farm

2

BUCKINGHAM RD

Rosall
Farm

Prune
Farm

Greatmoor

1

HM Prison
Springhill

HM Young
Offender Inst
Grendon

22

68

A

B

69

C

D

70

E

F

73
64

A **B** **C** **D** **E** **F**

8

QUEEN CATHERINE RD

Home Farm

TOWNSEND COTTS

Cemy

Middle Claydon

Weir

The Old Brick Yard (disused)

Claydon Park

Swan's Way

New Farm

SANDHILL RD

BRIARY CT

VERNEY FARM

VERNEY CT

Verney Farm

CHESTNUT CL

EMERALD CL

CHURCH WAY

CL

VIEW

ST MARYS CL

East Claydon

7

Catherine Farm

Claydon House

ST MARYS RD

Ivy Nook

25

South Lodge

East Claydon Sch

Phoenix Fruit Farm

Botolph Farm

6

THREE POINTS LA

BOTYL RD

Botolph Farm

Botolph Claydon

ORCHARD WAY

MK18

WEIR LA

Bernwood Farm

5

Home Wood

Muxwell Farm

24

4

Bernwood Jubilee Way

Claydon Lawn

Hogshaw Farm

3

Romer Wood

Balmore Wood

Runt's Wood

Coppice Lowhill Farm

Hogshaw Farm

23

Three Points La

Greatsea Wood

2

HP18

Finemerehill House

HP22

1

Kitehill Farm

22

71 **A** **B** 72 **C** **D** 73 **E** **F**

73
84

65
76

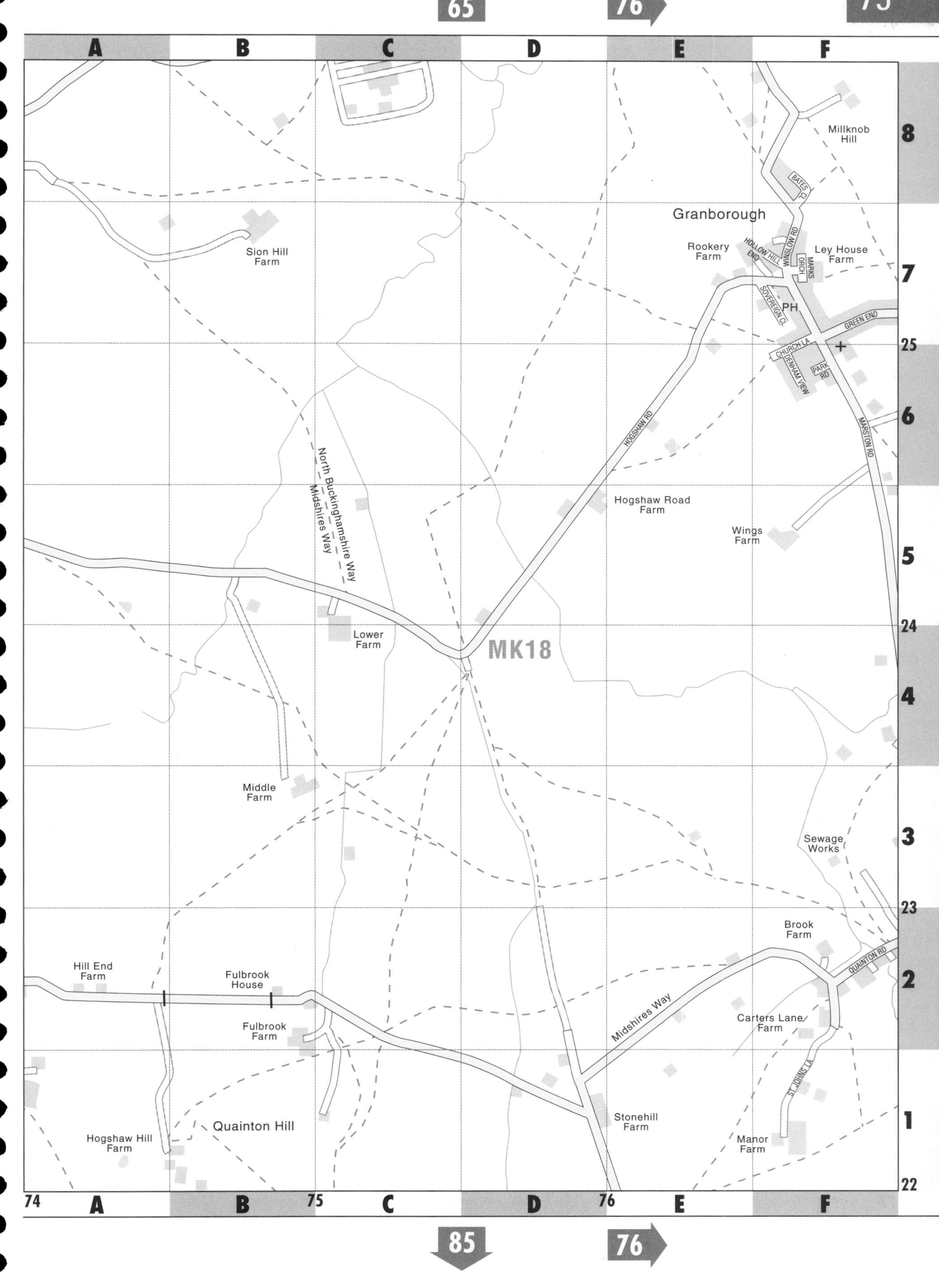
A
B
C
D
E
F
Millknob Hill
BATES CL
Granborough
Rookery Farm
HOLLOW HILL END
WINSLOW RD
MARKS ORCH
Ley House Farm
SOVEREIGN CL
PH
GREEN END
CHURCH LA
DENHAM VIEW
PARK RD
MARSTON RD
Sion Hill Farm
HOGSHAW RD
North Buckinghamshire Way
Midshires Way
Hogshaw Road Farm
Wings Farm
Lower Farm
MK18
Middle Farm
Sewage Works
Brook Farm
QUAINTON RD
Hill End Farm
Fulbrook House
Fulbrook Farm
Midshires Way
Carters Lane Farm
ST JOHNS LA
Quainton Hill
Hogshaw Hill Farm
Stonehill Farm
Manor Farm
8
7
25
6
5
24
4
3
23
2
1
22
74
75
76

85
76

75
66

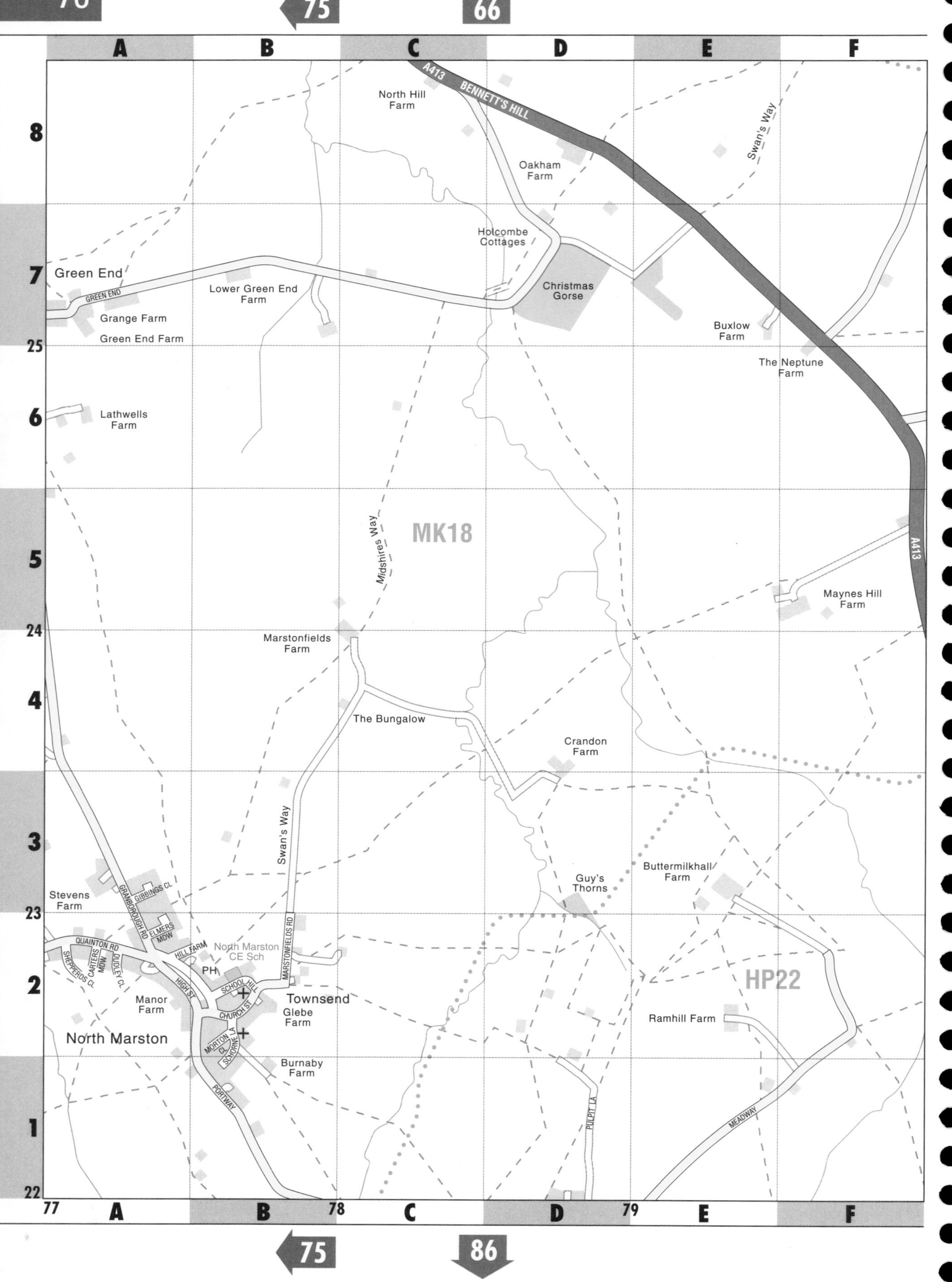
A
B
C
D
E
F
8
7
25
6
5
24
4
3
23
2
1
22
77
78
79
A413
BENNETT'S HILL
North Hill Farm
Oakham Farm
Swan's Way
Holcombe Cottages
Christmas Gorse
Green End
GREEN END
Lower Green End Farm
Grange Farm
Green End Farm
Buxlow Farm
The Neptune Farm
Lathwells Farm
MK18
Midshires Way
A413
Maynes Hill Farm
Marstonfields Farm
The Bungalow
Crandon Farm
Swan's Way
Guy's Thorns
Buttermilkhall Farm
Stevens Farm
GRANBOROUGH RD
GIBBINGS CL
ELMERS MDW
QUAINTON RD
SHEPPERDS CL
CARTERS MDW
DUDLEY CL
HILL FARM
North Marston CE Sch
PH
MARSTONFIELDS RD
SCHOOL HILL
HIGH ST
CHURCH ST
Townsend
Glebe Farm
HP22
Manor Farm
North Marston
MORTON CL
SCHORNE LA
Ramhill Farm
Burnaby Farm
PORTWAY
PULPIT LA
MEADWAY

75
86

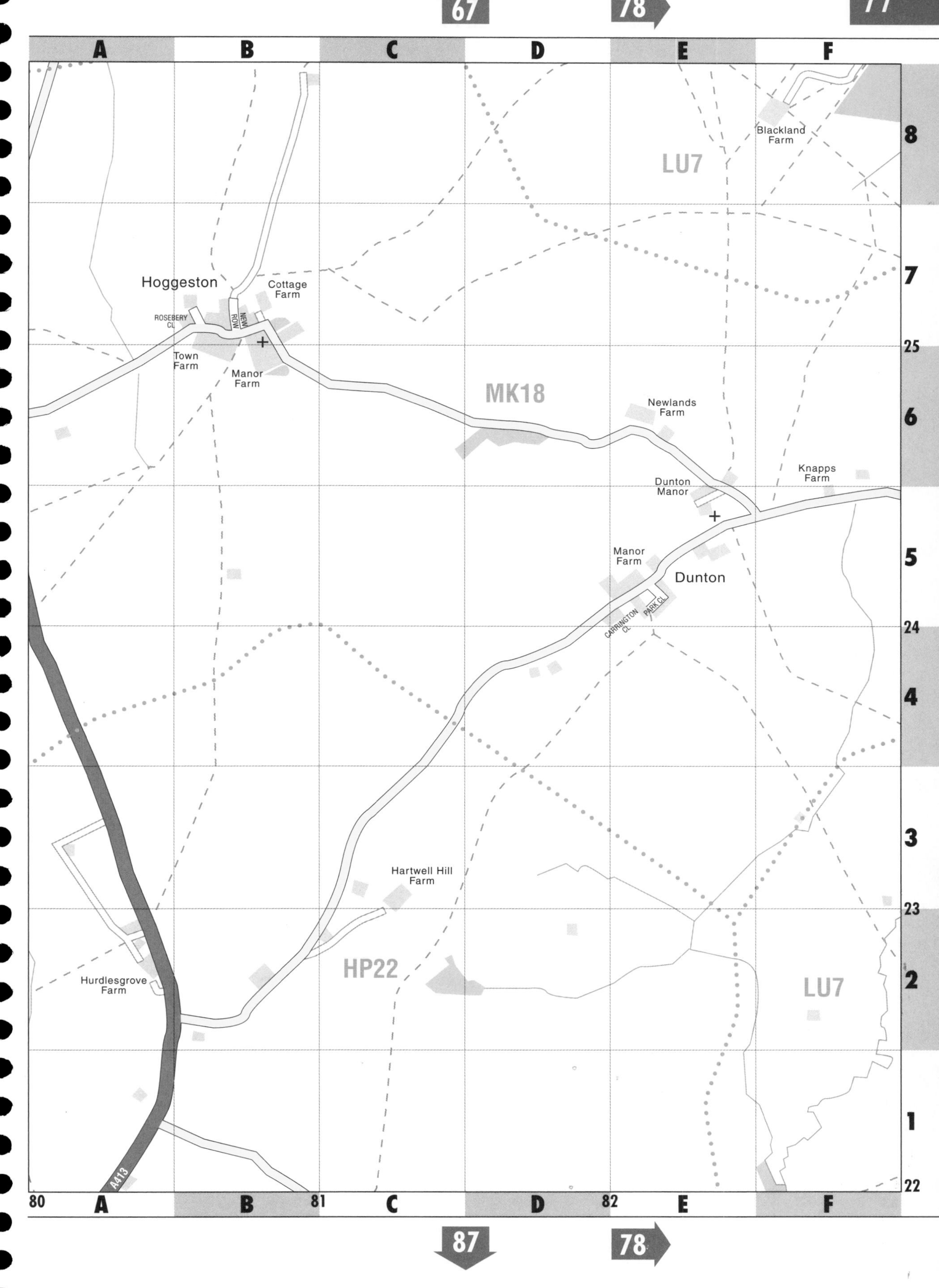

A B C D E F

8
LU7
Blackland
Farm

7
Hoggeston
Cottage
Farm
ROSEBERY
CL
NEW
ROW
25
Town
Farm
Manor
Farm
MK18
6
Newlands
Farm

Knapps
Farm
Dunton
Manor
Manor
Farm
Dunton
5
CARRINGTON
CL
PARK CL
24

4

3
Hartwell Hill
Farm
23
HP22
2
Hurdlesgrove
Farm
LU7

1
A413
22
80 A B 81 C D 82 E F

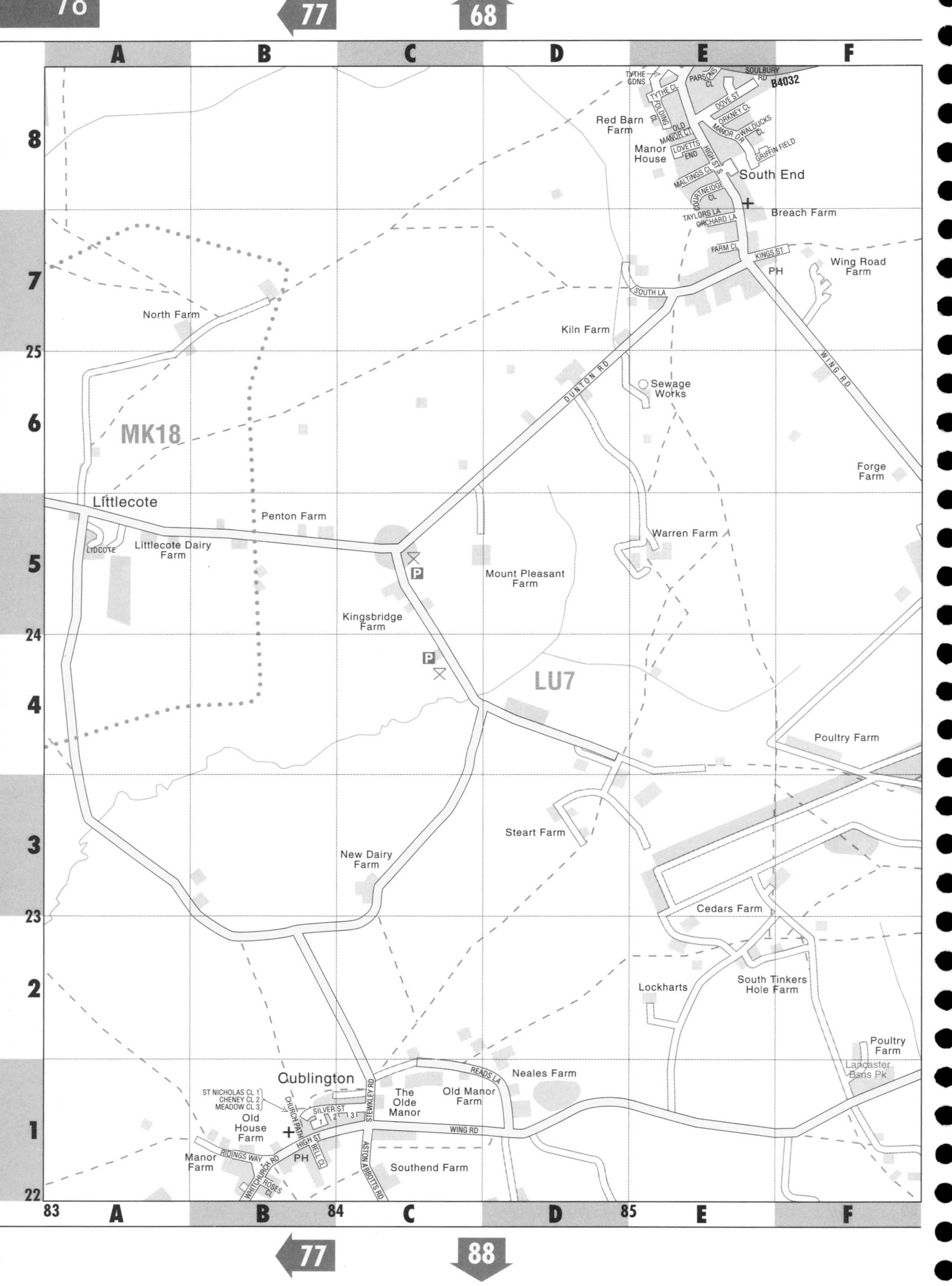

77
68

A   B   C   D   E   F

8

7

25

6

MK18

Littlecote

5

LIDCOTE

24

4

LU7

3

23

2

1

22

TYTHE GDNS

TYTHE CL

FOLLING

PARSONS CL

DOVE ST

ORKNEY CL

SOULBURY RD

B4032

Red Barn Farm

OLD MANOR CL

LOVETTS END

MALTINGS CL

HIGH ST

MANOR CR

WALDUCKS CL

GRIFFIN FIELD

Manor House

COURTNEIDGE CL

South End

TAYLORS LA

ORCHARD LA

FARM CL

Breach Farm

KINGS ST

PH

Wing Road Farm

SOUTH LA

Kiln Farm

DUNTON RD

Sewage Works

WING RD

Forge Farm

North Farm

Penton Farm

Littlecote Dairy Farm

Warren Farm

Kingsbridge Farm

Mount Pleasant Farm

Poultry Farm

New Dairy Farm

Steart Farm

Cedars Farm

Lockharts

South Tinkers Hole Farm

Poultry Farm

Lancaster Bsns Pk

Neales Farm

READS LA

Cublington

ST NICHOLAS CL 1
CHENEY CL 2
MEADOW CL 3

CHURCH PATH

SILVER ST

STEWKLEY RD

The Olde Manor

Old Manor Farm

Old House Farm

HIGH ST

HIGH BELL CL

ASTON ABBOTTS RD

WING RD

Manor Farm

RIDINGS WAY

WHITCHURCH RD

ROSES CL

PH

Southend Farm

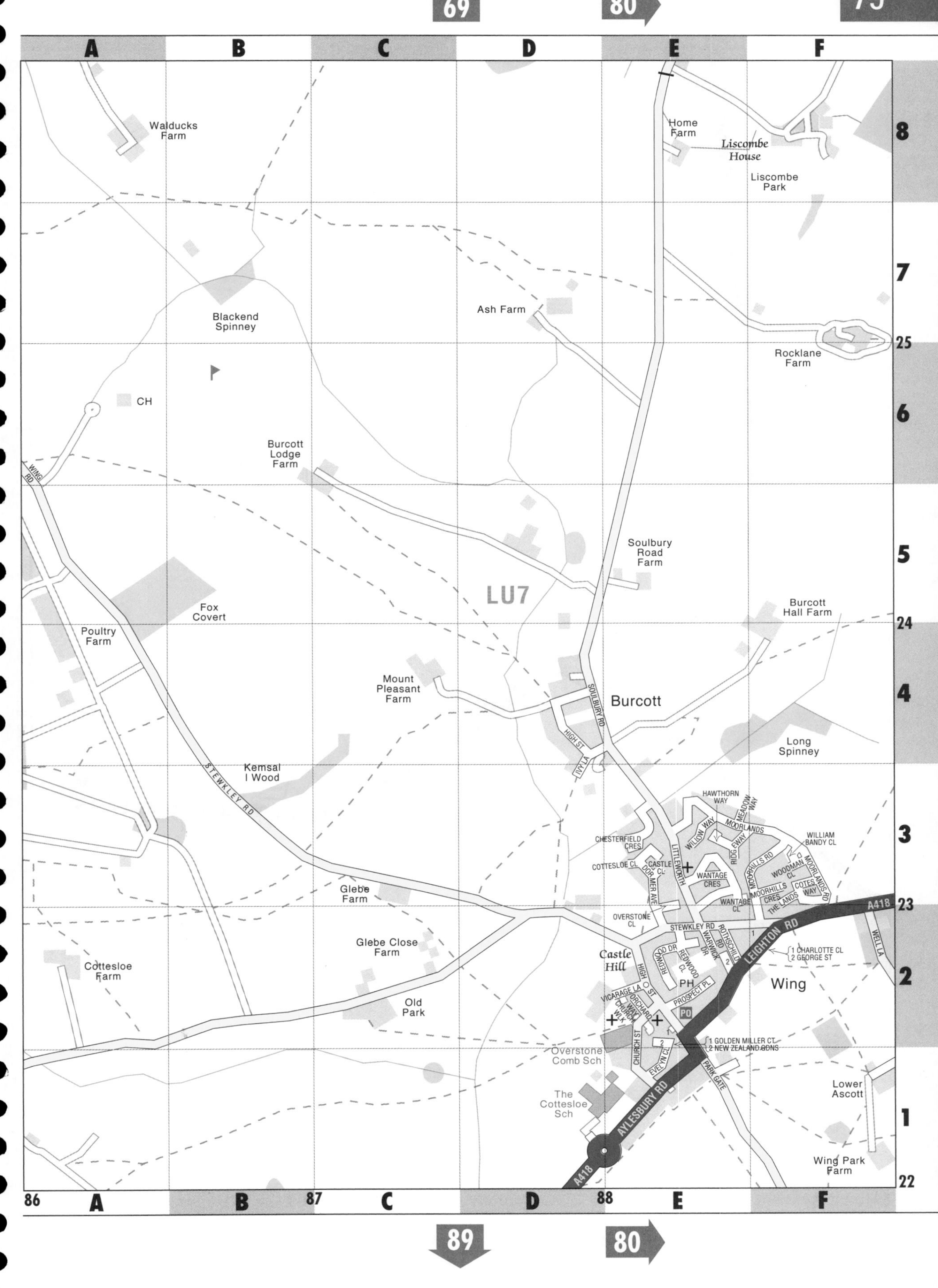

69
80
89
80

A   B   C   D   E   F

8
7
25
6
5
24
4
3
23
2
1
22

Walducks Farm

Blackend Spinney

CH

Burcott Lodge Farm

Fox Covert

Poultry Farm

STEWKLEY RD

Kemsal l Wood

Mount Pleasant Farm

Glebe Farm

Cottesloe Farm

Glebe Close Farm

Old Park

Ash Farm

Home Farm

Liscombe House

Liscombe Park

Rocklane Farm

Soulbury Road Farm

LU7

SOULBURY RD

Burcott

HIGH ST

IVY LA

Long Spinney

Burcott Hall Farm

HAWTHORN WAY

MEADOW WAY

MOORLANDS

CHESTERFIELD CRES

WILLOW WAY

RIDGE WAY

WILLIAM BANDY CL

COTTESLOE CL

CASTLE CL

LITTLEWORTH

CORNER AVE

WANTAGE CRES

MOORHILLS RD

WOODMAN CL

MOORLANDS RD

COTES WAY

MOORHILLS CRES

THE LANDS

WANTAGE CL

OVERSTONE CL

STEWKLEY RD

ROTHSCHILD

WARWICK RD

LEIGHTON RD

A418

WELL LA

1 CHARLOTTE CL
2 GEORGE ST

Castle Hill

HIGH ST

OLD DR

REDWOOD

PROSPECT PL

PH

Wing

VICARAGE LA

ORCHARD

CLARKE

CHURCH ST

WALK

PO

2

EVELYN CL

1 GOLDEN MILLER CT.
2 NEW ZEALAND GDNS

Overstone Comb Sch

The Cottesloe Sch

AYLESBURY RD

PARK GATE

Lower Ascott

A418

Wing Park Farm

WING RD

86   87   88

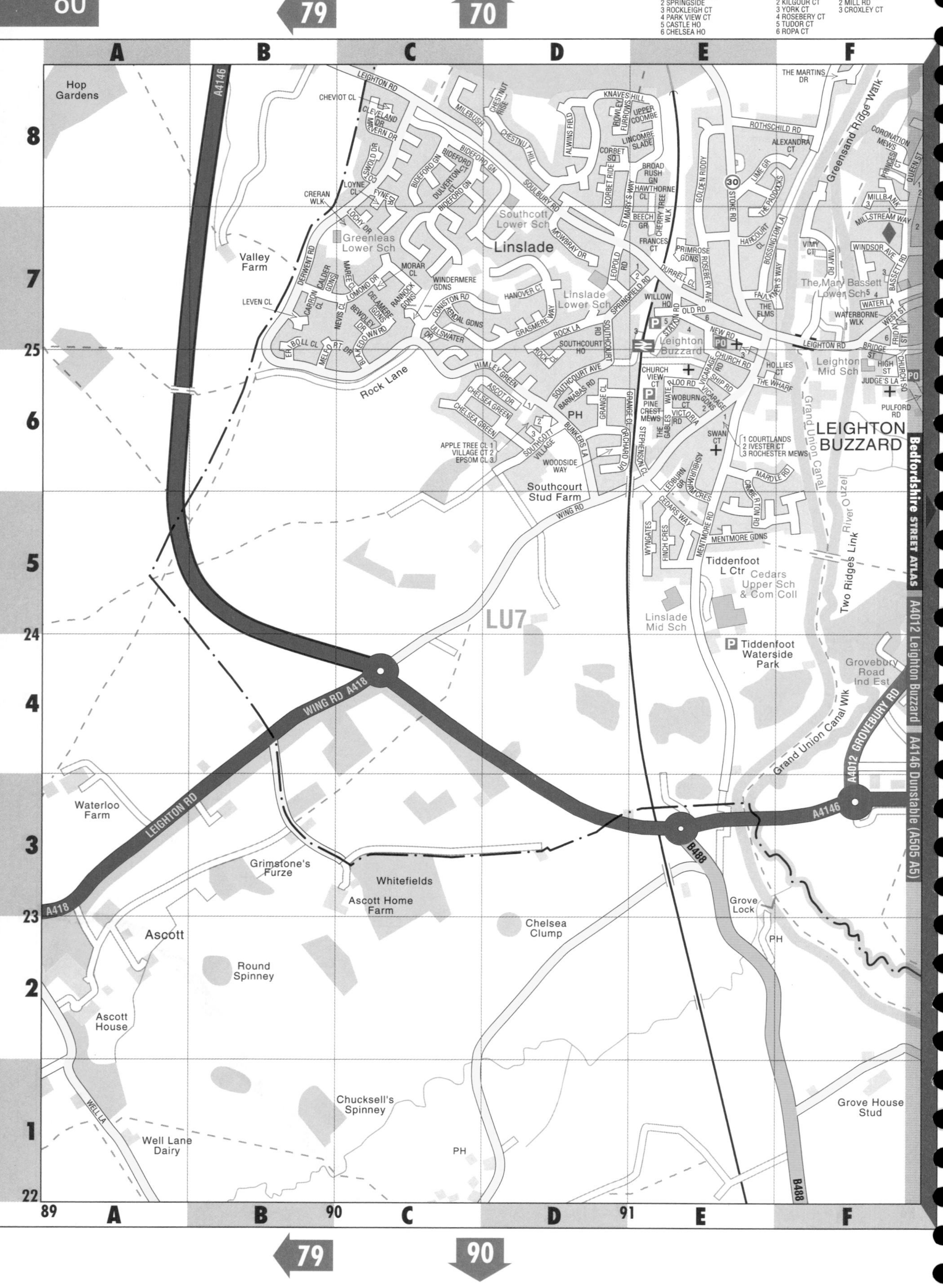

71
82

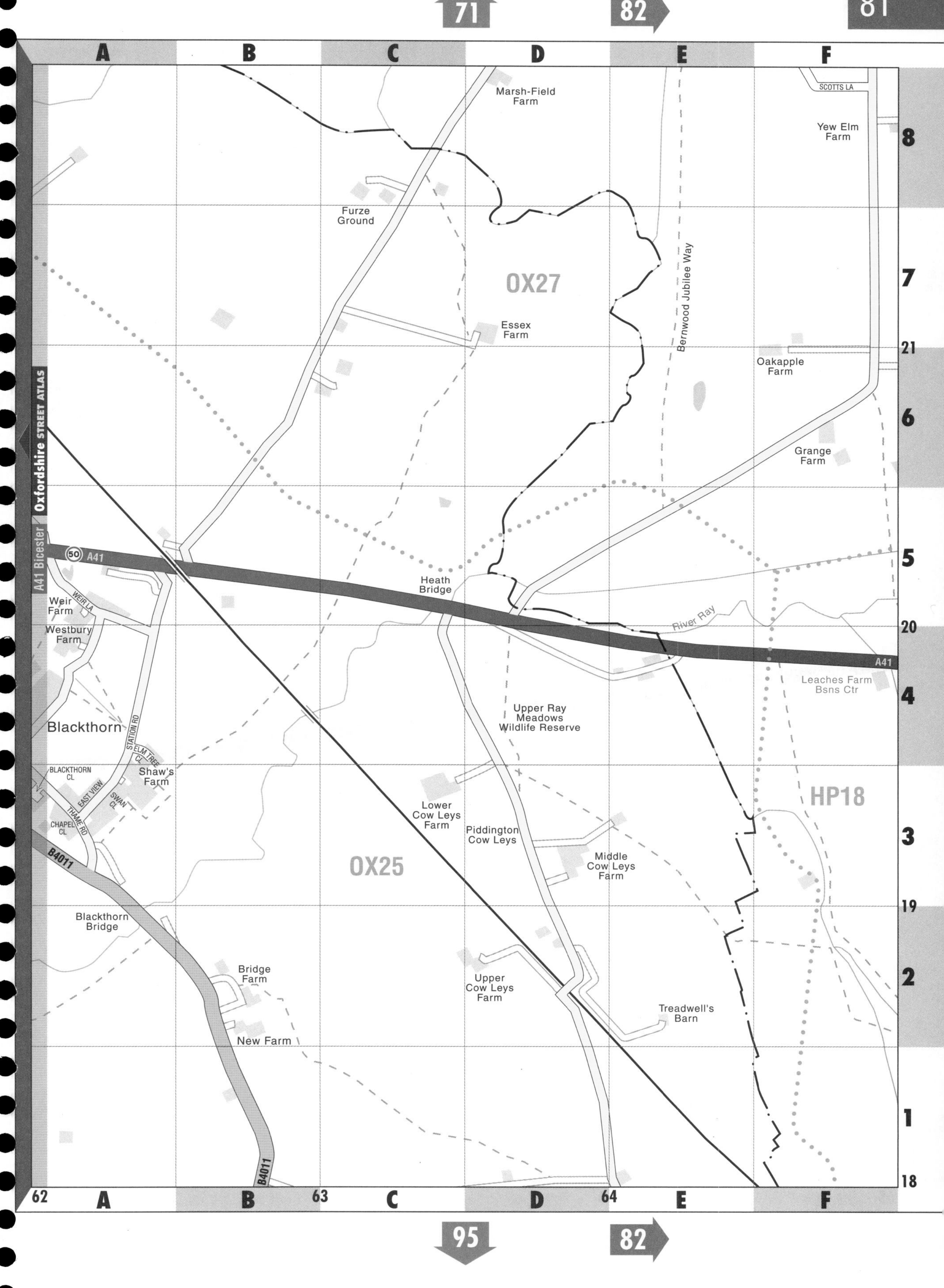
A
B
C
D
E
F
8
7
21
6
5
20
4
3
19
2
1
18
62
63
64
Oxfordshire STREET ATLAS
A41 Bicester
A41
50
A4011
B4011
SCOTTS LA
Marsh-Field Farm
Yew Elm Farm
Furze Ground
OX27
Bernwood Jubilee Way
Essex Farm
Oakapple Farm
Grange Farm
Heath Bridge
Weir Farm
WEIR LA
Westbury Farm
River Ray
Leaches Farm Bsns Ctr
Upper Ray Meadows Wildlife Reserve
Blackthorn
STATION RD
ELM TREE CL
BLACKTHORN CL
Shaw's Farm
EAST VIEW
SWAN CL
THAME RD
CHAPEL CL
HP18
Lower Cow Leys Farm
Piddington Cow Leys
Middle Cow Leys Farm
OX25
Blackthorn Bridge
Bridge Farm
Upper Cow Leys Farm
Treadwell's Barn
New Farm

95
82

81 72

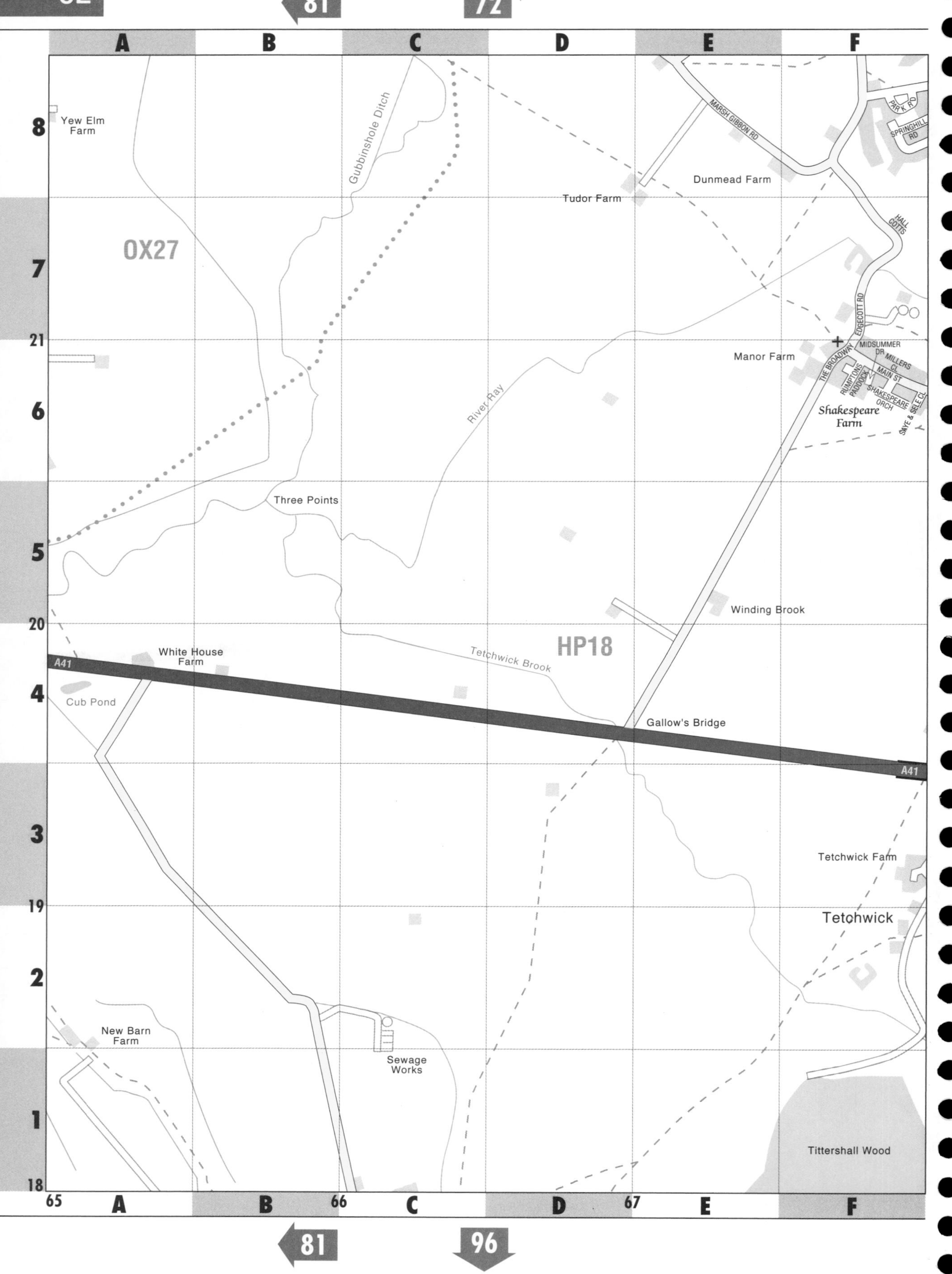
A
B
C
D
E
F
8
Yew Elm Farm
Gubbinshole Ditch
MARSH GIBBON RD
PARK RD
SPRINGHILL RD
Dunmead Farm
Tudor Farm
HALL COTTS
OX27
7
EDGECOTT RD
21
MIDSUMMER DR
MILLERS CL
Manor Farm
THE BROADWAY
MAIN ST
RUMPTONS PADDOCK
SHAKESPEARE ORCH
SAYE & SELE CL
River Ray
6
Shakespeare Farm
Three Points
5
Winding Brook
20
HP18
White House Farm
Tetchwick Brook
A41
4
Cub Pond
Gallow's Bridge
A41
3
Tetchwick Farm
19
Tetchwick
2
New Barn Farm
Sewage Works
1
Tittershall Wood
18
65
66
67

81 96

73
84

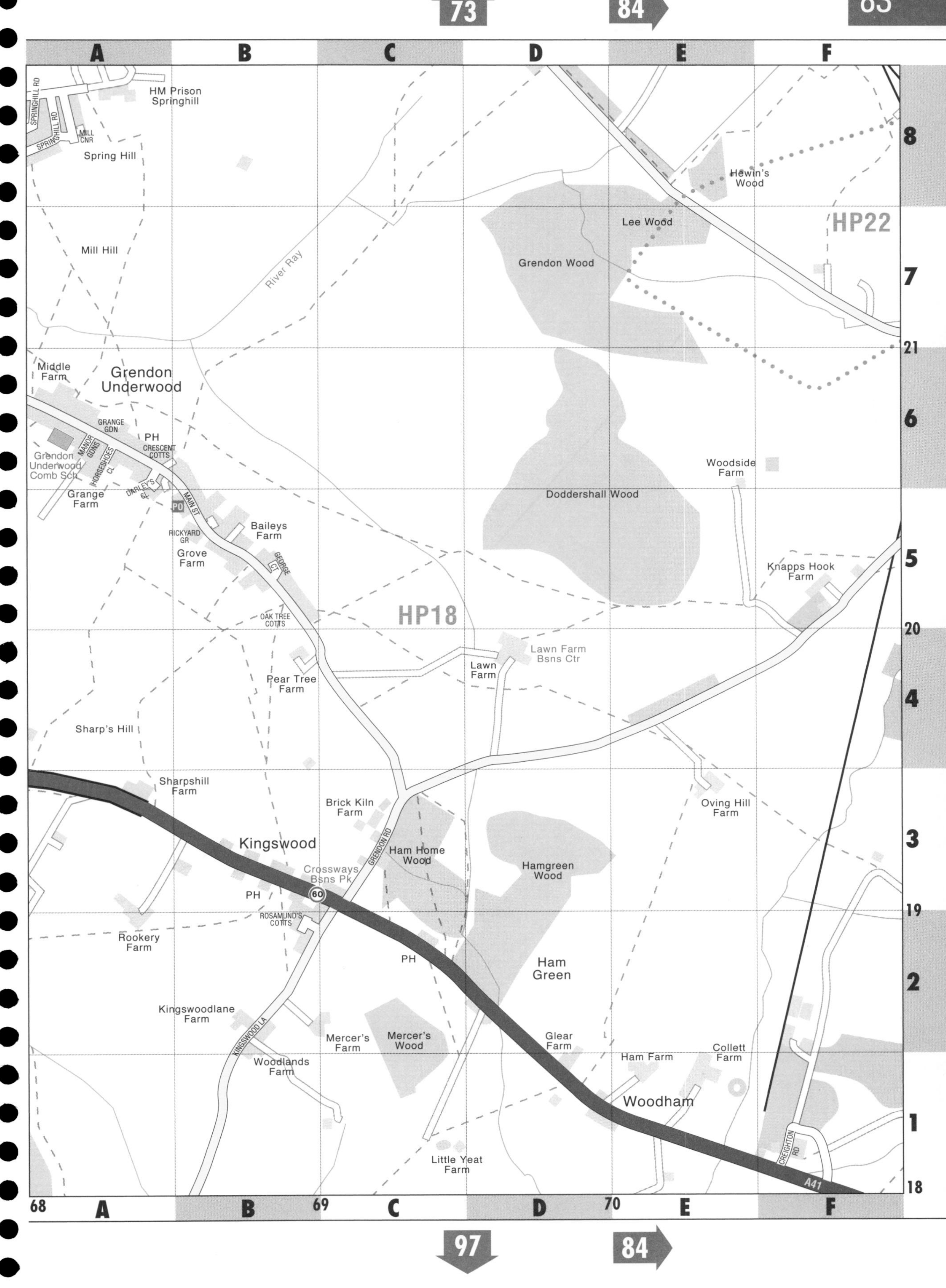
A
B
C
D
E
F
HM Prison Springhill
Spring Hill
Mill Hill
River Ray
Grendon Wood
Lee Wood
Hewin's Wood
HP22
Middle Farm
Grendon Underwood
GRANGE GDN
PH
CRESCENT COTTS
MANOR GDNS
HORSESHOES CL
DARLEY'S CL
Grendon Underwood Comb Sch
Grange Farm
MAIN ST
PO
Baileys Farm
RICKYARD GR
Grove Farm
GEORGE CT
OAK TREE COTTS
HP18
Doddershall Wood
Woodside Farm
Knapps Hook Farm
Lawn Farm Bsns Ctr
Lawn Farm
Pear Tree Farm
Sharp's Hill
Sharpshill Farm
Brick Kiln Farm
Oving Hill Farm
Kingswood
Ham Home Wood
GRENDON RD
Crossways Bsns Pk
Hamgreen Wood
PH
60
ROSAMUND'S COTTS
Rookery Farm
PH
Ham Green
Kingswoodlane Farm
KINGSWOOD LA
Mercer's Farm
Mercer's Wood
Glear Farm
Woodlands Farm
Ham Farm
Collett Farm
Woodham
CREIGHTON RD
Little Yeat Farm
A41
SPRINGHILL RD
SPRINGHILL RD
MILL CNR
8
7
21
6
5
20
4
3
19
2
1
18
68
69
70

97
84

MK18

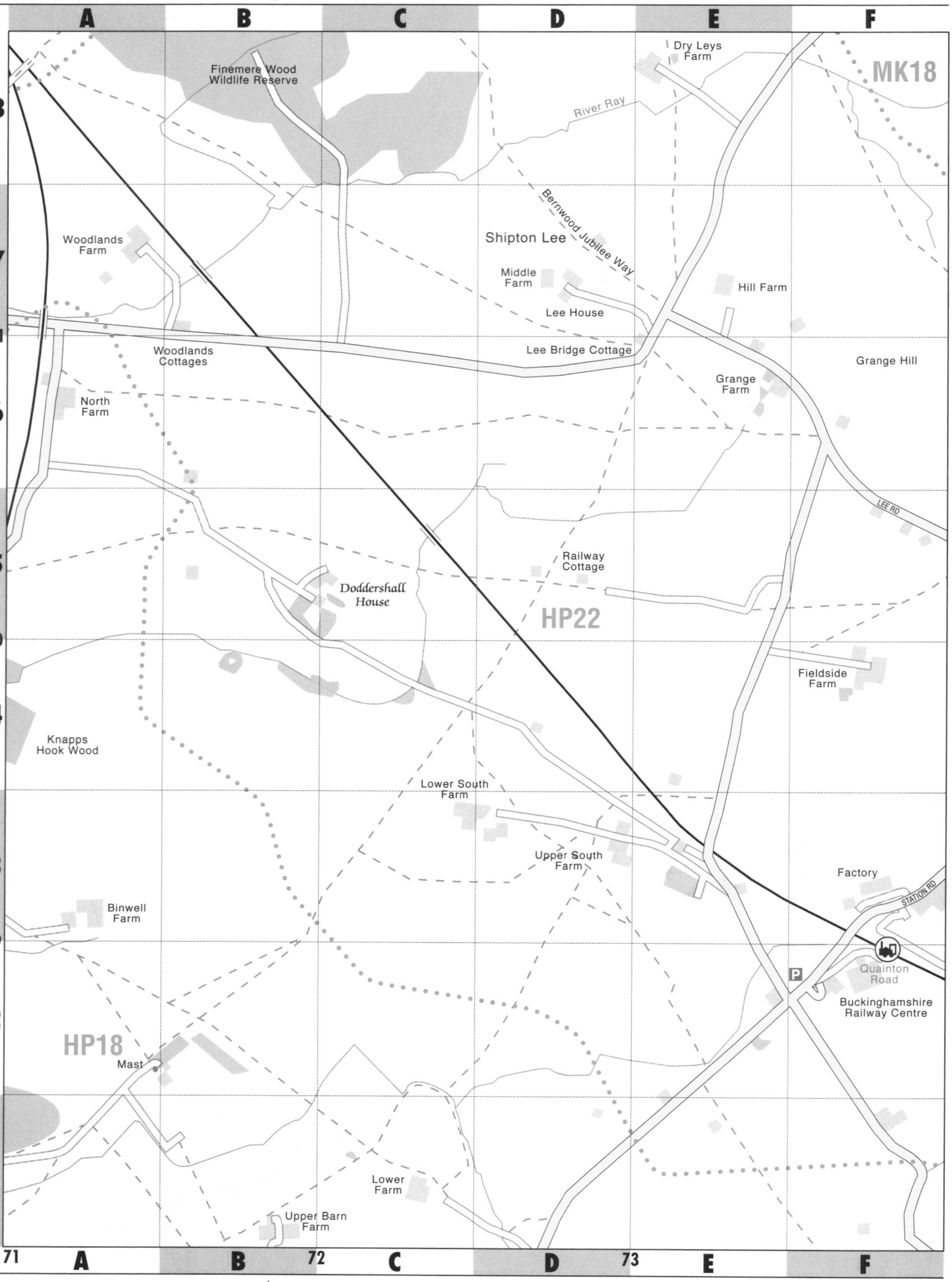

Dry Leys
Farm

River Ray

Finemere Wood
Wildlife Reserve

Shipton Lee

Bernwood Jubilee Way

Woodlands
Farm

Middle
Farm

Hill Farm

Lee House

Woodlands
Cottages

Lee Bridge Cottage

Grange Hill

North
Farm

Grange
Farm

Railway
Cottage

HP22

Doddershall
House

Fieldside
Farm

Knapps
Hook Wood

Lower South
Farm

Upper South
Farm

Factory

STATION RD

Binwell
Farm

Quainton
Road

HP18

Buckinghamshire
Railway Centre

Mast

Lower
Farm

Upper Barn
Farm

LEE RD

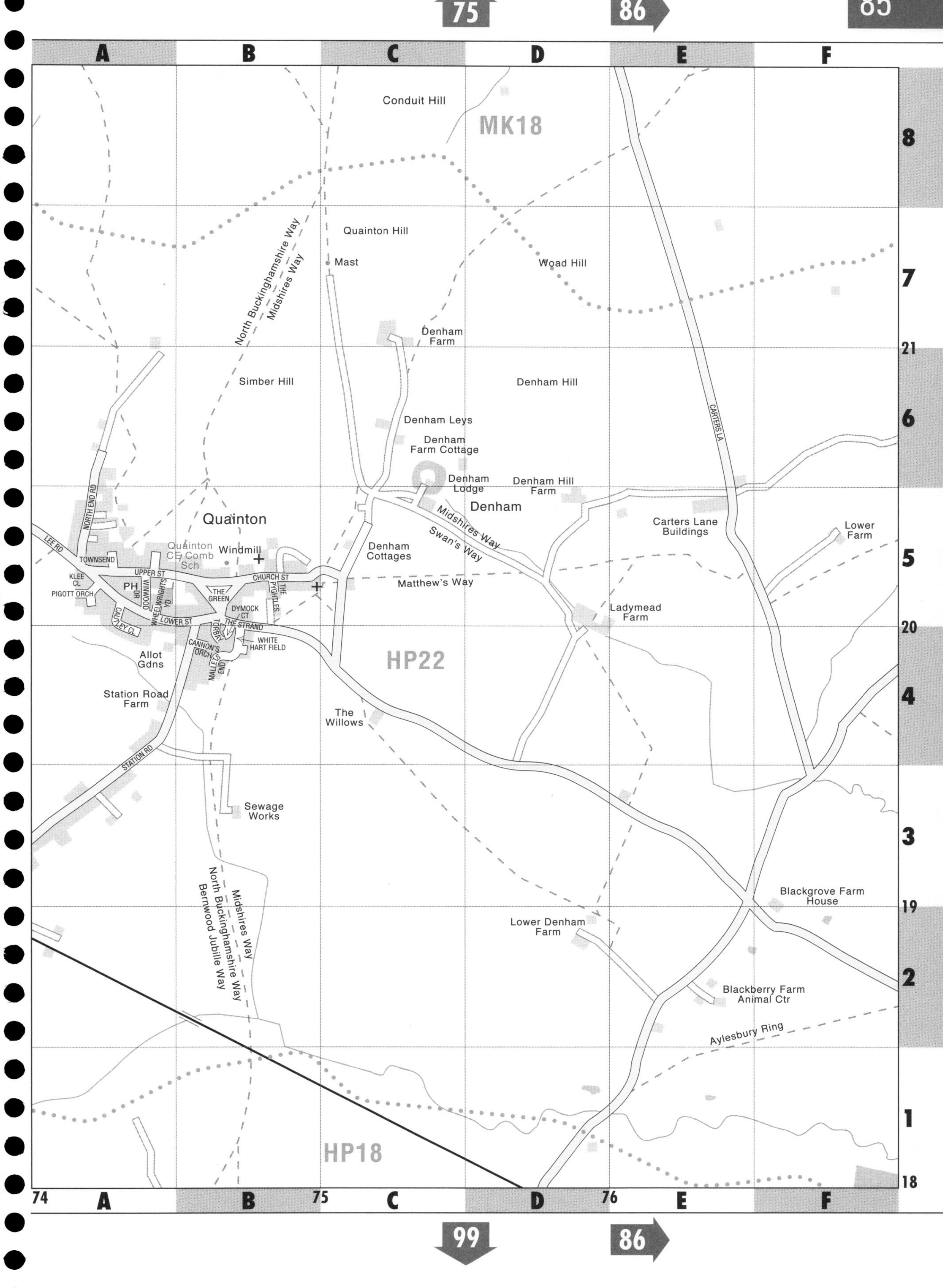

A B C D E F

8

Conduit Hill

MK18

Quainton Hill

7

Mast

Woad Hill

21

Denham Farm

Simber Hill

Denham Hill

6

Denham Leys

North Buckinghamshire Way
Midshires Way

Denham Farm Cottage

Denham Lodge

Denham Hill Farm

Denham

Carters Lane Buildings

CARTERS LA

Lower Farm

5

Quainton

Windmill

Denham Cottages

Midshires Way

Swan's Way

NORTH END RD

Quainton CE Comb Sch

LEE RD

TOWNSEND

KLEE CL

PIGOTT ORCH

PH

COLUMBIA

UPPER ST

WHEELWRIGHTS YD

THE GREEN

LOWER ST

CHURCH ST

THE PIGHTLES

Matthew's Way

Ladymead Farm

20

DYMOCK CT

CAUDLEY CL

MALL END

TURBER

THE STRAND

WHITE HART FIELD

CANNON'S ORCH

Allot Gdns

HP22

4

Station Road Farm

The Willows

STATION RD

3

Sewage Works

North Buckinghamshire Way
Midshires Way
Berwood Jubilee Way

Blackgrove Farm House

19

Lower Denham Farm

2

Blackberry Farm Animal Ctr

Aylesbury Ring

1

HP18

18

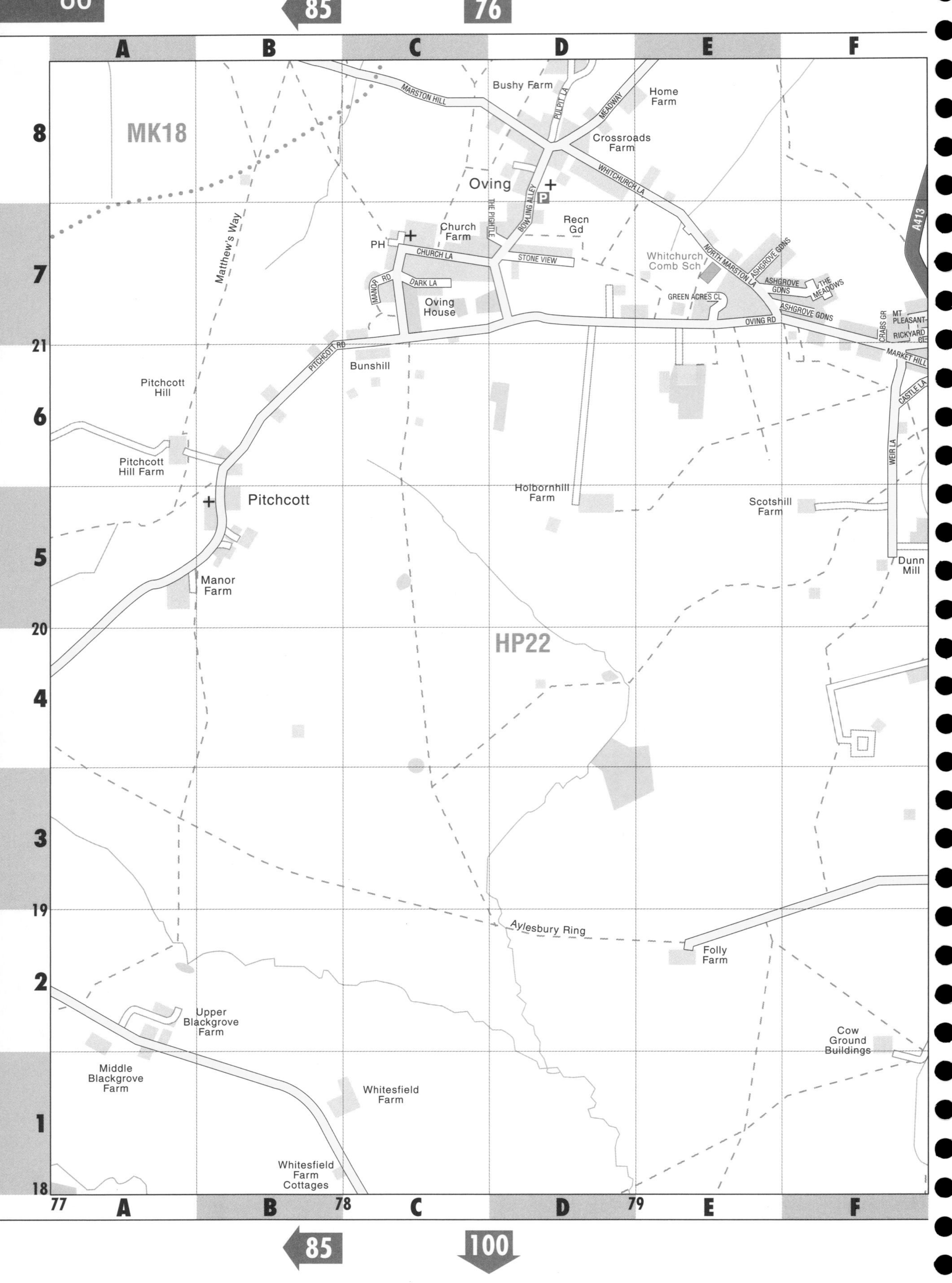

MK18

Marston Hill

Bushy Farm

Home Farm

Oving

Crossroads Farm

Whitchurch La

Matthew's Way

Church Farm

Recn Gd

PH

Church La

Stone View

Whitchurch Comb Sch

Ashgrove Gdns

Manor Rd

Dark La

Oving House

Green Acres Cl

Ashgrove Gdns

The Meadows

Crabs Gr

Mt Pleasant

Oving Rd

Rickyard

Pitchcott Rd

Bunshill

Market Hill

Pitchcott Hill

Castle La

Pitchcott Hill Farm

Holbornhill Farm

Scotshill Farm

Weir La

Pitchcott

HP22

Dunn Mill

Manor Farm

Aylesbury Ring

Folly Farm

Upper Blackgrove Farm

Cow Ground Buildings

Middle Blackgrove Farm

Whitesfield Farm

Whitesfield Farm Cottages

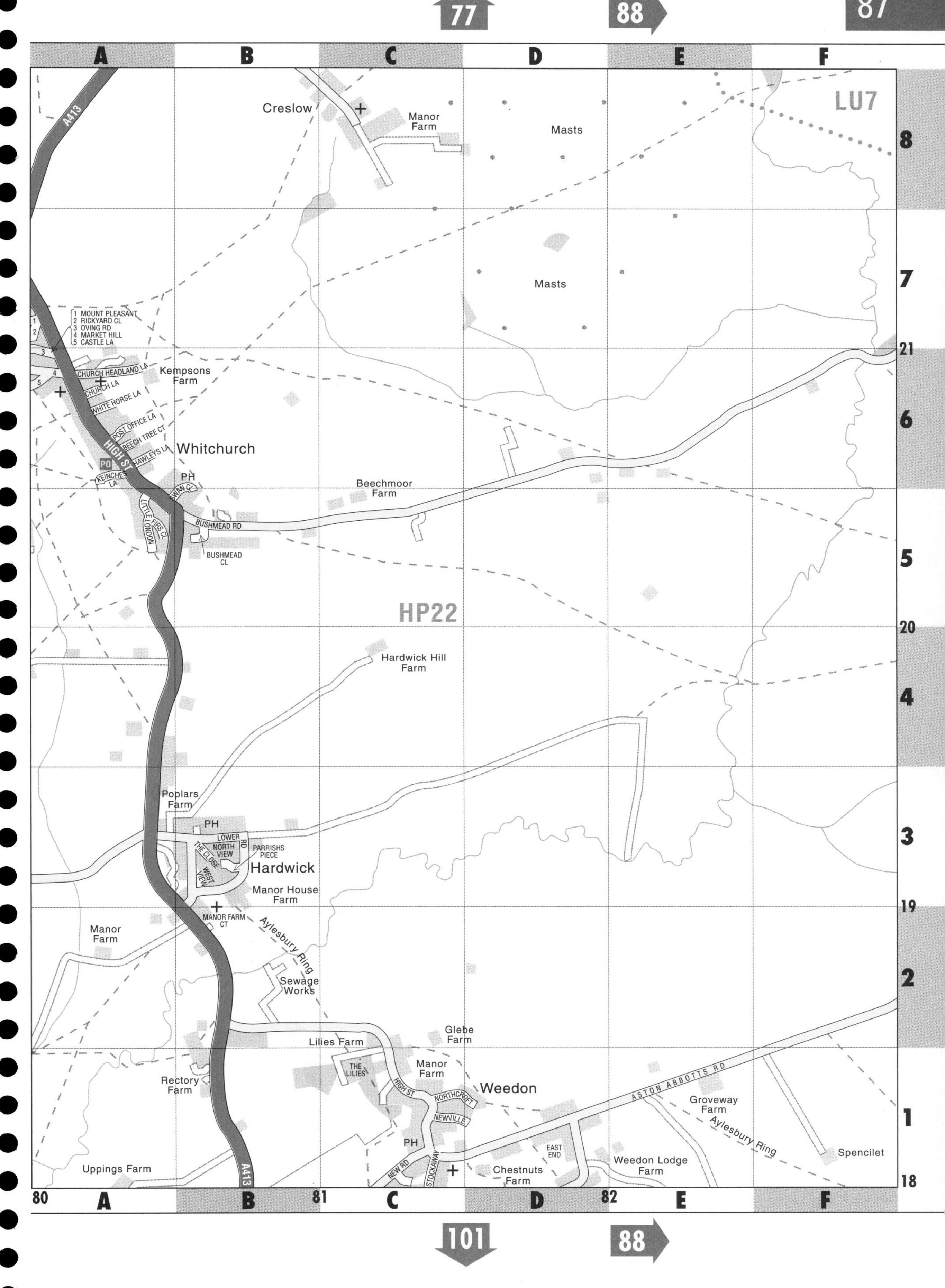

LU7

A B C D E F

Creslow

Manor
Farm

Masts

Masts

8

7

21

1 MOUNT PLEASANT
2 RICKYARD CL
3 OVING RD
4 MARKET HILL
5 CASTLE LA

CHURCH HEADLAND LA
CHURCH LA
WHITE HORSE LA
Kempsons
Farm

6

POST OFFICE LA
BEECH TREE CT
HAWLEYS LA

Whitchurch

HIGH ST
PO
KEINCHE
LA
PH

Beechmoor
Farm

SWAN CL
LITTLE LONDON
FIRS CL

BUSHMEAD RD

BUSHMEAD
CL

5

20

HP22

Hardwick Hill
Farm

4

Poplars
Farm

PH

NORTH RD
LOWER
NORTH
VIEW
THE CLOSE
WEST
VIEW
PARRISHS
PIECE

Hardwick

3

19

Manor House
Farm

Manor
Farm

MANOR FARM
CT

Aylesbury Ring

Sewage
Works

2

Lilies Farm

Glebe
Farm

Rectory
Farm

THE
LILIES

Manor
Farm

HIGH ST
NORTHCROFT
NEWVILLE

Weedon

ASTON ABBOTTS RD

Groveway
Farm

Aylesbury Ring

1

PH

NEW RD
STOCKAWAY

EAST
END

Chestnuts
Farm

Weedon Lodge
Farm

Spencilet

Uppings Farm

A413

18

87
78

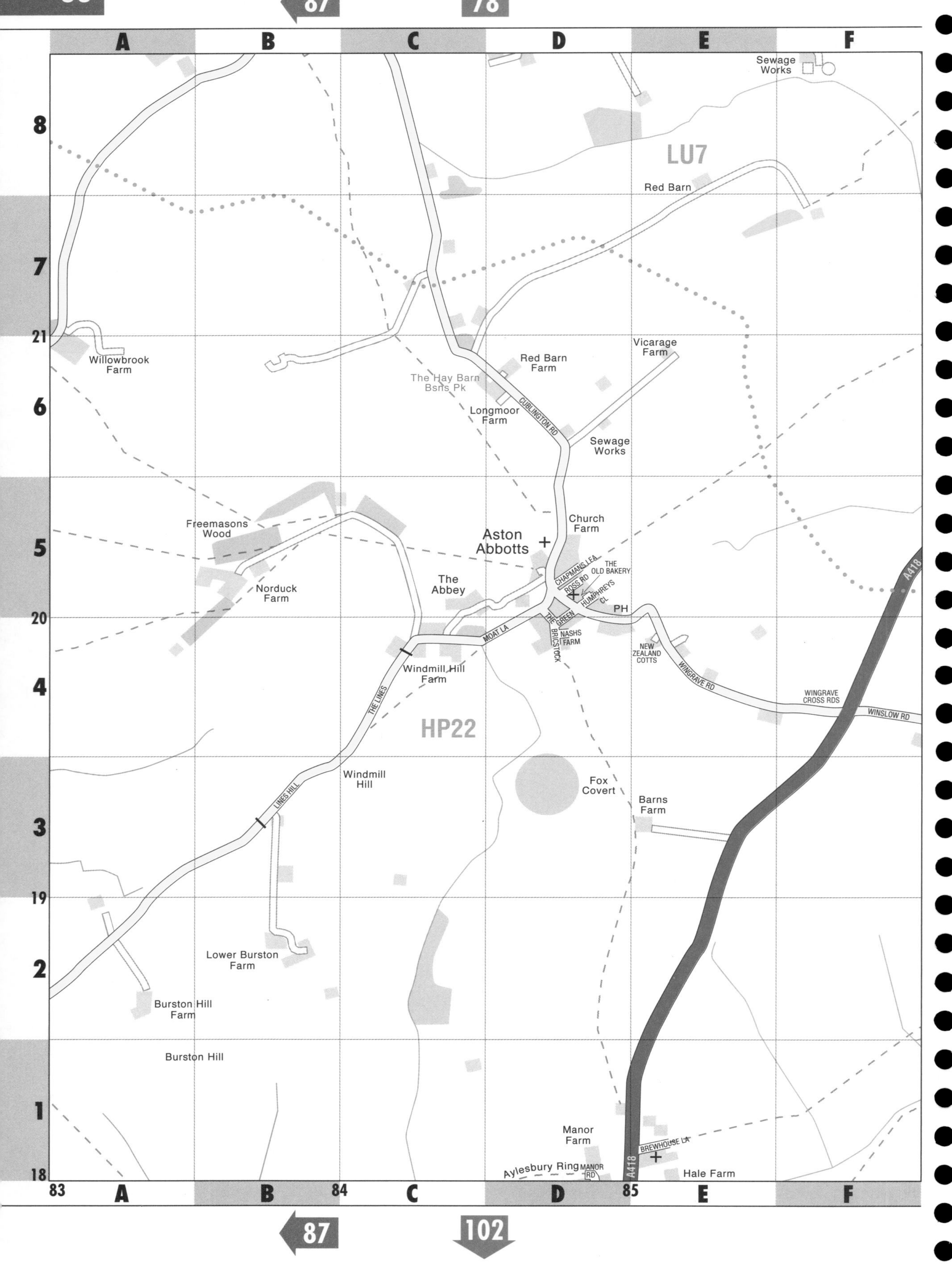
A
B
C
D
E
F
8
7
21
6
5
20
4
3
19
2
1
18
83
84
85
Sewage Works
LU7
Red Barn
Willowbrook Farm
The Hay Barn Bsns Pk
Red Barn Farm
Vicarage Farm
Longmoor Farm
CUBLINGTON RD
Sewage Works
Freemasons Wood
Church Farm
Aston Abbotts
Norduck Farm
The Abbey
CHAPMANS LEA
THE OLD BAKERY
ROSS RD
HUMPHREYS CL
PH
THE GREEN
MOAT LA
THE BRICSTOCK
NASHS FARM
NEW ZEALAND COTTS
WINGRAVE RD
A418
Windmill Hill Farm
THE LINES
HP22
WINGRAVE CROSS RDS
WINSLOW RD
Windmill Hill
LINES HILL
Fox Covert
Barns Farm
Lower Burston Farm
Burston Hill Farm
Burston Hill
Manor Farm
BREWHOUSE LA
Aylesbury Ring
MANOR RD
A418
Hale Farm

87
102

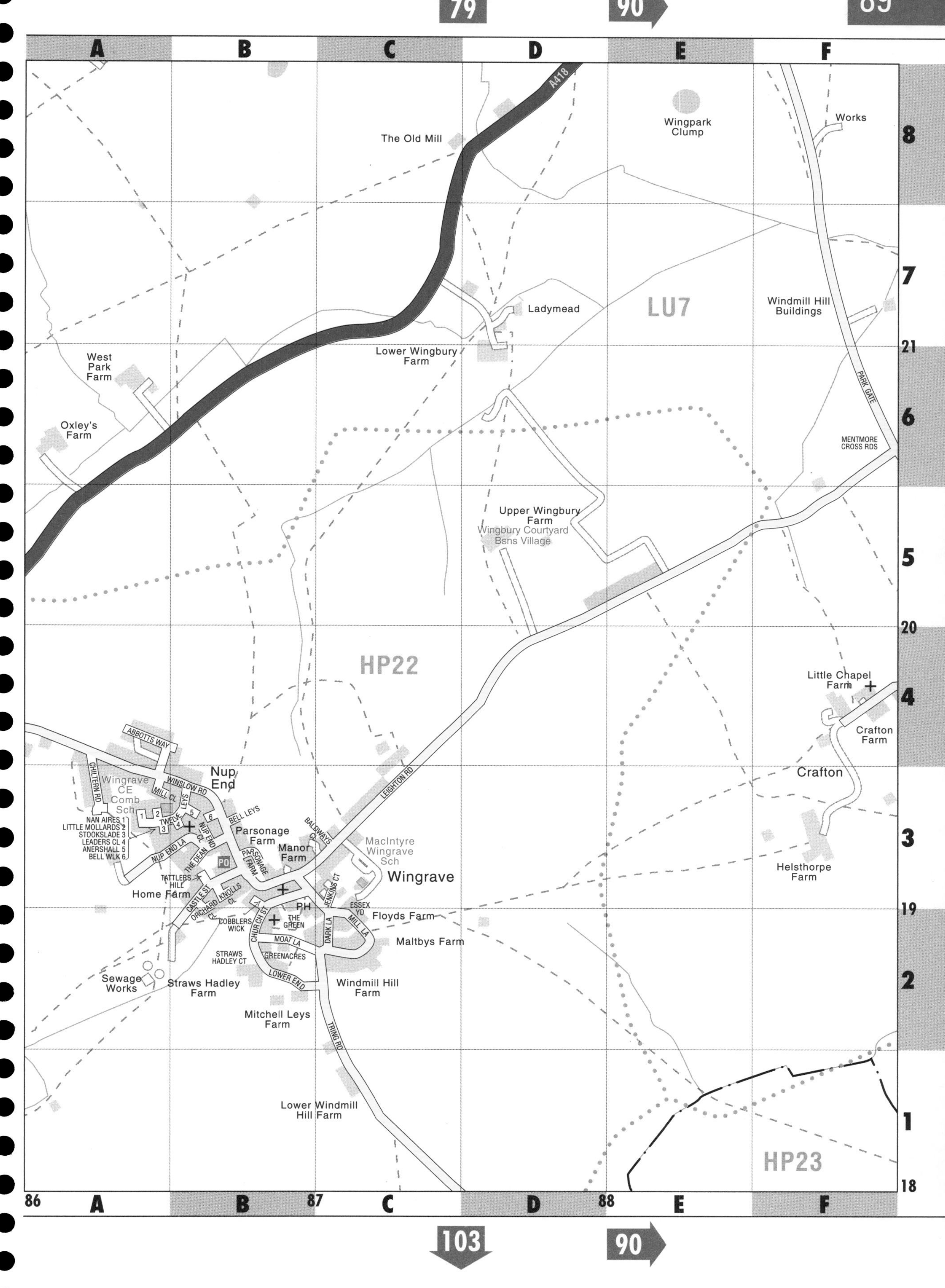

79
90

A   B   C   D   E   F

A418

The Old Mill

Wingpark Clump

Works

8

Ladymead

LU7

Windmill Hill Buildings

7

Lower Wingbury Farm

21

West Park Farm

PARK GATE

6

Oxley's Farm

MENTMORE CROSS RDS

Upper Wingbury Farm
Wingbury Courtyard Bsns Village

5

HP22

20

Little Chapel Farm

4

Crafton Farm

Crafton

ABBOTTS WAY

Nup End

CHILTERN RD

Wingrave CE Comb Sch

WINSLOW RD

MILL CL

Helsthorpe Farm

3

NAN AIRES 1
LITTLE MOLLARDS 2
STOOKSLADE 3
LEADERS CL 4
ANERSHALL 5
BELL WLK 6

TWELVE LEYS

NUP END

BELL LEYS

Parsonage Farm

BALDWAYS CL

LEIGHTON RD

Manor Farm

MacIntyre Wingrave Sch

THE DEAN

PO

PARSONAGE FARM

Wingrave

TATTLERS HILL

Home Farm

CASTLE ST

ORCHARD KNOLLS

JENKINS CT

ESSEX YD

19

COBBLERS WICK

CHURCH ST

PH

THE GREEN

DARK LA

MILL LA

Floyds Farm

MOAT LA

Maltbys Farm

STRAWS HADLEY CT

GREENACRES

Sewage Works

LOWER END

Straws Hadley Farm

Windmill Hill Farm

2

Mitchell Leys Farm

TRING RD

Lower Windmill Hill Farm

1

HP23

18

103
90

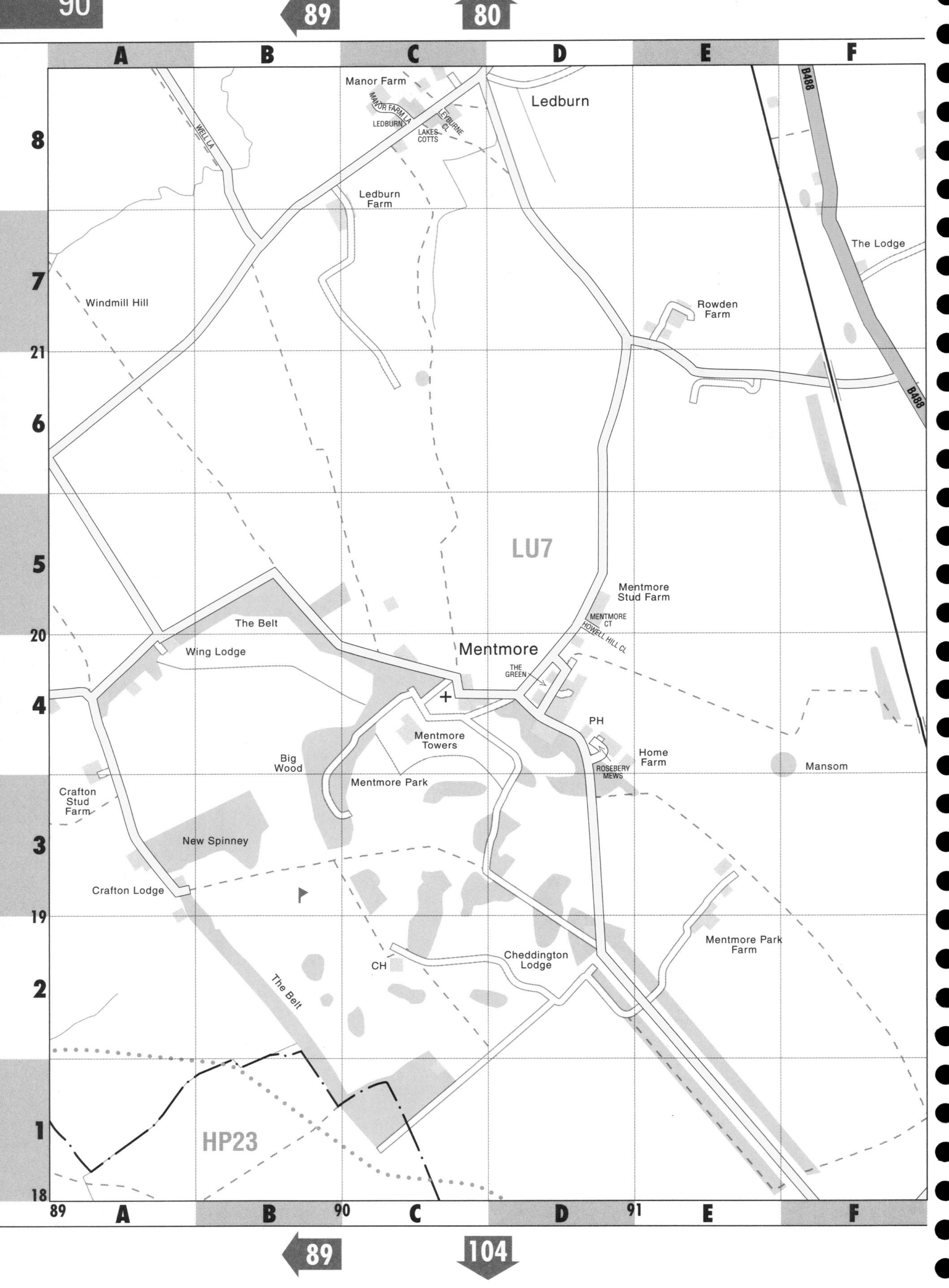

89
80

A   B   C   D   E   F

8

Manor Farm

Ledburn

MANOR FARM LA
LEDBURN

LETHORNE CL

LAKES
COTTS

The Lodge

B488

Ledburn
Farm

7

Windmill Hill

Rowden
Farm

21

6

B488

LU7

5

Mentmore
Stud Farm

The Belt

20

MENTMORE
CT

Wing Lodge

HOWELL HILL CL

Mentmore

THE
GREEN

4

Crafton
Stud
Farm

Big
Wood

Mentmore
Towers

PH

Home
Farm

Mansom

Mentmore Park

ROSEBERY
MEWS

3

New Spinney

Crafton Lodge

19

Mentmore Park
Farm

2

The Belt

CH

Cheddington
Lodge

1

HP23

18

89
104

92

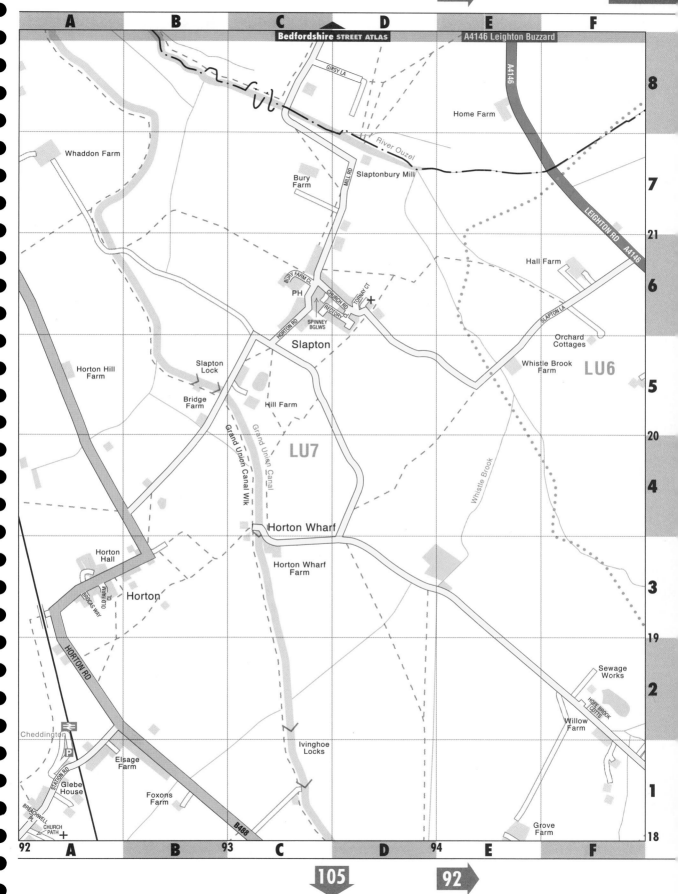
A B C D E F
Bedfordshire STREET ATLAS
A4146 Leighton Buzzard
8
7
21
6
5
20
4
3
19
2
1
18
Gipsy La
Home Farm
A4146
River Ouzel
Whaddon Farm
Slaptonbury Mill
Bury Farm
Mill Rd
Leighton Rd A4146
Hall Farm
Bury Farm Cl
Church Rd
Tornay Ct
PH
Rectory Cl
Spinney Bglws
Horton Rd
Slapton La
Orchard Cottages
Slapton
Horton Hill Farm
Slapton Lock
Whistle Brook Farm
LU6
Bridge Farm
Hill Farm
Grand Union Canal Wlk
Grand Union Canal
LU7
Whistle Brook
Horton Wharf
Horton Hall
Horton Wharf Farm
Brocas Way
Old Farm Cl
Horton
Horton Rd
Sewage Works
Hope Brook Cotts
Willow Farm
Cheddington
P
Ivinghoe Locks
Elsage Farm
Station Rd
Glebe House
Foxons Farm
Breachwell Pl
Church Path
B488
Grove Farm
92 A B 93 C D 94 E F

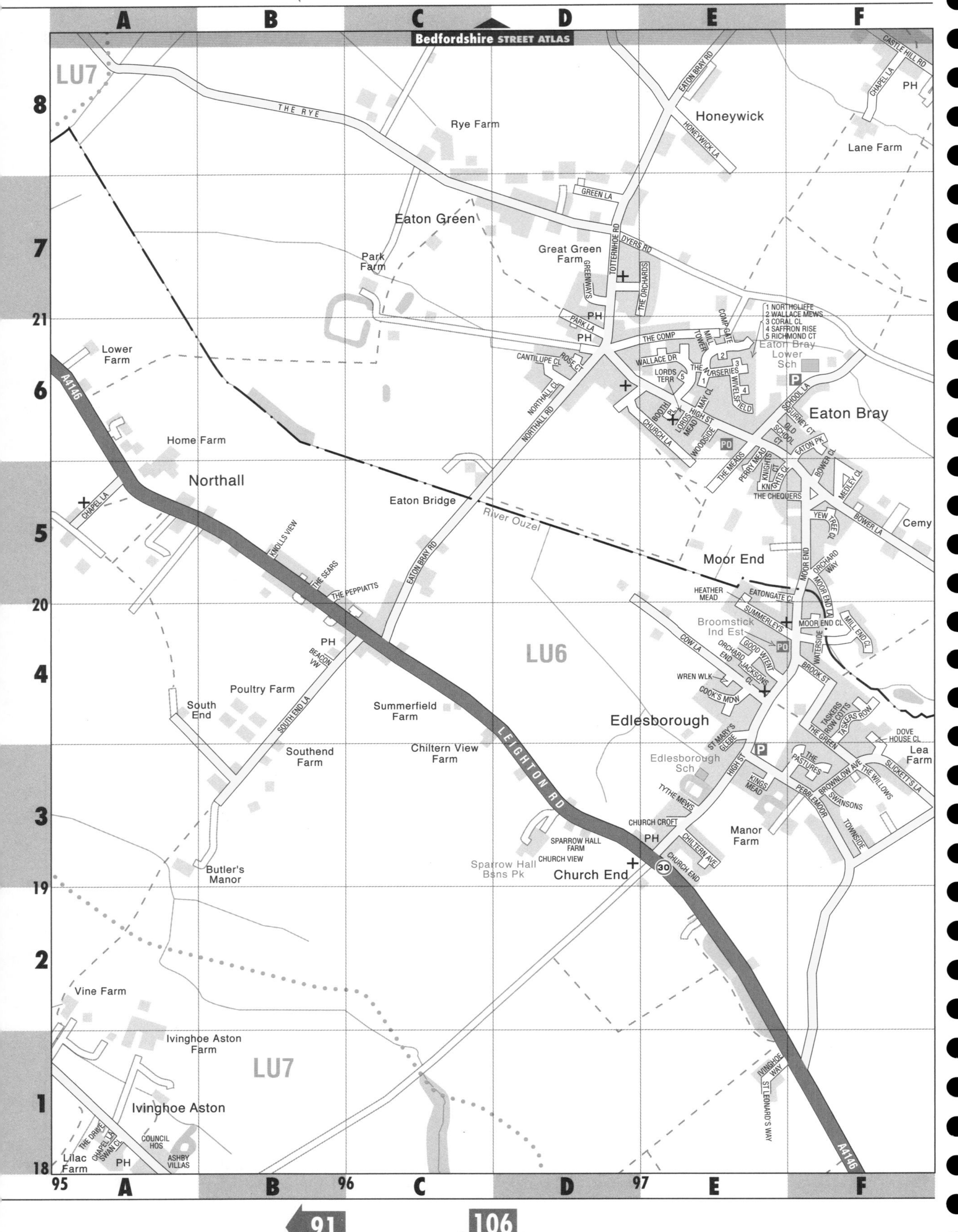

LU7

THE RYE

Rye Farm

Eaton Green

Park Farm

Great Green Farm

GREEN LA

Honeywick

EATON BRAY RD

CASTLE HILL RD

CHAPEL LA

PH

Lane Farm

HONEYWICK LA

DYERS RD

TOTTERNHOE RD

THE ORCHARDS

GREENWAYS

PARK LA

PH

PH

ROSS CT

CANTILUPE CL

NORTHALL RD

NORTHALL RD

THE COMP

WALLACE DR

1 NORTHCLIFFE
2 WALLACE MEWS
3 CORAL CL
4 SAFFRON RISE
5 RICHMOND CT

Eaton Bray Lower Sch

P

Eaton Bray

COMP GATE

NILL TOWER

THE NURSERIES

LORDS TERR

HIGH ST

LORDSMEAD

BOOTH

WIVELSFIELD

MAY CL

SCHOOL CT

OLD SCHOOL CT

SCHOOL LA

EATON PK

EATON CL

BOWER CL

McAULEY CT

YEW TREE CL TO

BOWER LA

Cemy

PO

CHURCH LA

WOODSIDE

THE MEARS

PERRY MEAD

KNIGHTS CL

KNS

THE CHEQUERS

Lower Farm

Home Farm

Northall

CHAPEL LA

KNOLLS VIEW

LINE SCARS

THE PEPPIATTS

Eaton Bridge

River Ouzel

EATON BRAY RD

Moor End

MOOR END

ORCHARD WAY

HEATHER MEAD

EATONGATE CL

SUMMERLEYS

MOOR END CL

MOOR END LA

MILL END CL

WATERSIDE

BROOK ST

PH

BEACON VW

SOUTH END LA

South End

Poultry Farm

Southend Farm

Summerfield Farm

Chiltern View Farm

LU6

Broomstick Ind Est

PO

COW LA

ORCHARD END

GOOD WYN

JACKSONS CL

WREN WLK

COOK'S MDN

Edlesborough

TASKERS ROW

HOW COTTS

TASKERS ROW

THE GREEN

DOVE HOUSE CL

Lea Farm

SLICKETT'S LA

ST MARY'S GLEBE

Edlesborough Sch

P

HIGH ST

KINGS MEAD

THE PASTURES

BROWNLOW AVE

THE WILLOWS

PEBBLEMOOR

SWANSONS

TOWNSIDE

LEIGHTON RD

TYTHE MEWS

CHURCH CROFT

CHURCH END

PH

CHILTERN AVE

CHURCH END

Manor Farm

Sparrow Hall Farm

CHURCH VIEW

Sparrow Hall Bsns Pk

Church End

30

Butler's Manor

Vine Farm

Ivinghoe Aston Farm

LU7

Ivinghoe Aston

IVINGHOE WAY

ST LEONARD'S WAY

A4146

Lilac Farm

THE DRIVE

CHAPEL LA

SWAN CL

PH

COUNCIL HOS

ASHBY VILLAS

A4146

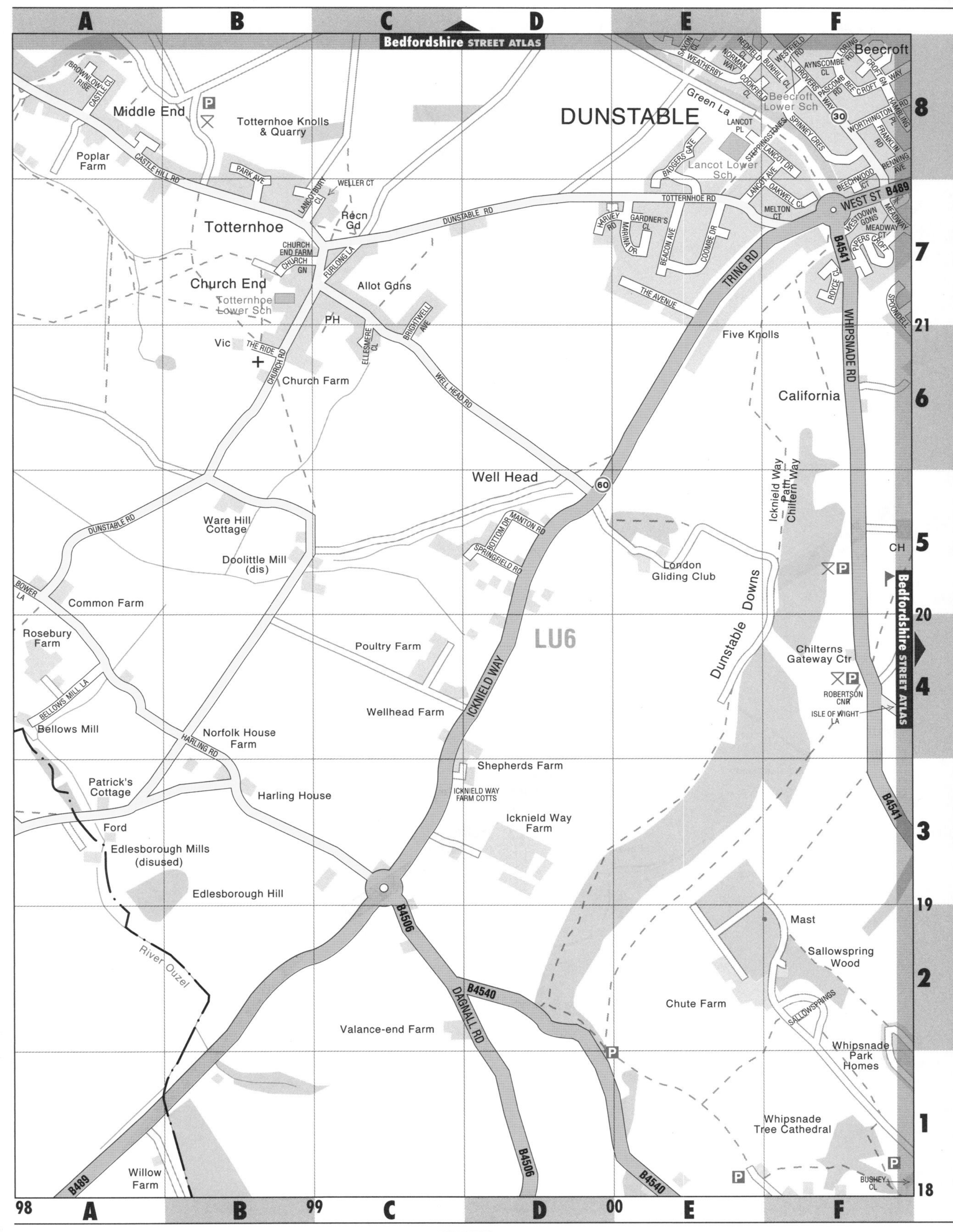

Bedfordshire STREET ATLAS

DUNSTABLE

Beecroft

Middle End

Totternhoe Knolls & Quarry

Poplar Farm

Totternhoe

Church End

Totternhoe Lower Sch

Vic

Church Farm

Recn Gd

Allot Gdns

PH

Dunstable Rd

Well Head Rd

Well Head

Five Knolls

California

Ware Hill Cottage

Doolittle Mill (dis)

Dunstable Rd

Common Farm

Rosebury Farm

Bellows Mill

Norfolk House Farm

Patrick's Cottage

Ford

Edlesborough Mills (disused)

Edlesborough Hill

Harling House

River Ouzel

Poultry Farm

Wellhead Farm

Shepherds Farm

Icknield Way Farm Cotts

Icknield Way Farm

Manton Rd

Springfield Rd

London Gliding Club

Dunstable Downs

Chilterns Gateway Ctr

ROBERTSON CNR

ISLE OF WIGHT LA

CH

LU6

Valance-end Farm

Chute Farm

Mast

Sallowspring Wood

Whipsnade Park Homes

Whipsnade Tree Cathedral

BUSHEY CL

Willow Farm

Bedfordshire STREET ATLAS

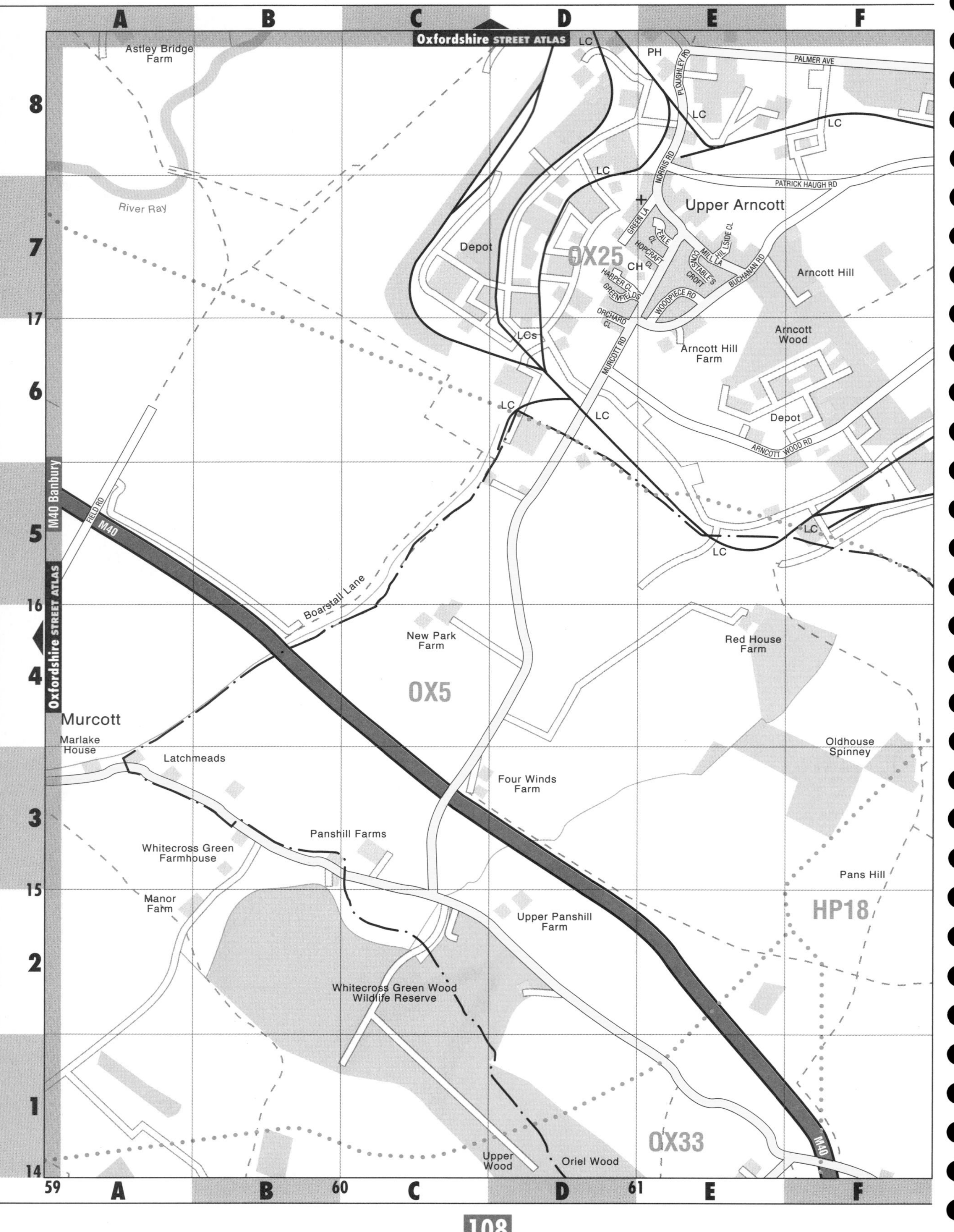
Oxfordshire STREET ATLAS
Astley Bridge Farm
River Ray
PH
PALMER AVE
PLOUGHLEY RD
LC
NORRIS RD
PATRICK HAUGH RD
Upper Arncott
Depot
OX25
CH
GREEN LA
HOPCRAFT CL
HARPER CL
GREENFIELDS
ORCHARD CL
WOODPIECE RD
CONSTABLE'S CROFT
MILL LA
HILLSIDE CL
BUCHANAN RD
Arncott Hill
Arncott Wood
Arncott Hill Farm
LCs
MURCOTT RD
Depot
ARNCOTT WOOD RD
M40 Banbury
FIELD RD
M40
Boarstall Lane
New Park Farm
Red House Farm
OX5
Murcott
Marlake House
Latchmeads
Oldhouse Spinney
Four Winds Farm
Panshill Farms
Whitecross Green Farmhouse
Pans Hill
Manor Farm
Upper Panshill Farm
HP18
Whitecross Green Wood Wildlife Reserve
OX33
Upper Wood
Oriel Wood
A
B
C
D
E
F
8
7
17
6
5
16
4
3
15
2
1
14
59
60
61

108

81
96

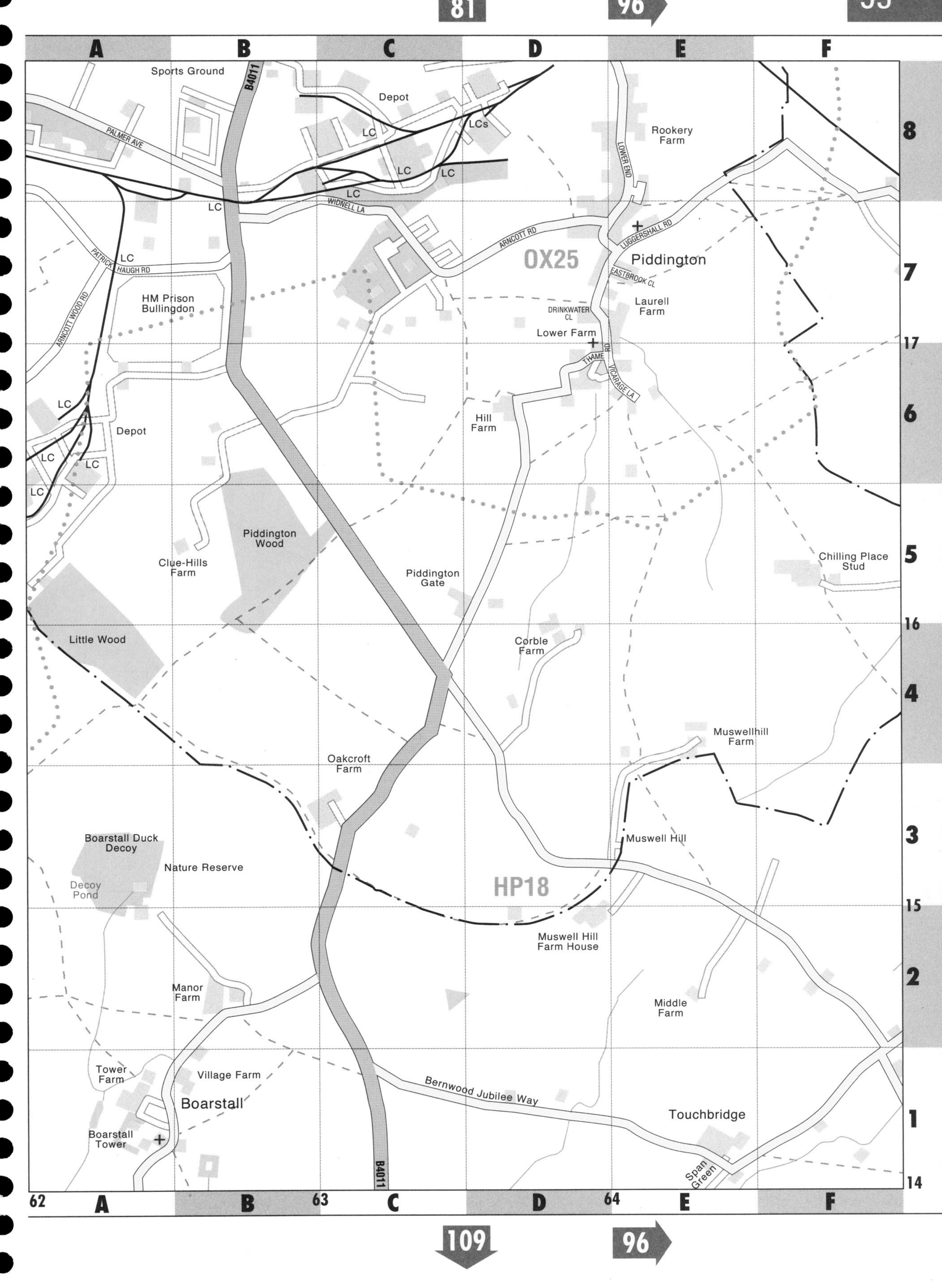
A
B
C
D
E
F
Sports Ground
B4011
Depot
LCs
LC
PALMER AVE
Rookery Farm
LOWER END
WIDNELL LA
ARNCOTT RD
LUGGERSHALL RD
OX25
Piddington
PATRICK HAUGH RD
EASTBROOK CL
HM Prison Bullingdon
ARNCOTT WOOD RD
Laurell Farm
DRINKWATER CL
Lower Farm
THAME RD
VICARAGE LA
Hill Farm
Depot
Piddington Wood
Clue-Hills Farm
Piddington Gate
Chilling Place Stud
Little Wood
Corble Farm
Muswellhill Farm
Oakcroft Farm
Boarstall Duck Decoy
Nature Reserve
Muswell Hill
Decoy Pond
HP18
Muswell Hill Farm House
Manor Farm
Middle Farm
Tower Farm
Village Farm
Bernwood Jubilee Way
Boarstall
Touchbridge
Boarstall Tower
Span Green
8
7
17
6
5
16
4
3
15
2
1
14
62
63
64

109
96

A B C D E F

Nursery
D'Oyley's Farm
Rookery Farm
The Green
Tittershall Wood
Kings Farm
BICESTER RD
Bridge Farm
PIDDINGTON RD
PH
DUCK LA
Ludgershall
SALTERS CL
Manor Farm
WHITE HART
BROOK CL
HIGH ST
SALTERS LA
Glebe Farm
Eastfield Farm
CHURCH LA
Ludgershall Farm
BRILL RD
WOTTON END
KINGSWOOD LA
The Lake

8

7

17

6

Clearfields Farm

Long Wood

5

The Warrells

Poletrees Farm
Lapland Farm
HP18
Fivearch Bridge
Fivearch Wood

16

4

Rushbeds Wood Wildlife Reserve
Grenville's Wood

Lawn Farm

3

Tramway Farm
Rid's Hill

15

Brillbury Hall Farm
Coldharbour Farm
TRAM HILL

2

Dorton Park Farm

Brill Common
NORCOTTS KILN COTTS
Chinkwell Wood

1

Windmill
NORTH HILLS
WINDMILL ST
THE LAWNS
TEMPLE ST
GODFREYS CL
Brill
Brill CE Comb Sch
Dorton
Brook Farm
SOUTH HILLS
PH
BRAE HILL
HIGH LAND CL
Ct

14
65 A B 66 C D 67 E F

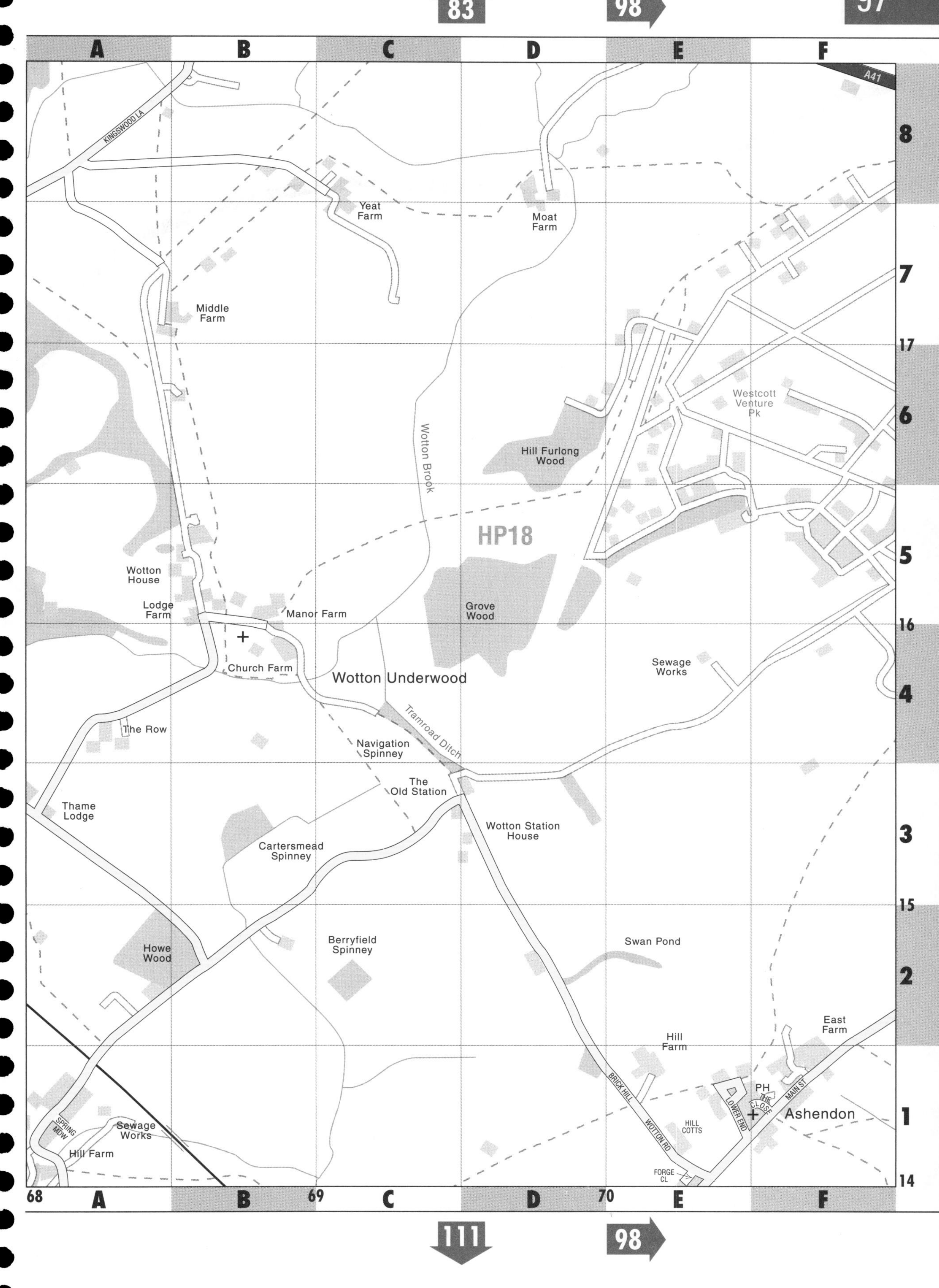

A41

A B C D E F

8
7
17
6
5
16
4
15
3
2
1
14

Kingswood La

Yeat Farm

Moat Farm

Middle Farm

Wotton Brook

Westcott Venture Pk

Hill Furlong Wood

HP18

Wotton House

Grove Wood

Lodge Farm

Manor Farm

Sewage Works

Church Farm

Wotton Underwood

The Row

Tramroad Ditch

Navigation Spinney

The Old Station

Wotton Station House

Thame Lodge

Cartersmead Spinney

Berryfield Spinney

Swan Pond

Howe Wood

Hill Farm

East Farm

Brick Hill

Wotton Rd

Lower End

Hill Cotts

The Close

PH

Main St

Ashendon

Spring Mdw

Sewage Works

Hill Farm

Forge Cl

68 A B 69 C D 70 E F

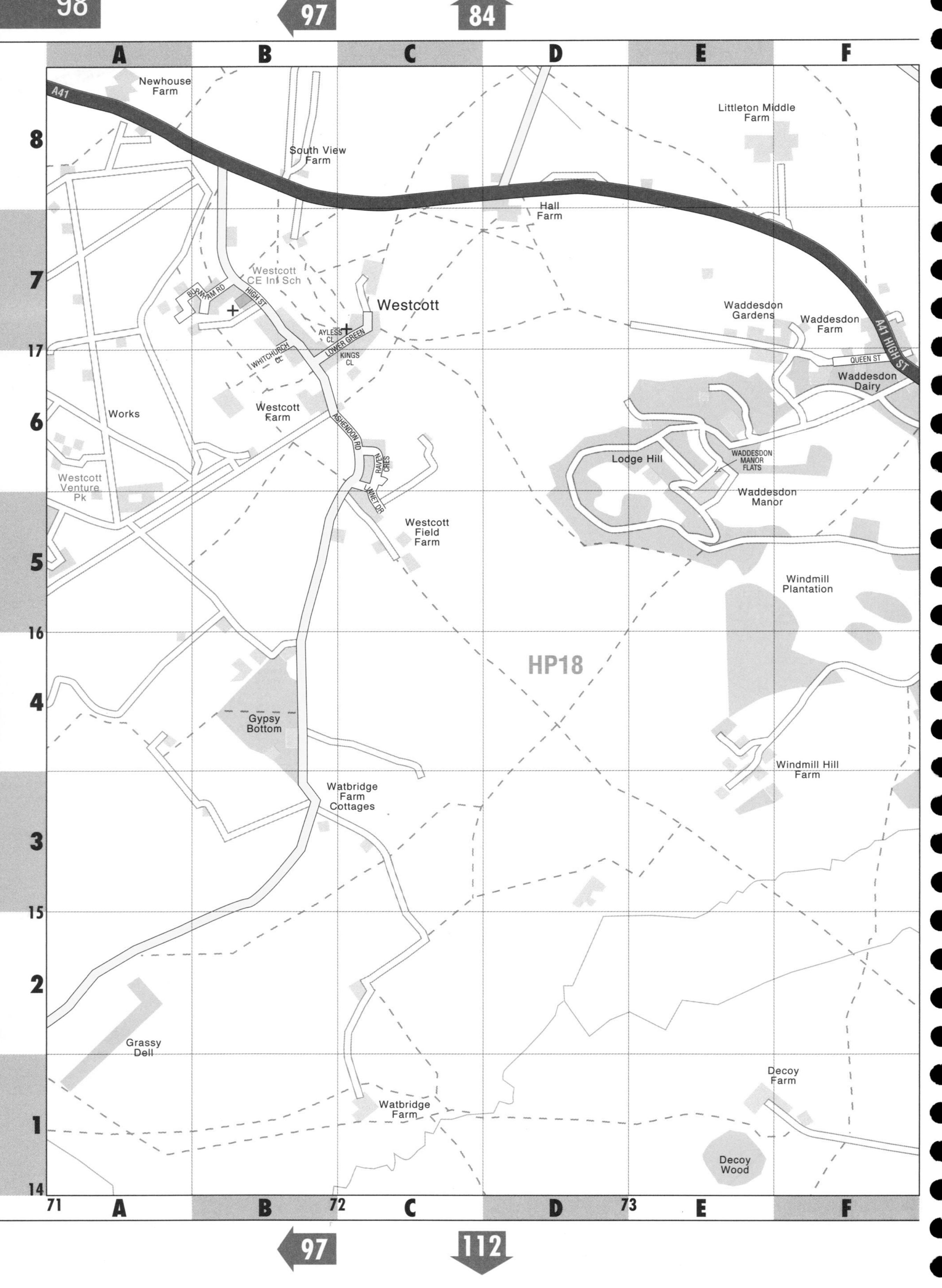

A41

Newhouse Farm

South View Farm

Littleton Middle Farm

Hall Farm

Westcott CE Inf Sch

BUCKINGHAM RD

HIGH ST

Westcott

Waddesdon Gardens

Waddesdon Farm

A41 HIGH ST

AYLESS CL

LOWER GREEN

WHITCHURCH CE

KINGS CL

QUEEN ST

Waddesdon Dairy

Works

Westcott Farm

ASHENDON RD

RAVEN CRES

Westcott Venture Pk

VINE DR

Lodge Hill

WADDESDON MANOR FLATS

Waddesdon Manor

Westcott Field Farm

Windmill Plantation

HP18

Gypsy Bottom

Windmill Hill Farm

Watbridge Farm Cottages

Grassy Dell

Decoy Farm

Watbridge Farm

Decoy Wood

85
100

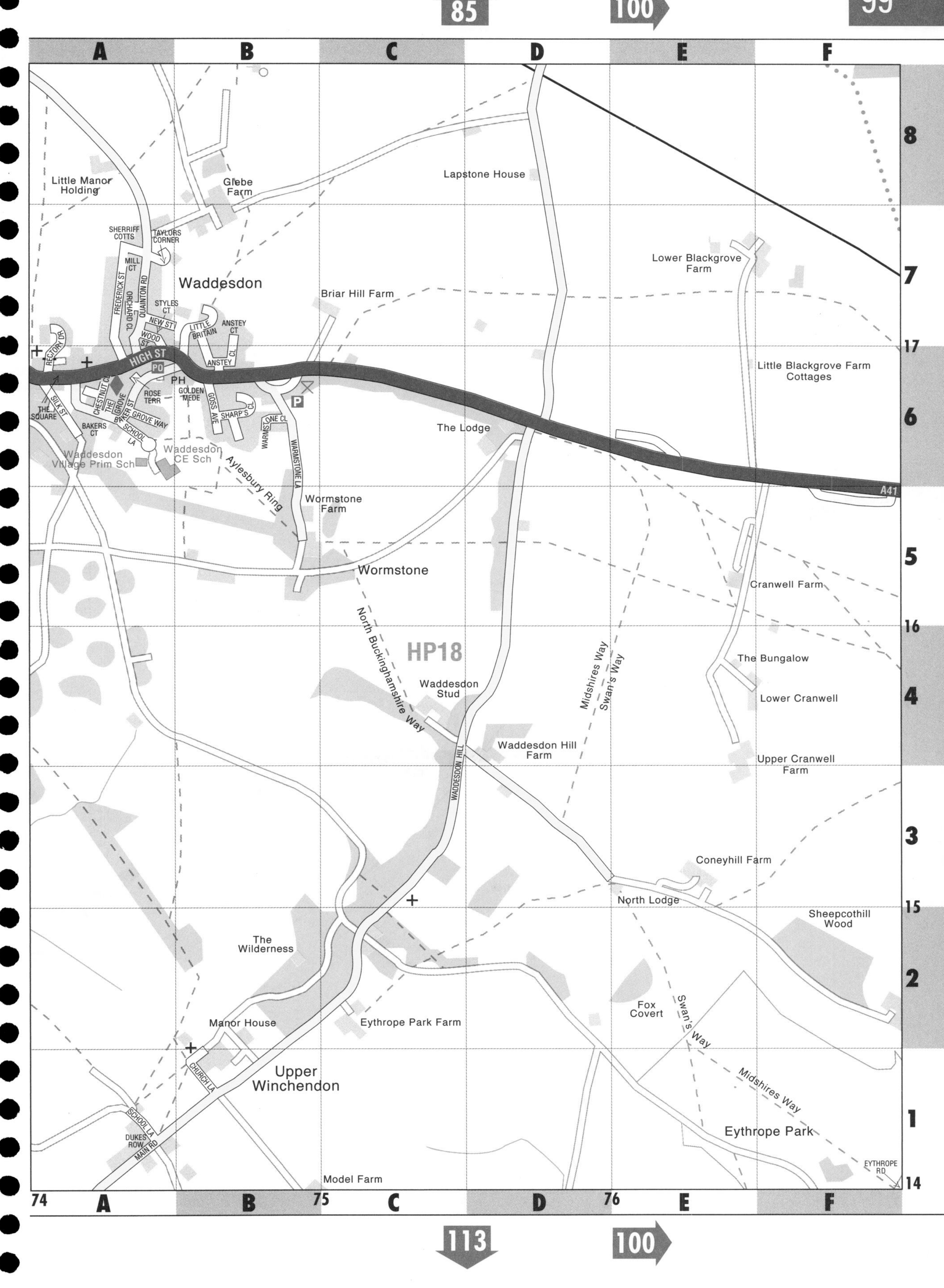
A
B
C
D
E
F
8
7
17
6
5
16
4
3
15
2
1
14
74
75
76
Little Manor Holding
Glebe Farm
Lapstone House
SHERRIFF COTTS
TAYLORS CORNER
MILL CT
Waddesdon
FREDERICK ST
ORCHARD CL
QUAINTON RD
STYLES CT
NEW ST
WOOD ST
LITTLE BRITAIN
ANSTEY CT
ANSTEY CL
ANSTEY
RECTORY DR
HIGH ST
PO
PH
CHESTNUT CL
THE GROVE
BAKER ST
ROSE TERR
GOLDEN MEDE
GOSS AVE
SHARP'S CL
WARMSTONE CL
WARMSTONE LA
GROVE WAY
SILK ST
THE SQUARE
BAKERS CT
SCHOOL LA
Waddesdon Village Prim Sch
Waddesdon CE Sch
Aylesbury Ring
Briar Hill Farm
Lower Blackgrove Farm
Little Blackgrove Farm Cottages
The Lodge
A41
Wormstone Farm
Wormstone
Cranwell Farm
North Buckinghamshire Way
HP18
Waddesdon Stud
Midshires Way
Swan's Way
The Bungalow
Lower Cranwell
Waddesdon Hill Farm
Upper Cranwell Farm
WADDESDON HILL
Coneyhill Farm
North Lodge
Sheepcothill Wood
The Wilderness
Fox Covert
Swan's Way
Manor House
Eythrope Park Farm
CHURCH LA
Upper Winchendon
Midshires Way
SCHOOL LA
DUKES ROW
MAIN RD
Eythrope Park
EYTHROPE RD
Model Farm

113
100

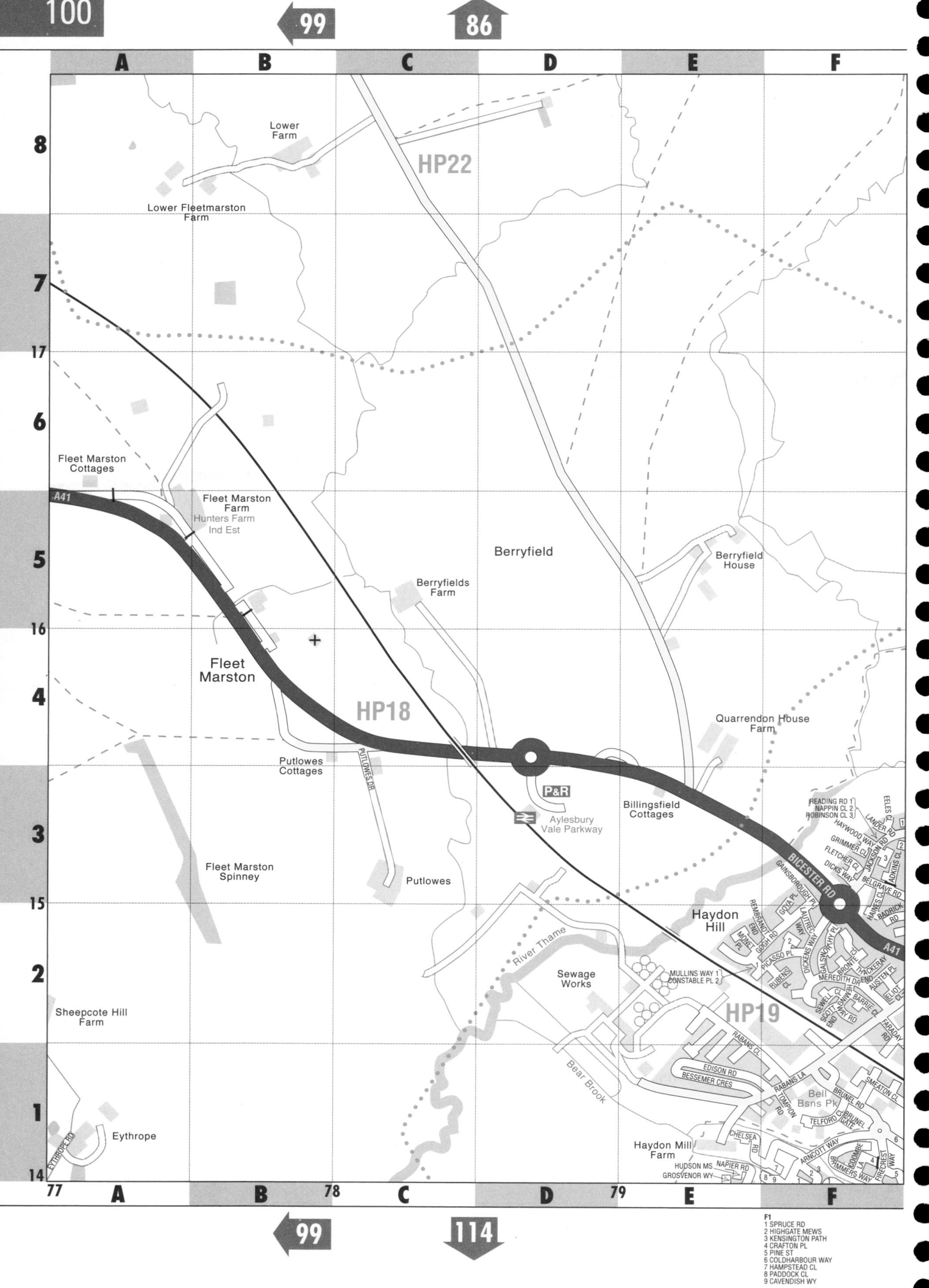

F1
1 SPRUCE RD
2 HIGHGATE MEWS
3 KENSINGTON PATH
4 CRAFTON PL
5 PINE ST
6 COLDHARBOUR WAY
7 HAMPSTEAD CL
8 PADDOCK CL
9 CAVENDISH WY

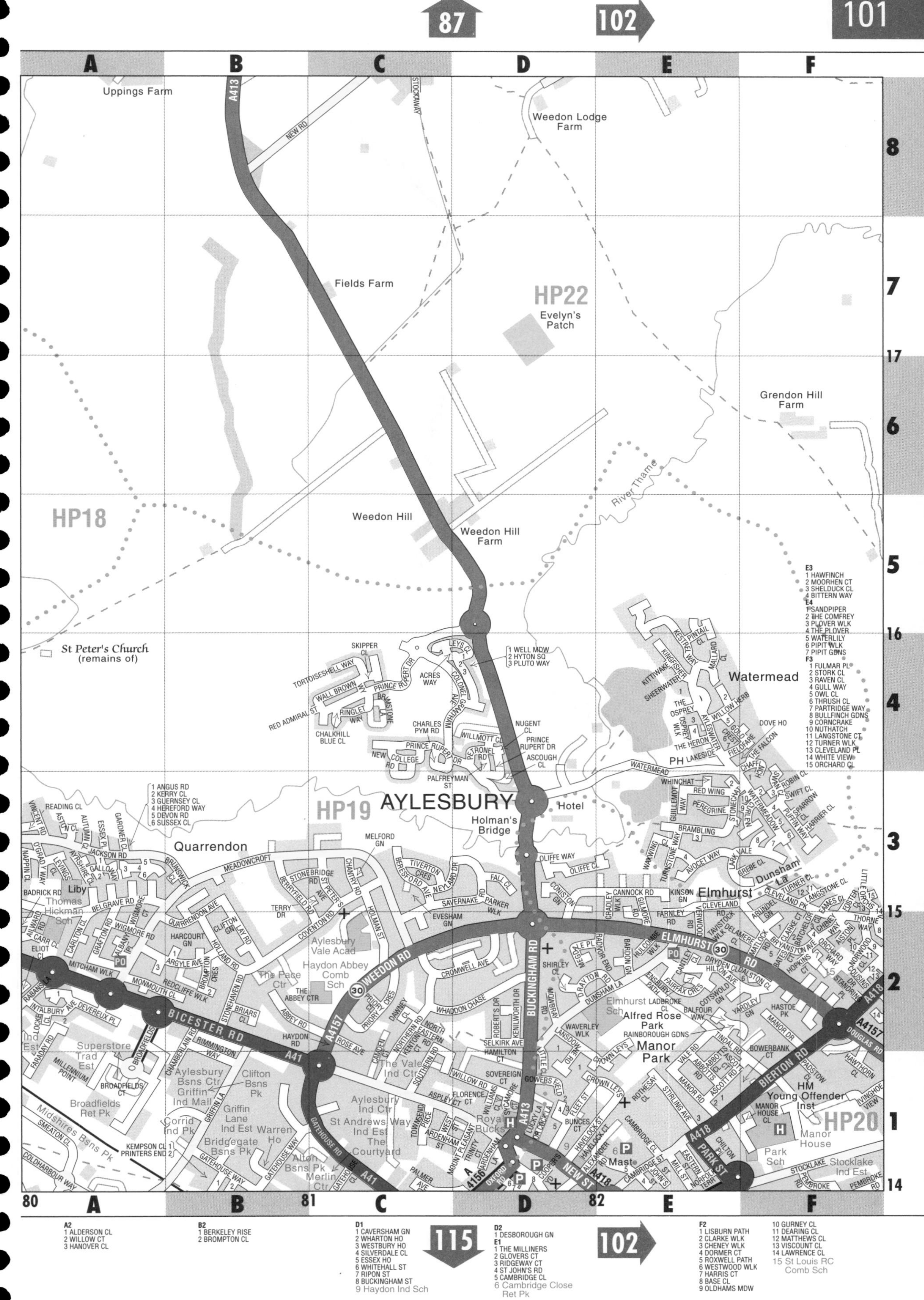

A B C D E F

8

7

17

6

HP22
Weedon Lodge Farm
Evelyn's Patch

Grendon Hill Farm

Uppings Farm
Fields Farm

HP18
Weedon Hill
Weedon Hill Farm
River Thame

5

16

St Peter's Church (remains of)

E3
1 HAWFINCH
2 MOORHEN CT
3 SHELDUCK CL
4 BITTERN WAY
E4
1 SANDPIPER
2 THE COMFREY
3 PLOVER WLK
4 THE PLOVER
5 WATERLILY
6 PIPIT WLK
7 PIPIT GDNS
F3
1 FULMAR PL
2 STORK CL
3 RAVEN CL
4 GULL WAY
5 OWL CL
6 THRUSH CL
7 PARTRIDGE WAY
8 BULLFINCH GDNS
9 CORNCRAKE
10 NUTHATCH
11 LANGSTONE CT
12 TURNER WLK
13 CLEVELAND PL
14 WHITE VIEW
15 ORCHARD CL

Watermead

SKIPPER CL
1 WELL MDW
2 HYTON SQ
3 PLUTO WAY

4

HP19
AYLESBURY
Quarrendon
Holman's Bridge
Hotel
Elmhurst
Dunsham La

1 ANGUS RD
2 KERRY CL
3 GUERNSEY CL
4 HEREFORD WAY
5 DEVON RD
6 SUSSEX CL

3

15

BICESTER RD
A41
WEEDON RD
A4157
BUCKINGHAM RD
ELMHURST RD
A418

Superstore Trad Est
Millennium Point
Broadfields Ret Pk
Midshires Bsns Pk
Aylesbury Bsns Ctr
Griffin Ind Mall
Clifton Bsns Pk
Griffin Lane Ind Est
Bridgegate Bsns Pk
Merlin Ctr
Alton Bsns Pk
The Courtyard
St Andrews Way Ind Est
Aylesbury Ind Ctr
The Vale Ind Ctr
Royal Bucks
Alfred Rose Park
Manor Park
Elmhurst Sch
Ladbroke Sch
Manor Park
HM Young Offender Inst
HP20
Manor House
Park Sch
Stocklake Ind Est

2

1

14

A2
1 ALDERSON CL
2 WILLOW CT
3 HANOVER CL

B2
1 BERKELEY RISE
2 BROMPTON CL

D1
1 CAVERSHAM GN
2 WHARTON HO
3 WESTBURY HO
4 SILVERDALE CL
5 ESSEX HO
6 WHITEHALL ST
7 RIPON ST
8 BUCKINGHAM ST
9 Haydon Ind Sch

D2
1 DESBOROUGH GN
E1
1 THE MILLINERS
2 GLOVERS CT
3 RIDGEWAY CT
4 ST JOHN'S RD
5 CAMBRIDGE CT
6 Cambridge Close Ret Pk

F2
1 LISBURN PATH
2 CLARKE WLK
3 CHENEY WLK
4 DORMER CT
5 ROXWELL PATH
6 WESTWOOD WLK
7 HARRIS CT
8 BASE CL
9 OLDHAMS MDW

10 GURNEY CL
11 DEARING CL
12 MATTHEWS CL
13 VISCOUNT CL
14 LAWRENCE CL
15 St Louis RC Comb Sch

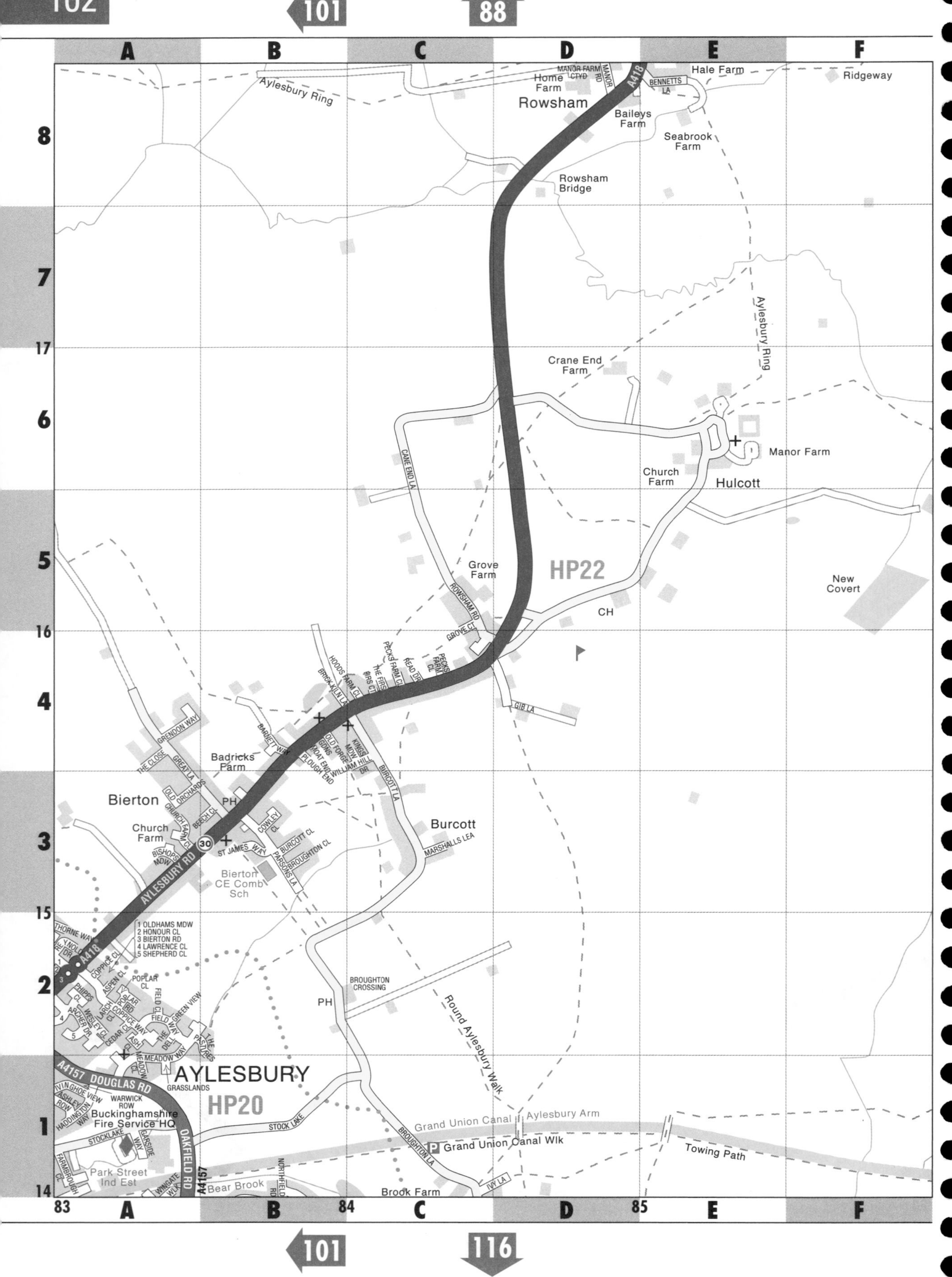

101

88

A   B   C   D   E   F

8

7

17

6

Aylesbury Ring

Home Farm

MANOR FARM CTYD

Rowsham

MANOR LA

A418

BENNETTS LA

Hale Farm

Ridgeway

Baileys Farm

Seabrook Farm

Rowsham Bridge

Crane End Farm

Aylesbury Ring

Manor Farm

Church Farm

Hulcott

5

Grove Farm

HP22

CH

New Covert

16

4

CANE END LA

ROWSHAM RD

GROVE CT

PECKS FARM CL

PECKS FARM LA

THE FIRS CL

HOODS FARM LA

BROOK MILL LA

GIB LA

BARRETT WAY

OLD FORGE CL

BURCOTT LA

3

Bierton

Church Farm

GRENDOON WAY

THE CLOSE

GREAT LA

OLD ORCHARDS

OLD CHURCH LA

BEECH CL

BISHOPS MDW

Badricks Farm

PH

COWLEY

PLOUGH END

WILLIAM HILL DR

KINGS MDW

ST JAMES WAY

BURCOTT CL

BROUGHTON CL

PARSONS LA

Burcott

MARSHALLS LEA

AYLESBURY RD

30

Bierton CE Comb Sch

15

2

THORNE WAY

A418

1 OLDHAMS MDW
2 HONOUR CL
3 BIERTON RD
4 LAWRENCE CL
5 SHEPHERD CL

COPPICE CL

ASPEN CL

POPLAR CL

FIELD CL

THE GREEN VIEW

FIELD WAY

THE PASTURES

BROUGHTON CROSSING

PH

Round Aylesbury Walk

A4157

DOUGLAS RD

AYLESBURY

HP20

GRASSLANDS

MEADOW WAY

CEDAR CL

WARWICK ROW

VIALGHOE VIEW

1

Buckinghamshire Fire Service HQ

STOCK LAKE

NORTHFIELD

BROUGHTON LA

Grand Union Canal

P

Aylesbury Arm

Grand Union Canal Wlk

IVY LA

Towing Path

OAKFIELD RD

A4157

14

Park Street Ind Est

WINGATE WAY

BASSIDE

STOCKLAKE

FARNBOROUGH

Bear Brook

Brook Farm

83   A   B   84   C   D   85   E   F

101

116

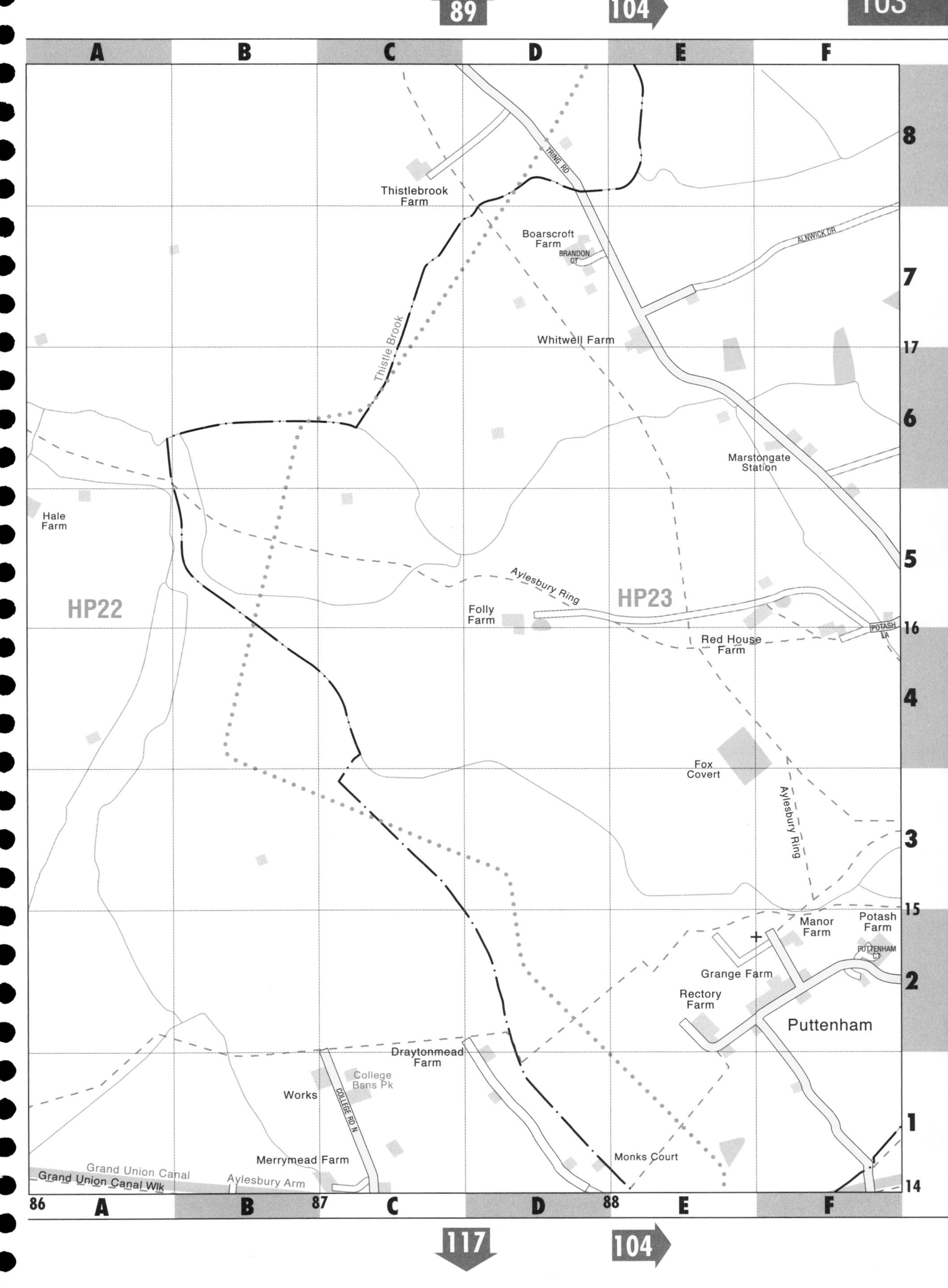
89
104
A
B
C
D
E
F
8
7
17
6
5
16
4
3
15
2
1
14
Thistlebrook Farm
TRING RD
Boarscroft Farm
BRANDON CT
ALNWICK DR
Whitwell Farm
Thistle Brook
Marstongate Station
Hale Farm
Aylesbury Ring
HP22
HP23
Folly Farm
Red House Farm
POTASH LA
Fox Covert
Aylesbury Ring
Manor Farm
Potash Farm
PUTTENHAM CT
Grange Farm
Rectory Farm
Puttenham
Draytonmead Farm
College Bsns Pk
Works
COLLEGE RD N
Merrymead Farm
Monks Court
Grand Union Canal
Grand Union Canal Wlk
Aylesbury Arm
86
87
88
117
104

103
90

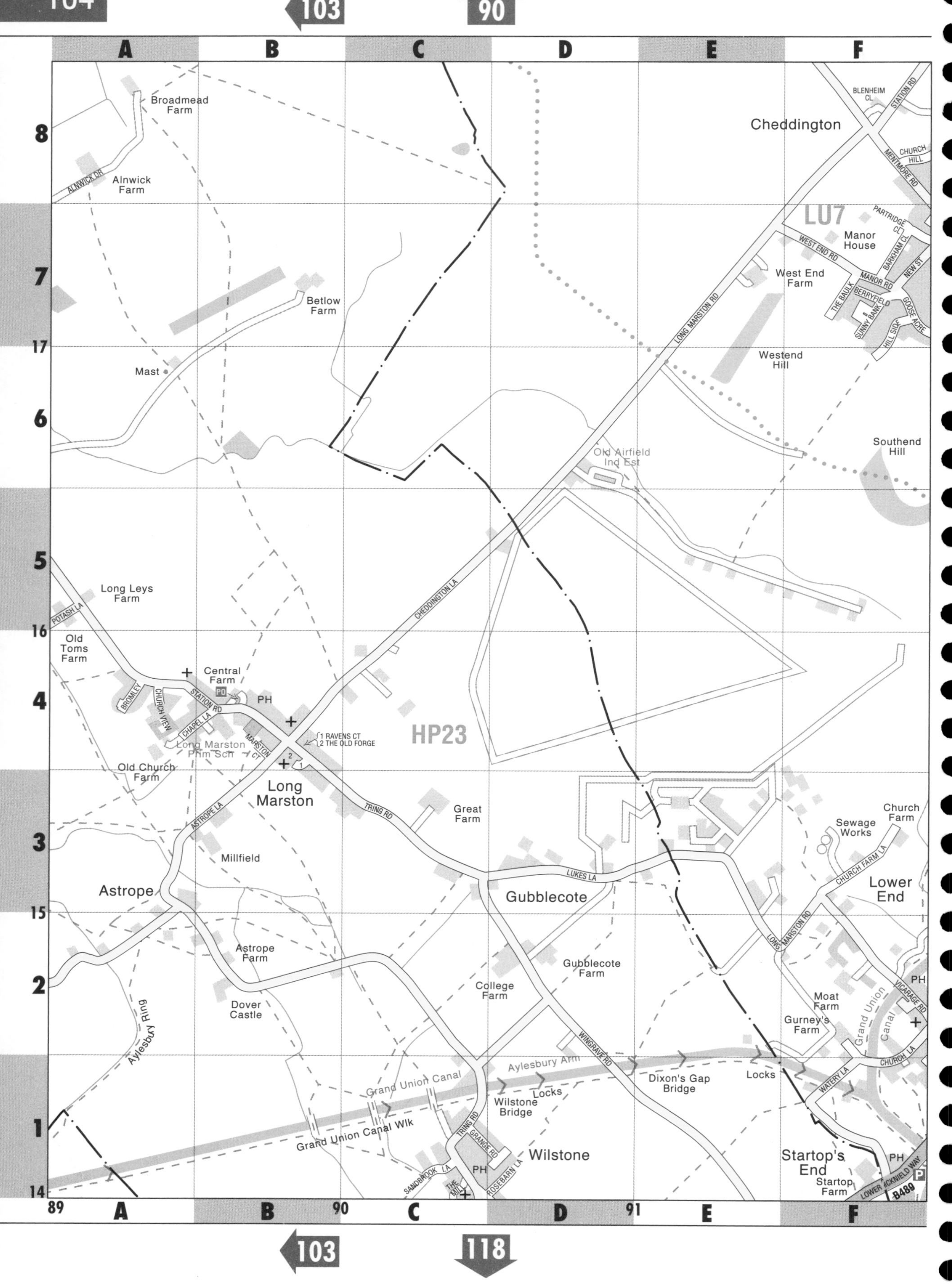
A
B
C
D
E
F
Broadmead Farm
Alnwick Farm
ALNWICK DR
Cheddington
BLENHEIM CL
STATION RD
CHURCH HILL
MENTMORE RD
LU7
PARTRIDGE CL
Manor House
WEST END RD
BARKHAM CL
West End Farm
MANOR RD
NEW ST
THE BAULK
BERRYFIELD
SUNNY BANK
GOOSE ACRE
HILL SIDE
LONG MARSTON RD
Betlow Farm
Mast
Westend Hill
Southend Hill
Old Airfield Ind Est
Long Leys Farm
POTASH LA
CHEDDINGTON LA
Old Toms Farm
Central Farm
PO
PH
BROMLEY
CHURCH VIEW
STATION RD
CHAPEL LA
MARSTON CT
1 RAVENS CT
2 THE OLD FORGE
HP23
Long Marston Prim Sch
Old Church Farm
Long Marston
ASTROPE LA
TRING RD
Great Farm
Church Farm
Sewage Works
CHURCH FARM LA
Millfield
LUKES LA
Lower End
Astrope
Gubblecote
LONG MARSTON RD
Astrope Farm
Gubblecote Farm
PH
College Farm
Dover Castle
Moat Farm
VICARAGE RD
Aylesbury Ring
Gurney's Farm
Grand Union Canal
WINGRAVE RD
Aylesbury Arm
Dixon's Gap Bridge
Locks
CHURCH LA
WATERY LA
Grand Union Canal
Wilstone Bridge
Locks
Grand Union Canal Wlk
TRING RD
GRANGE RD
Wilstone
Startop's End
PH
SANDBROOK LA
PH
ROSEBARN LA
THE MILL
Startop Farm
LOWER ICKNIELD WAY
P
B489
8
7
17
6
5
16
4
3
15
2
1
14
89
90
91

103
118

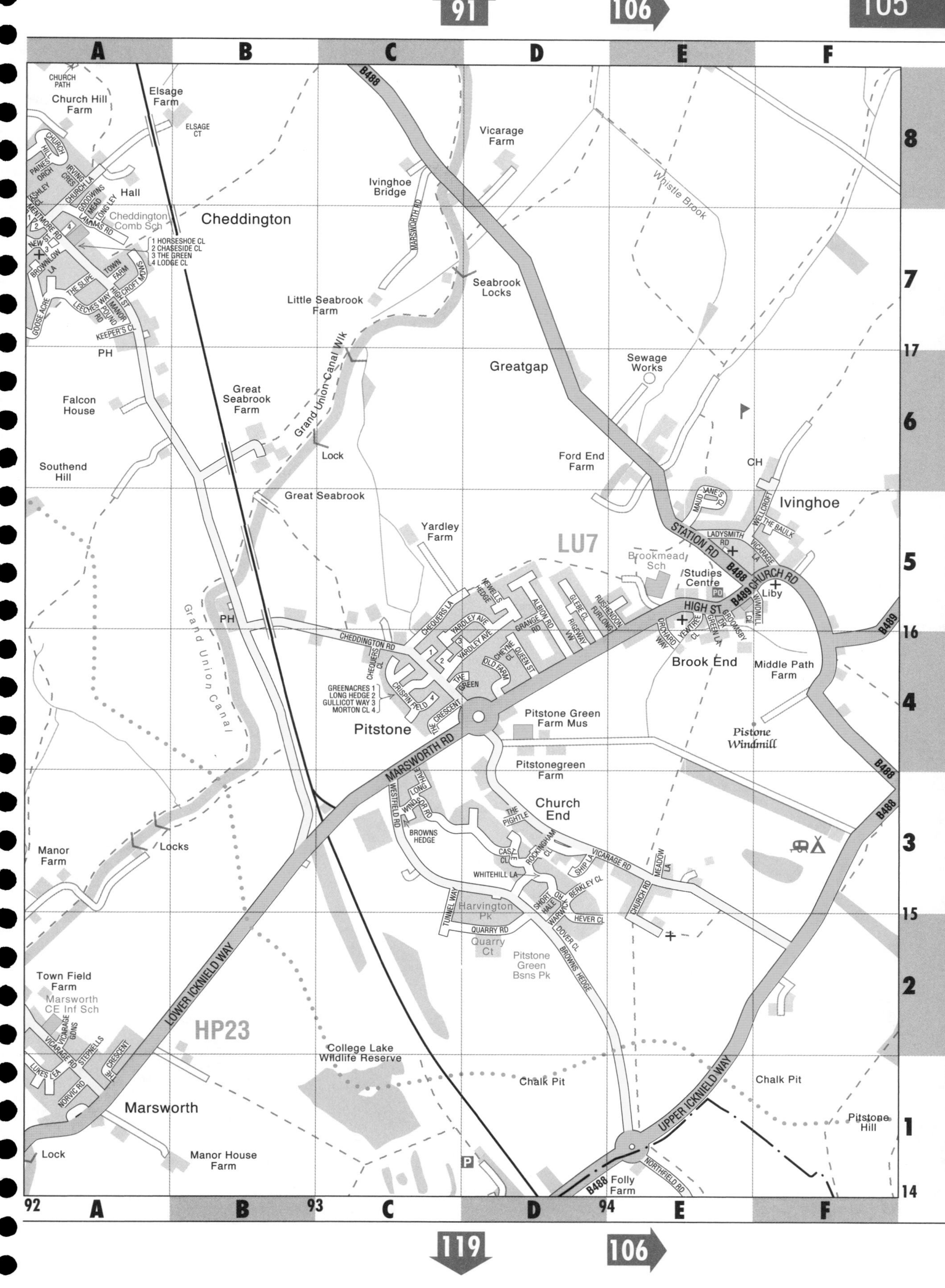
91
106
A
B
C
D
E
F
8
7
17
6
5
16
4
3
15
2
1
14
92
93
94
Church Hill Farm
Elsage Farm
Vicarage Farm
Ivinghoe Bridge
Cheddington
Cheddington Comb Sch
1 HORSESHOE CL
2 CHASESIDE CL
3 THE GREEN
4 LODGE CL
Whistle Brook
Seabrook Locks
Little Seabrook Farm
Grand Union Canal Wlk
Greatgap
Sewage Works
Falcon House
Great Seabrook Farm
Lock
Southend Hill
Ford End Farm
CH
Ivinghoe
Great Seabrook
Yardley Farm
LU7
Brookmead Sch
Studies Centre
Liby
PH
Grand Union Canal
Brook End
Middle Path Farm
GREENACRES 1
LONG HEDGE 2
GULLICOT WAY 3
MORTON CL 4
Pitstone
Pitstone Green Farm Mus
Pistone Windmill
Pitstonegreen Farm
Church End
Manor Farm
Locks
Harvington Pk
Quarry Ct
Pitstone Green Bsns Pk
Town Field Farm
Marsworth CE Inf Sch
HP23
College Lake Wildlife Reserve
Chalk Pit
Chalk Pit
Pitstone Hill
Marsworth
Lock
Manor House Farm
Folly Farm
B488
B489
LOWER ICKNIELD WAY
UPPER ICKNIELD WAY
MARSWORTH RD
HIGH ST
STATION RD
CHURCH RD
CHEDDINGTON RD
VICARAGE RD
119
106

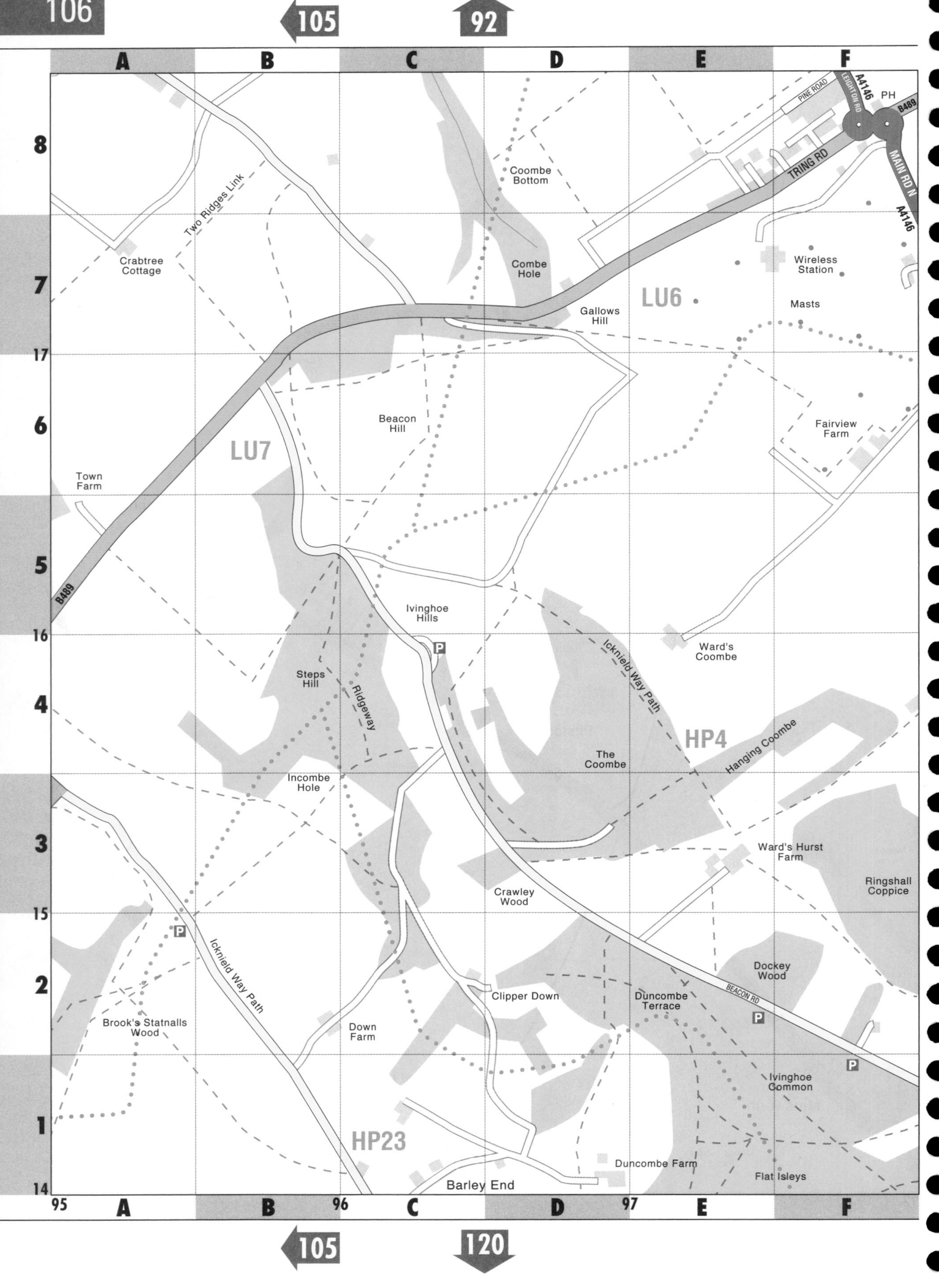

A B C D E F

8

7

17

6

5

16

4

3

15

2

1

14

Two Ridges Link

Crabtree
Cottage

Coombe
Bottom

Combe
Hole

Gallows
Hill

LU6

PINE ROAD

PH

TRING RD

B489

LEIGHTON RD

A4146

MAIN RD N

Wireless
Station

Masts

Fairview
Farm

Beacon
Hill

LU7

Town
Farm

B489

Ivinghoe
Hills

Icknield Way Path

Ward's
Coombe

P

Steps
Hill

Ridgeway

HP4

The
Coombe

Hanging Coombe

Incombe
Hole

Ward's Hurst
Farm

Ringshall
Coppice

Crawley
Wood

P

Icknield Way Path

Dockey
Wood

Clipper Down

Duncombe
Terrace

BEACON RD

P

Brook's Statnalls
Wood

Down
Farm

P

Ivinghoe
Common

HP23

Barley End

Duncombe Farm

Flat Isleys

93

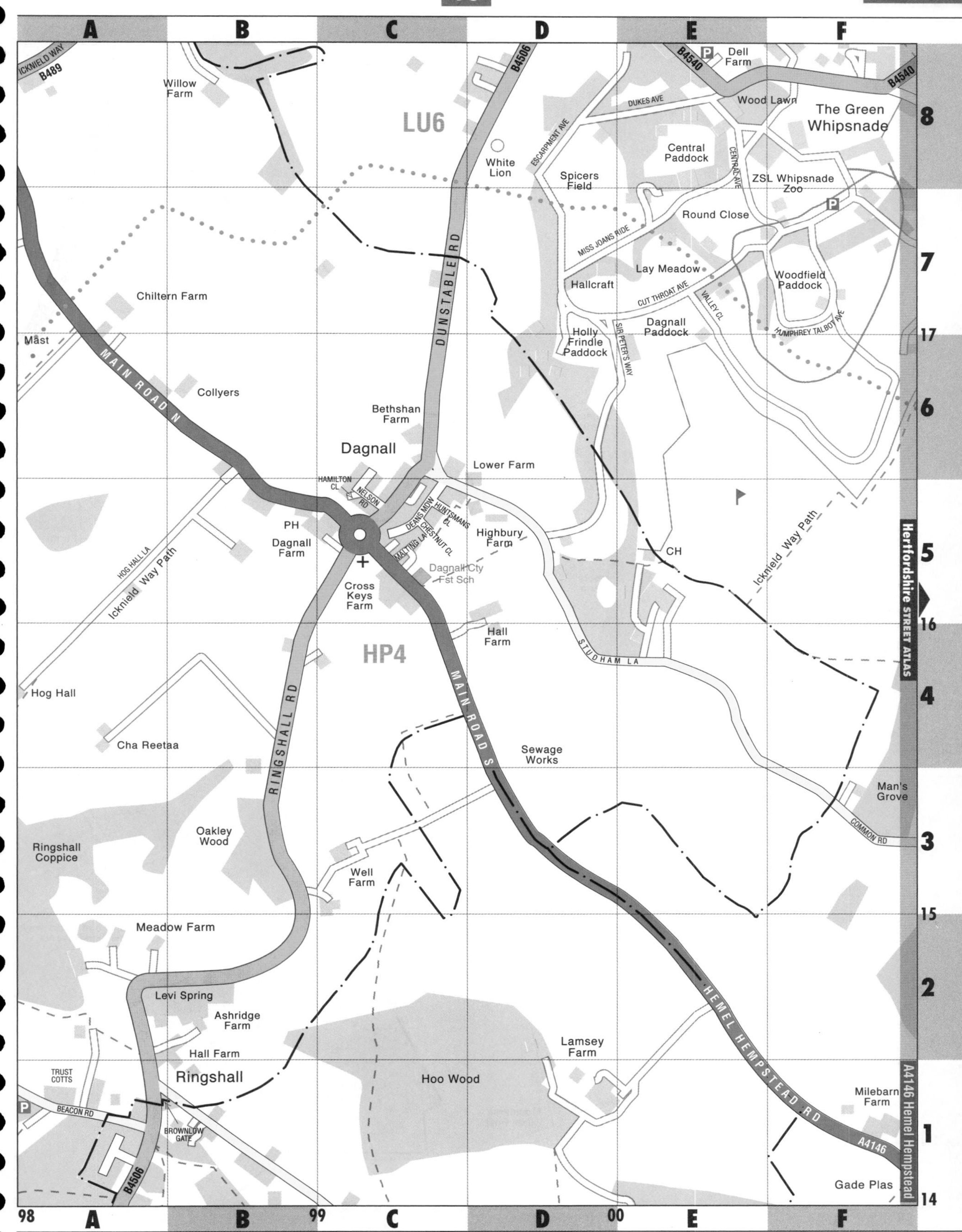
A
B
C
D
E
F
ICKNIELD WAY
B489
Willow Farm
B4506
LU6
B4540
Dell Farm
Wood Lawn
DUKES AVE
The Green
Whipsnade
ESCARPMENT AVE
White Lion
Central Paddock
CENTRAL AVE
Spicers Field
ZSL Whipsnade Zoo
Round Close
MISS JOANS RIDE
Lay Meadow
Woodfield Paddock
Hallcraft
CUT THROAT AVE
VALLEY CL
Dagnall Paddock
HUMPHREY TALBOT AVE
Holly Frindle Paddock
SIR PETER'S WAY
Chiltern Farm
DUNSTABLE RD
Mast
MAIN ROAD N
Collyers
Bethshan Farm
Dagnall
Lower Farm
HAMILTON CL
NELSON RD
DEANS MDW
HUNTSMANS CL
CHESTNUT CL
MALTING LA
PH
Dagnall Farm
Highbury Farm
HOG HALL LA
Icknield Way Path
Dagnall Cty Fst Sch
CH
Cross Keys Farm
Hall Farm
HP4
STUDHAM LA
Hog Hall
RINGSHALL RD
MAIN ROAD S
Cha Reetaa
Sewage Works
Man's Grove
COMMON RD
Oakley Wood
Ringshall Coppice
Well Farm
Meadow Farm
HEMEL HEMPSTEAD RD
Levi Spring
Ashridge Farm
Lamsey Farm
Hall Farm
TRUST COTTS
Ringshall
Hoo Wood
Milebarn Farm
BEACON RD
BROWNLOW GATE
A4146
B4506
Gade Plas
A4146 Hemel Hempstead
Hertfordshire STREET ATLAS
8
7
17
6
5
16
4
3
15
2
1
14
98
99
00

121

94

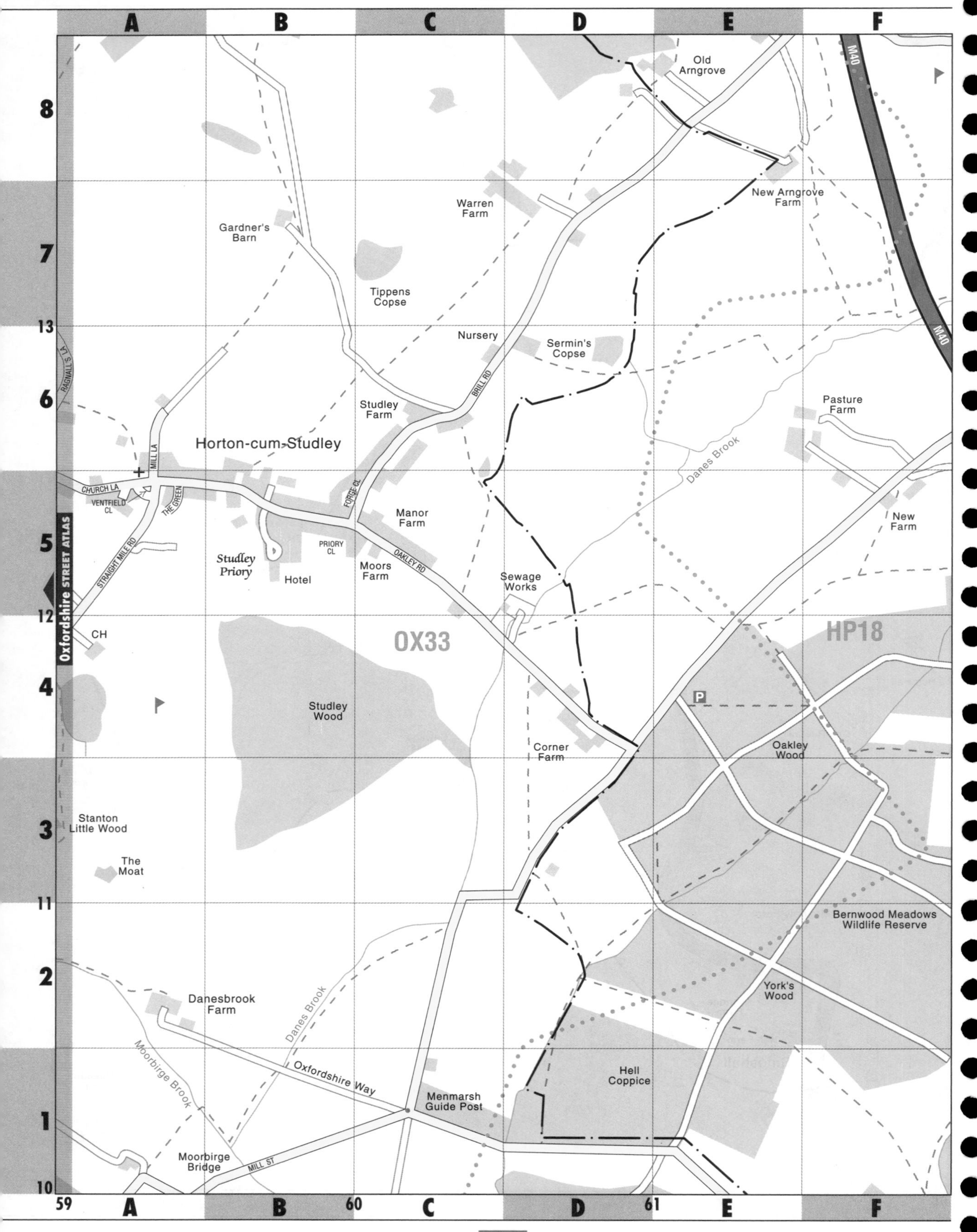

A
B
C
D
E
F
8
7
13
6
5
12
4
3
11
2
1
10
59
60
61
Old Arngrove
New Arngrove Farm
Warren Farm
Gardner's Barn
Tippens Copse
Nursery
Sermin's Copse
M40
Pasture Farm
Studley Farm
BRILL RD
Horton-cum-Studley
RAGNALL'S LA
MILL LA
CHURCH LA
VENTFIELD CL
THE GREEN
FORGE CL
Danes Brook
Manor Farm
New Farm
STRAIGHT MILE RD
Studley Priory
Hotel
PRIORY CL
Moors Farm
OAKLEY RD
Sewage Works
Oxfordshire STREET ATLAS
CH
OX33
HP18
Studley Wood
P
Oakley Wood
Corner Farm
Stanton Little Wood
The Moat
Bernwood Meadows Wildlife Reserve
York's Wood
Danesbrook Farm
Danes Brook
Moorbirge Brook
Oxfordshire Way
Hell Coppice
Menmarsh Guide Post
Moorbirge Bridge
MILL ST

122

95
110

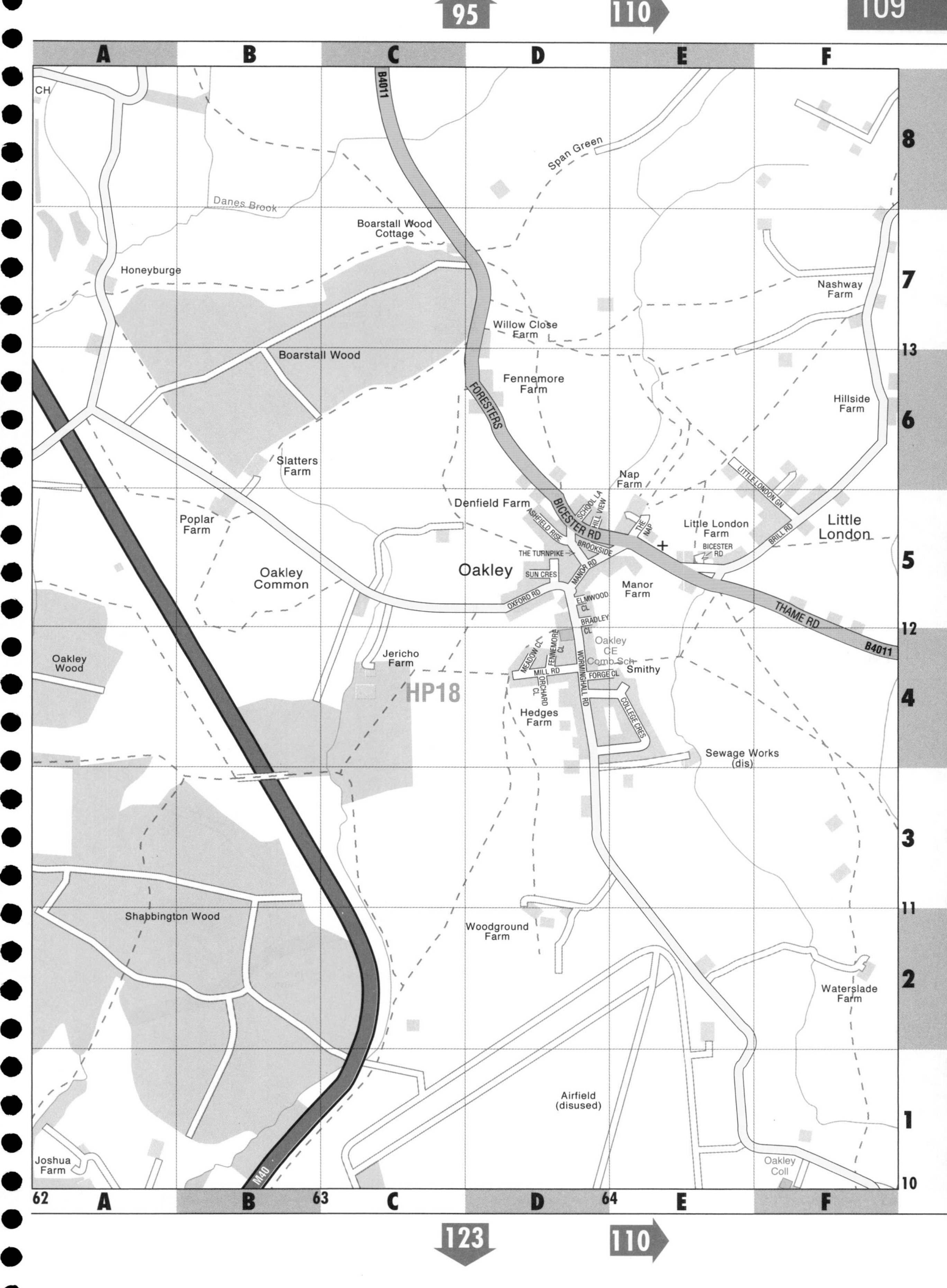
A
B
C
D
E
F
8
7
13
6
5
12
4
3
11
2
1
10
62
63
64
CH
B4011
Span Green
Danes Brook
Boarstall Wood
Cottage
Honeyburge
Willow Close
Farm
Nashway
Farm
Boarstall Wood
Fennemore
Farm
Hillside
Farm
FORESTERS
Slatters
Farm
Nap
Farm
LITTLE LONDON GN
Denfield Farm
SCHOOL LA
HILL VIEW
BICESTER RD
ASHFIELD RISE
THE NAP
Little London
Farm
Little
London
BRILL RD
Poplar
Farm
BROOKSIDE
BICESTER
RD
THE TURNPIKE
Oakley
MANOR RD
SUN CRES
Oakley
Common
Manor
Farm
OXFORD RD
ELMWOOD
CL
THAME RD
BRADLEY
CL
B4011
Oakley
Wood
Oakley
CE
Comb Sch
Jericho
Farm
MEADOW CL
FENNEMORE CL
WORMINGHALL RD
Smithy
MILL RD
FORGE CL
ORCHARD CL
HP18
Hedges
Farm
COLLEGE CRES
Sewage Works
(dis)
Shabbington Wood
Woodground
Farm
Waterslade
Farm
Airfield
(disused)
Joshua
Farm
M40
Oakley
Coll

123
110

109
96

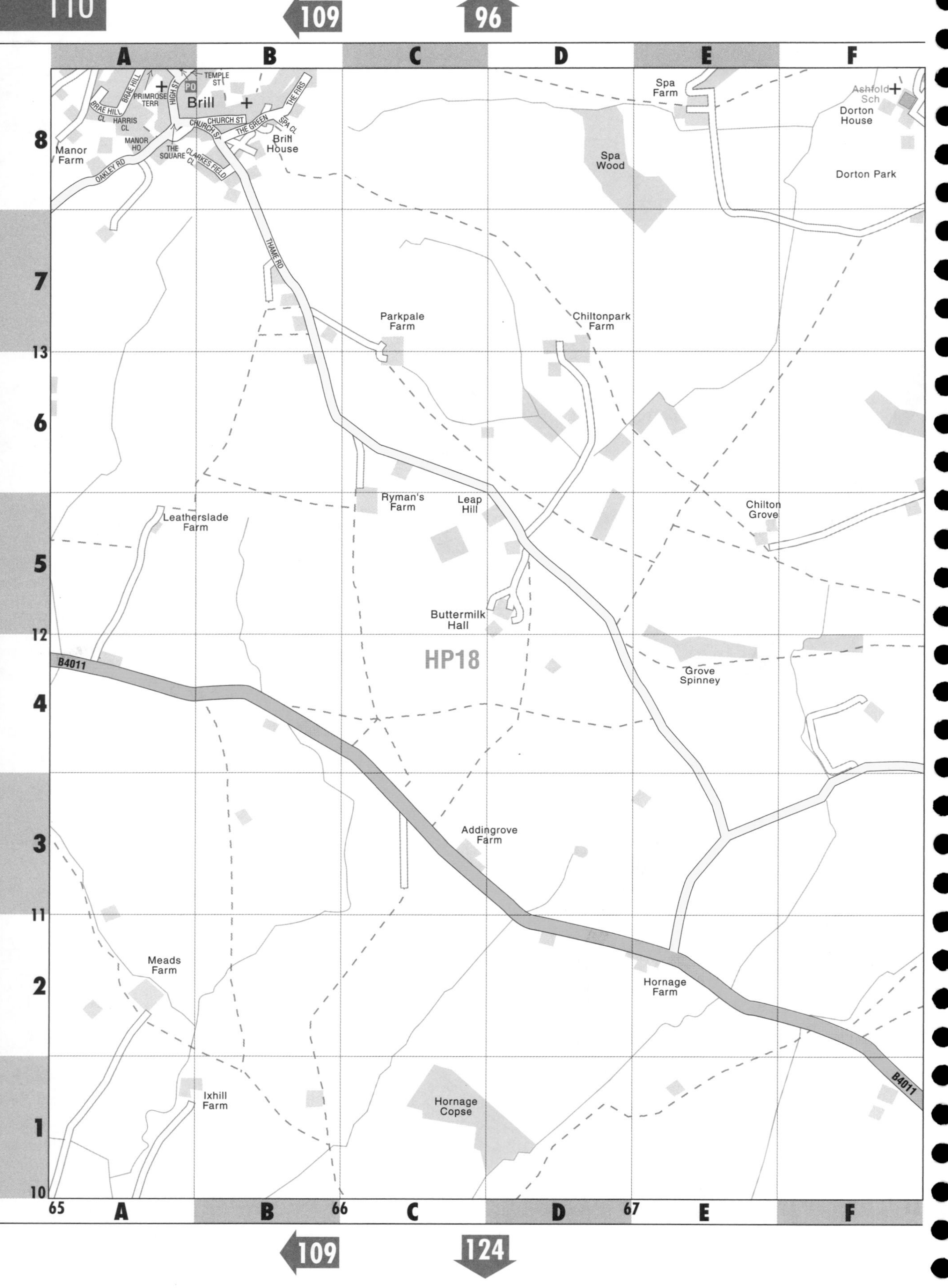
Brill
TEMPLE ST
PO
PRIMROSE TERR
HIGH ST
BRAE HILL
BRAE HILL CL
HARRIS CL
CHURCH ST
THE GREEN
THE FIRS
SPA CL
MANOR HO
THE SQUARE
CLARKES FIELD
CLARKES CL
Brill House
Manor Farm
OAKLEY RD
THAME RD
Spa Farm
Spa Wood
Ashfold Sch
Dorton House
Dorton Park
Parkpale Farm
Chiltonpark Farm
Ryman's Farm
Leap Hill
Chilton Grove
Leatherslade Farm
Buttermilk Hall
HP18
B4011
Grove Spinney
Addingrove Farm
Meads Farm
Hornage Farm
Ixhill Farm
Hornage Copse
A
B
C
D
E
F
8
7
13
6
5
12
4
3
11
2
1
10
65
66
67

109
124

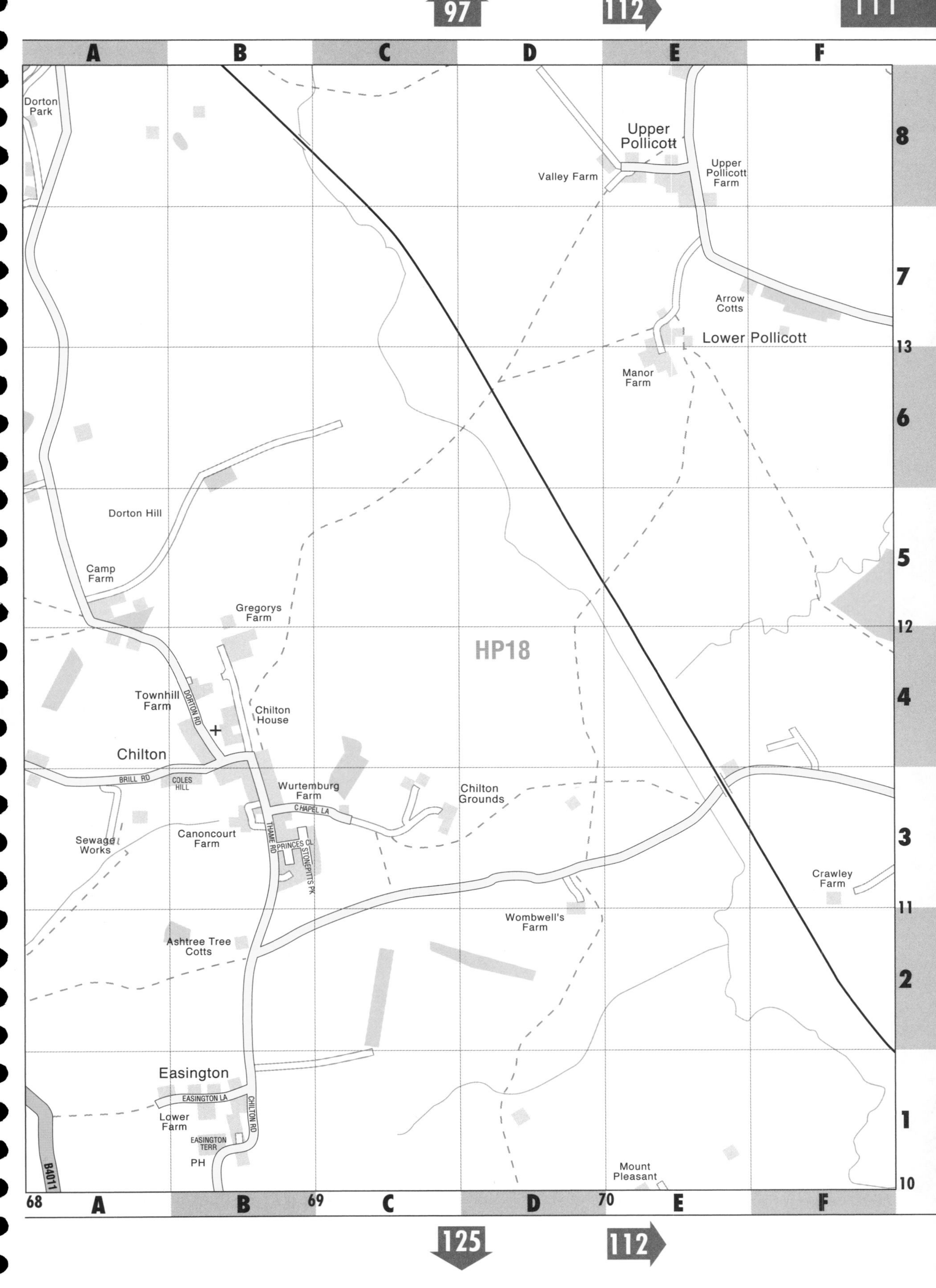

A B C D E F

Dorton Park

Upper Pollicott

Valley Farm

Upper Pollicott Farm

Arrow Cotts

Lower Pollicott

Manor Farm

Dorton Hill

Camp Farm

Gregorys Farm

HP18

Townhill Farm

Chilton House

Chilton

DORTON RD

Wurtemburg Farm

Chilton Grounds

BRILL RD

COLES HILL

CHAPEL LA

Canoncourt Farm

THAME RD

PRINCES CL

STONEPITS PK

Sewage Works

Crawley Farm

Ashtree Tree Cotts

Wombwell's Farm

Easington

EASINGTON LA

CHILTON RD

Lower Farm

EASINGTON TERR

PH

B4011

Mount Pleasant

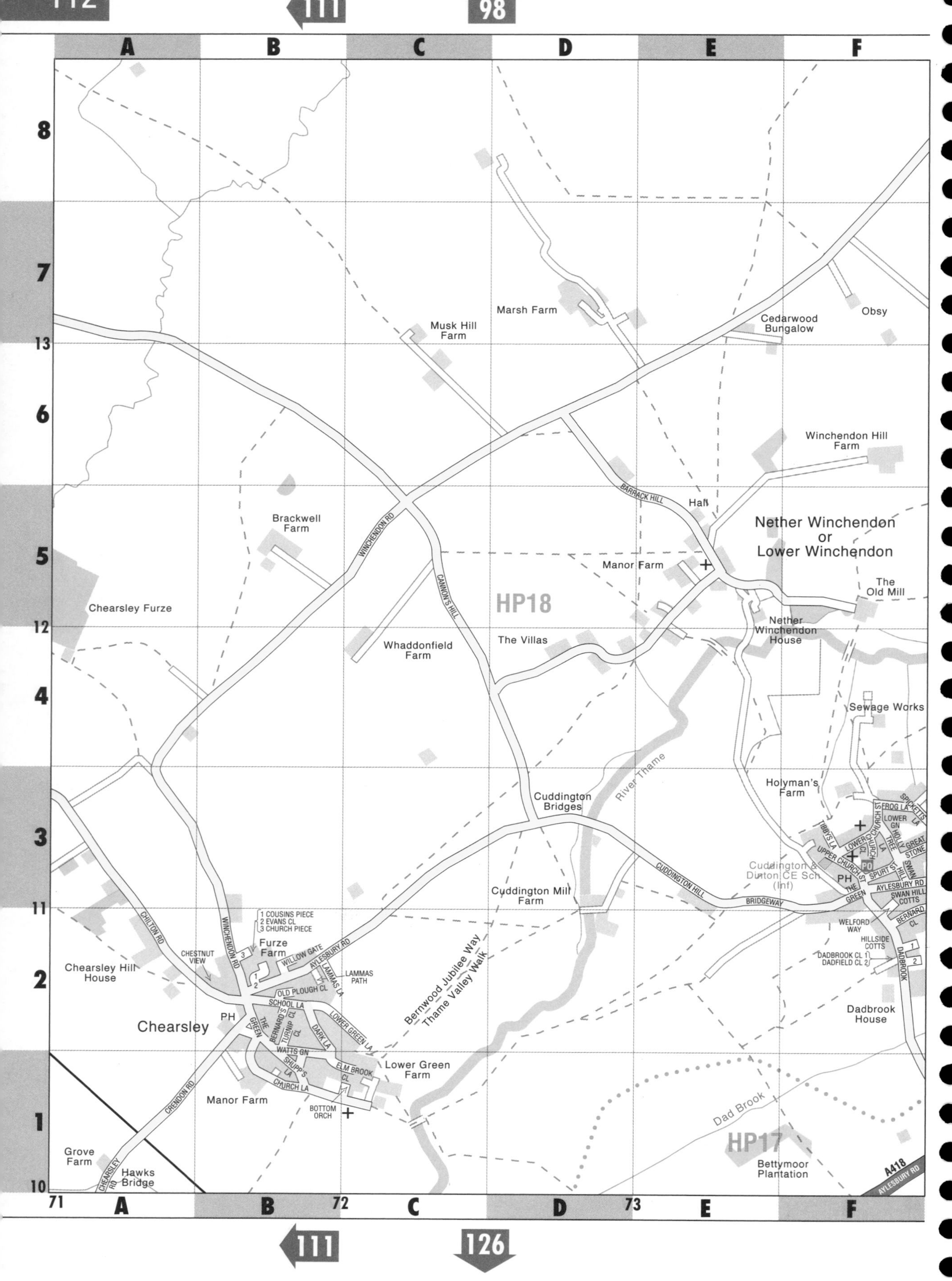

A B C D E F

8

7

13

6

5

12

4

3

11

2

1

10

Musk Hill Farm

Marsh Farm

Cedarwood Bungalow

Obsy

Winchendon Hill Farm

Brackwell Farm

Barrack Hill

Hall

Nether Winchendon
or
Lower Winchendon

Chearsley Furze

WINCHENDON RD

CANNON'S HILL

HP18

Manor Farm

The Old Mill

Nether Winchendon House

Whaddonfield Farm

The Villas

Sewage Works

River Thame

Holyman's Farm

Cuddington Bridges

Cuddington & Dinton CE Sch (Inf)

UPPER CHURCH ST
LOWER CHURCH ST
IBBS LA
FROG LA
LOWER GN
THE SWAN
SPURT ST
GREAT STONE
SPICKETTS LA

PH

Cuddington Mill Farm

Cuddington Hill

BRIDGEWAY

THE GREEN
SWAN HILL COTTS
AYLESBURY RD

Chearsley Hill House

CHILTON RD

WINCHENDON RD

1 COUSINS PIECE
2 EVANS CL
3 CHURCH PIECE

Furze Farm

CHESTNUT VIEW

WILLOW GATE

AYLESBURY RD

LAMMAS PATH

Bernwood Jubilee Way
Thame Valley Walk

WELFORD WAY

BERNARD CL
DADBROOK

HILLSIDE COTTS

DADBROOK CL 1
DADFIELD CL 2

OLD PLOUGH CL

Chearsley

SCHOOL LA
TURIP CL
THE BERNARDS

Dadbrook House

PH

THE GREEN

DARK LA

LOWER GREEN LA

WATTS GN
SHUPP'S LA
ELM BROOK CL
CHURCH LA

Lower Green Farm

CRENDON RD

Manor Farm

BOTTOM ORCH

Dad Brook

HP17

Grove Farm

CHEARSLEY RD

Hawks Bridge

Bettymoor Plantation

A418
AYLESBURY RD

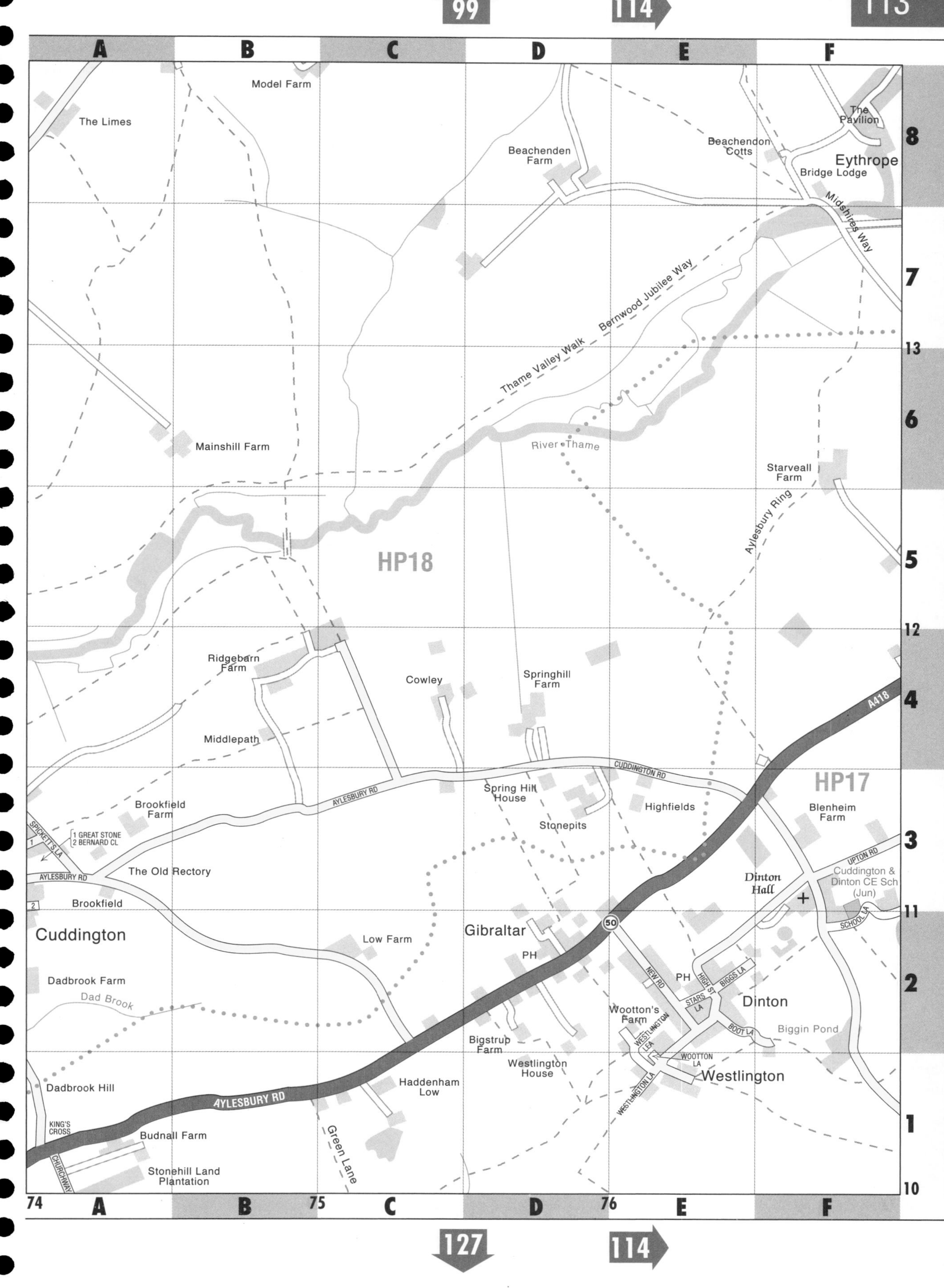

A   B   C   D   E   F

The Limes

Model Farm

Beachenden Farm

Beachendon Cotts

The Pavilion

Eythrope

Bridge Lodge

8

Midshires Way

7

Thame Valley Walk

Bernwood Jubilee Way

13

Mainshill Farm

6

River Thame

Starveall Farm

Aylesbury Ring

HP18

5

12

Ridgebarn Farm

Cowley

Springhill Farm

4

A418

Middlepath

HP17

Cuddington Rd

Blenheim Farm

Brookfield Farm

Spring Hill House

Highfields

1 GREAT STONE
2 BERNARD CL

Stonepits

Upton Rd

SOCKETT'S LA

Dinton Hall

Cuddington & Dinton CE Sch (Jun)

3

AYLESBURY RD

The Old Rectory

SCHOOL LA

AYLESBURY RD

Brookfield

Low Farm

Gibraltar

+

11

Cuddington

PH

50

PH

HIGH ST

BIGGS LA

2

Dadbrook Farm

NEW RD

STARS LA

Dinton

Dad Brook

Wootton's Farm

BOOT LA

Biggin Pond

WESTLINGTON LEA

WOOTTON LA

Bigstrup Farm

Westlington House

WESTLINGTON LA

Westlington

1

Dadbrook Hill

AYLESBURY RD

Haddenham Low

KING'S CROSS

Budnall Farm

Green Lane

CHURCH WAY

Stonehill Land Plantation

10

74   A   B   75   C   D   76   E   F

113
100

A B C D E F

8

HP18

Eythrope Park

Weir Lodge

River Thane

North Buckinghamshire Way

Littleworth Farm

Midshires Way

Whaddon Hill Farm

HP19

NAPIER RD

GROSVENOR WAY

NAPIER RD

PORTMAN MS

ARNCOTT WAY

SPRUCE LA

SWALLOW LA

WARBLER CL

CUCKOO WAY

BRIMMERS WAY

KINGSASH RD

CHALFORD WAY

GREAT MEADOW

COOKS RD

TREBAH SQ 1
WREN PATH 2
LOOSE PATH 3
WATERPERRY MEWS 4
CROWELL MEWS 5
LONGDOWN MEWS 6
ROSEMOOR MEWS 7
LOWNES PATH 8
WIXON PATH 9
PAKENHAM CL 10

7

Arthur's Gorse

Burn Hill

Lower Hartwell

Lower Hartwell Farm

13

6

The Nursery

Botts Furlong Farm

EYTHROPE RD

Cemy

Upper Hartwell

COTTAGE GROUNDS

CROMHAMSTONE

Barnet's Close

Griffiths Acre

Hartwell House

Park Hill

BELLE VUE

CHESTERFIELD CL

POPLARS CL

THE SPIERT

PO

A418

Beech Wlk

5

Long Furlong

DARVILL RD

FAITHFULL CL

JEFFERIES RD

OXFORD RD

BADGERS RISE

CHURCH WAY

STONE CROFT

MANOR FARM CL

CORN CL

ROUND HILL

LEE CRES

CHILTERN CL

CHILTERN AVE

PH

Stone CE Comb Sch

MAYLOWER CL

AMWAY MEADOW

12

Mast

WARREN CL

HAGGAR ST

BEACON CL

ST JOHN'S

CRESLOW WAY

WHITECHURCH CL

THE GLEBE

Stone

BISHOPSTONE RD

PH

SEDRUP LA

WILLOWMEAD

Calley Farm

4

A418

HP17

Stone House

Midshires Way

BITTENHAM CL

PORTWAY

Sedrup

Upton

TEMPLECROFT TERR

HOMESTEAD FARM

UPTON RD

Lower Farm

UPTON TERR

LOWER FARM GATE

Alwyn Lawn House

BISHOPSTONE

3

SCHOOL LA

Wallace Farm

11

Pasture Farm

Sewage Works

MEADOW COTTS

2

Chilboro Hill Farm

1

Aylesbury Ring

10

77 A 78 B C 79 D E F

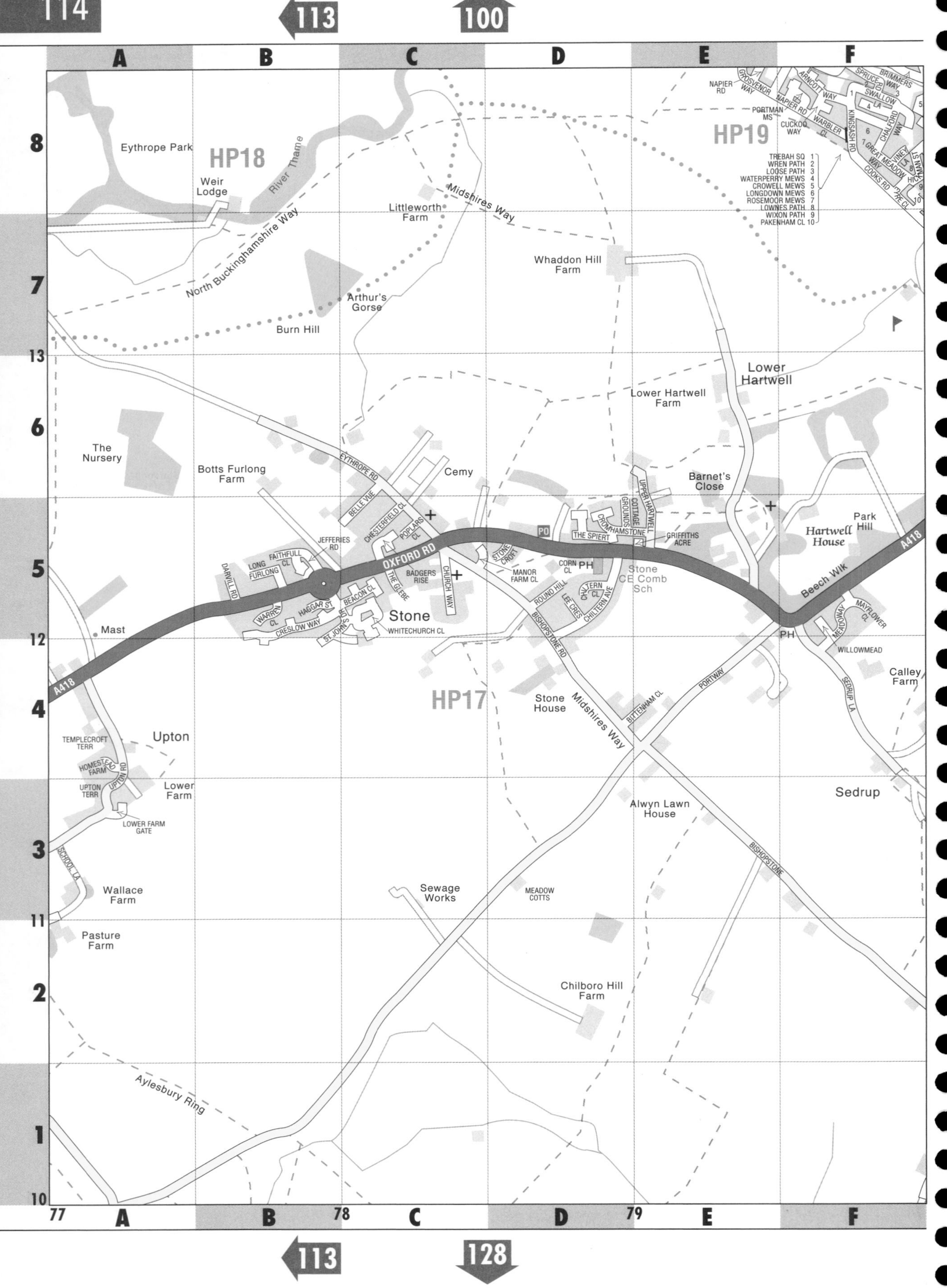

113
128

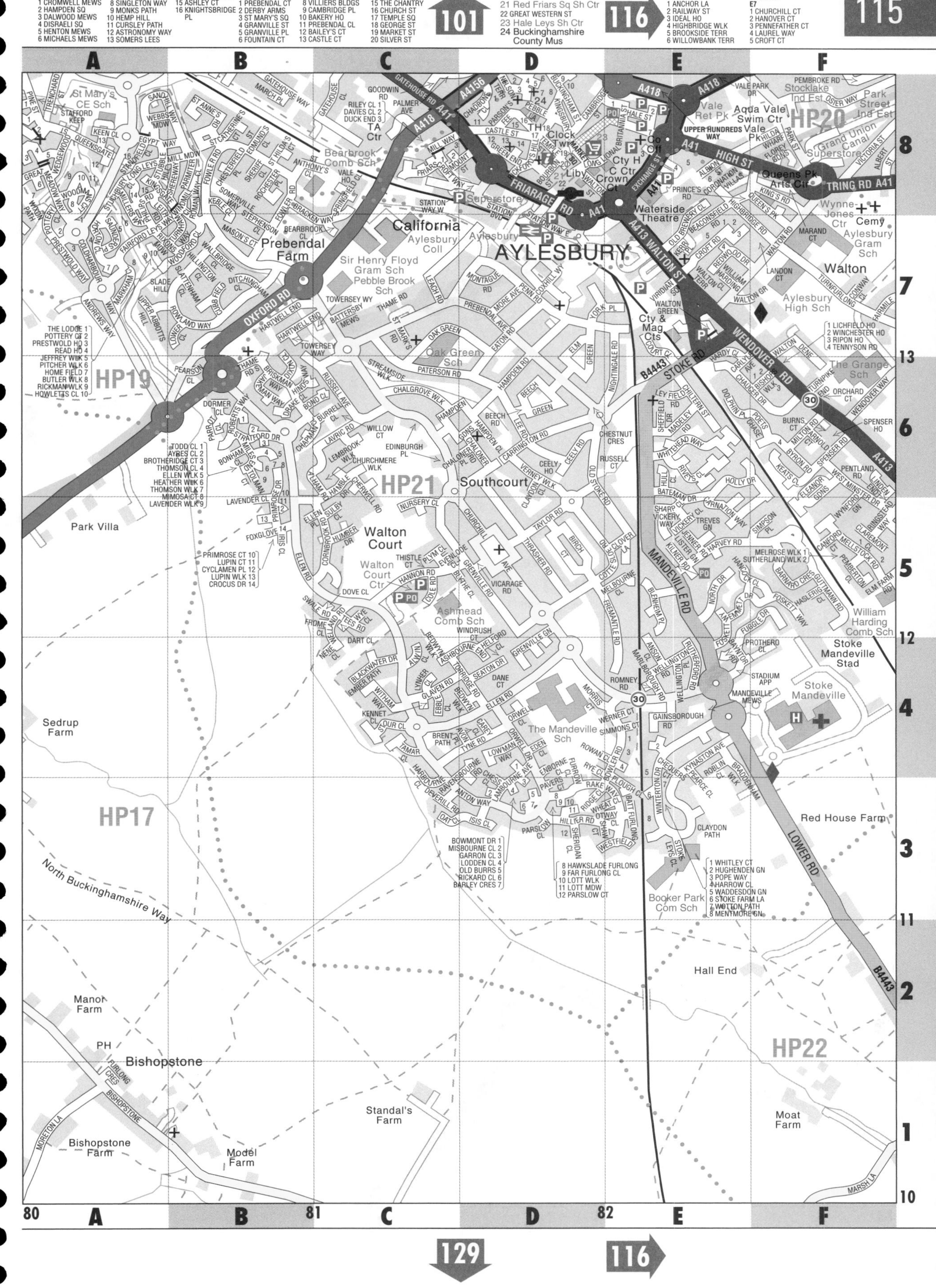

115
A8
1 CROMWELL MEWS
2 HAMPDEN SQ
3 DALWOOD MEWS
4 DISRAELI SQ
5 HENTON MEWS
6 MICHAELS MEWS
7 PHOENIX HO
8 SINGLETON WAY
9 MONKS PATH
10 HEMP HILL
11 CURSLEY PATH
12 ASTRONOMY WAY
13 SOMERS LEES
14 HOMESTEAD PL
15 ASHLEY CT
16 KNIGHTSBRIDGE PL
D8
1 PREBENDAL CT
2 DERBY ARMS
3 ST MARY'S SQ
4 GRANVILLE ST
5 GRANVILLE PL
6 FOUNTAIN CT
7 ST MARY'S ROW
8 VILLIERS BLDGS
9 CAMBRIDGE PL
10 BAKERY HO
11 PREBENDAL CL
12 BAILEY'S CT
13 CASTLE CT
14 ARCHWAYS
15 THE CHANTRY
16 CHURCH ST
17 TEMPLE SQ
18 GEORGE ST
19 MARKET ST
20 SILVER ST
101
D8
21 Red Friars Sq Sh Ctr
22 GREAT WESTERN ST
23 Hale Leys Sh Ctr
24 Buckinghamshire County Mus
116
E8
1 ANCHOR LA
2 RAILWAY ST
3 IDEAL HO
4 HIGHBRIDGE WLK
5 BROOKSIDE TERR
6 WILLOWBANK TERR
7 HIGH ST
E7
1 CHURCHILL CT
2 HANOVER CT
3 PENNEFATHER CT
4 LAUREL WAY
5 CROFT CT
AYLESBURY
California
Prebendal Farm
Southcourt
Walton Court
Walton
HP19
HP20
HP21
HP17
HP22
Park Villa
Sedrup Farm
Manor Farm
Bishopstone
Bishopstone Farm
Model Farm
Standal's Farm
Hall End
Moat Farm
Red House Farm
Stoke Mandeville Stad
Stoke Mandeville
North Buckinghamshire Way
80
81
82
129
116

115 102

A B C D E F
8 7 13 6 5 12 4 3 11 2 1 10
HP20
HP21
HP22
AYLESBURY
Victoria Park
Oak Farm
Broughton Manor Farm
Broughton Inf Sch
Broughton Jun Sch
St Joseph's RC Inf Sch
St Edward's RC Jun Sch
Turnfurlong Inf & Jun Schs
Bedgrove Jun Sch
Bedgrove Inf Sch
Bedgrove
Bedgrove Park
William Harding Comb Sch
Weston Mead Farm
Hotel
Calibre Audio Liby
Westend Ditch
Rectory Farm
CH
Weston Turville
Weston Turville CE Sch
Manor Farm
West End Farm
Stoke Mandeville
Malthouse Farm
Weston Wy Ind Est
Stoke Mandeville Comb Sch
Alberta Farm
Park Street Ind Est
Cemy
TRING RD
ASTON CLINTON RD
A41
A413
WENDOVER RD
STATION RD
A4010
B4443
LOWER RD
RISBOROUGH RD
NEW RD
MARROWAY
OAKFIELD RD A4157
1 JUNIPER DR
2 MAPLE END
3 SILVER BIRCH WY
4 ALMOND TREE DR
1 RINGSTEAD WAY
2 LYNWOOD RD
3 COPPIDWELL DR
4 HAVEN SHAW CL
MARSHAM CL 1
THORPE CL 2
LOWBROOK CL 3
83 84 85

115 130

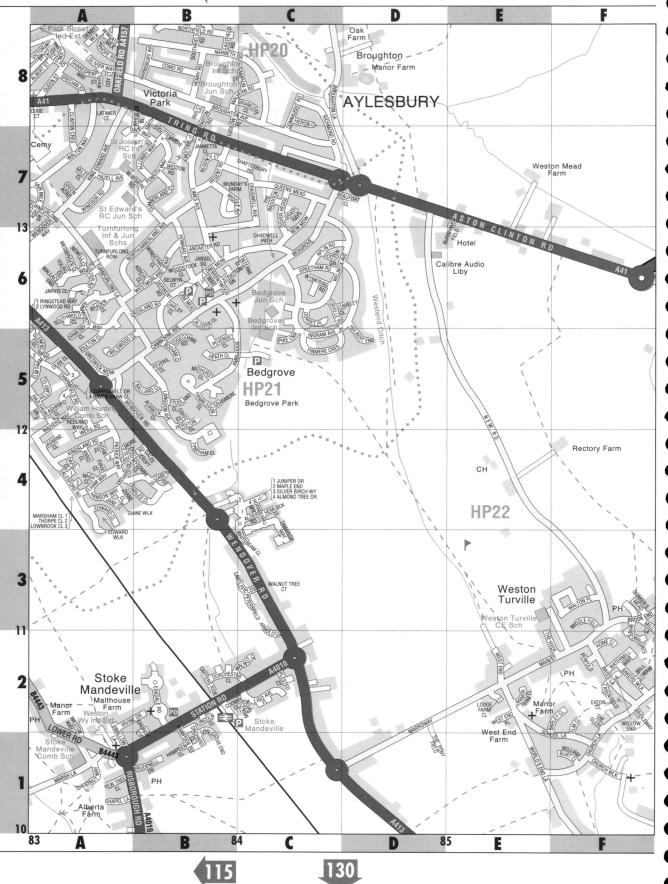

103
118

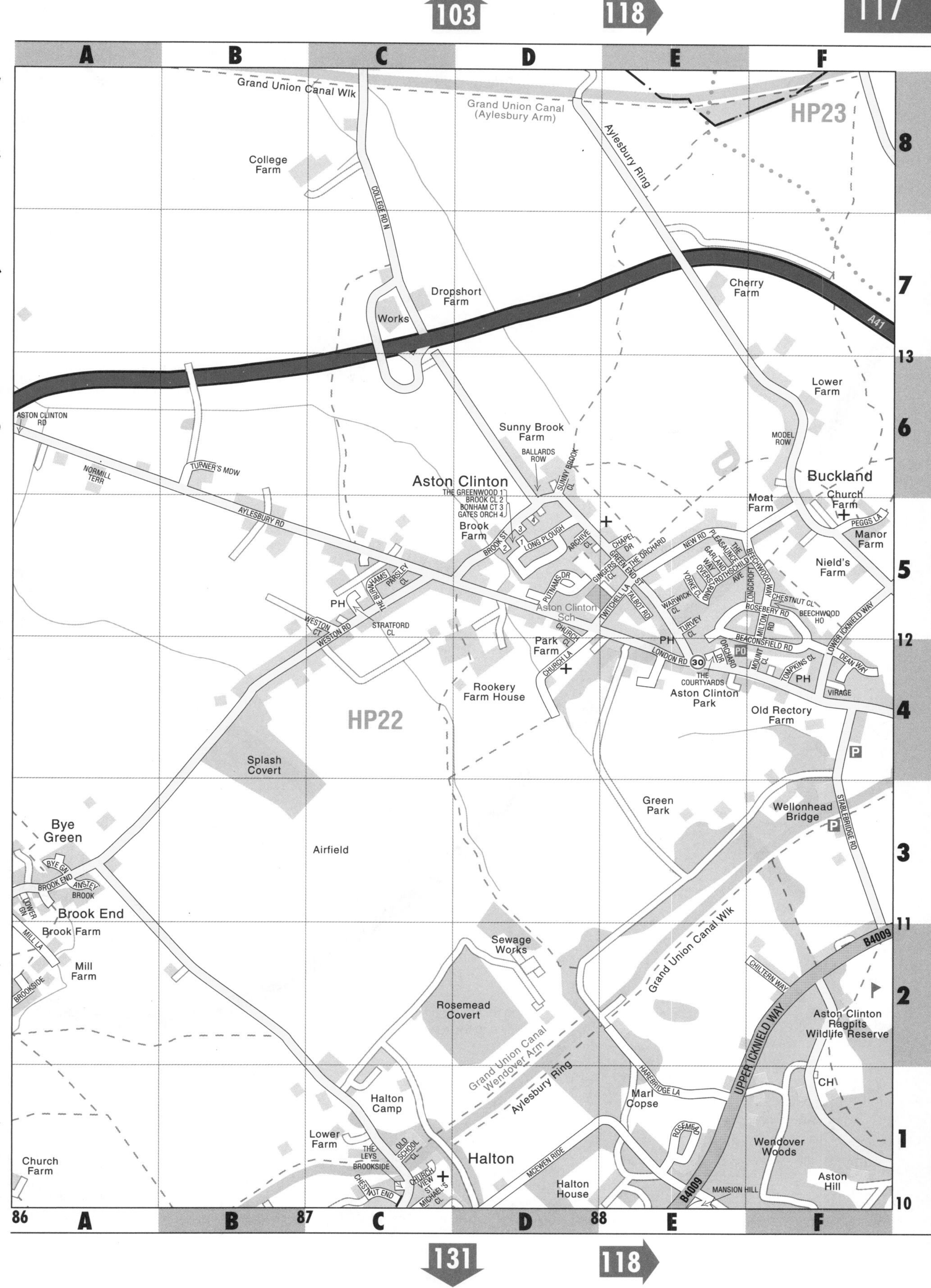
A
B
C
D
E
F
Grand Union Canal Wlk
Grand Union Canal
(Aylesbury Arm)
HP23
Aylesbury Ring
College
Farm
COLLEGE RD N
Dropshort
Farm
Works
Cherry
Farm
A41
Lower
Farm
ASTON CLINTON
RD
Sunny Brook
Farm
BALLARDS
ROW
SUNNY BROOK
CL
MODEL
ROW
Buckland
NORMILL
TERR
TURNER'S MDW
Aston Clinton
THE GREENWOOD 1
BROOK CL 2
BONHAM CT 3
GATES ORCH 4
Moat
Farm
Church
Farm
PEGGS LA
Manor
Farm
AYLESBURY RD
Brook
Farm
BROOK ST
LONG PLOUGH
ARCHIVE
CL
CHAPEL
DR
GREEN END ST
THE ORCHARD
NEW RD
PLEASAUNCE
THE
GARLAND
WAY
OVERSTRAND
ROTHSCHILD
AVE
BEECHWOOD
WAY
LONGCROFT
Nield's
Farm
THE BURKHAMS
PARSLEY
CL
PUTNAMS DR
GINGERS
CL
TWITCHELL LA
TALBOT RD
YORKE CL
WARWICK
CL
ROSEBERY RD
MILTON
RD
CHESTNUT CL
BEECHWOOD
HO
LOWER ICKNIELD WAY
PH
WESTON
CT
WESTON RD
STRATFORD
CL
Aston Clinton
Sch
CHURCH
CL
Park
Farm
PH
TURVEY
CL
BEACONSFIELD RD
CHURCH LA
LONDON RD
30
ORCHARD
DR
PO
MOUNT
CL
TOMPKINS CL
PH
DEAN WAY
THE
COURTYARDS
Aston Clinton
Park
VIRAGE
Rookery
Farm House
HP22
Old Rectory
Farm
P
Splash
Covert
Green
Park
Wellonhead
Bridge
P
STABLEBRIDGE RD
Bye
Green
BYE GN
BROOK END
ANSTEY
BROOK
Airfield
LOWER
GN
Brook End
Brook Farm
MILL LA
Mill
Farm
BROOKSIDE
Grand Union Canal Wlk
Sewage
Works
B4009
CHILTERN WAY
UPPER ICKNIELD WAY
Rosemead
Covert
Aston Clinton
Ragpits
Wildlife Reserve
Grand Union Canal
Wendover Arm
Aylesbury Ring
CH
HAREBRIDGE LA
Halton
Camp
Marl
Copse
ROSEMEAD
Lower
Farm
THE
LEYS
BROOKSIDE
OLD
SCHOOL
CL
Wendover
Woods
Church
Farm
CHURCH
VIEW
CHESTNUT END
ST
MICHAEL'S
CL
Halton
MCEWEN RIDE
Halton
House
B4009
MANSION HILL
Aston
Hill
8
7
13
6
5
12
4
3
11
2
1
10
86
87
88

131
118

117 104

A B C D E F

8 7 13 6 5 12 4 3 11 2 1 10

Chapel End
THE MILL
CHAPEL FIELDS
CHAPEL END LA
NEW RD
THE SCHOOL
Wilstone Great Farm
James Farm
WINGRAVE RD
B489
Startop's End Resr
Chapelend Farm
Manor Farm
TRING RD
NEW RD
Wilstone Green
BUCKLANDS CROFT
Tringford
TRING FORD RD
Wilstone Little Farm
Cemy
LOWER ICKNIELD WAY
WIGGLES LA
Tringford Resr
Wilstone Resr
Tring Reservoirs (Wildlife Trust Reserves)
Tringford Farm
A41
Landing Stage
Little Tring Farm
Little Tring
B489
LITTLE TRING RD
Lower Farm
Drayton Beauchamp
HP23
Grand Union Canal Wlk
Upper Farm
B488
DUNDALE RD
Miswell Farm
HOBSONS WLK
THE GREENWAY
MENTMORE VIEW
Miswell House
ASH RD
Bridge Farm
MILL VIEW RD
THORNTREE DR
BUCKLAND RD
HP22
Drayton Bridge
GREEN PATH
FANTAIL LA
LUDGATE
BUNSTRUX
BLACKAMORE GATE
Church Hill Farm
GREEN PATH
Broadview Farm
Icknield Farm
ICKNIELD WAY
CHRISTCHURCH RD
SANDON CL
LITTLE HOO
Windmill
Mast
WINDMILL WAY
DENNIS CL
BISHOPS FIELD
Bucklandwharf
Tring Bsns Ctr
OSMINGTON PL
THORNE WAY
WHARF ROW
THE HOLLOWAY
HEDLEY CL
LONDON RD
Rye Hill Farm
Icknield Way Ind Est
WEAVERS RD
OKEFORD CL
OKEFORD DR
Beeches Farm
Factories
AMIES CL
BUCKINGHAM RD
MISWELL LA
Goldfield Inf Sch
WENWELL CL
ACACIA WLK
HIGHFIELD RD
OKELEY LA
FAITHORN CL
ELLISON CT 1
POPE CT 2
BEECHWOOD CT
PH Hotel
B488
GOLDFIELD RD
UPPER ICKNIELD WAY
TRING HILL
BEACONSFIELD RD
CARMAN CT
ORCHARDS
THE
STANLEY GDNS
GRAVEL DR
B4009
B4635
CHERRY GDNS
CRABTREE CT
BARBERS WLK
COBBETTS RIDE
HILL
LONGFIELD RD
Lodge Farm
Cemy
B4635 WESTERN RD
CHAPEL ST
Icknield House
LONGFIELD GDNS
DONKEY LA
CONVENT CT
B4009
AYLESBURY RD
PARK RD
CHILTERN VILLAS
WOODLAND CL
HOME FARM
Francis House Prep Sch
WhiteCloud House
A41
Drayton Manor
DANCERS END LA
Fox Lane
West Leith
DUCKMORE LA
Daniel's Hole
West Leith Farm
WEST LEITH
Astonhill Coppice
Stud Farm
THE BARNS
Stubbing's Wood
Forest Wlk
LEAFY LA
BOTTOM RD
Buckland Hoo
Hastoe Hill
Aston Hill Farm
Deacon's Hill Wood
HASTOE HILL

89 90 91

117 132

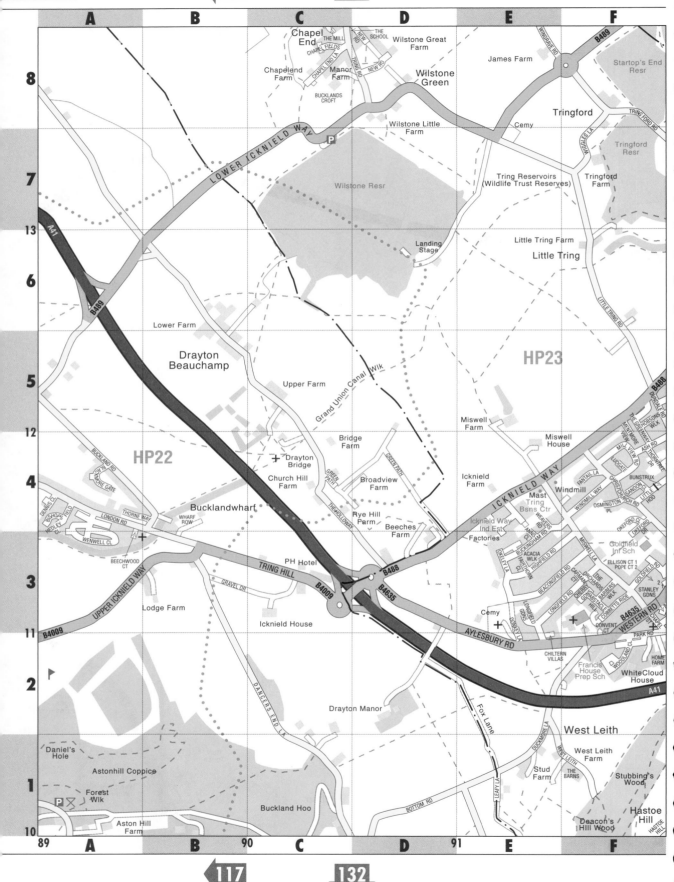

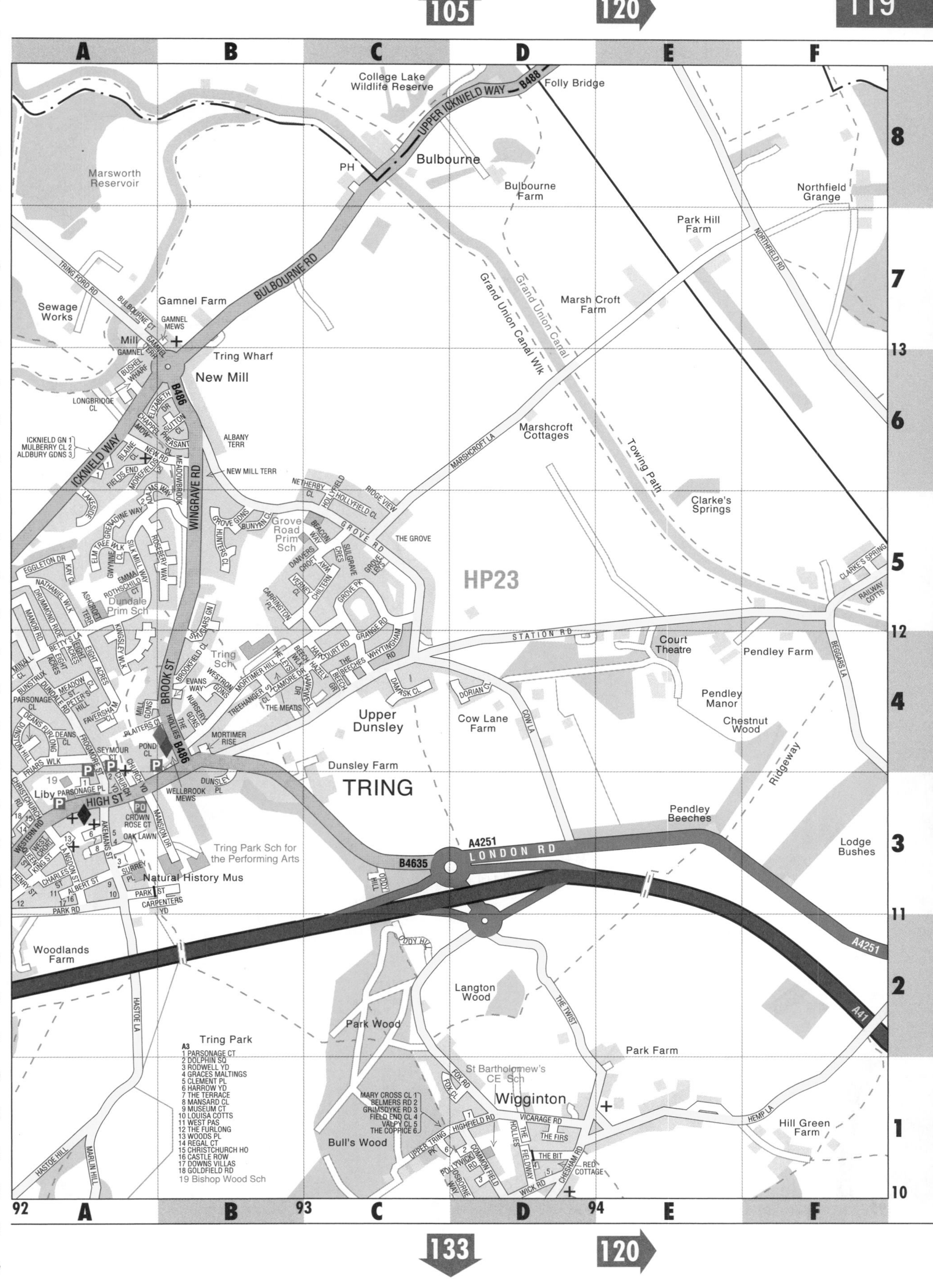

A B C D E F

8
7
13
6
5
12
4
11
3
2
1
10

Marsworth
Reservoir

College Lake
Wildlife Reserve

UPPER ICKNIELD WAY
B488
Folly Bridge

PH
Bulbourne

Bulbourne
Farm

Park Hill
Farm

Northfield
Grange

NORTHFIELD RD

BULBOURNE RD

Sewage
Works

Gamnel Farm

Marsh Croft
Farm

Grand Union Canal Wlk

Grand Union Canal

TRING FORD RD

BULBOURNE CT

GAMNEL TERR

GAMNEL
MEWS

Mill
GAMNEL
BUSHEL WHARF

LONGBRIDGE CL

Tring Wharf

New Mill

B486

ELIZABETH
DR
SUTTON
CHAPEL MDW
PHEASANT
NEW RD
BLAINE
FIELDS END
MOREFIELDS

ICKNIELD WAY

ICKNIELD GN 1
MULBERRY CL 2
ALDBURY GDNS 3

WINGRAVE RD

MEADOWBROOK RD

ALBANY
TERR

NEW MILL TERR

MS WAY
LAKESIDE
ELM TREE WLK
GRENADINE WAY
HUNTERS CL
SILK MILL WAY
GWYNNE
ROSEBERY WAY

EGGLETON DR
KAY CT
NATHANIEL WLK
ASHCROFT
DRUMMOND RIDE
MANOR RD
BETTY S LA
EIGHT ACRES
GMMA CL
ROTHSCHILD
KINGSLEY WK

Dundale
Prim Sch

NETHERBY
CL
HOLLYFIELD CL
HOLLYFIELD CL

RIDGE VIEW

MARSHCROFT LA

Marshcroft
Cottages

Towing Path

Clarke's
Springs

CLARKE'S SPRING

RAILWAY
COTTS

GROVE GDNS
BUNYAN CL

GROVE RD

THE GROVE

HP23

BRANDON WAY
DANVERS
CROFT
ATYA
CRES
SULGRAVE
GREEN
GROVE PK
CARRINGTON
VERNEY
CL
CHILTERN
CL

Grove
Road
Prim
Sch

MINAL
CL
BUNSTRUX
MEADOW
ST
ST PETER'S
PARSONAGE
PL
DUNDALE RD
DEANS FURLONG
FRONTMEAD
SEYMOUR
FROGMORE
DEANS
CL

BROOK ST

BROOKEFIELD CL

WESTERN
GDNS
EVANS
WAY

MORTIMER HILL

TREEHANGER CL

Tring
Sch

B486
CAMORE DR

THE MEADS

MILL
GDNS
PLAITERS CL
POND
CL

NURSERY
CL

MORTIMER
RISE

THE BEECHES

AMORE DR
COURT RD

HAZEL
GRANGE RD

WHYTINGHAM
RD

Upper
Dunsley

DAMASK CL

DORIAN CS

Cow Lane
Farm

COW LA

STATION RD

Court
Theatre

Pendley Farm

Pendley
Manor

Chestnut
Wood

BEGGARS LA
PENDLEY LA

RIDGEWAY

Lodge
Bushes

FRIARS WLK
CHRISTCHURCH PL
19
Liby PARSONAGE PL

P
P
P
P

HIGH ST

CROWN
ROSE CT

DUNSLEY
PL

WELLBROOK
MEWS

OAK LAWN

Dunsley Farm

TRING

Pendley
Beeches

WESTERN RD
AKEMANS CL
13
6
LANGDON ST
KING ST
CHARLES ST
ALBERT ST
HENRY ST
11
7
16
SURREY
PL
Natural History Mus

Tring Park Sch for
the Performing Arts

PARK ST
CARPENTERS
YD

B4635
A4251
LONDON RD
A4251
A41

CODDY
HILL

CODY HILL

Woodlands
Farm

HASTOE LA

Langton
Wood

THE TWIST

Park Wood

FOX CL
FOX CL

Park Farm

St Bartholomew's
CE Sch

VICARAGE RD
THE FIRS
THE ROLLIES
THE FIELDWAY
THE BIT

Hill Green
Farm

HEMP LA

Wigginton

RED
COTTAGE

HASTOE HILL
MARLIN HILL

HIGHFIELD RD
UPPER TRING PK
COMMON FIELD
POLLYWICK WAY
WICK RD
CHESHAM RD

Tring Park
A3
1 PARSONAGE CT
2 DOLPHIN SQ
3 RODWELL YD
4 GRACES MALTINGS
5 CLEMENT PL
6 HARROW YD
7 THE TERRACE
8 MANSARD CL
9 MUSEUM CT
10 LOUISA COTTS
11 WEST PAS
12 THE FURLONG
13 WOODS PL
14 REGAL CT
15 CHRISTCHURCH HO
16 CASTLE ROW
17 DOWNS VILLAS
18 GOLDFIELD RD
19 Bishop Wood Sch

MARY CROSS CL 1
BELMERS RD 2
GRIMSDYKE RD 3
FIELD END CL 4
VALPY CL 5
THE COPPICE 6

Bull's Wood

119
106

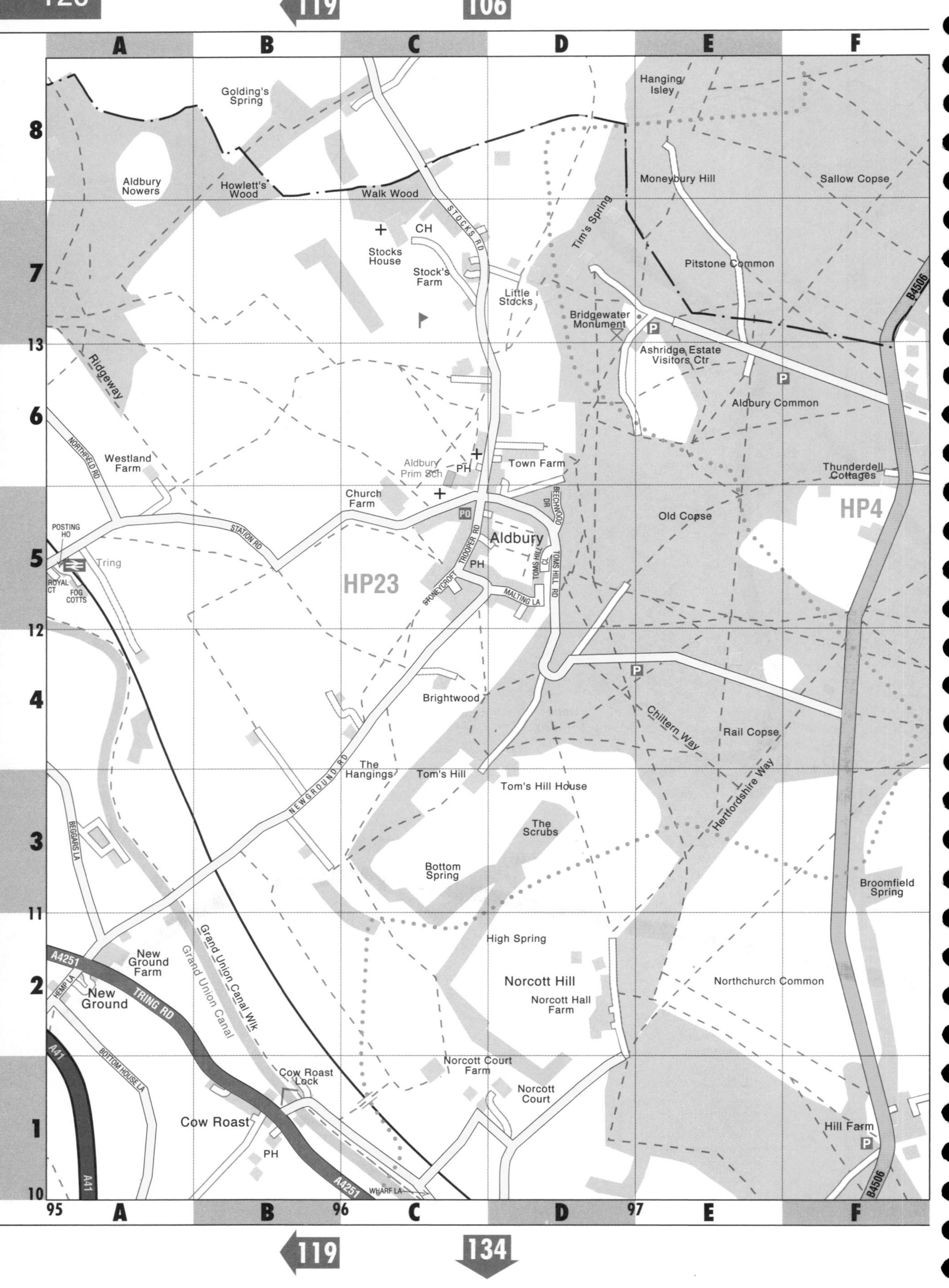
A
B
C
D
E
F
Golding's Spring
Hanging Isley
Aldbury Nowers
Howlett's Wood
Walk Wood
Moneybury Hill
Sallow Copse
STOCKS RD
CH
Stocks House
Stock's Farm
Tim's Spring
Pitstone Common
Little Stocks
Bridgewater Monument
Ashridge Estate Visitors Ctr
B4506
Ridgeway
Aldbury Common
NORTHFIELD RD
Westland Farm
Aldbury Prim Sch
PH
Town Farm
Thunderdell Cottages
Church Farm
BEECHWOOD DR
HP4
PO
Old Copse
POSTING HO
STATION RD
TROOPER RD
Aldbury
TOMS HILL CL
TOMS HILL RD
Tring
PH
HP23
ROYAL CT
FOG COTTS
STONEYCROFT
MALTING LA
Brightwood
Chiltern Way
Rail Copse
NEWGROUND RD
The Hangings
Tom's Hill
Tom's Hill House
Hertfordshire Way
BEGGARS LA
The Scrubs
Bottom Spring
Broomfield Spring
Grand Union Canal Wlk
Grand Union Canal
High Spring
A4251
New Ground Farm
Norcott Hill
Northchurch Common
HEMP LA
New Ground
TRING RD
Norcott Hall Farm
A41
BOTTOM HOUSE LA
Cow Roast Lock
Norcott Court Farm
Norcott Court
Cow Roast
Hill Farm
PH
A41
A4251
WHARF LA
B4506
8
7
13
6
5
12
4
3
11
2
1
10
95
96
97

119
134

107

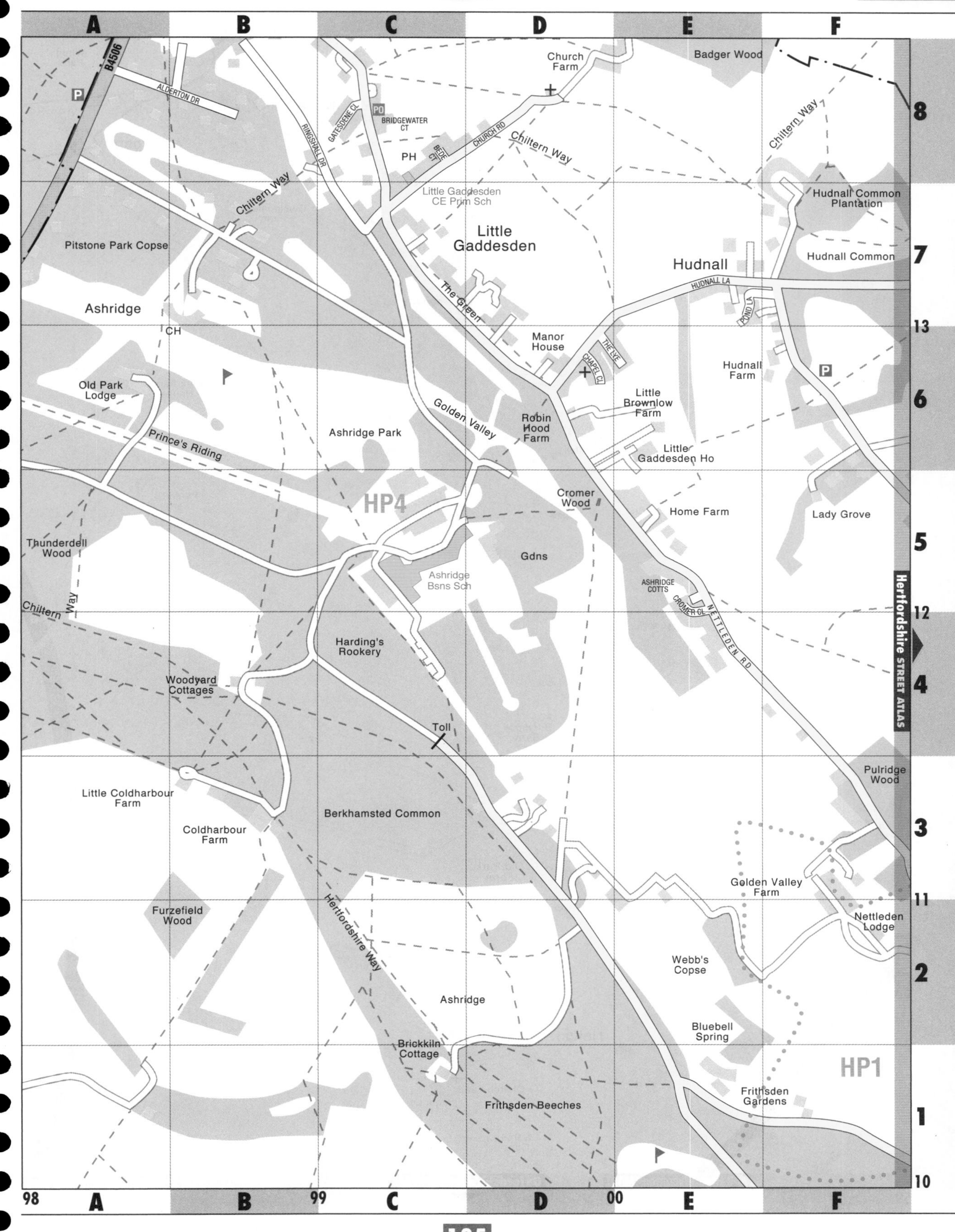

A B C D E F
B4506
ALDERTON DR
Church Farm
Badger Wood
GATESDENE CL
PO
BRIDGEWATER CT
RINGSHALL DR
CHURCH RD
BEDE CT
PH
Chiltern Way
Little Gaddesden CE Prim Sch
Little Gaddesden
Hudnall Common Plantation
Hudnall Common
Hudnall
HUDNALL LA
POND LA
Pitstone Park Copse
Ashridge
CH
The Green
Manor House
THE LYE
CHAPEL CL
Hudnall Farm
Old Park Lodge
Little Brownlow Farm
Golden Valley
Robin Hood Farm
Ashridge Park
Prince's Riding
Little Gaddesden Ho
Cromer Wood
HP4
Home Farm
Lady Grove
Thunderdell Wood
Gdns
Ashridge Bsns Sch
ASHRIDGE COTTS
CROMER CL
NETTLEDEN RD
Chiltern Way
Harding's Rookery
Woodyard Cottages
Toll
Pulridge Wood
Little Coldharbour Farm
Berkhamsted Common
Coldharbour Farm
Golden Valley Farm
Furzefield Wood
Hertfordshire Way
Nettleden Lodge
Webb's Copse
Ashridge
Bluebell Spring
Brickkiln Cottage
HP1
Frithsden Beeches
Frithsden Gardens
8 7 13 6 5 12 4 3 11 2 1 10
98 99 00
Hertfordshire STREET ATLAS

135

108

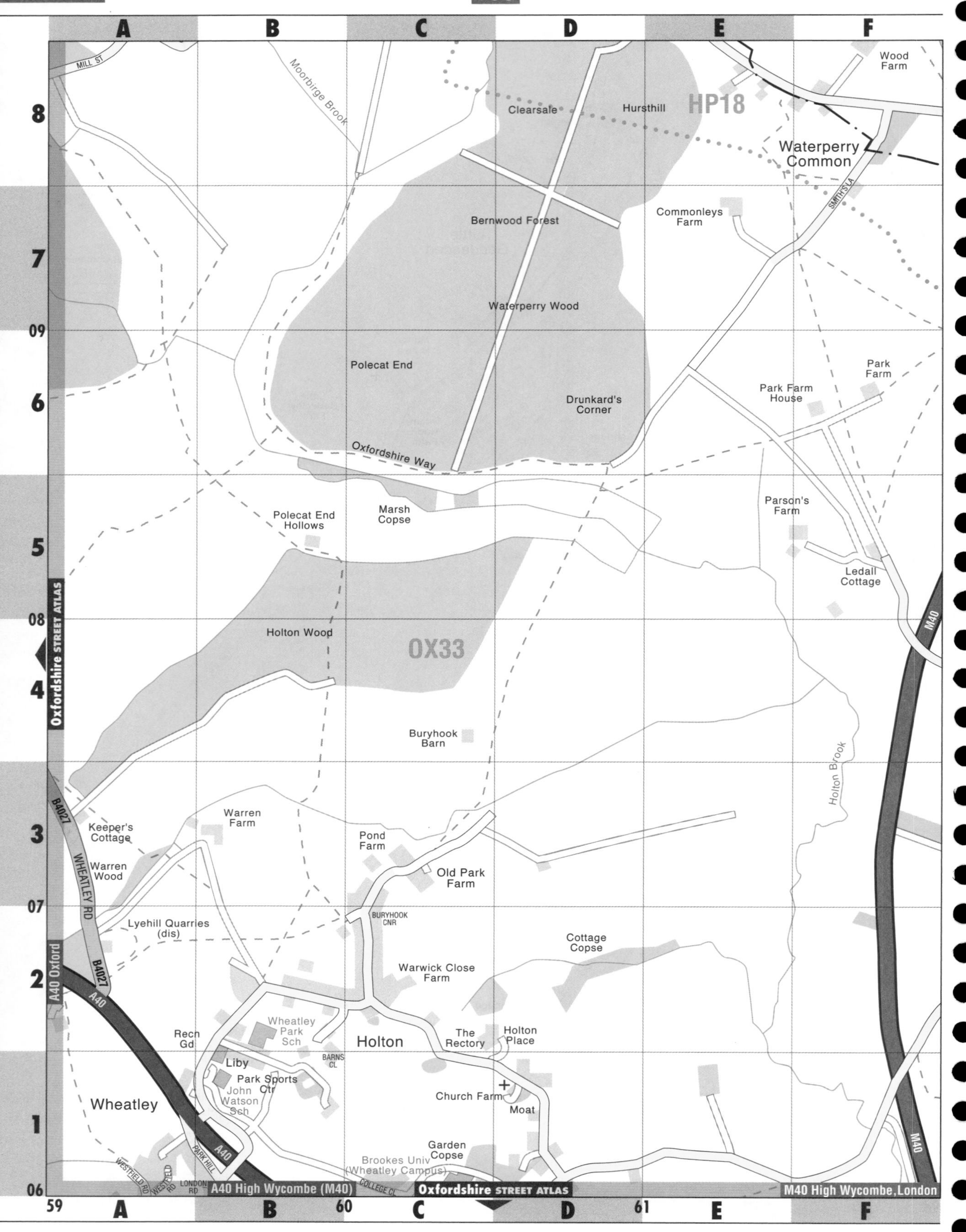

MILL ST

Moorbirge Brook

8

Clearsale

Hursthill

HP18

Wood Farm

Waterperry Common

SMITH'S LA

Bernwood Forest

Commonleys Farm

7

09

Waterperry Wood

Polecat End

Park Farm House

Park Farm

6

Drunkard's Corner

Oxfordshire Way

Parson's Farm

Polecat End Hollows

Marsh Copse

Ledall Cottage

5

08

Holton Wood

OX33

M40

4

Buryhook Barn

Holton Brook

Keeper's Cottage

Warren Farm

Pond Farm

3

Warren Wood

Old Park Farm

07

Lyehill Quarries (dis)

BURYHOOK CNR

Cottage Copse

B4027

Warwick Close Farm

2

A40 Oxford

Rech Gd

Wheatley Park Sch

Holton

The Rectory

Holton Place

Liby

Park Sports Ctr

BARNS CL

M40

John Watson Sch

Church Farm

Moat

Wheatley

1

Garden Copse

WESTFIELD RD

WESTF'LD RD

LONDON RD

PARK HILL

A40

Brookes Univ (Wheatley Campus)

COLLEGE CL

06

A40 High Wycombe (M40)

59   A   B   60   C   D   61   E   F

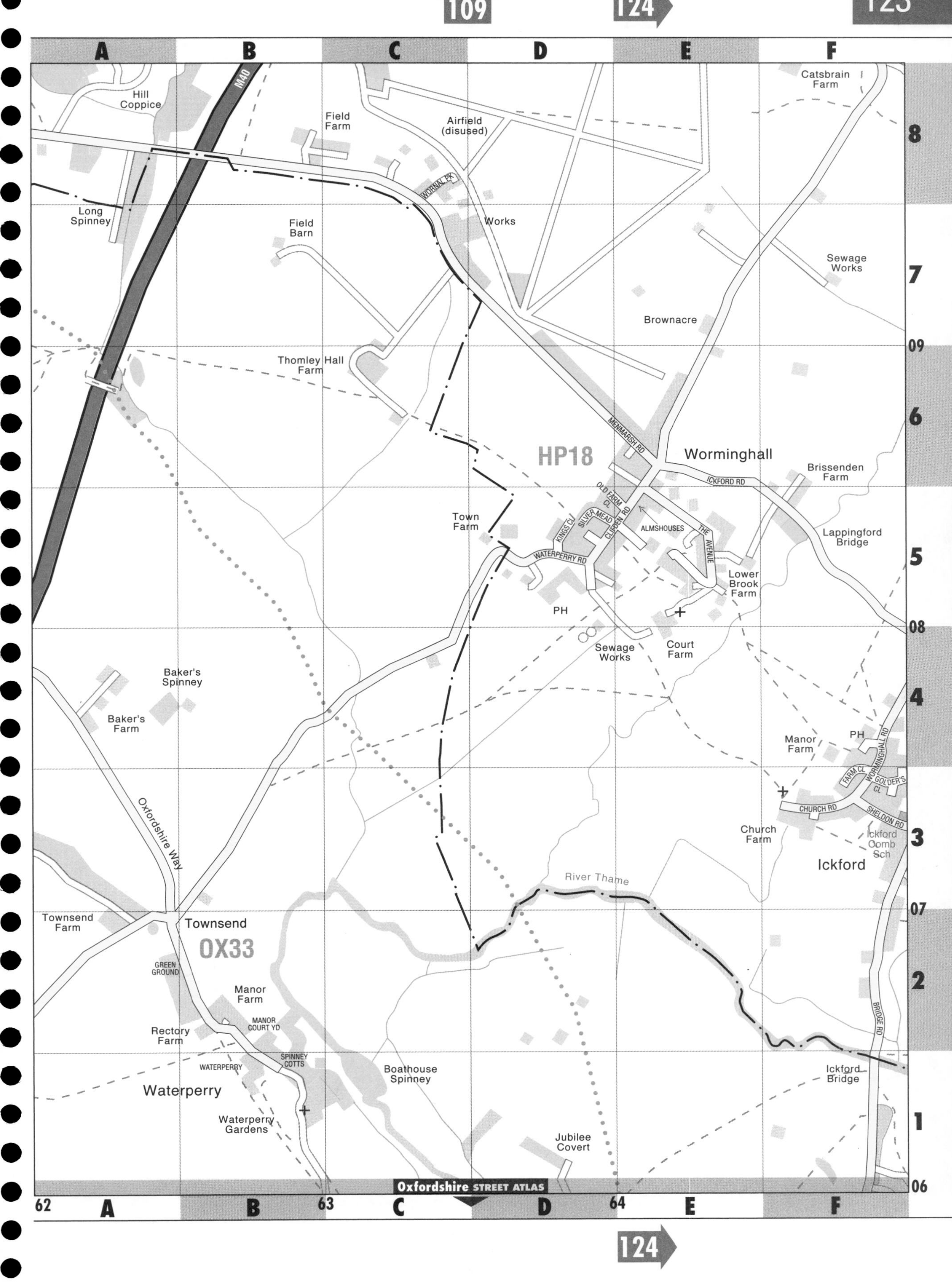
109
124
A
B
C
D
E
F
M40
Hill Coppice
Field Farm
Airfield (disused)
Catsbrain Farm
WORNAL PK
Long Spinney
Field Barn
Works
Sewage Works
Brownacre
Thomley Hall Farm
MENMARSH RD
HP18
Worminghall
ICKFORD RD
Brissenden Farm
OLD FARM CL
SILVER MEAD
CLIFDEN RD
KINGS CL
ALMSHOUSES
THE AVENUE
Town Farm
Lappingford Bridge
WATERPERRY RD
Lower Brook Farm
PH
Sewage Works
Court Farm
Baker's Spinney
Baker's Farm
Manor Farm
PH
WORMINGHALL RD
FARM CL
GOLDER'S CL
CHURCH RD
SHELDON RD
Oxfordshire Way
Church Farm
Ickford Comb Sch
Ickford
River Thame
Townsend Farm
Townsend
OX33
GREEN GROUND
Manor Farm
Rectory Farm
MANOR COURT YD
BRIDGE RD
SPINNEY COTTS
WATERPERRY
Waterperry
Boathouse Spinney
Ickford Bridge
Waterperry Gardens
Jubilee Covert
Oxfordshire STREET ATLAS
8
7
09
6
5
08
4
3
07
2
1
06
62
63
64
124

123
110

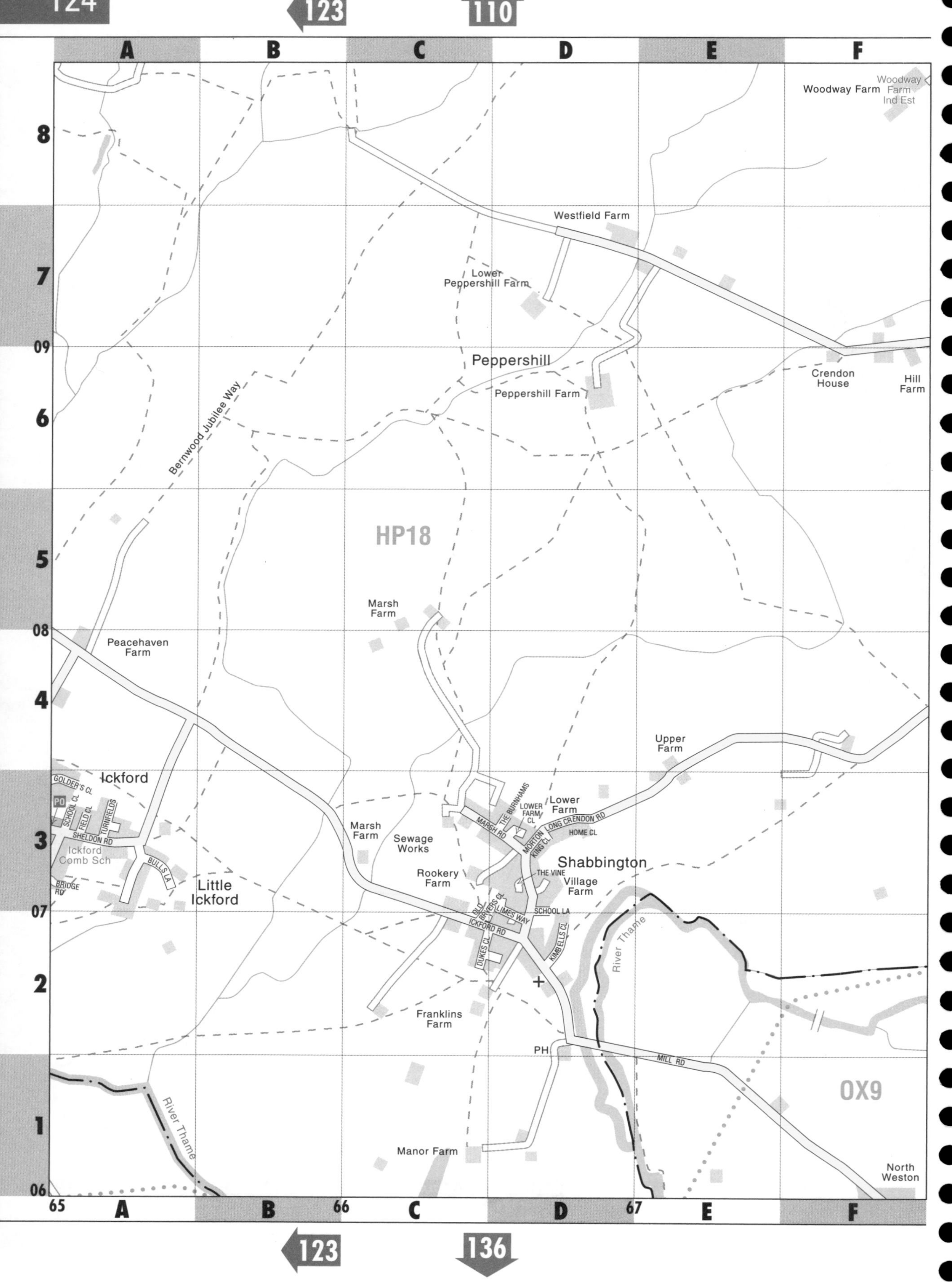
Woodway Farm
Woodway Farm Ind Est
Westfield Farm
Lower Peppershill Farm
Peppershill
Peppershill Farm
Crendon House
Hill Farm
Bernwood Jubilee Way
HP18
Marsh Farm
Peacehaven Farm
Upper Farm
Ickford
GOLDER'S CL
PO
SCHOOL CL
FIELD CL
TURNFIELDS
SHELDON RD
Ickford Comb Sch
BULLS LA
BRIDGE RD
Little Ickford
Marsh Farm
Sewage Works
Rookery Farm
THE BURNHAMS
LOWER FARM CL
Lower Farm
LONG CRENDON RD
HOME CL
MARSH RD
MORTON KING CL
Shabbington
THE VINE
Village Farm
OLD BREWERS CL
LIMES WAY
SCHOOL LA
ICKFORD RD
DUKES CL
KIMBELLS CL
River Thame
Franklins Farm
PH
MILL RD
OX9
River Thame
Manor Farm
North Weston
A
B
C
D
E
F
8
7
09
6
5
08
4
3
07
2
1
06
65
66
67

123
136

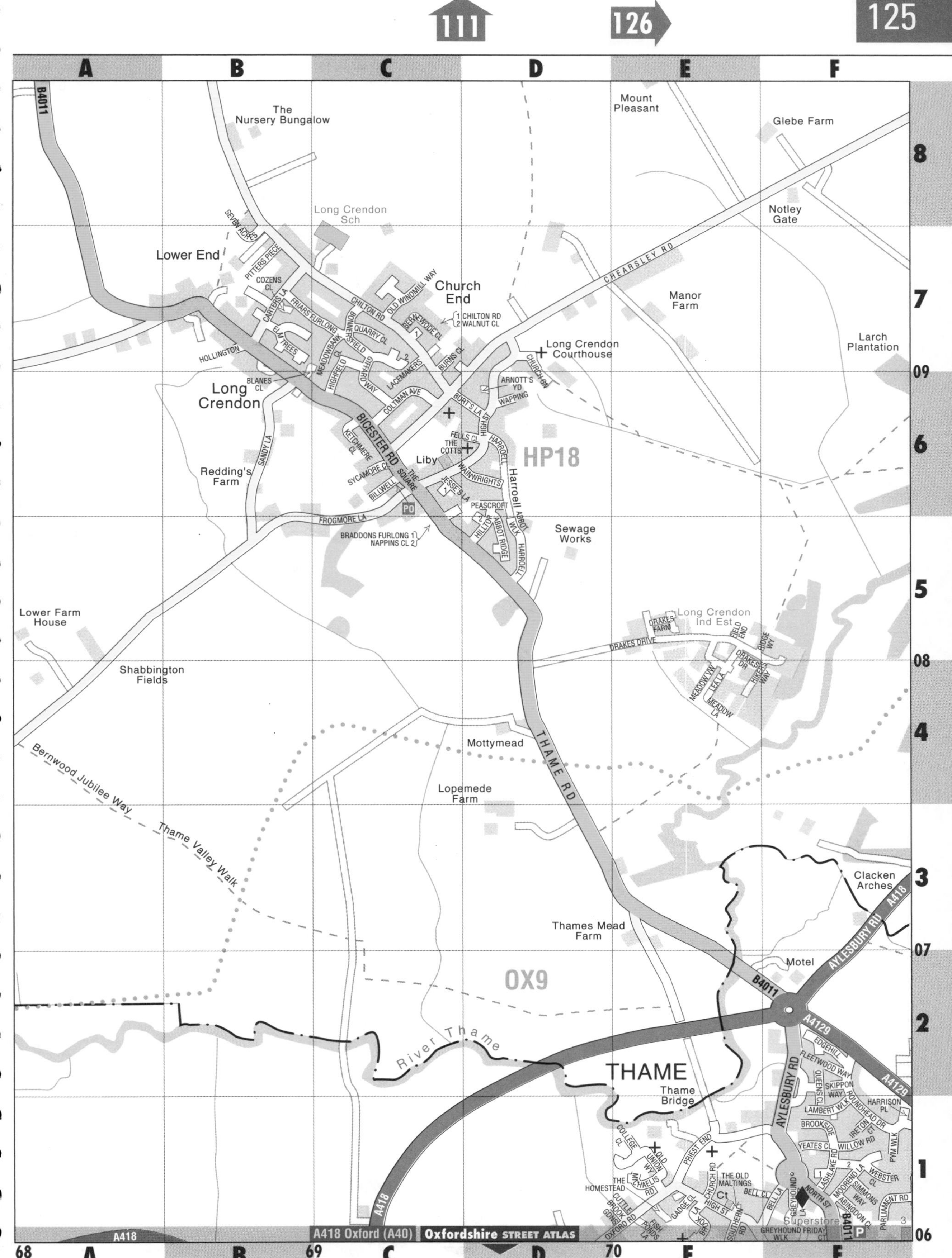
A
B
C
D
E
F
8
7
09
6
5
08
4
3
07
2
1
06
68
69
70
B4011
The Nursery Bungalow
Mount Pleasant
Glebe Farm
Long Crendon Sch
Notley Gate
Lower End
Church End
Manor Farm
CHEARSLEY RD
Long Crendon Courthouse
Larch Plantation
Long Crendon
HP18
Liby
Redding's Farm
Harroell
Sewage Works
BICESTER RD
FROGMORE LA
Lower Farm House
Long Crendon Ind Est
DRAKES DRIVE
Shabbington Fields
Mottymead
THAME RD
Lopemede Farm
Bernwood Jubilee Way
Thame Valley Walk
Clacken Arches
Thames Mead Farm
Motel
AYLESBURY RD
A418
OX9
A4129
River Thame
THAME
Thame Bridge
Superstore
A418 Oxford (A40)

F1
1 MEADOW WAY
2 GREENWAY
3 Barley Hill Prim Sch

125
112

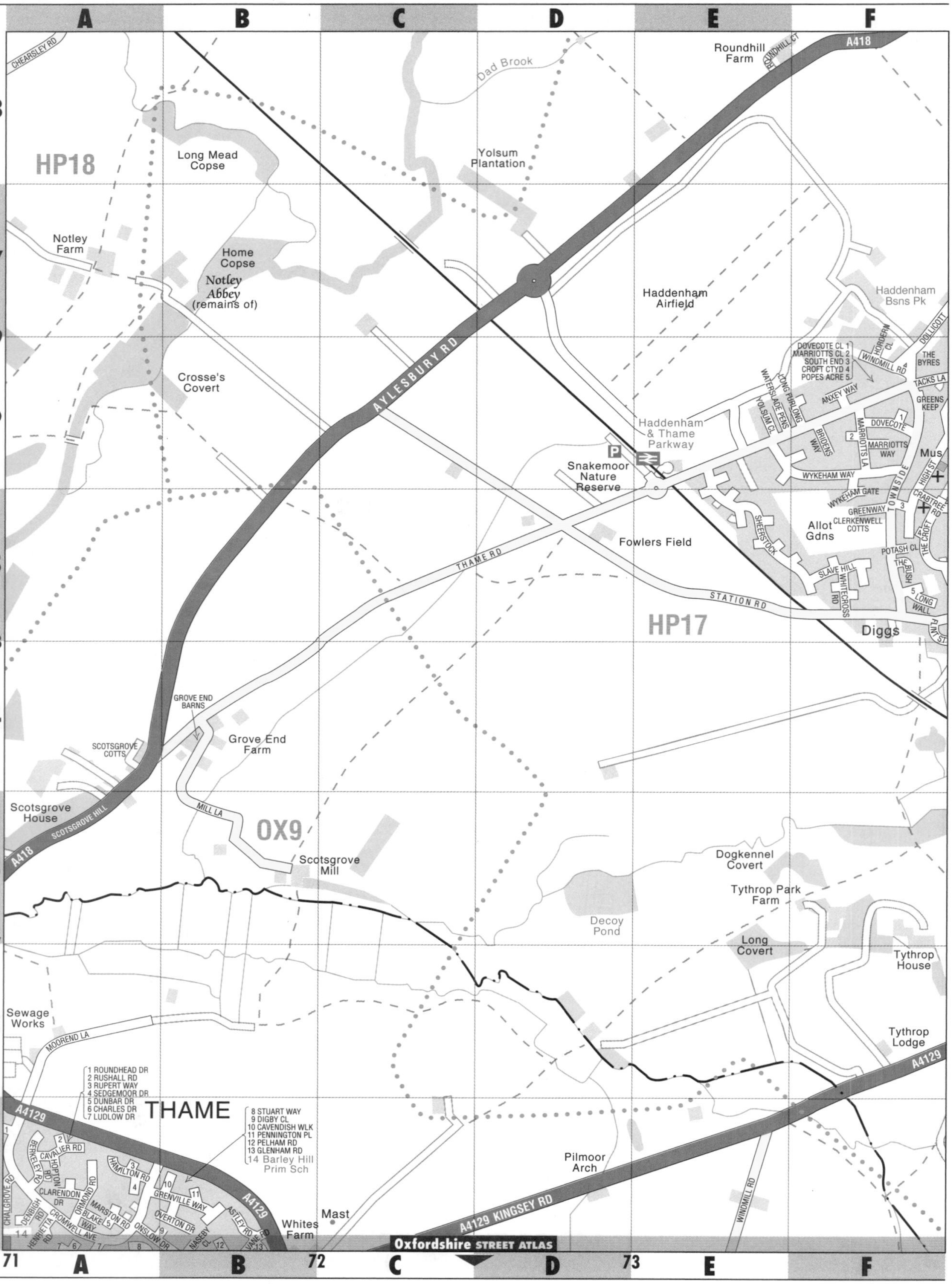

A   B   C   D   E   F

CHEARSLEY RD

Dad Brook

Roundhill Farm

ROUNDHILL CT

A418

8

HP18

Long Mead Copse

Yolsum Plantation

7

Notley Farm

Home Copse

Notley Abbey (remains of)

Haddenham Airfield

Haddenham Bsns Pk

DOLLICOTT

09

DOVECOTE CL 1
MARRIOTTS CL 2
SOUTH END 3
CROFT CTYD 4
POPES ACRE 5

THE BYRES

TACKS LA

LONG FURLONG

WINDMILL RD

NORBURN CL

Crosse's Covert

WATERSLADE FENS

YOLSUM CL

ANXEY WAY

GREENS KEEP

6

AYLESBURY RD

Haddenham & Thame Parkway

P

Snakemoor Nature Reserve

PEUDENS WAY

MARRIOTTS LA

DOVECOTE

WYKEHAM WAY

Mus

MARRIOTTS WAY

WOWSIDE

HIGH ST

CRABTREE RD

WYKEHAM GATE

GREENWAY

THE CROFT

THAME RD

Fowlers Field

SHEERSTOCK

CLERKENWELL COTTS

Allot Gdns

POTASH CL

THE BUSH

5

STATION RD

SLAVE HILL

WHITECROSS RD

LONG WALL

08

HP17

Diggs

FINS ST

4

GROVE END BARNS

Grove End Farm

Scotsgrove Cotts

Dogkennel Covert

3

A418

SCOTSGROVE HILL

Scotsgrove House

MILL LA

OX9

Scotsgrove Mill

Decoy Pond

Tythrop Park Farm

Long Covert

Tythrop House

07

2

Sewage Works

MOOREND LA

Tythrop Lodge

A4129

1 ROUNDHEAD DR
2 RUSHALL RD
3 RUPERT WAY
4 SEDGEMOOR DR
5 DUNBAR DR
6 CHARLES DR
7 LUDLOW DR

THAME

8 STUART WAY
9 DIGBY CL
10 CAVENDISH WLK
11 PENNINGTON PL
12 PELHAM RD
13 GLENHAM RD
14 Barley Hill Prim Sch

Pilmoor Arch

1

A4129

CHALGROVE RD

BERKELEY RD

CAVALIER RD

CLARENDON DR

HAMILTON RD

ORMOND RD

BLAKE

MARSTON RD

CROMWELL WAY

ONSLOW DR

GRENVILLE WAY

OVERTON DR

ASTLEY RD

RAMSEY

A4129

KINGSEY RD

Mast

Whites Farm

WINDMILL RD

06

OBERON

HENRIETTA

CROMWELL AVE

Oxfordshire STREET ATLAS

71 A   B 72 C   D 73 E   F

125

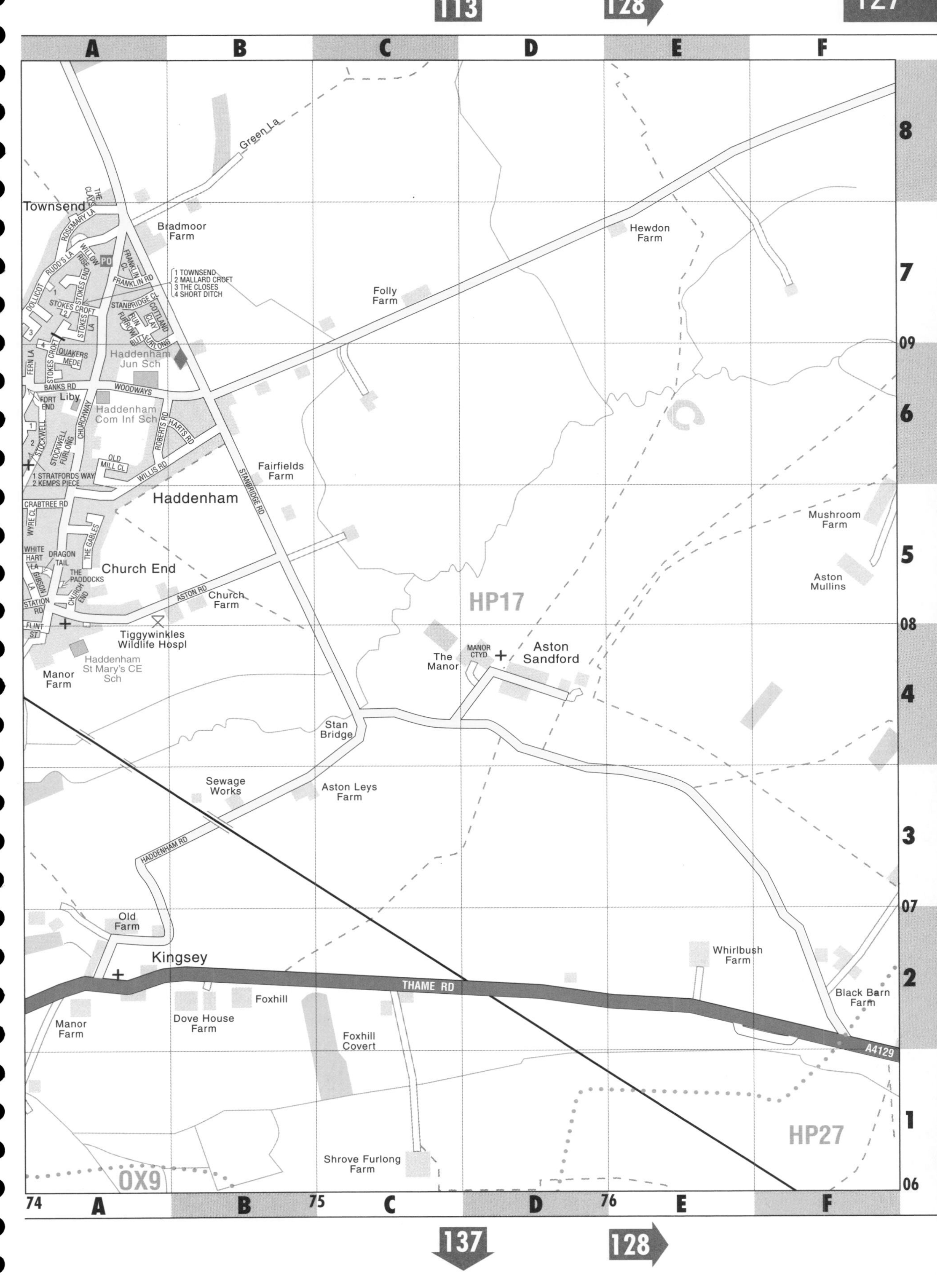
113
128
A
B
C
D
E
F
8
7
09
6
5
08
4
3
07
2
1
06
74
75
76
137
Green La
Townsend
Bradmoor Farm
Hewdon Farm
Folly Farm
1 TOWNSEND
2 MALLARD CROFT
3 THE CLOSES
4 SHORT DITCH
Haddenham Jun Sch
Liby
Haddenham Com Inf Sch
Fairfields Farm
Haddenham
Mushroom Farm
Church End
Aston Mullins
HP17
Church Farm
Tiggywinkles Wildlife Hospl
The Manor
MANOR CTYD
Aston Sandford
Manor Farm
Haddenham St Mary's CE Sch
Stan Bridge
Sewage Works
Aston Leys Farm
Old Farm
Kingsey
Whirlbush Farm
Black Barn Farm
THAME RD
Foxhill
Dove House Farm
Manor Farm
Foxhill Covert
A4129
HP27
Shrove Furlong Farm
OX9
STANBRIDGE RD
ASTON RD
HADDENHAM RD
WOODWAYS
BANKS RD
CRABTREE RD
WILLIS RD
ROBERTS RD
HARTS RD
OLD MILL CL
CHURCHWAY
STOCKWELL
STOCKWELL FURLONG
1 STRATFORDS WAY
2 KEMPS PIECE
WYRE CL
WHITE HART LA
DRAGON TAIL
THE GABLES
THE PADDOCKS
CHURCH END
GIBSON LA
STATION RD
FLINT ST
FORT END
FERN LA
STOKES CROFT
QUAKERS MEDE
STOKES LA
STOKES END
DOLLICOT
RUDD'S LA
ROSEMARY LA
THE CLAYS
WILLOW RISE
FRANKLIN CL
FRANKLIN RD
STANBRIDGE CL
COTTLAND CLAY
RUN FURROW
BUTT FURLONG
PO

127
114

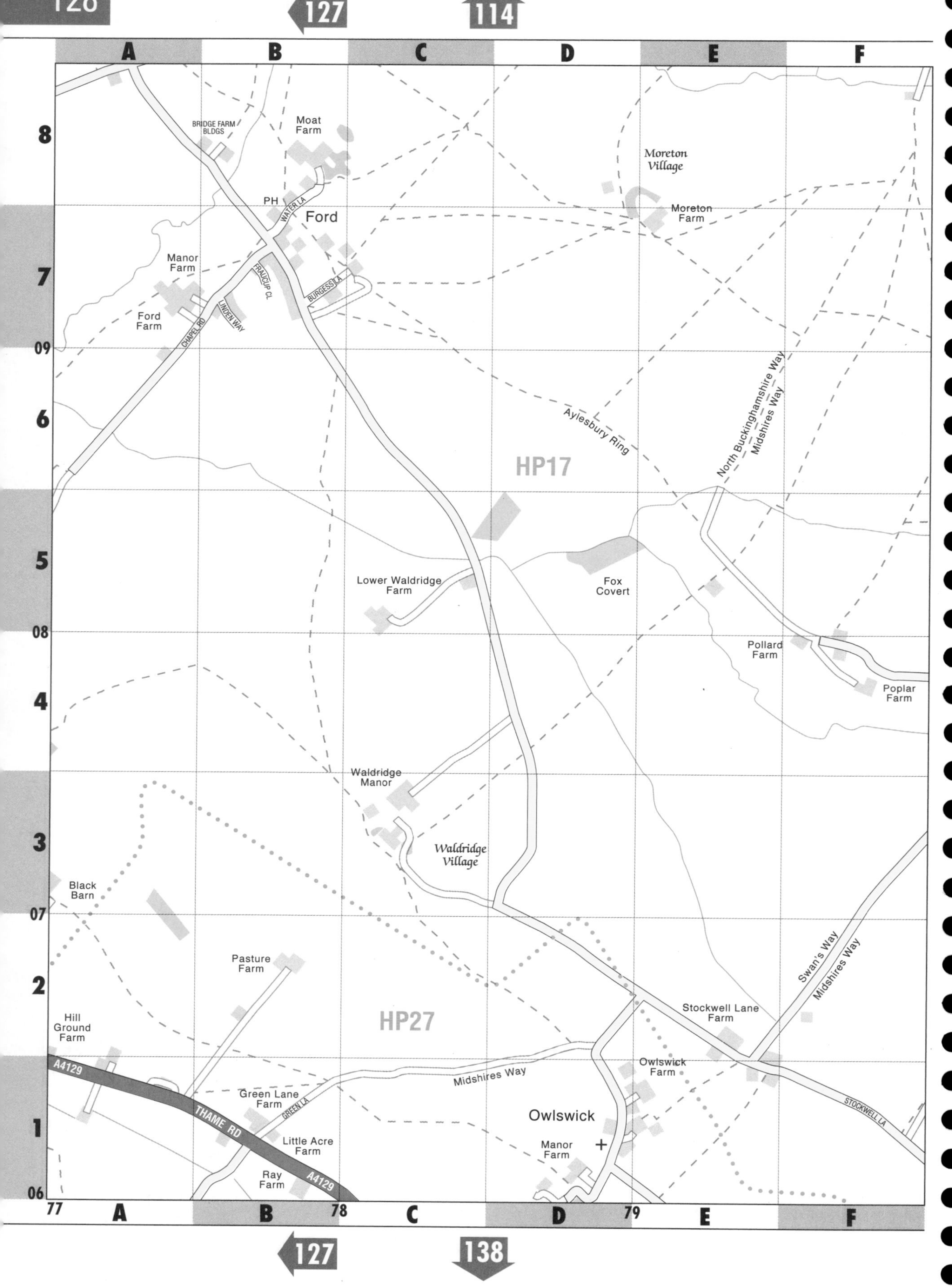
A
B
C
D
E
F
8
7
09
6
5
08
4
3
07
2
1
06
77
78
79
BRIDGE FARM BLDGS
Moat Farm
Moreton Village
PH
WATER LA
Ford
Moreton Farm
Manor Farm
FRAUCUP CL
BURGESS LA
Ford Farm
LINDEN WAY
CHAPEL RD
Aylesbury Ring
North Buckinghamshire Way
Midshires Way
HP17
Lower Waldridge Farm
Fox Covert
Pollard Farm
Poplar Farm
Waldridge Manor
Waldridge Village
Black Barn
Pasture Farm
Swan's Way
Midshires Way
Hill Ground Farm
HP27
Stockwell Lane Farm
A4129
Owlswick Farm
Midshires Way
Green Lane Farm
GREEN LA
THAME RD
STOCKWELL LA
Owlswick
Little Acre Farm
Manor Farm
Ray Farm
A4129

127
138

115
130

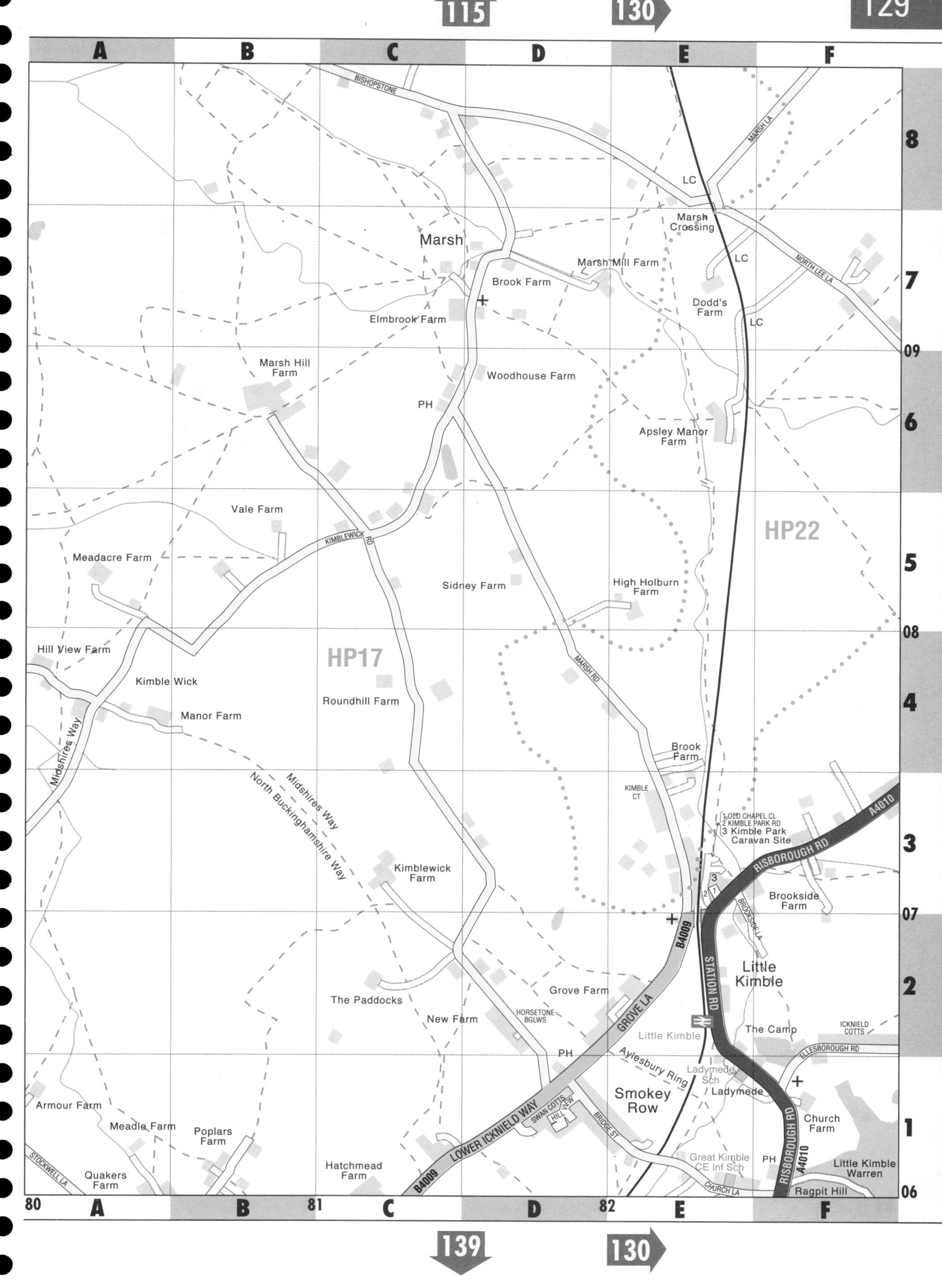
A
B
C
D
E
F
8
7
09
6
5
08
4
3
07
2
1
06
80
81
82
Marsh
Brook Farm
Elmbrook Farm
Marsh Mill Farm
Marsh Crossing
LC
Dodd's Farm
NORTH LEE LA
MARSH LA
BISHOPSTONE
Marsh Hill Farm
Woodhouse Farm
PH
Apsley Manor Farm
Vale Farm
HP22
KIMBLEWICK RD
Meadacre Farm
Sidney Farm
High Holburn Farm
Hill View Farm
HP17
Kimble Wick
MARSH RD
Roundhill Farm
Manor Farm
Midshires Way
North Buckinghamshire Way
Brook Farm
KIMBLE CT
1 OLD CHAPEL CL
2 KIMBLE PARK RD
3 Kimble Park Caravan Site
A4010
RISBOROUGH RD
Kimblewick Farm
Brookside Farm
BROOKSIDE LA
B4009
STATION RD
Little Kimble
The Paddocks
New Farm
Grove Farm
HORSETONE BGLWS
GROVE LA
The Camp
ICKNIELD COTTS
ELLESBOROUGH RD
Aylesbury Ring
Ladymede Sch
Ladymede
Smokey Row
Armour Farm
Meadle Farm
Poplars Farm
LOWER ICKNIELD WAY
SWAN COTTS
HILL VIEW
BRIDGE ST
Church Farm
STOCKWELL LA
Quakers Farm
Hatchmead Farm
Great Kimble CE Inf Sch
Little Kimble Warren
CHURCH LA
Ragpit Hill

139
130

129
116

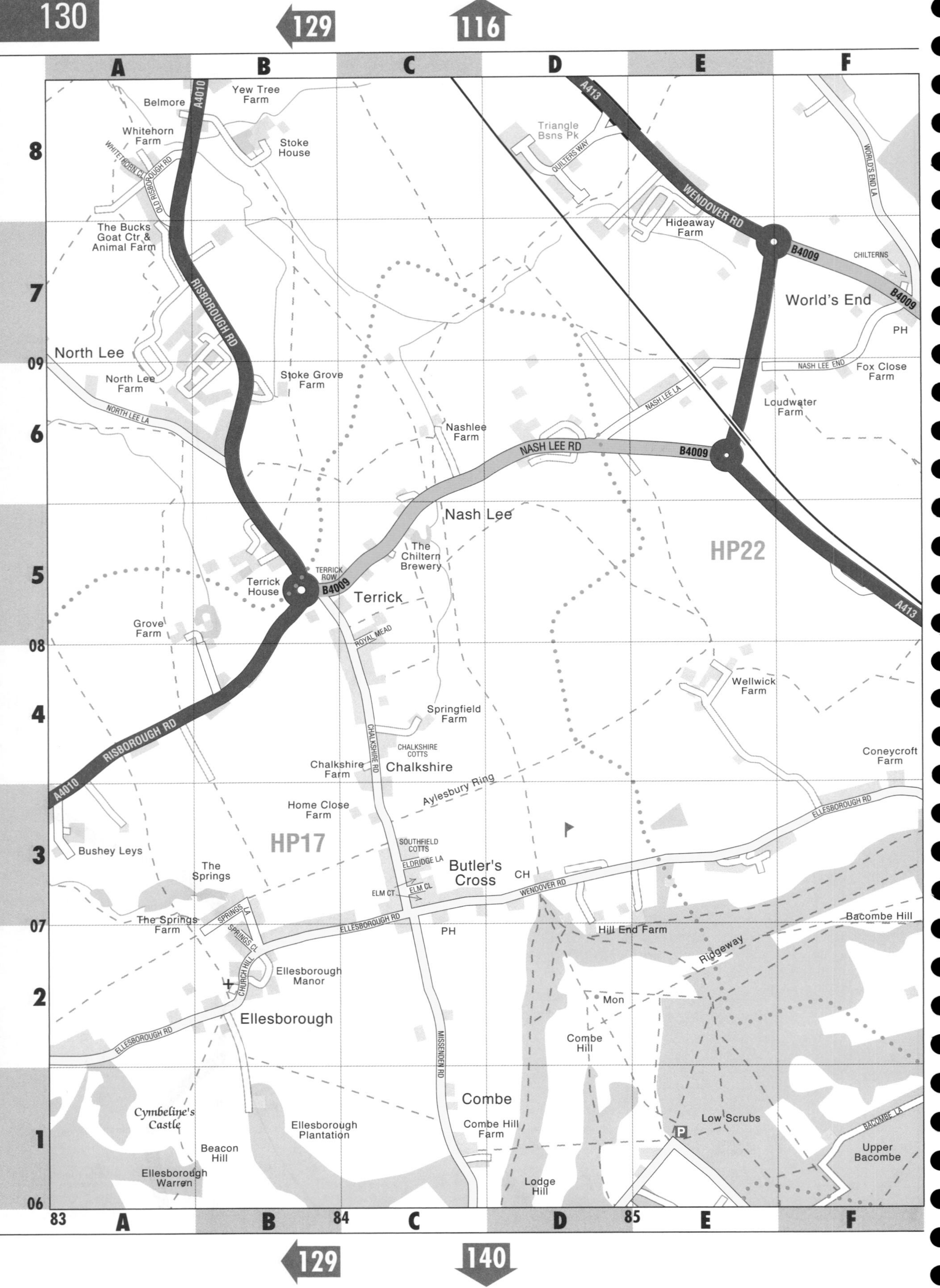
A
B
C
D
E
F
Belmore
Yew Tree Farm
A4010
A413
Whitehorn Farm
WHITEHORN CL
OLD RISBOROUGH RD
Stoke House
Triangle Bsns Pk
QUILTERS WAY
WENDOVER RD
WORLD'S END LA
The Bucks Goat Ctr & Animal Farm
Hideaway Farm
B4009
CHILTERNS
World's End
RISBOROUGH RD
PH
North Lee
Stoke Grove Farm
NASH LEE END
Fox Close Farm
North Lee Farm
NORTH LEE LA
NASH LEE LA
Loudwater Farm
Nashlee Farm
NASH LEE RD
Nash Lee
The Chiltern Brewery
HP22
TERRICK ROW
Terrick House
Terrick
Grove Farm
ROYAL MEAD
Wellwick Farm
Springfield Farm
CHALKSHIRE RD
CHALKSHIRE COTTS
Chalkshire Farm
Chalkshire
Coneycroft Farm
Aylesbury Ring
Home Close Farm
ELLESBOROUGH RD
Bushey Leys
HP17
SOUTHFIELD COTTS
ELDRIDGE LA
The Springs
Butler's Cross
CH
ELM CT
ELM CL
The Springs Farm
SPRINGS LA
SPRINGS CL
PH
Hill End Farm
Bacombe Hill
Ridgeway
CHURCH HILL
Ellesborough Manor
Mon
Ellesborough
MISSENDEN RD
Combe Hill
Combe
Cymbeline's Castle
Ellesborough Plantation
Combe Hill Farm
Low Scrubs
BACOMBE LA
Beacon Hill
Upper Bacombe
Ellesborough Warren
Lodge Hill
8
7
09
6
5
08
4
3
07
2
1
06
83
84
85

129
140

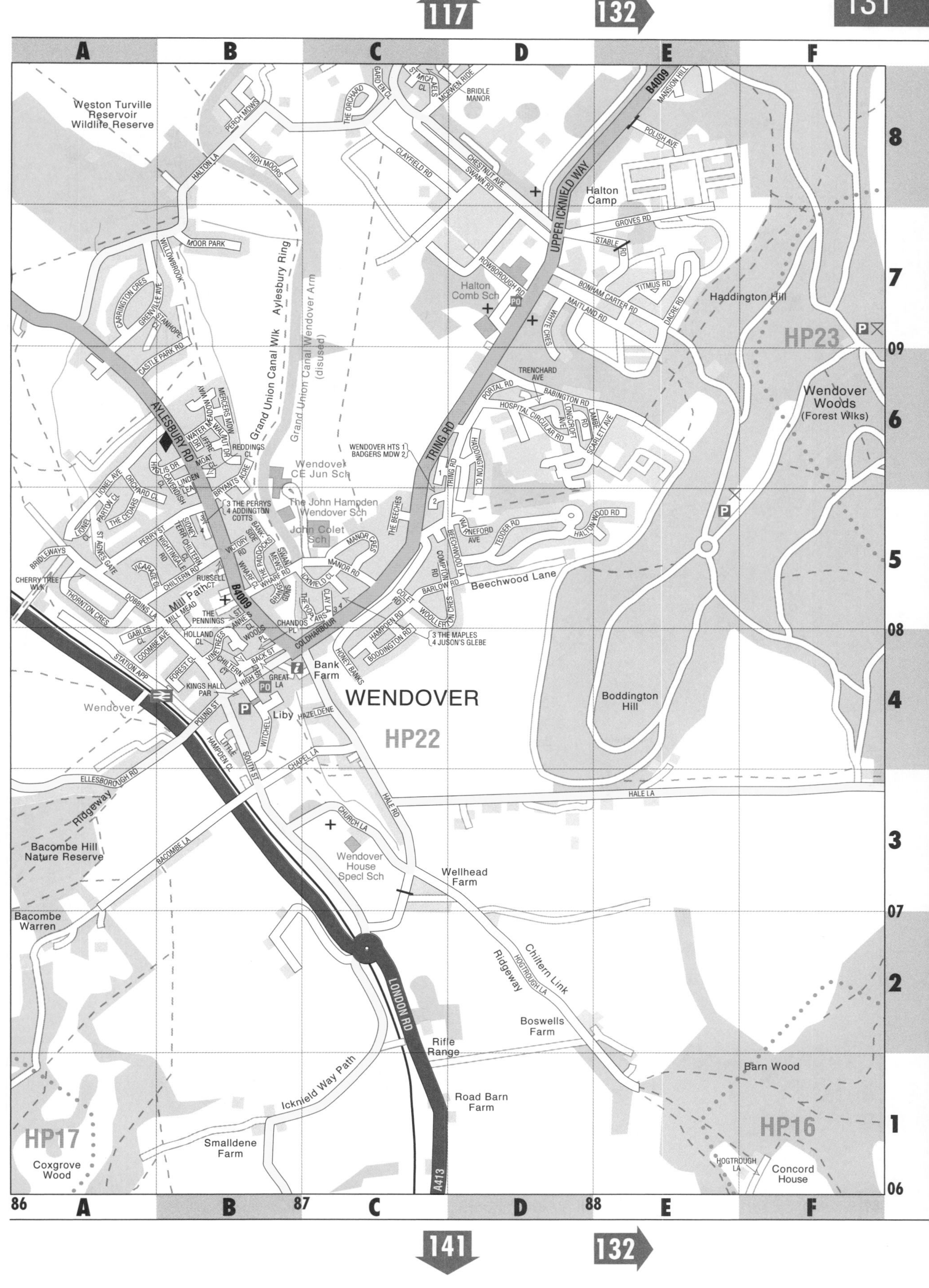
117
132
Weston Turville Reservoir Wildlife Reserve
Halton Camp
Haddington Hill
HP23
Wendover Woods (Forest Wlks)
Halton Comb Sch
Wendover CE Jun Sch
The John Hampden Wendover Sch
John Colet Sch
Grand Union Canal Wlk
Aylesbury Ring
Grand Union Canal Wendover Arm (disused)
UPPER ICKNIELD WAY
TRING RD
AYLESBURY RD
B4009
Beechwood Lane
WENDOVER
HP22
Bank Farm
Boddington Hill
Wendover
Liby
HALE LA
Ridgeway
Bacombe Hill Nature Reserve
Wendover House Specl Sch
Wellhead Farm
Bacombe Warren
Chiltern Link
LONDON RD
Boswells Farm
Rifle Range
Barn Wood
Icknield Way Path
Road Barn Farm
HP17
Coxgrove Wood
Smalldene Farm
HP16
Concord House
A413
141
132

131 118

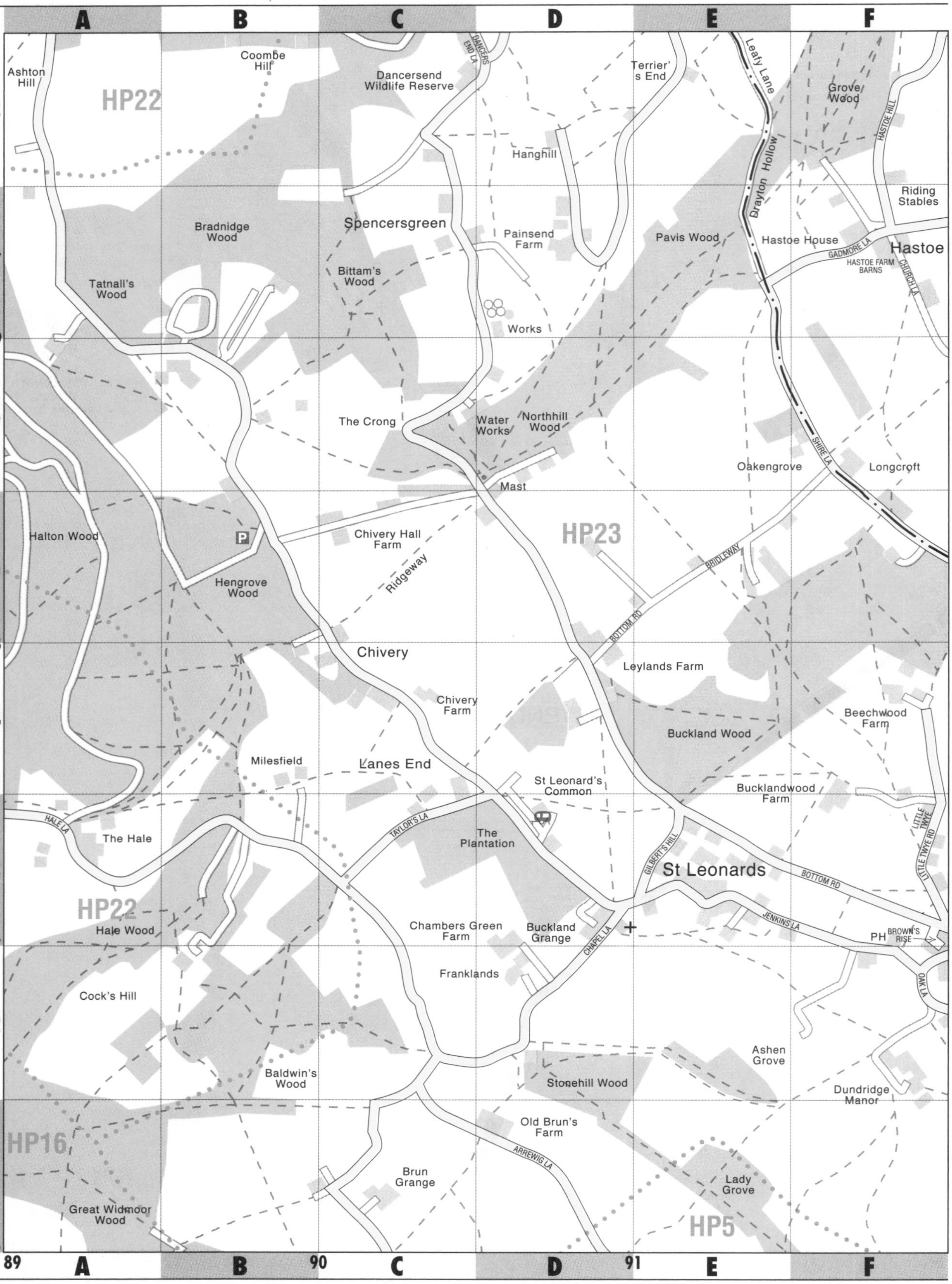

| | A | B | C | D | E | F |

8
Ashton Hill
HP22
Coombe Hill
Dancersend Wildlife Reserve
Terrier's End
Grove Wood
Riding Stables
Hanghill
Leafy Lane
Drayton Hollow
Hastoe House
Hastoe
HASTOE FARM BARNS
GADMORE LA
CHURCH LA
HASTOE HILL

7
Bradnidge Wood
Spencersgreen
Painsend Farm
Pavis Wood
Tatnall's Wood
Bittam's Wood
Works

09
The Crong
Water Works
Northhill Wood
Oakengrove
Longcroft
SHIRE LA

6
Mast

5
Halton Wood
P
Hengrove Wood
Chivery Hall Farm
Ridgeway
HP23
BRIDLEWAY
BOTTOM RD

08
Chivery
Leylands Farm

4
Chivery Farm
Buckland Wood
Beechwood Farm
Milesfield
Lanes End
St Leonard's Common
Bucklandwood Farm
LITTLE TWYE RD

3
The Hale
TAYLOR'S LA
The Plantation
St Leonards
BOTTOM RD
HP22
Hale Wood
Chambers Green Farm
Buckland Grange
CHAPEL LA
GILBERT'S HILL
JENKINS LA
PH BROWN'S RISE
OAK LA

07
Cock's Hill
Franklands

2
Baldwin's Wood
Ashen Grove
Dundridge Manor
Stonehill Wood

HP16
Old Brun's Farm
ARREWIG LA

1
Great Widmoor Wood
Brun Grange
Lady Grove
HP5

06
89 90 91

| A | B | C | D | E | F |

131 142

119
134

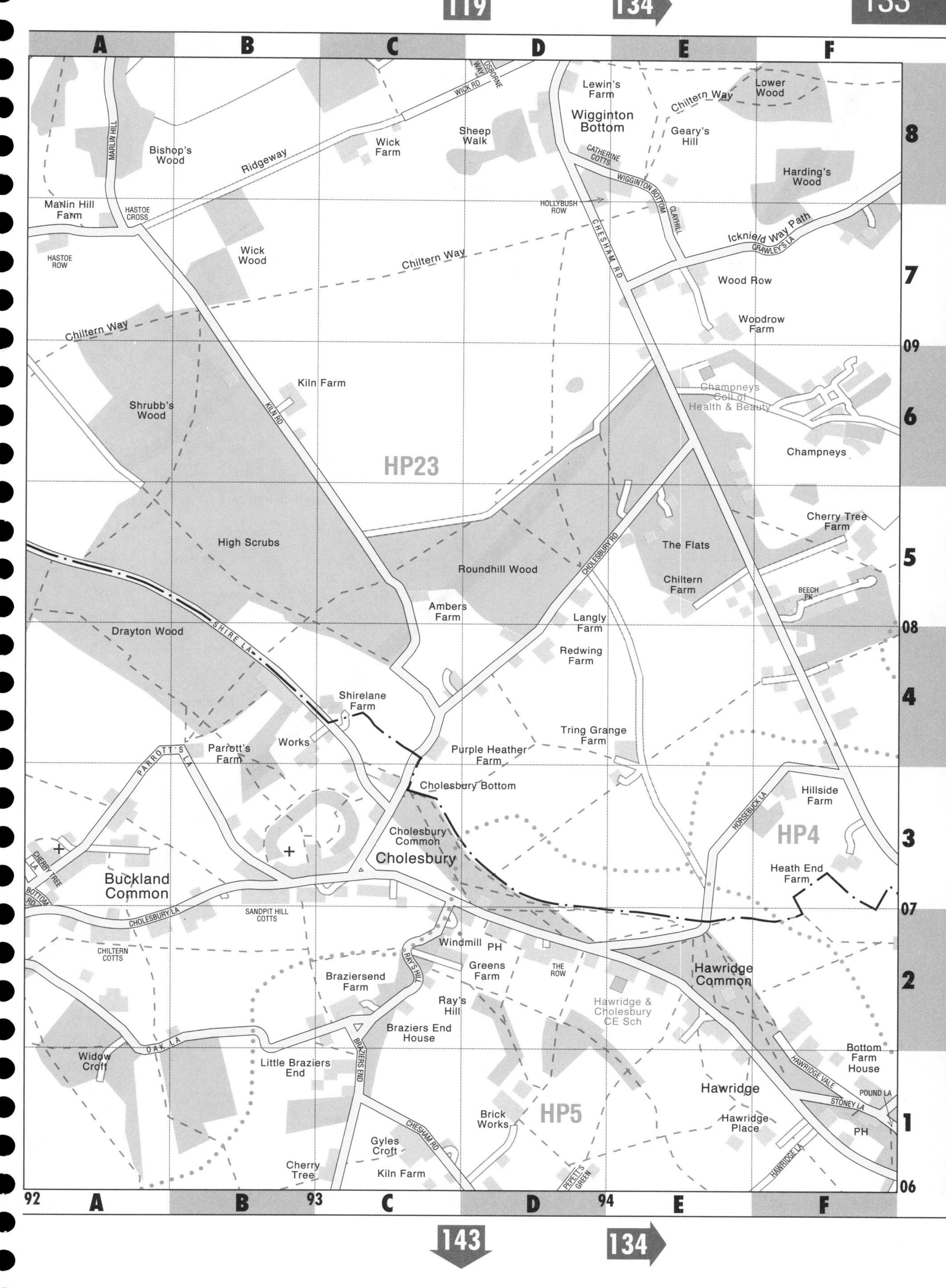
A
B
C
D
E
F
8
7
09
6
5
08
4
3
07
2
1
06
92
93
94
Lewin's Farm
Wigginton Bottom
Chiltern Way
Lower Wood
Geary's Hill
Harding's Wood
Bishop's Wood
Ridgeway
Wick Farm
Sheep Walk
WICK RD
OSBORNE WAY
MARLIN HILL
Marlin Hill Farm
HASTOE CROSS
HASTOE ROW
CATHERINE COTTS
WIGGINTON BOTTOM
CLAYHILL
HOLLYBUSH ROW
CHESHAM RD
Icknield Way Path
CRAWLEY'S LA
Wick Wood
Chiltern Way
Wood Row
Woodrow Farm
Kiln Farm
KILN RD
Shrubb's Wood
Champneys Coll of Health & Beauty
Champneys
HP23
Cherry Tree Farm
High Scrubs
Roundhill Wood
CHOLESBURY RD
The Flats
Chiltern Farm
BEECH PK
Ambers Farm
Langly Farm
Drayton Wood
SHIRE LA
Redwing Farm
Shirelane Farm
Works
Parrott's Farm
PARROTT'S LA
Tring Grange Farm
Purple Heather Farm
Cholesbury Bottom
HORSEBUCK LA
Hillside Farm
Cholesbury Common
Cholesbury
HP4
Heath End Farm
Buckland Common
CHERRY TREE LA
BOTTOM RD
CHOLESBURY LA
SANDPIT HILL COTTS
Windmill
PH
Greens Farm
THE ROW
CHILTERN COTTS
RAY'S HILL
Braziersend Farm
Hawridge Common
Rays Hill
Hawridge & Cholesbury CE Sch
Braziers End House
Widow Croft
OAK LA
Little Braziers End
BRAZIERS END
Bottom Farm House
HAWRIDGE VALE
POUND LA
Hawridge
STONEY LA
Brick Works
HP5
Hawridge Place
PH
CHESHAM RD
Gyles Croft
Cherry Tree
Kiln Farm
PEPETT'S GREEN
HAWRIDGE LA

143
134

133 120

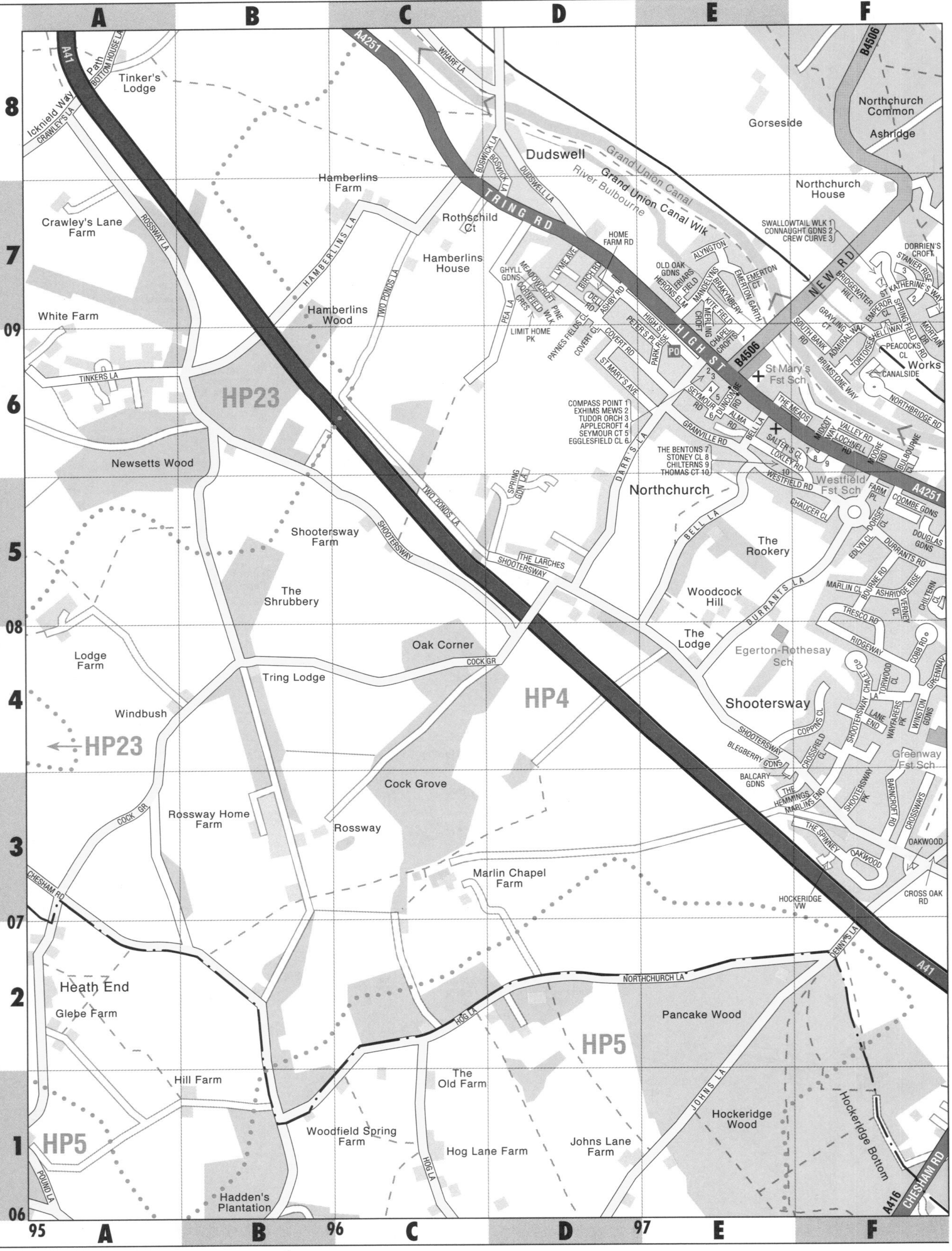

A B C D E F

8
7
09
6
5
08
4
08
07
3
2
07
1
06

95 A B 96 C D 97 E F

133 144

A41
Path
BOTTOM HOUSE LA
Icknield Way
CRAWLEY'S LA
Tinker's Lodge

A4251
WHARF LA

B4506
Northchurch Common
Ashridge

Gorseside

Dudswell
Grand Union Canal
Grand Union Canal Wlk
River Bulbourne

Northchurch House

Crawley's Lane Farm
ROSSWAY LA

Hamberlins Farm
HAMBERLINS LA
BOSSNICK LA
RESSWELL LA
BUSHMELLIA
TRING RD

Rothschild Ct

SWALLOWTAIL WLK 1
CONNAUGHT GDNS 2
CREW CURVE 3

DORRIEN'S CROFT
STANIER RISE
ST KATHERINE'S WAY

White Farm

Hamberlins House

TWO PONDS LA

Hamberlins Wood

GHYLL GDNS
PEA LA
MEADOWCROFT PINE
CANFIELD WAY
CRES

HOME FARM RD
OLD OAK GDNS
HERONS ELM
ALYNGTON
EMERTON CT

NEW RD
HIGH ST

B4506

Works

PEACOCKS CL
TORTOISES
CANALSIDE

HP23

TINKERS LA

LIMIT HOME PK
PAYNES FIELDS
COVERT RD
COVERT

ST MARY'S AVE

St Mary's Fst Sch

COMPASS POINT 1
EXHIMS MEWS 2
TUDOR ORCH 3
APPLECROFT 4
SEYMOUR CT 5
EGGLESFIELD CL 6

SEYMOUR RD
DUNCOMBE RD
ALMA RD
BELL LA

THE MEADS

VALLEY RD
LOCHNELL RD
NORTHBRIDGE RD

Newsetts Wood

SPRING GDN LA
DARR LA

GRANVILLE RD
THE BENTONS 7
STONEY CL 8
CHILTERNS 9
THOMAS CT 10

TORLEY RD
WESTFIELD RD

COOMBE GDNS

Northchurch

Westfield Fst Sch

FARM PL
DOUGLAS GDNS

Shootersway Farm
SHOOTERSWAY

The Shrubbery

THE LARCHES
SHOOTERSWAY

BELL LA
BURRANTS LA

The Rookery

Woodcock Hill

The Lodge

CHAUCER CL

MARLIN LA
BOURNE RD
ASHRIDGE RISE
CHILTERN CL

TRESCO RD
RIDGEWAY

COBB RD
GREENWAY

Lodge Farm

Tring Lodge

Oak Corner
COCK GR

Egerton-Rothesay Sch

LANE END
WAYFARERS PK
WINSTON GDNS

Windbush

HP23

HP4

Shootersway
SHOOTERSWAY
BLEGBERRY GDNS
COPPINS CL
CROSSFIELD CL

Greenway Fst Sch

Cock Grove

BALCARY GDNS
THE HEMMINGS
MARLIN END

OAKWOOD
THE SPINNEY

OAKWOOD

Rossway Home Farm

Rossway

CHESHAM RD

HOCKERIDGE VW

CROSS OAK RD

Marlin Chapel Farm

NORTHCHURCH LA

PENNYS LA

A41

Heath End

Glebe Farm

HOG LA

Pancake Wood

HP5

Hill Farm

The Old Farm

Woodfield Spring Farm

Hog Lane Farm

Johns Lane Farm

JOHNS LA

Hockeridge Wood

Hockeridge Bottom

A416
CHESHAM RD

HP5

POUND LA

Hadden's Plantation

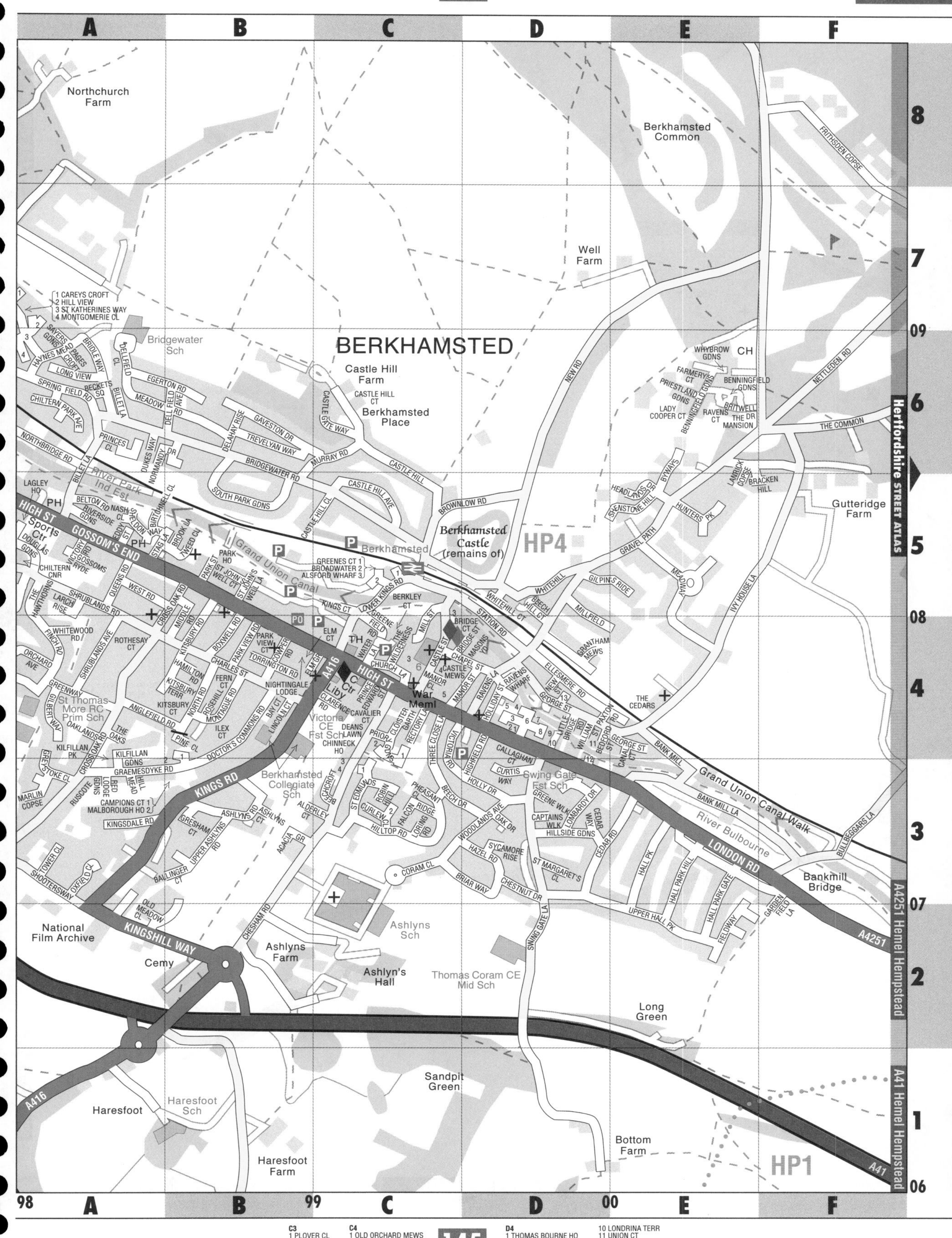

BERKHAMSTED

HP4

Hertfordshire STREET ATLAS

A4251 Hemel Hempstead

A41 Hemel Hempstead

HP1

C3
1 PLOVER CL
2 KESTREL CL
3 DAVIS HO
4 FROST HO

C4
1 OLD ORCHARD MEWS
2 PRIORY CT
3 CHURCHGATES
4 WILLIAM FISKE HO
5 DOWER MEWS
6 Berkhamsted Sch

D4
1 THOMAS BOURNE HO
2 AUGUSTUS SMITH HO
3 COOPER WAY
4 GLASSMILL HO
5 NEW PROVIDENT PL
6 ROBERTSON RD
7 COSTINS WLK
8 MCDOUGALL RD
9 LONDRINA CT
10 LONDRINA TERR
11 UNION CT
12 OLD MILL GDNS
13 CAMBRIDGE TERR

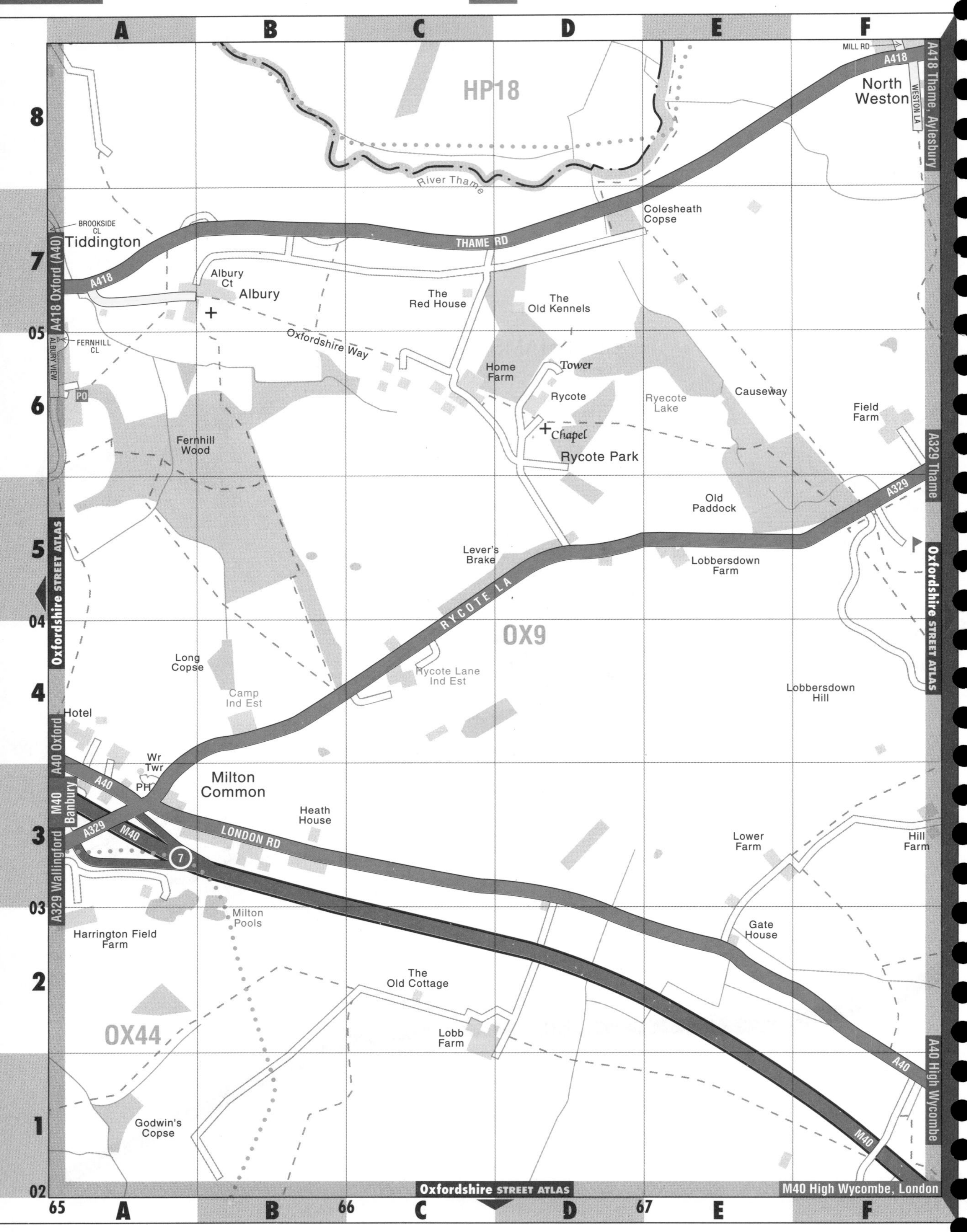

A B C D E F

8

HP18

North
Weston

MILL RD

A418

River Thame

THAME RD

A418 Thame, Aylesbury

WESTON LA

7

BROOKSIDE
CL

Tiddington

A418 Oxford (A40)

Albury
Ct

Albury

The
Red House

The
Old Kennels

Colesheath
Copse

05

FERNHILL
CL

Oxfordshire Way

Home
Farm

Tower

Rycote

Ryecote
Lake

Causeway

Field
Farm

A329 Thame

ALBURY VIEW

PO

6

Fernhill
Wood

+ Chapel

Rycote Park

Old
Paddock

A329

Oxfordshire STREET ATLAS

5

Lever's
Brake

Lobbersdown
Farm

04

RYCOTE LA

OX9

Lobbersdown
Hill

4

Long
Copse

Camp
Ind Est

Rycote Lane
Ind Est

Hotel

A40 Oxford

Wr
Twr

Milton
Common

Heath
House

Lower
Farm

Hill
Farm

M40 Banbury

PH

3

A329

A40

M40

LONDON RD

7

03

A329 Wallingford

Milton
Pools

Gate
House

Harrington Field
Farm

2

The
Old Cottage

OX44

Lobb
Farm

A40 High Wycombe

1

Godwin's
Copse

M40

02

M40 High Wycombe, London

65 A B 66 C D 67 E F

127
138

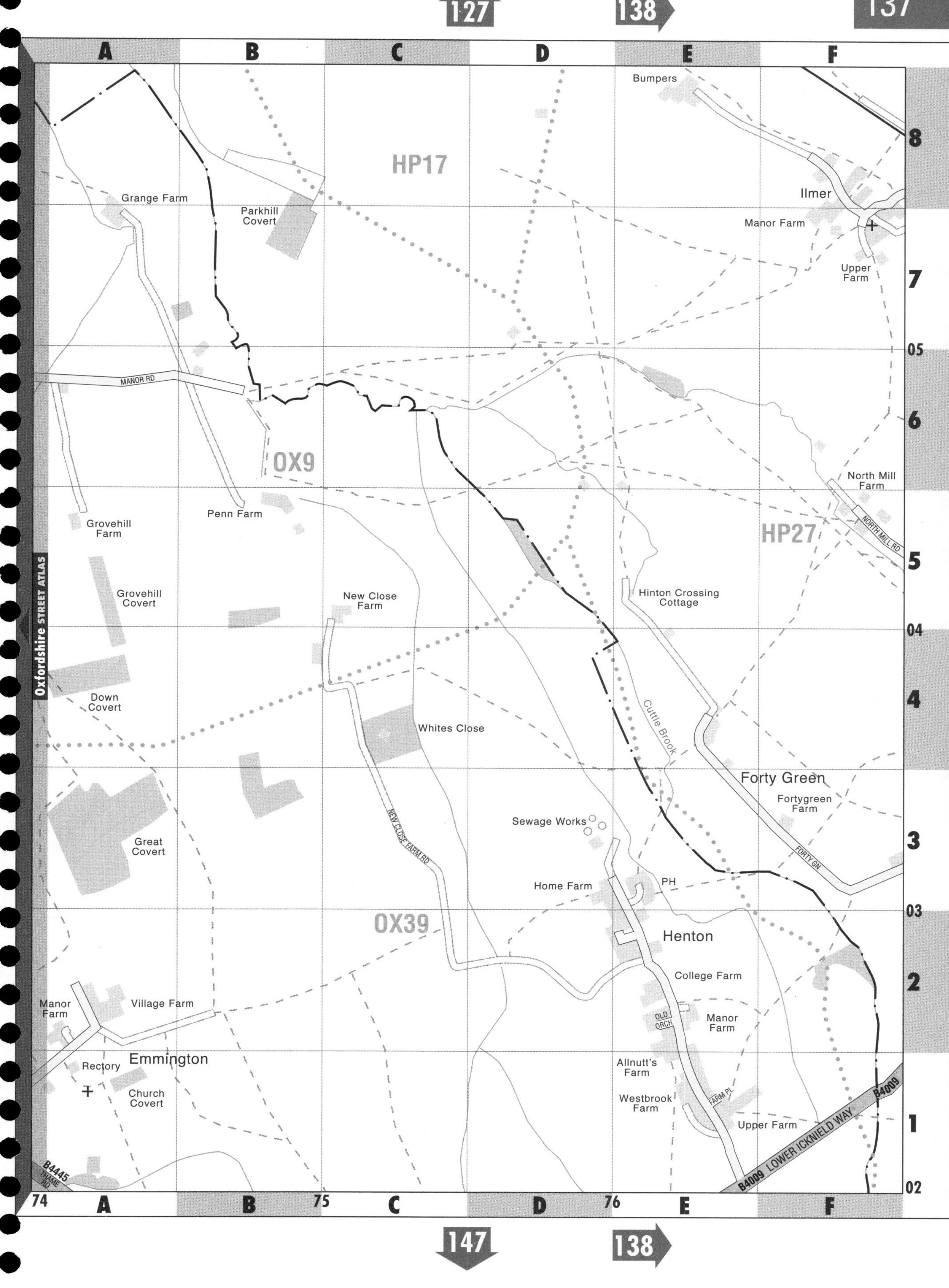
A
B
C
D
E
F
Bumpers
HP17
Grange Farm
Parkhill
Covert
Ilmer
Manor Farm
Upper
Farm
MANOR RD
OX9
North Mill
Farm
NORTH MILL RD
HP27
Grovehill
Farm
Penn Farm
Grovehill
Covert
New Close
Farm
Hinton Crossing
Cottage
Oxfordshire STREET ATLAS
Down
Covert
Whites Close
Cuttle Brook
Forty Green
Fortygreen
Farm
Sewage Works
Great
Covert
NEW CLOSE FARM RD
FORTY GN
Home Farm
PH
OX39
Henton
College Farm
Manor
Farm
Village Farm
OLD
ORCH
Manor
Farm
Emmington
Rectory
Allnutt's
Farm
Church
Covert
Westbrook
Farm
FARM PL
Upper Farm
B4009
LOWER ICKNIELD WAY
B4445
THAME
RD
B4009
8
7
05
6
5
04
4
3
03
2
1
02
74
75
76

147
138

137
128

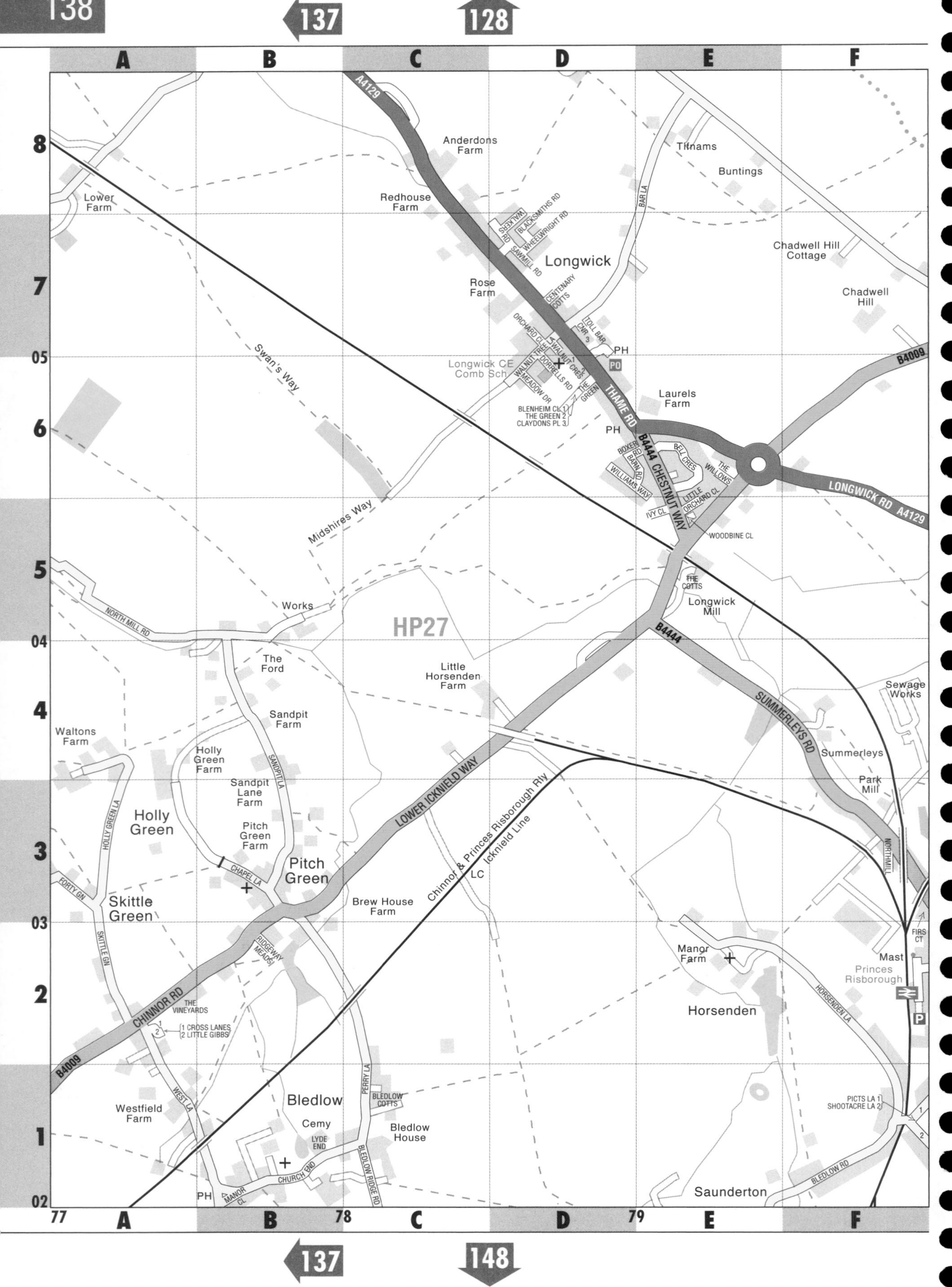
A
B
C
D
E
F
8
7
05
6
5
04
4
3
03
2
1
02
77
78
79
A4129
Anderdons Farm
Tifnams
Buntings
Lower Farm
Redhouse Farm
WALKERS RD
BLACKSMITHS RD
WHEELWRIGHT RD
SAWMILL RD
BAR LA
Longwick
Chadwell Hill Cottage
Rose Farm
CENTENARY COTTS
Chadwell Hill
ORCHARD CL
TOLL BAR CNR
WALNUT TREE
PH
PO
Swan's Way
Longwick CE Comb Sch
DORRELLS RD
MEADOW DR
THE GREEN
B4009
THAME RD
Laurels Farm
BLENHEIM CL 1
THE GREEN 2
CLAYDONS PL 3
BOXER RD
BARN RD
B4444
CHESTNUT WAY
BELL CRES
THE WILLOWS
WILLIAMS WAY
LITTLE ORCHARD CL
IVY CL
LONGWICK RD A4129
Midshires Way
WOODBINE CL
THE COTTS
Longwick Mill
NORTH MILL RD
Works
HP27
The Ford
Little Horsenden Farm
SUMMERLEYS RD
Sewage Works
Sandpit Farm
Waltons Farm
Holly Green Farm
SANDPIT LA
Summerleys
LOWER ICKNIELD WAY
Chinnor & Princes Risborough Rly
Icknield Line
Park Mill
Sandpit Lane Farm
Holly Green
HOLLY GREEN LA
Pitch Green Farm
Pitch Green
NORTHMILL
CHAPEL LA
LC
FORTY GN
Skittle Green
Brew House Farm
FIRS CT
RIDGEWAY MEADS
SKITTLE GN
Manor Farm
Mast
Princes Risborough
HORSENDEN LA
CHINNOR RD
THE VINEYARDS
Horsenden
1 CROSS LANES
2 LITTLE GIBBS
P
B4009
WEST LA
PERRY LA
BLEDLOW COTTS
Bledlow
PICTS LA 1
SHOOTACRE LA 2
Westfield Farm
Cemy
Bledlow House
LYDE END
CHURCH END
BLEDLOW RIDGE RD
MANOR CL
BLEDLOW RD
PH
Saunderton

137
148

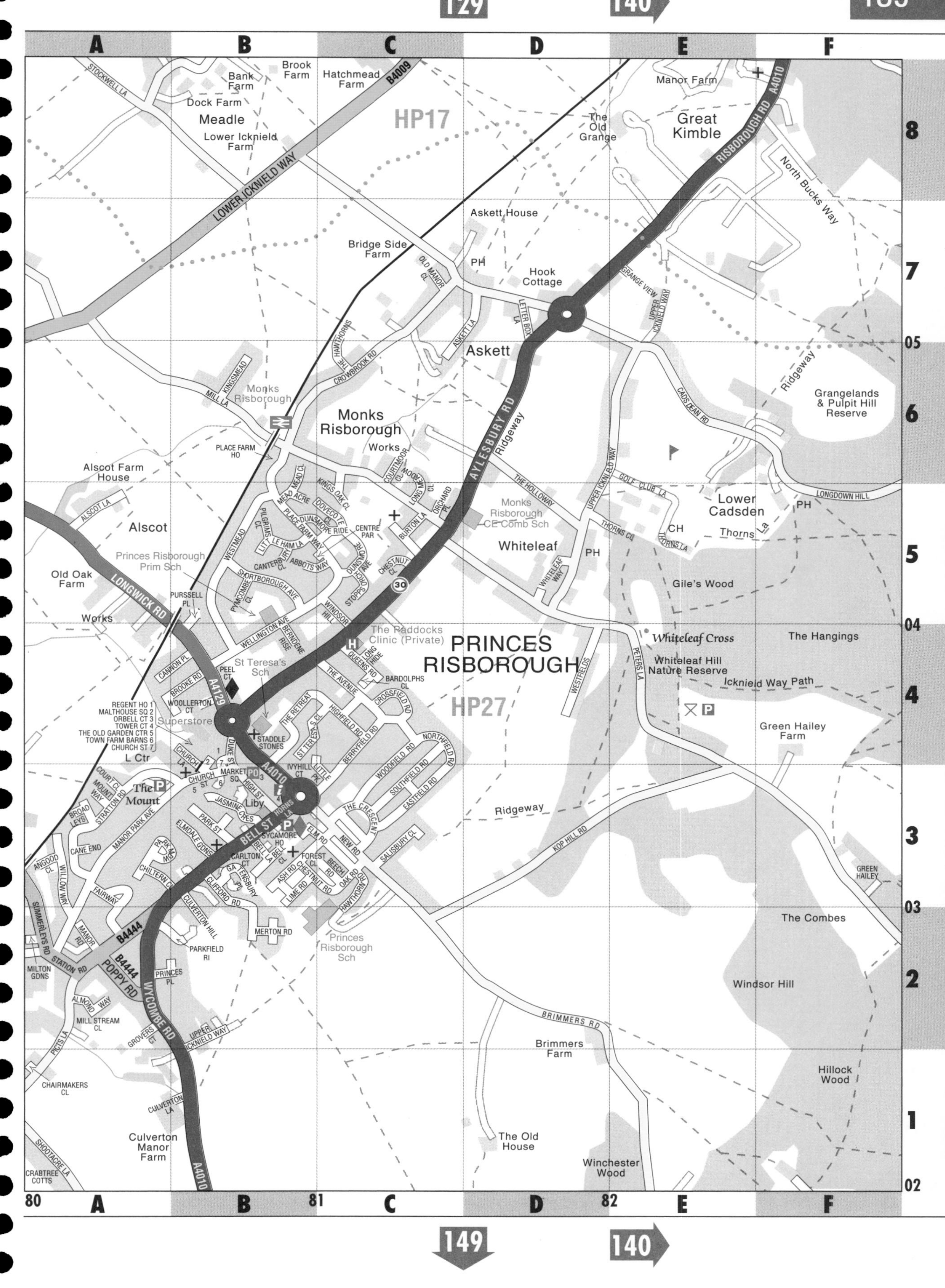
129
140
A
B
C
D
E
F
Brook Farm
Bank Farm
Hatchmead Farm
Dock Farm
Meadle
Lower Icknield Farm
HP17
LOWER ICKNIELD WAY
B4009
Manor Farm
The Old Grange
Great Kimble
RISBOROUGH RD
A4010
North Bucks Way
Askett House
Bridge Side Farm
Hook Cottage
Askett
Monks Risborough
Alscot Farm House
Alscot
Princes Risborough Prim Sch
Old Oak Farm
LONGWICK RD
Works
Grangelands & Pulpit Hill Reserve
Ridgeway
AYLESBURY RD
Monks Risborough CE Comb Sch
Whiteleaf
Lower Cadsden
Thorns La
Gile's Wood
The Paddocks Clinic (Private)
PRINCES RISBOROUGH
Whiteleaf Cross
The Hangings
Whiteleaf Hill Nature Reserve
Icknield Way Path
St Teresa's Sch
HP27
Green Hailey Farm
Superstore
L Ctr
The Mount
Liby
BELL ST
KOP HILL RD
The Combes
Windsor Hill
Princes Risborough Sch
BRIMMERS RD
Brimmers Farm
Hillock Wood
WYCOMBE RD
Culverton Manor Farm
The Old House
Winchester Wood
A4010
80
81
82
02
03
04
05
1
2
3
4
5
6
7
8
149
140

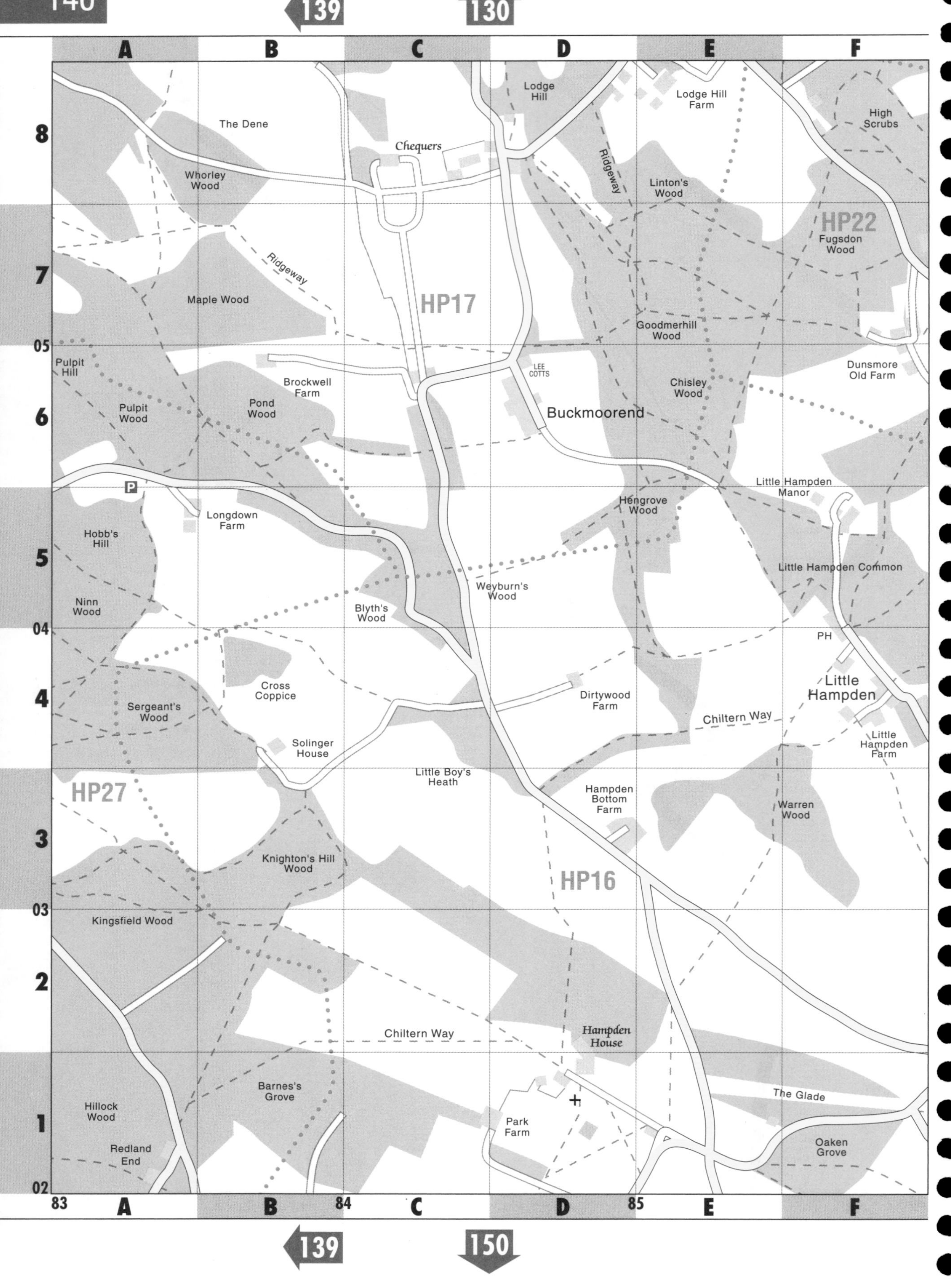

139
130

A   B   C   D   E   F

8

The Dene

Chequers

Lodge
Hill

Lodge Hill
Farm

High
Scrubs

Whorley
Wood

Ridgeway

HP22

Linton's
Wood

7

Ridgeway

Maple Wood

HP17

Fugsdon
Wood

05

Pulpit
Hill

Brockwell
Farm

Goodmerhill
Wood

LEE
COTTS

Dunsmore
Old Farm

6

Pulpit
Wood

Pond
Wood

Chisley
Wood

Buckmoorend

Little Hampden
Manor

P

Longdown
Farm

Hengrove
Wood

5

Hobb's
Hill

Little Hampden Common

Ninn
Wood

Weyburn's
Wood

04

Blyth's
Wood

PH

Little
Hampden

4

Sergeant's
Wood

Cross
Coppice

Dirtywood
Farm

Chiltern Way

Little
Hampden
Farm

Solinger
House

Little Boy's
Heath

HP27

Hampden
Bottom
Farm

Warren
Wood

3

Knighton's Hill
Wood

HP16

03

Kingsfield Wood

2

Chiltern Way

Hampden
House

Barnes's
Grove

The Glade

1

Hillock
Wood

Park
Farm

Oaken
Grove

Redland
End

02

83   A   B   84   C   D   85   E   F

131
142

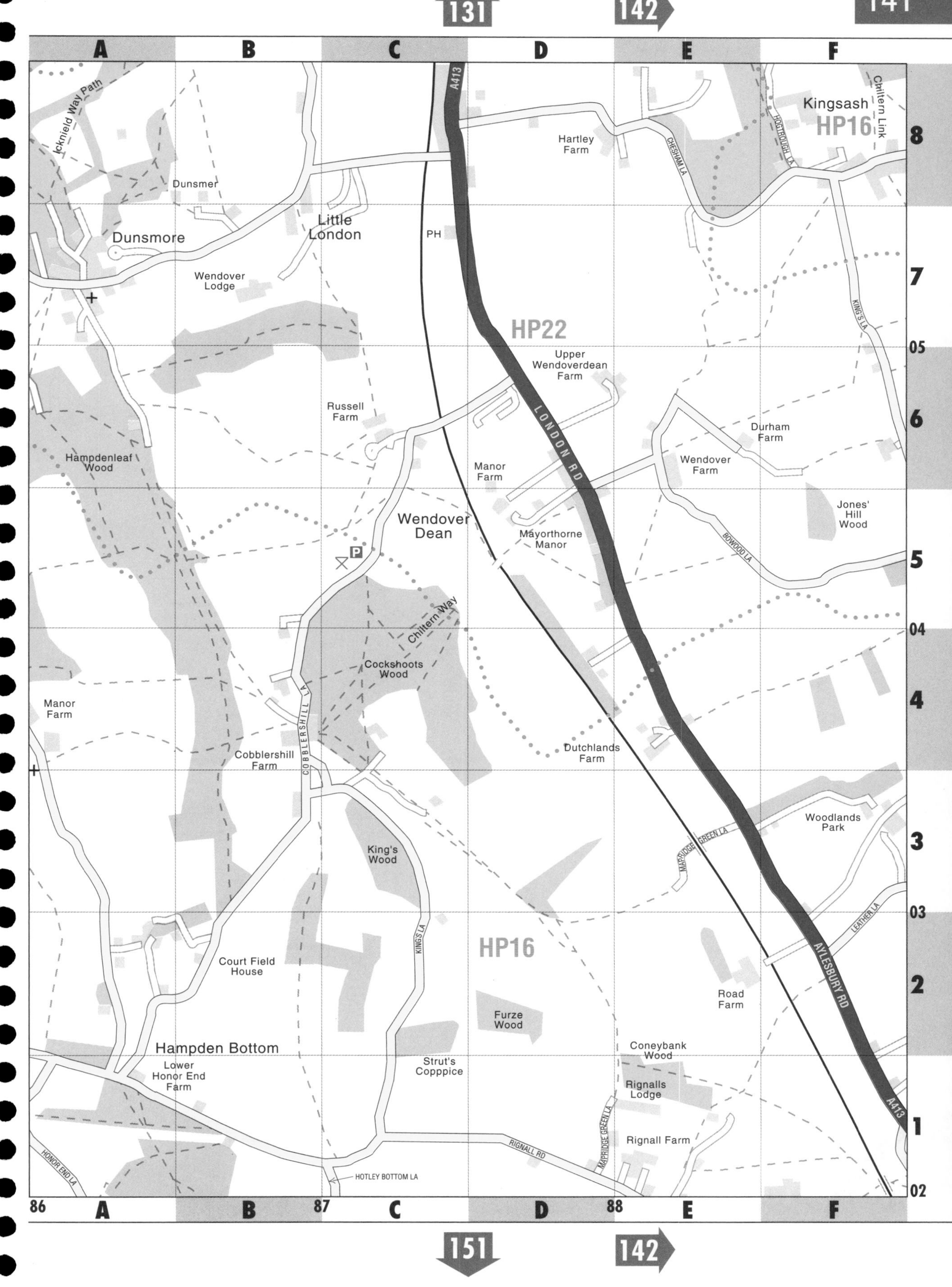
A
B
C
D
E
F
A413
Icknield Way Path
Kingsash
Chiltern Link
HP16
Hartley Farm
CHESHAM LA
HOGTROUGH LA
Dunsmer
Dunsmore
Little London
PH
Wendover Lodge
HP22
KING'S LA
Upper Wendoverdean Farm
Russell Farm
LONDON RD
Durham Farm
Hampdenleaf Wood
Manor Farm
Wendover Farm
Wendover Dean
Mayorthorne Manor
Jones' Hill Wood
BOWOOD LA
Chiltern Way
Cockshoots Wood
Manor Farm
COBBLERSHILL LA
Cobblershill Farm
Dutchlands Farm
Woodlands Park
MAPRIDGE GREEN LA
King's Wood
LEATHER LA
KING'S LA
HP16
Court Field House
AYLESBURY RD
Road Farm
Furze Wood
Hampden Bottom
Strut's Copppice
Coneybank Wood
Lower Honor End Farm
Rignalls Lodge
MAPRIDGE GREEN LA
Rignall Farm
RIGNALL RD
HONOR END LA
HOTLEY BOTTOM LA
A413
8
7
05
6
5
04
4
3
03
2
1
02
86
87
88

151
142

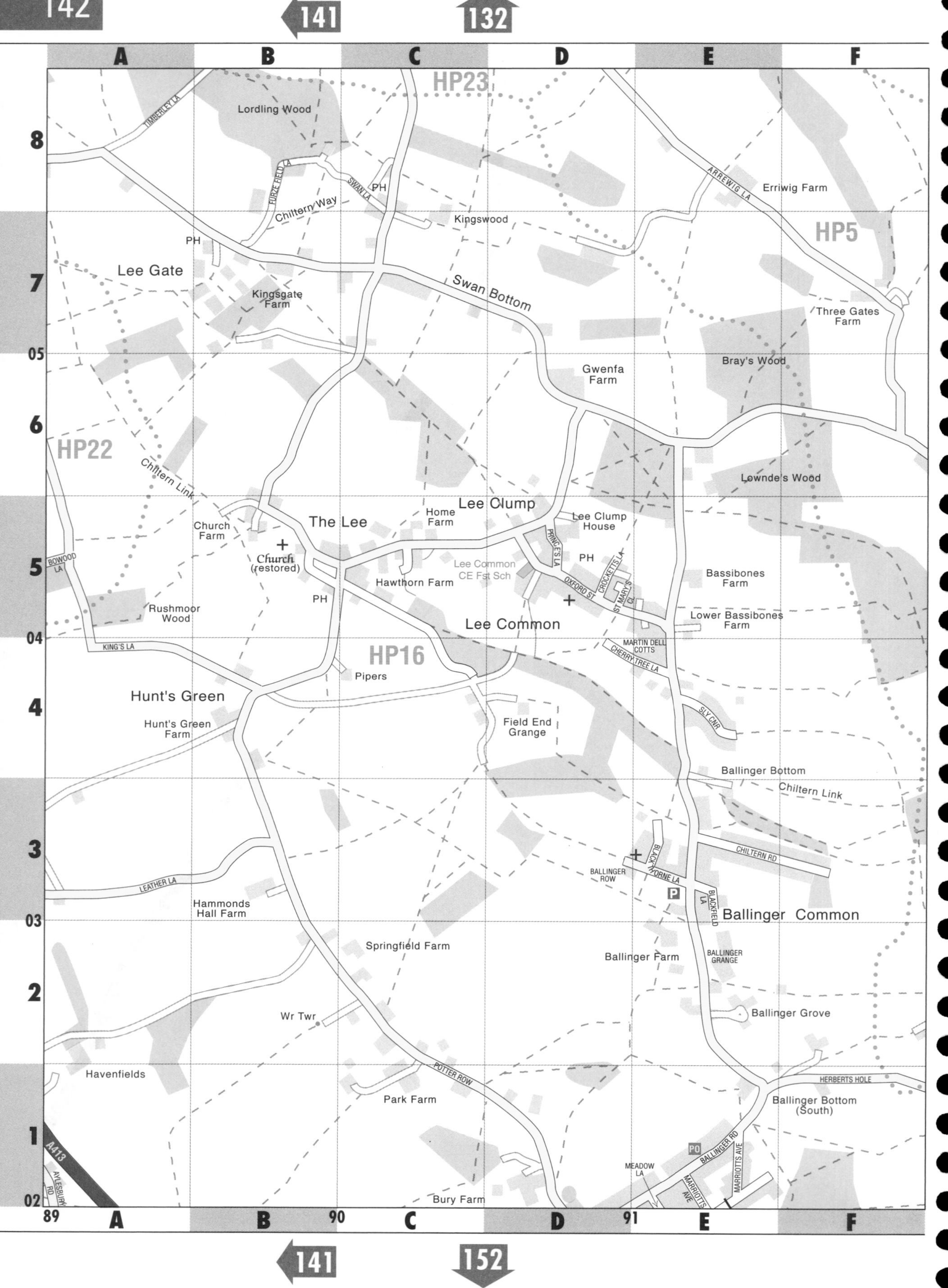

141
132

A   B   C   D   E   F

HP23

Lordling Wood

8

Chiltern Way

PH
SWAN LA
Kingswood

ARREWIG LA
Erriwig Farm

HP5

7   Lee Gate
PH
Kingsgate Farm
Swan Bottom
Three Gates Farm

05
Bray's Wood

Gwenfa Farm

6   HP22
Chiltern Link
Lownde's Wood

Lee Clump
Lee Clump House
Church Farm
The Lee
Home Farm
5   Church (restored)
Hawthorn Farm
PRINCE'S LA
Lee Common CE Fst Sch
PH
CRICKETTS LA
ST MARY'S
Bassibones Farm
BOWOOD LA
OXFORD ST
PH
Rushmoor Wood
Lower Bassibones Farm

04   KING'S LA
Lee Common
MARTIN DELL COTTS
CHERRY TREE LA

HP16
Pipers
SLY CNR

4   Hunt's Green
Hunt's Green Farm
Field End Grange
Ballinger Bottom
Chiltern Link

3   LEATHER LA
BLACKTHORNE LA
Ballinger Row
CHILTERN RD

03   Hammonds Hall Farm
P
BLACKFIELD LA
Ballinger Common

Springfield Farm
Ballinger Farm
Ballinger Grange

2   Wr Twr
Ballinger Grove

Havenfields
POTTER ROW
Park Farm
HERBERTS HOLE
Ballinger Bottom (South)

1   A413
PO
BALLINGER RD
MARRIOTTS AVE
AYLESBURY RD
MEADOW LA
MARRIOTTS AVE

02   Bury Farm
89   A   B   90   C   D   91   E   F

141
152

133
144

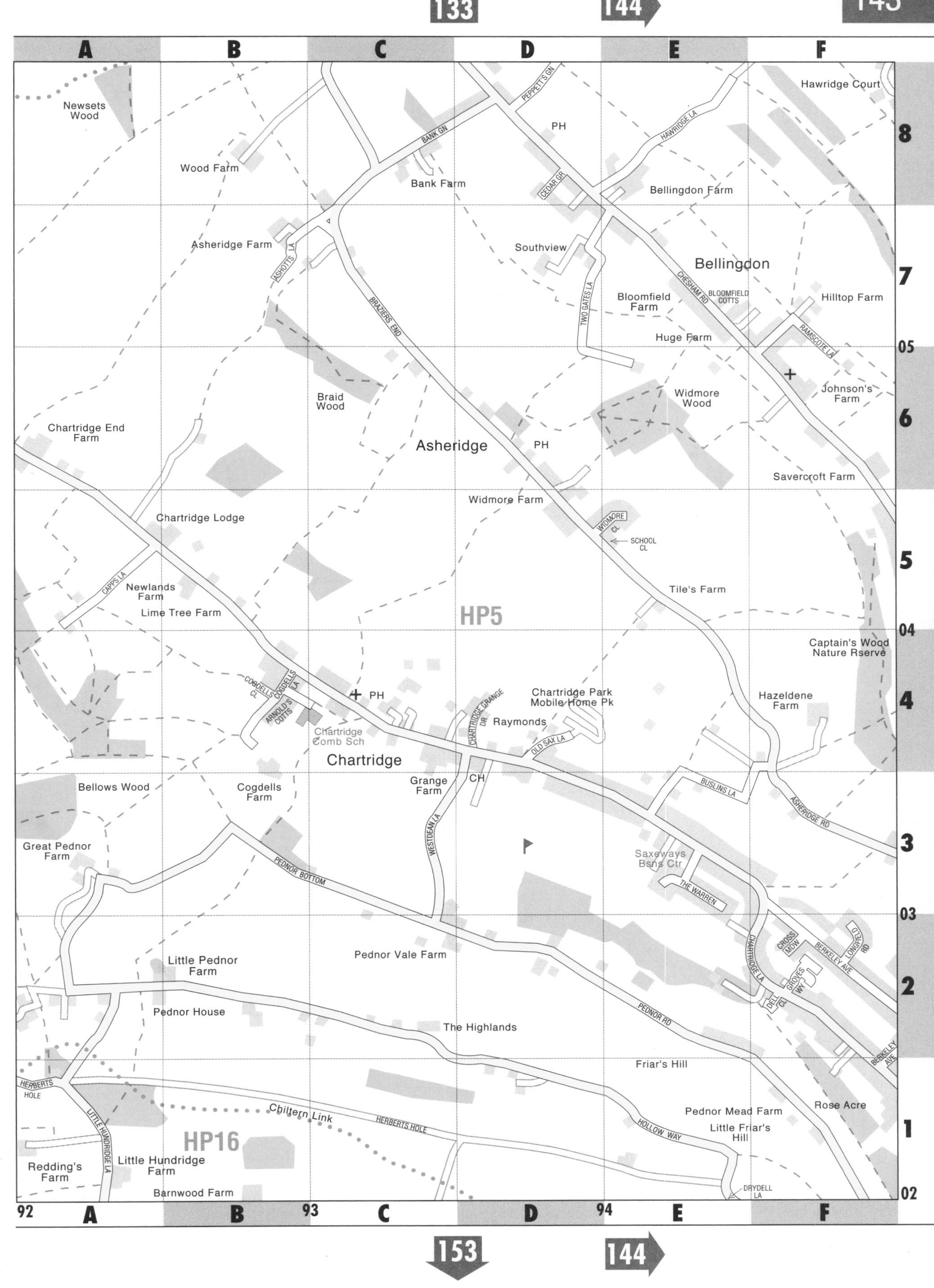
A
B
C
D
E
F
Newsets Wood
Wood Farm
Bank Farm
PH
Hawridge Court
Bellingdon Farm
Asheridge Farm
Southview
Bellingdon
Bloomfield Farm
Hilltop Farm
Huge Farm
Braid Wood
Widmore Wood
Johnson's Farm
Chartridge End Farm
Asheridge
PH
Savercroft Farm
Widmore Farm
Chartridge Lodge
Newlands Farm
Lime Tree Farm
Tile's Farm
HP5
Captain's Wood Nature Rserve
PH
Chartridge Park Mobile Home Pk
Hazeldene Farm
Raymonds
Chartridge Comb Sch
Chartridge
Grange Farm
CH
Bellows Wood
Cogdells Farm
Great Pednor Farm
Saxeways Bsns Ctr
Little Pednor Farm
Pednor Vale Farm
Pednor House
The Highlands
Friar's Hill
Chiltern Link
Pednor Mead Farm
Rose Acre
Little Friar's Hill
HP16
Redding's Farm
Little Hundridge Farm
Barnwood Farm
PEPPETT'S GN
BANK GN
HAWRIDGE LA
CEDAR GR
ASHOTTS LA
CHESHAM RD
BLOOMFIELD COTTS
TWO GATES LA
BRAZIERS END
RAMSCOTE LA
WIDMORE CL
SCHOOL CL
CAPPS LA
COGDELLS CL
COGDELLS LA
ARNOLD'S COTTS
CHARTRIDGE GRANGE DR
OLD SAX LA
BUSLINS LA
ASHERIDGE RD
WESTDEAN LA
PEDNOR BOTTOM
THE WARREN
CROSS MDW
BERKELEY AVE
LONGFIELD RD
CHARTRIDGE LA
GROVES WY
DELL CL
PEDNOR RD
HERBERTS HOLE
LITTLE HUNDRIDGE LA
HOLLOW WAY
DRYDELL LA
8
7
05
6
5
04
4
3
03
2
1
02
92
93
94

153
144

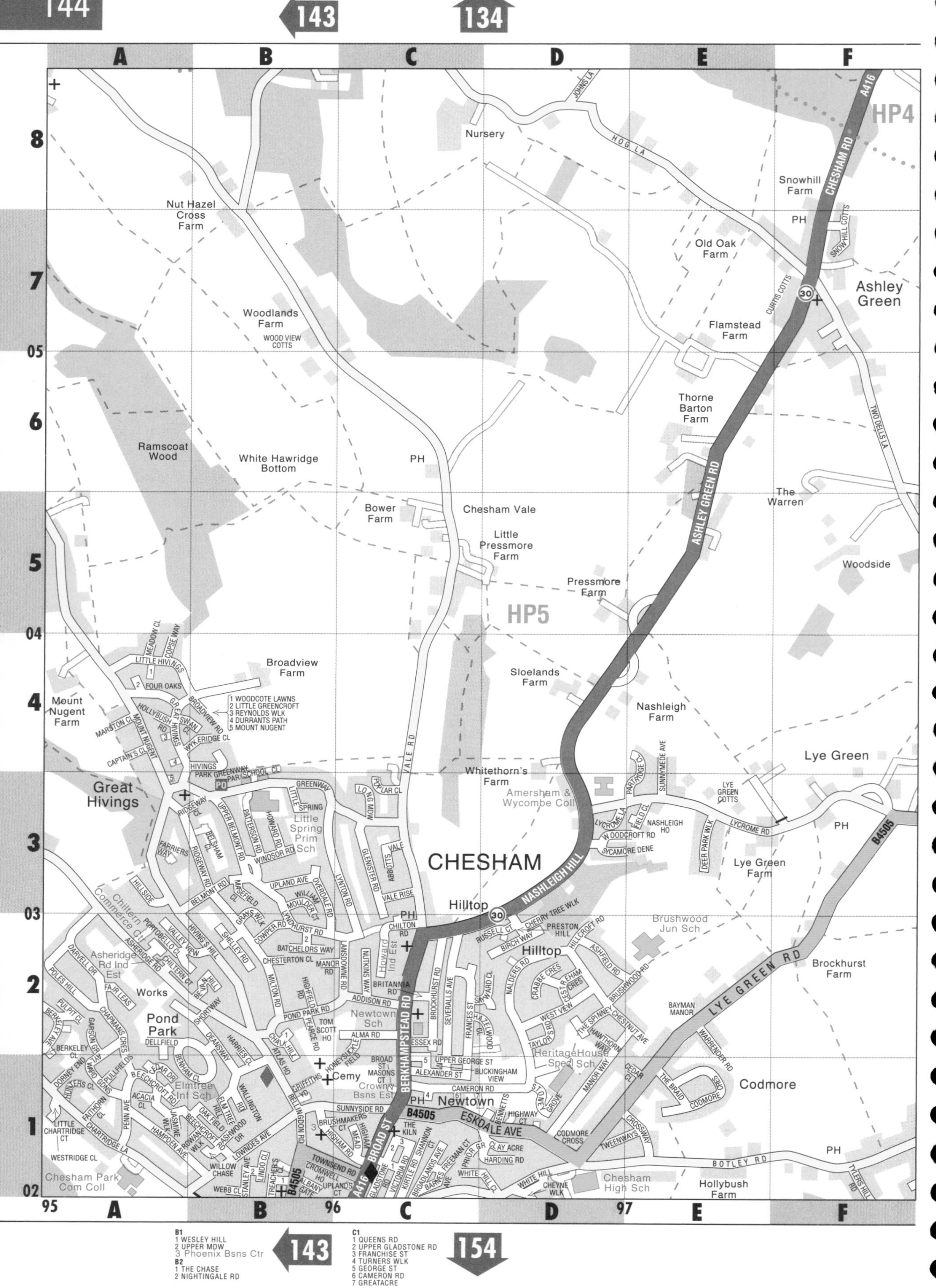

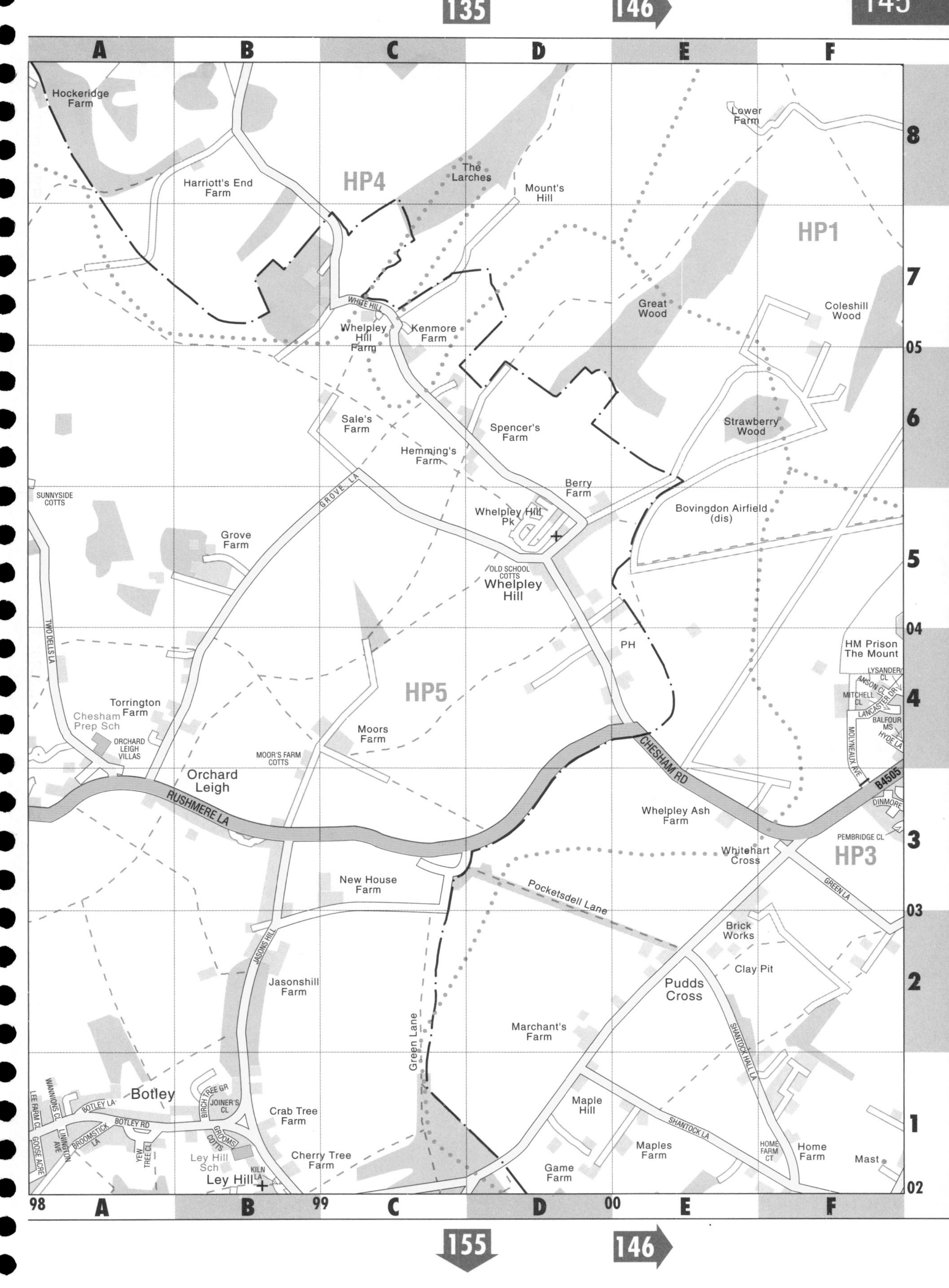
135
146
A
B
C
D
E
F
8
7
05
6
5
04
4
3
03
2
1
02
98
99
00
Hockeridge Farm
Harriott's End Farm
HP4
The Larches
Mount's Hill
Lower Farm
HP1
WHITE HILL
Whelpley Hill Farm
Kenmore Farm
Great Wood
Coleshill Wood
Strawberry Wood
Sale's Farm
Spencer's Farm
Hemming's Farm
Berry Farm
Bovingdon Airfield (dis)
SUNNYSIDE COTTS
GROVE LA
Grove Farm
Whelpley Hill Pk
OLD SCHOOL COTTS
Whelpley Hill
TWO DELLS LA
PH
HM Prison The Mount
LYSANDER CL
ANSON CL
MITCHELL CL
LANCASTER DR
BALFOUR MS
HYDE LA
MOLYNEAUX AVE
HP5
Torrington Farm
Chesham Prep Sch
ORCHARD LEIGH VILLAS
Moors Farm
MOOR'S FARM COTTS
CHESHAM RD
Orchard Leigh
RUSHMERE LA
B4505
DINMORE
Whelpley Ash Farm
PEMBRIDGE CL
Whitehart Cross
HP3
New House Farm
Pocketsdell Lane
GREEN LA
JASONS HILL
Brick Works
Clay Pit
Jasonshill Farm
Pudds Cross
Marchant's Farm
SHANTOCK HALL LA
Green Lane
Botley
BIRCH TREE GR
JOINER'S CL
WANNIONS CL
LEE FARM CL
BOTLEY LA
BOTLEY RD
BROOMSTICK LA
LINNINGTON AVE
GOOSE ACRE
YEW TREE CL
GROOMS COTTS
Ley Hill Sch
Ley Hill
KILN LA
Crab Tree Farm
Cherry Tree Farm
Maple Hill
Maples Farm
SHANTOCK LA
Game Farm
HOME FARM CT
Home Farm
Mast
155
146

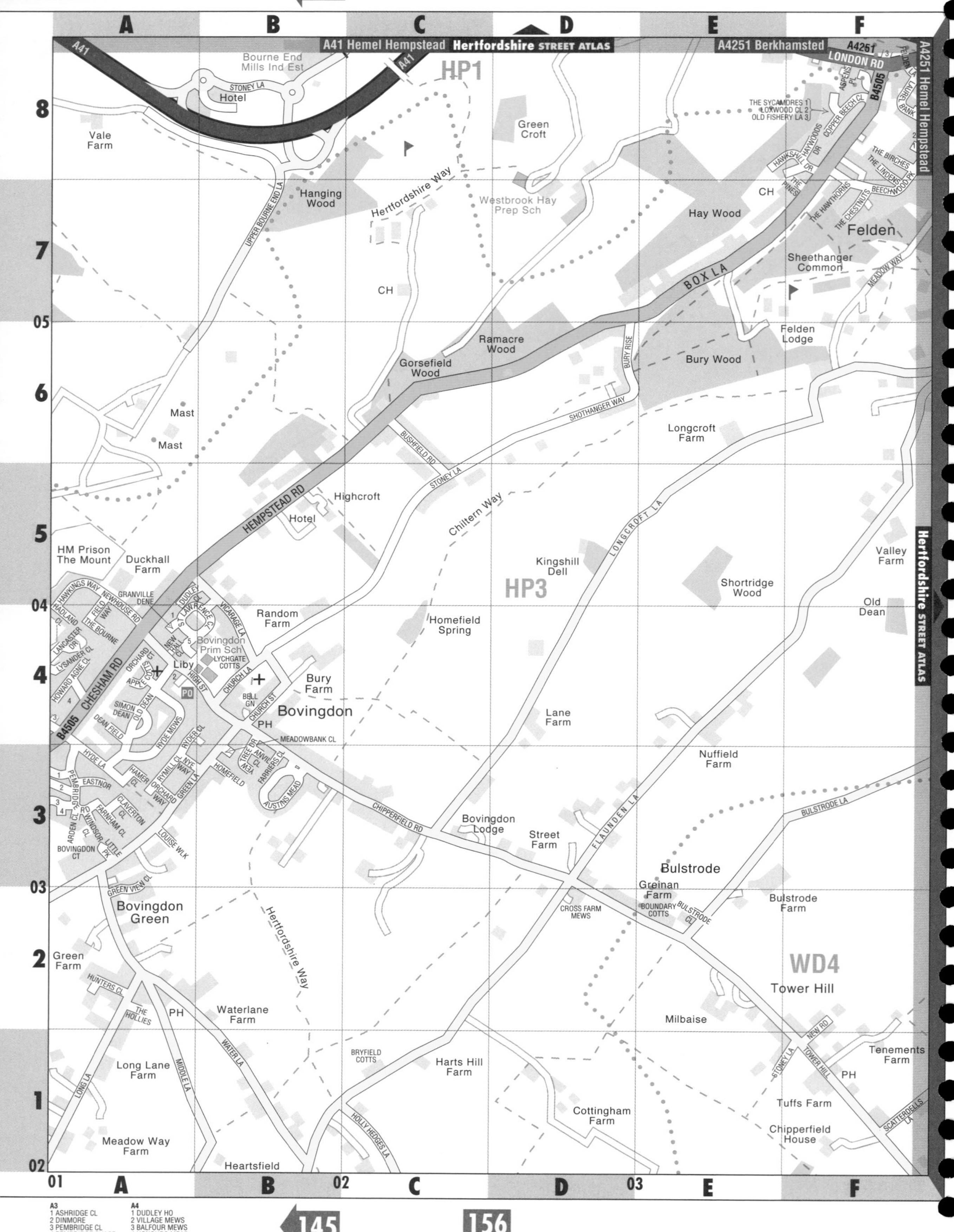

A41 Hemel Hempstead **Hertfordshire** STREET ATLAS   A4251 Berkhamsted

A3
1 ASHRIDGE CL
2 DINMORE
3 PEMBRIDGE CL
4 PEMBRIDGE CHASE

A4
1 DUDLEY HO
2 VILLAGE MEWS
3 BALFOUR MEWS
4 HONOURS MEAD
5 HAMILTON MD

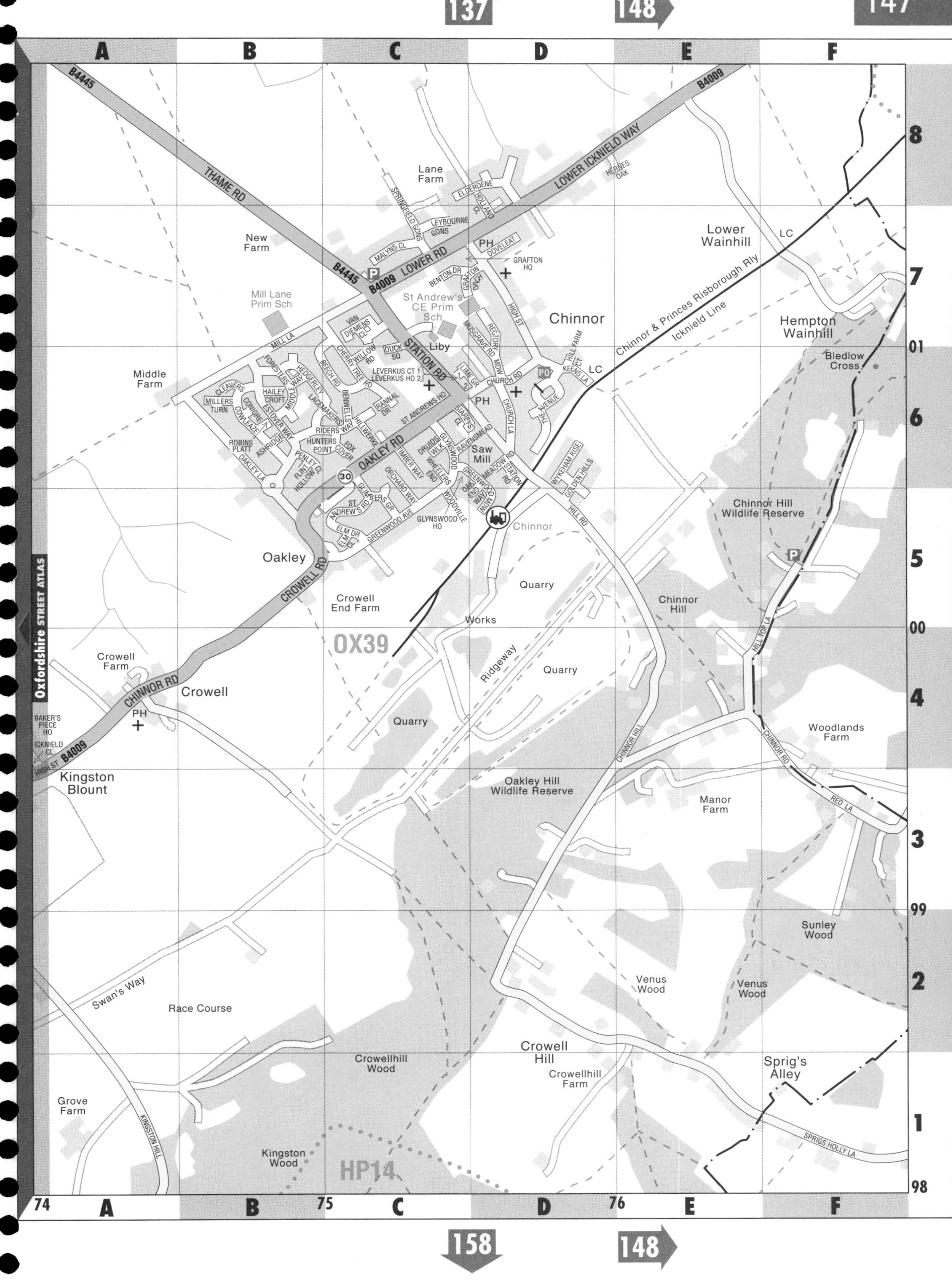
137
148
A
B
C
D
E
F
B4445
B4009
THAME RD
LOWER ICKNIELD WAY
Lane Farm
New Farm
Lower Wainhill
Mill Lane Prim Sch
St Andrew's CE Prim Sch
Chinnor
Hempton Wainhill
Chinnor & Princes Risborough Rly
Icknield Line
Bledlow Cross
Middle Farm
STATION RD
LOWER RD
OAKLEY RD
Saw Mill
Chinnor
Oakley
CROWELL RD
Crowell End Farm
Quarry
Works
OX39
Chinnor Hill Wildlife Reserve
Chinnor Hill
HILL TOP LA
Crowell Farm
Crowell
CHINNOR RD
Ridgeway
Quarry
Woodlands Farm
Kingston Blount
Oakley Hill Wildlife Reserve
Manor Farm
RED LA
Sunley Wood
Swan's Way
Race Course
Venus Wood
Venus Wood
Crowell Hill
Crowellhill Farm
Crowellhill Wood
Sprig's Alley
Grove Farm
KINGSTON HILL
Kingston Wood
HP14
SPRIGS HOLLY LA
CHINNOR HILL
HILL RD
Oxfordshire STREET ATLAS
8
7
01
6
5
00
4
3
99
2
1
98
74
75
76
158
148

147 138

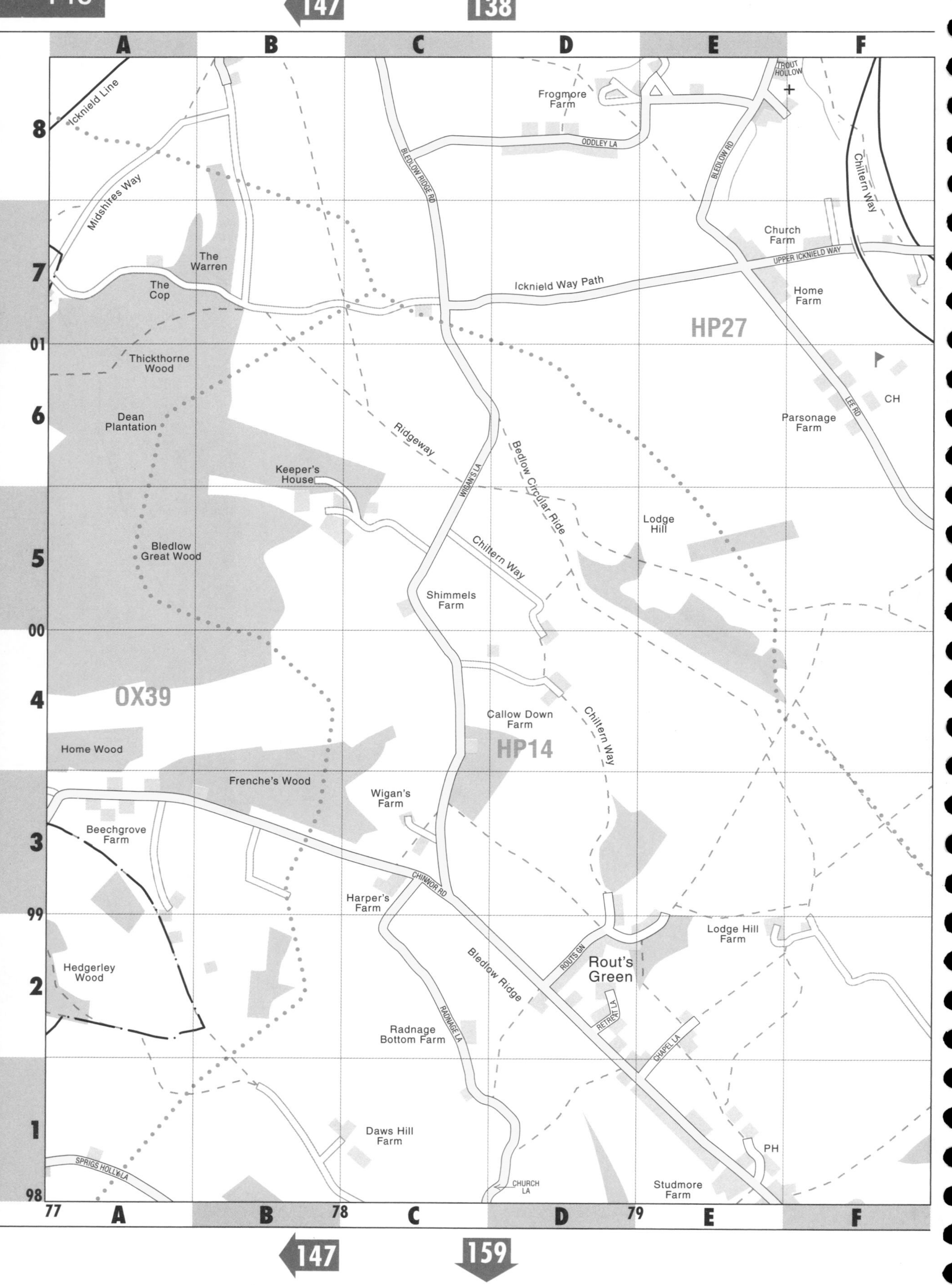
Icknield Line
Midshires Way
The Warren
The Cop
Thickthorne Wood
Dean Plantation
Keeper's House
Bledlow Great Wood
OX39
Home Wood
Frenche's Wood
Beechgrove Farm
Hedgerley Wood
SPRIGS HOLLY LA
Frogmore Farm
ODDLEY LA
BLEDLOW RIDGE RD
BLEDLOW RD
TROUT HOLLOW
Chiltern Way
Church Farm
UPPER ICKNIELD WAY
Icknield Way Path
Home Farm
HP27
LEE RD
CH
Parsonage Farm
Ridgeway
WIGAN'S LA
Bedlow Circular Ride
Lodge Hill
Chiltern Way
Shimmels Farm
Callow Down Farm
HP14
Chiltern Way
Wigan's Farm
CHINNOR RD
Harper's Farm
Bledlow Ridge
ROUTS GN
Rout's Green
RETREAT LA
CHAPEL LA
Lodge Hill Farm
RADNAGE LA
Radnage Bottom Farm
Daws Hill Farm
CHURCH LA
Studmore Farm
PH
A
B
C
D
E
F
8
7
01
6
5
00
4
3
99
2
1
98
77
78
79

147 159

139
150

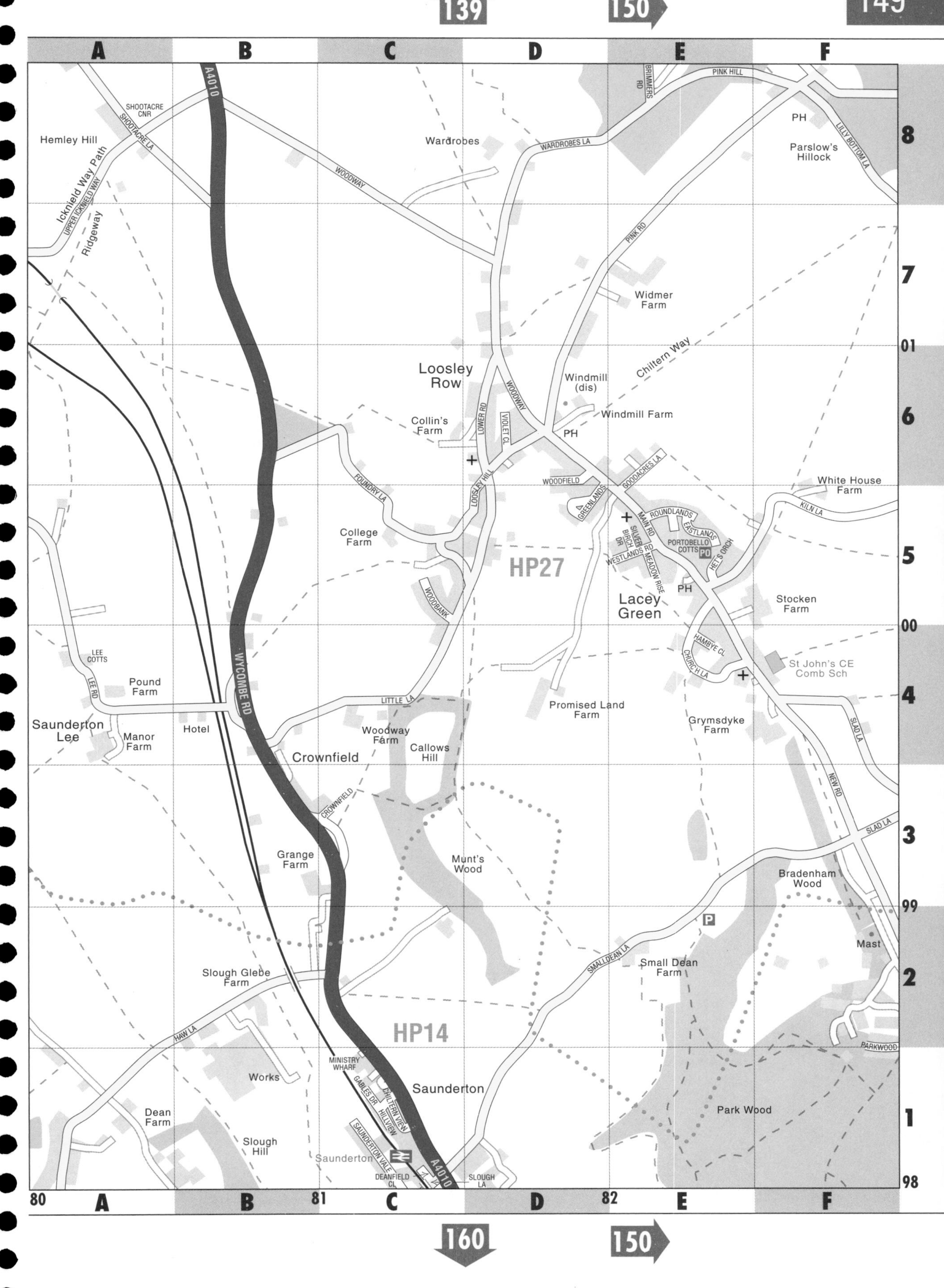
A
B
C
D
E
F
8
7
01
6
5
00
4
3
99
2
1
98
80
81
82
Hemley Hill
SHOOTACRE CNR
SHOOTACRE LA
Icknield Way Path
UPPER ICKNIELD WAY
Ridgeway
A4010
WOODWAY
Wardrobes
WARDROBES LA
BRIMMERS RD
PINK HILL
PH
Parslow's Hillock
LILLY BOTTOM LA
PINK RD
Widmer Farm
Chiltern Way
Loosley Row
Windmill (dis)
Windmill Farm
Collin's Farm
LOWER RD
VIOLET CL
WOODWAY
PH
LOOSLEY HILL
FOUNDRY LA
WOODFIELD
GOODACRES LA
GREENLANDS
White House Farm
KILN LA
MAIN RD
ROUNDLANDS
EASTLANDS
BIRCH DR
SILVER
PORTOBELLO COTTS
PO
HET'S ORCH
WESTLANDS RD
MEADOW RISE
College Farm
HP27
WOODBANK
Lacey Green
PH
Stocken Farm
HAMBYE CL
CHURCH LA
St John's CE Comb Sch
LEE COTTS
LEE RD
Pound Farm
WYCOMBE RD
LITTLE LA
Promised Land Farm
Grymsdyke Farm
SLAD LA
Saunderton Lee
Manor Farm
Hotel
Woodway Farm
Callows Hill
Crownfield
NEW RD
CROWNFIELD
SLAD LA
Grange Farm
Munt's Wood
Bradenham Wood
P
Mast
SMALLDEAN LA
Small Dean Farm
Slough Glebe Farm
HAW LA
HP14
PARKWOOD
MINISTRY WHARF
Works
GABLES DR
CHILTERN VIEW
HILLVIEW
Saunderton
Park Wood
Dean Farm
Slough Hill
SAUNDERTON VALE
Saunderton
DEANFIELD CL
A4010
SLOUGH LA

160
150

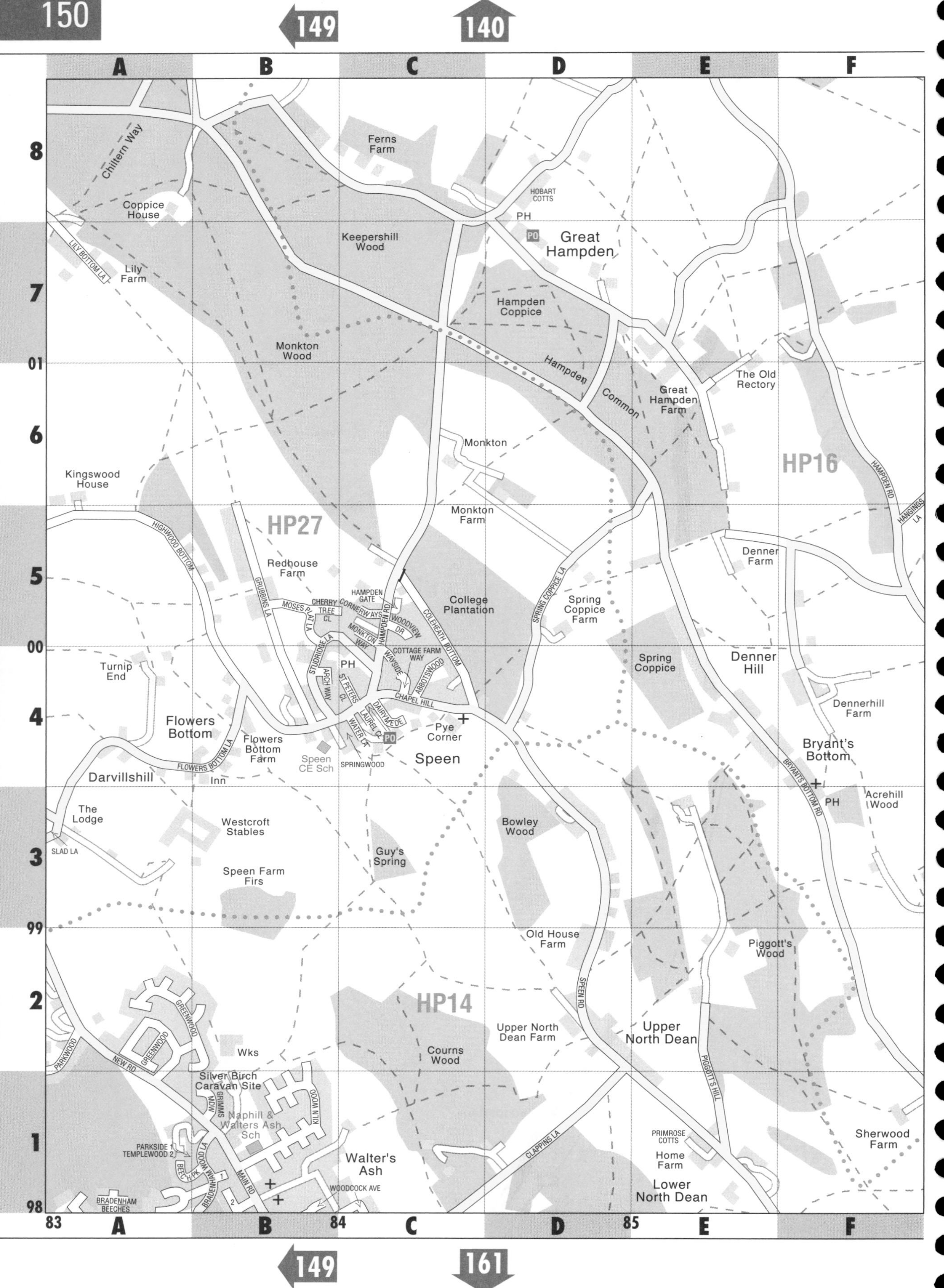

149
140

A **B** **C** **D** **E** **F**

8

Chiltern Way

Coppice House

Ferns Farm

Keepershill Wood

HOBART COTTS

PH

PO

Great Hampden

Lily Farm

LILY BOTTOM LA

7

Monkton Wood

Hampden Coppice

01

Hampden

Common

Great Hampden Farm

The Old Rectory

6

Kingswood House

Monkton

Monkton Farm

Great Hampden Farm

HP16

HAMPDEN RD

HANGINGS LA

HP27

Redhouse Farm

HIGHWOOD BOTTOM

GRUBBINS LA

MOSES A LA

CHERRY TREE CL

CORNER

HAMPDEN GATE

NEW WAY S

WOODVIEW DR

COLEHEATH BOTTOM

SPRING COPPICE LA

College Plantation

Spring Coppice Farm

Denner Farm

5

MONKTON WAY

BAYSIDE

ABBOTS WOOD

COTTAGE FARM WAY

Spring Coppice

Denner Hill

00

Turnip End

ARCH WAY

PH

ST PETERS CL

LAUREL CL

WATER LA

LAUREL DE

CHAPEL HILL

Pye Corner

Dennerhill Farm

4

Flowers Bottom

Flowers Bottom Farm

Speen CE Sch

SPRINGWOOD

PO

Speen

Bryant's Bottom

PH

Acrehill Wood

BRYANTS BOTTOM RD

Darvillshill

FLOWERS BOTTOM LA

Inn

The Lodge

SLAD LA

Westcroft Stables

Guy's Spring

Bowley Wood

3

Speen Farm Firs

99

Old House Farm

Piggott's Wood

2

HP14

Courns Wood

Upper North Dean Farm

Upper North Dean

SPEEN RD

PIGGOTTS HILL

PARKWOOD

NEW RD

GREENWOOD

GREENWOOD

Wks

Silver Birch Caravan Site

GRIMMS

MAIN RD

Naphill & Walters Ash Sch

1

PARKSIDE

TEMPLEWOOD

BEECH PK

BRADENHAM WD LA

DOWN TR LA

DOWN N TR LA

Walter's Ash

WOODCOCK AVE

CLAPPINS LA

PRIMROSE COTTS

Home Farm

Lower North Dean

Sherwood Farm

98

BRADENHAM BEECHES

83 **A** **B** 84 **C** **D** 85 **E** **F**

149
161

141 152

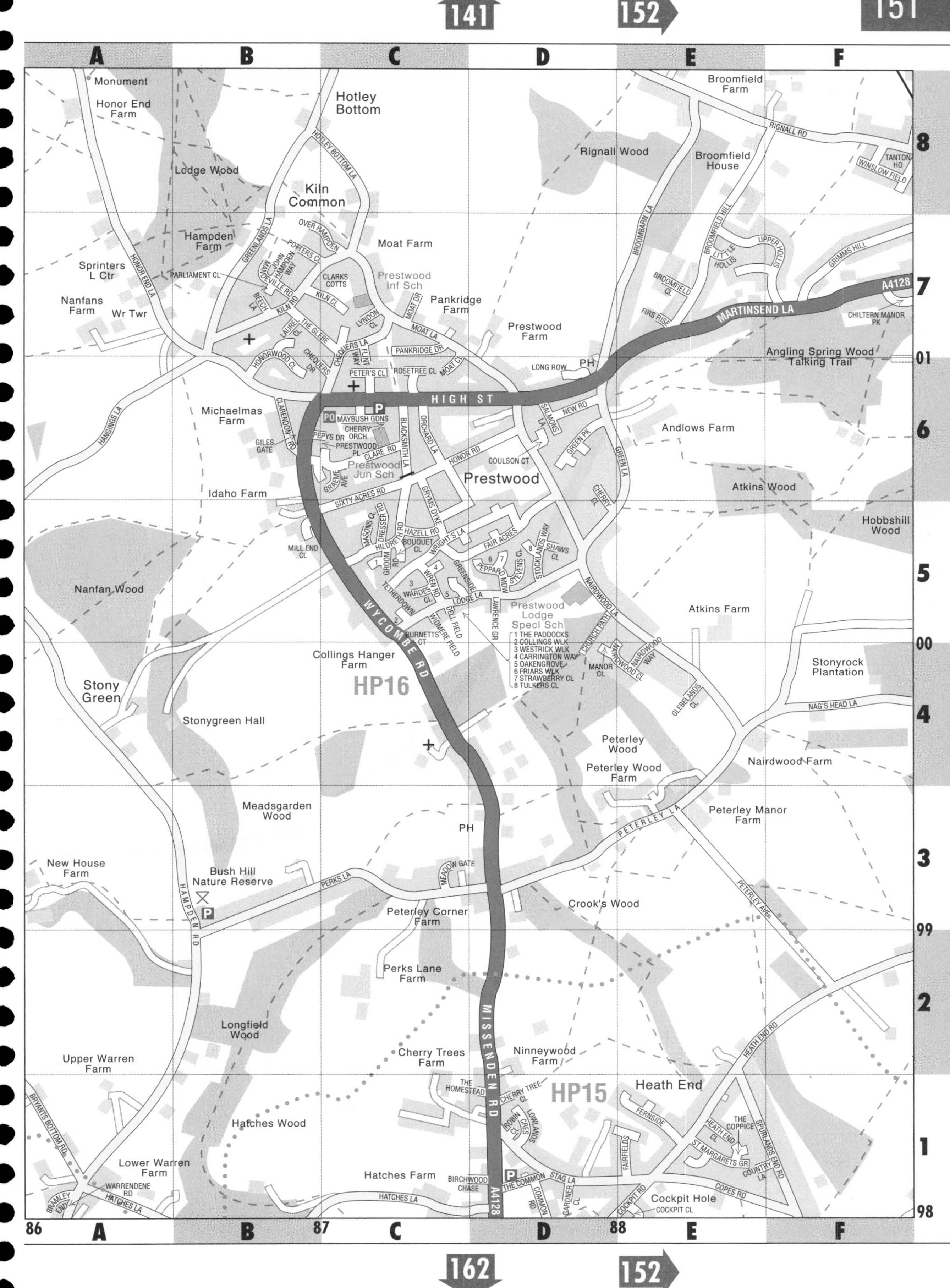
A B C D E F
8 7 01 6 5 00 4 3 99 2 1 98
86 87 88
Monument
Honor End Farm
Hotley Bottom
Broomfield Farm
RIGNALL RD
Rignall Wood
Broomfield House
TANTON HO
WINSLOW FIELD
Lodge Wood
Kiln Common
HOTLEY BOTTOM LA
Hampden Farm
Moat Farm
Sprinters L Ctr
Nanfans Farm
Wr Twr
Prestwood Inf Sch
Pankridge Farm
Prestwood Farm
MARTINSEND LA
A4128
CHILTERN MANOR PK
Angling Spring Wood Talking Trail
HIGH ST
Michaelmas Farm
Andlows Farm
Prestwood
Prestwood Jun Sch
Idaho Farm
Atkins Wood
Hobbshill Wood
Nanfan Wood
Atkins Farm
Prestwood Lodge Specl Sch
1 THE PADDOCKS
2 COLLINGS WLK
3 WESTRICK WLK
4 CARRINGTON WAY
5 OAKENGROVE
6 FRIARS WLK
7 STRAWBERRY CL
8 TULKERS CL
WYCOMBE RD
Collings Hanger Farm
HP16
Stony Green
Stonygreen Hall
Stonyrock Plantation
NAG'S HEAD LA
Peterley Wood
Peterley Wood Farm
Nairdwood Farm
Meadsgarden Wood
PH
Peterley Manor Farm
PETERLEY LA
New House Farm
Bush Hill Nature Reserve
PERKS LA
HAMPDEN RD
Peterley Corner Farm
Crook's Wood
Perks Lane Farm
MISSENDEN RD
Longfield Wood
Upper Warren Farm
Cherry Trees Farm
Ninneywood Farm
HP15
Heath End
HEATH END RD
Hatches Wood
Lower Warren Farm
Hatches Farm
Cockpit Hole
HATCHES LA
BRYANTS BOTTOM RD

162 152

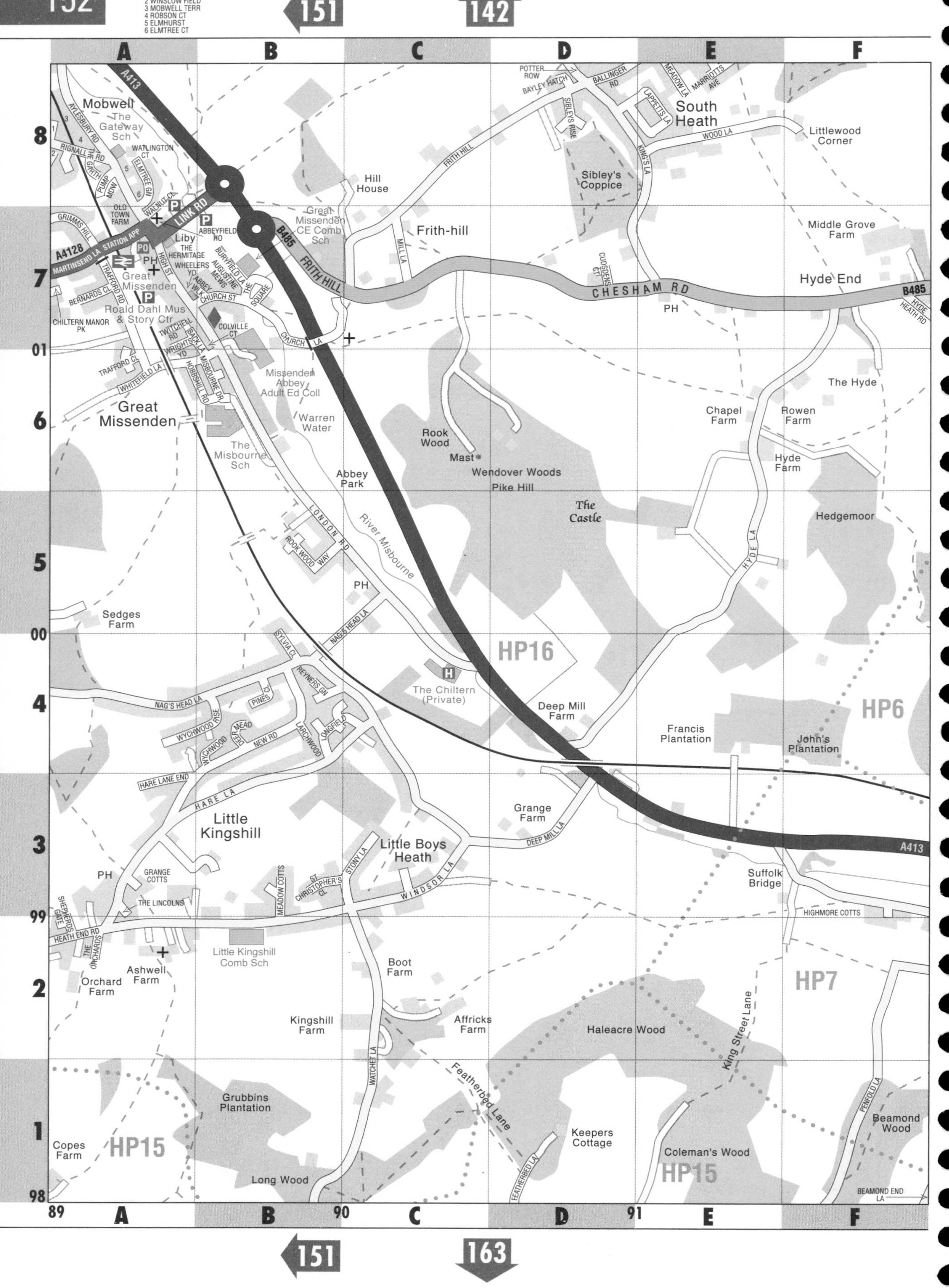

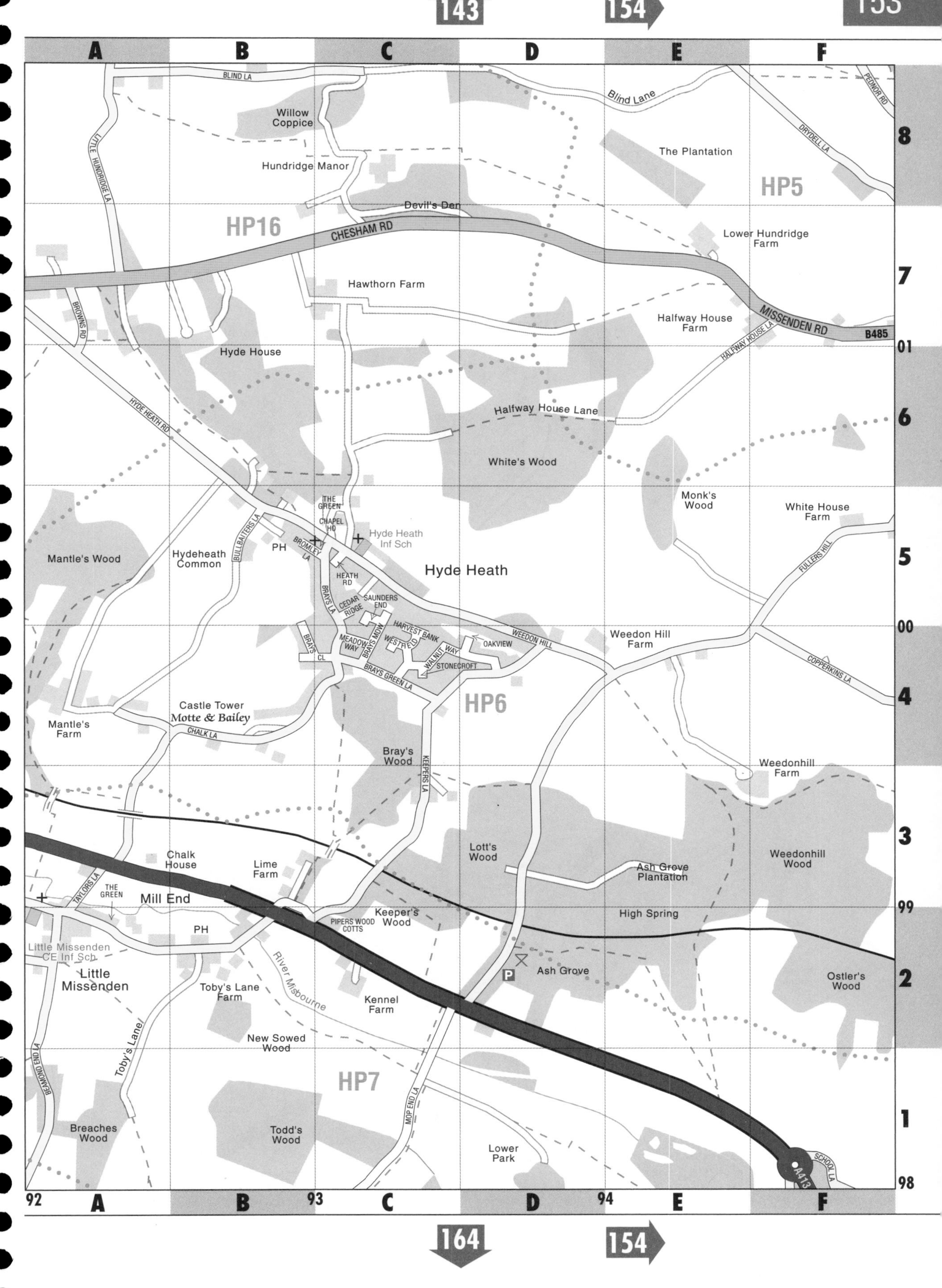
143
154
A
B
C
D
E
F
BLIND LA
Blind Lane
PEDNOR RD
Willow Coppice
DRYDELL LA
The Plantation
Hundridge Manor
LITTLE HUNDRIDGE LA
HP5
Devil's Den
HP16
CHESHAM RD
Lower Hundridge Farm
Hawthorn Farm
BROWNS RD
MISSENDEN RD
B485
Halfway House Farm
HALFWAY HOUSE LA
Hyde House
HYDE HEATH RD
Halfway House Lane
White's Wood
Monk's Wood
White House Farm
THE GREEN
CHAPEL HO
BULLBAITERS LA
Hyde Heath Inf Sch
PH
BROMLEY LA
Mantle's Wood
Hydeheath Common
HEATH RD
Hyde Heath
FULLERS HILL
BRAYS LA
CEDAR RIDGE
SAUNDERS END
Weedon Hill Farm
BRAYS CL
MEADOW WAY
BRAYS MDW
WESTFIELD
HARVEST BANK
WALNUT WAY
OAKVIEW
WEEDON HILL
STONECROFT
COPPERKINS LA
BRAYS GREEN LA
HP6
Castle Tower
Motte & Bailey
Mantle's Farm
CHALK LA
Bray's Wood
KEEPERS LA
Weedonhill Farm
Chalk House
Lime Farm
Lott's Wood
Ash Grove Plantation
Weedonhill Wood
TAYLORS LA
THE GREEN
Mill End
High Spring
PH
PIPERS WOOD COTTS
Keeper's Wood
Little Missenden CE Inf Sch
River Misbourne
Ash Grove
Little Missenden
Toby's Lane Farm
Kennel Farm
Ostler's Wood
New Sowed Wood
Toby's Lane
BEAMOND END LA
HP7
MOP END LA
Breaches Wood
Todd's Wood
Lower Park
SCHOOL LA
A413
8
7
01
6
5
00
4
3
99
2
1
98
92
93
94
164
154

153
144

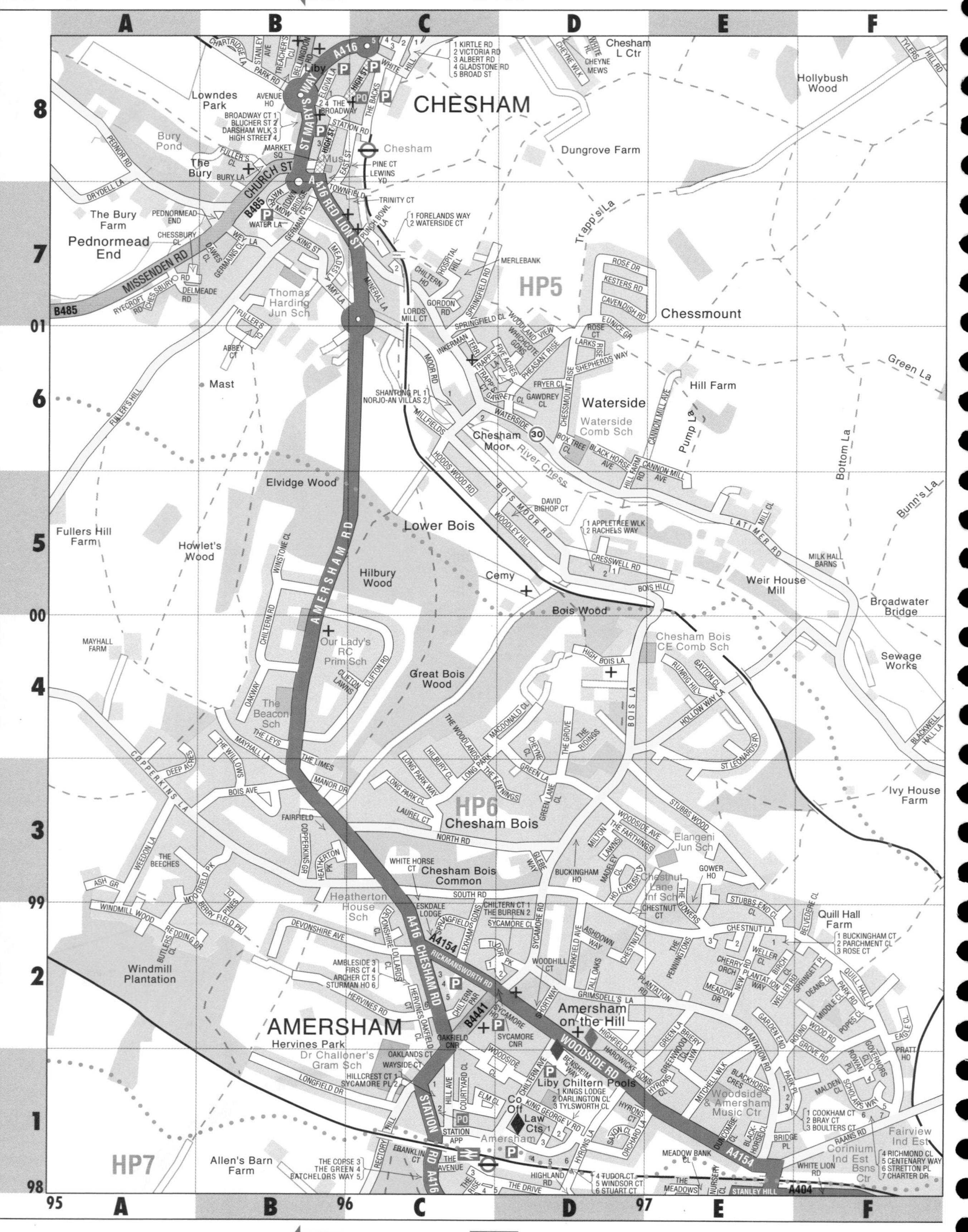
A
B
C
D
E
F
8
7
01
6
5
00
4
3
99
2
1
98
95
96
97
CHESHAM
Chesham L Ctr
Hollybush Wood
Lowndes Park
Bury Pond
The Bury
Chesham
Dungrove Farm
1 KIRTLE RD
2 VICTORIA RD
3 ALBERT RD
4 GLADSTONE RD
5 BROAD ST
CHEYNE MEWS
ST MARY'S WAY
A416
Liby
HIGH ST
THE BACKS
THE BROADWAY
STATION RD
BROADWAY CT 1
BLUCHER ST 2
DARSHAM WLK 3
HIGH STREET 4
MARKET SQ
CHURCH ST
BURY LA
PINE CT
LEWINS YD
TOWNFIELD
TRINITY CT
A416 RED LION ST
1 FORELANDS WAY
2 WATERSIDE CT
The Bury Farm
PEDNORMEAD END
Pednormead End
CHESSBURY CL
MISSENDEN RD
B485
WATER LA
GERMAIN ST
KING ST
Trapp's La
HP5
ROSE DR
KESTERS RD
CAVENDISH RD
Chessmount
EUNICE GR
MERLEBANK
Thomas Harding Jun Sch
DELMEADE RD
RYECROFT RD
FULLER'S CL
ABBEY CT
MINERAL LA
LORDS MILL CT
GORDON RD
SPRINGFIELD RD
SPRINGFIELD CL
INKERMAN TERR
TRAPP'S LA
FIVE ACRES
WOODLAND VIEW
WHICHCOTE GDNS
PHEASANT RISE
ROSE CT
LARKS RISE
SHEPHERDS WAY
Green La
Mast
FULLER'S HILL
MOOR RD
SHANTUNG PL 1
NORJO-AN VILLAS 2
FRYER CL
GAWDREY CL
CHESSMOUNT RISE
Waterside
Waterside Comb Sch
Hill Farm
CANNON MILL AVE
Pump La
MILLFIELDS
Chesham Moor
WATERSIDE
30
River Chess
BOX TREE CL
BLACK HORSE AVE
HILL FARM RD
CANNON MILL AVE
Bottom La
Elvidge Wood
HODDS WOOD RD
BOIS MOOR RD
DAVID BISHOP CT
Bunn's La
Lower Bois
WOODLEY HILL
1 APPLETREE WLK
2 RACHELS WAY
LATIMER RD
MILL CL
Fullers Hill Farm
Howlet's Wood
AMERSHAM RD
WINSTONE CL
Hilbury Wood
Cemy
CRESSWELL RD
BOIS HILL
MILK HALL BARNS
Weir House Mill
Broadwater Bridge
Bois Wood
MAYHALL FARM
CHILTERN RD
Our Lady's RC Prim Sch
CLIFTON RD
CLIFTON LAWNS
Chesham Bois CE Comb Sch
HIGH BOIS LA
RUNRIG HILL
GAYTON CL
Sewage Works
Great Bois Wood
HOLLOW WAY LA
BOIS LA
OAKWAY
The Beacon Sch
THE LEYS
THE WOODLANDS
MACDONALD CL
CHEYNE CL
THE GROVE
THE RIDINGS
ST LEONARDS RD
BLACKWELL HALL LA
COPPERKINS LA
DEEP ACRES
THE WILLOWS
MAYHALL LA
THE LIMES
HILBURY CL
LONG PARK
GREEN LA
LONG PARK WAY
THE PENNINGS
GREEN LANE CL
MANOR DR
BOIS AVE
LONG PARK CL
Ivy House Farm
HP6
Chesham Bois
LAUREL CT
FAIRFIELD
COPPERKINS GR
NORTH RD
STUBBS WOOD
WOODSIDE AVE
THE FARTHINGS
Elangeni Jun Sch
WEEDON LA
THE BEECHES
HEATHERTON PK
WHITE HORSE CT
Chesham Bois Common
GLEBE WAY
BUCKINGHAM HO
MILTON LAWNS
MADELEY CL
HOLLYBUSH LA
Chestnut Lane Inf Sch
GOWER HO
ASH GR
WOODFIELD PK
PINES CL
SOUTH RD
Heatherton House Sch
THE BOWERS
STUBBS END CL
BELVEDERE CL
Quill Hall Farm
WINDMILL WOOD
BERRY FIELD PK
ESKDALE LODGE
CHILTERN CT 1
THE BURREN 2
CHESTNUT CT
CHESTNUT LA
1 BUCKINGHAM CT
2 PARCHMENT CL
3 ROSE CT
REDDING DR
DEVONSHIRE AVE
DEVONSHIRE CL
SPRINGFIELDS
LEXHAM GDNS
SYCAMORE CL
SYCAMORE RD
PARKFIELD AVE
ASHDOWN WAY
CHESTNUT CL
THE PENNINGTONS
CHERRY ORCH
WELLER CL
BIRCH
SPRINGETT PL
QUILL HALL LA
BUTLERS CL
A4154
TUDOR PK
WOODHILL CT
PLANTATION WAY
NEW RD
WELLER RD
DEANS CL
PARK RD
Windmill Plantation
AMBLESIDE 3
FIRS CT 4
ARCHER CT 5
STURMAN HO 6
LOLLARDS
A416 CHESHAM RD
RICKMANSWORTH RD
TALL OAKS
PLANTATION RD
MEADOW DR
MIDDLE CL
SHORTWAY
GRIMSDELL'S LA
Amersham on the Hill
HERVINES RD
HERVINES CT
CHILTERN PAR
B4441
SYCAMORE HO
GREEN LA
BRIERY WAY
GARDEN END
ROUND WOOD RD
POPES CL
EAGLE CL
AMERSHAM
Hervines Park
OAKFIELD CL
OAKFIELD CNR
SYCAMORE CNR
HIGHFIELD CL
HARDWICK GDNS
WOODSIDE RD
GROVE RD
ROWAN CL
GOVERNORS CL
PRATT HO
Dr Challoner's Gram Sch
OAKLANDS CT
WAYSIDE CT
WOODSIDE
CHILTERN AVE
BENSHEIM WAY
HYRONS CT
GREENWOOD
PLANTATION RD
LONGFIELD DR
HILLCREST CT 1
SYCAMORE PL 2
HILL AVE
COURTYARD CL
Liby Chiltern Pools
1 KINGS LODGE
2 DARLINGTON CL
3 TYLSWORTH CL
MITCHELL WLK
BLACKHORSE CRES
Woodside & Amersham Music Ctr
PARK PL
MALDEN CL
SCHOLARS WAY
ELM CL
Co Off
KING GEORGE V RD
HYRONS CL
1 COOKHAM CT
2 BRAY CT
3 BOULTERS CT
Fairview Ind Est
STATION
Law Cts
SAXON CL
ORCHARD LA
DUNCOMBE CL
BLACKHORSE CL
RAANS RD
HILL
STATION APP
Amersham
HYRONS LA
BRIDGE PL
Corinium Ind Est
Bsns Ctr
4 RICHMOND CL
5 CENTENARY WAY
6 STRETTON PL
7 CHARTER DR
HP7
Allen's Barn Farm
THE COPSE 3
THE GREEN 4
BATCHELORS WAY 5
RECTORY
FRANKLIN CT
THE AVENUE
STATION RD A416
THE RISE
THE DRIVE
HIGHLAND RD
4 TUDOR CT
5 WINDSOR CT
6 STUART CT
MEADOW BANK CL
THE MEADOWS
NURSERY CL
A4154
WHITE LION RD
STANLEY HILL
A404

153
165

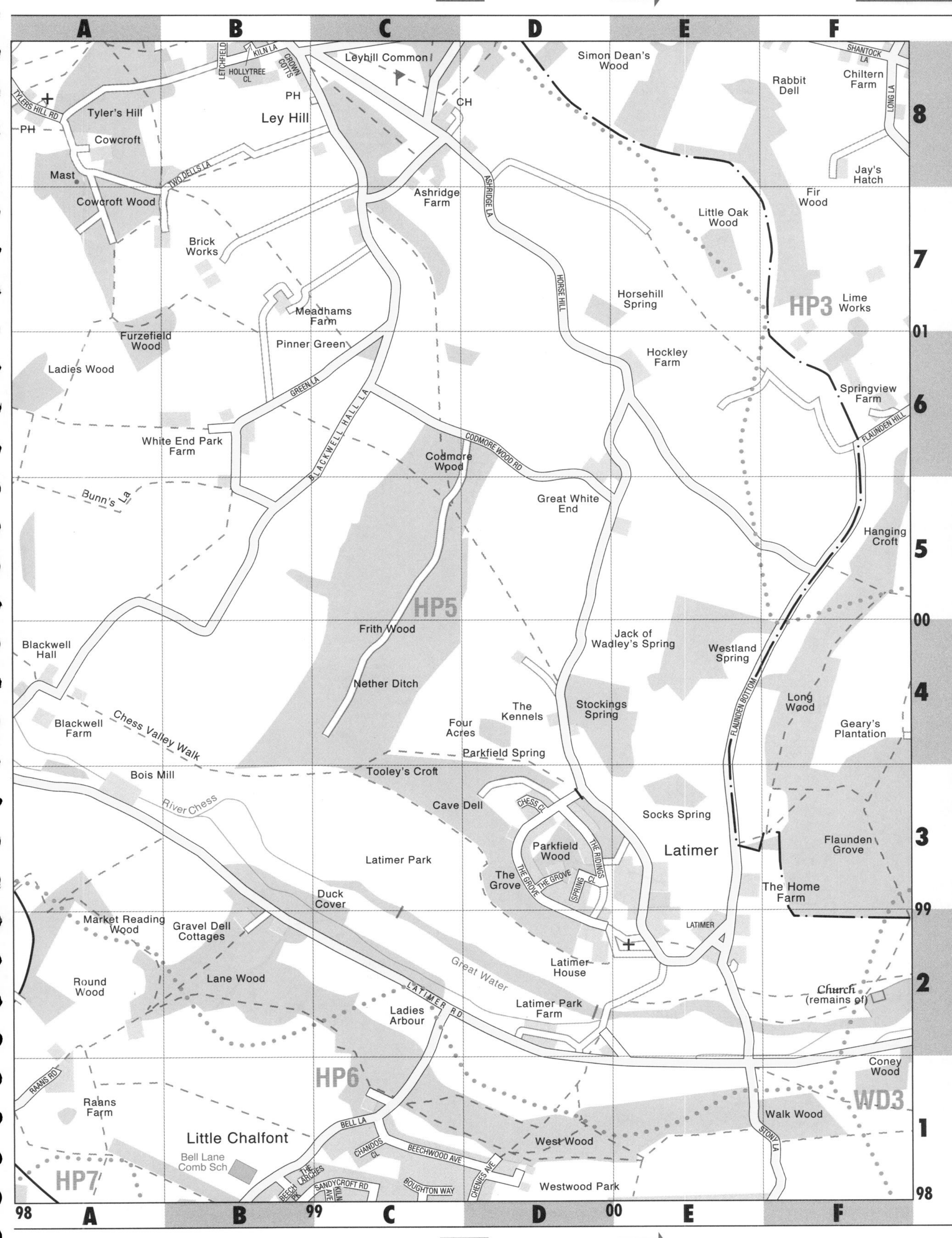
A B C D E F
8 7 01 6 5 00 4 3 99 2 1 98
Leyhill Common
Simon Dean's Wood
Rabbit Dell
Chiltern Farm
Tyler's Hill
Ley Hill
Cowcroft
Mast
Cowcroft Wood
Ashridge Farm
Jay's Hatch
Fir Wood
Little Oak Wood
Brick Works
Horsehill Spring
Meadhams Farm
HP3
Lime Works
Furzefield Wood
Pinner Green
Hockley Farm
Ladies Wood
Springview Farm
White End Park Farm
Codmore Wood
Great White End
Bunn's La
Hanging Croft
HP5
Frith Wood
Jack of Wadley's Spring
Westland Spring
Blackwell Hall
Nether Ditch
Long Wood
Blackwell Farm
Chess Valley Walk
The Kennels
Four Acres
Stockings Spring
Geary's Plantation
Parkfield Spring
Bois Mill
Tooley's Croft
River Chess
Cave Dell
Socks Spring
Parkfield Wood
Latimer
Flaunden Grove
Latimer Park
The Grove
The Home Farm
Duck Cover
Market Reading Wood
Gravel Dell Cottages
Latimer House
Great Water
Round Wood
Lane Wood
Church (remains of)
Ladies Arbour
Latimer Park Farm
Coney Wood
HP6
WD3
Raans Farm
Walk Wood
Little Chalfont
West Wood
Bell Lane Comb Sch
HP7
Westwood Park
98 99 00

155
146

A B C D E F

8 7 01 6 5 00 4 3 99 2 1 98

Oxgate Farm
Venus Hill
Venus Hill Dairy Farm
MIDDLE LA
VENUS HILL
HOLLY HEDGES LA
Hollow Hedge
Braziers Farm
TOWER HILL
Chipperfield
New Maulden Farm
Chiltern Way
Woodman's Wood
WD4
Rose Farm
Caravan Site
Hogpits Bottom
FLAUNDEN LA
Woodman's Farm
LONG LA
HOGPITS BOTTOM
PH
OLLEBERRIE LA
DUNNY LA
WINDMILL HILL
THE COMMON
Lower Plantation
Cherry Trees Farm
WINDMILL HILL
LITTLE WINDMILL HILL
BIRCH LA
Dale Farm
Holly Hedges
Perman's Green
Sharlow's Farm
BELSIZE COTTS
PH
HP3
Belsize
FLAUNDEN HILL
PH
Whitedell Farm
FLAUNDEN LA
POLES HILL
BRAGMANS LA
PLOUGH LA
Newhouse Farm
Flaunden
Rose Hall Farm
Bragman's Farm
Rosehall Wood
Hollin's Hall
Moonshine Farm
Hertfordshire STREET ATLAS
Wireless Station
Great Sarratt Hall
Mast
Chiltern Way
Mast
Oldcroft Wood
Sarratt
HP5
Hanginglane Wood
Bramble Croft
Martin Top Farm
Oldfield Spring
MOOR LA
Limeshill Wood
Baldwin's Wood
DAWES LA
Dawes Common
WARDS DR
DOWNER DR
Valley Farm
Wallace's Wood
WD3
Old Rectory
Ford
Mill Farm
Chenies Bottom
River Chess
Mount Wood
Sarratt Bottom
HOLLOWAY LA
Chenies Place
Chenies
PH
CHURCH LA
Church End
Manor House
Mountwood Farm
CHURCH END COTTS
Chenies Comb Sch
Goldingtons
Nicholas Spring
Hotel
Greathouse Farm
BEDFORD CL
PH
Turveylane Wood
Wyburn Wood
NEW RD
Chiltern Way

01 A B 02 C D 03 E F

155
167

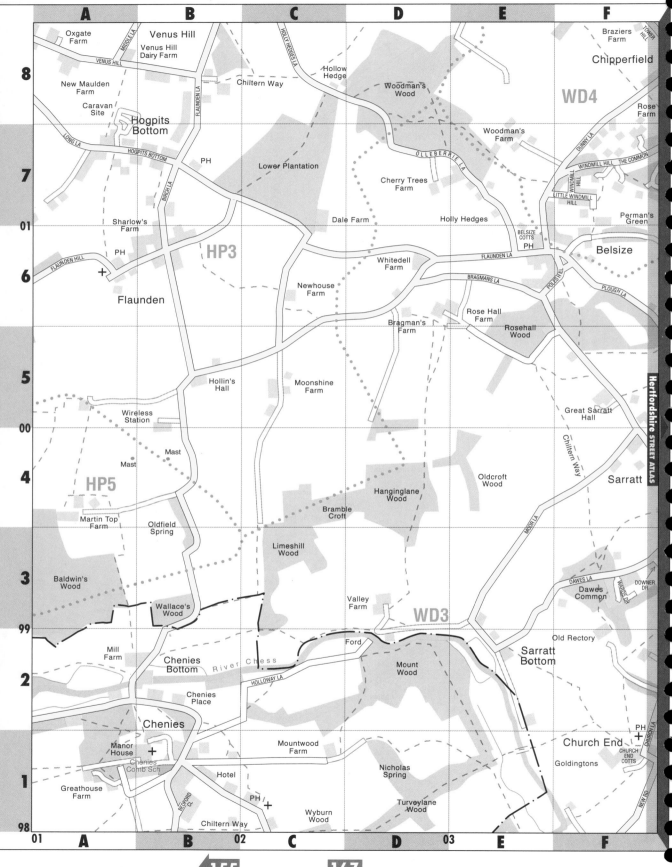

158

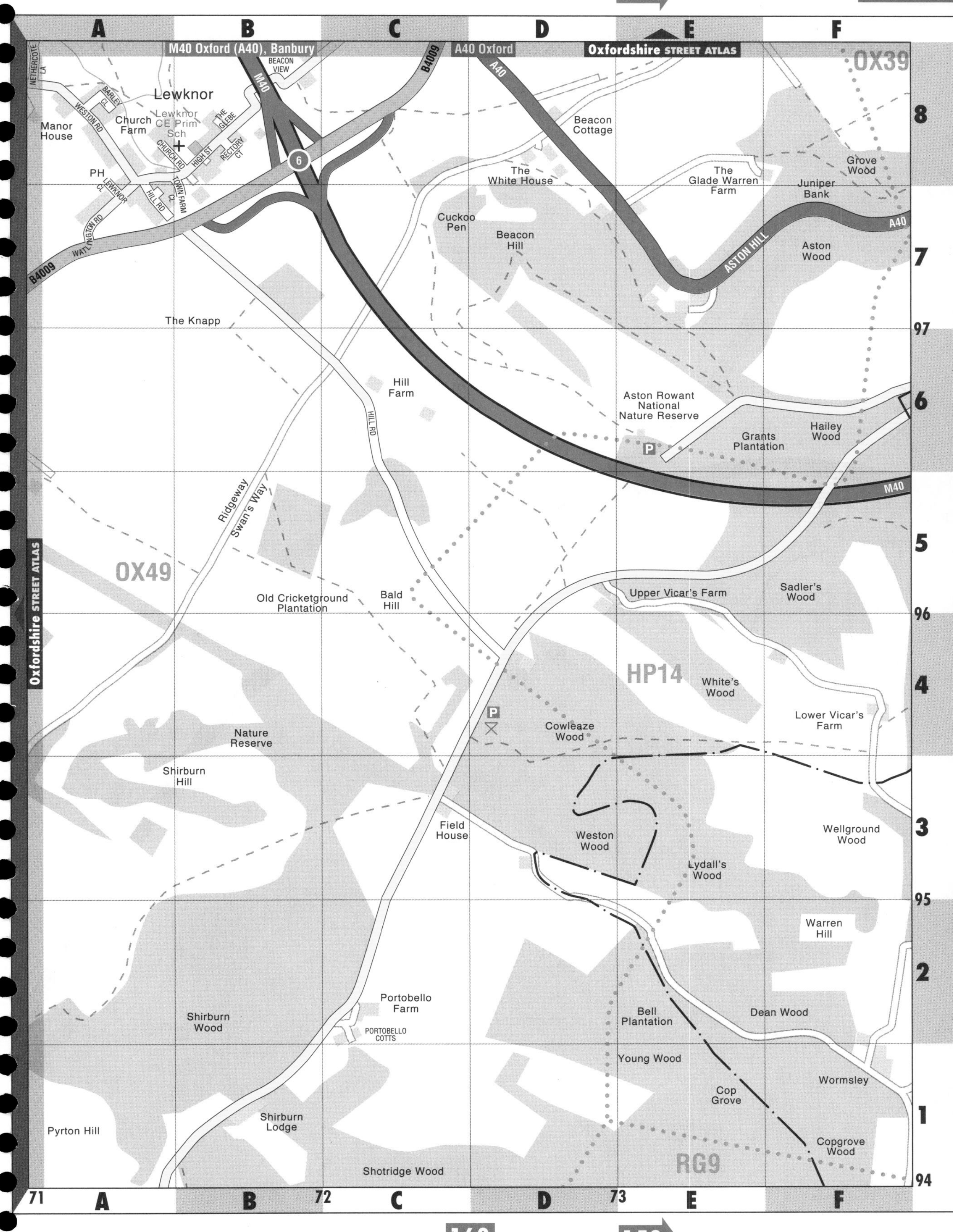
A
B
C
D
E
F
M40 Oxford (A40), Banbury
A40 Oxford
Oxfordshire STREET ATLAS
OX39
8
7
97
6
5
96
4
3
95
2
1
94
Lewknor
Lewknor CE Prim Sch
Manor House
Church Farm
PH
BARLEY CL
WESTON RD
THE GLEBE
CHURCH RD
HIGH ST
RECTORY CT
LEWKNOR CL
HILL RD
TOWN FARM CL
WATLINGTON RD
B4009
NETHERCOTE LA
BEACON VIEW
M40
A40
6
Beacon Cottage
The White House
The Glade Warren Farm
Grove Wood
Juniper Bank
Cuckoo Pen
Beacon Hill
ASTON HILL
Aston Wood
The Knapp
Hill Farm
HILL RD
Aston Rowant National Nature Reserve
Grants Plantation
Hailey Wood
P
M40
Ridgeway
Swan's Way
OX49
Old Cricketground Plantation
Bald Hill
Upper Vicar's Farm
Sadler's Wood
HP14
White's Wood
Lower Vicar's Farm
P
Cowleaze Wood
Nature Reserve
Shirburn Hill
Field House
Weston Wood
Lydall's Wood
Wellground Wood
Warren Hill
Portobello Farm
PORTOBELLO COTTS
Shirburn Wood
Bell Plantation
Dean Wood
Young Wood
Wormsley
Cop Grove
Shirburn Lodge
Pyrton Hill
Copgrove Wood
Shotridge Wood
RG9
71
72
73
Oxfordshire STREET ATLAS

168
158

157 147

OX39
Kingston Grove
Grove Wood

Collier's Lane
High Wood
Crowell Wood
OX39

Gurdon's Farm
Lott Wood
Collier's Lane
Beechwood Shaw

A40
ASTON HILL
Aston Wood
Hawing Wood
Stockfield Wood
Hallbottom Farm

Hill Farm
BUTTERLY RD

Mast
Radio Station
OXFORD RD
Kiln Farm

Mallard's Court

M40
Wood Farm
BOWLING GN 1
CHURCH PATH 2
LOWER CHURCH ST 3
PARK LANE CT 4
KARENZA 5
STOCKFIELDS PL 6

PARK LA
Stokenchurch

North Remlets Wood
Stokenchurch Prim Sch

Hailey Wood
OXFORD RD
1 CURZON GATE CT
2 BRITNELL CT
3 MILESTONE CL
4 FERNDALE CL
5 HART MOOR CL
6 FOWLERS FARM RD

Langleygreen Plantation
CRICKET GROUND
COOPER'S COURT RD
PH
Lib
GEORGE RD
TIPPING WAY

MILL LA
GREEN LA
Independent Bsns Pk
PO
C R Bates Ind Est
B482
WYCOMBE RD
A40

CHILTERN RISE
HORNSLEY GDNS
STUDDRIDGE CT
Coopers Court Farm
COLLIER RD
PARRS RD
SLADE RD

Wallace Hill
HP14
Little Studdridge
Chiltern Way
Bissomhill Shaw
ST HUGH'S CL

BISTONE ROAD
HARCOURT RD
MARLOW RD

Wellground Farm
Studdridge Farm
Saunders Wood Copse
JUBILEE RD
NEW RD
EASTWOOD RD

Bowley's Wood
M40

Coombe Wood
Commonhill Wood
Penley Farm
PENDLES PADDOCK
B482

Commonhill Wood
Hartmoor Wood
Penley Wood

74
75
76

157 169

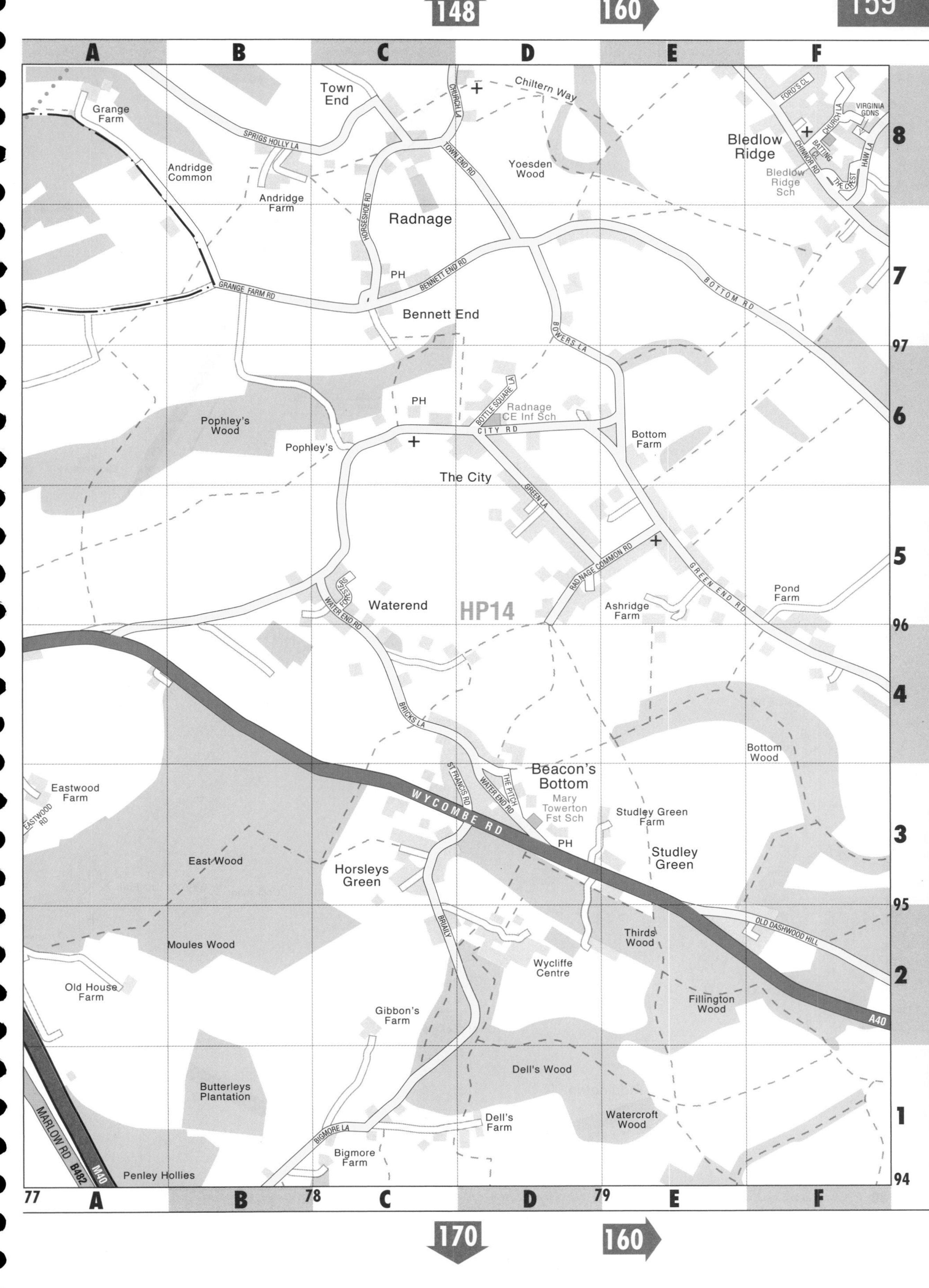

A **B** **C** **D** **E** **F**

Grange Farm

Town End

Chiltern Way

Sprigs Holly La

Andridge Common

Andridge Farm

Yoesden Wood

Bledlow Ridge

Fords Cl

Virginia Gdns

Church Rd

Batting

Haw La

The Crest

Virginia Gdns

Bledlow Ridge Sch

Cannon Rd

8

Radnage

Horseshoe Rd

Town End Rd

Churchla

Bottom Rd

7

PH

Grange Farm Rd

Bennett End Rd

Bennett End

Bowers La

97

Pophley's Wood

PH

Bottle Square La

Radnage CE Inf Sch

City Rd

Bottom Farm

6

Pophley's

The City

Green La

Radnage Common Rd

Green End Rd

5

Waterend

HP14

Ashridge Farm

Pond Farm

Water End Rd

96

Bricks La

Bottom Wood

4

Eastwood Farm

Eastwood Rd

East Wood

St Francis Rd

Wycombe Rd

The Pitch

Water End Rd

Beacon's Bottom

Mary Towerton Fst Sch

Studley Green Farm

Studley Green

3

Horsleys Green

PH

95

Moules Wood

Braily

Thirds Wood

Old Dashwood Hill

2

Old House Farm

Gibbon's Farm

Wycliffe Centre

Fillington Wood

A40

Butterleys Plantation

Dell's Wood

Watercroft Wood

1

Marlow Rd

B482

M40

Bigmore La

Dell's Farm

Penley Hollies

Bigmore Farm

94

159
149

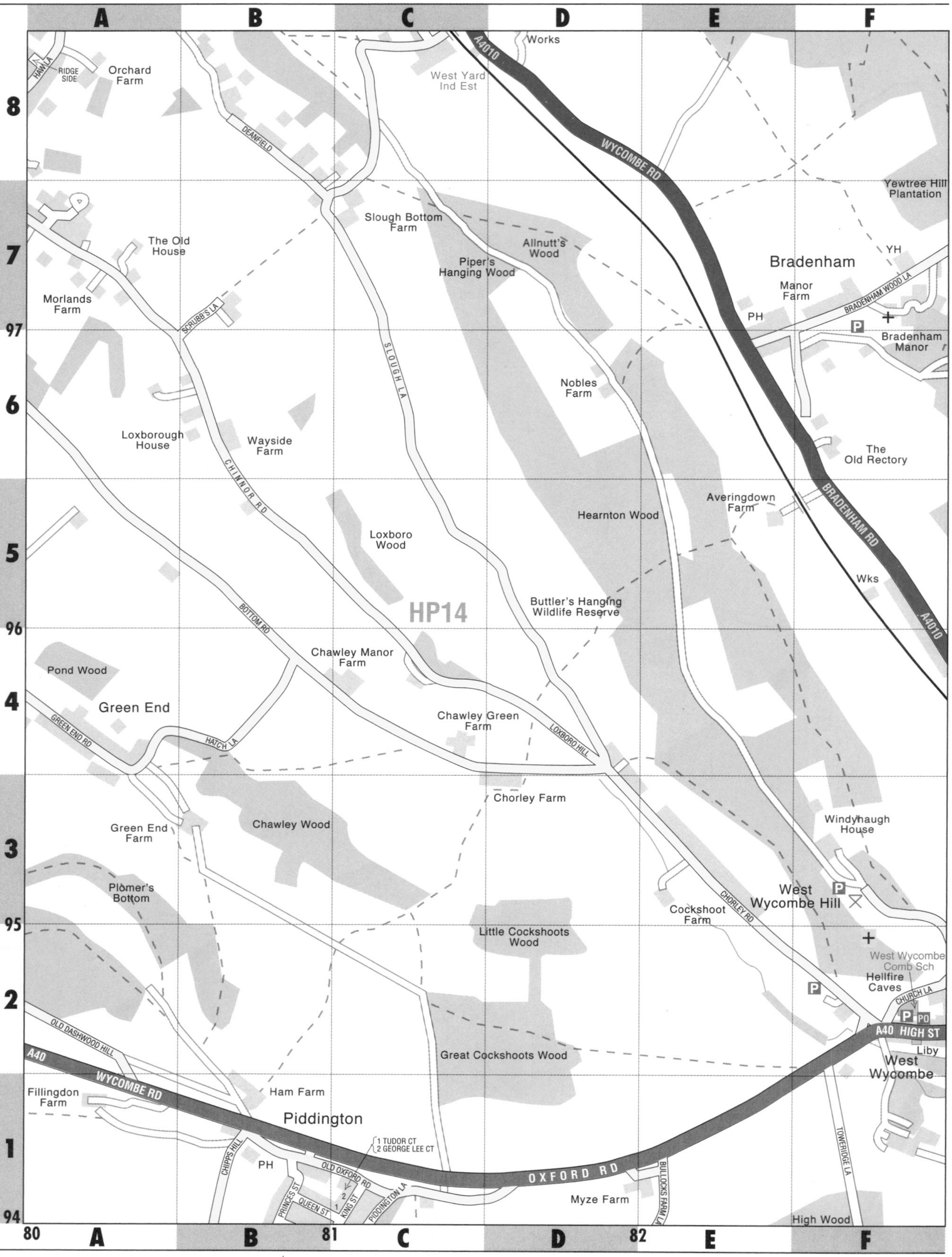

A   B   C   D   E   F

8

7

97

6

96

5

96

4

95

2

1

94

HP14

Works

West Yard Ind Est

WYCOMBE RD

A4010

RIDGE SIDE

HAM LA

Orchard Farm

DEANFIELD

Slough Bottom Farm

Piper's Hanging Wood

Allnutt's Wood

Bradenham

Yewtree Hill Plantation

YH

The Old House

Morlands Farm

SCRUBBS LA

Manor Farm

PH

BRADENHAM WOOD LA

Bradenham Manor

Nobles Farm

Loxborough House

Wayside Farm

SLOUGH LA

CHINNOR RD

The Old Rectory

Loxboro Wood

Hearnton Wood

Averingdown Farm

BRADENHAM RD

A4010

Pond Wood

BOTTOM RD

Chawley Manor Farm

Buttler's Hanging Wildlife Reserve

Wks

Green End

GREEN END RD

HATCH LA

Chawley Green Farm

LOXBORO HILL

Chawley Wood

Chorley Farm

Windyhaugh House

Green End Farm

Plomer's Bottom

Little Cockshoots Wood

Cockshoot Farm

CHORLEY RD

West Wycombe Hill

P

West Wycombe Comb Sch

Hellfire Caves

CHURCH LA

OLD DASHWOOD HILL

A40

WYCOMBE RD

Ham Farm

Great Cockshoots Wood

P

A40 HIGH ST

Liby

West Wycombe

Fillingdon Farm

CHIPPS HILL

PH

PRINCES ST

QUEEN ST

KING ST

OLD OXFORD RD

PIDDINGTON LA

Piddington

1 TUDOR CT
2 GEORGE LEE CT

OXFORD RD

BULLOCKS FARM LA

TOWERIDGE LA

Myze Farm

High Wood

80   A   B   81   C   D   82   E   F

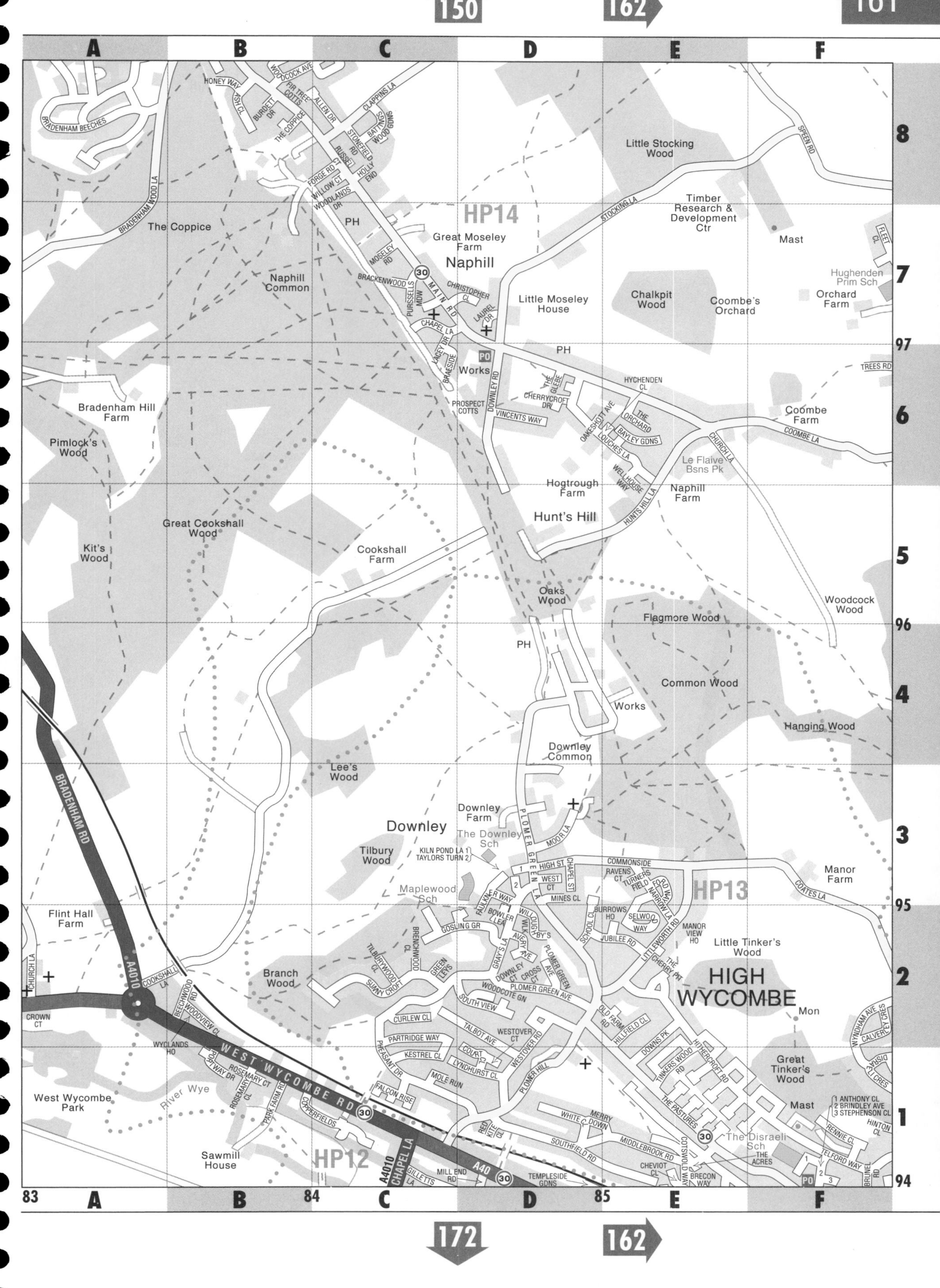
150
162
A
B
C
D
E
F
8
7
97
6
5
96
4
3
95
2
1
94
83
84
85
HP14
HP13
HP12
Naphill
Naphill Common
The Coppice
Great Moseley Farm
Little Moseley House
Little Stocking Wood
Timber Research & Development Ctr
Mast
Hughenden Prim Sch
Orchard Farm
Chalkpit Wood
Coombe's Orchard
Works
Bradenham Hill Farm
Pimlock's Wood
Coombe Farm
Le Flaive Bsns Pk
Naphill Farm
Hogtrough Farm
Hunt's Hill
Great Cookshall Wood
Kit's Wood
Cookshall Farm
Oaks Wood
Flagmore Wood
Woodcock Wood
Common Wood
Hanging Wood
Downley Common
Lee's Wood
Downley Farm
Downley
The Downley Sch
Tilbury Wood
Maplewood Sch
Manor Farm
Flint Hall Farm
Little Tinker's Wood
Branch Wood
HIGH WYCOMBE
Mon
Great Tinker's Wood
West Wycombe Park
River Wye
Sawmill House
The Disraeli Sch
BRADENHAM RD
WEST WYCOMBE RD
A4010
A40
STOCKING LA
SPEEN RD
MAIN RD
DOWNLEY RD
CHURCH LA
COOMBE LA
HUNTS HILL LA
PLOMER GREEN LA
HIGH ST
COMMONSIDE
COATES LA
KILN POND LA 1
TAYLORS TURN 2
1 ANTHONY CL
2 BRINDLEY AVE
3 STEPHENSON CL
172
162

HP16

Longrove Plantations

Hatches La

New Rd
A4128 MISSENDEN RD
Limmers Mead
Timpson Ct
Oak View
Cockpit Rd
Common Rd
Lime Tree Cl

1 HOMELANDS GDNS
2 OLD HEATHERDENE COTTS
3 HOPPERS WAY
4 COCKPIT CL

Great Kingshill

Pipers La
Pipers Corner Sch

Cherry Tree Cl
PH
South Mainith
Warrendene Rd
Tegsmore Rd
Spring Way
Friars Gdns
Orchard Cl
Hughenden Prim Sch

Springfields

Hoppers Farm

Hawbushes Farm

Primrose Farm

Spurlands End Rd

Boss La
Lodge

Hughenden Valley

Trees Rd
Trees Ave
Wrigwood Rd
Coombe Rdg
Coombe La
Whitfield Rd
Widmer Rd

Gomms Wood

Great Kingshill CE Comb Sch

Mews Cotts
Lisley's Field
PH
PO
+ Cryers Hill

Sladmore Farm

Binders Ind Est

Widmer End

Windmill La
Honeysuckle Rd
Lavender Rd
Snowdrop Way
Cowslip Rd
Primrose Gn
Windmill Dr
Haines Rd
Georges Cl
Larkspur Way
Marigold Rd
Estcourt Rd
Dashfield Dr
Columbine Rd
Campion Rd
Candytuft Gn
Windmill Par
Sunny Bank
Primrose Hill
Harebell Way
Bluebell Way
+

Boss Lane Farm
Provost Wood

Cryers Hill La

Widmer End Farm

Brimmers Hill
Yew Tree La
Upper Lodge La
Widmer End Comb Sch
Roberts Ride
Maurice Mount
Copes Shroves
Fox Field
Cedar Ave
Shepherds La

CRYERS HILL RD

School Cl

Cemy

HP14

VALLEY RD

Four Ashes Rd

Town Wood

HP15

North Rd

PH

Rec Gd

Grange Rd

Cedar Park Sch

Lone Warts Mead
Turnpike La
Finlays Cres
Retreat

Church Farm
+

Uplands

Four Ashes

Grange Farm

Church La

Cockshoot Wood

Beaumont Way

Grange Rd

Green St

Beaumont Gr

Millfield Wood Wildlife Reserve

Brands House

Masts

Kingshill Rd

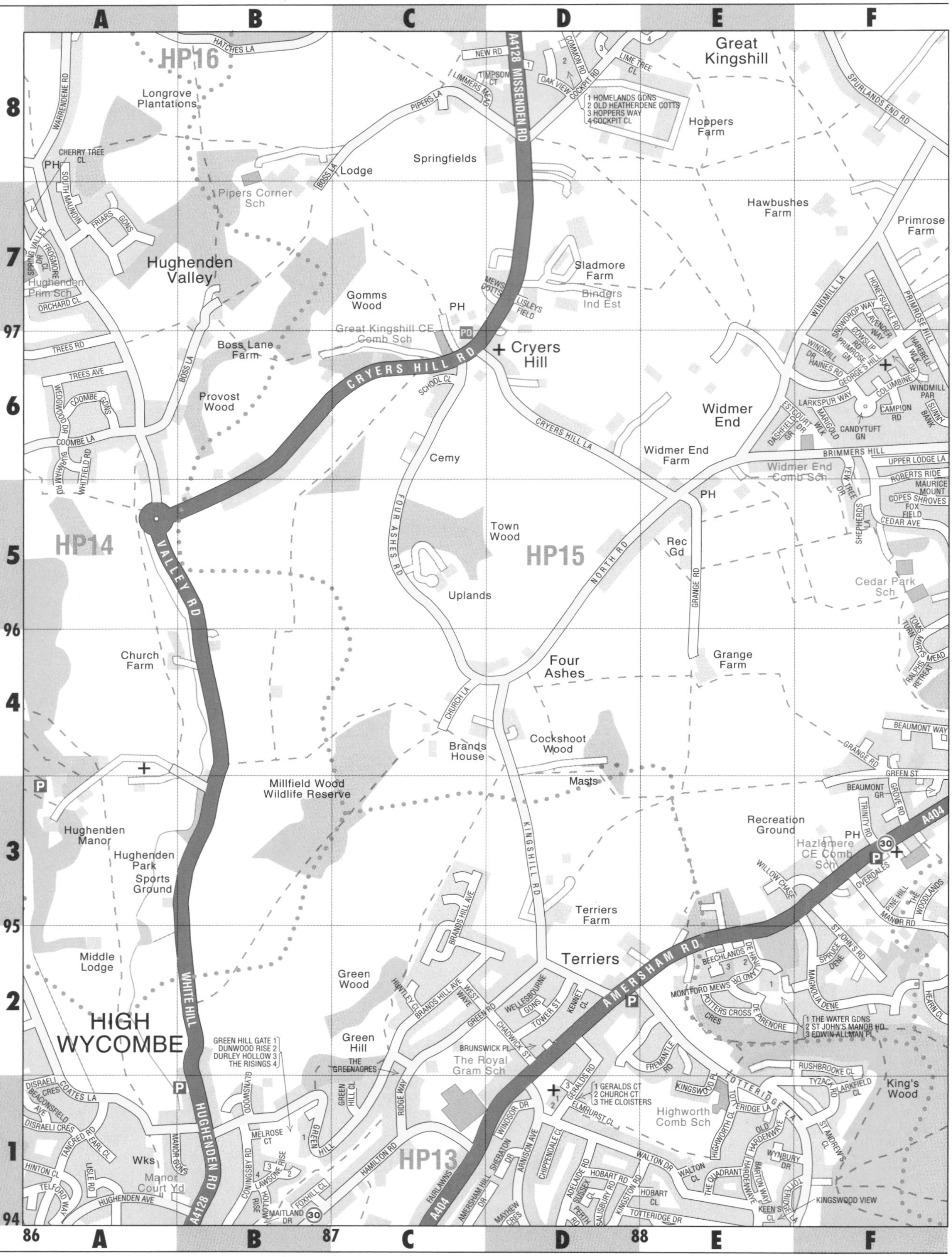

Recreation Ground

Hazlemere CE Comb Sch

PH

A404

Trinity Rd
Grove Rd
30
+
Overdales
Pine Hill Rd
Woodlands
Manor Rd

Willow Chase

P
Hughenden Manor

Hughenden Park Sports Ground

WHITE HILL

Terriers Farm

Terriers

AMERSHAM RD

St John's Rd
Spruce Dene
Magnolia Dene
Beechlands
De Havilland Dr
Montford Mews
Potters Cross Cres

1 THE WATER GDNS
2 ST JOHN'S MANOR RD
3 EDWIN-ALLMAN PL

Middle Lodge

HIGH WYCOMBE

HUGHENDEN RD A4128

GREEN HILL GATE 1
DUNWOOD RISE 2
DURLEY HOLLOW 3
THE RISINGS 4

Green Wood

Green Hill

The Greenacres

Hamilton Rd
Ridge Way
Green Hill
Brands Hill Ave
Brands Hill Cl
Hawksley Rd
West Wane
Green Rd
Tower St
Wellesbourne Gdns
Chadwick St
Kennet Rd

Brunswick Pl

The Royal Gram Sch

P
Fremantle Rd
Windsor Dr
Chippendale Cl
Adelaide Rd
Salisbury Rd
Perth Rd
Hobart Rd
Hobart Cl
Walton Dr
Walton Cl

Highworth Comb Sch

1 GERALDS CT
2 CHURCH CT
3 THE CLOISTERS

Gerald's Cl
Sheraton Dr
Elmhurst Cl
+

Kingswood Dr
Kingswo

TOTTERIDGE LA

Rushbrooke Cl

Tyzack Rd

Starkfield Cl

King's Wood

P
Disraeli Cres
Coates La
Beaconsfield Ave
Disraeli Cres

Wks
Manor Court Yd

Manor Rd
Cowingsby Rd
Conisby Rd
Melrose Ct
Lawshine Rise
Maitland Dr
Foxhill Cl
30

Green Hill Cl
Green Hill

HP13

The Quadrant
Montrose Way
Old Oxbridge La
St Andrews
The Quadrant
Barton Way
Hardenwaye
Wynbury Dr
Keen Cl
Kingswood View

Hinton Cl
Telford Way
Tancred Rd
Lisle Rd
Earl Rd
Hughenden Ave

A404
Mayhew Cres
Amersham Ibc Rd
Totteridge Dr

8 7 97 6 5 96 4 95 2 1 94

A B C D E F

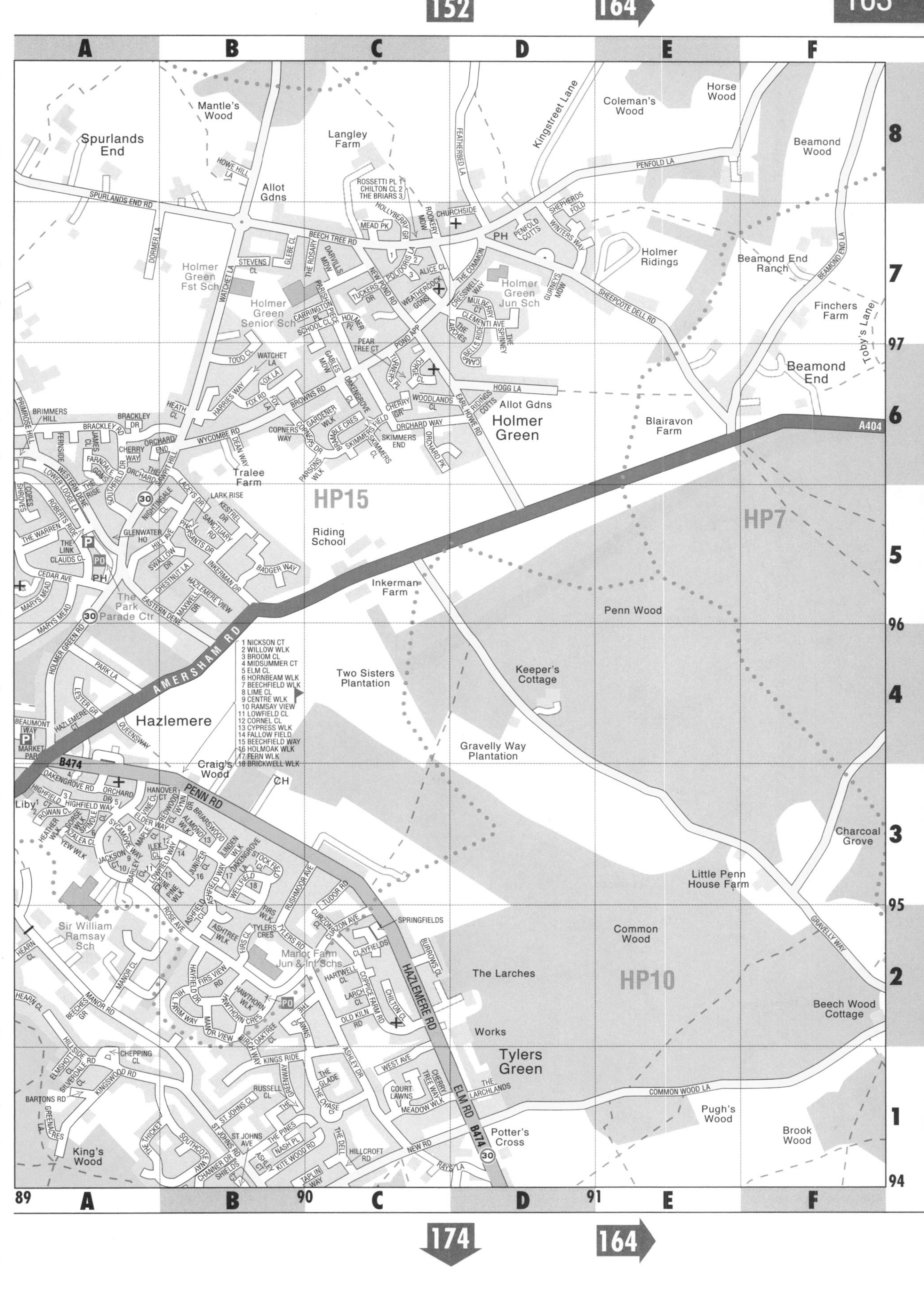
152
164
A B C D E F
Spurlands End
Mantle's Wood
Langley Farm
Coleman's Wood
Horse Wood
Beamond Wood
Kingstreet Lane
Allot Gdns
Holmer Green Fst Sch
Holmer Green Senior Sch
Holmer Green Jun Sch
Holmer Ridings
Beamond End Ranch
Finchers Farm
Toby's Lane
Beamond End
Allot Gdns
Holmer Green
Blairavon Farm
A404
Tralee Farm
HP15
Riding School
HP7
Inkerman Farm
Penn Wood
The Park Parade Ctr
AMERSHAM RD
1 NICKSON CT
2 WILLOW WLK
3 BROOM CL
4 MIDSUMMER CT
5 ELM CL
6 HORNBEAM WLK
7 BEECHFIELD WLK
8 LIME CL
9 CENTRE WLK
10 RAMSAY VIEW
11 LOWFIELD CL
12 CORNEL CL
13 CYPRESS WLK
14 FALLOW FIELD
15 BEECHFIELD WAY
16 HOLMOAK WLK
17 FERN WLK
18 BRICKWELL WLK
Two Sisters Plantation
Keeper's Cottage
Hazlemere
Gravelly Way Plantation
Craig's Wood
B474
PENN RD
Charcoal Grove
Little Penn House Farm
Sir William Ramsay Sch
Manor Farm Jun & Inf Schs
Common Wood
HP10
The Larches
HAZLEMERE RD
Beech Wood Cottage
Works
Tylers Green
COMMON WOOD LA
Pugh's Wood
Brook Wood
King's Wood
Potter's Cross
ELM RD
8 7 6 5 4 3 2 1
97 96 95 94
89 90 91
174
164

163 153

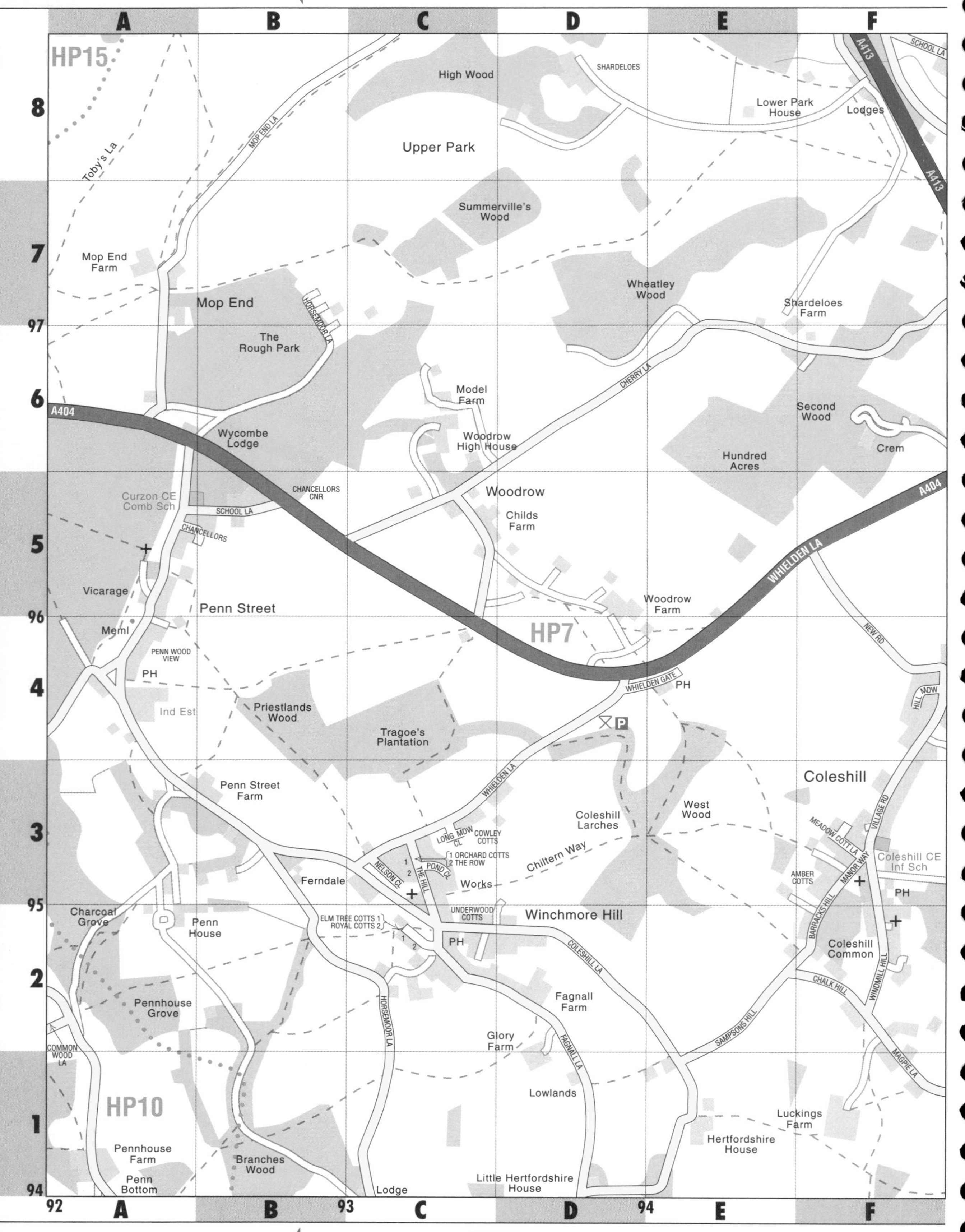

A B C D E F
8 7 97 6 5 96 4 3 95 2 1 94
92 93 94
HP15
HP7
HP10
High Wood
SHARDELOES
Lower Park House
Lodges
SCHOOL LA
A413
Toby's La
MOP END LA
Upper Park
Summerville's Wood
Mop End Farm
Mop End
HORSEMOOR LA
The Rough Park
Wheatley Wood
Shardeloes Farm
Model Farm
CHERRY LA
Second Wood
Crem
A404
Wycombe Lodge
Woodrow High House
Hundred Acres
Curzon CE Comb Sch
SCHOOL LA
CHANCELLORS CNR
Woodrow
Childs Farm
CHANCELLORS
WHIELDEN LA
Vicarage
Penn Street
Woodrow Farm
Meml
PENN WOOD VIEW
PH
WHIELDEN GATE
NEW RD
Ind Est
Priestlands Wood
Tragoe's Plantation
HILL MDW
Penn Street Farm
Coleshill
Coleshill Larches
West Wood
VILLAGE RD
MEADOW COTT LA
LONG MDW CL
COWLEY COTTS
1 ORCHARD COTTS
2 THE ROW
POND CL
Chiltern Way
NELSON CL
THE HILL
Ferndale
Works
Coleshill CE Inf Sch
AMBER COTTS
MANOR WAY
Charcoal Grove
Penn House
ELM TREE COTTS 1
ROYAL COTTS 2
UNDERWOOD COTTS
Winchmore Hill
BARRACKS HILL
Coleshill Common
COLESHILL LA
CHALK HILL
WINDMILL HILL
Pennhouse Grove
Fagnall Farm
HORSEMOOR LA
Glory Farm
FAGNALL LA
SAMPSONS HILL
COMMON WOOD LA
MAGPIE LA
Lowlands
Luckings Farm
Hertfordshire House
Pennhouse Farm
Branches Wood
Penn Bottom
Lodge
Little Hertfordshire House

163 175

154
166

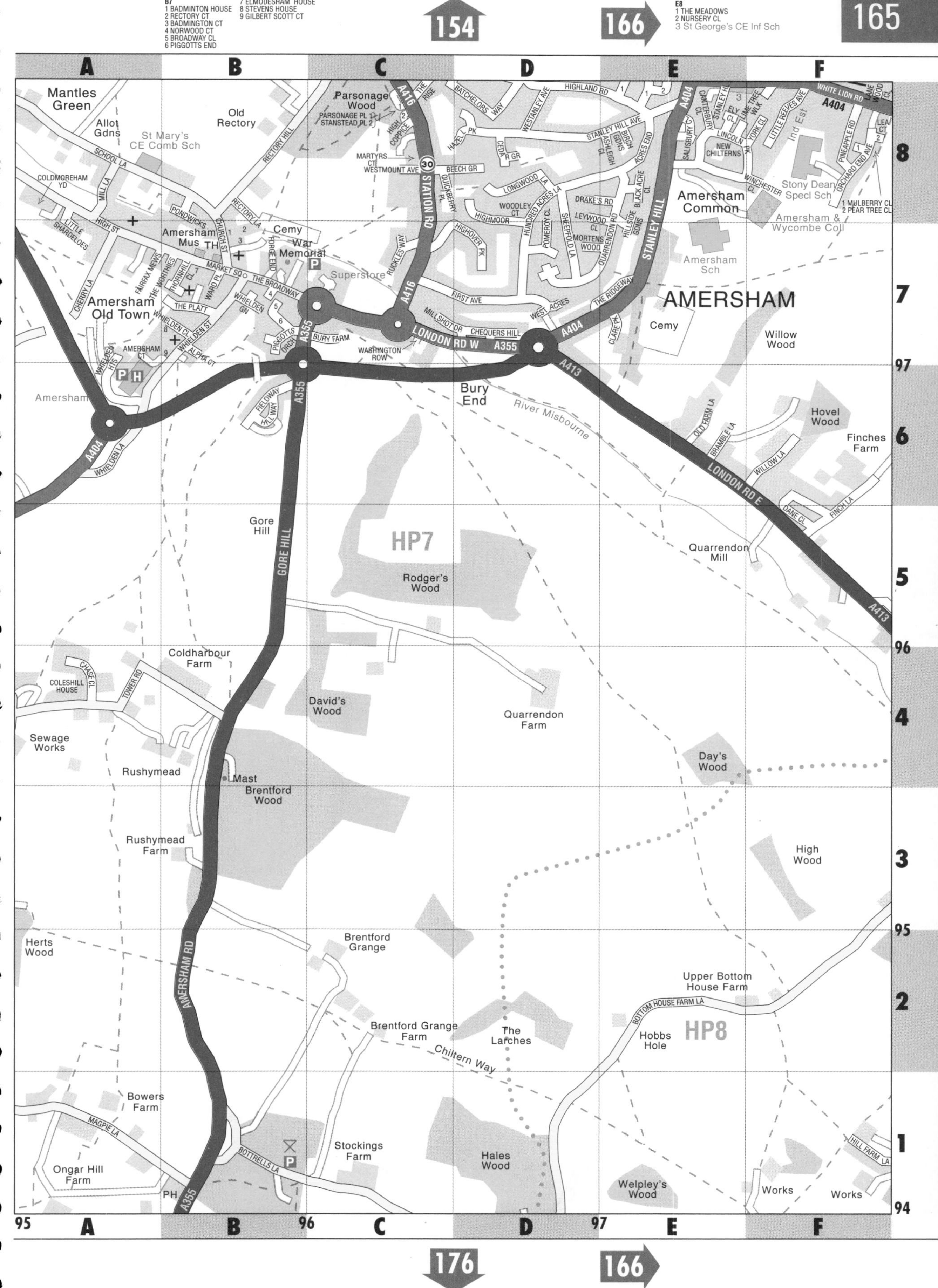
B7
1 BADMINTON HOUSE
2 RECTORY CT
3 BADMINGTON CT
4 NORWOOD CT
5 BROADWAY CL
6 PIGGOTTS END
7 ELMODESHAM HOUSE
8 STEVENS HOUSE
9 GILBERT SCOTT CT
E8
1 THE MEADOWS
2 NURSERY CL
3 St George's CE Inf Sch
A
B
C
D
E
F
Mantles Green
Allot Gdns
St Mary's CE Comb Sch
Old Rectory
Parsonage Wood
PARSONAGE PL
STANSTEAD PL
MARTYRS CT
WESTMOUNT AVE
BEECH GR
STATION RD
BATCHELORS WAY
WESTANLEY AVE
HIGHLAND RD
STANLEY HILL AVE
HAZEL PK
CEDAR GR
ASHLEIGH CL
BIRCH GDNS
ACRES END
SALISBURY CL
CANTERBURY CL
STANLEY HL
ELY CL
LIME TREE WLK
LINCOLN PK
YORK CL
NEW CHILTERNS
LITTLE REEVES AVE
WHITE LION RD
LANE WOOD
A404
Ind Est
PINEAPPLE RD
ORCHARD END AVE
LEA CL
Stony Dean Specl Sch
WINCHESTER CL
1 MULBERRY CL
2 PEAR TREE CL
Amersham Common
Amersham & Wycombe Coll
Amersham Sch
SCHOOL LA
COLDMOREHAM YD
MILL LA
PONDWICKS
RECTORY HILL
RECTORY LA
Cemy
War Memorial
Amersham Mus
TH
CHURCH ST
HIGH ST
LITTLE SHARDELOES
FORGE END
MARKET SQ
THE BROADWAY
Superstore
RUCKLES WAY
A416
LONGWOOD LA
WOODLEY CT
HIGHMOOR
HIGHOVER PK
HUNDRED ACRES LA
POMEROY CL
SHEEPFOLD LA
DRAKE'S RD
LEYWOOD CL
MORTENS WOOD
QUARRENDON RD
HILLSIDE GDNS
BLACK ACRE CL
STANLEY HILL
AMERSHAM
FAIRFAX MEWS
THE WORTHIES
THORNHILL CL
WARD PL
CHERRY LA
Amersham Old Town
THE PLATT
WHIELDEN GN
WHIELDEN CL
WHIELDEN ST
AMERSHAM CT
ALPHA CT
PIGGOTTS ORCH
BURY FARM
A355
WASHINGTON ROW
FIRST AVE
MILLSHOT DR
CHEQUERS HILL
LONDON RD W
WEST ACRES
THE RIDGEWAY
A404
CLARE PK
Cemy
Willow Wood
WHIELDEN HTS
Amersham
A413
FIELDWAY
HILL WAY
Bury End
River Misbourne
OLD FARM LA
BRAMBLE LA
Hovel Wood
Finches Farm
WILLOW LA
LONDON RD E
DANE CL
FINCH LA
WHIELDEN LA
Gore Hill
GORE HILL
HP7
Rodger's Wood
Quarrendon Mill
Coldharbour Farm
CHASE CL
COLESHILL HOUSE
TOWER RD
David's Wood
Quarrendon Farm
Sewage Works
Rushymead
Mast
Brentford Wood
Day's Wood
Rushymead Farm
High Wood
Herts Wood
Brentford Grange
AMERSHAM RD
Upper Bottom House Farm
BOTTOM HOUSE FARM LA
Brentford Grange Farm
The Larches
Hobbs Hole
HP8
Chiltern Way
Bowers Farm
MAGPIE LA
Stockings Farm
Hales Wood
HILL FARM LA
BOTTRELLS LA
Ongar Hill Farm
PH
Welpley's Wood
Works
Works
8
7
97
6
5
96
4
3
95
2
1
94
95
96
97

176
166

165 155

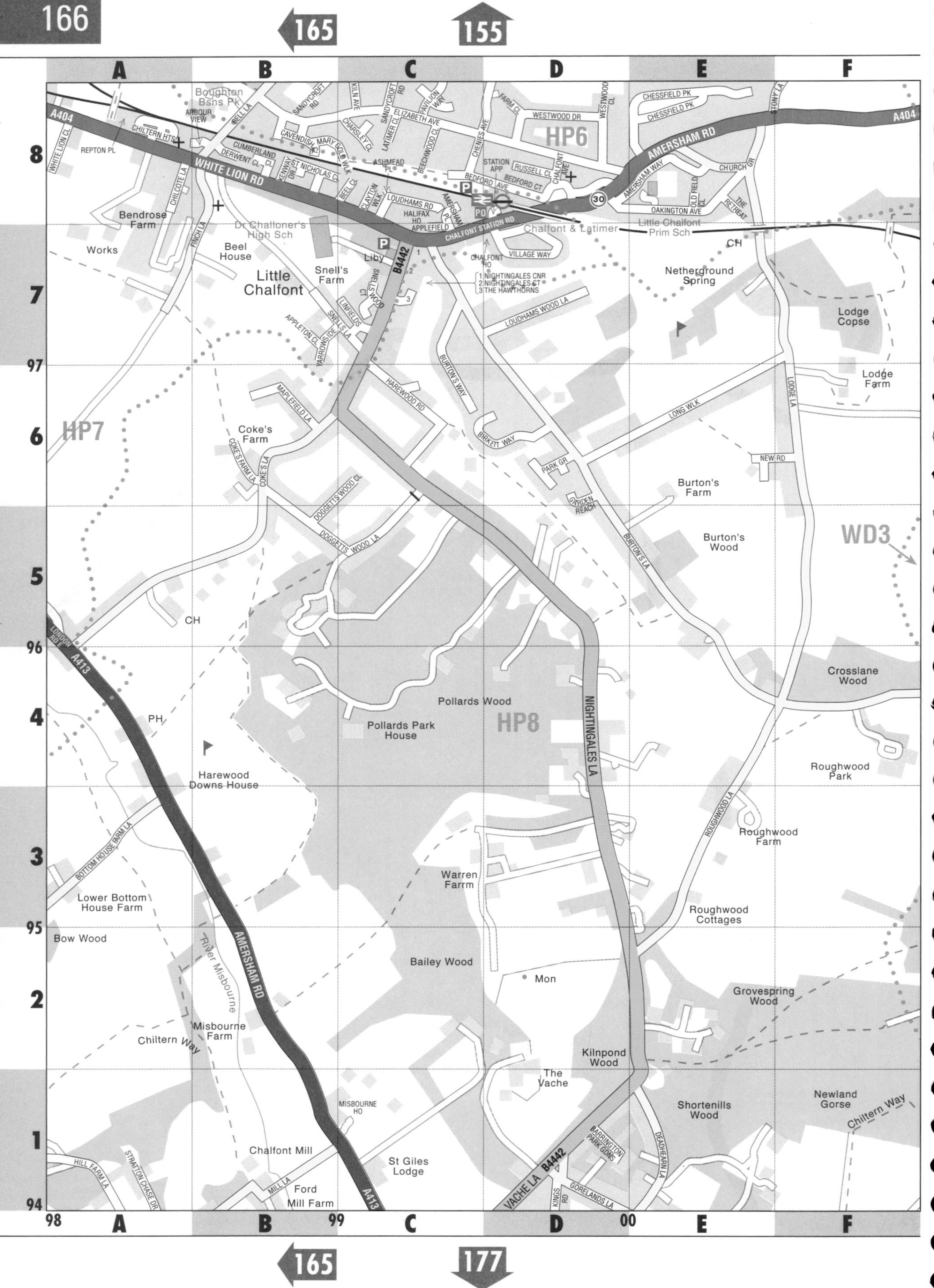

A B C D E F
8 7 6 5 4 3 2 1
97 96 95 94
98 99 00
A404
Boughton Bsns Pk
ARBOUR VIEW
BELL LA
CHILTERN HTS
REPTON PL
WHITE LION CL
CUMBERLAND CL
DERWENT CL
WHITE LION RD
CAVENDISH CL
MARY BOLD WLK
KENWAY DR
ST NICHOLAS CL
SANDYCROFT RD
KILN AVE
CHARSLEY CL
LATIMER CL
SANDYCROFT RD
ELIZABETH AVE
PAVILION WAY
BEECHWOOD CL
CHENIES AVE
FARM CL
WESTWOOD DR
WESTWOOD CL
HP6
CHESSFIELD PK
AMERSHAM RD
AMERSHAM WAY
STONY LA
CHURCH GR
OLD FIELD CL
THE RETREAT
OAKINGTON AVE
STATION APP
RUSSELL CL
BEDFORD AVE
BEDFORD CT
CHALFONT AVE
ASHMEAD PL
BEEL CL
CLAYTON WLK
LOUDHAMS RD
HALIFAX HO
APPLEFIELD
AMERSHAM PL
CHALFONT STATION RD
Chalfont & Latimer
Little Chalfont Prim Sch
CHILCOTE LA
FINCH LA
Bendrose Farm
Works
Dr Challoner's High Sch
Beel House
Little Chalfont
Snell's Farm
Liby
B4442
CHALFONT HO
VILLAGE WAY
1 NIGHTINGALES CNR
2 NIGHTINGALES CT
3 THE HAWTHORNS
SNELLS WOOD CT
LINFIELDS
SNELLS LA
APPLETON CL
YARROWSIDE
LOUDHAMS WOOD LA
Netherground Spring
CH
Lodge Copse
Lodge Farm
LODGE LA
BURTON'S WAY
HAREWOOD RD
MAPLEFIELD LA
HP7
Coke's Farm
COKE'S FARM LA
COKE'S LA
BIRKETT WAY
LONG WLK
PARK GR
NEW RD
Burton's Farm
GARDEN REACH
DOGGETTS WOOD CL
DOGGETTS WOOD LA
BURTON'S LA
Burton's Wood
WD3
CH
LONDON RD E
A413
Crosslane Wood
Pollards Wood
Pollards Park House
HP8
NIGHTINGALES LA
PH
Harewood Downs House
Roughwood Park
ROUGHWOOD LA
Roughwood Farm
BOTTOM HOUSE FARM LA
Lower Bottom House Farm
Warren Farm
Roughwood Cottages
Bow Wood
River Misbourne
AMERSHAM RD
Bailey Wood
Mon
Grovespring Wood
Misbourne Farm
Chiltern Way
Kilnpond Wood
The Vache
Shortenills Wood
Newland Gorse
Chiltern Way
MISBOURNE HO
HILL FARM LA
STRATTON CHASE DR
Chalfont Mill
St Giles Lodge
BARRINGTON PARK GDNS
DEADHEARN LA
MILL LA
Ford Mill Farm
A413
VACHE LA
B4442
KINGS RD
GORELANDS LA

165 177

156

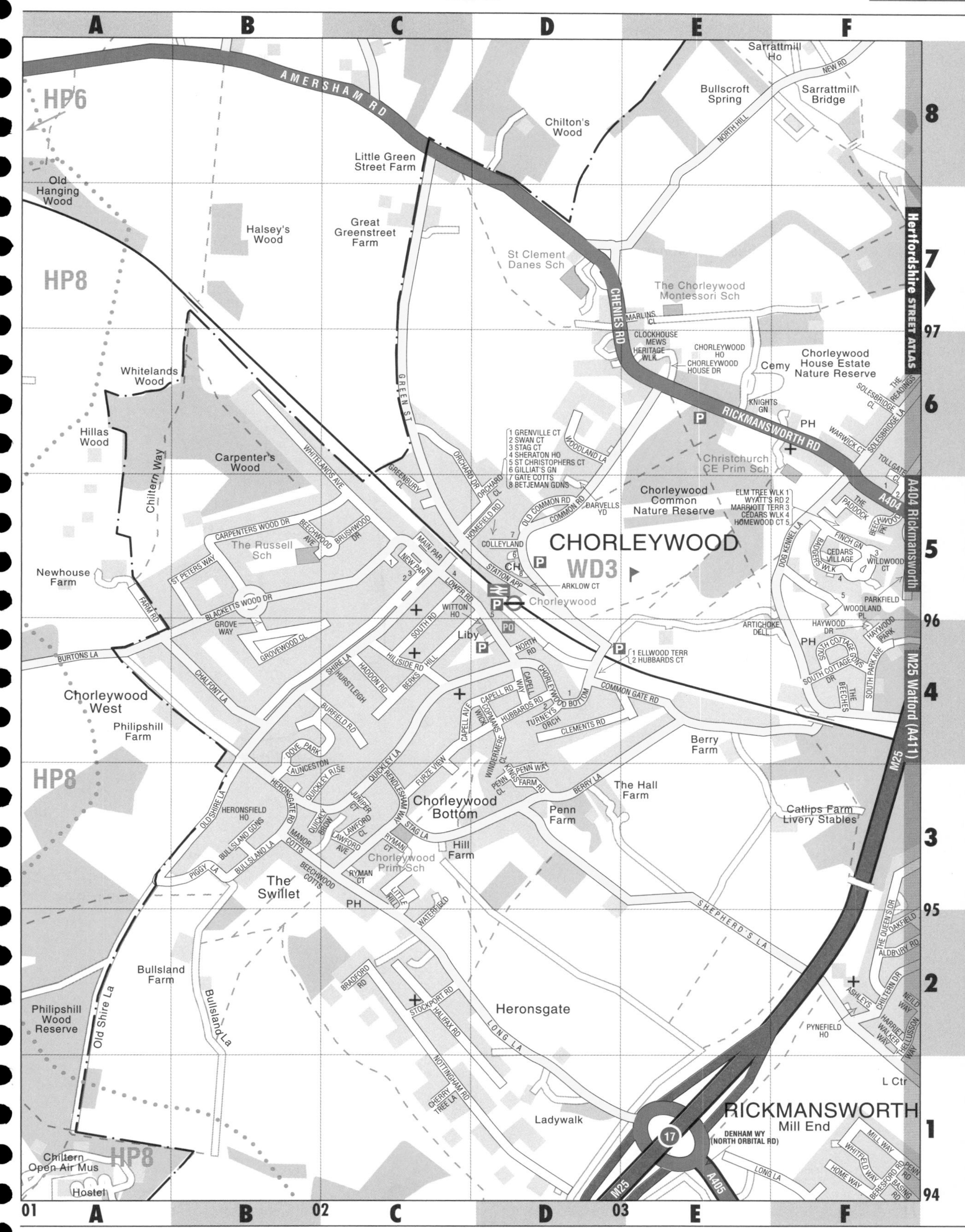

A
B
C
D
E
F
AMERSHAM RD
HP6
HP8
Old Hanging Wood
Little Green Street Farm
Halsey's Wood
Great Greenstreet Farm
Chilton's Wood
Bullscroft Spring
Sarrattmill Ho
Sarrattmill Bridge
NEW RD
NORTH HILL
St Clement Danes Sch
The Chorleywood Montessori Sch
CHENIES RD
MARLINS CL
CLOCKHOUSE MEWS
HERITAGE WLK
CHORLEYWOOD HO
CHORLEYWOOD HOUSE DR
Cemy
Chorleywood House Estate Nature Reserve
KNIGHTS GN
RICKMANSWORTH RD
PH
Christchurch CE Prim Sch
Whitelands Wood
Hillas Wood
Chiltern Way
Carpenter's Wood
GREEN ST
GREENBURY CL
ORCHARD DR
ORCHARD CL
1 GRENVILLE CT
2 SWAN CT
3 STAG CT
4 SHERATON HO
5 ST CHRISTOPHERS CT
6 GILLIAT'S GN
7 GATE COTTS
8 BETJEMAN GDNS
WOODLAND LA
OLD COMMON RD
COMMON RD
DARVELLS YD
Chorleywood Common Nature Reserve
ELM TREE WLK 1
WYATT'S RD 2
MARRIOTT TERR 3
CEDARS WLK 4
HOMEWOOD CT 5
DOG KENNEL LA
THE PADDOCK
A404
Hertfordshire STREET ATLAS
A404 Rickmansworth
M25 Watford (A411)
WHITELANDS AVE
CARPENTERS WOOD DR
BEECHWOOD AVE
BRUSHWOOD DR
The Russell Sch
HOMEFIELD RD
COLLEYLAND
MAIN PAR
NEW PAR
CHORLEYWOOD
WD3
CH
STATION APP
ARKLOW CT
Chorleywood
FINCH GN
CEDARS VILLAGE
BADGERS WLK
WILDWOOD CT
PARKFIELD
WOODLAND PL
Newhouse Farm
ST PETERS WAY
BLACKETTS WOOD DR
GROVE WAY
GROVEWOOD CL
FARM RD
LOWER RD
WITTON HO
SOUTH RD
Liby
PO
NORTH RD
1 ELLWOOD TERR
2 HUBBARDS CT
ARTICHOKE DELL
HAYWOOD DR
HAYWOOD PARK
SOUTH COTTAGE GDNS
SOUTH COTTAGE DR
SOUTH PARK AVE
THE BEECHES
BURTONS LA
CHALFONT LA
SHIRE LA
HURSTLEIGH
HADDON RD
HILLSIDE RD
BERKS HILL
CAPELL WAY
CAPELL RD
CHORLEYWOOD BOTTOM
COMMON GATE RD
Chorleywood West
Philipshill Farm
BURFIELD RD
HUBBARDS RD
TURNEYS ORCH
CLEMENTS RD
Berry Farm
DOVE PARK
LAUNCESTON
QUICKLEY RISE
QUICKLEY LA
FURZE VIEW
WINDERMERE CL
PENN CL
KINGS FARM RD
PENN WAY
BERRY LA
The Hall Farm
M25
HP8
HERONSFIELD HO
HERONSGATE RD
OLDSHIRE LA
BULLSLAND GDNS
BULLSLAND LA
MANOR COTTS
QUICKLY BROW
JUNIPER CT
LAWFORD CL
LAWFORD AVE
RENDLESHAM WAY
Chorleywood Bottom
STAG LA
Penn Farm
Catlips Farm Livery Stables
RYMAN CT
Hill Farm
Chorleywood Prim Sch
PIGGY LA
The Swillet
BEECHWOOD COTTS
PH
LITTLE HILL
WATERFIELD
SHEPHERD'S LA
THE QUEEN'S DR
OAKFIELD
ALDBURY RD
Bullsland Farm
Bullsland La
BRADFORD RD
STOCKPORT RD
HALIFAX RD
Heronsgate
LONG LA
ASHLEYS
CHILTERN DR
NEILD WAY
HARRIET WALKER WAY
TELLUSSON WAY
PYNEFIELD HO
Philipshill Wood Reserve
Old Shire La
NOTTINGHAM RD
CHERRY TREE LA
L Ctr
RICKMANSWORTH
Mill End
Ladywalk
17
DENHAM WY (NORTH ORBITAL RD)
A405
MILL WAY
WHITFIELD WAY
PENN RD
BERESFORD RD
BASING RD
HOME WAY
LONG LA
Chiltern Open Air Mus
Hostel
HP8
8
7
97
6
5
96
4
3
95
2
1
94
01
02
03

178

157

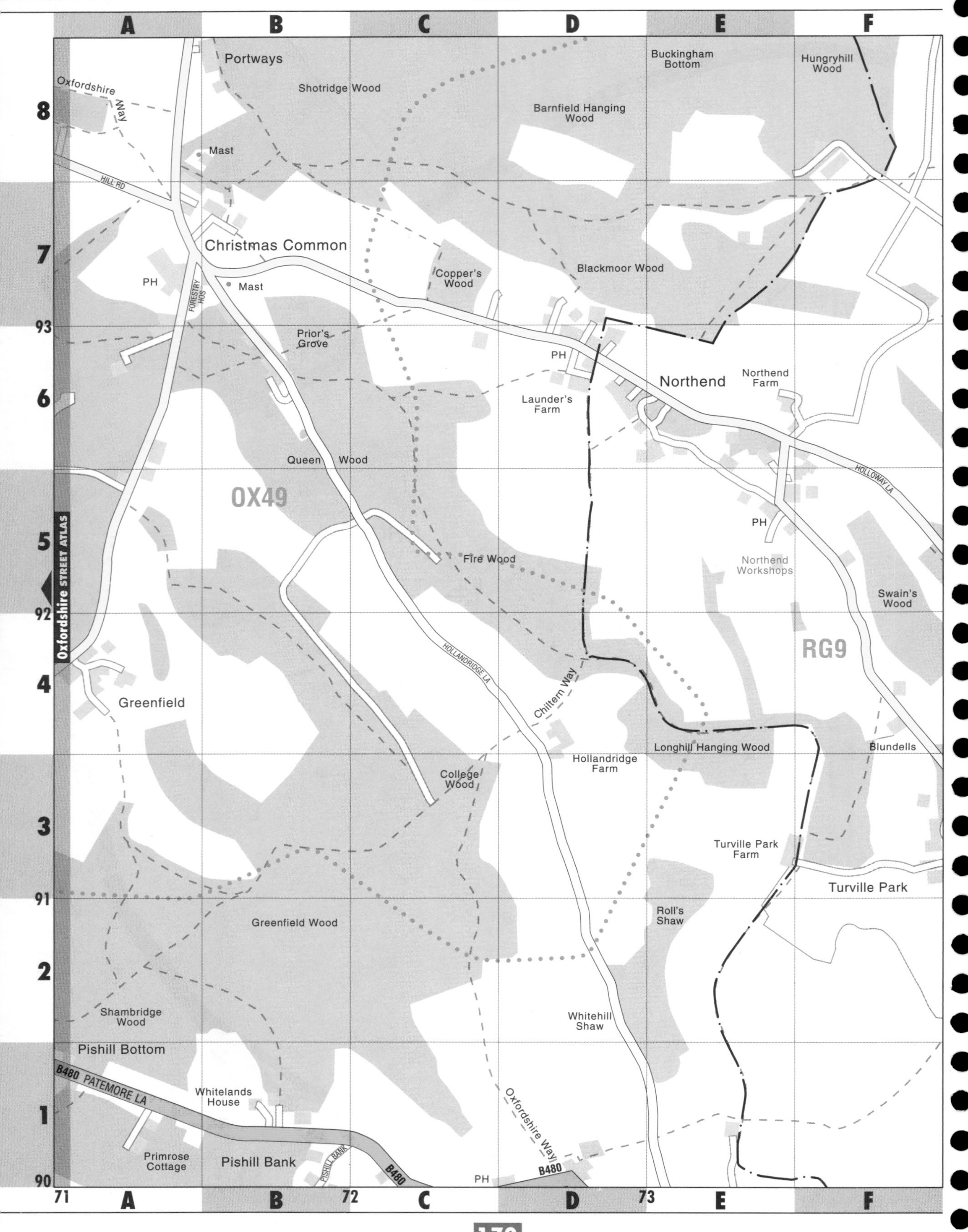

A
B
C
D
E
F
8
7
93
6
5
92
4
3
91
2
1
90
71
72
73
Portways
Shotridge Wood
Buckingham Bottom
Hungryhill Wood
Barnfield Hanging Wood
Oxfordshire Way
Mast
HILL RD
Christmas Common
PH
FORESTRY HOS
Mast
Copper's Wood
Blackmoor Wood
Prior's Grove
PH
Northend
Northend Farm
Launder's Farm
Queen Wood
HOLLOWAY LA
OX49
PH
Fire Wood
Northend Workshops
Swain's Wood
RG9
HOLLANDRIDGE LA
Chiltern Way
Greenfield
Longhill Hanging Wood
Blundells
Hollandridge Farm
College Wood
Turville Park Farm
Turville Park
Roll's Shaw
Greenfield Wood
Shambridge Wood
Whitehill Shaw
Pishill Bottom
B480 PATEMORE LA
Whitelands House
Oxfordshire Way
Primrose Cottage
Pishill Bank
PISHILL BANK
B480
PH
B480
Oxfordshire STREET ATLAS

179

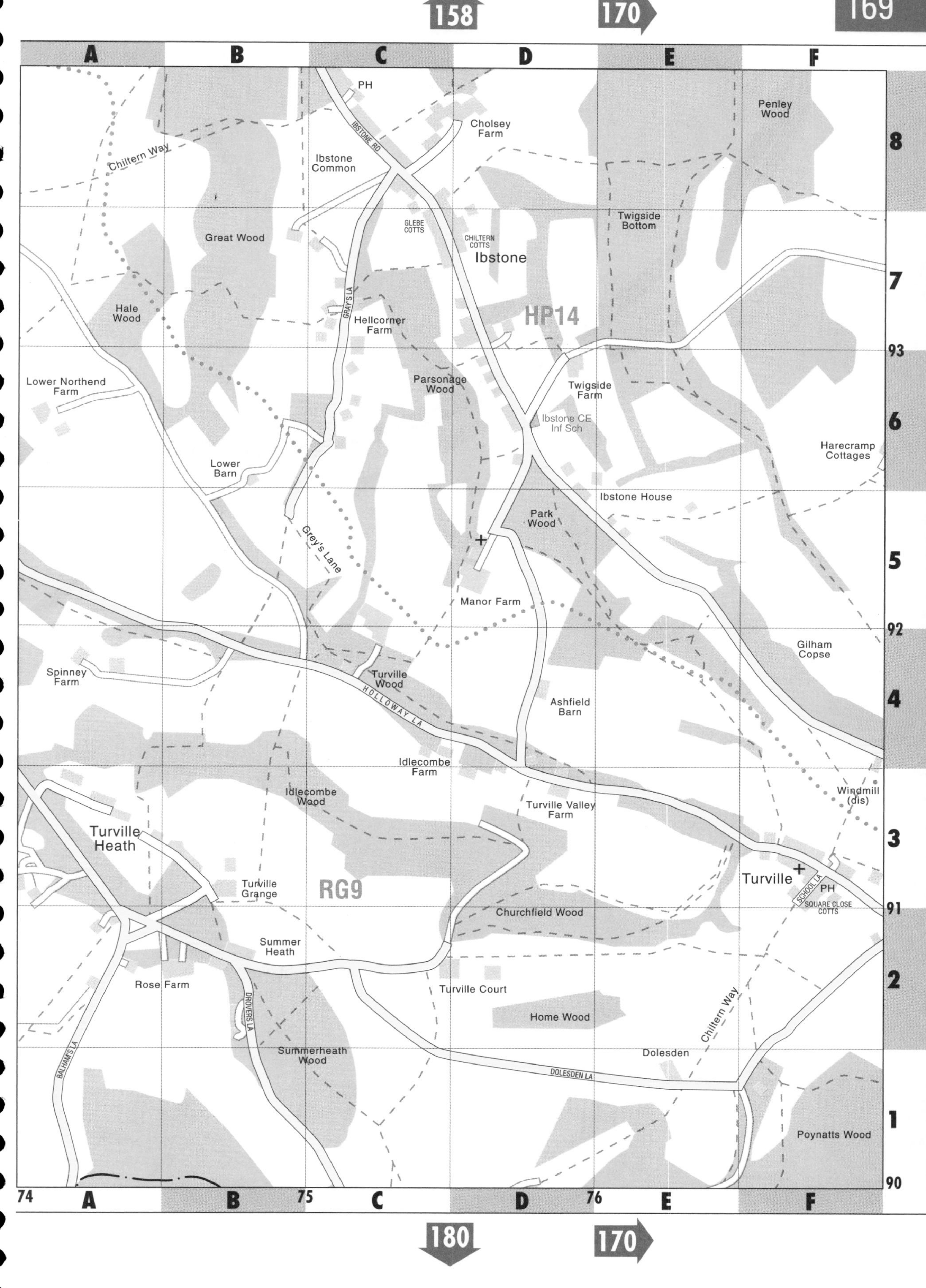

Chiltern Way

PH

Cholsey Farm

Penley Wood

Ibstone Common

Ibstone Common

Great Wood

GLEBE COTTS

CHILTERN COTTS

Ibstone

Twigside Bottom

HP14

Hale Wood

GRAY'S LA

Hellcorner Farm

Lower Northend Farm

Parsonage Wood

Twigside Farm

Ibstone CE Inf Sch

Harecramp Cottages

Lower Barn

Ibstone House

Park Wood

Grey's Lane

Manor Farm

Gilham Copse

Spinney Farm

Turville Wood

HOLLOWAY LA

Ashfield Barn

Idlecombe Farm

Windmill (dis)

Idlecombe Wood

Turville Valley Farm

Turville Heath

RG9

Turville Grange

Turville

PH

SCHOOL LA

SQUARE CLOSE COTTS

Churchfield Wood

Summer Heath

Rose Farm

DROVERS LA

Turville Court

Home Wood

Chiltern Way

Summerheath Wood

Dolesden

DOLESDEN LA

BALHAM'S LA

Poynatts Wood

169
159

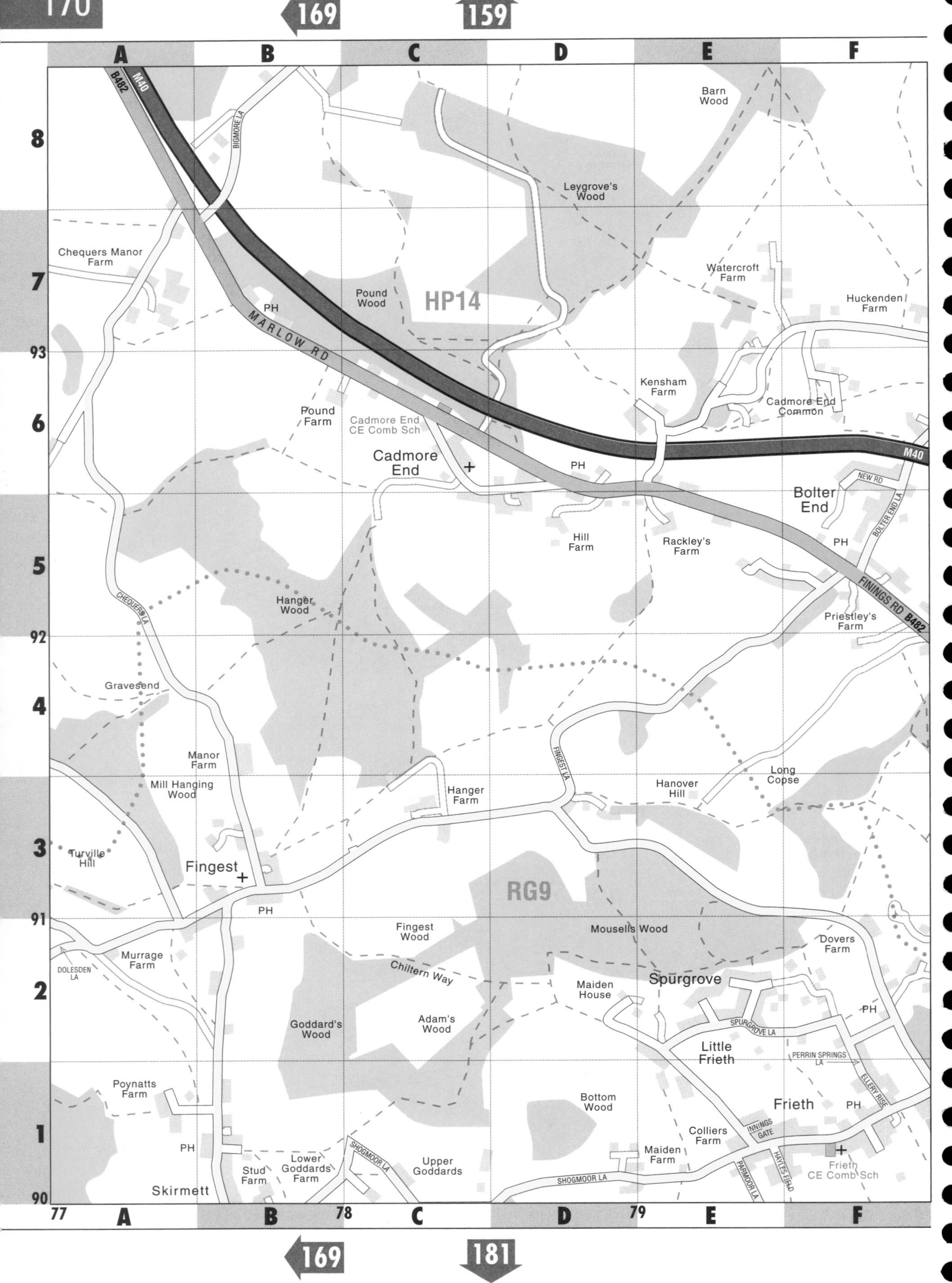

A
B
C
D
E
F
8
7
93
6
5
92
4
3
91
2
1
90
77
78
79
B482
M40
BIGMORE LA
Barn Wood
Leygrove's Wood
Chequers Manor Farm
Watercroft Farm
Pound Wood
HP14
PH
Huckenden Farm
MARLOW RD
Kensham Farm
Cadmore End Common
Pound Farm
Cadmore End CE Comb Sch
Cadmore End
PH
NEW RD
Bolter End
BOLTER END LA
Hill Farm
Rackley's Farm
PH
FININGS RD
Hanger Wood
CHEQUERS LA
Priestley's Farm
Gravesend
FINGEST LA
Manor Farm
Long Copse
Mill Hanging Wood
Hanger Farm
Hanover Hill
Turville Hill
Fingest
RG9
PH
Fingest Wood
Mousells Wood
Dovers Farm
Murrage Farm
DOLESDEN LA
Chiltern Way
Maiden House
Spurgrove
PH
SPURGROVE LA
Goddard's Wood
Adam's Wood
Little Frieth
PERRIN SPRINGS LA
ELLERY RISE
Poynatts Farm
Bottom Wood
Frieth
PH
INNINGS GATE
Colliers Farm
PH
SHOGMOOR LA
Upper Goddards
Maiden Farm
Frieth CE Comb Sch
Lower Goddards Farm
Stud Farm
Skirmett
SHOGMOOR LA
PARMOOR LA
HAYLES FIELD

169
181

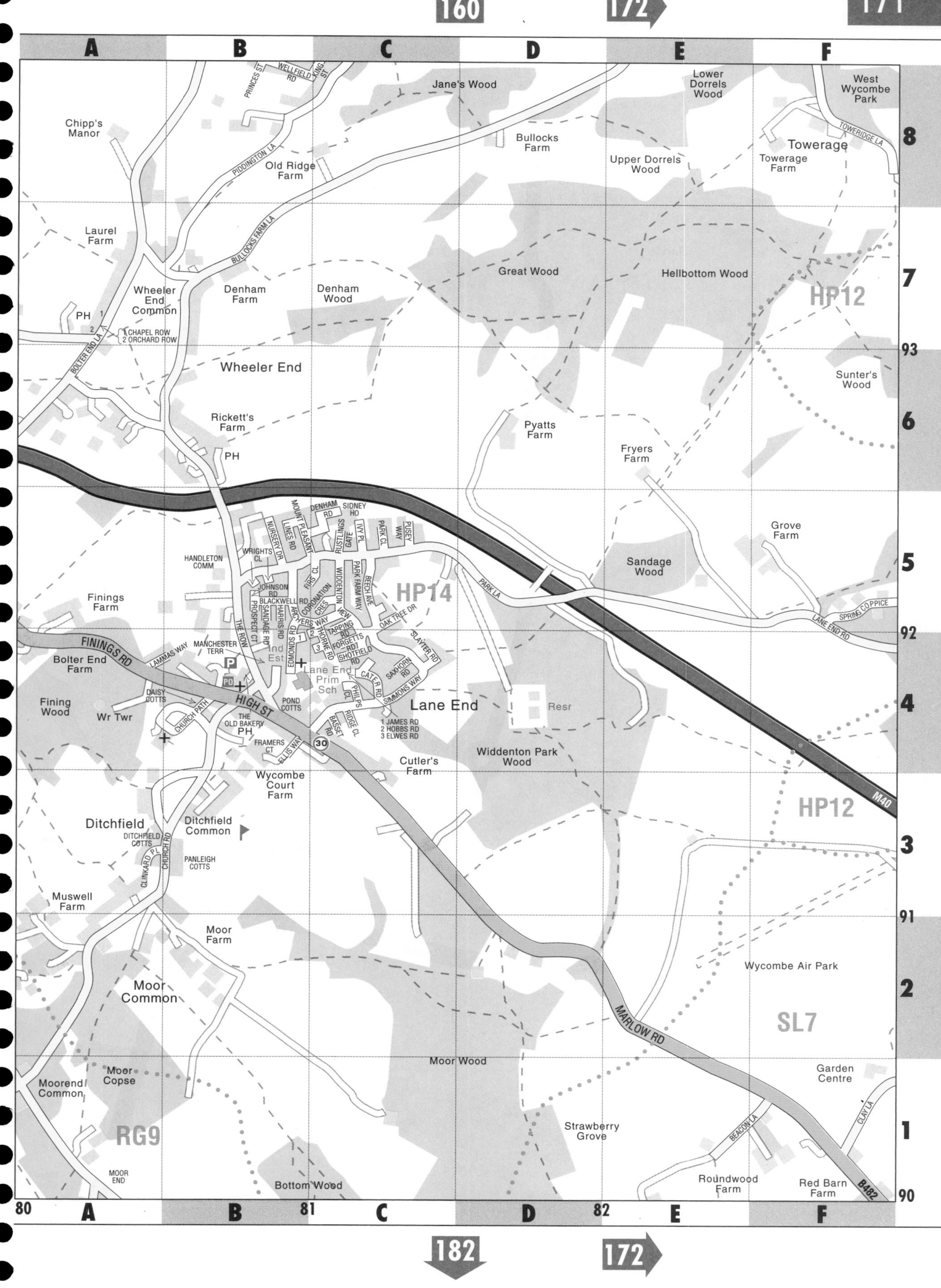
160
172
A
B
C
D
E
F
Jane's Wood
Lower Dorrels Wood
West Wycombe Park
Chipp's Manor
Bullocks Farm
Towerage
Towerage Farm
Upper Dorrels Wood
Old Ridge Farm
PIDDINGTON LA
BULLOCKS FARM LA
TOWERIDGE LA
Laurel Farm
Great Wood
Hellbottom Wood
HP12
Wheeler End Common
Denham Farm
Denham Wood
PH
1 CHAPEL ROW
2 ORCHARD ROW
BOLTER END LA
Wheeler End
Sunter's Wood
Rickett's Farm
Pyatts Farm
Fryers Farm
Grove Farm
Sandage Wood
HANDLETON COMM
Finings Farm
HP14
PARK LA
LANE END RD
SPRING COPPICE
Bolter End Farm
FININGS RD
LAMMAS WAY
MANCHESTER TERR
Fining Wood
Wr Twr
HIGH ST
Lane End Prim Sch
Lane End
Resr
1 JAMES RD
2 HOBBS RD
3 ELWES RD
THE OLD BAKERY
FRAMERS CT
ELLIS WAY
Widdenton Park Wood
Cutler's Farm
Wycombe Court Farm
M40
HP12
Ditchfield
Ditchfield Common
DITCHFIELD COTTS
CHURCH RD
CLINKARD PL
PANLEIGH COTTS
Muswell Farm
Moor Farm
Wycombe Air Park
Moor Common
MARLOW RD
SL7
Moer Copse
Moor Wood
Moorend Common
Garden Centre
RG9
Strawberry Grove
BEACON LA
CLAY LA
MOOR END
Bottom Wood
Roundwood Farm
Red Barn Farm
B482
8
7
93
6
5
92
4
3
91
2
1
90
80
81
82
182
172

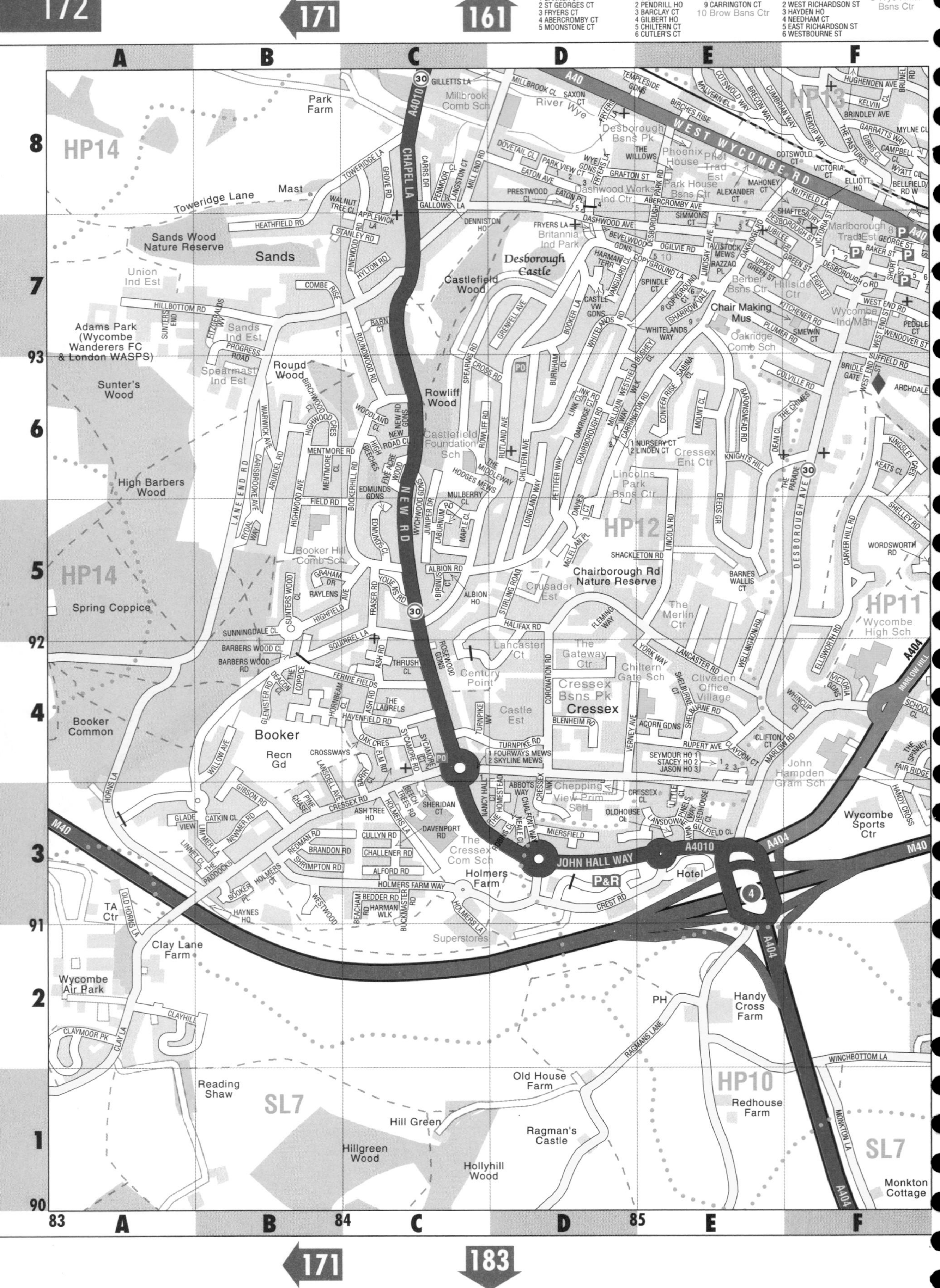

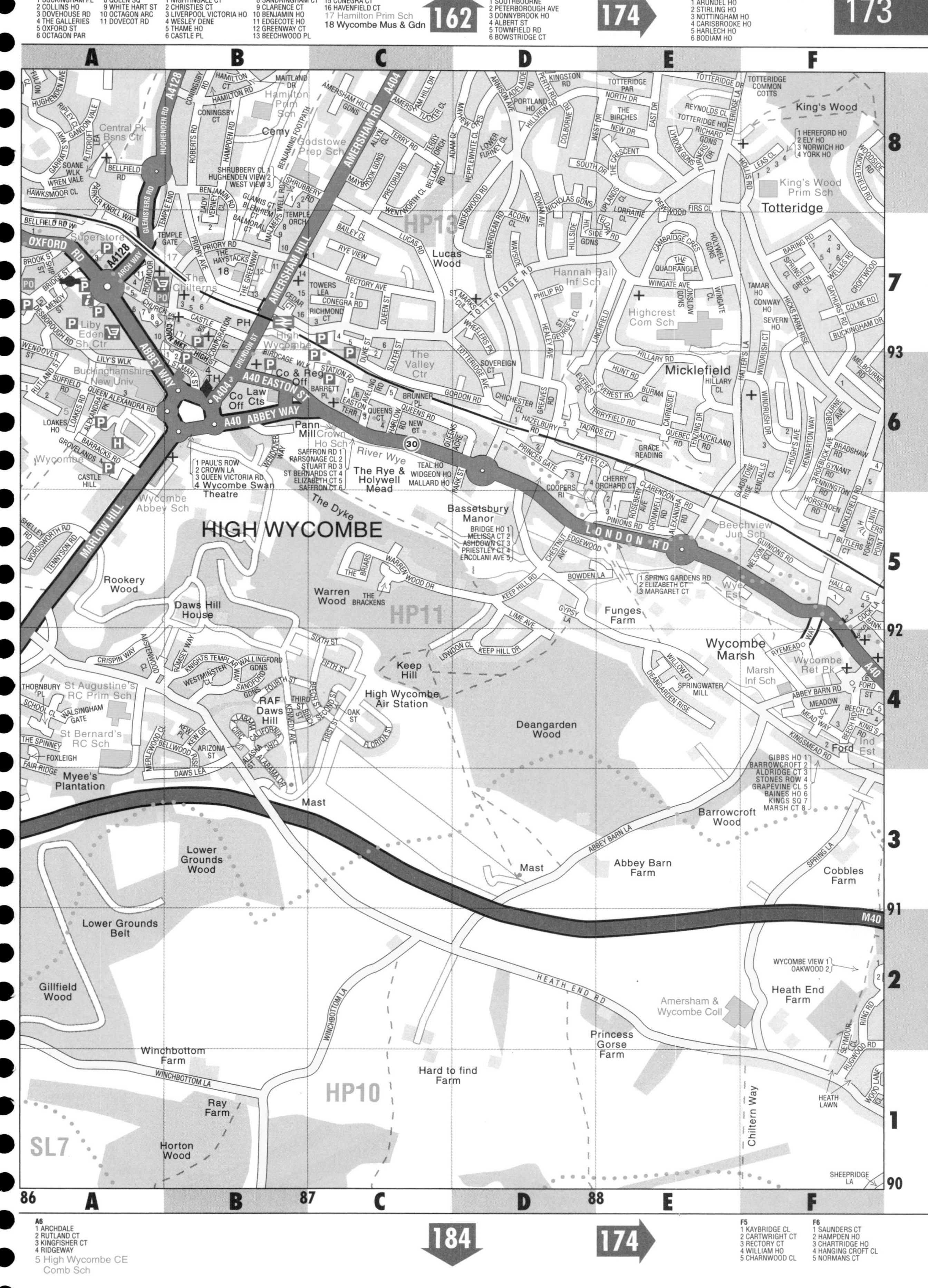

173
A7
1 BUCKINGHAM PL
2 COLLINS HO
3 DOVEHOUSE RD
4 THE GALLERIES
5 OXFORD ST
6 OCTAGON PAR
7 BULL LA
8 QUEEN SQ
9 WHITE HART ST
10 OCTAGON ARC
11 DOVECOT RD
B7
1 NIGHTINGALE CT
2 CHRISTIES CT
3 LIVERPOOL VICTORIA HO
4 WESLEY DENE
5 THAME HO
6 CASTLE PL
7 CHURCH SQ
8 SANDRINGHAM CT
9 CLARENCE CT
10 BENJAMIN HO
11 EDGECOTE HO
12 GREENWAY CT
13 BEECHWOOD PL
14 DESBOROUGH HO
15 CONEGRA CT
16 HAVENFIELD CT
17 Hamilton Prim Sch
18 Wycombe Mus & Gdn
162
C7
1 SOUTHBOURNE
2 PETERBOROUGH AVE
3 DONNYBROOK HO
4 ALBERT ST
5 TOWNFIELD RD
6 BOWSTRIDGE CT
174
F7
1 ARUNDEL HO
2 STIRLING HO
3 NOTTINGHAM HO
4 CARISBROOKE HO
5 HARLECH HO
6 BODIAM HO
7 WARWICK HO
A B C D E F
HIGH WYCOMBE
HP13
HP11
HP10
SL7
Totteridge
Micklefield
Wycombe Marsh
King's Wood
Lucas Wood
Rookery Wood
Warren Wood
Daws Hill House
Keep Hill
High Wycombe Air Station
RAF Daws Hill
Deangarden Wood
Funges Farm
Barrowcroft Wood
Abbey Barn Farm
Cobbles Farm
Lower Grounds Wood
Lower Grounds Belt
Gillfield Wood
Winchbottom Farm
Ray Farm
Horton Wood
Hard to find Farm
Princess Gorse Farm
Heath End Farm
Amersham & Wycombe Coll
Myee's Plantation
Bassetsbury Manor
The Rye & Holywell Mead
River Wye
The Dyke
M40
A40 LONDON RD
A40 EASTON ST
A40 ABBEY WAY
A404 AMERSHAM HILL
MARLOW HILL
A4128
8 7 93 6 5 92 4 3 91 2 1 90
86 87 88
A6
1 ARCHDALE
2 RUTLAND CT
3 KINGFISHER CT
4 RIDGEWAY
5 High Wycombe CE Comb Sch
184
174
F5
1 KAYBRIDGE CL
2 CARTWRIGHT CT
3 RECTORY CT
4 WILLIAM HO
5 CHARNWOOD CL
F6
1 SAUNDERS CT
2 HAMPDEN HO
3 CHARTRIDGE HO
4 HANGING CROFT CL
5 NORMANS CT

173
163

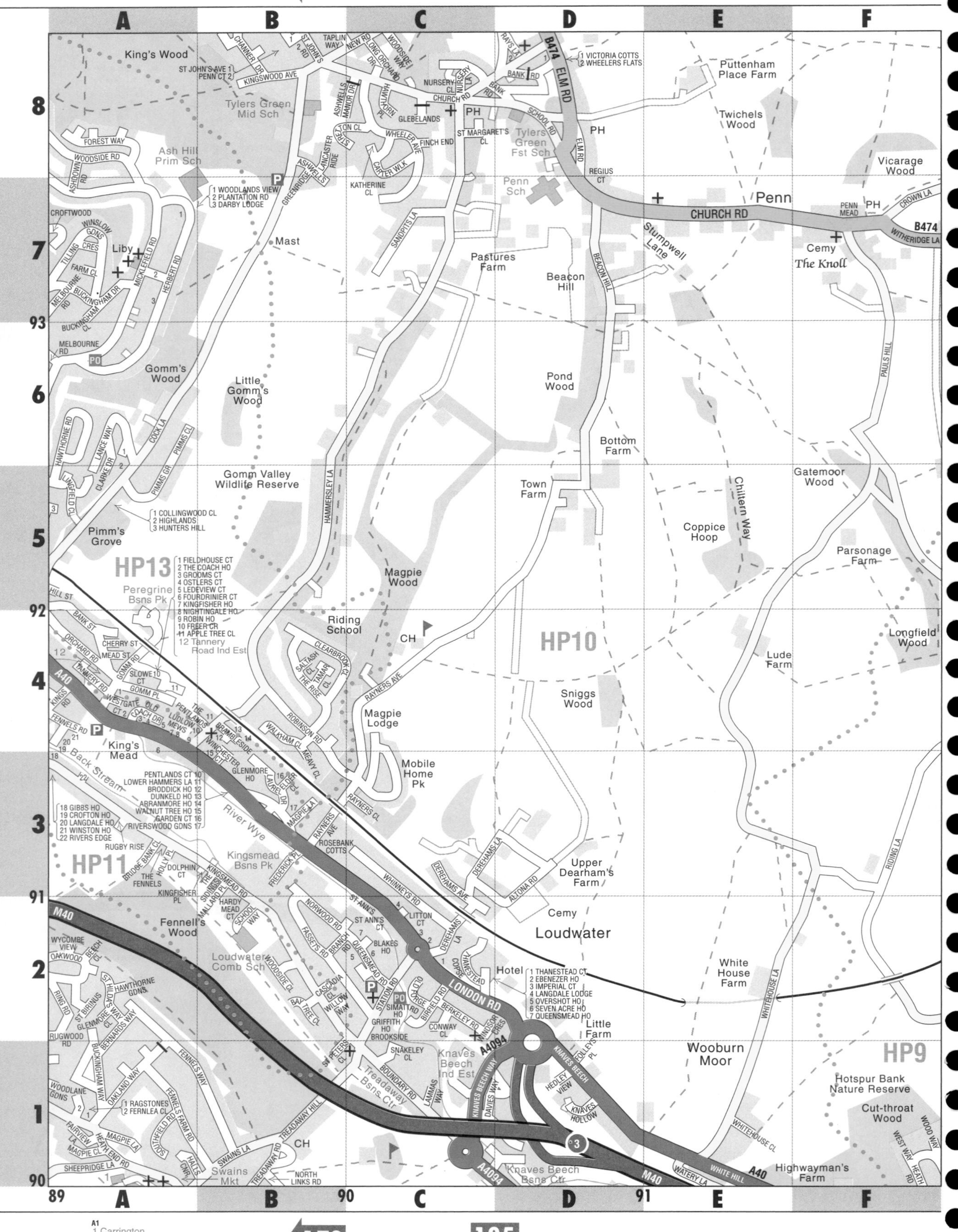
A
B
C
D
E
F
8
7
93
6
5
92
4
3
91
2
1
90
89
90
91
King's Wood
Tylers Green Mid Sch
Ash Hill Prim Sch
1 WOODLANDS VIEW
2 PLANTATION RD
3 DARBY LODGE
Mast
Liby
Gomm's Wood
Little Gomm's Wood
Gomm Valley Wildlife Reserve
Pimm's Grove
1 COLLINGWOOD CL
2 HIGHLANDS
3 HUNTERS HILL
HP13
Peregrine Bsns Pk
1 FIELDHOUSE CT
2 THE COACH HO
3 GROOMS CT
4 OSTLERS CT
5 LEDEVIEW CT
6 FOURDRINIER CT
7 KINGFISHER HO
8 NIGHTINGALE HO
9 ROBIN HO
10 FREER CR
11 APPLE TREE CL
12 Tannery Road Ind Est
1 VICTORIA COTTS
2 WHEELERS FLATS
Tylers Green Fst Sch
Penn Sch
Puttenham Place Farm
Twichels Wood
Vicarage Wood
Penn
CHURCH RD
ELM RD
B474
Stumpwell Lane
Cemy
The Knoll
Pastures Farm
Beacon Hill
Pond Wood
Bottom Farm
Town Farm
Gatemoor Wood
Chiltern Way
Coppice Hoop
Parsonage Farm
Magpie Wood
Riding School
CH
HP10
Longfield Wood
Lude Farm
Sniggs Wood
Magpie Lodge
Mobile Home Pk
King's Mead
Back Stream
River Wye
PENTLANDS CT 10
LOWER HAMMERS LA 11
BRODDICK HO 12
DUNKELD HO 13
ARRANMORE HO 14
WALNUT TREE HO 15
GARDEN CT 16
RIVERSWOOD GDNS 17
18 GIBBS HO
19 CROFTON HO
20 LANGDALE HO
21 WINSTON HO
22 RIVERS EDGE
HP11
Kingsmead Bsns Pk
Upper Dearham's Farm
Cemy
Loudwater
Fennell's Wood
Loudwater Comb Sch
Hotel
1 THANESTEAD CT
2 EBENEZER HO
3 IMPERIAL CT
4 LANGDALE LODGE
5 OVERSHOT HO
6 SEVEN ACRE HO
7 QUEENSMEAD HO
White House Farm
LONDON RD
A4094
Little Farm
Wooburn Moor
HP9
Hotspur Bank Nature Reserve
Cut-throat Wood
Knaves Beech Ind Est
Treadaway Bsns Ctr
1 RAGSTONES
2 FERNLEA CL
M40
A40
Swains Mkt
Knaves Beech Bsns Ctr
WHITE HILL
Highwayman's Farm

A1
1 Carrington Inf Sch

173
185

164 176

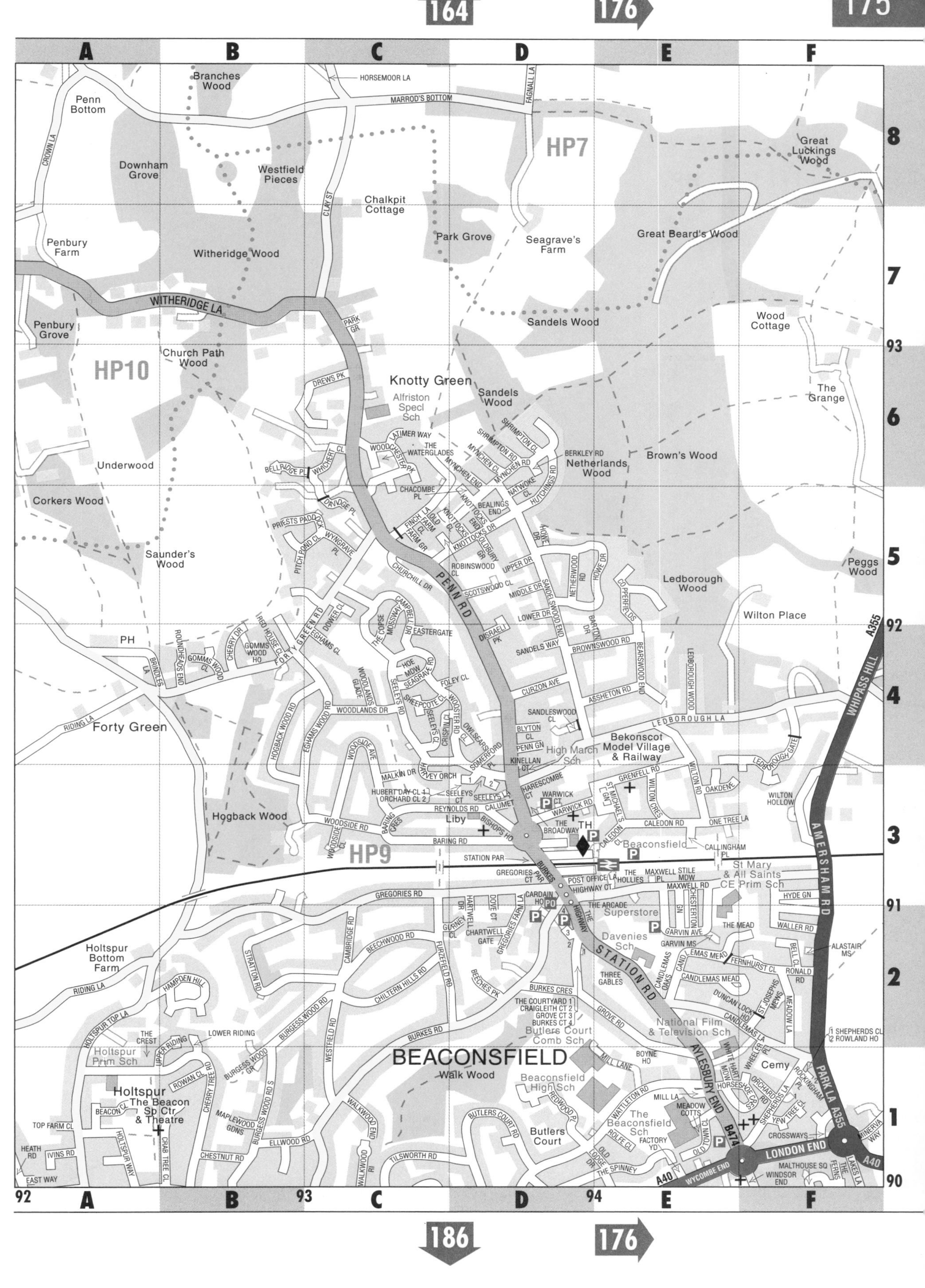

Branches Wood
Penn Bottom
HORSEMOOR LA
MARROD'S BOTTOM
FAGNALL LA
HP7
Downham Grove
Westfield Pieces
Chalkpit Cottage
Great Luckings Wood
Penbury Farm
Witheridge Wood
Park Grove
Seagrave's Farm
Great Beard's Wood
WITHERIDGE LA
Penbury Grove
Sandels Wood
Wood Cottage
HP10
Church Path Wood
Knotty Green
Alfriston Specl Sch
Sandels Wood
The Grange
Underwood
Netherlands Wood
Brown's Wood
Corkers Wood
Saunder's Wood
Ledborough Wood
Peggs Wood
Wilton Place
PENN RD
PH
Forty Green
Bekonscot Model Village & Railway
High March Sch
LEDBOROUGH LA
WHIPASS HILL
A355
Hogback Wood
Liby
TH
Beaconsfield
HP9
St Mary & All Saints CE Prim Sch
Superstore
Davenies Sch
AMERSHAM RD
Holtspur Bottom Farm
STATION RD
National Film & Television Sch
Butlers Court Comb Sch
BEACONSFIELD
Walk Wood
Beaconsfield High Sch
Cemy
Holtspur Prim Sch
Holtspur
The Beacon Sp Ctr & Theatre
The Beaconsfield Sch
Butlers Court
AYLESBURY END
LONDON END
WYCOMBE END
PARK LA
A40
B474
A B C D E F
8 7 93 6 5 92 4 3 91 2 1 90
92 93 94

186 176

175 165

A B C D E F

8

HP7

Hill's Wood
Barnhurst
Red Barn Farm
Highfield Grove
Hodgemoor Woods
BOTTOM HOUSE FARM LANE
P
BOTTRELLS LA

HP8

Owlsears Wood
7
Three Households

93
Starveacre Wood
Widmer Farm
RAWLINGS LA
Rawlings Farm
Piggery
Newbarn
Highclere
CH

6
Bottom Wood
Big Copse
PRINCESS GR
NEWBARN LA
Butlers Cross

South Lodge
West Riding
The Princess Marina Centre
TWITCHELLS LA

Birchen Spring
Cleare Craft Wood
HIGHLANDS RD
PARK PL
Recreation Ground
Harmony Nurseries
Austens

5
Blue Close Wood
Oldfields Farm
HOWARD CRES
HOWARD RD
ORCHARD CT
MANOR RD
WORLEY PL
MANOR PCH

92
BOTTOM LA
GURNELLS RD
WYNDSWICK
RASELDE RD
CHERRYWOOD CL
CHURCH RD
PO
PH
HEARNE'S CL
HEARNE'S MDW
HP9

Drummer's Yard
Young's Wood
GODOLPHIN RD
DEAN TREE
LESS DROVERS WAY
WOOL POND
CULVERS CROFT
FARMERS WAY
BARRARDS
COAT WINDS
STABLE
SEER MDW
Seer Green
Hall Place
Cemy
Jordans Sch
PUERS FIELD
LONG WOOD DR

4
Long Grove Wood Wildlife Reserve
LONG GROVE
Seer Green CE Comb Sch
SCHOOL LA
SEER
1 PADDOCKS END
2 MOSS CT
3 ORCHARD MEWS
4 MANOR FARM WAY
5 GREENWOOD CL
6 THE COPPICE
WILTON LA
PUERS LA
CRUTCHES LA
JORDANS WAY
MEADOWSIDE
Jordans

3
LONGBOTTOM LA
VICARAGE CL
BARNE HILL CL
BAYNE HILL
COPSE LA
SEER GREEN LA
GREEN WEST RD
GREEN NORTH
GREEN EAST RD
PO
JORDANS LA
Crutches Wood
BEECH LA
Jordans Farm

91
Seer Green & Jordans
CH
FARM LA
DEAN WOOD RD
YH
WELDERS LA
Meeting House
Welders House

The Mount
Wheatsheaf Wood
Stone Dean Farm
SL9

2
Walk Wood
Wilton Park

MINERVA WAY
MAUDE RD
MAUDE CL
Wilton Park
GORELL RD
CUPRE CRES
WAKELL RD
BALDWIN RD
BERWICK CL
Sports Field
POTKILN LA
Birchland Wood
Thirty Acre Knoll

1
LONDON END
MINERVA WAY

90
A40 LONDON RD
BURNHAM AVE
A40

95 A B 96 C D 97 E F

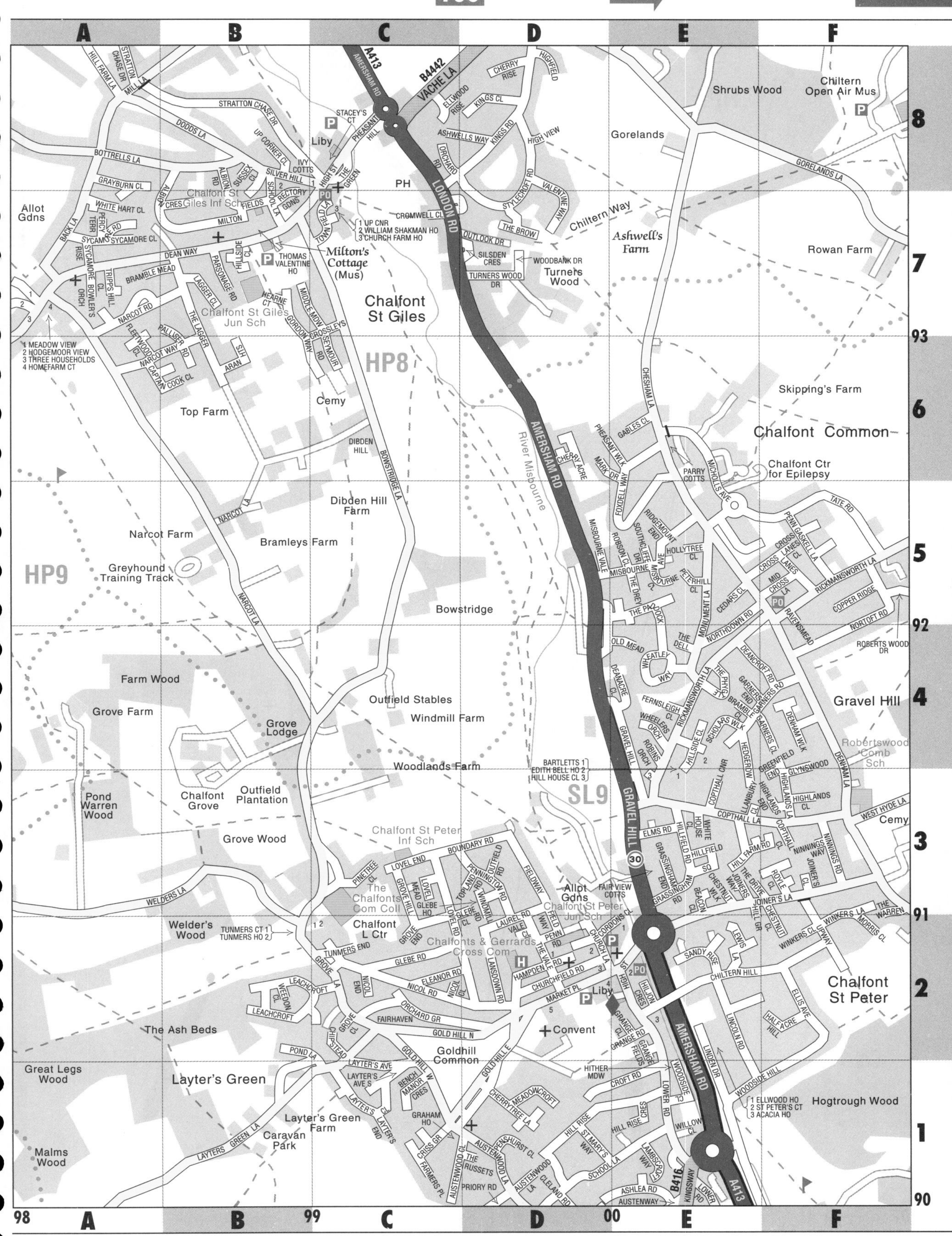

D2
1 STRINGERS COTTS
2 ADSTOCK MEWS
3 THE BROADWAY
4 BUCKINGHAM PAR
5 MARKET HO

A   B   C   D   E   F

8

HP8

Bottom Wood

Ladywalk Wood

BASING RD

KENWOOD

FOTHERLEY RD

PLASTWICK CRES

LONG LA

UXBRIDGE RD

A412   A412

A412 Rickmansworth, Watford

Becks New University

Newland Park

Five Plantations

Pollardshill Wood

CHALFONT RD

M25

DENHAM WY (NORTH ORBITAL RD)

A405

A405

UXBRIDGE RD

Froghall Farm

GORELANDS LA

7

Model Farm

Woodoaks Farm

A412

93

Brawlings Farm

BRAWLINGS LA

SHIRE LA

Maple Cross

PH
PO

OAKHILL RD   OAKHILL CL

FRANK SKS

MAPLE LODGE CL

LONGMORE

Maplelodge Farm

River Colne

6

Hillview

HAZEL CT

DUMBLETONS

Springwell Lake

Horn Hill

Beechen Wood

Sewage Works

RICKMANSWORTH LA

PH

Longlees

POLLARDSRY

BRADBERY

BEECHEN WOOD RD

DOWNING

TICHBORNE

WOODRICKS

PINCH FIELD

ADAWALK

P

Recn Gd

+

5

Springview Farm

ROBERTS LA

Mast

BUTTLEHIDE

LONG CROFT RD

HORSLEYS

HORNHILL RD

WOOD

WOODLAND RD

BY-WOOD END

ROBERTS WOOD DR

ASH VALE

Franklin's Spring

Lynsters

92

SL9

THE HAWTHORNS

THE BIRCH DR

WD3

Maple Cross JMI Sch

Round Rocket Plantation

+

WEST HYDE LA

DENHAM WY (NORTH ORBITAL RD)

Lynsters Lake

4

Cemy

SUNNYHILL RD

CHALFONT LA

OLD UXBRIDGE RD

PH

COPPERMILL LA

P

Bloom Wood

Butterfield Cotts

PLEASANT PL

PH

3

Warren Farm

West Hyde

Pynesfield Lake

DENHAM LA

91

2

Chalfont Heights Scout Camp

TILEHOUSE LA

Mopes Farm

UB9

1

West Hyde House

A412

M25

90

Hertfordshire STREET ATLAS

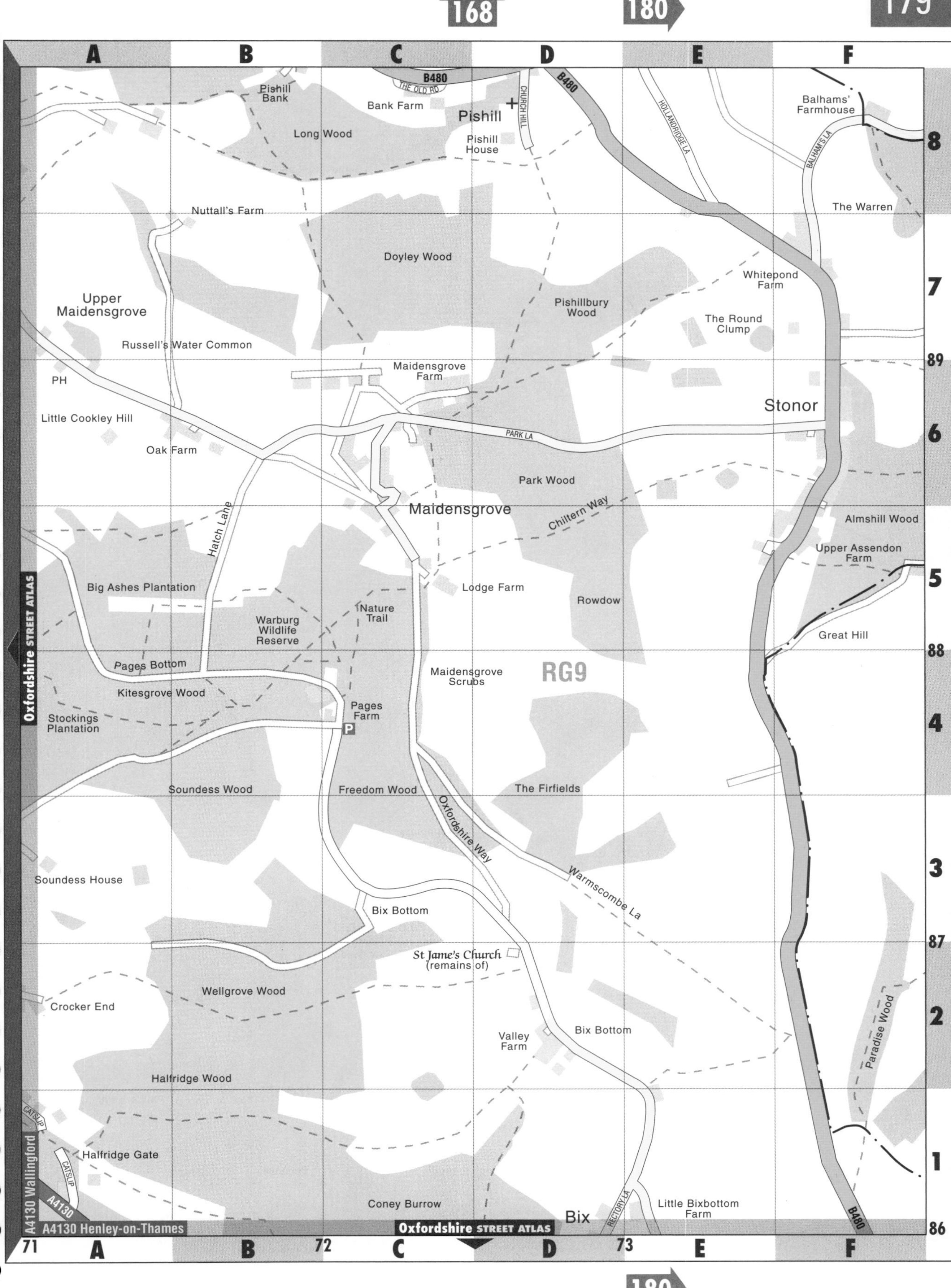

A B C D E F

8

7

89

6

5

88

4

3

87

2

1

86

B480
THE OLD RD.
Pishill Bank
Bank Farm
Pishill
+ CHURCH HILL
Pishill House
B480
HOLLANDRIDGE LA
Balhams' Farmhouse
BALHAMS LA
The Warren

Long Wood

Nuttall's Farm

Doyley Wood

Whitepond Farm

Upper Maidensgrove

Pishillbury Wood

The Round Clump

Russell's Water Common

Maidensgrove Farm

Stonor

PH

Little Cookley Hill

PARK LA

Oak Farm

Park Wood

Maidensgrove

Chiltern Way

Almshill Wood

Hatch Lane

Upper Assendon Farm

Big Ashes Plantation

Lodge Farm

Rowdow

Great Hill

Nature Trail

Warburg Wildlife Reserve

Pages Bottom

Maidensgrove Scrubs

RG9

Kitesgrove Wood

Pages Farm
P

88

Stockings Plantation

Soundess Wood

Freedom Wood

The Firfields

Oxfordshire Way

Warmscombe La

Soundess House

Bix Bottom

Wellgrove Wood

St Jame's Church (remains of)

Paradise Wood

Crocker End

Valley Farm

Bix Bottom

Halfridge Wood

CATSLIP

A4130 Wallingford

Halfridge Gate

CATSLIP

A4130

Coney Burrow

Bix

RECTORY LA

Little Bixbottom Farm

B480

71 A 72 B C 73 D E F

179
169

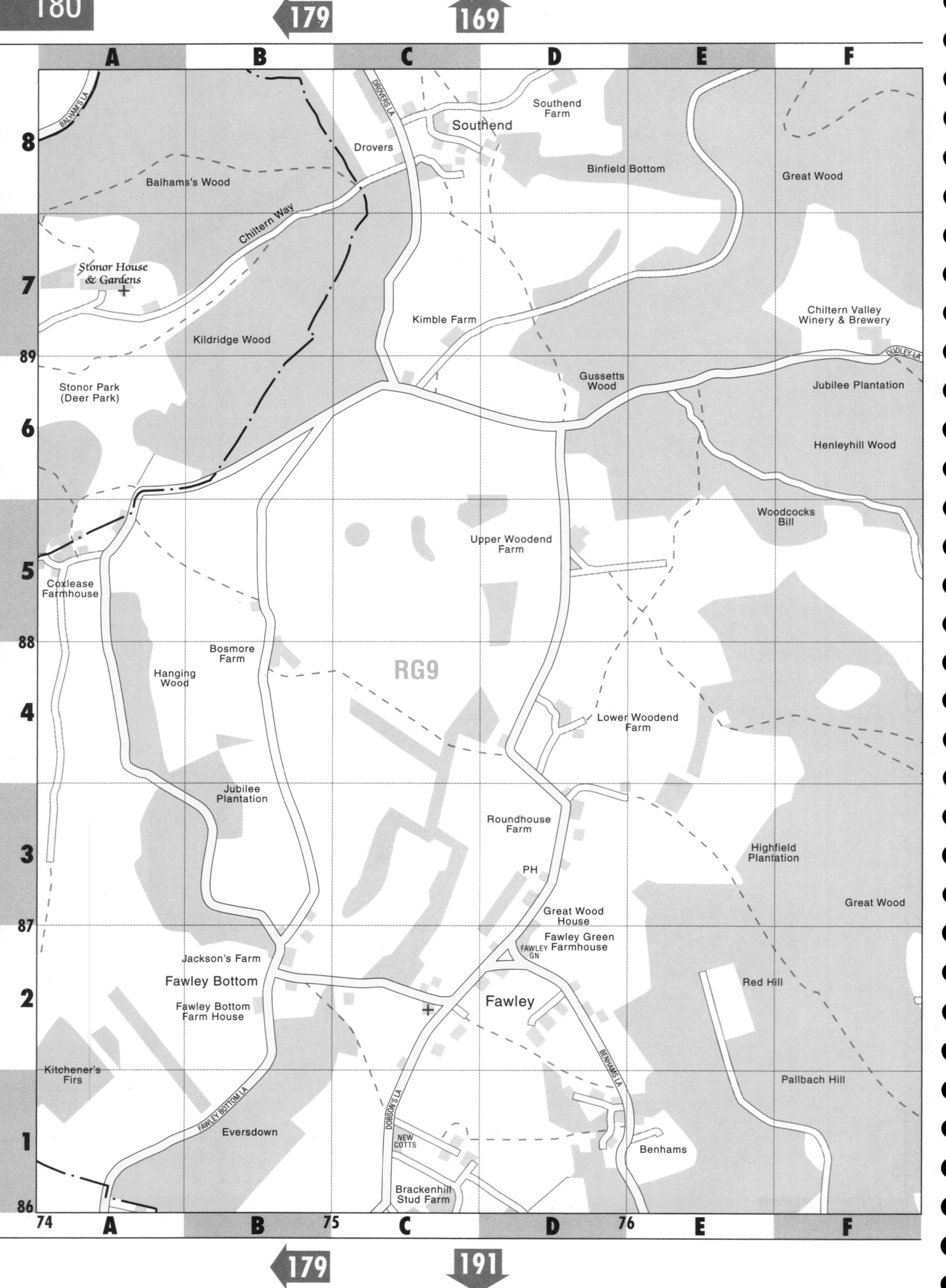
A
B
C
D
E
F
8
7
89
6
5
88
4
3
87
2
1
86
74
75
76
BALHAM'S LA
DROVERS LA
Southend
Southend Farm
Drovers
Binfield Bottom
Great Wood
Balhams's Wood
Chiltern Way
Stonor House & Gardens
Kimble Farm
Chiltern Valley Winery & Brewery
Kildridge Wood
DUDLEY LA
Stonor Park (Deer Park)
Gussetts Wood
Jubilee Plantation
Henleyhill Wood
Woodcocks Bill
Upper Woodend Farm
Coxlease Farmhouse
Bosmore Farm
Hanging Wood
RG9
Lower Woodend Farm
Jubilee Plantation
Roundhouse Farm
Highfield Plantation
PH
Great Wood House
Great Wood
Fawley Green Farmhouse
FAWLEY GN
Jackson's Farm
Fawley Bottom
Red Hill
Fawley
Fawley Bottom Farm House
BENHAMS LA
Kitchener's Firs
Pallbach Hill
FAWLEY BOTTOM LA
DOBSON'S LA
Eversdown
NEW COTTS
Benhams
Brackenhill Stud Farm

179
191

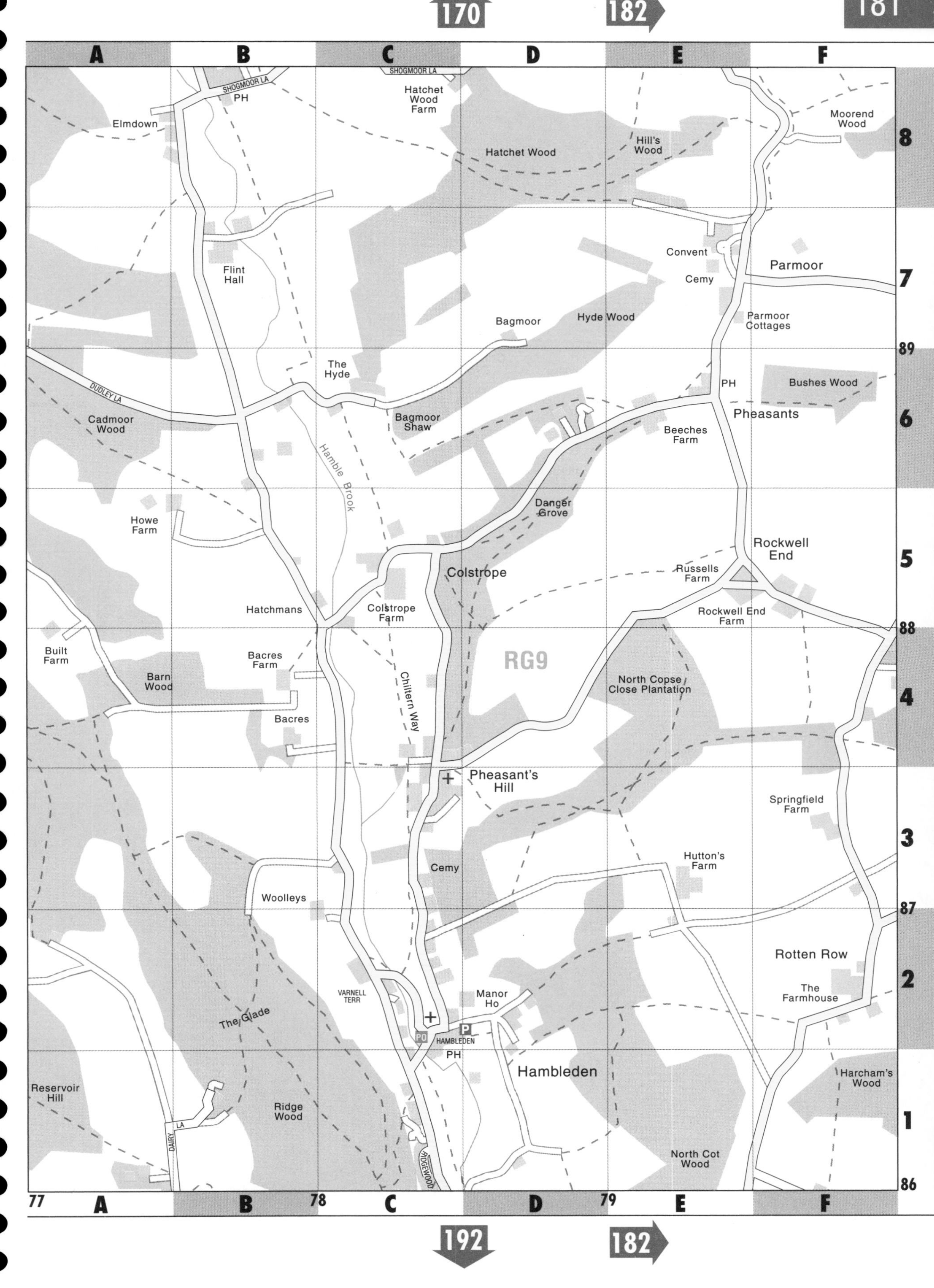
170
182
A
B
C
D
E
F
SHOGMOOR LA
PH
Elmdown
Hatchet Wood Farm
Hatchet Wood
Hill's Wood
Moorend Wood
8
Flint Hall
Convent
Cemy
Parmoor
7
Bagmoor
Hyde Wood
Parmoor Cottages
89
The Hyde
DUDLEY LA
PH
Bushes Wood
Pheasants
6
Cadmoor Wood
Bagmoor Shaw
Beeches Farm
Hamble Brook
Howe Farm
Danger Grove
Rockwell End
5
Russells Farm
Colstrope
Hatchmans
Colstrope Farm
Rockwell End Farm
88
Built Farm
Bacres Farm
RG9
Barn Wood
Chiltern Way
North Copse Close Plantation
4
Bacres
Pheasant's Hill
Springfield Farm
3
Cemy
Hutton's Farm
Woolleys
87
Rotten Row
2
VARNELL TERR
Manor Ho
The Farmhouse
The Glade
P
PO
HAMBLEDEN
PH
Hambleden
Harcham's Wood
Reservoir Hill
Ridge Wood
1
LA
DAIRY
RIDGEWOOD
North Cot Wood
86
77
78
79
192
182

181
171

A   B   C   D   E   F

8

Moorend
Wood

HP14

Bottom Wood

Beacon
Farm

Finnamore La

Beacon La

B482

7

Finnamore
Wood

Bluey's
Farm

The Roost

89

Chisbridge

Chisbridge
Cross

6

Shillingridge Wood

Copy Green

Woodlands

Holme Wood
Cottage

Holme
Wood

SHILLINGRIDGE
PK

Denelands
Farm

FRIETH RD

Oaklands
Farm

Holme Wood

5

Kent's
Wood

Hawkins
Farm

Mundaydean
Bottom

MUNDAYDEAN LA

88

Bottom House

RG9

Woodend
House

SL7

4

Fountain's

Woodend Farm

Holywick

Arbon

Lower
Woodend

3

Heath Wood

Walnut
Tree
Farm

Lord's
Wood

Marlow
Common

MARLOW COMM

87

Homefield Wood
Wildlife Reserve

Rogues Plantation

2

Chiltern Way

Davenport Wood

Bockmer End
Farm

1

Woodland Plain

Bockmer
House

BOCKMER LA

Bockmer End

Pullingshill
Wood

Hook's Farm

86

Widefield

80   A   B   81   C   D   82   E   F

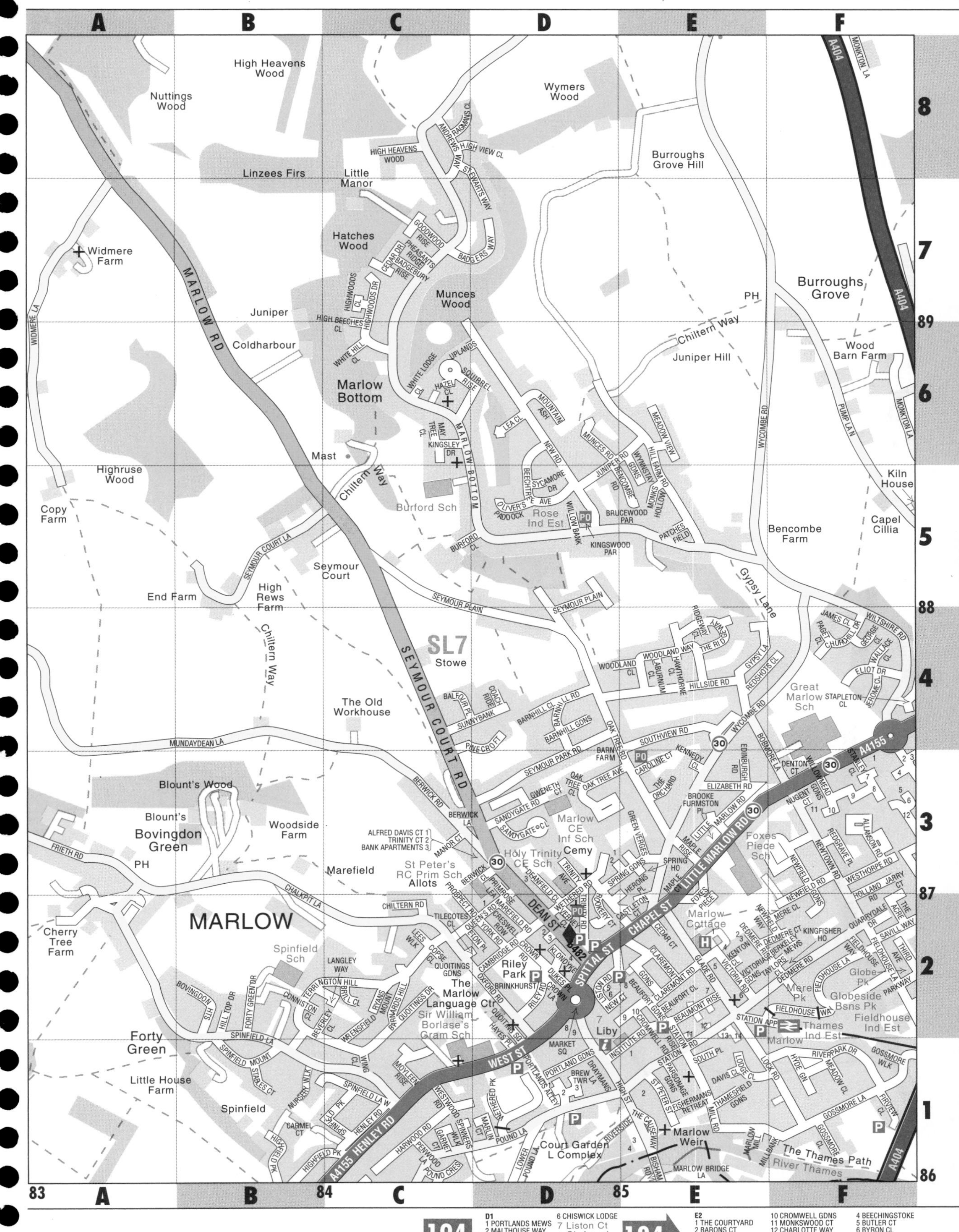

183
173

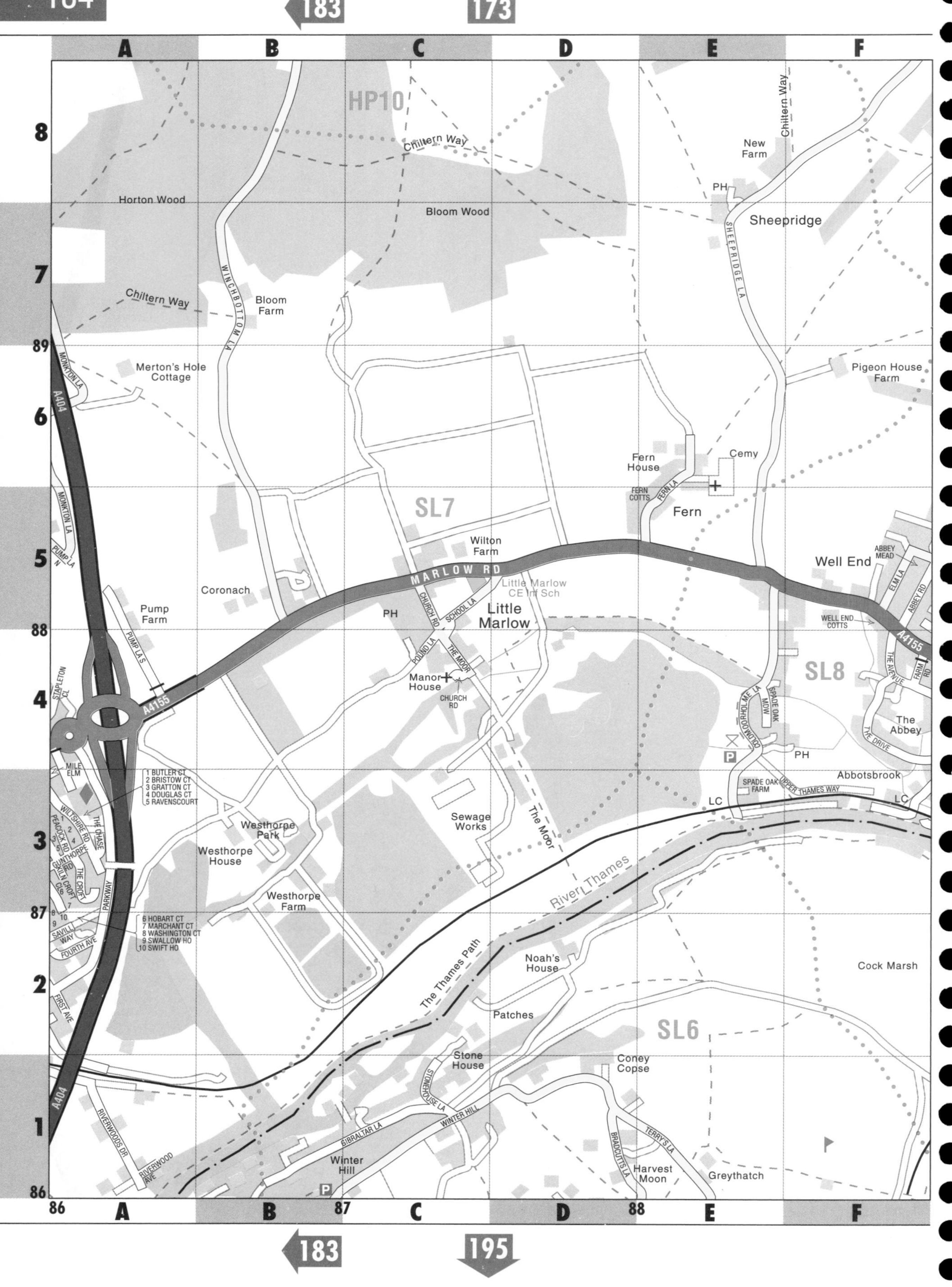
A B C D E F
8 7 6 5 4 3 2 1
89 88 87 86
HP10
SL7
SL8
SL6
Chiltern Way
Horton Wood
Bloom Wood
New Farm
PH
Sheepridge
SHEEPRIDGE LA
Bloom Farm
WINCHBOTTOM LA
Merton's Hole Cottage
MONKTON LA
A404
Pigeon House Farm
Fern House
Cemy
FERN COTTS
FERN LA
Fern
Wilton Farm
MARLOW RD
Little Marlow CE Inf Sch
Little Marlow
Well End
ABBEY MEAD
ELM LA
ABBEY RD
WELL END COTTS
A4155
Coronach
Pump Farm
PUMP LA
PUMP LA S
CHURCH RD
SCHOOL LA
POUND LA
THE MOOR
Manor House
CHURCH RD
STAPLETON CL
COLDMOORHOLME LA
SPADE OAK MDW
THE AVENUE
FARM RD
The Abbey
THE DRIVE
PH
Abbotsbrook
SPADE OAK FARM
UPPER THAMES WAY
LC
MILE ELM
1 BUTLER CT
2 BRISTOW CT
3 GRATTON CT
4 DOUGLAS CT
5 RAVENSCOURT
WILTSHIRE RD
THE CHASE
PEACOCK RD
GUNTHORPE RD
THE CROFT
PARKWAY
Westhorpe Park
Westhorpe House
Sewage Works
The Moor
River Thames
Westhorpe Farm
6 HOBART CT
7 MARCHANT CT
8 WASHINGTON CT
9 SWALLOW HO
10 SWIFT HO
SAVILL WAY
FOURTH AVE
FIRST AVE
The Thames Path
Noah's House
Cock Marsh
Patches
Stone House
Coney Copse
STONEHOUSE LA
WINTER HILL
GIBRALTAR LA
RIVERWOODS DR
RIVERWOOD AVE
Winter Hill
Harvest Moon
Greythatch
BRADCUTTS LA
TERRY'S LA
P
86 87 88

183
195

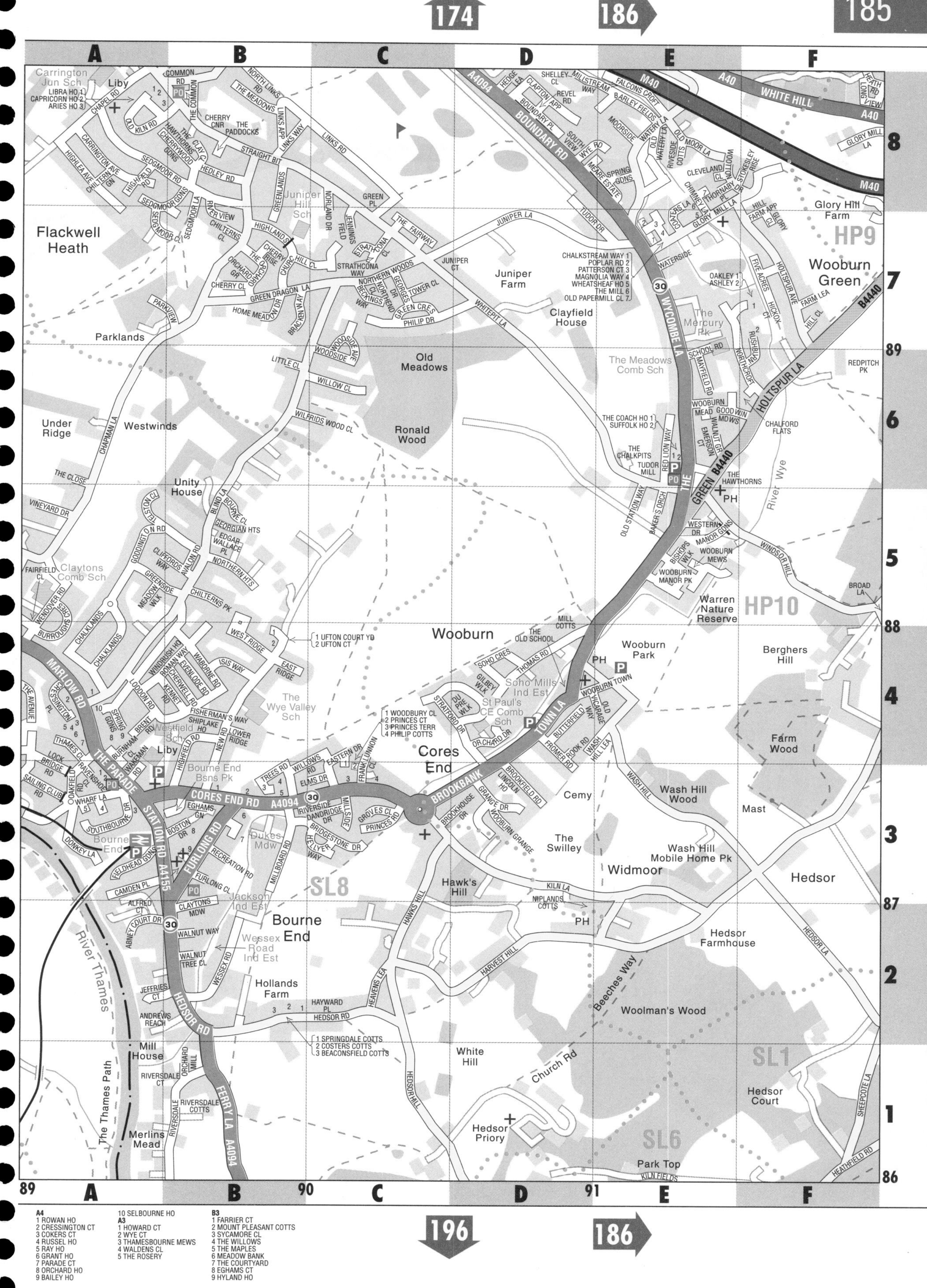

174
186
A
B
C
D
E
F
Carrington Jun Sch
Liby
LIBRA HO 1
CAPRICORN HO 2
ARIES HO 3
CHAPEL RD
OLD KILN RD
COMMON RD
THE COMMON
NORTH LINKS RD
THE MEADOWS
CHERRY CNR
THE PADDOCKS
LINKS APP
LINKS WAY
LINKS RD
STRAIGHT BIT
CARRINGTON AVE
CHILTERN AVE
HIGHLEA AVE
SEDGMOOR RD
HEDLEY RD
GREENLANDS
Juniper Hill Sch
NORLAND DR
GREEN PL
JENNINGS FIELD
HIGHLANDS
SEDGMOOR GDNS
SEDGMOOR LA
RIVER VIEW
CHILTERNS CL
SEDGMOOR CL
Flackwell Heath
THE FAIRWAY
JUNIPER LA
HEDGE LA
CLAPTON APP
SHELLEY CL
REVEL RD
MILLSTREAM WAY
FALCONS CROFT
BARLEY FIELDS
M40
A40
WHITE HILL
HEATH RD
LONG VIEW
GLORY MILL LA
A4094
BOUNDARY RD
BOUNDARY PL
SOUTH VIEW
WYE RD
MEARE ESTATE
SPRING GDNS
MOORSIDE
WATERY LA
OLD WATERY LA
RIVERSIDE COTTS
OLD MOOR LA
CLEVELAND CL
WOOTTON DR
STOKESLEY RISE
THORNABY PL
GLORY MILL LA
HILL FARM APP
GLORY CL
Glory Hill Farm
HP9
TUDOR DR
COATERS LA
CHIMNEY LA
STRATHCONA CL
STRATHCONA WAY
NORTHERN WOODS
JUNIPER CT
Juniper Farm
CHALKSTREAM WAY 1
POPLAR RD 2
PATTERSON CT 3
MAGNOLIA WAY 4
WHEATSHEAF HO 5
THE MILL 6
OLD PAPERMILL CL 7
WATERSIDE
OAKLEY 1
ASHLEY 2
FIVE ACRES
HOLTSPUR AVE
Wooburn Green
FARM LEA
HILL CL
B4440
CHERRY RISE
THE ORCHARD
ORCHARD GR
CHURCH HILL CL
CHERRY CL
GREEN DRAGON LA
HOME MEADOW DR
BRACKEN WAY
GEORGES DR
NORTHEND CL
BECKINGS WAY
TOWER CL
GREEN CRES
PHILIP DR
WHITEPIT LA
Clayfield House
WYCOMBE LA
The Mercury Pk
HICKOX CT
PARKVIEW
Parklands
LITTLE CL
WOODSIDE
WOODSIDE AVE
Old Meadows
WILLOW CL
SCHOOL RD
RUSHBURN
NORTHCROFT
The Meadows Comb Sch
MAYFIELD RD
REDPITCH PK
WOOBURN MEAD
GOODWIN MDWS
HOLTSPUR LA
THE COACH HO 1
SUFFOLK HO 2
CHALFORD FLATS
Under Ridge
Westwinds
CHAPMAN LA
WILFRIDS WOOD CL
Ronald Wood
RED LION WAY
WALNUT GR
EMERSON CT
THE CHALKPITS
TUDOR MILL
THE GREEN
THE HAWTHORNS
PH
River Wye
THE CLOSE
Unity House
BLIND LA
BOURNE CL
GEORGIAN HTS
EDGAR WALLACE PL
NORTHERN HTS
TILSTON CL
VINEYARD DR
GODDINGTON RD
CLIFFORDS WAY
AVALON RD
OLD STATION WAY
BAKER'S ORCH
WESTERN DR
MANOR GDNS
BISHOPS WLK
WOOBURN MEWS
WOOBURN MANOR PK
WINDSOR HILL
FAIRFIELD CL
Claytons Comb Sch
GREENSIDE
MEADOW WLK
CHILTERNS PK
WENDOVER RD
BURROUGHS CRES
CHALKLANDS
Warren Nature Reserve
HP10
BROAD LA
WEST RIDGE
1 UFTON COURT YD
2 UFTON CT
Wooburn
THE OLD SCHOOL
MILL COTTS
Wooburn Park
Berghers Hill
MARLOW RD
THE AVENUE
CRESSINGTON PL
WINDRUSH HO
BOWAN WAY
EVENLODE RD
WABORNE RD
ISIS WAY
CHERWELL RD
KENNET RD
EAST RIDGE
SOHO CRES
THOMAS RD
GILBEY WLK
Soho Mills Ind Est
WOOBURN TOWN
LODDON RD
SPRING GDNS
FISHERMAN'S WAY
The Wye Valley Sch
1 WOODBURY CL
2 PRINCES CT
3 PRINCES TERR
4 PHILIP COTTS
DU PRE WLK
STRATFORD DR
St Paul's CE Comb Sch
TOWN LA
BUTTERFIELD
VICARAGE WAY
OLD WASH HILL LEA
Farm Wood
THAMES CL
THE PARADE
BURNHAM CL
WAKEMAN RD
BRENT RD
Westfield Sch
SHIPLAKE HO
HIGHFIELD RD
NEW RD
LOWER RIDGE
Liby
EASTERN DR
FRANK LUNNON CL
Cores End
ORCHARD DR
FROMER RD
BROOK RD
LOCK BRIDGE RD
RAVENSHOE CL
SAILING CLUB RD
COAKFIELD
WHARF LA
PO
P
Bourne End Bsns Pk
TREES RD
WILLOWS RD
ELMS DR
CORES END RD
A4094
BROOKBANK
LINCOLN HO
BROOKFIELD RD
WASH HILL
Cemy
Wash Hill Wood
Mast
SOUTHBOURNE DR
DONKEY LA
Bourne End
STATION RD
EGHAMS GN
BOSTON DR
FURLONG RD
RIVERSIDE
DANDRIDGE DR
MILLSIDE
GROVES CL
PRINCES RD
BRIDGESTONE DR
HELLYER WAY
Dukes Mdw
BROOKHOUSE DR
GRANGE DR
WOOBURN GRANGE
The Swilley
Wash Hill Mobile Home Pk
Widmoor
Hedsor
FIELDHEAD GDNS
A4155
RECREATION RD
MILLBOARD RD
SL8
Hawk's Hill
KILN LA
NIPLANDS COTTS
CAMDEN PL
FURLONG CL
Jackson Ind Est
ALFRED CT
CLAYTONS MDW
ABNEY COURT DR
WALNUT WAY
Bourne End
HAWKS HILL
PH
Hedsor Farmhouse
River Thames
WALNUT TREE CL
Wessex Road Ind Est
WESSEX RD
HARVEST HILL
JEFFRIES CT
HEDSOR RD
Hollands Farm
HAYWARD PL
HEAVENS LEA
Beeches Way
HEDSOR LA
ANDREWS REACH
HEDSOR RD
Woolman's Wood
1 SPRINGDALE COTTS
2 COSTERS COTTS
3 BEACONSFIELD COTTS
Mill House
The Thames Path
ORCHARD MILL
RIVERSDALE CT
FERRY LA
White Hill
HEDSOR HILL
Church Rd
SL1
Hedsor Court
SHEEPCOTE LA
RIVERSDALE
RIVERSDALE COTTS
A4094
Merlins Mead
Hedsor Priory
SL6
Park Top
KILN FIELDS
HEATHFIELD RD
8
7
89
6
5
88
4
3
87
2
1
86
89
90
91
A4
1 ROWAN HO
2 CRESSINGTON CT
3 COKERS CT
4 RUSSEL HO
5 RAY HO
6 GRANT HO
7 PARADE CT
8 ORCHARD HO
9 BAILEY HO
10 SELBOURNE HO
A3
1 HOWARD CT
2 WYE CT
3 THAMESBOURNE MEWS
4 WALDENS CL
5 THE ROSERY
B3
1 FARRIER CT
2 MOUNT PLEASANT COTTS
3 SYCAMORE CL
4 THE WILLOWS
5 THE MAPLES
6 MEADOW BANK
7 THE COURTYARD
8 EGHAMS CT
9 HYLAND HO
196
186

185
175

BEACONSFIELD

HP9

HP10

A40 WYCOMBE END

M40

A355

A **B** **C** **D** **E** **F**

8

HOLTSPUR CL
HEATH RD
MAYFLOWER WAY
KINGS CL
SKELTON
3 CL
NORTH DR
KILN CT
BURKES
WOOD RD S
KILN CT
PENINGTON RD
BURKES CL
BURKES RD
WALKWOOD RISE
TILSWORTH RD
TILSWORTH RD
BUTLERS COURT RD
THE SPINNEY
THE SPINNEY
CROSBY RD
MALTHOUSE SQ
WINDSOR RD
LAKES LA
HEDGERLY LA
CROSS LA
Cts

St ANTHONY'S CT
WATTLETON RD

WHITE HILL
GLORY HILL LA
A40
SOUTH DR

B4440

1 FREDERICKS CT
2 HOLTSPUR TOP LA
3 BEACONSFIELD MEWS
4 HOLTSPUR PAR
5 HOLTSPUR CT

1 CHERRY TREE RD
2 NORTH CL

M40

HOLTSPUR LA
WOOBURN GREEN LA

Cemy

7

P

Springfield

Obelisk

Home Farm

Hall Barn

89

The Grove

Over's Farm

BURNHAM RD

The Bungalow

6

Mill Wood

BROAD LA

Fairview House

Lillyfee Farm

Hill Wood

LILLYFEE FARM LA

5

Dipple Wood

Woodlands Farm

WOODLANDS HILL

Hollybush Wood

88

Castleman's Farm

Dipple Lodge

SHIP HILL

4

Odds Farm Park

GREEN COMMON LA

Jennings Farm

PH

SALTERS ROW

ODDS FARM EST

Hicknaham Plantation

Wooburn Common

HAREHATCH LA

3

Sheepcote Farm

Ashen Coppice

SL1

Little Jennings Farm

Hicknaham Farm

Boveney Wood

ABBEY PARK LA

Akroyd Cottages

87

WOOBURN COMMON RD

Hales Cottage

Healy's Gorse

SHEEPCOTE LA

2

Abbey Park Farm

Saw Mill

Bristles Wood

Boveney Wood Farm

PARK LA

HEDSOR LA

PH

Johnson's Coppice

Dropmore Inf Sch

Boveney Wood La

Dorney Wood

Staplefurze Wood

HEATHFIELD RD

Hollybush Wood

DROPMORE RD

LITTLEWORTH RD

Littleworth Common

DORNEY WOOD RD

PH

COMMON LA

1

SL2

86

The Lake

Dropmore

A **B** **C** **D** **E** **F**

92 93 94

176 188

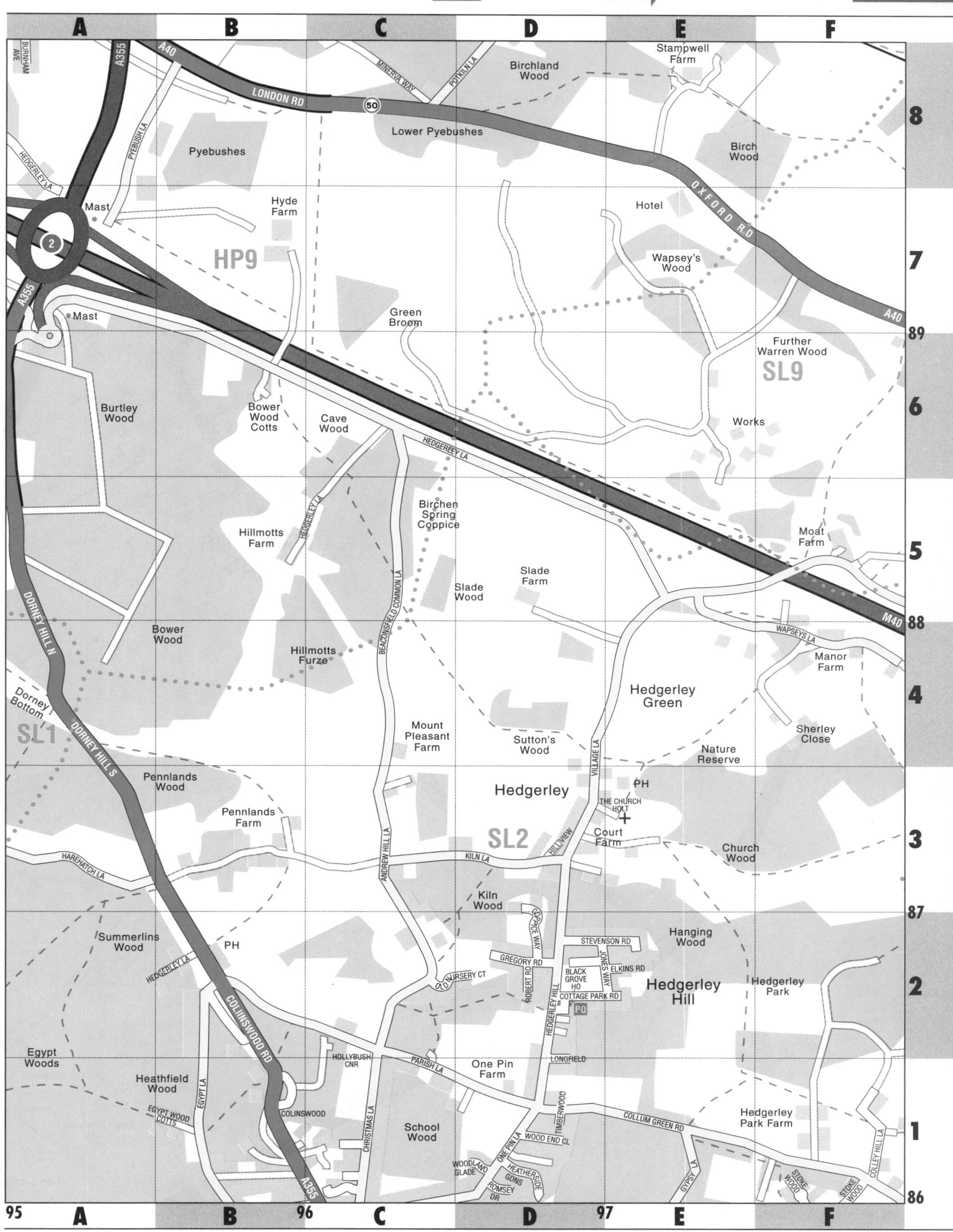
A
B
C
D
E
F
Stampwell Farm
Birchland Wood
BURNHAM AVE
A355
A40
LONDON RD
MINERVA WAY
POTKILN LA
50
Lower Pyebushes
PYEBUSH LA
Pyebushes
Birch Wood
HEDGERLEY LA
OXFORD RD
Mast
Hyde Farm
Hotel
2
HP9
Wapsey's Wood
Mast
Green Broom
A40
Further Warren Wood
SL9
Burtley Wood
Bower Wood Cotts
Cave Wood
Works
HEDGERLEY LA
Birchen Spring Coppice
Hillmotts Farm
HEDGERLEY LA
Moat Farm
Slade Farm
Slade Wood
BEACONSFIELD COMMON LA
M40
WAPSEYS LA
Bower Wood
Hillmotts Furze
Manor Farm
DORNEY HILL N
Hedgerley Green
Dorney Bottom
SL1
DORNEY HILL S
Mount Pleasant Farm
Sutton's Wood
Sherley Close
Nature Reserve
Pennlands Wood
VILLAGE LA
PH
Hedgerley
THE CHURCH HOLT
Pennlands Farm
ANDREW HILL LA
SL2
HILLVIEW
Court Farm
Church Wood
HAREHATCH LA
KILN LA
Kiln Wood
Summerlins Wood
PH
COPPICE WAY
STEVENSON RD
Hanging Wood
GREGORY RD
JONES WAY
ELKINS RD
HEDGERLEY LA
OLD NURSERY CT
BLACK GROVE HO
Hedgerley Hill
Hedgerley Park
ROBERT RD
HEDGERLEY HILL
COTTAGE PARK RD
PO
COLLINSWOOD RD
Egypt Woods
HOLLYBUSH CNR
PARISH LA
One Pin Farm
LONGFIELD
Heathfield Wood
EGYPT LA
TIMBERWOOD
EGYPT WOOD COTTS
COLINSWOOD
COLLUM GREEN RD
Hedgerley Park Farm
School Wood
CHRISTMAS LA
ONE PIN LA
WOOD END CL
WOODLAND GLADE
HEATHERSIDE GDNS
ROMSEY DR
GYPSY LA
STOKE WOOD
STOKE WOOD
COLLEY HILL LA
A355
8
7
89
6
5
88
4
3
87
2
1
86
95
96
97

198 188

187 177

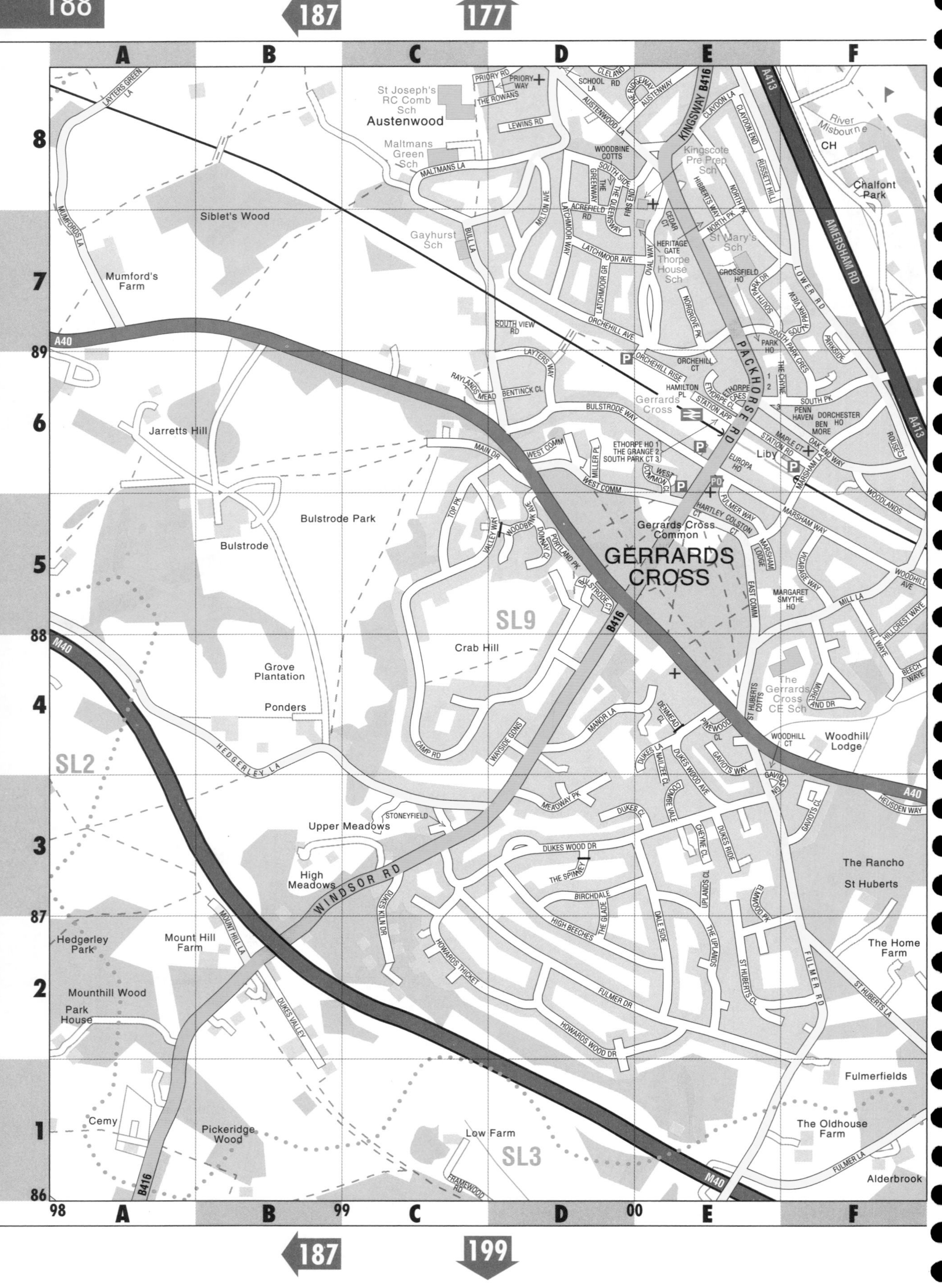
Austenwood
St Joseph's RC Comb Sch
Maltmans Green Sch
Siblet's Wood
Gayhurst Sch
Mumford's Farm
Kingscote Pre Prep Sch
St Mary's Sch
Thorpe House Sch
Chalfont Park
River Misbourne
Jarretts Hill
Gerrards Cross
Bulstrode Park
Bulstrode
Gerrards Cross Common
GERRARDS CROSS
SL9
Crab Hill
Grove Plantation
Ponders
The Gerrards Cross CE Sch
Woodhill Lodge
SL2
Upper Meadows
High Meadows
The Rancho
St Huberts
Hedgerley Park
Mount Hill Farm
The Home Farm
Mounthill Wood
Park House
Fulmerfields
Cemy
Pickeridge Wood
Low Farm
SL3
The Oldhouse Farm
Alderbrook
A40
M40
A413
B416
WINDSOR RD
PACKHORSE RD
KINGSWAY
AMERSHAM RD
FULMER RD
HEDGERLEY LA
MUMFORDS LA
LAYTERS GREEN LA
BULL LA
MALTMANS LA
LEWINS RD
THE ROWANS
PRIORY RD
PRIORY WAY
SCHOOL LA
CLELAND RD
AUSTENWOOD LA
AUSTENWAY
THE RIDGEWAY
CLAYDON LA
CLAYDON END
RUSSETT HILL
NORTH PK
HIBBERTS WAY
WOODBINE COTTS
SOUTH SIDE
THE GREENWAY
THE QUEENSWAY
FIRS END
ACREFIELD RD
LATCHMOOR WAY
LATCHMOOR AVE
LATCHMOOR GR
MILTON AVE
CEDAR CT
HERITAGE GATE
OVAL WAY
CROSSFIELD HO
NORGROVE PK
SOUTH PARK DR
PARK VIEW
LOWER RD
ORCHEHILL AVE
ORCHEHILL RISE
ORCHEHILL CT
SOUTH VIEW RD
LAYTERS WAY
PARK HO
SOUTH PARK CRES
THE CHYNE
PARKSIDE
RAYLANDS MEAD
BENTINCK CL
HAMILTON PL
ETHORPE CRES
ETHORPE CL
STATION APP
BULSTRODE WAY
PENN HAVEN
DORCHESTER HO
BEN MORE
SOUTH PK
MAPLE CT
OAK END WAY
STATION RD
ROUSE CT
ETHORPE HO 1
THE GRANGE 2
SOUTH PARK CT 3
MILLER PL
EUROPA HO
Liby
MARSHAM LA
WEST COMM
MAIN DR
WEST COMMON CL
PO
FULMER WAY
HARTLEY CT
COLSTON CT
MARSHAM WAY
WOODLANDS
TOP PK
VALLEY WAY
WOODBANK AVE
DONNAY CL
PORTLAND PK
BULSTRODE CT
MARSHAM LODGE
EAST COMM
VICARAGE WAY
MARGARET SMYTHE HO
MILL LA
WOODHILL AVE
HILLCREST WAYE
HILL WAYE
BEECH WAYE
MORELAND DR
ST HUBERTS COTTS
CAMP RD
WAYSIDE GDNS
MANOR LA
DENMEAD CL
PINEWOOD CL
DUKES LA
NALZEE CL
DUKES WOOD AVE
GAVIOTS WAY
GAVIOTS GN
WOODHILL CT
GAVIOTS CL
HEUSDEN WAY
STONEYFIELD
MEADWAY PK
DUKES CL
COOMBE VALE
CHEYNE CL
DUKES RIDE
DUKES WOOD DR
THE SPINNEY
UPLANDS CL
BIRCHDALE
HIGH BEECHES
THE GLADE
DALE SIDE
THE UPLANDS
ELMWOOD PK
DUKES KILN DR
HOWARDS THICKET
FULMER DR
ST HUBERTS CL
ST HUBERTS LA
HOWARDS WOOD DR
MOUNT HILL LA
DUKES VALLEY
FRAMEWOOD RD
FULMER LA
CH
P
A
B
C
D
E
F
8
7
6
5
4
3
2
1
89
88
87
86
98
99
00

187 199

178 190

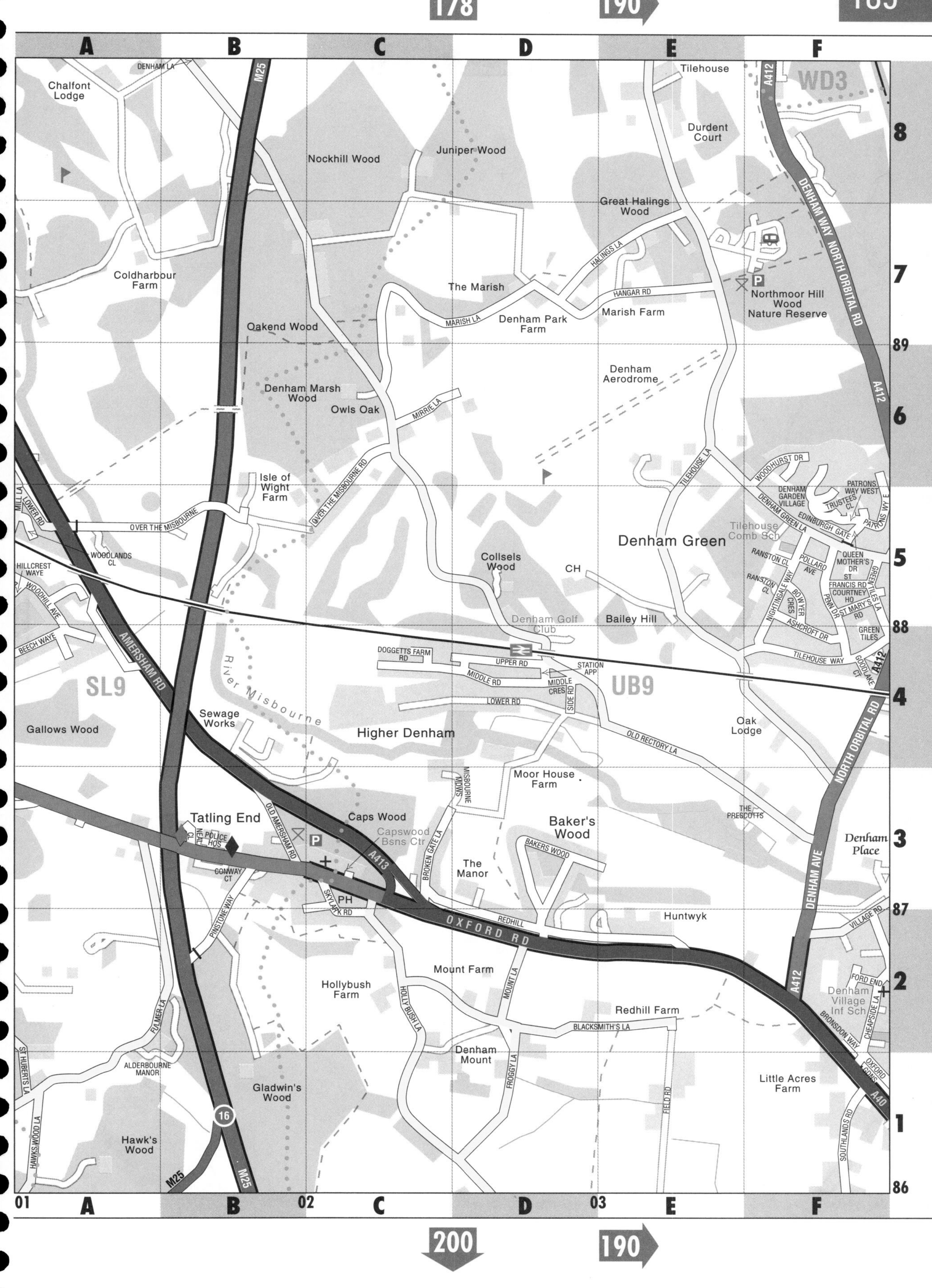
A
B
C
D
E
F
Chalfont Lodge
DENHAM LA
M25
Tilehouse
A412
WD3
Durdent Court
Nockhill Wood
Juniper Wood
Great Halings Wood
Coldharbour Farm
HALINGS LA
The Marish
HANGAR RD
Northmoor Hill Wood Nature Reserve
MARISH LA
Denham Park Farm
Marish Farm
Oakend Wood
DENHAM WAY NORTH ORBITAL RD
Denham Aerodrome
Denham Marsh Wood
Owls Oak
MIRRIE LA
OVER THE MISBOURNE RD
Isle of Wight Farm
MILL LA
LOWER RD
OVER THE MISBOURNE
TILEHOUSE LA
WOODHURST DR
DENHAM GARDEN VILLAGE
PATRONS WAY WEST
TRUSTEES CL
DENHAM GREEN LA
EDINBURGH GATE
PATRONS WY E
Tilehouse Comb Sch
Denham Green
WOODLANDS CL
HILLCREST WAYE
WOODHILL AVE
Collsels Wood
CH
RANSTON CL
POLLARD AVE
QUEEN MOTHER'S DR
ST FRANCIS RD
COURTNEY HO
ST MARY'S RD
GREEN TILES LA
NIGHTINGALE WAY
BOWYER CRES
PENN DR
ASHCROFT DR
GREEN TILES
Denham Golf Club
Bailey Hill
BEECH WAYE
AMERSHAM RD
DOGGETTS FARM RD
UPPER RD
STATION APP
TILEHOUSE WAY
GOODLAKE CT
MIDDLE RD
MIDDLE CRES
SIDE RD
SL9
River Misbourne
UB9
LOWER RD
Sewage Works
Gallows Wood
Higher Denham
OLD RECTORY LA
Oak Lodge
NORTH ORBITAL RD
MISBOURNE MDWS
Moor House Farm
Tatling End
OLD AMERSHAM RD
Caps Wood
Capswood Bsns Ctr
Baker's Wood
THE PRESCOTTS
Denham Place
NEAL CL
POLICE HQS
A413
BAKERS WOOD
BROKEN GATE LA
The Manor
DENHAM AVE
CONWAY CT
SKYLARK RD
PH
OXFORD RD
REDHILL
Huntwyk
VILLAGE RD
PINSTONE WAY
Mount Farm
MOUNT LA
Hollybush Farm
HOLLY BUSH LA
FORD END
Denham Village Inf Sch
Redhill Farm
BLACKSMITH'S LA
BRONSDON WAY
CHEAPSIDE LA
FULMER LA
Denham Mount
FROGGY LA
ST HUBERTS LA
ALDERBOURNE MANOR
OXFORD GDNS
Little Acres Farm
Gladwin's Wood
FIELD RD
A40
HAWKS WOOD LA
16
SOUTHLANDS RD
Hawk's Wood
M25
8
7
89
6
5
88
4
3
87
2
1
86
01
02
03

200 190

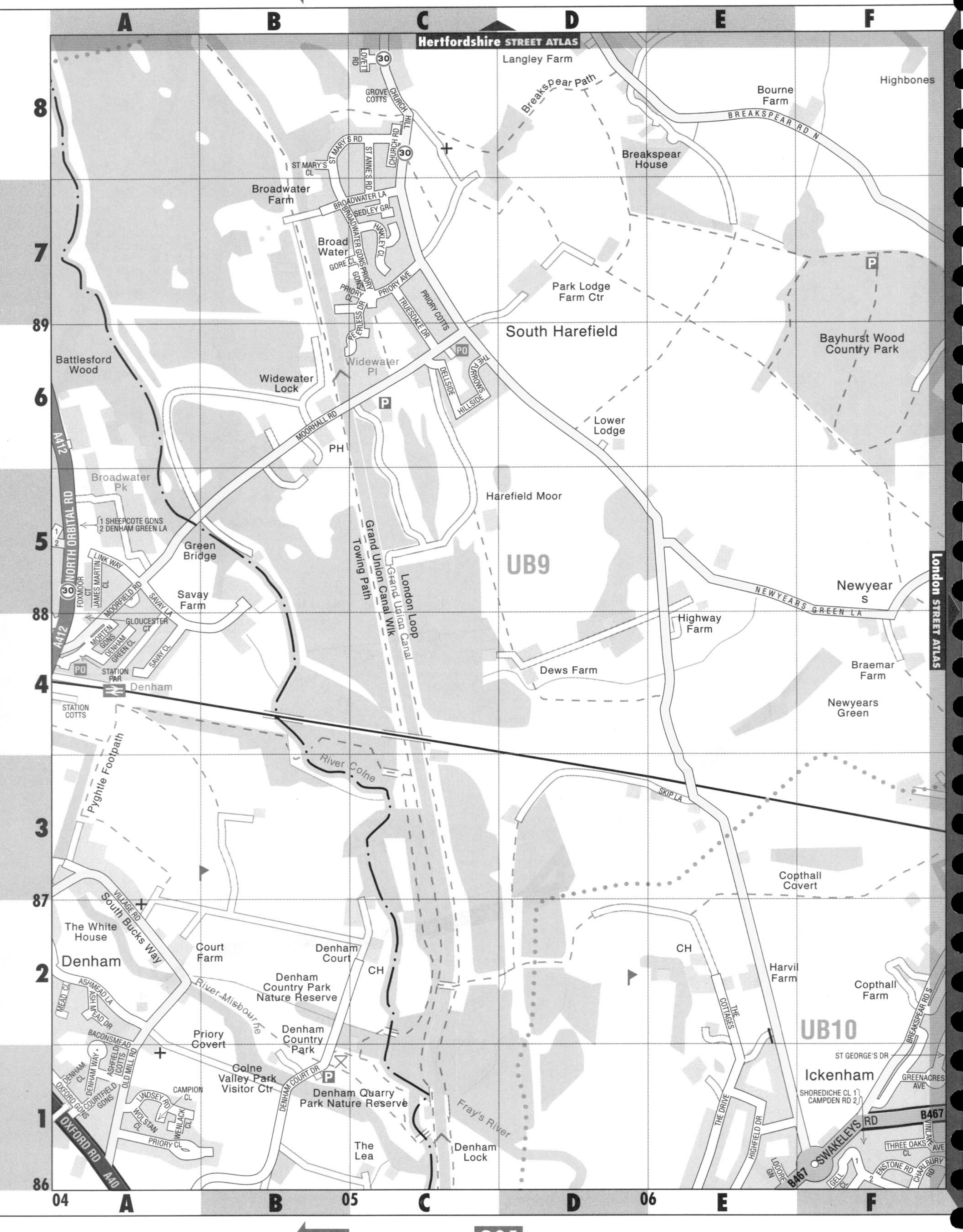

Hertfordshire STREET ATLAS

London STREET ATLAS

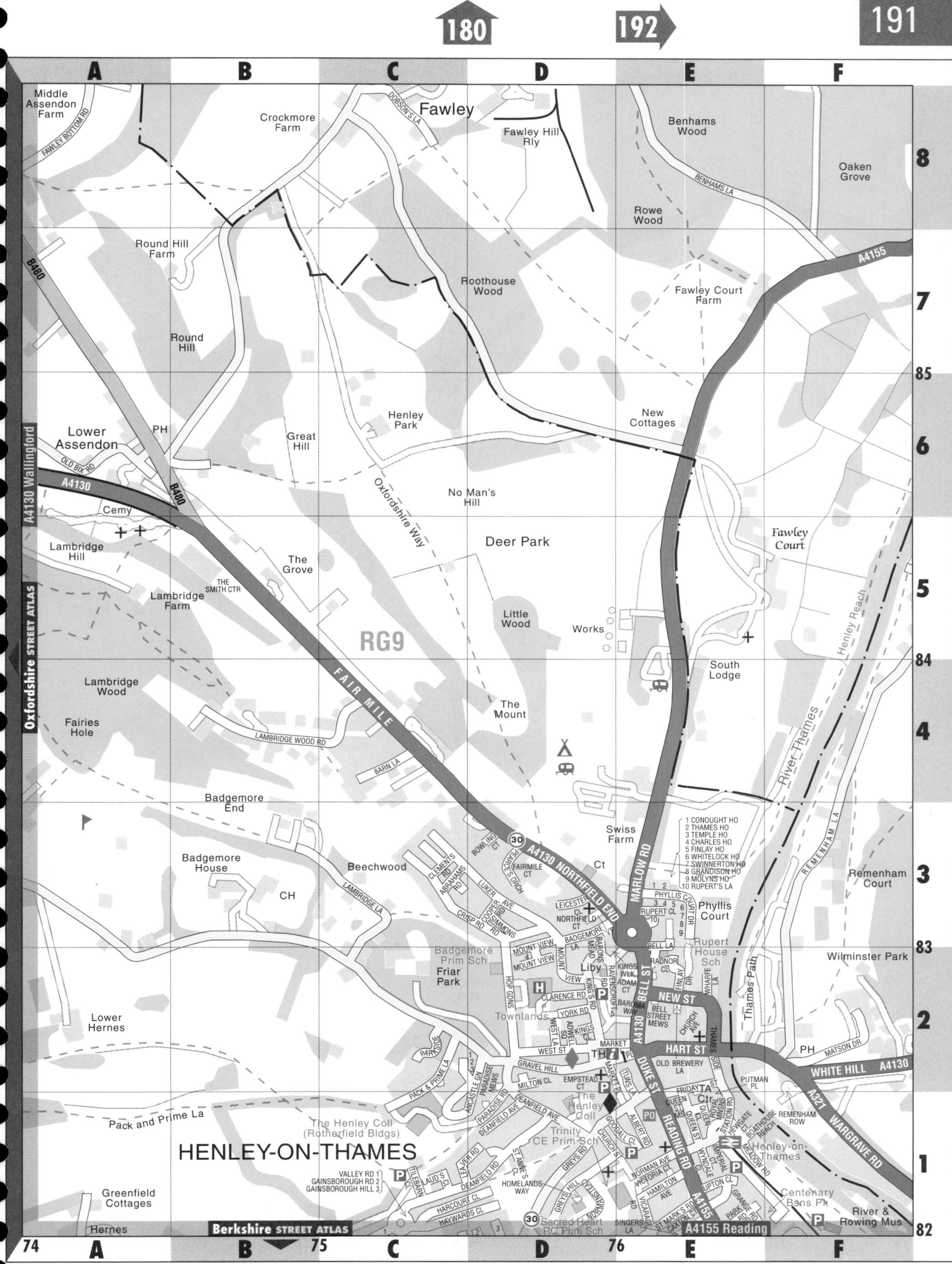

D2
1 CEDAR
2 BEECH
3 ACACIA
4 MOUNT VIEW CT
5 MARKET PLACE MEWS

191
181

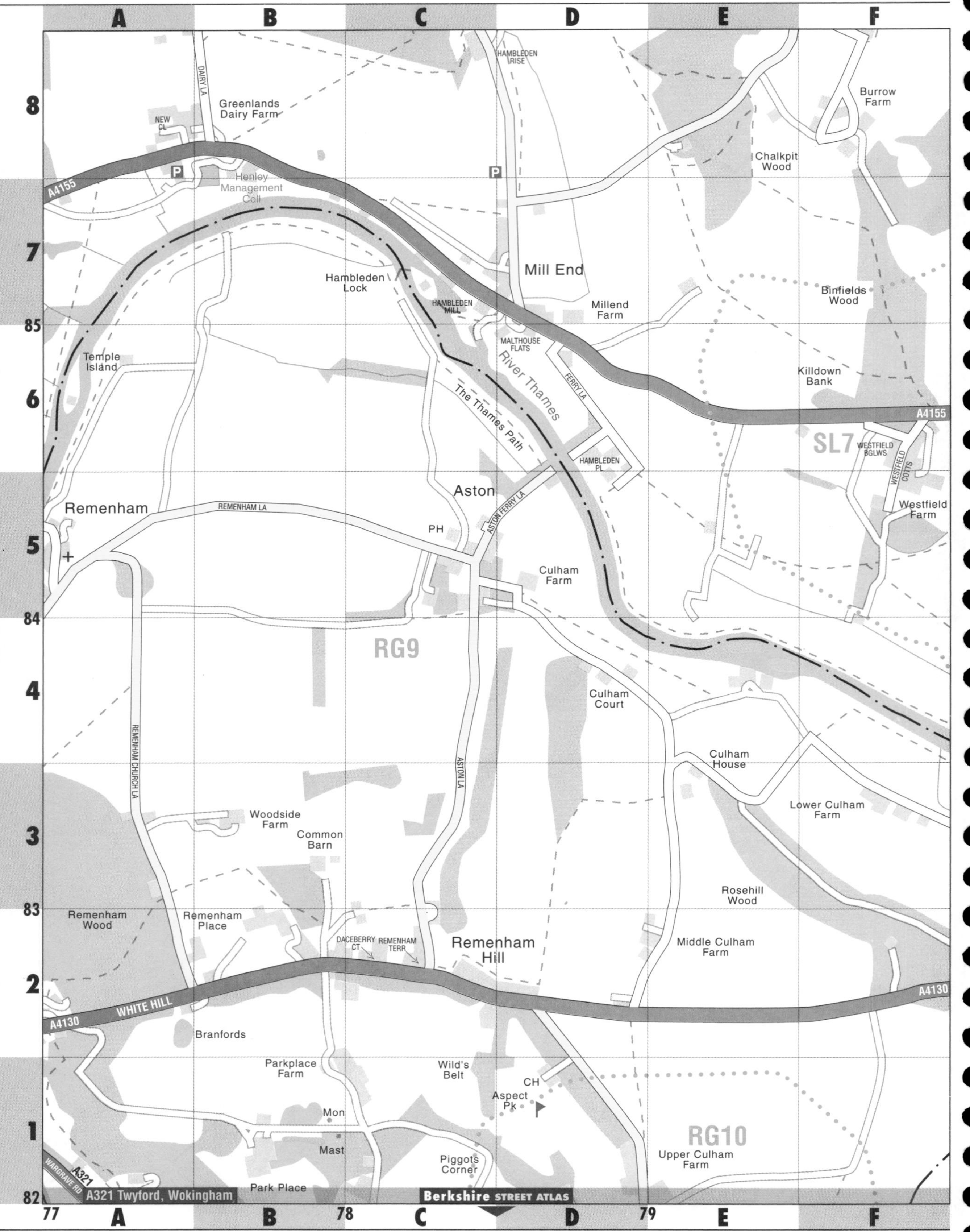

A
B
C
D
E
F
8
7
85
6
5
84
4
3
83
2
1
82
77
78
79
Greenlands Dairy Farm
DAIRY LA
NEW CL
A4155
Henley Management Coll
HAMBLEDEN RISE
Burrow Farm
Chalkpit Wood
Hambleden Lock
HAMBLEDEN MILL
Mill End
Millend Farm
Binfields Wood
MALTHOUSE FLATS
River Thames
FERRY LA
Temple Island
Killdown Bank
The Thames Path
A4155
SL7
WESTFIELD BGLWS
WESTFIELD COTTS
HAMBLEDEN PL
Westfield Farm
Aston
Remenham
REMENHAM LA
ASTON FERRY LA
PH
Culham Farm
RG9
Culham Court
REMENHAM CHURCH LA
ASTON LA
Culham House
Woodside Farm
Common Barn
Lower Culham Farm
Rosehill Wood
Remenham Wood
Remenham Place
DACEBERRY CT
REMENHAM TERR
Remenham Hill
Middle Culham Farm
WHITE HILL
A4130
A4130
Branfords
Parkplace Farm
Wild's Belt
CH
Aspect Pk
Mon
Mast
RG10
Upper Culham Farm
Piggots Corner
WARGRAVE RD
A321
A321 Twyford, Wokingham
Park Place

191

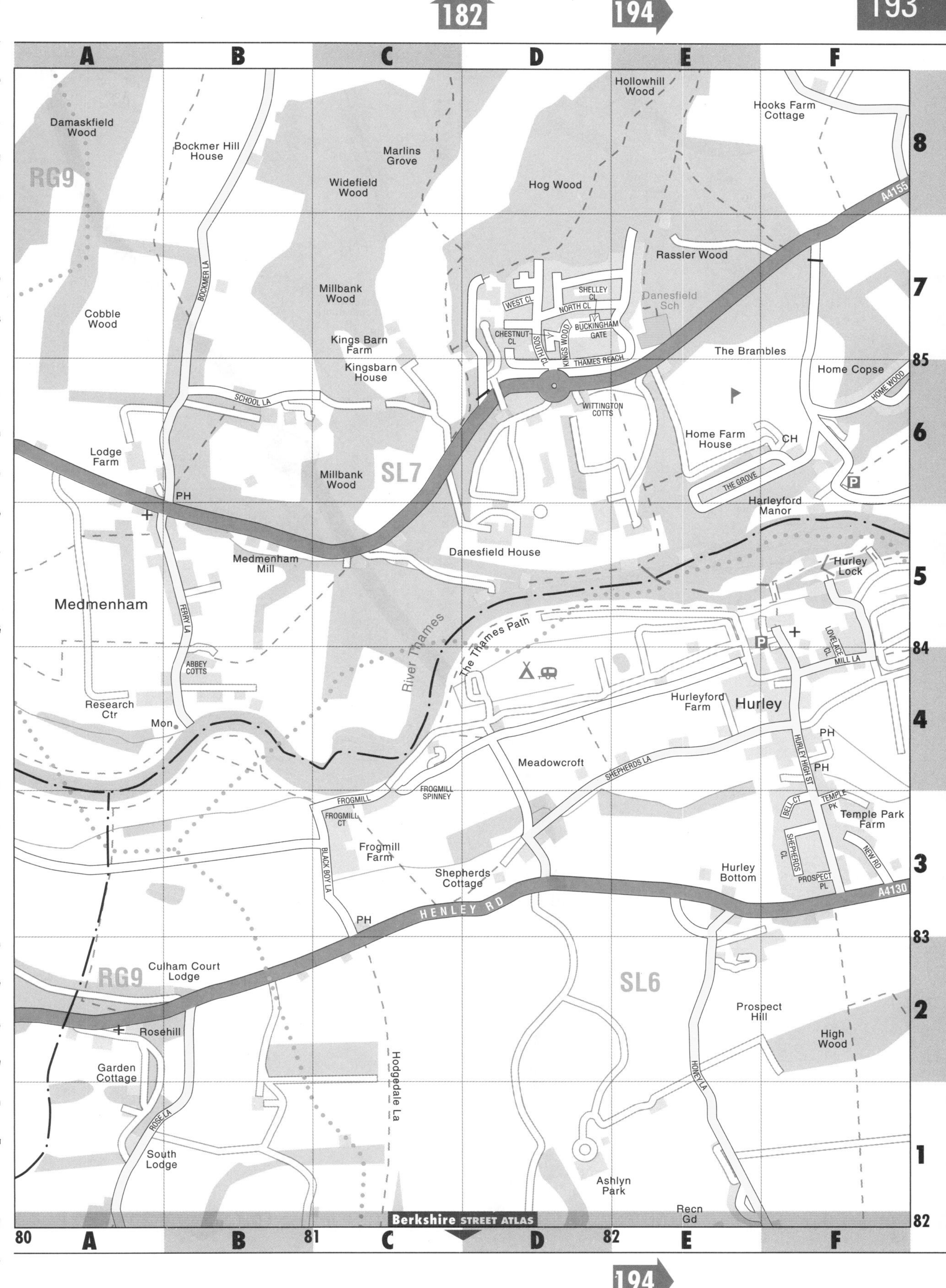
182
194
Damaskfield Wood
Bockmer Hill House
Marlins Grove
Widefield Wood
Hog Wood
Hollowhill Wood
Hooks Farm Cottage
RG9
Cobble Wood
Millbank Wood
Rassler Wood
Danesfield Sch
West Cl
Shelley Cl
North Cl
Chestnut Cl
South Cl
Kings Wood
Buckingham Gate
Thames Reach
Kings Barn Farm
Kingsbarn House
The Brambles
Home Copse
Home Wood
A4155
Bockmer La
School La
Wittington Cotts
Lodge Farm
Home Farm House
CH
SL7
Millbank Wood
PH
The Grove
Harleyford Manor
Danesfield House
Medmenham Mill
Hurley Lock
Medmenham
Ferry La
River Thames
The Thames Path
Lovelace Cl
Mill La
Abbey Cotts
Research Ctr
Hurleyford Farm
Hurley
Mon
PH
Meadowcroft
Shepherds La
Hurley High St
PH
Frogmill
Frogmill Spinney
Frogmill Ct
Temple Pk
Temple Park Farm
Bell Ct
Frogmill Farm
Black Boy La
Shepherds Cl
New Rd
Shepherds Cottage
Hurley Bottom
Prospect Pl
A4130
Henley Rd
PH
Culham Court Lodge
RG9
SL6
Prospect Hill
Rosehill
High Wood
Garden Cottage
Hodgedale La
Honey La
Rose La
South Lodge
Ashlyn Park
Recn Gd
Berkshire STREET ATLAS
194

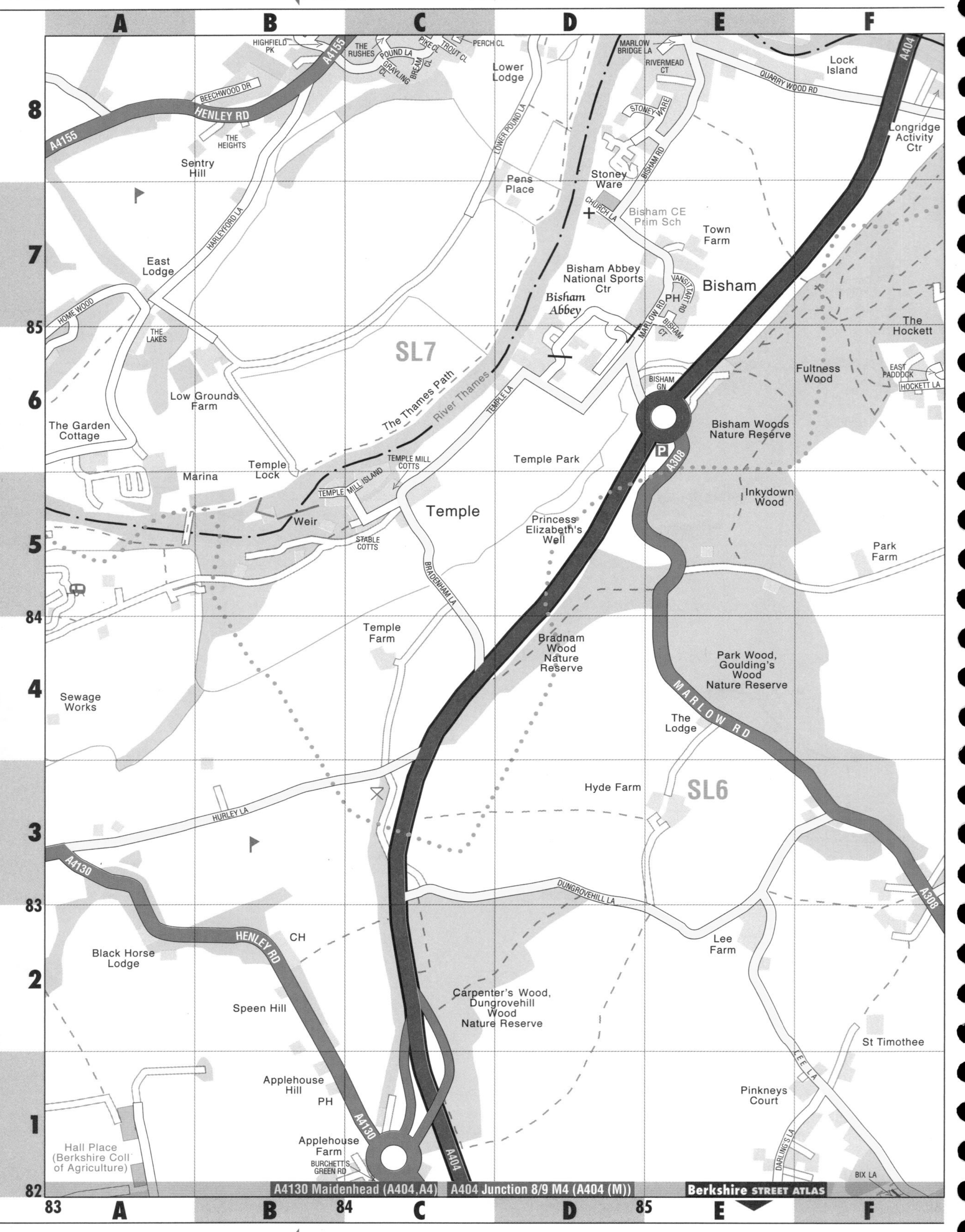

A4130 Maidenhead (A404,A4)   A404 Junction 8/9 M4 (A404 (M))   **Berkshire** STREET ATLAS

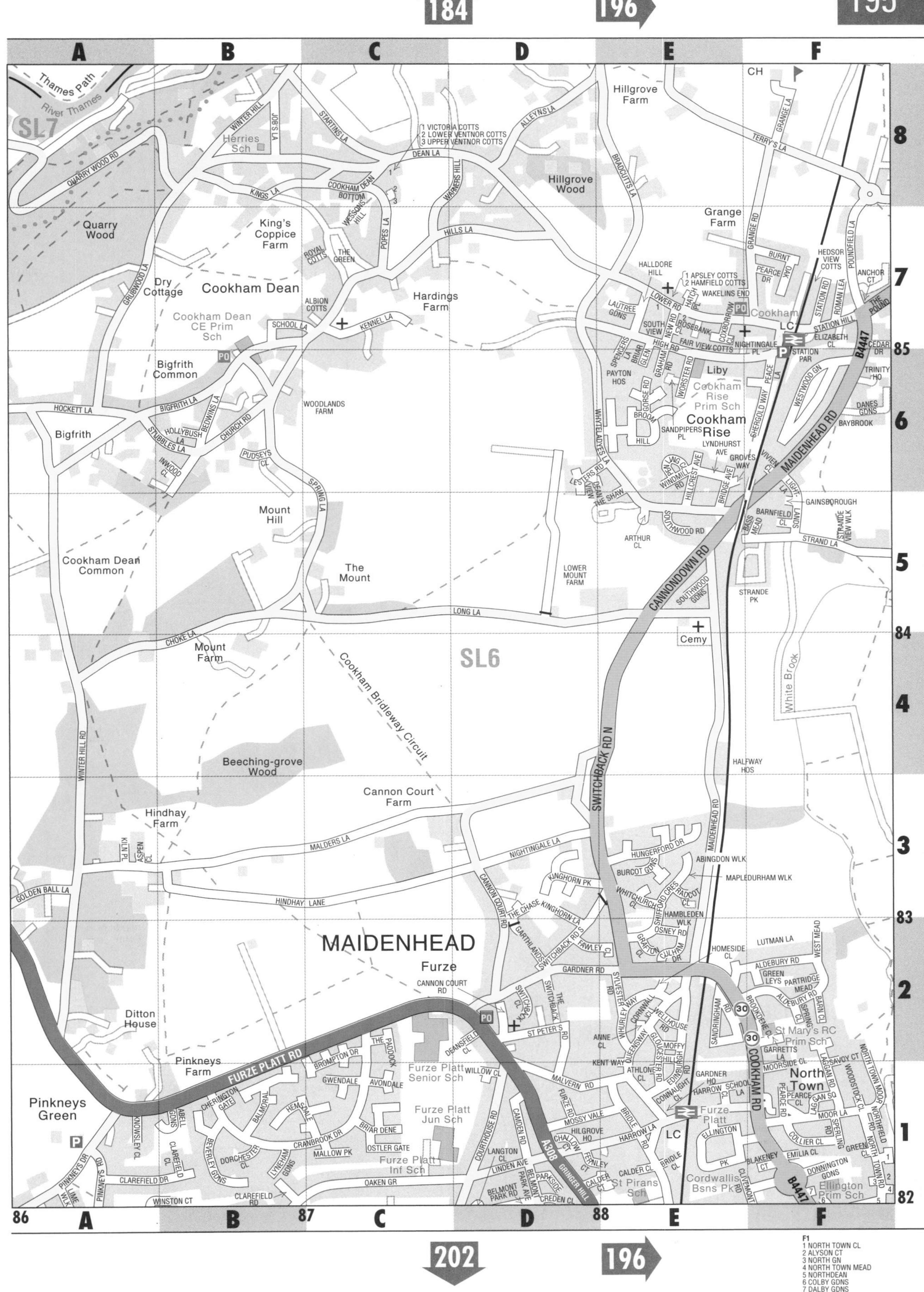

F1
1 NORTH TOWN CL
2 ALYSON CT
3 NORTH GN
4 NORTH TOWN MEAD
5 NORTHDEAN
6 COLBY GDNS
7 DALBY GDNS

195
185

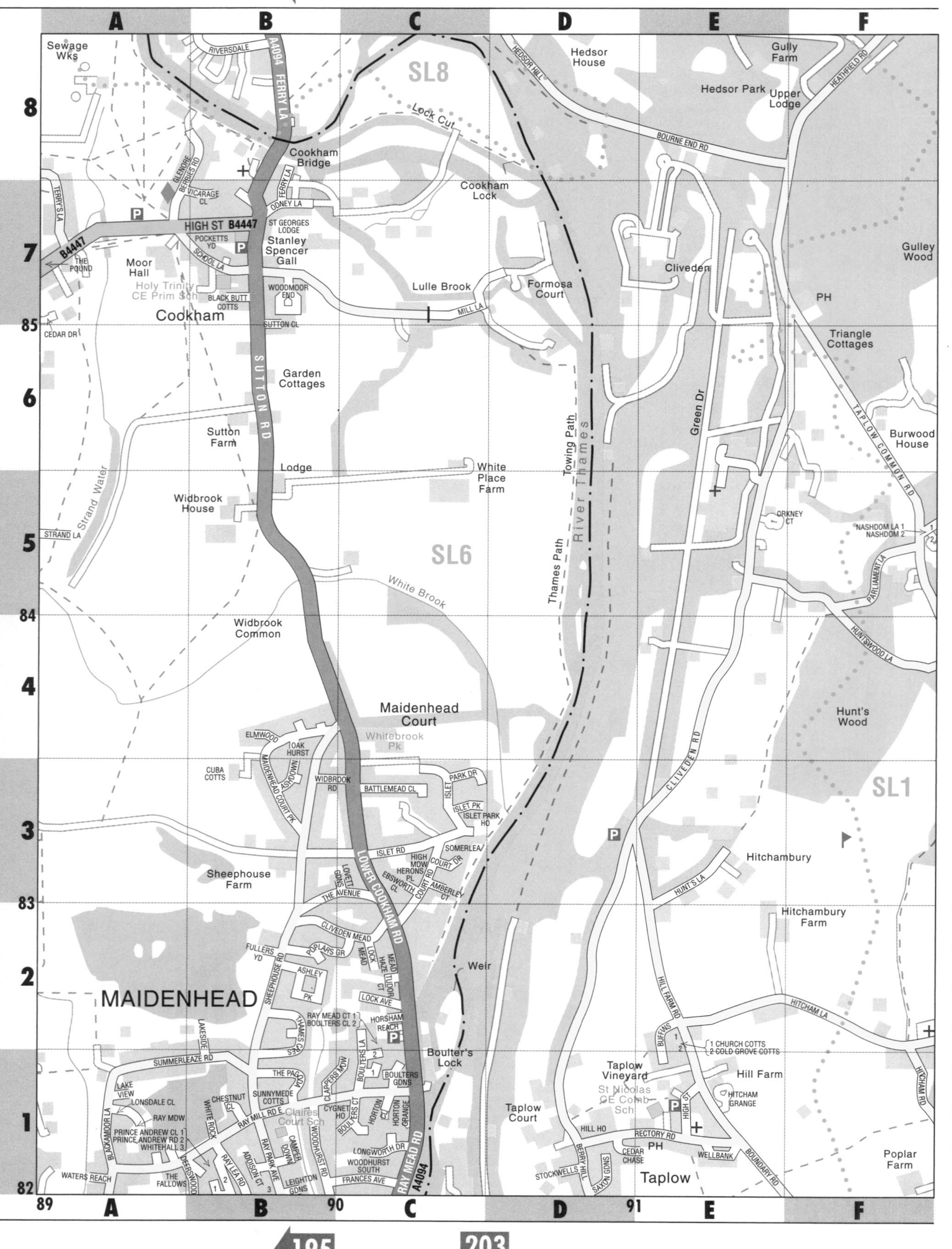
A
B
C
D
E
F
8
7
85
6
5
84
4
3
83
2
1
82
89
90
91
Sewage Wks
RIVERSDALE
A4094 FERRY LA
SL8
HEDSOR HILL
Hedsor House
Gully Farm
Hedsor Park
Upper Lodge
HEATHFIELD RD
Lock Cut
BOURNE END RD
Cookham Bridge
Cookham Lock
GLENORE
BERRIES RD
VICARAGE CL
FERRY LA
ODNEY LA
TERRY'S LA
HIGH ST B4447
ST GEORGES LODGE
POCKETTS YD
Stanley Spencer Gall
B4447
THE POUND
Moor Hall
SCHOOL LA
Holy Trinity CE Prim Sch
BLACK BUTT COTTS
WOODMOOR END
Lulle Brook
Formosa Court
Cliveden
Gulley Wood
PH
MILL LA
Cookham
SUTTON CL
CEDAR DR
Triangle Cottages
SUTTON RD
Garden Cottages
Green Dr
TAPLOW COMMON RD
Burwood House
Sutton Farm
Towing Path
River Thames
Lodge
White Place Farm
Strand Water
Widbrook House
ORKNEY CT
NASHDOM LA 1
NASHDOM 2
STRAND LA
SL6
Thames Path
PARLIAMENT LA
White Brook
Widbrook Common
HUNTSWOOD LA
Hunt's Wood
Maidenhead Court
ELMWOOD
OAK HURST
Whitebrook Pk
CLIVEDEN RD
CUBA COTTS
MAIDENHEAD COURT PK
ASHDOWN
WIDBROOK RD
BATTLEMEAD CL
ISLET PARK DR
SL1
ISLET PK
ISLET PARK HO
ISLET RD
SOMERLEA
HIGH MDW
HERONS PL
COURT DR
Hitchambury
Sheephouse Farm
LOVETT GDNS
LOWER COOKHAM RD
EBSWORTH CL
COURT RD
AMBERLEY CT
HUNT'S LA
THE AVENUE
Hitchambury Farm
CLIVEDEN MEAD
FULLERS YD
POPLARS GR
LOCK MEAD
HAZE MEAD
SHEEPHOUSE RD
ASHLEY PK
TUDOR CT
Weir
MAIDENHEAD
LOCK AVE
HILL FARM RD
HITCHAM LA
RAY MEAD CT 1
BOULTERS CL 2
HORSHAM REACH
LAKESIDE
THAMES CRES
BUFFINS
1 CHURCH COTTS
2 COLD GROVE COTTS
Boulter's Lock
SUMMERLEAZE RD
BOULTERS LA
Taplow Vineyard
Hill Farm
THE PAGODA
CLAPPERS MDW
BOULTERS GDNS
St Nicolas CE Comb Sch
HITCHAM GRANGE
LAKE VIEW
CHESTNUT CL
SUNNYMEDE COTTS
HIGH ST
HITCHAM RD
LONSDALE CL
Claires Court Sch
CYGNET HO
BOULTERS CT
HORTON CT
HORTON GRANGE
Taplow Court
RAY MDW
WHITE ROCK
RAY MILL RD E
HILL HO
PRINCE ANDREW CL 1
PRINCE ANDREW RD 2
WHITEHALL 3
BLACKAMOOR LA
CAMPER DOWN
WOODHURST RD
RECTORY RD
PH
Poplar Farm
LONGWORTH DR
CEDAR CHASE
WELLBANK
ADDISON CT
RAY PARK AVE
RAY LEA RD
DEERSWOOD
WOODHURST SOUTH
RAY MEAD RD
A4094
BERRY HILL
STOCKWELLS
SAXON GDNS
BOUNDARY RD
WATERS REACH
THE FALLOWS
LEIGHTON GDNS
FRANCES AVE
Taplow

195
203

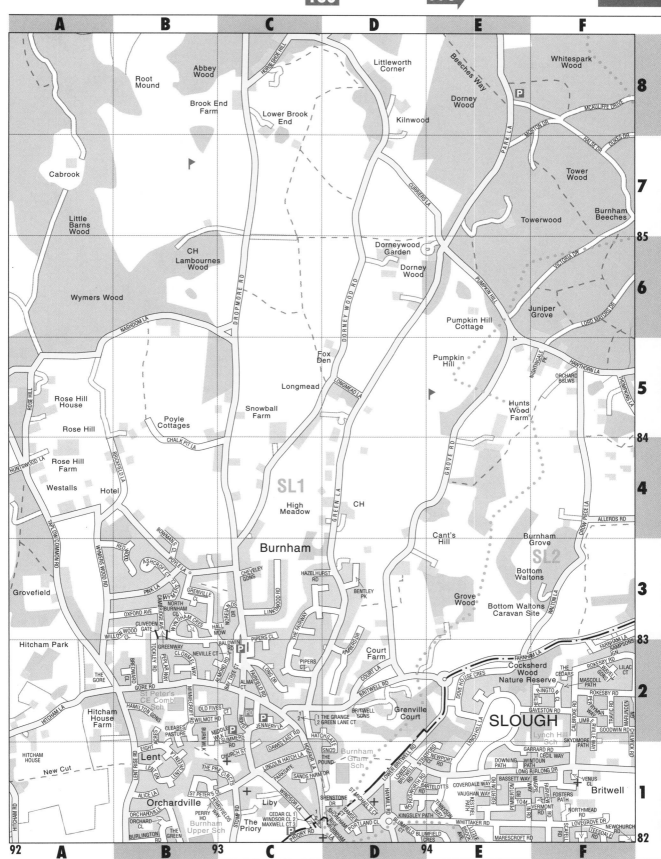

186 198

A **B** **C** **D** **E** **F**

8
7
85
6
5
84
4
3
83
2
1
82

92 93 94

Whitespark Wood
Littleworth Corner
Beeches Way
Dorney Wood
McAULIFFE DRIVE
Abbey Wood
Root Mound
Brook End Farm
Lower Brook End
Kilnwood
PARK LA
MORTON DR
HALSE DR
DUKES DR
Tower Wood
Cabrook
Little Barns Wood
Towerwood
Burnham Beeches
CH Lambournes Wood
Dorneywood Garden
VICTORIA DR
Wymers Wood
Dorney Wood
PUMPKIN HILL
Juniper Grove
LORD MAYORS DR
HAWTHORN LA
NASHDOM LA
DROPMORE RD
DORNEY WOOD RD
CURRIERS LA
Pumpkin Hill Cottage
NIGHTINGALE PK
ORCHARD BGLWS
THOMPKINS LA
Fox Den
Pumpkin Hill
Rose Hill
Rose Hill House
Poyle Cottages
Snowball Farm
Longmead
LONGMEAD LA
Hunts Wood Farm
ROSE HILL
BROOKFIELD LA
CHALK PIT LA
GREEN LA
CROW PIECE LA
ALLERDS RD
Rose Hill
HUNTSWOOD LA
Rose Hill Farm
SL1
CH
GROVE RD
Burnham Grove
Westalls
Hotel
High Meadow
SL2
Bottom Waltons
Grovefield
TAPLOW COMMON RD
Burnham
Cant's Hill
Bottom Waltons Caravan Site
WALTON LA
Grove Wood
BOWMAN'S CT
POYLE LA
RED COTT
ASHCROFT CT
CHEVELEY GDNS
LINKSWOOD RD
HAZELHURST RD
BENTLEY PK
FARNHAM LA
SAMPSONS
Hitcham Park
WYMERS WOOD RD
PINK LA
CAMBRIDGE AVE
OXFORD AVE
NORTH BURNHAM
NORGAN DS
HALL MDW
THE FAIRWAY
KINGERS DR
Court Farm
Cocksherd Wood Nature Reserve
THE CEDARS
ROKESBY RD
MASCOLL PATH
LILAC CT
CLIVEDEN GATE
WILLOW WOOD CL
WYNDHAM CRES
PIPERS CL
PIPERS CT
COURT LA
BRITWELL RD
DOVE HOUSE CRES
LYNCHBALL LA
GAVESTON RD
ROKESBY RD
TRAVIC RD
The Gore
BREDWARD CL
TOCKLEY RD
PEPLAR WAY
GREENWAY
CLONMEL WAY
NEVILLE CT
ALMOND RD
BAY TREE CT
FAIRFIELD RD
LONG TR
BALDWIN RD
Grenville Court
SLOUGH
Lynch Hill Sch
SKYDMORE PATH
GOODWIN RD
CHILWICK RD
Hitcham House Farm
HAMILTON GDNS
MINNIECROFT RD
OLD FIVES CT
WILMOT RD
DAWES EAST RD
CT
BRITWELL GDNS
GRENVILLE COURT
HATCHGATE
GARRARD RD
CECIL WAY
LONG FURLONG DR
DOWNING PATH
WINTOUN PATH
CALBROKE RD
HETHE CT
Lent
EIGHT ACRES
CLEABES PASTURE
BURN WLK
SUMMERS RD
THE GRANGE
GREEN LANE CT
LOWER BRITWELL RD
LOWER BRITWELL RD
WORDSWORTH RD
BARTELOTTS RD
NEWPORT RD
STRATFORD RD
COVERDALE WAY
BASSETT WAY
EGERTON RD
MAGPIE WAY
VERMONT RD
FAIRVIEW RD
FOSTERS PATH
Venus CL
Britwell
Hitcham House
New Cut
HITCHAM LA
LENT RISE RD
LENT GN
LENT GN
ALICE LA
THE PRECINCTS
PERRYFIELDS
CHURCH ST
LINCOLN HATCH LA
HIGRAM LA
SANDS FARM DR
PARKGATE
Burnham Gram Sch
THE POUND
SNG9
ST MICHAEL'S C
HAYMILL RD
KINGSLEY PATH
PEMBERTON RD
TOM RD
DOWNING PATH
NORTHMEAD RD
LOVEGROVE DR
NEWCHURCH RD
Orchardville
ORCHARDVILLE RD
ORCHARD CL
BURLINGTON RD
PERRY HO
STUMP RD
ST PETER'S CL
THE GREEN
Liby
WINDSOR LA
The Priory
Burnham Upper Sch
CEDAR CL
WINDSOR CL
MAXWELL RD
PRIORY RD
SHENSTONE DR
RAMSEY
BURNHAM LA
SHORTFERN
PORTLAND CL
BLUMFIELD CRES
WHITTAKER RD
LITTLE BROOK AVE
SCAFELL RD
TEESDALE RD
MARESCROFT RD
St Peter's CE Comb Sch
PO

197
187

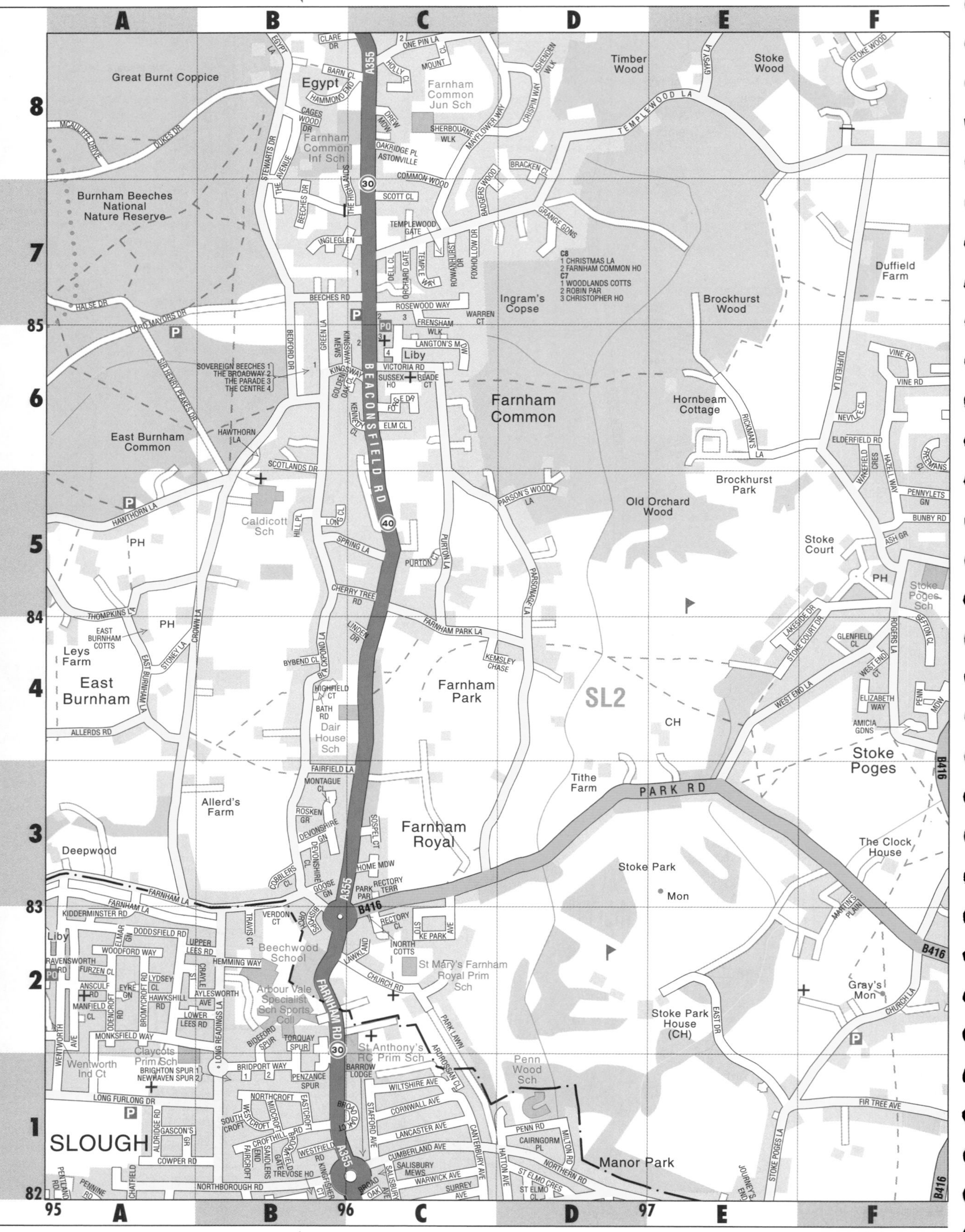
A
B
C
D
E
F
8
7
85
6
5
84
4
3
83
2
1
82
95
96
97
Great Burnt Coppice
Egypt
Farnham Common Jun Sch
Timber Wood
Stoke Wood
TEMPLEWOOD LA
Farnham Common Inf Sch
Burnham Beeches National Nature Reserve
MCAULIFFE DRIVE
DUKES DR
STEWARTS DR
THE AVENUE
BEECHES DR
THE HIGHLANDS
SCOTT CL
COMMON WOOD
BRACKEN CL
BADGERS WOOD
GRANGE GDNS
TEMPLEWOOD GATE
INGLEGLEN
DELL CL
ORCHARD GATE
TEMPLE WAY
ROWANHURST DR
FOXHOLLOW DR
C8
1 CHRISTMAS LA
2 FARNHAM COMMON HO
C7
1 WOODLANDS COTTS
2 ROBIN PAR
3 CHRISTOPHER HO
Ingram's Copse
Brockhurst Wood
Duffield Farm
BEECHES RD
HALSE DR
LORD MAYORS DR
ROSEWOOD WAY
WARREN CT
FRENSHAM WLK
LANGTON'S MDW
Liby
VICTORIA RD
SUSSEX HO
READE CT
SOVEREIGN BEECHES 1
THE BROADWAY 2
THE PARADE 3
THE CENTRE 4
SIR HENRY PEAKES DR
BEDFORD DR
GREEN LA
KINGSWAY MEWS
BEACONSFIELD RD
Farnham Common
Hornbeam Cottage
RICKMAN'S LA
DUFFIELD LA
VINE RD
NEVILLE CL
ELDERFIELD RD
WAKEFIELD CRES
HAZELL WAY
FREEMANS CL
ELM CL
East Burnham Common
HAWTHORN LA
SCOTLANDS DR
PARSON'S WOOD LA
Brockhurst Park
Old Orchard Wood
PENNYLETS GN
BUNBY RD
Caldicott Sch
PH
HILL PL
SPRING LA
PURTON CT
PURTON LA
Stoke Court
ASH GR
Stoke Poges Sch
PARSONAGE LA
CHERRY TREE RD
THOMPKINS LA
EAST BURNHAM COTTS
CROWN LA
LINDEN DR
FARNHAM PARK LA
LAKESIDE DR
STOKE COURT DR
GLENFIELD CL
ROGERS LA
SEFTON CL
Leys Farm
East Burnham
STONEY LA
EAST BURNHAM LA
BYBEND CL
BLACKPOND LA
KEMSLEY CHASE
Farnham Park
SL2
WEST END CT
WEST END LA
ELIZABETH WAY
PENN MDW
HIGHFIELD CT
BATH RD
Dair House Sch
CH
AMICIA GDNS
ALLERDS RD
FAIRFIELD LA
Tithe Farm
PARK RD
Stoke Poges
B416
MONTAGUE CL
Allerd's Farm
ROSKEN GR
DEVONSHIRE GN
GOSPEL CT
Farnham Royal
Deepwood
The Clock House
HOME MDW
Stoke Park
COBBLERS CL
GOOSE GN
A355
RECTORY TERR
PARK PAR
Mon
MARTIN'S PLAIN
FARNHAM LA
KIDDERMINSTER RD
VERDON CT
TRAVIS CT
RECTORY CL
STOKE PARK AVE
Liby
DODDSFIELD RD
UPPER LEES RD
WOODFORD WAY
Beechwood School
NORTH COTTS
St Mary's Farnham Royal Prim Sch
RAVENSWORTH RD
FURZEN CL
HEMMING WAY
CRAYLE ST
CHURCH RD
Gray's Mon
CHURCH LA
PO
ANSCULF RD
EYRE GN
LYDSEY CL
AYLESWORTH AVE
Arbour Vale Specialist Sch Sports Coll
MANFIELD CL
HAWKSHILL RD
LOWER LEES RD
Stoke Park House (CH)
EAST DR
MONKSFIELD WAY
BIDEFORD SPUR
TORQUAY SPUR
FARNHAM RD
PARK LAWN
WENTWORTH AVE
Claycots Prim Sch
St Anthony's RC Prim Sch
ARDROSSAN CL
Wentworth Ind Ct
BRIGHTON SPUR 1
NEWHAVEN SPUR 2
LONG READINGS LA
BRIDPORT WAY
PENZANCE SPUR
BARROW LODGE
WILTSHIRE AVE
Penn Wood Sch
LONG FURLONG DR
NORTHCROFT
EASTCROFT
CORNWALL AVE
FIR TREE AVE
SOUTH CROFT
WESTCROFT
MIDCROFT
BROAD OAK CT
STAFFORD AVE
LANCASTER AVE
PENN RD
CAIRNGORM PL
MILTON RD
SLOUGH
ALDRIDGE RD
GASCON'S GR
CROFTHILL RD
FAIRCROFT
SANDLERS END
BROOKFIELD
WESTFIELD RD
CUMBERLAND AVE
CANTERBURY AVE
HATTON AVE
Manor Park
NORTHERN RD
STOKE POGES LA
COWPER RD
TREVOSE HO
SALISBURY MEWS
WARWICK AVE
ST ELMO CRES
ST ELMO CL
JOURNEY'S END
PENTLAND RD
PENNINE RD
CHATFIELD
NORTHBOROUGH RD
KINGFISHER CT
BROAD OAK AVE
SALISBURY AVE
SURREY AVE
30
40

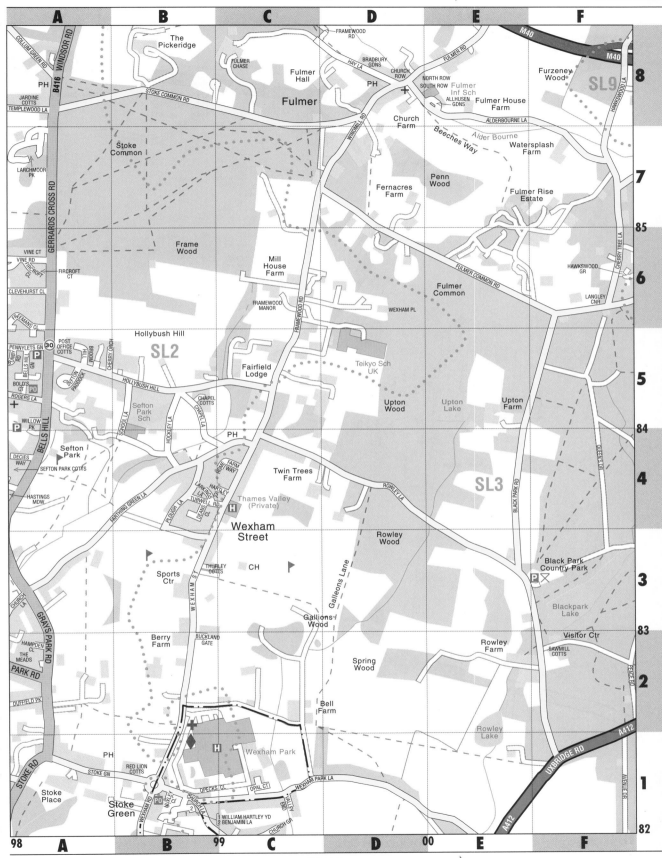

A B C D E F

The Pickeridge

FRAMEWOOD RD

FULMER CHASE

Fulmer Hall

HAY LA

BRADBURY GDNS

CHURCH ROW

FULMER RD

M40

M40

Furzeney Wood

SL9

HAWKSWOOD LA

8

WINDSOR RD

B416

COLLUM GREEN RD

STOKE COMMON RD

PH

NORTH ROW
SOUTH ROW

Fulmer Inf Sch

Fulmer

PH

Church Row

ALLHUSEN GDNS

Fulmer House Farm

Church Farm

ALDERBOURNE LA

JARDINE COTTS

TEMPLEWOOD LA

Stoke Common

Beeches Way

Alder Bourne

Watersplash Farm

Fulmer Rise Estate

LARCHMOOR PK

GERRARDS CROSS RD

Fernacres Farm

Penn Wood

7

VINE CT

Frame Wood

85

VINE RD

FIRCROFT CL

FIRCROFT CT

Mill House Farm

FULMER COMMON RD

HAWKSWOOD GR

CHERRY TREE LA

6

CLEVEHURST CL

FRAMEWOOD MANOR

WEXHAM PL

Fulmer Common

LANGLEY CNR

FREEMANS CL

PENNYLETS GN

30

POST OFFICE COTTS

Hollybush Hill

SL2

Teikyo Sch UK

P

PO

BELLS HILL GN

SEFTON PADDOCK

CHERRY ORCH

Fairfield Lodge

FRAMEWOOD RD

WINDMILL RD

5

BOLD'S CT

ROGERS LA

HOLLYBUSH HILL

Sefton Park Sch

HOCKLEY LA

CHAPEL LA

CHAPEL COTTS

Upton Wood

Upton Lake

Upton Farm

84

WILLOW PK

P

Sefton Park

SCHOOL LA

PH

Twin Trees Farm

SL3

4

DECIES WAY

BELLS HILL

SEFTON PARK COTTS

FARTHING GREEN LA

FARM HOUSE WAY

HARTLEY

LARKINS CL

Thames Valley (Private)

H

ROWLEY LA

BLACK PARK RD

HASTINGS MDW

PLOUGH LA

DEANS CT

TUBWELL RD

Wexham Street

Rowley Wood

QUEENS DR

CHURCH LA

Sports Ctr

THURLEY COTTS

CH

Galleons Lane

Black Park Country Park

P

3

GRAYS PARK RD

Berry Farm

BUCKLAND GATE

Gallions Wood

Rowley Farm

Blackpark Lake

Visitor Ctr

83

HAMPDEN CL

THE MEADS

PARK RD

WEXHAM ST

Spring Wood

SAWMILL COTTS

PEACE RD

2

DUFFIELD PK

Bell Farm

Rowley Lake

A412

UXBRIDGE RD

AVENUE DR

STOKE RD

PH

Wexham Park

H

1

STOKE GN

RED LION COTTS

OPECKS CL

OPAL CT

WEXHAM PARK LA

A412

Stoke Place

WEXHAM RD

PO

NULLEY CL

CHURCH LA

VALLEY END

CHURCH GR

Stoke Green

1 WILLIAM HARTLEY YD
2 BENJAMIN LA

82

98 A B 99 C D 00 E F

199
189

A **B** **C** **D** **E** **F**

8

HAWKSWOOD LA
SOUTHLANDS RD

M40
M40

1a
16

Alderbourne Arches
SL9

Rush Green

New House Farm

WILLETTS LA
HOLLYBUSH LA
FIELD RD

Gossams Wood

UB9

7

Brown's Wood
Ways Farm

Oldhouse Wood

Kingcup Farm

WILLETTS LA
A412

Alderbourne Farm

ALDERBOURNE LA

Blanchards Farm

85

Alder Bourne

6

HAWKSWOOD GR
FULMER COMMON RD

SEVENHILLS RD

Belle Farm

Sevenhills Farm

Long Coppice

LADY YORKE PK

Southlands Manor

Strawberry Wood

The Clump

Dromenagh Farm

DENHAM RD

5

Black Park Nature Reserve

Pinewood Film Studios

BOND CL
PINEWOOD GN
PINEWOOD RD
PINEWOOD CL
KINGS CL
CEDAR CL
ASHFORD RD
THORNBRIDGE RD

SL0

Round Coppice Farm

84

PEACE RD

PEACE RD

Park Lodge Farm

HEATHERDEN GN

COPSE WOOD
LAUREL CT

Mansfield Farm

M25
A4007

4

Park Lodge

AVE PARKWAY
LONGSTO NE

RD

Iver Heath

Black Park Country Park

ST DAVID'S CL
Recn Gd
BIRCH CL
ANSLOW GDNS
BANGORS RD N

Chandlers Hill

3

CHURCH RD
ROWAN GDNS
WARREN
ALDER RD
GLASIER RD
ROSTREVOR GDNS
BOOLEY WAY
TREWARDEN AVE
ST MARGARET'S
KEITH WAY
ST LAURELS RD
KEENS CRES

1 ST MARGARET'S GATE
2 ST MARGARETS CT

83

SL3

Warren House

Liby
PO

SLOUGH RD

30

Beeches Way

HAWTHORN CL

Iver Heath Jun Sch

MEAD HO
MEAD POST

POTTERS CROSS

2

UXBRIDGE RD
A412
A4007
FIVE POINTS

PLEASANT COTTS
PH
WOOD LANE CL

THE CLOSE
WHITEHOUSE WAY
SWALLOWDALE
LOWER MEAD

Iver Heath Inf Sch

Home Cottage Farm

BANGORS RD S

Moorwards Farm

White Lodge

HARDINGS CL
HARDINGS ROW

1

A412

Langley Park Country Park

BILLET LA
WOOD LA

COOPERS ROW
SWALLOW ST
PH
SWALLOW FIELDS

NORWOOD LA

BANGOR COTTS

Bangors Park Farm

82

MARTINDALE
COPPINS LA

01 **A** **B** 02 **C** **D** 03 **E** **F**

190

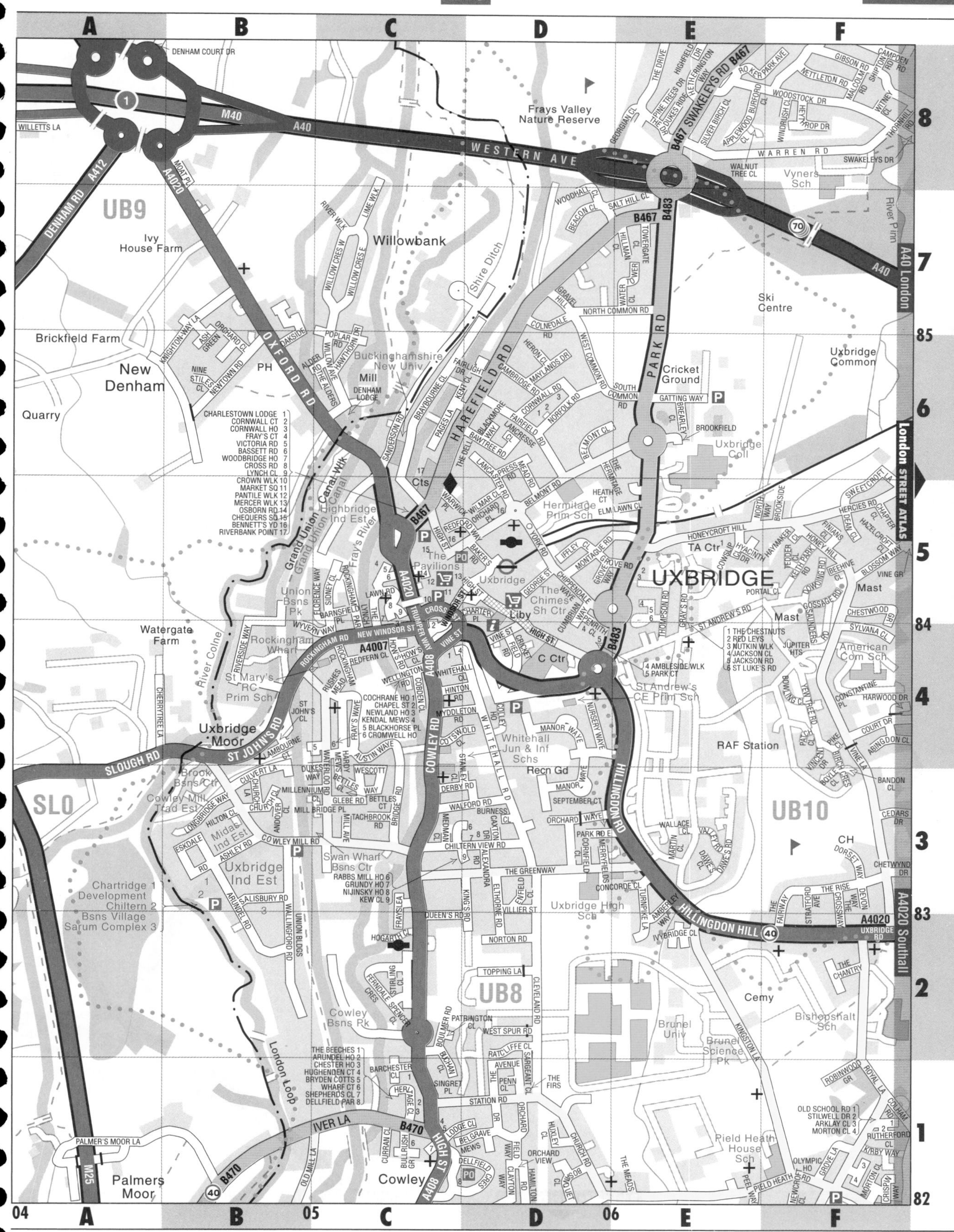

A
B
C
D
E
F
8
7
85
6
5
84
4
3
83
2
1
82
04
05
06
DENHAM COURT DR
WILLETTS LA
M40
A40
WESTERN AVE
DENHAM RD
A412
A4020
MOAT PL
UB9
Ivy House Farm
Brickfield Farm
New Denham
Quarry
OXFORD RD
PH
Willowbank
RIVER WLK
LIME WLK
WILLOW CRES W
WILLOW CRES E
Shire Ditch
Frays Valley Nature Reserve
Buckinghamshire New Univ
Mill
DENHAM LODGE
POPLAR RD
HAWTHORN DR
WILLOW AVE
THE ALDERS
ALDER
KNIGHTON-WAY LA
ORCHARD CL
ASH GREEN
NINE STILES CL
NEWTOWN RD
OAKSIDE
CHARLESTOWN LODGE 1
CORNWALL CT 2
CORNWALL HO 3
FRAY'S CT 4
VICTORIA RD 5
BASSETT RD 6
WOODBRIDGE HO 7
CROSS RD 8
LYNCH CL 9
CROWN WLK 10
MARKET SQ 11
PANTILE WLK 12
MERCER WLK 13
OSBORN RD 14
CHEQUERS SQ 15
BENNETT'S YD 16
RIVERBANK POINT 17
Grand Union Canal Wlk
Grand Union Canal
Highbridge Ind Est
Frays River
B467
HAREFIELD RD
PARK RD
B467 SWAKELEYS RD
B483
THE DRIVE
PINE TREES DR
DUKES RIDE
HIGHFIELD DR
HETHERINGTON WAY
GEORGIAN CL
ROKER PARK AVE
GIBSON RD
CAMPDEN RD
NETTLETON RD
MALCOLM RD
SHIPTON CL
WITNEY CL
THORNHILL RD
WOODSTOCK DR
HEYTHROP DR
WINDRUSH CL
APPLEWOOD CL
BURFORD CL
SILVER BIRCH CL
WARREN RD
SWAKELEYS DR
WALNUT TREE CL
Vyners Sch
River Pinn
A40 London
WOODHALL CL
BEACON CL
SALT HILL CL
HILLMAN CL
TOWERGATE CL
WATER TOWER CL
GRAVEL HILL
NORTH COMMON RD
COLNEDALE RD
HERON CL
MAYLANDS DR
WEST COMMON RD
SOUTH COMMON RD
CAMBRIDGE RD
CORNWALL RD
NORFOLK RD
BLACKMORE WAY
LANCRESSE CL
FAIRFIELD RD
BAWTREE RD
BELMONT CL
BELMONT RD
LANCASTER RD
PRESS RD
MEAD RD
THE HERMITAGE
HEATH CT
ELM LAWN CL
Hermitage Prim Sch
WARWICK PL
WILMAR CL
ORCHARD PL
SANDERSON RD
BRAYBOURNE CL
PAGES LA
KENT CL
FAIRLIGHT DR
THE DELL
REDFORD WAY
HIGH ST
BAKER'S RD
Cts
GATTING WAY
BREARLEY CL
BROOKFIELD
Uxbridge Coll
Cricket Ground
Ski Centre
Uxbridge Common
London STREET ATLAS
NORTH WAY
BROOKSIDE
SWEETCROFT LA
HERCIES RD
CHAPTER CL
DEAN CL
HAZELCROFT CL
PINIANS
HONEY HILL
HONEYCROFT HILL
HYACINTH DR
HAYMAKER CL
COWSLIP CL
FEDDER CL
KELLY CL
PARK RD
BEEHIVE CL
BLOSSOM WAY
VINE GR
TA Ctr
UXBRIDGE
PORTAL CL
Mast
GOSSAGE RD
CHESTWOOD GR
SYLVANA CL
American Com Sch
JUPITER HTS
1 THE CHESTNUTS
2 RED LEYS
3 NUTKIN WLK
4 JACKSON CL
5 JACKSON RD
6 ST LUKE'S RD
ST ANDREW'S RD
GRAY'S RD
THOMPSON RD
4 AMBLESIDE WLK
5 PARK CT
The Pavilions
Uxbridge
The Chimes Sh Ctr
Liby
C Ctr
IFFLEY CL
MONTAGUE RD
GROVE RD
YORK RD
GEORGE ST
CHIPPENDALE WAY
CUMBRIAN WAY
PENRITH CL
HIGH ST
VINE ST
CRICKET FIELD RD
CHARTER PL
CROSS ST
WINDSOR ST
NEW WINDSOR ST
TRUMPER WAY
LAWN RD
A4007
ROCKINGHAM RD
ROCKINGHAM CL
WYVERN WAY
BARNSFIELD PL
SIDNEY CL
FLORENCE WAY
Union Bsns Pk
Rockingham Wharf
Watergate Farm
RIVERSIDE WAY
River Colne
St Mary's RC Prim Sch
REDFERN CL
HOWS RD
HOW'S CL
WELLINGTON RD
COBDEN CL
WHITEHALL CL
HINTON RD
COCHRANE HO 1
CHAPEL ST 2
NEWLAND HO 3
KENDAL MEWS 4
5 BLACKHORSE PL
6 CROMWELL HO
ST JOHN'S CL
RUSHES MEAD
FRAY'S WAYE
AUSTIN WAYE
MYDDLETON RD
COTSWOLD CL
COLLEY HO
WHITEHALL RD
Whitehall Jun & Inf Schs
MANOR WAYE
NURSERY WAYE
St Andrew's CE Prim Sch
RAF Station
Recn Gd
STANLEY CL
DERBY RD
COWLEY RD
A408
ST JOHN'S RD
SLOUGH RD
Uxbridge Moor
AMBOURNE
CHERRYTREE LA
SL0
Brook Bsns Ctr
Cowley Mill Trad Est
CULVERT LA
CHURCH LA
LONGBRIDGE WAY
HILTON CL
ANDOVER CL
Midas Ind Est
ESKDALE
ASHLEY RD
COWLEY MILL RD
Uxbridge Ind Est
MILLENNIUM CL
MILL BRIDGE PL
DUKES WAY
WESCOTT WAY
BETTLES CL
GLEBE RD
TACHBROOK RD
MILL AVE
BRIDGE RD
Swan Wharf Bsns Ctr
RABBS MILL HO 6
GRUNDY HO 7
NIJINSKY HO 8
KEW CL 9
Chartridge Development 1
Chiltern Bsns Village 2
Sarum Complex 3
SALISBURY RD
ARUNDEL RD
WALLINGFORD RD
UNION BLDGS
WALFORD RD
BURNESS CL
CAXTON RD
MEDMAN CL
CHILTERN VIEW RD
ALEXANDRA RD
THE GREENWAY
KING'S RD
ELTHORNE RD
ENFIELD CL
VILLIER ST
QUEEN'S RD
NORTON RD
SEPTEMBER CT
ORCHARD WAYE
PARK RD E
CORNFIELD CL
MERRYFIELDS
CONCORDE CL
Uxbridge High Sch
HILLINGDON RD
HILLINGDON HILL
AMBERLEY WAY
TURNPIKE LA
IVYBRIDGE CL
WALLACE CL
MARTIN CL
VALLEY RD
DAWE'S CL
DAWE'S RD
UB10
BOWLING CL
YEW TREE RD
CONSTANTINE PL
HARWOOD DR
COURT DR
ABINGDON CL
VINCENT DR
PIKE CL
BIRCH CRES
BOYLE CL
VINE LA
BANDON CL
CEDARS DR
CH
DORSET WAY
CHETWYND DR
THE RISE
STRATFORD AVE
THE CROSSWAY
DEVON WAY
THE FAIRWAY
A4020
UXBRIDGE RD
A4020 Southall
THE CHANTRY
Cemy
Bishopshalt Sch
FRAYSLEA
HOGARTH CL
STIRLING CL
FERNDALE CRES
SPENCER CL
TOPPING LA
CLEVELAND RD
UB8
HAMILTON RD
PATRINGTON CL
BOULMER RD
WEST SPUR RD
RATCLIFFE CL
Brunel Univ
Brunel Science Pk
KINGSTON LA
Cowley Bsns Pk
THE BEECHES 1
ARUNDEL HO 2
CHESTER HO 3
HUGHENDEN CT 4
BRYDEN COTTS 5
WHARF CT 6
SHEPHERDS CL 7
DELLFIELD PAR 8
BARCHESTER CL
BUCHAN CL
SINGRET PL
HERITAGE CL
THE AVENUE
PENN CL
SARGEANT CL
THE FIRS
STATION RD
ORCHARD DR
IVER LA
B470
HIGH ST
LODGE CL
BELGRAVE MEWS
CURLAN CL
BULLRUSH GR
DELLFIELD CRES
FIELD WAY
CLAYTON WAY
ORCHARD VIEW
HAMILTON RD
HUXLEY CL
CHURCH RD
THE MEADS
Pield Heath House Sch
PIELD HEATH RD
PEEL WAY
NEWCROFT CL
ROBINWOOD GR
ROYAL LA
COLHAM AVE
OLD SCHOOL RD 1
STILWELL DR 2
ARKLAY CL 3
MORTON CL 4
RUTHERFORD CL
KIRBY WAY
OLYMPIC HO
GROVE LA
MORTON CL
CRISPIN WAY
OLD MILL LA
Cowley
PALMER'S MOOR LA
M25
Palmers Moor
London Loop

208

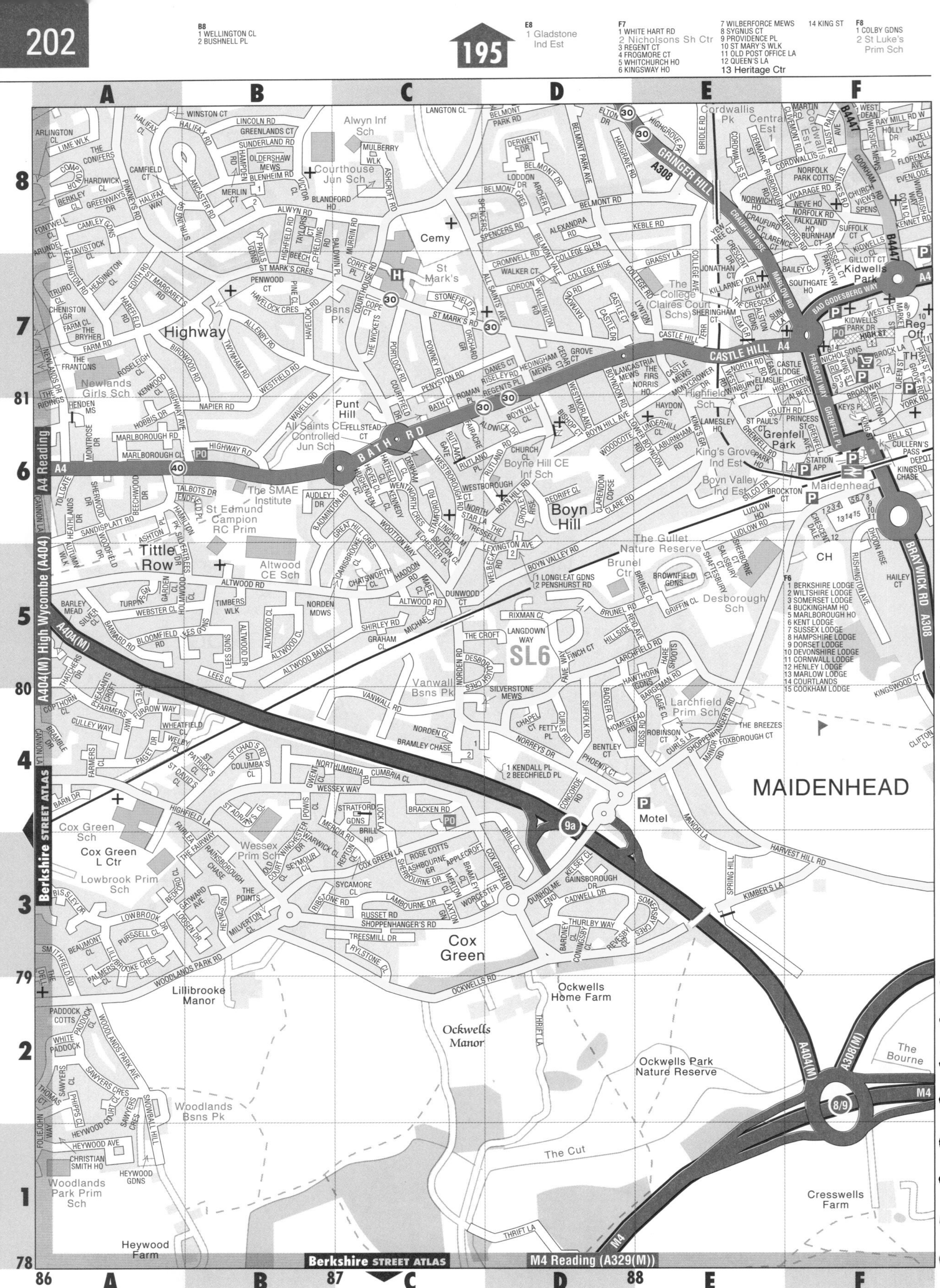

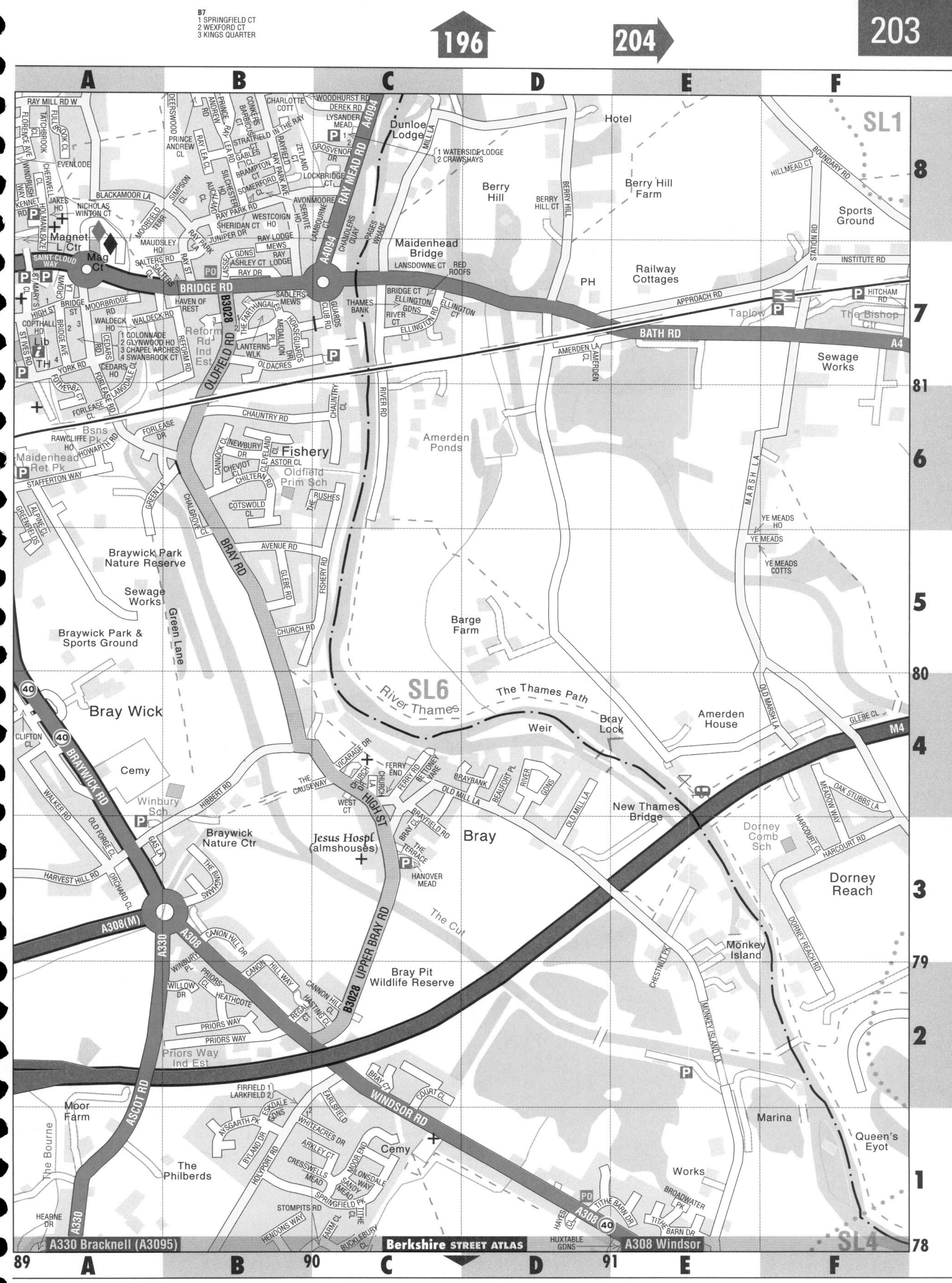

B7
1 SPRINGFIELD CT
2 WEXFORD CT
3 KINGS QUARTER

196

204

203

SL1

8

7

81

6

5

80

4

3

79

2

1

78

A   B   90   C   D   91   E   F

Berkshire STREET ATLAS

A330 Bracknell (A3095)   A308 Windsor   SL4

RAY MILL RD W
TATCHBROOK
FULLER CL
RAY MILL RD
FLORENCE AVE
WINDRUSH WAY
CHERWELL
KENNET RD
HOLMANLEAZE
EVENLODE
BLACKAMOOR LA
JAKES HO
NICHOLAS WINTON CT
Magnet L Ctr
Mag Ct
SAINT-CLOUD WAY
ST MARY'S
ST IVES RD
HIGH ST
Bridge
MOORBRIDGE
MOORBRIDGE RD
WALDECK
BRIDGE AVE
WALDECK RD
COPTHALL
CEDARS
LANGDALE CL
YORK RD
FORLEASE RD
FORLEASE DR
ALPINE CL
GREENACRES
STAFFERTON WAY
Maidenhead Ret Pk
Bsns Pk
RAWLCLIFFE HO
HOWARTH RD
FORLEASE DR
GREEN LA
CHALGROVE RD

Reform Rd Ind Est
1 COLONNADE
2 GLYNWOOD HO
3 CHAPEL ARCHES
4 SWANBROOK CT
Lib
TH

DEERSWOOD
PRINCE ANDREW CL
RAY LEA CL
PRINCES RD
BARBICON
CONIFERS
STRATFIELD
RAYFIELD
GABLES
BRAMPTON
SOMERFORD CL
CHARLOTTE COTT
IN THE RAY
ZETLAND CT
AUCKLAND CL
RAY PARK AVE
LASSEL GDNS
SHERIDAN CT
JUNIPER DR
RAY PARK RD
RAY DR
ASHLEY CT
RAY LODGE
WESTCOIGN CT
RAY MEWS
PO
BRIDGE RD
B3028
OLDFIELD RD

WOODHURST RD
DEREK RD
A4094
LYSANDER MEAD
GROSVENOR DR
CAMBOURNE
CHANDLERS QUAY
PAGES WHARF
LOCKBRIDGE
AVONMORE RD
CLUB RD
MEDALLION PL
HORSEGUARDS
THE FARTHINGALES
LANTERNS WLK
OLDACRES
SADLERS MEWS
HAVEN OF REST

Dunloe Lodge
1 WATERSIDE LODGE
2 CRAWSHAYS
RAY MEAD RD
A4094
MILLA
Maidenhead Bridge
LANSDOWNE CT
RED ROOFS
Thames Bank
BRIDGE CT
ELLINGTON GDNS
ELLINGTON CT
ELLINGTON RD
River CT

Hotel
Berry Hill
Berry Hill CT
Berry Hill Farm
PH
Railway Cottages
HILLMEAD CT
APPROACH RD
STATION RD
BOUNDARY RD
INSTITUTE RD
HITCHAM RD
Taplow
The Bishop Ctr
BATH RD
A4
Sewage Works

Sports Ground

CHAUNTRY RD
CHAUNTRY CL
CANNICK CL
NEWBURY CL
CHEVIOT
CLEVELAND
ASTOR CL
Fishery
Oldfield Prim Sch
CHILTERN
COTSWOLD CL
THE RUSHES
RIVER RD
AMERDEN LA
AMERDEN
Amerden Ponds

AVENUE RD
GLEBE RD
FISHERY RD
BRAY RD
CHURCH RD
Green Lane
Braywick Park Nature Reserve
Sewage Works
Braywick Park & Sports Ground

MARSH LA
YE MEADS HO
YE MEADS
YE MEADS COTTS

Barge Farm

SL6
River Thames
The Thames Path
Weir
Bray Lock
Amerden House
OLD MARSH LA
GLEBE CL
M4
Amerden House

40
CLIFTON CL
Bray Wick
Cemy
WALKER RD
BRAYWICK RD
OLD FORGE CL
GAS LA
Winbury Sch
Braywick Nature Ctr
THE BINGHAMS
HARVEST HILL RD
ORCHARD CL
HIBBERT RD
VICARAGE DR
THE CAUSEWAY
WEST CT
CHURCH LA
CHURCH
HIGH ST
FERRY END
FERRY RD
BETTONS HARE
OLD MILL LA
BRAYBANK
BEAUFORT PL
RIVER GDNS
OLD MILL LA
New Thames Bridge
Bray
Jesus Hospl (almshouses)
BRAYFIELD RD
BRAN CL
THE TERRACE
HANOVER MEAD
UPPER BRAY RD
B3028
The Cut

Dorney Comb Sch
HARCOURT CL
MEADOW WAY
OAK STUBBS LA
HARCOURT RD
Monkey Island
Dorney Reach
DORNEY REACH RD
CHESTNUT PK

A308(M)
A330
A308
WINBURY PL
CANON HILL DR
PRIORS CL
CANON HILL WAY
CANON HILL
HEATHCOTE
HASTING CL
REGAL CT
WILLOW DR
PRIORS WAY
PRIORS WAY
Priors Way Ind Est
Bray Pit Wildlife Reserve
MONKEY ISLAND LA

Moor Farm
ASCOT RD
The Bourne
HEARNE DR
A330
The Philberds
RYSGARTH PK
BYLAND DR
HOLYPORT RD
FIRFIELD 1
LARKFIELD 2
EARLSFIELD
WHITEACRES DR
ARKLEY CT
CRESSWELLS MEAD
LONSDALE
SANDY MEAD
GLOVESDALE
STOMPITS RD
HENDONS WAY
FARM CL
BUCKLEBURY RD
SPRINGFIELD PK
Cemy
WINDSOR RD
BRAY CT
COURT CL
P
PO
A308
40
HAYES
HUXTABLE GDNS
TITHE BARN DR
A308
BROADWATER PK
Works
Marina
Queen's Eyot
SL4

The Philberds

HARVEST HILL RD

203 197

Lent Rise

Burnham Upper Sch

THE GREEN

Our Lady of Peace Jun & Inf Schs

Priory Sch

SL2

NORTHMEAD RD
MARESCROFT RD
GREYSTOKE RD
SCAFELL RD
NEWCHURCH
AMBERLEY RD
SANDHOLM
FLYFOOT RD
YEOVIL
Yeovil Ent Ctr

HANBURY CL
BYWAYS
HITCHAM RD
BINGHAM RD
BAY
MILNER RD
ALDBOURNE RD
HARKNESS RD
OPPENHEIM RD
STOMP RD
PRIORY RD
PRIORY GDNS
STOMP RD
LEAHOLME GDNS
LAMMAS RD
HURST RD
PHIPPS
PHIPPS RD
BLUMFIELD CRES
Haymill Valley Nature Reserve
BANBURY AVE
Slough Trad Est

EASTFIELD RD
LENT RISE RD
CHILTERN RD
WENDOVER RD
SOUTHFIELD GDNS
Ct
COULSON RD
WETHERED RD
ANSLOW PL
HUNTER AVE
CONISTON CRES
ULLSWATER AVE
DERWENT DR
ORCHARD AVE
LITHWAITE WAY
MAYBURY
MEAD WAY
THE SPUR
ROYSTON WAY
ATTWOOD CL
BERKELEY MEWS
PARKVIEW CHASE
WESTON RD
OXFORD AVE

Lent Rise Comb Sch
PO
MAYPOLE RD
MANS WAY
POOL
FAIRVIEW RD
MISSENDEN GDNS
BARR'S RD
HUNTERCOMBE LA
ST JAMES PL
GREENFERNS AVE
CARDINALS
BURNHAM HTS
Sandringham Ct
Burnham
Progress Bsns Ctr
STANHOPE RD
Recn Gd
COMPTON CT
BROOK CRES
BUCKINGHAM AVE
DEAL AVE

Marshgate Trad Est
HAG HILL RISE
TAPLOW RD
GREEN CL
NURSERY RD
CONWAY RD
BRIAR CL
RAMBLER CL
HURST FIELD DR
STAFFORD CL
CHILTON CT
KINNAIRD
WINTERMERE WAY
SUMMERDALE CRES
BUTTERMERE AVE
MOCK CL
EATON AVE
BOSWORTH CT
CLARE RD
FRANCIS WAY
WHITTLE PARKWAY
Works
HOLYHEAD MEWS
BALMORAL CL
PO
MARLBOROUGH CT
IONA CRES
PETTY CROSS
SUFFOLK CL
MASON'S CT
GOSFORTH CT
BROOK PTH
CARDIGAN CL
HENLEY RD

A4
HAG HILL LA
CAVENDISH
LAKE END CT
FERN DR
ALVISTA
WESTLANDS AVE
LONGFT DR
BATH RD
WASHINGTON DR
LINCOLN WAY
AVON CL
LUNDY CT
STOWE RD
MASONS RD
CENTRAL
LEWINS RD
DOVER RD
WESTGATE CL

81
ROCKFORD WAY
ABBEY GATE
B3026
Superstore
SL6
Pondleys Cottage
M4
HUNTERCOMBE SPUR
St GEORGES CRES
FRANCIS WAY
MARINA WAY
ANTHONY WAY
St ANDREWS WAY
Cippenham Inf & Jun Schs
STROMA CT
Liby
PATRICIA CL
ABBEY CL
HINTON RD
SHERIDAN CL
ERICA CL
BERNERS CL
BOWER WAY
CHARTER RD
LEWINS FARM CT
RIDGEBANK CL
CIPPENHAM LA
IVY CRES
BOARLANDS

6
West Town Farm
LAKE END RD
HUNTERCOMBE LA
The Huntercombe
H
Burnham Abbey
SOUTH CL
ABBOTTS WAY
HARRISON WAY
THE GREENWAY
PLACKETT WAY
DENNIS WAY
BOWYER DR
FRENCHUM GDNS
ROXWELL CL
LOWER CL
ALDER
COLLEGE
PEARTREE
TRUMPER WAY
ALUMNI

5
BLYTHE HOS
BARNFIELD
LANGTON CL
LILLOWAY LA
MERCIAN WAY
MORETON WAY
SL1
Robin Hood CL
SAXON LODGE
WATERMAN CT
LODGE DUCHESS ST
SHAKESPEARE LODGE
EARLS LA
GERVAISE CL

80
M4
7
Recn Gd
1 Kennedy Ho
2 Harborough Cl
MOOR FURLONG
LILLEY WAY
FEHRERS CL
WARNER CL
MOLYNS MEWS
NICKOLAS
DUPRE CL
GOODWIN
MILLSTREAM LA
STREAMSIDE
Western Ho Prim Sch
Cippenham
LANGTREE AVE
ELTHAM AVE
ST MARGARET WY
GRAYLANDS CL
DAYLESFORD GR
FRIMLEY DR
AMESBURY RD

4
Lake End
PH
LAKE END RD
ASHFORD LA
Lake End Farm
NEPTUNE WAY
ELTHAM AVE
MOUNDSFIELD WAY
HOLME WAY
CHILBYE MEWS
Sewage Works
M4

3
MARSH LA
COURT LA
Dorney Court
Roundmoor Ditch
Elm View Farm
Pigeonhouse Farm

2
Dorney
VILLAGE RD
PH
SOUTH FIELD CL
Court Farm
Manor Farm
ALMA CT 1
VAUGHAN GDNS 2
BELLSFIELD CT 3
THE WHEATBUTTS 4
GLENORTON CRES
BOVENEY NEW RD
STOCKDALES RD
MOORS LA
NORTHFIELD RD
INKERMAN
ALMA RD
BELL LA
COMMON RD
SL4
Dorney Common
TILSTONE CL
TILSTONE AVE
LEESON GDNS
CORNWALL AVE
VICTORIA RD
PRINCES CL
QUEENS RD
Liby
Eton Wick Rd
B3026
PO
HAYWARDS MEAD

79

1
Riding School
Elm Farm Bungalow
Cress Brook
Boveney Ditch
Recn Gd
SL6
Dorney Lake
River Thames
Roasthill La
Eton Wick

78
92 A B 93 C D 94 E F

203 209

A4
1 Ashmount Cres
2 Mathecombe Rd
3 Darie Cl

E3
1 Eton Wlk
2 St Andrews Ct
3 Lincoln Ct
4 Locksley Ct

E4
1 Burlington Ct
2 Burlington Rd
3 Hilperton Rd
4 Tower Ho
5 Ashbourne Ho
6 Shaftesbury Ct
7 Moorstown Ct

F3
1 Eton Ho
2 Stoke Ho
3 Datchet Ho
4 Windsor Ho
5 Upton Cl
6 Manor Ct
7 Spruce Ct
8 Charter Cl
9 Albert Cl

10 Dartmouth Ct
11 Benison Ct
F4
1 Prudential Bldgs
2 Mackenzie St
3 Mackenzie Mall
4 Observatory Sh Ctr
5 Leopold Mall
6 Curzon Mall
7 Chandos Mall

8 Town Sq
9 Victoria St
10 Bisham Ct
11 Bembridge Ct
12 Stephenson Ct
13 Shamaa Ho
14 Hencroft Mews

Grid columns: A B C D E F
Grid rows: 8 7 81 6 5 80 4 3 79 2 1 78
Eastings: 98 99 00

SL2   SL1   SL3

SLOUGH

George Green · Middle Green · Upton Lea · Upton · Stone's Wood · Home Farm · Lavender Farm · Nursery · Convent · Trenches Farm · The Pippins · The Orchards

Upton Court Park · Cricket Gd · Ditton Park · Longmead Bridge · Kedermister Park · Parry Green

Khalsa Prim Sch · St Joseph's RC High Sch · St Ethelbert's RC Prim Sch · Wexham Sch Sports Coll · Wexham Court Prim Sch · IQRA Slough Islamic Prim Sch · St Johns Rd · Business Village · Works · St Bernard's Prep Sch · St Bernard's RC Gram Sch · Slough Gram Sch · St Mary's CE Prim Sch · Langley Manor Sch · Slough Interchange Ind Est · Marish Wharf Ind Est · Middlegreen Trad Est · Deseronto Wharf Ind Est · Langley Bsns Pk · Ryvers Sch · Langley Acad · Castleview Comb Sch · Langley Gram Sch · Holy Family RC Sch · Ditton Park Cvn Site · Long Close Sch · Parkstone Lodge

Slough Mus · Superstore · Mobile Home Site · Liby

Grand Union Canal · Slough Arm · Grand Union Canal Wlk

Roads: Uxbridge Rd · Wellington St · Sussex Pl · Yew Tree Rd · London Rd · Upton Court Rd · Slough Rd · Datchet Rd · Westfield Lane · Wexham Park La · Coronation Ave · George Green Rd · George Green Dr · Avenue Dr · Norway Dr · M4

A4 · A412 · B376 · B470 · B3026

A3
1 GROVE CL
2 CHATHAM CT
3 EASTFIELD CL
4 ALBERT ST
5 PRIORS CL
6 NIGHTINGALE CT
7 MOUNTBATTEN CL
8 HORNBEAM GDNS
9 CHURCH VIEW

A4
1 COLONIAL RD
2 QUEENSMERE RD
3 ALPHA ST N
4 MILFORD CT
5 CLIFTON RD
6 BELGRAVE PL
7 CLIFTON LODGE
8 LASCELLES HO
9 RYE CT
10 ELIZABETH CT

B4
1 AUSTRALIA RD
2 PRINCES ST
3 CONNAUGHT RD
4 SELIM CT
5 CLEMENTS CL
6 CHESHIRE CT
7 SUSSEX KEEP

C3
1 STARWOOD CT
2 BLACKTHORN DELL
3 APPLETREE LA
4 LA ROCHE CL
5 KINGSWAY
6 RED COTTAGE MEWS
7 FLEMING CT

F1
1 CALDER CT
2 BESSEMER CL
3 TYLER WLK
4 OWEN CL
5 BECKETT CHASE
6 DAVIDSON RD
7 CHAPLIN MEWS
8 SHARMAN ROW
9 GIBSON CT
10 SHERWOOD CT
11 SHAW GDNS
12 JAMES MDW
13 HARDING SPUR
14 HUDSON PL
15 DALTON GN

200
208

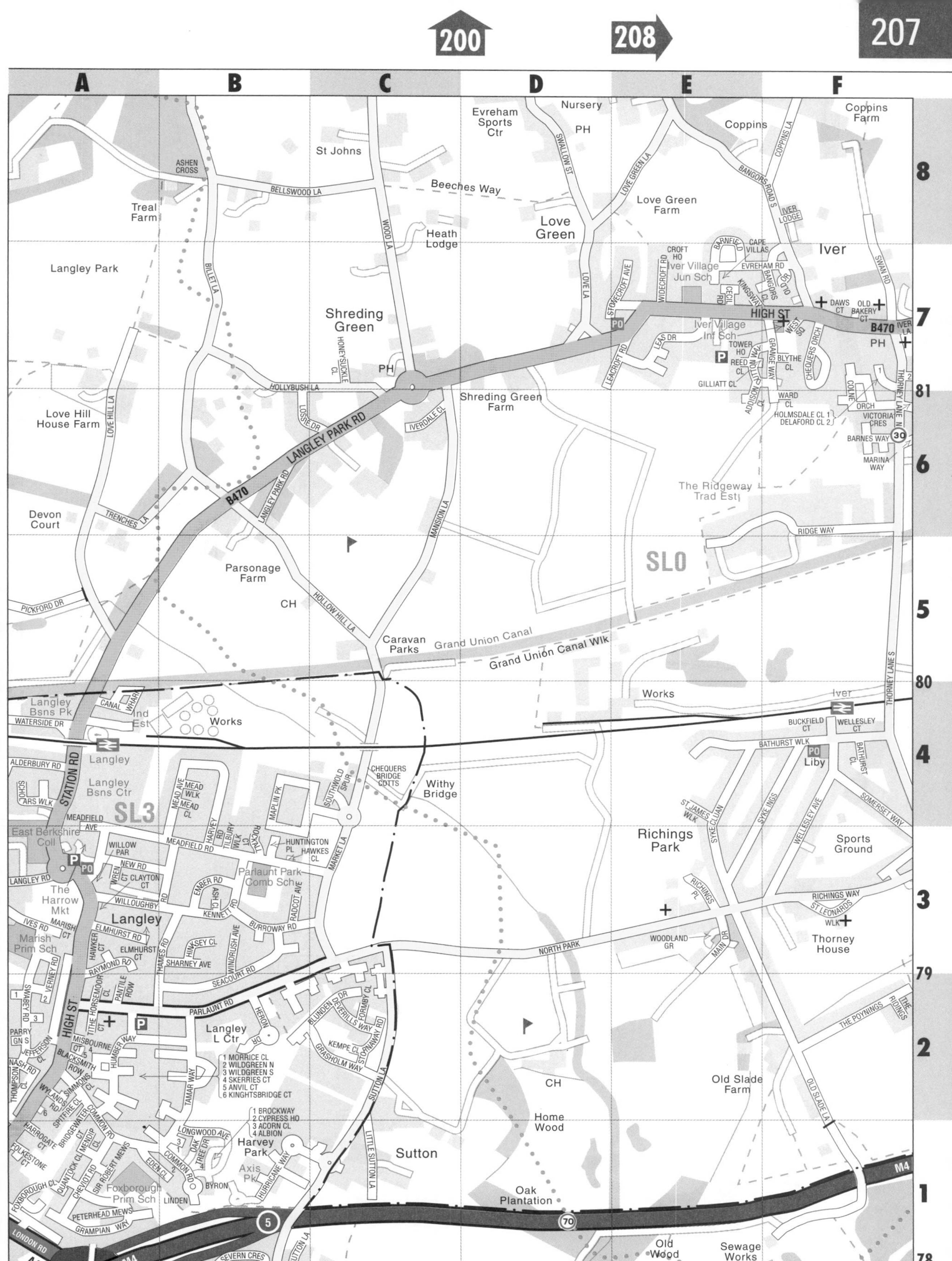
A
B
C
D
E
F
8
7
81
6
5
80
4
3
79
2
1
78
01
02
03
Ashen Cross
Bellswood La
St Johns
Evreham Sports Ctr
Nursery
PH
Coppins
Coppins Farm
Beeches Way
Treal Farm
Wood La
Heath Lodge
Love Green
Love Green Farm
Iver
Langley Park
Billet La
Shreding Green
Iver Village Jun Sch
Iver Village Inf Sch
High St
B470
Langley Park Rd
Hollybush La
Love Hill House Farm
Shreding Green Farm
Devon Court
Trenches La
Mansion La
The Ridgeway Trad Est
Ridge Way
Parsonage Farm
SL0
CH
Hollow Hill La
Pickford Dr
Caravan Parks
Grand Union Canal
Grand Union Canal Wlk
Works
Langley Bsns Pk
Canal Wharf
Ind Est
Waterside Dr
Langley
Alderbury Rd
Station Rd
Langley Bsns Ctr
SL3
Chequers Bridge Cotts
Withy Bridge
Liby
Richings Park
Sports Ground
East Berkshire Coll
Meadfield Rd
Parlaunt Park Comb Sch
Market La
The Harrow Mkt
North Park
Richings Way
Thorney House
Marish Prim Sch
Parlaunt Rd
Seacourt Rd
Langley L Ctr
Old Slade Farm
Old Slade La
Home Wood
Harvey Park
Sutton
Sutton La
Little Sutton La
Foxborough Prim Sch
Oak Plantation
M4
London Rd
A4
Old Wood
Sewage Works

212
208

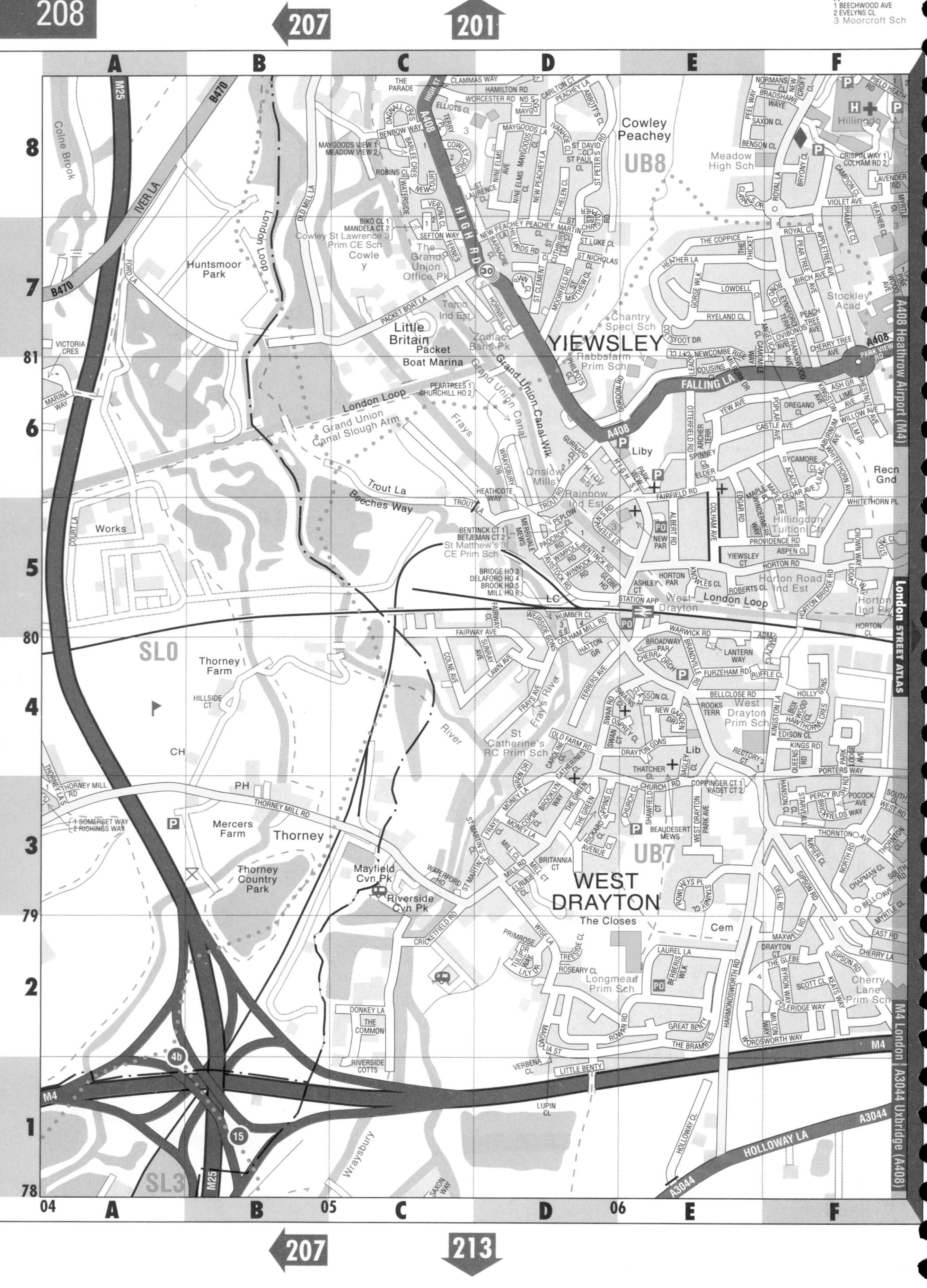

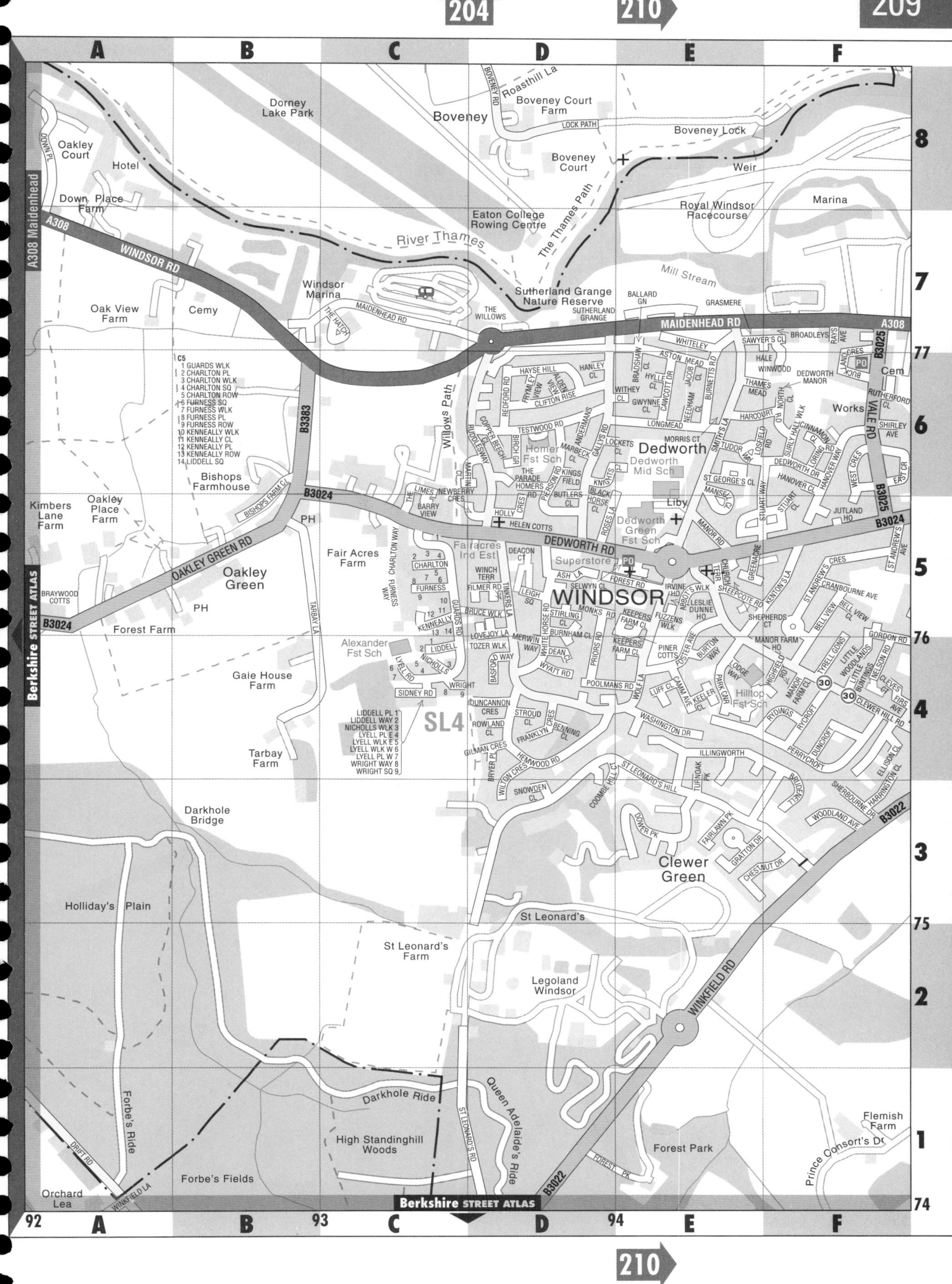
204
210
A
B
C
D
E
F
8
7
77
6
5
76
4
3
75
2
1
74
92
93
94
Dorney Lake Park
Boveney
Boveney Court Farm
Roasthill La
Boveney Lock
Boveney Court
Weir
Marina
Royal Windsor Racecourse
Oakley Court
Hotel
Down Place Farm
Eaton College Rowing Centre
River Thames
The Thames Path
Mill Stream
Windsor Marina
Sutherland Grange Nature Reserve
Oak View Farm
Cemy
A308 Maidenhead
WINDSOR RD
MAIDENHEAD RD
A308
Dedworth
WINDSOR
Oakley Green
B3024
B3383
B3025
B3022
OAKLEY GREEN RD
DEDWORTH RD
Kimbers Lane Farm
Oakley Place Farm
Bishops Farmhouse
Fair Acres Farm
Forest Farm
Gaie House Farm
Tarbay Farm
Alexander Fst Sch
SL4
C5
1 GUARDS WLK
2 CHARLTON PL
3 CHARLTON WLK
4 CHARLTON SQ
5 CHARLTON ROW
6 FURNESS SQ
7 FURNESS WLK
8 FURNESS PL
9 FURNESS ROW
10 KENNEALLY WLK
11 KENNEALLY CL
12 KENNEALLY PL
13 KENNEALLY ROW
14 LIDDELL SQ
LIDDELL PL 1
LIDDELL WAY 2
NICHOLLS WLK 3
LYELL PL E 4
LYELL WLK E 5
LYELL WLK W 6
LYELL PL W 7
WRIGHT WAY 8
WRIGHT SQ 9
Darkhole Bridge
Clewer Green
St Leonard's
Holliday's Plain
St Leonard's Farm
Legoland Windsor
WINKFIELD RD
Darkhole Ride
Queen Adelaide's Ride
High Standinghill Woods
Forbe's Ride
Forbe's Fields
Orchard Lea
Forest Park
Flemish Farm
Prince Consort's Dr
Works
Cem
Liby
Superstore
Hilltop Fst Sch
Dedworth Green Fst Sch
Dedworth Mid Sch
Homer Fst Sch
Fairacres Ind Est
Berkshire STREET ATLAS

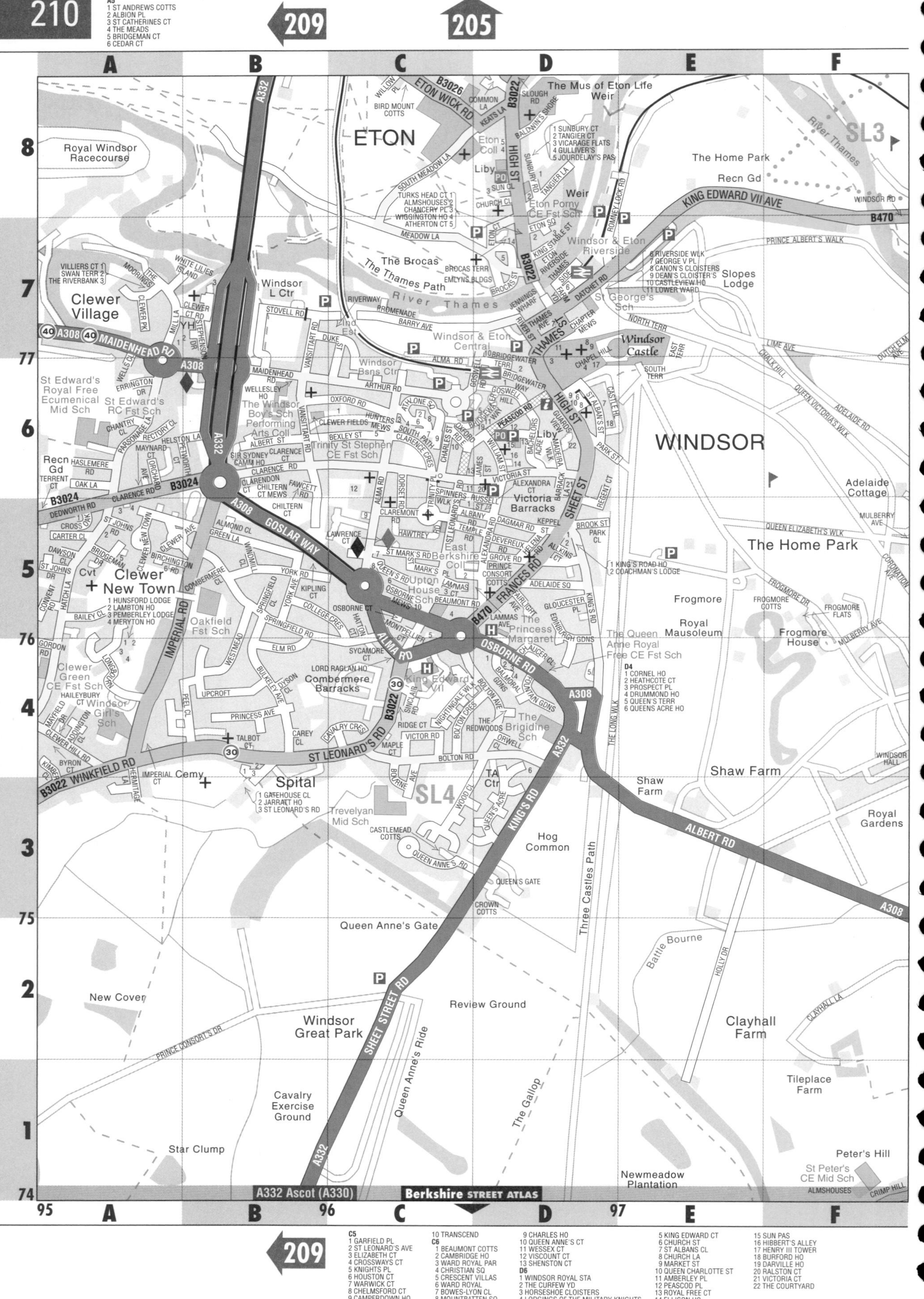

210

A5
1 ST ANDREWS COTTS
2 ALBION PL
3 ST CATHERINES CT
4 THE MEADS
5 BRIDGEMAN CT
6 CEDAR CT

209   205

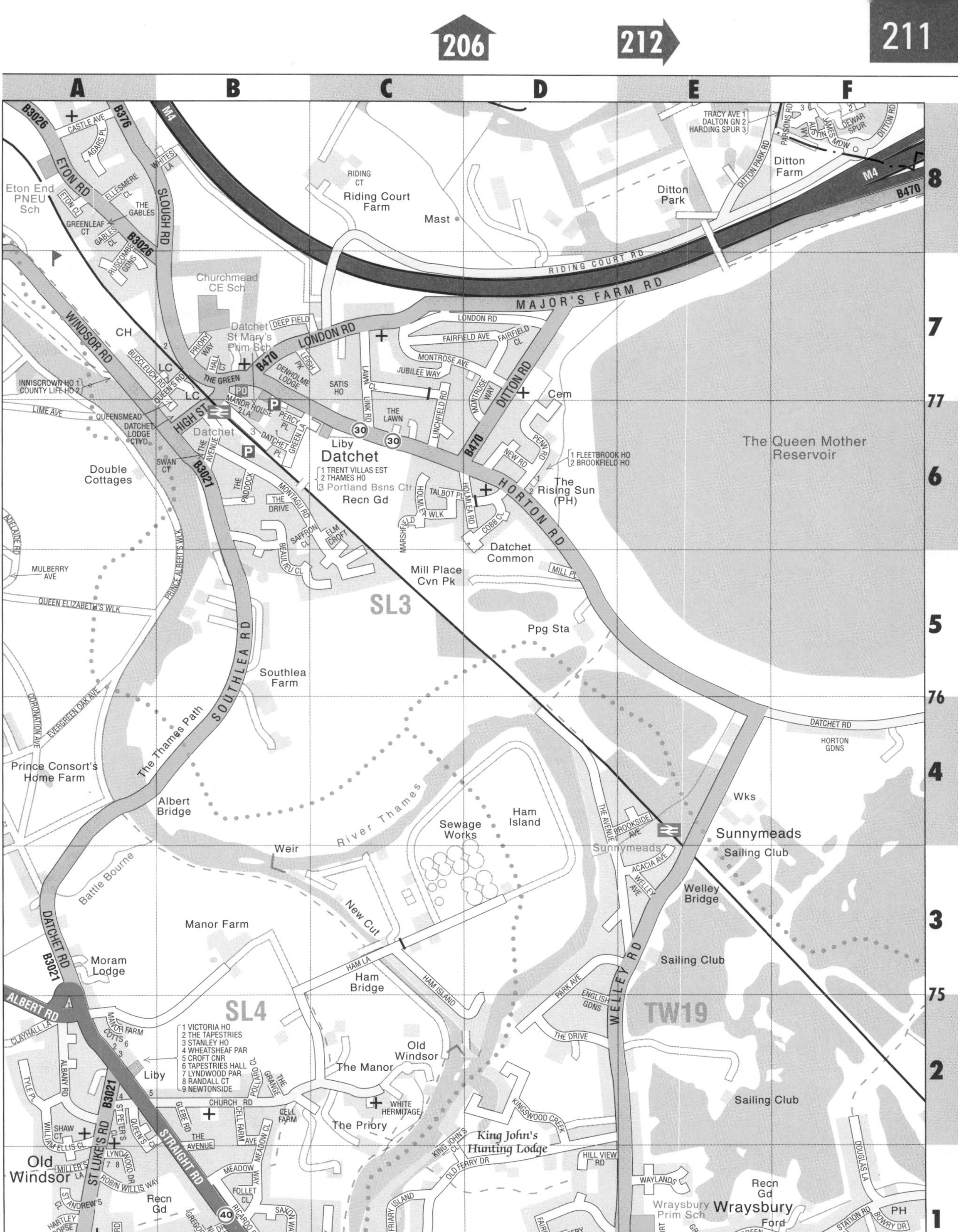
206
212
A
B
C
D
E
F
8
7
77
6
5
76
4
3
75
2
1
74
98
99
00
B3026
B376
M4
CASTLE AVE
AGARS PL
ETON RD
ETON CL
WHITES LA
ELLESMERE CL
THE GABLES
SLOUGH RD
Eton End PNEU Sch
GREENLEAF CT
GABLES CL
RUSCOMBE GDNS
B3026
RIDING CT
Riding Court Farm
Mast
Ditton Park
TRACY AVE 1
DALTON GN 2
HARDING SPUR 3
PARSONS RD
DITTON PARK RD
AUSTIN WY
JAMES MDW
DEWAR SPUR
DITTON RD
Ditton Farm
B470
RIDING COURT RD
MAJOR'S FARM RD
Churchmead CE Sch
WINDSOR RD
CH
PRIORY WAY
HALL CT
Datchet St Mary's Prim Sch
DEEP FIELD
LONDON RD
B470
LONDON RD
FAIRFIELD AVE
FAIRFIELD CL
MONTROSE AVE
JUBILEE WAY
BUCCLEUCH RD
QUEEN'S RD
THE GREEN
LC
LC
INNISCROWN HO 1
COUNTY LIFE HO 2
LEIGH PK
DENHOLME LODGE
SATIS HO
LAWN CL
LINK RD
LINCHFIELD RD
MONTROSE WAY
DITTON RD
Cem
LIME AVE
QUEENSMEAD
DATCHET LODGE CTYD
HIGH ST
MANOR HOUSE LA
PERCY PL
DATCHET PL
GREEN LA
THE LAWN
Datchet
Liby
Datchet
SWAN CT
THE AVENUE
B3021
30
30
B470
NEW RD
PENN RD
1 FLEETBROOK HO
2 BROOKFIELD HO
Double Cottages
THE PADDOCK
THE DRIVE
MONTAGU RD
1 TRENT VILLAS EST
2 THAMES HO
3 Portland Bsns Ctr
Recn Gd
TALBOT PL
HOLMLEA WLK
HOLMLEA RD
HORTON RD
The Rising Sun (PH)
COBB CL
ADELAIDE RD
SAFFRON CL
ELM CROFT
MARSHFIELD
Datchet Common
MULBERRY AVE
PRINCE ALBERT'S WLK
BEAULIEU CL
Mill Place Cvn Pk
MILL PL
QUEEN ELIZABETH'S WLK
SL3
Ppg Sta
The Queen Mother Reservoir
SOUTHLEA RD
Southlea Farm
CORONATION AVE
EVERGREEN OAK AVE
The Thames Path
DATCHET RD
HORTON GDNS
Prince Consort's Home Farm
Albert Bridge
Sewage Works
Ham Island
Wks
River Thames
THE AVENUE
BROOKSIDE AVE
Sunnymeads
Sunnymeads
Sailing Club
Weir
ACACIA AVE
WELLEY AVE
Battle Bourne
New Cut
Welley Bridge
Manor Farm
DATCHET RD
B3021
Moram Lodge
HAM LA
Ham Bridge
HAM ISLAND
WELLEY RD
Sailing Club
PARK AVE
ENGLISH GDNS
ALBERT RD
SL4
TW19
MANOR FARM COTTS
CLAYHALL LA
1 VICTORIA HO
2 THE TAPESTRIES
3 STANLEY HO
4 WHEATSHEAF PAR
5 CROFT CNR
6 TAPESTRIES HALL
7 LYNDWOOD PAR
8 RANDALL CT
9 NEWTONSIDE
Old Windsor
THE DRIVE
TYLE PL
ALBANY RD
Liby
POLLARD CL
THE GRANGE
The Manor
Sailing Club
B3021
CHURCH RD
GLEBE RD
CELL FARM
WHITE HERMITAGE
KINGSWOOD CREEK
SHAW CT
ST PETER'S CL
QUEEN'S CL
CELL FARM AVE
MEADOW CL
The Priory
WILLIAM ELLIS CL
THE AVENUE
King John's Hunting Lodge
STRAIGHT RD
KING JOHN'S CL
LYNDWOOD DR
MILLER'S LA
Old Windsor
ST LUKE'S RD
ROBIN WILLIS WAY
MEADOW WAY
FOLLET CL
OLD FERRY DR
HILL VIEW RD
DOUGLAS LA
WAYLANDS
Recn Gd
ST ANDREW'S CL
Recn Gd
SAXON WAY
FRIARY ISLAND
Wraysbury Prim Sch
Wraysbury
PH
HARTLEY COPSE
SETTERS
GREGORY DR
NURSERY PL
RICARDO RD
40
NURSERY WAY
Ford
STATION RD
BOWRY DR
THE FRIARY
FRIARY RD
FAIRFIELD APP
HARCOURT
THE GRANGE
GRANGE CL
THE GREEN
The Green
THE WORPLE
PH
CORNWELL RD
GRIMP HILL
NEWTON CT
KINGSBURY DR
NEWTON LA
A308
PO
FARM DR
POULCOTT
FAIRFIELD RD
OUSELEY RD
HIGH ST
NEWTON SIDE ORCH
BURFIELD RD
B3021
ORCHARD RD
A308 Staines
WINDSOR RD
B376
ST ANDREW'S CL
PO

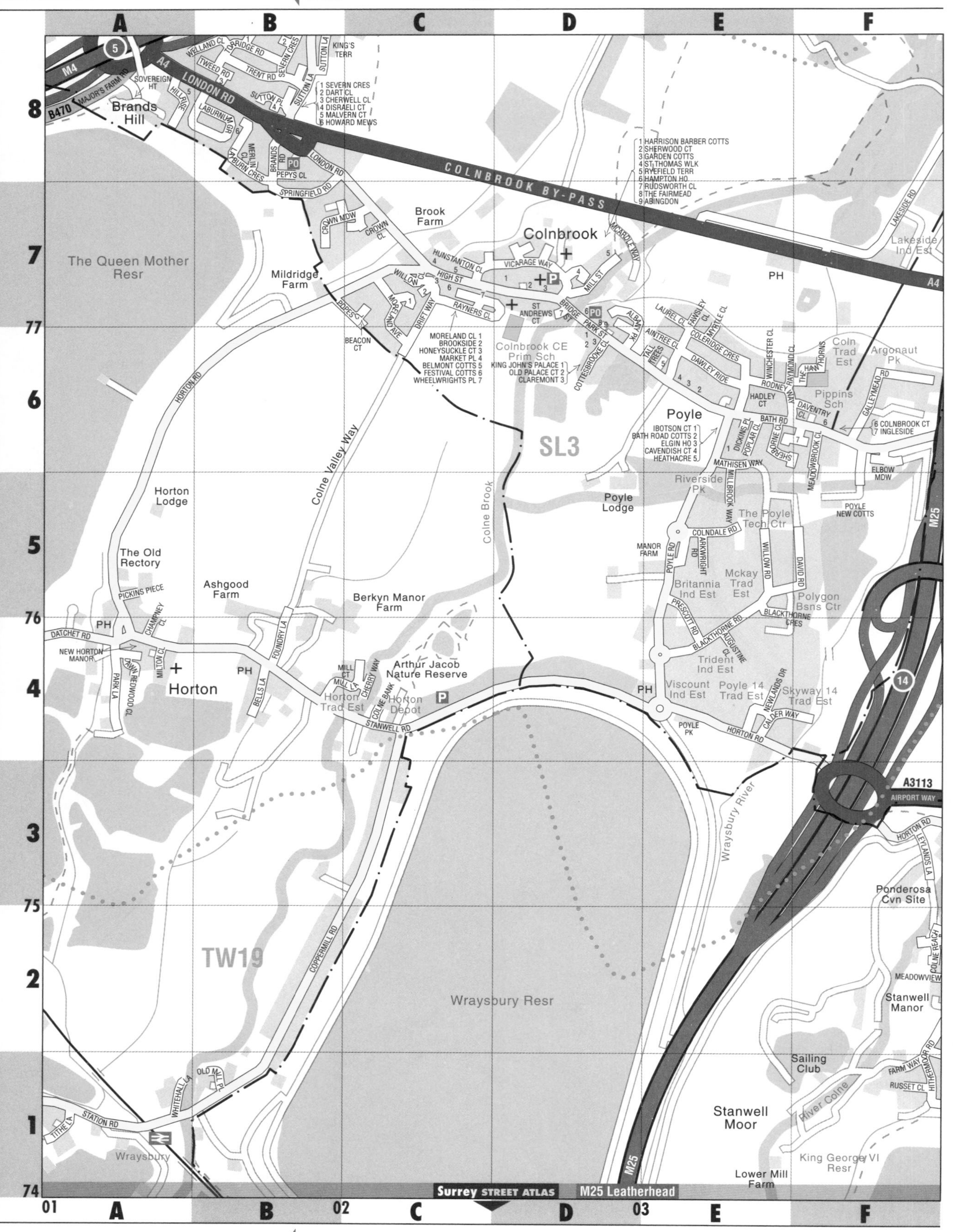

A   B   C   D   E   F

8

Brands Hill

1 SEVERN CRES
2 DART CL
3 CHERWELL CL
4 DISRAELI CT
5 MALVERN CT
6 HOWARD MEWS

1 HARRISON BARBER COTTS
2 SHERWOOD CT
3 GARDEN COTTS
4 ST.THOMAS WLK
5 RYEFIELD TERR
6 HAMPTON HO
7 RUDSWORTH CL
8 THE FAIRMEAD
9 ABINGDON

LONDON RD

COLNBROOK BY-PASS

Brook Farm

7

The Queen Mother Resr

Mildridge Farm

Colnbrook

PH

Lakeside Ind Est

77

BEACON CT

MORELAND CL 1
BROOKSIDE 2
HONEYSUCKLE CT 3
MARKET PL 4
BELMONT COTTS 5
FESTIVAL COTTS 6
WHEELWRIGHTS PL 7

Colnbrook CE Prim Sch

KING JOHN'S PALACE 1
OLD PALACE CT 2
CLAREMONT 3

Coln Trad Est

Argonaut Pk

6

Horton Lodge

Colne Valley Way

Colne Brook

SL3

Poyle

IBOTSON CT 1
BATH ROAD COTTS 2
ELGIN HO 3
CAVENDISH CT 4
HEATHACRE 5.

Pippins Sch

6 COLNBROOK CT
7 INGLESIDE

5

The Old Rectory

Ashgood Farm

Berkyn Manor Farm

Poyle Lodge

Riverside Pk

MANOR FARM

The Poyle Tech Ctr

POYLE NEW COTTS

ELBOW MDW

76

PICKINS PIECE

DATCHET RD   PH

NEW HORTON MANOR

Britannia Ind Est

Mckay Trad Est

Polygon Bsns Ctr

4

Horton

PH

Arthur Jacob Nature Reserve

Horton Trad Est   Horton Depot

STANWELL RD

Viscount Ind Est

Trident Ind Est

Poyle 14 Trad Est

Skyway 14 Trad Est

PH

POYLE PK

HORTON RD

14

A3113

3

AIRPORT WAY

75

Ponderosa Cvn Site

TW19

2

Wraysbury Resr

Stanwell Manor

Sailing Club

1

OLD M

Stanwell Moor

King George VI Resr

Lower Mill Farm

Wraysbury

74

01   A   02   B   C   02   D   03   E   F

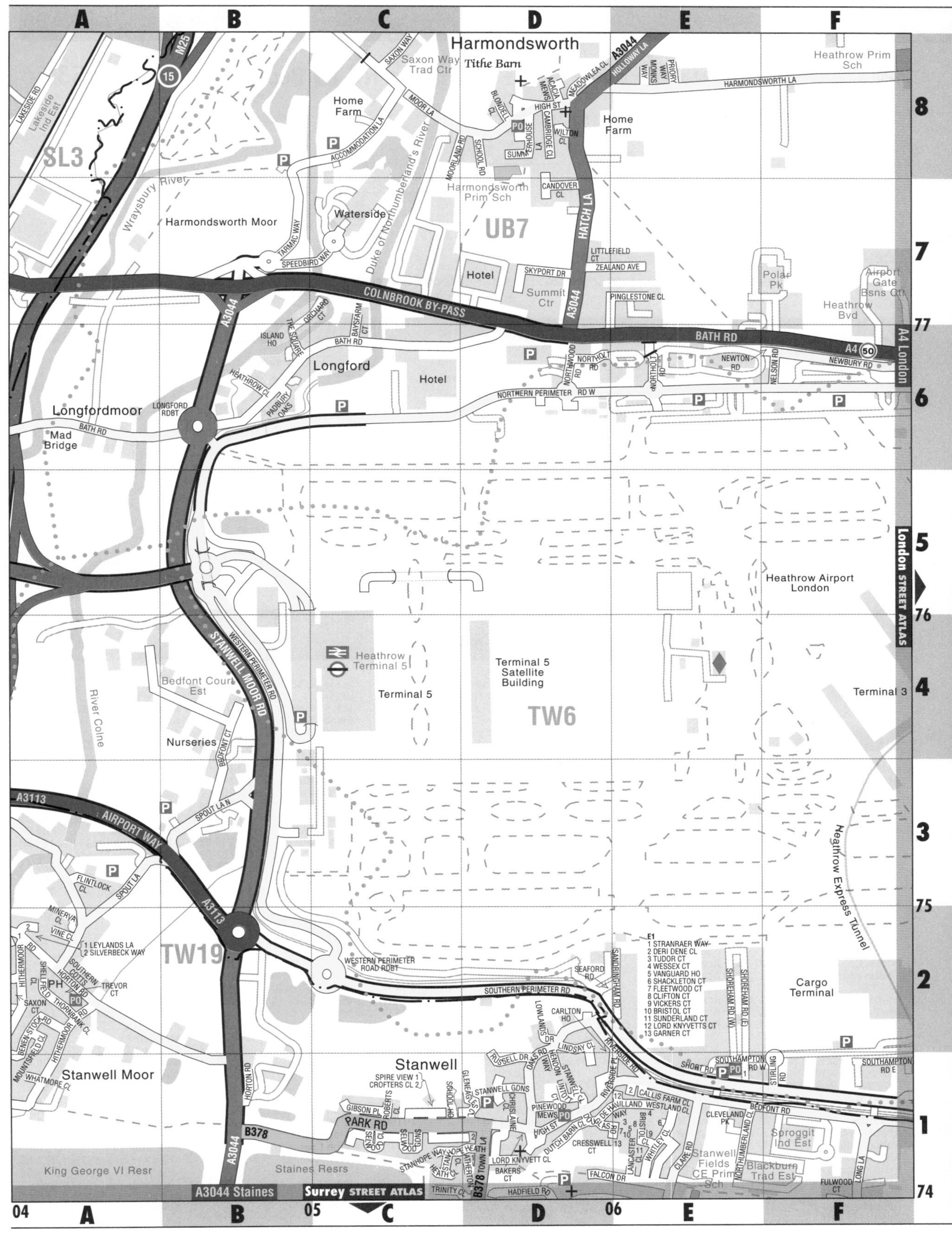

A   B   C   D   E   F

8

Heathrow Prim Sch

Harmondsworth

Tithe Barn

HARMONDSWORTH LA

SL3

Home Farm

Home Farm

Harmondsworth Moor

Waterside

Harmondsworth Prim Sch

UB7

CANDOVER CL

7

77

Longfordmoor   Longford

Hotel

Heathrow Blvd

Airport Gate Bsns Ctr

Polar Pk

COLNBROOK BY-PASS

BATH RD   A4   50

Longford

Hotel

Summit Ctr

A4 London

Mad Bridge

Longfordmoor

BATH RD

NORTHERN PERIMETER RD W

6

5

76

Heathrow Airport London

London STREET ATLAS

River Colne

Bedfont Court Est

Heathrow Terminal 5

Terminal 5 Satellite Building

Terminal 5

TW6

Terminal 3

4

Nurseries

75

A3113   AIRPORT WAY

FLINTLOCK CL

A3113

3

STANWELL MOOR RD   WESTERN PERIMETER RD

Heathrow Express Tunnel

TW19

WESTERN PERIMETER ROAD RDBT

SEAFORD RD

E1
1 STRANRAER WAY
2 DERI DENE CL
3 TUDOR CT
4 WESSEX CT
5 VANGUARD HO
6 SHACKLETON CT
7 FLEETWOOD CT
8 CLIFTON CT
9 VICKERS CT
10 BRISTOL CT
11 SUNDERLAND CT
12 LORD KNYVETTS CT
13 GARNER CT

Cargo Terminal

2

SOUTHERN PERIMETER RD

SOUTHAMPTON RD W

SOUTHAMPTON RD E

Stanwell Moor

Stanwell

Stanwell Gdns

BEDFONT RD

Stanwell Ind Est

Sproggit Ind Est

1

PARK RD

B378

Stanwell Fields CE Prim Sch

Blackburn Trad Est

King George VI Resr

A3044   B378

Staines Resrs

74

04   A   B   05   C   D   06   E   F

Index

Place name May be abbreviated on the map	Church Rd
Location number Present when a number indicates the place's position in a crowded area of mapping	6
Locality, town or village Shown when more than one place has the same name	Beckenham
Postcode district District for the indexed place	BR2
Page and grid square Page number and grid reference for the standard mapping	53 C6

Example: **Church Rd** 6 Beckenham BR2..........**53** C6

Cities, towns and villages are listed in CAPITAL LETTERS

Public and commercial buildings are highlighted in magenta **Places of interest** are highlighted in blue with a star

Abbreviations used in the index

Acad	Academy	Comm	Common	Gd	Ground	L	Leisure	Prom	Promenade
App	Approach	Cott	Cottage	Gdn	Garden	La	Lane	Rd	Road
Arc	Arcade	Cres	Crescent	Gn	Green	Liby	Library	Recn	Recreation
Ave	Avenue	Cswy	Causeway	Gr	Grove	Mdw	Meadow	Ret	Retail
Bglw	Bungalow	Ct	Court	H	Hall	Meml	Memorial	Sh	Shopping
Bldg	Building	Ctr	Centre	Ho	House	Mkt	Market	Sq	Square
Bsns, Bus	Business	Ctry	Country	Hospl	Hospital	Mus	Museum	St	Street
Bvd	Boulevard	Cty	County	HQ	Headquarters	Orch	Orchard	Sta	Station
Cath	Cathedral	Dr	Drive	Hts	Heights	Pal	Palace	Terr	Terrace
Cir	Circus	Dro	Drove	Ind	Industrial	Par	Parade	TH	Town Hall
Cl	Close	Ed	Education	Inst	Institute	Pas	Passage	Univ	University
Cnr	Corner	Emb	Embankment	Int	International	Pk	Park	Wk, Wlk	Walk
Coll	College	Est	Estate	Intc	Interchange	Pl	Place	Wr	Water
Com	Community	Ex	Exhibition	Junc	Junction	Prec	Precinct	Yd	Yard

Index of towns, villages, streets, hospitals, industrial estates, railway stations, schools, shopping centres, universities and places of interest

Abb–Ale

A

Abbey Barn La HP10 . . . 173 E3
Abbey Barn Rd HP11 . . . 173 F4
Abbey Cl SL1 . . . 204 E6
Abbey Cotts SL7 . . . 193 B4
Abbey Ct HP5 . . . 154 B6
Abbey Ctr The HP19 . . . 101 B2
Abbeydore Gr MK10 . . . 35 F1
Abbeyfield Ho HP16 . . . 152 A7
Abbey Gate SL6 . . . 204 A7
Abbeyhill Rdbt MK12 . . . 33 E4
Abbey Mead SL8 . . . 184 F5
Abbey Park La SL1 . . . 186 E2
Abbey Rd
  Aylesbury HP19 . . . 101 B2
  Bourne End SL8 . . . 184 F5
  Milton Keynes, Bradwell MK13 . . . 34 A4
  Milton Keynes, Simpson MK6 . . . 47 E5
  Syresham NN13 . . . 27 C7
Abbey's Prim Sch MK3 . . . 47 A2
Abbey Sq MK43 . . . 8 E5
Abbey Terr MK16 . . . 22 D4
Abbey Way
  High Wycombe HP11 . . . 173 A6
  Milton Keynes MK13 . . . 34 B6
  Ravenstone MK46 . . . 5 E2
Abbey Wlk HP16 . . . 152 B7
Abbot Ridge HP18 . . . 125 D5
Abbotsbury MK4 . . . 45 E2
Abbots Cl MK13 . . . 34 B6
Abbotsfield MK6 . . . 47 B8
Abbots Way
  High Wycombe HP12 . . . 172 D3
  Monks Risborough HP27 139 C5
Abbot's Wlk SL4 . . . 209 E5
Abbotswood HP27 . . . 150 C4
Abbotts Cl HP20 . . . 101 E1
Abbott's Cl UB8 . . . 208 D8
Abbotts Rd HP20 . . . 101 E1
Abbotts Vale HP5 . . . 144 C3
Abbotts Way
  Slough SL1 . . . 204 D5
  Wingrave HP22 . . . 89 A4
Abbot Wlk HP18 . . . 125 D5
Abell Gdns SL6 . . . 195 B1
Abercromby Ave HP12 . 172 E8
Abercromby Ct 4 HP12 . . . 172 D8
Aberdeen Ave SL1 . . . 205 A6
Aberdeen Cl MK3 . . . 46 F2
Abingdon Cl
  Thame OX9 . . . 125 F1
  Uxbridge UB10 . . . 201 F4
Abingdon Wlk SL6 . . . 195 E3
Abington SL3 . . . 212 D7
Abney Court Dr SL8 . . . 185 A2
Abraham Cl MK15 . . . 35 C6
Abrahams Rd RG9 . . . 191 C3
Abstacle Hill HP23 . . . 118 F3
Acacia 3 RG9 . . . 191 D2
Acacia Ave
  West Drayton UB7 . . . 208 F6
  Wraysbury TW19 . . . 211 E3
Acacia Cl HP5 . . . 144 A1
Acacia Gr HP4 . . . 135 B3
Acacia Ho SL9 . . . 177 E2
Acacia Mews UB7 . . . 213 D8
Acacia Wlk HP23 . . . 118 E3
Accommodation La UB7 . . . 213 C8
Ackerman Cl MK18 . . . 52 F8
Ackroyd Pl MK5 . . . 46 B5
Acorn Cl
  High Wycombe HP13 . . . 173 D7
  Slough SL3 . . . 207 B1
Acorn Gdns HP12 . . . 172 E4
Acorn Ho MK9 . . . 34 D2
Acorn Wlk MK9 . . . 34 E2
Acrefield Rd SL9 . . . 188 D8
Acre Pas SL4 . . . 210 D6
Acres End HP7 . . . 165 E8
Acres The HP13 . . . 161 E1
Acres Way HP19 . . . 101 C4
Acre The SL7 . . . 183 F2
Adam Cl
  High Wycombe HP13 . . . 173 D8
  Slough SL1 . . . 205 A5
Adam Ct RG9 . . . 191 E2
Adams Cl MK18 . . . 41 C1
Adams Ct MK6 . . . 47 C8
Adams Pk (Wycombe Wanderers FC & London Wasps) HP12 . . . 172 A7
Adams Way HP23 . . . 119 B6
Addenbrookes MK16 . . . 22 F3
ADDINGTON . . . 65 A6
Addington Cl SL4 . . . 210 A4
Addington Cotts HP22 . . 131 B5
Addington Rd MK18 . . . 41 D1
Addington Terr MK18 . . . 41 D1
Addison Cl SL0 . . . 207 E6
Addison Ct SL6 . . . 196 B1
Addison Rd
  Chesham HP5 . . . 144 C2
  Steeple Claydon MK18 . . . 63 D2
Adelaide Cl SL1 . . . 205 A4
Adelaide Rd
  High Wycombe HP13 . . . 162 D1
  Windsor SL4 . . . 210 F6
Adelaide Sq SL4 . . . 210 D5
Adelphi Gdns SL1 . . . 205 E4
Adelphi St MK9 . . . 34 F4
Adkins Cl HP19 . . . 100 F3
Adkins Ct HP14 . . . 158 E5
Admiralty Cl UB7 . . . 208 F4
Admiral Way HP4 . . . 134 F6
Adrians Wlk SL2 . . . 205 F5
ADSTOCK . . . 53 F1
Adstock Mews 2 SL9 . . 177 D2
Adwell Sq RG9 . . . 191 D2
Agars Pl SL3 . . . 211 A8
Agora Ctr MK12 . . . 33 D7
Agora Ctr (Sh Ctr) 7 MK2 . . . 58 C8
Aidan Cl HP21 . . . 116 A4
Ailward Rd HP19 . . . 101 A2
Ainsdale Cl MK3 . . . 46 D1
Aintree Cl
  Milton Keynes MK3 . . . 57 C6
  Poyle SL3 . . . 212 E6
Airport Gate Bsns Ctr UB7 . . . 213 F7
Airport Way TW19 . . . 213 A3
Aiston Pl HP20 . . . 101 F2
Ajax Ave SL1 . . . 205 B6
AKELEY . . . 41 E8
Akeley Wood Jun Sch MK19 . . . 31 A1
Akeley Wood Lower Sch MK18 . . . 29 B4
Akeley Wood Sch MK18 . 41 C7
Akeman St HP23 . . . 119 A3
Akerlea Cl MK6 . . . 47 C6
Akerman Cl MK12 . . . 33 B5
Akister Cl MK18 . . . 52 E8
Alabama Circ HP11 . . . 173 B4
Alabama Dr HP11 . . . 173 B3
Alan Way SL3 . . . 206 E7
Alaska St HP11 . . . 173 B4
Alastair Mews HP9 . . . 175 F2
Albany Ct MK14 . . . 34 D7
Albany Gate HP5 . . . 144 B1
Albany Pk SL3 . . . 212 D7
Albany Pl HP19 . . . 101 A2
Albany Rd
  Old Windsor SL4 . . . 211 A2
  Windsor SL4 . . . 210 D5
Albany Terr HP23 . . . 119 B6
Albert Cl 9 SL1 . . . 205 F3
Albert Pl SL4 . . . 205 A1
Albert Rd
  Chesham HP5 . . . 154 C8
  Henley-on-Thames RG9 . . 191 E1
  West Drayton UB7 . . . 208 E5
  Windsor SL4 . . . 210 E3
Albert St
  Aylesbury HP20 . . . 116 A8
  4 High Wycombe HP13 . 173 C7
  Maidenhead SL6 . . . 202 F7
  Milton Keynes MK2 . . . 58 C8
  Slough SL1 . . . 205 F3
  Tring HP23 . . . 119 A3
  Windsor SL4 . . . 210 B6
Albion SL3 . . . 207 B1
Albion Cl SL2 . . . 206 A5
Albion Cotts SL6 . . . 195 C7
Albion Cres HP8 . . . 177 B7
Albion Ho HP12 . . . 172 C5
Albion Pl
  Milton Keynes MK9 . . . 35 A3
  2 Windsor SL4 . . . 210 A5
Albion Rd
  Chalfont St Giles HP8 . . . 177 B8
  High Wycombe HP12 . . . 172 C5
  Pitstone LU7 . . . 105 D5
Albion St HP20 . . . 115 E8
ALBURY . . . 136 B7
Albury Ct 3 MK8 . . . 33 F1
Albury View OX9 . . . 136 A6
Aldborough Spur SL1 . . 205 E7
Aldbourne Rd SL1 . . . 204 B8
ALDBURY . . . 120 D5
Aldbury Gdns HP23 . . . 119 B6
Aldbury Prim Sch HP23 . . . 120 C6
Aldbury Rd WD3 . . . 167 F2
Aldebury Rd SL6 . . . 195 F2
Aldene Rd MK19 . . . 11 B3
Aldenham MK6 . . . 47 D5
Alden View SL4 . . . 209 D6
Alderbourne La SL3 . . . 199 E8
Alderbourne Manor SL9 . . . 189 A1
Alderbury Rd SL3 . . . 207 A4
Alderbury Road W SL3 . 206 F4
Alder Cl SL1 . . . 204 F5
Aldergill MK13 . . . 34 C5
Alderley Ct HP4 . . . 135 C3
Aldermead MK12 . . . 33 E5
Alderney Pl MK5 . . . 45 F4
Alder Rd
  Aylesbury HP22 . . . 116 C4
  Iver Heath SL0 . . . 200 D3
  New Denham UB9 . . . 201 C6
Alderson Cl 1 HP19 . . . 101 A2
Alders The UB9 . . . 201 C6
ALDERTON . . . 9 A2
Alderton Dr HP4 . . . 121 B8
Aldin Avenue N SL1 . . . 206 A4
Aldin Avenue S SL1 . . . 206 A4
Aldrich Dr MK15 . . . 35 E7
Aldridge Ct HP11 . . . 173 F4
Aldridge Rd SL2 . . . 198 A1
Aldwick Dr SL6 . . . 202 D6
Aldwycks Cl MK5 . . . 45 F6
Alexander Ct
  High Wycombe HP12 . . . 172 E8
  Slough SL1 . . . 205 C4
Alexander Fst Sch SL4 . 209 C4
Alexander Ho 1 MK2 . . . 58 C8
Alexander Rd HP20 . . . 101 D1
Alexander St HP5 . . . 144 C1
Alexandra Ct
  Leighton Buzzard LU7 . . . 80 F8
  4 Milton Keynes MK13 . . . 34 A4
  Windsor SL4 . . . 210 D5

Alexandra Dr MK16 22 C2
Alexandra Pk HP11 173 A6
Alexandra Rd
High Wycombe HP13 173 E5
Maidenhead SL6 202 D8
Slough SL1 205 D3
Uxbridge UB8 201 D3
Windsor SL4 210 D5
Alford Pl MK3 47 B1
Alford Rd HP12 172 C3
Alfred Ct SL8 185 B3
Alfred Davis Ct SL7 183 D3
Alfriston Specl Sch HP9 175 C6
Alham Rd HP21 115 C6
Alice Cl HP15 163 C7
Alice La SL1 197 B1
Alladale Pl MK12 33 D4
Allanson Rd SL7 183 F3
Allenby Rd SL6 202 B7
Allen Cl MK2 58 C5
Allen Dr HP14 161 C8
Allerds Rd SL2 198 A4
Allerford Ct MK4 46 C4
Alleyns La SL6 195 D8
Allhusen Gdns SL3 199 E8
Allington Circ MK4 45 E1
Allington Ct SL2 205 F6
Allison Ct MK15 35 C1
Allkins Ct SL4 210 D5
Allonby Way HP21 116 B7
All Saints' Ave SL6 202 D7
All Saints CE Controlled Jun Sch SL6 202 C6
All Saints View MK5 46 B8
All Souls Cotts SL3 206 E8
Allyn Cl HP13 173 C8
Alma Ct
Burnham SL1 197 C2
Eton Wick SL4 204 F2
Alma Rd
Berkhamsted HP4 134 E6
Chesham HP5 144 C2
Eton Wick SL4 204 F2
Windsor SL4 210 C6
Almhouses MK14 21 E1
Almond Cl
Newport Pagnell MK16 22 B3
Windsor SL4 210 B5
Almond Rd SL1 197 C2
Almond Tree Dr HP22 116 C4
Almond Way HP27 139 A2
Almond Wlk HP15 163 B3
Almons Way SL2 206 B8
Almshouses
Eton SL4 210 D7
Old Windsor SL4 210 F1
Worminghall HP18 123 E5
Almshouses The MK46 5 E2
Alnwick Dr HP23 103 F7
Alpha Ct HP7 165 B7
Alpha Street N 3 SL1 206 A4
Alpha Street S SL1 205 F3
Alpine Cl SL6 203 A6
Alpine Croft MK5 46 A3
ALSCOT 139 A5
Alscot La HP27 139 A5
Alsford Wharf HP4 135 C5
Alston Dr MK13 33 F3
Alstonefield 1 MK4 46 B3
Alston Gdns SL6 202 E7
Althorpe Cres MK13 34 B6
Altona Rd HP10 174 D3
Altona Way SL1 205 B7
Alton Bsns Pk HP19 101 B1
Alton Gate MK4 45 F3
Altwood Bailey SL6 202 B5
Altwood CE Sch SL6 202 B5
Altwood Cl
Maidenhead SL6 202 B5
Slough SL1 204 E8
Altwood Dr SL6 202 B5
Altwood Rd SL6 202 B5
Alverton MK14 34 F8
Alvista Ave SL6 204 B7
Alvric Way 3 MK12 33 A6
Alwin Cl HP21 115 C4
Alwins Field LU7 80 D8
Alwyn Inf Sch SL6 202 C8
Alwyn Rd SL6 202 B8
Alyngton HP4 134 E7
Alyson Ct 2 SL6 195 F1
Amanda Ct SL3 206 D3
Amber Cotts HP7 164 F3
Ambergate MK16 36 B4
Amberley Ct SL6 196 C3
Amberley Pl 11 SL4 210 D6
Amberley Rd SL2 204 E8
Amberley Way UB10 201 E3
Amberley Wlk MK4 45 E1
Amblers Way MK18 53 A1
Ambleside
Amersham HP6 154 C2
Aylesbury HP21 116 B5
Ambleside Wlk UB8 201 D4
Ambridge Gr MK6 35 C1
Ambrose Ct MK15 35 C2
Amelias La MK9 35 A3
Amerden Cl SL6 203 D7
Amerden La SL6 203 D7
Amerden Way SL1 205 A4
American Com Sch UB10 201 F4
AMERSHAM 154 B2
AMERSHAM COMMON 165 E8
Amersham Ct HP7 165 A7
Amersham Hill HP13 173 B7
Amersham Hill Dr HP13 173 C8
Amersham Hill Gdns HP13 173 C8
Amersham Hospl HP7 165 A6
Amersham Mus★ HP7 165 B7
AMERSHAM OLD TOWN 165 A7
AMERSHAM ON THE HILL 154 D2
Amersham Pl HP7 166 C8
Amersham Rd
Beaconsfield HP7 176 A6
Chalfont Common HP8, SL9 177 D6
Chalfont St Giles HP8 166 B2
Chalfont St Peter SL9 177 E2
Chesham HP6 154 B5
Chorleywood WD3 167 C8
Denham Green SL9 189 A4
Gerrards Cross SL9 188 F7
Hazlemere HP15 162 E2
High Wycombe HP13 173 C8
Little Chalfont HP6 166 E8
Amersham Sch HP7 165 E7
Amersham Sta/U Sta HP6 154 C1
Amersham Way HP6 166 E8
Amersham & Wycombe Coll
Amersham HP7 165 F8
Chesham HP5 144 D3
Flackwell Heath HP10 173 E2
Amesbury Rd SL1 204 F4
Ames Cl MK6 46 F8
Amherst Ct MK15 35 C7
Amicia Gdns SL2 198 F4
Amos Ct MK13 34 A6
Amy La HP5 154 B7
Ancastle Gn RG9 191 D1
Ancell Rd MK11 32 E5
Anchor Ct SL6 195 F7
Anchor La 1 HP20 115 E8
Ancona Gdns MK5 45 F3
Andermans SL4 209 D6
Andersen Gate MK4 57 A7
Anderson Cl HP14 158 F4
Anding Cl MK46 6 E4
Andover Cl UB8 201 B3
Andrewes Croft MK14 34 F8
Andrew Hill La SL2 187 C3
Andrews Cl LU7 69 E3
Andrews Reach SL8 185 A2
Andrews Way
Aylesbury HP19 115 A7
Marlow Bottom SL7 183 C8
Anershall HP22 89 B3
Angel Cl MK15 35 A7
Angelica Cl UB7 208 F7
Angelica Ct MK7 48 A5
Angels Cl MK18 65 F4
Anglefield Rd HP4 135 B4
Anglesey Ct
Milton Keynes MK8 46 A8
Stokenchurch HP14 158 E5
Angling Spring Wood Talking Trail★ HP16 151 F7
Angood Cl HP27 139 A3
Angora Cl MK5 46 A3
Angstrom Cl MK5 46 B5
Angus Dr MK3 46 F2
Angus Rd HP19 101 A3
Anne Cl SL6 195 E2
Annes Gr MK14 21 D1
Annesley Rd MK16 22 B3
Anns Cl
Aylesbury HP21 116 A4
Tring HP23 118 E3
Ansculf Rd SL2 198 A2
Anslow Gdns SL0 200 D3
Anslow Pl SL1 204 C8
Anson Cl
Aylesbury HP21 115 E4
Bovingdon HP3 145 F4
Anson Rd MK12 33 C6
Anstey Brook HP22 117 A3
Anstey Cl HP18 99 B6
Anstey Ct HP18 99 B7
Anthony Cl HP13 161 F1
Anthony Ct MK11 32 D5
Anthony Way SL1 204 D6
Anton Way HP21 115 D3
Anvil Cl HP3 146 B3
Anvil Ct SL3 207 A2
Anxey Way HP17 126 F6
Aplin Rd HP21 116 C6
Appleacres MK17 69 D8
Appleby Heath MK2 58 D6
Apple Cotts HP3 146 A4
Applecroft
Berkhamsted HP4 134 E6
Maidenhead SL6 202 C3
Applecroft *continued*
Newton Longville MK17 57 D4
Applefield HP7 166 C7
Appleton Cl HP7 166 B7
Appleton Mews 4 MK4 46 B3
Appletree Ave UB7, UB8 208 F7
Apple Tree Cl
Leighton Buzzard LU7 80 D6
Loudwater HP13 174 A4
Appletree La 3 SL3 206 C3
Appletree Wlk HP5 154 D5
Applewick La HP12 172 C8
Applewood Cl UB10 201 E8
Appleyard Pl 1 MK6 34 E1
Approach Rd SL6 203 E7
Approach The MK8 33 E2
Apsley Cotts SL6 195 E7
Apsley Ho SL1 206 A4
Aqua Vale Swimming & Fitness Ctr HP20 115 F8
Aran Hts HP8 177 B6
Arborfield Cl SL1 205 E3
Arbour Vale Specialist Sch Sports Coll SL2 198 B2
Arbour View HP7 166 B8
Arbroath Cl MK3 46 E3
Arbrook Ave MK13 34 D3
Arcade The HP9 175 E3
Archdale 1 HP11 173 A6
Archer Cl SL6 202 D8
Archer Ct HP6 154 C2
Archer Dr HP20 102 A2
Archers Way HP14 171 B5
Archers Wells MK3 47 B2
Archer Terr UB7 208 E6
Archford Croft MK4 46 C3
Archive Cl HP22 117 D5
Arch Way
High Wycombe HP13 173 A7
Speen HP27 150 B4
Archways 14 HP20 115 D8
Arden Cl HP3 146 A3
Ardenham La HP19 101 D1
Ardenham St HP19 101 C1
Arden Park MK12 33 B7
Ardley Mews 7 MK10 36 B3
Ardrossan Cl SL2 198 C1
Ardwell La MK12 33 B5
Ardys Ct MK5 46 B8
Argonaut Pk SL3 212 F6
Argyle Ave HP19 101 B2
Argyll Ave SL1 205 A6
Argyll Ho MK3 46 F1
Aries Ho HP10 185 A8
Aris Way MK18 52 D6
Arizona St HP11 173 B4
Arklay Cl UB8 201 F1
Arkley Ct SL6 203 C1
Arklow Ct WD3 167 D5
Arkwright Rd SL3 212 E5
Arlington Cl SL6 202 A8
Arlington Ct MK4 46 E3
Arlott Cres MK6 46 F8
Armourer Dr MK14 34 F6
Armstrong Cl MK8 45 E7
Armstrong Ho SL2 206 C7
Arncliffe Dr MK13 34 B5
Arncott Rd OX25 95 D7
Arncott Way HP19 100 F1
Arncott Wood Rd OX25 94 E6
Arne La MK7 48 D5
Arnison Ave HP13 162 D1
Arnold Cl HP22 116 C2
Arnold Cott MK19 32 C7
Arnold Ct HP21 115 F6
Arnolds Cl MK18 53 A1
Arnold's Cotts HP5 143 B4
Arnos Gr MK10 35 F1
Arnott's Yd HP18 125 D6
Arranmore Ho HP11 174 B4
Arrewig La HP5 142 E8
Arrow Pl MK2 58 D4
Arthur Cl SL6 195 E5
Arthur Jacob Nature Reserve★ SL3 212 C4
Arthur Rd
Slough SL1 205 D4
Windsor SL4 210 C6
Artichoke Dell WD3 167 E4
Arundel Cl SL6 202 A8
Arundel Ct SL3 206 D2
Arundel Gn HP20 101 F2
Arundel Gr MK3 57 E7
Arundel Ho
1 High Wycombe HP13 173 F7
Uxbridge UB8 201 C1
Arundel Rd
High Wycombe HP12 172 B6
Uxbridge UB8 201 B2
Ascot Dr LU7 80 D6
Ascot Ho MK9 34 C2
Ascot Pl MK3 57 D7
Ascot Rd SL6 203 A1
ASCOTT 80 A2
Ascott Ct HP20 101 E1
Ascott House★ LU7 80 A2
Ascott Rd HP20 101 E1
Ascough Cl HP19 101 D3
Ashbourne End HP21 115 D4
Ashbourne Gr SL6 202 C3
Ashbourne Ho 5 SL1 205 E4
Ashbrook Sch MK8 33 E1
Ashburnham Cl 2 MK3 46 D1
Ashburnham Cres LU7 80 E6
Ashby MK6 47 A8
Ashby Rd HP4 134 D7
Ashby Villas LU7 92 A1
Ash Cl
Aylesbury HP20 102 A2
Slough SL3 207 B3
Walter's Ash HP14 161 B8
Ashcroft Ct SL1 197 B3
Ashcroft Dr UB9 189 F4
Ashcroft Rd SL6 202 C8
Ashcroft Terr HP23 119 A5
Ashdown SL6 196 B3
Ashdown Cl MK14 35 A8
Ashdown Ct HP13 173 D6
Ashdown Rd HP13 174 A8
Ashdown Way HP6 154 D2
Ashen Cross SL3 207 B8
Ashenden Wlk SL2 198 D8
ASHENDON 97 F1
Ashendon Rd HP18 98 C6
ASHERIDGE 143 C6
Asheridge Rd HP5 144 A2
Asheridge Rd Ind Est HP5 144 A2
Ashfield MK14 34 D8
Ashfield Cl HP15 163 B2
Ashfield Cotts UB9 190 A1
Ashfield Gr MK2 58 C7
Ashfield Rd HP5 144 D2
Ashfield Rise HP18 109 D5
Ashfield Way HP15 163 B3
Ashfold Sch HP18 110 F8
Ashford Cl HP21 116 A5
Ashford Cres MK8 45 D6
Ashford La SL4 204 B4
Ashford Rd SL0 200 C4
Ash Gn UB9 201 B6
Ash Gr
Amersham HP6 154 A3
Aylesbury HP21 116 A7
Stoke Poges SL2 198 F5
West Drayton UB7 208 F6
Ashgrove MK18 63 D2
Ashgrove Gdns HP22 86 E7
Ash Hill Prim Sch HP13 174 A7
Ash Hill Rd MK16 22 B4
Ash La SL4 209 D5
Ashland Rdbt MK1 47 C5
Ashlea MK46 6 E3
Ashlea Rd SL9 177 E1
Ashleigh Cl HP7 165 E8
Ashley HP10 185 F7
Ashley Cl LU7 105 A8
Ashley Ct
15 Aylesbury HP19 115 A8
Maidenhead SL6 203 B7
Tylers Green HP10 163 B1
West Drayton UB7 208 E5
Ashley Dr HP10 163 C1
ASHLEY GREEN 144 F7
Ashley Green Rd HP5 144 E5
Ashley Pk SL6 196 B2
Ashley Rd UB8 201 B3
Ashley Row HP20 102 A1
Ashleys WD3 167 F2
Ashlyns Ct HP4 135 B3
Ashlyns Rd HP4 135 B3
Ashlyns Sch HP4 135 C2
Ashmead Comb Sch HP21 115 C5
Ash Mead Dr UB9 190 A2
Ashmead La UB9 190 A2
Ashmead Pl HP7 166 C8
Ashmount Cres 1 SL1 205 A4
Ashotts La HP5 143 B7
Ashover MK10 36 C4
Ashpole Furlong MK5 46 B7
Ash Rd
High Wycombe HP12 172 C4
Princes Risborough HP27 139 B3
Tring HP23 118 F4
Ashridge OX39 147 B6
Ashridge Bsns Sch HP4 121 C5
Ashridge Cl
1 Bovingdon HP3 146 A3
Milton Keynes MK3 57 D7
Ashridge Coll Gdns★ HP4 121 D5
Ashridge Cotts HP4 121 E5
Ashridge Est Visitor Ctr★ HP4 120 E6
Ashridge La HP5 155 D7
Ashridge Rise HP4 134 F5
ASHTON 9 E8
Ashton Pl SL6 202 A6
Ashton Rd NN12 9 D8
Ash Tree Ho HP12 172 C4
Ashtree Wlk HP15 163 B2
Ash Vale WD3 178 D5
Ashwells HP10 174 B8
Ashwells Manor Dr HP10 174 C8
Ashwell St 1 LU7 80 F8
Ashwells Way HP8 177 D8
Ashwood MK13 34 A7
Ashwood Dr HP5 144 B1
ASKETT 139 D6
Askett La HP27 139 D7
Aspen Cl
Aylesbury HP20 102 A2
Maidenhead SL6 195 A3
Slough SL2 205 B8
West Drayton UB7 208 F5
Aspens Pl HP1 146 F8
Aspery Pl SL1 205 F5
Asplands Cl MK17 49 B4
Aspley Ct
Aylesbury HP19 101 C1
Woburn Sands MK17 49 C3
ASPLEY GUISE 49 F4
Aspley Guise Lower Sch MK17 49 F4
Aspley Guise Sta MK17 49 D6
ASPLEY HEATH 49 A2
Aspley Hill MK17 49 C4
Aspley La MK17 49 E2
Aspreys MK46 6 E4
Assheton Rd HP9 175 E4
Astlethorpe MK8 33 F2
Astley Rd OX9 126 B1
ASTON 192 C5
ASTON ABBOTTS 88 D5
Aston Abbotts Rd
Cublington LU7 78 C1
Weedon HP22 87 E1
Aston Cl
Aylesbury HP19 101 A3
Milton Keynes MK5 46 B5
ASTON CLINTON 117 D6
Aston Clinton Ragpits Wildlife Reserve★ HP22 117 F2
Aston Clinton Rd HP22 116 E6
Aston Clinton Sch HP22 117 D5
Aston Ferry La RG9 192 D5
Aston Hill OX49 157 E7
Aston La RG9 192 C3
Aston Mead SL4 209 E6
Aston Rd HP17 127 B5
Aston Rowant National Nature Reserve★ HP14 157 E6
ASTON SANDFORD 127 D4
Astonville SL2 198 C8
Astor Cl SL6 203 B6
Astronomy Way 12 HP19 115 A8
ASTROPE 104 A3
Astrope La HP23 104 B3
ASTWOOD 16 A3
Astwood Rd MK43 25 C7
Atherstone Ct MK8 33 C2
Atherton Cl TW19 213 D1
Atherton Ct SL4 210 D7
Athlone Cl SL6 195 E1
Athlone Sq SL4 210 C5
Atkins Cl MK13 34 B3
Atlas Ho HP5 144 B1
Atterbrook MK13 34 A4
ATTERBURY 36 A4
Attingham Hill
6 Milton Keynes MK8 33 F1
Milton Keynes MK8 34 A1
Atwell Cl MK8 45 E7
Auckland Cl SL6 203 B8
Auckland Pk MK1 47 D4
Auckland Rd HP13 173 E6
Auden Cl MK16 22 A5
Audley Dr SL6 202 B6
Audley Mead MK13 34 B3
August End SL3 206 E7
Augustine Cl SL3 212 E4
Augustine Mews HP16 152 B7
Augustus Rd MK11 32 E4
Augustus Smith Ho 2 HP4 135 D4
Austen Ave MK46 7 A4
Austen Pl HP19 100 F2
Austenway SL9 188 E8
AUSTENWOOD 188 C8
Austenwood Cl
Chalfont St Peter SL9 177 C1
High Wycombe HP11 173 A4
Austenwood La
Chalfont St Peter SL9 177 D1
Gerrards Cross SL9 188 D8
Austins Mead HP3 146 B3
Austin Way SL3 211 F8
Austin Waye UB8 201 C4
Australia Ave SL6 202 F8
Australia Rd 1 SL1 206 B4
Austwick La MK4 46 B2
Autumn Cl
Aylesbury HP19 101 A3
Slough SL1 204 F5

Autumn Wlk SL6 202 A5
Avalon Rd SL8 185 B5
Avant Bsns Ctr MK1 47 C2
Avebury SL1 205 A6
Avebury Bvd MK9 34 E2
Avebury Rdbt MK9 34 D1
Aveling Rd HP13 173 C6
Avenue Cl UB7 208 D3
Avenue Dr
Iver Heath SL3 199 F1
Slough SL3 206 F8
Avenue Ho HP5 154 B8
Avenue Rd
Buckingham MK18 41 E3
Maidenhead SL6 203 B5
Winslow MK18 65 F4
Avenue The
Amersham HP7 154 C1
Bourne End SL8 184 F4
Chinnor OX39 147 D6
Datchet SL3 211 B6
Dunstable LU6 93 E7
Farnham Common SL2 198 B8
Maidenhead SL6 196 C3
Old Windsor SL4 211 B2
Princes Risborough HP27 139 C4
Uxbridge UB8 201 D1
Whitfield NN13 26 D4
Worminghall HP18 123 E5
Wraysbury TW19 211 D4
Averil Ct SL6 204 C7
Avery Ave HP13 161 D2
Avery Ct MK16 22 C2
Avington MK8 33 E1
Avocet Way HP19 101 E3
Avonbury Ct NN13 38 A5
Avon Cl
Newport Pagnell MK16 22 D3
Slough SL1 204 E6
Avondale SL6 195 C1
Avon Gr MK3 57 E8
Avonmoore SL6 203 B8
Avon Pl HP21 115 D4
Axis Pk SL3 207 B1
AYLESBURY 115 D7
Aylesbury Bsns Ctr HP19 101 B1
Aylesbury Coll HP21 115 C7
Aylesbury Cres SL1 205 D6
Aylesbury End HP9 175 E1
Aylesbury Gram Sch HP21 115 F7
Aylesbury High Sch HP21 115 F7
Aylesbury Ind Ctr HP19 101 C1
Aylesbury Rd
Aston Clinton HP22 117 B5
Bierton HP22 102 B3
Chearsley HP18 112 B2
Cuddington HP18 113 A3
Great Missenden HP16 141 F2
Haddenham HP17, OX9 126 C6
Monks Risborough HP27 139 D6
Thame OX9 125 F2
Tring HP23 118 E2
Wendover HP22 131 B6
Wing LU7 79 E1
Aylesbury St
Milton Keynes, Bletchley MK2 58 E8
Milton Keynes, Wolverton MK12 33 D6
Aylesbury Sta HP20 115 D7
Aylesbury Street W MK12 33 C6
Aylesbury Vale Acad HP19 101 C2
Aylesbury Vale Parkway Sta HP18 100 D3
Aylesbury Waterside Theatre HP20 115 E8
Aylesford Gr MK10 36 A1
Ayless Cl HP18 98 B7
Aylesswater HP19 101 E4
Aylesworth Ave SL2 198 B2
Aylward Gdns HP5 144 A1
Aynho Ct MK8 45 F8
Aynscombe Cl LU6 93 F8
Ayres Cl HP21 115 B6
Ayrshire Cl HP19 101 A3
Ayrton Cl MK8 45 D6
Ayr Way MK3 46 E2
Aysgarth Pk SL6 203 B1
Azalea Cl HP15 163 A3
Azalea Way SL3 206 E7

B

Babington Cl MK10 36 A3
Babington Rd HP22 131 D6
Babylon Gr 10 MK4 45 F1
Baccara Gr MK2 58 C7
Bachelors Acre SL4 210 D6
Back Dr MK16 12 F3
Back La
Chalfont St Giles HP8 177 A7
Great Missenden HP16 152 B7
Tingewick MK18 51 A6
Backleys MK7 48 A2
Back St
Gawcott MK18 51 F4
Thornborough MK18 54 A8
Wendover HP22 131 B4
Backs The HP5 154 C8
Bacombe Hill Nature Reserve* HP22 131 A3
Bacombe La HP22 131 B3
Bacon Hill MK46 6 E3
Baconsmead UB9 190 A2
Bader Gdns SL1 205 A4
Badgebury Rise SL7 183 C7
Badgemore Ct MK8 33 C2
Badgemore La RG9 191 D3
Badgemore Prim Sch RG9 191 D2
Badger Cl SL6 202 D4
Badgers Gate LU6 93 E8
Badgers Mdw HP22 131 C5
Badgers Oak MK7 48 B7
Badgers Rise HP17 114 C5
Badgers Way
Buckingham MK18 52 E7
Marlow Bottom SL7 183 D7
Badgers Wlk WD3 167 F5
Badgers Wood SL2 198 C7
Badger Way HP15 163 B5
Bad Godesberg Way SL6 202 F7
Badmington Ct 3 HP7 165 B7
Badminton Ho 1 HP7 165 B7
Badminton Rd SL6 202 B6
Badminton View MK8 34 A1
Badrick Rd HP19 100 F2
Bagley Cl UB7 208 E4
Bagshot Ct MK2 58 C7
Bailey Cl
High Wycombe HP13 173 C7
Maidenhead SL6 202 F7
Windsor SL4 210 A5
Bailey Ho 9 SL8 185 A4
Bailey's Ct 12 HP20 115 D8
Baily Ct MK5 46 A5
Baines Ho HP11 173 F4
Baird Cl SL1 205 B4
Baisley Ho MK2 58 D8
Bakers Cl
Stoke Goldington MK16 12 B5
Turvey MK43 8 E5
Bakers Ct
Stanwell TW19 213 D1
Waddesdon HP18 99 A6
Bakers La NN12 9 A8
Baker's Orch HP10 185 E5
Baker's Piece Ho OX39 147 A4
Baker's Rd UB8 201 D5
Baker St
High Wycombe HP11 172 F7
Waddesdon HP18 99 A6
BAKER'S WOOD 189 D3
Bakers Wood UB9 189 D3
Bakery Cl MK43 25 B1
Bakery Ho 10 HP20 115 D8
Bala Cl MK2 58 D5
Bala Lake Cres MK10 36 B4
Bala Way MK2 58 C5
Balcary Gdns HP4 134 F3
Balcary Gr MK4 56 F8
Baldways Cl HP22 89 C3
Baldwin Cres MK16 22 C3
Baldwin Pl SL6 202 C7
Baldwin Rd
Beaconsfield HP9 176 B1
Burnham SL1 197 C2
Baldwin's Shore SL4 210 D8
Balfe Mews MK7 48 D4
Balfour Mews 3 HP3 146 A4
Balfour Pl SL7 183 D4
Balfour Way HP20 101 E2
Balham's La RG9 179 F8
Ballard Cl HP21 116 B5
Ballard Gn SL4 209 E7
Ballards Row HP22 117 D6
BALLINGER COMMON 142 E3
Ballinger Ct HP4 135 B3
Ballinger Grange HP16 142 E2
Ballinger Rd HP16 142 E1
Ballinger Row HP16 142 D3
Ball Moor MK18 52 D6
Balmer Bridge MK18 52 E5
Balmer Cut MK18 52 E6
Balmerino Cl MK10 36 B2
Balmoral SL6 195 B1
Balmoral Cl SL1 204 E7
Balmoral Ct
High Wycombe HP13 173 B7
Newport Pagnell MK16 22 B3
Balmoral Gdns SL4 210 D4
Balsam Cl MK7 48 B6
Bamfords La MK43 8 E6
Bamfords Yd MK43 8 E5
Bampton Cl MK4 46 E2
Banburies Cl MK3 47 A3
Banbury Ave SL1 204 F8
BANCROFT 33 F5
Bancroft Rdbt MK13 34 A5
Bandon Cl UB10 201 F3
Bangor Cotts SL0 200 D1
Bangors Cl SL0 207 F7
Bangors Road N SL0 200 D3
Bangors Road S SL0 207 E8
Bank Apartments SL7 183 D3
Bank Court Mews MK12 33 D7
Bankfield Rdbt MK9 35 A2
Bank Gn HP5 143 C8
Bank Mill HP4 135 E4
Bank Mill La HP4 135 E3
Bank Rd HP10 174 D8
Bankside HP22 131 B5
Banks Rd HP17 127 A6
Banks Spur SL1 205 B4
Bank St HP13 174 A4
Banktop Pl MK4 46 C3
Bannard Rd SL6 202 A5
Banner Ct 1 HP12 172 D8
Bannister Cl SL3 206 E4
Bantock Cl MK7 48 C5
Bantry Rd SL1 204 F4
Barbers Mews MK14 34 F6
Barbers Wlk HP23 118 F3
Barbers Wood Cl HP12 172 B4
Barbers Wood Rd HP12 172 B4
Barbicus Ct SL6 203 B8
Barbury Ct MK14 35 A8
Barchester Cl UB8 201 C1
Barchester Rd SL3 206 F4
Barclay Cl OX27 72 E6
Barclay Ct 3 HP12 172 E7
Bardney Cl SL6 202 D3
Bardolphs Cl HP27 139 C4
Bardon Gn HP20 101 E2
Bardsey Ct MK10 36 A2
Barford MK11 32 F4
Bargeman Rd SL6 202 E5
Barham Lodge MK18 52 C8
Baring Cres HP9 175 C3
Baring Rd
Beaconsfield HP9 175 D3
High Wycombe HP13 173 F7
Barkers Croft MK12 33 C4
Barkestone Cl MK4 46 C1
Barkham Cl LU7 104 F7
Barkus Way HP14 158 F5
Bar La HP27 138 E7
Barlee Cres UB8 208 C8
Barley Cl
Hazelmere HP15 163 A3
Lewknor OX49 157 A8
Weston Turville HP22 116 F2
Barley Cres HP21 115 D3
Barleycroft MK4 46 E4
Barley Fields HP10 185 E8
Barley Hill Prim Sch OX9 126 A1
Barleyhurst Park Prim Sch MK3 46 F1
Barley Mead SL6 202 A5
Barley Way 3 SL7 183 D1
Barlow Rd HP22 131 C5
Barnabas Rd LU7 80 D6
Barnacre Cl UB8 208 D7
Barnard Cres HP21 115 F5
Barnards Hill SL7 183 C2
Barn Cl
Farnham Common SL2 198 B8
Maidenhead SL6 195 F2
Barncroft MK43 8 E6
Barncroft Rd HP4 134 F3
Barn Ct HP12 172 C7
Barn Dr SL6 202 A4
Barnes Ave HP5 144 C1
Barnes Pl MK6 46 E8
Barnes Wallis Ct HP12 172 E5
Barnes Way SL0 207 F6
Barnet Cl MK5 45 D5
Barnett Way HP22 102 B4
Barn Farm SL7 183 D3
Barnfield
Iver SL0 207 E7
Slough SL1 204 D5
Barnfield Cl SL6 195 F5
Barnfield Dr MK6 47 C5
Barnhill Cl SL7 183 D4
Barnhill Gdns SL7 183 D4
Barnhill Rd SL7 183 D4
Barn La RG9 191 C4
Barn Rd HP27 138 E6
Barnsbury Ave HP20 116 B8
Barnsbury Gdns MK16 22 C3
Barns Cl OX33 122 B1
Barnsdale Dr MK4 45 F2
Barnsfield Pl UB8 201 C5
Barnstable Ct MK4 46 D3
Barns The HP23 118 F1
Baroma Way RG9 191 E2
Barons Cl MK2 58 C8
Barons Ct 2 SL7 183 E2
Baronsmead RG9 191 D2
Baronsmead Rd HP12 172 E6
Barrack Hill HP18 112 E5
Barrack La SL4 210 D6
Barracks Hill HP7 164 F2
Barracks Rd HP11 173 A6
Barrards Way HP9 176 C4
Barrett Pl
High Wycombe HP11 173 C6
Milton Keynes MK5 45 F6
BARRETTS END 42 F7
Barrie Cl HP19 100 F2
Barrington Ct NN13 38 A5
Barrington Mews 4 MK6 34 E1
Barrington Park Gdns HP8 166 D1
Barrowcroft HP11 173 F4
Barrow Lodge SL2 198 C1
Barr Piece MK12 33 C6
Barr's Rd SL6 204 B7
Barry Ave
Eton SL4 210 C7
Milton Keynes MK14 34 C7
Barry Cl HP12 172 C4
Barry View SL4 209 C5
Bartelotts Rd SL2 197 E1
Bartholomew Cl MK7 48 A5
Bartholomew Tipping Way HP14 158 F5
Bartlett Pl MK18 41 E1
Bartletts SL9 177 E3
Barton Dr HP9 175 E4
BARTON HARTSHORN 50 D2
Barton Rd
Milton Keynes MK2 58 C6
Slough SL3 206 F4
Bartons Rd HP10 163 A1
Barton Way HP13 162 E1
Bascote MK6 47 D5
Base Cl 8 HP20 101 F2
Basford Way SL4 209 D4
Basildon Ct
1 Leighton Buzzard LU7 80 F7
Milton Keynes MK8 45 F8
Basing Rd WD3 167 F1
Baskerfield Gr MK6 47 C8
Basset Rd HP14 171 C4
Bassetsbury La HP11 173 D5
Bassett Ct MK16 22 C4
Bassett Rd
Leighton Buzzard LU7 80 F7
Uxbridge UB8 201 C5
Bassett Way SL2 197 E1
Bass Mead SL6 195 F5
Batchelor Cl HP20 101 F2
Batchelors Way
Amersham HP7 165 D8
Chesham HP5 144 B2
Bateman Croft MK5 45 F6
Bateman Dr HP21 115 E5
Bates Cl
Granborough MK18 75 F8
Milton Keynes MK15 35 D7
Slough SL3 206 E7
Bates Ct HP20 101 F2
Bates Gdns MK17 68 B6
Bates La HP22 116 F2
Bath Ct SL6 202 C6
Bath La MK18 52 C8
Bath Lane Terr MK18 52 C8
Bath Rd
Harmondsworth UB7 213 C6
Maidenhead SL6 202 C6
Poyle SL3 212 E6
Slough SL1, SL6 204 D6
Slough SL2 198 B4
Taplow SL6 203 E7
Bath Road Cotts SL3 212 E6
Bathurst Cl SL0 207 F4
Bathurst Wlk SL0 207 F4
Battersby Mews HP21 115 C7
Batt Furlong HP21 115 E3
Batting Cl HP14 159 F8
Battings Wood Gdns HP14 161 C8
Battle Cl MK46 13 F8
Battlemead Cl SL6 196 C3
Battoney Vare SL6 203 C4
Baulk The
Cheddington LU7 104 F7
Ivinghoe LU7 105 F5
Bawtree Rd UB8 201 D6
Baxter Cl
Milton Keynes MK8 45 E7
Slough SL1 205 E3
Baybrook SL6 195 F6
Bay Ct HP4 135 B4
Bayhurst Wood Ctry Pk* UB9 190 F6
Bay La MK46 5 D2
Bayley Cres SL1 204 A8
Bayley Gdns HP14 161 E6
Bayley Hatch HP16 152 D8
Baylis Bsns Ctr SL1 205 D6
Baylis Court Sch SL1 205 D8
Baylis Par SL1 205 E7
Baylis Rd SL1 205 E6
Bayman Manor HP5 144 E2
Bayne Hill HP9 176 D3
Bayne Hill Cl HP9 176 D3
Baynham Mead MK7 48 B8
Bayntor Rd HP21 115 E4
Baysfarm Ct UB7 213 C6
Bay Tree Cl
Loudwater HP11 174 B2
Newton Longville MK17 57 D4
Bay Tree Ct SL1 197 C2
BEACHAMPTON 44 B6
Beachampton Bsns Pk MK19 44 C4
Beacham Rd HP12 172 C3
Beachborough Sch NN13 39 A4
Beacon Ave LU6 93 E7
Beacon Cl
Beaconsfield HP9 175 A1
Chalfont St Peter SL9 177 E3
Stone HP17 114 C5
Uxbridge UB8 201 D7
Beacon Ct
Colnbrook SL3 212 C7
Milton Keynes MK4 46 D2
Beacon Hill HP10 174 D7
Beacon La SL7 171 E1
Beacon Rd HP4 106 E2
BEACON'S BOTTOM 159 D3
Beacon Sch The HP6 154 B4
BEACONSFIELD 175 D1
Beaconsfield Ave HP13 162 A1
Beaconsfield Common La SL2 187 C5
Beaconsfield Cotts SL8 185 B2
Beaconsfield High Sch HP9 175 D1
Beaconsfield Mews HP9 186 A8
Beaconsfield Pl MK16 22 C4
Beaconsfield Rd
Aston Clinton HP22 117 F4
Aylesbury HP21 115 E8
Farnham Common SL2 198 C5
Tring HP23 118 E3
Beaconsfield Sch The HP9 175 E1
Beaconsfield Sta HP9 175 E3
Beacon Sports Ctr & Theatre The HP9 175 A1
Beacon View
Dunstable LU6 92 B4
Lewknor OX49 157 B8
Beacon Way HP23 119 C5
Beadlemead MK6 47 C6
Beales La MK7 48 A5
Bealings End HP9 175 D5
Beamish Way MK18 66 B5
BEAMOND END 163 F6
Beamond End La HP7, HP15 163 F7
Beanfare MK6 47 B4
BEANHILL 47 B4
Bearbrook Cl HP21 115 C7
Bearbrook Comb Sch HP19 115 C8
Bearswood End HP9 175 E4
Beatrice Cl OX27 72 E6
Beauchamp Cl MK14 34 E6
Beauchamp Ct SL1 205 E6
Beaudesert Mews UB7 208 E4
Beaufort Cl
Aylesbury HP21 116 D7
Marlow SL7 183 E2
Beaufort Dr MK15 35 C7
Beaufort Gdns SL7 183 E2
Beaufort Pl SL6 203 D4
Beaulieu Cl SL3 211 B5
Beaumaris Ct SL1 205 C8
Beaumaris Gr MK5 46 A6
Beaumont Cl SL6 202 A3
Beaumont Cotts 1 SL4 210 C6
Beaumont Ct SL3 206 D7
Beaumont Gr HP15 162 F3
Beaumont Rd
Slough SL2 205 D8
Windsor SL4 210 C5
Beaumont Rise SL7 183 E2
Beaumont Way HP15 162 F4
Beaverbrook Ct MK3 46 F1
Beaver Cl MK18 52 E7
Beckets Sq HP4 135 A6
Beckett Chase 5 SL3 206 F1
Beckings Way HP10 185 C7
Beckinsale Gr MK8 45 E7
Beckton Rise MK10 35 E1
Beckwell Rd SL1 205 C4
Bec La MK15 35 B7
Bedder Rd HP12 172 C3
Beddoes Croft MK5 45 E4
Bede Ct HP4 121 C8
Bedfont Court Est TW19 213 B4
Bedfont Rd TW19 213 F1
Bedford Ave
Little Chalfont HP6 166 D8
Slough SL1 205 A7
Bedford Cl
Chenies WD3 156 B1
Maidenhead SL6 202 A3
Bedford Ct HP6 166 D8
Bedford Dr SL2 198 B6

Bedford Rd
Aspley Guise MK17 . . . . . . 49 F5
Cold Brayfield MK46 . . . . . . 8 B5
Cranfield MK43 . . . . 25 C2
Sherington MK16 . . . . 14 A1
Bedford Road E NN7 . . . . . 1 D5
Bedford Road W NN7 . . . . 1 A6
Bedford St
Berkhamsted HP4 . . . . . . .135 D4
Milton Keynes, Bletchley
MK2 . . . . .58 C8
Milton Keynes, Wolverton
MK12 . . . . .33 D6
Woburn MK17 . . . . .60 F7
Bedgebury Pl MK7 . . . . 48 A8
BEDGROVE 116 C5
Bedgrove HP21 . . . . .116 C6
Bedgrove Inf Sch HP21 116 C5
Bedgrove Jun Sch
HP21 . . . . .116 C6
BEDLAM 14 C1
Bedlam La MK16 . . . . . . 14 C1
Bedlam Wlk MK16 . . . . . . 14 C1
Bedwins La SL6 . . . . . . .195 B6
Bedwyn Wlk HP21 . . . . . .115 D4
Beech 2 RG9 . . . . .191 D2
Beechams The MK17 . . . . 67 D6
Beech Ave
Lane End HP14 . . . . .171 C5
Olney MK46 . . . . 6 E3
Beech Cl
Bierton HP22 . . . . .102 B3
Buckingham MK18 . . . . . . 41 D2
Flackwell Heath HP10 . . . .174 A2
High Wycombe HP11 . . . . .173 F4
Maidenhead SL6 . . . . . . .202 B8
Stokenchurch HP14 . . . . .158 F3
Beechcroft HP4 . . . . . . .135 C3
Beechcroft Rd
Chesham HP5 . . . . .144 B1
Milton Keynes MK3 . . . . . 57 E6
Beech Ct
Berkhamsted HP4 . . . . . .135 D4
3 Marlow SL7 . . . . .183 E2
Beech Dr HP4 . . . . .135 D4
Beechen Wood WD3 . . . .178 D5
Beeches Dr SL2 . . . . . . .198 B7
Beeches Gr HP10 . . . . . .163 A2
Beeches Pk HP9 . . . . . . .175 D2
Beeches Rd SL2 . . . . . . .198 B7
Beeches The
Amersham HP6 . . . . .154 A3
Chorleywood WD3 . . . . . .167 F4
Deanshanger MK19 . . . . . 31 E3
Milton Keynes MK1 . . . . . 47 E1
Tring HP23 . . . . .119 C4
Uxbridge UB8 . . . . .201 C1
Wendover HP22 . . . . .131 C5
Beeches Way SL1 . . . . . .197 C2
Beech Fern MK7 . . . . 48 A5
Beechfield Pl SL6 . . . . . .202 C4
Beechfield Way HP15 . . . .163 B3
Beechfield Wlk HP15 . . . .163 A3
Beech Gn HP21 . . . . .115 D6
Beech Gr
Amersham HP7 . . . . .165 D8
Leighton Buzzard LU7 . . . . 80 E7
Tring HP23 . . . . .119 C4
Beech Hill Ct HP4 . . . . . .135 D5
Beech House Dr NN12 . . . 18 F4
Beechingstoke 4 SL7 . .183 F3
Beech La
Prestwood HP16 . . . . . . .151 B7
Seer Green HP9 . . . . .176 E3
Beechlands HP15 . . . . . .162 E2
Beech Leys MK18 . . . . . . 63 E3
Beech Pk
Little Chalfont HP6 . . . . . .155 B1
Naphill HP14 . . . . .150 A1
Wigginton HP23 . . . . .133 F5
Beech Rd
Aylesbury HP21 . . . . .115 D6
Chinnor OX39 . . . . .147 C6
High Wycombe HP11 . . . . .173 F4
Newport Pagnell MK16 . . . 22 B3
Princes Risborough
HP27 . . . . .139 C3
Slough SL3 . . . . .206 E4
Beech St HP11 . . . . .173 C4
Beechtree Ave SL7 . . . . .183 D5
Beech Tree Cl MK19 . . . . 20 D2
Beech Tree Ct HP22 . . . . . 87 A6
Beech Tree Rd HP15 . . . . .163 C7
Beech Trees Rd HP12 . . . .172 C5
Beechview Jun Sch
HP13 . . . . .173 E5
Beech Waye SL9 . . . . . . .189 A4
Beech Wlk HP23 . . . . . . .119 B4
Beechwood Ave
Chorleywood WD3 . . . . . .167 B5
Little Chalfont HP6 . . . . . .155 C1
1 Uxbridge UB8 . . . . . . .208 F7
Beechwood Cl HP6 . . . . .166 C8
Beechwood Cotts WD3 167 B3
Beechwood Ct
Aston Clinton HP22 . . . . .118 A3
Dunstable LU6 . . . . 93 F7
Beechwood Dr
Aldbury HP23 . . . . .120 D5

Beechwood Dr continued
Maidenhead SL6 . . . . . . .202 A6
Marlow SL7 . . . . .194 B8
Beechwood Gdns SL1 . .205 E4
Beechwood Ho HP22 . . . .117 F5
Beechwood La HP22 . . . .131 D5
Beechwood Pk
Chorleywood WD3 . . . . . .167 F5
Felden HP3 . . . . .146 F8
Beechwood Pl 13 HP13 173 B7
Beechwood Rd
Beaconsfield HP9 . . . . . . .175 C2
High Wycombe HP12 . . . . .161 B2
Slough SL2 . . . . .205 D8
Beechwood Sch SL2 . . . .198 B3
Beechwood Way HP22 . . .117 F5
BEECROFT 93 F8
Beecroft Lower Sch LU6 93 F8
Beecroft Way LU6 . . . . . . 93 F8
Beehive Cl UB10 . . . . . . .201 F5
Beel Cl HP7 . . . . .166 C8
Beethoven Cl MK7 . . . . . . 48 E4
Beeward Cl MK12 . . . . . . 33 A5
Beggars La HP23 . . . . . . .119 F4
Bekonscot Ct MK14 . . . . . 21 F1
Bekonscot Model Village &
Railway★ HP9 . . . . .175 D4
Belfast Ave SL1 . . . . . . .205 D7
Belgrave Par SL1 . . . . . .205 E6
Belgrave Pl 6 SL1 . . . . .206 A4
Belgrave Rd
Aylesbury HP19 . . . . .101 A3
Slough SL1 . . . . .205 F6
Bellamy Mews 5 MK4 . . . 45 E3
Bellamy Rd HP13 . . . . . .173 C8
Bell Ave UB7 . . . . .208 F3
Bell Bsns Pk HP19 . . . . . .100 F1
Bell Cl
Beaconsfield HP9 . . . . . . .175 F2
Cublington LU7 . . . . 78 B1
Drayton Parslow MK17 . . . 68 B6
Princes Risborough
HP27 . . . . .139 B3
Slough SL2 . . . . .206 B8
Thame OX9 . . . . .125 C1
Bellclose Rd UB7 . . . . . .208 E4
Bell Cres HP27 . . . . .138 E6
Bell Ct SL6 . . . . .193 F3
Belle Vue HP17 . . . . .114 C5
Bellfield Rd HP13 . . . . . .173 A8
Bellfield Road W HP11 . . .172 F7
Bellfounder Ho MK13 . . . . 34 B4
Bell Gn HP3 . . . . .146 B4
BELLINGDON 143 E7
Bellingdon Rd HP5 . . . . .144 B1
Bellini Cl MK7 . . . . 48 D5
Bellis Gr MK6 . . . . 47 C8
Bell La
Berkhamsted HP4 . . . . . .134 E5
Eton Wick SL4 . . . . .204 F2
Henley-on-Thames RG9 . . .191 E3
Little Chalfont HP6 . . . . . .155 C1
Princes Risborough
HP27 . . . . .139 B3
Syresham NN13 . . . . 27 B8
Thame OX9 . . . . .125 F1
Bell Lane Comb Sch
HP6 . . . . .155 B1
Bell Leys HP22 . . . . 89 B3
Bellows Mill La LU6 . . . . . 93 A4
Bellridge Pl HP9 . . . . . . .175 B6
Bellsfield Ct SL4 . . . . . . .204 F2
Bells Hill SL2 . . . . .199 A4
Bells Hill Gn SL2 . . . . . . .199 A5
Bells La SL3 . . . . .212 B4
Bells Mdw MK15 . . . . 35 B7
Bell St
Henley-on-Thames RG9 . . .191 E2
Maidenhead SL6 . . . . . . .202 F6
Princes Risborough
HP27 . . . . .139 B3
Bell Street Mews RG9 . . .191 E2
Bellswood La SL0 . . . . . .207 B8
Bell View SL4 . . . . .209 F5
Bell View Cl SL4 . . . . . . .209 F5
Bellway MK17 . . . . 49 A6
Bellwether MK11 . . . . 33 A4
Bell Wlk
Wingrave HP22 . . . . 89 B3
Winslow MK18 . . . . 65 F3
Bellwood Rise HP11 . . . . .173 B4
Belmers Rd HP23 . . . . . .119 D1
Belmont SL2 . . . . .205 A8
Belmont Cl UB8 . . . . . . .201 D6
Belmont Cotts SL3 . . . . .212 C7
Belmont Cres SL6 . . . . . .202 D8
Belmont Ct MK8 . . . . 33 C2
Belmont Dr SL6 . . . . .202 D8
Belmont Park Ave SL6 . .202 D8
Belmont Park Rd SL6 . . .202 D8
Belmont Rd
Chesham HP5 . . . . .144 B3
Maidenhead SL6 . . . . . . .202 D8
Uxbridge UB8 . . . . .201 D5
Belmont Vale SL6 . . . . . .202 D8
Belsham Cl HP5 . . . . .144 B3
BELSIZE 156 F6
Belsize Ave MK6 . . . . 35 B1

Belsize Cotts WD3 . . . . .156 E6
Belton Rd HP4 . . . . .135 A5
Belvedere Cl HP6 . . . . . .154 F2
Belvedere La MK17 . . . . . 58 F8
Belvedere Mans SL1 . . . .205 D4
Belvedere Rdbt MK9 . . . . 34 F4
Belvoir Ave MK4 . . . . 46 C1
Bembridge Ct 11 SL1 . . .205 F4
Benacre Croft MK4 . . . . . 57 A8
Benbow Cl MK5 . . . . 46 A7
Benbow Way UB8 . . . . . .208 C8
Bench Manor Cres SL9 177 C1
Bencombe Rd SL7 . . . . . .183 E5
Benen-Stock Rd TW19 .213 A2
Benham Cl HP5 . . . . .144 B1
Benhams La RG9 . . . . . . .180 D2
Benison Ct 11 SL1 . . . . .205 F3
Benjamin Ho 10 HP13 . . .173 B7
Benjamin La SL3 . . . . . . .199 B1
Benjamin Rd HP13 . . . . . .173 B8
Benjamins Footpath
HP13 . . . . .173 B8
Ben More SL9 2 . . . . . . .188 F6
Benmore Rise 2 MK4 . . . 45 E2
Bennet Cl MK11 . . . . 32 D4
Bennet's Yd UB8 . . . . . . .201 D5
BENNETT END 159 C7
Bennett End Rd HP14 . . . .159 C7
Bennetts HP5 . . . . .144 D1
Bennetts Cl
Padbury MK18 . . . . 53 B1
Slough SL1 . . . . .205 A5
Bennetts La HP22 . . . . . .102 E8
Bennett's Hill MK18 . . . . . 76 C8
Benning Ave SL4 . . . . . . .209 D4
Benning Cl SL4 . . . . .209 D4
Benningfield Gdns HP4 135 E6
Bens Cl MK19 . . . . 19 F5
Bensheim Way HP6 . . . . .154 D1
Benson Cl
Slough SL2 . . . . .206 A1
Uxbridge UB8 . . . . .208 E8
Bentall Cl MK15 . . . . 35 C7
Bentinck Cl SL9 . . . . .188 D6
Bentinck Ct UB7 . . . . . . .208 D5
Bentinck Rd UB7 . . . . . . .208 D5
Bentley Cl SL6 . . . . .202 D5
Bentley Pk SL1 . . . . .197 D3
Bentley Rd SL1 . . . . .205 A5
Benton Dr OX39 . . . . .147 C7
Bentons The HP4 . . . . . . .134 F6
Benwell Cl MK13 . . . . 33 F5
Benwells OX39 . . . . .147 C6
Berber Bsns Ctr HP11 . . .172 E7
Berberis Cl MK7 . . . . 48 A5
Berberis Wlk UB7 . . . . . .208 E2
Bercham MK8 . . . . 33 E2
Beresford Ave
Aylesbury HP19 . . . . .101 C3
Slough SL2 . . . . .206 C6
Beresford Cl MK4 . . . . . . 46 B3
Beresford Rd WD3 . . . . . .167 F1
Beretun MK8 . . . . 33 E1
Bereville Cl MK10 . . . . . . 35 E3
Berevilles La MK10 . . . . . 35 E3
Bergamot Gdns MK7 . . . . 48 B5
Bergman Cl 1 MK4 . . . . . 45 D2
Berkeley Ave HP5 . . . . . .143 F1
Berkeley Cl
Chesham HP5 . . . . .144 A1
Stoke Goldington MK16 . . . 12 B6
Berkeley Mews
Marlow SL7 . . . . .183 F2
Slough SL1 . . . . .204 E7
Berkeley Rd
Loudwater HP10 . . . . .174 C2
Thame OX9 . . . . .126 A1
Berkeley Rise 1 HP19 . . .101 B2
Berkhampstead Rd
HP5 . . . . .144 C1
BERKHAMSTED 135 C6
Berkhamsted Castle★
HP4 . . . . .135 D5
Berkhamsted Collegiate
Sch HP4 . . . . .135 B4
Berkhamsted Sch 6
HP4 . . . . .135 C4
Berkhamsted Sta HP4 . .135 C5
Berkley Cl
Maidenhead SL6 . . . . . . .202 A8
Pitstone LU7 . . . . .105 D3
Berkley Ct HP4 . . . . .135 C4
Berkly Rd HP9 . . . . .175 D6
Berks Hill WD3 . . . . .167 C4
Berkshire Ave SL1 . . . . . .205 B7
Berkshire Cl MK5 . . . . 45 F3
Berkshire Lodge 1
SL6 . . . . .202 F6
Berling Rd MK4 . . . . 33 F2
Bernard Cl HP18 . . . . . . .112 F2
Bernardines Way MK18 . . 52 F7
Bernards Cl HP16 . . . . . .152 A7
Bernard's Cl HP18 . . . . . .112 B2
Bernards Way HP10 . . . . .174 A2
Bernay Gdns MK15 . . . . . 35 B7
Berndene Rise HP27 . . . . .139 B4
Berners Cl SL1 . . . . .204 E6
Bernewode Cl HP18 . . . . .125 C7
Bernstein Cl MK7 . . . . 48 C4

Bernwood Mdws Wildlife
Reserve★ HP18 . . . . . . .108 F2
Berrell's Ct 2 MK46 . . . . .6 F3
Berries Rd SL6 . . . . .196 A8
Berrington Gr 4 MK4 . . . 45 E2
BERRYFIELD 100 D5
Berryfield LU7 . . . . .104 F7
Berry Field SL2 . . . . .206 C7
Berry Field Pk HP6 . . . . . .154 F6
Berryfield Rd
Aylesbury HP19 . . . . .101 B3
Princes Risborough
HP27 . . . . .139 C4
Berry Hill HP18 . . . . .203 D8
Berry Hill Ct SL6 . . . . . . .203 D8
Berry La
Aspley Guise MK17 . . . . . 49 F6
Chorleywood WD3 . . . . . .167 D3
Berrystead MK7 . . . . 48 B3
Berry Way MK17 . . . . 57 D4
Bertram Cl MK13 . . . . 34 B8
Berwald Cl MK7 . . . . 48 D4
Berwick Ave SL1 . . . . . . .205 B6
Berwick Cl
Beaconsfield HP9 . . . . . . .176 B1
Marlow SL7 . . . . .183 D3
Berwick Dr MK3 . . . . 46 F2
Berwick La SL7 . . . . .183 D3
Berwick Rd SL7 . . . . .183 C3
Bessemer Cl 2 SL3 . . . . .206 F1
Bessemer Cres HP19 . . . .100 E1
Bessemer Ct MK14 . . . . . 22 A1
Bestobell Rd SL1 . . . . . . .205 C7
Betjeman Cl HP7 . . . . . . .208 D5
Betjeman Gdns WD3 . . . .167 D5
Bettina Gr MK2 . . . . 58 C7
Bettles Cl UB8 . . . . .201 C3
Bettles Ct UB8 . . . . .201 C3
Betty's Hill HP17 . . . . 57 D3
Betty's La HP23 . . . . .119 A4
Bevan Ct MK18 . . . . 65 F4
Bevan Hill MK5 . . . . .144 B2
Bevelwood Gdns HP12 172 D7
Beverley Cl MK7 . . . . . . .183 B2
Beverley Cl SL1 . . . . .206 B4
Beverley Gdns SL6 . . . . .195 B1
Beverley Pl MK6 . . . . 35 B2
Bewcastle Row MK4 . . . . 45 E1
Bewdley Dr LU7 . . . . 80 C7
Bewdley Gr MK10 . . . . . . 36 A4
Bexley St SL4 . . . . .210 C6
Bicester Rd
Aylesbury HP19 . . . . .101 B2
Long Crendon HP18 . . . . .125 C6
Ludgershall HP18 . . . . 96 C8
Marsh Gibbon OX27 . . . . . 71 E3
Oakley HP18 . . . . .109 D5
Twyford MK18 . . . . 62 C1
Bickleigh Cres MK4 . . . . . 46 D3
Biddles Cl SL1 . . . . .204 E5
BIDDLESDEN 27 D5
Biddlesden Rd NN13 . . . . 39 A5
Bideford Cl LU7 . . . . 80 C8
Bideford Gn LU7 . . . . 80 C8
Bideford Spur SL2 . . . . . .198 B2
BIERTON 102 A3
Bierton CE Comb Sch
HP22 . . . . .102 B3
Bierton Rd HP20 . . . . .101 F1
Bigfrith La SL6 . . . . .195 B6
Biggs La HP17 . . . . .113 E2
Bigmore La
Beacon's Bottom HP14 . . .170 B8
Stokenchurch HP14 . . . . .159 C1
Bignell Croft MK5 . . . . . . 34 B1
Bigton Chase 2 MK10 . . 36 B2
Biko Cl UB8 . . . . .208 C7
Bilbrook La MK4 . . . . 46 C4
Billet La
Berkhamsted HP4 . . . . . .135 A6
Iver SL0, SL3 . . . . .207 B7
Billings Cl HP14 . . . . .158 F5
Billingwell Pl MK6 . . . . . . 35 B2
Billwell HP18 . . . . .125 C6
Bilton Rd MK1 . . . . 47 D2
Binders Ind Est HP15 . . . .162 D7
Bingham Cl MK4 . . . . 46 C1
Bingham Rd SL1 . . . . . . .204 A8
Binghams The SL6 . . . . . .203 B3
Birch Ave UB7 . . . . .208 F7
Birch Cl
Amersham HP6 . . . . .154 E2
Bedford MK43 . . . . 25 C3
Iver Heath SL0 . . . . .200 D3
Birch Cres UB10 . . . . . . .201 F6
Birch Ct HP21 . . . . .115 D5
Birchdale SL9 . . . . .188 D3
Birch Dr WD3 . . . . .178 D5
Birchen Lee MK4 . . . . 46 C2
Birches Rise HP12 . . . . . .172 E8
Birches The
Felden HP3 . . . . .146 F8
High Wycombe HP13 . . . . .173 E8
Birchfield Gr MK2 . . . . . . 58 C7
Birch Gdns HP7 . . . . .165 E8
Birch Gr
Slough SL2 . . . . .205 B8
Windsor SL4 . . . . .209 D6
Birchington Rd SL4 . . . . .210 A5

Bed–Bla 217

Birch La HP3 . . . . .156 B7
Birchmoor Gn MK17 . . . . 60 F8
BIRCHMOOR GREEN . . . 60 E8
Birch Rd HP4 . . . . .134 D7
Birch St HP11 . . . . .173 B3
Birch Tree Gr HP5 . . . . . .145 B1
Birch Way
Chesham HP5 . . . . .144 D2
Tylers Green HP10 . . . . . .163 B1
Birchwood Chase
HP15 . . . . .151 D1
Birchwood Cl HP12 . . . . .172 B6
Birdcage Wlk HP13 . . . . .173 B6
Birdlip La MK7 . . . . 48 B7
Bird Mount Cotts SL4 . . .210 C8
Birdwood Rd SL6 . . . . . . .202 B7
Birfield Rd HP10 . . . . .174 C2
Birinus Ct HP12 . . . . .172 C5
Birkdale Cl MK3 . . . . 57 D7
Birkett Way HP8 . . . . .166 D6
Birley Rd SL1 . . . . .205 D7
Birtchnell Cl HP4 . . . . . . .135 A5
BISHAM 194 E7
Bisham Abbey National
Sports Ctr SL7 . . . . . . .194 D7
Bisham CE Prim Sch
SL7 . . . . .194 D7
Bisham Ct
Bisham SL7 . . . . .194 E6
10 Slough SL1 . . . . .205 F4
Bisham Gn SL7 . . . . .194 E6
Bisham Rd
Bisham SL7 . . . . .194 E8
Marlow SL7 . . . . .183 E1
Bisham Woods Nature
Reserve★ SL6 . . . . . . .194 E6
Bishop Ct SL6 . . . . .202 D6
Bishop Ctr The SL6 . . . . .203 F7
Bishop Parker RC Comb
Sch MK2 . . . . .58 C6
Bishops Ct MK18 . . . . 52 C7
Bishops Farm Cl SL4 . . . .209 B6
Bishops Field HP22 . . . . .118 A4
Bishopshalt Sch UB8 . . . .201 F2
Bishops Ho HP9 . . . . .175 D3
Bishops Mdw HP22 . . . . .102 A3
Bishops Orch SL2 . . . . . .198 B2
Bishops Rd SL1 . . . . .206 A4
BISHOPSTONE 115 A1
Bishopstone
Milton Keynes MK13 . . . . . 34 B5
Stone HP17 . . . . .115 A1
Bishopstone Rd HP17 . . .114 D5
Bishops Wlk
Aylesbury HP21 . . . . .115 F6
Woburn Sands MK17 . . . . . 49 B3
Wooburn Green HP10 . . . .185 E5
Bishop Wood Sch 19
HP23 . . . . .119 A3
Bissley Dr SL6 . . . . .202 A3
Bittenham Cl HP17 . . . . . .114 D4
Bittern Way 4 HP20 . . . . .101 D3
Bit The HP23 . . . . .119 D1
BIX 179 D1
Bix La SL6 . . . . .194 F1
Black Acre Cl HP7 . . . . . .165 E8
Blackamoor La SL6 . . . . .196 A1
Blackberry Ct MK7 . . . . . . 48 B6
Black Boy La SL6 . . . . . . .193 C3
Blackburn Trad Est
TW19 . . . . .213 F1
Black Butt Cotts SL6 . . . .196 B7
Blackdown MK11 . . . . 32 F4
Blacketts Wood Dr
WD3 . . . . .167 B5
Blackfield La HP12 . . . . . .142 E3
Blackheath Cres MK13 . . . 34 D3
Blackhill Dr MK12 . . . . 33 A6
Black Horse Ave HP5 . . . .154 D6
Black Horse Cl SL4 . . . . .209 D5
Blackhorse Cres HP6 . . . .154 E1
Blackhorse Pl UB8 . . . . . .201 C4
Black Horse Pl UB8 . . . . .201 C4
Blackmoor Gate MK4 . . . . 46 E2
Blackmore Gate HP22 . . .118 A4
Blackmore Way UB8 . . . .201 D6
Black Park Ctry Pk★ SL0,
SL3 . . . . .199 F3
Black Park Ctry Pk Visitor
Ctr★ SL3 . . . . .199 F2
Black Park Nature
Reserve★ SL0 . . . . . . .200 A5
Black Park Rd SL3 . . . . . .199 E4
Blacksmith La HP16 . . . . .151 C6
Blacksmith Row SL3 . . . .207 A2
Blacksmith's La SL9 . . . .189 D2
Blacksmiths Rd HP27 . . . .138 D7
Blacksmiths Way MK17 . . 49 B5
BLACKTHORN 81 A4
Blackthorn Cl OX25 . . . . . 81 A3
Blackthorn Dell 2 SL3 206 C2
Blackthorne Cres SL3 . . .212 D4
Blackthorne Ind Pk
SL3 . . . . .212 E5

Blackthorne La HP16 142 E3
Blackthorne Rd SL3 212 E4
Blackthorn Gr MK17 49 A4
Blackwater Dr HP21 115 C4
Blackwell End NN12 18 C3
Blackwell Hall La HP5 155 C6
Blackwell Pl MK5 46 A4
Blackwell Rd HP14 171 B5
Blackwells Yd NN7 1 B6
Blackwood Cres MK13 33 E6
Blaine Cl HP23 119 A6
Blairmont St MK9 34 F4
Blair Rd SL1 205 E5
Blakedown Rd LU7 80 C6
BLAKELANDS 22 B1
Blakeney Ct
Maidenhead SL6 195 F1
Milton Keynes MK4 57 B8
Blakes Ho HP10 174 C2
Blake Way OX9 126 A1
Blanchland Circ MK10 36 A1
Blandford Cl SL3 206 D3
Blandford Ho SL6 202 C8
Blandford Road N SL3 206 D3
Blandford Road S SL3 206 D3
Blanes Cl HP18 125 C6
Blansby Chase MK4 46 C3
Blatherwick Ct MK5 45 F7
Blaydon Cl MK3 57 D6
BLEAK HALL 46 F5
Bleak Hall Rdbt MK6 47 A5
Bleasdale MK13 34 C5
BLEDLOW 138 B1
Bledlow Cotts HP27 138 C1
Bledlow Rd HP27 148 E8
BLEDLOW RIDGE 159 F8
Bledlow Ridge Rd
HP14 148 C8
Bledlow Ridge Sch
HP14 159 F8
Blegberry Gdns HP4 134 E4
Blenheim Ave MK11 32 E4
Blenheim Cl
Cheddington LU7 104 F8
Longwick HP27 138 D6
Slough SL3 206 F5
Blenheim Ct HP13 173 B7
Blenheim Pl
Aylesbury HP21 115 E5
Syresham NN13 27 C7
Blenheim Rd
High Wycombe HP12 172 D4
Maidenhead SL6 202 B8
Slough SL3 206 D2
Bletcham Rdbt MK1 47 E3
Bletcham Way
Milton Keynes MK1 47 C2
Milton Keynes MK1 47 E2
Walton Park MK7 48 B4
BLETCHLEY 58 A7
Bletchley Com Hospl
MK3 47 A1
Bletchley L Ctr MK2 58 C8
Bletchley Park National
Codes Ctr★ MK3 58 A8
Bletchley Rd
Milton Keynes MK5 46 B4
Newton Longville MK17 57 D4
Stewkley LU7 68 D3
Bletchley Sta MK3 58 B8
Blinco La SL3 206 E7
Blind La
Bourne End HP10, SL8 185 B5
South Heath HP16 153 B8
Blind Pond Ind Est
MK17 48 D2
Bliss Ave MK43 25 C2
Bliss Ct MK7 48 C4
Blisworth MK6 47 D5
Blondell Cl UB7 213 D8
Bloomfield Cotts HP5 143 E7
Bloomfield Rd SL6 202 A5
Bloomsbury Cl MK17 60 F6
Blossom Way UB10 201 F5
Blucher St HP5 154 B8
Blue Anchor Ave 1
MK10 36 B3
Bluebell Cl MK18 52 C7
Bluebell Croft MK7 48 B6
Blue Lagoon Nature
Reserve★ MK3 58 B7
Blumfield Cres SL1 204 E8
Blumfield Ct SL1 197 D1
Blundells Rd MK13 34 C6
Blunden Dr SL3 207 C2
Blyth Ct MK4 57 A8
Blythebridge MK10 36 C3
Blythe Cl
Aylesbury HP21 115 C5
Iver SL0 207 F7
Newport Pagnell MK16 22 D3
Blythe Hos SL1 204 D5
Blyton Cl HP9 175 D4
Boadicea Cl SL1 204 E5
Boarlands Cl SL1 204 F6
BOARSTALL 95 B1
Boarstall Duck Decoy★
HP18 95 A3
Boarstall Tower★ HP18 95 A1
Boathouse Reach RG9 191 E1
Bobmore La SL7 183 F3
BOCKMER END 182 C1
Bockmer La SL7 193 B7
Boddington Rd HP22 131 C4
Bodenham Cl MK18 52 F8
Bodiam Cl
Aylesbury HP21 116 B5
Milton Keynes MK5 46 A5
Bodiam Ho 6 HP13 173 F7
Bodle Cl MK15 35 A7
Bodley Ho SL0 200 D3
Bodmin Ave SL2 205 A8
Bodnant Ct MK4 45 F2
Bogart Pl MK4 45 D2
Bois Ave HP6 154 B3
Bois Hill HP5 154 E5
Bois La HP6 154 D4
Bois Moor Rd HP5 154 D5
Bolan Ct MK8 45 E6
BOLBECK PK 35 A7
Bold's Ct SL2 199 A5
BOLTER END 170 F5
Bolter End La HP14 171 A6
Bolton Ave SL4 210 D4
Bolton Cres SL4 210 C4
Bolton Rd SL4 210 C4
Boltwood Gr MK5 45 E5
Bond Ave MK1 47 D3
Bond Cl
Aylesbury HP21 115 B6
Iver Heath SL0 200 B5
West Drayton UB7 208 F7
Bone Hill MK18 52 C7
Bonham Carter Rd
HP22 131 E7
Bonham Cl HP21 115 B6
Bonham Ct HP22 117 D5
Bonnards Rd MK17 57 D4
Bonnersfield HP18 125 C7
BOOKER 172 B4
Booker Ave MK13 34 D4
Booker Hill Comb Sch
HP12 172 B5
Bookerhill Rd HP12 172 C6
Booker La HP12 172 D7
Booker Park Com Sch
HP21 115 E3
Booker Pl HP12 172 B3
Booth Pl LU6 92 E6
Boot La HP17 113 E2
Borderside SL2 206 A7
Borodin Ct MK7 48 D5
Boroma Way RG9 191 E2
Borough Ct NN13 38 A5
Borough Rd NN13 38 A5
Borough Wlk MK9 34 E3
Bosanquet Cl UB8 201 D1
Bossiney Pl MK6 34 F1
Bossington La LU7 80 E7
Boss La
Great Kingshill HP15 162 B8
Hughenden Valley HP14 162 B6
Bostock Ct MK18 52 C8
Boston Dr SL8 185 B3
Boston Gr SL1 205 C7
Boswell Ct MK18 41 E2
Boswell La MK19 31 E4
Boswick La HP4 134 D8
Bosworth Cl MK3 46 E2
Bosworth Ct SL1 204 C6
Botham Dr SL1 205 E3
BOTLEY 145 A1
Botley La HP5 145 A1
Botley Rd HP5 144 E1
BOTOLPH CLAYDON 74 F6
Bottesford Cl MK3 46 D1
Bottle Dump Rdbt MK17 56 E6
Bottle Square La HP14 159 D6
Bottom Dr LU6 93 D5
Bottom House Farm La
HP8 165 E2
Bottom House La HP23 120 A1
Bottom La HP9 176 C5
Bottom Orch HP18 112 C1
Bottom Rd
Bledlow Ridge HP14 160 B5
Buckland Common HP23 132 F3
Bottom Waltons Caravan
Site SL2 197 F3
Bottrells La HP8 176 E8
Botyl Rd MK18 74 E6
Boughton Bsns Pk HP6 166 B8
Boughton Way HP6 155 C1
Boulevard The MK9 34 E2
Boulmer Rd UB8 201 C2
Boulters Cl
Maidenhead SL6 196 C1
Slough SL1 205 A4
Boulters Ct
Amersham HP6 154 E1
Maidenhead SL6 196 C1
Boulters Gdns SL6 196 C1
Boulters La SL6 196 C1
Boulters Lock MK14 21 F2
Boundary Cotts WD4 146 E2
Boundary Cres MK11 32 E6
Boundary Pl HP10 185 D8
Boundary Rd
Brackley NN13 38 A6
Chalfont St Peter SL9 177 D3
Loudwater HP10 174 C1
Taplow SL6 203 F8
Wooburn Green HP10 185 D8
Boundary The 1 MK6 34 F1
Bounds Croft MK12 33 C4
Bounty St MK13 33 F7
Bouquet Cl HP16 151 C5
Bourbon St HP20 115 D8
Bourne Ave SL4 210 C3
Bourne Cl SL8 185 B5
BOURNE END 185 B2
Bourne End MK43 25 C6
Bourne End Bsns Pk
SL8 185 B3
Bourne End Mills Ind Est
HP1 146 B8
Bourne End Rd
Bourne End SL6, SL8 196 E8
Cranfield MK43 25 C4
Bourne End Sta SL8 185 A3
Bourne Rd
Berkhamsted HP4 134 F5
Slough SL1 205 D4
Bourne The HP3 146 A4
BOURTON 52 F8
Bourton Low MK7 48 B5
Bourton Meadow Sch
MK18 52 F8
Bourton Rd MK18 52 E8
Bourtonville MK18 52 D8
Bouverie Way SL3 206 E2
BOVENEY 209 D8
Boveney Cl SL1 205 A4
Boveney New Rd SL4 204 E2
Boveney Rd SL4 204 C1
Boveney Wood La SL1 186 D1
BOVINGDON 146 B4
Bovingdon Ct HP3 146 A3
BOVINGDON GREEN 146 A2
Bovingdon Hts SL7 183 B2
Bovingdon Prim Sch
HP3 146 B4
BOW BRICKHILL 48 C1
Bow Brickhill Prim Sch
MK17 48 D2
Bow Brickhill Rd MK17 48 F3
Bow Brickhill Sta MK7 48 B2
Bowden La HP11 173 D5
Bowen Cl MK7 48 C5
Bowerbank Ct HP20 101 F1
Bower Cl LU6 92 F5
Bower Ct SL1 204 F6
Bowerdean Rd HP13 173 D7
Bower La LU6 92 F5
Bowers La HP14 159 D7
Bower Way SL1 204 E6
Bowes Cl MK16 22 C3
Bowes-Lyon Cl 7 SL4 210 C6
Bowland Dr MK4 46 B1
Bowler Lea HP13 161 D2
Bowler Rd HP21 115 E4
Bowler's Orch HP8 177 A7
Bowles Pl MK6 47 D7
Bowling Alley HP22 86 D7
Bowling Cl UB10 201 F4
Bowling Ct RG9 191 D3
Bowling Gn HP14 158 D5
Bowling Green Rd MK43 25 C1
Bowling Leys MK10 36 A2
Bowl Rdbt The MK4 46 D5
Bowmans Cl SL1 197 B3
Bowmont Dr HP21 115 D4
Bowood Ct 5 MK8 33 F1
Bowood La HP22 141 E5
Bowry Dr TW19 211 F1
Bowstridge Ct 6 HP13 173 C7
Bowstridge La HP8 177 C5
Bowyer Cres UB9 189 F5
Bowyer Dr SL1 204 E6
Bowyers Mews MK14 34 F6
Boxberry Gdns MK7 48 A6
Boxer Rd HP27 138 E6
Boxgrove Ct MK10 36 A1
Box La HP3 146 E7
Box Tree Cl HP5 154 D6
Boxwell Rd HP4 135 B4
Boxwood Cl UB7 208 F4
Boyce Cres MK7 48 E5
Boycott Ave MK6 34 E1
Boyle Cl UB10 201 F3
Boyndon Rd SL6 202 D7
BOYNE HILL 202 D6
Boyne Hill CE Inf Sch
SL6 202 D6
Boyne Ho HP9 175 E1
Boyn Hill Ave SL6 202 D6
Boyn Hill Cl SL6 202 D6
Boyn Hill Rd SL6 202 D6
Boyn Valley Ind Est
SL6 202 E6
Boyn Valley Rd SL6 202 D5
Bozenham Mill La NN7 9 F5
Bracken Cl SL2 198 D8
Brackenforde SL3 206 C4
Bracken Hill HP4 135 E5
Bracken Rd SL6 202 C4
Brackens The HP11 173 C5
Bracken Way
Aylesbury HP21 115 B8
Flackwell Heath HP10 185 B7
Brackenwood HP14 161 C7
BRACKLEY 38 A8
Brackley Dr HP15 163 A6
Brackley La MK18 73 B6
Brackley Rd
Chackmore MK18 41 B1
Hazelmere HP15 163 A6
Westbury NN13 39 B5
Bradbery WD3 178 D5
Bradbourne Dr MK7 48 C3
Bradbury Cl MK13 34 A3
Bradbury Gdns SL3 199 D8
Bradcutts La SL6 195 E8
Braddenham Wlk HP21 115 E4
Braddons Furlong
HP18 125 C6
Braden Cl HP21 116 A6
BRADENHAM 160 F7
Bradenham Beeches
HP14 161 A8
Bradenham La SL7 194 C5
Bradenham Rd HP14 161 A3
Bradenham Wood La
Naphill HP14 150 B1
Walter's Ash HP14 161 A7
Bradfield Ave MK18 41 D2
Bradford Gdns MK5 46 B4
Bradford Rd
Heronsgate WD3 167 C2
Slough SL1 205 A7
Bradley Cl HP18 109 D5
Bradley Gr MK4 46 B2
Bradley Rd SL1 205 E6
Bradnam Wood Nature
Reserve★ SL6 194 D4
Bradshaw Cl SL4 209 E6
Bradshawe Waye UB8 208 F8
Bradshaw Rd HP13 173 F6
BRADVILLE 34 B7
Bradvue Cres MK13 34 B6
BRADWELL 34 A4
BRADWELL ABBEY 33 F3
BRADWELL COMMON 34 B3
Bradwell Common Bvd
MK13 34 C3
Bradwell Rd
Milton Keynes, Bradville
MK13 34 A6
Milton Keynes, Loughton
MK5 46 B8
Milton Keynes MK5, MK8 34 A1
Bradwell Village Sch
MK13 34 B4
Braeburn Ct SL1 205 C4
Brae Hill HP18 110 A8
Brae Hill Cl HP18 110 A8
Braemar Ct 5 SL7 183 D2
Braemar Gdns SL1 205 A4
Braeside HP14 161 C6
Braford Gdns MK5 46 B4
BRAGENHAM 70 C6
Bragenham La LU7,
MK17 70 D5
Bragenham Side MK17 69 F7
Bragmans La WD4 156 E6
Brahms Cl MK7 48 C5
Braid The HP5 144 E1
Brakynbery HP4 134 E7
Bramber Cl MK3 57 E7
Bramber Ct SL1 205 A5
Bramble Ave MK14 34 E4
Bramble Cl
Chalfont St Peter SL9 177 E4
Uxbridge UB8 208 F7
Bramble Cres HP15 163 C6
Bramble Dr SL6 202 A4
Bramble La HP7 165 E6
Bramble Mead HP8 177 B7
Brambleside HP11 174 B4
Brambles The UB7 208 E2
Brambling HP19 101 E3
Bramcote Cl HP20 116 C8
Bramley Chase SL6 202 C4
Bramley Cl SL6 202 C3
Bramley Ct MK43 3 F6
Bramley End HP14 151 A1
Bramley Grange MK2 58 D4
Bramley Mdws MK16 22 B3
Bramley Rd MK1 47 D3
Brammas Cl SL1 205 C3
Brampton Ct
Maidenhead SL6 203 B8
Milton Keynes MK13 34 A6
Branch Rd HP10 174 B2
Brandon Ct HP23 103 D7
Brandon Rd HP12 172 B3
BRANDS HILL 212 A8
Brands Hill Ave HP13 162 C2
Brands Rd SL3 212 B8
Brandville Rd UB7 208 E4
Bransgill Ct MK13 34 B4
Bransworth Ave MK10 48 C8
Brantham Cl MK7 48 A3
Brantwood Cl 7 MK4 45 F1
Braunston MK6 47 D6
Bravenfield MK18 53 C2
Brawlings La SL9 178 A6
BRAY 203 D3
Braybank SL6 203 D4
Braybourne Cl UB8 201 C6
Braybrooke Dr MK4 46 E4
Bray Cl SL6 203 C3
Bray Ct
Amersham HP6 154 E1
Maidenhead SL6 203 C2
Brayfield Ho MK46 8 B5
Brayfield Rd SL6 203 C4
Bray Pit Wildlife Reserve★
SL6 203 C2
Bray Rd SL6 203 B5
Brays Cl HP6 153 C4
Brays Green La HP6 153 C4
Brays La HP6 153 C5
Brays Mdw HP6 153 C4
Brayton Ct MK5 46 C6
BRAY WICK 203 A4
Braywick Nature Ctr★
SL6 203 B3
Braywick Park Nature
Reserve★ SL6 203 A5
Braywick Park & Sports Gd
SL6 203 A5
Braywick Rd SL6 203 A4
Braywood Cotts SL4 209 A5
Braziers End HP5 133 C1
Breachwell Pl LU7 91 A1
Breakspear Road N
UB9 190 E8
Breakspear Road S
UB10 190 F2
Bream Cl SL7 194 C8
Breamore Ct MK8 45 F8
Brearley Ave MK6 46 E7
Brearley Cl UB8 201 E6
Breckland MK14 34 D6
Brecon Ct
Milton Keynes MK10 35 F1
Slough SL1 205 C4
Brecon Way HP13 172 E8
Bredward Cl SL1 197 B2
Breezes The SL6 202 E4
Bremen Gr MK5 46 A4
Brenchwood Cl HP13 161 C2
Brendon Ct MK4 46 D2
Brent MK6 47 D5
Brent Path HP21 115 D4
Brent Rd SL8 185 A4
Brentwood Way HP21 116 B6
Bretby Chase MK4 45 F3
Breton MK11 32 E6
Brewhouse La HP22 88 E1
Brewster Cl MK5 45 D5
Brew Twr SL7 183 D1
Briaily HP14 159 C2
Briar Cl SL6 204 B7
Briar Dene SL6 195 C1
Briar Glen SL6 195 E6
Briar Hill MK12 33 E4
Briar Lodge MK12 33 D5
Briars Cl HP19 101 B2
Briars The
High Wycombe HP11 173 C5
Holmer Green HP15 163 C7
Slough SL3 206 F1
Briarswood HP15 163 B3
Briarswood Cl HP14 158 E5
Briar Way
Berkhamsted HP4 135 D3
Slough SL2 205 B8
Briary Ct MK18 74 F8
Briary View MK17 56 C8
Brices Mdw MK5 46 A3
Brick Cl MK11 33 C2
Brickfield La SL1 197 B4
Brickfields Way UB7 208 F3
Brick Hill HP18 97 E1
Brickhill Manor Ct
MK17 59 D5
Brickhill St
Giffard Park MK14 22 A1
Milton Keynes, Monkston Park
MK10 35 E2
Milton Keynes, Willen Park
MK15 35 C6
Walton Park MK7 48 A4
Brickhill Way MK18 73 B5
Brick Kiln La HP22 102 B4
Bricks La HP14 159 C4
Brickwell Wlk HP15 163 B3
Bricstock HP22 88 D4
Bridens Way HP17 126 F6
Bridge Ave
Cookham Rise SL6 195 E6
Maidenhead SL6 203 A7
Bridge Bank Cl HP11 174 A3
Bridge Cl SL1 204 F6
Bridge Ct
Berkhamsted HP4 135 D4
Maidenhead SL6 203 C7
Bridge Farm Bldgs
HP17 128 B8
Bridgeford Ct MK6 46 E8

Bridgegate Bsns Pk HP19 . . . 101 B1
Bridge Ho
High Wycombe HP13 . . . 173 D6
West Drayton UB7 . . . 208 D5
Bridge Hook Cl 4 MK12 . 33 A6
Bridgeman Ct 5 SL4 . . . 210 A5
Bridgeman Dr SL4 . . . 210 A5
Bridge Pl HP6 . . . 154 F1
Bridge Rd
Cosgrove MK19 . . . 19 E2
Ickford HP18 . . . 123 F2
Maidenhead SL6 . . . 203 B7
Stoke Bruerne NN12 . . . 9 A8
Uxbridge UB8 . . . 201 C3
Bridge St
Berkhamsted HP4 . . . 135 D4
Buckingham MK18 . . . 52 D8
Colnbrook SL3 . . . 212 D7
Great Kimble HP17 . . . 129 D1
High Wycombe HP11 . . . 173 A7
Leighton Buzzard LU7 . . . 80 F7
Maidenhead SL6 . . . 203 A7
Milton Keynes MK13 . . . 33 F7
Olney MK46 . . . 6 F2
Thornborough MK18 . . . 54 B8
Turvey MK43 . . . 8 D5
Bridgestone Dr SL8 . . . 185 C3
Bridgeturn Ave MK12 . . . 33 D8
Bridgewater Ct
Little Gaddesden HP4 . . . 121 C8
Slough SL3 . . . 207 A2
Bridgewater Hill HP4 . . . 134 F7
Bridgewater Ho MK18 . . . 52 C8
Bridgewater Monument★ HP4 . . . 120 E7
Bridgewater Rd HP4 . . . 135 B5
Bridgewater Sch HP4 . . . 135 A6
Bridgewater Terr SL4 . . . 210 D6
Bridgewater Way SL4 . . . 210 D6
Bridgeway
Cuddington HP18 . . . 112 E3
Milton Keynes MK13 . . . 34 A7
Bridge Wlk MK19 . . . 31 E4
Bridgnorth Dr MK4 . . . 45 E1
Bridle Cl
Maidenhead SL6 . . . 195 E1
Milton Keynes MK13 . . . 34 B6
Bridle Gate HP11 . . . 172 F6
Bridle Manor HP22 . . . 131 C8
Bridle Rd SL6 . . . 195 E1
Bridleway
Buckland Common HP22 . . . 132 E5
Weston Turville HP22 . . . 116 F2
Bridle Way HP4 . . . 135 A6
Bridleways HP22 . . . 131 A5
Bridlington Cres MK10 . . . 36 A1
Bridlington Spur SL1 . . . 205 B4
Bridport Way SL2 . . . 198 B1
Briery Way HP6 . . . 154 E1
Brighton Spur SL2 . . . 198 B1
Brightwell Ave LU6 . . . 93 C7
Brigidine Sch The SL4 . . 210 D4
BRILL . . . 96 B1
Brill CE Comb Sch HP18 . 96 B1
Brill Cl
Maidenhead SL6 . . . 202 D3
Marlow SL7 . . . 183 C2
Brill Ho SL6 . . . 202 C3
Brill Pl MK13 . . . 34 C3
Brill Rd
Chilton HP18 . . . 111 A3
Horton-cum-S OX33 . . . 108 C6
Ludgershall HP18 . . . 96 B7
Oakley HP18 . . . 109 F5
Brimmers Hill HP15 . . . 162 F6
Brimmers Rd HP27 . . . 139 D2
Brimmers Way HP19 . . . 114 F8
Brimstone La HP19 . . . 101 C4
Brimstone Way HP4 . . . 134 F6
Brindlebrook MK8 . . . 33 E1
Brindles Cl MK18 . . . 73 B5
Brindles La HP9 . . . 175 A4
Brindley Ave HP13 . . . 161 F1
Brinkburn Chase MK10 . . 36 A1
Brinkhurst SL7 . . . 183 D2
Brinklow Rdbt MK10 . . . 36 C1
Briskman Way HP21 . . . 115 B6
Bristle Hill MK18 . . . 52 C8
Bristol Cl TW19 . . . 213 E1
Bristol Ct 10 TW19 . . . 213 E1
Bristol Way SL1 . . . 205 F5
Bristow Cl MK2 . . . 47 E1
Britannia Ct UB7 . . . 208 D3
Britannia Ind Est
High Wycombe HP12 . . . 172 D7
Poyle SL3 . . . 212 E5
Britannia Rd 6 HP5 . . . 144 C2
Britannia St HP20 . . . 115 E8
Britnell Ct HP14 . . . 158 E5
Britten Gr MK7 . . . 48 D5
Brittens Ct MK46 . . . 7 C3
Brittons La MK17 . . . 37 C3
BRITWELL . . . 197 F1
Britwell Dr HP4 . . . 135 E6
Britwell Gdns SL1 . . . 197 D2
Britwell Rd SL1 . . . 197 D2
Broad Arrow Cl MK14 . . . 34 E7
Broad Dean MK6 . . . 47 A8
Broadfields HP19 . . . 101 A1
Broadfields Ct HP19 . . . 101 A1
Broadfields Ret Pk HP19 . . . 101 A1
Broad Gn MK43 . . . 25 C3
BROAD GREEN . . . 25 B3
Broad La HP9, HP10 . . . 186 A6
Broadlands MK6 . . . 47 C5
Broadlands Ave HP5 . . . 144 C1
Broadleys SL4 . . . 209 F7
Broad Leys HP27 . . . 139 A3
Broadmark Rd SL2 . . . 206 B6
Broad Oak SL2 . . . 198 C1
Broad Oak Ct SL2 . . . 198 C1
Broadpiece MK15 . . . 35 A7
Broad Platts SL3 . . . 206 D3
Broad Rush Gn LU7 . . . 80 E8
Broad St
Chesham HP5 . . . 144 C1
Newport Pagnell MK16 . . . 22 C4
Syresham NN13 . . . 27 B8
Broadview Rd HP5 . . . 144 B4
Broadwater
Berkhamsted HP4 . . . 135 C5
Milton Keynes MK6 . . . 47 D6
Broadwater Gdns UB9 . . 190 C7
Broadwater La UB9 . . . 190 C7
Broadwater Pk UB9 . . . 190 A5
Broadwater Pk SL6 . . . 203 E1
Broadway SL6 . . . 202 F7
Broadway Ave MK14 . . . 21 F2
Broadway Cl 5 HP7 . . . 165 B7
Broadway Ct HP5 . . . 154 B8
Broadway Par UB7 . . . 208 E4
Broadway The
Amersham HP7 . . . 165 B7
Beaconsfield HP9 . . . 175 D3
3 Chalfont St Peter SL9 177 D2
Chesham HP5 . . . 154 B8
Farnham Common SL2 . . . 198 C6
Grendon Underwood HP18 82 F6
Brocas St SL4 . . . 210 D7
Brocas Terr SL4 . . . 210 D7
Brocas Way LU7 . . . 91 A3
Brockhampton MK15 . . . 35 B6
Brockhurst Rd HP5 . . . 144 C2
Brock La SL6 . . . 202 F7
Brockton Ct SL6 . . . 202 F6
Brockway SL3 . . . 207 B1
Brockwell MK16 . . . 22 C4
Broddick Ho HP11 . . . 174 B4
Broken Furlong SL4 . . . 205 B1
Broken Gate La UB9 . . . 189 C3
Bromham Mill MK14 . . . 21 F2
Bromley HP23 . . . 104 A4
Bromley La HP6 . . . 153 C5
Brompton Cl 2 HP19 . . 101 B2
Brompton Cres HP19 . . . 101 B2
Brompton Dr SL6 . . . 195 C2
Bromycroft Rd SL2 . . . 198 A2
Bronsdon Way UB9 . . . 189 F2
Bronte Cl
Aylesbury HP19 . . . 100 F2
Slough SL1 . . . 205 E4
Brookbank HP10 . . . 185 D3
Brook Bsns Ctr UB8 . . . 201 B3
Brook Cl
Aston Clinton HP22 . . . 117 D5
Ludgershall HP18 . . . 96 C8
Brook Cres SL1 . . . 204 E7
Brookdene Cl SL6 . . . 195 F2
Brooke Cl MK3 . . . 57 F7
Brooke Furmston Pl SL7 . . . 183 E3
BROOK END
Ivinghoe . . . 105 E4
North Crawley . . . 23 F5
Weston Turville . . . 117 A3
Brook End
North Crawley MK16 . . . 24 A6
Weston Turville HP22 . . . 117 A3
Brook End Sp Ctr MK5 . . 46 A3
Brooke Rd HP27 . . . 139 B4
Brookes Univ (Wheatley Campus) OX33 . . . 122 C1
Brook Farm Cl MK18 . . . 62 C1
Brookfield UB8 . . . 201 E6
Brookfield Cl HP23 . . . 119 B4
Brookfield Ho SL3 . . . 211 D6
Brookfield La MK18 . . . 52 D7
Brookfield Rd
Haversham MK19 . . . 20 D2
Newton Longville MK17 . . . 57 D3
Wooburn HP10 . . . 185 D3
Brook Ho
Slough SL1 . . . 205 D3
West Drayton UB7 . . . 208 D5
Brookhouse Dr HP10 . . . 185 C3
Brook La
Berkhamsted HP4 . . . 135 B5
Harrold MK43 . . . 3 F7
Newton Blossomville MK43 . 8 B3
Thame OX9 . . . 125 E1
Brooklands Rd MK2 . . . 58 C7
Brooklyn Way UB7 . . . 208 D3
Brookmead Sch LU7 . . . 105 E5
Brook Path SL1 . . . 204 F6
Brooks Ct MK18 . . . 52 D8
Brookside
Colnbrook SL3 . . . 212 C7
Halton HP22 . . . 117 C1
Lillingstone Lovell MK18 . . 30 A6
Loudwater HP10 . . . 174 C2
Milton Keynes MK12 . . . 33 D4
Oakley HP18 . . . 109 D5
Slough SL3 . . . 206 E7
Thame OX9 . . . 125 F1
Uxbridge UB10 . . . 201 F5
Weston Turville HP22 . . . 117 A2
Brookside Ave TW19 . . . 211 E4
Brookside Cl
Old Stratford MK19 . . . 32 B6
Tiddington OX9 . . . 136 A7
Brookside La HP17 . . . 129 E3
Brookside Terr 5 HP21 . . . 115 E8
Brook St
Aston Clinton HP22 . . . 117 D5
Edlesborough LU6 . . . 92 F4
High Wycombe HP11 . . . 173 A7
Tring HP23 . . . 119 B4
Windsor SL4 . . . 210 D5
Brooksward Comb Sch MK14 . . . 34 F7
Brookway MK19 . . . 31 E4
Broombarn La HP16 . . . 151 E7
Broom Cl HP15 . . . 163 A3
Broomfield MK12 . . . 33 D4
Broomfield Cl HP16 . . . 151 E7
Broomfield Gate SL2 . . . 198 B1
Broomfield Hill HP16 . . . 151 E7
Broom Hill
Cookham Rise SL6 . . . 195 E6
Stoke Poges SL2 . . . 199 A5
Broom Ho SL3 . . . 206 F2
Broomlee MK13 . . . 34 A5
Broomstick Ind Est LU6 . 92 E4
Broomstick La HP5 . . . 145 A1
Brora Cl MK2 . . . 58 C5
Brotheridge Ct HP21 . . . 115 B6
Brough Cl MK5 . . . 46 A5
BROUGHTON
Aylesbury . . . 116 D8
Milton Keynes . . . 36 A3
Broughton Ave HP20 . . . 116 B8
Broughton Cl HP22 . . . 102 B3
Broughton Crossing HP22 . . . 102 C2
Broughton Fields Prim Sch MK10, MK16 . . . 36 B4
Broughton Grounds Com Woodlands★ MK16 . . . 36 E6
Broughton Inf Sch HP20 . . . 116 B8
Broughton Jun Sch HP20 . . . 116 B8
Broughton La HP20, HP22 . . . 116 C8
Broughton Manor Bsns Pk MK16 . . . 36 B4
Broughton Manor Prep Sch MK10 . . . 36 C4
Broughton Rd
Milton Keynes MK10 . . . 36 B4
Salford MK17 . . . 37 C3
Brow Bsns Ctr 10 HP11 172 E7
Brownbaker Ct MK14 . . . 34 F6
Browne Willis Cl MK2 . . . 58 D8
Brownfield Gdns SL6 . . . 202 E5
Browning Cl MK16 . . . 22 A4
Browning Cres MK3 . . . 58 A7
Brownlow Ave LU6 . . . 92 F3
Brownlow Gate HP4 . . . 107 A1
Brownlow La LU7 . . . 105 A7
Brownlow Rd HP4 . . . 135 C5
Brownlow Rise LU6 . . . 93 A8
Browns Ct SL1 . . . 204 E6
Brownset Dr MK4 . . . 45 E1
Brownsfield Rd NN12 . . . 18 E6
Browns Hedge
Leighton Buzzard LU7 . . . 105 D2
Pitstone LU7 . . . 105 C3
Browns Rd
Holmer Green HP15 . . . 163 C6
South Heath HP16 . . . 153 A7
Brown's Rise HP23 . . . 132 F3
Browns Way MK17 . . . 49 E5
BROWNS WOOD . . . 48 C4
Brownswood Dr NN12 . . . 18 D3
Brownswood Rd HP9 . . . 175 E4
Browns Wood Rdbt MK7 . 48 C5
Brow The HP8 . . . 177 D7
Broxbourne Cl MK14 . . . 21 F2
Bruce Cl SL1 . . . 205 A5
Bruce Wlk SL4 . . . 209 D5
Brucewood Par SL7 . . . 183 E5
Bruckner Gdns MK7 . . . 48 D5
Brudenell SL4 . . . 209 F3
Brudenell Dr
Milton Keynes MK10 . . . 48 C8
Stoke Mandeville HP22 . . 116 B1
Brunel Cl SL6 . . . 202 E5
Brunel Ctr SL6 . . . 202 D5
Brunel Ctr (Sh Ctr) MK2 . 58 C8
Brunel Gate HP19 . . . 100 F1
Brunel Rd
Aylesbury HP19 . . . 100 F1
Brunel Rd *continued*
High Wycombe HP13 . . . 161 F1
Maidenhead SL6 . . . 202 D5
Brunel Rdbt SL1 . . . 205 F5
Brunel Science Pk UB8 201 E2
Brunel Univ UB8 . . . 201 E2
Brunel Way SL1 . . . 205 F5
Brunleys MK11 . . . 33 B3
Brunner Pl HP13 . . . 173 C6
Brunswick Cl HP19 . . . 101 B3
Brunswick Pl HP13 . . . 162 D2
Brushford Cl MK4 . . . 46 D3
Brush Hill Nature Reserve★ HP16 . . . 151 B3
Brushmakers Ct HP5 . . . 144 B1
Brushwood Dr WD3 . . . 167 C5
Brushwood Jun Sch HP5 . . . 144 E2
Brushwood Rd HP5 . . . 144 E2
Bryans Cres MK16 . . . 24 A6
Bryanston Ave HP20 . . . 101 F2
Bryant Ave SL2 . . . 205 E8
Bryants Acre HP22 . . . 131 B6
BRYANT'S BOTTOM . . . 150 F4
Bryants Bottom Rd HP16 . . . 150 F4
Bryden Cotts UB8 . . . 201 C1
Bryer Pl SL4 . . . 209 D4
Bryfield Cotts HP3 . . . 146 C1
Bryher The SL6 . . . 202 A7
Bryne La MK18 . . . 53 B2
Bryony Cl UB8 . . . 208 F8
Bryony Pl MK14 . . . 34 E5
Buccleuch Rd SL3 . . . 211 B7
Buchanan Rd OX25 . . . 94 E7
Buchan Cl UB8 . . . 201 C2
Buckby MK6 . . . 47 D6
Buckfast Ave MK3 . . . 47 A2
Buckfield Ct SL0 . . . 207 F4
BUCKINGHAM . . . 41 D2
Buckingham Ave SL1 . . . 205 B7
Buckingham Avenue E SL1 . . . 205 C7
Buckingham Canal Wildlife Reserve★ MK18 . . . 42 D3
Buckingham Chantry Chapel MK18 . . . 41 D1
Buckingham Cl HP13 . . . 174 A7
Buckingham Ct
Amersham HP6 . . . 154 E2
Brackley NN13 . . . 38 A6
Newport Pagnell MK16 . . . 22 B3
Buckingham Ctr 8 MK18 . . . 41 D1
Buckingham Dr HP13 . . 174 A7
Buckingham Gate
Medmenham SL7 . . . 193 D7
Milton Keynes MK6 . . . 35 B1
Buckingham Gdns SL1 . 205 F4
Buckingham Ho
Amersham HP6 . . . 154 D3
4 Maidenhead SL6 . . . 202 F6
Buckingham Hospl MK18 . . . 41 D1
Buckingham Ind Pk MK18 . . . 52 D5
Buckingham Par 4 SL9 . . . 177 D2
Buckingham Pl 1 HP13 . . . 173 A7
Buckingham Prim Sch MK18 . . . 41 E2
Buckingham Rd
Aylesbury HP19, HP20 . . . 101 D3
Brackley NN13 . . . 38 A6
Deanshanger MK19 . . . 31 E2
Edgcott HP18 . . . 72 F2
Gawcott MK18 . . . 52 A5
Milton Keynes, Church Hill MK17 . . . 56 E6
Milton Keynes MK3 . . . 57 D7
Steeple Claydon MK18 . . . 63 E3
Tring HP23 . . . 118 E3
Winslow MK18 . . . 65 F5
Buckingham Road Ind Est NN13 . . . 38 A6
Buckingham Sch MK18 . . 52 D7
Buckinghamshire County Mus★ HP20 . . . 115 D8
Buckinghamshire New Univ
Chalfont St Peter HP8 . . . 178 A8
High Wycombe HP11 . . . 173 A6
Uxbridge UB8 . . . 201 C6
Buckinghamshire Railway Ctr★ HP22 . . . 84 F2
Buckingham Sq 1 MK9 . 34 C2
Buckingham St
8 Aylesbury HP20 . . . 101 D1
Milton Keynes MK12 . . . 33 D7
Tingewick MK18 . . . 51 B6
Buckingham View HP5 . 144 C1
Buckingham Way HP10 174 A1
BUCKLAND . . . 117 F6
Buckland Ave SL3 . . . 206 B3
BUCKLAND COMMON . . . 133 A3
Buckland Cres SL4 . . . 209 F6
Buckland Dr MK6 . . . 47 C6
Buckland Gate SL3 . . . 199 B2
Buckland Lodge MK6 . . . 47 B6
Buckland Rd HP22 . . . 118 A4
Bucklands Croft HP23 . . 118 C8
BUCKLANDWHARF . . . 118 B4
Bucklebury Cl SL6 . . . 203 C1
Buckley Ct MK11 . . . 32 F4
Buckman Cl MK12 . . . 33 B5
Buckmaster Rd HP12 . . . 172 C3
BUCKMOOREND . . . 140 D6
Bucks Goat Ctr & Animal Farm The★ HP22 . . . 130 A7
Buckthorn MK12 . . . 33 E5
Budge Rd NN12 . . . 18 F5
Buffins SL6 . . . 196 E2
BUFFLER'S HALT . . . 40 C3
BULBOURNE . . . 119 C8
Bulbourne Cl HP4 . . . 134 F6
Bulbourne Ct HP23 . . . 119 A7
Bulbourne Rd HP23 . . . 119 B7
Bulkeley Ave SL4 . . . 210 B4
Bullbaiters La HP6 . . . 153 B5
Bullbeggars La HP4 . . . 135 F3
Bullfinch Gdns 8 HP19 . 101 F3
BULLINGTON END . . . 20 C7
Bullington End Rd MK19 . 20 A6
Bull La
Gerrards Cross SL9 . . . 188 C7
7 High Wycombe HP11 . 173 A7
Milton Keynes MK2 . . . 58 D8
Bullocks Farm La HP14 171 B7
Bullrush Gr UB8 . . . 201 C1
Bulls La HP18 . . . 124 A3
Bullsland Gdns WD3 . . . 167 B3
Bullsland La WD3 . . . 167 B3
Bulmer Cl MK10 . . . 36 B3
BULSTRODE . . . 146 E3
Bulstrode Cl WD4 . . . 146 E2
Bulstrode Ct SL9 . . . 188 D5
Bulstrode La WD4 . . . 146 F3
Bulstrode Pl SL1 . . . 205 F3
Bulstrode Way SL9 . . . 188 D6
Bunby Rd SL2 . . . 198 F5
Bunces Cl SL4 . . . 205 B1
Bunces Ct HP20 . . . 101 D1
Bungalows The MK18 . . . 51 A6
Bunhill Cl LU6 . . . 93 F8
Bunkers La LU7 . . . 80 D6
Bunsen Pl MK5 . . . 46 C4
Bunstrux HP23 . . . 119 A4
Bunsty Ct MK11 . . . 32 F5
Bunten Meade SL1 . . . 205 B5
Bunyan Cl HP23 . . . 119 B5
Burano Cl MK7 . . . 48 C6
Burchard Cres MK5 . . . 46 A6
Burchett's Green Rd SL6 . . . 194 C1
Burcot Gdns SL6 . . . 195 E3
BURCOTT . . . 79 E4
Burcott Cl HP22 . . . 102 B3
Burcott La HP22 . . . 102 C3
Burdeleys La MK5 . . . 46 A4
Burdett Dr HP14 . . . 161 B8
Burdock Ct MK16 . . . 21 F4
Burewelle MK8 . . . 33 D1
Burfield Rd
Chorleywood WD3 . . . 167 C4
Old Windsor SL4 . . . 211 A1
Burford Cl
Ickenham UB10 . . . 201 E8
Marlow Bottom SL7 . . . 183 C5
Burford Gdns SL1 . . . 204 C8
Burford Ho 18 SL4 . . . 210 D6
Burford Sch SL7 . . . 183 C5
Burgess Gdns MK16 . . . 22 B2
Burgess La HP17 . . . 128 B7
Burgess Wood Gr HP9 . . 175 B1
Burgess Wood Rd HP9 . 175 B2
Burgess Wood Road S HP9 . . . 175 B1
Burgett Rd SL1 . . . 205 B3
Burghley Ct MK8 . . . 45 F8
Burholme MK4 . . . 46 C3
Burke Rd HP22 . . . 131 C5
Burkes Cl HP9 . . . 186 B8
Burkes Cres HP9 . . . 175 D2
Burkes Ct HP9 . . . 175 D2
Burkes Par HP9 . . . 175 D3
Burkes Rd HP9 . . . 175 C2
Burleigh Ct MK18 . . . 52 F8
Burleigh Piece MK18 . . . 41 F1
Burleys Rd MK18 . . . 65 F4
Burlington Ave SL1 . . . 205 E4
Burlington Ct 1 SL1 . . . 205 E4
Burlington Rd
Burnham SL1 . . . 197 B1
2 Slough SL1 . . . 205 E4
Burma Cl HP13 . . . 173 E6
Burners La MK11 . . . 33 B4
Burners Lane S MK11 . . . 33 B3
Burness Cl UB8 . . . 201 D3
Burnet MK14 . . . 34 C7
Burnetts Ct HP16 . . . 151 C5
Burnetts Rd SL4 . . . 209 E6
BURNHAM . . . 197 C3
Burnham Ave HP9 . . . 176 A1
Burnham Beeches National Nature Reserve★ SL2 . 198 A7

Burnham Cl
Bourne End SL8 . . . 185 A4
High Wycombe HP12 . . . 172 D6
Windsor SL4 . . . 209 D5
Burnham Ct SL6 . . . 202 F8
Burnham Dr MK13 . . . 34 C3
Burnham Gram Sch SL1 . . . 197 D1
Burnham Hts SL1 . . . 204 C7
Burnham La SL1 . . . 204 E7
Burnham Pl NN13 . . . 27 B8
Burnham Rd
Beaconsfield HP9 . . . 186 F6
Hughenden Valley HP14 . 162 A6
Westcott HP18 . . . 98 B7
Burnhams Field HP22 . . 116 E7
Burnham Sta SL1 . . . 204 D7
Burnhams The
Aston Clinton HP22 . . . 117 C5
Shabbington HP18 . . . 124 D3
Burnham Upper Sch SL1 . . . 204 B8
Burnmoor Cl MK2 . . . 58 D4
Burns Cl
Long Crendon HP18 . . . 125 D7
Newport Pagnell MK16 . . . 22 A4
Burns Ct HP21 . . . 115 F6
Burns Rd MK3 . . . 58 A7
Burnt Oak SL6 . . . 195 F7
Burn Wlk SL1 . . . 197 B1
Burrell Cl HP21 . . . 115 C6
Burren The HP6 . . . 154 D2
Burroughs Cres SL8 . . . 185 A4
Burrow Ash Cl MK19 . . . 10 F2
Burroway Rd SL3 . . . 207 B3
Burrows Cl
Tylers Green HP10 . . . 163 C2
Woburn Sands MK17 . . . 49 B5
Burrows Ho HP13 . . . 161 E2
Burton La HP27 . . . 139 C5
Burtons La WD3 . . . 167 A4
Burton's La HP8 . . . 166 E5
Burton's Way HP8 . . . 166 C7
Burton Way SL4 . . . 209 E4
Burtree Cl MK12 . . . 33 D5
Burt's La HP18 . . . 125 D6
Bury Ave MK16 . . . 22 C4
Bury Cl MK16 . . . 22 C4
BURY END . . . 165 D6
Bury Farm HP7 . . . 165 C7
Bury Farm Cl LU7 . . . 91 C6
Buryfield La HP16 . . . 152 B7
Buryhook Cnr OX33 . . . 122 C2
Bury La HP5 . . . 154 B8
Bury Lawn Sch MK14 . . . 34 D7
Bury Rise HP3 . . . 146 D6
Bury St MK16 . . . 22 C4
Busby Cl MK18 . . . 41 F1
Buscot Pl MK8 . . . 45 F8
Bushel Wharf HP23 . . . 119 A6
Bushes La MK18 . . . 51 C1
Bushey Bartrams MK5 . . . 46 A3
Bushey Cl
Buckingham MK18 . . . 41 F1
High Wycombe HP12 . . . 172 E7
Whipsnade LU6 . . . 93 F1
Bushfield Rd HP3 . . . 146 C6
Bushfields MK12 . . . 33 D6
Bushfield Sch MK12 . . . 33 D6
Bushmead Cl HP22 . . . 87 B5
Bushmead Rd HP22 . . . 87 B5
Bushnell Pl 2 SL6 . . . 202 B8
Bush The HP17 . . . 126 F5
Bushy Cl MK3 . . . 47 A3
Business Ctr The HP6 . . 154 F1
Business Village SL2 . . . 206 B5
Buslins La HP5 . . . 143 E3
Butcher La MK5 . . . 45 F3
Bute Brae MK3 . . . 46 E2
Butler Ct 5 SL7 . . . 183 F3
Butlers Cl
Amersham HP6 . . . 154 A2
Windsor SL4 . . . 209 D6
Butlers Court Comb Sch HP9 . . . 175 D1
Butlers Court Rd HP9 . . 175 D1
BUTLERS CROSS . . . 176 F6
BUTLER'S CROSS . . . 130 C3
Butlers Ct HP13 . . . 173 F5
Butlers Gr MK14 . . . 34 D8
Butler Wlk HP19 . . . 115 A7
Butterfield HP10 . . . 185 D4
Butterfield Cl MK15 . . . 35 C2
Butterfield Cotts WD3 . . . 178 E3
Butterfly Gate 5 MK10 . . 36 B3
Butterly Rd
High Wycombe HP14 . . . 158 B6
Stokenchurch HP14 . . . 158 F4
Buttermere HP21 . . . 116 B7
Buttermere Ave SL1 . . . 204 C8
Buttermere Cl MK2 . . . 58 D6
Butterton Gdns MK10 . . . 36 C3
Buttfurlong HP17 . . . 127 A7
Buttlehide WD3 . . . 178 D5
Buttler's Hanging Wildlife Reserve★ HP14 . . . 160 D5
Button Gr MK6 . . . 47 A7
Buzzacott La MK4 . . . 46 C3
Bybend Cl SL2 . . . 198 B4
Bycell Rd MK18 . . . 41 C6
Bye Gn HP22 . . . 117 A3
BYE GREEN . . . 117 A3
Byerly Ho MK14 . . . 34 F5
Byerly Pl MK14 . . . 34 F5
Byford Way MK18 . . . 65 F4
Byland Dr SL6 . . . 203 B1
Byrd Cres MK7 . . . 48 D6
Byres The HP17 . . . 126 F6
Byron SL3 . . . 207 B1
Byron Cl
6 Marlow SL7 . . . 183 F3
Milton Keynes MK3 . . . 57 F7
Byron Ct SL4 . . . 210 A4
Byron Dr MK16 . . . 22 A4
Byron Rd HP21 . . . 115 F6
Byron Way UB7 . . . 208 F2
Byward Cl MK14 . . . 34 E7
Byways
Berkhamsted HP4 . . . 135 E5
Burnham SL1 . . . 204 A8
Bywell Ct MK4 . . . 56 E8
By-Wood End SL9 . . . 178 A5

C

Cabair Coll of Air Training MK43 . . . 24 E1
Cable Cres MK17 . . . 49 B5
Cadeby Ct MK10 . . . 36 B3
Cadman Sq MK5 . . . 46 C5
CADMORE END . . . 170 C6
Cadmore End CE Comb Sch HP14 . . . 170 C6
Cadsdean Rd HP27 . . . 139 E6
Cadwell Dr SL6 . . . 202 D3
Caernarvon Cres MK3 . . . 57 E7
Caesars Cl MK13 . . . 34 A5
Caesars Gate MK13 . . . 38 A6
Cages Wood Dr SL2 . . . 198 B8
Cagney Cres 1 MK4 . . . 45 E3
Cairngorm Gate MK6 . . . 46 D8
Cairngorm Pl SL2 . . . 198 D1
Cairnside HP13 . . . 173 E6
Caister Ct MK4 . . . 56 E8
Caithness Ct MK3 . . . 46 E2
Calamus Ct MK7 . . . 48 B6
Calbroke Rd SL2 . . . 197 F2
CALDECOTE . . . 22 E1
Caldecote La MK16 . . . 22 F2
Caldecote St MK16 . . . 22 C4
CALDECOTTE . . . 48 A2
Caldecotte La MK7 . . . 48 A3
Caldecotte Lake Dr MK7 . 48 A2
Caldecotte Rdbt MK7 . . . 47 F3
Calder Cl SL6 . . . 195 E1
Calder Ct
Maidenhead SL6 . . . 195 D1
1 Slough SL3 . . . 206 F1
Calder Gdns LU7 . . . 80 B7
Calder Vale MK3 . . . 46 E1
Calder Way SL3 . . . 212 E4
Caldewell MK8 . . . 33 D1
Caldicot Cl HP21 . . . 116 B6
Caldicott Sch SL2 . . . 198 B5
Caledon Cl HP9 . . . 175 E3
Caledonian Rd MK13 . . . 33 E7
Caledon Rd HP9 . . . 175 E3
Calewen MK8 . . . 33 E1
CALIFORNIA
Aylesbury . . . 115 C7
Dunstable . . . 93 F6
California Circ HP11 . . . 173 B4
Callaghan Ct HP4 . . . 135 D4
Callingham Pl HP9 . . . 175 E3
Callis Farm Cl TW19 . . . 213 E1
Calluna Dr MK3 . . . 47 A3
Calumet HP9 . . . 175 D3
Calvards Croft MK12 . . . 33 C4
Calverleigh Cres MK4 . . . 46 D3
Calverley Cres HP13 . . . 161 F2
CALVERT . . . 73 B6
Calvert Cotts MK18 . . . 73 D7
Calvert Jubilee Wildlife Reserve★ MK18, OX27 . . 73 A7
CALVERTON . . . 32 E3
Calverton La MK19 . . . 33 B1
Calverton Lane Rdbt MK11 . . . 33 B2
Calverton Rd MK11 . . . 32 D4
Calves Cl MK5 . . . 46 A3
Calvie Croft MK12 . . . 33 D4
Cambell Sq MK9 . . . 35 A3
Camber Cl MK3 . . . 57 E7
Camberton Rd LU7 . . . 80 E6
Camborne Ave HP21 . . . 116 B5
Cambria Ct SL3 . . . 206 C4
Cambridge Ave
Burnham SL1 . . . 197 B3
Slough SL1 . . . 205 A7
Cambridge Cl
Aylesbury HP20 . . . 101 E1
5 Aylesbury HP20 . . . 101 E1
Harmondsworth UB7 . . . 213 D8
Cambridge Close Ret Pk 6 HP20 . . . 101 E1
Cambridge Cres HP13 . . 173 E7
Cambridge Ho 2 SL4 . . 210 C6
Cambridge Pl 9 HP20 . . 115 D8
Cambridge Rd
Beaconsfield HP9 . . . 175 C2
Marlow SL7 . . . 183 D2
Uxbridge UB8 . . . 201 D6
Cambridge St
Aylesbury HP20 . . . 101 E1
Milton Keynes, Bletchley MK2 . . . 58 C8
Milton Keynes, Wolverton MK12 . . . 33 C6
Cambridge Terr 13 HP4 . . . 135 D4
Cambron MK8 . . . 33 D2
Cam Ct MK3 . . . 57 E8
Camden Ct HP19 . . . 101 C1
Camden Pl SL8 . . . 185 A3
Camden Rd SL6 . . . 195 D1
Cameron Rd 6 HP5 . . . 144 C1
Camfield Ct SL6 . . . 202 A8
Camlet Gr MK14 . . . 34 D7
Camley Gdns SL6 . . . 202 A8
Camm Ave SL4 . . . 209 E4
Cam Mead HP21 . . . 116 B6
Camomile Ct MK7 . . . 48 C5
Camomile Way UB7 . . . 208 E6
Campania Cl MK10 . . . 36 A2
Campbell Cl
Buckingham MK18 . . . 52 F8
High Wycombe HP13 . . . 172 F8
Campbell Dr HP9 . . . 175 C5
CAMPBELL PARK . . . 35 A3
Campbell Park Rdbt MK9 . . . 34 F3
Campbells Ride HP15 . . 163 D7
Campden Rd UB10 . . . 190 F1
Camperdown SL6 . . . 196 B1
Camperdown Ho 9 SL4 . . . 210 C5
Camp Ind Est OX9 . . . 136 B4
Campion MK14 . . . 21 E2
Campion Cl
Aylesbury HP20 . . . 116 C8
Denham UB9 . . . 190 A1
Uxbridge UB8 . . . 208 F8
Campion Rd HP15 . . . 162 F6
Campions Ct HP4 . . . 135 B3
Camp Rd SL9 . . . 188 C4
Canada Rd SL1 . . . 206 B4
Canal Ct HP4 . . . 135 E4
Canal La MK19 . . . 31 F4
Canalside
Berkhamsted HP4 . . . 134 F6
Old Stratford MK19 . . . 32 C7
Stoke Bruerne NN12 . . . 9 A8
Canalside Rdbt MK9 . . . 35 B4
Canal Wharf SL3 . . . 207 A4
Candlemas La HP9 . . . 175 E2
Candlemas Mead HP9 . . 175 E2
Candlemas Oaks HP9 . . 175 E2
Candlewicks MK7 . . . 48 B6
Candover Cl UB7 . . . 213 D7
Candy La MK5 . . . 46 B4
Candytuft Gn HP15 . . . 162 F6
Cane End HP27 . . . 139 A3
Cane End La HP22 . . . 102 C6
Canford Ct HP21 . . . 115 F5
Cannock Cl SL6 . . . 203 B6
Cannock Rd HP20 . . . 101 E3
Cannon Court Rd SL6 . . 195 D3
Cannondown Rd SL6 . . . 195 E5
Cannon Gate SL2 . . . 206 C6
Cannon Hill Cl SL6 . . . 203 C2
Cannon La SL6 . . . 202 A6
Cannon Mill Ave HP5 . . . 154 E5
Cannon Pl HP27 . . . 139 B4
Cannon's Hill HP18 . . . 112 C5
Cannon's Orch HP22 . . . 85 B4
Canonbury MK10 . . . 35 E1
Canon Harnett Ct MK12 . 32 F6
Canon Hill Dr SL6 . . . 203 B3
Canon Hill Way SL6 . . . 203 B2
Canon's Cloisters SL4 . . 210 D7
Canons Rd MK12 . . . 33 C7
Canons The MK16 . . . 22 E3
Cantell Cl MK18 . . . 41 D1
Canterbury Ave SL2 . . . 198 C1
Canterbury Cl
Amersham HP7 . . . 165 E8
Monks Risborough HP27 139 B5
Cantilupe Cl LU6 . . . 92 D6
Cantle Ave MK14 . . . 35 A5
Cantley Cl HP20 . . . 101 E2
Capel Cl MK18 . . . 41 F7
Capel Dr MK14 . . . 34 F5
Capell Ave WD3 . . . 167 C4
Capell Rd WD3 . . . 167 D4
Capell Way WD3 . . . 167 D4
Cape Villas SL0 . . . 207 E7
Capian Wlk MK8 . . . 33 E1
Capital Dr MK14 . . . 34 E6
Capps La HP5 . . . 143 A5
Capricorn Ho HP10 . . . 185 A8
Capron MK6 . . . 47 B5
Capswood Bsns Ctr UB9 . . . 189 C3
Captain Cook Cl HP8 . . . 177 B6
Captain's Cl HP5 . . . 144 A4
Captains Wlk HP4 . . . 135 D3
Captain's Wood Nature Reserve★ HP5 . . . 143 F4
Caraway Cl MK7 . . . 48 B4
Cardain Ho HP9 . . . 175 D3
Cardigan Cl
Milton Keynes MK3 . . . 46 F1
Slough SL1 . . . 204 F6
Cardinals Wlk SL6 . . . 204 C7
Cardwell Cl MK4 . . . 46 C2
Carey Cl
Aylesbury HP21 . . . 115 D4
Windsor SL4 . . . 210 B4
Careys Croft HP4 . . . 135 A7
Careys Rd NN12 . . . 17 A8
Carey Way MK46 . . . 7 A4
Carhampton Ct MK4 . . . 46 D3
Carisbrooke Ave HP12 . . 172 B6
Carisbrooke Cl SL6 . . . 202 C6
Carisbrooke Ct
Buckingham MK18 . . . 41 E2
Slough SL1 . . . 205 F6
Carisbrooke Ho 4 HP13 . . . 173 F7
Carisbrooke Way MK4 . . . 45 E1
Carleton Gate MK15 . . . 35 E7
Carlina Pl MK14 . . . 34 D3
Carlisle Rd SL1 . . . 205 D6
Carlton Cl
Aylesbury HP19 . . . 101 A2
Newport Pagnell MK16 . . . 22 E4
Carlton Ct HP27 . . . 139 B3
Carlton Ho TW19 . . . 213 D2
Carlton Rd
Slough SL2 . . . 206 B6
Turvey MK43 . . . 8 E7
Carlyle Ave HP21 . . . 115 F7
Carlyle Cl MK16 . . . 22 A4
Carman Ct HP23 . . . 118 F3
Carmarthen Rd SL1 . . . 205 E6
Carmel Ct SL7 . . . 183 B1
Carnation Way HP21 . . . 115 E5
Carne The MK11 . . . 32 E5
Carnot Cl MK5 . . . 46 C4
Carnoustie Cl MK3 . . . 57 C7
Carnweather Ct MK4 . . . 57 B8
Caroline Cl UB7 . . . 208 D4
Caroline Ct SL7 . . . 183 E3
Caroline Haslett Comb Sch MK5 . . . 46 B4
Carolus Creek MK15 . . . 35 A7
Carpenter Ct MK14 . . . 34 F6
Carpenters Wood Dr WD3 . . . 167 B5
Carpenter's Wood, Dungrove Wood Nature Reserve★ SL6 . . . 194 C2
Carpenters Yd HP23 . . . 119 B3
Carr Cl HP19 . . . 101 A2
Carrick Rd MK6 . . . 34 F1
Carriers Cl MK19 . . . 11 A2
Carrington Ave HP10 . . . 185 A8
Carrington Cl MK18 . . . 77 E5
Carrington Cres HP22 . . 131 A7
Carrington Ct 9 HP12 . . 172 E7
Carrington Hall Rd MK17 . . . 68 C6
Carrington Inf Sch 1 HP10 . . . 174 A1
Carrington Jun Sch HP10 . . . 185 A8
Carrington Pl
Holmer Green HP15 . . . 163 C7
Tring HP23 . . . 119 B5
Carrington Rd
Aylesbury HP21 . . . 115 D6
High Wycombe HP12 . . . 172 D6
Newport Pagnell MK16 . . . 22 B3
Slough SL1 . . . 205 E6
Carrington Way HP16 . . 151 C5
Carroll Cl MK16 . . . 22 A5
Carron Cl LU7 . . . 80 B7
Carron Ct MK2 . . . 58 C4
Carrs Dr HP12 . . . 172 C8
Carter Cl SL4 . . . 210 A5
Carteret Cl MK15 . . . 35 E7
Carters Cl MK16 . . . 13 F1
Carters La
Long Crendon HP18 . . . 125 B7
Milton Keynes MK11 . . . 33 A3
Quainton HP22, MK18 . . . 85 E6
Carters Mdw MK18 . . . 76 A2
Carters Ride HP22 . . . 116 B2
Carter Wlk HP10 . . . 174 C8
Cartmel Cl MK3 . . . 57 C6
Cartwright Ct 2 HP13 . . 173 F5
Cartwright Pl MK6 . . . 46 E8
Carver Hill Rd HP11 . . . 172 F5
Carvers Mews MK14 . . . 34 F6
Cascadia Cl HP11 . . . 174 B2
Cashmere Cl MK5 . . . 46 A4
Casterton Cl MK13 . . . 34 C4
Castle Acre MK10 . . . 35 F1
Castle Ashby Rd NN7 . . . 1 B7
Castle Ave
Datchet SL3 . . . 211 A8
West Drayton UB7 . . . 208 F6
Castle Cl
Marsh Gibbon OX6 . . . 72 A3
Pitstone LU7 . . . 105 D3
Totternhoe LU6 . . . 93 A8
Wing LU7 . . . 79 E3
Castle Ct
13 Aylesbury HP20 . . . 115 D8
Buckingham MK18 . . . 52 D8
Maidenhead SL6 . . . 202 D7
Castle Dr SL6 . . . 202 D7
Castle Est HP12 . . . 172 D4
Castlefield Foundation Sch HP12 . . . 172 C6
Castlefields HP22 . . . 116 C3
Castle Gate Way HP4 . . . 135 C6
Castle Hill
Berkhamsted HP4 . . . 135 C5
High Wycombe HP11 . . . 173 A6
Maidenhead SL6 . . . 202 E7
Windsor SL4 . . . 210 D6
Castle Hill Ave HP4 . . . 135 C5
Castle Hill Cl HP4 . . . 135 C5
Castle Hill Ct HP4 . . . 135 C6
Castle Hill Rd LU6 . . . 93 A8
Castle Hill Terr SL6 . . . 202 E7
Castle Ho 5 LU7 . . . 80 E7
Castle La HP22 . . . 86 F6
Castle Lodge SL6 . . . 202 F7
Castlemead Cotts SL4 . . 210 C3
Castle Meadow Cl MK16 . 22 E4
Castle Mews
Berkhamsted HP4 . . . 135 C4
Maidenhead SL6 . . . 202 E7
Castle Park Rd HP22 . . . 131 B6
Castle Pl 6 HP13 . . . 173 B7
Castle Rd MK46 . . . 2 F1
Castle Rose MK6 . . . 47 D6
Castle Row 16 HP23 . . . 119 A3
Castle St
Aylesbury HP20 . . . 115 D8
Berkhamsted HP4 . . . 135 C4
Buckingham MK18 . . . 52 D8
High Wycombe HP13 . . . 173 B7
Marsh Gibbon OX27 . . . 72 A3
Slough SL1 . . . 205 F3
Wingrave HP22 . . . 89 B3
Castlesteads MK13 . . . 33 F5
CASTLETHORPE . . . 19 E5
Castlethorpe Fst Sch MK19 . . . 19 F5
Castlethorpe Rd MK19 . . . 11 A2
Castleton Ct SL7 . . . 183 E2
Castleview Comb Sch SL3 . . . 206 D2
Castle View Gdns HP12 . . . 172 D7
Castleview Ho SL4 . . . 210 D7
Castleview Rd SL3 . . . 206 C2
Caswell La MK17 . . . 60 F7
Catchpole Cl MK12 . . . 33 B5
Cater Rd HP14 . . . 171 C4
Catesby Croft MK5 . . . 46 C8
Cathay Cl MK3 . . . 58 B7
Cathedral of Trees★ MK15 . . . 35 C5
Catherine Cotts HP23 . . . 133 E8
Catherine Ct MK18 . . . 41 E2
Catherines Cl UB7 . . . 208 D4
Catkin Cl HP12 . . . 172 B3
Catslip RG9 . . . 179 A1
Causeway The
Bray SL6 . . . 203 C4
Marlow SL7 . . . 183 E1
Causey Arch MK10 . . . 36 C3
Cautley Cl HP22 . . . 85 A5
Cavalier Ct HP4 . . . 135 C4
Cavalier Rd OX9 . . . 126 A1
Cavalry Cres SL4 . . . 210 C4
Cavan Way MK10 . . . 36 A4
Cavendish Cl
Burnham SL6 . . . 204 A7
Little Chalfont HP6 . . . 166 B8
Wendover HP22 . . . 131 B6
Cavendish Ct
Milton Keynes MK5 . . . 46 A7
Poyle SL3 . . . 212 E6
Cavendish Rd HP5 . . . 154 D7
Cavendish Way 9 HP19 . . . 100 F1
Cavendish Wlk OX9 . . . 126 B1
Cavenham MK8 . . . 33 F2
Caversham Gn 1 HP20 . . . 101 D1
Cawardon MK14 . . . 34 C7
Cawcott Dr SL4 . . . 209 E6
Cawdor Rise MK4 . . . 45 E2
Cawkwell Way MK2 . . . 58 C8
Caxton Ct RG9 . . . 191 E1
Caxton Dr UB8 . . . 201 D3
Caxton Rd MK12 . . . 33 B7
Cecil Rd SL0 . . . 207 E7
Cecils Yd 7 MK18 . . . 41 D1
Cecil Way SL2 . . . 197 F1
Cecily Ct MK5 . . . 46 A5
Cedar 1 RG9 . . . 191 D2

Cedar Ave
Hazelmere HP15 .... 163 A5
West Drayton UB7 .... 208 F6
Cedar Chase SL6 .... 196 D1
Cedar Cl
Aylesbury HP20 .... 102 A2
Burnham SL1 .... 197 C1
Chesham HP5 .... 144 E1
Iver Heath SL0 .... 200 C4
Milton Keynes MK19 ..... 32 B7
Cedar Ct
Gerrards Cross SL9 ..... 188 E7
High Wycombe HP13 .... 173 B7
Maidenhead SL6 .... 202 D7
Marlow SL7 .... 183 E2
6 Windsor SL4 .... 210 A5
Cedar Dr
Chesham HP5 .... 144 A1
Cookham Rise SL6 ...... 195 F7
Cookham SL6 .... 196 A7
Marlow Bottom SL7 ..... 183 C7
Cedar Gr
Amersham HP7 .... 165 D8
Bellingdon HP5 .... 143 D8
Cedar Lodge Dr MK12 ... 33 D7
Cedar Park Sch HP15 .. 162 F5
Cedar Rd HP4 .... 135 D3
Cedar Ridge HP6 ...... 153 C5
Cedars Cl
Akeley MK18 .... 41 F8
Chalfont St Peter SL9 ... 177 E5
Cedars Comb Sch MK16 . 22 C4
Cedars Dr UB10 .... 201 F3
Cedars Ho SL6 .... 203 A7
Cedars Rd SL6 .... 203 A7
Cedars The
Berkhamsted HP4 ...... 135 E4
Slough SL2 .... 197 F2
Wendover HP22 .... 131 A5
Cedars Upper Sch & Com Coll LU7 .... 80 E5
Cedars Village WD3 .... 167 F5
Cedars Way
Leighton Buzzard LU7 .... 80 E5
Newport Pagnell MK16 ... 22 C4
Cedars Wlk WD3 .... 167 F5
Cedar Terr 1 HP11 .... 172 F7
Cedar Way
Berkhamsted HP4 ...... 135 D3
Slough SL3 .... 206 E2
Ceely Ho HP21 .... 115 D6
Ceely Rd HP21 .... 115 D6
Celandine Ct MK7 .... 48 A5
Celina Cl MK2 .... 58 C7
Cell Farm SL4 .... 211 B2
Cell Farm Ave SL4 ..... 211 B2
Centenary Bsns Pk RG9 .... 191 F1
Centenary Cotts HP27 .. 138 D7
Centenary Way HP6 .... 154 F1
Central Ave
Cranfield MK43 .... 24 E2
Whipsnade LU6 .... 107 E8
Central Dr SL1 .... 204 F6
Central Est SL6 .... 202 E7
Central Est SL6 .... 202 E8
CENTRAL MILTON KEYNES 34 D1
Central Park Bsns Ctr HP13 .... 173 A8
Centre Par HP27 .... 139 C5
Centre The SL2 .... 198 C6
Centre Wlk HP15 .... 163 A3
Centurion Ct MK11 ...... 33 C2
Centurion Rdbt MK1 .... 47 C2
Century Ave
Milton Keynes MK6 ...... 46 E7
Oldbrook MK6 .... 46 E8
Century Point HP12 .... 172 C4
Cestreham Cres HP5 ... 144 D2
CHACKMORE 41 B4
Chacombe Pl HP9 ...... 175 D5
Chadbone Cl HP20 ..... 115 D8
Chadds La MK6 .... 47 C8
Chadwell Path HP21 ... 116 C6
Chadwick Dr MK6 .... 47 B7
Chadwick St HP13 ..... 162 D2
Chaffinch HP19 .... 101 F4
Chaffron Way
Leadenhall MK6 .... 46 F7
Milton Keynes, Oakgrove MK6, MK10, MK15 .... 35 D1
Milton Keynes, Shenley Lodge MK4, MK5, MK6 .... 46 C5
Chairborough Rd HP12 172 D6
Chairborough Rd Nature Reserve★ HP12 .... 172 D5
Chairmakers Cl HP27 ... 139 A1
Chalcot Pl MK8 .... 45 F8
Chalcott SL1 .... 205 E3
Chalet Cl HP4 .... 134 F4
Chalfont Ave HP6 ...... 166 D8
Chalfont Cl MK13 .... 34 A6
CHALFONT COMMON 177 F6
Chalfont & Gerrards Cross Com Hospl SL9 .... 177 D2
Chalfont Ho HP7 .... 166 D7
Chalfont La
Chorleywood WD3 ...... 167 B4
Chalfont La *continued*
Maple Cross WD3 ...... 178 D3
Chalfont & Latimer Sta/U Sta HP7 .... 166 C8
Chalfont L Ctr SL9 ..... 177 C2
Chalfont Rd
Maple Cross SL9 .... 178 C7
Seer Green HP9 .... 176 D5
CHALFONT ST GILES 177 C7
Chalfont St Giles Inf Sch HP8 .... 177 B7
Chalfont St Giles Jun Sch HP8 .... 177 B7
CHALFONT ST PETER 177 F2
Chalfont St Peter Inf Sch SL9 .... 177 C3
Chalfont St Peter Jun Sch SL9 .... 177 D2
Chalfonts Com Coll The SL9 .... 177 C3
Chalfont Station Rd HP7 .... 166 C7
Chalfont Way HP12 .... 172 D3
Chalford Flats HP10 .... 185 F6
Chalford Way HP19 .... 114 F8
Chalgrove Cl SL6 ...... 203 B6
Chalgrove End HP22 ... 116 B1
Chalgrove Rd OX9 ..... 126 A1
Chalgrove Wlk HP21 ... 115 C6
Chalkdell Dr MK5 .... 45 F4
Chalk Farm Rd HP14 ... 158 D5
Chalk Hill
Chesham HP5 .... 144 B2
Coleshill HP7 .... 164 F2
Windsor SL4 .... 210 F6
Chalkhill Blue Cl HP19 . 101 C4
Chalk La HP6, HP7 ..... 153 B4
Chalklands SL8 .... 185 A4
Chalkpit La SL7 .... 183 B3
Chalk Pit La SL1 .... 197 B4
Chalkpits The HP10 .... 185 E6
CHALKSHIRE 130 C4
Chalkshire Cotts HP17 . 130 C4
Chalkshire Rd HP17 .... 130 C4
Chalkstream Way HP10 185 E7
Challacombe MK4 ...... 46 D2
Challener Rd HP12 ..... 172 C3
Challenge Ho MK3 ...... 47 B1
Challow Ct SL6 .... 195 D1
Chalmers Ave MK19 ..... 20 D2
Chaloner Pl HP21 ..... 115 D6
Chaloner Rd HP21 ..... 115 D6
Chaloners Hill MK18 .... 63 D3
CHALVEY 205 C3
Chalvey Gdns SL1 ...... 205 E4
Chalvey Gr SL1 .... 205 B4
Chalvey Pk SL1 .... 205 E4
Chalvey Road E SL1 .... 205 E4
Chalvey Road W SL1 ... 205 D4
Chalwell Ridge MK5 .... 46 B4
Chamberlain Rd HP19 .. 101 B1
Champflower MK4 ...... 46 D3
Champney Cl SL3 ...... 212 A4
Champneys Coll of Health & Beauty HP23 .... 133 E6
Chancellors HP7 .... 164 B5
Chancellors Cnr HP7 ... 164 B5
Chancery Cl MK13 ...... 34 A6
Chancery Pl SL4 .... 210 D7
Chandlers Ct MK6 .... 47 E5
CHANDLERS HILL 200 E3
Chandlers Quay SL6 .... 203 C8
Chandos Cl
Buckingham MK18 .... 52 D7
Little Chalfont HP6 ..... 155 C1
Chandos Ct MK18 .... 52 D7
Chandos Mall 7 SL1 .... 205 F4
Chandos Pl
Milton Keynes MK2 ...... 58 B8
Wendover HP22 .... 131 B4
Chandos Rd MK18 .... 52 D8
Channer Dr HP10 .... 163 B1
Channory Cl MK4 .... 46 A1
Chantry Cl
Windsor SL4 .... 210 A6
Woburn Sands MK17 ..... 49 A6
Chantry Rd HP19 .... 101 C3
Chantry Rise 8 MK46 ..... 6 F3
Chantry Specl Sch UB7 208 E6
Chantry The
15 Aylesbury HP20 ..... 115 D8
Uxbridge UB8 .... 201 F2
Chapel Arches SL6 ..... 203 A7
Chapel Cl
Blackthorn OX25 .... 81 A3
Little Gaddesden HP4 ... 121 D6
Chapel Cotts SL2 ...... 199 B5
Chapel Crofts HP4 ..... 134 E6
Chapel Ct SL6 .... 202 D4
Chapel Dr HP22 .... 117 E5
CHAPEL END 118 C8
Chapel End La HP23 .... 118 C8
Chapel Farm NN7 .... 10 C6
Chapel Fields HP23 .... 118 C8
Chapel Hill
Soulbury LU7 .... 69 E3
Speen HP27 .... 150 C4
Windsor SL4 .... 210 D6
Chapel Ho HP6 .... 153 C5
Chapel La
Akeley MK18 .... 41 F8
Chilton HP18 .... 111 B3
Drayton Parslow MK17 ... 68 B5
High Wycombe HP12 .... 172 C8
Ivinghoe Aston LU7 ...... 92 A1
Long Marston HP23 ..... 104 B4
Northall LU6 .... 92 A5
Pitch Green HP27 ...... 138 B3
Rout's Green HP14 ..... 148 E2
St Leonards HP23 ...... 132 D3
Stoke Bruerne NN12 ...... 9 A8
Stoke Mandeville HP22 .. 116 A1
Stoke Poges SL2 .... 199 B5
Thornborough MK18 ..... 54 B8
Totternhoe LU6 .... 92 F8
Turweston NN13 .... 38 B7
Walter's Ash HP14 ..... 161 C7
Wendover HP22 .... 131 B4
Whitfield NN13 .... 26 D3
Chapel Rd
Flackwell Heath HP10 ... 185 A8
Ford HP17 .... 128 A7
Chapel Row HP14 ...... 171 A7
Chapels Cl SL1 .... 204 E5
Chapel Sq LU7 .... 68 E1
Chapel St
Berkhamsted HP4 ...... 135 D4
High Wycombe HP13 .... 161 D3
Marlow SL7 .... 183 E2
Slough SL1 .... 205 F4
Tring HP23 .... 118 F3
Uxbridge UB8 .... 201 C4
Woburn Sands MK17 ..... 49 B4
Chaplin Gr MK8 .... 45 D7
Chaplin Mews 7 SL3 ... 206 F1
Chapman Ave MK14 ..... 35 A6
Chapman Cl
Aylesbury HP21 .... 115 B6
West Drayton UB7 ...... 208 F3
Chapman La HP8, HP10 . 185 A6
Chapmans Cres HP5 ... 144 A2
Chapmans Dr MK19 ..... 32 B7
Chapmans Lea HP22 .... 88 D5
Chappel Mdw HP23 .... 119 B6
Chapter MK6 .... 47 A5
Chapter Cl UB10 .... 201 F5
Chapter Ho MK6 .... 47 A5
Chapter Mews SL4 ...... 210 D7
Charbray Cres MK5 ..... 46 A4
Chardacre MK8 .... 33 E1
Charlbury Rd UB10 ..... 190 F1
Charles Cl HP21 .... 116 B4
Charles Dr OX9 .... 126 A1
Charles Gdns SL2 ...... 206 A7
Charles Ho
Henley-on-Thames RG9 .. 191 E3
9 Windsor SL4 .... 210 C6
Charles Pym Rd HP19 .. 101 C4
Charles St
Berkhamsted HP4 ...... 135 B4
Tring HP23 .... 119 A3
Windsor SL4 .... 210 C6
Charlestown Lodge UB8 .... 201 D6
Charles Way MK16 ...... 22 C4
Charlewood Ho MK17 ... 49 B3
Charlock Ct MK16 .... 21 F4
Charlotte Ave SL2 ...... 205 F6
Charlotte Cl LU7 .... 79 F2
Charlotte Cott SL6 ...... 203 B8
Charlotte Way 12 SL7 .. 183 E2
Charlton SL4 .... 209 C5
Charlton Cl
Slough SL1 .... 205 B4
Swanbourne MK17 .... 66 F3
Charlton Pl 2 SL4 ..... 209 C5
Charlton Row 5 SL4 ... 209 C5
Charlton Sq 4 SL4 ..... 209 C5
Charlton Way SL4 ...... 209 C5
Charlton Wlk 3 SL4 ... 209 C5
Charmfield Rd HP21 .... 116 A5
CHARNDON 72 E6
Charnwood Cl 5 HP13 . 173 F5
Charsley Cl HP6 .... 166 C8
Charter Cl 8 SL1 ...... 205 F3
Charter Dr HP6 .... 154 F1
Charter Pl UB8 .... 201 D5
Charter Rd SL1 .... 204 E6
Chartley Ct MK5 .... 46 B4
CHARTRIDGE 143 C4
Chartridge Comb Sch HP5 .... 143 C4
Chartridge Development UB8 .... 201 B3
Chartridge Grange Dr HP5 .... 143 D4
Chartridge Ho 3 HP13 . 173 F6
Chartridge La HP5 ..... 143 F2
Chartridge Park Mobile Home Pk HP5 .... 143 D4
Chartwell Gate HP9 .... 175 D2
Chartwell Rd MK16 ..... 22 E4
Chase Ave MK7 .... 48 A4
Chase Cl HP7 .... 165 A4
Chase Farm Barns MK17. 56 C4
Chase Park Rd NN7 ...... 1 A5
Chaseport Cl MK46 .... 5 D2
Chaseside Cl LU7 ...... 105 A7
Chase The
1 Chesham HP5 .... 144 B2
Maidenhead SL6 .... 195 D3
Marlow SL7 .... 184 A3
Tylers Green HP10 ..... 163 C1
Chasewater Cres MK10 .. 36 B3
Chatfield SL2 .... 205 A8
Chatham Ct 2 SL1 ..... 206 A3
Chatsworth MK8 .... 33 F1
Chatsworth Cl SL6 ..... 202 C5
Chaucer Cl
Berkhamsted HP4 ...... 134 F5
Newport Pagnell MK16 ... 22 A4
Windsor SL4 .... 210 D4
Chaucer Dr HP21 ...... 115 F6
Chaucer Rd MK3 .... 58 A7
Chaucer Way SL1 ...... 205 F5
Chauntry Cl SL6 .... 203 C6
Chauntry Rd SL6 .... 203 B6
Chawton Cres MK8 ...... 33 F1
Cheapside La UB9 ..... 189 F2
CHEARSLEY 112 A2
Chearsley Rd HP18 ..... 125 E7
CHEDDINGTON 105 B7
Cheddington Comb Sch LU7 .... 105 A7
Cheddington La HP23 .. 104 C5
Cheddington Rd LU7 ... 105 C4
Cheddington Sta LU7 .... 91 A2
Chelmsford Ct 8 SL4 .. 210 C5
Chelsea Gn LU7 .... 80 D6
Chelsea Ho 6 LU7 ...... 80 E7
Chelsea Rd HP19 .... 100 E1
Cheltenham Gdns MK3 .. 57 D6
Cheney Cl LU7 .... 78 B1
Cheneys Wlk MK3 .... 47 A2
Cheney Way HP20 ...... 101 E1
Cheney Wlk 3 HP20 ... 101 F2
CHENIES 156 B2
Chenies Ave HP6 .... 166 D8
CHENIES BOTTOM 156 B2
Chenies Comb Sch WD3 .... 156 B1
Chenies Manor Ho★ WD3 .... 156 A1
Chenies Par HP7 .... 166 C7
Chenies Rd WD3 .... 167 D7
Cheniston Gr SL6 ...... 202 A7
Chepping Cl HP10 ...... 163 A1
Chepping View Prim Sch HP12 .... 172 D3
Chepstow Dr MK3 .... 57 D6
Chequers Bridge Cotts SL0 .... 207 C4
Chequers Cl LU7 .... 105 C4
Chequers Ct HP21 ...... 115 E4
Chequers Dr HP16 ..... 151 C6
Chequers End MK18 ..... 66 A4
Chequers Hill HP7 ..... 165 D7
Chequers La
Ibstone HP14, RG9 ..... 170 A5
North Crawley MK16 ..... 24 B6
Pitstone LU7 .... 105 C3
Prestwood HP16 .... 151 C7
Chequers Orch SL0 .... 207 F7
Chequers Sq UB8 ...... 201 C5
Chequers The
Castlethorpe MK19 ...... 19 F5
Eaton Bray LU6 .... 92 F5
Cherington Gate SL6 ... 195 B1
Cheriton MK4 .... 46 E3
Cherleton MK8 .... 33 E1
Cherries The SL2 ...... 206 B7
Cherry Acre SL9 .... 177 D6
Cherry Ave SL3 .... 206 D4
Cherry Cl
Flackwell Heath HP10 ... 185 B7
Prestwood HP16 .... 151 D6
Cherry Cnr HP10 .... 185 B8
Cherrycroft Dr HP14 ... 161 D6
Cherry Dr HP9 .... 175 B4
Cherry Gdns HP23 ..... 118 F3
Cherry Gr HP15 .... 163 C6
Cherry La
Amersham HP7 .... 165 A7
West Drayton UB7 ...... 208 F2
Woodrow HP7 .... 164 D6
Cherry Lane Prim Sch UB7 .... 208 F2
Cherry Leys MK18 .... 63 E3
Cherry Orch
Amersham HP6 .... 154 E2
Olney MK46 .... 6 E4
Prestwood HP16 .... 151 C6
Stoke Poges SL2 .... 199 A5
West Drayton UB7 ...... 208 E4
Cherry Orchard Ct HP13 .... 173 E6
Cherry Pit The HP13 ... 161 E2
Cherry Rd MK16 .... 22 B3
Cherry Rise
Chalfont St Giles HP8 ... 177 D8
Flackwell Heath HP10 ... 185 B7
Cherry St HP13 .... 174 A4
Cherry Tree Ave UB7 ... 208 F7
Cherry Tree Cl
Great Kingshill HP15 .... 151 D1
Hughenden Valley HP14 . 162 A7
Speen HP27 .... 150 B5
Cherry Tree Ho 4 SL7 . 183 D2
Cherrytree La
Chalfont St Peter SL9 ... 177 D1
Iver Heath SL0 .... 201 A4
Cherry Tree La
Buckland Common HP23 .... 133 A3
Fulmer SL3 .... 199 F6
Heronsgate WD3 .... 167 C1
Lee Common HP16 ..... 142 E4
Cherry Tree Rd
Beaconsfield HP9 ...... 175 B1
Chinnor OX39 .... 147 C6
Farnham Common SL2 ... 198 C5
Cherry Tree Way HP10 . 163 C1
Cherry Tree Wlk
Chesham HP5 .... 144 D2
Leighton Buzzard LU7 .... 80 E7
Wendover HP22 .... 131 A5
Cherry Way
Hazelmere HP15 .... 163 A6
Horton SL3 .... 212 C4
Cherrywood Cl HP9 .... 176 D5
Cherrywood Gdns HP10 .... 185 B8
Chervil MK6 .... 47 B5
Cherwell Cl
Maidenhead SL6 .... 203 A8
Slough SL3 .... 212 B8
Cherwell Ho MK3 .... 57 E8
Cherwell Rd
Aylesbury HP21 .... 115 C6
Bourne End SL8 .... 185 B4
CHESHAM 154 C8
Chesham Ave MK13 ..... 34 C3
CHESHAM BOIS 154 C3
Chesham Bois CE Comb Sch HP6 .... 154 D4
Chesham High Sch HP5 .... 144 D1
Chesham La
Chalfont St Peter SL9 ... 177 E6
Wendover HP22, HP16 ... 141 E8
Chesham L Ctr HP5 .... 154 D8
Chesham Mus★ HP5 ... 154 B8
Chesham Park Com Coll HP5 .... 144 A1
Chesham Prep Sch HP5 .... 145 A4
Chesham Rd
Amersham HP6 .... 154 C2
Ashley Green PH4, PH5 .. 144 F8
Bellingdon HP5 .... 143 E7
Berkhamsted HP4 ...... 135 B2
Bovingdon HP3, HP5 .... 145 E4
Hyde Heath HP16 ...... 153 C7
Wigginton HP23 .... 133 D7
Chesham U Sta HP5 .... 154 C8
Cheshire Cotts OX27 .... 72 F6
Cheshire Ct 6 SL1 ..... 206 B4
Cheshire Rise MK3 ...... 46 E1
Cheslyn Gdns MK14 ..... 35 A8
Chesney Wold MK6 ..... 46 F5
Chessbury Cl HP5 ..... 154 A7
Chessbury Rd HP5 ..... 154 A7
Chess Cl
Aylesbury HP21 .... 115 D3
Latimer HP5 .... 155 D3
Chessfield Pk HP6 ..... 166 E8
CHESSMOUNT 154 E7
Chessmount Rise HP5 .. 154 D6
Chester Cl MK3 .... 57 D7
Chesterfield Cl HP17 ... 114 C5
Chesterfield Cres LU7 .. 79 E3
Chesterfield Pl HP19 ... 115 B8
Chester Ho UB8 .... 201 C1
Chesterholm MK13 ...... 33 F5
Chester Rd SL1 .... 205 D7
Chesterton Cl HP5 ..... 144 B2
Chesterton Gn HP9 .... 175 E2
Chestnut Ave
Chesham HP5 .... 144 E2
Halton HP22 .... 131 D8
High Wycombe HP11 .... 173 D5
Slough SL3 .... 206 E4
West Drayton UB7 ...... 208 F6
Chestnut Cl
Amersham HP6 .... 154 D2
Aston Clinton HP22 ..... 117 F5
Chalfont St Peter SL9 ... 177 F2
Dagnall HP4 .... 107 C5
Maidenhead SL6 .... 196 B1
Medmenham SL7 .... 193 D7
Milton Keynes MK11 ...... 32 D5
Monks Risborough HP27 139 C5
Newton Longville MK17 ... 57 D2
Waddesdon HP18 .... 99 A6
Chestnut Comb Sch MK3 .... 57 E7
Chestnut Cotts MK18 .... 52 C7
Chestnut Cres
Aylesbury HP21 .... 115 D6
Milton Keynes MK2 ...... 58 D7
Chestnut Ct HP6 .... 154 D2
Chestnut Dr
Berkhamsted HP4 ...... 135 D3

Chestnut Dr *continued*
Windsor SL4 209 F3
Chestnut End HP22 117 C1
Chestnut Gn NN13 26 E4
Chestnut Hill LU7 80 D8
Chestnut La
Amersham HP6 154 E2
Hazlemere HP15 163 B5
Chestnut Lane Inf Sch HP6 154 E3
Chestnut Leys MK18 63 E3
Chestnut Pk SL6 203 E3
Chestnut Rd
Beaconsfield HP9 175 B1
Princes Risborough HP27 139 C3
Yardley Gobion NN12 18 F6
Chestnut Rise LU7 80 D8
Chestnuts The
Castlethorpe MK19 19 F5
Felden HP3 146 F7
Uxbridge UB10 201 E5
Chestnut View
Chearsley HP18 112 B2
East Claydon MK18 74 F7
Chestnut Way
Longwick HP27 138 E6
Stoke Mandeville HP22 116 A1
Chestnut Wlk SL9 177 E3
Chestwood Gr UB10 201 F5
Chettle Pl NN12 18 E2
CHETWODE 61 E8
Chetwode Ave MK10 36 B1
Chetwode Cl MK18 41 E2
Chetwynd Dr UB10 201 F3
Chevalier Gr MK8 45 D7
Cheveley Gdns SL1 197 C3
Cheviot Cl
High Wycombe HP13 161 E1
Leighton Buzzard LU7 80 C8
Maidenhead SL6 203 B6
Cheviot Rd SL3 207 A1
Cheyne Cl
Amersham HP6 154 D3
Buckingham MK18 41 F1
Gerrards Cross SL9 188 E3
Pitstone LU7 105 D4
Cheyne Mews HP5 154 D8
Cheyne Wlk HP5 154 D8
CHICHELEY 23 C8
Chicheley Hall MK16 23 D8
Chicheley Hill MK16 23 A8
Chicheley Rd MK16 23 E7
Chicheley St MK16 22 E4
Chichester Cl HP13 173 D6
Chichester Ct SL1 206 A4
Chicksands Ave MK10 36 A2
Chievely Ct MK4 46 C1
Chilcote La HP7 166 A8
Childs Way MK4, MK5, MK6, MK10 46 C7
Chillery Leys MK15 35 E7
Chillingham Ct MK5 46 A4
Chiltern Ave
Amersham HP6 154 D1
Edlesborough LU6 92 E3
High Wycombe HP12 172 D6
Stone HP17 114 D5
Chiltern Brewery The★ HP17 130 C5
Chiltern Bsns Village UB8 201 B3
Chiltern Cl
Berkhamsted HP4 134 F5
Princes Risborough HP27 139 A3
Stone HP17 114 D5
Wendover HP22 131 B5
Chiltern Cnr HP4 135 A5
Chiltern Commerce Ctr HP5 144 A2
Chiltern Cotts
Buckland Common HP23 133 A2
Ibstone HP14 169 D7
Chiltern Court Mews SL4 210 B6
Chiltern Ct
Amersham HP6 154 C2
Chesham HP5 144 A2
5 High Wycombe HP12 172 E7
Wendover HP22 131 B4
Windsor SL4 210 B6
Winslow MK18 65 F3
Chiltern Dr WD3 167 F2
Chiltern Gate Sch HP12 172 E4
Chiltern Gn HP10 185 A8
Chiltern Hill SL9 177 E2
Chiltern Hills Rd HP9 175 C2
Chiltern Ho HP5 154 C7
Chiltern Hospl The (private) HP16 152 C4
Chiltern Hts HP7 166 A8
Chiltern Manor Pk HP16 152 A7
Chiltern Open Air Mus★ HP8 177 F8
Chiltern Par HP6 154 C2
Chiltern Park Ave HP4 135 A6
Chiltern Pools The HP6 154 D1
Chiltern Rd
Amersham HP6 154 B4
Ballinger Common HP16 142 E3
Burnham SL1 204 B8
Maidenhead SL6 203 B6
Marlow SL7 183 C2
Wendover HP22 131 B5
Wingrave HP22 89 A3
Chiltern Ridge HP14 158 C4
Chilterns
Berkhamsted HP4 134 F6
World's End HP22 130 F7
Chilterns Cl HP10 185 B7
Chilterns Gateway Ctr★ LU6 93 F4
Chilterns Pk SL8 185 B5
Chiltern St HP21 115 E6
Chilterns The (Sh Ctr) HP13 173 A7
Chiltern Valley Winery & Brewery★ RG9 180 F7
Chiltern View HP14 149 C1
Chiltern View Rd UB8 201 D3
Chiltern Villas HP23 118 E2
Chiltern Way
Aston Clinton HP22 117 F2
Tring HP23 119 C5
CHILTON 111 A4
Chilton Cl
Holmer Green HP15 163 C7
Tylers Green HP10 163 C2
Chilton Ct SL6 204 C7
Chilton Pl HP20 101 E1
Chilton Rd
Chearsley HP18 112 A2
Chesham HP5 144 C2
Long Crendon HP18 125 C7
Chilwick Rd SL2 197 F1
Chimes Sh Ctr The UB8 201 D5
Chimes The HP12 172 E6
Chimney La HP10 185 E8
Chinalls Cl MK18 50 D6
Chingle Croft MK4 46 C2
Chinneck Ho HP4 135 C4
CHINNOR 147 D7
Chinnor Hill OX39 147 E4
Chinnor Hill Wildlife Reserve★ OX39 147 F5
Chinnor & Princes Risborough Rly★ OX39 147 E7
Chinnor Rd
Bledlow HP27 138 A2
Bledlow Ridge HP14 148 C3
Chinnor OX39 147 A4
Chinnor Sta★ OX39 147 D5
Chippendale Cl HP13 162 D1
Chippendale Waye UB8 201 D5
Chippenham Dr MK10 36 C1
CHIPPERFIELD 156 F8
Chipperfield Cl MK13 34 A7
Chipperfield Rd HP3 146 C3
Chipping Vale MK4 46 C2
Chipstead SL9 177 C2
Chirbury Cl MK10 35 F1
CHISBRIDGE CROSS 182 D6
Chislehampton MK15 35 C3
Chiswick Cl MK4 45 F2
Chiswick Lodge 6 SL7 183 D2
CHIVERY 132 C4
Choke La SL6 195 B4
CHOLESBURY 133 C3
Cholesbury La HP23 133 A2
Cholesbury Rd HP23 133 D5
Chorley Rd HP14 160 E3
CHORLEYWOOD 167 D5
CHORLEYWOOD BOTTOM 167 C3
Chorleywood Bottom WD3 167 D4
Chorleywood Comm Nature Reserve★ WD3 167 E5
Chorleywood Ho WD3 167 E6
Chorleywood House Dr WD3 167 E6
Chorleywood House Est Nature Reserve★ WD3 167 F6
Chorleywood Montessori Sch The WD3 167 E7
Chorleywood Prim Sch WD3 167 C3
Chorleywood Sta/U Sta WD3 167 D5
CHORLEYWOOD WEST 167 A4
Chrislaine Cl TW19 213 D1
Christchurch CE Prim Sch WD3 167 F6
Christchurch Gr MK12 33 B6
Christchurch Ho 15 HP23 119 A3
Christchurch Rd HP23 118 F4
Christian Ct MK15 35 D7
Christian Smith Ho SL6 202 A1
Christian Sq 4 SL4 210 C6
Christie Cl MK16 22 A5
Christies Ct 2 HP13 173 B7
Christine Ho 3 MK2 58 C8
CHRISTMAS COMMON 168 B7
Christmas La 1 SL2 198 C8
Christopher Cl HP14 161 D7
Christopher Ho 3 SL2 198 C7
Christ the Sower Ecumenical Prim Sch MK8 45 D6
Church Ave RG9 191 E2
Church Cl
Aston Clinton HP22 117 D5
Cuddington HP18 112 F3
Eton SL4 210 D8
Maidenhead SL6 202 D6
Maids Moreton MK18 41 F3
Uxbridge UB8 201 B3
West Drayton UB7 208 E3
Wicken MK19 31 B3
Church Cotts SL6 196 E2
Church Croft LU6 92 E3
Church Ct
Aylesbury HP22 116 B2
High Wycombe HP13 162 D1
Church Dr SL6 203 C4
CHURCH END
Chorley Wood 156 F1
Drayton Parslow 68 B5
Haddenham 127 A5
Hanslope 11 A2
Long Crendon 125 C7
Pitstone 105 D3
Steeple Claydon 63 E2
Totternhoe 93 B7
Church End
Adstock MK18 53 F1
Bledlow HP27 138 B1
Drayton Parslow MK17 68 B5
Edlesborough LU6 92 E3
Haddenham HP17 127 A5
Hillesden MK18 63 B6
Leckhampstead MK18 42 D8
Newton Longville MK17 57 D3
Potterspury NN12 18 E3
Sherington MK16 14 A2
Syresham NN13 27 C8
Wavendon MK17 48 E7
Church End Cotts WD3 156 F1
Church End Farm LU6 93 B7
Church End Rd MK5 46 A4
Church Farm Cl HP22 102 B3
Church Farm Cres MK14 34 E8
Church Farm Ho HP8 177 C7
Church Farm La HP23 104 F3
Churchfield Mews SL2 206 A7
Churchfield Rd SL9 177 D2
Churchgates 3 HP4 135 C4
Church Gn
Long Crendon HP18 125 D7
Totternhoe LU6 93 B7
Church Gr
Little Chalfont HP6 166 E8
Slough SL3 206 C8
Church Green Rd MK3 58 A8
Church Headland La HP22 87 A6
CHURCH HILL 56 A8
Church Hill
Akeley MK18 41 F8
Aspley Guise MK17 49 E5
Cheddington LU7 105 A8
Ellesborough HP17 130 B2
Milton Keynes MK8 33 F2
Pishill RG9 179 D8
South Harefield UB9 190 C8
Whaddon MK17 45 B1
Church Holt The SL2 187 E3
Churchill Ave HP21 115 D5
Churchill Cl HP10 185 B7
Churchill Ct 1 HP21 115 E7
Churchill Dr
Beaconsfield HP9 175 C5
Marlow SL7 183 F4
Churchill Ho UB7 208 D6
Churchill Rd SL3 206 F2
Church La
Alderton NN12 9 A2
Aston Clinton HP22 117 D4
Berkhamsted HP4 135 C4
Bisham SL7 194 D7
Bledlow Ridge HP14 159 F8
Bovingdon HP3 146 B4
Bray SL6 203 C4
Chalfont St Peter SL9 177 D2
Chearsley HP18 112 B1
Cheddington LU7 105 A8
Chinnor OX39 147 D6
Clifton Reynes MK46 7 C3
Cryers Hill HP15 162 C4
Deanshanger MK19 31 E4
Eaton Bray LU6 92 E6
Church La *continued*
Edgcott HP18 72 F2
Emberton MK46 13 F7
Grafton Regis NN12 9 D2
Granborough MK18 75 F6
Great Horwood MK17 55 A3
Great Kimble HP17 129 E1
Great Missenden HP16 152 B7
Hastoe HP23 132 F7
Horton-cum-S OX33 108 A5
Lacey Green HP27 149 E4
Lillingstone Lovell MK18 30 A6
Ludgershall HP18 96 C7
Marsworth HP23 104 F1
Milton Keynes MK5 46 B8
Mixbury NN13 38 D1
Mursley MK17 67 D5
Newport Pagnell MK16 22 D7
Oving HP22 86 C7
Padbury MK18 53 C2
Potterspury NN12 18 E3
Princes Risborough HP27 139 B4
Radnage HP14 159 D8
Sarratt WD3 156 F1
Slough SL2, SL3 206 C8
Soulbury LU7 69 E2
Stoke Bruerne NN12 9 A8
Stoke Goldington MK16 12 A7
Stoke Poges SL2 198 F2
Thornborough MK18 54 A8
Tingewick MK18 51 B7
Upper Winchendon HP18 99 B1
Uxbridge UB8 201 B3
Walter's Ash HP14 161 E6
Walton MK7 47 F6
Wendover HP22 131 C3
Weston Turville HP22 116 F1
West Wycombe HP14 161 A2
Whaddon MK17 45 B1
Whitchurch HP22 87 A6
Wicken MK19 31 B3
8 Windsor SL4 210 D6
Yardley Hastings NN7 1 B7
Church Lees MK14 21 D1
Churchmead CE Sch SL3 211 B7
Churchmere Wlk HP21 115 C6
Church Pas MK16 22 D4
Church Path
Cheddington LU7 91 A1
Cublington LU7 78 B1
Lane End HP14 171 B4
Prestwood HP16 151 D5
Stokenchurch HP14 158 D5
Church Piece HP18 112 B2
Church Rd
Aspley Heath MK17 49 B3
Bow Brickhill MK17 48 D1
Brackley NN13 38 A7
Chinnor OX39 147 D6
Cookham Dean SL6 195 B6
Farnham Royal SL2 198 C2
Ickford HP18 123 F3
Iver Heath SL0 200 C3
Ivinghoe LU7 105 F5
Lane End HP14 171 B3
Leighton Buzzard LU7 80 E6
Lewknor OX49 157 B8
Little Gaddesden HP4 121 D8
Little Marlow SL7 184 C5
Maidenhead SL6 203 B5
Old Windsor SL4 211 B2
Penn HP10 174 E7
Pitstone LU7 105 E3
Seer Green HP9 176 D4
Sherington MK16 13 F2
Slapton LU7 91 D6
South Harefield UB9 190 C8
Stoke Hammond MK17 69 D8
Stokenchurch HP14 158 D5
Thame OX9 125 E1
Totternhoe LU6 93 B6
Tylers Green HP10 174 C8
Uxbridge UB8 201 D1
West Drayton UB7 208 E3
Church Row SL3 199 D8
Churchside HP15 163 D7
Church Sq
7 High Wycombe HP11 173 B7
Leighton Buzzard LU7 80 F6
Church St
Amersham HP7 165 B7
Aspley Guise MK17 49 E5
16 Aylesbury HP20 115 D8
Bovingdon HP3 146 B4
Brill HP18 110 B8
Buckingham MK18 52 C8
Burnham SL1 197 C1
Chesham HP5 154 B7
Gawcott MK18 52 A4
Great Missenden HP16 152 B7
Henley-on-Thames RG9 191 D1
High Wycombe HP11 173 B7
Little Horwood MK17 55 E2
Maids Moreton MK18 41 F3
Marsh Gibbon OX27 71 F3
Church St *continued*
Milton Keynes, Fenny Stratford MK2 47 E1
Milton Keynes, New Bradwell MK13 33 F7
Milton Keynes, Stony Stratford MK11 32 D5
Milton Keynes, Wolverton MK12 33 D7
North Marston MK18 76 B2
6 Olney MK46 6 F3
Olney MK46 7 A3
Princes Risborough HP27 139 B3
Quainton HP22 85 B5
Slough, Chalvey SL1 205 D4
Slough, Upton Park SL1 205 F4
Stokenchurch HP14 158 D5
Twyford MK18 62 C2
6 Windsor SL4 210 D6
Wing LU7 79 E2
Wingrave HP22 89 B2
Winslow MK18 65 F4
Church Terr
Turvey MK43 8 E5
Windsor SL4 209 E5
Church View
Brackley NN13 38 A7
Edlesborough LU6 92 D3
Halton HP22 117 C1
Long Marston HP23 104 A4
Newport Pagnell MK16 22 D4
9 Slough SL1 206 A3
Steeple Claydon MK18 63 E2
Church View Ct LU7 80 E6
Church Views SL6 202 F8
Churchway HP17 127 A6
Church Way
East Claydon MK18 74 F8
Stone HP17 114 C5
Church Wlk
Milton Keynes MK3 57 F7
North Crawley MK16 24 B6
Weston Turville HP22 116 F1
Wing LU7 79 E2
Winslow MK18 65 F4
Church Yd HP23 119 A3
Chyne The SL9 188 F6
Cinnamon Cl SL4 209 F6
Cinnamon Gr MK7 48 A5
CIPPENHAM 204 F4
Cippenham Cl SL1 204 F6
Cippenham Inf Sch SL1 204 D6
Cippenham Jun Sch SL1 204 D6
Cippenham La SL1 205 B5
City Rd HP14 159 D6
Clailey Ct MK11 32 F5
Claires Court Sch SL6 196 B1
Clammas Way UB8 208 D8
Clapham Pl MK13 34 C2
Clappers Mdw SL6 196 B1
Clappins La
Naphill HP14 150 D1
Walter's Ash HP14 161 C8
Clapton App HP10 185 D8
Clare Croft MK10 36 A3
Clare Dr SL2 198 B8
Clarefield Cl SL6 195 B1
Clarefield Dr SL6 195 A1
Clarefield Rd SL6 195 A1
Claremont SL3 212 D6
Claremont Ave MK11 32 E4
Claremont Cl HP21 115 F5
Claremont Gdns SL7 183 E2
Claremont Rd
Marlow SL7 183 E2
Windsor SL4 210 C5
Clarence Cres SL4 210 C6
Clarence Ct
9 High Wycombe HP13 173 B7
Maidenhead SL6 202 E8
Windsor SL4 210 B6
Clarence Ho 2 MK9 34 C2
Clarence Rd
Berkhamsted HP4 135 C4
Henley-on-Thames RG9 191 D2
Milton Keynes MK11 32 E5
Windsor SL4 210 B6
Clarendon Copse SL6 202 D6
Clarendon Ct
Slough SL2 206 B6
Windsor SL4 210 B6
Clarendon Dr
Milton Keynes MK8 33 F2
Thame OX9 126 A1
Clarendon Rd
High Wycombe HP13 173 E5
Prestwood HP16 151 B6
Clare Park HP7 165 E7
Clare Rd
Maidenhead SL6 202 D6
Prestwood HP16 151 C6
Slough SL6 204 C7
Stanwell TW19 213 E1
Claridge Dr MK10 36 A2
Clarke Ct HP20 101 F2

Clarke Dr HP13 174 A6
Clarke Rd MK1 47 D4
Clarkes Dr UB8 208 E8
Clarkes Field Cl HP18 110 B8
Clarkes Orch MK16 12 B5
Clarke's Spring HP23 119 F5
Clarke Wlk 2 HP20 101 F2
Clarks Cotts HP16 151 C7
Classon Cl UB7 208 E4
Clauds Cl HP15 163 A5
Claverton Cl HP3 146 A3
Clay Acre HP5 144 D1
Clay Cl HP10 185 B8
Claycots Prim Sch SL2 198 A1
Claycutters MK18 66 A4
Claydon Cl HP21 115 D6
Claydon Ct HP12 172 E4
Claydon End SL9 188 E8
Claydon Ho★ MK18 74 C7
Claydon La SL9 188 E8
Claydon Path HP21 115 E3
Claydons Pl HP27 138 D7
Clayfield Rd HP22 131 C8
Clayfields HP10 163 C2
Clayhall La SL4 210 F2
Clayhill
Marlow Bottom SL7 172 A2
Wigginton HP23 133 E7
Clay Hill MK8 33 E2
Clay La
Calvert MK18 73 A5
Marlow Bottom SL7 172 A2
Wendover HP22 131 C5
Claymoor Pk SL7 172 A2
Clay Pit La 9 MK46 6 F3
Clays La MK17 55 E2
Clay St HP7, HP9 175 C7
Clays The HP17 127 A7
Clayton Ct SL3 207 A3
Clayton Gate MK14 35 A8
Claytons Comb Sch
SL8 185 A5
Claytons Mdw SL8 185 B2
Clayton Way UB8 201 D1
Clayton Wlk HP7 166 C8
Clearbrook Cl HP13 174 B4
Cleares Pasture SL1 197 B2
Cleavers OX39 147 B6
Cleavers Ave MK14 34 E3
Cleeve Cres MK3 47 A2
Clegg Sq MK5 46 B5
Cleland Rd SL9 177 D1
Clementi Ave HP15 163 D7
Clement Pl 5 HP23 119 A3
Clements Cl 5 SL1 206 B4
Clements La OX27 71 F2
Clements Rd
Chorleywood WD3 167 D4
Henley-on-Thames RG9 191 C3
Clerkenwell Cotts
HP17 126 F5
Clerkenwell Pl MK6 35 B2
Clevehurst Cl SL2 199 A6
Cleveland MK13 34 B6
Cleveland Cl
Maidenhead SL6 203 B6
Wooburn Green HP10 185 E8
Cleveland Dr LU7 80 C8
Cleveland Pk
Aylesbury HP20 101 F3
Stanwell TW19 213 E1
Cleveland Pl 13 HP20 101 F3
Cleveland Rd
Aylesbury HP20 101 E3
Uxbridge UB8 201 D2
Cleves Ct SL4 209 F4
Clewer Ave SL4 210 A5
Clewer Court Rd SL4 210 B7
Clewer Fields SL4 210 C6
CLEWER GREEN 209 E3
Clewer Green CE Fst Sch
SL4 210 A4
Clewer Hill Rd SL4 209 F4
CLEWER NEW TOWN 210 A5
Clewer New Town SL4 210 A5
Clewer Pk SL4 210 A7
CLEWER VILLAGE 210 A7
Clicker Yd MK46 6 F4
Clifden Rd HP18 123 E5
Clifford Ave MK2 58 C7
Clifford Rd HP27 139 B3
Cliffords Way SL8 185 B5
Clifton Bsns Pk HP19 101 B1
Clifton Cl SL6 203 A4
Clifton Ct
High Wycombe HP11 172 E4
Olney MK46 7 A3
8 Stanwell TW19 213 E1
Clifton Gn HP19 101 B2
Clifton Lawns HP6 154 C4
Clifton Lodge
Eton Wick SL4 205 A1
7 Slough SL1 206 A4
Clifton Moor MK5 45 D5
Clifton Rd
Amersham HP6 154 C4
Newton Blossomville MK43 8 A4
5 Slough SL1 206 A4
CLIFTON REYNES 7 C3
Clifton Rise SL4 209 D6
Cline Ct MK8 45 E6
Clinkard Pl HP14 171 A3
Clinton Cres HP21 116 A8
Clipstone Brook Way 4
MK10 36 B3
Clive Ct SL1 205 D4
Cliveden★ SL6 196 E7
Cliveden Gate SL1 197 B3
Cliveden Mead SL6 196 C2
Cliveden Office Village
HP12 172 E4
Cliveden Pl MK4 45 F2
Cliveden Rd SL6 196 E4
Clivemont Rd SL6 202 F8
Clock Ho The MK17 59 D6
Clockhouse Mews
WD3 167 E6
Cloebury Paddock MK15 35 C3
Cloister Garth HP4 135 C4
Cloisters The
High Wycombe HP13 162 D2
Slough SL1 205 D4
Clonmel Way SL1 197 B2
Closes The HP17 127 A7
Close The
Akeley MK18 42 A8
Ashendon HP18 97 F1
Bierton HP22 102 A4
Bourne End SL8 185 A6
Great Horwood MK17 55 B3
Hardmead MK16 15 D4
Hardwick HP22 87 B3
Iver Heath SL0 200 C2
Lathbury MK16 22 D7
Milton Keynes, Bradwell
MK13 34 A4
Milton Keynes, The Green
MK6 47 D7
Newton Blossomville MK43 7 F3
Ravenstone MK46 5 E2
Slough SL1 204 D6
Weston Underwood MK46 6 A1
Cloudberry MK7 48 A6
Cloutsham Cl MK4 46 D3
Clover Cl MK5 46 B8
Clover End MK18 52 C7
Clover La HP21 115 E5
Club Cotts MK17 49 B4
Cluny Ct MK7 48 D6
Clyde Pl MK3 46 E1
Clydesdale Pl MK14 34 F4
Coach Ho The
Loudwater HP11 174 A4
Wooburn Green HP10 185 E6
Coachmaker Ct MK14 34 F6
Coachman's Lodge SL4 210 D5
Coach Ride SL7 183 D4
Coach Yd NN12 18 E3
Coalmans Way SL1 204 A8
Coaters La HP10 185 E7
Coates La HP13 162 A1
Coat Wicks HP9 176 C4
Cobb Cl SL3 211 D6
Cobbetts Mount MK18 63 D2
Cobbetts Ride HP23 118 F3
Cobb Hall Rd MK17 57 C3
Cobblers Cl SL2 198 B3
Cobblershill La HP16 141 B4
Cobblers Wick HP22 89 B3
Cobb Rd HP4 134 F4
Cobbs Gdn MK46 6 F4
Cobden Cl UB8 201 C4
Coberley Cl MK15 35 B6
Cobham Cl
Buckingham MK18 41 C1
Slough SL1 204 F5
Cochran Cl MK8 45 E7
Cochrane Ho UB8 201 C4
Cockerell Gr MK5 46 C5
Cockett Rd SL3 206 E3
Cock Gr HP4 134 D4
Cock La HP10 174 A6
Cockpit Cl HP15 151 E1
Cockpit Rd HP15 162 D8
Cocksherd Wood Nature
Reserve★ SL2 197 E2
Coddimoor La MK17 56 B7
CODMORE 144 E1
Codmore Cres HP5 144 E1
Codmore Cross HP5 144 D1
Codmore Wood Rd
HP5 155 D6
Coe Spur SL1 205 B3
COFFEE HALL 46 F7
Coffee Hall Rdbt MK6 47 B6
Cofferidge Cl MK11 32 D5
Coftards SL2 206 C7
Cogan Ct MK8 45 E7
Cogdells Cl HP5 143 B4
Cogdells La HP5 143 B4
Coggeshall Gr MK7 48 C7
Coin Cl MK10 35 F3
Cokers Ct 3 SL8 185 A4
Coke's Farm La HP8 166 B6
Coke's La HP8 166 B6
Colborne Rd HP13 173 D8
Colby Gdns 1 SL6 202 F8
Colchester Ct MK3 57 E7
Colchester Wlk MK3 57 E7
COLD BRAYFIELD 8 B5
Coldeaton La MK4 46 B3
Cold Grove Cotts SL6 196 E2
Coldharbour HP22 131 C4
Cold Harbour CE Comb Sch
MK3 46 F3
Coldharbour Way
HP19 115 A7
Coldmoorholme La
SL8 184 E4
Coldmoreham Yd HP7 165 A8
Coleheath Bottom
HP27 150 C5
Colenorton Cres SL4 204 E2
Cole Rd HP21 115 C5
Coleridge Cl
Milton Keynes MK3 58 A7
Newport Pagnell MK16 21 F4
Coleridge Cres SL3 212 E6
Coleridge Way UB7 208 F2
Coles Ave MK6 46 F6
Colesbourne Dr MK15 35 B6
COLESHILL 164 F3
Coles Hill HP18 111 B3
Coleshill CE Inf Sch
HP7 164 F3
Coleshill Ho HP7 165 A4
Coleshill La HP7 164 D2
Coleshill Pl MK13 34 C3
Colet Rd HP22 131 C5
Colgrain St MK9 35 A4
Colham Ave UB7 208 E5
Colham Mill Rd UB7 208 D5
Colham Rd UB8 201 F1
Colindale St MK10 35 E1
Colinswood SL2 187 B1
Colin Way SL1 205 B3
College Ave
Maidenhead SL6 202 E7
Slough SL1 205 E3
College Bsns Pk HP22 103 C1
College Cl
Holton OX33 122 C1
Thame OX9 125 E1
College Cres
Oakley HP18 109 E4
Windsor SL4 210 B5
College Glen SL6 202 D7
College Lake Wildlife
Reserve★ HP23 105 C1
College Rd
Cranfield MK43 24 E2
Maidenhead SL6 202 E7
Slough SL1 204 F5
College Rise SL6 202 D7
College Road N HP22 117 C6
College The OX27 71 F3
College The (Claires Court
Schs) SL6 202 E7
Colley Hill MK13 34 A4
Colley Hill La SL2 187 F1
Colley Ho UB8 201 D4
Colleyland WD3 167 D5
Collier Cl SL6 195 F1
Colliers Wood MK10 35 E8
Collings Walk HP16 151 C5
Collingwood Cl HP13 174 A6
Collins Ho 2 HP11 173 A7
Collins Wlk MK16 22 A4
Collinswood Rd SL2 187 B2
Collum Green Rd SL2 187 E1
Collyer Rd HP14 158 E4
COLNBROOK 212 D7
Colnbrook By-Pass
Colnbrook SL3 212 D7
Harmondsworth UB7 213 C7
Colnbrook CE Prim Sch
SL3 212 D6
Colnbrook Ct SL3 212 F6
Coln Cl SL6 202 F8
Colndale Rd SL3 212 E5
Colne MK6 47 D6
Colne Ave UB7 208 C4
Colne Bank SL3 212 C4
Colnedale Rd UB8 201 D7
Colne Orch SL0 207 F6
Colne Park Cvn Site
UB7 208 C2
Colne Rd HP13 173 F7
Colne Reach TW19 212 F2
Colne Valley Park Visitor
Ctr★ UB9 190 B1
Coln Trad Est SL3 212 F6
Colonel Grantham Ave
HP19 101 D4
Colonial Rd 1 SL1 206 A4
Colonnade SL6 203 A7
Colossus Way MK3 47 A1
Colsons Way MK46 6 F5
Colston Bassett MK4 46 C1
Colston Ct SL9 188 E5
COLSTROPE 181 D5
Coltman Ave HP18 125 C6
Coltsfoot Dr UB7 208 E7
Coltsfoot Pl MK14 34 D3
Colts Holm Rd MK12 33 C8
Columbia Pl MK9 35 A3
Columbine Rd HP15 162 F6
Colville Ct HP16 152 B7
Colville Rd HP11 172 F6
COMBE 130 C1
Combe Martin MK4 46 D3
Combe Rise HP12 172 B7
Combermere Cl SL4 210 B5
Combes Cres MK6 46 F6
Comerford Way MK18 66 A5
Comfrey Cl MK7 48 A5
Comfrey The 2 HP19 101 E4
Common Field HP23 119 D1
Common Gate Rd WD3 167 E4
Common La
Eton SL4 205 D1
Hedgerley SL1 186 D1
Milton Keynes, Bradwell
MK13 34 A4
Milton Keynes MK5 46 C8
Common Rd
Chorleywood WD3 167 D5
Dagnall LU6 107 F3
Dorney SL4 204 D2
Eton Wick SL4 205 A2
Flackwell Heath HP10 185 B8
Great Kingshill HP15 151 D1
Slough SL3 207 A1
Commonside HP13 161 E3
Common St MK46 5 D1
COMMON THE 55 B4
Common The
Berkhamsted HP4 135 F6
Chipperfield WD4 156 F7
Flackwell Heath HP10 185 B8
Great Kingshill HP15 151 D1
Holmer Green HP15 163 D7
Stokenchurch HP14 158 E5
West Drayton UB7 208 C2
Common Wood SL2 198 C8
Common Wood La
HP10 163 E1
Como Rd HP20 116 B8
Compass Point HP4 134 E6
Comp Gate LU6 92 E6
Comp The LU6 92 E6
Compton Ct
Moulsoe MK16 36 D8
Slough SL1 204 E7
Compton Dr SL6 202 A8
Compton Rd HP22 131 D5
Concorde Cl UB10 201 E3
Concorde Rd SL6 202 D4
Concorde Way SL1 205 C4
Concourse The 6 MK2 58 C8
Concra Pk MK17 49 C4
Concrete Cows★ MK13 33 F4
Condor Cl MK6 47 A8
Conduit La SL3 206 E1
Conegar Ct SL1 205 E5
Conegra Ct 15 HP13 173 B7
Conegra Rd HP13 173 C7
Coneygere MK46 7 A3
Congreve MK6 47 D5
Conifer Rise HP12 172 E6
Conifers The SL6 202 A8
Conigre OX39 147 B6
Coningsby Cl SL6 202 D3
Coningsby Ct HP13 173 B8
Coningsby Rd HP13 162 B1
Coniston Cres SL1 204 C8
Coniston Gn HP20 101 D3
Coniston Rd LU7 80 C7
Coniston Way MK2 58 D6
Conkers SL6 203 B8
Connaught Cl SL6 195 E1
Connaught Gdns HP4 134 F7
Connaught Rd
Aylesbury HP20 116 C8
3 Slough SL1 206 B4
CONNIBURROW 34 E4
Conniburrow Bvd MK14 34 E4
Conniston Cl SL7 183 B2
Conought Ho RG9 191 E3
Constable Cl MK14 34 F7
Constable Pl HP19 100 F2
Constable's Croft OX25 94 E7
Constantine Pl UB10 201 F4
Constantine Way MK13 33 F5
Convent Ct HP23 118 F3
Convent Rd SL4 210 A5
Conway Cl
Aylesbury HP21 115 F7
Loudwater HP10 174 C2
Milton Keynes MK3 57 F8
Conway Cres MK3 57 E8
Conway Ct SL9 189 B3
Conway Ho HP13 173 F7
Conway Rd SL6 204 B7
Cook Cl MK7 48 B4
Cookfield Cl LU6 93 E8
COOKHAM 196 A7
Cookham Ct HP6 154 E1
COOKHAM DEAN 195 B7
Cookham Dean Bottom
SL6 195 C8
Cookham Dean CE Prim
Sch SL6 195 B7
Cookham Lodge 15
SL6 202 F6
Cookham Rd SL6 195 F1
COOKHAM RISE 195 E6
Cookham Rise Prim Sch
SL6 195 E6
Cookham Sta SL6 195 F7
Cooks Cl NN7 9 F8
Cookshall La HP12 161 A2
Cooks La MK17 67 E6
Cook's Mdw LU6 92 E4
Cooks Rd HP19 114 F8
Coombe Ave HP22 131 B4
Coombe Cl HP22 116 C2
Coombe Dr LU6 93 E7
Coombe Gdns
Berkhamsted HP4 134 F5
Hughenden Valley HP14 162 A6
Coombe Hill Ct SL4 209 D4
Coombe La
Aylesbury HP19 100 F1
Walter's Ash HP14 161 F6
Coombes Quarry Nature
Reserve★ MK18 53 E6
Coombe Vale SL9 188 E3
Cooper Rd RG9 191 D3
Cooper's Court Rd
HP14 158 D5
Coopers Ct MK16 22 C4
Coopers Mews MK14 34 F6
Coopers Rise HP13 173 D5
Coopers Row SL0 200 D1
Cooper's Yd HP20 101 D1
Cooper Way
3 Berkhamsted HP4 135 D4
Slough SL1 205 B3
Coots Cl MK18 52 E7
Cope Ct SL6 202 C7
Copeland Cl MK7 48 C5
Copes Rd HP15 151 E1
Copes Shroves HP15 162 F5
Copmans Wick WD3 167 D4
Copners Dr HP15 163 C6
Copners Way HP15 163 B6
Copper Beech Cl
Felden HP3 146 F8
Windsor SL4 209 D6
Copperfields
Beaconsfield HP9 175 E5
High Wycombe HP12 161 B1
Copperfield Terr SL2 206 B6
Copperhouse Ct MK7 48 A2
Copperkins Gr HP6 154 B3
Copperkins La HP6 154 A3
Coppermill La WD3 178 F3
Coppermill Rd TW19 212 B2
Copper Ridge SL9 177 F5
Coppice Cl HP20 102 A2
Coppice Farm Rd HP10 163 C2
Coppice The
Great Kingshill HP15 151 E1
High Wycombe HP12 172 B4
Seer Green HP9 176 D4
Stokenchurch HP14 158 E5
Walter's Ash HP14 161 B8
West Drayton UB7 208 E7
Wigginton HP23 119 C1
Coppice Way
Aylesbury HP20 102 A2
Hedgerley SL2 187 D2
Coppidwell Dr HP21 116 A5
Coppinger Ct UB7 208 E4
Coppin La MK13 34 A3
Coppins Cl HP4 134 F4
Coppins La SL0 207 F8
Copse Cl
Marlow SL7 183 C2
Slough SL1 204 F5
West Drayton UB7 208 D3
Copse Gate MK18 66 A4
Copse La HP9 176 E3
Copse The
Amersham HP7 154 C1
Beaconsfield HP9 175 C4
Copse Way HP5 144 A4
Copse Wood SL0 200 D4
Copthall Cl SL9 177 F3
Copthall Cnr SL9 177 E3
Copthall Ho SL6 203 A7
Copthall La SL9 177 E3
Copthorn Cl SL6 202 A4
Copthorne Pl MK7 48 B8
Copyground Ct HP12 172 E7
Copyground La HP12 172 E7
Coral Cl LU6 92 E6
Coram Cl HP4 135 C3
Corbet Ride LU7 80 D8
Corbet Sq LU7 80 D8
Corbett Cl MK15 35 D7
Cordons Cl SL9 177 D2
Cordwainer Ct MK14 34 F6
Cordwallis Bsns Pk
SL6 195 E1
Cordwallis Est SL6 202 F8
Cordwallis Pk SL6 202 E8
Cordwallis Rd SL6 202 F8
Cordwallis St SL6 202 E8
CORES END 185 C4
Cores End Rd SL8 185 B3

Corfe Cl HP21 ....116 B5
Corfe Cres MK3.........57 F8
Corfe Gdns SL1 ....205 A6
Corfe Pl SL6.............202 C7
Coriander Ct MK7......48 B5
Corin Cl MK2 ....58 D5
Corin Way MK2 ....58 D5
Corinium Ind Est HP6 .154 F1
Cork Pl MK3 ....46 E2
Cornbrook Rd HP21 ...115 C5
Cornbury Cres MK15 ...35 A6
Corn Cl HP17 ....114 D5
Corncrake 9 HP19......101 F3
Cornel Cl HP15 ....163 B3
Cornel Ho 1 SL4 ....210 D4
Cornelia Cl MK2 ....58 C6
Cornerways HP27.......150 C5
Cornfield Cl UB8.......201 D3
Cornfield Cres HP4 ....134 D7
Cornflower Pl MK18....52 C7
Corn Hill MK8...........33 E1
Corn Mkt HP11 ....173 B7
Cornwall Ave SL2 ......198 C1
Cornwall Cl
  Eton Wick SL4 ....204 E1
  Maidenhead SL6 ....195 E2
Cornwall Cl UB8.........201 D6
Cornwall Gr MK3........46 F1
Cornwall Ho UB8........201 D6
Cornwall Lodge 11 SL6. 202 F6
Cornwall Pl MK18.......41 D1
Cornwall Rd UB8........201 D6
Cornwalls Mdw 3
  MK18.....................41 D1
Cornwell Rd SL4 ....211 A1
Coronation Ave
  Slough SL3..............206 E7
  Windsor SL4 ....211 A4
Coronation Cotts MK18...41 F8
Coronation Cres HP14..171 C5
Coronation Mews LU7...80 F8
Coronation Pl MK18.....63 D2
Coronation Rd
  Cranfield MK43 ....25 B1
  High Wycombe HP12...172 D4
  Milton Keynes MK11 ....32 E5
Coronation St HP13 ....173 B7
Coronation Villas HP21 115 E8
Corporation St HP13 ...173 B7
Corrid Ind Pk HP19 ....101 B1
Corrigan Cl MK3........58 A8
Corsewall Pl 6 MK4 ...45 F1
Corsham Ct 4 MK8 ....33 F1
COSGROVE................19 D2
Cosgrove Prim Sch
  MK19.....................19 E2
Cosgrove Rd MK19.....32 C7
Costers Cotts SL8......185 B2
Costins Wlk 7 HP4 ....135 D4
Cosway Pl MK8..........45 D6
Cotes Way LU7 ....79 F3
Cotman Cl MK12........33 B5
Cotswold Cl
  Maidenhead SL6 ....203 B6
  Slough SL1...............205 B3
  Uxbridge UB8...........201 C4
Cotswold Ct HP12.......172 F8
Cotswold Dr LU7........80 C8
Cotswold Gn HP20......101 E2
Cotswolds Way MK18...73 B8
Cotswold Way HP13...172 E8
Cottage Comm MK6....46 B8
Cottage Farm Way
  HP27......................150 C4
Cottage Grounds HP17 .114 D5
Cottage Park Rd SL2 ..187 D2
Cottages The
  Ickenham UB10........190 E2
  Syresham NN13..........27 C5
Cottesbrooke Cl SL3 ..212 D6
Cottesloe Cl LU7........79 E3
Cottesloe Ct MK11 .....32 F5
Cottesloe Rd HP21.....115 E5
Cottesloe Sch The LU7 .79 D1
Cottingham Gr MK3....58 A7
Cottisford Cres MK14 ...21 F1
Cottland Clay HP17 ....127 A7
Cotts The
  Long Crendon HP18.....125 C6
  Longwick HP27.........138 E5
Coulson Ave MK8, MK5...45 E6
Coulson Ct HP16 ....151 D6
Coulson Way SL1 ....204 B8
Council Hos LU7 ....92 A1
Countisbury MK4 ....46 D2
Country La HP15 ....151 F1
Country Life Ho SL3....211 B7
County Rd NN13 ....38 A6
Cours La Ville Cl MK18 ..65 E3
Court Cl
  Aylesbury HP21........115 E7
  High Wycombe HP13...161 D1
  Maidenhead SL6 ....203 C3
  Princes Risborough
    HP27...................139 A3
Court Cnr MK46..........6 E3
Court Cres SL1 ....205 D7

Court Dr
  Maidenhead SL6 ....196 C3
  Uxbridge UB10.........201 F4
Courteneys Lodge MK4..46 E3
Court Farm Cl SL1 .....205 B5
Courtfield Dr SL6.......202 C6
Courtfield Gdns UB9 ..190 A1
Court Garden L Complex
  SL7.......................183 D1
Courthouse Cl MK18 ...65 F5
Courthouse Jun Sch
  SL6.......................202 B8
Courthouse Mews MK16. 22 C4
Courthouse Rd SL6 ....202 C8
Court La
  Burnham SL1 ....197 D2
  Dorney SL4.............204 B3
  Iver SL0.................208 A5
Courtlands
  Leighton Buzzard LU7 ..80 E6
  14 Maidenhead SL6...202 F6
Courtlands Ave SL3 ....206 D2
Court Lawns HP10 .....163 C5
Courtmoor Cl HP27 ....139 C6
Courtneidge Cl LU7 ....78 E8
Courtney Ho UB9 ......189 F5
Court Rd
  Cranfield MK43 ....25 B1
  Maidenhead SL6 ....196 C3
Court The MK17.........37 C3
Courtyard Arts Ctr★
  MK14.....................21 E1
Courtyard Cl HP6 ......154 C1
Courtyards The HP22...117 E4
Courtyard The HP19...101 C1
Courtyard The
  Beaconsfield HP9......175 D2
  7 Bourne End SL8....185 B3
  8 Marlow SL7.........183 D2
  1 Marlow SL7.........183 D2
  22 Windsor SL4.......210 D6
Cousins Cl UB7..........208 E6
Cousins Dr HP20........101 F2
Cousins Piece HP18....112 B2
Coventon Rd HP19.....101 C2
Coverack Pl MK4........57 B8
Coverdale MK13.........34 C5
Coverdale Way SL2 ....197 E1
Covert Cl HP4 ....134 D6
Covert Rd HP4 ....134 D6
Cowdray Cl MK15 ......35 C3
Cow La
  Edlesborough LU6 ......92 E4
  Gawcott MK18.........51 F4
  Tring HP23.............119 D4
Cowleaze OX39 ....147 B6
COWLEY..................201 C1
Cowley Bsns Pk UB8...201 C2
Cowley Cl HP22.........102 B3
Cowley Cotts HP7......164 C3
Cowley Cres UB8.......208 C8
Cowley Mill Rd UB8....201 B3
Cowley Mill Trad Est
  UB8.......................201 B3
COWLEY PEACHEY....208 E8
Cowley Rd UB8..........201 C4
Cowley St Laurence Prim
  CE Sch UB8 ....208 D8
Cowper Cl MK46........22 A4
Cowper & Newton Mus
  The★ MK46............6 F3
Cowper Rd
  Berkhamsted HP4 .....135 B4
  Chesham HP5..........144 B2
  Slough SL2.............198 A1
Cowpers Orch MK46...6 A1
Cowper St MK46........7 A5
COW ROAST............120 B1
Cowslip Cl UB10........201 E5
Cowslip Rd HP15.......162 F6
Coxborrow Cl SL6......195 E2
Coxfield Cl HP14........158 F5
COX GREEN.............202 C3
Cox Green La SL6......202 A3
Cox Green L Ctr SL6...202 A3
Cox Green Rd SL6......202 D3
Cox Green Sch SL6.....202 A4
Coxhill Way HP21......115 D7
Coxwell Cl MK18........41 F1
Coy Ct HP20.............116 A8
Cozens Cl HP18.........125 B7
Crabbe Cres HP5.......144 D2
Crabs Gr HP22..........86 F7
Crab Tree Cl
  Beaconsfield HP9......175 B1
  Olney MK46............6 E5
Crabtree Cotts HP27 ..139 A1
Crabtree La MK17......49 C8
Crabtree Rd HP27 .....127 A5
Craddocks Cl MK13....34 B3
Cradley Wlk HP20......101 E3
CRAFTON.................89 F3
Crafton Pl 4 HP19 ....100 F1
Craigleith Ct HP9......175 D2
Craigmore Ave MK3...57 F8
Craigwell Ave HP21....116 C7
Cranborne Ave MK4....45 E2
Cranbourne Ave SL4 ..209 F5
Cranbourne Cl SL1.....205 C5

Cranbourne Rd SL1 ...205 C5
Cranbrook MK17........49 B5
Cranbrook Dr SL6......195 C1
Crane Cl MK5............34 B1
Cranesbill Pl MK14.....34 E4
Cranes Cl MK43.........8 E5
Crane Way MK43.......25 C2
Cranfield Airport MK43..24 F1
CRANFIELD...............25 B1
Cranfield Innovation Ctr
  MK43.....................37 D8
Cranfield Lower Sch
  MK43.....................25 B1
Cranfield Rd
  Astwood MK16, MK43..16 B2
  Cranfield MK43 ....25 F3
  Moulsoe MK16.........36 E8
  Salford MK17..........37 D5
  Wavendon MK17.......49 B7
Cranfield Tech Pk MK43..37 C8
Cranfield Univ MK43...24 E2
Cranwell Cl MK5........46 B3
Craufurd Ct SL6.........202 E8
Craufurd Rise SL6......202 E8
Craven The MK13......34 C4
Crawford Way 3 MK4..45 D2
Crawley Rd
  Cranfield MK43 ....25 B3
  Woburn MK17..........60 F8
Crawley's La HP23.....133 F1
Crawshays SL6..........203 C8
Crayle St SL2............198 B2
CR Bates Ind Est HP14.158 E5
Creden Cl SL6...........195 D1
Creed St MK12..........33 D7
Creighton Rd HP18.....83 F1
Crendon Rd HP18......112 A1
Crendon St HP13.......173 B7
Creran Wlk LU7........80 C7
Crescent Cotts HP18...83 A6
Crescent Dale SL6......202 F6
Crescent Dr SL6........202 E7
Crescent The
  Cranfield MK43 ....24 E2
  Haversham MK19 .....20 E2
  High Wycombe HP13...173 E8
  Maidenhead SL6 ....202 E7
  Marsworth HP23.......105 A1
  Milton Keynes, Fenny Stratford
    MK2....................47 C1
  Milton Keynes, Giffard Park
    MK14...................21 E2
  Pitstone LU7...........105 C4
  Princes Risborough
    HP27...................139 C3
  Slough SL1.............205 E4
Crescent Villas 5 SL4..210 C6
CRESLOW................87 B8
Creslow Ct MK11.......32 F5
Creslow Way MK17....114 B5
CRESSEX.................172 D4
Cressex Bsns Pk HP12.172 E4
Cressex Cl HP12........172 D3
Cressex Com Sch The
  HP12.....................172 C3
Cressex Ent Ctr HP12 .172 E6
Cressex Link HP11 ....172 D3
Cressex Rd HP12.......172 D3
Cressey Ave MK5.......46 B4
Cressington Ct 2 SL8..185 A4
Cressington Pl SL8.....185 A4
Cress Rd SL1............205 B4
Cresswell Ct TW19.....213 D1
Cresswell Rd HP5......154 D5
Cresswells Mead SL6..203 C1
Cresswell Way HP15...163 D7
Crest Rd HP11..........172 D3
Crest The
  Beaconsfield HP9......175 A1
  Bledlow Ridge HP14 ..159 F8
Creswell Row SL7......183 D2
Creswick Mdw HP21...116 A5
Crew Curve HP4........134 F7
Cricketers Row MK18...66 A4
Cricketfield Rd UB7....208 C2
Cricket Field Rd UB8...201 D4
Cricket Green Rdbt MK9. 35 B4
Cricket Ground HP14...158 D5
Cricklebeck MK13......34 B5
Crimp Hill SL4...........211 A1
Crispin Cl HP9..........175 C4
Crispin Field LU7 .....105 C4
Crispin Rd MK13........34 B7
Crispin Way
  Farnham Common SL2..198 D8
  High Wycombe HP11...173 A4
  Uxbridge UB8..........208 F8
Crisp Rd RG9...........191 C3
Criss Gr SL9.............177 C1
Crocketts La HP16.....142 D5
Crocus Dr HP21.........115 B5
Croft Cnr SL4...........211 A2
Croft Ct 5 HP21........115 E7
Croft Ctyd HP17........126 F6
Crofters SL4.............211 A1
Crofters Cl TW19.......213 D1
Croft Gn LU6............93 F8
Crofthill Rd SL2.........198 B1
Croft Ho SL0............207 E7

Croft Mdws LU7........105 A7
Crofton Ho HP11.......174 A4
Croft Rd
  Aylesbury HP21.......115 E7
  Chalfont St Peter SL9 ..177 E1
CROFTS END.............14 A1
Crofts End MK16........14 A1
Crofts La MK17.........57 D3
Croft The
  Haddenham HP17......126 F5
  Maidenhead SL6 ....202 C5
  Marlow SL7............184 A3
Croftwood HP13........173 F7
Cromarty Ct MK3......46 E3
Cromer Cl HP4..........121 C5
Cromer Ct SL1..........205 E7
Cromhamstone HP17...114 D5
Cromwell Ave
  Aylesbury HP19........101 D2
  Newport Pagnell MK16 ..22 A3
  Thame OX9............126 A1
Cromwell Cl HP8........177 C7
Cromwell Ct MK18......41 E2
Cromwell Dr SL1........205 E2
Cromwell Gdns 10 SL7.183 E2
Cromwell Ho
  Chesham HP5..........144 B1
  Uxbridge UB8..........201 C4
Cromwell Mews 1
  HP19.....................115 A8
Cromwell Rd
  High Wycombe HP13...173 E5
  Maidenhead SL6 ....202 D7
  Marlow SL7............183 E2
Cropredy Ct MK18......41 E2
Cropton Rise MK4......46 A2
Cropwell Bishop MK4..46 C1
Crosby Cl HP9..........186 F8
Crosby Ct MK8..........45 E6
Crosland Rd HP21......116 B6
Cross Ct HP13..........161 D2
Cross End MK17........48 F7
Cross Farm Mews HP3 .146 D2
Crossfield Cl HP4.......134 F4
Crossfield Ho SL9......188 E7
Crossfield Rd HP27 ...139 C4
Crosshills MK11..........32 D4
Cross La
  Beaconsfield HP9......186 F8
  Tingewick MK18.......51 B6
  Weston Underwood MK46..6 B2
Crosslands MK14.......34 E8
Cross Lanes
  Bledlow HP27..........138 A2
  Chalfont St Peter SL9 ..177 F5
Cross Lanes Cl SL9....177 F5
Crossleys HP8...........177 C7
Crosslow Bank MK4....46 C3
Cross Mdw HP5.........143 F2
Cross Oak SL4...........210 A5
Cross Oak Rd HP4......135 A4
Cross Rd
  High Wycombe HP12...172 C6
  Uxbridge UB8..........201 C5
Cross St
  Newport Pagnell MK16 ..22 C4
  Uxbridge UB8..........201 C5
Cross Tree Rd MK19...31 B3
Crossway HP5...........144 E1
Crossways
  Beaconsfield HP9......175 F1
  Berkhamsted HP4 .....134 F3
  High Wycombe HP12...172 C4
Crossways Bsns Pk
  HP18.....................83 C3
Crossways Ct 4 SL4...210 C5
Crossway The UB10....201 F3
Crosthwaite Way SL1 ..204 D8
Crowborough La MK7 ...48 A8
Crowbrook Rd HP27....139 C6
CROWELL.................147 B4
CROWELL HILL.........147 D2
Crowell Mews HP19....114 F8
Crowell Rd OX39.......147 B5
CROWFIELD..............26 F1
Crow La MK17..........49 B8
Crown Bsns Est HP5...144 C1
Crown Cl SL3............212 C7
Crown Cotts
  Botley HP5..............155 B8
  Windsor SL4 ....210 D3
Crown Ct HP14.........161 A2
CROWNFIELD............149 B4
Crownfield HP27........149 C3
CROWNHILL..............45 E7
Crownhill Rdbt MK8....45 E8
Crown House Sch
  HP11.....................173 C6
Crown La
  East Burnham SL2.....198 A4
  High Wycombe HP11...173 B6
  Maidenhead SL6 ....203 A7
  Marlow SL7............183 D2
  Penn HP10.............174 F7
Crown Leys HP20......101 E1
Crown Mdw SL3........212 B7
Crown Rd SL7...........183 D2
Crown Rose Ct HP23...119 A3
Crown Way UB7........208 F5

Crown Wlk
  Milton Keynes MK9 ....34 E3
  Uxbridge UB8..........201 C5
Crow Piece La SL2 .....197 F4
Crowther Ct MK5.......46 E3
Croxley Ct 3 LU7......80 F8
Croxley Rise SL6.......202 D6
Croydon Cl MK4........46 C3
Cruickshank Gr MK8...45 E7
Crummock Cl SL1......204 C3
Crummock Pl MK2......58 D6
Crusader Est HP12.....172 D5
Crutches La HP9........176 E4
CRYERS HILL...........162 D6
Cryers Hill La HP15....162 D6
Cryers Hill Rd HP15...162 C6
Cuba Cotts SL6.........196 B3
Cubb Field HP19........115 B7
CUBLINGTON.............78 B1
Cublington Rd HP22...88 D6
Cuckoo Hill Rise MK19.. 10 F2
Cuckoo Way HP19 .....114 F8
CUDDINGTON............113 A2
Cuddington & Dinton CE
  Sch (Inf) HP18.........112 F3
Cuddington & Dinton CE
  Sch (Jun) HP17........113 F3
Cuddington Hill HP18..112 E3
Cuddington Rd HP17,
  HP18.....................113 E3
Cudsdens Ct HP16.....152 D7
Cuff La MK17............59 D1
Culbertson La MK13...33 E6
Culham Dr SL6..........195 E2
Cullen Pl MK2...........58 D5
Cullern's Pass SL6.....202 F6
Culley Way SL6.........202 A4
Cullyn Rd HP12........172 C5
Culmstock Cl MK4......46 D2
Culrain Pl MK12........33 C4
Culross Gr MK10.......36 A2
Culvers Croft HP9......176 C4
Culvert La UB8..........201 B3
Culverton Hill HP27...139 B3
Culverton La HP27.....139 B1
Cumberland Ave SL2 ..198 C1
Cumberland Cl
  Aylesbury HP21........116 B7
  Little Chalfont HP7....166 B8
Cumbrae Cl SL2........206 A5
Cumbria Cl
  Maidenhead SL6 ....202 C4
  Milton Keynes MK3 ....46 F1
Cumbrian Way
  High Wycombe HP13...172 F8
  Uxbridge UB8..........201 D5
Curfew Yd The 2 SL4..210 D6
Curlew HP19.............101 F3
Curlew Cl
  Berkhamsted HP4 .....135 C3
  High Wycombe HP13...161 C2
Curls La SL6.............202 E4
Curls Rd SL6............202 D4
Curran Cl UB8..........201 C1
Currier Dr MK14........34 F6
Curriers La SL1.........197 D7
Cursley Path 11 HP19..115 A8
Curtis Cotts HP5.......144 F7
Curtis Croft MK5.......46 B3
Curtis Way HP4........135 D3
Curzon Ave
  Beaconsfield HP9......175 D4
  Tylers Green HP15....163 C2
Curzon CE Comb Sch
  HP7.......................164 A5
Curzon Cl HP15........163 C2
Curzon Gate Ct HP14..158 E5
Curzon Mall 6 SL1....205 F4
Curzon Pl MK7..........48 E4
Cushing Dr 7 MK4....45 E2
Cutler's Ct 6 HP12....172 E7
Cutlers Mews MK14....34 F6
Cut Throat Ave HP4....107 E7
Cuttle Brook Gdns OX9 125 E1
Cyclamen Pl HP21.....115 B5
Cygnet Ho SL6..........196 C1
Cypress MK16...........22 A3
Cypress Ho SL3.........207 B1
Cypress Wlk HP15.....163 B3

D

Daceberry Ct RG9......192 C2
Dacre Rd HP22.........131 E7
Dadbrook HP18.........112 F2
Dadbrook Ho HP18 ....112 F2
Dadfield Cl HP18........112 F2
DADFORD.................28 D1
Dadford Rd MK18......28 D5
Dag La MK16............12 A7
Dagmar Rd SL4.........210 D5
DAGNALL.................107 C6
Dagnall Cres UB8......208 C8
Dagnall Cty Fst Sch
  HP4.......................107 C5
Dagnall Rd
  Olney MK46............6 E3
  Whipsnade LU6........93 D2

Dair House Sch SL2....198 B4
Dairy La RG9....192 B8
Dairymede HP27....150 C4
Daisy Cotts HP14....171 B4
Dalby Gdns 7 SL6....195 F1
Dale Cl NN13....38 A7
Dale Ct SL1....205 C4
Dalegarth Way MK10....36 C3
Dalesford Rd HP21....116 A4
Dale Side SL9....188 E2
Dalgin Pl MK9....35 A3
Dalston Cl HP20....101 F2
Dalston End MK10....35 E1
Dalton Gate MK10....35 F4
Dalton Gn 15 SL3....206 F1
Dalvina Pl MK12....33 D4
Dalwood Mews 3 HP19....115 A8
Daly Way HP20....116 B7
Damask Cl HP23....119 C4
Damson Gr SL1....205 C4
Danbury Ct MK14....34 E5
Dancers End La HP22, HP23....118 C2
Dancersend Wildlife Reserve★ HP23....132 C8
Dandridge Cl SL3....206 D2
Dandridge Ct MK8....45 C6
Dandridge Dr SL8....185 C3
Dane Cl HP7....165 F6
Dane Ct HP21....115 D4
Dane Rd MK1....47 E2
Danesborough Dr MK17....49 A2
Danesbrook Cl MK4....46 D4
Danes Ct SL6....202 D7
Danesfield Sch SL7....193 E7
Danes Gdns SL6....195 F6
Daneswood MK17....49 A1
Daniels Welch MK6....47 A6
Dansteed Way
Milton Keynes, Bradwell Common MK8, MK13, MK14, MK15....34 C4
Milton Keynes, Crownhill MK8....45 D7
Danvers Croft HP23....119 C5
Darby Cl
Milton Keynes MK5....46 B5
Milton Keynes MK13....34 C2
Darby Lodge HP13....174 A7
Darie Cl 3 SL1....205 A4
Darin Ct MK8....45 F8
Dark La
Chearsley HP18....112 B2
Oving HP22....86 C7
Wingrave HP22....88 C2
Darley Cl HP21....116 B6
Darley Gate MK14....35 A5
Darley's Cl HP18....83 A6
Darling's La SL6....194 E1
Darlington Cl HP6....154 D1
Darnel Cl MK6....47 A5
Darrell Cl SL3....206 F2
Darr's La HP4....134 D6
Darsham Wlk HP5....154 B8
Dart Cl
Aylesbury HP21....115 C5
Newport Pagnell MK16....22 D4
Slough SL3....212 B8
Dartington Pl 2 MK4....45 F1
Dartmouth Ct 10 SL1....205 F3
Dartmouth Rd MK46....6 F4
Darvell Dr HP5....144 A2
Darvells Yd WD3....167 D5
Darville Ho 19 SL4....210 D6
Darvill Rd HP17....114 B5
DARVILLSHILL....150 A4
Darvill's La SL1....205 D4
Darvills Mdw HP15....163 C7
Darwin Cl MK5....45 E5
Darwin Rd SL3....206 F4
Dashfield Gr HP15....162 F6
Dashwood Ave HP12....172 D7
Dashwood Cl SL3....206 C2
Dashwood Works Ind Est HP12....172 D7
DATCHET....211 C6
Datchet Ho 3 SL1....205 F3
Datchet Lodge Ctyd SL3....211 B6
Datchet Pl SL3....211 B6
Datchet Rd
Eton SL4....205 F2
Horton SL3....211 F4
Old Windsor SL4....211 A3
Windsor SL4....210 D7
Datchet St Mary's CE Prim Sch SL3....211 B6
Datchet Sta SL3....211 B6
Daubeney Gate MK5....45 F6
Davenies Sch HP9....175 E2
Davenport Lea MK7....48 E5
Davenport Rd HP12....172 C3
Daventry Cl SL3....212 F6
David Bishop Ct HP5....154 D5
David Cl HP21....116 A4
Davidge Pl HP9....175 C5
David Rd SL3....212 F5
Davidson Rd 6 SL3....206 F1
Davies Cl HP20....115 D8
Davies Ct HP12....172 D5
Davies Way HP10....174 C1
Davis Cl SL7....183 E1
Davis Gr MK4....45 E3
Davis Ho 3 HP4....135 C3
Davison Ct MK8....45 D6
Davy Ave MK5....46 D6
Dawes Cl HP5....154 B7
Dawe's Cl UB10....201 E3
Dawes East Rd SL1....197 C2
Dawes La WD3....156 F3
Dawes Moor Cl SL2....206 C7
Dawe's Rd UB10....201 E3
Dawley Ride SL3....212 E6
Dawney Cl HP19....101 C2
Dawn Redwood Cl SL3....212 A4
Daws Ct SL0....207 F7
Daws Hill La HP11....173 A4
Daws Lea HP11....173 B3
Dawson Cl SL4....210 A5
Dawson Rd MK1....47 D3
Daylesford Ct MK15....35 B5
Daylesford Gr SL1....204 F4
Deacon Cl HP12....172 B4
Deacon Ct SL4....209 D5
Deacon Pl MK10....35 F3
Deadhearn La HP8....166 E1
Deal Ave SL1....204 F7
Deanacre Cl SL9....177 E4
Dean Cl
Aylesbury HP21....116 A5
High Wycombe HP12....172 E6
Uxbridge UB10....201 F5
Windsor SL4....209 D4
Deancroft Rd SL9....177 E4
Dean Farm La LU7....69 E4
Deanfield HP14....160 B8
Dean Field HP3....146 A4
Deanfield Ave RG9....191 D1
Deanfield Cl
Marlow SL7....183 D2
Saunderton HP14....149 C1
Deanfield Rd RG9....191 D1
Dean Forest Way MK10....36 A5
Deangarden Rise HP11....173 E4
Dean La SL6....195 C8
Dean Rd LU7....68 B2
Deans Cl
Amersham HP6....154 F2
Tring HP23....119 A4
Wexham Street SL2....199 B4
Dean's Cloisters SL4....210 D7
Deansfield Cl SL6....195 D2
Deans Furlong HP23....119 A4
DEANSHANGER....31 D4
Deanshanger Dr NN12....17 F1
Deanshanger Prim Sch MK19....31 E3
Deanshanger Rd
Old Stratford MK19....32 B6
Wicken MK19....31 B3
Deans Lawn HP4....135 C4
Deans Mdw HP4....107 C5
Dean's Rd MK12....33 C7
Dean St SL7....183 D2
Deansway HP5....144 B2
Dean The HP22....89 B3
Dean View SL6....195 D6
Dean Way
Aston Clinton HP22....117 F4
Chalfont St Giles HP8....177 B7
Holmer Green HP15....163 B6
Dean Wood Rd HP9....176 D2
Dearing Cl 11 HP20....101 F2
Debbs Cl MK11....32 E5
Deben Cl MK16....22 E3
Decies Way SL2....199 A4
De Clare Ct MK18....41 E1
Dedmere Ct SL7....183 F2
Dedmere Rd SL7....183 F2
Dedmere Rise SL7....183 E2
DEDWORTH....209 E6
Dedworth Dr SL4....209 F6
Dedworth Green Fst Sch SL4....209 E5
Dedworth Manor SL4....209 F6
Dedworth Mid Sch SL4....209 E6
Dedworth Rd SL4....209 D5
Deeds Gr HP12....172 E5
Deena Cl SL1....204 E6
Deep Acres HP6....154 A3
Deepdale MK13....34 C5
Deep Field SL3....211 B7
Deep Mill La HP16....152 D3
Deerfern Cl MK14....21 E1
Deerfield Cl MK18....52 E7
Deermead HP16....152 B4
Deer Park Wlk HP5....144 E3
Deerswood SL6....196 A1
Deer Wlk MK9....34 F3
Deethe Cl MK17....49 B6
De Havilland Dr HP15....162 E2
De Havilland Way TW19....213 E1
Delafield Cl HP14....158 F4
Delaford Cl SL0....207 F7
Delaford Ho UB7....208 D5
Delahay Rise HP4....135 B6
Delamere Cl HP20....101 F2
Delamere Gdns LU7....80 C7
Delaware Dr
Milton Keynes MK15....35 B8
Tongwell MK15, MK16....22 B1
Delius Cl MK7....48 C4
Dell Cl
Chesham HP5....143 F2
Farnham Common SL2....198 C7
Dellfield HP5....144 A2
Dell Field HP16....151 C5
Dell Field Ave HP4....135 B6
Dellfield Cl HP4....135 A6
Dellfield Cres UB8....201 C1
Dellfield Par UB8....201 C1
Dell Lees HP9....176 C4
Dell Rd
Berkhamsted HP4....134 D7
West Drayton UB7....208 F3
Dells MK46....6 F4
Dellside UB9....190 C6
Dell The
Aylesbury HP20....102 A2
Chalfont St Peter SL9....177 E4
Maidenhead SL6....202 A2
Stokenchurch HP14....158 F3
Tylers Green HP10....163 C1
Uxbridge UB8....201 C6
Delmeade Rd HP5....154 A7
Deltic Ave MK13....34 B2
Demoram Cl MK18....65 F3
Denbigh East Ind Est MK1....47 D2
Denbigh Hall MK3....46 F3
Denbigh Hall Dr MK3....46 F3
Denbigh Hall Ind Est MK3....46 F3
Denbigh Rd
Milton Keynes MK1....47 B2
Thame OX9....126 A1
Denbigh Rdbt MK1....47 C2
Denbigh Sch MK5....46 A6
Denbigh Way MK2....47 C1
Denbigh West Ind Est MK1....47 B2
Denby Walk HP20....116 A8
Denchworth Ct 2 MK4....46 C2
Dene Cl
Winslow MK18....66 A3
Woburn Sands MK17....49 C4
Dene The MK18....63 D3
Denewood HP13....173 E8
DENHAM
Denham Green....190 A2
Quainton....85 D5
Denham Aerodrome UB9....189 E6
Denham Ave UB9....189 F3
Denham Cl
Denham UB9....190 A1
Maidenhead SL6....202 C6
Milton Keynes MK3....57 D8
Denham Court Dr UB9....190 B1
Denham Ctry Park Nature Reserve★ UB9....190 B2
Denham Ctry Pk★ UB9....190 B2
Denham Garden Village UB9....189 F5
Denham Golf Club Sta UB9....189 D4
DENHAM GREEN....189 E5
Denham Green Cl UB9....190 A4
Denham Green La UB9....189 F5
Denham La SL9....178 A2
Denham Lodge UB9....201 C6
Denham Quarry Park Nature Reserve★ UB9....190 C1
Denham Rd
Iver Heath SL0....200 E5
Lane End HP14....171 C5
Denham Sta UB9....190 A4
Denham View MK18....75 F6
Denham Village Inf Sch UB9....189 F2
Denham Way UB9....190 A1
Denham Way (North Orbital Rd)
Denham Green UB9....189 F7
Maple Cross WD3....178 E4
Denham Wlk SL9....177 F4
Denholme Lodge SL3....211 B7
Denison Ct MK7....48 D6
Denmark St
Maidenhead SL6....202 E8
Milton Keynes MK2....58 E8
Denmead MK8....33 E2
Denmead Cl SL9....188 E4
DENNER HILL....150 E4
Dennis Cl HP22....118 A4
Denniston Ho HP12....172 C8
Dennis Way SL1....204 D6
Denny Rd SL3....206 F2
Denny's La HP4....134 F2
Denton Ct SL7....183 F3
De Pirenore HP15....162 E2
Depot Rd SL6....203 A6
Derby Arms 2 HP20....115 D8
Derby Rd UB8....201 D3
Derehams Ave HP10....174 C3
Derehams La HP10....174 C2
Derek Rd SL6....203 C8
Dere Pl MK2....58 E4
Deri Dene Cl 2 TW19....213 E1
Derwent Cl
Little Chalfont HP7....166 B8
Newport Pagnell MK16....22 D4
Derwent Dr
Maidenhead SL6....202 D8
Milton Keynes MK3....57 E8
Slough SL1....204 C8
Derwent Rd
Aylesbury HP21....116 B6
Leighton Buzzard LU7....80 B7
Desborough Ave HP11....172 F6
Desborough Bsns Pk HP12....172 E8
Desborough Cres SL6....202 D5
Desborough Gn 1 HP20....101 D2
Desborough Ho 14 HP13....173 B7
Desborough Park Rd HP12....172 E8
Desborough Rd HP11....172 F7
Desborough Sch SL6....202 E5
Desborough St HP11....172 F7
Deseronto Wharf Ind Est SL3....206 E4
Develin Cl MK14....34 F7
Devereux Pl
Aylesbury HP19....101 A2
Milton Keynes MK6....46 F7
Devereux Rd SL4....210 D5
Deverill Rd HP21....115 C3
Deverills Way SL3....207 C2
Devon Ave SL1....205 C7
Devon Cl MK3....46 F1
Devon Rd HP19....101 A3
Devonshire Ave HP6....154 B2
Devonshire Cl
Amersham HP6....154 C2
Farnham Royal SL2....198 B3
Devonshire Gn SL2....198 B3
Devonshire Lodge 10 SL6....202 F6
Devon Way UB10....201 F3
Dewar Spur SL3....211 B8
Dexter Ave MK6....46 F8
Dexter Ho MK6....46 F8
Dhoon Rise SL6....202 F6
Diamond Rd SL1....206 A4
Diana Cl SL3....206 E7
Diane Cl HP21....116 A4
Diane Wlk HP21....116 A4
Dibden Hill HP8....177 C6
Dickens Cl MK43....3 F6
Dickens Dr MK19....32 B6
Dickens Pl SL3....212 E6
Dickens Rd MK12....33 C8
Dickens Spinney MK46....6 E4
Dickens Way HP19....100 F2
Dickins Pl SL3....212 E6
Dicks Way HP19....100 F3
Diddington Cl MK2....58 C3
Digby Cl OX9....126 B1
Digby Croft MK10....35 E3
DIGGS....126 F5
Dilwyn Ct 1 HP12....172 E7
Dingle Dell LU7....70 F2
Dingledery MK46....6 F4
Dinmore 2 HP3....145 F3
DINTON....113 F2
Disraeli Cres HP13....161 F1
Disraeli Ct SL3....212 B8
Disraeli Pk HP9....175 D4
Disraeli Sch The HP13....161 F1
Disraeli Sq 4 HP19....115 A8
Diswell Brook Way MK19....31 E5
DITCHFIELD....171 A3
Ditchfield Cotts HP14....171 A3
Ditchingham Cl HP19....115 B7
Ditton Park Cvn Site SL3....206 F1
Ditton Park Rd SL3....211 E8
Ditton Rd
Datchet SL3....211 D7
Slough SL3....211 F8
Dixie Ct HP20....116 A8
Dixie La MK7....48 C6
Dixon Ct HP21....115 B6
Dobbins La HP22....131 B5
Dobson's La RG9....191 C8
Docton Mill 3 MK4....45 E2
Doctor's Commons Rd HP4....135 B4
Doddsfield Rd SL2....198 A2
Dodds La HP8....177 B8
Dodkin MK6....47 B5
Dodman Gn MK4....57 B8
Doggetts Farm Rd UB9....189 C4
Doggetts Wood Cl HP8....166 B6
Doggetts Wood La HP8....166 B5
Dog Kennel La WD3....167 F5
Dolben Ct MK15....35 D8
Dolesden La RG9....169 D1
Dollicot HP17....126 F6
Dolphin Ct
Loudwater HP11....174 A3
Slough SL1....206 B4
Dolphin Pl HP21....115 E6
Dolphin Rd SL1....206 B4
Dolphin Sq 2 HP23....119 A3
Donkey Dr SL8....185 A3
Donkey La
Bourne End SL8....185 A3
Tring HP23....118 E2
West Drayton UB7....208 C2
Donnay Cl SL9....188 D5
Donnington MK13....34 B6
Donnington Gdns SL6....195 F1
Donnybrook Ho 3 HP13....173 C7
Don The MK3....46 D1
Doon Way MK2....58 C5
Dorchester Ave MK3....47 A2
Dorchester Cl
Maidenhead SL6....195 B1
Stoke Mandeville HP22....116 B2
Dorchester Ho SL9....188 F6
Doreen Cl MK2....58 C7
Dorian Cl HP23....119 D4
Dorking Pl MK5....46 B4
Dormans Cl MK10....36 A2
Dormer Ave LU7....79 E3
Dormer Cl HP21....115 B6
Dormer Ct 4 HP20....101 F2
Dormer La HP15....163 B7
Dornels SL2....206 C7
DORNEY....204 C3
Dorney Comb Sch SL6....203 F3
Dorney Court★ SL4....204 B3
Dorney End HP5....144 A1
Dorney Hill N SL1, HP9....187 A4
Dorney Hill S SL2....187 A4
Dorney Lake Pk★ SL4....209 B8
Dorney Pl MK13....34 C3
DORNEY REACH....203 F3
Dorney Reach Rd SL6....203 F3
Dorneywood Gdn★ SL1....197 D6
Dorney Wood Rd
Burnham SL1....197 D6
Littleworth Common SL1....186 C1
Dorrells Rd HP27....138 D6
Dorrien's Croft HP4....134 F7
Dorset Cl
Berkhamsted HP4....134 F5
Milton Keynes MK3....46 F1
Dorset Lodge 9 SL6....202 F6
Dorset Pl HP21....116 C6
Dorset Rd SL4....210 C6
Dorset Way UB10....201 F3
Dorsey Cl MK8....45 E6
DORTON....96 F1
Dorton Cl MK8....33 F1
Dorton Rd HP18....111 B4
Douglas Ct SL7....184 A3
Douglas Gdns HP4....135 A5
Douglas La TW19....211 F1
Douglas Pl MK6....46 E8
Douglas Rd
Aylesbury HP20....102 A1
Slough SL2....205 D8
Stanwell TW19....213 D1
Doune Ho MK3....46 F2
Dove Cl
Aylesbury HP21....115 C5
Buckingham MK18....52 E7
Newport Pagnell MK16....22 D4
Dovecote
Haddenham HP17....126 F6
Newport Pagnell MK16....22 C4
Dovecote Cft MK14....21 E1
Dovecote Cl
Haddenham HP17....126 F6
Monks Risborough HP27....139 C5
Dovecote Cotts MK5....46 A4
Dovecot Rd 11 HP13....173 A7
Dove Ct HP9....175 D3
Dove Ho HP19....101 F4
Dove House Cl
Edlesborough LU6....92 F4
Winslow MK18....66 A4
Dove House Cres SL2....197 E2
Dovehouse Mews MK16....12 B6
Dovehouse Rd 3 HP11....173 A7
Doveleat OX39....147 D7
Dove Pk WD3....167 B4
Dover Cl LU7....105 D2
Dover Gate MK3....57 F8
Dover Hedge HP21....116 C7
Dover Rd SL1....204 F7
Dove St LU7....78 E8
Dovetail Cl HP12....172 D8
Dowding Rd UB10....201 F5
Dower Cl HP9....175 C5
Dower Mews 5 HP4....135 C4
Dower Pk SL4....209 E3
Downdean MK6....47 A8
Downderry Croft MK4....57 B8
Downer Cl MK18....52 F8
Downer Dr WD3....156 F3

Downham Rd MK17 49 C4
DOWNHEAD PARK 35 B5
Downing Cl MK3 58 B8
Downing Path SL2 197 E1
Downings Wood WD3 178 D5
Downland MK8 33 E2
DOWNLEY 161 C3
Downley Ave MK13 34 C3
Downley Ct HP13 161 D2
Downley Rd HP14 161 D6
Downley Sch The HP13 161 D3
Down Pl SL4 209 A8
DOWNS BARN 35 A5
Downs Barn Bvd MK14 34 F5
Downs Barn Rdbt MK14 34 F5
Downs Barn Sch MK14 34 F5
Downs Field MK16 22 F3
Downs Pk HP13 161 E2
Downs Rd SL3 206 D4
Downs View MK17 48 C2
Downs Villas 17 HP23 119 A3
Dragon Tail HP17 127 A5
Drake Ave SL3 206 D2
Drake Cl HP21 115 B6
Drakeloe Cl MK17 60 F8
Drakes Dr HP18 125 E5
Drakes Farm HP18 125 E5
Drakes Mews MK8 45 F7
Drake's Rd HP7 165 E8
Drakewell Rd MK17 48 D1
Draymans La SL7 183 D1
DRAYTON BEAUCHAMP 118 B5
Drayton Ct UB7 208 F2
Drayton Gdns UB7 208 E4
Drayton Park Sch MK2 58 D5
DRAYTON PARSLOW 68 C6
Drayton Parslow Village Sch MK17 68 C6
Drayton Rd
Aylesbury HP20 101 D2
Milton Keynes MK2 58 C5
Newton Longville MK17 57 C2
Dr Challoner's Gram Sch HP6 154 C1
Dr Challoner's High Sch HP7 166 B7
Dresser Rd HP16 151 C5
Drew Ct MK3 47 A4
Drew Mdw SL2 198 C8
Drews Pk HP9 175 C6
Drey The SL9 177 E5
Drift Rd SL4 209 A1
Drift Way
Colnbrook SL3 212 C7
Olney MK46 6 F5
Drinkwater Cl OX25 95 D7
Drive The
Amersham HP7 154 D1
Bourne End SL8 184 F4
Chalfont St Peter SL9 177 F3
Cranfield MK43 24 D2
Datchet SL3 211 B6
Ickenham UB10 190 E1
Ivinghoe Aston LU7 92 A1
Slough SL3 206 E4
Wraysbury TW19 211 D2
Dropmore Inf Sch SL1 186 C1
Dropmore Rd
Burnham SL1 197 C5
Littleworth Common SL1 186 C1
Drovers Croft MK12 33 B4
Drovers La RG9 169 B2
Drovers Way
Dunstable LU6 93 F8
Newton Longville MK17 57 D2
Seer Green HP9 176 C4
Druce End NN12 18 E6
Druids Wlk OX39 147 C6
Drummond Ho 4 SL4 210 D4
Drummond Ride HP23 119 A5
Drummound Hay MK15 35 C7
Drydell La HP5 153 F8
Dryden Cl
Aylesbury HP20 101 E2
Newport Pagnell MK16 22 A4
Duchess Gdns NN12 18 D3
Duchess Gr MK7 48 C7
Duchess St SL1 204 E5
DUCK END
Akeley 42 A8
Swanbourne 66 F4
Duck End
Aylesbury HP20 115 C8
Great Brickhill MK17 59 D1
Duck La
Ludgershall HP18 96 C8
Woburn MK17 60 F7
Duck Lake MK18 41 E3
Duck Lake Cl MK18 41 E4
Duckmore La HP23 118 E2
Duck Sq OX39 147 C6
Duckworth Ct MK6 46 E7
Dudley Cl MK18 76 A2
Dudley Ct SL1 206 A3
Dudley Hill MK5 46 A6
Dudley Ho 1 HP3 146 A4
Dudley La RG9 181 A6
DUDSWELL 134 D8
Dudswell La HP4 134 D7
Duffield La SL2 198 F6
Duffield Pk SL2 199 A2
Dukes Ave LU6 107 E8
Dukes Cl
Gerrards Cross SL9 188 E3
Shabbington HP18 124 C2
Dukes Dr
Farnham Common SL2 198 A8
Milton Keynes MK2 47 C1
Dukes Kiln Dr SL9 188 C3
Dukes La SL9 188 E4
Dukes Mdw SL8 185 B3
Dukes Piece MK18 52 F8
Dukes Pl
Marlow SL7 183 D2
Slough SL1 205 F6
Dukes Ride
Gerrards Cross SL9 188 E3
Ickenham UB10 201 E8
Leighton Buzzard LU7 70 F3
Dukes Row HP18 99 A1
Duke St
Aspley Guise MK17 49 D4
Eton SL4 210 C7
Henley-on-Thames RG9 191 E2
High Wycombe HP13 173 C6
Princes Risborough HP27 139 B4
Dukes Valley SL9 188 B2
Dukes Way
Berkhamsted HP4 135 A6
Uxbridge UB8 201 C4
Dukes Wood Ave SL9 188 E3
Dukes Wood Dr SL9 188 D3
Dulverton Ct LU7 80 C8
Dulverton Dr MK4 46 D3
Dulwich Cl MK16 22 C2
Dumbletons WD3 178 E6
Dumfries Cl MK3 46 F3
Dunbar Cl
Milton Keynes MK3 57 D8
Slough SL2 206 A6
Dunbar Dr OX9 126 A1
Duncan Gr MK5 45 F6
Duncan Lock Ho HP9 175 F2
Duncannon Cres SL4 209 D4
Duncan Rd MK43 24 E2
Dunchurch Dale MK7 48 B5
Duncombe Cl HP6 154 E1
Duncombe Rd HP4 134 E6
Duncombe St MK2 58 C7
Duncroft SL4 209 F4
Dundale Prim Sch HP23 119 A5
Dundale Rd HP23 119 A4
Dundee Rd SL1 205 A8
Dungeness Ct MK4 46 A1
Dungrovehill La SL7 194 D3
Dunholme End SL6 202 D3
Dunkeld Ho HP11 174 B4
Dunkery Beacon MK4 46 D3
Dunnet Cl MK4 57 A8
Dunny La WD4 156 F7
Dunsby Rd MK6 47 A4
Dunsham La HP20 101 E2
Dunsley Pl HP23 119 B3
DUNSMORE 141 A7
Dunsmore Ave HP27 139 C5
Dunsmore Ride HP27 139 C5
DUNSTABLE 93 E8
Dunstable Downs★ LU6 93 E4
Dunstable Ho 4 SL7 183 E1
Dunstable Rd
Dagnall HP4 107 C7
Eaton Bray LU6 93 A5
Totternhoe LU6 93 D7
Dunster Ct MK4 46 E3
Dunster Gdns SL1 205 A6
Dunston Hill HP23 119 A4
Dunthorne Way MK8 45 D6
DUNTON 77 E5
Dunton Rd LU7 78 D6
Dunvedin Pl MK12 33 D4
Dunvegan Cl MK2 58 D4
Dunwood Ct SL6 202 C5
Dunwood Rise HP13 162 B1
Duparc Cl MK7 48 C5
Dupre Cl SL1 204 E4
Dupre Cres HP9 176 B1
Du Pre Wlk HP10 185 D4
Durgate MK7 48 A8
Durham Ave SL1 205 A7
Durham Ho 1 MK3 46 F1
Durley Hollow HP13 162 B1
Durlston End MK4 57 A8
Durrans Ct MK2 47 E1
Durrans Ho MK2 47 E1
Durrants La HP4 134 F5
Durrants Path HP5 144 A4
Durrants Rd HP4 134 F5
Durrell Cl LU7 80 E7
Dutch Barn Cl TW19 213 D1
Dutch Elm Ave SL4 210 F7
Dutton Way SL0 207 E7
Dyersdale MK13 34 C5
Dyers Mews MK14 34 F6
Dyers Rd LU6 92 D7
Dymock Ct HP22 85 B4
Dyson Cl SL4 210 B4

E

Eagle Cl HP6 154 F2
Eagles Rd HP20 116 A8
EAGLESTONE 47 B7
Eaglestone Rdbt MK6 47 A8
Eagle Way MK43 3 F6
Eagle Wlk MK9 34 F3
EAKLEY LANES 4 D2
Ealing Chase MK10 47 F8
Eames Cl HP20 101 F3
Eardley Pl MK8 45 D6
Earl Cl HP13 162 A1
Earl Howe Rd HP15 163 D6
Earls Cl MK2 58 C8
Earlsfield SL6 203 C2
Earls La SL1 204 F5
Earls Willow MK13 34 A8
Earlswood Cl HP21 116 A5
Easby Gr MK10 36 A1
Eascote Rd HP21 116 B4
EASINGTON 111 B1
Easington La HP18 111 B1
Easington Terr HP18 111 B1
East Berkshire Coll
Slough SL3 207 A3
Windsor SL4 210 C5
Eastbourne Rd SL1 205 A7
Eastbridge SL2 206 B5
Eastbrook Cl OX25 95 E7
EAST BURNHAM 198 A4
East Burnham Cotts SL2 198 A4
East Burnham La SL2 198 A4
Eastbury Ct MK4 46 D1
East Chapel MK4 57 B8
EAST CLAYDON 74 E8
East Claydon Rd MK18 65 D2
East Claydon Sch MK18 74 E7
East Comm SL9 188 E5
East Cres SL4 209 F6
Eastcroft SL2 198 B1
East Dales MK13 34 C5
East Dr
High Wycombe HP13 173 E8
Stoke Poges SL2 198 E2
EAST END
Cranfield 25 C1
North Crawley 24 F6
East End HP22 87 D1
Eastergate HP9 175 C4
Eastern Dene HP15 163 B5
Eastern Dr SL8 185 C4
Eastern St HP20 101 E1
Eastfield Cl 3 SL1 206 A3
Eastfield Cres NN12 18 F5
Eastfield Dr MK19 11 A3
Eastfield Rd
Aylesbury HP20 116 B8
Burnham SL1 204 A8
Princes Risborough HP27 139 C3
East Green Cl MK5 45 F6
East Hills MK43 25 B1
East La MK7 47 F7
Eastlands HP27 149 E5
Eastnor HP3 146 A3
Eastoke Pl MK4 57 A8
Easton St HP11 173 B6
Easton Terr HP13 173 C6
East Paddock SL6 194 F6
East Rd
Cranfield MK43 24 E2
Maidenhead SL6 202 E7
West Drayton UB7 208 F2
East Richardson St 5 HP11 172 F7
East Ridge SL8 185 B4
East Spur MK7 47 F7
East St
Adstock MK18 53 F1
Chesham HP5 154 B8
Olney MK46 7 A4
East Terr SL4 210 E7
East View OX25 81 A3
East Walk N MK9 34 E2
East Walk S MK9 34 E2
East Way HP9 175 A1
Eastwick Cres WD3 178 F8
Eastwood Ct 1 SL7 183 F3
Eastwood Rd HP14 158 F3
Eaton Ave
High Wycombe HP12 172 D8
Milton Keynes MK2 58 D7
Slough SL1 204 C6
EATON BRAY 92 F6
Eaton Bray Lower Sch LU6 92 F6
Eaton Bray Rd
Edlesborough LU6 92 C5
Honeywick LU6 92 E8
Eaton Cl HP22 116 F2
Eatongate Cl LU6 92 E5
EATON GREEN 92 C7
Eaton Mill Prim Sch MK2 58 D6
Eaton Pk LU6 92 F6
Eaton Pl HP12 172 D8
Eaton Rd HP21 115 D7
Ebble Cl HP21 115 C4
Ebbsgrove MK5 34 B1
Ebenezer Ho HP10 174 C2
Ebsworth Cl SL6 196 C3
Eddington Ct MK4 46 D1
Eddy St HP4 135 A5
Eden Cl
Aylesbury HP21 115 D4
Slough SL3 207 A1
Eden Sh Ctr HP11 173 A7
Eden Wlk MK3 46 E1
Edgar Rd UB7 208 E5
Edgar Wallace Pl SL8 185 B5
EDGCOTT 72 F2
Edgecombe Rd HP21 116 B5
Edgecote MK8 46 A8
Edgecote Ho 11 HP13 173 B7
Edgecott Rd HP18 82 F7
Edgehill OX9 125 F2
Edge Hill Ct MK18 41 E2
Edgewood HP11 173 D5
Edinburgh Ave SL1 205 B7
Edinburgh Gate UB9 189 F5
Edinburgh Gdns SL4 210 D5
Edinburgh Ho MK3 57 D7
Edinburgh Pl HP21 115 C6
Edinburgh Rd
Maidenhead SL6 195 E1
Marlow SL7 183 E3
Edison Cl UB7 208 F4
Edison Rd HP19 100 E1
Edison Sq MK5 46 C5
Edith Bell Ho SL9 177 E4
Edith Rd SL6 202 A7
EDLESBOROUGH 92 E4
Edlesborough Sch LU6 92 E3
Edlyn Cl HP4 134 F5
Edmonds Cl MK18 41 F1
Edmonds Rd HP14 171 B4
Edmund Ct
Beaconsfield HP9 186 A8
Milton Keynes MK5 45 F7
Edmunds Cl HP12 172 C5
Edmunds Gdns HP12 172 C5
Edmunds Way SL2 206 B7
Edrich Ave MK6 46 F8
Edstone Pl MK4 46 C3
Edward Cl HP21 116 A4
Edwards Croft MK13 34 A7
Edward Wlk HP21 116 A4
Edwin Allman Pl HP15 162 E2
Edwin Cl MK17 48 D2
Edy Ct MK5 34 A1
Edzell Cres MK4 45 E2
Eelbrook Ave MK13 34 C2
Eeles Cl HP19 100 F3
Egerton Cl NN13 38 A7
Egerton Gate MK5 46 B4
Egerton Rd
Berkhamsted HP4 135 B6
Slough SL2 197 E1
Egerton-Rothesay Sch HP4 134 E4
Egglesfield Cl HP4 134 E6
Eggleton Dr HP23 119 A5
Eghams Cl HP9 175 C4
Eghams Ct 8 SL8 185 B3
Eghams Gn SL8 185 B3
Eghams Wood Rd HP9 175 C4
Egmont Ave MK11 32 E4
Egremont Gdns SL1 205 A5
EGYPT 198 B8
Egypt La SL2 187 B1
Egypt Way HP19 115 A8
Egypt Wood Cotts SL2 187 B1
Eider Cl MK18 52 E8
Eight Acres
Burnham SL1 197 B1
Tring HP23 119 A4
Elangeni Jun Sch HP6 154 E3
Elbow Mdw SL3 212 F6
Elder Cl
Loudwater HP11 174 B3
West Drayton UB7 208 E6
Elderdene OX39 147 D8
Elderfield Rd SL2 198 F6
Elder Gate
Milton Keynes, Rooksley MK9 34 C1
Milton Keynes, Winterhill MK9 46 C8
Elder Way HP15 163 B3
Eldridge La HP17 130 C3
Eleanor Cl MK17 60 F7
Eleanor Gdns HP21 115 F6
Eleanor Rd SL9 177 C2
Eleanor Wlk MK17 60 F7
Elfords MK6 47 A6
Elgar Gr MK7 48 C4
Elgin Ho SL3 212 E6
Elgiva La HP5 154 B8
Elham Way HP21 116 A4
Eliot Cl
Aylesbury HP19 100 F2
Newport Pagnell MK16 21 F5
Eliot Dr SL7 183 F4
Elizabeth Ave HP6 166 C8
Elizabeth Cl
Aylesbury HP21 116 B4
Cookham Rise SL6 195 F7
Elizabeth Ct
High Wycombe HP13 173 C6
High Wycombe, Wycombe Marsh HP13 173 E5
10 Slough SL1 206 A4
3 Windsor SL4 210 C5
Elizabeth Dr HP23 119 B6
Elizabeth Rd
Marlow SL7 183 E3
Stokenchurch HP14 158 F4
Elizabeth Sq MK2 58 C8
Elizabeth Way SL2 198 F4
Elkins Rd SL2 187 E2
Ellen Pl HP21 115 C5
Ellen Rd HP21 115 C5
Ellenstow MK13 34 A4
Ellen Wlk HP21 115 B6
Ellerburn Pl MK4 46 B3
Ellery Rise RG9 170 F1
ELLESBOROUGH 130 B2
Ellesborough Gr MK8 33 D3
Ellesborough Rd
Butler's Cross HP17 130 C2
Ellesborough HP17 130 A2
Wendover HP22 131 A3
Ellesmere Cl
Datchet SL3 211 A8
Totternhoe LU6 93 C6
Ellesmere Rd HP4 135 D4
Elliman Ave SL2 205 F6
Ellington Ct SL6 203 C7
Ellington Gdns SL6 203 C7
Ellington Pk SL6 195 E1
Ellington Prim Sch SL6 195 F1
Ellington Rd SL6 203 C7
Elliots Cl UB8 208 C8
Elliott Ho HP11 172 F8
Ellis Ave
Chalfont St Peter SL9 177 F2
Slough SL1 205 E4
Ellisgill Ct MK13 34 B4
Ellison Cl SL4 209 F4
Ellison Ct HP23 118 F3
Ellison Ho 14 SL4 210 D6
Ellis Way HP14 171 B4
Ellsworth Rd HP11 172 F4
Ellwood Ho SL9 177 E2
Ellwood Rd HP9 175 B1
Ellwood Rise HP8 177 C8
Ellwood Terr WD3 167 D4
Elmar Gn SL2 198 A2
Elm Brook Cl HP18 112 C1
Elm Cl
Amersham HP6 154 C1
Butler's Cross HP17 130 C3
Chinnor OX39 147 C5
Farnham Common SL2 198 C6
Hazelmere HP15 163 A3
Newton Longville MK17 57 C2
Weston Turville HP22 116 F2
Elm Croft SL3 211 C6
Elm Ct
Berkhamsted HP4 135 B4
Butler's Cross HP17 130 C3
Elmdale Gdns HP27 139 B3
Elm Dr
Chinnor OX39 147 C5
Deanshanger MK19 31 D5
Elmers Cl MK19 44 A6
Elmers Mdw MK18 76 A2
Elmers Pk MK3 58 A8
Elm Farm Rd HP21 116 A5
Elmfield Cl NN12 18 D3
Elmfields Gate MK18 66 A4
Elm Gn HP21 115 D7
Elm Gr
Berkhamsted HP4 135 C4
Maidenhead SL6 202 E7
West Drayton UB7 208 F6
Woburn Sands MK17 49 B4
ELMHURST 101 E3
Elmhurst 5 HP16 152 A8
Elmhurst Cl
High Wycombe HP13 162 D1
Milton Keynes MK4 46 F4
Elmhurst Ct SL3 207 A3
Elmhurst Rd
Aylesbury HP20 101 E2
Slough SL3 207 A3
Elmhurst Sch HP20 101 E2
Elm La SL8 184 F5
Elm Lawn Cl UB8 201 E5
Elmlea Dr MK46 6 E3
Elmodesham Ho 7 HP7 165 B7
Elm Rd
High Wycombe HP12 172 C4
Princes Risborough HP27 139 C3
Tylers Green HP10 174 D8
Windsor SL4 210 B4

Elmridge Ct MK4 46 C2
Elms Dr SL8 185 C3
Elmshott Cl HP10 163 A1
Elmshott La SL1 204 E6
Elmside MK18 66 A4
Elmslie Ct SL6 202 E7
Elms Rd SL9 177 E3
Elm St MK18 52 D8
Elms The
Leighton Buzzard LU7 80 E7
Milton Keynes MK3 57 F8
Preston Bissett MK18 51 B1
Elm Tree Cl OX25 81 A4
Elm Tree Cotts HP7 164 C2
Elmtree Ct 6 HP16 152 A8
Elmtree Gn HP16 152 A8
Elmtree Hill HP5 144 B1
Elmtree Inf Sch HP5 144 B1
Elm Trees HP18 125 B7
Elm Tree Wlk
Chorleywood WD3 167 F5
Tring HP23 119 A5
Elmwood
Maidenhead SL6 196 B4
Turvey MK43 8 E6
Elmwood Cl HP18 109 D5
Elmwood Pk SL9 188 E3
Elmwood Rd SL2 206 B6
Elora Rd HP13 173 E7
Elruge Cl UB7 208 D3
Elsage Ct LU7 105 B8
Elsmore Cl HP21 116 A4
Eltham Ave SL1 204 E6
Elthorne Rd UB8 201 D3
Elthorne Way MK16 22 C2
Elton MK6 47 D7
Elton Dr SL6 202 D8
Elwes Rd HP14 171 C4
Ely Ave SL1 205 C8
Ely Cl HP7 165 E8
Ely Ho HP13 173 F8
Ember Path HP21 115 C4
Ember Rd SL3 207 B3
EMBERTON 13 E8
Emberton Ctry Pk* MK46 6 E1
Emberton Fst Sch MK46 13 F8
Embleton Way MK18 52 C7
Emerald Cl MK18 74 F8
Emerald Ct SL1 205 E4
Emerald Gate MK15 35 E5
Emerson Ct HP10 185 E6
EMERSON VALLEY 46 B2
Emerson Valley Comb Sch MK4 46 C2
Emerton Ct HP4 134 E7
Emerton Garth HP4 134 E7
Emerton Gdns MK11 32 E5
Emilia Cl SL6 195 F1
Emlyns Bldgs SL4 210 D7
Emma Rothschild Ct HP23 119 A5
Emmett Cl MK4 46 C1
Emmett Dr HP21 115 E5
EMMINGTON 137 A1
Emperor Cl HP4 134 F7
Empingham Cl MK2 58 D4
Empstead Ct RG9 191 D2
Enborne Cl HP21 115 D4
Enders Ct MK5 45 E5
Endfield Pl SL6 202 B6
Enfield Chase MK14 34 D5
Enfield Cl UB8 201 D3
Engaine Dr MK5 45 F7
English Gdns TW19 211 D2
Enigma Ctr The MK1 47 E2
Enmore Gate MK9 35 A3
Enmore Rdbt MK9 35 A3
Ennell Gr MK2 58 C5
Ennerdale Cl MK2 58 D6
Ennerdale Cres SL1 204 C8
Ensbury Path HP20 101 E2
Enstone Rd UB10 190 F1
Enterprise La MK9 35 A3
Epsom Cl LU7 80 D6
Epsom Gr MK3 57 D6
Ercolani Ave HP13 173 D6
Eriboll Cl LU7 80 B6
Erica Cl SL1 204 E6
Erica Rd MK12 33 E4
Eridge Gn MK7 48 A8
Errington Dr SL4 210 A6
Escarpment Ave LU6 107 D8
Eskan Ct MK9 35 B4
Eskdale Ave HP5 144 D1
Eskdale Gdns SL6 203 B2
Eskdale Lodge HP6 154 C2
Eskdale Rd
Stoke Mandeville HP22 116 B2
Uxbridge UB8 201 B3
Eskdale Way MK10 36 B3
Esk Way MK3 46 E1
Essenden Ct MK11 32 F5
Essex Ave SL2 205 C8
Essex Cl MK3 46 F1
Essex Ho 5 HP20 101 D1
Essex Pl HP19 101 A3
Essex Rd HP5 144 C2
Essex Yd HP22 89 C2
Estcourt Dr HP15 162 F6
Esther Cl MK13 34 A6
Eston Ct MK13 34 A5
Estover Way OX39 147 B6
Etheridge Ave MK10 48 C8
Ethorpe MK8 33 E1
Ethorpe Cl SL9 188 E6
Ethorpe Cres SL9 188 E6
Ethorpe Ho SL9 188 E6
ETON 210 C8
Eton Cl SL3 211 A8
Eton Coll SL4 210 D8
Eton College Rowing Ctr* SL4 204 D7
Eton Cres MK12 33 C6
Eton Ct SL4 210 D7
Eton End PNEU Sch SL3 211 A8
Eton Ho 1 SL1 205 F3
Eton Pl SL7 183 D2
Eton Porny CE Fst Sch SL4 210 D8
Eton Rd SL3 211 A8
Eton Riverside SL4 210 D7
Eton Sq SL4 210 D7
ETON WICK 204 F1
Eton Wick CE Fst Sch SL4 205 A1
Eton Wick Rd SL4 205 B1
Eton Wlk 1 SL1 205 E3
Eunice Gr HP5 154 D7
Europa Bsns Pk MK10 36 C2
Europa Ho SL9 188 E6
Evans Cl
Aylesbury HP21 116 A4
Chearsley HP18 112 B2
Evans Gate MK6 46 E8
Evans Way HP23 119 B4
Evelyn Cl LU7 79 E1
Evelyn Pl MK13 34 A7
Evelyns Cl 2 UB8 208 F7
Evenley Rd NN13 38 D1
Evenlode SL6 202 F8
Evenlode Cl HP21 115 C5
Evenlode Rd SL8 185 B4
Everard Ave SL1 205 E4
Everest Cl HP13 173 D6
Everest Rd HP13 173 E6
Everglade MK6 47 A8
Evergreen Oak Ave SL4 211 A4
Everley Cl MK4 46 C3
Evesham Gn HP19 101 C3
Evesham Way MK5 45 D5
Evreham Rd SL0 207 E7
Evreham Sp Ctr SL0 207 D8
Exbury La MK4 45 F1
Exchange Ho MK9 34 E2
Exchange St HP20 115 E8
Exebridge MK4 46 C3
Exhims Mews HP4 134 E6
Exmoor Gate MK4 46 E2
Eynsford Terr UB7 208 F7
Eynsham Ct MK15 35 C2
Eyre Cl HP19 114 F8
Eyre Gn SL2 198 A2
EYTHROPE 113 F8
Eythrope Rd
Eythrope HP18 100 A1
Stone HP17 114 C6

F

Factory Yd HP9 175 E1
Fadmoor Pl 3 MK4 46 B3
Fagnall La HP7 164 D2
Fairacre SL6 202 C6
Fair Acres HP16 151 D5
Fairacres Ind Est SL4 209 D5
Faircroft SL2 198 B1
Fairfax MK13 34 C6
Fairfax Cres HP20 101 E2
Fairfax Mews HP7 165 A7
Fairfield HP6 154 B3
Fairfield App TW19 211 D1
Fairfield Ave SL3 211 D7
Fairfield Cl
Bourne End SL8 185 A5
Datchet SL3 211 D7
Olney MK46 7 A3
Fairfield La SL2 198 B3
Fairfield Rd
Burnham SL1 197 C2
Paulerspury NN12 17 B7
Uxbridge UB8 201 D6
West Drayton UB7 208 E6
Wraysbury TW19 211 D1
Fairfields HP15 151 E1
Fairford Cres MK15 35 B6
Fairford Leys Way HP19 115 A7
Fairford Rd SL6 202 F8
Fairhaven SL9 177 C2
Fairlawn Pk SL4 209 E3
Fairlawns HP13 162 C1
Fairlea SL6 202 B3
Fair Leas HP5 144 A2
Fairlie Rd SL1 205 A8
Fairlight Ave SL4 210 D5
Fairlight Dr UB8 201 D6
Fair Mdw MK18 66 A4
Fairmead The SL3 212 D7
Fair Mile
Aylesbury HP21 116 A7
Henley-on-Thames RG9 191 C4
Fairmile Ct RG9 191 D3
Fair Ridge HP11 172 F4
Fairthorn Cl HP23 118 E3
Fair View Cotts
Chalfont St Peter SL9 177 E3
Cookham Rise SL6 195 E7
Fairview Ind Est
Amersham HP6 154 F1
High Wycombe HP11 173 F4
Fairview La HP10 174 A1
Fairview Rd
Burnham SL6 204 A7
Slough SL2 197 F1
Fairway HP27 139 A3
Fairway Ave UB7 208 D5
Fairway Cl UB7 208 D5
Fairways MK8 33 C2
Fairways Rdbt MK8 33 C2
Fairway The
Burnham SL1 197 C3
Flackwell Heath HP10 185 C7
Maidenhead SL6 202 B3
Uxbridge UB10 201 F3
Faithfull Cl HP17 114 B5
Faithorn Cl HP5 144 A1
Faith Terr MK19 11 A2
Falaise MK15 35 B7
Falcon Ave MK6 35 B2
Falcon Dr
Milton Keynes MK19 32 B7
Stanwell TW19 213 E1
Falconhurst Comb Sch MK6 47 B8
Falcon Ridge HP4 135 C3
Falcon Rise HP13 161 C1
Falcons Croft HP10 185 E8
Falcon The HP19 101 F4
Falkland Ho SL6 202 F8
Falklands Cl MK18 63 D2
Fall Cl HP19 101 D3
Falling La UB7 208 E6
Fallow Field HP15 163 B3
Fallows The SL6 196 A1
Falmouth Pl MK6 34 F1
Falmouth Rd SL1 205 A7
Fane Way SL6 202 D5
Fantail La HP23 118 F4
Faraday Cl SL2 205 B8
Faraday Dr MK5 46 C5
Faraday Rd
Aylesbury HP19 101 A1
Slough SL2 205 B8
FAR BLETCHLEY 57 D7
Far Furlong Cl HP21 115 D3
Farinton MK8 33 F2
Farjeon Ct MK7 48 D4
Farmborough MK6 47 C6
Farmbrough Cl HP20 102 A1
Farm Cl
High Wycombe HP13 174 A7
Ickford HP18 123 F3
Little Chalfont HP6 166 D8
Maidenhead, Highway SL6 202 A7
Maidenhead SL6 203 C1
Stewkley LU7 78 E7
Farm Cres SL2 206 C8
Farm Dr SL4 211 B1
Farmers Cl SL6 202 A4
Farmers Pl SL9 177 C1
Farmers Way
Maidenhead SL6 202 A4
Seer Green HP9 176 C4
Farmery Ct HP4 135 E6
Farm Gr HP9 175 C5
Farm La HP9 176 D3
Farm Lea HP10 185 F7
Farm Pl
Berkhamsted HP4 134 F5
Henton OX39 137 E1
Farm Rd
Bourne End SL8 184 F4
Brackley NN13 38 A6
Burnham SL6 204 A5
Chorleywood WD3 167 A5
Maidenhead SL6 202 A7
Farm Way TW19 212 F1
Farm Yd SL4 210 D7
Farnburn Ave SL1 205 B8
Farndale Gdns HP15 163 A6
Farnell Ct MK5 46 C8
Farnham Cl HP3 146 A3
FARNHAM COMMON 198 D6
Farnham Common Ho 2 SL2 198 C8
Farnham Common Inf Sch SL2 198 B8
Farnham Common Jun Sch SL2 198 C8
Farnham Ct MK8 33 F1
Farnham La SL2 198 A2
FARNHAM PARK 198 C4
Farnham Park La SL2 198 C4
Farnham Rd SL1, SL2 205 C7
FARNHAM ROYAL 198 C3
Farnley Rd HP20 101 E2
Farrer Cl NN13 26 D4
Farrer Theatre Eton* SL4 205 C1
Farrier Ct 1 SL8 185 B3
Farrier Pl MK14 35 A5
Farriers Cl HP3 146 B3
Farriers Way HP5 144 A3
Farringdon St MK10 35 F1
Farthingales The SL6 203 B7
Farthing Ent Ctr The MK6 47 C6
Farthing Gr MK6 47 C6
Farthing Green La SL2 199 B4
Farthings The HP6 154 A3
Fassets Rd HP10 174 B2
Faulkner Dr MK3 47 B1
Faulkner's Way LU7 80 E7
Faulkner Way HP13 161 D3
Favell Dr MK4 46 F4
Faversham Cl HP23 119 A4
Fawcett Rd SL4 210 B6
FAWLEY 191 C8
FAWLEY BOTTOM 180 B2
Fawley Bottom La RG9 180 B1
Fawley Cl SL6 195 D2
Fawley Court* RG9 191 E5
Fawley Gn RG9 180 D2
Fawley Hill Rly* RG9 191 D8
Fawsley Cl SL3 212 E7
Featherbed La HP15 163 D8
Featherstone Rd MK12 33 A5
Fedden Ho MK43 24 D3
Fegans Ct MK11 32 D6
Felbridge MK7 48 A7
FELDEN 146 F7
Felden La HP3 146 F8
Fells Cl HP18 125 D6
Fellstead Ct SL6 202 C6
Felstar Wlk MK6 47 C4
Felsted MK7 48 A3
Fences La MK16 13 A2
Fennel Dr MK14 34 E4
Fennels Farm Rd HP10 174 A1
Fennels Rd HP11 174 A4
Fennels The HP11 174 A3
Fennels Way HP10 174 A1
Fennemore Cl HP18 109 D4
Fennings The HP6 154 D3
Fenny House Tuition Service MK6 47 A6
FENNY LOCK 47 E2
Fennymere MK8 33 D1
Fenny Rd MK17 69 E8
FENNY STRATFORD 47 D1
Fenny Stratford Sta MK1 47 E1
Fen St MK17 36 F1
Fenton Ct MK8 45 F8
FERN 184 E5
Fernan Dell MK8 45 D7
Fernborough Haven 4 MK4 46 C2
Fern Cotts SL7 184 E5
Fern Ct HP4 135 B4
Ferndale MK6 35 B1
Ferndale Cl HP14 158 F4
Ferndale Cres UB8 201 C2
Fern Dr SL6 204 B7
Ferne Furlong MK46 6 F5
Fernes Cl UB8 208 C7
Fernfield MK17 56 A5
Fern Gr MK2 58 D5
Fernhill Cl OX9 136 A6
Fernhurst Cl HP9 175 F2
Fernie Fields HP12 172 C4
Fern La
Fern SL7 184 E5
Haddenham HP17 127 A6
Fernlea Cl HP10 174 A1
Fernley Ct SL6 195 D1
Fernside
Great Kingshill HP15 151 E1
Hazelmere HP15 163 A6
Fernsleigh Cl SL9 177 E4
Ferns The HP9 175 F1
Fern Wlk HP15 163 B3
Fernwood Sch MK17 49 B2
Ferrers Ave UB7 208 D4
Ferrers Cl SL1 204 E5
Ferry End SL6 203 C4
Ferry La
Bourne End SL8 196 B8
Medmenham SL7 193 B5
Mill End RG9 192 D6
Ferry Mdws Cl MK10 36 A4
Ferry Rd SL6 203 C4
Festival Cotts SL3 212 C7
Fetty Pl SL6 202 D4
Field Cl
Aylesbury HP20 102 A2
Buckingham MK18 51 B6
Chesham HP5 144 E3
Ickford HP18 124 A3
Sherington MK16 14 A2
Field Ct MK5 46 B8
Field End HP18 125 F5
Field End Cl HP23 119 D1
Fieldfare HP19 101 E4
Field Farm Bsns Ctr OX26 71 A5
Fieldhead Gdns SL8 185 A3
Fieldhouse Ct HP13 174 A4
Fieldhouse Ind Est SL7 183 F2
Fieldhouse La SL7 183 F2
Fieldhouse Way SL7 183 F2
Field Hurst SL3 206 F1
Fielding Gdns SL3 206 C4
Fielding Rd SL6 202 B8
Field La MK12 33 B5
Field Rd
Denham, Rush Green UB9 200 E8
Denham UB9 189 E1
High Wycombe HP12 172 B5
Murcott OX5 94 A5
Fields End HP23 119 A6
Fields The SL1 205 D4
Fieldway
Amersham HP7 165 B6
Berkhamsted HP4 135 E2
Chalfont St Peter SL9 177 D3
Wigginton HP23 119 D1
Field Way
Aylesbury HP20 102 A2
Bovingdon HP3 146 A4
Chalfont St Peter SL9 177 D2
Uxbridge UB8 201 D1
Field Wlk MK9 34 F3
Fife Ct MK4 57 A8
Fife Ho MK3 46 F1
Fifth St HP11 173 C4
Filey Spur SL1 205 B4
FILGRAVE 13 C5
Filgrave Sch MK16 13 C5
Filmer Rd SL4 209 D5
Finch Cl MK10 35 F3
Finch Cres LU7 80 E5
Finch Ct SL6 202 D5
Finch End HP10 174 C8
Finch Gn WD3 167 F5
Finch La
Amersham HP7 165 F5
Beaconsfield HP9 175 C5
Little Chalfont HP7 166 B7
Finch Rd HP4 135 A4
Findlay Way MK2 58 C8
Finemere Wood Wildlife Reserve* HP22 84 B8
Fingest La RG9 170 D4
Fingle Dr MK13 33 E7
Finians Cl UB10 201 F5
Finings Rd HP14 171 A4
Finlay Dr RG9 191 E2
Finlay Ho RG9 191 E3
FINMERE 50 D7
Finmere CE Prim Sch MK18 50 D6
Finmere Cres HP21 116 C5
Finsbury Chase MK10 47 F8
Fircroft Cl SL2 199 A6
Fircroft Ct SL2 199 A6
Firecrest Way HP19 100 F1
Fire La MK17 57 D4
Firemans Run MK17 49 B5
Firfield SL6 203 B1
Firs Ave SL4 209 F4
Firs Cl
Hazelmere HP15 163 B2
High Wycombe HP13 173 E8
Iver Heath SL0 200 C4
Lane End HP14 171 C5
Whitchurch HP22 87 A5
Firs Ct
Amersham HP6 154 C2
Bierton HP22 102 C4
Princes Risborough HP27 138 F3
Firs Dr SL3 206 F5
Firs End SL9 188 D8
Firs Rise HP16 151 E7
First Ave
Amersham HP7 165 D7
Marlow SL7 184 A2
Milton Keynes MK1 47 C1
First Cres SL1 205 C8
Firs The
Bierton HP22 102 C4
Brill HP18 110 B8
Maidenhead SL6 202 E7
Uxbridge UB8 201 D1
Wigginton HP23 119 D1
First St HP11 173 C3
Firs View Rd HP15 163 B2
Firs Wlk HP15 163 B2
Fir Tree Ave SL2 198 F1
Fir Tree Cotts HP14 161 B8
Firview Cl SL7 183 F1
Fishermans Cl MK46 6 E4
Fishermans Retreat SL7 183 E1
Fisherman's Way SL8 185 B4
FISHERMEAD 35 A1

Fishermead Bvd **2** MK6. **34** F1
Fishermead Rdbt MK1... **47** B2
Fishers Field MK18..... **52** C8
Fishery Rd SL6......... **203** C5
Fishguard Spur SL1.. **206** B4
Fish Ponds La OX9.... **125** E1
Fishweir LU7............ **68** D1
Fitzgeralds Way HP12.. **172** B7
Fitzhamon Cl MK3...... **33** A5
Fitzwilliam St MK3..... **58** B8
Five Acres
  Chesham HP5.........**154** D6
  Wooburn Green HP10 ...**185** F7
Five Acre Wood HP12 ..**172** C6
Five Points SL0.........**200** C2
FLACKWELL HEATH **185** A7
Flaggs Mdw MK46....... **6** E4
Flambard Cl MK15...... **35** A7
Flamborough Spur SL1 **205** A4
Flamstead Gate MK5.... **45** E5
FLAUNDEN...............**156** A6
Flaunden Bottom HP5.. **155** E4
Flaunden Hill HP3.. **156** A6
Flaunden La
  Bovingdon HP3 ....**146** D3
  Chipperfield WD3.......**156** E6
Flavius Gate NN13..... **38** A7
Flaxbourne Ct MK7..... **48** C7
Flaxen Field HP22...... **116** F2
Flaxley Gate MK10..... **36** A2
Fledgelings Wlk MK5... **66** A5
Fleetbrook Ho SL3......**211** D6
Fleet Cl
  Buckingham MK18....... **41** F2
  Walter's Ash HP14.......**161** F7
FLEET MARSTON.........**100** B4
Fleet St HP20...........**101** D1
Fleet The MK6.......... **35** B2
Fleetwood Cl HP8.......**177** A6
Fleetwood Ct **7** TW19 .**213** E1
Fleetwood Rd SL2......**205** F6
Fleetwood Way OX9....**125** F2
Fleming Ct **7** SL3......**206** C3
Fleming Dr MK6........ **47** B6
Fleming Way HP12......**172** D5
Fletcher Cl HP19.......**100** F3
Fletchers Mews MK14... **34** F6
Flexerne Cres MK6..... **47** D5
Flintergill Ct MK13..... **34** B4
Flint Ho **7** MK3........ **46** F1
Flint Hollow OX39......**147** B6
Flintlock Cl TW19......**213** A3
Flint St HP17...........**127** A5
Flint Way HP16.........**151** C7
Flitcroft Lea HP13......**173** A6
Flitt Leys Cl MK43..... **25** B2
Flitton Ct MK11........ **32** F5
Flora Thompson Dr
  MK16................. **21** F6
Florence Ave SL6.......**203** C5
Florence Ct HP19.......**101** D1
Florence Way UB8......**201** C5
Florey Gdns HP20......**115** F8
Florida St HP11.........**173** C4
Florin Cl MK15......... **35** A7
FLOWERS BOTTOM......**150** A4
Flowers Bottom La
  HP27.................**150** B4
Flynn Croft MK4........ **45** D1
Fog Cotts HP23.........**120** A5
Folding Cl LU7.......... **78** E8
Foley Cl HP9............**175** C4
Foliejohn Way SL6......**202** A1
Folkestone Ct SL3......**207** A1
Follet Cl SL4............**211** B1
Folleys Pl HP10.........**174** D1
Folly La
  Hartwell NN7.......... **10** C8
  North Crawley MK16.... **24** B5
Folly Rd MK19.......... **31** D4
Fonda Mdws MK4....... **45** D3
Fontwell Cl SL6.........**202** A8
Fontwell Dr MK3........ **57** C6
Forbes Pl MK5.......... **45** E4
Forches Cl MK4........ **46** D2
FORD...................**128** B7
Fordcombe Lea MK7.... **48** B8
Ford End UB9...........**189** F2
Ford La SL0.............**208** A4
Ford's Cl HP14.........**159** F8
Ford St
  Buckingham MK18...... **52** D8
  High Wycombe HP11.....**173** F4
Ford Way HP15.........**161** E3
Forelands Way HP5.....**154** C7
Forest Cl
  Princes Risborough
    HP27.................**139** B3
  Slough SL3............**206** B8
  Wendover HP22.........**131** B4
Foresters
  Beacon's Bottom HP14 .**159** C5
  Chinnor OX39..........**147** B6
  Oakley HP18...........**109** D6
Forest Pk SL4...........**209** E1
Forest Point HP13 .....**173** F5

Forest Rd
  Hanslope MK19 .... **10** F5
  Piddington (Northants) NN7 **4** A8
  Windsor SL4............**209** E5
Forest Rise MK6........ **47** B8
Forestry Hos OX49......**168** A7
Forest Way HP13.......**174** A8
Forfar Dr MK3.......... **46** F2
Forge Cl
  Ashendon HP18........ **97** E1
  Holmer Green HP15.....**163** C6
  Horton-cum-S HP15.....**108** B5
  Marsh Gibbon OX27..... **71** F3
  Oakley HP18...........**109** D4
  Steeple Claydon MK18... **63** E2
Forge Dr SL7...........**183** B2
Forge End HP7..........**165** B7
Forge Rd HP14..........**161** C6
Forge The MK46........ **13** F8
Forgetts Rd HP14.......**171** C4
Forlease Cl SL6.........**203** A6
Forlease Dr SL6.........**203** A6
Forlease Rd SL6........**203** A6
Formby Cl
  Milton Keynes MK3..... **57** C7
  Slough SL3............**207** C2
Forrabury Ave MK13.... **34** C3
Forsythia Gdns SL3.....**206** B1
Fort End HP17..........**127** A6
Fortescue Dr MK5...... **46** B6
Forthill Pl MK5......... **45** F7
Fortuna Ct MK7........ **48** C6
Forty Gn HP27.........**137** F3
FORTY GREEN
  Beaconsfield..........**175** A4
  Princes Risborough....**137** F3
Forty Green Dr SL7....**183** B2
Forty Green Rd HP9....**175** C4
Forum The MK14....... **34** E5
FOSCOTE............... **42** B4
Foscote Cotts MK18.... **42** B4
Foscote Rd MK18...... **41** F3
Foscot Way MK18...... **41** E2
Foskett Way HP21......**115** E5
Fossey Cl MK5.......... **45** F3
Foster Ave SL4.........**209** E4
Foster La MK13........ **34** A3
Fosters Path MK13......**197** F1
Fotherby Ct SL6........**203** A6
Fotheringay Gdns SL1...**205** A6
Fotherley Rd WD3......**178** F8
Founders Mews MK14... **34** F6
Foundry La
  Horton SL3............**212** B4
  Lacey Green HP27......**149** C5
Fountain Ct
  6 Aylesbury HP20....**115** D8
  1 Olney MK46........ **6** F3
Fountaine Cl MK14..... **34** E7
Fountain Gdns SL4......**210** D4
FOUR ASHES............**162** D4
Four Ashes Rd HP15....**162** C5
Fourdrinier Ct HP11....**174** A4
Four Oaks HP5.........**144** A4
Fourth Ave SL7.........**184** A2
Fourth St MK11........ **33** B4
Fourways Mews HP12...**172** C4
Fowler MK14........... **34** C7
Fowler Rd HP19........**115** B8
Fowlers Farm Rd HP14 **158** E4
Foxborough Cl SL3......**207** A1
Foxborough Ct SL6......**202** E4
Foxborough Prim Sch
  SL3..................**207** A1
Fox Cl HP23............**119** D1
Fox Cover OX39........**147** C6
Fox Covert La MK19.... **20** A5
Foxcovert Rd MK5...... **45** F4
Foxdell Way SL9........**177** C5
Foxes Piece SL7........**183** E2
Foxes Piece Sch SL7....**183** E3
Fox Farm Rd MK17..... **59** D6
Foxfield MK10.......... **36** B3
Fox Field HP15.........**162** F5
Foxgate MK16.......... **22** B4
Foxglove HP21.........**115** B5
Foxglove Cl MK18...... **52** C7
Foxglove Ct MK16...... **21** F4
Foxgoles Cl MK19...... **31** F5
Foxherne SL3...........**206** C4
Foxhill MK46........... **6** E5
Foxhill Cl HP13.........**162** B1
Foxhollow Dr SL2.......**198** C2
Foxhunter Dr MK14.... **34** E6
Fox La HP15............**163** B6
Foxleigh HP11..........**173** A4
Foxley Pl MK5.......... **46** C8
FOX MILNE............. **35** F4
Fox Milne Rdbt MK10... **35** F4
Foxmoor Ct UB9........**190** A5
Fox Rd
  Holmer Green HP15.....**163** B6
  Slough SL3............**206** D2
  Wigginton HP23........**119** C2
Foxton MK6............ **47** D6
Fox Way MK18......... **52** E7
Fraderica Cotts MK16... **22** C3
Framers Ct HP14........**171** B4

Framewood Manor
  SL2..................**199** C6
Framewood Rd
  Slough SL3............**188** C1
  Wexham Street SL2, SL3 **199** C6
Framlingham Ct MK5... **46** A5
Frampton Ct **11** MK4.. **45** F1
France Furlong MK14... **34** F8
Frances Ave SL6.......**196** C1
Frances Ct LU7......... **80** E7
Frances Rd SL4.........**210** D5
Frances St HP5.........**144** C2
Franchise St **3** HP5...**144** C1
Francis Ct MK5......... **46** B6
Francis House Prep Sch
  HP23.................**118** F3
Francis Way SL1........**204** D6
Frank Atter Croft MK12.. **33** C5
Frank Howe Ct MK6.... **35** A1
Franklin Ave SL2.......**205** B8
Franklin Cl HP17.......**127** A7
Franklin Cl HP7.........**154** C1
Franklin Rd
  Dunstable LU6........ **93** F8
  Haddenham HP17.......**127** A7
Franklins Croft MK12....**33** C5
FRANKLIN'S SPRING.....**178** D5
Frank Lunnon Cl SL8...**185** C3
Franklyn Cres SL4......**209** D4
Frankston Ave MK11.... **32** F5
Frank Sutton Way SL1..**205** D6
Frankswood Ave UB7 ..**208** F7
Frantons The SL6.......**202** A7
Frascati Way SL6.......**202** F7
Fraser Rd HP12.........**172** C5
Fraucup Cl HP17........**128** B7
Fraunchies Ct SL1......**205** E6
Frays Ave UB7..........**208** D4
Frays Cl UB7...........**208** D3
Fray's Ct UB8..........**201** C5
Frayslea UB8...........**201** C3
Frays Valley Nature
  Reserve★ UB10........**201** D8
Fray's Waye UB8........**201** C4
Frederick Pl HP11......**174** B3
Fredericks Ct HP9·.....**186** A8
Frederick Smith Ct
  MK12................. **33** D4
Frederick St HP18...... **99** A7
Freeman Cl MK12...... **33** B5
Freeman Ct HP5........**144** C1
Freemans Cl SL2.......**199** A6
Freemans Gdns MK46... **7** A3
Freer Cres HP13........**174** A4
Fremantle Rd
  Aylesbury HP21........**115** E5
  High Wycombe HP13....**162** E2
Frenchum Gdns SL1....**204** D5
Frensham Dr MK2....... **58** C7
Frensham Wlk SL2......**198** C6
Freshfield Ave **1** MK10.. **36** A3
Friarage Rd HP20.......**115** D8
Friarscroft Way HP20...**115** D8
Friars Field HP4........**134** E7
Friars Furlong HP18....**125** B7
Friars Gdns HP14.......**162** A7
Friars Walk HP15.......**151** D5
Friars Wlk HP23........**119** A4
Friary Gdns MK16...... **22** C2
Friary Island TW19.....**211** C2
Friary Rd TW19.........**211** C1
Friary The SL4..........**211** C1
Friday Ct OX9..........**125** F1
Friday St
  Henley-on-Thames RG9..**191** E2
  Leighton Buzzard LU7... **80** F7
FRIETH.................**170** F1
Frieth CE Comb Sch
  RG9..................**170** F1
Frieth Rd SL7..........**182** E5
Frimley Dr SL1.........**204** F4
Fripp Gdns MK8........ **45** D6
Frithe The SL2..........**206** B7
FRITH-HILL.............**152** C7
Frith Hill
  Great Missenden HP16..**152** B7
  South Heath HP16......**152** C8
Frithsden Copse HP4...**135** F8
Frithwood Cres MK7.... **48** B7
Froggy La UB9..........**189** D1
Frog La HP18...........**112** F3
Frogmill SL6...........**193** C3
Frogmill Ct SL6.........**193** C3
Frogmill Spinney SL6...**193** C4
Frogmoor HP13.........**173** C4
Frogmore Cl
  Hughenden Valley
    HP14.................**162** A7
  Slough SL1............**205** A4
Frogmore Cotts SL4.....**210** D5
Frogmore Ct **4** SL6....**202** F7
Frogmore Dr SL4........**210** F5
Frogmore Flats SL4.....**210** D5
Frogmore Ho★ SL4....**210** F5
Frogmore La HP18......**125** D1
Frogmore St HP23......**119** A3
Frome Cl HP21..........**115** C6
Fromer Rd HP10........**185** D4
Frost Ho **4** HP4.......**135** C3

Froxfield Ct MK4........ **46** C1
Fryday St MK6.......... **46** F2
Fryer Cl HP5...........**154** D6
Fryers Ct **3** HP12.....**172** D8
Fryers La HP12.........**172** D8
Frymley View SL4.......**209** D6
Fuggle Dr HP21.........**115** E5
Fulbrook Mid Sch MK17.. **49** B5
Fullbrook Cl SL6.......**203** A8
Fuller's Cl HP5..........**154** B6
Fuller's Hill HP5, HP6...**154** C1
FULLERS SLADE......... **33** A4
Fullers Yd SL6..........**196** B2
Fulmar Pl **1** HP19......**101** F3
FULMER.................**199** C8
Fulmer Chase SL3......**199** C8
Fulmer Common Rd SL3,
  SL0..................**199** E6
Fulmer Dr SL9..........**188** D2
Fulmer Inf Sch SL3......**199** E8
Fulmer La SL9..........**189** A2
Fulmer Rd SL3..........**188** F2
Fulmer St
  Milton Keynes, Emerson
    Valley MK4............ **46** C3
  Milton Keynes, Medbourne MK8,
    MK5................. **45** E6
Fulmer Way SL9........**188** D5
Fulton Cl HP13.........**173** A8
FULWELL................ **39** A4
Fulwell Ct MK14........ **34** E8
Fulwell Rd
  Finmere MK18......... **50** C7
  Westbury MK13........ **39** A4
Fulwood Ct TW19.......**213** F1
Fulwoods Dr MK6...... **47** A8
Furlong Cl SL8.........**185** B3
Furlong Cres HP17......**115** A1
Furlong La LU6......... **93** C7
Furlong Rd SL8.........**185** B3
Furlong The **12** HP23...**119** A3
Furness SL4............**209** C5
Furness Cres MK3...... **47** A1
Furness Pl **8** SL4......**209** C5
Furness Row **9** SL4....**209** C5
Furness Sq **6** SL4......**209** C5
Furness Wlk **7** SL4....**209** C5
Furnival Ave SL2.......**205** B8
Furrow Cl HP21.........**115** C6
Furrows The UB9.......**190** C6
Furrow Way SL6........**202** A4
FURTHO................ **19** A3
Furtho Ct MK19........ **32** B7
Furtho La NN12........ **18** E3
Fury Ct MK8........... **45** F7
Furze Down Specl Sch
  MK18................. **65** E4
Furze Field La HP16....**142** B8
Furzefield Rd HP9......**175** C4
Furzeham Rd UB7.......**208** E4
Furze La MK18......... **65** E5
Furzen Cl SL2..........**198** A2
FURZE PLATT...........**195** C2
Furze Platt Inf Sch SL6 **195** C1
Furze Platt Jun Sch
  SL6..................**195** C1
Furze Platt Rd SL6.....**195** B1
Furze Platt Senior Sch
  SL6..................**195** C2
Furze Platt Sta SL6.....**195** E1
Furze Rd SL6...........**195** D1
Furze View WD3........**167** C4
Furze Way MK12....... **33** C6
FURZTON............... **46** B4
Furzton Rdbt MK4...... **46** C4
Fuzzens Wlk SL4.......**209** E5
Fyfield Barrow MK7.... **48** C6
Fyne Dr LU7............ **80** C8

G

Gables Cl
  Chalfont St Peter SL9 ...**177** E6
  Datchet SL3...........**211** A8
  Maidenhead SL6.......**203** B8
  Wendover HP22........**131** A4
Gables Dr HP14.........**149** C1
Gables Mdw HP15......**163** C6
Gables The
  Datchet SL3...........**211** A8
  Haddenham HP17.......**127** A5
  Leighton Buzzard LU7... **80** E6
Gable Thorne MK7...... **48** D6
Gabriel Cl MK7......... **48** C5
Gaddesden Cres MK7... **48** C6
Gadge Cl OX9..........**125** E1
Gadmore La HP23......**132** F7
Gadsden Cl MK43...... **25** D3
Gadsden Ct MK17...... **69** E8
Gage Cl SL6............**202** E4
Gainsborough SL6......**195** F5
Gainsborough Cl MK8... **45** D6
Gainsborough Dr SL6...**202** D3
Gainsborough Hill RG9 **191** D1
Gainsborough Pl HP19 **100** F3
Gainsborough Rd
  Aylesbury HP21........**115** E4

Gainsborough Rd continued
  Henley-on-Thames RG9..**191** D1
Gairloch Ave MK2...... **58** D5
Galahad Cl SL1.........**205** A4
Gallagher Cl MK8...... **45** D6
Galleries The **4** HP13..**173** A7
Galley Hill MK11....... **32** F5
Galley La MK17........ **59** F4
Galleymead Rd SL3.....**212** F6
Galloway HP19.........**101** A3
Galloway Chase SL2....**206** A6
Galloway Cl MK3....... **46** E2
Gallows La HP12.......**172** C8
Gallys Rd SL4..........**209** D6
Galsworthy Pl HP19....**100** F3
Galvin Rd SL1..........**205** C6
Gamnel HP23...........**119** A6
Gamnel Mews HP23....**119** B7
Gamnel Terr HP23......**119** A6
Gandon Vale HP13......**173** A8
Ganton Cl MK3......... **46** D1
Garamonde Dr MK8.... **33** F2
Garbo Cl MK8.......... **45** D7
Garden Cl
  Halton HP22...........**131** C8
  Maidenhead SL6.......**202** A5
Garden Cotts SL3.......**212** D7
Garden Ct HP11........**174** B3
Garden End HP6........**154** E2
Gardener Wlk HP15.....**163** C6
Garden Field La HP4....**135** F2
Garden Mews SL1......**205** F5
Garden Reach HP8......**166** D6
Gardens Cl HP14.......**158** F4
Gardens The MK18..... **53** F1
Gardiner Ct MK13...... **33** E4
Gardner Cl
  Aylesbury HP19........**101** A3
  Great Kingshill HP15....**151** D1
Gardner Ho SL6........**195** E1
Gardner Rd SL6........**195** D2
Gardner's Cl SL6....... **93** E7
Garfield Pl **1** SL4......**210** C5
Garland Cl MK8........ **45** E8
Garland Way HP22......**117** C5
Garner Ct **13** TW19....**213** E1
Garners Cl SL9.........**177** F4
Garners End SL9.......**177** F4
Garners Rd SL9........**177** F4
Garnet Cl SL1..........**205** A4
Garnet St SL7..........**183** C1
Garrard Rd SL2.........**197** F1
Garraways MK6........ **47** A6
Garrett Cl HP5.........**154** D6
Garretts La SL6........**195** F2
Garrick Wlk MK9....... **34** F3
Garron Cl HP21.........**115** D3
Garrowmore Gr MK2... **58** D5
Garry Cl MK2.......... **58** C5
Garside Way HP20......**102** A1
Garson Gr HP5.........**144** A2
Garston MK8........... **33** F1
Garthlands SL6.........**195** D2
Garth The HP16........**152** A8
Garthwaite Cres MK5... **46** A4
Garvin Ave HP9.........**175** E2
Garvin Mews HP9.......**175** E2
Garwood Cres MK8..... **45** C6
Gascon's Gr SL2........**198** A1
Gaskin Ct MK14........ **35** A5
Gas La SL6.............**203** A3
Gatcombe MK8......... **33** F1
Gate Cotts WD3........**167** D5
Gatehouse Cl
  Aylesbury HP19........**115** C8
  Windsor SL4...........**210** B4
Gatehouse Sch The
  MK14................. **34** D7
Gatehouse Way HP19...**101** B1
Gatensbury Pl HP27....**139** B3
Gatesdene Cl HP4......**121** C8
Gates Orch HP22.......**117** D5
Gateway Ctr The HP12..**172** D4
Gateway Sch The HP16 **152** A8
Gatewick Cl SL1........**205** E5
Gatewick La MK7....... **48** A3
Gatting Way UB8.......**201** E6
Gatward Ave SL6.......**202** A3
Gaveston Dr HP4.......**135** B6
Gaveston Rd SL2.......**197** D8
Gaviots Cl SL9.........**188** F3
Gaviots Gn SL9.........**188** F3
Gaviots Way SL9.......**188** E4
GAWCOTT............... **51** F4
Gawcott Fields MK18....**52** B7
Gawcott Rd MK18...... **52** B6
Gawcott Road Ind Pk
  MK18................. **52** B7
Gawdrey Cl HP5........**154** D6
Gayal Croft MK5....... **46** B4
GAYHURST............. **12** D2
Gayhurst Ho MK16..... **12** D1
Gayhurst Rd HP13......**173** F7
Gayhurst Sch SL9......**188** C7
Gayton Cl HP6.........**154** E4
Gees Farm Cl NN7..... **1** A5
Gell Cl UB10...........**190** F1
George Cl SL7..........**183** F4
George Ct HP18........ **83** B5

GEORGE GREEN 206 E8
George Green Dr SL3 206 F7
George Green Rd SL3 206 E7
George Inn Pl MK16 12 B6
George Lee Ct HP14 160 C1
George Rd HP14 158 E5
Georges Dr HP10 185 C7
George's Hill HP15 162 F6
George St
 18 Aylesbury HP20 115 D8
 Berkhamsted HP4 135 D4
 5 Chesham HP5 144 C1
 High Wycombe HP11 172 F7
 Milton Keynes MK2 47 E1
 Uxbridge UB8 201 D5
 Wing LU7 79 E2
 Woburn MK17 60 F7
George V Pl SL4 210 D7
George Yd MK11 32 D5
Georgian Cl UB10 201 E8
Georgian Hts SL8 185 B5
Geralds Ct HP13 162 D1
Geralds Rd HP13 162 D2
Gerard Cl MK13 34 A7
Germains Cl HP5 154 B7
Germain St HP5 154 B7
Germander Park First Sch MK14 34 D4
Germander Pl MK14 34 D4
GERRARDS CROSS 188 E5
Gerrards Cross CE Sch The SL9 188 F4
Gerrards Cross Rd SL2 199 A6
Gerrards Cross Sta SL9 188 E6
Gershwin Ct MK7 48 C4
Gervaise Cl SL1 204 F5
Ghyll Gdns HP4 134 D7
Gibbings Cl MK18 76 A3
Gibbs Cl HP13 172 F8
Gibbs Ho HP11 173 F4
Gibbwin MK14 34 E8
Gib La HP22 102 D4
GIBRALTAR 113 D2
Gibraltar La SL6 184 C1
Gibson Ct 9 SL3 206 F1
Gibson La HP17 127 A5
Gibson Pl TW19 213 C1
Gibson Rd
 High Wycombe HP12 172 B3
 Ickenham UB10 201 F8
Gibsons Gn MK13 34 C4
Gibsons Green MK13 34 C4
GIFFARD PARK 22 A2
Giffard Park Prim Sch MK14 22 A2
Giffard Park Rdbt MK14 21 F3
Giffard Rd MK2 58 C6
Giffard Way HP18 125 C7
Gifford Gate MK14 34 E7
Gifford Pl MK18 41 E1
Gilbert Cl MK3 58 B7
Gilbert Ho 4 HP11 172 E7
Gilbert Scott Ct 9 HP7 165 B7
Gilbert Scott Gdns MK18 52 A4
Gilbert Scott Rd MK18 41 D2
Gilbert's Hill HP23 132 E3
Gilbert Way
 Berkhamsted HP4 135 A4
 Slough SL3 206 F1
Gilbey Wlk HP10 185 D4
Gilders Mews MK14 34 F6
Giles Brook Comb Sch MK4 57 A7
Giles Gate HP16 151 B6
Gillamoor Cl 2 MK4 46 B3
Gilletts La HP12 161 C1
Gillfield Cl HP11 172 E3
Gilliat Rd SL1 205 E6
Gilliat's Gn WD3 167 D5
Gilliatt Cl SL0 207 E7
Gillions Pl HP21 116 B7
Gillott Ct SL6 202 F8
Gilman Cres SL4 209 D4
Gilmore Cl SL3 206 C4
Gilmore Rd HP20 101 E3
Gilpin's Ride HP4 135 D5
Gilpin Way MK46 7 A4
Gingers Cl HP22 117 E5
Gipsy La LU7 91 D8
Girton Way MK3 58 B8
Gisburn Cl MK13 34 B5
Glade Ho 5 SL7 183 E2
Glade Rd SL7 183 E2
Glade The
 Gerrards Cross SL9 188 D2
 Tylers Green HP10 163 C1
Glade View HP12 172 A3
Gladstone Cl MK16 22 D3
Gladstone Ind Est 1 SL6 202 E8
Gladstone Rd HP5 144 C1
Gladstone Rise HP13 173 F6
Gladstone Way SL1 205 A5
Glaisyer Way SL0 200 D3
Glamis Ct HP13 173 B8
Glamis Ho MK3 57 E7
Glamorgan Cl MK3 46 F1
Glanmor Rd SL2 206 B6
Glassmill Ho 4 HP4 135 D4
Glastonbury Cl MK3 47 A2
Glastonbury Thorn Fst Sch MK5 46 B6
Glaven Rd HP21 115 C4
Glazier Dr MK14 34 F6
Glebe Cl
 Chalfont St Peter SL9 177 D3
 Dorney SL6 203 F4
 Holmer Green HP15 163 B7
 Maids Moreton MK18 41 F3
 Milton Keynes MK5 46 A8
 Pitstone LU7 105 D5
Glebe Cotts HP14 169 C7
Glebe Dr NN13 38 A7
Glebe Ho SL9 177 D3
Glebe House Dr MK18 39 E6
Glebe La MK19 10 E5
Glebelands HP10 174 C8
Glebelands Cl HP16 151 E4
Glebe Rd
 Chalfont St Peter SL9 177 C2
 Deanshanger MK19 31 E5
 Maidenhead SL6 203 B5
 Old Windsor SL4 211 B2
 Uxbridge UB8 201 C3
Glebe Rdbt MK9 35 B4
Glebe Terr MK18 41 F3
Glebe The
 Lavendon MK46 7 F8
 Lewknor OX49 157 B8
 Prestwood HP16 151 C7
 Stone HP17 114 C5
 Walter's Ash HP14 161 D6
 West Drayton UB7 208 F2
 Weston Turville HP22 116 F2
Glebe Way HP6 154 D3
Gledfield Pl MK12 33 D4
Gleeman Cl MK12 33 A5
Glenavon Gdns SL3 206 C3
Glenduragan Ct 9 MK4 45 F1
Gleneagles Cl
 Milton Keynes MK3 57 D7
 Stanwell TW19 213 D1
Glenfield MK16 22 D1
Glenfield Cl
 Aylesbury HP21 116 A5
 Stoke Poges SL2 198 F4
Glenham Rd OX9 126 B1
Glenister Rd
 Chesham HP5 144 C3
 High Wycombe HP12 172 B4
Glenisters Rd HP13 173 A8
Glenmore Cl HP10 174 A2
Glenmore Ho HP11 174 B3
Glenore SL6 196 A8
Glenstal Pl MK9 35 A3
Glen The SL3 206 C2
Glentworth Pl SL1 205 C5
Glenwater Ho HP15 163 A5
Glenwoods MK16 22 C3
Glimbers Gr OX39 147 C5
Globe Ho UB7 208 D5
Globe La LU7 70 E1
Globe Pk (Bsns Ctr) SL7 183 F2
Globeside Bsns Pk SL7 183 F2
Glory Cl HP10 185 F7
Glory Mill La
 Beaconsfield HP9 185 F8
 Wooburn Green HP10 185 E7
Gloucester Ave SL1 205 C8
Gloucester Ct UB9 190 A4
Gloucester Pl SL4 210 D5
Gloucester Rd
 Maidenhead SL6 195 E2
 Milton Keynes MK12 33 D5
Glovers Ct 2 HP20 101 E1
Glovers La MK13 34 B4
Glyn Sq MK12 33 D7
Glyn St MK13 34 A7
Glynswood
 Chalfont St Peter SL9 177 F3
 Chinnor OX39 147 C6
 High Wycombe HP13 162 B1
Glynswood Ho OX39 147 C6
Glynswood Rd MK18 41 C1
Glynwood Ho SL6 203 A7
Goathland Croft 2 MK4 46 B2
Goddards Croft MK12 33 C5
Goddington Rd SL8 185 A5
Godfreys Cl HP18 96 B1
GODLINGTON 61 E3
Godolphin Inf Sch SL1 205 C7
Godolphin Jun Sch SL1 205 D7
Godolphin Rd
 Seer Green HP9 176 C4
 Slough SL1 205 D6
Godrevy Gr MK4 57 B8
Godstowe Prep Sch HP13 173 B8
Godwin Cl MK7 48 C7
Gogh Rd HP19 100 F2
Gold Crest HP19 101 F4
Golden Ball La SL6 195 A3
Golden Dr MK6 47 B8
Golden Hills OX39 147 D6
Golden Mede HP18 99 B6
Golden Miller Ct LU7 79 E2
Golden Oak Cl SL2 198 C6
Golden Riddy LU7 80 E8
Golder's Cl HP18 123 F3
Goldfield Inf Sch HP23 118 F3
Goldfield Rd HP23 118 F3
Goldhawk Rd MK10 47 E8
Gold Hill E SL9 177 D1
Gold Hill N SL9 177 C2
Gold Hill W SL9 177 C1
Goldilocks MK7 48 B6
Goldmark Cl MK7 48 D5
Gold Oak Wlk MK9 34 F3
Goldsmith Dr MK16 21 F4
Gold St MK19 11 A2
Goldsworthy Way SL1 204 C7
Golf Club La HP27 139 E5
Golspie Croft MK12 33 C4
Gomez Cl MK4 45 D3
Gomm Pl HP13 174 A4
Gomm Rd HP13 174 A4
Gomms Wood Cl HP9 175 B4
Gomms Wood Ho HP9 175 B4
Gomm Valley Wildlife Reserve★ HP13 174 B5
Goodacres La HP27 149 E6
Goodall Cl RG9 191 E1
Good Intent LU6 92 E4
Goodlake Ct UB9 189 F4
Goodman Gdns MK6 47 D8
Goodman Pk SL2 206 C5
Goodrich Gn MK4 56 E8
Goodrington Pl 2 MK10 36 A4
Goodwick Gr MK4 57 B8
Goodwin Mdws HP10 185 E6
Goodwin Rd
 Aylesbury HP19 115 C8
 Slough SL2 197 F2
Goodwins Mead LU7 105 A7
Goodwin Villas SL1 204 F5
Goodwood MK8 45 F8
Goodwood Rise SL7 183 C7
Goose Acre
 Botley HP5 145 A1
 Cheddington LU7 105 A7
Goose Gn SL2 198 B3
Goosemere MK19 31 E4
Goosen Gn HP21 116 C6
Goran Ave MK11 32 E4
Gordale MK13 34 C5
Gordon Rd
 Chesham HP5 154 C7
 High Wycombe HP13 173 D6
 Maidenhead SL6 202 D7
 West Drayton UB7 208 E6
 Windsor SL4 209 F5
Gordon Way HP8 177 B7
Gore Cl UB9 190 C7
Gore Hill HP7 165 B5
Gorelands La HP8 177 F8
Gorell Rd HP9 176 B1
Gore Rd SL1 197 B2
Gore The SL1 197 A2
Goring MK14 34 C7
Gorman Pl MK2 58 E4
Gorrell Cl MK18 51 B6
Gorrell La MK18 51 B6
Gorricks MK11 32 D4
Gorse Meade SL1 205 B5
Gorse Rd SL6 195 E6
Gorse Wlk
 Hazelmere HP15 163 A3
 West Drayton UB7 208 E7
Gosforth Pl SL1 204 F6
Goslar Way SL4 210 B5
Gosling Gn SL3 206 E3
Gosling Gr HP13 161 D2
Gosling Rd SL3 206 E3
Gossage Rd UB10 201 F5
GOSSARD'S GREEN 25 C4
Goss Ave HP18 99 B6
Gossmore Cl SL7 183 F1
Gossmore La SL7 183 F1
Gossmore Wlk SL7 183 F1
Gossom's End HP4 135 A5
Gossoms Ryde HP4 135 A5
Goswell Hill SL4 210 D6
Goswell Rd SL4 210 D6
Goudhurst Ct MK7 48 B7
Governors Cl HP6 154 F1
Gower Ho HP6 154 E3
Gowers Field HP19, HP20 101 D1
Gowers The HP6 154 E2
Gowings Gn SL1 204 E4
Goya Pl HP19 100 F2
Grable Ave MK4 45 E3
Grace Ave MK6 46 E8
Grace Ct SL1 205 C5
Grace Reading HP13 173 E6
Grace Reading Cl HP13 173 E6
Graces Cl MK43 25 C3
Graces Maltings 4 HP23 119 A3
Graeme Ave HP16 151 C6
Grafham Cl MK14 35 A8
Grafton Cl
 Maidenhead SL6 195 E2
 Potterspury NN12 18 E3
Grafton Cl *continued*
 Slough SL3 206 E7
Grafton Ct NN7 4 A8
Grafton Gate MK9 34 C1
Grafton Ho OX39 147 C7
Grafton Orch OX39 147 D7
Grafton Park MK9 34 D1
Grafton Rd
 Aylesbury HP19 101 A2
 Yardley Gobion NN12 18 F6
GRAFTON REGIS 9 D2
Grafton St
 High Wycombe HP12 172 D8
 Milton Keynes, Bradwell MK13 34 B4
 Milton Keynes, Granby MK1 47 B3
 Milton Keynes, New Bradwell MK12, MK13, MK19 33 E8
 Milton Keynes, Winterhill MK6 46 E7
Graham Cl SL6 202 C5
Graham Dr HP12 172 B5
Graham Ho SL9 177 C1
Graham Rd SL6 195 E6
Grainge Chase MK17 55 A3
Grainge Cl NN13 39 A5
Grampian Gate MK6 46 E7
Grampian Way SL3 207 A1
Gramwell MK5 45 F7
Granary Cl MK19 21 A3
GRANBOROUGH 75 E7
Granborough Rd
 North Marston MK18 76 A2
 Winslow MK18 65 E2
GRANBY 47 B3
Granby Ct MK1 47 A3
Granby Ind Est MK1 47 B3
Granby Rdbt MK1 47 C3
Grandison Ho RG9 191 E3
Grand Union Office Pk The UB8 208 C7
Granes End MK14 34 E8
Grange Chase MK17 55 A3
Grange Cl
 Chalfont St Peter SL9 177 E2
 Leighton Buzzard LU7 80 D6
 Maids Moreton MK18 41 E3
 Twyford MK18 62 D2
 Wraysbury TW19 211 E1
Grange Cotts HP16 152 A3
Grange Dr HP10 185 D3
Grange Farm Rd HP14 159 B7
Grange Farm Rdbt MK8 45 D7
Grange Fields SL9 177 E2
Grange Gdn HP18 83 A6
Grange Gdns
 Farnham Common SL2 198 D7
 Wendover HP22 131 B5
Grange La SL6 195 F8
Grangelands & Pulpit Hill Reserve★ HP27 139 F6
Grange Rd
 Chalfont St Peter SL9 177 E2
 Cookham Rise SL6 195 F7
 Hazlemere HP15 162 F4
 Hazlemere, Widmer End HP15 162 E5
 Henley-on-Thames RG9 191 E1
 Milton Keynes MK3 57 F7
 Pitstone LU7 105 D5
 Tring HP23 119 C4
 Wilstone HP23 104 D1
Grangers Croft MK12 33 C4
Grange Sch The HP21 115 F6
Grange The
 Burnham SL1 197 C2
 Gerrards Cross SL9 188 E6
 Old Windsor SL4 211 B2
 Wraysbury TW19 211 E1
Grange View HP27 139 E7
Grange Way SL0 207 F7
Grangewood SL3 206 C8
Grant Ave SL1 205 E7
Grantham Ct MK5 46 C5
Grantham Mews HP4 135 D4
Grant Ho 6 SL8 185 A4
Granville Ave SL2 205 D8
Granville Dene HP3 146 A4
Granville Pl 5 HP20 115 D8
Granville Rd HP4 134 E6
Granville Sq MK15 35 C7
Granville St 4 HP20 115 D8
Grapevine Cl HP11 173 F4
Grasholm Way SL3 207 C2
Grasmere
 Aylesbury HP21 116 B5
 Windsor SL4 209 E7
Grasmere Ave SL2 206 A6
Grasmere Par SL2 206 B6
Grasmere Way
 Leighton Buzzard LU7 80 D7
 Milton Keynes MK2 58 D6
Grasscroft MK4 46 E4
Grass Hays HP21 116 C7
Grassingham End SL9 177 E3
Grassingham Rd SL9 177 E3
Grassington MK13 34 A5
Grasslands HP20 102 A1
Grassy La SL6 202 E7
Grattan Ct SL7 184 A3
Gratton Ct MK4 46 C3
Gratton Dr SL4 209 E3
Gravel Dr HP23 118 B3
GRAVEL HILL 177 F4
Gravel Hill
 Chalfont St Peter SL9 177 E3
 Henley-on-Thames RG9 191 D2
 Uxbridge UB8 201 D7
Gravelly Way HP10 163 F2
Gravel Path HP4 135 E5
Gravel Wlk MK46 13 F7
Graveney Pl MK6 35 B2
Grayburn Cl HP8 177 A8
Graylands Cl SL1 204 F5
Grayling Cl SL7 194 C8
Grayling Ct HP4 134 F6
Grays Cl NN12 17 D8
Grays La
 Paulerspury NN12 17 D8
 Yardley Gobion NN12 18 E6
Gray's La
 High Wycombe HP13 161 D2
 Ibstone HP14 169 C7
Gray's Mon★ SL2 198 F2
Grays Park Rd SL2 199 A3
Gray's Pl SL2 205 F5
Gray's Rd
 Slough SL1 205 F5
 Uxbridge UB10 201 E5
Grays Wlk HP5 144 B2
Greamesdyke Rd HP4 135 A3
Greatacre 7 HP5 144 C1
Great Benty UB7 208 E2
GREAT BRICKHILL 59 D2
Great Brickhill La MK17 59 D5
Greatchesters MK13 33 F5
Great Denson MK6 47 A8
GREATGAP 105 D6
Great Ground MK14 34 E7
GREAT HAMPDEN 150 D7
Greatheed Dell MK7 48 D4
Great Hill Cres SL6 202 C6
GREAT HIVINGS 144 A3
Great Hivings HP5 144 A4
GREAT HOLM 45 E8
GREAT HORWOOD 55 A1
Great Horwood CE Comb Sch MK17 55 A3
Great Horwood Rd MK18 65 F7
GREAT KIMBLE 139 E8
Great Kimble CE Inf Sch HP17 129 E1
GREAT KINGSHILL 162 E8
Great Kingshill CE Comb Sch HP15 162 C6
Great La
 Bierton HP22 102 A4
 Wendover HP22 131 B4
Great Linch MK10 36 A2
GREAT LINFORD 34 E8
Great Linford Comb Sch MK14 34 E8
Great Linford Lakes★ MK14 21 D3
Great Marlow Sch SL7 183 F4
Great Meadow Way HP19 114 F8
GREAT MISSENDEN 152 A6
Great Missenden CE Comb Sch HP16 152 B7
Great Missenden Sta HP16 152 A7
Great Monks St
 Milton Keynes, Wolverton MK12 33 C5
 Milton Keynes, Wymbush MK8 33 E2
Great Ormes MK4 56 F8
Great Pasture MK10 35 F3
Great Slade MK18 52 D6
Great Stone HP18 112 F3
Great Western St 22 HP20 115 D8
Greaves Rd HP13 173 D6
Grebe Cl HP19 101 F3
Grecian St HP20 116 A8
Greenacre SL4 209 E5
Green Acre HP21 116 A7
Greenacres
 Aylesbury HP22 89 B2
 Pitstone LU7 105 C4
Greenacres Ave UB10 190 F1
Green Acres Cl HP22 86 E7
Greenacres La HP10 163 A1
Greenacres The HP13 162 C1
Greenbury Cl WD3 167 C5
Green Cl
 Burnham SL6 204 A7
 High Wycombe HP13 173 F7
 Maidenhead SL6 195 F1
Green Common La HP10, HP9, SL1 186 C4
Green Cres HP10 185 C7
Greendale Mews SL2 206 A6

Green Dragon La HP10 185 B7
Green East Rd HP9 176 E3
Greene Field Rd HP4 135 C4
GREEN END
Granborough 76 A7
High Wycombe 160 A4
Green End
Aylesbury HP20 115 D8
Granborough MK18 76 A7
Great Brickhill MK17 59 D2
Green End La MK19 11 A3
Green End Rd HP14 159 E5
Green End St HP22 117 E5
Greenes Ct HP4 135 C5
Greene Wlk HP4 135 D3
Green Farm Rd MK16 22 C4
Greenfern Ave SL1 204 C7
GREENFIELD 168 A4
Greenfield End SL9 177 F3
Greenfield Rd MK16 22 A4
Greenfields
Adstock MK18 53 F1
Maidenhead SL6 203 A5
Upper Arncott OX6 94 D7
Green Ground OX33 123 A2
Green Hailey HP27 139 F3
Green Hill HP13 162 B1
Greenhill Cl MK5 46 A8
Green Hill Cl HP13 162 C1
Green Hill Gate HP13 162 B1
Green La
Amersham HP6 154 E2
Aspley Guise MK17 49 E4
Botley HP5 155 B6
Bovingdon HP3 146 A3
Burnham SL1 197 D4
Chesham Bois HP6 154 D3
Datchet SL3 211 B6
Eaton Bray LU6 92 D7
Farnham Common SL2 198 B6
Ivinghoe LU7 105 E5
Maidenhead SL6 203 A6
Milton Keynes MK12 33 D6
Owlswick HP27 128 B1
Prestwood HP16 151 E6
Radnage HP14 159 D5
Stokenchurch HP14 158 C5
Upper Arncott OX6 94 E7
Windsor SL4 210 B5
Greenlands
Flackwell Heath HP10 185 B8
Lacey Green HP27 149 D5
Greenlands Cl MK16 22 A3
Greenlands Ct SL6 202 B8
Greenlands La HP16 151 B7
Green Lane Cl HP6 154 D3
Green Lane Ct SL1 197 C2
Green Lane Rdbt MK9 35 B5
Greenlaw Pl MK3 47 A3
Greenleaf Ct SL3 211 A8
Greenleas Lower Sch LU7 80 C7
GREENLEYS 33 B5
Green Leys
High Wycombe HP13 161 C2
Maidenhead SL6 195 F2
Greenleys Fst Sch MK12 33 C5
Greenleys Jun Sch MK12 33 C5
Greenleys La MK12 33 C4
Greenleys Rdbt MK12 33 B6
Green North Rd HP9 176 E4
Greenock Rd SL1 205 A7
Green Park Dr MK16 22 C3
Green Park Sch MK16 22 B3
Green Path HP22, HP23 118 D4
Green Pk HP16 151 D6
Green Pl HP10 185 C8
Green Rd HP13 162 C2
Greenridge HP10 174 B8
Greensand View MK17 49 B5
Greenside
Bourne End SL8 185 A5
Prestwood HP16 151 C5
Slough SL2 205 A8
Greenside Hill MK4 46 B1
Greens Keep HP17 126 F6
Green St
Chorleywood WD3 167 C6
Hazlemere HP15 162 F4
High Wycombe HP11 172 F7
Green The
Amersham HP7 154 C1
Aston Abbotts HP22 88 D4
Brill HP18 110 B8
Burnham SL1 197 B1
Chalfont St Giles HP8 177 C8
Chearsley HP18 112 B2
Cheddington LU7 105 A7
Cosgrove MK19 19 F2
Cranfield MK43 24 E2
Cuddington HP18 112 F3
Deanshanger MK19 31 E4
Edlesborough LU6 92 F4
Great Horwood MK17 55 A3
Hanslope MK19 11 A2
Green The *continued*
Horton-cum-S OX33 108 A5
Hyde Heath HP6 153 C5
Little Missenden HP7 153 A2
Longwick HP27 138 D6
Maidenhead SL6 195 C7
Mentmore LU7 90 D4
Milton Keynes, Loughton MK5 46 A8
Milton Keynes, The Green MK6 47 C8
Newport Pagnell MK16 22 C4
Paulerspury NN12 17 B7
Pitstone LU7 105 D4
Quainton HP22 85 B5
Slough SL1 205 D4
Soulbury LU7 69 E3
Stoke Hammond MK17 69 E7
Thornborough MK18 54 A8
Turvey MK43 8 E5
West Drayton UB7 208 D3
Wingrave HP22 89 B2
Wooburn Green HP10 185 E5
Wraysbury TW19 211 E1
Green Tiles UB9 189 F4
Green Tiles La UB9 189 F5
Green Verges SL7 183 E3
Green View HP20 102 A2
Green View Cl HP3 146 A2
Greenway
Berkhamsted HP4 135 A4
Burnham SL1 197 B3
Chesham HP5 144 B3
Great Horwood MK17 55 A2
Haddenham HP17 126 F5
Milton Keynes MK10 36 C3
2 Thame OX9 125 F1
Green Way MK17 57 D4
Greenway Bsns Pk MK17 55 A1
Greenway Ct 12 HP13 173 B7
Greenway Fst Sch HP4 134 F4
Greenway Par HP5 144 B3
Greenways
Bow Brickhill MK17 48 C2
Eaton Bray LU6 92 D7
Greenways Dr SL6 202 A8
Greenway The
Gerrards Cross SL9 188 D8
High Wycombe HP13 173 B7
Slough SL1 204 D5
Tring HP23 118 F5
Tylers Green HP10 163 B1
Uxbridge UB8 201 D3
Greenway Wlk MK18 41 F1
Green West Rd HP9 176 E3
Greenwich Gdns MK16 22 C2
Greenwood HP14 150 A2
Greenwood Ave OX39 147 C5
Greenwood Cl
Amersham HP6 154 E1
Seer Green HP9 176 D4
Greenwood Mdw OX39 147 D6
Greenwood Pl MK18 63 D3
Greenwood The HP22 117 D5
Greenyard The NN7 1 B7
Greetham Rd HP21 116 C6
Gregories Ct HP9 175 D3
Gregories Dr MK7 48 D6
Gregories Farm La HP9 175 D2
Gregories Rd HP9 175 C3
Gregory Dr SL4 211 B1
Gregory Rd SL2 187 D2
Grenadine Way HP23 119 A5
Grendon Rd
Edgcott HP18 72 F1
Kingswood HP18 83 C3
GRENDON UNDERWOOD 83 A6
Grendon Underwood Comb Sch HP18 83 A6
Grendon Way HP22 102 A4
Grenfell Ave
High Wycombe HP12 172 D7
Maidenhead SL6 202 F6
Grenfell Pl SL6 202 F6
Grenfell Rd
Beaconsfield HP9 175 E3
Maidenhead SL6 202 E6
Grenville Ave HP22 131 A7
Grenville Cl SL1 197 B3
Grenville Comb Sch MK18 52 D7
Grenville Ct WD3 167 C5
Grenville Gn HP21 115 D4
Grenville Rd
Aylesbury HP21 115 D5
Buckingham MK18 41 C1
Grenville Way OX9 126 B1
Gresham Ct HP4 135 B3
Gresham Rd SL1 205 A7
Greyfriars Ct MK10 36 B2
Greyhound Ct MK18 66 A4
Greyhound La
Thame OX9 125 F1
Winslow MK18 66 A4
Greyhound Wlk OX9 125 F1
Greys Hill RG9 191 D1
Greys Rd RG9 191 D1
Greys The MK6 47 C8
Greystoke Cl HP4 135 A3
Greystoke Rd SL2 204 F8
Greystonley 1 MK4 46 C2
Griffin Cl
Maidenhead SL6 202 E5
Slough SL1 205 C4
Griffin Field LU7 78 E8
Griffin Ind Mall HP19 101 B1
Griffin La HP19 101 B1
Griffin Lane Ind Est HP19 101 B1
Griffith Gate MK10 36 A3
Griffith Gate Rdbt MK10 36 A2
Griffith Ho HP10 174 C2
Griffiths Acre HP17 114 E5
Griffiths Yd HP5 144 B1
Griffon Cl MK6 47 A7
Grigby Rise MK6 47 A7
Griggs Orch MK16 14 A2
Grimbold Ct MK15 35 C7
Grimmer Cl HP19 100 F3
Grimms Hill HP16 151 F7
Grimms Mdw HP14 150 B1
Grimsby Rd SL1 204 F4
Grimsdell's La HP6 154 D2
Grimsdyke Rd HP23 119 D1
Gringer Hill SL6 202 E8
Grizedale MK13 34 B5
Groombridge MK7 48 A7
Groom Rd HP16 151 C5
Groomsby Dr LU7 105 E5
Grooms Cotts HP5 145 B1
Grooms Ct HP11 174 A4
Grosmont Cl 1 MK4 46 B2
Grosvenor Cl SL0 200 D2
Grosvenor Ct SL1 205 E7
Grosvenor Dr SL6 203 C8
Grosvenor Way HP19 114 E8
Groundsel Cl MK7 48 B6
Grove Ash MK1 47 D3
Grovebury Rd LU7 80 F4
Grove Cl
Chalfont St Peter SL9 177 C2
1 Slough SL1 206 A3
Grove Cotts UB9 190 C8
Grove Ct
Beaconsfield HP9 175 D2
Bierton HP22 102 C5
Maidenhead SL6 202 D7
Turvey MK43 8 E6
Grove End SL9 177 C2
Grove End Barns OX9 126 B4
Grove Gdns HP23 119 B5
Grove Hill SL9 177 C3
Grove Ind Sch The MK5 46 C7
Grove La
Ashley Green HP5 145 C5
Chalfont St Peter SL9 177 C2
Little Kimble HP17 129 E2
Uxbridge UB8 201 F1
Grovelands HP11 173 A6
Grove Leys HP23 119 C5
Grove Pk HP23 119 C5
Grove Rd
Amersham HP6 154 F1
Beaconsfield HP9 175 E2
Burnham SL1, SL2 197 E4
Hazlemere HP15 162 F3
High Wycombe HP12 172 C8
Maidenhead SL6 202 F7
Tring HP23 119 C5
Turvey MK43 8 E6
Uxbridge UB8 201 D5
Windsor SL4 210 D5
Grove Road Prim Sch HP23 119 C5
Grovers Ct HP27 139 A2
Grovesbrook MK17 48 D2
Groves Cl SL8 185 C3
Groves Rd HP22 131 E7
Groves Way
Chesham HP5 143 F2
Cookham Rise SL6 195 E6
Grove The
Amersham HP6 154 D4
Latimer HP5 155 D3
Medmenham SL7 193 E6
Milton Keynes, Bradwell MK13 34 A4
Milton Keynes, Rickley Park MK3 58 A8
Newport Pagnell MK16 22 B3
Slough SL1 206 A4
Tring HP23 119 C5
Waddesdon HP18 99 A6
Groveway
Bow Brickhill MK7 48 B7
Milton Keynes, Redmoor MK3 47 A3
Milton Keynes, Simpson MK6 47 D5
Grove Way
Chorleywood WD3 167 B4
Uxbridge UB8 201 D5
Waddesdon HP18 99 A6
Grovewood Cl WD3 167 B4
Grubbins La HP27 150 B5
Grubbs Cl LU7 68 D2
Grubwood La SL6 195 A7
Grundy Ho UB8 201 D3
Gryms Dyke HP16 151 D6
Guards Club Rd SL6 203 C7
Guards Rd SL4 209 C5
Guards View SL4 210 D6
Guards Wlk 1 SL4 209 C5
GUBBLECOTE 104 D3
Guernsey Cl HP19 101 A3
Guest Gdns MK13 34 B8
Guildford Ave MK4 45 E1
Guildford Cl MK18 52 A4
Guillemot Way HP19 101 E3
Guinea Orch MK46 6 E4
Guinions Rd HP13 173 F5
Guise Ct MK17 49 F4
Gullet Nature Reserve The★ SL6 202 E5
Gullicot Way LU7 105 C4
Gulliver's SL4 210 D8
Gulliver's Dinosaur & Farm Park★ MK15 35 C4
Gulliver's Land★ MK15 35 C4
Gull Way 4 HP19 101 F3
Gundale Ct MK4 46 B2
Gun La MK16 14 A2
Gunmaker Ct MK14 34 F6
Gunthorpe Rd SL7 184 A3
Gunver La MK4 57 B8
Gurnard Cl UB7 208 D6
Gurnards Ave MK6 35 A2
Gurnells Rd HP9 176 C5
Gurney Cl
10 Aylesbury HP20 101 F2
Beaconsfield HP9 175 D2
Milton Keynes MK5 46 A7
Gurney Ct LU6 92 F6
Gurneys Mdw HP15 163 D7
Guttmann Rd HP21 115 F5
Gwendale SL6 195 C1
Gweneth Ct SL7 183 D3
Gwent Cl SL6 202 B4
Gwynant Ct MK2 58 C3
Gwynne Cl
Tring HP23 119 A5
Windsor SL4 209 E6
Gynant Rd HP13 173 F6
Gyosei International Sch UK MK15 35 C5
Gypsy La
Aspley Guise MK17 49 F3
High Wycombe HP11 173 D5
Marlow SL7 183 E4
Stoke Poges SL2 187 E1

H

Haberley Mead MK13 34 B3
Hackett Pl MK16 24 A6
HADDENHAM 127 B5
Haddenham Airfield HP17 126 E7
Haddenham Bsns Pk HP17 126 F7
Haddenham Com Inf Sch HP17 127 A6
Haddenham Jun Sch HP17 127 A6
Haddenham Mus★ HP17 126 F6
Haddenham Rd HP17 127 A3
Haddenham St Mary's CE Sch HP17 127 A4
Haddenham & Thame Parkway Sta HP17 126 E6
Haddington Cl
Milton Keynes MK3 46 E2
Wendover HP22 131 D6
Haddington Way HP20 102 A1
Haddon MK8 45 F8
Haddon Rd
Chorleywood WD3 167 C4
Maidenhead SL6 202 C5
Hadfield Rd TW19 213 D1
Hadland Cl HP3 146 A4
Hadley Ct SL3 212 E6
Hadley Pl MK13 34 C3
Hadlow Ct SL1 205 C5
Hadrians Dr MK13 34 A5
Hadrian's Gate NN13 38 A7
Haggar St HP17 114 B5
Hag Hill La SL6 204 A7
Hag Hill Rise SL6 204 A7
Haglis Dr HP22 131 B6
Haig Dr SL1 205 B4
Haileybury Ct SL4 210 A4
Hailey Croft OX39 147 B6
Hailey Ct SL6 202 F5
Hainault Ave MK14 22 A1
Haines Cl HP19 100 F2
Haines Rd HP15 162 F6
Haithewaite MK8 33 D1
Haldene MK8 33 E2
Hale SL4 209 F6
Hale Ave MK11 32 E5
Hale La HP22 131 E3
Hale Leys Sh Ctr 23 HP20 115 D8
Hale Rd HP22 131 C3
Hales Croft HP21 116 B4
Hale St HP20 115 E8
Halfacre Hill SL9 177 F2
Halfway Hos
Hanslope MK19 10 F4
Maidenhead SL6 195 E4
Halfway House La HP5 153 F7
Halifax Cl SL6 202 A8
Halifax Ho HP7 166 C8
Halifax Rd
Heronsgate WD3 167 C2
High Wycombe HP12 172 D5
Maidenhead SL6 202 A8
Halifax Way SL6 202 A8
Halings La UB9 189 E7
Halkingcroft SL3 206 C4
Hall Cl
High Wycombe HP13 173 F5
Maids Moreton MK18 41 F3
Old Stratford MK19 32 B6
Hall Cotts HP18 82 F7
Hall Ct SL3 211 B7
Halldore Hill SL6 195 E7
Hall La MK16 23 C8
Hall Mdw SL1 197 C3
Hall Park Gate HP4 135 E3
Hall Park Hill HP4 135 E3
Hall Pk HP4 135 E3
Hall Place (Berkshire Coll of Agriculture) SL6 194 A1
Halls Cnr HP10 174 A1
Halse Dr SL1 197 F7
Halswell Pl MK10 36 A3
HALTON 117 D1
Haltonchesters MK13 33 F6
Halton Comb Sch HP22 131 D7
Halton La HP22 131 B8
Halton Wood Forest Wlks★ HP23 132 A5
Halton Wood Rd HP22 131 D5
Haly Cl MK13 34 B4
Hamberlins La HP4, HP23 134 B7
HAMBLEDEN 181 D1
Hambleden RG9 181 C2
Hambleden Mill RG9 192 C7
Hambleden Pl RG9 192 D6
Hambleden Rise RG9 192 D8
Hambleden Wlk SL6 195 E3
Hambledon Cl HP21 116 B5
Hamble Dr HP21 115 C6
Hambleton Gr MK4 46 B2
Hambling Pl LU6 93 F8
Hamburg Croft MK5 46 B3
Hambye Cl HP27 149 E4
Hamer Cl HP3 146 A3
Hamfield Cotts SL6 195 E7
HAM GREEN 83 D2
Hamilton Ave RG9 191 E1
Hamilton Cl HP4 107 C5
Hamilton Ct
Aylesbury HP19 101 D1
High Wycombe HP13 173 B8
Hamilton Gdns SL1 197 B2
Hamilton La MK3 57 C6
Hamilton Mead 5 HP3 146 A4
Hamilton Pk SL6 202 A6
Hamilton Pl SL9 188 E6
Hamilton Prim Sch 17 HP13 173 B7
Hamilton Prim Sch (Annexe) HP13 173 B8
Hamilton Rd
Berkhamsted HP4 135 B4
High Wycombe HP13 162 C1
Slough SL1 205 A7
Thame OX9 126 A1
Uxbridge UB8 201 D1
Ham Island SL4 211 C3
Ham La SL4 211 C3
Hamlins MK6 47 A6
Hammersley La HP10, HP11 174 B5
Hammerwood Gate MK7 48 A7
Hammond Cres MK15 35 B6
Hammond End SL2 198 B8
Hamon Way 2 MK12 33 A6
Hampden Ave HP5 144 A1
HAMPDEN BOTTOM 141 B2
Hampden Cl
Aylesbury HP21 115 D6
Aylesbury HP22 116 B1
Stoke Mandeville HP22 116 B1
Stoke Poges SL2 199 A2
Hampden Gate HP27 150 C5
Hampden Gdns HP21 115 D6
Hampden Hill
Beaconsfield HP9 175 B2
Charndon OX27 72 E6
Hampden Ho 2 HP13 173 F6
Hampden Rd
Aylesbury HP21 115 D6
Chalfont St Peter SL9 177 D2
High Wycombe HP13 173 B8
Hughenden Valley HP16 151 B3

Hampden Rd *continued*
Maidenhead SL6 202 B8
Slough SL3 206 F3
Speen HP27 150 C5
Stoke Mandeville HP22 116 B1
Wendover HP22 131 C5
Hampden Sq 2 HP19 115 A8
Hampden Villas OX27 71 F7
Hampshire Ave SL1 205 C8
Hampshire Ct MK3 46 F2
Hampshire Lodge 8 SL6 202 F6
Hampson Cl MK13 34 A5
Hampstead Cl 7 HP19 100 F1
Hampstead Gate MK13 34 C3
Hampton 7 MK8 45 F8
Hampton Ho SL3 212 D7
Hanbury Cl SL1 204 A8
Hancock Cl HP21 115 E5
Handel Mead MK7 48 E5
Handleton Comm HP14 171 B5
Handley Page Cl MK43 24 E2
Handy Cross HP11 172 F3
Hangar Rd UB9 189 E7
Hanging Croft Cl 4 HP13 173 F6
Hangings La HP16 151 A6
Hanley Cl SL4 209 D6
Hanmer Rd MK6 47 E5
Hannah Ball Inf Sch HP13 173 D7
Hannon Rd HP21 115 C5
Hanover Cl
3 Aylesbury HP19 101 A2
Slough SL1 206 A3
Windsor SL4 209 F6
Hanover Ct
2 Aylesbury HP21 115 E7
Hazlemere HP15 163 B3
Leighton Buzzard LU7 80 D7
Milton Keynes MK14 34 D7
Hanover Mead SL6 203 C3
Hanover Way SL4 209 F6
Hanscomb Cl MK15 35 C2
Hansen Croft MK5 46 B5
HANSLOPE 11 B3
Hanslope Comb Sch MK19 11 A3
Hanslope Rd MK19 19 F6
Hanson Cl UB7 208 F3
Hanson Way HP21 116 A4
Harborne Ct MK8 33 C2
Harborough Cl SL1 204 D5
Harbourne Cl HP21 115 C3
Harby Cl MK4 46 C1
Harcourt
Milton Keynes MK13 34 A3
Wraysbury TW19 211 E1
Harcourt Cl
Dorney SL6 203 F3
Henley-on-Thames RG9 191 C1
Leighton Buzzard LU7 80 E7
Harcourt Gn HP19 101 B2
Harcourt Rd
Dorney SL4 203 F3
Tring HP23 119 C4
Windsor SL4 209 F6
Hardenwaye HP13 162 E1
Harding Rd
Chesham HP5 144 D1
Milton Keynes MK10 48 C8
Hardings Cl SL0 200 C2
Harding Spur 13 SL3 206 F1
Hardings Row SL0 200 D2
HARDMEAD 15 D3
Hardmead Rd MK43 8 A3
HARDWICK 87 B3
Hardwick Cl SL6 202 A8
Hardwicke Gdns HP6 154 E1
Hardwick Mews MK17 49 B3
Hardwick Pl MK17 49 B4
Hardwick Rd MK17 49 B4
Hardy Cl
Aylesbury HP21 115 E7
Slough SL1 205 A5
Hardy Mead Ct HP11 174 B2
Hardy Mews UB8 201 C3
Harebell Cl MK7 48 B5
Harebell Wlk HP15 162 F6
Harebridge La HP22 117 E1
Hare Cl MK18 52 E7
Hareden Croft MK4 46 B2
Harefield Rd
Maidenhead SL6 202 A7
Uxbridge UB8 201 D6
Harehatch La SL1 186 F3
Hare La HP16 152 B3
Hare Lane End HP16 152 A3
Harescombe Ct HP9 175 D3
Haresfoot Sch HP4 135 B1
Hare Shoots SL6 202 E5
Harewood Pl SL1 206 A3
Harewood Rd HP8 166 C6
Hargrave Rd SL6 202 D8
Hargreaves Nook MK14 22 B2
Harkness Cl MK2 58 D6
Harkness Rd SL1 204 B8
Harlans Cl MK6 47 B8
Harlech Ho 5 HP13 173 F7
Harlech Pl MK3 57 E7
Harlequin Pl MK5 45 F3
Harlesden Cl MK10 35 E1
Harle Stone Ct MK14 22 A1
Harley Ct SL1 205 C4
Harleyford La SL7 194 B7
Harling Rd LU6 93 B4
Harlow Cres 6 MK4 45 E2
Harlow Rd HP13 173 C6
Harmans Cross MK10 36 B3
Harman Terr HP12 172 D7
Harman Wlk HP12 172 C3
HARMONDSWORTH 213 D8
Harmondsworth La UB7 213 E8
Harmondsworth Prim Sch UB7 213 D8
Harmondsworth Rd UB7 208 E2
Harnett Dr MK12 32 F6
Harper Cl OX25 94 D7
Harpers La MK14 34 F8
Harrier Cl HP20 101 F3
Harrier Ct MK6 47 A8
Harrier Dr MK6 47 A8
Harries Cl HP5 144 B1
Harries Way HP15 163 B6
Harriet Walker Way WD3 167 F2
Harrington Cl SL4 209 F3
Harris Cl HP18 110 A8
Harris Ct 7 HP20 101 F2
Harris Gdns SL1 205 C4
Harrison Barber Cotts SL3 212 D7
Harrison Cl MK5 46 D6
Harrison Pl OX9 125 F1
Harrison Way SL1 204 D5
Harris Rd HP14 171 B5
Harroell
Long Crendon, Church End HP18 125 D6
Long Crendon HP18 125 D5
Harrogate Ct SL3 207 A1
HARROLD 3 F6
Harrold Lower Sch MK43 3 F6
Harrold Priory Mid Sch MK43 3 F6
Harrold Rd MK46 3 B1
Harrow Cl
Aylesbury HP21 115 E4
Maidenhead SL6 195 E1
Harrowden MK13 34 B7
Harrow La SL6 195 E1
Harrow Mkt The SL3 207 A3
Harrow Rd SL3 206 F3
Harrow Yd 6 HP23 119 A3
Hartdames MK5 46 A3
Hartfield Cl MK7 48 A7
Hartington Gr 5 MK4 46 B3
Hartland Ave MK4 57 B8
Hartland Cl SL1 205 D5
Hartley MK14 34 E8
Hartley Cl SL3 199 C4
Hartley Copse SL4 211 A1
Hartley Ct SL9 188 E5
Hart Moor Cl HP14 158 E4
Harts Rd HP17 127 B6
Hart St RG9 191 E2
HARTWELL 10 D8
Hartwell Cl HP10 163 C2
Hartwell Dr HP9 175 D3
Hartwell End HP21 115 B7
Hartwell Rd
Ashton NN7 9 F8
Hanslope MK19 10 E5
Hartwort Cl MK7 48 B5
Harvard Cl MK14 21 F2
Harvest Bank HP6 153 C4
Harvester Cl MK12 33 B5
Harvest Hill HP10 185 D2
Harvest Hill Rd SL6 202 F3
Harvey Dr MK46 6 F1
Harvey Ho SL3 206 E7
Harvey Orch HP9 175 C3
Harvey Rd
Aylesbury HP21 115 E5
Dunstable LU6 93 D7
Slough SL3 207 B4
Harvil Rd UB9, UB10 190 E4
Harvington Pk LU7 105 D3
Harwich Rd SL1 205 A7
Harwood Dr UB10 201 F4
Harwood Rd SL7 183 C1
Harwood St MK13 34 A7
Hasgill Ct MK13 34 B4
Haslemere Rd SL4 210 A6
Haslerig Cl HP21 115 F5
Haslow Ct MK8 33 E3
Hasting Cl SL6 203 C2
Hastings MK11 32 E5
Hastings Mdw SL2 199 A4
HASTOE 132 F7
Hastoe Cross HP23 133 A7
Hastoe Farm Barns HP23 132 F7
Hastoe Hill HP23 132 F8
Hastoe La HP23 119 A2
Hastoe Pk HP20 101 F2
Hastoe Row HP23 133 A7
Hatches La
Great Kingshill HP15 151 C1
Hughenden Valley HP15 162 B8
Hatchet Leys La MK18 53 F8
Hatchgate Gdns SL1 197 D1
Hatch La
Harmondsworth UB7 213 D7
Radnage HP14 160 B4
Windsor SL4 210 A5
Hatchlands MK8 33 F1
Hatch Pl SL6 195 E7
Hatch The SL4 209 C7
Hatfield Cl SL6 202 C6
Hatfield Rd SL1 206 A4
Hathaway Ct MK8 45 E8
Hatter's La HP13 173 F6
Hatton MK6 47 D6
Hatton Ave SL2 198 D1
Hatton Ct SL4 210 C5
Hatton Gr UB7 208 D4
Hauksbee Gdns MK5 46 D5
Havelock Bsns Pk SL6 202 C7
Havelock Cres SL6 202 B7
Havelock Ct HP20 101 D1
Havelock Rd SL6 202 B7
Havelock St HP20 101 D1
Havenfield Ct 16 HP13 173 B7
Havenfield Rd HP12 172 C4
Haven of Rest SL6 203 B7
Haven Shaw Cl HP21 116 A5
Haven St MK10 36 C3
HAVERSHAM 20 E2
Haversham Rd MK19 20 D1
Haversham Village Sch MK19 20 E2
Hawfinch 1 HP19 101 E3
Hawker Ct SL3 207 A3
Hawkes Cl SL3 207 B3
Hawkhurst Gate MK7 47 F7
Hawkings Way HP3 146 A5
Hawkins Cl MK11 32 D5
Hawkmoor Cl MK6 47 B8
Hawkridge MK4 46 E3
Hawkshead Dr MK4 46 C3
Hawks Hill SL8 185 C3
Hawkshill Dr HP3 146 F8
Hawkshill Rd SL2 198 A2
Hawkslade Furlong HP21 115 D3
Hawksmoor Cl HP13 173 A8
Hawkswood MK46 6 F5
Hawkswood Gr SL3 199 F6
Hawkswood La SL3, SL9 199 F8
Hawkwell Dr HP23 119 C4
Hawkwell Est MK19 32 B7
Haw La HP14 149 A2
Hawleys La HP22 87 A6
Haworth Croft 2 MK10 36 B3
HAWRIDGE 133 E1
Hawridge & Cholesbury CE Sch HP5 133 E2
HAWRIDGE COMMON 133 E2
Hawridge La HP5 143 E8
Hawridge Vale HP5 133 F1
Hawthorn Ave MK2 58 E8
Hawthorn Cl
Aylesbury HP20 101 F2
Iver Heath SL0 200 C2
Turvey MK43 8 E6
Hawthorn Cres HP15 163 B2
Hawthorn Dr UB9 201 C6
Hawthorne Cl
Leighton Buzzard LU7 80 E8
Marlow SL7 183 E4
Hawthorne Cres
Slough SL1 205 F7
West Drayton UB7 208 F4
Hawthorne Gdns HP10 174 A2
Hawthorne Rd HP13 174 A6
Hawthorn Gdns SL6 202 E5
Hawthorn La SL2 198 A5
Hawthorn Pl HP10 174 C8
Hawthorn Rd HP27 139 C3
Hawthorns The
Berkhamsted HP4 135 A5
Cranfield MK43 25 B1
Felden HP3 146 F7
Little Chalfont HP8 166 C7
Maple Cross WD3 178 D5
Monks Risborough HP27 139 C6
Poyle SL3 212 F6
Wooburn Green HP10 185 E6
Hawthorn Way
Chesham HP5 144 D2
Wing LU7 79 E3
Hawthorn Wlk HP15 163 B2
Hawtrey Cl SL1 206 B4
Hawtrey Rd SL4 210 C5
Hay Barn Bsns Pk The HP22 88 C6
Hayden Ho 3 HP11 172 F7
Haydock Cl MK3 57 C6
Haydon Abbey Comb Sch HP19 101 C2
Haydon Ct SL6 202 E6
HAYDON HILL 100 E2
Haydon Ind Sch 9 HP20 101 D1
Haydon Rd HP19 101 C2
Hayes Cl SL6 203 D1
Hayes Pl SL7 183 D1
Hayes Rd MK19 31 F5
Hayfield Dr HP15 163 B2
Hay La SL3 199 D8
Hayles Field RG9 170 E1
Hayling Cl SL1 205 B5
Haymaker Cl UB10 201 F5
Hayman Rise MK8 45 D6
Haymill Rd SL1, SL2 197 D1
Haymill Valley Nature Reserve★ SL2 204 E8
Haynes Cl
Bow Brickhill MK17 48 D2
Slough SL3 206 F1
Haynes Ho HP12 172 B3
Haynes Mead HP4 135 A6
Hayse Hill SL4 209 D6
Haystacks The HP13 173 B7
Haythrop Cl MK15 35 B6
Hayward Pl SL8 185 C2
Haywards Cl RG9 191 C1
Haywards Croft MK12 33 B5
Haywards Mead SL4 204 F1
Haywood Dr WD3 167 F4
Haywood Pk
Chorleywood WD3 167 F4
Stewkley LU7 68 C3
Haywoods Dr HP3 146 F8
Haywood Way HP19 100 F3
Hayworth Pl 2 MK4 45 D2
Hazelbury Rd HP13 173 D6
Hazel Cl SL7 183 C6
Hazelcroft Cl UB10 201 F5
Hazel Ct WD3 178 E5
Hazeldene HP22 131 C4
HAZELEY 45 D5
Hazeley Sch The MK8 45 D5
Hazel Gr MK2 58 D7
Hazelhurst 7 MK4 46 B2
Hazelhurst Rd SL1 197 D3
Hazell Ave HP21 116 A7
Hazell Cl SL6 202 F8
Hazell Pk HP7 165 D8
Hazell Rd HP16 151 C5
Hazell Way SL2 198 F6
HAZELMERE 163 B4
Hazel Rd HP4 135 D3
Hazelwood MK14 34 F8
Hazelwood Cl HP5 144 D2
Hazely HP23 119 C4
Hazlehurst Dr HP21 116 A5
Hazlemere CE Comb Sch HP15 162 F3
Hazlemere Ct HP15 163 A4
Hazlemere Rd
Slough SL2 206 B5
Tylers Green HP10 163 C2
Hazlemere View HP15 163 B5
Hazley Wlk MK18 41 F1
Headington Cl SL6 202 A7
Headington Pl SL2 205 F5
Headington Rd SL6 202 A7
Headland Cl 1 HP16 152 A8
Headlands Dr HP4 135 E5
Healey Ave HP13 173 D7
Heaney Cl MK16 22 A5
Hearn Cl HP10 162 F2
Hearne Ct HP8 177 B7
Hearne Dr SL6 203 A1
Hearne Pl MK6 46 F8
Hearnes Cl HP9 176 D5
Hearne's Mdw HP9 176 D5
Heathacre SL3 212 E6
Heath Cl
Aylesbury HP21 116 B5
Holmer Green HP15 163 B6
Stanwell TW19 213 C1
Woburn Sands MK17 49 C3
Heathcote SL6 203 B2
Heathcote Ct 2 SL4 210 D4
Heathcote Way UB7 208 D5
Heath Ct
Leighton Buzzard LU7 70 E3
Uxbridge UB8 201 D5
HEATH END
Cholesbury 134 A2
Prestwood 151 E1
Heath End Cl HP15 151 E1
Heath End Rd
Flackwell Heath HP10 174 A1
Great Kingshill HP15, HP16 151 E2
Little Marlow HP10 173 D2
Heather Cl
Buckingham MK18 52 C7
Uxbridge UB8 208 F8
Heathercroft MK14 34 E7
Heatherden Gn SL0 200 D4
Heather La UB7 208 E7
Heather Mead LU6 92 E5
Heathers Cl MK18 73 B5
Heatherside Gdns SL2 187 D1
Heatherton House Sch HP6 154 C3
Heatherton Pk HP6 154 B3
Heather Wlk
Aylesbury HP21 115 B6
Heather Wlk *continued*
Hazelmere HP15 163 A3
Heathfield MK12 33 E4
Heathfield Rd
High Wycombe HP12 172 B7
Taplow SL1 186 A1
Heath La MK17 49 A2
Heathlands Dr SL6 202 A6
Heath Lawn HP10 173 F1
Heath Rd
Beaconsfield HP9 186 A8
Great Brickhill MK17, LU7 59 E1
Hyde Heath HP6 153 C5
Heathrow Bvd UB7 213 F7
Heathrow Cl UB7 213 B6
Heathrow Prim Sch UB7 213 F8
Heathrow T5 Sta/U Sta TW6 213 C4
Heath The LU7 70 E4
Heath Way SL0 200 D3
Heavens Lea SL8 185 C2
Hedge Lea HP10 185 D8
HEDGERLEY 187 D3
Hedgerley OX39 147 B6
HEDGERLEY GREEN 187 E4
HEDGERLEY HILL 187 E2
Hedgerley Hill SL2 187 D2
Hedgerley La
Beaconsfield HP9 186 F8
Gerrards Cross SL9 188 B4
Hedgerley SL2 187 D6
Hedgerow SL9 177 E4
Hedgerows The MK4 46 E4
Hedges Ct MK5 46 B6
Hedingham Ct MK5 46 A5
Hedingham Mews SL6 202 D7
Hedley Cl HP22 118 A4
Hedley Rd HP10 185 B8
Hedley View HP10 174 D1
HEDSOR 185 F3
Hedsor Hill SL8 185 C1
Hedsor La
Hedsor HP10 185 F2
Taplow SL1 186 A2
Hedsor Rd SL8 185 B2
Hedsor View Cotts SL6 195 F7
HEELANDS 34 C4
Heelands Fst Sch MK13 34 B4
Heights The SL7 194 B8
Hele Ct MK7 48 B3
Helena Rd SL4 210 D5
Helen Cotts SL4 209 D5
Helford Cl HP21 115 D4
Helford Pl MK6 35 A1
Heligan Pl MK4 45 F1
Hellfire Caves★ HP14 160 F2
Hellyer Way SL8 185 C3
Helmsley Rise MK4 45 E1
Helston La SL4 210 B6
Helston Pl 3 MK6 34 F1
Hemel Hempstead Rd HP4 107 F1
Hemingway Cl MK16 21 F5
Hemingway Rd HP19 100 F2
Hemlock Cl HP22 116 C4
Hemmings The HP4 134 F3
Hemming Way SL2 198 B2
Hemp Hill 10 HP19 115 A8
Hemp La HP23 119 F1
Hempson Ave SL3 206 C3
Hempstead Rd HP3 146 B5
HEMPTON WAINHILL 147 F7
Hemsdale SL6 195 B1
Hemwood Rd SL4 209 D4
Hencroft Mews 14 SL1 205 F4
Hencroft Street N SL1 205 F4
Hencroft Street S SL1 205 F3
Henden Mews SL6 202 A6
Henders MK11 32 E5
Hendon Ct 5 MK10 35 F1
Hendons Way SL6 203 B1
Hendon Way TW19 213 D1
Hendrix Dr MK8 45 D7
Hengistbury La MK4 46 A1
Henley Coll The RG9 191 D1
Henley Coll The (Rotherfield Bldgs) RG9 191 C1
Henley Lodge 12 SL6 202 F6
Henley Management Coll RG9 192 B7
HENLEY-ON-THAMES 191 B1
Henley-on-Thames Sta RG9 191 E1
Henley Rd
Hurley SL6 193 D3
Maidenhead SL6, SL7 194 B2
Marlow SL7 194 B8
Slough SL1 204 F7
Hennerton Way HP13 173 F6
Henrietta Rd OX9 126 A1
Henry III Tower 17 SL4 210 D6
Henry Rd
Aylesbury HP20 116 B8
Slough SL1 205 D4

Henry St HP23 119 A3
Hensman Gate MK10 35 F4
Henson Cl MK43 24 E3
HENTON 137 E2
Henton Mews 5 HP19 115 A8
Hepburn Cres MK4 45 E3
Hepleswell MK8 33 E1
Hepplewhite Cl HP13 173 D8
Herbert Rd HP13 174 A7
Herberts Hole
  Chesham HP5 143 C1
  South Heath HP5, HP16 142 F1
Hercies Rd UB10 201 F5
Herdman Cl MK12 33 B5
Herd's Hill MK18 64 A4
Hereford Ho HP13 173 F8
Hereford Way HP19 101 A3
Heritage Cl UB8 201 C1
Heritage Gate SL9 188 E7
Heritage House Specl Sch HP5 144 D1
Heritage Wlk WD3 167 E6
Hermitage Cl SL3 206 C3
Hermitage La SL4 210 A4
Hermitage Prim Sch UB8 201 D5
Hermitage The
  Great Missenden HP16 152 A7
  Uxbridge UB8 201 D6
Hernes Oak OX39 147 D8
Heron Cl
  Aylesbury HP20 116 C8
  Uxbridge UB8 201 D6
Heron Dr SL3 207 B2
Heron Lodge MK14 34 C6
Herons Elm HP4 134 E7
Heronsfield Ho WD3 167 B3
HERONSGATE 167 D2
Heronsgate Rd WD3 167 B3
Heronsgate Sch MK7 48 B5
Heronshaw Sch MK7 48 B5
Herons Pl
  Maidenhead SL6 196 C3
  Marlow SL7 183 E3
Heron The HP19 101 E4
Herries Sch SL6 195 B8
Herriot Cl MK16 22 A5
Herschel Gram Sch SL1 205 C7
Herschel Sports SL1 205 C7
Herschel St SL1 205 F4
Herston Cl HP21 116 B5
Hertford Pl MK3 46 F2
Hervines Ct HP6 154 C2
Hervines Rd HP6 154 C2
Hesketh Rd NN12 18 E6
Hetherington Cl SL2 197 F2
Hetherington Way UB10 201 E8
Het's Orch HP27 149 E5
Hetton Cl MK13 34 C4
Heusden Way SL9 188 F3
Hever Cl
  Maidenhead SL6 202 C6
  Pitstone LU7 105 D2
Hewgate Ct RG9 191 E1
Hexham Gdns MK3 57 D6
Heybridge Cres MK7 48 B3
Heydon Ct MK13 34 A7
Heynes Gn SL6 202 B3
Heythrop Dr UB10 201 F8
Heyward Gate MK6 47 C5
Heywood Ave SL6 202 A1
Heywood Court Cl SL6 202 A2
Heywood Gdns SL6 202 A1
Hibbert Rd SL6 203 B4
Hibbert's Alley 16 SL4 210 D6
Hibberts Way SL9 188 E8
Hickmans Cl MK18 51 B6
Hickman St HP19 114 F8
Hickox Ct HP10 185 F7
Hicks Farm Rise HP13 173 F7
Hidcote Dr MK4 45 F1
Hide The MK6 47 C6
Higgs Ct MK5 46 A8
HIGHAM CROSS 10 D3
Higham Cross Rd MK19 10 E4
Higham Mead HP5 144 C1
Higham Rd HP5 144 C1
High Ash CE Comb Sch MK17 59 D2
High Beeches
  Gerrards Cross SL9 188 D2
  High Wycombe HP12 172 C6
High Beeches Cl SL7 183 C7
High Bois La HP6 154 D4
Highbridge Ind Est UB8 201 C5
Highbridge Rd HP21 115 E8
Highbridge Wlk 4 HP21 115 E8
Highbury La MK9 35 B3
High Coppice HP7 165 C8
Highcrest Com Sch HP13 173 E7
Highcroft Cl NN12 18 E6
HIGHER DENHAM 189 C4
Highfield
  Chalfont St Giles HP8 177 D8
  Long Crendon HP18 125 C7
Highfield Ave HP12 172 B5
Highfield Cl
  Amersham HP6 154 D2
  Milton Keynes MK3 47 B2
  Newport Pagnell MK16 22 E4
Highfield Ct
  Farnham Royal SL2 198 B4
  Hazelmere HP15 163 A3
Highfield Dr UB10 190 E1
Highfield La SL6 202 A4
Highfield Pk SL7 183 B1
Highfield Rd
  Berkhamsted HP4 135 D4
  Bourne End SL8 185 B4
  Chesham HP5 144 B2
  Flackwell Heath HP10 185 A8
  Maidenhead SL6 202 B8
  Princes Risborough HP27 139 C4
  Tring HP23 118 E3
  Wigginton HP23 119 D1
  Windsor SL4 209 F4
  Winslow MK18 65 F5
Highfield Sch SL6 202 E7
Highfield Way
  Hazelmere HP15 163 A3
  Yardley Hastings NN7 1 B6
Highgate Mews 2 HP19 100 F1
Highgate Over MK7 48 B6
Highgrove Hill MK8 45 F8
Highgrove Pk SL6 202 E8
High Halden MK7 48 B8
High Heavens Wood SL7 183 C8
Highland Cl MK3 46 F3
High Land Cl HP18 96 A1
Highland Rd HP7 165 D8
Highlands
  Flackwell Heath HP10 185 B7
  High Wycombe HP13 174 A5
Highlands Cl SL9 177 F3
Highlands End SL9 177 F3
Highlands La SL9 177 F3
Highlands Rd
  Buckingham MK18 41 E2
  Seer Green HP9 176 C5
Highlands The SL2 198 C7
Highlea Ave HP10 185 A8
Highley Gr MK10 36 B3
High March Sch HP9 175 D4
High Mdw SL6 196 C3
Highmoor HP7 165 D8
High Moors HP22 131 B8
Highmore Cotts HP7 152 F3
Highmore Croft MK8 45 D6
Highover Pk HP7 165 D7
High Park Dr MK12 33 A6
High Rd
  Cookham Rise SL6 195 E7
  Soulbury LU7 69 E2
  Uxbridge UB8 208 C7
High St The MK8 33 E1
High St
  Amersham HP7 165 A7
  Aylesbury HP20 115 E8
  Berkhamsted HP4 135 C4
  Berkhamsted, Northchurch HP4 134 E6
  Bovingdon HP3 146 A4
  Bray SL6 203 C4
  Brill HP18 110 A8
  Buckingham MK18 28 D1
  Buckingham MK18 41 D1
  Burcott LU7 79 D4
  Burnham SL1 197 C2
  Chalfont St Giles HP8 177 C8
  Chalfont St Peter SL9 177 E2
  Chalvey SL1 205 D3
  Cheddington LU7 105 A7
  Chesham HP5 154 B8
  Chinnor, Kingston Blount OX39 147 A4
  Chinnor OX39 147 D7
  Colnbrook SL3 212 C7
  Cookham SL6 196 B7
  Cranfield MK43 25 B1
  Cublington LU7 78 B1
  Datchet SL3 211 B6
  Deanshanger MK19 31 E4
  Dinton HP17 113 E2
  Downley HP13 161 D3
  Eaton Bray LU6 92 E6
  Edlesborough LU6 92 E3
  Emberton MK46 13 F7
  Eton SL4 210 D8
  Great Horwood MK17 55 A3
  Great Missenden HP16 152 A7
  Haddenham HP17 126 F6
  Hanslope MK19 11 A2
  Harmondsworth UB7 213 D8
  Harrold MK43 3 F6
  Haversham MK19 21 A3
  High Wycombe HP11 173 B6
  Iver SL0 207 F7
High St *continued*
  Ivinghoe LU7 105 E5
  Lane End HP14 171 B4
  Lavendon MK46 7 F8
  Leighton Buzzard LU7 80 F6
  Lewknor OX49 157 B8
  Long Crendon HP18 125 D6
  Ludgershall HP18 96 B8
  14 Maidenhead SL6 202 F7
  Marlow SL7 183 E1
  Milton Keynes, Great Linford MK14 21 E1
  Milton Keynes MK2 47 E1
  Milton Keynes, New Bradwell MK13 34 A7
  Milton Keynes, Stony Stratford MK11 32 D6
  Nash MK17 44 C1
  Newport Pagnell MK16 22 D4
  North Crawley MK16 24 B6
  North Marston MK18 76 A2
  Olney MK46 6 F3
  Paulerspury NN12 17 C8
  Potterspury NN12 18 D3
  Prestwood HP16 151 D6
  Princes Risborough HP27 139 B3
  Sherington MK16 13 F2
  Slough SL3 207 A2
  Slough, Upton SL1 205 F4
  Stanwell TW19 213 D1
  Stoke Goldington MK16 12 B6
  Syresham NN13 27 B7
  Taplow SL6 196 E1
  Thame OX9 125 E1
  Thornborough MK18 54 A8
  Tring HP23 119 A3
  Turvey MK43 8 E5
  Uxbridge, Cowley UB8 201 C1
  Uxbridge UB8 201 D5
  Waddesdon HP18 99 A6
  Weedon HP22 87 C1
  Wendover HP22 131 B4
  Westcott HP18 98 B7
  West Drayton UB7 208 E6
  Weston Underwood MK46 6 B2
  West Wycombe HP14 160 F2
  Whaddon MK17 45 B1
  Whitchurch HP22 87 A6
  Windsor SL4 210 D6
  Wing LU7 79 E2
  Winslow MK18 65 F4
  Woburn Sands MK17 49 B4
  Wraysbury TW19 211 F1
  Yardley Gobion NN12 18 F6
  Yardley Hastings NN7 1 B6
High Street N LU7 68 D2
High Street S
  Olney MK46 6 F3
  Stewkley LU7 78 E8
High Town Rd SL6 202 F7
High Trees MK6 47 B8
Highveer Croft MK4 46 B1
High View
  Chalfont St Giles HP8 177 D8
  Deanshanger MK19 31 E5
High View Cl SL7 183 C8
HIGHWAY 202 B7
Highway MK17 68 C6
Highway Ave SL6 202 A6
Highway Ct
  Beaconsfield HP9 175 D3
  Chesham HP5 144 D1
Highway Rd SL6 202 B6
Highway The HP9 175 D2
Highwood Ave HP12 172 B5
Highwood Bottom HP27 150 A5
Highwood Cres HP12 172 B6
Highwoods Cl SL7 183 C7
Highwoods Dr SL7 183 C7
Highworth Cl HP13 162 E1
Highworth Comb Sch HP13 162 E1
HIGH WYCOMBE 173 B5
High Wycombe CE Comb Sch 5 HP11 173 A6
High Wycombe Sta HP13 173 B7
Hikers Way HP18 125 F4
Hilbre Ct 5 MK4 45 F1
Hilbury Cl HP6 154 C3
Hilda Wharf HP20 115 F8
Hildreth Rd HP16 151 C5
Hilgrove Ho SL6 195 D1
Hiljon Cres SL9 177 E2
Hillary Cl
  Aylesbury HP21 116 A5
  High Wycombe HP13 173 E6
Hillary Rd
  High Wycombe HP13 173 E6
  Slough SL3 206 E4
Hill Ave
  Amersham HP6 154 C1
  Hazelmere HP15 163 B5
Hillbeck Gr MK10 35 E3
Hillbottom Rd HP12 172 B7
Hill Cl HP10 185 F7
Hill Cotts HP18 97 E1
Hillcrest MK43 25 C2
Hillcrest Ave SL6 195 E6
Hillcrest Cl MK5 46 B6
Hillcrest Ct HP6 154 C1
Hillcrest Rise MK18 52 E6
Hillcrest Way MK18 52 E5
Hillcrest Waye SL9 188 F5
Hillcroft Rd
  Chesham HP5 144 D2
  Tylers Green HP10 163 C1
Hillersdon SL2 206 B8
Hillersdon Chase MK17 69 D8
HILLESDEN 63 A6
HILLESDEN HAMLET 51 F1
Hillesden Hamlet MK18 51 F1
Hillesden Way MK18 41 E1
Hill Farm MK18 76 A2
Hill Farm App HP10 185 F7
Hill Farm Ct OX39 147 D6
Hill Farm La
  Chalfont St Giles HP8 166 A1
  Little Horwood MK17 55 E2
Hill Farm Rd
  Chalfont St Peter SL9 177 E3
  Chesham HP5 154 D5
  Marlow Bottom SL7 183 E5
  Taplow SL6 196 E2
Hill Farm Way HP15 163 B2
Hillfield Cl HP13 161 E2
Hillfield Rd SL9 177 E3
Hillfield Sq SL9 177 E3
Hill Gr SL9 177 E3
Hill Ho SL6 196 D1
Hill House Cl SL9 177 E3
Hilliard Dr MK13 34 A3
Hilliards Rd UB8 208 D7
Hillier Rd HP21 115 D3
Hillingdon Hill UB10 201 E2
Hillingdon Hospl UB8 208 F8
Hillingdon Rd UB10 201 E3
Hillingdon Tuition Ctr UB7 208 E5
Hillington Cl HP19 115 B7
Hillman Cl UB8 201 E7
Hill Mdw HP7 164 F4
Hill Mead HP4 135 A3
Hillmead Ct SL6 203 F8
Hill Pl SL2 198 B5
Hill Rd
  Chinnor OX39 147 D5
  Christmas Common OX49 168 A8
  Lewknor OX49 157 C6
Hillrise SL3 212 A8
Hill Rise SL9 177 D1
Hill Rise Cres SL9 177 E1
Hills Cl MK14 34 E7
Hillside
  Chesham HP5 144 A3
  Gawcott MK18 51 F4
  High Wycombe HP13 173 D7
  Maidenhead SL6 202 D5
  Slough SL1 205 E4
  South Harefield UB9 190 C6
  Tingewick MK18 51 B6
Hill Side LU7 104 F7
Hillside Cl
  Chalfont St Giles HP8 177 B7
  Chalfont St Peter SL9 177 E4
  Upper Arncott OX25 94 E7
Hillside Cotts HP18 112 F2
Hillside Ct SL0 208 B4
Hillside Ctr HP11 172 F7
Hillside Gdns
  Amersham HP7 165 E7
  Berkhamsted HP4 135 D3
  High Wycombe HP13 173 D7
Hillside Rd
  Chorleywood WD3 167 C4
  Marlow SL7 183 E4
  Tylers Green HP10 163 A2
Hills La SL6 195 D7
Hill St HP13 174 A5
Hill The
  Syresham NN13 27 B8
  Winchmore Hill HP7 164 C3
HILLTOP 144 D2
Hilltop HP18 125 D5
Hilltop Ave MK18 41 E2
Hill Top Dr SL7 183 B2
Hilltop Fst Sch SL4 209 E4
Hill Top La OX39 147 F4
Hilltop Rd HP4 135 C3
Hillview
  Saunderton HP14 149 C1
  Sherington MK16 14 A1
Hill View
  Berkhamsted HP4 135 A6
  Great Kimble HP17 129 D1
  Hedgerley SL2 187 D3
  Newport Pagnell MK16 22 A3
  Oakley HP18 109 D5
Hillview Rd HP13 173 D8
Hill View Rd TW19 211 D1
Hillway MK17 49 A6
Hill Way HP7 165 B6
Hill Waye SL9 188 F4
Hillwerke OX39 147 C6
Hillyer Ct MK6 35 C1
Hilperton Rd 3 SL1 205 E4
Hilton Ave HP20 101 E2
Hilton Cl UB8 201 B3
Himley Gn LU7 80 D6
Hindemith Gdns MK7 48 D5
Hindhay La SL6 195 B3
Hindhead Knoll MK7 48 B6
Hinds Way HP21 115 B6
Hinkley Cl UB9 190 C7
Hinksey Cl SL3 207 B3
Hinton Cl HP13 162 A1
Hinton Ct MK3 46 F1
Hinton Rd
  Slough SL1 204 E6
  Uxbridge UB8 201 C4
Hipwell Ct MK46 6 F3
Hitcham Grange SL6 196 E1
Hitcham House SL1 197 A1
Hitcham La SL6, SL1 196 F2
Hitcham Rd SL1, SL6 204 A8
Hithercroft Rd HP13 161 E1
Hither Mdw SL9 177 E1
Hithermoor Rd TW19 213 A2
Hiving's Hill HP5 144 A2
Hivings Pk HP5 144 B4
Hoathly Mews MK7 48 B8
Hobart Cl HP13 162 E1
Hobart Cotts HP16 150 D8
Hobart Cres MK15 35 B7
Hobart Ct SL7 184 A3
Hobart Rd HP13 162 D1
Hobbis Dr SL6 202 A6
Hobbshill Rd HP16 152 B6
Hobbs Rd HP14 171 C4
Hobsons Wlk HP23 118 F5
Hockeridge View HP4 134 F3
Hockett La SL6 195 A6
Hockley La SL2 199 B4
Hockliffe Brae MK7 48 C5
Hodder La MK4 46 C2
Hodds Wood Rd HP5 154 C6
Hodge Lea La MK12 33 D4
Hodgemoor View HP8 177 A7
Hodgemore Ct MK14 21 F2
Hodges Cl HP14 158 F4
Hodges Mews HP12 172 C6
Hoe Mdw HP9 175 C4
Hogarth Cl
  Slough SL1 204 E6
  Uxbridge UB8 201 C2
Hogarths Ct 9 MK8 33 F1
Hogback Wood Rd HP9 175 B4
Hogfair La SL1 197 C1
HOGGESTON 77 B7
Hogg La HP15 163 D6
Hog Hall La HP4 107 A5
Hog La
  Ashley Green HP5 144 D8
  Berkhamsted HP5 134 C2
HOGPITS BOTTOM 156 B7
Hogpits Bottom HP3 156 B7
Hogshaw Rd MK18 75 E6
Hogtrough La
  Great Missenden HP16 141 F8
  Wendover HP22 131 D2
Holborn Cres MK4 57 A8
Holdom Ave MK1 47 D2
Holes La MK46 6 F4
Holiday La MK19 10 F4
Holland Cl
  Chinnor OX39 147 D7
  Wendover HP22 131 B4
Holland Rd
  Aylesbury HP19 101 B2
  Marlow SL7 183 F3
Hollandridge La OX49, RG9 168 D4
Holland Way MK16 22 C3
Holliday Cl MK8 45 E7
Holliday St HP4 135 D4
Hollies Ct LU7 80 E7
Hollies The
  Beaconsfield HP9 175 E3
  Bovingdon HP3 146 A2
  Tring HP23 119 D1
HOLLINGDON 69 C3
Hollingdon Depot LU7 69 D3
Hollingdon Rd LU7 69 C3
Hollington HP18 125 B7
Hollin La MK12 33 E4
Hollinwell Cl 3 MK4 46 D1
Hollis Rd HP13 173 F8
Hollister Chase MK5 46 B4
Holloway Cl UB7 208 E1
Holloway Dr MK18 41 E2
Holloway La
  Chenies WD3 156 C2
  Turville Heath RG9 169 C4
  West Drayton UB7 208 F1
Holloway The
  Monks Risborough HP27 139 D5
  Tring HP22, HP23 118 C4
Hollow Hill End MK18 75 F7
Hollow Hill La SL0 207 C5
Hollow Rise HP13 162 B1
Hollow Way HP5 143 E1

Hollow Way La HP5,
HP6 . . . . .154 E4
Hollow Wood MK46 . . . . . . 6 E3
Hollyberry Gr HP15 . . . .163 C7
Hollybush Cnr SL2 . . . . .187 C2
Hollybush Hill SL2 . . . .199 B5
Hollybush La
　Amersham HP6 . . . . . .154 D3
　Cookham Dean SL6 . . . .195 B6
　Denham UB9 . . . . .200 E8
　Iver SL0, SL3 . . . . . . .207 B7
Hollybush Rd HP5. . . . . .144 A4
Hollybush Row HP23 . . .133 D8
Holly Cl
　Farnham Common SL2. . .198 C8
　Milton Keynes MK8 . . . . .45 E6
Holly Cres SL4 . . . . .209 D6
Holly Dr
　Aylesbury HP21 . . . . . .115 E6
　Berkhamsted HP4 . . . . .135 D3
　Maidenhead SL6 . . . . . .202 F8
　Windsor SL4 . . . . .210 E2
Holly End HP14 . . . . . . .161 C8
Hollyfield HP23 . . . . . . .119 C5
Hollyfield Cl HP23. . . . . .119 C5
Holly Gdns UB7 . . . . . . .208 F4
HOLLY GREEN 138 A3
Holly Green La HP27 . . . .138 A3
Holly Hedges La HP3. . . .156 C8
Holly Pl HP11 . . . . .174 A3
Hollytree Cl
　Botley HP5. . . . . .155 B8
　Chalfont St Peter SL9 . . .177 E5
Holly Tree La HP18. . . . . .112 F3
Holly Wlk MK17 . . . . .49 B2
Holmanleaze SL6 . . . . . .203 A8
Holman St HP19 . . . . . . .101 C2
Holmedale SL2 . . . . .206 C6
HOLMER GREEN 163 D6
Holmer Green Fst Sch
　HP15. . . . . .163 B7
Holmer Green Jun Sch
　HP15. . . . . .163 D7
Holmer Green Rd
　HP15. . . . . .163 A4
Holmer Green Senior Sch
　HP15. . . . . .163 B3
Holmers Ct HP12. . . . . . .172 B3
Holmers Farm Way
　HP12 . . . . .172 C3
Holmers La HP12 . . . . . .172 C3
Holmewood MK4. . . . . . . .46 E4
Holmfield Cl MK6 . . . . . . .47 D5
Holm Gate MK5 . . . . .46 A8
Holmlea Rd SL3. . . . . . . .211 D6
Holmlea Wlk SL3 . . . . . . .211 C6
Holmoak Wlk HP15 . . . . .163 B3
Holmsdale SL0 . . . . .207 F7
Holmwood Cl SL6. . . . . . .202 B5
Holmwood Sch **10** MK8. . .33 F1
Holne Chase Prim Sch
　MK3 . . . . .58 A7
Holst Cres MK7 . . . . .48 D4
Holt Gr MK5 . . . . .46 A8
HOLTON 122 C2
Holton Hill MK4. . . . . .46 C2
Holton Rd MK18 . . . . .41 D2
Holts Gn MK17. . . . . .59 C1
HOLTSPUR 175 A1
Holtspur Ave HP9. . . . . . .185 F7
Holtspur Cl HP9 . . . . .186 A8
Holtspur Ct HP9 . . . . .186 A8
Holtspur La HP10 . . . . . . .185 F6
Holtspur Par HP9 . . . . . . .186 A8
Holtspur Prim Sch
　HP9. . . . . .175 A1
Holtspur Top La HP9 . . . .175 A2
Holtspur Way HP9 . . . . . .175 A1
Holt The MK18. . . . . .52 E7
Holy Family RC Sch
　SL3 . . . . .206 F1
Holyhead Cres MK3 . . . . . .57 C8
Holyhead Mews SL3. . . . .204 D7
Holyport Rd SL6. . . . . . . .203 B1
Holyrood MK8 . . . . .45 E8
Holy Thorn La MK5. . . . . . .46 A5
Holy Trinity CE Prim Sch
　SL6 . . . . .196 B7
Holy Trinity CE Sch
　SL7 . . . . .183 D3
Holywell Gdns HP13. . . . .173 E7
Holywell Pl MK6 . . . . .35 C2
Holywell Rd MK43. . . . . . .25 C1
Holywell Sch MK43. . . . . .25 B1
Home Cl
　Milton Keynes MK3 . . . . .47 B2
　Shabbington HP18. . . . .124 D3
　Weston Turville HP22. . . .116 F2
Home Ct MK10. . . . . .36 A3
Home Farm
　Newton Longville MK17. . .57 D4
　Tring HP23. . . . . .118 F2
Home Farm Cl MK19 . . . . .31 E4
Homefarm Ct HP8 . . . . . .177 A7
Home Farm Ct
　Bovingdon HP3 . . . . . .145 F1
　Emberton MK46. . . . . . .13 E8
Home Farm La MK17 . . . . .59 D2

Home Farm Rd HP4. . . .134 D7
Home Farm Way SL3 . . .199 C4
Homefield HP3 . . . . .146 B3
Home Field
　Aylesbury HP19 . . . . . .115 A7
　Bow Brickhill MK7 . . . . . .48 B3
Homefield Cl HP14. . . . . .158 E4
Homefield Rd WD3. . . . . .167 D5
*Homefield Wood Wildlife
Reserve★* SL7 . . . . .182 C2
Homeground MK18 . . . . . .52 E6
Homelands Gdns HP15 . .162 D8
Homelands Way RG9 . . . .191 D1
Homeleigh Terr SL2. . . . .206 A7
Home Mdw SL2. . . . . . . .198 C3
Home Meadow Dr
　HP10 . . . . .185 B7
Homer Fst Sch SL4 . . . . .209 D6
Homeridings Ho MK13 . . .34 B4
Homers Rd SL4. . . . . . . .209 D6
Homeside Cl SL6. . . . . . .195 E2
Homestall MK18 . . . . .52 D6
Homestall Cl MK5. . . . . . .46 A7
Homestead Cl HP17 . . . . .114 A4
Homestead Pl **14** HP19 . .115 A8
Homestead Rd SL6. . . . . .202 D4
Homestead The
　Great Kingshill HP15 . . .151 D1
　High Wycombe HP12 . . . .172 D3
　Milton Keynes MK5 . . . . .46 A6
　Thame OX9 . . . . .125 E4
Homestead Way NN12. . . .18 E3
Homeward Ct MK5. . . . . . .46 B7
Home Way WD3 . . . . . . .167 F1
Homewood SL3. . . . . . . .206 D7
Home Wood SL7 . . . . . . .193 F6
Homewood Ct WD3 . . . . .167 F5
Honey Banks HP22. . . . . .131 C4
Honeycroft Hill UB10. . . .201 E5
Honey Hill
　Emberton MK46. . . . . . . .13 F7
　Uxbridge UB10. . . . . . .201 E5
Honey Hill Dr MK19. . . . . .31 E5
Honey La SL6. . . . . .193 E2
Honeypot Cl MK13. . . . . . .34 B4
Honeysuckle Cl SL3 . . . . .207 C7
Honeysuckle Ct SL3. . . . .212 C7
Honeysuckle Field HP5 . .144 C2
Honeysuckle Rd HP15. . . .162 F7
Honey Way HP14. . . . . . .161 B8
HONEYWICK 92 E8
Honeywick La LU6. . . . . . .92 E8
Honiton Ct MK7. . . . . .48 C7
Honor End La HP16 . . . . .151 A7
Honor Rd HP16 . . . . .151 D6
Honorwood Cl HP16. . . . .151 B6
Honour Cl HP20. . . . . . . .102 A2
Honours Mead **4** HP3. . .146 A4
Hoods Farm Cl HP22 . . . .102 C4
Hooke The MK15. . . . . . . .35 D7
Hooper Gate MK15 . . . . . .35 C7
Hopcraft Cl OX25 . . . . . . .94 E7
Hope Brook Cotts LU7. . . .91 F2
Hop Gdns RG9 . . . . .191 D2
Hopkins Cl MK10. . . . . . . .36 A2
Hopkins Ct HP20. . . . . . . .101 F2
Hoppers Hill MK46. . . . . . .6 F5
Hoppers Mdw MK5. . . . . . .46 A8
Hoppers Way HP15. . . . . .162 D8
Hopton Gr MK16 . . . . .22 F3
Hopton Rd OX9 . . . . .126 A1
Hordern Cl HP17. . . . . . . .126 F6
Hornbeam MK16 . . . . .22 A3
Hornbeam Cl HP12. . . . . .172 B4
Hornbeam Gdns **8**
　SL1. . . . . .206 A3
Hornbeam Way HP22. . . . .116 C4
Hornbeam Wlk HP15. . . . .163 A3
Hornbill Cl UB8. . . . . . . .208 D7
Hornby Chase MK4. . . . . . .46 B2
Horners Croft MK12. . . . . .33 C5
HORN HILL 178 B6
Hornhill Rd WD3. . . . . . .178 D5
Horn La MK11. . . . . .32 D5
Horns La
　High Wycombe HP12 . . . .172 A3
　Princes Risborough
　HP27 . . . . .139 B3
Horn St MK18. . . . . .65 F4
Horsebuck La HP23 . . . . .133 E3
Horsefair La MK11. . . . . . .32 D5
Horseguards Dr SL6. . . . .203 B7
Horse Hill HP5. . . . . .155 D7
Horsemoor Cl SL3 . . . . . .207 A2
Horsemoor La HP7. . . . . .164 C2
HORSENDEN 138 E2
Horsenden La HP27 . . . . .138 F2
Horsenden Rd HP13. . . . .173 F5
Horsepond MK17. . . . . . . .59 C2
Horsepool La MK17. . . . . .49 F4
Horseshoe Cl LU7. . . . . . .105 A7
Horseshoe Cloisters **3**
　SL4. . . . . .210 D6
Horseshoe Cres MK5 . . . .175 F1
Horseshoe Hill SL1. . . . . .197 C8
Horseshoe Rd HP14 . . . . .159 C2
Horseshoes Cl HP18. . . . . .83 A6
Horsetone Bglws HP17 . .129 D2
Horsham Reach SL6. . . . .196 C2

Horsleys WD3 . . . . .178 D5
HORSLEYS GREEN. 159 C3
HORTON
　Cheddington. 91 B3
　Wraysbury. 212 A4
Horton Bridge Rd UB7 . . .208 F5
Horton Cl
　Aylesbury HP19 . . . . . .115 A7
　Maidenhead SL6 . . . . . .196 C1
　West Drayton UB7. . . . . .208 F5
**HORTON-CUM-
　STUDLEY**. 108 B6
Horton Depot SL3. . . . . . .212 C4
Horton Gate MK14 . . . . . .21 F2
Horton Gdns SL3. . . . . . .211 F4
Horton Grange SL6 . . . . .196 C1
Horton Ind Pk UB7. . . . . .208 F5
Horton Par. UB7. . . . . . . .208 E5
Horton Rd
　Datchet SL3. . . . . .211 D6
　Horton SL3. . . . . .212 A6
　Ivinghoe LU7. . . . . .91 A2
　Poyle SL3. . . . . .212 E4
　Slapton LU7. . . . . .91 C6
　Stanwell TW19. . . . . . . .213 A4
　West Drayton UB7. . . . . .208 F5
Horton Road Ind Est
　UB7. . . . . .208 F5
Hortonsfield Rd NN12. . . .18 F5
Horton Trad Est SL3. . . . .212 B4
HORTON WHARF. 91 C4
Horwood Ct MK1. . . . . . . .47 D2
Hospital Circular Rd
　HP22 . . . . .131 D6
Hospital Hill HP5 . . . . . . .154 C7
Hospital Rdbt MK6. . . . . . .47 B6
Hotch Croft MK43. . . . . . .25 C3
HOTLEY BOTTOM 151 C8
Hotley Bottom La HP16 . .151 C8
**Hotspur Bank Nature
Reserve★** HP13 . . . . . . .174 F1
Houghton Ct **4** MK8. . . . .45 F8
Housman Cl MK16. . . . . . .22 A5
Houston Ct SL4 . . . . .210 C5
Howard Agne Cl HP3. . . . .146 A4
Howard Ave
　Aylesbury HP21 . . . . . .116 B6
　Slough SL2. . . . . .205 E8
Howard Cres HP9 . . . . . . .176 D5
Howard Ct **1** SL8. . . . . . .185 A3
Howard Ind Est HP5. . . . . .144 C2
Howard Mews SL3 . . . . . .212 B8
Howard Rd
　Chesham HP5 . . . . . . .144 B3
　Seer Green HP9. . . . . . .176 D5
Howards Thicket SL9. . . .188 C2
Howards Wood Dr SL9 . . .188 D2
Howarth Rd SL6 . . . . . . .203 A6
Howe Ct MK10. . . . . .36 A3
Howe Dr HP9 . . . . .175 E5
Howe Hill La HP15 . . . . . .163 B8
Howell Hill Cl LU7. . . . . . .90 D5
Howe Park Sch MK4. . . . . .46 B1
Howe Rock Pl MK4. . . . . . .46 B1
Howitt Dr MK13. . . . . .34 B8
Howland Pl MK17 . . . . . . .60 F7
Howletts Cl HP19 . . . . . . .115 A7
How's Cl HP18. . . . . .201 C4
How's Rd UB8 . . . . .201 C4
Hoylake Cl
　Milton Keynes MK3 . . . . .57 D7
　Slough SL1. . . . . .204 E4
Hoyton Gate MK8 . . . . . . .45 D6
Hubbard Cl MK18. . . . . . . .41 F1
Hubbards Ct WD3. . . . . . .167 D4
Hubbards Rd WD3. . . . . . .167 D4
Hubert Day Cl HP9. . . . . .175 D3
Hubert Rd SL3. . . . . .206 D3
Huckleberry Cl MK7. . . . . .48 B6
Hudnall La HP4. . . . . .121 E7
Hudson La MK8. . . . . .45 D7
Hudson Mews HP19 . . . . .100 E1
Hudson Pl **14** SL3. . . . . .206 D1
Hughenden Ave HP13 . . . .173 A8
Hughenden Cl SL6. . . . . . .202 C6
Hughenden Ct UB8. . . . . .201 C1
Hughenden Gn HP21 . . . .115 E4
Hughenden Manor★
　HP14. . . . . .162 A3
Hughenden Prim Sch
　HP14. . . . . .162 A7
Hughenden Rd
　High Wycombe HP13 . . . .162 B1
　Slough SL1. . . . . .205 D7
HUGHENDEN VALLEY. . . .162 A7
Hughenden View HP13 . .173 B8
Hughes Croft **3** MK3. . . . .57 F7
Hugh Park Cl MK5 . . . . . . .46 C8
Hulbert End HP21. . . . . . .116 D5
Hulcombe Wlk HP20 . . . . .101 E2
HULCOTE. 37 E2
HULCOTT. 102 E6
Hull Cl
　Aylesbury HP21 . . . . . .115 E6
　Slough SL1. . . . . .205 C4
Hulton Dr MK46. . . . . .13 F8
Humber Cl UB7. . . . . .208 D5
Humber Dr HP21. . . . . . . .115 C5

Humber Way
　Milton Keynes MK3 . . . . .46 E1
　Slough SL3. . . . . .207 A2
Hume Cl MK13. . . . . .34 B7
Humphreys Cl HP22. . . . . .88 D5
Humphrey Talbot Ave
　LU6. . . . . .107 F7
Hundred Acres La HP7 . . .165 D8
Hungerford Ave SL2 . . . . .205 E8
Hungerford Dr SL6. . . . . .195 E3
Hungerford Ho **1** MK4. . . .46 D1
Hunsbury Chase MK10. . . .36 A3
Hunsdon Cl MK14. . . . . . . .34 D6
Hunsford Lodge SL4. . . . .210 A4
Hunstanton Cl SL3. . . . . .212 C7
Hunstanton Way MK3 . . . .57 D8
Hunt Ct HP14. . . . . .158 F4
Huntercombe Cl SL1 . . . .204 C7
Huntercombe Hospl The
　SL6. . . . . .204 C6
Huntercombe Lane N
　SL6. . . . . .204 C7
Huntercombe Lane S
　SL6. . . . . .204 C6
Huntercombe Spur
　SL6. . . . . .204 C6
Hunter Ct SL1 . . . . .204 C8
Hunter Dr MK2. . . . . .58 C6
Hunters Cl
　Bovingdon HP3 . . . . . .146 A2
　Chesham HP5 . . . . . . .144 A1
　Tring HP23. . . . . .119 B5
Hunters Farm Ind Est
　HP18. . . . . .100 B5
Hunters Hill HP13. . . . . . .173 F5
Hunters Mews SL4 . . . . . .210 C6
Hunters Pk HP4. . . . . .135 E5
Hunters Point OX39. . . . . .147 C6
Hunters Reach MK13 . . . . .34 A3
Hunter St MK18. . . . . .52 C8
Hunters Way SL1 . . . . . . .204 E4
HUNTGATE END 10 D2
Huntingbrooke **6** MK8. . . .45 F8
Huntingdon Cres MK3. . . .57 D6
Huntington Pl SL3. . . . . . .207 B3
Huntley Cl HP13 . . . . .162 C2
Huntley Cres MK9 . . . . . . .35 A3
Hunt Rd HP13. . . . . .173 E6
HUNT'S HILL 161 D5
Hunts Hill La HP14 . . . . . .161 E5
Hunt's La SL6. . . . . .196 E3
Huntsman Gr MK14 . . . . . .22 A2
Huntsmans Cl HP4. . . . . . .107 C5
Huntswood La SL6, SL1 . . .196 F4
HURLEY 193 E4
Hurley Croft MK10. . . . . . .36 B1
Hurley High St SL6 . . . . . .193 F4
Hurley La SL7. . . . . .194 B3
Hurlstone Gr MK4. . . . . . . .46 D3
Hurricane Way SL3 . . . . . .207 B1
HURST END 24 A3
Hurstfield Dr SL6. . . . . . . .204 B7
Hurstleigh WD3. . . . . .167 C4
Hurst Rd SL1. . . . . .204 D8
Hurworth Ave SL3 . . . . . . .206 C3
Hutchings Cl MK5. . . . . . . .46 A8
Hutchings Rd HP9 . . . . . . .175 D5
Hutton Ave MK6 . . . . .34 F1
Hutton Ct MK1 . . . . .49 B5
Hutton Way MK17. . . . . . . .49 B5
Huxley Cl
　Newport Pagnell MK16 . . .21 F4
　Slough SL3. . . . . .199 B1
　Uxbridge UB8. . . . . . . .201 D1
Huxtable Gdns SL6. . . . . .203 E1
Hyacinth Dr UB10 . . . . . . .201 E5
Hychenden Cl HP14. . . . . .161 E6
Hyde Cl MK16. . . . . .22 C2
HYDE END. 152 F7
Hyde Gn
　Beaconsfield HP9. . . . . .175 F3
　Marlow SL7. . . . . .183 F1
HYDE HEATH. 153 C5
Hyde Heath Inf Sch
　HP6. . . . . .153 C5
Hyde Heath Rd HP6,
　HP10 . . . . .153 A6
Hyde La
　Bovingdon HP3 . . . . . .146 A3
　South Heath HP16 . . . . .152 E5
Hyde Mdws HP3 . . . . . . .146 A4
Hyde The HP22. . . . . .116 F2
Hyland Ho **9** SL8 . . . . . . .185 B3
Hylle Cl SL4. . . . . .209 E6
Hylton Rd HP12. . . . . .172 C2
Hyrons Cl HP6. . . . . .154 E1
Hyrons Ct HP6. . . . . .154 E1
Hyrons La HP6. . . . . .154 D1
Hythe The MK8 . . . . .33 E3
Hyton Sq HP19. . . . . .101 D4

I

Ibotson Ct SL3. . . . . .212 E6
IBSTONE 169 D7
Ibstone Ave MK13. . . . . . .34 D4
Ibstone CE Inf Sch
　HP14. . . . . .169 D6

Ibstone Rd HP14 . . . . . . .158 C3
ICKENHAM 190 F1
ICKFORD 124 A3
Ickford Comb Sch
　HP18. . . . . .124 A3
Ickford Rd
　Shabbington HP18. . . . .124 C2
　Worminghall HP18. . . . .123 E6
Icknield Cl
　Chinnor OX39. . . . . . . .147 A4
　Wendover HP22. . . . . . .131 C5
Icknield Cotts HP17 . . . . .129 F2
Icknield Gn HP23 . . . . . . .119 A6
Icknield Way
　Dunstable LU6. . . . . . . .93 D4
　Tring HP23. . . . . .118 E4
Icknield Way Farm Cotts
　LU6. . . . . .93 C3
Icknield Way Ind Est
　HP23. . . . . .118 E4
Ideal Ho **3** HP20. . . . . . . .115 E8
Iffley Cl SL3. . . . . .201 D5
Ilchester Cl SL6. . . . . . . .202 C5
Ilex Cl HP15 . . . . .163 B3
Ilex Ct HP4 . . . . .135 B4
Illingworth SL4 . . . . .209 E4
Illingworth Pl MK6 . . . . . . .46 F8
ILMER 137 F8
Imperial Ct
　Henley-on-Thames RG9 . .191 E1
　Loudwater HP10 . . . . . .174 C2
　Windsor SL4 . . . . .210 A4
Imperial Rd SL4. . . . . . . .210 A5
Independent Bsns Pk
　HP14. . . . . .158 C5
India Rd SL1. . . . . .206 B4
Ingleglen SL2. . . . . .198 B7
Ingleside SL3 . . . . .212 F6
Ingleton Cl MK13. . . . . . . .34 C4
Ingram Ave HP21 . . . . . . .116 C5
Inkerman Dr HP15 . . . . . .163 B5
Inkerman Rd SL4. . . . . . . .204 F2
Inkerman Terr HP5 . . . . . .154 C6
Innes Ct MK8 . . . . .45 D6
Inn Farm Ct MK16 . . . . . . .22 D7
Innholder Ct MK4. . . . . . . .34 F6
Innings Gate RG9 . . . . . . .170 E1
Inniscrown Ho SL3. . . . . . .211 B7
Institute Rd
　Marlow SL7. . . . . .183 E1
　Taplow SL6. . . . . .203 F7
Intalbury Ave HP19. . . . . .101 A2
In the Ray SL6. . . . . .203 B8
Inverewe Pl **1** MK4. . . . . .45 E2
Inverness Cl MK3 . . . . .46 F2
Inwood Cl SL6. . . . . .195 B6
Iona Cres SL1. . . . . .204 E7
Ipswich Rd SL1. . . . . .205 A7
*IQRA Slough Islamic Prim
Sch* SL2. . . . . .206 B6
Ireland Cl MK7. . . . . .48 D4
Ireton Ct OX9. . . . . .125 F1
Iris Cl HP21. . . . . .115 B5
Iris Ct HP20. . . . . .116 B8
Ironmonger Ct MK14 . . . . .34 F6
Irvine Dr HP22 . . . . .116 A2
Irvine Ho SL4. . . . . .209 E5
Irving Cres LU7 . . . . .105 A8
Irving Dale MK7. . . . . .48 E5
Isaacson Dr MK7. . . . . . . .48 C7
Isis Cl HP21. . . . . .115 D3
Isis Way SL8. . . . . .185 B4
Isis Wlk MK3. . . . . .46 E1
Island Ho UB7 . . . . .213 B6
Island The MK18 . . . . .63 D2
Isle of Wight La LU6. . . . . .93 F4
Islet Park Dr SL6. . . . . . . .196 C3
Islet Park Ho SL6 . . . . . . .196 C3
Islet Pk SL6. . . . . .196 C3
Islet Rd SL6. . . . . .196 C3
Isling Brook MK5 . . . . .46 B3
Islington Gr **6** MK10. . . . . .35 F1
Ivanhoe Cl UB8. . . . . .208 D8
IVER 207 F7
Iver Ct MK18. . . . . .52 C7
Iverdale Cl SL0 . . . . .207 C6
IVER HEATH. 200 D4
Iver Heath Inf Sch SL0 . . .200 D4
Iver Heath Jun Sch
　SL0 . . . . .200 D3
Iver La SL0. . . . . .208 A8
Iver Lodge SL0. . . . . .207 F8
Iver Sta SL0 . . . . .207 F8
Iver Village Inf Sch SL0. . .207 F7
Iver Village Jun Sch
　SL0 . . . . .207 E7
Ives Rd SL3. . . . . .207 A3
Ivester Ct LU7. . . . . .80 E6
IVINGHOE. 105 F5
IVINGHOE ASTON 92 A1
Ivinghoe View HP20. . . . . .101 F1
Ivinghoe Way LU6. . . . . . .92 E1
Ivins Rd HP9. . . . . .175 A1
Ivybridge Cl UB8. . . . . . . .201 E2
Ivy Cl
　Buckingham MK18. . . . . .41 F8

Ivy Cl *continued*
Longwick HP27 138 E5
Newport Pagnell MK16 22 E4
Ivy Cotts HP8 177 B8
Ivy Cres SL1 204 F6
Ivyhill Ct HP27 139 B3
Ivy House La HP4 135 E5
Ivy La
Bierton HP22 102 D1
Burcott LU7 79 D4
Great Brickhill MK17 70 C8
Newton Longville MK17 57 C3
Stewkley LU7 68 E1
Ivy Pl HP14 171 C5

J

Jacks Cl MK46 7 E7
Jack's La MK43 8 E5
Jackson Cl
Slough SL3 206 E3
Uxbridge UB10 201 E5
Jackson Ct HP15 163 A3
Jackson Ind Est SL8 185 B2
Jackson Rd
Aylesbury HP19 101 A3
Uxbridge UB10 201 E5
Jacksons Cl LU6 92 E4
Jacob Cl SL4 209 E6
Jacobs Cl MK14 34 D7
Jakeman Way HP21 115 B6
Jakes Ho SL6 203 A8
Jamaica MK6 47 A6
James Cl
Hazlemere HP15 163 A6
Marlow SL7 183 F4
James Elliman Sch SL2 205 E6
James Martin Cl UB9 190 A5
James Mdw SL3 211 F8
James Rd HP14 171 B4
James St SL4 210 D6
James Way MK1 47 B1
Jane Cl HP21 116 A4
Jannetta Cl HP20 116 B7
Jansel Sq HP21 116 B6
Japonica La MK15 35 C6
Jardine Cotts SL2 199 A8
Jarman Cl MK18 52 F8
Jarratt Ho SL4 210 B4
Jarry Ct SL7 183 F3
Jarvis Cl HP21 116 A6
Jasmine Cl HP21 116 A4
Jasmine Cres HP27 139 B3
Jasmine Wlk HP5 144 A1
Jason Ho HP12 172 E4
Jasons Hill HP5 145 B2
Jeeves Cl MK6 47 C7
Jefferies Rd HP17 114 B5
Jefferson Cl SL3 207 A2
Jeffrey Wlk HP19 115 A7
Jeffries Ct SL8 185 B2
Jellicoe Cl SL1 205 B4
Jenkins Cl MK5 45 F5
Jenkins Ct HP22 89 C3
Jenkins La HP23 132 E3
Jenna Way MK16 23 A3
Jenner Rd HP21 115 E5
Jennery La SL1 197 C2
Jennings MK14 34 C7
Jennings Field HP10 185 C7
Jennings Wharf SL4 210 D7
Jerome Cl SL7 183 F4
Jersey Rd MK12 33 C6
Jesse's La HP18 125 D6
Job's La SL6 195 B8
John Colet Sch HP22 131 C5
John Hall Way HP11 172 D3
John Hampden Gram Sch HP11 172 F4
John Hampden Way HP16 151 B7
John Hampden Wendover Sch The HP22 131 B5
John Hellins Prim Sch NN12 18 D3
Johns La HP5 134 E1
Johnson Rd HP14 171 B5
Johnsons Field MK46 6 E4
Johnston Pl MK6 46 E8
John Taylor Ct SL1 205 C5
John Watson Sch OX33 122 B1
Joiner's Cl
Botley HP5 145 B1
Chalfont St Peter SL9 177 F3
Joiners La SL9 177 F3
Joiner's La SL9 177 E3
Joiners Way
Chalfont St Peter SL9 177 E3
Lavendon MK46 7 F8
Jonathan Ct SL6 202 E7
Jonathans MK6 47 A6
Jonathans Ct MK6 47 A6
Jones Way SL2 187 E2
Joplin Ct MK8 45 F7
JORDANS 176 F3
Jordans La HP9 176 E3
Jordans Sch HP9 176 F4
Jordans Way HP9 176 F4
Joules Ct MK5 46 C5
Jourdelay's Pas SL4 210 D8
Journeys End SL2 205 E8
Jubilee Cotts MK18 64 F3
Jubilee Rd
High Wycombe, Downley HP13 161 E2
High Wycombe HP11 172 E7
Stokenchurch HP14 158 F3
Jubilee Terr MK11 32 E5
Jubilee Way SL3 211 C7
Judge's La LU7 80 F6
Juniper Cl HP15 163 B3
Juniper Ct
Flackwell Heath HP10 185 C7
Rickmansworth WD3 167 C3
Slough SL1 204 E6
Slough SL1 206 B4
Juniper Dr
Aylesbury HP22 116 C4
High Wycombe HP12 172 C5
Maidenhead SL6 203 B8
Juniper Gdns MK7 48 B7
Juniper Hill Sch HP10 185 B7
Juniper La HP10 185 D7
Juniper Rd SL7 183 D5
Jupiter Hts UB10 201 F4
Juson's Glebe HP22 131 C5
Jutland Ho SL4 209 F5

K

Kalman Gdns MK7 48 D5
Kaplan Cl MK5 46 B5
Karenza HP14 158 E5
Katherine Cl
Tylers Green HP10 174 C8
Walton MK7 48 A4
Katrine Pl MK2 58 D5
Kaybridge Cl 1 HP13 173 F5
Kay Cl HP23 119 A5
Kaywood Cl SL3 206 C3
Keach Cl MK18 66 A5
Keasden Ct MK4 46 B2
Keaton Cl MK8 45 D7
Keats Cl
Aylesbury HP21 115 F6
High Wycombe HP11 172 F6
Newport Pagnell MK16 22 A4
Keats La SL4 210 C8
Keats Way
2 Milton Keynes MK3 57 F7
West Drayton UB7 208 F2
Keble Cl HP19 115 B8
Keble Rd SL6 202 E8
Keel Dr SL1 205 C4
Keeler Cl SL4 209 E4
Keel Way MK4 45 D3
Keen Cl HP19 115 A8
Keensacre SL0 200 D3
Keen's Ct HP13 162 E1
Keens La OX39 147 D6
Keepers Cl LU7 105 A7
Keepers Farm Cl SL4 209 E5
Keepers La HP6, HP7 153 C3
Keep Hill Dr HP11 173 D4
Keep Hill Rd HP11 173 D5
Keinches La HP22 87 A6
Keith Park Rd UB10 201 F5
Kellan Dr MK6 35 A1
Keller Cl MK11 33 B2
Kelling Way 3 MK10 36 A4
Kelmarsh Ct 11 MK8 33 F1
Kelpatrick Rd SL1 204 D7
Kelsey Cl
Maidenhead SL6 202 D3
Milton Keynes MK4 56 F8
Kelso Cl MK3 57 D6
Kelvin Cl HP13 172 F8
Kelvin Dr MK5 46 D6
Kemble Ct MK15 35 B6
Kempe Cl SL3 207 C2
Kempson Cl HP19 101 B1
Kemps Piece HP17 127 A6
Kempton Gdns MK3 57 D6
Kemsley Chase SL2 198 D4
Kemsley Cres MK10 36 A4
Kenchester MK13 33 F5
Kendal Cl
Aylesbury HP21 116 B6
Slough SL2 206 A6
Kendal Dr SL2 206 A6
Kendal Gdns LU7 80 C7
Kendall Pl
Maidenhead SL6 202 C4
Milton Keynes MK5 45 E5
Kendalls Cl HP13 173 F6
Kendal Mews UB8 201 C4
Kendrick Rd SL3 206 B3
Kenilworth Cl SL1 205 F3
Kenilworth Dr
Aylesbury HP19 101 D2
Milton Keynes MK3 57 E8
Kenneally SL4 209 C5
Kenneally Cl 11 SL4 209 C5
Kenneally Pl 12 SL4 209 C5
Kenneally Row 13 SL4 209 C5
Kenneally Wlk 10 SL4 209 C5
Kennedy Ave HP11 173 B4
Kennedy Cl
Farnham Common SL2 198 C6
Maidenhead SL6 202 C6
Marlow SL7 183 E3
Kennedy Ho SL1 204 D5
Kennel La SL6 195 C7
Kennels Dr NN12 17 D3
Kennet Cl
Aylesbury HP21 115 C4
High Wycombe HP13 162 D2
Kennet Dr MK3 57 E8
Kennet Pl MK3 57 F8
Kennet Rd
Bourne End SL8 185 B4
Maidenhead SL6 202 F8
Kennett Rd SL3 207 B3
Kennington Cl MK16 22 C3
Kennish Cl MK18 65 F4
Kensal Gn MK10 35 E1
Kensington Dr
Great Holm MK8 46 A8
Milton Keynes MK8 33 F1
Kensington Path 3 HP19 100 F1
Kensington Pl MK46 6 F5
Kent Ave SL1 205 C8
Kent Cl UB8 201 C6
Kent Ho MK3 46 F2
Kent Lodge 6 SL6 202 F6
Kentmere Rd HP21 116 B7
Kenton Cl SL7 183 E2
Kenton Ct HP19 101 C2
Kenton's La SL4 209 F5
KENTS HILL 48 A7
Kents Hill Park Rdbt MK10 47 E8
Kents Hill Rdbt MK10 47 F8
Kents Hill Sch MK7 48 A7
Kents Rd MK14 34 D8
Kent Way SL6 195 E1
Kenway Dr HP7 166 B8
Kenwell Ct MK15 35 C3
Kenwood Cl SL6 202 A7
Kenwood Dr WD3 178 F8
Kenwood Gate MK6 35 B2
Keppel Ave MK19 20 D2
Keppel St SL4 210 D5
Kepwick MK8 33 E1
Kercroft MK8 33 E2
Kernow Cres MK6 35 A1
Kerria Pl MK3 47 A3
Kerr Pl HP21 115 E7
Kerry Cl HP19 101 A3
Kersey MK14 34 C8
Kesters Rd HP5 154 D7
Kestrel Cl
2 Berkhamsted HP4 135 C3
High Wycombe HP13 161 C1
Kestrel Dr HP15 163 B5
Kestrel Path SL2 197 E1
Kestrel Way
Aylesbury HP19 101 E4
Buckingham MK18 52 F7
Keswick Ct SL2 205 F6
Keswick Rd MK19 11 B2
Ketchmere Cl HP18 125 C6
Ketelbey Nook MK7 48 E5
Ketton Cl MK15 35 D7
Kew Cl UB8 201 D3
Kew Ct MK8 33 F1
Kew Gr HP11 173 B4
Kew Pl HP11 173 B4
Keyes Way MK18 41 E2
Keynes Cl MK16 22 E4
Keys Pl SL6 202 F6
Khalsa Prim Sch SL2 206 A7
Khasiaberry MK7 48 B5
Kidd Cl MK8 45 E6
Kidderminster Rd SL2 198 A2
Kidderminster Wlk 3 MK10 36 B2
Kidwells Cl SL6 202 F8
Kidwells Park Dr SL6 202 F7
Kildonan Pl MK12 33 D4
Kilfillan Gdns HP4 135 A4
Kilfillan Pk HP4 135 A3
Kilgour Ct 2 LU7 80 F7
Kilkenny Ho MK4 45 E2
Killarney Dr SL6 202 E7
Killerton Cl MK4 45 F2
Kiln Ave HP6 155 C1
Kiln Cl
Calvert MK18 73 B5
Prestwood HP16 151 C7
KILN COMMON 151 B8
Kiln Croft Cl SL7 184 A3
Kiln Ct HP9 186 B8
Kilner Rd HP21 115 E5
KILN FARM 33 B3
Kiln Farm Ind Est MK11 33 B3
Kiln Farm Rdbt MK11 33 A3
Kiln Fields SL6 185 E1
Kiln La
Botley HP5 155 B8
Cores End SL8, HP10 185 D3
Kiln La *continued*
Hedgerley SL2 187 D3
Lacey Green HP27 149 F5
Kiln Pl SL6 195 A3
Kiln Pond La HP13 161 D3
Kiln Rd
Hastoe HP23 133 B6
Prestwood HP16 151 B7
Kiln The HP5 144 C1
Kilnwood HP14 150 B1
Kilpin Gn MK16 24 B6
Kilwinning Dr MK10 35 F1
Kimbells Cl HP18 124 D2
Kimber Cl SL4 210 A4
Kimberley Cl SL3 206 F2
Kimbers Dr SL1 197 D2
Kimber's La SL6 202 E3
Kimble Ct HP22 129 E3
Kimble Park Rd HP17 129 E3
Kimblewick Rd HP17 129 C5
Kimbolton Ct MK14 35 A8
Kincardine Dr MK3 46 F3
Kindermann Ct MK5 46 B5
Kindleton MK14 34 F8
Kinellan Ct HP9 175 D3
King Charles Cl MK18 41 E2
King Edward Ave HP21 116 A7
King Edward Ct 5 SL4 210 D6
King Edward St
Milton Keynes MK13 33 F7
Slough SL1 205 D4
King Edward VII Ave SL4 210 E8
King Edward VII Hospl SL4 210 C4
Kingfisher HP19 101 E4
Kingfisher Ct
3 High Wycombe HP11 173 A6
Slough SL2 198 B1
Kingfisher Ctr The MK16 22 C3
Kingfisher Ho
Loudwater HP11 174 A4
Marlow SL7 183 F2
Kingfisher Pl HP11 174 B3
Kingfisher Rd MK18 52 F7
King George Cres MK11 32 E6
King George V Rd HP6 154 D1
Kinghorn La SL6 195 D3
Kinghorn Pk SL6 195 D3
King John's Cl TW19 211 C2
King Johns Palace SL3 212 D6
Kingsash Rd HP19 114 F8
Kingsbridge MK4 46 D2
Kingsbrook Specialist Bsns & Ent Coll MK19 31 F4
Kingsbury HP20 115 D8
Kingsbury Dr SL4 211 B1
Kings Chase SL6 202 F6
Kings Cl
Beaconsfield HP9 186 A8
Chalfont St Giles HP8 177 D8
Henley-on-Thames RG9 191 D2
Westcott HP18 98 C6
Worminghall HP18 123 D5
Kingscote Pre Prep Sch SL9 188 E8
King's Cross HP18 113 A1
Kings Ct HP4 135 C5
Kingsdale Rd HP4 135 A3
KINGSEY 127 B2
Kingsey Rd OX9 126 D1
Kings Farm Rd WD3 167 D3
Kingsfield SL4 209 D6
Kingsfold MK13 34 B7
Kingsgate HP19 115 B8
King's Gr SL6 202 E6
King's Grove Ind Est SL6 202 E6
Kings Hall Par HP22 131 B4
Kingshill Dr MK19 31 E5
Kingshill Rd HP13, HP15 162 D3
Kingshill Way HP4 135 B2
Kings La SL6 195 B8
King's La
Great Missenden HP16 141 C2
Lee Common HP16, HP22 141 F7
South Heath HP16 152 E8
Kingsland Rd HP21 116 A4
Kingsley Cl MK16 21 F4
Kingsley Cres HP11 172 F6
Kingsley Dr SL7 183 C6
Kingsley Path SL2 197 D1
Kingsley Wlk HP23 119 A4
Kings Lodge
Amersham HP6 154 D1
Finmere MK18 50 D6
Kings Mdw HP22 102 C4
Kingsmead HP27 139 B6
Kings Mead LU6 92 E3
Kingsmead Bsns Pk HP11 174 B3
Kingsmead Ho SL1 205 C5
Kingsmead Rd HP11 174 B3
Kingsmead Rdbt MK4 56 F8
Kings Oak Cl HP27 139 C5
Kingsoe Leys MK10 36 A2
Kings Quarter 3 SL6 203 B7
Kings Rd
Berkhamsted HP4 135 B3
Chalfont St Giles HP8 177 D8
Henley-on-Thames RG9 191 D2
West Drayton UB7 208 F4
King's Rd
Aylesbury HP21 115 F8
Henley-on-Thames RG9 191 D2
High Wycombe HP11 173 F4
Loudwater HP11 174 A4
Slough SL1 205 E3
Uxbridge UB8 201 D3
Windsor SL4 210 D3
Windsor SL4 210 D5
Kings Ride HP10 163 B1
King's Road Ho SL4 210 D5
Kings Sq HP11 173 F4
Kings St LU7 78 E7
King St
Chesham HP5 154 B7
Maidenhead SL6 202 F6
Maidenhead SL6 202 F7
Milton Keynes MK11 32 E6
Piddington HP14 160 C1
Tring HP23 119 A3
King Stable St SL4 210 D7
King's Terr SL3 212 B8
KINGSTON 36 C2
Kingston Ave
Milton Keynes MK11 32 E5
West Drayton UB7 208 F6
KINGSTON BLOUNT 147 A3
Kingston Gymnastics & Fitness Ctr MK10 36 C1
Kingston Hill OX39, HP14 158 B8
Kingston La
Uxbridge UB8 201 E2
West Drayton UB7 208 F4
Kingston Rd HP13 162 D1
Kingston Rdbt MK10 36 D1
Kingsway
Farnham Common SL2 198 C6
Gerrards Cross SL9 188 E8
Iver SL0 207 E7
5 Slough SL3 206 C3
Kingsway Ho 6 SL6 202 F7
Kingsway Mews SL2 198 C6
Kingswear Dr MK10 36 B4
Kings Wlk RG9 191 D2
KINGSWOOD 83 B3
Kings Wood SL7 193 D7
Kingswood Ave HP10 174 B8
Kingswood Creek TW19 211 D2
Kingswood Ct SL6 202 F5
Kingswood Ho SL2 205 C8
Kingswood La
Kingswood HP18 83 B2
Ludgershall HP18 96 F6
Kings Wood National Nature Reserve★ MK17 60 B1
Kingswood Par SL7 183 D5
Kingswood Pl HP13 162 E1
King's Wood Prim Sch HP13 173 F8
Kingswood Rd HP10 163 A1
Kingswood View HP13 162 E1
Kinloch Pl MK2 58 E5
Kinnaird Cl SL1 204 C7
Kinnear Cl MK8 45 E7
Kinross Dr MK3 46 E2
Kinson Gn HP20 101 E3
Kipling Ct SL4 210 B5
Kipling Dr MK16 21 F4
Kipling Rd MK3 58 A7
Kippell Hill MK46 6 F5
Kirby Est UB7 208 D6
Kirby Way UB8 201 F1
Kirkeby Cl MK14 34 D6
Kirke Cl MK5 46 A5
Kirkham Ct MK5 46 C8
Kirkstall Pl MK6 46 D8
Kirkwall Spur SL1, SL2 205 E8
Kirkwood Gr MK5 45 D5
Kirtle Rd HP5 144 C1
Kirtlington MK15 35 B5
Kitchener Cl MK46 7 A3
Kitchener Rd HP11 172 E7
Kite Field HP4 134 E7
Kite Hill MK6 47 B8
Kitelee Cl MK19 11 A3
Kite Wood Rd HP10 163 B1
Kitsbury Ct HP4 135 B4
Kitsbury Rd HP4 135 B4
Kitsbury Terr HP4 135 B4
Kittiwake HP19 101 E4
Klee Cl HP22 85 A5
Klondyke SL7 183 D2
Knapp Gate MK5 45 F7
Knaresborough Ct MK3 57 D7
Knaves Beech HP10 174 D1
Knaves Beech Bsns Ctr HP10 174 D1
Knaves Beech Ind Est HP10 174 C1

Knaves Beech Way
HP10 ... 174 C1
Knaves Hill LU7 ... 80 D8
Knaves Hollow HP10 ... 174 D1
Knebworth Gate MK14 ... 22 A1
Knighton-Way La UB9 ... 201 B6
Knightsbridge Ct SL3 ... 207 A2
Knightsbridge Pl 16
HP19 ... 115 A8
Knights Cl
Eaton Bray LU6 ... 92 E5
Great Brickhill MK17 ... 59 D1
Windsor SL4 ... 209 D6
Knights Ct LU6 ... 92 E5
Knights Gn WD3 ... 167 E6
Knights Hill HP12 ... 172 E6
Knights Pl 5 SL4 ... 210 C5
Knights Templar Way
HP11 ... 173 B4
Knoll Cl MK16 ... 13 F2
Knolls Cl HP22 ... 89 B3
Knolls View LU6 ... 92 B5
Knoll The
Aspley Heath MK17 ... 49 A1
Sherington MK16 ... 13 F2
Knolton Way SL2 ... 206 C7
Knottocks Cl HP9 ... 175 D5
Knottocks Dr HP9 ... 175 D5
Knottocks End HP9 ... 175 D5
KNOTTY GREEN ... 175 C6
Knowles Cl UB7 ... 208 E5
Knowles Gn MK2 ... 58 C8
Knowles Inf Sch MK2 ... 58 D8
Knowles Jun Sch MK2 ... 58 D8
Knowl Gate MK5 ... 46 C7
KNOWLHILL ... 46 D6
Knowlhill Rdbt MK5 ... 46 C6
Knowsley Cl SL6 ... 195 A1
Knox Bridge MK7 ... 48 B8
Kola Ho SL2 ... 206 B6
Kop Hill Rd HP27 ... 139 D3
Kramer Ct MK8 ... 45 D6
Krohn Cl MK18 ... 52 F8
Krypton Cl MK5 ... 46 C6
Kynaston Ave HP21 ... 115 E4

L

Laburnham Cotts LU7 ... 69 E3
Laburnham Rd SL6 ... 202 E6
Laburnum Ave UB7 ... 208 F6
Laburnum Cl SL7 ... 183 E4
Laburnum Gr
Milton Keynes MK2 ... 58 E7
Slough SL3 ... 212 B8
Laburnum Rd HP12 ... 172 C5
Lacemakers
Chinnor OX39 ... 147 C6
Long Crendon HP18 ... 125 C7
Lace Mews MK46 ... 7 A4
Lacey Dr HP14 ... 161 C7
LACEY GREEN ... 149 E5
Laceys Dr HP15 ... 163 B5
Ladbroke Cl HP20 ... 101 E2
Ladbroke Gr MK10 ... 47 F8
Ladbrooke Rd SL1 ... 205 D3
Ladybridge Terr MK43 ... 8 E5
Lady Cooper Ct HP4 ... 135 E6
Ladyday Pl SL1 ... 205 C5
Lady Dr MK15 ... 35 A8
Ladymead Cl MK17 ... 56 B8
Ladymeadow Ct MK10 ... 35 E3
Ladymede Sch HP17 ... 129 E1
Ladysmith Rd LU7 ... 105 E5
Lady Verney Cl HP13 ... 173 B8
Ladywalk WD3 ... 178 E6
Lady Yorke Pk SL0 ... 200 D6
Laggan Ct MK2 ... 58 D4
Laggan Rd SL6 ... 195 F1
Laggan Sq SL6 ... 195 F1
Lagger Cl HP8 ... 177 B7
Lagger The HP8 ... 177 B7
Lagley Ho HP4 ... 135 A5
Lagonda Cl MK16 ... 22 E4
Laidon Cl MK2 ... 58 D4
Lake Ave SL1 ... 205 D6
Lake Cl MK18 ... 66 B6
LAKE END ... 204 B4
Lake End Ct SL6 ... 204 A7
Lake End Rd SL4, SL6 ... 204 B5
Laker Ct MK6 ... 46 E7
Lakes Cotts LU7 ... 90 C8
Lakeside
Aylesbury HP19 ... 101 E4
Maidenhead SL6 ... 196 B1
Tring HP23 ... 119 A5
Lakeside Dr SL2 ... 198 F4
Lakeside Est SL3 ... 212 F7
Lakeside Rd SL3 ... 212 F7
Lakes La
Beaconsfield HP9 ... 186 F8
Newport Pagnell MK16 ... 22 B5
Lakes The SL7 ... 194 A6
Lake View SL6 ... 196 A1
Lamb Cl MK16 ... 22 A4
Lambe Rd HP22 ... 131 C5
Lamberhurst Gr MK7 ... 48 A8
Lambert Ave SL3 ... 206 E3
Lamberts Croft MK12 ... 33 C5
Lambert Wlk OX9 ... 125 F1
Lamb La MK7 ... 48 C7
Lambourn Ct MK4 ... 46 D2
Lambourne Ave HP21 ... 115 D3
Lambourne Ct
Maidenhead SL6 ... 203 C8
Uxbridge UB8 ... 201 B4
Lambourne Dr SL6 ... 202 C3
Lambridge La RG9 ... 191 C3
Lambridge Wood Rd
RG9 ... 191 B4
Lambscroft Way SL9 ... 177 E1
Lambton Ho SL4 ... 210 A4
Lambtons Way MK18 ... 66 B5
Lamesley Ho SL6 ... 202 E6
Lammas MK6 ... 47 A5
Lammas Ave SL4 ... 210 D5
Lammas Ct SL4 ... 210 C5
Lammas La HP18 ... 112 B2
Lammas Path HP18 ... 112 B2
Lammas Rd
Cheddington LU7 ... 105 A7
Slough SL1 ... 204 D8
Lammas Way
Lane End HP14 ... 171 A4
Loudwater HP10 ... 174 C1
Lampitts Cross MK6 ... 47 B6
Lamport Ct MK8 ... 46 A8
Lamva Ct MK11 ... 32 F5
Lanark Ho MK3 ... 46 F1
Lancaster Ave SL2 ... 198 C1
Lancaster Bsns Park
LU7 ... 78 F1
Lancaster Cl TW19 ... 213 E1
Lancaster Ct HP12 ... 172 D4
Lancaster Dr HP3 ... 145 F4
Lancaster Gate MK3 ... 57 E7
Lancaster Rd
Aylesbury HP21 ... 116 B6
High Wycombe HP12 ... 172 E4
Maidenhead SL6 ... 202 B8
Uxbridge UB8 ... 201 D5
Lancaster Ride HP10 ... 174 B8
Lancastria Mews SL6 ... 202 D7
Lancelot Cl SL1 ... 205 A4
Lance Way HP13 ... 174 A6
Lanchester Rd MK43 ... 24 D2
Lancot Ave LU6 ... 93 F8
Lancotbury Cl LU6 ... 93 C7
Lancot Dr LU6 ... 93 F8
Lancot Lower Sch LU6 ... 93 E8
Lancot Pl LU6 ... 93 E8
Lancresse Cl UB8 ... 201 D6
Lander Rd HP19 ... 100 F3
Landon Ct HP21 ... 115 F7
Landrace Ct MK5 ... 45 F3
Landsborough Gate
MK15 ... 35 C7
Lands End Gr MK4 ... 56 F8
Lands The LU7 ... 79 F3
LANE END ... 171 C4
Lane End HP4 ... 134 F4
Lane End Ind Est HP14 ... 171 B4
Lane End Prim Sch
HP14 ... 171 B4
Lane End Rd HP12 ... 172 B6
Lanercost Cres MK10 ... 36 B1
LANES END ... 132 C4
Lane The
Grafton Regis NN12 ... 9 D2
Mursley MK17 ... 67 D6
Lane Wood Cl HP7 ... 165 F8
Lanfranc Gdns MK15 ... 35 B7
Langcliffe Dr MK13 ... 34 C5
Langdale Cl
Maidenhead SL6 ... 203 A6
Milton Keynes MK2 ... 58 D4
Langdale Ho HP11 ... 174 A4
Langdale Lodge HP10 ... 174 C2
Langdon Ave HP21 ... 116 B5
Langdon St HP23 ... 119 A3
Langdown Way SL6 ... 202 D5
Langerstone La MK4 ... 46 B1
Langford Pl MK7 ... 48 A3
Langham Way MK6 ... 47 C4
Langland Ho MK6 ... 47 C6
Langland Rd MK6 ... 47 C6
Langlands MK46 ... 7 E7
Langland Sch MK6 ... 47 C6
LANGLEY ... 207 A3
Langley Acad SL3 ... 206 E3
Langley Broom SL3 ... 206 F1
Langley Bsns Ctr SL3 ... 207 A4
Langley Bsns Pk SL3 ... 207 A4
Langley Cl MK18 ... 65 E4
Langley Cnr SL3 ... 199 F6
Langley Gram Sch SL3 ... 206 F2
Langley L Ctr SL3 ... 207 B2
Langley Manor Sch
SL3 ... 206 E5
Langley Park Ctry Pk★ SL0,
SL3 ... 200 A1
Langley Park Rd SL3 ... 207 B6
Langley Rd SL3 ... 206 E3
Langley Sta SL3 ... 207 A4
Langley Way SL7 ... 183 C2
Langmuir Ct MK5 ... 46 C4
Langney Gn MK4 ... 57 A8
Langport Cres MK5 ... 45 D5
Langston Ct HP12 ... 172 C8
Langstone Ct HP20 ... 101 F3
Langstone Ct 11 HP20 ... 101 F3
Langton Cl
Maidenhead SL6 ... 202 D8
Slough SL1 ... 204 D5
Langton Dr MK8 ... 33 E3
Langton's Mdw SL2 ... 198 C6
Langtree Ave SL1 ... 204 F4
Lanner Wlk MK6 ... 47 B8
Lanrick Copse HP4 ... 135 E5
Lansdell Ave HP12 ... 172 B3
Lansdowne Ave SL1 ... 205 E5
Lansdowne Ct
Maidenhead SL6 ... 203 C7
Slough SL1 ... 205 E5
Lansdowne Rd
Aylesbury HP20 ... 101 D2
Chesham HP5 ... 144 C2
Lansdowne Way HP11 ... 172 E3
Lansdown Rd SL9 ... 177 D2
Lanterns Wlk SL6 ... 203 B7
Lantern Way UB7 ... 208 E4
Lanthorn Cl MK14 ... 34 E6
Lappetts La HP16 ... 152 E8
Larch Cl
Aylesbury HP20 ... 102 A2
Slough SL2 ... 205 B8
Tylers Green HP10 ... 163 C2
Larches The
Berkhamsted HP4 ... 134 D5
Holmer Green HP15 ... 163 D7
Little Chalfont HP6 ... 155 B1
Larchfield Prim Sch
SL6 ... 202 E4
Larchfield Rd SL6 ... 202 E5
Larch Gr MK2 ... 58 E7
Larchlands The HP10 ... 163 D1
Larchmoor Pk SL2 ... 199 A7
Larch Rise HP4 ... 135 A5
Larchwood HP16 ... 152 B4
Lark Cl MK18 ... 52 E7
Larkfield SL6 ... 203 B1
Larkfield Cl HP13 ... 162 F1
Larkin Cl MK16 ... 22 A5
Larkings La SL2 ... 199 B4
Lark Rise HP15 ... 163 B5
Larkspur Ave MK14 ... 34 E5
Larkspur Way HP15 ... 162 F6
Larks Rise HP5 ... 154 D6
Lark Vale HP19 ... 101 E3
La Roche Cl 4 SL3 ... 206 C3
Larwood Pl MK6 ... 34 F1
Lasborough Rd MK10 ... 36 C1
Lascelles Cl MK15 ... 35 B7
Lascelles Ho 8 SL1 ... 206 A4
Lascelles Rd SL3 ... 206 B3
Laser Cl MK5 ... 46 C6
Lashlake Rd OX9 ... 125 F1
Lassell Gdns SL6 ... 203 B7
Lastingham Gr MK4 ... 46 B2
Latchmoor Ave SL9 ... 188 D7
Latchmoor Gr SL9 ... 188 D7
Latchmoor Way SL9 ... 188 D7
LATHBURY ... 22 C7
LATIMER ... 155 E3
Latimer
Latimer HP5 ... 155 E2
Milton Keynes MK11 ... 32 E4
Latimer Cl HP6 ... 166 C8
Latimer Ct HP20 ... 116 A8
Latimer Rd
Chesham HP5 ... 154 E5
Little Chalfont HP5 ... 155 C2
Latimer Way HP9 ... 175 C6
Laud's Cl RG9 ... 191 C1
Launceston WD3 ... 167 B3
Launceston Ct MK5 ... 46 B6
Launde 1 MK10 ... 36 B1
Laurance Ct 2 SL7 ... 183 D2
Laurel Ave SL3 ... 206 E4
Laurel Bank HP3 ... 146 F8
Laurel Cl
Milton Keynes MK8 ... 45 D7
Poyle SL3 ... 212 E7
Prestwood HP16 ... 151 B7
Speen HP27 ... 150 C4
Laurel Ct
Amersham HP6 ... 154 C3
Iver Heath SL0 ... 200 D5
Laurel Dr
Loudwater HP11 ... 174 B3
Walter's Ash HP14 ... 161 D7
Laurel La UB7 ... 208 E2
Laurel Rd SL9 ... 177 D2
Laurels Rd SL0 ... 200 D3
Laurels The
High Wycombe HP12 ... 172 C4
Milton Keynes MK1 ... 47 D1
Laurel Way 4 HP21 ... 115 E7
Lautrec Way HP19 ... 100 F2
Lautree Gdns SL6 ... 195 E7
Lavender Cl HP21 ... 115 B5
Lavender Gr MK7 ... 48 A5
Lavender Rd UB8 ... 208 F8
Lavender Way HP15 ... 162 F7
Lavender Wlk HP21 ... 115 B6
LAVENDON ... 7 F7
Lavendon Comb Sch
MK46 ... 7 F8
Lavendon Rd MK46 ... 7 A5
Lavric Rd HP21 ... 115 C6
Lawford Ave WD3 ... 167 C3
Lawford Cl WD3 ... 167 C3
Lawkland SL2 ... 198 C2
Lawn Ave UB7 ... 208 D4
Lawn Cl SL3 ... 211 C7
Lawn Farm Bsns Ctr
HP18 ... 83 D4
Lawn Hill HP18 ... 73 A2
Lawn House La HP18 ... 72 F1
Lawn Rd UB8 ... 201 C5
Lawnsmead Gdns MK16 ... 22 D5
Lawns The
Brill HP18 ... 96 B1
Tylers Green HP10 ... 163 B2
Lawn The SL3 ... 211 C6
Lawrence Cl
14 Aylesbury HP20 ... 101 F2
Aylesbury HP20 ... 102 A2
Lawrence Ct SL4 ... 210 C5
Lawrence Gr HP16 ... 151 D5
Lawrence Way SL1 ... 204 D8
Lawrence Wlk MK16 ... 21 F5
Laws Cl MK43 ... 8 E6
Lawsone Rise HP13 ... 162 B1
Lawson Pl MK5 ... 46 B5
Laxfield Dr MK10 ... 36 A4
Laxton Gn SL6 ... 202 C3
Layburn Cres SL3 ... 212 B8
Lay Rd HP19 ... 101 B2
Layter's Ave SL9 ... 177 C1
Layter's Avenue S SL9 ... 177 C1
Layter's Cl SL9 ... 177 C1
Layter's End SL9 ... 177 C1
LAYTER'S GREEN ... 177 B1
Layters Green La SL9 ... 177 B1
Layters Way SL9 ... 188 D6
Leaberry MK13 ... 34 A8
Leachcroft SL9 ... 177 B2
Leaches Farm Bsns Ctr
HP18 ... 81 F4
Leach Rd HP21 ... 115 C7
Lea Cl SL7 ... 183 D6
Leacroft Cl UB7 ... 208 E6
Leacroft Rd SL0 ... 207 E7
Lea Ct HP7 ... 165 F8
LEADENHALL ... 47 A8
Leadenhall Rdbt MK6 ... 46 E7
Leaders Cl HP22 ... 89 B3
Leafield Rise MK8 ... 33 D2
Leafy La HP23 ... 118 E1
Leaholme Gdns SL1 ... 204 D8
Lea La HP18 ... 125 F4
Leapingwell La MK18 ... 66 B5
Leary Cres MK16 ... 22 E4
Leas Cl HP13 ... 173 F8
Leas Dr SL0 ... 207 E7
Leaside MK16 ... 12 B6
Leasowe Pl MK13 ... 34 C3
Leather La HP16 ... 142 A3
Leaver Rd RG9 ... 191 C1
LECKHAMPSTEAD ... 42 E7
Leckhampstead Rd
MK18 ... 42 A8
Leckhamstead Rd MK19 ... 31 A3
Ledborough Gate HP9 ... 175 F4
Ledborough La HP9 ... 175 E4
Ledborough Wood
HP9 ... 175 E4
LEDBURN ... 90 D8
Ledburn LU7 ... 90 C8
Ledburn Gr LU7 ... 80 E6
Ledbury MK14 ... 21 E1
Ledeview Ct HP11 ... 174 A4
Ledger's Rd SL1 ... 205 D4
Leeches Way LU7 ... 105 A7
LEE COMMON ... 142 D5
Lee Common CE Fst Sch
HP16 ... 142 D5
Lee Cotts
Buckmoorend HP17 ... 140 D6
Lacey Green HP27 ... 149 A4
Lee Cres HP17 ... 114 D5
Lee Ct 7 HP12 ... 172 E7
Leeds Rd SL1 ... 205 E6
Lee Farm Cl HP5 ... 145 A1
LEE GATE ... 142 A7
Lee Ho 2 MK2 ... 58 C8
Lee La SL6 ... 194 F1
Lee Rd
Aylesbury HP21 ... 115 D6
Quainton HP22 ... 84 F5
Saunderton HP27 ... 148 F6
Lees Cl SL6 ... 202 B5
Lees Gdns SL6 ... 202 B5
Leeson Gdns SL4 ... 204 E2
Lees Wlk SL7 ... 183 C2
Le Flaive Bsns Pk HP14 ... 161 E6
Legoland Windsor★
SL4 ... 209 D2
Leicester Cl RG9 ... 191 D3
Leigh Hill MK4 ... 46 D2
Leigh Pk SL3 ... 211 B7
Leigh Rd SL1 ... 205 B6
Leigh Sq SL4 ... 209 D5
Leigh St HP11 ... 172 F7
LEIGHTON BUZZARD ... 80 F6
Leighton Buzzard Sta
LU7 ... 80 E7
Leighton Gdns SL6 ... 196 B1
Leighton Ho 7 SL7 ... 183 E2
Leighton Mid Sch LU7 ... 80 F6
Leighton Rd
Edlesborough LU6 ... 92 D4
Leighton Buzzard LU7 ... 80 F7
Soulbury LU7 ... 70 B1
Stoke Hammond MK17 ... 69 E7
Wing LU7 ... 80 A3
Wingrave HP22 ... 89 C3
Leighton St MK17 ... 60 E6
Leiston Spur SL1 ... 205 E7
Leisure Plaza★ MK9 ... 46 C8
Leith Cl SL1 ... 206 A5
Leith Rd HP19 ... 115 A8
Lembrook Wlk HP21 ... 115 C6
Lemmon Wlk 5 MK4 ... 45 E2
LENBOROUGH ... 52 D3
Lenborough Cl MK18 ... 52 C7
Lenborough Ct MK15 ... 35 C2
Lenborough Rd MK18 ... 52 C7
Lennon Dr MK8 ... 45 E7
Lennox Rd MK2 ... 58 D7
LENT ... 197 B1
Lent Gn SL1 ... 197 B1
Lent Green La SL1 ... 197 B1
Lenthall Cl MK13 ... 34 A5
LENT RISE ... 204 A8
Lent Rise Comb Sch
SL1 ... 204 B8
Lent Rise Rd SL1 ... 204 B8
Leominster Gate 4
MK10 ... 36 A1
Leonards Cl HP18 ... 72 F2
Leonardslee MK4 ... 45 F2
Leon Ave MK2 ... 58 D8
Leon L Ctr MK2 ... 58 C4
Leon Sch & Sports Coll
MK2 ... 58 C5
Leopard Dr MK15 ... 35 A7
Leopold Mall 5 SL1 ... 205 F4
Leopold Rd LU7 ... 80 D7
Lerwick Dr SL1 ... 205 E8
Leslie Dunne Ho SL4 ... 209 E5
Lester Gr HP15 ... 163 A4
Lesters Rd SL6 ... 195 D6
Letchfield HP5 ... 155 B8
Letter Box La HP27 ... 139 D7
Leven Cl
Leighton Buzzard LU7 ... 80 B7
Milton Keynes MK2 ... 58 D5
Levens Hall Dr MK4 ... 45 F1
Leverkus Ct OX39 ... 147 C6
Leverkus Ho OX39 ... 147 C6
Levings Cl HP19 ... 101 A3
Lewens Croft MK16 ... 16 A3
Lewes Ct SL1 ... 205 C4
Lewes Ho MK3 ... 57 D7
Lewins Farm Ct SL1 ... 204 F6
Lewins Rd SL9 ... 188 D8
Lewins Way SL1 ... 204 F6
Lewins Yd HP5 ... 154 B8
Lewis Cl MK16 ... 21 F5
Lewis La SL9 ... 177 E2
LEWKNOR ... 157 B8
Lewknor CE Prim Sch
OX49 ... 157 B8
Lewknor Cl OX49 ... 157 A7
Lexham Gdns HP6 ... 154 C2
Lexington Ave SL6 ... 202 D5
Leybourne Gdns OX39 ... 147 C7
Leyburn Ct MK13 ... 34 C5
Leyburne Cl LU7 ... 90 C8
Ley Field Rd HP21 ... 115 E6
LEY HILL ... 145 B1
Ley Hill Sch HP5 ... 145 B1
Leyland Cl MK18 ... 51 F4
Leyland Pl 3 MK6 ... 34 E1
Leylands La TW19 ... 213 A2
Leys Cl HP19 ... 101 C4
Leys Ct MK5 ... 46 B8
Leys La MK18 ... 62 B8
Leys Rd MK5 ... 46 B8
Leys The
Amersham HP6 ... 154 B4
Buckingham MK18 ... 41 F3
Halton HP22 ... 117 C1
Tring HP23 ... 119 B4
Woburn Sands MK17 ... 49 B4
Yardley Hastings NN7 ... 1 A6
Leys View MK16 ... 13 F1
Leywood Cl HP7 ... 165 E7
Libra Ho HP10 ... 185 A8
Lichfield Down MK7 ... 48 B5
Lichfield Ho HP21 ... 115 F6
Lidcote LU7 ... 78 A5
Liddall Way UB7 ... 208 F5
Liddell SL4 ... 209 C4
Liddell Pl SL4 ... 209 C4
Liddell Sq 14 SL4 ... 209 C5
Liddell Way SL4 ... 209 C4
Liffre Dr HP22 ... 131 B6
Lightfoot Ct MK7 ... 47 F5

Lightlands La SL6 195 F5
Ligo Ave HP22 116 C2
Lilac Cl MK17 57 C3
Lilac Ct SL2 197 F2
Lilac Pl UB7 208 F6
Lilies The HP22 87 C1
Lilleshall Ave MK10 35 F1
Lilley Way SL1 204 E5
Lillibrooke Cres SL6 202 A3
LILLINGSTONE DAYRELL 29 F4
LILLINGSTONE LOVELL 30 B5
Lillyfee Farm La HP10 186 B5
Lilly Hill MK46 6 F5
Lily Bottom La HP27 150 A7
Lily Dr UB7 208 D2
Lily's Wlk HP11 173 A6
Limbaud Cl MK7 48 A5
Lime Ave
Buckingham MK18 52 F7
High Wycombe HP11 173 D5
West Drayton UB7 208 F6
Windsor SL4 210 F7
Lime Cl
Hazelmere HP15 163 A3
Newport Pagnell MK16 22 B3
Lime Gr
Chinnor OX39 147 D6
Leighton Buzzard LU7 80 E8
Woburn Sands MK17 49 B4
Lime Rd
Princes Risborough HP27 139 B3
Yardley Gobion NN12 18 E6
Limerick La MK9 35 B3
Limes Ave HP21 116 B7
Lime St MK46 6 F3
Limes The
Amersham HP6 154 B3
Milton Keynes, Fenny Stratford MK2 58 E8
Milton Keynes MK11 32 E5
Windsor SL4 209 C6
Limes Way HP18 124 D2
Lime Tree Cl HP15 162 D8
Lime Tree Wlk HP7 165 F8
Lime Wlk
Maidenhead SL6 202 A8
New Denham UB9 201 C7
Limit Home Pk HP4 134 D7
Limmer La HP12 172 B3
Limmers Mead HP15 162 D8
Linceslade Gr MK5 34 B1
Linchfield HP13 173 E7
Linchfield Rd SL3 211 C6
Lincoln MK14 34 C8
Lincoln Cl HP22 116 B2
Lincoln Ct
Berkhamsted HP4 135 B4
3 Slough SL1 205 E3
Lincoln Hatch La SL1 197 C1
Lincoln Ho HP10 185 D3
Lincoln Park Bsns Ctr HP12 172 D6
Lincoln Pk
Amersham HP7 165 E8
Brackley NN13 38 A5
Lincoln Rd
Chalfont St Peter SL9 177 E2
High Wycombe HP12 172 E5
Maidenhead SL6 202 B8
Lincolnshire Cl MK3 46 E1
Lincolns The HP16 152 A3
Lincoln Way SL1 204 D6
Lincombe Slade LU7 80 E8
Lincroft MK43 25 B1
Linden SL3 207 B1
Linden Ave SL6 195 D1
Linden Cl SL0 200 D3
Linden Ct HP12 172 D6
Linden Dr
Chalfont St Peter SL9 177 E1
Farnham Royal SL2 198 C4
Linden End HP21 115 F6
Linden Gr MK14 34 E8
Linden Lea HP22 131 B6
Lindens The HP3 146 F8
Linden Way HP17 128 B7
Linden Wlk HP15 163 B3
Lindisfarne Dr MK10 36 A1
Lindo Cl HP5 144 B1
Lindores Croft MK10 36 B1
Lindsay Ave HP12 172 E7
Lindsay Cl TW19 213 D2
Lindsey Rd UB9 190 A1
Lines Hill HP22 88 B3
Lines Rd HP14 171 B5
Lines The HP22 88 C4
Linfields HP7 166 C7
Linford Ave MK16 22 A4
Linford La
Milton Keynes, Willen MK15 35 D7
Milton Keynes, Woolstone MK15 35 C3
Lingfield MK12 33 E4
Lingfield Cl HP13 174 A5
Lingholm Cl SL6 202 C6
Linington Ave HP5 145 A1
Link Cl HP12 172 D6
Link Rd
Datchet SL3 211 C6
Great Missenden HP16 152 A7
High Wycombe HP12 172 D6
Links App HP10 185 B8
Links Rd HP10 185 C8
Links Way HP10 185 B8
Linkswood Rd SL1 197 C3
Link The
Hazelmere HP15 163 A5
Slough SL2 206 B7
Link Way UB9 190 A5
Linnet Cl HP12 172 B3
Linnet Dr HP18 98 C5
Linney Ct MK4 46 A1
LINSLADE 80 D7
Linslade Lower Sch LU7 80 D7
Linslade Mid Sch LU7 80 E5
Linslade Rd LU7 70 F4
Lintlaw Pl MK3 47 A3
Linton Cl MK13 34 C4
Lintott Ct TW19 213 D1
Linx The MK3 47 A2
Lionel Ave HP22 131 A6
Lionel Cl HP22 131 A5
Lipscombe Dr MK18 41 E1
Lipscomb La MK5 46 A7
Lisburn Path 1 HP20 101 F2
Lisle Rd HP13 162 A1
Lisleys Field HP15 162 D7
Lismore Pk SL2 205 F7
Lissel Rd MK6 47 E5
Lisset Rd SL6 203 A6
Lister Cl MK6 47 B6
Lister Gn HP21 115 E5
Liston Ct (Sh Arcade) 7 SL7 183 D2
Liston Ho 9 SL7 183 E2
Liston Rd SL7 183 D2
Litcham Spur SL1 205 D7
Little Balmer MK18 52 E6
Little Benty UB7 208 D1
Little Boltons 13 SL7 183 E2
LITTLE BOYS HEATH 152 C3
LITTLE BRICKHILL 59 E5
Little Bridge Rd HP4 135 D4
LITTLE BRITAIN 208 C7
Little Britain HP18 99 B7
Littlebrook Ave SL2 204 E8
Little Buntings SL4 209 F4
LITTLE CHALFONT 155 B1
Little Chalfont Prim Sch HP6 166 E8
Little Chapels Way SL1 205 A4
Little Chartridge Ct HP5 144 A1
Little Cl
Aylesbury HP20 101 D1
Flackwell Heath HP10 185 B6
High Wycombe HP12 172 E3
LITTLECOTE 78 A5
Littlecote MK8 34 A1
Littledown Rd SL1 205 F5
Littledown Specl Sch SL1 205 F6
Little Dunmow MK10 36 A1
LITTLE END 23 B8
Littlefield Ct UB7 213 D7
LITTLE FRIETH 170 E2
LITTLE GADDESDEN 121 D7
Little Gaddesden CE Prim Sch HP4 121 C8
Little Gaddesden Ho HP4 121 E5
Little Gibbs HP27 138 A2
Little Greencroft HP5 144 A4
Little Habton 3 MK4 46 B2
Little Hame MK10 35 F3
Little Ham La HP27 139 B5
LITTLE HAMPDEN 140 F4
Little Hampden Cl HP22 131 B4
Little Hill WD3 167 C3
Little Hivings HP5 144 A4
Little Hollis HP16 151 E7
Little Hoo HP23 118 F4
LITTLE HORWOOD 55 F2
Little Horwood Manor MK17 55 E4
Little Horwood Rd MK17 55 C3
Little Hundridge La HP16 153 A8
LITTLE KIMBLE 129 E2
Little Kimble Sta HP17 129 E2
LITTLE KINGSHILL 152 B3
Little Kingshill Comb Sch HP16 152 B2
Little La
Lacey Green HP27 149 C4
Yardley Hastings NN7 1 A7
LITTLE LINFORD 21 C5
Little Linford La MK16, MK19 21 E4
Little Linford Wood Wildlife Reserve★ MK16 21 B8
LITTLE LONDON
Oakley 109 F5
Wendover 141 C7
Little London
Deanshanger MK19 31 E4
Whitchurch HP22 87 A5
Little London Gn HP18 109 F5
LITTLE MARLOW 184 D5
Little Marlow CE Inf Sch SL7 184 C5
Little Marlow Rd SL7 183 E3
LITTLE MARSH 72 A3
Littlemarsh MK7 48 A5
Little Marsh Rd OX27 72 A3
Little Mdw MK5 46 C7
Littlemere MK8 33 D1
LITTLE MISSENDEN 153 A2
Little Missenden CE Inf Sch HP7 153 B2
Little Mollards HP22 89 A3
Little Orchard Cl HP27 138 E5
Little Orchs HP20 101 F3
Little Pk
Bovingdon HP3 146 A3
Princes Risborough HP27 139 C3
Littleport Spur SL1 205 E7
Little Reeves Ave HP7 165 F8
LITTLE ROW 202 A5
Little Shardeloes HP7 165 A8
Little Spinney MK43 25 C3
Little Spring HP5 144 B3
Little Spring Prim Sch HP5 144 B3
Little St NN7 1 B6
Little Stanton MK14 34 D8
Little Stocking MK5 46 A3
Littlestone Gate MK10 36 B3
Little Sutton La SL3 207 C1
LITTLE TINGEWICK 50 E6
LITTLE TRING 118 F6
Little Tring Rd HP23 118 F6
Little Twye HP23 132 F3
Little Twye Rd HP23 132 F3
Little Windmill Hill WD4 156 F7
Little Wood HP14 158 E5
Little Woodlands SL4 209 F4
Littleworth LU7 79 E3
LITTLEWORTH COMMON 186 D1
Littleworth Rd
Hedgerley SL1 186 C1
High Wycombe HP13 161 E2
Litton Ct HP10 174 C2
Liverpool Rd SL1 205 B7
Liverpool Victoria Ho 3 HP13 173 B7
Livesey Hill MK5 46 B5
Living Furniture Making Mus★ HP11 172 F7
Livingstone Dr MK15 35 C5
Llanbury Cl SL9 177 E3
Lloyds MK6 47 A7
Loakes Ho HP11 173 A6
Loakes Rd HP11 173 A6
Lochinvar Cl SL1 205 B4
Lochnell Rd HP4 134 F6
Lochy Dr LU7 80 C7
Lock Ave SL6 196 C2
Lockbridge Ct SL6 203 C8
Lock Bridge Rd SL8 185 A3
Locke Cl HP19 101 A2
Locke Gdns SL3 206 C4
Locke Rd MK2 58 C8
Lockets Cl SL4 209 D6
Lockhart Ave MK4 45 D2
Lock La
Cosgrove MK19 19 E2
Maidenhead SL6 202 C4
Lock Mead SL6 196 C2
Lock Path SL4 209 D8
Lock Rd SL7 183 F1
Locksley Ct 4 SL1 205 E3
Lockton Ct MK4 46 B3
Lockview Cotts MK1 47 E1
Lock View La MK1 47 E1
Lockwood Chase MK4 45 D2
Lodden Cl HP21 115 D3
Loddon Dr SL6 202 D8
Loddon Rd SL8 185 A4
Loddon Spur SL1 205 E7
Lodge Cl
Cheddington LU7 105 A7
Marlow SL7 183 E1
Padbury MK18 53 C2
Slough SL1 205 C4
Uxbridge UB8 201 C1
Lodge Farm Bsns Ctr MK19 20 C3
Lodge Farm Cl HP22 116 E2
Lodge Farm Ct MK19 19 F6
Lodge Gate MK14 34 E7
Lodge La
Little Chalfont HP8 166 F6
Prestwood HP16 151 D5
Stoke Hammond MK17 69 E7
Lodge Park The MK16 22 C4
Lodge Rd MK43 37 F8
Lodge The
Aylesbury HP19 115 A7
Slough SL2 206 B8
Lodge Way SL4 209 E4
Lodgings of the Military Knights 4 SL4 210 D6
Lodore Gn UB10 190 E1
Logan Rock MK4 57 B8
Lollards Cl HP6 154 C2
Lombardy Dr HP4 135 D3
Lomond Dr
Leighton Buzzard LU7 80 C7
Milton Keynes MK2 58 D4
London End
Beaconsfield HP9 175 F1
Newton Longville MK17 57 D4
Woburn MK17 60 F6
London End La MK17 48 D1
London Ho MK11 32 D5
London Rd
Aston Clinton HP22 117 E4
Beaconsfield HP9 187 B8
Berkhamsted HP4 135 E3
Buckingham MK18 52 E6
Chalfont St Giles HP8 177 C7
Datchet SL3 211 C7
Felden HP3 146 F8
High Wycombe HP11 173 E5
Little Kingshill HP16 152 B5
Loughton MK5 46 B7
Milton Common OX9 136 B3
Milton Keynes MK16 36 B5
Milton Keynes, Stony Stratford MK11 32 E5
Newport Pagnell MK16 22 F3
Old Stratford MK19 32 C7
Slough, Brands Hill SL3 212 B8
Slough, Langley SL3 206 D2
Slough SL3 212 B8
Tring HP23 119 C3
Wendover HP22 141 D6
Wheatley OX33 122 B1
London Road E HP7 165 E6
London Road W HP7 165 C7
Londrina Ct 9 HP4 135 D4
Londrina Terr 10 HP4 135 D4
Long Ayres MK7 48 A3
Longborns MK43 25 C2
Longbottom La HP9 176 C3
Longbourn SL4 210 A4
Longbridge Cl HP23 119 A6
Longbridge Way UB8 201 B3
Long Cl SL2 198 B5
Long Close Sch SL3 206 A2
LONG CRENDON 125 B6
Long Crendon Courthouse★ HP18 125 D7
Long Crendon Ind Est HP18 125 E5
Long Crendon Rd HP18 124 D3
Long Crendon Sch HP18 125 C7
Longcroft HP22 117 F5
Longcroft Ave HP22 131 D6
Longcroft La
Bovingdon HP3 146 D5
Paulerspury NN12 17 C8
Long Croft Rd WD3 178 D5
Longcross MK15 35 A6
Longdown Hill HP27 139 F5
Longdown Mews HP19 114 F8
Long Dr SL1 197 C2
Longfellow Dr MK16 22 A4
Longfield
Hedgerley SL2 187 D1
Little Kingshill HP16 152 B4
Longfield Dr HP6 154 B1
Longfield Gdns HP23 118 E3
Longfield Rd
Chesham HP5 143 F2
Tring HP23 118 F3
LONGFORD 213 C6
LONGFORDMOOR 213 A6
Longford Rdbt UB7 213 B6
Long Furlong
Haddenham HP17 126 F6
Stone HP17 114 B5
Long Furlong Dr SL2 197 E1
Long Gr HP9 176 C4
Long Grove Wood Wildlife Reserve★ HP9 176 C4
Long Hale LU7 105 C3
Longhedge MK7 48 A2
Long Hedge LU7 105 C4
Long Hide HP27 139 C4
Long La
Bovingdon HP3 155 F8
Cookham Rise SL6 195 D5
Heronsgate WD3 167 D2
Olney MK46 6 F4
Rickmansworth WD3 167 F1
Stanwell TW19 213 F1
Longlands Ct MK18 66 A5
Longlands Wlk MK18 66 A5
Longland Way HP12 172 D5
Longleat Ct 7 MK8 33 F1
Longleat Gdns SL6 202 D6
Longlees WD3 178 D5
Long Ley LU7 105 A7
Long Leys HP19 115 A8
Long Lional HP20 115 D8
LONG MARSTON 104 B3
Long Marston Prim Sch HP23 104 B4
Long Marston Rd
Cheddington LU7 104 E7
Marsworth LU7 104 F2
Long Massey MK46 6 E5
Long Mdw
Aylesbury HP21 116 B6
Chesham HP5 144 C3
Longmead SL4 209 E6
Longmead La SL1 197 D5
Long Meadow Cl
Amersham HP7 164 C3
Monks Risborough HP27 139 C5
Long Meadow Sch MK5 45 F3
Longmead Prim Sch UB7 208 E2
Longmire MK46 7 F8
Longmore Cl WD3 178 F6
Long Orchard Dr HP10 174 C8
Long Park Cl HP6 154 C3
Long Park Way HP6 154 C3
Longpeak Cl MK4 46 B1
Long Pk HP6 154 C3
Long Plough HP22 117 D5
Long Readings La SL2 198 B2
Long Ride HP27 139 C3
Longridge (Activity Ctr)★ SL7 194 F8
Long Row
Leckhampstead MK18 30 E1
Prestwood HP16 151 D6
Longstone Rd SL0 200 C4
LONG STREET 10 F4
Longview HP9 185 F8
Long View HP4 135 A6
Longville MK12 33 B7
Long Walk The★ SL4 210 D4
Long Wall HP17 126 F5
LONGWICK 138 D7
Longwick CE Comb Sch HP27 138 D6
Longwick Rd
Longwick HP27 138 F6
Monks Risborough HP27 139 A5
Long Wlk HP8 166 E6
Longwood Ave SL3 207 B1
Long Wood Dr HP9 176 F4
Longwood La HP7 165 D8
Longworth Dr SL6 196 C1
Lonsdale Cl SL6 196 A1
Lonsdale Way SL6 203 C1
Look Ahead SL1 205 E4
Loosen Dr SL6 202 A3
Loose Path HP19 114 F8
Loosley Hill HP27 149 D6
LOOSLEY ROW 149 C6
Lord Grey Sch The MK3 46 F1
Lord Knyvett Cl TW19 213 D1
Lord Knyvetts Ct 12 TW19 213 E1
Lord Mayors Dr SL2 198 A7
Lord Raglan Ho SL4 210 C4
Lords Cl MK2 47 C1
Lordsmead MK43 25 C2
Lords Mead LU6 92 E6
Lords Mill Ct HP5 154 C7
Lords Terr LU6 92 E6
Loriner Pl MK14 35 A6
Loring Rd
Berkhamsted HP4 135 C3
Dunstable LU6 93 F8
Windsor SL4 209 F6
Lorne Cl SL1 205 C3
Lorraine Cl HP13 173 E8
Lorre Mews MK4 45 E3
Loseley Ct MK8 33 F1
Losfield Rd SL4 209 E6
Lossie Dr SL3 207 B6
Lothersdale MK13 34 B5
Lothian Cl MK3 46 E2
Lott Mdw HP21 115 D3
Lott Wlk HP21 115 D3
Louches La HP14 161 E6
Loudhams Rd HP7 166 C8
Loudhams Wood La HP8 166 D7
LOUDWATER 174 D2
Loudwater Comb Sch HP11 174 B2
Loughborough Dr MK10 36 C4
LOUGHTON 46 A8
Loughton Manor First Sch MK5 46 A8
Loughton Rd MK13 34 A3
Loughton Rdbt MK8 45 F8
Loughton Sch MK5 46 A7
Loughton Valley Pk★ MK5 46 D7
Louisa Cotts 10 HP23 119 A3
Louise Wlk HP3 146 A3
Lovat Meadow Cl MK16 22 E3
Lovat St MK16 22 D4
Lovatt Dr MK3 57 E8

LOWER GREEN 207 D8
Love Green La SL0 . . . . 207 E8
Lovegrove Dr SL2 . . . . . 197 F1
Love Hill La SL3 . . . . . . 207 A6
Lovejoy La SL4 . . . . 209 D5
Love La SL0 . . . . 207 D7
Lovelace Cl SL6 . . . . . . 193 F4
Lovel End SL9 . . . . 177 C3
Lovel Mead SL9 . . . . . . 177 C3
Lovel Rd SL9 . . . . 177 C2
Love Row MK17 . . . . 68 D6
Lovett Gdns SL6 . . . . . . 196 C3
Lovett Rd UB9 . . . . 190 C8
Lovetts End LU7 . . . . 78 E8
Lovibonds Ave UB7 . . . . 208 F7
Lowbrook Cl HP21 . . . . 116 A4
Lowbrook Dr SL6 . . . . . 202 A3
Lowbrook Prim Sch
SL6 . . . . 202 A3
Lowdell Cl UB7 . . . . . . 208 E7
Lowdon Cl HP11 . . . . . . 173 D4
LOWER ASCOTT 79 F1
LOWER ASSENDON 191 A6
LOWER BOIS 154 C5
Lower Boyndon Rd SL6 202 E6
Lower Britwell Rd SL2 . . 197 D1
LOWER CADSDEN 139 E5
Lower Church St
Cuddington HP18 . . . . . . 112 F3
Stokenchurch HP14 . . . . 158 E5
Lower Cippenham La
SL1 . . . . 204 F6
Lower Cl HP19 . . . . 115 B7
Lower Cookham Rd
SL6 . . . . 196 C3
Lower Dr HP9 . . . . 175 D5
Lower Eighth St MK9 . . . . 34 E2
LOWER END
Long Crendon 125 B7
Marsworth 104 F3
Thornborough 53 F8
Woburn Sands 49 C8
Lower End
Ashendon HP18 . . . . 97 E1
Lower End MK18 . . . . 53 F8
Newton Longville MK17 . . . 57 C3
Piddington OX25 . . . . 95 E8
Wingrave HP22 . . . . 89 B2
Lower End Rd MK17 . . . . 49 A8
Lower Farm Cl HP18 . . . 124 D3
Lower Farm Gate HP17 114 A3
Lower Fourth St MK9 . . . 34 D1
Lower Furney Cl HP13 . . 173 D8
Lower Gn
Cuddington HP18 . . . . . . 112 F3
Westcott HP18 . . . . 98 C7
Weston Turville HP22 . . . 117 A3
Lower Green La HP18 . . 112 C2
Lower Hammersley La
HP13 . . . . 174 B4
LOWER HARTWELL 114 E6
Lower Icknield Way
Chinnor OX39 . . . . 147 D8
Great Kimble HP17 . . . . 129 D1
Marsworth HP23 . . . . . . 105 B1
Monks Risborough HP17 139 B8
Pitch Green HP27 . . . . . 138 C3
Wilstone HP22, HP23 . . . 118 C7
Lower Kings Rd HP4 . . . 135 C5
Lower Lees Rd SL2 . . . . 198 B2
Lower Lodge La HP15 . . 163 A5
Lower Mead SL0 . . . . . . 200 D2
Lower Mount Farm
SL6 . . . . 195 D5
Lower Ninth St MK9 . . . . 34 E2
LOWER NORTH DEAN 150 E1
LOWER POLLICOTT 111 F7
Lower Pound La SL7 . . . 194 D8
Lower Rd
Aylesbury HP21, HP22 . . . 115 F3
Blackthorn OX25 . . . . 81 A4
Chinnor OX39 . . . . 147 C7
Chorleywood WD3 . . . . . 167 D5
Cookham Rise SL6 . . . . . 195 E7
Denham UB9 . . . . 189 D4
Gerrards Cross SL9 . . . . 188 F7
Hardwick HP22 . . . . 87 B3
Lacey Green HP27 . . . . . 149 D6
Lower Ridge SL8 . . . . . . 185 B4
Lower Riding HP9 . . . . . 175 B2
Lower Second St MK9 . . . 34 D1
Lower St
Pury End NN12 . . . . 17 A7
Quainton HP22 . . . . 85 A5
Lower Stonehayes MK14 34 F7
Lower Tenth St MK9 . . . . 34 F2
Lower Third St MK9 . . . . . 34 D1
Lower Twelfth St MK9 . . . 34 F3
Lower Ventnor Cotts
SL6 . . . . 195 C8
LOWER WAINHILL 147 E7
Lower Ward SL4 . . . . . . 210 D7
Lower Way
Great Brickhill MK17 . . . . 59 C1
Padbury MK18 . . . . 53 C2
LOWER WEALD 32 E2
Lower Weald MK19 . . . . . 32 E2
Lower Wharf MK18 . . . . . 41 E1
LOWER WOODEND 182 D4
Lowes Cl HP14 . . . . 158 C5
Lowestoft Dr SL1 . . . . . 204 D7
Lowfield Cl HP15 . . . . . 163 B3
Lowfield Way HP15 . . . . 163 B3
Lowick Pl 4 MK4 . . . . . . 46 B2
Lowland Rd MK3 . . . . 57 C8
Lowlands Cres HP15 . . . 151 D1
Lowlands Dr TW19 . . . . 213 D2
Lowlands Rd TW19 . . . . 213 D2
Lowman Way HP21 . . . . 115 D4
Lowndes Ave HP5 . . . . . 144 B1
Lowndes Gr MK5 . . . . 45 F7
Lowndes Way MK18 . . . . . 66 A5
Lownes Path HP19 . . . . . 114 F8
Loxbeare Dr MK4 . . . . . . 46 C4
Loxboro Hill HP14 . . . . . 160 D4
Loxley Rd HP4 . . . . 134 F6
Loxwood Cl HP3 . . . . . . 146 F8
Loyne Cl LU7 . . . . 80 C8
Lucas Pl MK6 . . . . 47 D8
Lucas Rd HP13 . . . . 173 C7
Luccombe MK4 . . . . 46 D3
Lucky La or Cock La
HP20 . . . . 101 D1
Lucy La MK5 . . . . 46 B8
Ludgate
Milton Keynes MK6 . . . . . 46 E7
Tring HP23 . . . . 118 F4
LUDGERSHALL 96 D8
Ludlow Cl MK3 . . . . 57 F7
Ludlow Dr OX9 . . . . 126 A1
Ludlow Ho SL6 . . . . 202 E6
Ludlow Mews HP11 . . . . 174 A4
Ludlow Pl HP20 . . . . 116 B8
Ludlow Rd SL6 . . . . 202 E6
Luff Cl SL4 . . . . 209 E4
Lufford Pk MK14 . . . . 34 F8
Luggershall Rd OX25 . . . . 95 E7
Luke Pl MK10 . . . . 35 F3
Luker Ave RG9 . . . . 191 D3
Lukes La HP23 . . . . 104 D3
Lukes Lea HP23 . . . . . . 105 A1
Lullingstone Dr MK13 . . . 33 F5
Lumber La NN12 . . . . 17 B7
Lundholme MK13 . . . . 34 B5
Lundy Ct SL1 . . . . 204 E6
Lupin Cl UB7 . . . . 208 D1
Lupin Ct HP21 . . . . 115 B5
Lupin Wlk HP21 . . . . . . 115 B5
Lutman La SL6 . . . . 195 F2
Lutyens Gr MK7 . . . . 48 D5
Luxborough Gr MK4 . . . . . 46 C4
Lychgate Cotts HP3 . . . . 146 B4
Lycrome La HP5 . . . . . . 144 D3
Lycrome Rd HP5 . . . . . . 144 E3
Lydbrook La MK17 . . . . . . 49 B5
Lyde End HP27 . . . . 138 B1
Lydford Ave SL2 . . . . . . 205 D8
Lydiard MK8 . . . . 33 E1
Lydiard Cl HP21 . . . . . . 116 A4
Lydsey Cl SL2 . . . . 198 A2
LYE GREEN 144 F4
Lye Green Cotts HP5 . . . 144 E3
Lye Green Rd HP5 . . . . . 144 E2
Lyell Place E SL4 . . . . . 209 C4
Lyell Place W SL4 . . . . . 209 C4
Lyell Rd SL4 . . . . 209 C4
Lyell Walk E SL4 . . . . . . 209 C4
Lyell Walk W SL4 . . . . . 209 C4
Lye The HP4 . . . . 121 D6
Lyme Ave HP4 . . . . 134 D7
Lynch Cl UB8 . . . . 201 C5
Lynch Hill La SL2 . . . . . 197 E2
Lynch Hill Sch SL2 . . . . 197 F2
Lynch The UB8 . . . . 201 C5
Lyndhurst Ave SL6 . . . . . 195 E6
Lyndhurst Cl HP13 . . . . 161 D1
Lyndhurst Rd HP5 . . . . . 144 B2
Lyndon Cl HP16 . . . . . . 151 C7
Lyndon Gdns HP13 . . . . 173 E8
Lyndwood Dr SL4 . . . . . 211 A1
Lyndwood Par SL4 . . . . . 211 A2
Lyneham Gdns SL6 . . . . 195 B1
Lynher Cl HP21 . . . . 115 C4
Lynmouth Cres MK4 . . . . . 46 D4
Lynott Cl MK8 . . . . 45 E6
Lynton Gn SL6 . . . . 202 E7
Lynton Rd HP5 . . . . 144 C3
Lynwood Ave SL3 . . . . . 206 D3
Lynwood Rd HP21 . . . . . 116 A5
Lyon Rd MK1 . . . . 47 B2
Lysander Cl HP3 . . . . . . 146 A4
Lysander Mead SL6 . . . . 203 C8

M

McArdle Way SL3 . . . . . 212 D7
McAuliffe Dr SL1, SL2 . . 197 F8
McConnell Dr MK12 . . . . . 33 E6
McCorquodale Rd
MK12 . . . . 33 C7
MacDonald Cl HP6 . . . . . 154 D4
McDougall Rd 8 HP4 . . . 135 D4
McEwen Ride HP22 . . . . 117 D1
MacIntyre Wingrave Sch
HP22 . . . . 89 C3
McKay Trad Est SL3 . . . . 212 E5
McKenzie Cl MK18 . . . . . . 52 D8
Mackenzie Mall 3 SL1 . . 205 F4
Mackenzie St 2 SL1 . . . 205 F4
McLellan Pl HP12 . . . . . 172 D5
McLernon Way MK18 . . . . 66 A5
Maconi Croft MK5 . . . . . . 46 C5
Madeira Wlk SL4 . . . . . . 210 D6
Madeley Cl HP6 . . . . 154 D3
Madeley Rd HP21 . . . . . 115 E6
Magdalen Cl
Milton Keynes MK11 . . . . . 32 D6
Syresham NN13 . . . . 27 C8
Magdalen Ho MK11 . . . . . 32 D6
Magenta Cl MK2 . . . . 58 D6
Magnet L Ctr SL6 . . . . . 203 A8
Magnolia Dene HP15 . . . 162 F2
Magnolia Gdns SL3 . . . . 206 C3
Magnolia St UB7 . . . . . . 208 D2
Magnolia Way HP10 . . . . 185 E7
Magpie Cl
Flackwell Heath HP10 . . . 174 A1
Milton Keynes MK5 . . . . . 46 B3
Magpie La
Coleshill HP7 . . . . 165 A1
Flackwell Heath HP10 . . . 174 A1
Loudwater HP13 . . . . . . 174 B3
Magpie Way
Slough SL2 . . . . 197 F1
Winslow MK18 . . . . 66 B6
Mahler Cl MK7 . . . . 48 C5
Mahoney Ct
High Wycombe HP11 . . . . 172 F8
Milton Keynes MK8 . . . . . 45 D6
Maida Vale 3 MK10 . . . . . 35 F1
MAIDENHEAD 202 F4
Maidenhead Ave MK13 . . . 34 C3
MAIDENHEAD COURT . . . 196 C4
Maidenhead Court Pk
SL6 . . . . 196 B3
Maidenhead Heritage Ctr*
13 SL6 . . . . 202 F7
Maidenhead Rd
Cookham Rise SL6 . . . . . 195 F6
Windsor SL4 . . . . 209 E7
Maidenhead Ret Pk
SL6 . . . . 203 A6
Maidenhead Sta SL6 . . . 202 F6
MAIDENSGROVE 179 C5
MAIDS MORETON 41 E4
Maids Moreton CE Sch
MK18 . . . . 41 E3
Maidstone Rd MK10 . . . . . 36 C2
Maigno Way 1 MK12 . . . . 33 A6
Main Dr
Gerrards Cross SL9 . . . . 188 C6
Iver SL0 . . . . 207 E3
Potterspury NN12 . . . . . . 18 B2
Main Par WD3 . . . . 167 C5
Main Rd
Astwood MK16 . . . . 16 B3
Drayton Parslow MK17 . . . 68 B5
Lacey Green HP27 . . . . . 149 E5
Syresham NN13 . . . . 27 C7
Upper Winchendon HP18 . . 99 A1
Walter's Ash HP14 . . . . . 161 C7
Main Road N HP4 . . . . . 107 A6
Main Road S HP4 . . . . . 107 D4
Main St
Adstock MK18 . . . . 53 F1
Akeley MK18 . . . . 41 F8
Ashendon HP18 . . . . 97 F1
Beachampton MK19 . . . . . 44 A6
Buckingham MK18 . . . . . . 41 F3
Chackmore MK18 . . . . 41 B4
Charndon OX27 . . . . 72 E5
Cosgrove MK19 . . . . 19 E2
Gawcott MK18 . . . . 51 F4
Grendon Underwood HP18 83 B5
Mursley MK17 . . . . 67 D6
Padbury MK18 . . . . 53 B1
Poundon OX27 . . . . 71 F7
Preston Bissett MK18 . . . . 62 B8
Shalstone MK18 . . . . 39 E6
Tingewick MK18 . . . . 51 B6
Turweston NN13 . . . . 38 C8
Twyford MK18 . . . . 62 C1
Westbury NN13 . . . . 39 A4
Weston Turville HP22 . . . 116 E2
Maitland Dr HP13 . . . . . 173 B8
Maitland Rd HP22 . . . . . 131 D7
Major's Farm Rd
Datchet SL3 . . . . 211 E8
Slough SL3 . . . . 212 A8
Malbons Ct MK6 . . . . 46 E7
Malborough Ho HP4 . . . . 135 A3
Malborough Way NN12 . . . 18 F5
Malcolm Rd UB10 . . . . . . 201 F8
Malden Cl HP6 . . . . 154 F1
Malders La SL6 . . . . 195 C3
Malet Cl HP14 . . . . 158 F5
Malins Gate MK14 . . . . . . 34 E8
Malkin Dr HP9 . . . . 175 C3
Mallard Cl HP19 . . . . . . 101 E4
Mallard Croft HP17 . . . . 127 A7
Mallard Dr
Buckingham MK18 . . . . . . 52 E8
Slough SL1 . . . . 204 F6
Mallard Ho HP11 . . . . . . 173 C6
Mallard Pl HP11 . . . . 174 B3
Mallets End HP22 . . . . . . 85 B4
Malletts Cl MK11 . . . . 32 E5
Mallow Gate MK14 . . . . . . 34 E4
Mallow Pk SL6 . . . . 195 C1
Malmers Well Rd HP13 173 B7
Malpas Rd SL2 . . . . 206 B6
Malthouse Flats RG9 . . . 192 D6
Malthouse Sq
Beaconsfield HP9 . . . . . . 186 F8
Princes Risborough
HP27 . . . . 139 B4
Malthouse Way 2 SL7 . . 183 D1
Malting Cl MK16 . . . . 12 B6
Malting La
Aldbury HP23 . . . . 120 D5
Dagnall HP4 . . . . 107 C5
Maltings Cl
Cranfield MK43 . . . . 25 A1
Stewkley LU7 . . . . 78 E8
Maltings Field MK19 . . . . 19 F5
Maltings The
Chackmore MK18 . . . . 41 B4
Olney MK46 . . . . 7 A3
Tingewick MK18 . . . . 51 B6
Malt La NN13 . . . . 27 C8
Maltmans Green Sch
SL9 . . . . 188 C8
Maltmans La SL9 . . . . . . 188 C8
Malton Ave SL1 . . . . 205 B6
Malton Cl MK10 . . . . 35 F1
Malvern Cl HP13 . . . . . . 172 E8
Malvern Ct SL3 . . . . 212 A7
Malvern Dr
Leighton Buzzard LU7 . . . . 80 C8
Milton Keynes MK11 . . . . . 33 A4
Malvern Rd
Aylesbury HP20 . . . . 116 C8
Maidenhead SL6 . . . . . . 195 D1
Malyns Cl OX39 . . . . 147 C7
Manchester Terr HP14 . 171 B4
Mandela Ct UB8 . . . . 208 C7
Mandelyns HP4 . . . . 134 E7
Mandeville Dr MK10 . . . . . 36 C2
Mandeville Mews HP21 115 E4
Mandeville Rd
Aylesbury HP21 . . . . 115 E5
Prestwood HP16 . . . . 151 B7
Mandeville Sch The
HP21 . . . . 115 D4
Manfield Cl SL2 . . . . 198 A2
Manifold La MK4, MK5 . . . 46 B3
Manor Cl
Berkhamsted HP4 . . . . . . 135 C4
Bledlow HP27 . . . . 138 B1
Buckingham MK18 . . . . . . 53 C2
Cosgrove MK19 . . . . 19 E2
Hanslope MK19 . . . . 11 A2
Milton Keynes MK10 . . . . . 35 F3
Milton Keynes MK17 . . . . . 67 D6
Prestwood HP16 . . . . 151 D4
Salford MK17 . . . . 37 D3
Stoke Hammond MK17 . . . 69 E7
Tylers Green HP10 . . . . . 163 A2
Manor Cotts
Chorleywood WD3 . . . . . . 167 B3
Milton Keynes MK12 . . . . . 33 B7
Manor Court Yd HP13 . . . 162 A1
Manor Court Yd OX33 . . . 123 B2
Manor Cres
Seer Green HP9 . . . . 176 D5
Wendover HP22 . . . . 131 C5
Manor Ct
Emberton MK46 . . . . 13 F8
Leighton Buzzard LU7 . . . . 70 E2
Marlow SL7 . . . . 183 C3
Slough, Cippenham SL1 . . 204 F5
6 Slough, Upton Park
SL1 . . . . 205 F3
Twyford MK18 . . . . 62 C1
Manor Ctyd
Haddenham HP17 . . . . . . 127 D4
Sherington MK16 . . . . 13 F1
Manor Dr
Amersham HP6 . . . . 154 B3
Aylesbury HP20 . . . . 101 F2
Haversham MK19 . . . . 20 E2
Stewkley LU7 . . . . 78 E8
Manor Farm SL3 . . . . 212 E5
Manor Farm Cl
Soulbury LU7 . . . . 69 E2
Stone HP17 . . . . 114 C5
Weston Turville HP22 . . . 116 E2
Windsor SL4 . . . . 209 F4
Manor Farm Cotts SL4 . 211 A2
Manor Farm Ct HP22 . . . . 87 B2
Manor Farm Ctyd
HP22 . . . . 102 D8
Manor Farm Ho SL4 . . . . 209 F4
Manor Farm Inf Sch
HP15 . . . . 163 B2
Manor Farm Jun Sch
HP15 . . . . 163 B2
Manor Farm La LU7 . . . . . 90 C8
Manor Farm Way HP9 . . 176 D4
Manorfields Rd MK19 . . . 32 B6
Manor Gdns
Grendon Underwood
HP18 . . . . 83 A6
High Wycombe HP13 . . . . 162 A1
Manor Gdns *continued*
Maids Moreton MK18 . . . . 41 E2
Wooburn Green HP10 . . . 185 E5
Manor Ho
Brill HP18 . . . . 110 A8
Hambleden RG9 . . . . 181 D2
Manor House Cl HP20 . . 101 F1
Manor House Hospl
HP20 . . . . 101 F1
Manor House La SL3 . . . 211 B6
Manor La
Gerrards Cross SL9 . . . . 188 D4
Maidenhead SL6 . . . . . . 202 E4
MANOR PARK
Aylesbury 101 E2
Slough 198 D1
Manor Park Ave HP27 . . 139 A3
Manor Pk MK18 . . . . 41 F4
Manor Pound Rd LU7 . . 105 A7
Manor Rd
Akeley MK18 . . . . 41 F7
Aylesbury HP20 . . . . 101 E1
Cheddington LU7 . . . . . . 104 F7
Chesham HP5 . . . . 144 C2
Emmington OX9 . . . . 137 B6
Maidenhead SL6 . . . . . . 202 E4
Milton Keynes, Bletchley
MK2 . . . . 58 E8
Milton Keynes, Wolverton
MK12 . . . . 33 B7
Newport Pagnell MK16 . . . 22 A4
Newton Longville MK17 . . . 57 D3
Oakley HP18 . . . . 109 D5
Oving HP22 . . . . 86 C7
Princes Risborough
HP27 . . . . 139 A2
Rowsham HP22 . . . . 102 D8
Seer Green HP9 . . . . 176 D5
Tring HP23 . . . . 119 A5
Tylers Green HP10 . . . . . 163 A2
Wendover HP22 . . . . 131 C5
Windsor SL4 . . . . 209 E5
Manor St
Berkhamsted HP4 . . . . . . 135 D4
Buckingham MK18 . . . . . . 52 C8
Manor View HP15 . . . . . 163 B2
Manor View Ho HP13 . . . 161 E2
Manor Way
Chesham HP5 . . . . 144 D1
Coleshill HP7 . . . . 164 F3
Yardley Gobion NN12 . . . . 18 E6
Manor Waye UB8 . . . . . . 201 D4
Mansard Cl 8 HP23 . . . 119 A3
Manse Cl MK11 . . . . 32 D6
Mansel Cl
Cosgrove MK19 . . . . 19 E2
Slough SL2 . . . . 206 B8
Mansell Cl
Milton Keynes MK5 . . . . . 46 A6
Windsor SL4 . . . . 209 E6
Manshead Ct MK11 . . . . . 32 F5
Mansion Dr HP23 . . . . . 119 B3
Mansion Hill HP22 . . . . . 131 E8
Mansion La
Harrold MK43 . . . . 3 F6
Iver SL0 . . . . 207 C6
Mansion The HP4 . . . . . 135 E6
MANTLES GN 165 A8
Manton Rd LU6 . . . . 93 D5
Maple Ave UB7 . . . . 208 F5
Maple Cl
Hazelmere HP15 . . . . . . 163 A3
High Wycombe HP12 . . . 172 C5
Maidenhead SL6 . . . . . . 202 C5
Maple Cres SL2 . . . . 206 B6
MAPLE CROSS 178 D6
Maple Cross JMI Sch
WD3 . . . . 178 E5
Maple Ct
Gerrards Cross SL9 . . . . 188 F6
Marlow SL7 . . . . 183 E3
Windsor SL4 . . . . 210 C4
Mapledean MK12 . . . . 33 E4
Mapledurham MK7 . . . . . . 48 B3
Mapledurham Wlk SL6 . 195 E3
Maple End HP22 . . . . . . 116 C4
Maplefield La HP8 . . . . 166 B6
Maple Gr
Milton Keynes MK2 . . . . . 58 E8
Woburn Sands MK17 . . . . 49 B4
Maple Leys MK18 . . . . 63 E3
Maple Lodge Cl WD3 . . . 178 E6
Maple Pl UB7 . . . . 208 F5
Maple Rise SL7 . . . . 183 E3
Maples The
5 Bourne End SL8 . . . . 185 B3
Wendover HP22 . . . . 131 C5
Maplewood Gdns HP9 . . 175 B1
Maplewood Sch HP13 . . 161 D3
Maplin Pk SL3 . . . . 207 B4
Mapperton Cl 3 MK4 . . . 45 F1
Mapridge Green La
HP16 . . . . 141 D1
Marand Ct HP21 . . . . . . 115 F8
Mara Pl MK9 . . . . 35 A3
Marbeck Cl SL4 . . . . 209 D6

Marchant Ct SL7 . . . . .184 A3
March Edge MK18. . . . . .41 E1
Marches The SL4 . . . . . .205 D2
March Mdw MK7. . . . . . . .48 D7
March Pl HP19. . . . . .115 B8
Marcia Ct SL1 . . . . .204 F5
Marcourt Rd HP14 . . . . .158 F3
Mardle Rd LU7. . . . . .80 E6
Maree Cl
  Leighton Buzzard LU7 . . . .80 C7
  Milton Keynes MK2 . . . . . .58 C5
Marefield Rd SL7. . . . . . .183 D2
Mare Leys MK18 . . . . . . .52 F8
Marescroft Rd SL2 . . . . .197 E1
Margam Cres MK10 . . . . . .36 A1
Margaret Ct HP13 . . . . . .173 E5
Margaret Powell Sq
  MK9 . . . . .34 F3
Margaret Smythe Ho
  SL9 . . . . .188 F5
Marie Cl OX27 . . . . .71 F7
Marigold Pl MK14. . . . . . .34 E4
Marigold Wlk HP15 . . . . .162 F6
Marina Dr
  Dunstable LU6 . . . . .93 E7
  Milton Keynes MK12 . . . . .33 D6
Marina Rdbt MK6. . . . . . .47 C7
Marina Way
  Iver SL0. . . . . .208 A6
  Slough SL1. . . . . .204 D6
Marine Ct SL6. . . . . .46 F6
Marish Ct SL3. . . . . .207 A3
Marish La UB9 . . . . .189 D7
Marish Prim Sch SL3. . . .207 A3
Marish Wharf Ind Est
  SL3 . . . . .206 E4
Marjoram Pl MK14. . . . . .34 E4
Mark Dr SL9 . . . . .177 E6
Markenfield Pl MK4. . . . . .45 E1
Market Hill
  Buckingham MK18. . . . . . .41 D1
  Milton Keynes MK6 . . . . . .47 B8
  Whitchurch HP22. . . . . . . .86 F6
Market Ho 5 SL9 . . . . . .177 D2
Market La SL3 . . . . .207 C3
Market Par HP15. . . . . . .163 A4
Market Pl
  Chalfont St Peter SL9 . . . .177 D2
  Colnbrook SL3 . . . . .212 C7
  Henley-on-Thames RG9 . .191 D2
  4 Olney MK46 . . . . .6 F3
  Woburn MK17 . . . . .60 F7
Market Place Mews 5
  RG9 . . . . .191 D2
Market Sq
  Amersham HP7 . . . . .165 B7
  Aylesbury HP20 . . . . .115 D8
  5 Buckingham MK18. . . . .41 D1
  Chesham HP5 . . . . .154 B8
  Hanslope MK19 . . . . .11 A2
  Marlow SL7 . . . . .183 D2
  Milton Keynes MK11 . . . . .32 D5
  Princes Risborough
    HP27 . . . . .139 B3
  Uxbridge UB8 . . . . .201 C5
  Winslow MK18. . . . . .65 F4
Market St
  19 Aylesbury HP20 . . . . . .115 D8
  Maidenhead SL6 . . . . . . .202 F6
  9 Windsor SL4 . . . . .210 D6
Markham Cl HP15 . . . . . .115 A7
Markhams Cl MK18. . . . . .52 D8
Marks Orch HP7 . . . . .75 F7
Marlborough Cl SL6. . . . .202 A6
Marlborough Ct SL1 . . . .204 E7
Marlborough Gate MK9 . .34 F3
Marlborough Ho 5
  SL6. . . . . .202 F6
Marlborough Rd
  Aylesbury HP21 . . . . .115 E4
  Maidenhead SL6 . . . . . . .202 A6
  Slough SL3 . . . . .206 A3
Marlborough St
  Milton Keynes, Neath Hill
    MK14. . . . . .34 E6
  Milton Keynes, Tinkers Bridge
    MK6. . . . . .47 B6
Marlborough Trad Est
  HP11. . . . . .172 F7
Marley Gr MK8. . . . . .45 E7
Marlin Cl HP4. . . . . .134 F5
Marlin Copse HP4. . . . . .135 A3
Marlin Ct SL7. . . . . .183 D1
Marlin Hill HP23 . . . . . . .133 A8
Marlins Cl WD3 . . . . .167 E7
Marlins End HP4. . . . . . .134 F3
MARLOW 183 B2
MARLOW BOTTOM 183 C6
Marlow Bottom SL7. . . . .183 D6
Marlow Bridge La SL7. . .194 E8
Marlow CE Inf Sch SL7 183 D3
Marlow Comm SL7. . . . .182 F3
MARLOW COMMON 182 F3
Marlow Cottage Hospl
  SL7 . . . . .183 E2
Marlow Dr MK16. . . . . . .22 A4

Marlow Hill HP11 . . . . . .173 A5
Marlow Ho 1 SL7. . . . . .183 E1
Marlow Language Ctr The
  SL7 . . . . .183 D2
Marlow Lodge 13 SL6 . .202 F6
Marlow Mill SL7 . . . . . . .183 E1
Marlow Rd
  Bisham SL7 . . . . .194 E7
  Henley-on-Thames RG9 . .191 E3
  High Wycombe HP11. . . . .172 E4
  Lane End HP14, SL7. . . . .171 E2
  Little Marlow SL7. . . . . . .184 C5
  Maidenhead, Furze Platt
    SL6 . . . . .194 E4
  Maidenhead SL6 . . . . . . .202 F7
  Stokenchurch HP14 . . . . .170 B6
Marlow Sta SL7 . . . . . . .183 F2
Marquis Ct MK17. . . . . . .60 F7
Marram Ct MK6. . . . . . . .47 A5
Marriotts Ave HP16 . . . .142 E1
Marriott's Cl HP17 . . . . .126 F6
Marriott's La HP17 . . . . .126 F6
Marriott's Way HP17 . . .126 F6
Marriott Terr WD3 . . . . .167 F5
Marrod's Bottom HP7. . .175 D8
Marron La MK12 . . . . . . .33 C5
Marroway HP22. . . . . . . .116 D2
MARSH. 129 C7
Marshall Court Ind Pk
  MK1 . . . . .47 B1
Marshalls La MK15 . . . . .35 C2
Marshalls Lea HP22 . . . .102 C3
Marsham Ct HP21 . . . . .116 A4
Marsham La SL9 . . . . . . .188 F6
Marsham Lodge SL9 . . . .188 E5
Marsham Way SL9 . . . . .188 F5
Marshaw Pl 3 MK4 . . . . .46 C2
Marshcroft La HP23. . . . .119 D6
Marsh Ct HP11. . . . . . . .173 F4
Marsh Dr MK14. . . . . . . .21 E1
Marsh End Rd MK16. . . . .22 D3
Marshfield SL3 . . . . .211 C6
Marshgate Trad Est
  SL6. . . . . .204 A7
MARSH GIBBON 71 F3
Marsh Gibbon CE Sch
  OX27. . . . . .71 F3
Marsh Gibbon Rd HP18. .82 E8
Marsh Inf Sch HP11. . . .173 F4
Marsh La
  Stoke Mandeville HP22 . .129 F8
  Taplow SL6. . . . . .203 E6
Marshment Cl HP22 . . . .117 D5
Marsh Rd
  Great Kimble HP22 . . . . .129 D4
  Shabbington HP18. . . . . .124 D3
Marshworth MK6 . . . . . . .47 D6
Marston Cl HP5 . . . . . . .144 A4
Marston Ct HP23. . . . . . .104 B4
Marstonfields Rd MK18. .76 B2
Marston Hill
  Cranfield MK43 . . . . .25 F2
  Oving HP22 . . . . .86 C8
Marston Rd
  Granborough MK18 . . . . .75 F6
  Thame OX9 . . . . .126 A1
MARSWORTH 105 A1
Marsworth CE Inf Sch
  HP23. . . . . .105 A2
Marsworth Rd LU7. . . . . .105 D4
Marsworth Reservoir★
  HP23. . . . . .119 A8
Martell Cl MK7. . . . . .48 A3
Martin Cl
  Buckingham MK18. . . . . . .52 F7
  Milton Keynes MK14 . . . . .34 E6
  Uxbridge UB10. . . . . .201 E3
  Windsor SL4 . . . . .209 D6
Martindale SL0 . . . . .200 D1
Martin Dell Cotts HP16 .142 E4
Martingale Pl MK14. . . . .34 F5
Martin Rd
  Maidenhead SL6 . . . . . . .202 F8
  Slough SL3 . . . . .205 E3
Martins Dr The LU7 . . . . .80 F8
Martinsend La HP16. . . .151 E7
Martin's Plain SL2 . . . . .198 F3
Martlet The MK6. . . . . . .47 C4
Martyrs Ct HP7 . . . . . . .165 C8
Marunden Gn SL2. . . . . .197 F2
Marwood Cl MK4 . . . . . . .46 D3
Mary Bassett Lower Sch
  The LU7. . . . . .80 F7
Mary Cross Cl HP23. . . .119 D1
Marygold Wlk HP6 . . . . .166 C3
Maryland Rd MK15 . . . . .35 B8
Mary MacManus Dr
  MK18. . . . . .41 D1
Mary Morgan Ct SL2. . . .205 D8
Maryot Cl MK16. . . . . . . .13 F7
Maryside SL3 . . . . .206 E4
Marys Mead HP15. . . . . .163 A5
Mary Towerton Fst Sch
  HP14. . . . . .159 D3
Mascoll Path SL2 . . . . . .197 F2
Masefield
  Chesham HP5 . . . . .144 B3
  Newport Pagnell MK16 . . .22 A4
Masefield Gr MK3. . . . . . .58 A7

Maslin Dr MK6. . . . . .47 B5
Mason MK14. . . . . .34 C8
Masons Cl HP16 . . . . . . .151 C5
Masons Ct HP5 . . . . .144 C1
Mason's Ct
  Aylesbury HP19 . . . . .115 B7
  Slough SL1. . . . . .204 E6
Masons Rd SL1 . . . . .204 E6
Masons Yd HP4. . . . . . . .135 D4
Massie Cl MK15. . . . . . . .35 B6
Mathecombe Rd 2
  SL1. . . . . .205 A4
Mathiesen Rd MK13. . . . .34 A6
Mathisen Way SL3 . . . . .212 E6
Matilda Gdns MK5 . . . . . .46 B5
Matlock Rd HP20 . . . . . .101 F2
Matson Dr RG9 . . . . .191 F2
Matthau La MK4 . . . . . . .45 D3
Matthew Ct MK5. . . . . . . .46 B6
Matthews Cl 12 HP20. . .101 F2
Maude Cl HP9 . . . . .176 A1
Maude Rd HP9. . . . . .176 A1
Maud Jane's Cl LU7. . . . .105 E5
Maudsley Cl MK5. . . . . . .46 C6
Maudsley Ho SL6 . . . . . .203 A7
Mauduit St HP16. . . . . . .11 A3
Maulden Gdns MK14 . . . .35 A8
Maurice Mount HP15. . . .162 F5
Mavoncliff Dr MK4. . . . . .57 A8
Maxham MK5. . . . . .46 A3
Maxwell Cl SL1 . . . . .197 C1
Maxwell Dr HP15 . . . . . .163 B5
Maxwell Pl HP9 . . . . . . .175 E3
Maxwell Rd
  Beaconsfield HP9. . . . . . .175 E3
  West Drayton SL0 . . . . . .208 F2
Maybach Ct MK5. . . . . . .46 B5
Maybrook Gdns HP13 . . .173 C8
Maybury Cl SL1 . . . . .204 D7
Maybush Gdns HP16 . . . .151 C6
Maybush Wlk MK46 . . . . .6 E5
May Cl LU6. . . . . .92 E6
Mayditch Pl MK13. . . . . . .34 C3
Mayer Gdns MK5. . . . . . .46 C5
Mayfield Dr SL4. . . . . . . .210 A4
Mayfield Rd HP10 . . . . . .185 E6
Mayflower Cl HP17 . . . . .114 F5
Mayflower Way
  Beaconsfield HP9. . . . . . .186 A8
  Farnham Common SL2. . .198 C8
Maygoods Cl UB8 . . . . . .208 D8
Maygoods Gn UB8 . . . . . .208 D8
Maygoods La UB8. . . . . . .208 D8
Maygoods View UB8 . . . .208 C8
Mayhall Farm HP6 . . . . .154 A4
Mayhall La HP6 . . . . .154 B4
Mayhew Cres HP13 . . . . .173 D8
Maylands Dr UB8 . . . . . .201 D6
Maynard Cl SL4. . . . . . . .34 A3
Maynard Ct SL4. . . . . . . .210 A6
Mayorfield Ho 1 SL7. . . .183 D2
Maypole Rd SL6 . . . . . . .204 A8
Maypool Way 1 MK10 . . .36 B2
May Rd MK43 . . . . .8 E6
Mays Way NN12. . . . . . . .18 D3
May Tree Cl SL7 . . . . . . .183 C6
Mead Acre HP27 . . . . . . .139 B5
Mead Cl
  Denham UB9 . . . . .190 A2
  7 Marlow SL7 . . . . .183 F3
  Monks Risborough HP27 .139 B6
  Slough SL3. . . . . .207 B4
  Uxbridge UB8 . . . . .190 A2
Meades La HP5 . . . . .154 B7
Meadfield Ave SL3 . . . . .207 A3
Meadfield Rd SL3 . . . . . .207 B3
Meadfurlong Sch MK6 . . .34 F1
Mead Haze SL6 . . . . . . .196 C2
Mead Ho SL0 . . . . .200 D8
MEADLE. 139 B8
Meadoway
  Steeple Claydon MK18. . . .63 E3
  Stone HP17 . . . . .114 F5
Meadow Bank 6 SL8 . . .185 B3
Meadowbank Cl
  Bovingdon HP3. . . . . . . .146 B3
  Long Crendon HP18. . . . .125 C7
Meadow Bank Cl HP14 . .154 E1
Meadowbrook HP23. . . . .119 B6
Meadowbrook Cl SL3 . . .212 F6
Meadow Cl
  Aylesbury HP20 . . . . .102 A1
  Chesham HP5 . . . . .144 A4
  Cublington LU7 . . . . .78 C1
  High Wycombe HP11. . . . .173 F4
  Marlow SL7 . . . . .183 F1
  Oakley HP18 . . . . .109 D4
  Old Windsor SL4 . . . . . . .211 B2
  Tring HP23. . . . . .119 A4
Meadowcott La HP7. . . . .164 F3
Meadow Cotts
  Beaconsfield HP9. . . . . . .175 E1
  Little Kingshill HP16 . . . .152 B3
  Stone HP17 . . . . .114 F5
Meadowcroft
  Aylesbury HP19 . . . . .101 B3
  Berkhamsted HP4 . . . . . .134 D7
  Chalfont St Peter SL9 . . .177 D1

Meadow Ct MK46 . . . . . . .5 D2
Meadow Dr
  Amersham HP6 . . . . .154 E2
  Longwick HP27 . . . . .138 D6
Meadow Farm Rd HP43 .16 F1
Meadow Gate
  Padbury MK18 . . . . .53 B2
  Prestwood HP16 . . . . . . .151 C3
Meadow Gdns HP8. . . . . .52 E6
Meadow High Sch UB8 208 E8
Meadow La
  Beaconsfield HP9 . . . . . .175 F2
  Eton SL4. . . . . .210 C7
  Long Crendon HP18. . . . .125 E4
  Milton Keynes MK10 . . . . .36 A3
  Pitstone LU7 . . . . .105 E3
  South Heath HP16 . . . . . .152 E8
Meadowlea Cl UB7. . . . . .213 D8
Meadow Pk HP22 . . . . . .116 C2
Meadow Rd
  Berkhamsted HP4 . . . . . .135 B6
  Chinnor OX39. . . . . .147 D6
  Henley-on-Thames RG9 . .191 E1
  Slough SL3. . . . . .206 E3
Meadow Rise HP27. . . . . .149 E5
Meadow Row MK18 . . . . .41 D1
Meadow Sh Ctr 4 MK18 41 D1
Meadowside HP9 . . . . . .176 F4
Meadows Sch The
  HP10. . . . . .185 E7
Meadows The
  1 Amersham HP7 . . . . . .154 E1
  Flackwell Heath HP10 . . .185 B8
  Old Stratford MK19. . . . . .32 B6
  Whitchurch HP22. . . . . . . .86 F7
Meadowsweet MK7 . . . . . .48 B5
Meadowview TW19 . . . . .212 F2
Meadow View
  Aspley Guise MK17 . . . . . .49 D6
  Chalfont St Giles HP8 . . .177 A7
  Long Crendon HP18. . . . .125 E4
  Marlow Bottom SL7. . . . .183 E6
  Pottersbury NN12 . . . . . .18 D3
  Stanwell TW19 . . . . .213 A2
  Uxbridge UB8. . . . . .208 C8
Meadow Way
  Aylesbury HP20 . . . . .102 A1
  Dorney SL6 . . . . .203 F4
  Felden HP3 . . . . .146 F7
  Hyde Heath HP6 . . . . . . .153 C4
  Old Windsor SL4 . . . . . . .211 B1
  1 Thame OX9 . . . . .125 F1
  Wing LU7 . . . . .79 E3
Meadow Wlk
  Bourne End SL8 . . . . . . .185 A5
  Buckingham MK18. . . . . . .41 D1
  Tylers Green HP10. . . . . .163 C1
Meads The
  Berkhamsted HP4 . . . . . .134 F6
  Eaton Bray LU6 . . . . .92 E5
  Stoke Poges SL2 . . . . . .199 A2
  Tring HP23. . . . . .119 B4
  Uxbridge UB8 . . . . .201 E1
  4 Windsor SL4 . . . . .210 A5
Mead The
  Beaconsfield HP9. . . . . . .175 E2
  Soulbury LU7 . . . . .69 E3
Meadway
  Berkhamsted HP4 . . . . . .135 E5
  Buckingham MK18. . . . . . .52 D6
  Dunstable LU6 . . . . .93 F7
  Oving HP22 . . . . .76 C1
Mead Way
  High Wycombe HP11 . . . .173 F4
  Slough SL1. . . . . .204 D8
Meadway Cl SL6. . . . . . . .93 F7
Meadway Pk SL9. . . . . . .188 D3
Meadway The MK5. . . . . .46 A7
Mead Wlk SL3 . . . . .207 B4
Meare Estate HP10. . . . .185 E8
Meavy Cl HP13. . . . . . . .174 B3
Medale Rd MK6. . . . . . . .47 B5
Medallion Pl SL6. . . . . . .203 B7
MEDBOURNE. 45 E6
Medbourne Rdbt MK8. . . .45 E6
Medeswell MK4. . . . . .46 E3
Medhurst MK8. . . . . .33 E2
Medland MK6. . . . . .47 D7
Medley Cl LU6 . . . . .92 F5
Medman Cl UB8 . . . . . . .201 C3
MEDMENHAM 193 A5
Medway Cl MK16. . . . . . .22 E3
Medway Oak La MK18 . . .66 B5
Meeting Oak La MK18 . . .66 B5
Megdale Pl HP20 . . . . . .101 D2
Melbourne Ave SL1 . . . . .205 C7
Melbourne Cl HP21 . . . . .115 E5
Melbourne Rd HP13. . . .173 F6
Melbourne Terr MK13. . . .34 A7
Melford Gn HP19 . . . . . .101 C3
Melfort Dr
  Leighton Buzzard LU7 . . . .80 B6
  Milton Keynes MK2 . . . . . .58 D4
Melick Rd MK6 . . . . .47 B4

Melissa Ct HP13 . . . . . . .173 D6
Mellish Ct MK3 . . . . .47 A2
Mellstock Rd HP21 . . . . .115 F5
Melrose Ave MK3 . . . . . . .47 A3
Melrose Ct HP13 . . . . . . .162 B1
Melrose Wlk HP21 . . . . . .115 F5
Melton MK14 . . . . .34 C8
Melton Ct
  Dunstable LU6 . . . . .93 F7
  Maidenhead SL6 . . . . . . .202 F6
Mendelssohn Gr MK7 . . . .48 C4
Mendip Cl SL3 . . . . .207 A1
Mendip Way HP13 . . . . . .172 F8
Mendy St HP11 . . . . .173 A7
Menmarsh Rd HP18 . . . .123 E6
Menteith Cl MK2. . . . . . . .58 C5
MENTMORE 90 D4
Mentmore Cl HP12 . . . . .172 B6
Mentmore Cross Rds
  LU7. . . . . .89 F6
Mentmore Ct
  Mentmore LU7. . . . . .90 D5
  2 Milton Keynes MK8. . . .45 F8
Mentmore Gdns LU7 . . . .80 E5
Mentmore Gn HP21 . . . . .115 E3
Mentmore Rd
  Cheddington LU7 . . . . . . .104 F8
  High Wycombe HP12 . . . .172 B6
  Leighton Buzzard LU7 . . . .80 E5
Mentmore Towers★
  LU7. . . . . .90 C4
Mentmore View HP23 . . .118 D3
Mentone Ave MK17 . . . . .49 D4
Menzies Ct MK5 . . . . . . .46 B4
Mercers Dr MK13 . . . . . . .34 B6
Mercers Mdw MK2 . . . . .131 B6
Mercer Wlk UB8. . . . . . . .201 C5
Merchant La
  Cranfield MK43 . . . . .25 A1
  Cranfield, Wharley End
    MK43. . . . . .24 F2
Merchant Pl MK10 . . . . . .35 E3
Mercian Way SL1 . . . . . . .204 D5
Mercia Rd SL6. . . . . .202 C4
Mercury Gr MK8 . . . . .45 E7
Mercury Pk The HP10 . . .187 C3
Merebrook Sch MK4 . . . . .46 C3
Mere Cl SL7 . . . . .183 F2
Meredith Dr HP19. . . . . .100 F2
Mere La MK18 . . . . .50 E6
Mere Pk SL7. . . . . .183 F2
Mere Rd
  Finmere MK18. . . . . .50 D6
  Slough SL1. . . . . .205 F3
Meriland Ct MK2. . . . . . . .58 E4
Merlebank HP5 . . . . .154 C7
Merlewood Cl HP11. . . . .173 A4
Merlewood Dr MK5 . . . . . .45 F4
Merlin Cl SL3 . . . . .212 B8
Merlin Ct SL6. . . . . .202 B8
Merlin Dr HP19 . . . . .101 C1
Merlin Ctr The HP12 . . . .172 E5
Merling Croft HP4 . . . . . .134 E7
Merlin Wlk MK6 . . . . .47 B8
Merman Rise MK4 . . . . . .45 D2
Merrivale Mews UB7. . . .208 D5
Merrydown HP13 . . . . . .161 D1
Merryfields UB8 . . . . . . .201 D3
Mersey Cl MK3. . . . . .46 E1
Mersey Way MK3 . . . . . . .46 E1
Merthen Gr MK4 . . . . . . .57 B8
Merton Cl SL6. . . . . .202 C3
Merton Ct SL1 . . . . .206 A3
Merton Dr MK6 . . . . .47 A4
Merton Rd
  Princes Risborough
    HP27 . . . . .139 B2
  Slough SL1. . . . . .206 A3
Merwin Way SL4 . . . . . . .209 D4
Meryton Ho SL4 . . . . . . .210 A4
Messenger Cl HP21 . . . . .116 A6
Metcalfe Gr MK14. . . . . . .22 B2
Mews Cotts HP15 . . . . . .162 D7
Mews Gamnel HP23 . . . .119 B6
Mews The HP6. . . . . .154 D3
Michael Cl SL6. . . . . .202 C5
Michaelis Rd OX9 . . . . . .125 E1
Michaels Mews 6
  HP19 . . . . .115 A8
Michigan Dr
  Milton Keynes MK15 . . . . .35 C8
  Newport Pagnell MK15 . . .22 C1
Micholls Ave SL9 . . . . . .177 E5
MICKLEFIELD. 173 E6
Micklefield Rd HP13 . . . .174 A7
Mickleton MK15 . . . . .35 A6
Midas Ind Est UB8 . . . . .201 B3
Midbrook Ct MK14 . . . . . .22 A2
Midcot Way HP4 . . . . . . .134 F6
Midcroft SL2 . . . . .198 B1
Mid Cross La SL9 . . . . . .177 F5
Middlebrook Rd HP13 . . .161 E4
Middle Cl HP6 . . . . .154 F2
MIDDLE CLAYDON 74 C8
Middle Cres UB9 . . . . . . .189 D4
Middle Dr HP9. . . . . .175 D5
MIDDLE END
  Leckhampstead 42 D8
  Totternhoe. 93 A8

Middle Field HP22 . . . . . 116 F3
Middlefield Cl MK18. . . . . 41 F1
Middle Gn SL3 . . . . 206 E6
MIDDLE GREEN 206 E5
Middlegreen Rd SL3 . . . 206 D5
Middlegreen Trad Est
SL3 . . . . 206 D4
Middle La HP3 . . . . 146 A1
Middle Mdw HP8 . . . . . . 177 C7
Middle Rd
Aylesbury HP21 . . . . 116 B7
Berkhamsted HP4 . . . . . . 135 B4
Denham UB9 . . . . 189 D4
Middlesex Dr MK3 . . . . . . 46 F1
Middle Slade MK18 . . . . . 52 D6
MIDDLETON 35 E3
Middleton MK14 . . . . 34 E7
Middleton Prim Sch
MK10 . . . . 35 E3
Middleton Swimming Pool
MK16 . . . . 22 E3
Middle Way OX39 . . . . . . 147 B6
Middleway The HP12 . . . 172 C6
MIDDLE WEALD 32 E1
Middle Weald MK19 . . . . . 32 E2
Middle Wlk SL1 . . . . 197 C2
Midhurst Cl HP21 . . . . . . 116 B5
Midland Dr MK10 . . . . 36 C3
Midland Rd MK46 . . . . 7 A5
Midshires Bsns Pk
HP19 . . . . 101 A1
Midsumer Ct HP15 . . . . . 163 A3
Midsummer Arc MK9 . . . . 34 E3
Midsummer Bvd MK9 . . . . 34 E2
Midsummer Dr HP18 . . . . 82 F6
Midsummer Pl (Sh Ctr)
MK9 . . . . 34 E2
Midsummer Rdbt MK9 . . 34 C1
Miersfield HP11 . . . . 172 D3
Mikern Cl MK2 . . . . 58 C8
Milburn Ave MK6 . . . . 46 E8
Milburn Dr UB7 . . . . 208 E6
Mildenhall Rd SL1 . . . . . 205 E7
Milebush LU7 . . . . 80 C8
Milecastle MK13 . . . . 34 A5
Mile Elm SL7 . . . . 184 A3
Miles Cl
Aylesbury HP21 . . . . 116 A7
Milton Keynes MK14 . . . . . 22 A3
Miles Ct HP22 . . . . 102 B3
Miles End HP21 . . . . 115 B6
Milesmere MK8 . . . . 33 D1
Milestone Cl HP14 . . . . . 158 E5
Milfoil Ave MK14 . . . . 34 E4
Milford Ave MK11 . . . . 32 E4
Milford Ct 4 SL1 . . . . . . 206 A4
Milk Hall Barns HP5 . . . . 154 F5
Milland Way MK4 . . . . 45 D3
Millards Cl MK43 . . . . 25 C2
Millards Pl MK43 . . . . 25 C2
Mill Ave UB8 . . . . 201 C3
Millbank
Leighton Buzzard LU7 . . . . 80 F8
Marlow SL7 . . . . 183 F1
Millbank Pl MK7 . . . . 48 B8
Millboard Rd SL8 . . . . . . 185 B3
Mill Bridge Pl UB8 . . . . . 201 C3
Millbrook Cl HP12 . . . . . 172 D8
Millbrook Comb Sch
HP12 . . . . 172 D8
Millbrook Way SL3 . . . . . 212 E5
Mill Cl
Buckingham MK18 . . . . 65 F5
Chesham HP5 . . . . 154 E5
West Drayton UB7 . . . . . . 208 D3
Wingrave HP22 . . . . 89 A3
Mill Cnr HP18 . . . . 83 A8
Mill Cotts HP10 . . . . 185 D4
Mill Ct
Horton SL3 . . . . 212 C3
Milton Keynes MK12 . . . . . 33 A5
Waddesdon HP18 . . . . 99 A7
West Drayton UB7 . . . . . . 208 D3
Milldun Way HP12 . . . . . 172 D6
MILL END
Henley-on-Thames 192 D7
Little Missenden 153 A3
Rickmansworth 167 F1
Mill End Cl
Edlesborough LU6 . . . . 92 F4
Prestwood HP16 . . . . 151 B5
Mill End Rd HP12 . . . . . . 172 C8
Millennium Cl UB8 . . . . . 201 C3
Millennium Point HP19 101 A1
Miller Pl SL9 . . . . 188 D6
Millers Cl HP18 . . . . 82 F6
Miller's La SL4 . . . . 211 A1
Millers Turn OX39 . . . . . . 147 B6
Millers Way
Aylesbury HP19 . . . . 115 A8
Milton Keynes MK12 . . . . . 33 D5
Millfield HP4 . . . . 135 D5
Millfield Ave OX27 . . . . . . 71 F3
Millfield Cl
Cranfield MK43 . . . . 25 B2
Marsh Gibbon OX27 . . . . . . 71 F3
Millfields HP5 . . . . 154 C6
Millfield Wood Wildlife
Reserve★ HP14 . . . . 162 B3

Mill Gdns HP23 . . . . 119 B4
Mill Gn MK43 . . . . 8 D5
Millhayes MK14 . . . . 34 F8
Mill Ho
Buckingham MK18 . . . . 52 C8
West Drayton UB7 . . . . . . 208 D5
Millholm Rise MK6 . . . . . . 47 E5
Milliners The 1 HP20 . . 101 E1
Millington Gate MK15 . . . 35 D7
Mill La
Amersham HP7 . . . . 165 A8
Aspley Guise MK17 . . . . . . 49 C5
Beaconsfield HP9 . . . . . . 175 E1
Brackley NN13 . . . . 38 A6
Buckingham MK18 . . . . 52 C8
Chalfont St Giles HP8 . . . 166 B1
Chinnor OX39 . . . . 147 B7
Cookham SL6 . . . . 196 C7
Gerrards Cross SL9 . . . . . 188 F5
Great Brickhill MK17 . . . . . 58 F2
Horton-cum-S OX33 . . . . . 108 A6
Horton SL3 . . . . 212 C4
Hulcote MK17 . . . . 37 E1
Hurley SL6 . . . . 193 F4
Milton Keynes, Bradville
MK13 . . . . 34 A7
Milton Keynes, Stony Stratford
MK11 . . . . 32 C5
Milton Keynes, Woolstone
MK15 . . . . 35 C3
Monks Risborough HP27 139 B6
Salford MK17 . . . . 37 C3
South Heath HP16 . . . . . . 152 C7
Stokenchurch HP14 . . . . . 158 C5
Taplow SL6 . . . . 203 C8
Thame OX9 . . . . 126 B3
Turvey MK43 . . . . 8 D5
Twyford MK18 . . . . 62 C1
Upper Arncott OX25 . . . . . 94 E7
Westbury NN13 . . . . 39 A4
Weston Turville HP22 . . . . 117 A2
Windsor SL4 . . . . 210 A7
Wingrave HP22 . . . . 89 C2
Mill Lane Prim Sch
OX39 . . . . 147 B7
Mill Mdw HP19 . . . . 115 B8
Mill Mead HP22 . . . . 131 B5
Mill Pl SL3 . . . . 211 D5
Mill Rd
Cranfield MK43 . . . . 25 C2
2 Leighton Buzzard LU7 . . 80 F8
Marlow SL7 . . . . 183 E1
Milton Keynes MK2 . . . . . . 58 E7
Milton Keynes MK19 . . . . . 21 B4
Oakley HP18 . . . . 109 D4
Slapton LU7 . . . . 91 D7
Stokenchurch HP14 . . . . . 158 C5
Thame OX9 . . . . 124 E1
West Drayton UB7 . . . . . . 208 D3
Whitfield NN13 . . . . 26 E3
Millshot Dr HP7 . . . . 165 D7
Millside SL8 . . . . 185 C3
Mill Sq MK12 . . . . 33 A5
Mill St
Aylesbury HP20 . . . . 101 E1
Berkhamsted HP4 . . . . . . 135 C4
Colnbrook SL3 . . . . 212 D7
High Wycombe HP11 . . . . 172 F7
Newport Pagnell MK16 . . . 22 D5
Oxford OX33 . . . . 108 B1
Slough SL2 . . . . 205 F5
Millstream HP22 . . . . 116 F2
Mill Stream Cl HP27 . . . . 139 A2
Millstream La SL1 . . . . . 204 E5
Millstream Way
Leighton Buzzard LU7 . . . . 80 F7
Wooburn Green HP10 . . . 185 E8
Mill Terr MK12 . . . . 33 A6
Mill The
Milton Keynes MK12 . . . . . 32 E7
Tring HP23 . . . . 104 C1
Wooburn Green HP10 . . . 185 E8
Mill Tower LU6 . . . . 92 E6
Mill View Rd HP23 . . . . . 118 F4
Mill Way
Aspley Guise MK17 . . . . . . 49 D5
Aylesbury HP20 . . . . 115 C8
Rickmansworth WD3 . . . . 167 F1
Mill West SL2 . . . . 205 F5
Milner Rd SL1 . . . . 204 A8
Milton Ave SL9 . . . . 188 D8
Milton Cl
Henley-on-Thames
RG9 . . . . 191 D2
Horton SL3 . . . . 212 A4
MILTON COMMON 136 B3
Milton Dr MK16 . . . . 22 E4
Milton Fields HP8 . . . . . . 177 B7
Milton Gdns HP27 . . . . . . 139 A2
Milton Gr MK3 . . . . 57 F7
MILTON KEYNES 34 D5
Milton Keynes Acad The
MK6 . . . . 47 A7
Milton Keynes Central Sta
MK9 . . . . 34 C1
Milton Keynes Coll MK6 . 46 F7
Milton Keynes Coll
(Bletchley Ctr) MK3 . . . . 58 B8

Milton Keynes Hospl
MK6 . . . . 47 B7
Milton Keynes Materials
Recycling Factory★
MK12 . . . . 33 C8
Milton Keynes Mus★
MK12 . . . . 33 D5
Milton Keynes Prep Sch
MK3 . . . . 57 D8
Milton Keynes Theatre★
MK9 . . . . 34 F3
MILTON KEYNES
VILLAGE 35 E2
Milton Lawns HP6 . . . . . 154 D3
Milton Rd
Aston Clinton HP22 . . . . . 117 F5
Aylesbury HP21 . . . . 115 F6
Chesham HP5 . . . . 144 B2
Milton Keynes, Broughton
MK10 . . . . 36 B3
Milton Keynes, Willen
MK15 . . . . 35 D7
Slough SL2 . . . . 198 D1
Walton MK7 . . . . 47 F6
Milton's Cottage (Mus)★
HP8 . . . . 177 B7
Milton Way UB7 . . . . 208 F2
Milverton Cl SL6 . . . . 202 B3
Milward Dr MK2 . . . . 47 E1
Mimosa Ct HP21 . . . . 115 B6
Mina Ave SL3 . . . . 206 D4
Minall Cl HP23 . . . . 119 A4
Mineral La HP5 . . . . 154 C7
Minerva Cl TW19 . . . . 213 A2
Minerva Gdns MK7 . . . . . . 48 C7
Minerva Way HP9 . . . . . . 176 A1
Mines Cl HP13 . . . . 161 D3
Ministry Wharf HP14 . . . 149 C1
Minniecroft Rd SL1 . . . . 197 B2
Minorca Gr MK5 . . . . 46 A4
Minshull Cl MK18 . . . . 41 D1
Minster Way SL3 . . . . 206 F4
Minstrel Ct MK13 . . . . 34 B7
Minton Cl MK14 . . . . 22 A1
Minton Rise SL6 . . . . 204 B7
Mirador Cres SL2 . . . . . . 206 B6
Mirrie La UB9 . . . . 189 C6
Misbourne Ave
Chalfont St Peter SL9 . . . 177 E5
High Wycombe HP13 . . . . 173 F6
Misbourne Cl
Aylesbury HP21 . . . . 115 D3
Chalfont St Peter SL9 . . . 177 E5
Misbourne Ct SL3 . . . . . . 207 A2
Misbourne Dr HP16 . . . . 152 B6
Misbourne Ho HP8 . . . . . . 166 C1
Misbourne Mdws UB9 . . 189 D3
Misbourne Sch The
HP16 . . . . 152 B6
Misbourne Vale SL9 . . . . 177 D5
Miserden Cres MK4 . . . . . 45 F1
Missenden Abbey Adult Ed
Coll HP16 . . . . 152 B6
Missenden Cl MK18 . . . . . 65 F4
Missenden Gdns SL1 . . . 204 B7
Missenden Rd
Chesham HP5 . . . . 154 A7
Ellesborough HP17 . . . . . 130 C2
Great Kingshill HP15 . . . . 151 D2
Winslow MK18 . . . . 65 F4
Miss Joans Ride HP4 . . . 107 D7
Miswell La HP23 . . . . 118 F3
Mitcham Pl MK13 . . . . 34 D3
Mitcham Wlk HP19 . . . . . 101 A2
Mitchell Cl
Bovingdon HP3 . . . . 145 F4
Slough SL1 . . . . 205 A4
Mitchell Rd MK43 . . . . 24 E2
Mitchell Wlk HP6 . . . . . . 154 E1
Mithras Gdns MK7 . . . . . . 48 C6
Mitre Ct MK18 . . . . 52 C7
Mitre St MK18 . . . . 52 C7
MIXBURY 38 D1
Moat Cl
Prestwood HP16 . . . . 151 C6
Wendover HP22 . . . . 131 B6
Moat Dr
Prestwood HP16 . . . . 151 C7
Slough SL2 . . . . 206 C8
Moat End HP22 . . . . 102 B4
Moat House The MK18 . . 52 D8
Moat La
Aston Abbotts HP22 . . . . . 88 D4
Marsh Gibbon OX27 . . . . . . 71 F2
Prestwood HP16 . . . . 151 C7
Wingrave HP22 . . . . 89 B2
Moat Pl UB9 . . . . 201 B8
MOBWELL 152 A8
Mobwell Terr 3 HP16 . . 152 A8
Model Row HP22 . . . . 117 F6
Moeran Cl MK7 . . . . 48 C5
Moffy Hill SL6 . . . . 195 E2
Mole Run HP13 . . . . 161 C1
Molyneaux Ave HP3 . . . . 145 F4
Molyns Ho RG9 . . . . 191 E3
Molyns Mews SL1 . . . . . . 204 E5
Monellan Cres MK7 . . . . . 48 A3
Monellan Gr MK7 . . . . 48 A2
Monet Pl HP19 . . . . 100 E2

Money La UB7 . . . . 208 D3
Monkey Island La SL6 . . 203 E2
Monksfield Way SL2 . . . 198 A2
Monks Hollow SL7 . . . . . 183 E5
Monks Path 9 HP19 . . . 115 A8
Monks Rd SL4 . . . . 209 D5
MONKS RISBOROUGH 139 C6
Monks Risborough CE
Comb Sch HP27 . . . . . . 139 D5
Monks Risborough Sta
HP27 . . . . 139 B6
MONKSTON 36 A1
Monkston Comb Sch
MK10 . . . . 36 B1
MONKSTON PARK 35 E1
Monkston Rdbt MK10 . . . 36 B2
Monks Way
Harmondsworth UB7 . . . . 213 E8
Milton Keynes MK12, MK13,
MK14, MK15 . . . . 34 C6
Monkswood Ct 11 SL7 . . 183 E2
Monkton La SL7 . . . . 172 F1
Monkton Way HP27 . . . . 150 C5
Monmouth Cl HP19 . . . . 101 A2
Monmouth Gr MK4 . . . . . . 45 E1
Monro Ave MK8 . . . . 45 E7
Montabaur Rd NN13 . . . . 38 A7
Montagu Dr MK6 . . . . 47 B8
Montague Cl SL2 . . . . . . 198 B3
Montague Rd
Aylesbury HP21 . . . . 115 D7
Berkhamsted HP4 . . . . . . 135 B4
Slough SL1 . . . . 205 F6
Uxbridge UB8 . . . . 201 D5
Montagu Rd SL3 . . . . 211 B6
Montem La SL1 . . . . 205 D4
Montem L Ctr SL1 . . . . . 205 D4
Montem Prim Sch SL1 . 205 B4
Montford Mews HP15 . . 162 E2
Montgomerie Cl HP4 . . . 135 A6
Montgomery Cres MK15 . 35 B7
Montgomery Pl SL2 . . . . 206 C7
Montpellier Ct SL4 . . . . . 210 C5
Montrose Ave
Datchet SL3 . . . . 211 C7
Slough SL1 . . . . 205 B7
Montrose Dr SL6 . . . . 202 A6
Montrose Way SL3 . . . . . 211 C7
Monument La SL9 . . . . . . 177 E5
Monycrower Dr SL6 . . . . 202 E7
Moon St MK12 . . . . 33 D6
Moonstone Ct 5 HP12 . 172 D8
Moorbridge Rd SL6 . . . . 203 A7
MOOR COMMON 171 A2
Moorcroft Sch 3 UB8 . . 208 F7
Moore Cl SL1 . . . . 205 B4
MOOR END
Eaton Bray 92 E5
Yardley Gobion 18 D6
Moor End
Eaton Bray LU6 . . . . 92 F5
Frieth RG9 . . . . 171 A1
Maidenhead SL6 . . . . 203 C1
Moor End Cl LU6 . . . . 92 F4
Moorend La OX9 . . . . 125 F1
Moor End La LU6 . . . . 92 F5
Moorend Rd NN12 . . . . . . 18 E6
Moore Rd HP4 . . . . 134 F6
Moores Hill MK46 . . . . 6 F5
Moores La SL4 . . . . 204 F2
Moorfield MK17 . . . . 57 D3
Moorfield Rd
Denham Green UB9 . . . . . 190 A5
Uxbridge UB8 . . . . 208 D7
Moorfield Terr SL6 . . . . . 203 A8
Moorfoot MK11 . . . . 33 A4
Moor Furlong SL1 . . . . . . 204 E5
Moorgate MK6 . . . . 46 F7
Moorhall Rd UB9 . . . . . . 190 B6
Moorhen Ct 2 HP20 . . . . 101 E3
Moorhen Way MK18 . . . . . 52 E8
Moorhills Cres LU7 . . . . . 79 F3
Moorhills Rd LU7 . . . . 79 F3
Moorings The
Buckingham MK18 . . . . 52 C8
Windsor SL4 . . . . 210 A7
Moor La
Harmondsworth UB7 . . . . 213 C8
High Wycombe HP13 . . . . 161 D3
Maidenhead SL6 . . . . 195 F1
Sarratt WD3 . . . . 156 E3
Moorland Inf Sch MK6 . . . 47 B5
Moorland Rd UB7 . . . . . . 213 C8
Moorlands LU7 . . . . 79 E3
Moorlands Rd LU7 . . . . . . 79 F3
Moor Pk
Milton Keynes MK3 . . . . . . 57 D8
Wendover HP22 . . . . 131 B7
Moor Rd HP5 . . . . 154 C6
Moors Cl MK19 . . . . 31 E5
Moor's Farm Cotts HP5 145 B4
Moorside HP10 . . . . 185 E8
Moorside Cl SL6 . . . . 195 F1
Moorstown Ct 7 SL1 . . . 205 E4
Moor The SL7 . . . . 184 C4
MOP END 164 B7
Mop End La HP7 . . . . 164 B7
Morar Cl LU7 . . . . 80 C7
Moray Dr SL2 . . . . 206 A7

Moray Pl MK3 . . . . 46 F2
Mordaunt Cl MK43 . . . . 8 E6
Mordaunts Ct MK15 . . . . . 35 C2
Moreau Wlk SL3 . . . . 206 E7
More Ave HP21 . . . . 115 D7
Morebath Gr MK4 . . . . 46 C4
Morefields HP23 . . . . 119 A6
Moreland Ave SL3 . . . . . . 212 C7
Moreland Cl SL3 . . . . 212 C7
Moreland Dr SL9 . . . . 188 F4
Morello Dr SL3 . . . . 206 F5
Moreton Dr MK18 . . . . 41 E2
Moreton La HP17 . . . . 115 A1
Moreton Rd MK18 . . . . 41 D2
Moreton Way SL1 . . . . . . 204 D5
Morland Dr MK8 . . . . 45 D6
Morley Cl SL3 . . . . 206 F4
Morley Cres MK7 . . . . 48 D4
Morrell Cl MK5 . . . . 46 B5
Morrice Cl SL3 . . . . 207 A2
Morris Cl SL9 . . . . 177 F2
Morris Ct
Aylesbury HP21 . . . . 115 D4
Windsor SL4 . . . . 209 E6
Morrison Ct MK8 . . . . 45 E6
Morris Wlk MK16 . . . . 22 A4
Mortain Cl MK7 . . . . 48 B3
Mortain Dr HP4 . . . . 134 F6
Morten Gdns UB9 . . . . . . 190 A4
Mortens Wood HP7 . . . . . 165 E7
Mortimer Hill HP23 . . . . . 119 B4
Mortimer Rd SL3 . . . . 206 D3
Mortimer Rise HP23 . . . . 119 B4
Morton Cl
North Marston MK18 . . . . . 76 B2
Pitstone LU7 . . . . 105 C4
Uxbridge UB8 . . . . 201 F1
Morton Dr SL1 . . . . 197 E8
Morton King Cl HP18 . . . 124 D3
Mortons Fork MK13 . . . . . 33 F6
Moseley Rd HP14 . . . . . . 161 C7
Moses Plat La HP27 . . . . 150 B5
Moss Ct HP9 . . . . 176 D4
Mossdale MK13 . . . . 34 B5
Mossmans Cl MK2 . . . . 58 D7
Mossway HP9 . . . . 175 C5
Mossy Vale SL6 . . . . 195 D1
MOULSOE 36 D8
Moundsfield Way SL1 . . 204 E4
Mountain Ash SL7 . . . . . 183 D6
Mount Ave MK1 . . . . 47 E3
Mountbatten Cl 7 SL1 . 206 A3
Mountbatten Sq 8
SL4 . . . . 210 C6
Mount Cl
Aston Clinton HP22 . . . . . 117 F4
Farnham Common SL2 . . . 198 C8
High Wycombe HP12 . . . . 172 E6
Mount Farm Ind Est
MK1 . . . . 47 D4
Mount Farm Rdbt MK1 . . 47 D4
Mounthill Ave MK19 . . . . . 32 B7
Mount Hill La SL9 . . . . . . 188 B2
Mount La UB9 . . . . 189 D2
Mount Nugent HP5 . . . . . 144 A4
MOUNT PLEASANT
Buckingham 52 D7
Stoke Goldington 12 B7
Mount Pleasant
Aspley Guise MK17 . . . . . . 49 F4
Aylesbury HP19 . . . . 101 D1
Lane End HP14 . . . . 171 B5
Milton Keynes MK6 . . . . . . 47 E4
Soulbury LU7 . . . . 69 E3
Steeple Claydon MK18 . . . . 63 F2
Stoke Goldington MK16 . . . 12 B7
Stoke Hammond MK17 . . . 69 E7
Whitchurch HP22 . . . . 86 F7
Yardley Gobion NN12 . . . . . 18 F6
Mount Pleasant Cl
MK18 . . . . 52 C7
Mount Pleasant Cotts 2
SL8 . . . . 185 B3
Mountsfield Cl
Newport Pagnell MK16 . . . 22 C3
Stanwell TW19 . . . . 213 A2
Mount St HP20 . . . . 115 D8
Mount The
Aspley Guise MK17 . . . . . . 49 D4
Milton Keynes MK6 . . . . . . 47 E4
Mount View RG9 . . . . 191 D2
Mount View Ct 4 RG9 . 191 D2
Mount Way HP27 . . . . 139 A3
Mowbray Dr LU7 . . . . 80 D7
Mowbray Rd HP20 . . . . . 101 D2
Mowhills MK43 . . . . 3 F6
Mow Mead MK46 . . . . 6 F5
Moyleen Rise SL7 . . . . . . 183 C1
Mozart Cl MK7 . . . . 48 C4
Muddiford La MK4 . . . . . . 46 D4
Muirfield Dr MK3 . . . . 46 D1
Mulberry Ave SL4 . . . . . . 210 F5
Mulberry Cl
Amersham HP7 . . . . 165 F8
High Wycombe HP12 . . . . 172 C5
Tring HP23 . . . . 119 A5

Mulberry Ct HP15 . . . . . . .163 D7
Mulberry Dr SL3 . . . . . . .206 E1
Mulberry Wlk SL6 . . . . . . .202 C8
Mullen Ave MK14 . . . . . . .34 F4
Mullins Way HP19 . . . . . .100 E3
Mullion Pl MK6 . . . . .35 A1
Mumfords La SL9 . . . . . . .188 A3
Munces Rd SL7 . . . . .183 D6
MUNDAYDEAN
 BOTTOM 182 E5
Mundaydean La SL7 . . . . .183 B4
Munday's Farm HP21 . . . . .116 B3
Mundesley Spur SL1 . . . . .205 E7
MURCOTT 94 A4
Murcott Rd OX6 . . . . .94 D6
Murray Rd HP4 . . . . .135 C6
Murrey Cl MK5 . . . . .46 C5
Murrin Rd SL6 . . . . .202 C8
MURSLEY 67 D6
Mursley CE Sch MK17 . . . . .67 D6
Mursley Ct MK11 . . . . . . .32 F5
Mursley Rd
 Little Horwood MK17 . . . . .55 E2
 Swanbourne MK17 . . . . . .67 B3
Museum Ct 9 HP23 . . . . . .119 A3
Musgrave Rd OX39 . . . . . .147 D7
Musgrave Wlk HP14 . . . . . .158 F5
Musgrove Pl MK5 . . . . . . .45 F6
Mus of Eton Life The★
 SL4 . . . . .210 D8
Myddleton Rd UB8 . . . . . .201 C4
Mylne Cl HP13 . . . . .172 F8
Mynchen Cl HP9 . . . . . . .175 D6
Mynchen End HP9 . . . . . . .175 D6
Mynchen Rd HP9 . . . . . . .175 D6
MYRKE 205 F2
Myrke The SL3 . . . . .205 F2
Myrtle Cl
 Poyle SL3 . . . . .212 E6
 Uxbridge UB8 . . . . .208 F8
 West Drayton UB7 . . . . . .208 F3
Myrtle Cres SL2 . . . . . . .205 F6

N

Nag's Head La HP16 . . . . .152 A4
Nailzee Cl SL9 . . . . .188 E4
Nairdwood Cl HP16 . . . . . .151 E4
Nairdwood La HP16 . . . . . .151 D5
Nairdwood Way HP16 . . . . .151 E4
Nairn Ct MK3 . . . . .46 E2
Naisby Dr MK17 . . . . .59 C1
Nalders Rd HP5 . . . . .144 D2
Nan Aires HP22 . . . . .89 A3
Nancy Hall Ct HP12 . . . . . .172 D3
Nans Gdn MK17 . . . . .57 C4
NAPHILL 161 D7
Naphill Pl MK13 . . . . .34 C3
Naphill & Walters Ash Sch
 HP14 . . . . .150 A1
Napier Cl UB7 . . . . .208 F3
Napier Rd
 Aylesbury HP19 . . . . . . .114 F8
 Harmondsworth TW6 . . . . .213 D6
 Maidenhead SL6 . . . . . . .202 B6
Napier St MK2 . . . . .58 D8
Nappin Cl HP19 . . . . .101 A3
Nappins Cl HP18 . . . . . . .125 D5
Nap The HP18 . . . . .109 E5
Narbeth Dr HP20 . . . . . . .116 B8
Narcot La HP8 . . . . .177 B5
Narcot Rd HP8 . . . . .177 A7
Narcot Way HP8 . . . . . . .177 B6
Narrow La HP19 . . . . .161 E3
Narrow Path MK17 . . . . . . .49 B3
Naseby Cl
 Newport Pagnell MK16 . . . .22 A4
 Thame OX9 . . . . .126 B1
Naseby Ct
 Buckingham MK18 . . . . . .41 E2
 Milton Keynes MK13 . . . . .34 B6
NASH 44 C1
Nash Cl
 Aylesbury HP21 . . . . . . .116 A4
 Berkhamsted HP4 . . . . . .135 A5
Nash Croft MK4 . . . . .57 B8
Nashdom SL1 . . . . .196 F5
Nashdom La SL1 . . . . . . .197 B6
NASH LEE 130 C5
Nash Lee End HP22 . . . . . .130 E6
Nash Lee La HP22 . . . . . .130 E6
Nash Lee Rd
 Nash Lee HP17 . . . . . . .130 D6
 World's End HP22 . . . . . .130 F4
Nashleigh Hill HP5 . . . . . .144 D7
Nashleigh Ho HP5 . . . . . .144 E3
Nash Pl HP10 . . . . .163 B6
Nash Rd
 Great Horwood MK17 . . . . .55 A4
 Slough SL3 . . . . .207 A2
 Thornborough MK18 . . . . . .54 B8
 Whaddon MK17 . . . . . . .45 A1
Nashs Farm HP22 . . . . . . .88 D4
Nathanial Cl MK5 . . . . . . .46 B5

Nathaniel Wlk HP23 . . . .119 A5
National Badminton Ctr
 MK8 . . . . .34 A1
National Bowl The★
 MK6 . . . . .46 E5
National Film & Television
 Sch HP9 . . . . .175 E1
National Waterways Mus★
 NN12 . . . . .9 A8
Natural History Mus at
 Tring★ HP23 . . . . .119 A3
Natwoke Ct HP9 . . . . . .175 D5
Neal Cl SL9 . . . . .189 B3
Neale Cl HP12 . . . . . . .172 D3
Neapland MK6 . . . . .47 B5
NEARTON END 67 A3
Nearton End MK17 . . . . .67 A3
Near Town MK46 . . . . . . .7 A3
Near Town Gdns MK46 . . . .7 A3
Neath Cres MK3 . . . . . . .47 A2
NEATH HILL 34 F6
Neath Hill Rdbt MK15 . . . .35 A6
Needham Cl SL4 . . . . . .209 E4
Needham Ct 4 HP11 . . . .172 F7
Neild Way WD3 . . . . . . .167 F2
Neilson Ct MK18 . . . . . . .52 C8
Nelson Cl
 High Wycombe HP13 . . . .173 F5
 Milton Keynes MK8 . . . . .45 E6
 Slough SL3 . . . . .206 D2
 Winchmore Hill HP7 . . . .164 C3
Nelson Ct MK18 . . . . . . .52 C8
Nelson Rd
 Dagnall HP4 . . . . .107 C5
 Harmondsworth TW6 . . . .213 D6
 Windsor SL4 . . . . .209 F4
Nelson St MK18 . . . . . . .52 C8
Nelson Terr HP20 . . . . . .115 D8
Nene Cl
 Aylesbury HP21 . . . . . .115 C4
 Newport Pagnell MK16 . . .22 D3
Nene Dr MK3 . . . . .57 E8
Neptune Way SL1 . . . . . .204 E4
Ness Way MK2 . . . . .58 D5
Netherby Cl HP23 . . . . .119 C6
Nether Cl NN13 . . . . . . .38 A7
Nethercote La OX49 . . . .157 A8
NETHERFIELD 47 C6
Netherfield Rdbt MK6 . . . .47 C7
Nether Gr MK5 . . . . . . .46 B3
Nether Winchendon Ho★
 HP18 . . . . .112 C5
Netherwood Rd HP9 . . . .175 D5
Netley Ct MK10 . . . . . . .36 A1
Nettlecombe MK4 . . . . . .46 C3
Nettleden Rd
 Berkhamsted HP4 . . . . .135 F6
 Little Gaddesden HP4 . . . .121 E4
Nettleton Rd UB10 . . . . .201 F8
Neve Ho SL6 . . . . .202 F8
Nevill Cl MK19 . . . . .11 B2
Neville Cl SL2 . . . . .198 F6
Neville Ct SL1 . . . . .197 C2
Nevis Cl LU7 . . . . .80 C7
Nevis Gr MK2 . . . . .58 E4
Newark Ct MK7 . . . . .48 A3
Newbarn La HP9 . . . . . . .176 E6
Newberry Cres SL4 . . . . . .209 D5
Newbery Way SL1 . . . . . .205 D4
Newbolt Cl
 Newport Pagnell MK16 . . .21 F5
 Paulerspury NN12 . . . . . .17 B8
NEW BRADWELL 33 F8
New Bradwell Comb Sch
 MK13 . . . . .33 F7
Newbridge Oval MK4 . . . . .46 B3
Newbury Ct MK3 . . . . . . .57 D6
Newbury Dr SL6 . . . . . . .203 B6
Newby Rd UB7 . . . . .213 F6
Newby Pl MK4 . . . . .46 B2
New Chapter Prim sch
 MK6 . . . . .47 A5
New Chilterns HP7 . . . . . .165 E8
Newchurch Rd SL2 . . . . . .204 F8
New Cl RG9 . . . . .192 A8
New Cl Farm Rd OX39 . . . .137 C3
New College MK18 . . . . . .51 F8
New College Ct MK18 . . . . .41 B4
New Coll Rd HP19 . . . . . .101 C4
Newcombe Rise UB7 . . . . .208 E2
New Cotts RG9 . . . . . . .180 C1
Newcourt UB8 . . . . .208 E8
Newcroft Cl UB8 . . . . . . .208 F8
New Ct
 High Wycombe HP13 . . . .173 C6
 Marlow SL7 . . . . .183 D2
NEW DENHAM 201 D6
New Dr HP13 . . . . .173 E8
Newell Cl HP21 . . . . . . .116 A6
Newells Hedge LU7 . . . . .105 D5
Newfield Gdns SL7 . . . . .183 F3
Newfield Rd SL7 . . . . . . .183 F3
Newfield Way SL7 . . . . . .183 F2
New Garden Dr UB7 . . . . .208 E4
NEW GROUND 120 A2
Newground Rd HP23 . . . . .120 B3
New Hall Ln HP3 . . . . . . .146 A4
Newhaven Spur SL2 . . . . .198 B3

New Horton Manor
 SL3 . . . . .212 A4
Newhouse Rd HP3 . . . . .146 A4
Newington Gate MK6 . . . .47 D5
New Inn La MK18 . . . . . .51 F4
Newland Ho UB8 . . . . . .201 C4
NEWLAND PARK 178 A7
Newlands Dr
 Maidenhead SL6 . . . . . .202 A7
 Poyle SL3 . . . . .212 E4
Newlands Girls Sch
 SL6 . . . . .202 A7
Newlyn Pl MK6 . . . . .35 A2
Newmans Cl MK14 . . . . . .21 E1
Newmans Ctyd MK17 . . . . .68 C6
Newmarket Ct MK10 . . . . .36 C2
New Mdw HP21 . . . . . . .116 C7
Newmer Rd HP12 . . . . . .172 B3
NEW MILL 119 B6
New Mill Terr HP23 . . . . .119 B6
New Par
 Chorleywood WD3 . . . . .167 C5
 West Drayton UB7 . . . . .208 E5
New Peachey La UB8 . . . .208 B8
New Pond Rd HP15 . . . . .163 C7
NEWPORT PAGNELL 22 B5
Newport Pagnell Rd
 MK43 . . . . .16 C4
Newport Rd
 Astwood MK16 . . . . . . .15 C2
 Emberton MK46 . . . . . .13 F6
 Hanslope MK19 . . . . . . .11 D7
 Milton Keynes MK10 . . . . .36 D1
 Milton Keynes, New Bradwell
  MK13 . . . . .34 A8
 Milton Keynes, Oakgrove
  MK15 . . . . .35 C2
 Milton Keynes, Willen
  MK15 . . . . .35 D7
 Milton Keynes, Woughton on
  the Green MK6 . . . . . .35 D1
 Moulsoe MK16 . . . . . . .36 C7
 Slough SL2 . . . . .197 E1
 Wavendon MK17 . . . . . .48 E7
 Woburn MK17 . . . . .60 F8
 Woughton on the Green
  MK6 . . . . .47 D8
 Woughton Park MK6 . . . .47 D6
Newport Way MK19 . . . . .11 C3
New Provident Pl 5
 HP4 . . . . .135 D4
Newquay Cl 4 MK4 . . . . .45 F1
New Rd
 Amersham HP6 . . . . . . .154 E2
 Aston Clinton HP22 . . . . .117 E5
 Berkhamsted HP4 . . . . . .135 D6
 Berkhamsted, Northchurch
  HP4 . . . . .134 F7
 Bolter End HP14 . . . . . .170 F6
 Bourne End SL8 . . . . . . .185 B4
 Castlethorpe MK19 . . . . .19 F5
 Chipperfield WD4 . . . . . .146 F1
 Coleshill HP7 . . . . . . .164 F4
 Cookham Rise SL6 . . . . .195 E7
 Datchet SL3 . . . . .211 D6
 Dinton HP17 . . . . .113 E2
 Drayton Parslow MK17 . . . .68 C5
 Great Kingshill HP15 . . . .162 D8
 Harrold MK43 . . . . .3 E6
 High Wycombe HP12 . . . .172 C5
 Hurley SL6 . . . . .193 F3
 Leighton Buzzard LU7 . . . .80 E7
 Little Chalfont HP8 . . . . .166 F6
 Little Kingshill HP16 . . . . .152 B4
 Marlow Bottom SL7 . . . . .183 D6
 Naphill HP14 . . . . .150 A2
 Prestwood HP16 . . . . . .151 D6
 Princes Risborough
  HP27 . . . . .139 C3
 Sarratt HP8 . . . . .156 F1
 Slough SL3 . . . . .207 A3
 Stokenchurch HP14 . . . . .158 F4
 Tring HP23 . . . . .119 B6
 Tylers Green HP10 . . . . .163 C1
 Weedon HP22 . . . . . . .101 B8
 Weston Turville HP22 . . . .116 E5
 Wilstone HP23 . . . . . . .118 D8
New Road Cl HP12 . . . . .172 C6
New Road Gdns HP12 . . . .172 C6
New Row
 Hoggeston MK18 . . . . . .77 B7
 Lavendon MK46 . . . . . . .7 E8
New Sq SL1 . . . . .205 F4
New St
 Aylesbury HP20 . . . . . .101 D1
 Berkhamsted HP4 . . . . .135 D4
 Cheddington LU7 . . . . . .104 F7
 Henley-on-Thames RG9 . . .191 E2
 Milton Keynes MK11 . . . . .32 D5
 Tingewick MK18 . . . . . . .51 B6
 Waddesdon HP18 . . . . . .99 A7
NEWTON 144 C1
NEWTON
 BLOSSOMVILLE 8 A4
Newton Blossomville CE
 Sch MK43 . . . . .8 B4
Newton Cl SL3 . . . . . . .206 F4
Newton Ct SL4 . . . . . . .211 A1
Newton La SL4 . . . . . . .211 B1

NEWTON LONGVILLE 57 D3
Newton Longville CE Comb
 Sch MK17 . . . . .57 D3
NEWTON PURCELL 50 B2
Newton Rd
 Drayton Parslow MK17 . . . .68 D8
 Milton Keynes MK3 . . . . .57 E6
 Stoke Hammond MK17 . . . .69 D8
 Turvey MK43 . . . . .8 E5
 West Drayton UB7 . . . . .213 F6
Newtonside SL4 . . . . . . .211 A1
Newton Side Orch SL4 . . . .211 A1
Newton St MK46 . . . . . . .7 A4
Newtown Rd
 Marlow SL7 . . . . .183 F3
 New Denham SL9 . . . . . .201 B6
Newtown Sch HP5 . . . . . .144 C2
Newville HP22 . . . . .87 C1
New Windsor St UB8 . . . . .201 C4
NEWYEARS GREEN 190 F5
Newyears Green La
 UB9 . . . . .190 F5
New Zealand Cotts
 HP22 . . . . .88 E4
New Zealand Gdns LU7 . . . .79 E2
Neyland Dr HP19 . . . . . .101 D3
Nicholas Gdns
 High Wycombe HP13 . . . .173 D8
 Slough SL1 . . . . .205 C7
Nicholas Mead MK14 . . . . .34 F8
Nicholas Winton Ct
 SL6 . . . . .203 A8
Nicholls SL4 . . . . .209 C4
Nicholls Wlk SL4 . . . . . .209 C4
Nicholson Gr MK8 . . . . . .45 E6
Nicholsons La SL6 . . . . . .202 F7
Nicholsons Sh Ctr 2
 SL6 . . . . .202 F7
Nickson Ct HP15 . . . . . .163 A3
Nicol Cl SL9 . . . . .177 C2
Nicol End SL9 . . . . .177 C2
Nicol Rd SL9 . . . . .177 C2
Nielson Ct MK7 . . . . .48 D5
Nigel Ct NN13 . . . . .38 A5
Nightingale Cl
 Hazelmere HP15 . . . . . .163 B5
 Steeple Claydon MK18 . . . .63 E3
Nightingale Cres MK13 . . . .34 A7
Nightingale Ct
 1 High Wycombe
  HP13 . . . . .173 B7
 6 Slough SL1 . . . . . . .206 A3
Nightingale Ho HP11 . . . .174 A4
Nightingale La SL6 . . . . .195 D3
Nightingale Lodge HP4 . . .135 B4
Nightingale Pk SL2 . . . . .197 F5
Nightingale Pl
 Buckingham MK18 . . . . .41 E1
 Cookham Rise SL6 . . . . .195 F7
Nightingale Rd
 Aylesbury HP21 . . . . . .115 C6
 2 Chesham HP5 . . . . .144 B2
 Wendover HP22 . . . . . .131 B5
Nightingales Cnr HP7 . . . .166 C7
Nightingales Ct HP8 . . . . .166 C7
Nightingales La HP8 . . . . .166 D4
Nightingale Way UB9 . . . .189 D4
Nightingale Wlk SL4 . . . . .210 C4
Nijinsky Ho UB8 . . . . . .201 D3
Nine Acres SL1 . . . . . . .204 F5
Nine Elms Ave UB8 . . . . .208 D8
Nine Elms Cl UB8 . . . . . .208 D8
Nine Stiles Cl UB9 . . . . . .201 B6
Ninnings Rd SL9 . . . . . .177 F3
Ninnings Way SL9 . . . . . .177 F3
Niplands Cotts HP10 . . . . .185 D2
Niven La MK4 . . . . .45 E3
Nixey Cl SL1 . . . . .206 A4
Nixons Cl MK6 . . . . .46 E6
Noble Cl MK15 . . . . .35 A7
Noble Ct SL2 . . . . .205 F5
Noon Layer Dr MK10 . . . . .35 E3
Norbrek MK8 . . . . .33 E2
NORCOTT HILL 120 D2
Norcotts Kiln Cotts
 HP18 . . . . .96 A1
Norden Cl SL6 . . . . . . .202 C4
Norden Mdws SL6 . . . . . .202 C5
Norden Rd SL6 . . . . . . .202 C5
Norelands Dr SL1 . . . . . .197 C3
Norfolk Ave SL1 . . . . . . .205 C8
Norfolk Ho 6 MK3 . . . . . .46 F1
Norfolk Park Cotts SL6 . . . .202 F8
Norfolk Rd
 Maidenhead SL6 . . . . . .202 F8
 Turvey MK43 . . . . .8 E6
 Uxbridge UB8 . . . . . . .201 D6
Norfolk Terr HP20 . . . . . .101 E1
Norgrove Pk SL9 . . . . . .188 E7
Norjo-An Villas HP5 . . . . .154 C6
Norland Dr HP10 . . . . . .185 C8
Norman Ave RG9 . . . . . .191 E1
Norman Cres MK10 . . . . . .35 E3
Normandy Dr HP4 . . . . . .135 B6
Normandy Way MK3 . . . . . .46 E2
Normans Cl UB8 . . . . . .208 E8
Normans Ct 5 HP13 . . . . .173 F6
Normanstead RG9 . . . . . .191 D1
Normans The SL2 . . . . . .206 B7

Norman Way LU6 . . . . . .93 E8
Normill Terr HP22 . . . . .117 A6
Norreys Dr SL6 . . . . . . .202 D4
Norrington MK8 . . . . . . .33 E2
Norris Ho SL6 . . . . .202 E7
Norris Rd OX6 . . . . .94 E8
NORTHALL 92 B5
Northall Cl LU6 . . . . .92 D6
Northall Rd LU6 . . . . .92 D6
Northampton Ave SL1 . . . .205 C7
Northampton Rd
 Brackley NN13 . . . . . . .26 A1
 Cosgrove MK19 . . . . . . .19 C1
 Cosgrove MK19 . . . . . . .32 C8
 Grafton Regis NN12 . . . . .9 C3
 Lathbury MK16 . . . . . . .22 D6
 Lavendon MK46 . . . . . . .7 F8
 Yardley Hastings NN7 . . . .1 A6
Northborough Rd SL2 . . . .198 B1
Northbridge Rd HP4 . . . . .135 A6
North Burnham Cl SL1 . . . .197 B3
NORTHCHURCH 134 E5
Northchurch La HP5 . . . . .134 D2
North Cl
 Beaconsfield HP9 . . . . . .186 B8
 Drayton Parslow MK17 . . . .68 C5
 Medmenham SL7 . . . . . .193 D7
 Windsor SL4 . . . . .209 F6
Northcliffe LU6 . . . . .92 E6
North Common Rd
 UB8 . . . . .201 D7
North Cotts SL2 . . . . . . .198 C2
NORTH CRAWLEY 24 A6
North Crawley CE Sch
 MK16 . . . . .24 B6
North Crawley Rd MK16 . . .23 C4
Northcroft
 Milton Keynes MK5 . . . . .46 C6
 Slough SL2 . . . . .198 B1
 Weedon HP22 . . . . . . .87 C1
 Wooburn Green HP10 . . . .185 F6
North Croft MK18 . . . . . .66 A4
Northdean 5 SL6 . . . . . .195 F1
Northdown Rd SL9 . . . . . .177 E4
North Dr
 Aylesbury HP21 . . . . . .115 E5
 Beaconsfield HP9 . . . . . .186 B8
 High Wycombe HP13 . . . .173 E8
North Eastern Rd HP19 . . .101 C2
North Eighth St MK9 . . . . .34 E3
North Elder Rdbt MK9 . . . .34 C1
North Eleventh St MK9 . . . .34 E3
NORTHEND 168 E6
NORTH END
 Stagsden 16 E8
 Steeple Claydon 63 D3
 Stewkley 68 D3
Northend MK46 . . . . . . .5 E3
Northend Cl HP10 . . . . . .185 C7
Northend Ct 1 MK18 . . . . .41 D1
North End Rd
 Quainton HP22 . . . . . . .85 A5
 Steeple Claydon MK18 . . . .63 D3
Northend Sq 2 MK18 . . . .41 D1
Northend Workshops
 RG9 . . . . .168 E5
Northern Hts SL8 . . . . . .185 B5
Northern Perimeter Rd (W)
 TW6 . . . . .213 D6
Northern Rd
 Aylesbury HP19 . . . . . .101 C2
 Slough SL2 . . . . .198 D1
Northern Woods HP10 . . . .185 C7
NORTHFIELD 35 F5
Northfield Ct RG9 . . . . . .191 D3
Northfield Dr MK15 . . . . . .35 F5
Northfield End RG9 . . . . . .191 D3
Northfield Rd
 Aylesbury HP20 . . . . . .116 B8
 Eton Wick SL4 . . . . . . .204 F2
 Maidenhead SL6 . . . . . .195 F1
 Princes Risborough
  HP27 . . . . .139 C4
 Tring HP23 . . . . .119 F7
Northfield Rdbt MK10 . . . . .36 A5
North Fifth St MK9 . . . . . .34 D2
North Fourteenth St
 MK9 . . . . .34 F4
North Fourth St MK9 . . . . .34 D2
North Gate MK2 . . . . . . .47 C1
North Gn
 3 Maidenhead SL6 . . . . .195 F1
 Slough SL1 . . . . .205 E6
North Grafton Rdbt
 MK13 . . . . .34 C2
North Hill
 Buckingham MK18 . . . . . .28 D2
 Dadford MK18 . . . . . . .28 D2
 Sarratt WD3 . . . . .167 E8
North Hills HP18 . . . . . . .96 A1
North La MK7 . . . . .47 E7
Northlands Rd MK18 . . . . .53 F1
NORTH LEE 130 A7
North Lee La
 North Lee HP22 . . . . . .130 A6
 Stoke Mandeville HP22 . . .129 F7
Northleigh MK4 . . . . . . .46 D2
North Links Rd HP10 . . . .174 B1
NORTH MARSTON 76 A2

North Marston CE Sch
MK18 76 B2
North Marston La HP22 86 E7
Northmead Rd SL2 204 F8
Northmill HP27 138 F3
North Mill Rd HP27 138 A5
Northmoor Hill Wood Nature Reserve★
UB9 189 F7
North Ninth St MK9 34 E3
Northolt Rd TW6 213 E6
North Orbital Rd
Denham Green UB9 189 F4
Rickmansworth WD3 178 E7
North Overgate Rdbt
MK15 35 B5
North Pk
Gerrards Cross SL9 188 E8
Iver SL0 207 D3
North Rd
Amersham HP6 154 C3
Berkhamsted HP4 135 B4
Chorleywood WD3 167 D4
Cryers Hill HP15 162 D5
Maidenhead SL6 202 E7
West Drayton UB7 208 F3
North Ridge MK6 35 B1
North Row
Fulmer SL3 199 E8
Milton Keynes MK9 34 C2
North Saxon Rdbt MK14 34 D3
North Secklow Rdbt
MK14 34 E3
North Second St MK9 34 C2
North Seventh St MK9 34 D2
North Sixth St MK9 34 D2
North Skeldon Rdbt
MK9 35 A4
North Sq MK16 22 D5
North St
Castlethorpe MK19 19 F5
Milton Keynes, Bradville
MK13 34 A7
Milton Keynes, Fenny Stratford
MK2 47 C1
Thame OX9 125 F1
North Star La SL6 202 C6
North Tenth St MK9 34 E3
North Terr SL4 210 E7
North Third St MK9 34 C2
North Thirteenth St MK9 34 F3
NORTH TOWN 195 F1
North Town Cl 1 SL6 195 F1
North Town Mead 4
SL6 195 F1
North Town Moor SL6 195 F1
North Town Rd SL6 195 F1
North Twelfth St MK9 34 F3
Northumberland Ave
HP21 116 B6
Northumberland Cl
TW19 213 E1
Northumbria Rd SL6 202 B4
North View HP22 87 B3
North Way
Deanshanger NN12 31 E5
Potterspury NN12 18 E2
Uxbridge UB10 201 E5
NORTH WESTON 136 F8
Northwich MK6 47 D7
Northwick Rd MK10 35 F1
North Witan Rdbt MK13 34 D2
Northwood Rd TW6 213 D6
Nortoft Rd SL9 177 F5
Norton Leys MK7 48 C7
Norton Rd UB8 201 D2
Norton's Pl MK18 52 C8
Nortons The MK7 48 B3
Norvic Rd HP23 105 A1
Norway Dr SL2 206 B8
Norwich Ho
High Wycombe HP13 173 F8
Maidenhead SL6 202 E8
Norwood Cl HP20 101 F2
Norwood Ct 4 HP7 165 B7
Norwood La
Newport Pagnell MK16 22 C3
Uxbridge SL0 200 D1
Norwood Rd HP10 174 B2
Notley Farm HP18 126 A7
Nottingham Gr MK3 46 E2
Nottingham Ho 3
HP13 173 F7
Nottingham Rd WD3 167 C1
Nova Lodge MK4 46 B2
Novello Croft MK7 48 D4
Nugent Cl HP19 101 D4
Nugent Ct
Chesham HP5 144 A3
Marlow SL7 183 F3
Nuneham Gr MK4 45 F3
NUP END 89 B3
Nup End Cl HP22 89 B3
Nup End La HP22 89 B3
Nurseries The LU6 92 E6
Nursery Cl
2 Amersham HP7 165 E8
Aylesbury HP21 115 C5
Tylers Green HP10 174 C8
Nursery Ct HP12 172 D6
Nursery Dr HP14 171 B5
Nursery Gdns
Milton Keynes MK13 34 A4
Tring HP23 119 B4
Nursery La
Slough SL3 206 D5
Tylers Green HP10 174 C8
Nursery Pl SL4 211 B1
Nursery Rd SL6 204 B7
Nursery Way TW19 211 D1
Nursery Waye UB8 201 D4
Nursery Wlk SL7 183 B1
Nutfield La HP11 172 F8
Nuthatch 10 HP19 101 F3
Nutkins Way HP5 144 C2
Nutkin Wlk UB10 201 E5
Nutmeg Cl MK7 48 B5
Nye Way HP3 146 A3
Nymans Gate 8 MK4 45 F1

O

Oak Barn Cl MK43 25 A1
Oak Cres HP12 172 C4
Oak Ct MK9 34 E2
Oakdene HP9 175 E3
Oakdown Cres MK46 6 F3
Oak Dr HP4 135 D3
Oak End Dr SL0 200 C3
Oak End Way
Chinnor OX39 147 D5
Gerrards Cross SL9 188 F6
Oaken Gr SL6 195 C1
Oakengrove HP16 151 C5
Oakengrove Cl HP15 163 C6
Oakengrove La HP15 163 B3
Oakengrove Rd HP15 163 A3
Oaken Head MK4 46 C2
Oakeshott Ave HP14 161 D6
Oakfield WD3 167 F2
Oak Field HP5 144 B1
Oakfield Ave SL1 205 B5
Oakfield Cl HP6 154 C2
Oakfield Cnr HP6 154 C2
Oakfield Fst Sch SL4 210 B5
Oakfield Rd
Aylesbury HP20 116 A8
Bourne End SL8 185 A3
Oak Gn HP21 115 C7
Oak Green Sch HP21 115 C7
OAKGROVE 35 D2
Oakgrove L Ctr MK10 35 F2
Oakgrove Rdbt MK10 35 F2
Oakgrove Sch MK10 35 F2
Oakham Rise MK4 45 E1
OAKHILL 45 D4
Oakhill Cl
Maple Cross WD3 178 E6
Milton Keynes MK5 45 E6
Oakhill Rd
Maple Cross WD3 178 D6
Milton Keynes, Hazeley
MK5 45 D5
Milton Keynes, Shenley Church
End MK5 45 F6
Oakhill Rdbt MK5 45 D5
Oakhurst SL6 196 B4
Oakington Ave HP6 166 E8
Oak La
Buckland Common
HP23 133 A2
Windsor SL4 210 A6
Oaklands HP4 135 A4
Oaklands Ct HP6 154 C1
Oakland Way HP10 174 A1
Oak Lawn HP23 119 A3
OAKLEY
Brill 109 D5
Chinnor 147 B5
Oakley HP10 185 F7
Oakley CE Comb Sch
HP18 109 D4
Oakley Coll HP18 109 F1
Oakley Cres SL1 205 E6
Oakley Gdns MK15 35 B5
OAKLEY GREEN 209 B5
Oakley Green Rd SL4 209 B5
Oakley Hill Wildlife
Reserve★ OX39 147 D4
Oakley La OX39 147 B6
Oakley Rd
Brill HP18 110 A8
Chinnor OX39 147 C6
Horton-cum-S OX33 108 C5
Oak Rd HP27 139 C3
Oakridge MK4 46 E4
Oakridge Combined Sch
HP11 172 E7
Oakridge Ct HP12 172 D6
Oakridge Pl SL2 198 C8
Oakridge Rd HP11 172 E7
Oakside UB9 201 B6
Oaks Rd TW19 213 D2
Oak St HP11 173 C4
Oaks The HP4 135 A4
Oak Stubbs La SL6 203 F4
Oak Tree Ave SL7 183 D3
Oaktree Cl HP10 163 B2
Oak Tree Cl SL7 183 D3
Oak Tree Cotts HP18 83 B5
Oaktree Ct MK15 35 C7
Oak Tree Dr
Lane End HP14 171 C5
Slough SL3 207 B1
Oak Tree Rd SL7 183 D4
Oakview HP6 153 D4
Oak View
Great Kingshill HP15 162 D8
Towcester NN12 18 D3
Oakview Gdns SL3 206 F2
Oakway
Amersham HP6 154 B4
Winslow MK18 66 A4
Oakwell Cl LU6 93 F7
Oakwood HP10 174 A2
Oak wood HP4 134 F3
Oakwood Dr MK2 58 E7
Oakworth Ave MK10 36 A4
Oat Cl HP21 115 C3
Oatlands Dr SL1 205 D7
Oban Ct SL1 205 D4
Oberon Way MK4 45 D2
Observatory Sh Ctr 4
SL1 205 F4
Ockwells Nature Reserve★
SL6 202 E2
Ockwells Rd SL6 202 C2
Octagon Arc 10 HP11 173 A7
Octagon Par 6 HP11 173 A7
Octavian Dr MK13 33 F5
Octavian Way NN13 38 A7
Oddley La HP27 148 D8
Odds Farm Est HP10 186 B4
Odds Farm Park★
HP10 186 B4
Oddy Hill
Tring HP23 119 C3
Wigginton HP23 119 C2
Odell Cl MK6 47 C8
Odencroft Rd SL2 198 A2
Odney La SL6 196 B7
Offas La MK18 66 B5
Ogilvie Rd HP12 172 E7
O'Grady Way HP19 101 A3
Okeford Cl HP23 118 F4
Okeford Dr HP23 118 F4
Okeley La HP23 118 E3
Oldacres SL6 203 B7
Old Airfield Ind Est
HP23 104 D6
Old Amersham Rd SL9 189 B3
Old Bakery Ct SL0 207 F7
Old Bakery The
Aston Abbotts HP22 88 D5
Lane End HP14 171 B4
Old Barn Cl MK18 52 A4
Old Bix Rd RG9 191 A6
Old Brewery Cl HP21 115 E7
Old Brewery La RG9 191 E2
OLDBROOK 46 E8
Oldbrook Bvd MK6 46 E8
Oldbrook Fst Sch MK6 46 E8
Old Bryers Cl HP18 124 C2
Old Burrs HP21 115 D3
Oldbury Gr HP9 175 D5
Oldcastle Croft MK4 46 A1
Old Chapel Cl HP17 129 E3
Old Coach Dr HP11 174 A4
Old Common Rd WD3 167 D5
Old Court Cl SL6 202 B3
Old Dashwood Hill
HP14 159 F2
Old Dean HP3 146 A4
Olde Bell Cl MK17 69 E7
Olde Bell La MK5 46 A7
Old End MK18 53 B2
Old English Cl MK17 44 C1
Oldershaw Mews SL6 202 B8
Old Farm LU7 105 D4
Old Farm Cl
Beaconsfield HP9 175 C5
Slapton LU7 91 A3
Worminghall HP18 123 E5
Old Farm La HP7 165 E6
OLD FARM PARK 48 E5
Old Farm Rd
High Wycombe HP13 161 E2
West Drayton UB7 208 D4
Old Ferry Dr TW19 211 D1
Old Field Cl HP6 166 E8
Oldfield Prim Sch SL6 203 B6
Oldfield Rd SL6 203 B7
Old Fishery La HP1 146 F8
Old Fives Ct SL1 197 C2
Old Forge Cl
Maidenhead SL6 203 A3
Tingewick MK18 51 B6
Old Forge Gdns HP22 102 B4
Old Forge Rd HP10 174 C2
Old Forge The HP23 104 B4
Old Gaol Mus★ MK18 41 D1
Old Garden Ctr The
HP27 139 B3
Old Groveway MK6 47 D5
Oldham Rise MK5 45 E5
Oldhams Mdw 9 HP20 101 F2
Old Hardenwaye HP13 162 E1
Old Heatherdene Cotts
HP15 162 D8
Old Horns La SL7 172 A3
Oldhouse Cl HP11 172 E3
Old House Ct SL3 206 D7
Old Kiln Rd
Flackwell Heath HP10 185 A8
Tylers Green HP10 163 C2
OLD LINSLADE 70 D2
Old Linslade Rd LU7 70 E3
Old Lodge Dr HP9 175 E1
Old Maltings The
Buckingham MK18 52 C7
Thame OX9 125 E1
Old Manor Cl
Askett HP27 139 C7
Whaddon MK17 45 B1
Old Manor Ct LU7 78 E8
Old Marsh La SL6 203 F4
Old Mead SL9 177 E4
Old Meadow Cl HP4 135 A2
Old Mews The MK46 6 F4
Old Mill Cl HP17 127 A6
Old Mill Furlong MK18 66 A5
Old Mill Gdns 12 HP4 135 D4
Old Mill La
Maidenhead SL6 203 D4
Uxbridge UB8 208 B8
Old Mill Pl TW19 212 B1
Old Mill Rd UB9 190 A1
Old Moor La HP10 185 E8
Old Nursery Ct SL2 187 C2
Old Oak Gdns HP4 134 E7
Old Orch
Henton OX39 137 E2
Iver SL0 207 F7
Old Orchard Mews 1
HP4 135 C4
Old Orchards HP22 102 A3
Old Oxford Rd HP14 160 C1
Old Palace Ct SL3 212 D6
Old Papermill Cl HP10 185 E8
Old Plough Cl HP18 112 B2
Old Post Office La 11
SL6 202 F7
Old Rd LU7 80 E7
Old Rd The RG9 179 C8
Old Rectory La UB9 189 E4
Old Risborough Rd
HP22 130 A8
Old Sax La HP5 143 D4
Old School Cl HP22 117 C1
Old School Cotts HP5 145 D5
Old School Ct
Buckingham MK18 52 C8
Eaton Bray LU6 92 E6
Old School La MK17 69 E8
Old School La The MK18 63 D3
Old School Rd UB8 201 F1
Old School The HP10 185 D4
Old Shire La WD3 167 B3
Old Slade La SL0 207 F2
Old Springfields MK18 53 C2
Old Stable Yd MK19 32 C7
Old Stable Yd The MK18 65 F4
Old Station Cl MK18 66 A5
Old Station La TW19 212 A1
Old Station Way HP10 185 E5
Old Stoke Rd HP21 115 D6
OLD STRATFORD 32 B7
Old Stratford Prim Sch
MK19 32 B6
Old Tan Yard Cl MK18 65 F4
OLD TOWN 38 A7
Old Town NN13 38 A7
Old Town Cl HP9 175 E1
Old Town Farm HP16 152 A7
Old Union Way OX9 125 E1
Old Uxbridge Rd WD3 178 E3
Old Vicarage Way
HP10 185 D4
Old Watery La HP10 185 E8
Oldway La SL1 204 D5
Old Windmill Way
HP18 125 C7
OLD WINDSOR 211 A1
OLD WOLVERTON 33 D8
Old Wolverton Rd MK12 33 C8
Oliffe Cl HP20 101 D3
Oliffe Way HP20 101 D3
Oliver Rd MK2 58 C8
Oliver Row 4 MK4 45 E3
Oliver's Paddock SL7 183 D5
Olivia Dr SL3 206 F1
Olivier Way HP20 116 A8
Olleberrie La WD4 156 D7
OLNEY 6 E4
Olney Ind Est MK46 6 F6
Olney Inf Sch MK46 6 E3
Olney Mid Sch MK46 6 F5
Olney Rd
Emberton MK46 13 F8
Lavendon MK46 7 E7
Olson Cotts HP14 158 F4
Olympic Ho UB8 201 F1
O'Neill Rd MK8 45 D6
One Pin La SL2 187 D1
One Tree La HP9 175 E3
Onslow Ct MK7 48 A4
Onslow Dr OX9 126 B1
Onslow Gdns HP13 173 E7
Onslow Mills UB7 208 D6
Opal Ct SL3 199 C1
Opal Dr MK15 35 F4
Opecks Cl SL3 199 B1
Opendale Rd SL1 204 B8
Open University (Walton
Hall) The MK7 47 F7
Oram Ct 3 SL7 183 D2
Orbell Ct HP27 139 B3
Orbison Ct MK8 45 D7
Orchard Ave
Berkhamsted HP4 135 A4
Slough SL1 204 D8
Windsor SL4 210 A6
Orchard Bglws SL2 197 F5
Orchard Cl
15 Aylesbury HP20 101 F3
Beaconsfield HP9 175 D3
Chorleywood WD3 167 D5
Cranfield MK43 25 A1
Hughenden Valley HP14 162 A7
Longwick HP27 138 D7
Maidenhead SL6 203 A3
Milton Keynes MK3 57 F7
New Denham UB9 201 B6
Newton Longville MK17 57 C3
Oakley HP18 109 D4
Slough SL1 197 B1
Stoke Mandeville HP22 116 B1
Upper Arncott OX25 94 D6
Waddesdon HP18 99 A7
Wendover HP22 131 A5
Wingrave HP22 89 B3
Yardley Gobion NN12 18 F6
Orchard Ct
Aylesbury HP21 115 F6
Bovingdon HP3 146 A4
Harmondsworth TW6 213 C7
Seer Green HP9 176 C5
Orchard Dene MK18 41 D1
Orchard Dr
Aston Clinton HP22 117 E4
Chorleywood WD3 167 D5
Hazelmere HP15 163 A3
Leighton Buzzard LU7 80 D6
Uxbridge UB8 201 D1
Wooburn HP10 185 D4
Orchard End
Edlesborough LU6 92 E4
Hazelmere HP15 163 B6
Orchard End Ave HP7 165 F8
Orchard Gate SL2 198 C7
Orchard Gr
Chalfont St Peter SL9 177 C2
Flackwell Heath HP10 185 B7
Maidenhead SL6 202 C7
Orchard Ho
8 Bourne End SL8 185 A4
Milton Keynes MK12 33 D6
Orchard La
Amersham HP6 154 D1
Harrold MK43 3 F7
Prestwood HP16 151 C6
Stewkley LU7 78 E7
ORCHARD LEIGH 145 B3
Orchard Leigh Villas
HP5 145 A4
Orchard Lodge SL1 204 E5
Orchard Mews HP9 176 D4
Orchard Mill SL8 185 B1
Orchard Pk HP15 163 C6
Orchard Pl
Monks Risborough
HP27 139 C5
Uxbridge UB8 201 D5
Westbury NN13 39 A4
Orchard Rd
Beaconsfield HP9 175 F1
Chalfont St Giles HP8 177 C8
Loudwater HP13 174 A4
Old Windsor SL4 211 B1
Seer Green HP9 176 C5
Orchard Rise MK46 6 F3
Orchard Row HP14 171 A7
Orchard Sch MK6 35 B2
Orchards The
Eaton Bray LU6 92 E7
Little Kingshill HP16 152 A2
Slough SL3 206 F5
Tring HP23 118 F3
Orchard The
Aston Clinton HP22 117 E5
Flackwell Heath HP10 185 B7
Halton HP22 131 C8
Hazelmere HP15 163 A6
Hillesden MK18 63 A7
Marlow SL7 183 E3
Potterspury NN12 18 C3
Walter's Ash HP14 161 E6
Orchard View
Hillesden MK18 63 B7
Uxbridge UB8 201 D1
ORCHARDVILLE 197 B1

Orchardville SL1 197 B1
Orchard Way
Aylesbury HP20 101 F2
Bovingdon HP3 146 A3
Chinnor OX39 147 C5
Cranfield MK43 25 A1
East Claydon MK18 74 E6
Eaton Bray LU6 92 F5
Holmer Green HP15 163 C6
North Crawley MK16 24 A6
Pitstone LU7 105 E4
Slough SL3 206 F5
Stoke Goldington MK16 12 B7
Wing LU7 79 E2
Orchard Waye UB8 201 D3
Orchard Wlk MK46 7 F7
Orchehill Ave SL9 188 D7
Orchehill Ct SL9 188 E6
Orchehill Rise SL9 188 E6
Oregano Cl UB7 208 F6
Orford Ct MK5 46 B6
Oriel Cl MK12 33 B6
Oriel Cotts MK18 63 D2
Orkney Cl
Milton Keynes MK3 46 F2
Stewkley LU7 78 E8
Orkney Ct SL6 196 E5
Ormesby Cl HP21 116 A5
Ormonde MK14 34 D7
Ormond Rd OX9 126 A1
Ormsgill Ct MK13 34 B5
Orne Gdns MK15 35 A7
Orpington Gr MK5 46 B4
Ortensia Dr MK7 48 C7
Orwell Cl
Aylesbury HP21 115 D4
Newport Pagnell MK16 21 F5
Windsor SL4 210 D4
Orwell Dr HP21 115 D4
Osborne Ct SL4 210 C5
Osborne Mews SL4 210 C5
Osborne Rd SL4 210 D4
Osborne St
Milton Keynes MK2 58 C7
Slough SL1 205 F4
Osborne Way HP23 119 D1
Osborn Rd UB8 201 C5
Osborn's Ct 5 MK46 6 F3
Osbourne St MK12 33 D6
Osier La MK5 46 B4
Osier Way
Aylesbury HP20 115 F8
Buckingham MK18 52 C6
Osmington Pl HP23 118 F4
Osney Rd SL6 195 E2
Osprey Cl
Milton Keynes MK6 47 B8
West Drayton UB7 208 E4
Osprey The HP19 101 E4
Osprey Wlk
Aylesbury HP19 101 E4
Buckingham MK18 52 F7
Osterley Cl MK16 22 C3
Ostler Gate SL6 195 C1
Ostlers Ct HP11 174 A4
Ostlers La MK11 32 D6
Otterburn Cres MK5 45 D5
Otter Cl MK3 46 D1
Otterfield Rd UB7 208 E6
Otters Brook MK18 52 E7
Otway Cl HP21 115 E3
Oulton Cl HP21 116 A5
Our Lady of Peace RC Inf Sch SL1 204 C8
Our Lady of Peace RC Jun Sch SL1 204 C8
Our Lady's RC Prim Sch HP6 154 B4
Ousebank St MK16 22 D5
Ousebank Way MK11 32 D5
Ousedale Sch
Newport Pagnell MK16 22 B3
Olney MK46 6 E4
Ouseley Rd TW19 211 D1
Outfield Rd SL9 177 D3
Outlook Dr HP8 177 D7
Ouzel Cl MK3 46 E1
Oval The MK6 46 E7
Oval Way SL9 188 E7
Overdale Rd HP5 144 B3
Overdales HP15 162 F3
Overgate MK6, MK9, MK14 35 B4
Over Hampden HP16 151 C7
Overhills MK46 6 E4
Overn Ave MK18 41 C1
Overn Cl MK18 41 D1
Overn Cres MK18 41 C1
Overshot Ho HP10 174 C2
Oversley Ct MK14 22 A1
Overstone Cl LU7 79 E2
Overstone Comb Sch LU7 79 E2
Overstrand HP22 117 E5
Overstreet MK15 35 A6
Over the Misbourne UB9 189 B5
Over the Misbourne Rd UB9 189 C5
Overton Dr OX9 126 B1
Oville Ct MK5 46 B5
OVING 86 D8
Oving Rd HP22 86 E7
Ovitts Cl MK18 66 A5
Owen Cl 4 SL3 206 F1
Owl Cl 5 HP19 101 F3
Owlsears Cl HP9 175 D4
OWLSWICK 128 D1
Oxendon Ct LU7 70 F2
Oxenhope Way MK10 36 A4
Oxfield Cl HP4 135 A3
Oxfield Park Dr MK19 32 C7
Oxford Ave
Burnham SL1 197 B3
Slough SL1 204 F8
Oxford Gdns UB9 190 A1
Oxford Rd
Aylesbury HP17, HP21 115 B7
Denham UB9 189 D2
Gerrards Cross SL9 188 D5
High Wycombe HP11 173 A7
Marlow SL7 183 D2
Oakley HP18 109 D5
Piddington HP14 160 D1
Stokenchurch HP14 158 D5
Stone HP17 114 C5
Thame OX9 125 E1
Uxbridge UB8, UB9 201 B6
Windsor SL4 210 C6
Oxford Road E SL4 210 C6
Oxford St
5 High Wycombe HP11 173 A7
Lee Common HP16 142 D5
Milton Keynes, Fenny Stratford MK2 58 C8
Milton Keynes, Stony Stratford MK11 32 D5
Milton Keynes, Wolverton MK12 33 D6
Oxhouse Ct MK5 46 A3
OXLEY PARK 45 E3
Oxley Park Rdbt MK5 45 F3
Oxleys MK46 6 E4
Oxman La MK12 33 A5
Oxwich Gr MK4 57 B8

P

Pace Ctr The HP19 101 B2
Packet Boat La UB8 208 C7
Packhorse Rd SL9 188 E6
Pack & Prime La RG9 191 C2
PADBURY 53 B2
Padbury CE Fst Sch MK18 53 C2
Padbury Oaks UB7 213 B6
Padcroft Rd UB7 208 D5
Paddock Cl
8 Aylesbury HP19 100 F1
Maidenhead SL6 202 A2
Milton Keynes MK14 34 E8
Paddock Cotts SL6 202 A2
Paddocks Clinic The (private) HP27 139 C4
Paddocks End HP9 176 C4
Paddocks The
Chorleywood WD3 167 F5
Flackwell Heath HP10 185 B8
Haddenham HP17 127 A5
High Wycombe HP12 172 B3
Leighton Buzzard LU7 80 F8
Prestwood HP16 151 C5
Steeple Claydon MK18 63 E3
Wendover HP22 131 B5
Paddock The
Aylesbury HP21 116 C7
Chalfont St Peter SL9 177 E5
Datchet SL3 211 B6
Emberton MK46 13 E8
Maidenhead SL6 195 C2
Maids Moreton MK18 41 E4
Paddock Way MK2 47 D1
Padstow Ave MK6 34 F1
Padstow Cl
Aylesbury HP20 101 F1
Slough SL3 206 E3
PAGE HILL 41 F2
Page Hill Ave MK18 41 E1
Pages Croft HP4 135 A6
Pages La UB8 201 C6
Pages Wharf SL6 203 C8
Paget Cl SL7 183 F4
Paget Ct UB7 208 E4
Paget Dr SL6 202 A4
Paget Rd SL3 206 F2
Pagg's Ct MK16 22 D4
Pagoda Rdbt MK15 35 C5
Pagoda The SL6 196 B1
Paignton Way 2 MK10 36 A3
Paines Orch LU7 105 A8
Pakenham Cl HP19 114 F8
Palace Cl SL1 204 F5
Palace Sq MK6 46 F7
Palfreyman St HP19 101 D4
Palliser Rd HP8 177 B6
Palmer Ave
Aylesbury HP19 115 C8
Upper Arncott OX25 94 F8
Palmers Cl SL6 202 A3
PALMERS MOOR 201 A1
Palmers Moor MK18 54 A8
Palmer's Moor La SL0 201 A1
Palmers Rd MK46 7 A3
Palmerston Ave SL3 206 B3
Pankridge Dr HP16 151 C7
Panleigh Cotts HP14 171 B3
Pannier Pl MK14 35 A5
Pann Mill HP13 173 C6
Panters Cl MK17 44 C1
Pantile Row SL3 207 A2
Pantile Wlk UB8 201 C5
Paprika Ct MK7 48 B5
Papworth Cl MK16 22 F3
Parade Ct 7 SL8 185 A4
Parade The
Bourne End SL8 185 A3
Farnham Common SL2 198 C6
High Wycombe HP11 172 F6
Uxbridge UB8 208 C8
Windsor SL4 209 D6
Paradise MK17 57 D4
Paradise Mews RG9 191 D2
Paradise Rd RG9 191 C1
Parchment Cl HP6 154 E2
Parish La SL2 187 C1
Parish Piece HP15 163 C7
Park Ave
Newport Pagnell MK16 22 B4
Totternhoe LU6 93 B8
Wraysbury TW19 211 D3
Park Cl
Cosgrove MK19 19 F2
Dunton MK18 77 E5
Lane End HP14 171 C5
Windsor SL4 210 D5
Park Cnr SL4 209 E4
Park Ct UB8 201 D4
Parker Cl MK13 34 A6
Parker Knoll Way HP13 173 A7
Parker Wlk HP19 101 D3
Park Farm Rd HP12 161 B1
Park Farm Way HP14 171 C5
Parkfield WD3 167 F5
Parkfield Ave HP6 154 D2
Parkfield Rise HP27 139 B2
Parkgate SL1 197 C1
Park Gate LU7 79 E1
Park Gdns MK3 47 A1
Park Gr
Beaconsfield HP9 175 C7
Little Chalfont HP8 166 D6
Park Hill OX33 122 B1
Park Ho
Berkhamsted HP4 135 B5
Gerrards Cross SL9 188 E7
Maidenhead SL6 202 E6
Park House Bsns Ctr HP12 172 E8
Park House Dr MK5 45 F6
Park La
Beaconsfield HP9 175 F1
Burnham SL1 197 E7
Eaton Bray LU6 92 D6
Hazelmere HP15 163 A4
Horton SL3 212 A4
Lane End HP14 171 D5
Maidensgrove RG9 179 D6
Paulerspury NN12 17 B7
Slough SL3 206 B3
Stokenchurch HP14 158 E6
Parkland Ave SL3 206 D2
Parklands MK14 21 D1
Park Lane Ct HP14 158 E5
Park Lawn SL2 198 C2
Park Lodge Ave UB7 208 F4
Park Mdw HP27 139 A3
Parkminster MK10 36 A1
Park Parade SL2 198 C3
Park Parade Ctr The HP15 163 A5
Park Pl
Amersham HP6 154 F1
Seer Green HP9 176 D5
Park Rd
Amersham HP6 154 F2
Chesham HP5 154 B8
Farnham Royal SL2 198 E3
Granborough MK18 75 F6
Grendon Underwood HP18 82 F8
Hanslope MK19 11 B1
Hartwell NN7 10 C8
Henley-on-Thames RG9 191 E1
Milton Keynes MK11 32 D5
Sherington MK16 14 A2
Stanwell TW19 213 C1
Tring HP23 118 F2
Uxbridge UB8 201 E6
Winslow MK18 65 F5
Park Rise HP4 134 E6
Park Road E UB10 201 D3
Park Road S MK18 65 F4
Park Sch HP20 101 F1
Parkside
Gerrards Cross SL9 188 F7
Henley-on-Thames RG9 191 C2
Maidenhead SL6 195 D1
Milton Keynes MK4 46 E3
Naphill HP14 150 B1
Parkside Wlk SL1 206 A3
Park Sports Ctr OX33 122 B1
Park St
Aylesbury HP20 115 F8
Berkhamsted HP4 135 B5
High Wycombe HP11 173 D6
Maidenhead SL6 202 F7
Poyle SL3 212 D6
Princes Risborough HP27 139 B3
Slough SL1 205 F4
Tring HP23 119 A3
Windsor SL4 210 D6
Woburn MK17 60 F7
Parkstone Lodge SL3 206 A3
Park Street Ind Est HP20 115 F8
Parkview
Flackwell Heath HP10 185 B7
Maidenhead SL6 202 F7
Park View
Newport Pagnell MK16 22 D4
West Drayton UB7 208 E6
Parkview Chase SL1 204 E7
Park View Ct
Berkhamsted HP4 135 B4
High Wycombe HP12 172 D8
4 Leighton Buzzard LU7 80 E7
Park View Rd
Berkhamsted HP4 135 B4
Uxbridge UB8 208 F7
Parkway
Bow Brickhill MK17 48 D2
Marlow SL7 184 A3
Woburn Sands MK17 49 A6
Parkway The SL0 200 C4
Parkwood HP14 150 A2
Park Wood, Gouldings Wood Nature Reserve★ SL6 194 E4
Parlaunt Park Comb Sch SL3 207 B3
Parlaunt Rd SL3 207 B2
Parliament Cl HP16 151 B7
Parliament La SL6, SL1 196 F5
Parliament Rd OX9 125 F1
Parmiter Cl HP19 115 B8
PARMOOR 181 F7
Parmoor La RG9 170 E1
Parneleys MK10 35 F2
Parrishs Piece HP22 87 B3
Parrock La MK10 36 A2
Parrot Cl HP21 115 B6
Parrott's La HP23 133 A4
Parrs Rd HP14 158 E4
Parry Cotts SL9 177 E6
Parry Green N SL3 206 F2
Parry Green S SL3 207 A2
Parsley Cl
Aston Clinton HP22 117 C5
Walton MK7 48 B5
Parslow Cl HP21 115 D3
Parslow Ct HP21 115 D3
Parsonage Cl
High Wycombe HP13 173 C6
Tring HP23 119 A4
Parsonage Ct 1 HP23 119 A3
Parsonage Farm HP22 89 B3
Parsonage Gdns SL7 183 E1
Parsonage La
Farnham Common SL2 198 D5
Windsor SL4 210 A6
Parsonage Pl HP7 165 C8
Parsonage Rd HP8 177 B7
Parson Cl MK18 65 F4
Parsons Cl LU7 78 E8
Parsons Cres MK5 46 C5
Parson's Fee HP20 115 D8
Parsons La HP22 102 B3
Parsons Rd SL3 206 F1
Parsons Wlk HP15 163 C6
Parson's Wood La SL2 198 D5
Parton Cl HP22 131 A5
Parton Rd HP20 116 B8
Partridge Cl
Buckingham MK18 52 F7
Chesham HP5 144 E3
Leighton Buzzard LU7 104 F7
Partridge Mead SL6 195 F2
Partridge Piece MK43 25 C3
Partridge Way
7 Aylesbury HP19 101 F3
High Wycombe HP13 161 C2
Pascal Dr MK5 45 E5
Pascomb Rd LU6 93 F8
Passalewe La MK7 48 D7
PASSENHAM 32 C4
Passmore MK6 47 D6
Pastern Pl MK14 35 A5
Pastures The
Aylesbury HP20 102 B2
Edlesborough LU6 92 F3
High Wycombe HP13 161 E1
Patch Cl UB10 201 F4
Patches Field SL7 183 E5
Pateman Cl MK18 41 C1
Patemore La RG9 168 A1
Paterson Rd HP21 115 C6
Patricia Cl SL1 204 E6
Patrick Haugh Rd OX25 94 F7
Patricks La MK19 31 F4
Patrick Way HP21 116 A4
Patrington Cl UB8 201 C2
Patriot Dr MK13 34 B2
Patrons Way E UB9 189 F5
Patrons Way W UB9 189 F5
Patterson Ct HP10 185 E7
Patterson Rd HP5 144 B3
Pattison La MK15 35 C3
PAULERSPURY 17 B7
Paulerspury CE Prim Sch NN12 17 B8
Pauls Hill HP10 174 F6
Paul's Row HP11 173 B6
Pavers Ct HP21 115 D3
Pavilion Cl HP20 116 A8
Pavilions The (Sh Ctr) UB8 201 C5
Pavilion Way HP6 166 C8
Paxton Ave SL1 205 C3
Paxton Cl MK46 6 F3
Paxton Cres MK5 46 B5
Paxton Rd HP4 135 D4
Paynes Ct MK18 41 D1
Paynes Dr MK5 46 A8
Paynes Field Cl HP4 134 D7
Payton Hos SL6 195 E6
Peace La SL6 195 F6
Peace Rd SL0, SL3 200 A3
Peachey Cl UB8 208 D7
Peachey La UB8 208 D8
Peach Tree Ave UB7 208 F7
Peacock Hay MK4 46 C2
Peacock Rd SL7 184 A3
Peacocks Cl HP4 134 F6
Pea La HP4 134 D7
Pearce Cl
Aylesbury HP21 115 E4
Maidenhead SL6 195 F1
Pearce Dr SL6 195 F7
Pearce Rd
Chesham HP5 144 B2
Maidenhead SL6 195 F1
Pearce's Orch RG9 191 D3
Pearl Gdns SL1 205 B5
Pearse Gr MK7 48 A4
Pearson Cl HP19 115 B6
Pear Tree Ave UB7 208 F7
Peartree Cl SL1 204 F5
Pear Tree Cl
Amersham HP7 165 F8
Seer Green HP9 176 C4
Pear Tree Ct HP15 163 C6
Pear Tree Farm Ind Units OX27 71 E2
Peartrees UB7 208 D6
Peascod Pl 12 SL4 210 D6
Peascod St SL4 210 D6
Peascroft HP18 125 D6
Peatey Ct HP13 173 D6
Pebble Brook Sch HP21 115 C7
Pebble La
Aylesbury HP20 115 D8
Brackley NN13 38 A7
Pebblemoor LU6 92 F3
Pebody Pl 10 MK46 6 F3
Peckover Ct 8 MK8 33 F1
Pecks Farm Cl HP22 102 C4
Peddle Ct HP11 172 F7
Pednor Bottom HP5 143 B3
PEDNORMEAD END 154 A7
Pednormead End HP5 154 B7
Pednor Rd HP5 143 E2
Peebles Pl MK3 46 F3
Peel Cl SL4 210 B4
Peel Ct
Monks Risborough HP27 139 B4
Slough SL1 205 B8
Peel Rd MK12 33 C6
Peel Way UB8 208 E8
Peerless Dr UB9 190 C7
Peers Dr MK17 49 E3
Peers La MK5 46 B6
Peggs La HP22 117 F5
Pelham Ct SL6 202 E7
Pelham Pl MK14 34 F5
Pelham Rd OX9 126 B1
Pelton Ct MK5 46 C5
Pemberley Lodge SL4 210 A4
Pemberton Cl HP21 115 F5
Pemberton Rd SL2 197 E1
Pembridge Chase 4 HP3 146 A3
Pembridge Cl 3 HP3 146 A3
Pembridge Gr MK4 45 E1
Pembridge Rd HP3 146 A3
Pembroke Ho
2 Milton Keynes MK3 46 F1
7 Olney MK46 6 F3
Pembroke Rd HP20 101 F1

Pencarrow Pl MK6 . . . . . . 35 A1
Pendeen Ct SL1 . . . . 205 A5
Pendennis Ct MK4 . . . . . . 57 A8
Pendles Paddocks
HP14 . . . . 158 F2
Pendrill Ho 2 HP12 . . . . 172 E7
Penfold HP22 . . . . 116 F2
Penfold Cotts HP15 . . . . 163 D7
Penfold La
Holmer Green HP15 . . . . . 163 E8
Hyde Heath HP7, HP15 . . 152 F1
Pengelly Ct 2 MK6 . . . . . 35 A1
Penhale Cl MK4 . . . . 57 B8
Penhow Rise MK4 . . . . 45 E1
Penina Cl MK3 . . . . 46 D1
Penington Rd HP9 . . . . . 186 B8
Penlee Rise MK4 . . . . 57 B8
Penley Cl OX39 . . . . 147 B6
Penling Cl SL6 . . . . 195 E6
Penmon Cl MK10 . . . . 35 F1
Penmoor Cl HP12 . . . . . . 172 C8
PENN 174 E7
Penn Ave HP5 . . . . 144 A1
Penn Cl
Chorleywood WD3 . . . . . . 167 D3
Uxbridge UB8 . . . . 201 D1
Penn Ct
14 Marlow SL7 . . . . 183 E2
Tylers Green HP10 . . . . . . 174 B8
Penn Dr UB9 . . . . 189 F5
Pennefather Ct 3
HP21 . . . . 115 E7
Penn Gaskell La SL9 . . . 177 F5
Penn Gn HP9 . . . . 175 D4
Penn Haven SL9 . . . . 188 F6
Pennine Rd SL2 . . . . 205 A8
Pennings The HP22 . . . . . 131 B5
Pennington Pl OX9 . . . . . 126 B1
Pennington Rd
Chalfont St Peter SL9 . . . 177 D3
High Wycombe HP13 . . . 173 F6
Penningtons The HP6 . . 154 E2
Penn Mdw SL2 . . . . 198 F4
Penn Mead HP10 . . . . 174 F7
Penn Rd
Aylesbury HP21 . . . . 115 D7
Beaconsfield HP9 . . . . 175 C5
Chalfont St Peter SL9 . . . 177 D2
Chorleywood WD3 . . . . . . 167 F1
Datchet SL3 . . . . 211 D6
Hazlemere HP15 . . . . 163 B3
Milton Keynes MK2 . . . . . . 58 E8
Slough SL2 . . . . 198 D1
Penn Sch HP10 . . . . 174 D7
PENN STREET 164 B5
Penn Street Works Ind Est
HP7 . . . . 164 A4
Penn Way WD3 . . . . 167 D3
Penn Wood Sch SL2 . . . 198 D1
Penn Wood View HP7 . . 164 A4
Pennycress Way MK16 . . 21 F4
Pennycuik MK17 . . . . 59 C1
PENNYLAND 35 A6
Pennylets Gn SL2 . . . . . . 199 A5
Penny Pk Rd MK16 . . . . . . 22 F3
Pennyroyal MK7 . . . . 48 B7
Penrith Cl UB8 . . . . 201 D5
Penrith Way HP21 . . . . . . 116 B7
Penryn Ave MK6 . . . . 35 A2
Penshurst Cl SL9 . . . . . . 177 D1
Penshurst Cres MK6 . . . . 47 D4
Penshurst Rd SL6 . . . . . . 202 D5
Pentewan Gate MK6 . . . . 34 F2
Pentland Rd
Aylesbury HP21 . . . . 115 F6
Slough SL2 . . . . 205 A8
Pentlands MK11 . . . . 32 F4
Pentlands Ct HP13 . . . . . 174 B4
Pentlands The HP13 . . . . 174 B4
Penwith Sch MK6 . . . . 34 F1
Penwood Ct SL6 . . . . 202 B7
Penwood La SL7 . . . . 183 C1
Penyston Rd SL6 . . . . 202 C7
Penzance Spur SL2 . . . . 198 B1
Peplar Way SL1 . . . . 197 B2
Peplow Cl UB7 . . . . 208 D5
Peppard Mdw HP16 . . . . 151 D5
Pepper Hill Fst Sch
MK13 . . . . 34 A7
PEPPERSHILL 124 D6
Peppett's Gn HP5 . . . . . . 143 D8
Peppiatts The LU6 . . . . . . 92 B5
Pepys Cl SL3 . . . . 212 B8
Pepys Dr HP16 . . . . 151 C6
Perch Cl SL7 . . . . 194 C8
Percheron Pl MK14 . . . . . . 34 F5
Perch Mdws HP22 . . . . . 131 B8
Percy Bush Rd UB7 . . . . 208 F3
Percy Pl SL3 . . . . 211 B6
Percy Terr HP8 . . . . 177 A7
Peregrine HP19 . . . . 101 E3
Peregrine Bsns Pk
HP13 . . . . 174 A5
Peregrine Cl MK6 . . . . 47 B8
Perivale MK10 . . . . 35 E1
Perks La HP16 . . . . 151 C3
Permayne MK13 . . . . 34 A7
Perracombe MK4 . . . . 46 E3
Perran Ave MK6 . . . . 35 A1
Perrin Springs La RG9 . . 170 F1
Perrycroft SL4 . . . . 209 F4
Perryfields Way SL1 . . . . 197 B1
Perry Hill HP18 . . . . 73 A3
Perry Ho SL1 . . . . 197 B2
Perry La
Bledlow HP27 . . . . 138 C2
Sherington MK16 . . . . 14 B2
Perryman Way SL2 . . . . . 197 F2
Perry Mead LU6 . . . . 92 E6
Perry St HP22 . . . . 131 A5
Perrys The HP22 . . . . 131 B5
Pershore Croft 1 MK10 . 36 A1
Perth Ave SL1 . . . . 205 B7
Perth Cl MK3 . . . . 46 F2
Perth Rd HP13 . . . . 173 D8
Perth Trad Est SL1 . . . . . 205 B8
Peterborough Ave 2
HP13 . . . . 173 C7
Peterborough Gate
MK15 . . . . 35 C6
Peterhead Mews SL3 . . . 207 A1
Peterhill Cl SL9 . . . . 177 E5
Peterley Ave HP15,
HP16 . . . . 151 E3
Peterley La HP16 . . . . . . 151 E3
Peter's Cl HP16 . . . . 151 C6
Petersfield HP22 . . . . 116 C3
Petersfield Ave SL2 . . . . 206 A5
Petersfield Gn 5 MK9 . . 34 E1
Petersham Cl MK16 . . . . . 22 C2
Peters La HP27 . . . . 139 E4
Peter's Pl HP4 . . . . 134 E6
Petronel Rd HP19 . . . . . . 101 D4
PETSOE END 14 A7
Pettifer Way HP12 . . . . . 172 D6
Pettingrew Cl MK7 . . . . . . 48 B6
Petty Cross SL1 . . . . 204 E7
Petworth MK8 . . . . 33 E1
Petworth Ct SL4 . . . . 210 B6
Petworth Ho 2 MK8 . . . . 33 F1
Pevensey Cl
Aylesbury HP21 . . . . 116 B5
Milton Keynes MK3 . . . . . . 57 E7
Pevensey Rd SL2 . . . . 205 A8
Peverel Dr MK1 . . . . 47 B3
Peveril Cl HP21 . . . . 116 B5
Pevers La MK46 . . . . 6 A1
Pheasant Cl
Berkhamsted HP4 . . . . . . 135 C3
Tring HP23 . . . . 119 B6
Pheasant Dr HP13 . . . . . . 161 C1
Pheasant Hill HP8 . . . . . . 177 C8
Pheasant Rise HP5 . . . . . 154 D6
PHEASANTS 181 E6
Pheasants Croft SL6 . . . . 202 A4
Pheasants Dr HP15 . . . . . 163 B5
PHEASANT'S HILL 181 D3
Pheasants Ridge SL7 . . . 183 C7
Pheasant Wlk SL9 . . . . . . 177 E6
Phelps Rd MK2 . . . . 58 E6
Philbye Mews SL1 . . . . . 204 F4
Philip Cotts SL8 . . . . 185 C3
Philip Dr HP10 . . . . 185 C7
Philip Rd HP13 . . . . 173 D7
Philipshill Wood Reserve★
WD3 . . . . 167 A2
Philips Rd HP19 . . . . 115 A8
Phillimore Cl MK15 . . . . . . 35 B7
Phillip Ct MK5 . . . . 46 B6
Philpots Cl UB7 . . . . 208 D6
Philps Cl HP14 . . . . 171 C4
Phipps Cl
Aylesbury HP20 . . . . 102 A2
Maidenhead SL6 . . . . 202 A2
Phipps Rd SL1 . . . . 204 E8
Phoebe La MK17 . . . . 48 E6
Phoebe's Orch MK17 . . . . 69 E7
Phoenix Bsns Ctr 3
HP5 . . . . 144 B1
Phoenix Ct SL6 . . . . 202 D4
Phoenix Dr MK6 . . . . 46 E6
Phoenix Ho 7 HP19 . . . . 115 A8
Phoenix House Bsns Ctr
HP12 . . . . 172 E8
Phygtle The SL9 . . . . 177 E4
Phyllis Court Dr RG9 . . . 191 E3
Picasso Pl HP19 . . . . 100 F2
Piccadilly Mews MK18 . . . 66 A5
Pickering Dr MK4 . . . . 46 B2
Pickford Dr SL3 . . . . 207 A5
Pickfords Gdns SL1 . . . . 205 E5
Pickins Piece SL3 . . . . . . 212 A5
Pickwick Terr SL2 . . . . . 206 B6
Picton St MK4 . . . . 45 E1
Picts La HP27 . . . . 139 A2
PIDDINGTON
Blackthorn 95 E7
High Wycombe 160 B1
Northamptonshire 4 B8
Piddington La HP14 . . . . 171 B8
Piddington Rd HP18 . . . . . 96 A8
Pield Heath House Sch
UB8 . . . . 201 F1
Pield Heath Rd UB8 . . . . 201 F1
Pierson Rd SL4 . . . . 209 D6
Pigeon Farm Rd HP14 . . 158 E5
Piggotts End 6 HP7 . . . 165 B7
Piggott's Hill HP14 . . . . . 150 E1
Piggotts Orch HP7 . . . . . 165 B7
Piggy La WD3 . . . . 167 B3
Pightle Cres MK18 . . . . . . 41 D2
Pightle The
Buckingham MK18 . . . . 41 D1
Maids Moreton MK18 . . . . 41 F4
Oving HP22 . . . . 86 D7
Pitstone LU7 . . . . 105 D3
Pigott Dr MK5 . . . . 46 A5
Pigott Orch HP22 . . . . 85 A5
Pike Cl
Marlow SL7 . . . . 194 C8
Uxbridge UB10 . . . . 201 F4
Pike Cnr HP21 . . . . 116 C5
Pilch Field Wildlife
Reserve★ MK17 . . . . 54 B5
Pilch La MK17 . . . . 54 D4
Pilgrims Cl HP27 . . . . 139 B5
Pilgrim St MK15 . . . . 35 A4
Pilot Trad Est HP12 . . . . 172 E8
PIMLICO 26 F6
Pimlico Ct 4 MK10 . . . . . 35 F1
Pimms Cl HP13 . . . . 174 A6
Pimms Gr HP13 . . . . 174 A5
Pimpernel Gr MK7 . . . . . . 48 B6
Pinchfield WD3 . . . . 178 D5
Pinders Croft MK12 . . . . . 33 B5
PINDON END 10 C4
Pineapple Rd HP7 . . . . . . 165 F8
Pine Chase HP12 . . . . 172 B3
Pine Cl
Berkhamsted HP4 . . . . . . 135 B4
Buckingham MK18 . . . . 41 E3
Hazelmere HP15 . . . . 163 B3
Maidenhead SL6 . . . . 202 B7
Pine Crest Mews LU7 . . . 80 E6
Pinecroft SL7 . . . . 183 D4
Pine Ct HP5 . . . . 154 C8
Pine Gr MK17 . . . . 49 A4
PINEHAM 35 E7
Pineham Rdbt MK15 . . . . . 35 E5
Pine Hill HP15 . . . . 162 F3
Pinels Way HP11 . . . . 172 E3
Piner Cotts SL4 . . . . 209 E4
Pine Rd LU6 . . . . 106 F8
Pines Cl
Amersham HP6 . . . . 154 B2
Little Kingshill HP16 . . . . 152 B4
Pine St HP19 . . . . 115 A8
Pines The
Felden HP3 . . . . 146 F7
Slough SL3 . . . . 206 F5
Tylers Green HP10 . . . . . . 163 B1
Pinetree Cl SL9 . . . . 177 C3
Pine Trees Dr UB10 . . . . 201 E8
Pine Wlk
Berkhamsted HP4 . . . . . . 134 D7
Hazelmere HP15 . . . . 163 B3
Pinewood Ave UB8 . . . . . 208 F7
Pinewood Cl
Gerrards Cross SL9 . . . . . 188 E4
Iver Heath SL0 . . . . 200 C5
Pinewood Dr MK2 . . . . 58 E7
Pinewood Film Studios
SL0 . . . . 200 B5
Pinewood Gn SL0 . . . . . . 200 C5
Pinewood Mews TW19 . 213 D1
Pinewood Rd
High Wycombe HP12 . . . 172 C7
Iver Heath SL0 . . . . 200 B4
Pinfold MK7 . . . . 48 B6
PINFOLDPOND 60 E6
Pinfold Yd MK18 . . . . 51 B6
Pinglestone Cl UB7 . . . . 213 E7
Pinions Rd HP13 . . . . 173 E5
Pinkard Ct MK6 . . . . 47 C8
Pink Hill HP27 . . . . 149 E8
Pink La SL1 . . . . 197 B3
Pinkneys Dr SL6 . . . . 195 A1
PINKNEYS GREEN 195 A1
Pinkneys Rd SL6 . . . . 202 A8
Pink Rd HP27 . . . . 149 E7
Pinks Cl MK5 . . . . 46 C8
Pinkworthy MK4 . . . . 46 D4
Pinn Cl UB8 . . . . 208 D7
Pinstone Way SL9 . . . . . . 189 B2
Pintail Cl HP19 . . . . 101 E4
Pipard MK14 . . . . 34 E7
Pipers Cl SL1 . . . . 197 C2
Pipers Corner Sch
HP15 . . . . 162 B7
Pipers Croft LU6 . . . . 93 F7
Pipers Ct SL1 . . . . 197 C2
Pipers La HP15 . . . . 162 C8
Pipers Wood Cotts
HP7 . . . . 153 C2
Pipit Gdns 7 HP19 . . . . . 101 E4
Pipit Wlk 6 HP19 . . . . . . 101 E4
Pippin Cl MK16 . . . . 22 B3
Pippins Cl UB7 . . . . 208 D3
Pippins Sch SL3 . . . . 212 F6
Pippins The SL3 . . . . 206 F5
Pipston Gn
Milton Keynes MK7 . . . . . . 48 B7
Walton MK7 . . . . 48 B6
PISHILL 179 D8
PISHILL BANK 168 B1
Pishill Bank RG9 . . . . 168 B1
PISHILL BOTTOM 168 A1
Pistone Green Bsns Pk
LU7 . . . . 105 D2
Pistone Windmill★
LU7 . . . . 105 F4
PITCHCOTT 86 B5
Pitchcott Rd HP22 . . . . . . 86 B6
Pitcher La MK5 . . . . 46 B8
Pitcher Wlk HP19 . . . . . . 115 A7
Pitchford Ave MK18 . . . . . 41 E2
Pitchford Wlk MK18 . . . . . 41 F1
PITCH GREEN 138 B3
Pitch Pond Cl HP9 . . . . . 175 C5
Pitch The HP14 . . . . 159 D3
Pitfield MK11 . . . . 33 B3
PITSTONE 105 C4
Pitstone Green Farm Mus★
LU7 . . . . 105 D4
Pitters Piece HP18 . . . . . 125 B7
Pitt Gn MK18 . . . . 41 F1
Pitts Rd SL1 . . . . 205 C5
Place Farm Ho HP27 . . . 139 B6
Place Farm Way HP27 . . 139 B5
Plackett Way SL1 . . . . . . 204 D5
Plaines Cl SL1 . . . . 204 F5
Plaistow Cres MK10 . . . . . 35 F1
Plaiters Cl HP23 . . . . 119 B4
Plantain Ct MK7 . . . . 48 B6
Plantation Pl MK5 . . . . 46 A4
Plantation Rd
Amersham HP6 . . . . 154 E2
High Wycombe HP13 . . . . 174 A7
Leighton Buzzard LU7 . . . . 70 F3
Plantation Way HP6 . . . . 154 E2
Platt The HP7 . . . . 165 B7
Playing Field Rd NN13 . . . 39 A4
Pleasant Cotts SL0 . . . . . 200 B2
Pleasant Pl WD3 . . . . 178 E3
Pleasaunce The HP22 . . 117 E5
Pleshey Cl MK5 . . . . 46 B6
Plested Ct HP22 . . . . 116 C2
Plomer Green Ave
HP13 . . . . 161 D2
Plomer Green La HP13 . 161 D3
Plomer Hill HP13 . . . . 161 D1
Plough Cl HP21 . . . . 115 E3
Plough End HP22 . . . . . . 102 B4
Plough La
Sarratt WD4 . . . . 156 F6
Wexham Street SL2 . . . . 199 B4
Ploughlees La SL1 . . . . . 205 E6
Ploughley Rd OX25 . . . . . 94 E8
Plover Cl
1 Berkhamsted HP4 . . . 135 C3
Buckingham MK18 . . . . 52 E7
Newport Pagnell MK16 . . . 22 F3
Plover The 4 HP19 . . . . 101 E4
Plover Wlk 3 HP19 . . . . 101 E4
Plowman Cl MK12 . . . . 33 B5
Plumer Rd HP11 . . . . 172 E7
Plum Park La NN12 . . . . . 17 D8
PLUMPTON END 17 C7
Plumstead Ave MK13 . . . . 34 D3
Pluto Cl SL1 . . . . 204 E4
Pluto Way HP19 . . . . 101 D4
Plym Cl HP21 . . . . 115 C5
Plymouth Gr MK4 . . . . 46 B1
Plymouth Rd SL1 . . . . 204 E8
Pocketts Yd SL6 . . . . 196 B7
Pocock Ave UB7 . . . . 208 F3
Pococks La SL4 . . . . 205 E1
Poets Chase HP21 . . . . . . 115 F6
Points The SL6 . . . . 202 B3
Polar Pk UB7 . . . . 213 F7
Poles Hill
Chesham HP5 . . . . 144 A2
Sarratt WD4 . . . . 156 E6
Police Hos SL9 . . . . 189 B3
Polidoris La HP15 . . . . . . 163 C7
Polish Ave HP22 . . . . 131 E8
Pollard Ave UB9 . . . . 189 F5
Pollard Cl SL4 . . . . 211 B2
Pollards WD3 . . . . 178 D5
Pollys Yd MK14 . . . . 22 D5
Pollywick Rd HP23 . . . . . 119 D1
Polmartin Ct 1 MK6 . . . . 35 A1
Polruan Pl
Fishermead MK6 . . . . 47 A8
Milton Keynes MK6 . . . . . . 35 A1
Polygon Bsns Ctr SL3 . . 212 F5
Pomander Cres MK7 . . . . 48 B7
Pomeroy Cl HP7 . . . . 165 D7
Pond App HP15 . . . . 163 C7
Pond Cl
Newton Longville MK17 . . . 57 C2
Tring HP23 . . . . 119 A4
Winchmore Hill HP7 . . . . 164 C3
Pond Cotts HP14 . . . . 171 B4
Pondgate MK7 . . . . 48 B8
Pond La
Chalfont St Peter SL9 . . . 177 C2
Little Gaddesden HP4 . . . 121 E7
POND PARK 144 A2
Pond Park Rd HP5 . . . . . 144 B2
Pondwicks HP7 . . . . 165 B8
Pony Field The HP22 . . . 116 D1
Pool La SL1 . . . . 205 E6
Poolmans Rd SL4 . . . . . . 209 D4
Pope Ct HP23 . . . . 118 F3
Popes Acre HP17 . . . . . . 126 F5
Popes Cl
Amersham HP6 . . . . 154 F2
Colnbrook SL3 . . . . 212 C7
Popes La SL6 . . . . 195 C7
Pope Way HP21 . . . . 115 E4
Poplar Ave UB7 . . . . 208 F6
Poplar Cl
Aylesbury HP20 . . . . 102 A2
Chesham HP5 . . . . 144 C3
Milton Keynes MK6 . . . . . . 47 E5
Poyle SL3 . . . . 212 E6
Poplar Ho SL3 . . . . 206 F1
Poplar Rd
Aylesbury HP20 . . . . 102 A2
New Denham UB9 . . . . . . 201 C6
Wooburn Green HP10 . . . 185 E7
Poplars Cl HP17 . . . . 114 C5
Poplars Gr SL6 . . . . 196 B2
Poplars Rd MK18 . . . . 52 D8
Poplars The HP22 . . . . . . 131 C5
Poppy Ave MK10 . . . . 36 B4
Poppy Rd HP27 . . . . 139 A2
Porlock La MK4 . . . . 46 C4
Portal Cl UB10 . . . . 201 F5
Portal Rd HP22 . . . . 131 D6
Portchester Ct 1 MK8 . . 33 F1
Porter's Cl MK19 . . . . 31 E4
Porters Way UB7 . . . . 208 F4
Portfield Cl MK18 . . . . 52 E8
Port Field Farm MK16 . . . 21 F5
Portfields Comb Sch
MK16 . . . . 22 A5
Portfields Rd MK16 . . . . . 22 B4
Portfield Way MK18 . . . . . 52 E8
Porthcawl Gn MK3 . . . . . . 57 C8
Porthleven Pl MK6 . . . . . . 35 A2
Porthmellin Cl MK4 . . . . . 57 B8
Portishead Dr MK4 . . . . . . 56 F8
Portland Bsns Ctr SL3 . . 211 B6
Portland Cl SL2 . . . . 197 D1
Portland Dr MK15 . . . . 35 C7
Portland Gdns SL7 . . . . . 183 D1
Portland Ho HP13 . . . . . . 173 D8
Portland Pk SL9 . . . . 188 D5
Portlands Alley SL7 . . . . 183 D1
Portlands Mews 1
SL7 . . . . 183 D1
Portlock Rd SL6 . . . . 202 C7
Portman Mews HP19 . . . 114 F8
Portmarnock Cl MK3 . . . . 57 D8
Portnall Pl MK43 . . . . 25 B2
Portobello Cl HP5 . . . . . . 144 A2
Portobello Cotts
Lacey Green HP27 . . . . . . 149 E5
Lewknor OX49 . . . . 157 C2
Portrush Cl MK3 . . . . 57 D8
Portsmouth Ct SL1 . . . . . 205 E6
Portway
Milton Keynes, Bradwell
Common MK5, MK9, MK13,
MK14, MK15 . . . . 34 D2
Milton Keynes, Shenley Church
End MK8, MK5 . . . . 45 F6
North Marston MK18 . . . . . 76 B1
Stone HP17 . . . . 114 E4
Portway Dr HP12 . . . . 161 B1
Portway Rd
Stone HP17 . . . . 114 E4
Twyford MK18 . . . . 62 D1
Portway Rdbt MK5 . . . . . . 34 B1
PORTWAYS 168 B8
Posting Ho HP23 . . . . 120 A5
Post Mdw SL0 . . . . 200 D2
Post Office Cotts SL2 . . . 199 A5
Post Office La
Beaconsfield HP9 . . . . 175 D3
Slough SL3 . . . . 206 D7
Whitchurch HP22 . . . . 87 A6
Potash Cl HP17 . . . . 126 F5
Potash La HP23 . . . . 104 A5
Potkiln La HP9 . . . . 176 D1
Potter Row HP16 . . . . 142 C1
Potters Cl HP16 . . . . 151 B7
Potters Cross SL0 . . . . . . 200 E2
Potters Cross Cres
HP15 . . . . 162 E2
Potters Glen MK18 . . . . . . 53 B1
Potters La MK11 . . . . 33 B4
POTTERSPURY 18 D2
Potterspury Lodge Sch
NN12 . . . . 18 B6
Pottery Cl HP19 . . . . 115 A7
Pottery Ct HP19 . . . . 115 A7
Potts Pl 8 SL7 . . . . 183 D2
Poulcott TW19 . . . . 211 E1
Pound Cl
Steeple Claydon MK18 . . . . 63 D3
Wicken MK19 . . . . 31 A4
Pound Cres SL7 . . . . 183 C1
Poundfield La SL6 . . . . . . 195 F7
Poundfield Rd NN12 . . . . . 18 E2
Pound Hill MK17 . . . . 59 C1
Pound La
Heath End HP5 . . . . 134 A1
Little Marlow SL7 . . . . 184 C4
Marlow SL7 . . . . 183 D1

Pound La *continued*
North Crawley MK16 ..... 24 B7
Preston Bissett MK18 ..... 51 C1
POUNDON 71 E7
Pounds Cl MK43 ..... 25 B1
Pound St HP22 ..... 131 B4
Pound The
Cookham Rise SL6 ..... 195 F7
Cookham SL6 ..... 196 A7
Slough SL1 ..... 197 D1
Syresham NN13 ..... 27 B7
Powell Haven MK10 ..... 35 E3
Powis Cl SL6 ..... 202 B4
Powis La MK4 ..... 45 F2
Powney Rd SL6 ..... 202 C7
POYLE 212 E6
Poyle 14 Trad Est SL3 ..... 212 E4
Poyle La SL1 ..... 197 B3
Poyle New Cotts SL3 ..... 212 F5
Poyle Pk SL3 ..... 212 E4
Poyle Rd SL3 ..... 212 E5
Poyle Tech Ctr The
SL3 ..... 212 E5
Poynings The SL0 ..... 207 F2
Pratt Ho HP6 ..... 154 F1
Prebendal Ave HP21 ..... 115 D7
Prebendal Cl 11 HP20 ..... 115 D8
Prebendal Ct 1 HP20 ..... 115 D8
PREBENDAL FARM 115 B7
Precedent Dr MK13 ..... 34 B3
Precincts The SL1 ..... 197 C1
Prentice Gr MK5 ..... 46 B3
Prescott Rd SL3 ..... 212 E5
Prescotts The UB9 ..... 189 F3
Presley Way MK8 ..... 45 E7
Press Rd UB8 ..... 201 D6
PRESTON BISSETT 62 B8
Preston Ct MK15 ..... 35 B7
Preston Hill HP5 ..... 144 D2
Preston Rd SL2 ..... 206 C6
Prestwick Cl MK3 ..... 57 D7
Prestwold Ho HP19 ..... 115 A7
Prestwold Way HP19 ..... 115 A7
PRESTWOOD 151 D6
Prestwood SL2 ..... 206 B7
Prestwood Cl HP12 ..... 172 D8
Prestwood Inf Sch
HP16 ..... 151 C7
Prestwood Jun Sch
HP16 ..... 151 C6
Prestwood Lodge Specl Sch
HP16 ..... 151 D5
Prestwood Pl HP16 ..... 151 C6
Pretoria Rd HP13 ..... 173 C8
Priest End OX9 ..... 125 E1
Priestland Gdns HP4 ..... 135 E6
Priestley Ct HP13 ..... 173 D6
Priests Paddock HP9 ..... 175 B5
Primatt Cres MK5 ..... 46 B6
Primrose Cotts HP14 ..... 150 E1
Primrose Ct HP21 ..... 115 B6
Primrose Dr
Aylesbury HP21 ..... 115 B5
West Drayton UB7 ..... 208 D2
Primrose Gdns LU7 ..... 80 E7
Primrose Gn HP15 ..... 162 F6
Primrose Hill HP15 ..... 162 F7
Primrose La MK10 ..... 36 C3
Primrose Lea SL7 ..... 183 D2
Primrose Rd MK13 ..... 34 A4
Primrose Terr HP18 ..... 110 A8
Primrose Way MK18 ..... 52 C7
Prince Albert's Wlk SL3,
SL4 ..... 211 B5
Prince Andrew Cl SL6 ..... 203 B8
Prince Andrew Rd SL6 ..... 196 B1
Prince Consort Cotts
SL4 ..... 210 D5
Prince Consort's Dr
SL4 ..... 210 B2
Prince Edward St HP4 ..... 135 C4
Prince Philip Ave MK43 ..... 24 D2
Prince Rupert Dr HP19 ..... 101 C4
Princes Cl
Berkhamsted HP4 ..... 135 A6
Chilton HP18 ..... 111 B3
Eton Wick SL4 ..... 204 F1
Princes Ct
Bourne End SL8 ..... 185 C3
Leighton Buzzard LU7 ..... 80 F8
Princes Gate HP13 ..... 173 D6
Princes Gdns HP27 ..... 139 B3
Prince's La HP16 ..... 142 D5
Princes Pl HP27 ..... 139 B1
Princes Rd SL8 ..... 185 C3
Prince's Rd HP21 ..... 115 E8
PRINCES RISBOROUGH 139 D4
Princes Risborough Prim Sch HP27 ..... 139 B5
Princes Risborough Sch
HP27 ..... 139 C2
Princes Risborough Sta
HP27 ..... 138 F2
Princess Ave SL4 ..... 210 B4
Princess Gr HP9 ..... 176 D6
Princess Margaret Hospl The (private) SL4 ..... 210 D5
Princess St SL6 ..... 202 F6
Princes St
Piddington HP14 ..... 160 B1
2 Slough SL1 ..... 206 B4
Princes Terr SL8 ..... 185 C3
Princes Way MK2 ..... 58 C8
Princes Way Rdbt MK2 ..... 58 B8
Printers End HP19 ..... 101 B1
Prior Gr HP5 ..... 144 C1
Priors Cl
Maidenhead SL6 ..... 203 B2
5 Slough SL1 ..... 206 A3
Priors Pk MK4 ..... 46 D2
Priors Rd SL4 ..... 209 D4
Priors Way SL6 ..... 203 B2
Priors Way Ind Est SL6 ..... 203 B2
Priory Ave
High Wycombe HP13 ..... 173 B7
South Harefield UB9 ..... 190 C7
Priory Cl
Aylesbury HP19 ..... 101 C2
Denham UB9 ..... 190 A1
Horton-cum-S OX33 ..... 108 B5
Newport Pagnell MK16 ..... 22 E4
South Harefield UB9 ..... 190 C7
Priory Common Sch
MK13 ..... 34 B4
Priory Cotts UB9 ..... 190 C7
Priory Cres HP19 ..... 101 C2
Priory Ct 2 HP4 ..... 135 C4
Priory Farm Cotts OX27 ..... 71 E2
Priory Gdns
Berkhamsted HP4 ..... 135 C4
South Harefield UB9 ..... 190 C7
Priory Rd
Gerrards Cross SL9 ..... 188 D8
High Wycombe HP13 ..... 173 B7
Slough SL1 ..... 204 C8
Priory Rise Sch MK4 ..... 56 E7
Priory Sch SL1 ..... 204 D8
Priory St MK16 ..... 22 E4
Priory Way
Datchet SL3 ..... 211 B7
Gerrards Cross SL9 ..... 188 D8
Harmondsworth UB7 ..... 213 E8
Pritchard Ct MK14 ..... 34 E8
Proctor Rise MK8 ..... 45 D6
Progress Bsns Ctr SL1 ..... 204 D7
Progress Rd HP12 ..... 172 B7
Promenade SL4 ..... 210 C7
Prospect Cl MK17 ..... 68 D6
Prospect Cotts HP14 ..... 161 D6
Prospect Ct
Lane End HP14 ..... 171 B5
Yardley Gobion NN12 ..... 18 F6
Prospect Pl
Castlethorpe MK19 ..... 19 F5
Hurley SL6 ..... 193 F3
3 Windsor SL4 ..... 210 D4
Wing LU7 ..... 79 E2
Prospect Rd
Marlow SL7 ..... 183 D2
Milton Keynes MK11 ..... 32 C5
Prothero Cl HP21 ..... 115 E4
Protheroe Field MK7 ..... 48 D4
Providence Pl
9 Maidenhead SL6 ..... 202 F7
2 Milton Keynes MK13 ..... 34 A4
Providence Rd UB7 ..... 208 F5
Prudential Bldgs 1
SL1 ..... 205 F4
PUDDS CROSS 145 E2
Pudseys Cl SL6 ..... 195 B6
Puers Field HP9 ..... 176 E4
Puers La HP9 ..... 176 E4
Puffin Way HP19 ..... 101 F3
Pulborough Cl MK3 ..... 46 D1
Pulford Rd LU7 ..... 80 F6
Pullfields HP5 ..... 144 A1
Pulpit Cl HP5 ..... 144 A2
Pulpit La HP22 ..... 76 D1
Pumpkin Hill SL1 ..... 197 E6
Pump Lane N SL7 ..... 183 F6
Pump Lane S SL7 ..... 184 A4
Pump Mdw HP16 ..... 152 A8
Pump Pl MK19 ..... 32 B7
Pumpus Gn MK18 ..... 66 A4
Punch Bowl La HP5 ..... 154 C7
Purbeck MK13 ..... 34 C6
Purbeck Cl HP21 ..... 116 B5
Purcel Dr MK16 ..... 22 C3
Purse La MK16 ..... 11 F8
Pursers Ct SL1 ..... 205 E7
Pursell Cl SL6 ..... 202 A3
Purssell Pl HP27 ..... 139 B5
Purssells Mdw HP14 ..... 161 C7
Purton Ct SL2 ..... 198 C5
Purton La SL2 ..... 198 C5
PURY END 17 A7
Pury Rd
Alderton NN12 ..... 9 A2
Paulerspury NN12 ..... 17 D8
Pusey Way HP14 ..... 171 C5
Putlowes Dr HP18 ..... 100 C3
Putman Ho MK5 ..... 46 C5
Putman Pl RG9 ..... 191 E1
Putnams Dr HP22 ..... 117 D5
PUTTENHAM 103 F2
Puttenham Ct HP23 ..... 103 F2
PUXLEY 31 D7
Puxley Rd
Deanshanger MK19 ..... 31 D5
Milton Keynes MK19 ..... 32 A5
Pye Bridge End MK10 ..... 36 A4
Pyebush La HP9 ..... 187 A8
Pyghtles The HP22 ..... 85 B5
Pyghtle The
Olney MK46 ..... 6 F3
Turvey MK43 ..... 8 E6
Pyke Hayes MK8 ..... 33 D3
Pymcombe Cl HP27 ..... 139 B5
Pym Wlk OX9 ..... 125 F1
Pynefield Ho WD3 ..... 167 F2
Pyxe Ct MK7 ..... 48 A4

Q

Quadrangle The HP13 ..... 173 E7
Quadrans Cl MK15 ..... 35 A7
Quadrant The
High Wycombe HP13 ..... 162 E1
Maidenhead SL6 ..... 203 A6
QUAINTON 85 B5
Quainton CE Comb Sch
HP22 ..... 85 A5
QUAINTON HILL 75 B1
Quainton Rd
North Marston MK18 ..... 76 A2
Waddesdon HP18 ..... 99 A7
Quainton Road Sta*
HP22 ..... 84 F2
Quaker's Mead HP22 ..... 116 F3
Quakers Mede HP17 ..... 127 A6
Quantock Cl SL3 ..... 207 A1
Quantock Cres MK4 ..... 46 D2
QUARRENDON 101 B3
Quarrendon Ave HP19 ..... 101 B2
Quarrendon Rd HP7 ..... 165 E7
Quarry Cl HP18 ..... 125 C7
Quarry Ct LU7 ..... 105 D2
Quarrydale Dr SL7 ..... 183 F2
Quarry Green Cl MK19 ..... 31 B3
Quarry Rd LU7 ..... 105 D2
Quarry Wood Rd SL6,
SL7 ..... 195 A8
Quaves Rd SL3 ..... 206 C3
Quebec Rd HP13 ..... 173 E6
Queen Alexandra Rd
HP11 ..... 173 A6
Queen Anne Royal Free CE Fst Sch The SL4 ..... 210 D4
Queen Anne's Ct 10
SL4 ..... 210 C6
Queen Anne's Rd SL4 ..... 210 C3
Queen Anne St MK13 ..... 33 F7
Queen Catherine Rd
MK18 ..... 63 E2
Queen Charlotte St 10
SL4 ..... 210 D6
Queen Cl RG9 ..... 191 E1
Queen Eleanor Prim Sch
MK11 ..... 32 F4
Queen Eleanor St MK11 ..... 32 E6
Queen Elizabeth's Wlk
SL4 ..... 210 F5
Queen Mother's Dr
UB9 ..... 189 F5
Queens Acre
High Wycombe HP13 ..... 173 D6
Windsor SL4 ..... 210 D3
Queen's Acre SL4 ..... 210 D3
Queens Acre Ho 6
SL4 ..... 210 D4
Queen St Mews RG9 ..... 191 E1
Queens Ave MK16 ..... 22 C4
Queensbury La MK10 ..... 35 E1
Queens Cl OX9 ..... 125 F2
Queen's Cl SL4 ..... 211 A2
Queens Ct HP13 ..... 173 C6
Queen's Ct SL1 ..... 205 F6
Queen's Dr SL3 ..... 199 F4
Queen's Dr The WD3 ..... 167 F2
Queensgate HP19 ..... 115 A8
Queen's Gate SL4 ..... 210 D3
Queen's La 12 SL6 ..... 202 F7
Queensmead SL3 ..... 211 B6
Queens Mead HP21 ..... 116 C7
Queensmead Ho HP10 ..... 174 C2
Queensmead Rd HP10 ..... 174 C2
Queensmere Rd SL1 ..... 205 F4
Queensmere (Sh Ctr)
SL1 ..... 205 F4
Queens Park Arts Ctr
HP21 ..... 115 F8
Queen's Pk HP21 ..... 115 F8
Queen Sq 8 HP11 ..... 173 A7
Queens Rd
Berkhamsted HP4 ..... 135 A5
1 Chesham HP5 ..... 144 C1
Eton Wick SL4 ..... 204 F1
High Wycombe HP13 ..... 173 C6
Princes Risborough
HP27 ..... 139 C4
Slough SL1 ..... 205 F6
West Drayton UB7 ..... 208 F4
Queen's Rd
Datchet SL3 ..... 211 B7
Marlow SL7 ..... 183 D2
Uxbridge UB8 ..... 201 C2
Windsor SL4 ..... 210 C5
Queen St
Aylesbury HP20 ..... 116 A8
Henley-on-Thames RG9 ..... 191 E1
High Wycombe HP13 ..... 173 C7
Leighton Buzzard LU7 ..... 80 F8
Maidenhead SL6 ..... 202 F7
Milton Keynes MK11 ..... 32 E6
Piddington HP14 ..... 160 B1
Pitstone LU7 ..... 105 D4
Tring HP23 ..... 119 A3
Waddesdon HP18 ..... 98 F6
Queen's Terr 5 SL4 ..... 210 D4
Queensway
Bletchley MK2 ..... 58 C8
Hazelmere HP15 ..... 163 A4
Maidenhead SL6 ..... 195 E2
Milton Keynes MK2 ..... 58 D8
Queensway The SL9 ..... 188 D7
Queen Victoria Rd
HP11 ..... 173 B6
Queen Victoria's Wlk
SL4 ..... 210 F6
Quickberry Pl HP7 ..... 165 C8
Quickley La WD3 ..... 167 C3
Quickley Rise WD3 ..... 167 B3
Quickly Brow WD3 ..... 167 B3
Quill Hall La HP6 ..... 154 F2
Quilter Mdw MK7 ..... 48 D5
Quilters Way HP22 ..... 130 D8
Quinbrookes SL2 ..... 206 C7
Quince Cl MK7 ..... 48 B5
Quinton Dr MK13 ..... 34 B3
Quoitings Dr SL7 ..... 183 C2
Quoitings Gdns SL7 ..... 183 C2
Quoiting Sq SL7 ..... 183 D2

R

Raans Rd HP6 ..... 154 F1
Rabans Cl
Aylesbury HP19 ..... 100 E1
Olney MK46 ..... 6 E5
Rabans La HP19 ..... 100 F1
Rabbsfarm Prim Sch
UB7 ..... 208 E6
Rabbs Mill Ho UB8 ..... 201 D3
Rachels Way HP5 ..... 154 D5
Rackstraw Gr MK7 ..... 48 D5
Radcliffe Sch The MK12 ..... 33 B6
Radcliffe St MK12 ..... 33 D6
RADCLIVE 51 E8
Radclive Rd MK18 ..... 51 F7
Radcot Ave SL3 ..... 207 B3
Radcot Cl SL6 ..... 195 E3
Radcote Lodge MK8 ..... 33 E1
Radian Ct MK5 ..... 46 C7
Radman Gr MK12 ..... 33 B5
RADNAGE 159 C7
Radnage CE Inf Sch
HP14 ..... 159 D6
Radnage Common Rd
HP14 ..... 159 D5
Radnage La HP14 ..... 148 C2
Radnor Cl RG9 ..... 191 E2
Radnor End HP20 ..... 101 E2
Radnor Way SL3 ..... 206 E2
Radstock Cres MK10 ..... 36 A4
RADSTONE 26 A6
Radworthy MK4 ..... 46 C3
Raeside Cl HP9 ..... 176 C5
Raglan Dr MK4 ..... 45 E1
Ragmans Cl SL7 ..... 183 C8
Ragmans La HP10, SL7 ..... 172 D1
Ragnall's La OX33 ..... 108 A6
Ragstone Rd SL1 ..... 205 E3
Ragstones HP10 ..... 174 A1
Railway Cotts
Steeple Claydon MK18 ..... 64 A1
Wigginton HP23 ..... 119 F5
Railway St 2 HP20 ..... 115 E8
Railway Terr SL2 ..... 205 F5
Rainborough Gdns
HP20 ..... 101 E2
Rainbow Dr MK6 ..... 46 F7
Rainbow Ind Est UB7 ..... 208 D6
Rainsborough MK14 ..... 35 A8
Rainsborough Chase
SL6 ..... 202 B3
Rake Way HP21 ..... 115 D3
Raleigh Cl SL1 ..... 205 A5
Ralphs Retreat HP15 ..... 162 F4
Ralston Ct 20 SL4 ..... 210 D6
RAM ALLEY 12 B5
Ram Alley MK16 ..... 12 B6
Rambler Cl SL6 ..... 204 B7
Rambler La SL3 ..... 206 C3
Ramsay Cl MK13 ..... 34 B3
Ramsay View HP15 ..... 163 A3
Ramscote La HP5 ..... 143 F7
Ramsey Ct SL2 ..... 197 D1
Ramsgill Ct MK13 ..... 34 C5
Ramsons Ave MK14 ..... 34 E4
Ramsthorn Gr MK7 ..... 48 B6
Ramworth Way HP21 ..... 116 A6
Randall Cl SL3 ..... 206 F1
Randall Ct SL4 ..... 211 A1
Randall Dr MK4 ..... 45 D2
Randolph Cl MK13 ..... 34 A6
Randolph Rd SL3 ..... 206 E3
Ranelagh Gdns MK16 ..... 22 C2
Rangers Ct MK8 ..... 33 F1
Rannal Dr OX39 ..... 147 C6
Rannoch Cl MK2 ..... 58 D5
Rannock Gdns LU7 ..... 80 C7
Ranston Cl UB9 ..... 189 F5
Rashleigh Pl MK6 ..... 46 E7
Ratcliffe Cl UB8 ..... 201 D2
Rathbone Cl MK8 ..... 45 E7
Ravel Cl MK7 ..... 48 D6
Raven Cl 3 HP19 ..... 101 F3
Raven Cres HP18 ..... 98 C6
Raven Rd HP14 ..... 158 F4
Ravensbourne Pl MK6 ..... 35 B2
Ravensbourne Rd
HP21 ..... 115 D4
Ravenscar Ct MK4 ..... 46 C2
Ravenscourt SL7 ..... 184 A3
Ravenscroft Rd RG9 ..... 191 D2
Ravens Ct
Berkhamsted HP4 ..... 135 E6
High Wycombe HP13 ..... 161 E3
Long Marston HP23 ..... 104 B4
Ravens Field SL3 ..... 206 D4
Ravensglass Croft 6
MK10 ..... 36 B3
Ravenshoe Cl SL8 ..... 185 A3
Ravens La HP4 ..... 135 D4
Ravensmead
Chalfont St Peter SL9 ..... 177 F5
Chinnor OX39 ..... 147 C6
RAVENSTONE 5 D2
Ravenstone Mill Rd
MK46 ..... 12 E7
Ravens Wharf HP4 ..... 135 D4
Ravensworth Rd SL2 ..... 198 A2
Ravigill Pl MK12 ..... 33 D4
Rawcliffe Ho SL6 ..... 203 A6
Rawlings La HP9 ..... 176 D7
Rawlins Rd MK13 ..... 34 A4
Ray Dr SL6 ..... 203 B7
Rayfield SL6 ..... 203 B8
Ray Ho 5 SL8 ..... 185 A4
Raylands Mead SL9 ..... 188 C6
Ray Lea Cl SL6 ..... 203 B8
Ray Lea Rd SL6 ..... 203 B8
Rayleigh Cl MK5 ..... 46 B6
Raylens HP12 ..... 172 B5
Ray Lodge SL6 ..... 203 B7
Ray Lodge Mews SL6 ..... 203 B7
Ray Mdw SL6 ..... 196 A1
Ray Mead Ct SL6 ..... 196 C1
Ray Mead Rd SL6 ..... 203 C8
Ray Mill Road E SL6 ..... 196 B1
Ray Mill Road W SL6 ..... 203 A8
Raymond Cl SL3 ..... 212 E6
Raymond Rd
Maidenhead SL6 ..... 202 D7
Slough SL3 ..... 207 A3
Rayners Ave HP10 ..... 174 B3
Rayners Cl
Colnbrook SL3 ..... 212 C7
Loudwater HP10 ..... 174 C3
Rayners La MK9 ..... 35 E1
Ray Park Ave SL6 ..... 203 B8
Ray Park La SL6 ..... 203 B7
Ray Park Rd SL6 ..... 203 B8
Rays Ave SL4 ..... 209 F7
Rays Cl MK2 ..... 58 E6
Ray's Hill HP5 ..... 133 C2
Rays La HP10 ..... 163 C1
Ray St SL6 ..... 203 B7
Razzaq Pl HP12 ..... 172 E7
Read Dr HP22 ..... 102 C4
Reade Ct SL2 ..... 198 C6
Read Ho HP19 ..... 115 A7
Reading Cl HP19 ..... 101 A3
Reading Rd RG9 ..... 191 E1
Readings The WD3 ..... 167 F6
Reads La LU7 ..... 78 D1
Recreation Rd SL8 ..... 185 B3
Rectory Ave HP13 ..... 173 C7
Rectory Cl
Farnham Royal SL2 ..... 198 C2
Marsh Gibbon OX27 ..... 71 F3
Slapton LU7 ..... 91 D6
Windsor SL4 ..... 210 A6
Rectory Ct
2 Amersham HP7 ..... 165 B7
3 High Wycombe HP13 ..... 173 F5
Lewknor OX49 ..... 157 B8
West Drayton UB7 ..... 208 E4
Rectory Dr HP18 ..... 99 A6
Rectory Fields MK15 ..... 35 D3
Rectory Gdns HP8 ..... 177 B7
Rectory Hill HP7 ..... 165 B8
Rectory La
Amersham HP7 ..... 165 B7
Berkhamsted HP4 ..... 135 C4
Bix RG9 ..... 179 D1
Yardley Hastings NN7 ..... 1 A7
Rectory Mdw OX39 ..... 147 D6
Rectory Orch MK46 ..... 7 F8

Rectory Rd SL6 196 E1
Rectory Terr SL2 198 C3
Red Admiral St HP19 101 C4
Redbourne Ct MK11 32 F5
Redbridge MK14 34 D7
Redcliffe Wlk HP19 101 B2
Redcote Manor MK7 48 A4
Red Cottage HP23 119 D1
Red Cottage Mews 6
SL3 206 C3
Red Ct SL1 205 E5
Redding Dr HP6 154 A2
Redding Gr MK8 45 E6
Reddings Cl HP22 131 B6
Reddington Dr SL3 206 E2
Redfern Cl UB8 201 C4
Redfield Cl LU6 93 E8
Redford Rd SL4 209 D6
Redford Way UB8 201 D5
Red Friars Square Sh Ctr 21
HP20 115 D8
Redgrave Dr 2 MK4 45 E3
Redgrave Pl SL7 183 F3
Redhill UB9 189 D2
Redhouse Cl HP11 172 E3
Red House Cl
Beaconsfield HP9 175 B4
Newton Longville MK17 57 D4
Redhuish Cl MK4 46 D3
Red Kite Cl HP13 161 D1
Red La OX39 147 F3
Redland Cl MK18 63 D2
Redland Dr MK5 46 C7
Redland Way HP21 116 A5
Red Leaf Cl SL3 206 F5
Red Leys UB10 201 E5
Red Lion Cl MK43 25 B1
Red Lion Cotts SL2 199 B1
Red Lion Dr HP14 158 D5
Red Lion St HP5 154 B7
Red Lion Way HP10 185 E6
Red Lodge Gdns HP4 135 A3
Redman Rd HP12 172 B3
REDMOOR 47 A4
Redpitch Pk HP10 185 F6
Redriff Cl SL6 202 D6
Red Roofs SL6 203 C7
Redshaw Cl MK18 41 E1
Redshots Cl SL7 183 E4
Redvers Gate MK15 35 B7
Redway Sch The MK6 47 C6
Red Wing HP20 101 E3
Redwood SL1 197 B3
Redwood Cl
Hazlemere HP15 163 B3
Wing LU7 79 E2
Redwood Dr
Aylesbury HP21 115 E7
Wing LU7 79 E2
Redwood Gate MK5 46 C4
Redwood Gdns SL1 205 D6
Redwood Glade LU7 70 F3
Redwood Pl HP9 175 D1
Redwoods The SL4 210 D4
Reed Cl SL0 207 E7
Reeves Croft MK12 33 C4
Reform Rd SL6 203 B7
Reform Road Ind Est
SL6 203 B7
Regal Ct
Maidenhead SL6 203 B2
14 Tring HP23 119 A3
Regency Ct HP21 116 B7
Regent Ct
3 Maidenhead SL6 202 F7
Slough SL1 205 E7
Windsor SL4 210 D5
Regent Ho HP27 139 B4
Regent Rd HP21 116 B7
Regents Hall MK11 32 E5
Regents Pl SL6 202 D6
Regent St MK2 58 C8
Regius Ct HP10 174 D8
Reid Ave SL6 202 E5
Reliance La MK9 35 B3
Rembrandt End HP19 100 F2
REMENHAM 192 A5
Remenham Church La
RG9 192 A4
REMENHAM HILL 192 C2
Remenham La
Remenham Hill RG9 191 F3
Remenham RG9 192 B5
Remenham Row RG9 191 F2
Remenham Terr RG9 192 C2
Remus Gate NN13 38 A6
Rendlesham MK15 35 C3
Rendlesham Way WD3 167 C3
Renfrew Way MK3 46 F3
Rennie Cl HP13 161 F1
Repton Cl SL6 202 C3
Repton Pl HP7 166 A8
Retreat La HP14 148 D2
Retreat The
Little Chalfont HP6 166 E8
Milton Keynes MK11 32 D5
Princes Risborough
HP27 139 B4
Revel Rd HP10 185 D8
Revesby Cl SL6 202 D3
Reyners Gn HP16 152 B4
Reynold Dr HP20 102 A2
Reynolds Cl
Cranfield MK43 24 E2
High Wycombe HP13 173 E8
Reynolds Pl MK8 45 D6
Reynolds Rd HP9 175 D3
Reynolds Wlk HP5 144 A4
Rhodes Pl MK6 46 E7
Rhondda Cl MK1 47 E1
Rhoscolyn Dr MK3 57 C8
Rhuddlan Cl MK5 45 F7
Rhymer Cl MK19 10 F4
Ribble Cl MK16 22 E4
Ribble Cres MK3 57 D8
Ribstone Rd SL6 202 B3
Ricardo Rd SL4 211 B1
Richard Gdns HP13 173 E8
Richardson Pl 2 MK6 34 E1
Richards Way SL1 204 F5
Richborough MK13 34 A6
RICHINGS PARK 207 E3
Richings Pl SL0 207 E3
Richings Way SL0 207 F3
Richmond Cl
Amersham HP6 154 F1
Milton Keynes MK3 46 D1
Richmond Cres SL1 206 A5
Richmond Ct
Dunstable LU6 92 E6
High Wycombe HP13 173 C7
Richmond Rd HP20 116 C7
Richmond Way MK16 22 D3
Rickard Cl
Aylesbury HP21 115 D3
West Drayton UB7 208 D3
Rickford's Hill HP20 115 D8
Rickley La MK3 58 A8
Rickley Park Prim Sch
MK3 57 F8
Rickman's La SL2 198 E6
RICKMANSWORTH 167 F1
Rickmansworth La SL9 177 F5
Rickmansworth Rd
Amersham HP6 154 C2
Chorleywood WD3 167 F6
Rickman Wlk HP19 115 A7
Rickyard Cl
1 Milton Keynes MK13 34 A4
Whitchurch HP22 87 A7
Rickyard Gr HP18 83 B5
Rickyard The MK46 7 C3
Rick Yd The MK16 13 F1
Riders Way OX39 147 C6
Ride The LU6 93 B6
Ridgebank SL1 204 F6
Ridge Cl
Aylesbury HP21 115 D3
Lane End HP14 171 C4
Ridge Ct SL4 210 C4
Ridgemount End SL9 177 E5
Ridge Side HP14 160 A8
Ridge View HP23 119 C5
Ridgeway
Berkhamsted HP4 134 F4
4 High Wycombe HP11 173 A6
Milton Keynes, Stony Stratford
MK11 32 F4
Milton Keynes, Wolverton Mill
MK12 33 A5
Wing LU7 79 E3
Ridge Way
High Wycombe HP13 162 C1
Iver SL0 207 F6
Long Crendon HP18 125 F4
Ridgeway Cl
Chesham HP5 144 B3
Marlow SL7 183 E4
Ridgeway Cotts MK17 67 B3
Ridgeway Ct 3 HP20 101 E1
Ridgeway Meads HP27 138 B2
Ridgeway Rd HP5 144 B3
Ridgeway The
Amersham HP7 165 E7
Gerrards Cross SL9 188 D8
Marlow SL7 183 E4
Ridgeway Trad Est The
SL0 207 E6
Ridgewood RG9 181 C1
Ridgmont MK19 31 E5
Ridgmont Cl MK19 31 E5
Ridgway MK17 49 B6
Riding Court Rd SL3 211 D7
Riding Ct SL3 211 C8
Riding La HP9, HP10 174 F3
Ridings Cotts HP15 163 D6
Ridings The
Amersham HP6 154 D4
Iver SL0 207 F2
Latimer HP5 155 D3
Maidenhead SL6 202 A7
Ridings Way LU7 78 B1
Riding The MK19 31 E5
Rigby Lodge SL1 205 E7
Rigeway View LU7 105 D4
Rignall Rd HP16 151 E8
Riley Cl HP20 115 C8
Riley Rd SL7 183 D2
Rillington Gdns MK4 46 B3
Rimmington Way HP19 101 B1
Rimsdale Ct MK2 58 D3
Ringlet Way HP19 101 C4
Ring Rd HP10 173 F2
Ring Road E MK7 47 F7
Ring Road N MK7 47 F7
Ring Road W MK7 47 E7
RINGSHALL 107 B1
Ringshall Dr HP4 121 C8
Ringshall Rd HP4 107 B3
Ringstead Way HP21 116 A5
Ripley Cl
High Wycombe HP13 173 A8
Milton Keynes MK4 45 E1
Slough SL3 206 E2
Ripon Ho HP21 115 F6
Ripon St 7 HP20 101 D1
Risborough Rd
Great Kimble HP17,
HP27 139 E8
Maidenhead SL6 202 E8
Stoke Mandeville HP17 130 B7
Risborough Springs Swim &
Fitness Ctr HP27 139 A4
Rise Hag Hill SL6 204 A7
Riseley Rd SL6 202 D7
Rise The
Amersham HP7 165 C8
Gawcott MK18 51 F4
Hazelmere HP15 163 A5
Loudwater HP13 174 B4
Uxbridge UB10 201 F3
Risings The HP13 162 B1
Riverbank Point UB8 201 C6
Riverbank The SL4 210 B7
River Cl MK16 22 D4
Rivercrest Rd MK19 32 B6
River Ct SL6 203 C7
River Gdns SL6 203 D4
Rivermead Ct SL7 194 E8
Riverpark Dr SL7 183 F1
River Park Ind Est HP4 135 A5
River Rd SL6 203 C6
River & Rowing Mus★
RG9 191 F1
Riversdale SL8 185 B1
Riversdale Cotts SL8 185 B1
Riversdale Ct SL8 185 A1
Rivers Edge HP11 174 A3
Riverside SL7 183 D1
River Side MK16 22 D4
Riverside Cotts
West Drayton UB7 208 C1
Wooburn Green HP10 185 E8
Riverside Cvn Pk UB7 208 C3
Riverside Gdns HP4 135 A5
Riverside Mews MK18 52 D8
Riverside Pk SL3 212 E5
Riverside Pl TW19 213 E1
Riverside Rd TW19 213 E1
Riverside Way UB8 201 B4
Riverside Wlk SL4 210 D7
River St SL4 210 D7
Riverswood Gdns HP11 174 B3
River View HP10 185 B7
Riverway SL4 210 C7
River Wlk UB9 201 C7
Riverwood Ave SL7 184 A1
Riverwoods Dr SL7 184 A1
Rivets Cl HP21 115 E6
Rivetts Cl MK46 6 E4
Rixband Cl MK7 48 B4
Rixman Cl SL6 202 D5
Rixon Cl SL3 206 E7
Rixons Mdw HP19 115 B7
Roade Hill NN7 9 F8
Roald Dahl Mus & Story
Ctr★ HP16 152 A7
Robert Rd SL2 187 D2
Roberts Cl
Deanshanger MK19 31 E4
Stanwell TW19 213 C1
West Drayton UB7 208 E5
Robert's Dr HP19 101 D2
Roberts La SL9 178 B5
Robertson Cl MK5 45 F7
Robertson Cnr LU6 93 F4
Robertson Rd 6 HP4 135 D4
Roberts Rd
Haddenham HP17 127 B6
High Wycombe HP13 173 B8
Roberts Ride HP15 163 A5
Roberts Way HP21 115 B6
Robertswood Comb Sch
SL9 177 F3
Roberts Wood Dr SL9 177 F5
Robeson Pl MK8 45 E8
Robin Cl
Aylesbury HP19 101 F3
Buckingham MK18 52 F7
Great Kingshill HP15 151 D1
Robin Hill HP4 135 C3
Robin Ho HP11 174 A4
Robin Hood Cl SL1 204 F5
Robin Par 2 SL2 198 C7
Robins Cl
High Wycombe HP12 172 D3
Uxbridge UB8 208 C8
Robins Hill MK6 47 A6
Robinson Cl HP19 100 F3
Robinson Ct SL6 202 E4
Robinson Rd HP13 174 B4
Robins Orch SL9 177 E4
Robins Platt OX39 147 B6
Robinswood Cl
Beaconsfield HP9 175 C5
Leighton Buzzard LU7 70 F2
Robin Willis Way SL4 211 A1
Robinwood Gr UB8 201 F1
Roblin Cl HP21 115 E4
Robson Cl SL9 177 E5
Robson Ct 4 HP16 152 A8
Roche Gdns MK3 58 A8
Rochester Ct MK5 46 A5
Rochester Mews LU7 80 E6
Rochester Pl HP19 115 B8
Rochfords MK6 46 F6
Rochfords Gdns SL2 206 C5
Rochford Way SL6 204 A7
Rockall Ct SL3 207 B3
Rock Cl LU7 80 D6
Rockingham Cl
Pitstone LU7 105 D3
Uxbridge UB8 201 C4
Rockingham Dr MK14 34 E6
Rockingham Par UB8 201 C5
Rockingham Pl HP9 175 F1
Rockingham Rd UB8 201 C4
Rockingham Wharf
UB8 201 B4
Rock La LU7 80 D7
Rockleigh Ct 3 LU7 80 E7
Rockspray Gr MK7 48 B5
ROCKWELL END 181 F5
Rodney Way SL3 212 E6
Rodwell Gdns MK7 48 D4
Rodwell Yd 3 HP23 119 A3
Roebuck Ave HP13 173 F6
Roebuck Gn SL1 204 E5
Roebuck Way MK5 46 C6
Roeburn Cres MK4 46 C1
Rogers Croft MK6 47 D7
Rogers La SL2 198 F4
Roker Park Ave UB10 201 E8
Rokesby Rd SL2 197 F2
Rolfe Cl HP9 175 E1
Rolvenden Gr MK7 48 B7
Roman Lea SL6 195 F7
Roman Pl SL6 202 C6
Roman Rdbts MK1 47 C2
Romans Field Specl Sch
MK3 46 E1
Roman Way
Aylesbury HP19 115 B8
Bourne End SL8 185 B4
Brackley NN13 38 A7
Romar Ct MK1 47 C2
Romney Ct 11 SL7 183 F3
Romney Lock Rd SL4 210 D7
Romney Rd HP21 115 E4
Romsey Cl SL3 206 F3
Romsey Dr SL2 187 D1
Romsey Way HP11 173 B4
Romulus Way NN13 38 A6
Ronald Rd HP9 175 F2
Ronaldsay Spur SL1 205 E8
Rookery Ct SL7 183 D2
Rookery Mdw HP15 163 C7
Rookery Way MK18 63 F3
Rook Rd HP10 185 D4
ROOKSLEY 34 B2
Rooksley Rdbt MK13 34 B3
Rooks Terr UB7 208 E4
Rook Tree Farm Ind Est
MK17 37 F3
Rook Wood Way HP16 152 B5
Ropa Ct 6 LU7 80 F7
Ropley Way 3 MK10 36 B3
Rosamund's Cotts HP18 83 B2
Rosary The HP15 163 C7
Roseary Cl UB7 208 D2
Rose Ave
Aylesbury HP19 101 C2
Hazlemere HP15 163 B2
Rosebank Cl SL6 195 E7
Rosebank Cotts HP10 174 B3
Rosebarn La HP23 104 D1
Rosebay Cl MK7 48 B5
Rosebery Ave
High Wycombe HP13 173 E5
Leighton Buzzard LU7 80 E7
Rosebery Cl MK18 77 B7
Rosebery Ct 4 LU7 80 F7
Rosebery Mews LU7 90 D4
Rosebery Rd HP22 117 F5
Rosebery Way HP23 119 B5
Rose Cnr HP14 158 E5
Rosecomb Pl MK5 46 A4
Rose Cotts SL6 202 C3
Rose Ct
Amersham HP6 154 E2
Chesham HP5 154 D6
Eaton Bray LU6 92 D6
3 Olney MK46 6 F3
Rose Dr HP5 154 D7
Rosehill HP4 135 B4
Rose Hill SL1 197 A5
Rosehill Cres MK18 62 D1
Rosehill Ct SL1 206 A3
Rose Ind Est SL7 183 D5
Rose La RG9 193 A1
Roseleigh Cl SL6 202 A7
Rosemary Cl HP12 161 B1
Rosemary Ct
High Wycombe HP12 161 B1
Walton MK7 48 A5
Rosemary La HP17 127 A7
Rosemead HP22 117 E1
Rosemoor Mews HP19 114 F8
Rosemullion Ave MK4 57 B8
Rosery The 5 SL8 185 A3
Roses Cl LU7 78 B1
Roses La SL4 209 D5
Rose Terr HP18 99 A6
Rosetree Cl HP16 151 C6
Rose Wlk SL2 205 B8
Rosewood Gdns HP12 172 C4
Rosewood Way SL2 198 C7
Rosken Gr SL2 198 B3
Roslyn Ct MK15 35 D7
Rossal Pl MK12 33 D4
Rossendale MK14 34 D7
Rossetti Pl HP15 163 C7
Rossini Pl MK7 48 D5
Rossiter Cl SL3 206 E2
Ross Rd
Aston Abbotts HP22 88 D5
Maidenhead SL6 202 E4
Ross Way MK3 46 F2
Rossway La HP4 134 A7
Rostrevor Gdns SL0 200 D3
Rothersthorpe MK14 35 A8
Rothesay Cl HP20 101 E1
Rothesay Ct HP4 135 A4
Rothschild Ave HP22 117 E5
Rothschild Rd
Leighton Buzzard LU7 80 F8
Wing LU7 79 E2
ROTTEN ROW 181 F2
Rotten Row MK17 59 C2
Roughwood La HP8 166 E3
Roundhead Dr OX9 125 F1
Roundheads End HP9 175 B4
Round Hill HP17 114 D5
Roundhill Ct HP17 126 E8
Roundlands HP27 149 E5
Roundwood Prim Sch (Inf)
MK18 51 B6
Roundwood Prim Sch (Jun)
MK18 51 F4
Roundwood Rd HP12 172 C7
Round Wood Rd HP6 154 F2
Rouse Ct SL9 188 F6
Routs Gn HP14 148 D2
ROUT'S GREEN 148 D2
Roveley Ct MK11 32 F5
Rowan Ave HP13 173 D8
Rowan Cl
Aylesbury HP21 115 E4
Beaconsfield HP9 175 B1
Hazelmere HP15 163 A3
Rowan Dr MK19 20 D2
Rowan Gdns SL0 200 C3
Rowan Ho 1 SL8 185 A4
Rowanhurst Dr SL2 198 C7
Rowan Pl HP6 154 F1
Rowan Rd UB7 208 E2
Rowans The SL9 188 D8
Rowan Way SL2 205 B8
Rowan Wlk HP5 144 B1
Rowborough Rd HP22 131 D7
Rowland Cl SL4 209 D4
Rowland Ho HP9 175 F1
Rowlands Cl MK2 58 E8
Rowland Way HP19 115 B7
Rowle Cl MK14 34 E7
Rowley Furrows LU7 80 D8
Rowley La SL3 199 D4
Rowlheys Pl UB7 208 E3
Rowliff Rd HP12 172 C6
ROWSHAM 102 D8
Rowsham Dell MK14 21 F2
Rowsham Rd HP22 102 C5
Row The
Cholesbury HP5 133 D2
Cold Brayfield MK46 8 B6
Lane End HP14 171 B4
Newton Blossomville MK43 8 B3
Winchmore Hill HP7 164 C3
Rowton Heath MK5 45 C5
Roxburgh Way MK3 46 F3
Roxhill Rd MK43 25 F3
Roxwell Cl SL1 204 E5
Roxwell Path 5 HP20 101 F2
Royal Buckinghamshire
Hospl HP19 101 D1
Royal Cl UB7, UB8 208 F7
Royal Cotts SL6 195 C7
Royal Cotts HP7 164 C2
Royal Ct HP23 120 A5
Royal Free Ct 13 SL4 210 D6
Royal Gram Sch The
HP13 162 C1

Royal La UB8 ... 201 F1
Royal Latin Sch The MK18 ... 52 D7
Royal Mansions RG9 ... 191 E1
Royal Mead HP17 ... 130 C5
Royal Windsor Racecourse SL4 ... 209 E7
Royce Cl LU6 ... 93 F7
Royce Rd MK43 ... 24 D3
Royle Cl SL9 ... 177 F3
Royston Way SL1 ... 204 D8
Rubbra Cl MK7 ... 48 C5
Rubens Cl HP19 ... 100 F2
Ruby Cl SL1 ... 205 A4
Ruckles Way HP7 ... 165 C7
Rudchesters MK13 ... 33 F5
Ruddlesway SL4 ... 209 D6
Rudds Cl MK18 ... 66 A5
Rudd's La HP17 ... 127 A7
Rudsworth Cl SL3 ... 212 D7
Ruffle Cl UB7 ... 208 E4
Rugby Rise HP11 ... 174 A3
Rugwood Rd HP10 ... 173 F2
Rumptons Paddock HP18 ... 82 F6
Runford Ct MK5 ... 46 C5
Run Furrow HP17 ... 127 A7
Runnymede MK14 ... 21 F2
Runrig Hill HP6 ... 154 E4
Rupert Ave HP12 ... 172 E4
Rupert Cl RG9 ... 191 E3
Rupert House Sch RG9 191 E2
Rupert's La ... 191 E3
Rupert Way OX9 ... 126 A1
Ruscombe Gdns SL3 ... 211 A7
Ruscote HP4 ... 135 A3
Rushall Rd OX9 ... 126 A1
Rushbeds Wood Wildlife Reserve* HP18 ... 96 D4
Rushbrooke Cl HP13 ... 162 F2
Rushburn HP10 ... 185 F6
Rushendon Furlong LU7 ... 105 E5
Rushes Mead UB8 ... 201 C4
Rushes The
Maidenhead SL6 ... 203 C6
Marlow SL7 ... 194 C8
Rushfields Cl 12 MK4 ... 45 F1
RUSH GREEN ... 200 E8
Rushington Ave SL6 ... 202 F5
Rushleys Cl MK5 ... 46 A8
RUSHMERE ... 70 E4
Rushmere Cl MK17 ... 48 D2
Rushmere La HP5 ... 145 B3
Rushmere Ret Pk MK1 ... 47 D2
Rushmoor Ave HP15 ... 163 B3
Rushton Ct 5 MK8 ... 45 F8
Ruskin Ct MK16 ... 22 C2
Rusland Cir MK4 ... 46 C2
Russel Ct HP14 ... 161 C8
Russell Ave HP21 ... 115 C6
Russell Cl
Little Chalfont HP6 ... 166 D8
Tylers Green HP10 ... 163 B1
Russell Ct
Aylesbury HP21 ... 115 E6
Chesham HP5 ... 144 D2
Maidenhead SL6 ... 202 F7
Wendover HP22 ... 131 B5
Russell Dr TW19 ... 213 D1
Russell Ho 4 SL8 ... 185 A4
Russell Sch The WD3 ... 167 B5
Russell St
Milton Keynes MK11 ... 32 D5
Windsor SL4 ... 210 D6
Woburn Sands MK17 ... 49 B4
Russell Street Sch MK11 ... 32 D5
Russet Cl TW19 ... 212 F1
Russet Rd SL6 ... 202 C3
Russets The SL9 ... 177 D1
Russett Hill SL9 ... 188 E8
Russwell La MK17 ... 59 C6
Rustics Cl MK18 ... 73 B5
Rustlings Gate HP14 ... 171 C5
Rutherford Cl
Uxbridge UB8 ... 201 F1
Windsor SL4 ... 209 F6
Rutherford Gate MK5 ... 46 C5
Rutherford Rd HP21 ... 115 E4
Ruthven Cl MK2 ... 58 C4
Rutland Ave
High Wycombe HP12 ... 172 D6
Slough SL1 ... 205 C8
Rutland Ct 2 HP11 ... 173 A6
Rutland Gate SL6 ... 202 C6
Rutland Ho 3 MK3 ... 46 F1
Rutland Pl SL6 ... 202 C6
Rutland Rd SL6 ... 202 D6
Rutland St HP11 ... 173 A6
Ryans Mount SL7 ... 183 C2
Rycote La OX9 ... 136 D5
Rycote Lane Ind Est OX9 ... 136 C4
Rycroft
Milton Keynes MK4 ... 46 E3
Rycroft *continued*
Windsor SL4 ... 209 F4
Rydal Way
High Wycombe HP12 ... 172 B5
Milton Keynes MK2 ... 58 D5
Ryder Cl HP3 ... 146 A4
Rydings SL4 ... 209 F4
Ryding The MK5 ... 46 A4
Rye Cl
Aylesbury HP21 ... 115 D4
Maidenhead SL6 ... 202 A4
Ryecote Chapel* OX9 ... 136 D6
Ryecroft Rd HP5 ... 154 A7
Rye Ct 9 SL1 ... 206 A4
Ryefield Terr SL3 ... 212 D7
Ryeland MK11 ... 32 E6
Ryeland Cl UB7 ... 208 E7
Ryemead Way HP11 ... 173 F4
Rye The LU6, LU7 ... 92 B8
Rye View HP13 ... 173 C7
Rylstone Cl
Maidenhead SL6 ... 202 C3
Milton Keynes MK13 ... 34 B3
Ryman Ct WD3 ... 167 C3
Rymill Cl HP3 ... 146 A3
Ryton Pl MK4 ... 46 C3
Ryvers End SL3 ... 206 F3
Ryvers Rd SL3 ... 206 F3
Ryvers Sch SL3 ... 206 D3

S

Sabina Cl HP12 ... 172 E6
Sacred Heart RC Prim Sch RG9 ... 191 D1
Saddington MK6 ... 47 D6
Saddlers Pl MK14 ... 35 A5
Sadleirs Gn MK17 ... 49 B5
Sadlers Mews SL6 ... 203 B7
Saffron Cl SL3 ... 211 B6
Saffron Ct HP13 ... 173 C6
Saffron Rd HP13 ... 173 C6
Saffron Rise LU6 ... 92 E6
Saffron St MK2 ... 58 D7
Saham Croft Cl MK18 ... 65 E4
Sailing Club Rd SL8 ... 185 A3
St Abbs Ct MK4 ... 56 F8
St Adrian's Cl SL6 ... 202 B4
St Agnes Gate HP22 ... 131 A5
St Aidan's Cl MK3 ... 57 E6
St Albans Cl 7 SL4 ... 210 D6
St Alban's Rd MK18 ... 65 F4
St Alban's St SL4 ... 210 D6
St Andrew's Ave SL4 ... 209 F5
St Andrew's CE Inf Sch MK14 ... 34 E8
St Andrew's CE Prim Sch
Chinnor OX39 ... 147 C7
Uxbridge UB8 ... 201 D4
St Andrew's Cl
High Wycombe HP13 ... 162 F1
Old Windsor SL4 ... 211 A1
Wraysbury TW19 ... 211 E1
St Andrews Cotts 1 SL4 ... 210 A5
St Andrew's Cres SL4 ... 209 F5
St Andrews Ct
Colnbrook SL3 ... 212 D7
2 Slough SL1 ... 205 E3
St Andrews Ho OX39 ... 147 C6
St Andrew's Rd
Chinnor OX39 ... 147 C5
Milton Keynes MK3 ... 57 E7
Uxbridge UB10 ... 201 E5
St Andrews Way SL1 ... 204 D6
St Andrews Way Ind Est HP19 ... 101 C1
St Anne's Cl
Henley-on-Thames RG9 ... 191 D1
Wendover HP22 ... 131 B5
St Anne's Rd
Aylesbury HP19 ... 115 B8
South Harefield UB9 ... 190 C8
St Ann's HP10 ... 174 C2
St Ann's Ct HP10 ... 174 C2
St Anthony's Cl HP19 ... 115 B8
St Anthony's Ct HP9 ... 186 C8
St Anthony's Pl MK4 ... 57 B8
St Anthony's RC Prim Sch SL2 ... 198 C1
St Augustine's RC Prim Sch HP11 ... 173 A4
St Augustus Cl MK3 ... 57 E7
St Bartholomews MK10 ... 36 A1
St Bartholomew's CE Sch HP23 ... 119 D1
St Bees MK10 ... 36 B1
St Bernadettes RC Prim Sch MK10 ... 47 F8
St Bernards Ct HP13 ... 173 C6
St Bernard's Prep Sch SL1 ... 206 B4
St Bernard's RC Gram Sch SL3 ... 206 C4
St Bernard's RC Sch HP11 ... 173 A4
St Bernards Rd SL3 ... 206 C3
St Birinus HP10 ... 174 A2
St Botolphs 2 MK10 ... 36 B1
St Brides Cl MK6 ... 35 C2
St Catherine RC Prim Sch UB7 ... 208 D4
St Catherine's Ave MK3 ... 57 D6
St Catherines Ct 3 SL4 ... 210 A5
St Catherine's Ct HP19 ... 115 B8
St Chad's Rd SL6 ... 202 B4
St Christopher Rd UB8 ... 208 D8
St Christopher's Cl HP16 ... 152 B3
St Christophers Ct WD3 ... 167 D5
St Clement Cl UB8 ... 208 D7
St Clement Danes Sch WD3 ... 167 D7
St Clement's Dr MK3 ... 57 D6
Saint-Cloud Way SL6 ... 203 A7
St Columba's Cl SL6 ... 202 B4
St Cuthburt La UB8 ... 208 D7
St David Cl UB8 ... 208 D8
St David's Cl
Iver Heath SL0 ... 200 D4
Maidenhead SL6 ... 202 A4
St David's Ct NN13 ... 38 A8
St David's Par SL0 ... 200 D4
St David's Rd MK3 ... 57 E6
St Dunstans MK6 ... 47 A6
St Edmund Campion RC Prim Sch SL6 ... 202 B5
St Edmunds HP4 ... 135 C3
St Edmund's Cl HP19 ... 115 B8
St Edwards Ct MK14 ... 34 F7
St Edward's RC Fst Sch SL4 ... 210 A6
St Edward's RC Jun Sch HP21 ... 116 A7
St Edward's Royal Free Ecumenical Mid Sch SL4 ... 210 A6
St Elmo Cl SL2 ... 198 D1
St Elmo Cres SL2 ... 198 D1
St Ethelbert's RC Prim Sch SL2 ... 206 A7
St Faith's Cl MK17 ... 57 D3
St Francis Rd
Beacon's Bottom HP14 ... 159 D3
Denham Green UB9 ... 189 F5
St George's CE Inf Sch 3 HP7 ... 165 E8
St George's Cl
High Wycombe HP13 ... 173 D7
Windsor SL4 ... 209 E6
St Georges Cres SL1 ... 204 D6
St Georges Ct 2 HP12 ... 172 D8
St George's Dr UB10 ... 190 F1
St Georges Ind Est HP7 165 F8
St Georges Lodge SL6 ... 196 B7
St George's Rd MK3 ... 57 E6
St George's Sch SL4 ... 210 D7
St Georges Way ... 33 D7
St Giles Mews MK11 ... 32 D6
St Giles St MK13 ... 33 F7
St Govans Cl MK4 ... 57 B8
St Helena Ave
Milton Keynes MK3 ... 58 C3
Milton Keynes MK17 ... 58 C3
St Helen Cl UB8 ... 208 D8
St Helens Gr MK10 ... 47 F8
St Hilda's Ct HP19 ... 115 B8
St Hilda's Way HP10 ... 174 A2
St Huberts Cl SL9 ... 188 E2
St Huberts Cotts SL9 ... 188 E4
St Huberts La SL9 ... 188 F2
St Hugh's Ave HP13 ... 173 F6
St Hugh's Cl HP14 ... 158 F4
St Hugh's Pl HP14 ... 158 F4
St Ives Cres MK4 ... 57 B8
St Ives Rd SL6 ... 203 A7
St James Cl MK19 ... 11 A2
St James Ctyd 8 SL7 ... 183 E2
St James Pl SL1 ... 204 C7
St James & St John CE Prim Sch
Akeley MK18 ... 41 F8
Chackmore MK18 ... 41 B4
St James St MK13 ... 33 F7
St James Way HP22 ... 102 B3
St James Wlk SL0 ... 207 E4
St John's Ave HP10 ... 174 B8
St John's CE Comb Sch HP27 ... 149 F4
St Johns Cl HP10 ... 163 B1
St John's Cl UB8 ... 201 B4
St John's Cres MK12 ... 33 D5
St Johns Dr
Stone HP17 ... 114 B5
Windsor SL4 ... 210 A5
St Johns La MK18 ... 75 F2
St John's La MK19 ... 31 B4
St John's Manor Ho HP15 ... 162 E2
St Johns Rd
Slough SL2 ... 206 A6
Tylers Green HP10 ... 163 B1
Windsor SL4 ... 210 A5
St John's Rd
4 Aylesbury HP20 ... 101 E1
Hazlemere HP15 ... 162 F2
Milton Keynes MK3 ... 57 E6
Uxbridge UB8 ... 201 B4
St John's St HP20 ... 101 E1
St John St MK16 ... 22 D4
St John's Terr MK16 ... 22 D4
St John's Well Ct HP4 ... 135 B5
St John's Well La HP4 ... 135 B5
St Josephs Cl MK46 ... 6 F4
St Josephs Mews HP9 ... 175 F2
St Joseph's RC Comb Sch SL9 ... 188 C8
St Joseph's RC High Sch SL2 ... 206 A7
St Joseph's RC Inf Sch HP21 ... 116 A7
St Katherine's Way HP4 ... 134 F7
St Laurence Cl UB8 ... 208 C8
St Laurence Rd MK18 ... 65 F4
St Laurence Way SL1 ... 206 A3
St Lawrence Cl HP3 ... 146 A4
St Lawrence View MK13 ... 34 A4
St Leger Ct MK14 ... 34 E8
St Leger Dr MK14 ... 34 E7
ST LEONARDS ... 132 E3
St Leonard's Ave 2 SL4 ... 210 C5
St Leonard's Hill SL4 ... 209 E4
St Leonards Rd HP6 ... 154 E4
St Leonard's Rd
Oakley Green SL4 ... 209 D1
Windsor SL4 ... 210 C4
St Leonard's Way LU6 ... 92 E1
St Leonards Wlk SL0 ... 207 F3
St Louis RC Comb Sch 15 HP20 ... 101 F2
St Luke Cl UB8 ... 208 D7
St Luke's CE Prim Sch 2 SL6 ... 202 F8
St Luke's Rd
Maidenhead SL6 ... 202 F8
Old Windsor SL4 ... 211 A1
Uxbridge UB10 ... 201 E5
St Margaret Ct MK2 ... 58 E8
St Margarets Cl MK16 ... 22 E4
St Margaret's Cl
Berkhamsted HP4 ... 135 D3
Iver Heath SL0 ... 200 D3
Tylers Green HP10 ... 174 C8
St Margaret's Ct SL0 ... 200 D3
St Margaret's Gate SL0 200 D3
St Margarets Gr HP15 ... 151 E1
St Margaret's Rd SL6 ... 202 A7
St Margaret Way SL1 ... 204 F4
St Marks Cl HP13 ... 173 D7
St Mark's Cres SL6 ... 202 B7
St Mark's Hospl SL6 ... 202 C7
St Mark's Pl SL4 ... 210 C5
St Mark's Rd
Aylesbury HP21 ... 115 C7
Henley-on-Thames RG9 ... 191 E1
Maidenhead SL6 ... 202 D7
Windsor SL4 ... 210 C5
St Martin Cl UB8 ... 208 D7
St Martin's Cl UB7 ... 208 D3
St Martin's Rd UB7 ... 208 D3
St Martin's St MK2 ... 58 C8
St Mary & All Saints CE Prim Sch HP9 ... 175 E3
St Mary Magdalene RC Prim Sch MK12 ... 33 A5
St Mary & St Giles CE Sch MK11 ... 32 E6
St Mary's Ave
Berkhamsted HP4 ... 134 D6
Milton Keynes MK3 ... 57 E7
Milton Keynes, Stony Stratford MK11 ... 32 E6
St Mary's CE Comb Sch HP7 ... 165 A8
St Mary's CE Prim Sch SL1 ... 206 A3
St Mary's CE Sch HP19 115 A8
St Marys Cl
East Claydon MK18 ... 74 F8
Mursley MK17 ... 67 D6
St Mary's Cl
Lee Common HP16 ... 142 D5
Maidenhead SL6 ... 203 A7
South Harefield UB9 ... 190 B8
Wavendon MK17 ... 48 E7
St Marys Ct MK18 ... 51 B7
St Mary's Farnham Royal Prim Sch SL2 ... 198 C2
St Mary's Fst Sch HP4 ... 134 E6
St Mary's Glebe LU6 ... 92 E4
St Mary's RC Prim Sch
Maidenhead SL6 ... 195 F2
Uxbridge UB8 ... 201 C4
St Marys Rd MK18 ... 74 F7
St Mary's Rd
Denham Green UB9 ... 189 F5
Slough SL3 ... 206 E4
South Harefield UB9 ... 190 B8
St Mary's Row 7 HP20 115 D8
St Mary's Sch SL9 ... 188 E7
St Mary's Sq 3 HP20 ... 115 D8
St Mary St
High Wycombe HP11 ... 173 B6
Milton Keynes MK13 ... 33 F7
St Marys Wavendon Prim Sch MK17 ... 48 E7
St Mary's Way
Chalfont St Peter SL9 ... 177 D1
Chesham HP5 ... 154 B8
Leighton Buzzard LU7 ... 80 D7
St Mary's Wlk 10 SL6 ... 202 F7
St Matthew Cl UB8 ... 208 D7
St Matthew's CE Prim Sch UB7 ... 208 E5
St Matthews Ct MK3 ... 57 E6
St Michael's CE Comb Sch LU7 ... 68 E1
St Michaels Cl
Edgcott HP18 ... 72 F2
Halton HP22 ... 131 C8
Stewkley LU7 ... 68 E1
St Michael's Cl HP22 ... 117 C1
St Michael's Ct
Ashton NN7 ... 9 F8
Slough SL2 ... 197 D1
St Michaels Dr
Milton Keynes MK7 ... 47 F6
Walton MK7 ... 47 E7
St Michael's Gn HP9 ... 175 E3
St Michaels Way MK18 ... 63 E3
St Monica's RC Comb Sch MK14 ... 34 F6
St Nicholas CE Comb Sch SL6 ... 196 E1
St Nicholas Cl
Cublington LU7 ... 78 B1
Little Chalfont HP7 ... 166 B8
Uxbridge UB8 ... 208 D7
St Patrick's Cl SL6 ... 202 B4
St Patrick's Way MK3 ... 57 E6
St Paul Cl UB8 ... 208 D8
St Pauls Ave SL2 ... 206 A5
St Paul's CE Comb Sch HP10 ... 185 D4
St Pauls Ct MK11 ... 32 D6
St Paul's Ct SL6 ... 202 F6
St Pauls Gdns SL6 ... 202 B8
St Pauls RC Sch MK6 ... 46 F7
St Paul's Rd MK3 ... 57 E6
St Pauls Yd MK16 ... 22 D4
St Peter's Ave HP19 ... 101 C3
St Peter's CE Comb Sch SL1 ... 197 B2
St Peter's CE Mid Sch SL4 ... 210 F1
St Peters Cl
Loudwater HP11 ... 174 B1
Speen HP27 ... 150 C4
St Peter's Cl
Burnham SL1 ... 197 B1
Old Windsor SL4 ... 211 A2
St Peter's Ct SL9 ... 177 E2
St Peter's Gate NN13 ... 38 A7
St Peters Hill HP23 ... 119 A4
St Peter's RC Prim Sch SL7 ... 183 D3
St Peter's Rd
Brackley NN13 ... 38 A8
Maidenhead SL6 ... 195 D2
Uxbridge UB8 ... 208 D8
St Peter St SL7 ... 183 E1
St Peters Way
Chorleywood WD3 ... 167 B5
Milton Keynes MK13 ... 34 A8
St Pirans Sch SL6 ... 195 E1
St Rumbold's La MK18 ... 52 C8
St Stephens Dr MK15 ... 35 B7
St Stephen's Rd UB7 ... 208 D5
St Teresa's Cl HP27 ... 139 B4
St Teresa's Sch HP27 ... 139 B4
St Thomas Aquinas RC Comb Sch MK3 ... 57 E7
St Thomas Ct MK4 ... 45 F1
St Thomas More RC Prim Sch HP4 ... 135 A4
St Thomas Wlk SL3 ... 212 D7
St Vincents MK17 ... 49 C4
Sakura Wlk MK15 ... 35 C6
Salcey Forest Trail* MK16 ... 4 C2
SALCEY GREEN ... 11 B7
SALDEN ... 67 F8
Salden Cl
Drayton Parslow MK17 ... 68 C6
Milton Keynes MK5 ... 46 B6
SALFORD ... 37 C3
Salford Rd MK17 ... 49 D7
Salisbury Ave SL2 ... 205 C8
Salisbury Cl
Amersham HP7 ... 165 E8
Princes Risborough HP27 ... 139 C3
Salisbury Ct SL6 ... 202 E5
Salisbury Gr MK14 ... 21 F2
Salisbury Mews SL2 ... 198 C1
Salisbury Rd
High Wycombe HP13 ... 162 D1
Uxbridge UB8 ... 201 B3
Sallowsprings LU6 ... 93 F2

Salmons La HP16 ..... 151 D6
Salop Ho MK3 ..... 46 F2
Saltash Cl HP13 ..... 174 B4
Salters Cl
Ludgershall HP18 ..... 96 C8
Maidenhead SL6 ..... 203 A7
Salter's Cl HP4 ..... 134 F6
Salters La HP18 ..... 96 C8
Salters Mews MK14 ..... 34 F6
Salters Rd SL6 ..... 203 B7
Salters Row HP10 ..... 186 A4
SALT HILL 205 D5
Salt Hill Ave SL1 ..... 205 C5
Salt Hill Cl UB8 ..... 201 E7
Salt Hill Dr SL1 ..... 205 C5
Salt Hill Mans SL1 ..... 205 C5
Salt Hill Way SL1 ..... 205 D5
Salton Link MK4 ..... 46 B2
Saltwood Ave MK4 ..... 45 E1
Samphire Ct MK7 ..... 48 A6
Sampsons Gn SL2 ..... 197 F2
Sampsons Hill HP7 ..... 164 E2
Samuel Cl MK16 ..... 22 F3
Sanctuary Rd HP15 ..... 163 B5
Sandage Rd HP14 ..... 171 B5
Sandal Ct MK5 ..... 46 A5
Sandbrier Cl MK7 ..... 48 B6
Sandbrook La HP23 ..... 104 C1
Sandels Way HP9 ..... 175 D4
Sandelswood End HP9 ..... 175 D5
Sanders La NN12 ..... 18 D3
Sanderson Rd UB8 ..... 201 C6
Sandford Gdns HP11 ..... 173 B4
SANDHILL 64 E2
Sandhill Rd
Buckingham MK18 ..... 64 C4
East Claydon MK18 ..... 74 F8
Sandhill Way HP19 ..... 115 A8
Sandholme MK18 ..... 63 E2
Sandhurst Dr MK18 ..... 52 C7
Sandisplatt Rd SL6 ..... 202 A6
Sandlers End SL2 ..... 198 B1
Sandles The SL4 ..... 205 B1
Sandleswood Cl HP9 ..... 175 D4
Sandmartin Cl MK18 ..... 41 E1
Sandon Cl HP23 ..... 118 F4
Sandown Ct
8 High Wycombe HP12 ..... 172 E7
Milton Keynes MK3 ..... 57 D6
Sandown Rd SL2 ..... 204 F8
Sandpiper 1 HP19 ..... 101 E4
Sandpipers Pl SL6 ..... 195 E6
Sandpit Hill MK18 ..... 50 F6
Sandpit Hill Cotts HP23 ..... 133 B2
Sandpit La HP27 ..... 138 B4
Sandpits La HP10 ..... 174 C7
Sandringham Ct
8 High Wycombe HP13 ..... 173 B7
Newport Pagnell MK16 ..... 22 B3
Slough SL1 ..... 204 D7
Sandringham Pl MK2 ..... 58 C8
Sandringham Rd
Maidenhead SL6 ..... 195 E2
Stanwell TW6 ..... 213 E2
SANDS 172 B7
Sands Bank Nature Reserve* HP12 ..... 172 A7
Sands Farm Dr SL1 ..... 197 C1
Sands Ind Est HP12 ..... 172 B7
Sandstone Cl MK18 ..... 73 B5
Sandwell Ct MK8 ..... 33 C2
Sandy Cl
Buckingham MK18 ..... 52 F8
Milton Keynes MK14 ..... 34 D8
Sandycroft Rd HP6 ..... 155 C1
Sandygate Cl SL7 ..... 183 D3
Sandygate Rd SL7 ..... 183 D3
Sandy La
Aspley Heath MK17 ..... 49 B2
Leighton Buzzard LU7 ..... 70 F3
Long Crendon HP18 ..... 125 B6
Sandy Mead SL6 ..... 203 C1
Sandy Rd MK18 ..... 73 B5
Sandy Rise SL9 ..... 177 E2
Sandywell Dr MK15 ..... 35 A6
San Remo Rd MK17 ..... 49 F4
Santen Gr MK2 ..... 58 D4
Saracens' Wharf MK2 ..... 47 E1
Sargeant Cl UB8 ..... 201 D2
SARRATT 156 F4
Sarum Complex UB8 ..... 201 B3
Satis Ho SL3 ..... 211 C7
Saunders Cl MK7 ..... 48 D6
Saunders Ct 1 HP13 ..... 173 F6
Saunders End HP6 ..... 153 C5
Saunders Pl HP19 ..... 115 A7
Saunders Rd UB10 ..... 201 F4
Saunders Wood Copse HP14 ..... 158 F4
SAUNDERTON
Bledlow Ridge 149 C1
Princes Risborough 138 E1
SAUNDERTON LEE 149 A4
Saunderton Sta HP14 ..... 149 C1
Saunderton Vale HP14 ..... 149 C1
Savage Croft MK10 ..... 35 E3
Savay Cl UB9 ..... 190 A4
Savay La UB9 ..... 190 A5
Savernake Rd HP19 ..... 101 D3
Savill La MK4, MK5 ..... 45 F2
Savill Way SL7 ..... 183 F2
Savoy Cres MK9 ..... 34 F3
Savoy Ct SL6 ..... 195 F1
Sawley Ho 5 MK3 ..... 46 F1
Sawmill Cotts SL3 ..... 199 F2
Sawmill Rd HP27 ..... 138 D7
Sawpit Hill HP15 ..... 163 B5
Sawyers Cl SL6 ..... 202 A2
Sawyer's Cl SL4 ..... 209 E7
Sawyers Cres SL6 ..... 202 A2
Saxeways Bsns Ctr HP5 ..... 143 E3
Saxhorn Rd HP14 ..... 171 C4
Saxon Cl
Amersham HP6 ..... 154 D1
Dunstable LU6 ..... 93 E8
Milton Keynes MK19 ..... 11 B2
Slough SL3 ..... 206 F4
Uxbridge UB8 ..... 208 E8
Saxon Ct
High Wycombe HP12 ..... 172 D8
Stanwell TW19 ..... 213 A2
Saxon Gate MK9 ..... 34 E2
Saxon Gdns SL6 ..... 196 D1
Saxon Lodge SL1 ..... 204 F5
Saxon Park Ind Est MK1 ..... 47 D2
Saxon St
Milton Keynes, Ashland MK1, MK6 ..... 47 C4
Milton Keynes, Heelands MK6, MK13, MK14 ..... 34 C5
Milton Keynes MK2 ..... 58 C8
Saxon Way
Harmondsworth UB7 ..... 213 C8
Old Windsor SL4 ..... 211 B1
Saxon Way Trad Ctr UB7 ..... 213 C8
Sayers Gdns HP4 ..... 135 A6
Saye & Sele Cl HP18 ..... 82 F6
Sayward Cl HP5 ..... 144 D2
Scafell Rd SL2 ..... 204 F8
Scarborough Way SL1 ..... 205 B4
Scardale MK13 ..... 34 C5
Scarlett Ave HP22 ..... 131 E6
Scatterdells La WD4 ..... 146 F1
Scatterill Cl MK13 ..... 34 A4
Scholars Way HP6 ..... 154 F1
Scholars Wlk
Chalfont St Peter SL9 ..... 177 E4
Slough SL3 ..... 207 A4
School Cl
Asheridge HP5 ..... 143 E5
Brackley NN13 ..... 39 A4
Cryers Hill HP15 ..... 162 C6
High Wycombe, Downley HP13 ..... 161 D2
High Wycombe HP11 ..... 173 A4
Holmer Green HP15 ..... 163 C7
Ickford HP18 ..... 124 A3
School Dr MK17 ..... 57 C3
School End
Chetwode MK18 ..... 61 D8
Great Horwood MK17 ..... 55 A3
School Hill
Charndon OX27 ..... 73 A6
North Marston MK18 ..... 76 B2
School Ho TW19 ..... 213 C1
School La
Amersham HP7 ..... 165 A8
Buckingham MK18 ..... 52 C8
Castlethorpe MK19 ..... 19 F5
Chalfont St Giles HP8 ..... 177 B7
Chalfont St Peter SL9 ..... 177 D1
Chearsley HP18 ..... 112 B2
Cookham Dean SL6 ..... 195 B7
Cookham SL6 ..... 196 B7
Dinton HP17 ..... 113 F2
Eaton Bray LU6 ..... 92 F6
Leighton Buzzard LU7 ..... 68 E1
Little Marlow SL7 ..... 184 C5
Maidenhead SL6 ..... 195 E1
Medmenham SL7 ..... 193 B6
Milton Keynes MK5 ..... 46 B8
Oakley HP18 ..... 109 D5
Penn Street HP7 ..... 164 B5
Preston Bissett MK18 ..... 62 B8
Seer Green HP9 ..... 176 D4
Shabbington HP18 ..... 124 D3
Sherington MK16 ..... 14 A2
Slough SL2 ..... 205 F6
Turville RG9 ..... 169 F3
Twyford MK18 ..... 62 D2
Upper Winchendon HP18 ..... 99 A1
Waddesdon HP18 ..... 99 A6
Weston Turville HP22 ..... 116 F1
Wexham Street SL2 ..... 199 B5
Yardley Gobion NN12 ..... 18 E6
School Rd
Harmondsworth UB7 ..... 213 D8
Tylers Green HP10 ..... 174 D8
Wooburn Green HP10 ..... 185 E6
School St MK13 ..... 33 F7
School The HP23 ..... 118 C8
School Way HP11 ..... 174 B2
Schorne La MK18 ..... 76 B2
Schumann Cl MK7 ..... 48 C4
Scotch Firs MK7 ..... 48 C6
Scotlands Dr SL2 ..... 198 B6
Scotney Gdns MK3 ..... 57 E8
Scotsgrove Cotts OX9 ..... 126 A4
Scotsgrove Hill OX9 ..... 126 A3
Scotswood Cl HP9 ..... 175 D5
Scott Cl
Farnham Common SL2 ..... 198 C7
West Drayton UB7 ..... 208 F2
Scott Dr MK16 ..... 22 A5
Scott End HP19 ..... 100 F2
Scott Evans Ct MK18 ..... 66 A5
Scotts Cl
Marsh Gibbon OX27 ..... 72 A3
Stoke Hammond MK17 ..... 69 E8
Scotts Cnr NN13 ..... 39 A4
Scotts Farm Cl MK18 ..... 41 E4
Scotts La
Adstock MK18 ..... 53 F1
Buckingham MK18 ..... 41 E3
Marsh Gibbon OX27 ..... 71 E2
Scriven Ct MK15 ..... 35 E7
Scriveners La NN12 ..... 17 A8
Scrubb's La HP14 ..... 160 B7
Seabrooke Ct MK8 ..... 45 D6
Seacourt Rd SL3 ..... 207 B2
Seaford Rd TW6 ..... 213 D2
Seagrave Ct MK7 ..... 48 A4
Seagrave Rd HP9 ..... 175 C4
Sears The LU6 ..... 92 B5
Seaton Dr HP21 ..... 115 D4
Seaton Gr MK10 ..... 36 A4
Secklow Gate MK9 ..... 34 F3
Second Ave MK1 ..... 47 C2
Second Cres SL1 ..... 205 C8
Second St HP11 ..... 173 C4
Sedgemere MK8 ..... 33 D2
Sedgemoor Dr OX9 ..... 126 A1
Sedgmoor Cl HP10 ..... 185 A7
Sedgmoor Gdns HP10 ..... 185 A8
Sedgmoor La HP10 ..... 185 B7
Sedgmoor Rd HP10 ..... 185 A8
Sedley Gr UB9 ..... 190 C7
SEDRUP 114 F3
Sedrup La HP17 ..... 114 F4
Seebeck Cl MK5 ..... 46 C7
Seeleys Cl HP9 ..... 175 C4
Seeleys Ct HP9 ..... 175 D3
Seeleys La HP9 ..... 175 D3
Seeleys Rd HP9 ..... 175 C4
SEER GREEN 176 D4
Seer Green CE Comb Sch HP9 ..... 176 C4
Seer Green & Jordans Sta HP9 ..... 176 C3
Seer Green La HP9 ..... 176 E3
Seer Mead HP9 ..... 176 D4
Sefton Cl SL2 ..... 198 F4
Sefton Paddock SL2 ..... 199 A5
Sefton Park Cotts SL2 ..... 199 A4
Sefton Park Sch SL2 ..... 199 B5
Sefton Way UB8 ..... 208 C7
Selbourne Ave MK3 ..... 57 F7
Selbourne Ho 10 SL8 ..... 185 A4
Selby Gr MK5 ..... 46 B5
Selim Ct 4 SL1 ..... 206 B4
Selkirk Ave HP19 ..... 101 D2
Selkirk Gr MK3 ..... 46 F2
Selwood Cl TW19 ..... 213 C1
Selwood Gdns TW19 ..... 213 C1
Selwood Way HP13 ..... 161 E2
Selworthy MK4 ..... 46 D3
Selwyn Cl SL4 ..... 209 E5
Selwyn Ct HP21 ..... 116 B6
Selwyn Gr MK3 ..... 58 B8
Selwyn Pl SL1 ..... 204 F6
September Ct UB10 ..... 201 D3
Serjeants Gn MK14 ..... 34 F6
Serles Cl MK6 ..... 47 A6
Sermed Ct SL2 ..... 206 C5
Serpentine Ct MK2 ..... 58 D5
Servite Ho SL6 ..... 203 B8
Seven Acre Ho HP10 ..... 174 C2
Seven Acres HP18 ..... 125 B7
Seven Gables MK18 ..... 65 D6
Sevenhills Rd SL0 ..... 200 C6
Severalls Ave HP5 ..... 144 C2
Severn Cres SL3 ..... 207 B1
Severn Dr MK16 ..... 22 E4
Severn Ho HP13 ..... 173 F7
Severn Way MK3 ..... 57 D8
Sewell Cl HP19 ..... 100 F2
Seymour Cl
Flackwell Heath HP10 ..... 173 F2
Maidenhead SL6 ..... 202 B3
Seymour Court La SL7 ..... 183 B5
Seymour Court Rd SL7 ..... 183 C4
Seymour Ct
Berkhamsted HP4 ..... 134 E6
Tring HP23 ..... 119 A4
Seymour Ho
High Wycombe HP12 ..... 172 E4
Slough SL3 ..... 206 E4
Seymour Park Rd SL7 ..... 183 D3
Seymour Plain SL7 ..... 183 C5
Seymour Rd
Berkhamsted HP4 ..... 134 E6
Chalfont St Giles HP8 ..... 177 C6
Seymour Rd *continued*
Slough SL1 ..... 205 D4
SHABBINGTON 124 D3
Shackerstone Cl MK10 ..... 36 B4
Shackleton Ct 6 TW19 ..... 213 E1
Shackleton Pl MK6 ..... 34 E1
Shackleton Rd
High Wycombe HP12 ..... 172 E5
Slough SL1 ..... 205 F6
Shaftesbury Cres MK3 ..... 47 A1
Shaftesbury Ct
Maidenhead SL6 ..... 202 E5
6 Slough SL1 ..... 205 E4
Winslow MK18 ..... 65 F5
Shaftesbury Ho HP21 ..... 116 C7
Shaftesbury St HP11 ..... 172 F8
Shaggy Calf La SL2 ..... 206 A6
Shakespeare Cl MK16 ..... 22 A5
Shakespeare Lodge SL1 ..... 204 F5
Shakespeare Orch HP18 ..... 82 F6
Shakespeare Way HP20 ..... 116 A8
Shallowford Gr MK4 ..... 46 D4
SHALSTONE 39 E6
Shamaa Ho 13 SL1 ..... 205 F4
Shamrock Cl MK7 ..... 48 B6
Shannon Ct
Chesham HP5 ..... 144 C1
Milton Keynes MK14 ..... 35 A6
Shantock Hall La HP3 ..... 145 E1
Shantock La HP3 ..... 145 E1
Shantung Pl HP5 ..... 154 C6
Shardeloes HP7 ..... 164 D8
Sharkham Ct MK4 ..... 46 B1
Sharman Row 8 SL3 ..... 206 F1
Sharman Wlk MK13 ..... 34 A3
Sharney Ave SL3 ..... 207 B3
Sharp Cl HP21 ..... 115 E5
Sharp's Cl HP18 ..... 99 B6
Sharrow Vale HP12 ..... 172 E7
Shaw Cl
Aylesbury HP20 ..... 116 A8
Newport Pagnell MK16 ..... 22 A5
Shaw Ct
Aylesbury HP21 ..... 115 E3
Old Windsor SL4 ..... 211 A2
Shawfield Ct UB7 ..... 208 E3
Shaw Gdns 11 SL3 ..... 206 F1
Shaws Cl HP16 ..... 151 D5
Shaw The SL6 ..... 195 E6
Shearmans MK11 ..... 33 A4
Sheehy Way SL2 ..... 206 B6
Sheelin Gr MK2 ..... 58 D4
Sheepcoat Cl MK5 ..... 46 A5
Sheepcote Cl HP9 ..... 175 C4
Sheepcote Dell Rd HP15 ..... 163 E7
Sheepcote Gdns UB9 ..... 190 A5
Sheepcote La HP10, SL1 ..... 186 A2
Sheepcote Rd
Eton Wick SL4 ..... 205 A1
Windsor SL4 ..... 209 E5
Sheepfold La HP7 ..... 165 D7
Sheephouse Rd SL6 ..... 196 B2
SHEEPLANE 60 C2
Sheeplane MK17 ..... 60 C2
SHEEPRIDGE 184 E7
Sheepridge La SL7, SL8 ..... 184 E7
Sheep St MK18 ..... 66 A4
Sheering Gr MK13 ..... 34 B8
Sheerness Ct MK4 ..... 57 A8
Sheerstock HP17 ..... 126 E5
Sheerwater HP19 ..... 101 E4
Sheet St SL4 ..... 210 D6
Sheet Street Rd SL4 ..... 210 C2
Sheffield Dr HP21 ..... 115 E6
Sheffield Rd SL1 ..... 205 C7
Shelburne Ct HP12 ..... 172 E4
Shelburne Rd HP12 ..... 172 E4
Sheldon Ct MK8 ..... 33 F1
Sheldon Rd HP18 ..... 124 A3
Sheldon Way HP4 ..... 135 A5
Shelduck Cl 3 HP20 ..... 101 E3
Shelley Cl
Medmenham SL7 ..... 193 D7
Newport Pagnell MK16 ..... 22 B4
Slough SL3 ..... 206 F1
Wooburn Green HP10 ..... 185 E8
Shelley Dr MK3 ..... 57 F7
Shelley Rd
Chesham HP5 ..... 144 B2
High Wycombe HP11 ..... 172 F5
12 Marlow SL7 ..... 183 F3
Shellfield Cl TW19 ..... 213 A2
Shelsley Ave MK6 ..... 47 C5
Shelsmore MK14 ..... 35 A8
Shelton Ct
Slough SL3 ..... 206 C3
Woburn Sands MK17 ..... 49 B4
SHENLEY BROOK END 46 A2
Shenley Brook End Sch MK5 ..... 46 A2
SHENLEY CHURCH END 45 E6
Shenley L Ctr MK5 ..... 46 A7
SHENLEY LODGE 46 C5
Shenley Rd
Milton Keynes, Bletchley MK3 ..... 46 E1
Milton Keynes, Loughton MK5 ..... 46 A7
Whaddon MK17 ..... 56 C8
Shenley Rdbt MK5 ..... 46 A5
SHENLEY WOOD 45 F4
Shenston Ct 13 SL4 ..... 210 C6
Shenstone Dr SL1 ..... 197 D1
Shenstone Hill HP4 ..... 135 E5
Shenton MK10 ..... 36 C3
Shepherd Cl HP20 ..... 102 A2
Shepherds MK11 ..... 33 A4
Shepherds Cl
Beaconsfield HP9 ..... 175 F1
Hurley SL6 ..... 193 F3
Uxbridge UB8 ..... 201 C1
Shepherds Ct SL4 ..... 209 E5
Shepherds Fold HP15 ..... 163 D8
Shepherds Gate HP16 ..... 152 A2
Shepherds La
Beaconsfield HP9 ..... 175 F1
Hazlemere HP15 ..... 162 F5
Hurley SL6 ..... 193 E4
Shepherd's La WD3 ..... 167 E2
Shepherds Row MK18 ..... 66 A4
Shepherds Way HP5 ..... 154 D6
Shepherdswell Sch MK6 ..... 35 B2
Sheppards Cl MK16 ..... 22 C4
Shepperds Cl MK18 ..... 76 A2
Shepperds Gn MK5 ..... 45 F6
Shepperton Ct MK19 ..... 19 F5
Sheraton Dr HP13 ..... 162 D1
Sheraton Ho WD3 ..... 167 C5
Sherborne Cl SL3 ..... 212 E6
Sherborne Ct SL6 ..... 202 E5
Sherbourne Dr
Bow Brickhill MK7 ..... 48 B4
Maidenhead SL6 ..... 202 C3
Windsor SL4 ..... 209 F3
Sherbourne Wlk SL2 ..... 198 C8
Shereway HP19 ..... 115 B8
Shergold Way SL6 ..... 195 F6
Sheridan Cl HP21 ..... 115 D3
Sheridan Ct
High Wycombe HP12 ..... 172 C3
Maidenhead SL6 ..... 203 B8
Slough SL1 ..... 204 E6
Sheridan Gr MK4 ..... 45 D2
Sheriff Cl HP19 ..... 115 B8
Sheringham Ct SL6 ..... 202 E7
SHERINGTON 14 A2
Sherington CE Fst Sch MK16 ..... 14 A2
Sherington Rd MK16 ..... 22 E7
Sherman Rd SL1 ..... 205 E8
Shernfold MK7 ..... 48 B7
Sherriff Cotts HP18 ..... 99 A7
Sherwood Cl SL3 ..... 206 E3
Sherwood Ct
Colnbrook SL3 ..... 212 D7
10 Slough SL3 ..... 206 F1
Sherwood Dr
Maidenhead SL6 ..... 202 A6
Milton Keynes MK1, MK2, MK3 ..... 47 B1
Shields Ct HP10 ..... 163 B1
Shifford Cres SL6 ..... 195 E3
Shilling Cl MK15 ..... 35 A7
Shillingridge Pk SL7 ..... 182 E5
Shinfield Cl MK18 ..... 63 D2
Ship Hill SL1 ..... 186 E4
Ship La LU7 ..... 105 D3
Shiplake Ho SL8 ..... 185 B4
Shipley Rd MK16 ..... 22 B4
Shipman Ct MK15 ..... 35 B7
Ship Rd LU7 ..... 80 E6
Ship St HP11 ..... 173 A7
SHIPTON 66 B3
Shipton MK18 ..... 66 B3
Shipton Hill MK13 ..... 34 B6
SHIPTON LEE 84 D7
Shipton Rd UB10 ..... 201 F8
Shire Ct MK14 ..... 35 A5
Shire La
Chalfont St Peter HP8, SL9 ..... 178 B6
Cholesbury HP23 ..... 133 B4
Chorleywood WD3 ..... 167 C4
North Crawley MK16 ..... 24 E4
Shires Bsns Pk The NN13 ..... 38 A6
Shires Rd NN13 ..... 38 A6
Shirley Ave SL4 ..... 209 F6
Shirley Cl HP20 ..... 101 D2
Shirley Moor MK7 ..... 48 B8
Shirley Rd SL6 ..... 202 C5
Shirwell Cres MK4 ..... 46 D5
Shogmoor La RG9 ..... 170 C1
Shootacre Cnr HP27 ..... 149 A8
Shootacre La HP27 ..... 149 A8
SHOOTERSWAY 134 E4
Shootersway HP4 ..... 134 E4
Shootersway La HP4 ..... 134 F4
Shootersway Pk HP4 ..... 134 F3

Shop La NN7 1 B6
Shoppenhanger's Rd SL6 202 E4
Shorediche Cl UB10 190 F1
Shoreham Rise SL2 197 D1
Shoreham Road (E) TW6 213 E2
Shoreham Road (W) TW6 213 E2
Shorham Rise MK8 33 E2
Shortborough Ave HP27 139 B5
Short Ditch HP17 127 A7
Shortfern SL2 206 C7
Short Hale LU7 105 D3
Short Massey MK46 6 E5
Short Rd TW6 213 E1
Short St HP11 172 F7
Shortway
Amersham HP6 154 D2
Chesham HP5 144 B2
Shotfield Rd HP14 171 C4
Shothanger Way HP3 146 D6
Shouler Cl MK5 46 A5
SHREDING GREEN 207 C7
Shrewsbury Cl MK10 36 A2
Shrimpton Cl HP9 175 D6
Shrimpton Rd
Beaconsfield HP9 175 D6
High Wycombe HP12 172 B3
Shropshire Ct MK3 46 E1
Shrubbery Cl HP13 173 B8
Shrubbery Rd HP13 173 B8
Shrublands Ave HP4 135 A4
Shrublands Rd HP4 135 A5
Shucklow Hill MK17 55 E3
Shugars Gn HP23 119 B5
Shupp's La HP18 112 B1
Shutlanger Rd NN12 9 A8
Shuttleworth Gr MK7 48 D6
Siareys Cl OX39 147 C6
Sibleys Rise HP16 152 D8
Side Rd UB9 189 D4
Sidings Ind Est The NN13 38 A8
Sidings The
Loudwater HP11 174 B3
Milton Keynes MK2 47 E1
Sidlow Ct MK11 32 F4
Sidney Cl UB8 201 C5
Sidney Ho HP14 171 C5
Sidney Rd SL4 209 C4
Sidney Terr HP22 131 B5
Silbury Arc MK9 34 E3
Silbury Bvd MK9 34 D2
Silbury Rdbt MK9 34 C1
Silchester Ho SL6 203 B8
Silco Dr SL6 202 E6
Silicon Ct MK5 46 C5
Silk Mill Way HP23 119 A5
Silk St HP18 99 A6
Silkwood Ct SL1 205 F6
Sillswood MK46 6 E4
Silsden Cres HP8 177 D7
Silverbeck Way TW19 213 A2
Silver Birch Cl UB10 201 E8
Silver Birch Dr HP27 149 E5
Silverbirches La MK17 49 A2
Silver Birch Way HP22 116 B4
Silver Cl SL6 202 A5
Silverdale Cl
4 Aylesbury HP20 101 D1
Tylers Green HP10 163 A1
Silver End MK46 7 A3
Silver Hill HP8 177 B8
Silvermead HP18 123 D5
Silver St
20 Aylesbury HP20 115 D8
Cublington LU7 78 B1
Milton Keynes MK11 32 D5
Newport Pagnell MK16 22 D4
Silverstone Mews SL6 202 C4
Silverstone Motor Racing Circuit* MK18 28 F8
Silvertrees Dr SL6 202 A5
Silverweed Ct MK7 48 B5
Simatt Ho HP10 174 C2
Simdims MK43 25 A1
Simmons Cl SL3 207 A2
Simmons Ct
Aylesbury HP21 115 E4
High Wycombe HP12 172 E7
Simmons Rd RG9 191 D3
Simmons Way
Lane End HP14 171 C4
Thame OX9 125 F1
Simms Croft MK10 36 A2
Simnel MK6 47 B6
Simon Dean HP3 146 A4
Simonsbath MK4 46 D2
Simons Lea MK13 34 B4
Simon's Way MK18 39 E7
Simpson Cl SL6 203 B8
Simpson Dr MK6 47 E5
Simpson Pl HP21 115 F5
Simpson Rd MK1, MK2, MK6 47 E3
Simpson Rdbt MK6 47 D5
Simpson Sch MK6 47 D5
Simpsons Way SL1 205 E5
Sinatra Dr MK4 45 E3
Sinclair Ct MK1 47 B3
Sinclair Rd SL4 210 C4
Singers La RG9 191 E1
SINGLEBOROUGH 54 F5
Singleborough La MK17 54 F3
Singleton Dr MK8 45 D6
Singleton Way 8 HP19 115 A8
Singret Pl UB8 201 C1
Sion Terr MK18 51 B6
Sipson Rd UB7 208 F3
Sipthorp Cl MK7 48 C6
Sir Henry Floyd Gram Sch HP21 115 C7
Sir Henry Peakes Dr SL2 198 A6
Sir Peter's Way HP4 107 E6
Sir Robert Mews SL3 207 A1
Sir Sydney Camm Ho SL4 210 B6
Sir William Borlase's Gram Sch SL7 183 C1
Sir William Ramsay Sch HP15 163 A3
Sissinghurst Dr MK4 45 E2
Sitwell Cl MK16 21 F5
Six Cotts MK18 29 E5
Sixth St HP11 173 C4
Sixty Acres Rd HP16 151 C6
Skeats Wharf MK15 35 A7
Skeldon Gate MK14 35 A4
Skeldon Rdbt MK9 35 A4
Skelton Cl HP9 186 A8
Skene Cl MK2 58 C4
Skerries Ct SL3 207 A2
Skimmers Cl HP15 163 C6
Skimmers End HP15 163 C6
Skimmers Field HP15 163 C6
Skip La UB9 190 E3
Skipper Cl HP19 101 C4
Skippon Way OX9 125 F2
Skipton Cl MK15 35 C6
SKIRMETT 170 A1
Skittle Gn HP27 138 A2
SKITTLE GREEN 138 A3
Skydmore Path SL2 197 F1
Skye Cres
Milton Keynes MK17 58 C3
Milton Keynes MK17 58 C3
Skye Lodge SL1 205 E5
Skylark Rd UB9 189 C3
Skyline Mews HP12 172 C4
Skyport Dr UB7 213 D7
Skyway 14 Trad Est SL3 212 F4
Slade Hill
Aylesbury HP19 115 A7
Mixbury NN13 38 D1
Slade La MK11 33 A4
Slade Oak La UB9 189 C5
Slade Rd HP14 158 E4
Slade The MK17 57 D3
Slad La HP27 149 F3
SLAPTON 91 C5
Slapton La LU6 91 F6
Slated Row MK12 33 B7
Slated Row Specl Sch MK12 33 A7
Slatepits Croft MK46 6 E5
Slater St HP13 173 C6
Slattenham Cl HP19 115 B7
Slave Hill HP17 126 F5
Slayter Rd HP14 171 C4
Slickett's La LU6 92 F3
Slipe The LU7 105 A7
SLOUGH 205 D5
Slough & Eton CE Sch SL1 205 D3
Slough Gram Sch SL3 206 B3
Slough Ice Arena SL1 205 D4
Slough Interchange Ind Est SL2 206 A5
Slough La HP14 160 C6
Slough Mus* SL1 206 A4
Slough Rd
Datchet SL3 211 B8
Iver Heath SL0 200 E3
Slough SL4 205 E2
Slough Sta SL1 205 F5
Slough Trad Est SL1 205 B7
Sly Corner HP16 142 E4
Smabridge Wlk MK15 35 D7
SMAE Inst The SL6 202 B6
Small Cres MK18 52 F8
Smalldean La HP27 149 E2
Smarden Bell MK7 48 B8
Smeaton Cl
Aylesbury HP19 101 A1
Blakelands MK14 22 A2
Smewin Ct HP11 172 E7
Smith Cl HP20 116 B7
Smith Ctr The RG9 191 B5
Smithergill Ct MK13 34 C5
Smithfield End MK17 66 F4
Smithfield Rd SL6 202 A3
Smith's La
Waterperry Common OX33 122 F7
Windsor SL4 209 E6
Smithsons Pl MK9 35 B3
Smithy The MK19 31 E4
Snaith Cres MK5 46 B7
Snakeley Cl HP10 174 C1
Snakemoor Nature Reserve* HP17 126 D6
Snape Spur SL1 205 E7
Snells La HP7 166 C7
Snells Wood Ct HP7 166 C7
SNELSHALL EAST 57 B7
Snelshall St MK4 56 F8
SNELSHALL WEST 57 A7
Snowball Hill SL6 202 A1
Snowberry Cl MK12 33 D5
Snowden Cl SL4 209 D3
Snowdon Dr MK6 46 D7
Snowdrop Way HP15 162 F7
Snowhill Cotts HP5 144 F7
Snowshill Ct MK14 21 F2
Soames Cl MK46 7 F7
Soane Wlk HP13 173 A8
Soho Cres HP10 185 D4
Soho Mills Ind Est HP10 185 D4
Sokeman Cl MK12 33 A5
Solar Ct MK14 21 E1
Solesbridge Cl WD3 167 F6
Solesbridge La WD3 167 F6
Somerford Cl SL6 203 B8
Somerford Pl HP9 175 D3
Somerlea SL6 196 C3
Somersby Cres SL6 202 E3
Somerset Cl MK3 46 F1
Somerset Lodge 3 SL6 202 F6
Somerset Way SL0 207 F4
Somers Lees 13 HP19 115 A8
Somerville Rd SL4 205 C1
Somerville Way HP19 115 B8
Sophie Gdns SL3 206 D4
Sorensen Ct MK5 45 E4
Sorrell Dr MK16 21 F4
Soskin Dr MK14 34 D6
Sospel Ct SL2 198 C3
SOULBURY 69 E3
Soulbury LU7 69 E2
Soulbury Rd
Burcott LU7 79 D4
Leighton Buzzard LU7 80 D7
Stewkley LU7 68 F1
Southampton Road E TW6 213 F1
Southampton Road W TW6 213 E1
South Bank NN13 38 C7
South Bank Rd HP4 134 F6
Southbourne 1 HP13 173 C7
Southbourne Dr SL8 185 A3
Southbridge Gr MK7 48 A7
South Cl
Medmenham SL7 193 D7
Slough SL1 204 D6
West Drayton UB7 208 F3
Southcliffe Dr SL9 177 E5
South Common Rd UB8 201 E6
Southcote Way HP10 163 B1
South Cottage Dr WD3 167 F4
South Cottage Gdns WD3 167 F4
Southcott Lower Sch LU7 80 D8
Southcott Village LU7 80 D6
Southcott Way MK6 47 D5
SOUTHCOURT 115 D6
Southcourt Ave LU7 80 D6
Southcourt Ho LU7 80 D7
Southcourt Rd LU7 80 D7
Southcroft SL2 198 B1
South Dr
Beaconsfield HP9 186 B8
High Wycombe HP13 173 D8
South Eighth St MK9 34 E2
SOUTHEND 180 C8
SOUTH END
Leckhampstead 42 E7
Stewkley 78 E8
South End HP17 126 F5
South End La LU6 92 B4
South Enmore Rdbt MK6 35 B3
Southern Cotts TW19 213 A2
Southern Perimeter Rd TW6, TW19 213 D2
Southern Rd
Aylesbury HP19 101 C1
Thame OX9 125 E1
Southern Way MK12 33 D5
Southfield Cl MK15 35 E7
South Field Cl SL4 204 C3
Southfield Cotts HP17 130 C3
Southfield Dr HP15 163 A6
Southfield Gdns SL1 204 B8
Southfield Rd
Aylesbury HP20 116 B8
Flackwell Heath HP10 174 A1
High Wycombe HP13 161 D1
Princes Risborough HP27 139 C3
South Fifth St MK9 34 E1
South Fourth St MK9 34 D1
Southgate Ho SL6 202 F8
South Gn SL1 205 E6
South Hall MK18 41 E3
SOUTH HAREFIELD 190 D6
SOUTH HEATH 152 E8
South Hills HP18 96 A1
South Ho MK1 47 D3
South La LU7 78 E7
Southland Dr MK2 58 E6
Southlands Rd UB9 189 F1
South Lawne MK3 57 F8
Southlea Rd SL3, SL4 211 B5
South Maundin HP14 162 A7
South Meadow La SL4 210 C8
South Ninth St MK9 34 F2
South Overgate Rdbt MK6 35 B3
South Park Ave WD3 167 F4
South Park Cres SL9 188 F7
South Park Ct SL9 188 E6
South Park Dr SL9 188 E7
South Park Gdns HP4 135 B5
South Park View SL9 188 F7
South Path SL4 210 C5
South Pk SL9 188 F6
South Pl SL7 183 E1
South Rd
Amersham HP6 154 C3
Chorleywood WD3 167 C4
Maidenhead SL6 202 E6
West Drayton UB7 208 F3
South Row
Fulmer SL3 199 E8
Milton Keynes MK9 34 E1
Milton Keynes MK9 46 D8
South Saxon Rdbt MK9 34 F1
South Secklow Rdbt MK6 34 F2
South Second St MK9 34 D1
South Seventh St MK9 34 E1
South Side SL9 188 D8
South Sixth St MK9 34 E1
South St
Castlethorpe MK19 19 F5
Wendover HP22 131 B4
South Tenth St MK9 34 F2
South Terr
Milton Keynes MK2 58 C8
Windsor SL4 210 E6
South Vale NN7 1 A5
South View
Cookham Rise SL6 195 E7
Eton SL4 205 B1
High Wycombe HP13 161 D2
Wooburn Green HP10 185 D8
Southview Rd SL7 183 E4
South View Rd SL9 188 D7
South Way HP9 186 A8
Southwick Ct MK8 45 F8
South Witan Rdbt MK6 34 E1
Southwold Cl HP21 116 A6
Southwold Spur SL3 207 C4
Southwood Gdns SL6 195 E5
Southwood Rd SL6 195 E5
Southwood Sch MK14 34 E5
Sovereign Beeches SL2 198 B6
Sovereign Cl MK18 75 F7
Sovereign Ct
Aylesbury HP19 101 D1
High Wycombe HP13 173 D6
Sovereign Dr MK15 35 A7
Sovereign Hts SL3 212 A8
Sovereign Lodge MK15 35 A7
Spackmans Way SL1 205 D3
Spa Cl HP18 110 B8
Spade Oak Farm SL8 184 E3
Spade Oak Mdw SL8 184 E4
Spark Way MK16 21 F5
Sparrow Cl HP19 101 F3
Sparrow Hall Bsns Pk LU6 92 D3
Sparrow Hall Farm LU6 92 D3
Sparsholt Cl 5 MK4 46 C2
Spearing Rd HP12 172 C7
Spearmast Ind Est HP12 172 B6
Spearmint Cl MK7 48 B5
Specklands MK5 46 A8
Speedbird Way UB7 213 B7
Speedwell Pl MK14 34 E4
SPEEN 150 C4
Speen CE Sch HP27 150 B4
Speen Rd HP14, HP16, HP27 150 D2
Speldhurst Ct MK7 48 B7
Spencer MK14 34 C8
Spencer Cl UB8 201 C2
Spencer Gdns OX27 72 E5
Spencer Rd SL3 206 F3
Spencers Cl SL6 202 D8
SPENCERSGREEN 132 C7
Spencers La SL6 195 E6
Spencers Rd SL6 202 D8
Spencer St MK13 33 F7
Spencer Villas SL1 204 F5
Spenlows Rd MK3 47 A3
Spens SL6 202 F8
Spenser Ho HP21 115 F6
Spenser Rd HP21 115 F6
Sperling Rd SL6 195 F1
Spickett's La HP18 113 A3
Spier's La OX27 71 F2
Spiert The HP17 114 D5
Spindle Cl HP15 163 A3
Spindle Ct HP12 172 E7
Spinfield La SL7 183 B2
Spinfield Lane W SL7 183 C1
Spinfield Mount SL7 183 B1
Spinfield Pk SL7 183 C1
Spinfield Sch SL7 183 B2
Spinners Wlk
Marlow SL7 183 C1
Windsor SL4 210 C6
Spinney SL1 205 B5
Spinney Bglws LU7 91 C6
Spinney Cl
Steeple Claydon MK18 63 E2
West Drayton UB7 208 E6
Spinney Cotts OX33 123 B1
Spinney Cres LU6 93 F8
Spinney Hill Rd MK46 6 E3
Spinney La MK17 49 F4
Spinney The
Beaconsfield HP9 175 E1
Berkhamsted HP4 134 F3
Chesham HP5 144 D2
Gerrards Cross SL9 188 D3
High Wycombe HP11 173 A4
Holmer Green HP15 163 D7
Milton Keynes MK13 34 A4
Winslow MK18 66 A6
Spire View TW19 213 D1
SPITAL 210 B3
Spitfire Cl SL3 207 A2
Spittal St SL7 183 D2
Spoondell LU6 93 F7
Spoonley Wood MK13 33 E5
Sportsman Cl MK18 63 D3
Spout La TW19 213 A3
Spout Lane N TW19 213 B3
SPRIG'S ALLEY 147 F1
Sprigs Holly La HP14 159 B8
Springate Field SL3 206 E4
Springbank Ct MK16 12 B7
Spring Cl
High Wycombe HP13 173 F7
Latimer HP5 155 D3
Maidenhead SL6 195 F2
Milton Keynes MK17 55 A2
Spring Coppice HP14 171 F5
Spring Coppice La HP27 150 D5
Springdale Cotts SL8 185 B2
Springett Pl HP6 154 F2
SPRINGFIELD 35 B2
Springfield SL1 206 A3
Springfield Bvd MK6 35 B2
Springfield Cl
Aylesbury HP21 115 C8
Chesham HP5 154 C7
Windsor SL4 210 B5
Springfield Ct
1 Leighton Buzzard LU7 80 E7
1 Maidenhead SL6 203 B7
Milton Keynes MK6 35 B2
Springfield Gdns
Chinnor OX39 147 C7
Deanshanger MK19 31 E4
Springfield Hollow HP14 158 E5
Springfield Pk SL6 203 C1
Springfield Rd
Chesham HP5 154 C7
Dunstable LU6 93 D5
Leighton Buzzard LU7 80 E7
Olney MK46 6 F4
Slough SL3 212 B7
Stokenchurch HP14 158 F4
Windsor SL4 210 B5
Spring Field Rd HP4 135 A6
Springfield Rdbt MK6 35 A2
Springfields
Amersham HP6 154 C2
Padbury MK18 53 C1
Tylers Green HP10 163 C2
Springfields Cl MK18 53 C2
Springfields Ct MK18 53 C1
Springfield Way MK43 25 C2
Spring Gardens Rd HP13 173 E5
Spring Gdn La HP4 134 D5
Spring Gdns
Bourne End SL8 185 A4
Marlow SL7 183 E3
Newport Pagnell MK16 22 C4
Wooburn Green HP10 185 E8
Spring Gr MK17 49 B5
Spring Hill SL6 202 E3
Springhill Rd HP18 83 A8

Spring Ho SL7 . . . . 183 E3
Spring La
Alderton NN12. . . . . 9 A2
Clifton Reynes MK46 . . . . . . 7 C3
Cookham Dean SL6 . . . . . 195 C5
Farnham Common SL2. . . 198 C5
Flackwell Heath HP10 . . . 173 F3
Great Horwood MK17 . . . . 55 A2
Olney MK46. . . . . 6 F3
Slough SL1. . . . . 204 F5
Spring Mdw HP18. . . . . . . 97 A1
Springs Cl HP17 . . . . 130 B2
Springside 2 LU7 . . . . . . 80 E7
Springs La HP17 . . . . 130 B3
Spring Valley Dr HP14. . 162 A7
Springwater Mill HP11 . 173 E4
Springwood HP27. . . . . . 150 C4
Sprinters L Ctr HP16 . . . 151 A7
Sproggit Ind Est TW19. . 213 F1
Spruce Ct 7 SL1. . . . . . . 205 F3
Spruce Dene HP15 . . . . . 162 F2
Spruce Rd 1 HP19. . . . . 100 F1
SPURGROVE 170 E2
Spurgrove La RG9. . . . . . 170 E2
SPURLANDS END 163 A8
Spurlands End Rd
HP15 . . . . 163 A8
Spur The SL1 . . . . 204 D8
Spurt St HP18. . . . . 112 F3
Square Close Cotts
RG9 . . . . 169 F3
Square The
Akeley MK18 . . . . 41 F8
Aspley Guise MK17 . . . . . . 49 E4
Brill HP18. . . . . 110 A8
Great Missenden HP16 . . 152 B7
Harmondsworth UB7 . . . 213 B6
Long Crendon HP18. . . . . 125 C6
Milton Keynes MK12 . . . . . 33 D6
Preston Bissett MK18 . . . . 62 B8
Waddesdon HP18 . . . . 99 A6
Yardley Hastings NN7 . . . . . 1 A6
Squires Cl MK6 . . . . 47 A6
Squirrel La HP12. . . . . . . 172 C5
Squirrel Rise SL7 . . . . . . 183 D6
Squirrels Way MK18. . . . . . 52 E7
Stablebridge Rd HP22. . 117 F3
Stable Cl MK18 . . . . 50 C7
Stable Cotts SL7 . . . . 194 C5
Stable La HP9 . . . . 176 C4
Stable Rd HP22 . . . . 131 E7
Stables Ct SL7 . . . . 183 B1
Stables The MK19. . . . . . . 20 F3
Stacey Ave MK12. . . . . 33 D6
STACEY BUSHES 33 E4
Stacey Bushes Trad Ctr
MK12 . . . . 33 E4
Stacey Ho HP12. . . . . 172 E4
Stacey's Ct HP8. . . . . 177 C8
Staddle Stones HP27. . . . 139 B4
Stadium App HP21 . . . . . 115 E4
StadiumMK (MK Dons FC)
MK1 . . . . 47 C3
Stafferton Way SL6 . . . . 203 A6
Stafford Ave SL2. . . . . . . 198 C1
Stafford Cl SL6 . . . . 204 B7
Stafford Gr MK5 . . . . 46 B6
Stafford Keep HP19 . . . . 115 A8
Stag Ct WD3. . . . . 167 C5
Stag La
Berkhamsted HP4 . . . . . . 135 B5
Chorleywood WD3 . . . . . 167 C3
Great Kingshill HP15. . . . 151 D1
STAGSDEN WEST END 16 F4
Stagshaw Gr 5 MK4 . . . . 46 B2
Stainby Cl UB7. . . . . 208 E3
Stainton Dr MK13 . . . . 34 C4
Stamford Ave MK6 . . . . . . 35 B2
Stamford Rd SL6. . . . . . . 202 C6
Stanbridge Cl HP17 . . . . 127 A7
Stanbridge Ct MK11. . . . . 32 F5
Stanbridge Rd HP17. . . . 127 B6
Stanbrook Pl MK10. . . . . . 36 A1
Standfield Cl HP19 . . . . . 115 A8
Standing Way
Milton Keynes, Coldharbour Spinney MK3, MK4 . . . . . 46 E3
Milton Keynes, Kingston MK10. . . . . 36 C1
Milton Keynes, Peartree Bridge MK10, MK4, MK6 . . . . . . 47 C7
Milton Keynes, Snelshall East MK4. . . . . 57 B7
Standring Pl HP20 . . . . . 101 F2
Stanhope Cl HP22. . . . . . 131 B7
Stanhope Heath TW19. . 213 C1
Stanhope Rd
Aylesbury HP20 . . . . 116 A8
Slough SL1. . . . . 204 D7
Stanhope Way TW19 . . . 213 C1
Stanier Rise HP4. . . . . . . 134 F7
Stanier Sq 5 MK2 . . . . . . 58 C8
Stanley Ave HP5 . . . . 154 B8
Stanley Cl
Marlow SL7 . . . . 183 F3
Uxbridge UB8. . . . . 201 D3
Stanley Cotts SL2 . . . . . . 205 F5
Stanley Ct MK46 . . . . 6 F3
Stanley Gdns HP23. . . . . 118 F3
Stanley Green E SL3 . . . 206 F2
Stanley Green W SL3. . . 206 F2
Stanley Hill HP7 . . . . 165 E7
Stanley Hill Ave HP7 . . . 165 E8
Stanley Ho SL4 . . . . 211 A2
Stanley Rd HP12 . . . . 172 C7
Stanley Spencer Gall★
SL6 . . . . 196 B7
Stanmore Gdns MK16 . . . 22 B2
Stanstead Pl HP7 . . . . . . 165 C8
Stanton Ave MK13 . . . . . . 34 A6
STANTONBURY 34 D7
Stantonbury Campus
MK14 . . . . 34 C7
Stantonbury Campus L Ctr
MK14 . . . . 34 C7
Stantonbury Cl MK13. . . . 34 A8
Stanton Gate MK14. . . . . . 34 D8
Stanton Mid Sch MK13 . . . 34 B7
Stanton Way SL3. . . . . . . 206 E2
Stanton Wood Rdbt
MK14 . . . . 34 D4
Stanway Cl MK15 . . . . 35 B6
STANWELL. 213 C1
Stanwell Cl TW19 . . . . . . 213 D1
Stanwell Fields CE Prim Sch TW19 . . . . 213 E1
Stanwell Gdns TW19 . . . 213 D1
STANWELL MOOR. 212 E1
Stanwell Moor Rd TW6, TW19, UB7 . . . . 213 B4
Stanwell Rd SL3 . . . . 212 C4
Stanwyck La 4 MK4 . . . . 45 D2
Stapeley Ct 1 MK4 . . . . . 45 F1
Stapleford Mill★ LU7. . . . 70 B5
Staple Hall Rd MK1 . . . . . 47 E1
Stapleton Cl SL7 . . . . 183 F4
Stars La HP17. . . . . 113 E2
Startins La SL6 . . . . 195 C8
STARTOP'S END 104 F1
Starveall Cl UB7 . . . . 208 F3
Starwood Ct 1 SL3 . . . . 206 C3
Staters Pound MK15 . . . . 35 A7
Statham Pl MK6. . . . . 46 F8
Station App
Amersham HP6 . . . . 154 C1
Chorleywood WD3 . . . . . . 167 D5
Denham UB9 . . . . 189 D4
Gerrards Cross SL9. . . . . . 188 E6
Great Missenden HP16 . . 152 A7
Little Chalfont HP7. . . . . 166 D8
Maidenhead SL6 . . . . 202 F6
Marlow SL7 . . . . 183 E2
Wendover HP22. . . . . 131 B4
West Drayton UB7. . . . . . 208 E5
Station Bvd HP20 . . . . . . 115 D8
Station Cotts
Denham UB9 . . . . 190 A4
Winslow MK18. . . . . 66 A5
Station Hill SL6 . . . . 195 F7
Station Par
Beaconsfield HP9. . . . . . . 175 D3
Cookham Rise SL8 . . . . . . 195 F6
Denham Green UB9 . . . . . 190 A4
Station Rd
Aldbury HP23. . . . . 120 B5
Amersham HP7 . . . . 165 C8
Beaconsfield HP9. . . . . . . 175 E2
Berkhamsted HP4 . . . . . . 135 D4
Blackthorn OX25 . . . . 81 A4
Bourne End SL8. . . . . 185 A3
Bow Brickhill MK17 . . . . . . 48 C2
Buckingham MK18. . . . . . . 52 C7
Castlethorpe MK19 . . . . . . 19 F5
Cheddington LU7 . . . . 91 A1
Chesham HP5 . . . . 154 C8
Chinnor OX39. . . . . 147 C6
Cookham Rise SL6. . . . . . 195 F7
Gerrards Cross SL9. . . . . . 188 E6
Haddenham HP17 . . . . . . 126 E5
Henley-on-Thames RG9 . . 191 E1
High Wycombe HP13 . . . . 173 C6
Ivinghoe LU7 . . . . 105 E5
Leighton Buzzard LU7 . . . . 80 E7
Little Kimble HP17. . . . . . 129 E2
Long Marston HP23. . . . . 104 B4
Loudwater HP10 . . . . 174 C2
Marlow SL7 . . . . 183 E1
Marsh Gibbon OX27. . . . . . 71 F3
Mursley MK17 . . . . 67 B7
Newport Pagnell MK16 . . . 22 C4
Padbury MK18 . . . . 53 B1
Princes Risborough HP27. . . . . 139 A2
Quainton HP22. . . . . 85 A4
Slough, Langley SL3. . . . . 207 A4
Slough SL1. . . . . 204 E7
Stoke Mandeville HP22 . . 116 B2
Swanbourne MK17. . . . . . . 67 A4
Taplow SL6. . . . . 203 F7
Tring HP23. . . . . 119 D4
Uxbridge UB8. . . . . 201 D1
West Drayton UB7. . . . . . 208 E4
Winslow MK18. . . . . 66 A5
Woburn Sands MK17. . . . . . 49 B5
Wraysbury TW19. . . . . 212 A1
Station Rd Ind Est MK18. 66 A5
Station Rise SL7 . . . . 183 E2
Station Sq MK9 . . . . 34 C1
Station Terr
Buckingham MK18. . . . . . . 52 C7
Milton Keynes MK14 . . . . . 21 E2
Station Way E HP20 . . . . 115 D7
Station Way W HP20 . . . . 115 D7
Staunton Ho MK17 . . . . . . 60 F7
Staunton Rd SL2. . . . . . . 205 D8
Staveley Cl HP21. . . . . . . 116 C6
Staverton Gr MK10 . . . . . . 36 B2
Stavordale 2 MK10. . . . . . 36 A1
Stayning La MK14 . . . . 34 F6
Steeple Cl MK4 . . . . 57 A8
STEEPLE CLAYDON. 63 C3
Steeple Claydon Sch
MK18 . . . . 63 E3
Steinbeck Cres MK4. . . . . 56 F7
Stephenson Cl
Aylesbury HP19 . . . . 115 B7
High Wycombe HP13 . . . . 161 F1
Leighton Buzzard LU7 . . . . 80 E6
Stephenson Ct 12 SL1. . 205 F4
Stephenson Dr SL4 . . . . 210 B7
Stepnells HP23 . . . . 105 A1
Steppingstones LU6. . . . . 93 F8
Sterling Bus Pk MK18 . . . 52 D6
Sterling Cl MK15. . . . . 35 A6
Stevens Cl
Holmer Green HP15. . . . . 163 B7
Prestwood HP16 . . . . 151 D5
Stevens Field MK7 . . . . . . 48 D6
Stevens Ho 8 HP7. . . . . 165 B7
Stevenson Rd SL2. . . . . . 187 D2
Stewart Ave SL1 . . . . 205 F8
Stewarts Dr SL2 . . . . 198 B7
Stewarts Way SL7. . . . . . 183 D7
STEWKLEY. 68 E2
STEWKLEY DEAN 68 B1
Stewkley La MK17. . . . . . . 67 E4
Stewkley Rd
Cublington LU7 . . . . 78 C1
Hollingdon LU7 . . . . 69 C2
Wing LU7. . . . . 79 B3
Stilebrook Rd MK46 . . . . . . 6 F6
Stile Mdw HP9. . . . . 175 E3
Stile Rd SL3 . . . . 206 D3
Stilliters Farm Rd MK43 . 37 E8
Stilwell Dr UB8 . . . . 201 F1
Stirling Ave HP20 . . . . . . 101 E1
Stirling Cl
Uxbridge UB8. . . . . 201 C2
Windsor SL4 . . . . 209 D5
Stirling Gr SL6. . . . . 202 A8
Stirling Ho
2 High Wycombe HP13. . . . . 173 F7
Milton Keynes MK3 . . . . . . 57 D7
Stirling Rd
High Wycombe HP12 . . . . 172 D5
Slough SL1. . . . . 205 A8
Stanwell TW6. . . . . 213 F1
Stockaway HP22 . . . . 87 C1
Stockdale MK13. . . . . 34 C5
Stockdales Rd SL4 . . . . . 204 F2
Stocken Cl MK46. . . . . 6 E4
Stock Field Cl HP15 . . . . 163 B3
Stockfields Pl HP14 . . . . 158 D5
Stockgrove Ctry Pk★
LU7 . . . . 70 F7
Stockgrove Park Ho LU7 70 F8
Stockhall Cres LU7. . . . . . 68 D2
Stocking Green Cl MK19. 11 A3
Stocking La HP14 . . . . . . 161 E7
Stock La MK17. . . . . 45 B1
Stocklake HP20. . . . . 101 F1
Stocklake Ind Est HP20. 101 F1
Stocklands Way HP16 . . 151 D5
Stockley Academy UB8. 208 F7
Stockleys La MK18 . . . . . . 51 B6
Stockport Rd WD3 . . . . . 167 C2
Stocks Cl MK18 . . . . 65 F4
Stocks Rd HP23. . . . . 120 C7
Stocks The MK19 . . . . 19 E2
Stockwell HP17 . . . . 127 A6
Stockwell Furlong
HP17 . . . . 127 A6
Stockwell La
Longwick HP17 . . . . 139 A8
Wavendon MK17 . . . . 48 D7
Stockwells SL6 . . . . 196 D1
STOKE BRUERNE. 9 B8
Stoke Bruerne CE Prim Sch
NN12. . . . . 9 A8
Stoke Common Rd SL2, SL3. . . . . 199 B8
Stoke Court Dr SL2 . . . . 198 F4
Stoke Farm La HP21 . . . 115 E3
Stoke Gdns SL1. . . . . 205 F5
Stoke Gn SL2 . . . . 199 A1
STOKE GOLDINGTON 12 A6
Stoke Goldington CE Fst Sch MK16 . . . . 12 B6
STOKE GREEN. 199 B1
STOKE HAMMOND 69 E8
Stoke Ho 2 SL1 . . . . 205 F3
Stoke La MK17. . . . . 59 C1
Stoke Leys Cl HP21. . . . . 115 E3
STOKE MANDEVILLE. 116 A2
Stoke Mandeville Comb Sch
HP22. . . . . 116 A1
Stoke Mandeville Hospl
HP21. . . . . 115 F4
Stoke Mandeville Sta
HP22. . . . . 116 B2
STOKENCHURCH. 158 E5
Stokenchurch Pl MK13 . . 34 C3
Stokenchurch Prim Sch
HP14. . . . . 158 E5
Stoke Park Ave SL2 . . . . 198 C2
STOKE POGES 198 F4
Stoke Poges La SL1. . . . 205 E7
Stoke Poges Sch SL2. . . 198 F5
Stoke Rd
Ashton NN7 . . . . 9 E8
Aylesbury HP21 . . . . 115 E6
Leighton Buzzard LU7 . . . . 70 D1
Milton Keynes MK2 . . . . . . 58 E5
Newton Longville MK17. . . 57 F3
Slough SL2. . . . . 205 F7
Stokesay SL2 . . . . 205 F6
Stokesay Ct MK4. . . . . 45 E2
Stokes Croft HP17 . . . . . 127 A6
Stokes End HP17. . . . . . . 127 A7
Stokes La HP17 . . . . 127 A7
Stokesley Rise HP10 . . . 185 E8
Stoke View SL1 . . . . 205 F5
Stoke Wood SL2 . . . . 198 F8
Stolford Rise MK4. . . . . . . 46 B1
Stompits Rd SL6. . . . . . . 203 C1
Stomp Rd SL1 . . . . 204 B8
STONE 114 C5
STONEBRIDGE. 33 F7
Stonebridge Field SL4 . 205 B1
Stonebridge Gr MK10 . . . 35 E1
Stonebridge Rd HP19 . . 101 B3
Stonebridge Rdbt MK13 . 33 E8
Stone CE Comb Sch
HP17. . . . . 114 D5
Stonechat HP19. . . . . 101 E3
Stone Cl UB7 . . . . 208 F5
Stonecroft HP6 . . . . 153 C4
Stone Croft HP17 . . . . . . 114 D5
Stonecroft Ave SL0 . . . . 207 E7
Stonecrop Pl MK14. . . . . . 34 E4
Stone Ct MK46. . . . . 13 E8
Stonefield Pk SL6. . . . . . 202 C7
Stonefield Rd HP14 . . . . 161 C8
Stonegate MK13 . . . . 34 A5
Stonehaven Rd HP19. . . . 101 B2
Stone Hill MK8. . . . . 33 D1
Stone House La SL6. . . . 184 C1
Stoneleigh Ct MK4 . . . . . . 45 E1
Stonemasons Cl 11 MK46 . . 6 F3
Stone Pit Cl MK46. . . . . 6 E3
Stonepitts Pk HP18 . . . . 111 B3
Stones Row HP11 . . . . . . 173 F4
Stones Way MK17 . . . . 68 C6
Stone View HP22 . . . . 86 D7
Stoney Cl HP4 . . . . 134 F6
Stoneycroft HP23 . . . . . . 120 C5
Stoney Dean Specl Sch
HP7. . . . . 165 F8
Stoneyfield SL9. . . . . 188 C3
Stoney Gr HP5 . . . . 144 D1
Stoney Grove HP5 . . . . . 144 C1
Stoney La
Berkhamsted HP1 . . . . . . 146 B8
Bovingdon HP3 . . . . 146 C5
Chipperfield WD4. . . . . . . 146 F1
Cholesbury HP5. . . . . 133 F1
East Burnham SL2 . . . . . . 198 A4
Stoney Meade SL1 . . . . . 205 B5
Stoney Ware SL7 . . . . . . 194 E8
STONOR. 179 F6
Stonor RG9. . . . . 179 F6
Stonor Ct MK8. . . . . 45 F8
Stonor Ho & Gdns★
RG9. . . . . 180 A7
STONY GREEN. 151 A4
Stony Hill NN12. . . . . 17 C8
Stony La
Little Chalfont HP6. . . . . . 155 F1
Little Kingshill HP16 . . . . 152 C3
Stookslade HP22. . . . . 89 A3
Stopps Orch HP27. . . . . . 139 C5
Stork Cl 2 HP19. . . . . . . 101 F3
Stornaway Rd SL3 . . . . . 207 C2
Stotfold Ct MK11. . . . . 32 E4
Stour Cl
Aylesbury HP21 . . . . 115 C4
Milton Keynes MK3 . . . . . . 57 E8
Newport Pagnell MK16 . . . 22 E3
Slough SL1. . . . . 205 B3
Stourhead Gate MK4 . . . . 45 E2
Stovell Rd SL4 . . . . 210 B7
Stowe Ave MK18 . . . . 41 B3
Stowe Cl MK18. . . . . 41 C1
Stowe Ct MK14 . . . . 34 C8
Stowe Landscape Gdns★
MK18 . . . . 40 F7
STOWE PARK. 40 F7
Stowe Rd SL1. . . . . 204 E6
Stowe Rise MK18 . . . . 41 C1
Stowe Sch MK18. . . . . 40 F7
Stowe View MK18. . . . . 51 A7
Straight Bit HP10 . . . . . . 185 B8
Straight Mile Rd OX33. . 108 A5
Straight Rd SL4. . . . . 211 B1
Strande Pk SL6 . . . . 195 F5
Strande View Wlk SL6. . 195 F5
Strand La SL6. . . . . 195 F5
Strand The HP22. . . . . 85 B5
Strangers La MK18 . . . . . . 51 A6
Strangford Dr MK2. . . . . . 58 C4
Stranraer Gdns SL1 . . . . 205 E5
Stranraer Rd TW19. . . . . 213 E1
Stranraer Way 1 TW6 . 213 E1
Stratfield Ct
Maidenhead SL6 . . . . 203 B8
Milton Keynes MK8 . . . . . . 33 F1
Stratfield Rd SL1. . . . . . . 206 A4
Stratford Arc MK11 . . . . . 32 D6
Stratford Ave UB10. . . . . 201 F3
Stratford Cl
Aylesbury HP22 . . . . 117 C5
Slough SL2. . . . . 197 D1
Stratford Dr
Aylesbury HP21 . . . . 115 B6
Wooburn HP10. . . . . 185 D4
Stratford Gdns SL6. . . . . 202 C4
Stratford Rd
Buckingham MK18 . . . . 41 E1
Cosgrove MK19 . . . . 19 D1
Deanshanger MK19 . . . . . . 31 F4
Maids Moreton MK18 . . . . 42 C2
Milton Keynes MK12 . . . . . 33 C7
Nash MK17 . . . . 44 C1
Old Stratford MK19 . . . . . . 32 B5
Whaddon MK17 . . . . 45 A2
Stratfords Way HP17 . . . 127 A6
Strathcona Cl HP10 . . . . 185 C7
Strathcona Way HP10 . . 185 C7
Strathnaver Pl MK12 . . . . 33 D4
Strathspey Gate MK10. . . 36 C3
Stratton Chase Dr
Chalfont St Giles HP8 . . . 177 B8
Chalfont St Peter HP8 . . . 177 A8
Stratton Gn HP21 . . . . . . 116 B6
Stratton Rd
Beaconsfield HP9. . . . . . . 175 B2
Princes Risborough HP27. . . . . 139 A3
Strauss Gr MK7 . . . . 48 C4
Strawberry Cl HP16 . . . . 151 D5
Straws Hadley Ct HP22. . 89 B2
Streamside SL1. . . . . 204 F5
Streamside Wlk HP21 . . 115 C6
Streatham Pl MK13. . . . . . 34 C2
Stretton Cl HP10 . . . . 174 C8
Stretton Pl HP6 . . . . 154 F1
Stringers Cotts 1 SL9. . 177 D2
Stringfellow Cl MK43. . . . 24 E2
Stroma Ct SL1 . . . . 204 D6
Stroud Cl SL4. . . . . 209 D4
Strudwick Dr MK6 . . . . . . 46 F8
Stuart Cl
Milton Keynes MK2 . . . . . . 47 D1
Windsor SL4 . . . . 209 F5
Stuart Ct HP6. . . . . 154 D1
Stuart Rd HP13 . . . . 173 C6
Stuart Way
Thame OX9 . . . . 126 A1
Windsor SL4 . . . . 209 F5
Stubble Hill HP19 . . . . . . 115 A8
Stubbles La SL6. . . . . 195 B6
Stubbs End Cl HP6 . . . . . 154 E2
Stubbs Field MK5 . . . . 46 A3
Stubbs Wood HP6. . . . . . 154 E3
Stuchbury Cl HP19 . . . . . 115 A8
Studdridge Ct HP14 . . . . 158 C4
Studham La HP4. . . . . 107 D4
Studland Cl HP21 . . . . . . 116 B5
STUDLEY GREEN. 159 E3
Studley Knapp
Milton Keynes MK7 . . . . . . 48 B5
Walnut Tree MK7 . . . . 48 B7
Studridge La HP27 . . . . . 150 B4
Sturges Cl MK7 . . . . 48 A5
Sturman Ho HP6. . . . . 154 C2
Stylecroft Rd HP8. . . . . . 177 D8
Styles Cl OX27. . . . . 71 E2
Styles Ct HP18. . . . . 99 A7
Sudbury Chase MK10. . . . 35 E1
Sudgrove Ho MK15. . . . . . 35 A6
Suffield Rd HP11. . . . . . . 172 F6
Suffolk Cl
Milton Keynes MK3 . . . . . . 46 F1
Slough SL1. . . . . 204 E7
Suffolk Ct
Maidenhead SL6 . . . . 202 F8
Marsh Gibbon OX27. . . . . . 71 F3
Suffolk Ho HP10 . . . . 185 E6
Suffolk Rd SL6. . . . . 202 D4
Sulby Cl HP21 . . . . 115 C5
Sulgrave Cres HP23. . . . 119 C5
Sulgrave Ct 3 MK8 . . . . . 45 F8
Sullivan Cres MK7 . . . . . . 48 C5
Sultan Croft MK5 . . . . 46 A4
Sumburgh Way SL1 . . . . 205 E8
Summerfield Sch MK13 . . 34 C3
Summergill Ct MK13 . . . . 34 C5
Summerhayes MK14 . . . . . 34 F7
Summerhouse La UB7. . 213 D8
Summerlea SL1. . . . . 205 B5
Summerleaze Rd SL6 . . 196 B1

- Summerleys LU6 92 E4
- Summerleys Rd HP27 138 F4
- Summerlin Dr MK17 49 B5
- Summerson Ct MK6 46 F5
- Summerson Rd
  - Bleak Hall MK6 47 A5
  - Milton Keynes MK6 46 F5
- Summers Rd SL1 197 C2
- SUMMERSTOWN 72 B2
- Summit Ctr UB7 213 D7
- Sumner Ct MK5 46 A8
- Sunbury Cl MK13 34 A6
- Sunbury Ct SL4 210 D8
- Sunbury Rd SL4 210 D8
- Sun Cl SL4 210 D8
- Sun Cres HP18 109 D5
- Sunderland Ct
  - Milton Keynes MK4 45 F1
  - 11 Stanwell TW19 213 E1
- Sunderland Rd SL6 202 B8
- Sun La SL6 202 F7
- Sunningdale Cl HP12 172 B5
- Sunningdale Way MK3 57 D8
- Sunnybank SL7 183 D4
- Sunny Bank
  - Cheddington LU7 104 F7
  - Hazlemere HP15 162 F6
- Sunny Brook Cl HP22 117 D6
- Sunny Croft HP13 161 C2
- Sunnyhill Rd WD3 178 D4
- SUNNYMEADS 211 E4
- Sunnymeads Sta TW19 211 E4
- Sunnymede Ave HP5 144 E3
- Sunnymede Cotts SL6 196 B1
- Sunnyside Cotts HP5 145 A5
- Sunnyside Rd HP5 144 C1
- Sunny View NN7 1 B6
- Sun Pas 15 SL4 210 D6
- Sunray Ave UB7 208 D4
- Sunridge Cl MK16 22 C3
- Sunrise Parkway MK14 34 E6
- Sunset Cl MK2 58 C7
- Sunset Wlk MK9 34 E2
- Sunters End HP12 172 A7
- Sunters Wood Cl HP12 172 B5
- Surly Hall Wlk SL4 209 F6
- Surrey Ave SL2 198 C1
- Surrey Pl
  - Milton Keynes MK3 46 F2
  - Tring HP23 119 A3
- Surrey Rd MK3 46 F2
- Sussex Cl
  - Aylesbury HP19 101 A3
  - Chalfont St Giles HP8 177 B8
  - High Wycombe HP13 162 D1
  - Slough SL1 206 B4
- Sussex Ho SL2 198 C6
- Sussex Keep 7 SL1 206 B4
- Sussex Lodge 7 SL6 202 F6
- Sussex Pl SL1 206 B4
- Sussex Rd MK3 46 F1
- Sutcliffe Ave MK6 34 E1
- Sutherland Gr MK3 46 F3
- Sutherland Grange SL4 209 D7
- Sutherland Grange Nature Reserve* SL4 209 D7
- Sutherland Wlk HP21 115 F5
- Sutleye Ct MK5 46 A5
- SUTTON 207 C1
- Sutton Ave SL3 206 C4
- Sutton Cl
  - Cookham SL6 196 B7
  - Maidenhead SL6 202 C5
  - Tring HP23 119 B6
- Sutton Ct MK4 46 C1
- Sutton La SL3 207 B1
- Sutton Pl SL3 212 B8
- Sutton Rd SL6 196 B6
- Swabey Rd SL3 207 A2
- Swains Cl UB7 208 E4
- Swains La HP10 174 B1
- Swains Mkt HP10 174 A1
- Swakeleys Dr UB10 201 F8
- Swakeleys Rd UB10 201 E8
- Swale Rd HP21 115 C5
- Swallow Cl MK18 52 E7
- Swallowdale SL0 200 D2
- Swallow Dr HP15 163 B5
- Swallowfield MK8 33 E1
- Swallowfield Lower Sch MK17 49 B5
- Swallow Fields SL0 200 D1
- Swallow Ho SL7 184 A2
- Swallow La
  - Aylesbury HP19 114 F8
  - Stoke Mandeville HP22 116 A1
- Swallow St
  - Iver Heath SL0 200 D1
  - Iver SL0 207 D8
- Swallowtail Wlk HP4 134 F7
- SWANBOURNE 67 B3
- Swanbourne CE Fst Sch MK17 67 A3
- Swanbourne House Sch MK17 66 F3
- Swanbourne Rd MK17 67 D4
- Swanbrook Ct SL6 203 A7
- Swan Bsns Pk MK18 52 C6
- Swan Cl
  - Aylesbury HP19 101 F3
  - Blackthorn OX25 81 A3
  - Buckingham MK18 52 E7
  - Chesham HP5 144 B4
  - Ivinghoe Aston LU7 92 A1
  - Whitchurch HP22 87 B5
- Swan Cotts HP17 129 D1
- Swan Ct
  - Buckingham MK18 65 F5
  - Chorleywood WD3 167 C5
  - Datchet SL3 211 B6
  - Leighton Buzzard LU7 80 E6
  - Olney MK46 7 A4
  - West Drayton UB7 208 D4
- Swan Hill HP18 112 F3
- Swan Hill Cotts HP18 112 F3
- Swan La
  - Lee Gate HP16 142 C8
  - Marsh Gibbon OX6 72 A3
- Swan Mews HP22 131 B5
- Swann Rd HP22 131 D8
- Swan Pool & L Ctr MK18 52 D7
- Swan Rd
  - Iver SL0 207 F7
  - West Drayton UB7 208 D4
- Swanson Dr MK4 45 D3
- Swansons LU6 92 F3
- Swan Terr
  - Milton Keynes MK11 32 D5
  - Windsor SL4 210 A7
- Swan Wharf Bsns Ctr UB8 201 C3
- Swanwick La MK10 36 B3
- Swayne Rise MK10 36 A2
- Sweetcroft La UB10 201 F6
- Sweetlands Cnr MK7 48 B8
- Swift Cl
  - Aylesbury HP19 101 F3
  - Newport Pagnell MK16 22 A5
- Swift Ho SL7 184 A2
- Swimbridge La MK4 46 D4
- Swinden Ct MK13 34 B4
- Swing Gate Fst Sch HP4 135 D3
- Swing Gate La HP4 135 D2
- Swinnerton Ho RG9 191 E3
- Switchback Cl SL6 195 D2
- Switchback Road N SL6 195 D3
- Switchback Road S SL6 195 D2
- Switchback The SL6 195 D2
- Sycamore Ave MK2 58 E8
- Sycamore Cl
  - Amersham HP6 154 D2
  - 3 Bourne End SL8 185 B3
  - Buckingham MK18 52 F7
  - Chalfont St Giles HP8 177 A7
  - Long Crendon HP18 125 C6
  - Maidenhead SL6 202 C3
  - Stewkley LU7 68 D2
  - West Drayton UB7 208 F6
- Sycamore Cnr HP6 154 D2
- Sycamore Ct
  - Aylesbury HP19 101 D1
  - High Wycombe HP12 172 C4
  - Windsor SL4 210 C4
- Sycamore Dene HP5 144 D3
- Sycamore Dr
  - Marlow Bottom SL7 183 D5
  - Tring HP23 119 B4
- Sycamore Ho
  - Amersham HP6 154 D2
  - Princes Risborough HP27 139 B3
- Sycamore Leys MK18 63 E3
- Sycamore Pl HP6 154 C1
- Sycamore Rd
  - Amersham HP6 154 D2
  - Chalfont St Giles HP8 177 A7
  - High Wycombe HP12 172 C4
- Sycamore Rise
  - Berkhamsted HP4 135 D3
  - Chalfont St Giles HP8 177 A7
- Sycamores The HP3 146 F8
- Sycamore Way HP15 163 A3
- Sycamore Wlk SL3 206 E7
- Sydney Gr SL1 205 C7
- Sygnus Ct 8 SL6 202 F7
- Syke Cluan SL0 207 E4
- Syke Ings SL0 207 E4
- Sykes Croft MK4 46 C1
- Sykes Rd SL1 205 B8
- Sylvana Cl UB10 201 F4
- Sylvester Rd SL6 195 E2
- Sylvia Cl HP16 152 B4
- Symington Ct MK5 46 B5
- Syon Gdns MK16 22 C2
- SYRESHAM 27 B8
- Syresham St James CE Prim Sch NN13 27 C8

T

- Tabard Gdns MK16 22 C2
- Tachbrook Rd UB8 201 C3
- Tacknell Dr MK5 46 A4
- Tacks La HP17 126 F6
- Tadmarton MK15 35 A6
- Tadmere MK8 33 D1
- Tadros Ct HP13 173 D6
- Talbot Ave
  - High Wycombe HP13 161 D2
  - Slough SL3 206 F4
- Talbot Ct
  - Milton Keynes MK15 35 C1
  - Windsor SL4 210 B4
- Talbot Pl SL3 211 C6
- Talbot Rd HP22 117 E5
- Talbots Dr SL6 202 B6
- Talbots Hyde MK46 6 E4
- Talland Ave MK6 34 F1
- Tallis La MK7 48 C5
- Tall Oaks HP6 154 D2
- Tall Pines LU7 70 F2
- Tall Trees SL3 212 E6
- Tamar Cl
  - Aylesbury HP21 115 C4
  - Loudwater HP13 174 B4
- Tamar Ho
  - High Wycombe HP13 173 F7
  - Milton Keynes MK3 46 E1
- Tamarisk Ct MK7 48 B5
- Tamarisk Way
  - Aylesbury HP22 116 C4
  - Slough SL1 205 B5
- Tamar Way SL3 207 B2
- Tamworth Stubb MK7 48 A5
- Tancred Rd HP13 162 A1
- Tandra MK6 47 B5
- Tandy Rise MK8 45 D6
- Tandys Cl MK43 8 E5
- Tanfield La MK10 36 A3
- Tangier Ct SL4 210 D8
- Tangier La SL4 210 D8
- Tankard Cl MK16 22 C4
- Tank House Rd MK18 66 B6
- Tanners Dr MK14 22 A2
- Tannery Rd HP13 174 A4
- Tannery Road Ind Est HP13 174 A4
- Tannery The MK18 65 F4
- Tansley La MK17 49 B5
- Tansman La MK7 48 D5
- Tanton Ho HP16 151 F8
- Tapestries Hall SL4 211 A2
- Tapestries The SL4 211 A2
- Taplin Way HP10 163 C1
- TAPLOW 196 E1
- Taplow Common Rd SL1 197 A3
- Taplow Rd SL6 204 A7
- Taplow Sta SL6 203 F7
- Tapping Rd HP14 171 C5
- Taranis Cl MK7 48 C7
- Tarbay La SL4 209 B5
- Tarbert Cl MK2 58 C5
- Tarmac Way UB7 213 B7
- Tarnbrook Cl 6 MK4 46 B2
- Tarragon Cl
  - Milton Keynes MK7 48 B6
  - Walton MK7 48 A6
- Tarry Ct MK13 34 B6
- Taskers Row LU6 92 F4
- Taskers Row Cotts LU6 92 F4
- Task The MK46 7 A4
- Tatchbrook Cl SL6 203 A8
- Tate Rd SL9 177 F5
- TATHALL END 11 E2
- TATLING END 189 B3
- Tatling Gr MK7 48 A6
- Tattam Cl MK15 35 C2
- Tattams La MK17 67 B3
- TATTENHOE 57 A8
- Tattenhoe La MK3 57 D8
- Tattenhoe Pavilion MK4 57 A8
- Tattenhoe St MK5 45 E4
- Tattershall Cl MK5 46 A6
- Tattlers Hill HP22 89 B3
- Taunton Deane MK4 46 D2
- Taurus Cl MK18 63 D2
- Tavelhurst MK8 33 E1
- Taverner Cl MK7 48 D5
- Tavistock Cl
  - Maidenhead SL6 202 A8
  - Woburn Sands MK17 49 B6
- Tavistock Mews HP12 172 E7
- Tavistock Rd UB7 208 D5
- Tavistock St MK2 47 D1
- Tavistock Wlk HP20 101 E2
- Taylor Rd HP21 115 D5
- Taylors Cl SL7 183 F2
- Taylors Cnr HP18 99 A7
- Taylors Ct SL6 202 B8
- Taylors La
  - Little Missenden HP7 153 A3
  - Stewkley LU7 78 E7
  - St Leonards HP23 132 C3
- Taylors Mews MK14 34 F6
- Taylors Rd HP5 144 D2
- Taylor's Ride LU7 70 F2
- Taylors Turn HP13 161 D3
- Taymouth Pl MK9 35 B3
- Tay Rd MK3 46 E1
- Teale Cl OX25 94 E7
- Teal Ho HP11 173 C6
- Teasel Ave MK14 34 E5
- Tedder Cl UB10 201 F5
- Tedder Rd HP22 131 D5
- Teesdale Rd SL2 204 F8
- Tees Rd HP21 115 C5
- Tees Way MK3 46 D1
- Teign Cl MK16 22 D4
- Teikyo Sch UK SL2 199 D5
- Telford Cl HP19 100 F1
- Telford Dr SL1 205 A4
- Telford Way
  - High Wycombe HP13 162 A1
  - Milton Keynes MK14 22 B1
- Telston Cl SL8 185 A5
- Temperance Terr MK11 32 C6
- Templars Pl 2 SL7 183 E1
- TEMPLE 194 C5
- Temple MK14 34 C7
- Temple Cl
  - Buckingham MK18 41 E2
  - Milton Keynes MK3 57 D7
- Templecroft Terr HP17 114 A4
- Temple End HP13 173 A8
- Temple Gate HP13 173 A7
- Temple Ho RG9 191 E3
- Temple La SL7 194 D6
- Temple Mill Cotts SL7 194 C5
- Temple Mill Island SL7 194 C5
- Temple Orch HP13 173 B7
- Temple Pk SL6 193 F3
- Temple Rd SL4 210 D5
- Templeside Gdns HP12 172 E8
- Temple Sq 17 HP20 115 D8
- Temple St
  - Aylesbury HP20 115 D8
  - Brill HP18 96 B1
- Temple Way SL2 198 C7
- Templewood HP14 150 B1
- Templewood Gate SL2 198 C7
- Templewood La SL2 198 E8
- Tenby Gr MK4 45 D1
- Tene Acres MK5 45 F6
- Tennant Cl MK8 45 D6
- Tennis La MK18 66 A3
- Tennyson Dr MK16 22 A4
- Tennyson Gr 1 MK3 57 F7
- Tennyson Rd
  - Aylesbury HP21 115 F6
  - High Wycombe HP11 173 A5
- Tennyson Way SL2 197 E1
- Tenterden Cres MK7 48 B7
- Tenzing Dr HP13 173 E6
- Terrace The
  - Aspley Guise MK17 49 E5
  - Bray SL6 203 C3
  - 7 Tring HP23 119 A3
- Terrent Ct SL4 210 A5
- TERRICK 130 C5
- Terrick Row HP17 130 B5
- TERRIERS 162 D2
- Terrington Hill SL7 183 B2
- Terry Dr HP19 101 C3
- Terryfield Rd HP13 173 E6
- Terry Orch HP13 173 C8
- Terry Pl UB8 208 C8
- Terry Rd HP13 173 C8
- Terry's La SL6 195 F8
- Testwood Rd SL4 209 D6
- TETCHWICK 82 F2
- Tetherdown HP16 151 C5
- Tewkesbury La 1 MK10 35 F1
- TEW'S END 17 C8
- Tews End La NN12 17 B8
- Thackeray End HP19 100 F2
- THAME 125 E2
- Thame Ho 5 HP13 173 B7
- Thame Rd
  - Aylesbury HP17 127 C2
  - Aylesbury HP21 115 D7
  - Blackthorn OX25 81 A3
  - Brill HP18 110 B7
  - Chilton HP18 111 B3
  - Chinnor OX39 147 B8
  - Haddenham HP17 126 D5
  - Long Crendon HP18, OX9 125 D4
  - Longwick HP27 138 E6
  - Piddington OX25 95 D6
  - Thame OX9 136 C7
- Thame Road S HP21 115 B6
- Thames Ave SL4 210 D7
- Thames Bank SL6 203 C7
- Thamesbourne Mews 3 SL8 185 A3
- Thames Cl
  - Bourne End SL8 185 A4
  - Milton Keynes MK3 57 E8
- Thames Cres SL6 196 B2
- Thames Dr MK16 22 E3
- Thamesfield Gdns SL7 183 E1
- Thames Ho
  - Datchet SL3 211 B6
  - Henley-on-Thames RG9 191 E3
- Thames Ind Est SL7 183 F2
- Thames Mead SL4 209 E6
- Thames Rd SL3 207 B3
- Thames Reach SL7 193 D6
- Thames Side
  - Henley-on-Thames RG9 191 E2
  - Windsor SL4 210 D7
- Thames St SL4 210 D7
- Thames Valley Athletics Ctr SL4 205 E1
- Thames Valley Hospl (private) SL3 199 C4
- Thames Valley Univ (Slough Campus) SL1 205 E5
- Thane Ct MK14 34 C7
- Thanestead Copse HP10 174 C2
- Thanestead Ct HP10 174 C2
- Thatcher Cl UB7 208 E4
- Thatchers Dr SL6 202 A5
- Theatre Wlk MK9 34 F3
- thecentre:mk (Sh Ctr) MK9 34 E3
- THE CITY 159 D6
- THE GREEN
  - Milton Keynes 47 D8
  - Newport Pagnell 22 C3
  - Whipsnade 107 F8
- Thellusson Way WD3 167 F2
- THE SWILLET 167 B3
- Theydon Ave MK17 49 B4
- Thicket The
  - Tylers Green HP10 163 A1
  - West Drayton UB7 208 E7
- Third Ave
  - Marlow SL7 183 F2
  - Milton Keynes MK1 47 B2
- Third Cres SL1 205 C8
- Third St HP11 173 B4
- Thirkleby Cl SL1 205 C5
- Thirlby La MK5 46 A6
- Thirlmere Ave
  - Milton Keynes MK2 58 D6
  - Slough SL1 204 C8
- Thirsk Gdns MK3 57 C6
- Thistle Ct HP21 115 C5
- Thomas Bourne Ho 1 HP4 135 D4
- Thomas Coram CE Mid Sch HP4 135 D2
- Thomas Ct
  - Berkhamsted HP4 134 E6
  - Maidenhead SL6 202 A2
- Thomas Dr MK16 22 A6
- Thomas Harding Jun Sch HP5 154 B7
- Thomas Hickman Sch HP19 101 A3
- Thomas Rd HP10 185 D4
- Thomas Valentine Ho HP8 177 B7
- Thompkins La SL2 198 A5
- Thompson Cl SL3 207 A2
- Thompson Rd UB10 201 E5
- Thompson St MK13 34 A7
- Thomson Cl HP21 115 B6
- Thomson Wlk HP21 115 B6
- Thornaby Pl HP10 185 E8
- Thornbank Cl TW19 213 A2
- THORNBOROUGH 54 A8
- Thornborough Inf Sch MK18 54 A8
- Thornborough Rd MK17 55 B8
- Thornbridge Rd SL0 200 C4
- Thornbury Pl HP11 173 A4
- Thorncliffe MK8 33 D1
- Thorndike SL2 205 B8
- Thorn Dr SL3 206 E7
- Thorne Rd HP14 171 C4
- Thorne Way
  - Aston Clinton HP22 118 A4
  - Aylesbury HP20 101 F2
- THORNEY 208 B3
- Thorneycroft La MK15 35 B5
- Thorney Ctry Pk* UB7 208 B3
- Thorney Lane N SL0 207 F6
- Thorney Lane S SL0 207 F5
- Thorney Mill Rd SL0, UB7 208 B3
- Thornhill MK18 54 B8
- Thornhill Cl HP7 165 B7
- Thornhill Rd UB10 201 F8
- Thornlea Croft MK46 6 F3
- Thornley Croft MK4 46 C2
- Thorns Cl HP27 139 D5
- Thorns La HP27 139 E5
- THORNTON 43 C4
- Thornton Ave UB7 208 F3
- Thornton Chase MK14 34 E6
- Thornton Cl UB7 208 F3
- Thornton Coll Convent of Jesus & Mary MK17 43 C5
- Thornton Cres HP22 131 A5
- Thornton Rd MK17 44 A1
- Thorntree Dr HP23 118 F4
- Thorpe Cl HP21 116 A4
- Thorpe House Sch SL9 188 E7
- Thorpeness Croft MK4 56 F8
- Thorwold Pl MK5 46 B6

Thrasher Rd HP21 115 D5
Three Close La HP4 135 C4
Three Gables HP9 175 E2
THREE HOUSEHOLDS 176 F7
Three Households HP8 176 F6
Three Oaks Cl UB10 190 F1
Three Points La MK18 74 A6
Thresher Gr MK12 33 A5
Thrift La SL6 202 D1
Thrift View MK43 25 C2
Thrupp Cl MK19 20 A6
Thrush Cl
6 Aylesbury HP19 101 F3
High Wycombe HP12 172 C4
Thurlby Way SL6 202 D3
Thurley Cotts SL2 199 B3
Thurne Cl MK16 22 E3
Thursby Cl MK15 35 D7
Thurston Rd SL1 205 E7
Thyme Cl MK16 21 F5
Tibbys La HP18 112 F3
Ticehirst Cl MK7 48 B7
Ticehurst Cl MK7 48 B7
Tichborne WD3 178 D5
Tickford Arc MK16 22 D4
TICKFORD END 22 F4
Tickford Park Prim Sch MK16 22 D3
Tickford St MK16 22 E4
Tidbury Cl MK17 49 A4
Tiddenfoot Waterside Pk* LU7 80 E4
TIDDINGTON 136 A7
Tierney 5 MK4 45 D2
Tierney Ct 3 SL7 183 E1
Tiffany Cl MK2 58 D6
Tiggywinkles Wildlife Hospl* HP17 127 A4
TILBROOK 48 C3
Tilbrook Ind Est MK7 48 B3
Tilbrook Rdbt MK7 48 B2
Tilbury Wlk SL3 207 B3
Tilburywood Cl HP13 161 C2
Tilebarn Cl RG9 191 C1
Tilecotes Cl SL7 183 C2
Tilehouse Comb Sch UB9 189 F5
Tilehouse La UB9 189 E6
Tilehouse Way UB9 189 F4
Tilers Rd MK11 33 B2
Tilling Cres HP13 174 A7
Tillman Cl MK12 33 C5
Tilstone Ave SL4 204 E2
Tilstone Cl SL4 204 E1
Tilsworth Rd HP9 175 C1
Timber La MK17 60 F7
Timberley La HP16 142 A8
Timberscombe MK4 46 D3
Timbers Wlk SL6 202 B5
Timber Way OX39 147 C6
Timberwood SL2 187 D1
Timbold Dr MK7 48 A7
Timor Ct MK11 32 D6
Timothy's Cl MK12 33 C7
Timpson Ct HP15 162 D8
Timpson La MK46 7 C3
Timpsons Row MK46 7 A3
Tindal Rd HP20 101 E2
TINGEWICK 51 B7
Tingewick Rd
Buckingham MK18 52 B8
Radclive MK18 51 E7
Tingewick Road Ind Est MK18 52 B8
TINKERS BRIDGE 47 D6
Tinkers Dr MK18 65 F3
TINKERS END 65 F3
Tinkers La
Berkhamsted HP23 134 A6
Windsor SL4 209 D5
Tinkers Wood Rd HP13 161 E1
Tintagel Ct MK6 47 A8
Tintagel Ho SL1 205 C5
Tintern Cl SL1 205 C3
Tinterne Cl HP21 116 C6
Tippet Cl MK7 48 D4
Tiree Ct
Milton Keynes MK3 58 C3
Milton Keynes MK3 58 C3
Tiree Ho SL2 205 B8
Titchmarsh Ct MK6 46 E8
Tithe Barn Dr SL6 203 E1
Tithe Cl SL6 203 C1
Tithe Ct SL3 207 A2
Tithe La TW19 212 A1
Titmus Rd HP22 131 E7
Tiverton Cres
Aylesbury HP19 101 C3
Milton Keynes MK4 45 E1
Tobermory Cl SL3 206 E2
Tockley Rd SL1 197 B2
Todd Cl
Aylesbury HP21 115 B6
Holmer Green HP15 163 B6
Tolcarne Ave MK6 35 A1
Toll Bar Cnr HP27 138 D7
Tollgate SL6 202 A6
Tollgate Cl WD3 167 F5
Tolman Ct HP21 115 B6
Tomlin Rd SL2 197 E1
Tomo Ind Est UB8 208 C7
Tompion Rd HP19 100 F1
Tompkins Cl
Aston Clinton HP22 117 F4
Milton Keynes MK5 46 B3
Tompkins La OX27 71 E2
Tom Scott Ho HP5 144 B2
Toms Hill Cl HP23 120 D5
Toms Hill Rd HP23 120 D5
Toms Turn HP15 162 F5
TONGWELL 35 C8
Tongwell La MK15, MK16 22 C2
Tongwell Rdbt MK15 35 D8
Tongwell St
Milton Keynes, Broughton MK10 36 A3
Milton Keynes, Northfield MK15 35 F5
Milton Keynes, Pineham MK15 35 E7
Walnut Tree MK7 48 C6
Toot Hill Cl MK5 46 A5
Top Angel MK18 52 D5
Topaz Cl SL1 205 B5
Top Farm Cl HP9 175 A1
Topland Rd SL9 177 D3
Top Mdw
Bow Brickhill MK7 48 B3
Milton Keynes MK3 47 A3
Topping La UB8 201 D2
Top Pk SL9 188 C5
Top Station Rd NN13 38 A8
Top Station Road Ind Est NN13 38 A8
Torbay HP22 85 B4
Tornay Ct LU7 91 D6
Torquay Spur SL2 198 B2
Torre Cl MK3 47 A2
Torridge Rd
Aylesbury HP21 115 D4
Slough SL3 212 B8
Torridon Ct MK2 58 D4
Torrington Rd HP4 135 B4
Tortoiseshell Way
Aylesbury HP19 101 C4
Berkhamsted HP4 134 F6
Torwood Cl HP4 134 F4
TOTTERIDGE 173 F8
Totteridge Ave HP13 173 D6
Totteridge Common Cotts HP13 173 F8
Totteridge Dr HP13 162 E1
Totteridge Ho HP13 173 E8
Totteridge La HP13 162 E1
Totteridge Par HP13 173 E8
Totteridge Rd HP13 173 D7
TOTTERNHOE 93 B7
Totternhoe Knolls & Quarry* LU6 93 B8
Totternhoe Lower Sch LU6 93 B7
Totternhoe Rd
Dunstable LU6 93 E7
Eaton Bray LU6 92 D7
TOUCHBRIDGE 95 E1
Towan Ave
Fishermead MK6 47 A8
Milton Keynes MK6 35 A1
Towcester Dr NN12 18 B3
Towcester Rd
Buckingham MK18 41 E4
Old Stratford MK19 32 B7
TOWERAGE 171 F8
Tower Cl
Berkhamsted HP4 135 A3
Emberton MK16 13 C5
Flackwell Heath HP10 185 C7
Tower Cres MK14 34 F6
Tower Ct HP27 139 B3
Tower Dr MK14 34 F7
Towergate Cl UB8 201 E7
TOWER HILL 146 F2
Tower Hill WD4 146 F1
Tower Hill Bsns Pk OX27 71 D7
Tower Ho
Iver SL0 207 E7
4 Slough SL1 205 E4
Toweridge La
High Wycombe HP12 172 C8
West Wycombe HP14 160 F1
Tower Rd HP7 165 A4
Towersey Way HP21 115 B7
Towers Lea HP13 173 C7
Tower St HP13 162 D2
Town Bridge Ct HP5 154 B7
Town Cl MK18 50 D6
TOWN END 159 C8
Town End Cres MK16 12 B5
Town End Rd HP14 159 C8
Town Farm LU7 105 A7
Town Farm Barns HP27 139 B3
Town Farm Cl OX49 157 B8
Townfield HP5 154 C7
Town Field La HP8 177 C7
Townfield Rd 5 HP13 173 C7
Town La
Stanwell TW19 213 D1
Wooburn HP10 185 D4
Townlands Hospl RG9 191 D2
TOWNSEND
Haddenham 127 A7
North Marston 76 B2
TOWN'S END 71 D2
Townsend
Haddenham HP17 127 A7
Marsh Gibbon OX27 71 E2
Quainton HP22 85 A5
Townsend Cl MK43 37 F8
Townsend Cotts
Great Horwood MK17 55 B3
Middle Claydon MK18 74 C8
Townsend Gr MK13 34 B8
Townsend La OX27 71 E2
Townsend Piece HP19 101 C1
Townsend Rd HP5 144 C1
Townside
Edlesborough LU6 92 F3
Haddenham HP17 126 F5
Town Sq 8 SL1 205 F4
Tozer Wlk SL4 209 D4
Tracy Ave SL3 206 F1
Tracy Way 3 MK4 45 E3
Trafalgar Ave MK3 46 E2
Trafford Cl HP16 152 A6
Trafford Rd HP16 152 A7
Tram Hill HP18 96 B2
Tranlands Brigg MK13 34 B4
Transcend 10 SL4 210 C5
Trapp's Ct HP5 154 C6
Trapp's La HP5 154 C6
Travell Ct MK13 34 B3
Travic Rd SL2 197 F2
Travis Ct SL2 198 B2
Travis Gr MK3 58 A8
Treacher's Cl HP5 154 B8
Treadaway Bsns Ctr HP10 174 C1
Treadaway Hill HP10 174 B1
Treadaway Rd HP10 174 B1
Trebah Sq HP19 114 F8
Treborough MK4 46 D2
Tredington Gr MK7 48 B4
Treefields MK18 52 E8
Treehanger Cl HP23 119 B4
Trees Ave HP14 162 A6
Treeside Cl UB7 208 D2
Treesmill Dr SL6 202 C3
Trees Rd
Bourne End SL8 185 B3
Hughenden Valley HP14 162 A6
Trelawney Ave SL3 206 E3
Tremayne Ct MK6 47 A8
Trenchard Ave HP22 131 D6
Trenchard St HP19 115 A8
Trenches La SL3 207 A6
Trengothal Ct NN13 26 D4
Trent Dr MK16 22 D4
Trentishoe Cres MK4 46 D3
Trent Rd
Milton Keynes MK3 46 E1
Slough SL3 212 B8
Trent Villas Est SL3 211 B6
Tresco Rd HP4 134 F5
Tresham Ct MK5 46 A7
Tressell The SL6 202 D6
Trevelyan Mid Sch SL4 210 C3
Trevelyan Way HP4 135 B6
Treves Gn HP21 115 E5
Trevithick La MK5 46 B5
Trevone Ct MK6 47 A8
Trevor Ct TW19 213 A2
Trevose Ho SL2 198 B1
Trewarden Ave SL0 200 D3
Triangle Bsns Pk HP22 130 D8
Trident Ind Est SL3 212 E4
TRING 119 C3
Tring Bsns Ctr HP23 118 E4
TRINGFORD 118 F8
Tring Ford Rd HP23 119 A7
Tring Hill HP23 118 C3
Tring Park Sch for the Performing Arts HP23 119 B3
Tring Rd
Aylesbury HP21 116 B7
Berkhamsted HP4 134 D7
Dunstable LU6 93 E7
Edlesborough LU6 106 E8
Long Marston HP23 104 C3
Wendover HP22 131 C5
Wilstone HP23 104 C1
Wingrave HP22 89 C1
Tring Reservoirs (Wildlife Trust Reserves)* HP23 118 E7
Tring Sch HP23 119 B4
Tring Sta HP23 120 A5
Trinity Ave SL7 183 D3
Trinity CE Prim Sch RG9 191 D1
Trinity Cl
Old Stratford MK19 32 B7
Stanwell TW19 213 C1
Trinity Ct
Aylesbury HP19 101 D1
Chesham HP5 154 C7
Marlow SL7 183 D3
Trinity Ho SL8 195 F6
Trinity Pl SL4 210 C5
Trinity Rd
Hazlemere HP15 162 F3
Marlow SL7 183 D2
Milton Keynes MK12 33 B7
Trinity St Stephen CE Fst Sch SL4 210 B6
Tripps Hill Cl HP8 177 A7
Trispen Ct MK6 47 A8
Trooper Rd HP23 120 C5
Troutbeck MK6 47 C8
Troutbeck Cl SL2 206 A6
Trout Cl SL7 194 C8
Trout Hollow HP27 148 E8
Trout La UB7 208 C5
Trout Rd UB7 208 D6
Trubys Gdn MK6 47 A2
Trueman Pl MK6 46 F8
Truesdale Dr UB9 190 C7
Trumper Way
Slough SL1 204 F5
Uxbridge UB8 201 C4
Trumpton La MK7 48 C7
Trunk Furlong MK17 49 D6
Truro Cl SL6 202 A7
Trust Cotts HP4 107 A1
Trustees Cl UB9 189 F5
Tubwell Rd SL2 199 B4
Tucker Cl HP13 173 C8
Tuckers Dr HP15 163 C7
Tudeley Hale MK7 48 B8
Tudor Ct
Amersham HP6 154 D1
5 Leighton Buzzard LU7 80 F7
Maidenhead SL6 196 C2
Piddington HP14 160 C1
3 Stanwell TW19 213 E1
Tudor Dr HP10 185 D7
Tudor Gdns
Milton Keynes MK11 32 E4
Slough SL1 204 C8
Steeple Claydon MK18 63 D3
Tudor Mill HP10 185 E6
Tudor Orch HP4 134 E6
Tudor Pk HP6 154 D2
Tudor Rd HP15 163 C3
Tudors Cl MK18 73 B4
Tudor Way SL4 209 E6
Tuffnell Cl MK15 35 E7
Tuffnell Gn MK10 35 E1
Tulip Way UB7 208 D2
Tulkers Cl HP16 151 D5
Tulla Ct MK2 58 C4
Tummell Way MK2 58 C6
Tunbridge Gr MK7 48 B8
Tunmers Ct SL9 177 C2
Tunmers End SL9 177 C2
Tunmers Ho SL9 177 C2
Tunnel Way LU7 105 C2
Tuns La
Henley-on-Thames RG9 191 E2
Slough SL1 205 C4
Turks Head Ct SL4 210 C7
Turnberry Cl MK3 57 D7
Turner Cl HP20 101 F3
Turner Rd SL3 206 C4
Turners Dr HP13 173 E8
Turners Field HP13 161 E3
Turner's Mdw HP22 117 B6
Turners Mews MK14 34 F6
Turners Pl HP15 163 C6
Turners Wlk 4 HP5 144 C1
Turners Wood Dr HP8 177 D7
Turner Wlk 12 HP20 101 F3
Turneys Dr MK12 33 A6
Turneys Orch WD3 167 D4
Turnfields HP18 124 A3
Turnfurlong HP21 115 F7
Turnfurlong Inf Sch HP21 116 A6
Turnfurlong Jun Sch HP21 116 A6
Turnfurlong La HP21 116 A6
Turnfurlong Row HP21 116 A6
Turnham Way HP19 115 B7
Turnip Cl HP18 112 B2
Turnmill Ave MK6 35 B2
Turnmill Ct MK6 35 B2
Turnoak Pk SL4 209 E3
Turnpike Ct MK17 49 A5
Turnpike End HP21 115 F6
Turnpike La UB10 201 E3
Turnpike Rd HP12 172 D4
Turnpike The HP18 109 D5
Turnpike Way HP12 172 C4
Turnstone Way HP19 101 E3
Turpins Gn SL6 202 A5
Turpyn Ct MK6 47 D8
Turton Way SL1 205 D3
TURVEY 8 F6
Turvey Cl HP22 117 E5
Turvey Lower Sch MK43 8 E6
Turvey Mill MK43 8 D5
Turvey Rd
Astwood MK16 15 F5
Turvey MK43 3 E2
TURVILLE 169 F3
TURVILLE HEATH 169 A3
Turvill End MK5 46 B8
Turville Rd HP21 116 C6
TURWESTON 38 C8
Turweston Rd NN13 26 A1
Tuscans Cl MK18 73 B5
Tweedale Cl MK17 67 C7
Tweed Cl HP4 135 B5
Tweed Dr MK3 46 D1
Tweed Rd SL3 212 B8
Tweenways HP5 144 E1
Twelve Leys HP22 89 B3
Twinches La SL1 205 B5
Twinflower MK7 48 B6
Twist The HP23 119 D2
Twitchell La HP22 117 E5
Twitchell Rd HP16 152 A7
Twitchell's La HP9 176 F5
Twitchen La MK4 46 D3
Twizel Cl MK13 33 E6
Two Dells La
Ashley Green HP5 145 A4
Chesham HP5 155 B8
Two Gates La HP5 143 D7
TWO MILE ASH 33 D2
Two Mile Ash Sch MK8 33 E1
Two Mile Dr SL1 204 E4
Two Ponds La HP4 134 C7
TWYFORD 62 C1
Twyford CE Fst Sch MK18 62 C2
Twyford La MK7 48 C5
Twynham Rd SL6 202 B7
Tyburn Ave MK6 35 B2
Tyhurst MK10 36 A2
Tyle Pl SL4 211 A2
Tylers Cres HP15 163 B2
Tylers Gn MK13 34 D3
TYLERS GREEN 163 D1
Tylers Green Fst Sch HP10 174 D8
Tylers Green Mid Sch HP10 174 B8
Tylers Hill Rd HP5 154 F8
Tylers Rd HP15 163 B2
Tyler Wlk 3 SL3 206 F1
Tylsworth Cl HP6 154 D1
Tyndale Mews SL1 205 B4
Tyneham Cl HP21 116 B4
Tynemouth Rise 3 MK10 36 A1
Tyne Rd HP21 115 D4
Tyne Sq MK3 46 D1
Tyrell Cl
Buckingham MK18 52 C7
Milton Keynes MK19 20 A5
Tyrell Gdns SL4 209 F4
Tyrells Gdns MK17 69 E8
Tyrells Rd MK17 69 E8
Tyrill MK14 34 C7
TYRINGHAM 12 F2
Tyson Pl MK6 46 E8
Tythe Cl LU7 78 E8
Tythe Gdns LU7 78 E8
Tythe Mews LU6 92 E3
Tyzack Rd HP13 162 F1

U

Ufton Court Yd SL8 185 B4
Ufton Ct SL8 185 B4
Ullswater Cl SL1 204 C8
Ullswater Dr LU7 80 C7
Ultra Ave MK3 47 A1
Ulverscroft MK10 36 B2
Ulverston Cres MK10 36 B2
Ulyett Pl MK6 46 E8
Umberville Way SL2 197 F2
Underhill Cl SL6 202 E6
Underwood Cotts HP7 164 C2
Underwood Pl MK6 46 E8
Underwood Rd HP13 173 D8
Union Bldgs UB8 201 B2
Union Bsns Pk UB8 201 B5
Union Ct 11 HP4 135 D4
Union Ind Est HP12 172 A7
Union St MK16 22 D5
University Way MK43 24 D1
Univ of Buckingham The MK18 52 C7
Univ of Buckingham The (Verney Pk) MK18 52 E7
Up Corner HP8 177 C8
Up Corner Cl HP8 177 B8
Upcroft SL4 210 B4
UP END 24 A8
Upland Ave HP5 144 B3
Uplands SL7 183 D6
Uplands Cl
Gerrards Cross SL9 188 E3
High Wycombe HP13 173 E8

Uplands Ct HP5 .... 144 C1
Uplands The SL9 .... 188 E2
Upminster Cl MK10 ...... 35 E1
Upper Abbotts Hill HP19 .... 115 A7
UPPER ARNCOTT 94 E7
Upper Ashlyns Rd HP4 . 135 B3
Upper Barn Farm HP18 . . 84 B1
Upper Belmont Rd HP5 144 B3
Upper Bourne End La HP1 .... 146 B7
Upper Bray Rd SL6 ..... 203 C3
Upper Church St HP18 . 112 F3
Upper Coombe LU7 ..... 80 E8
Upper Dr HP9 .... 175 D5
UPPER DUNSLEY 119 C4
Upper Fifth St MK9 ...... 34 D2
Upper Fourth St MK9 .... 34 D2
Upper George St HP5 . . 144 C1
Upper Gladstone Rd 2 HP5 .... 144 C1
Upper Green St HP11 . . . 172 E7
Upper Hall Pk HP4 ..... 135 E2
Upper Hartwell HP17 . . . 114 E5
Upper Hollis HP16 ..... 151 F7
Upper Hundreds Way HP20 .... 115 E8
Upper Icknield Way
Askett HP27 .... 139 E7
Halton HP22 .... 117 F2
Monks Risborough HP27 139 D6
Pitstone HP23, LU7 ..... 105 E1
Princes Risborough HP27 .... 139 B2
Saunderton HP27 .... 148 F7
Upper Lees Rd SL2 ...... 198 B2
Upper Lodge La HP15 . . 162 F6
UPPER MAIDENSGROVE 179 A7
Upper Mdw 2 HP5 ..... 144 B1
UPPER NORTH DEAN 150 E2
UPPER POLLICOTT 111 E8
Upper Ray Mdws Wildlife Reserve★ OX25 .... 81 D4
Upper Rd UB9 .... 189 D4
Upper Riding HP9 ...... 175 B2
Upper Second St MK9 . . . 34 D1
Upper St
Quainton HP22 .... 85 A5
Tingewick MK18 .... 51 B6
Upper Stonehayes MK14 . 34 F8
Upper Thames Way SL8 .... 184 F3
Upper Third St MK9 ..... 34 D1
Upper Tring Pk HP23 . . . 119 D1
Upper Ventnor Cotts SL6 .... 195 C8
Upper Way MK17 .... 59 C2
Upper Weald MK19 ...... 45 A8
UPPER WINCHENDON 99 B1
Upperwood Cl 1 MK5 ... 46 A3
Upper Wood Cl MK5 .... 45 F3
UPTON
Slough 206 B3
Stone 114 A4
Upton Cl
Henley-on-Thames RG9 . . 191 E1
5 Slough SL1 .... 205 F3
Upton Court Rd SL3 .... 206 B2
Upton Gr MK5 .... 46 C4
Upton Hospl SL1 .... 205 F4
Upton House Sch SL4 . . 210 C5
UPTON LEA 206 A7
Upton Lea Par SL2 ...... 206 B6
UPTON PARK 205 F3
Upton Pk SL1 .... 205 F3
Upton Rd
Dinton HP17 .... 114 A3
Slough SL1 .... 206 A3
Upton Terr HP17 .... 114 A3
Upway SL9 .... 177 F2
Ushercombe View MK18 50 D6
UXBRIDGE 201 E5
Uxbridge Coll UB8 ..... 201 E6
Uxbridge High Sch UB8 .... 201 D3
Uxbridge Ind Est UB8 . . 201 B3
UXBRIDGE MOOR 201 B4
Uxbridge Rd
Iver Heath SL0, SL3 .... 200 B2
Rickmansworth WD3 ...... 178 F7
Slough SL1, SL3 .... 206 C7
Uxbridge UB10 .... 201 F2
Uxbridge U Sta UB8 .... 201 D5

V

Vache La
Chalfont St Giles HP8 . . . 177 C8
Milton Keynes MK5 ...... 45 F6
Vale Cl SL9 .... 177 D2
Vale Ct MK43 .... 25 D2
Vale Gr SL1 .... 205 E3
Vale House HP19 .... 115 C8
Vale Ind Ctr The HP19 . . 101 C1
Valens Cl MK8 .... 45 E7
Valentine Ct MK8 .... 45 E7
Valentine Way HP8 ..... 177 D7
Vale Park Dr HP20 ..... 115 E8
Vale Rd
Aylesbury HP20 .... 101 E2
Chesham HP5 .... 144 C4
Windsor SL4 .... 209 F6
Vale Ret Pk HP20 ...... 115 E8
Valerian Pl MK16 .... 21 F4
Vale Rise HP5 .... 144 C3
Vale The SL9 .... 177 D2
Valley Cl
Brackley NN13 .... 38 A8
Whipsnade HP4 .... 107 E7
Valley Cres NN13 .... 38 A8
Valley Ctr The HP13 .... 173 C6
Valley End SL3 .... 199 C1
Valley Rd
Berkhamsted HP4 ...... 134 F6
Brackley NN13 .... 38 A8
Buckingham MK18 .... 52 F8
Finmere MK18 .... 50 D6
Henley-on-Thames RG9 . . 191 C1
Hughenden Valley HP14 . 162 A5
Uxbridge UB10 .... 201 E3
Valley Rise NN13 .... 38 A8
Valley View HP5 .... 144 B2
Valley Way SL9 .... 188 D5
Valpy Cl HP23 .... 119 D1
Van Der Bilt Ct MK13 .... 33 F6
Van Diemens Cl OX39 . . 147 C7
Vandyke Cl MK17 .... 49 B6
Vane Rd OX9 .... 126 B1
Vanguard Cl HP12 ...... 172 D7
Vanguard Ho 5 TW19 . . 213 E1
Vansittart Rd
Bisham SL7 .... 194 E7
Windsor SL4 .... 210 B6
Vantage Ct MK16 .... 22 F3
Vantage Rd SL1 .... 205 B5
Vanwall Bsns Pk SL6 . . 202 C5
Vanwall Rd SL6 .... 202 C4
Varnell Terr RG9 .... 181 C2
Vaughan Copse SL4 .... 205 D2
Vaughan Gdns SL4 ...... 204 F2
Vaughan Way SL2 ...... 197 E1
Vauxhall MK13 .... 34 B6
Vellan Ave MK6 .... 35 B1
Venables La MK15 ...... 35 B7
Venetian Ct MK7 .... 48 C7
Ventfield Cl OX33 ...... 108 A5
Venus Cl SL2 .... 197 F1
VENUS HILL 156 B8
Venus Hill HP3 .... 156 A8
Verbena Cl UB7 .... 208 D1
Verdi Cl MK7 .... 48 D5
Verdon Ct SL2 .... 198 B2
Verdon Dr MK15 .... 35 B7
Verity Pl MK6 .... 34 F1
Verley Cl MK6 .... 47 C8
Vermont Pl MK15 .... 22 C1
Vermont Rd SL2 .... 197 F1
Verney Ave HP12 .... 172 D4
Verney Cl
Berkhamsted HP4 ...... 134 F5
6 Buckingham MK18 .... 41 D1
Marlow SL7 .... 183 D2
Tring HP23 .... 119 C5
Verney Farm Cl MK18 . . . 74 F8
Verney Junc Bsns Pk MK18 .... 64 E3
VERNEY JUNCTION 64 F4
Verney Rd
Slough SL3 .... 207 A2
Winslow MK18 .... 65 E4
Verney Wlk HP21 .... 115 D6
Vernier Cres MK5 .... 45 E5
Vernon Bldg 7 HP11 . . . 172 F7
Verona Cl UB8 .... 208 C7
Verwood Rd HP20 ...... 101 E2
Veryan Pl MK6 .... 35 B1
Vicarage Cl
Cookham SL6 .... 196 B7
Seer Green HP9 .... 176 D3
Steeple Claydon MK18 .... 63 D2
Wendover HP22 .... 131 B5
Vicarage Ct
Hanslope MK19 .... 11 B2
Steeple Claydon MK18 .... 63 D3
Vicarage Dr SL6 .... 203 C4
Vicarage Flats SL4 ...... 210 D8
Vicarage Gdns
Leighton Buzzard LU7 .... 80 E6
Marsworth HP23 .... 105 A2
3 Milton Keynes MK13 . . . 34 A4
Vicarage La
Bovingdon HP3 .... 146 B4
Ivinghoe LU7 .... 105 F5
Piddington OX25 .... 95 E6
Steeple Claydon MK18 .... 63 D2
Wing LU7 .... 79 E2
Vicarage Rd
Aylesbury HP21 .... 115 D5
Henley-on-Thames RG9 . . 191 E1
Leighton Buzzard LU7 .... 80 E6
Maidenhead SL6 .... 202 F8
Milton Keynes, Bradwell MK13 .... 34 A4
Vicarage Rd *continued*
Milton Keynes, Fenny Stratford MK2 .... 58 E8
Milton Keynes, Stony Stratford MK13 .... 32 D6
Pitstone LU7 .... 105 D2
Whaddon MK17 .... 56 B8
Wigginton HP23 .... 119 D1
Winslow MK18 .... 65 F4
Yardley Gobion NN12 ..... 18 E6
Vicarage St MK17 .... 49 C4
Vicarage Way
Colnbrook SL3 .... 212 D7
Gerrards Cross SL9 ..... 188 F5
Vicarage Wlk MK11 ..... 32 D6
Vickers Ct 9 TW19 .... 213 E1
Vickery Cl HP21 .... 115 E5
Vickery Way HP21 ...... 115 E5
Victor Cl SL6 .... 202 B8
Victoria CE Fst Sch Berkhamsted HP4 .... 135 C4
Victoria Cotts SL6 ...... 195 C8
Victoria Cres SL0 ...... 208 A6
Victoria Ct
Henley-on-Thames RG9 . . 191 E1
High Wycombe HP11 .... 172 F8
4 Marlow SL7 .... 183 E2
Slough SL1 .... 205 E5
21 Windsor SL4 .... 210 D6
Victoria Dr SL1, SL2 ..... 197 F6
Victoria Gdns
High Wycombe HP11 .... 172 F4
Marlow SL7 .... 183 E2
Victoria Ho SL4 .... 211 A2
VICTORIA PARK 116 B8
Victoria Rd
Berkhamsted HP4 ...... 135 C4
Chesham HP5 .... 144 C1
Eton Wick SL4 .... 204 F1
Farnham Common SL2 . . . 198 C6
Leighton Buzzard LU7 .... 80 E6
Marlow SL7 .... 183 E2
Milton Keynes MK2 ...... 47 E1
Slough SL2 .... 206 B5
Uxbridge UB8 .... 201 C5
Victoria Row MK18 ...... 52 D8
Victoria St
Aylesbury HP20 .... 115 F8
High Wycombe HP11 .... 172 F7
Milton Keynes MK12 ...... 33 D6
9 Slough SL1 .... 205 F4
Windsor SL4 .... 210 D6
Victor Rd SL4 .... 210 C4
Victory Ct MK1 .... 47 B2
Victory Rd
Berkhamsted HP4 ...... 135 A5
Steeple Claydon MK18 .... 63 D2
Wendover HP22 .... 131 B5
Vienna Gr MK13 .... 33 E6
Village Cl MK16 .... 13 F2
Village Ct LU7 .... 80 D6
Village La SL2 .... 187 D4
Village Mews 2 HP3 . . . 146 A4
Village Rd
Coleshill HP7 .... 164 F3
Denham UB9 .... 190 A2
Dorney SL4 .... 204 B3
Village Way HP7 .... 166 D7
Villa Park (Mobile Home Pk) MK43 .... 37 F7
Villiers Bldgs 8 HP20 . . 115 D8
Villiers Cl MK18 .... 41 E2
Villiers Ct SL4 .... 210 A7
Villiers Rd SL2 .... 205 D8
Villier St UB8 .... 201 D3
Vimy Ct LU7 .... 80 F7
Vimy Rd LU7 .... 80 F7
Vincent Ave MK8 .... 45 F8
Vincent Dr UB10 .... 201 F4
Vincent Rd HP19 .... 101 A3
Vincents Way HP14 .... 161 D6
Vine Cl
Hazelmere HP15 .... 163 A3
Stanwell TW19 .... 213 A2
Vine Ct SL2 .... 199 A6
Vine Gr UB10 .... 201 F5
Vine La UB10 .... 201 F4
Vine Rd SL2 .... 198 F6
Vine Row MK43 .... 8 E6
Vine St UB8 .... 201 C4
Vine The HP18 .... 124 D3
Vinetrees HP22 .... 131 B4
Vineyard Dr SL8 .... 185 A5
Vineyards The HP27 .... 138 A2
Viney La HP19 .... 114 F8
Vinlake Ave UB10 ...... 190 F1
Vintners Mews MK14 .... 34 F6
Violet Ave UB8 .... 208 F8
Violet Cl HP27 .... 149 D6
Violets Cl MK16 .... 24 B6
Virage HP22 .... 117 F4
Virginia MK6 .... 47 A7
Virginia Gdns HP14 .... 159 F8
Viridian Sq HP21 .... 115 E7
Viscount Cl 13 HP20 . . . . 101 F2
Viscount Ct 12 SL4 ..... 210 C6
Viscount Ind Est SL3 .... 212 E4
Viscount Way MK2 ...... 47 C1
Vitalograph Bsns Pk MK18 .... 41 F4
Vivaldi Ct MK7 .... 48 D5
Vivien Cl SL6 .... 195 F6
Volta Rise MK5 .... 46 C4
Vyne Cres MK8 .... 33 F1
Vyners Sch UB10 .... 201 F8

W

Waborne Rd SL8 .... 185 B4
WADDESDON 99 B7
Waddesdon CE Sch HP18 .... 99 A6
Waddesdon Cl 8 MK8 . . . 45 F8
Waddesdon Green HP21 .... 115 E4
Waddesdon Hill HP18 . . . 99 C3
Waddesdon Manor★ HP18 .... 98 E5
Waddesdon Manor Flats HP18 .... 98 E6
Waddesdon Village Prim Sch HP18 .... 99 A6
Wade Dr SL1 .... 205 A5
Wadesmill La MK7 ...... 48 A4
Wadhurst La MK10 ...... 36 B1
Wadworth Holme MK10 . 35 E3
Waglands Gdn MK18 .... 52 D7
Wagner Cl MK7 .... 48 C4
Wagstaff Way 12 MK46 . . . . 6 F3
Waine Cl MK18 .... 52 D7
Wainers Croft MK12 ..... 33 B4
Wainwrights HP18 ..... 125 D6
Waivers Way HP21 ...... 116 A5
Wakefield Cl MK14 ...... 34 F7
Wakefield Cres SL2 .... 198 F6
Wakelins End SL6 ...... 195 E7
Wakeman Rd SL8 ...... 185 A3
Walbank Gr MK5 .... 46 A3
Walbrook Ave MK6 ...... 35 B3
Waldeck Ho SL6 .... 203 A7
Waldeck Rd SL6 .... 203 A7
Walden Croft MK6 ...... 47 E4
Waldens Cl 4 SL8 ..... 185 A3
Waldcks Cl LU7 .... 78 E8
Walford Rd UB8 .... 201 D3
Walgrave Dr MK13 ...... 34 B4
Walker Ave MK12 .... 33 A6
Walker Cres SL3 .... 206 F1
Walker Ct SL6 .... 202 D7
Walker Rd SL6 .... 203 A4
Walkers Rd HP27 ...... 138 D7
Walkham Cl HP13 ...... 174 B4
Walkhampton Ave MK13 . 34 C3
Walk House Cl MK43 .... 25 B1
Walk The
Eton Wick SL4 .... 205 A1
Winslow MK18 .... 65 F4
Walkwood End HP9 .... 175 C1
Walkwood Rise HP9 .... 186 C8
Wallace Cl
Marlow SL7 .... 183 F4
Uxbridge UB10 .... 201 E3
Wallace Dr LU6 .... 92 E6
Wallace End HP21 ...... 116 A6
Wallace Mews LU6 ...... 92 E6
Wallace St MK13 .... 33 E7
Wallace Wlk SL4 .... 205 F1
Wallbridge Cl HP19 .... 115 B7
Wall Brown Way HP19 . . 101 C4
Waller Rd HP9 .... 175 F2
Wallinger Dr MK5 .... 46 A3
Wallingford MK13 .... 34 B5
Wallingford Gdns HP11 173 B4
Wallingford Rd UB8 .... 201 B2
Wallington Rd HP5 ..... 144 B1
Wallis Ct SL1 .... 206 A3
Wallmead Gdns MK5 .... 46 B7
Walney Pl MK4 .... 45 F1
Walnut Cl
Great Missenden HP16 . . 152 A7
Long Crendon HP18 ...... 125 C7
Newport Pagnell MK16 . . . 22 A3
Stoke Mandeville HP22 . . 116 C2
Walnut Cres HP27 ...... 138 D7
Walnut Dr
Maids Moreton MK18 .... 41 F4
Milton Keynes MK2 ...... 58 E8
Wendover HP22 .... 131 B6
Walnut Gr HP10 .... 185 E6
Walnut Lodge SL1 ..... 205 D4
Walnuts Sch The MK8 . . . 45 D5
WALNUT TREE 48 C6
Walnut Tree Cl
Bourne End SL8 .... 185 B2
High Wycombe HP12 .... 172 C8
Uxbridge UB10 .... 201 E8
Walnut Tree Ct HP22 . . . 116 C3
Walnut Tree Ho HP11 . . 174 B3
Walnut Tree La HP27 . . . 138 D6
Walnut Tree Rdbt MK7 . . 48 C7
Walnut Way
Bourne End SL8 .... 185 B2
Hyde Heath HP6 .... 153 C4
Walpole Rd SL1 .... 204 D7
Walsh's Manor MK14 .... 34 D7
Walsingham Gate HP11 .... 173 A4
WALTER'S ASH 150 C1
Waltham Dr MK10 .... 36 A1
Waltham Ho 4 MK3 .... 46 F1
WALTON
Aylesbury 115 F7
Milton Keynes 47 F5
Walton Cl HP13 .... 162 E1
WALTON COURT 115 C5
Walton Court Ctr HP21 115 C5
Walton Dene HP21 ..... 115 F7
Walton Dr
High Wycombe HP13 .... 162 E1
Walton MK7 .... 47 F6
Walton End MK7 .... 48 C6
Walton Gn HP21 .... 115 E7
Walton Gr HP21 .... 115 E7
Walton Heath MK3 ...... 57 D7
Walton High Sch MK7 . . . 48 C6
Walton La SL2 .... 197 F3
WALTON MANOR 48 A6
WALTON PARK 48 A4
Walton Park Rdbt MK7 . . 48 B4
Walton Pl HP22 .... 116 F3
Walton Rd
Aylesbury HP21 .... 115 F7
Caldecotte MK7 .... 48 B3
Milton Keynes MK10 ..... 36 A2
Walton MK7 .... 48 B6
Wavendon MK10, MK17 . . . 48 D7
Walton St HP21 .... 115 E7
Walton Terr HP21 .... 115 E7
Walton Way HP21 ...... 116 A7
Wandlebury MK14 .... 35 A8
Wandsworth Pl MK13 .... 34 D3
Wannions Cl HP5 ...... 145 A1
Wantage Cl LU7 .... 79 E3
Wantage Cres LU7 ...... 79 E3
Wappenham Rd NN13 . . . 27 B8
Wapping HP18 .... 125 D6
Wapseys La SL2 .... 187 F4
Warbler Cl HP19 .... 114 F8
Warburg Nature Reserve★ RG9 .... 179 B5
Ward Cl SL0 .... 207 F7
Wardes Cl HP16 .... 151 C5
Ward Gdns SL1 .... 204 E5
Wardle Pl MK6 .... 46 E8
Ward Pl HP7 .... 165 B7
Ward Rd
Brackley NN13 .... 38 A5
Milton Keynes MK1 ...... 47 E3
Wardrobes La HP27 .... 149 D8
Ward Royal 6 SL4 ..... 210 C6
Ward Royal Parade 3 SL4 .... 210 C6
Wards Dr WD3 .... 156 F3
Wardstone End MK4 .... 46 B2
Ware Leys Cl OX27 ..... 71 E3
Wargrave Rd RG9 ...... 191 F1
Warmington Gdns MK15 . 35 B5
Warmstone Cl HP18 ..... 99 B6
Warmstone La HP18 .... 99 B6
Warneford Ave HP22 . . . 131 D5
Warner Cl SL1 .... 204 E5
Warners Cl MK17 .... 59 D1
Warners Hill SL6 .... 195 D8
Warners Rd MK17 .... 57 D3
Warren Bank MK6 .... 47 E5
Warren Cl
Buckingham MK18 .... 52 E7
Slough SL3 .... 206 E3
Stone HP17 .... 114 B5
Warren Ct
Farnham Common SL2 . . . 198 C7
Little Horwood MK17 ..... 55 E5
Warrendene Rd HP14 . . 162 A8
Warrender Rd HP5 ..... 144 E2
Warren Farm Cotts MK18 .... 50 A7
Warren Field SL0 ...... 200 C3
Warren Ho HP19 .... 101 B1
Warren Nature Reserve★ HP10 .... 185 E5
Warren Parade SL2 .... 206 C5
Warren Rd
Ickenham UB10 .... 201 F8
Little Horwood MK17 ..... 55 F5
Yardley Gobion NN12 ..... 18 F6
Warren The
Chalfont St Peter SL9 . . . 177 F3
Chartridge HP5 .... 143 E3
Hazelmere HP15 .... 163 A5
Warren Wood Dr HP11 . 173 C5
Warren Yd MK12 .... 33 A6
WARRINGTON 2 B1
Warrington Ave SL1 .... 205 C7
Warrington Rd MK46 ..... 7 B7
Warwick Ave
High Wycombe HP12 .... 172 B6
Milton Keynes MK10 ..... 36 C3
Slough SL2 .... 198 C1
Warwick Cl
Aston Clinton HP22 ..... 117 E5
Maidenhead SL6 .... 202 B4
Warwick Ct
Beaconsfield HP9 .... 175 D3
Chorleywood WD3 ...... 167 F6

Warwick Ct continued
  7 Windsor SL4 . . . . **210** C5
Warwick Dr LU7 . . . . **79** E2
Warwick Ho 7 HP13 . . **173** F7
Warwick Pl
  Milton Keynes MK3 . . . **57** E7
  Uxbridge UB8 . . . . **201** C5
Warwick Rd
  Beaconsfield HP9 . . . . . **175** D3
  Hanslope MK19 . . . . **11** A3
  Milton Keynes MK3 . . . . **57** F7
  Pitstone LU7 . . . . **105** D2
  West Drayton UB7 . . . . . **208** E5
Warwick Row HP20 . . **102** A1
Washfield MK4 . . . . **46** D3
Wash Hill HP10 . . . . . . **185** E3
Wash Hill Lea HP10 . . **185** E3
Wash Hill Mobile Home Pk
  HP10 . . . . **185** E3
Washingleys MK43 . . . . **25** C2
Washington Ct SL7 . . . **184** A3
Washington Dr
  Slough SL1 . . . . **204** D6
  Windsor SL4 . . . . **209** E4
Washington Row HP7 . **165** C7
Wastel MK6 . . . . **47** B5
Watchcroft Dr MK18 . . . **41** E2
Watchet Ct MK4 . . . . . . **46** D3
Watchet La
  Holmer Green HP15 . . . . **163** B7
  Little Kingshill HP16 . . **152** C1
Waterbeach Cl SL1 . . . **205** D7
Waterbeach Rd SL1 . . . **205** D7
Waterborne Wlk LU7 . . . **80** F7
Water Cl MK19 . . . . **32** B7
Watercress Way MK10 . . **36** B3
WATER EATON **58** D5
Water Eaton Rd MK2,
  MK3 . . . . **58** C7
WATEREND **159** C5
Water End Rd
  Beacon's Bottom HP14 . . **159** D3
  Beacon's Bottom, Waterend
  HP14 . . . . **159** C5
Waterfield WD3 . . . . **167** C2
Waterford Cl MK3 . . . . . **46** E1
Waterford Ho UB7 . . . . **208** C3
Water Gdns The HP15 . . **162** E2
Waterglades The HP9 . . **175** C6
Water Hall Comb Sch
  MK2 . . . . **58** D4
Waterhouse Cl MK16 . . . **22** D4
Water La
  Berkhamsted HP4 . . . . . **135** C4
  Bovingdon HP3 . . . . **146** B1
  Ford HP17 . . . . **128** B7
  Leighton Buzzard LU7 . . . **80** F7
  Sherington MK16 . . . . . . **13** E1
  Speen HP27 . . . . **150** C4
Waterlily 5 HP19 . . . . . **101** E4
Waterloo Ct MK3 . . . . . . **46** E2
Waterloo Rd
  Leighton Buzzard LU7 . . . **80** E6
  Uxbridge UB8 . . . . **201** C4
Waterlow Cl MK16 . . . . . **22** C2
Waterman Ct SL1 . . . . . **204** E5
Water Mdw HP5 . . . . . . **154** B7
WATERMEAD **101** F4
Watermead HP19 . . . . . **101** E4
Watermeadow HP19 . . . **101** F3
Water Meadow Way
  HP22 . . . . **131** B6
Watermill Way HP22 . . **116** F2
WATERPERRY **123** B1
Waterperry OX33 . . . . . **123** B1
WATERPERRY
  COMMON **122** F8
Waterperry Gdns★
  OX33 . . . . **123** B1
Waterperry Mews
  HP19 . . . . **114** F8
Waterperry Rd HP18 . . **123** D5
WATERSIDE **154** D6
Waterside
  Berkhamsted HP4 . . . . . **135** D4
  Chesham HP5 . . . . **154** D6
  Edlesborough LU6 . . . . . **92** F4
  Milton Keynes MK6 . . . . **47** C8
  Uxbridge UB8 . . . . **208** C8
  Wooburn Green HP10 . . **185** E7
Waterside Comb Sch
  HP5 . . . . **154** D6
Waterside Ct HP5 . . . . . **154** C7
Waterside Dr SL3 . . . . . **207** A4
Waterside Lodge SL6 . . **203** C8
Waterslade Pk MK12 . . . **33** C7
Waterslade Pens HP17 . **126** F6
Waters Reach SL6 . . . . **196** A1
WATER STRATFORD **40** A1
Water Stratford Rd
  MK18 . . . . **51** A7
Water Tower Cl UB8 . . . **201** E7
Watery La
  Beachampton MK19 . . . . **44** B6
  Brackley NN13 . . . . **38** A7
  Marsworth HP23 . . . . . . **104** F1
  Wooburn Green HP10 . . **185** E8
Watling St
  Bletchley MK2 . . . . **47** D1

Watling St continued
  Bow Brickhill MK17 . . . . . **58** F8
  Granby MK6 . . . . **47** A3
  Milton Keynes, Kiln Farm MK8,
  MK11 . . . . **33** B2
  Milton Keynes, Shenley Lodge
  MK6 . . . . **46** C6
  Potterspury NN12 . . . . . . **18** C3
Watling Terr MK2 . . . . . **47** E1
Watlington Ct HP16 . . . **152** A8
Watlington Rd OX49 . . . **157** A7
Watling Way Pool MK11 . **32** F4
Watlow Gdns MK18 . . . . **41** E2
Watson Cl MK8 . . . . **45** D6
Watten Cl MK2 . . . . **58** E4
Wattleton Rd HP9 . . . . **175** E1
Watts Cl MK13 . . . . **11** A3
Watts Gn HP18 . . . . **112** B2
Wavell Cl MK15 . . . . **35** B7
Wavell Gdns SL2 . . . . . **197** F2
Wavell Rd
  Beaconsfield HP9 . . . . . **176** B1
  Maidenhead SL6 . . . . . . **202** B6
WAVENDON **48** E7
Wavendon Fields MK17 . **48** F6
WAVENDON GATE **48** D6
Wavendon Gate Comb Sch
  MK7 . . . . **48** D6
Wavendon House Dr
  MK17 . . . . **49** B8
Wavendon Rd MK17 . . . . **37** C2
Waveney Cl MK16 . . . . . . **22** E3
Waverley Croft MK10 . . . **36** A1
Waverley Rd SL1 . . . . . **205** C8
Waverley Wlk HP20 . . . **101** D2
Waxwing Cl HP19 . . . . . **101** E3
Wayfarers Pk HP4 . . . . **134** F4
Waylands TW19 . . . . . . **211** E1
Wayside
  High Wycombe HP13 . . . **173** D7
  Speen HP27 . . . . **150** C4
Wayside Ct HP6 . . . . . . **154** C1
Wayside Gdns SL9 . . . . **188** C3
Wayside Mews SL6 . . . **202** F8
Wealdstone Pl MK6 . . . . **35** A2
Weasel La MK3 . . . . **57** C6
Weatherby LU6 . . . . **93** E8
Weathercock Cl MK17 . . **49** B5
Weathercock Gdns
  HP15 . . . . **163** C7
Weathercock La MK17 . . **49** C4
Weavers End MK19 . . . . **11** B2
Weavers Hill MK11 . . . . **33** A4
Weavers Rd HP23 . . . . . **118** E4
Webb Cl
  Chesham HP5 . . . . **144** B1
  Slough SL3 . . . . **206** D2
Webber Heath MK7 . . . . **48** D4
Webbs Home Cl MK10 . . **36** A2
Webbs Mdw HP19 . . . . . **115** A8
Webster Cl
  Maidenhead SL6 . . . . . . **202** A5
  Thame OX9 . . . . **125** F1
Webster Rd HP21 . . . . . **116** A6
Websters Mdw MK4 . . . . **46** C1
Wedgewood St HP19 . . **115** A8
Wedgwood Ave MK14 . . . **22** A1
Wedgwood Dr HP14 . . . **162** A6
WEEDON **87** D1
Weedon Cl SL9 . . . . **177** B2
Weedon Hill HP6 . . . . . **153** D4
Weedon La HP6 . . . . **154** A3
Weedon Rd HP19 . . . . . **101** D2
Weekes Dr SL1 . . . . **205** B4
Weill Rd HP21 . . . . **116** A4
Weir La
  Blackthorn OX25 . . . . . . **81** A4
  East Claydon MK18 . . . . . **74** E5
  Whitchurch HP22 . . . . . . **86** F6
Weirside Gdns UB7 . . . **208** D5
Welbeck Ave HP21 . . . . **116** C6
Welbeck Cl MK10 . . . . . . **35** F1
Welbeck Rd SL6 . . . . . . **202** D5
Welburn Gr MK4 . . . . . . **46** B2
Welby Cl SL6 . . . . **202** A4
Welden SL2 . . . . **206** C7
Welders La
  Chalfont St Giles SL9 . . **177** A3
  Seer Green SL9 . . . . **177** B3
Weldon Rise MK5 . . . . . . **46** B8
Welford Way HP18 . . . . **112** F3
Welland Cl SL3 . . . . **212** B8
Welland Dr MK16 . . . . . . **22** E3
Welland Ho MK3 . . . . . . **57** E8
Welland Rd HP21 . . . . . **115** C5
Wellbank SL6 . . . . **196** E1
Wellbrook Mews HP23 . **119** B4
Wellcroft LU7 . . . . **105** F5
Wellcroft Rd SL1 . . . . . **205** B5
WELL END **184** F5
Well End Cotts SL8 . . . **184** F5
Weller Cl HP6 . . . . **154** E2
Weller Ct LU6 . . . . **93** C7
Weller Rd HP6 . . . . **154** E2
Wellesbourne Gdns
  HP13 . . . . **162** D2
Welles La MK4 . . . . **45** D3
Wellesley Ave SL0 . . . . **207** F4
Wellesley Ct SL0 . . . . . **207** F4

Wellesley Ho SL4 . . . . . **210** B6
Wellesley Path SL1 . . . **206** A4
Wellesley Rd SL1 . . . . . **206** A4
Welles Rd HP13 . . . . . . **173** F7
Welley Ave TW19 . . . . . **211** E3
Welley Rd SL3, TW19 . . . **211** E3
Wellfield HP15 . . . . **163** B3
Wellfield Ct MK15 . . . . . **35** D8
Wellfield Rd HP14 . . . . **171** B8
Wellhayes MK14 . . . . . . **34** F8
Wellhouse Rd SL6 . . . . **195** C2
Wellhouse Way HP4 . . . **134** F8
Wellingborough Rd MK46 . **6** F5
Wellington Ave HP27 . . **139** B4
Wellington Cl 1 SL6 . . **202** B8
Wellington Pl
  Aylesbury HP21 . . . . . . **115** E4
  Milton Keynes MK3 . . . . **58** B7
Wellington Rd
  Aylesbury HP21 . . . . . . **115** E4
  High Wycombe HP12 . . . **172** E4
  Maidenhead SL6 . . . . . . **202** D7
  Uxbridge UB8 . . . . **201** C4
Wellington St SL1 . . . . **206** A4
Well La MK17 . . . . **80** A1
Well Mdw HP19 . . . . . . **101** D4
Wells Cl SL4 . . . . **210** A7
Well St MK18 . . . . **52** D8
Welsh La MK18 . . . . **40** C5
Welsummer Gr MK5 . . . . **46** A3
Welton Rd HP21 . . . . . . **116** B7
WENDOVER **131** C4
Wendover CE Jun Sch
  HP22 . . . . **131** B6
WENDOVER DEAN **141** C5
Wendover House Specl Sch
  HP22 . . . . **131** C3
Wendover Hts HP22 . . . **131** C6
Wendover Rd
  Bourne End SL8 . . . . . . **185** A5
  Burnham SL1 . . . . **204** B8
  Ellesborough HP17 . . . . **130** D3
Wendover St HP11 . . . . **172** F7
Wendover Sta HP22 . . . **131** B4
Wendover Way
  Aylesbury HP21 . . . . . . **115** F6
  High Wycombe HP11 . . . **173** B6
Wendover Woods (Forest
  Wlks)★ HP23 . . . . **131** F6
Wenford MK10 . . . . **36** C3
Wenlack Cl UB9 . . . . . . **190** A1
Wenning La MK4 . . . . . . **46** B2
Wentworth Ave SL2 . . . **198** A2
Wentworth Cl HP13 . . . **173** C8
Wentworth Cres SL6 . . **202** C6
Wentworth Ind Ctr SL2 **198** A1
Wentworth Way MK3 . . . **57** C7
Wenwell Cl HP22 . . . . . **118** A3
Werner Ct HP21 . . . . . . **115** E4
Werner Terr MK18 . . . . . **73** B6
Werth Dr MK17 . . . . **49** B2
Wescott Way SL8 . . . . . **201** C3
Wesley Cl HP20 . . . . . . **102** A2
Wesley Dene 4 HP13 . . **173** B7
Wesley Hill 1 HP5 . . . . **144** B1
Wessex Ct
  4 Stanwell TW19 . . . . **213** E1
  11 Windsor SL4 . . . . . . **210** C6
Wessex Prim Sch SL6 . **202** B4
Wessex Rd SL8 . . . . **185** B2
Wessex Road Ind Est
  SL8 . . . . **185** B2
Wessex Way SL6 . . . . . **202** B4
Wessons Hill SL6 . . . . . **195** C2
West Acres HP4 . . . . . . **165** D7
Westanley Ave HP7 . . . **165** D8
West Ave HP10 . . . . **163** C1
Westborne Ct MK13 . . . . **34** A6
Westborough Ct SL6 . . **202** C6
Westborough Rd SL6 . . **202** C6
Westbourne St 6
  HP11 . . . . **172** F7
Westbrook End MK17 . . . **57** C3
Westbrook Hay Prep Sch
  HP1 . . . . **146** D7
WESTBURY **39** B4
Westbury Cl
  Bicester OX27 . . . . **71** E2
  Newport Pagnell MK16 . . **22** B4
Westbury Court Bsns Ctr
  OX27 . . . . **71** C4
Westbury Ho 3 HP20 . . **101** D1
Westbury La MK16 . . . . . **22** A5
Westbury Mill NN13 . . . . **38** F4
Westbury Terr OX27 . . . . **71** F2
West Cl SL7 . . . . **193** D7
Westcliffe MK8 . . . . **33** C2
Westcoign Ho SL6 . . . . **203** B8
West Comm SL9 . . . . . . **188** D6
West Common Cl SL9 . . **188** E6
West Common Rd UB8 . **201** D6
WESTCOTT **98** C7
Westcott CE Sch HP18 . **98** A7
Westcott Venture Pk
  HP18 . . . . **98** A6
West Cres SL4 . . . . **209** F6
WESTCROFT **45** E2

Westcroft
  Slough SL2 . . . . **198** B1
  Tring HP23 . . . . **119** A3
Westcroft Rdbt MK4 . . . . **46** A2
Westcroft Stables★
  HP27 . . . . **150** B3
West Ct
  Bray SL6 . . . . **203** C4
  High Wycombe HP13 . . . **161** D3
West Dales MK13 . . . . . . **34** C5
West Dean SL6 . . . . **202** F8
Westdean La HP5 . . . . . **143** C3
Westdown Gdns LU6 . . . **93** F7
West Dr HP13 . . . . **173** D8
WEST DRAYTON **208** D4
West Drayton Park Ave
  UB7 . . . . **208** E4
West Drayton Prim Sch
  UB7 . . . . **208** E4
West Drayton Sta UB7 . **208** D5
West Edge OX27 . . . . **71** E2
WEST END **63** C2
West End HP22 . . . . **116** E2
West End Cl MK18 . . . . . . **63** C2
West End Ct SL2 . . . . . . **198** F4
West End La SL2 . . . . . . **198** F4
West End Pl HP22 . . . . . **116** E2
West End Rd
  Cheddington LU7 . . . . . **104** F7
  High Wycombe HP11 . . . **172** F7
West End St HP11 . . . . . **172** F7
Western Ave
  Buckingham MK18 . . . . . **41** C1
  New Denham UB9 . . . . . **201** D8
Western Dene HP15 . . . **163** A5
Western Dr
  Hanslope MK19 . . . . **11** A3
  Wooburn Green HP10 . . **185** E5
Western House Prim Sch
  SL1 . . . . **204** F5
Western La MK18 . . . . . . **65** F3
Western Perimeter Rd
  TW6 . . . . **213** B5
Western Perimeter Road
  Rdbt TW19 . . . . **213** B5
Western Rd
  Great Horwood MK17 . . . **55** A3
  Milton Keynes, Fenny Stratford
  MK2 . . . . **47** D1
  Milton Keynes, Wolverton
  MK12 . . . . **33** C6
  Tring HP23 . . . . **118** F3
West Farm Way MK46 . . **13** E8
Westfield
  Aylesbury HP21 . . . . . . **115** E3
  Hyde Heath HP6 . . . . . . **153** C4
Westfield Ave MK19 . . . . **31** D5
Westfield Bglws SL7 . . . **192** F6
Westfield Cotts SL7 . . . **192** F5
Westfield Fst Sch HP4 . **134** F5
Westfield Rd
  Beaconsfield HP9 . . . . . **175** C1
  Berkhamsted HP4 . . . . . **134** E6
  Dunstable LU6 . . . . **93** F8
  Maidenhead SL6 . . . . . . **202** B7
  Milton Keynes MK2 . . . . **58** C7
  Pitstone LU7 . . . . **105** C3
  Slough SL2 . . . . **198** B1
  Wheatley OX33 . . . . **122** A1
Westfields
  Buckingham MK18 . . . . . **52** C8
  Princes Risborough
  HP27 . . . . **139** D4
Westfield Sch SL8 . . . . **185** A3
Westfield Wlk HP12 . . . **172** D6
West Furlong MK18 . . . . **53** A1
Westgate Cres SL1 . . . **204** F6
Westgate Ct HP13 . . . . **174** A4
Westgate Ret 2 SL1 . . . **205** A6
Westgate Sch The SL1 . **205** A4
Westhill MK14 . . . . **34** D8
West Hill MK17 . . . . **49** D4
Westhorpe Rd SL7 . . . . **183** F3
WEST HYDE **178** E3
West Hyde La SL9 . . . . . **178** A4
West La
  Bledlow HP27 . . . . **138** B1
  Emberton MK46 . . . . **13** E8
  Henley-on-Thames RG9 . **191** D2
Westland Cl TW19 . . . . **213** E1
Westlands Ave SL1 . . . **204** C7
Westlands Cl SL1 . . . . . **204** C7
Westlands Rd HP27 . . . **149** E5
WEST LEITH **118** F2
West Leith HP23 . . . . . . **118** F1
WESTLINGTON **113** E1
Westlington La HP17 . . **113** E1
Westlington Lea HP17 . **113** E1
Westmead
  Monks Risborough
  HP27 . . . . **139** B5
  Windsor SL4 . . . . **210** B4
West Mead SL6 . . . . **195** F2
Westminster Cl
  Brackley NN13 . . . . **38** A7
  High Wycombe HP11 . . . **173** B4
Westminster Cres NN13 . **38** A7
Westminster Dr
  Aylesbury HP21 . . . . . . **115** F6

Westminster Dr continued
  Milton Keynes MK3 . . . . **47** A2
Westmorland Ave
  HP21 . . . . **116** B6
Westmorland Ho MK3 . . . **46** F2
Westmorland Rd SL6 . . **202** D6
Westmount Ave HP7 . . . **165** C8
Weston Ct HP22 . . . . . . **117** C5
Weston La OX9 . . . . **136** F8
Weston Rd
  Aston Clinton HP22 . . . . **117** C5
  Lewknor OX49 . . . . **157** A8
  Olney MK46 . . . . **6** E3
  Ravenstone MK46 . . . . . . **5** E2
  Slough SL1 . . . . **204** F8
WESTON TURVILLE **116** E3
Weston Turville CE Sch
  HP22 . . . . **116** E3
Weston Turville Resr
  Wildlife Reserve★
  HP22 . . . . **130** F8
WESTON UNDERWOOD **6** B1
Weston Way HP22 . . . . . **116** A2
Weston Way Ind Est
  HP22 . . . . **116** A2
Westover Ct HP13 . . . . . **161** D1
Westover Rd HP13 . . . . **161** D1
West Pas 11 HP23 . . . . . **119** A3
Westpits MK46 . . . . **13** E8
West Point SL1 . . . . **204** D5
West Puxley Cl MK19 . . . **31** D5
West Rd
  Berkhamsted HP4 . . . . . **135** A5
  Cranfield MK43 . . . . **24** D2
  Maidenhead SL6 . . . . . . **202** E7
  West Drayton UB7 . . . . . **208** F3
  Woburn Sands MK17 . . . . **49** B5
West Richardson St 2
  HP11 . . . . **172** F7
Westrick Walk HP16 . . . **151** C5
West Ridge SL8 . . . . . . **185** B4
Westridge Cl HP5 . . . . . **144** A3
Westron Gdns HP23 . . . **119** B4
Westside La MK16 . . . . . **12** B6
West Side Rise MK46 . . . . **6** F4
West Spur Rd UB8 . . . . **201** D2
West Sq SL0 . . . . **207** F7
West St
  Adstock MK18 . . . . **53** F1
  Aylesbury HP19 . . . . . . **101** C1
  Buckingham MK18 . . . . . **41** C1
  Dunstable LU6 . . . . **93** F7
  Henley-on-Thames RG9 . **191** D2
  Leighton Buzzard LU7 . . . **80** F7
  Maidenhead SL6 . . . . . . **202** F7
  Marlow SL7 . . . . **183** D1
  Olney MK46 . . . . **6** F4
  Steeple Claydon MK18 . . **63** D2
West View
  Chesham HP5 . . . . **144** D2
  Hardwick HP22 . . . . **87** B3
  High Wycombe HP13 . . . **173** B8
West Way HP9 . . . . **174** F1
West Waye HP13 . . . . . . **162** C2
West Well Cl MK18 . . . . . **51** A6
West Well La MK18 . . . . . **51** A6
West Wlk MK9 . . . . **34** E2
Westwood HP12 . . . . . . **172** B3
Westwood Cl
  Little Chalfont HP6 . . . . **166** D8
  Milton Keynes MK8 . . . . **45** F8
Westwood Dr HP6 . . . . . **166** D8
Westwood Gn SL6 . . . . . **195** F6
Westwood Rd SL7 . . . . . **183** C1
Westwood Wlk 6
  HP20 . . . . **101** F2
WEST WYCOMBE **160** F2
West Wycombe Comb Sch
  HP14 . . . . **160** F2
West Wycombe Park★
  HP14 . . . . **161** A1
West Wycombe Rd
  HP12 . . . . **161** C1
West Yard Ind Est
  HP14 . . . . **160** C8
Wetherby Gdns MK3 . . . **57** D6
Wethered Pk SL7 . . . . . **183** D1
Wethered Rd
  Burnham SL1 . . . . **204** B8
  Marlow SL7 . . . . **183** D2
Wexford Ct 2 SL6 . . . . **203** B7
Wexham Court Prim Sch
  SL3 . . . . **206** C8
Wexham Park Hospl
  SL3 . . . . **199** C1
Wexham Park La SL3 . . **199** C1
Wexham Pl SL2 . . . . **199** D6
Wexham Rd SL1, SL2 . . **206** B6
Wexham Sch Sports Coll
  SL2 . . . . **206** C8
Wexham St SL3 . . . . . . **199** B3
WEXHAM STREET **199** C1
Wexham Woods SL3 . . . **206** C8
Weybourne Rd 1 MK10 . **36** A4
Wey La HP5 . . . . **154** B7
WHADDON **45** A1

Whaddon CE Sch MK17 . 56 B8
Whaddon Chase HP19 . . 101 D2
Whaddon Hall MK17 . . . . 45 B2
Whaddon Rd
Milton Keynes, Shenley Brook End MK5 . . . 46 A3
Mursley MK17 . . . . 56 C3
Nash MK17 . . . . 44 D2
Newport Pagnell MK16 . . . 22 B3
Newton Longville MK17 . . . 57 D3
Whaddon Way MK3 . . . . 46 F2
Whales La OX27 . . . . 71 E2
Whalley Dr MK3 . . . . 47 A2
Wharf Cl
Old Stratford MK19 . . . . 32 B7
Wendover HP22 . . . . 131 B5
Wharf Ct UB8 . . . . 201 C1
Wharfe La RG9 . . . . 191 E2
Wharf La
Berkhamsted HP4 . . . . 134 C8
Bourne End SL8 . . . . 185 A3
Old Stratford MK19 . . . . 32 C7
Wharf Rd HP22 . . . . 131 B5
Wharf Row HP22 . . . . 118 B4
Wharfside MK2 . . . . 47 E1
Wharfside Pl MK18 . . . . 41 E1
Wharf The
Leighton Buzzard LU7 . . . . 80 E6
Milton Keynes, Giffard Park MK14 . . . . 21 E2
Milton Keynes MK2 . . . . 58 E6
Wharf View MK18 . . . . 41 E1
WHARLEY END 24 D1
Wharton Ho 2 HP20 . . . 101 D1
Whatmore Cl TW19 . . . . 213 A1
Wheatbutts The SL4 . . . 204 F2
Wheat Cl HP21 . . . . 115 E3
Wheatcroft Cl MK6 . . . . 47 A5
Wheatfield Cl SL6 . . . . 202 A4
Wheathouse Copse MK17 . . . . 55 A3
Wheatlands Rd SL3 . . . . 206 C3
WHEATLEY 122 A1
Wheatley Cl MK4 . . . . 46 C2
Wheatley Park Sch OX33 . . . . 122 B2
Wheatley Rd OX33 . . . . 122 A3
Wheatley Way SL9 . . . . 177 E4
Wheatsheaf Ho HP10 . . . 185 E7
Wheatsheaf Par SL4 . . . 211 A2
Wheatstone Cl SL3 . . . . 206 A3
Wheeler Ave HP10 . . . . 174 C8
Wheeler Cl HP20 . . . . 116 B8
WHEELER END 171 B6
Wheeler Pl HP9 . . . . 175 F2
Wheelers End OX39 . . . 147 C6
Wheelers Flats HP10 . . . 174 D8
Wheelers La MK13 . . . . 34 A6
Wheelers Orch SL9 . . . . 177 E4
Wheelers Pk HP13 . . . . 173 D7
Wheelers Yd HP16 . . . . 152 A7
Wheelwright Mews MK14 . . . . 34 F6
Wheelwright Rd HP27 . . 138 D7
Wheelwrights HP22 . . . . 116 F2
Wheelwrights Pl SL3 . . . 212 C7
Wheelwrights Way MK19 . . . . 32 C7
Wheelwrights Yd HP22 . . 85 A5
WHELPLEY HILL 145 D5
Whelpley Hill Pk HP5 . . 145 D5
Whet Stone Cl MK13 . . . . 34 B4
Whichcote Gdns HP5 . . . 154 D6
Whichert Cl HP9 . . . . 175 C6
Whichford MK14 . . . . 22 A1
Whielden Cl HP7 . . . . 165 B7
Whielden Gate HP7 . . . . 164 E4
Whielden Gn HP7 . . . . 165 B7
Whielden Hts HP7 . . . . 165 A7
Whielden La
Coleshill HP7 . . . . 164 E5
Winchmore Hill HP7 . . . . 164 D3
Whielden St HP7 . . . . 165 B7
Whinchat HP19 . . . . 101 E3
Whincup Cl HP11 . . . . 172 F4
Whinneys Rd HP10 . . . . 174 C3
Whipass Hill HP9 . . . . 176 A5
WHIPSNADE 107 F8
Whipsnade Park Homes LU6 . . . . 93 F1
Whipsnade Rd LU6 . . . . 93 F6
Whipsnade Tree Cathedral★ LU6 . . . . 93 F1
Whitby Cl MK3 . . . . 47 A2
Whitby Rd SL1 . . . . 205 C6
WHITCHURCH 87 B6
Whitchurch Cl
Maidenhead SL6 . . . . 195 E3
Westcott HP18 . . . . 98 B7
Whitchurch Comb Sch HP22 . . . . 86 E7
Whitchurch Ho 5 SL6 . . 202 F7
Whitchurch La HP22 . . . 86 D8
Whitchurch Rd LU7 . . . . 78 B1
Whiteacres Dr SL6 . . . . 203 B1
White Alder MK12 . . . . 33 E5
Whitebaker Ct MK14 . . . . 34 F6
Whitebeam Cl HP22 . . . . 116 C3
Whitebrook Pk SL6 . . . . 196 C4
Whitechurch Cl HP17 . . 114 C5
White Cl
High Wycombe HP13 . . . . 161 D1
Slough SL1 . . . . 205 D5
White Cotts MK18 . . . . 29 D4
White Cres HP22 . . . . 131 D7
Whitecross Green Wood Wildlife Reserve★ OX5 . . . . 94 C2
Whitecross Rd HP17 . . . 126 F5
Whitefield La HP16 . . . . 152 A6
Whiteford Rd SL2 . . . . 205 E8
Whitegate Ct MK6 . . . . 47 B6
Whitehall SL6 . . . . 196 B1
Whitehall Ave MK10 . . . . 36 D1
Whitehall Cl UB8 . . . . 201 D4
Whitehall Inf Sch UB8 . . 201 C4
Whitehall Jun Sch UB8 201 C4
Whitehall La TW19 . . . . 212 A1
Whitehall Rd UB8 . . . . 201 D3
Whitehall St 6 HP20 . . . 101 D1
White Hart Cl
Chalfont St Giles HP8 . . . 177 A7
Ludgershall HP18 . . . . 96 B8
White Hart Field HP22 . . . 85 B4
White Hart La HP17 . . . . 127 A5
White Hart Mdw HP9 . . . 175 E1
White Hart Rd
1 Maidenhead SL6 . . . . 202 F7
Slough SL1 . . . . 205 D3
White Hart St 9 HP11 . . 173 A7
Whitehaven SL1 . . . . 205 F6
Whitehead Way HP21 . . . 115 E6
White Hermitage SL4 . . 211 C2
Whitehill
Berkhamsted HP4 . . . . 135 D5
Olney MK46 . . . . 6 E5
White Hill
Ashley Green HP4, HP5 . . . . 145 C7
Beaconsfield HP9, HP10 . 185 F8
Chesham HP5 . . . . 144 D1
High Wycombe HP13 . . . 162 B2
Remenham Hill RG9 . . . . 192 A2
White Hill Cl
Chesham HP5 . . . . 144 D1
Marlow Bottom SL7 . . . . 183 C6
Whitehill Ct HP4 . . . . 135 D5
Whitehill La LU7 . . . . 105 D3
White Hill La LU7 . . . . 105 D3
White Horse Ct HP6 . . . 154 C2
White Horse Dr MK4 . . . . 46 C2
White Horse La HP22 . . . 87 A6
White Horse Rd SL4 . . . 209 D5
Whitehorse Yd MK11 . . . 32 D5
White Hos MK18 . . . . 50 D6
Whitehouse Cl HP10 . . . 174 E1
White House Cl SL9 . . . . 177 E3
Whitehouse La HP10 . . . 174 E2
Whitehouse Way
Iver Heath SL0 . . . . 200 D2
Slough SL3 . . . . 206 D3
Whitelands Ave WD3 . . . 167 C5
Whitelands Rd HP12 . . . 172 D7
Whitelands Way HP12 . . 172 D7
WHITELEAF 139 D5
Whiteleaf Hill Nature Reserve★ HP27 . . . 139 E4
Whiteleaf Way HP27 . . . 139 D5
Whiteley SL4 . . . . 209 E7
Whiteley Cres MK3 . . . . 57 F6
White Lilies Island SL4 . 210 B7
White Lion Cl HP7 . . . . 166 A8
White Lion Rd HP7 . . . . 166 B8
Whitelock Ho RG9 . . . . 191 E3
White Lodge Cl SL7 . . . . 183 C6
White Paddock SL6 . . . . 202 A2
Whitepit La HP10 . . . . 185 D7
White Rock SL6 . . . . 196 B1
Whites Cl MK18 . . . . 63 D3
Whites Croft MK6 . . . . 46 F6
Whites La SL3 . . . . 211 B8
White Spire Specl Sch MK3 . . . . 46 F1
Whitethorn Ave UB7 . . . 208 F6
Whitethorn Cl HP22 . . . . 130 A8
Whitethorn Pl UB7 . . . . 208 F5
Whitethorns MK16 . . . . 22 B3
White View 14 HP20 . . . . 101 F3
Whitewood Rd HP4 . . . . 135 A4
WHITFIELD 26 D3
Whitfield Rd HP14 . . . . 162 A6
Whitfield Way WD3 . . . . 167 F1
Whitley Cl TW19 . . . . 213 E1
Whitley Ct HP21 . . . . 115 E4
Whitmees Cl MK46 . . . . 6 E4
Whitney Rdbt MK4 . . . . 45 E2
Whitsun Pasture MK15 . . 35 B7
Whittaker Rd SL2 . . . . 197 E1
Whittenham Cl SL2 . . . . 206 A5
Whittington Chase MK4 . 45 E1
Whittle Ct MK5 . . . . 46 C7
Whittle Parkway SL1 . . . 204 D7
Whitton Way MK16 . . . . 22 C3
Whitworth La MK5 . . . . 46 B7
Whurley Way SL6 . . . . 195 E2
Whybrow Gdns HP4 . . . . 135 E6
Whyteladyes La SL6 . . . . 195 E6
Whytingham Rd HP23 . . 119 C4
WICKEN 31 B3
Wicken Park Rd MK19 . . . 31 B2
Wicken Rd MK18 . . . . 30 E1
Wickets The SL6 . . . . 202 C7
Wicket The SL1 . . . . 205 E3
Wick Rd HP23 . . . . 133 D8
Wickstead Ave MK8 . . . . 45 D6
Widbrook Rd SL6 . . . . 196 B3
Widdenton View HP14 . . 171 C5
Widecroft Rd SL0 . . . . 207 E7
Widewater Pl UB9 . . . . 190 C6
Widgeon Ho HP11 . . . . 173 C6
Widmere Field HP16 . . . 151 C5
Widmere La SL7 . . . . 183 A6
WIDMER END 162 E6
Widmer End Comb Sch HP15 . . . . 162 F6
WIDMOOR 185 E3
Widmore Cl HP5 . . . . 143 E5
Widnell La OX25 . . . . 95 C7
Wigan's La HP14 . . . . 148 C6
Wiggington Ho SL4 . . . . 210 D7
WIGGINTON 119 D1
WIGGINTON BOTTOM . . . 133 D8
Wigginton Bottom HP23 . . . . 133 E8
Wiggles La HP23 . . . . 118 F7
Wigmore Ct HP19 . . . . 101 A2
Wigmore Rd HP19 . . . . 101 A2
Wigwell Gdns MK17 . . . . 55 A2
Wilberforce Mews 7 SL6 . . . . 202 F7
Wildacre Rd MK5 . . . . 46 A4
Wilderness The HP4 . . . 135 C4
Wildgreen N SL3 . . . . 207 A2
Wildgreen S SL3 . . . . 207 A2
Wildwood Ct WD3 . . . . 167 F5
Wilford Cl MK15 . . . . 35 C2
Wilford Rd SL3 . . . . 206 F2
Wilfrids Wood Cl HP10 . 185 B6
Wilks Croft MK5 . . . . 45 F7
WILLEN 35 D7
Willen La MK14 . . . . 34 F8
WILLEN PARK 35 C6
Willen Park Ave MK15 . . . 35 B6
Willen Prim Sch MK15 . . 35 C7
Willen Rd
Milton Keynes MK10 . . . . 35 F3
Newport Pagnell MK16 . . . 22 D3
Willets Rise MK5 . . . . 46 A5
Willetts La UB9 . . . . 200 F7
Willey Ct MK11 . . . . 32 F4
William Bandy Cl LU7 . . . 79 F3
William Burt Cl HP22 . . . 116 F1
William Ellis Cl SL4 . . . . 211 A1
William Fiske Ho 4 HP4 . . . . 135 C4
William Harding Cl HP21 . . . . 115 E7
William Harding Comb Sch HP21 . . . . 116 A5
William Hartley Yd SL3 199 B1
William Hill Dr HP22 . . . 102 C4
William Ho 4 HP13 . . . . 173 F5
William Moulder Ct HP5 . . . . 144 B3
Williams Circ MK7 . . . . 48 A4
Williams Cl
Aylesbury HP19 . . . . 101 D1
Hanslope MK19 . . . . 10 F3
William Shakman Ho HP8 . . . . 177 B8
William Smith Cl MK15 . . 35 C3
William St
Berkhamsted HP4 . . . . 135 D4
Slough SL1 . . . . 205 F5
Windsor SL4 . . . . 210 D6
William Sutton Ho MK5 . 46 A6
Williams Way HP27 . . . . 138 D6
Willis Rd HP17 . . . . 127 A6
Willmott Cl HP19 . . . . 101 D4
Willoners SL2 . . . . 205 A8
Willoughby Rd SL3 . . . . 207 B3
Willoughby's Wlk HP13 161 D2
Willow Ave
High Wycombe HP12 . . . 172 B4
New Denham UB9 . . . . 201 C6
West Drayton UB7 . . . . 208 F6
WILLOWBANK 201 C7
Willow Bank SL7 . . . . 183 D5
Willowbank Terr 6 HP21 . . . . 115 E8
Willowbrook
Slough SL4 . . . . 205 D2
Wendover HP22 . . . . 131 B7
Willow Chase
Chesham HP5 . . . . 144 B1
Hazlemere HP15 . . . . 162 E3
Willow Cl
Chalfont St Peter SL9 . . . 177 E1
Colnbrook SL3 . . . . 212 C7
Flackwell Heath HP10 . . . 185 C6
Maidenhead SL6 . . . . 195 D1
Moulsoe MK16 . . . . 36 E8
Willow Crescent E UB9 201 C7
Willow Crescent W UB9 . . . . 201 C7
Willow Ct
2 Aylesbury, Quarrendon HP19 . . . . 101 A2
Aylesbury, Walton Court HP21 . . . . 115 C6
High Wycombe HP11 . . . . 173 E4
Walter's Ash HP14 . . . . 161 C8
Willow Dr
Buckingham MK18 . . . . 52 F7
Maidenhead SL6 . . . . 203 B2
Willow End HP22 . . . . 116 F2
Willowford MK13 . . . . 33 E5
Willow Gate HP18 . . . . 112 B2
Willow Gr MK19 . . . . 32 B6
Willow Herb HP19 . . . . 101 E4
Willow Ho LU7 . . . . 80 E7
Willow La
Amersham HP7 . . . . 165 F6
Milton Keynes MK11 . . . . 32 C5
Willowmead HP17 . . . . 114 F5
Willowmead Cl 10 SL7 . . 183 F3
Willowmead Gdns SL7 . . 183 F3
Willowmead Rd 8 SL7 . . 183 F3
Willowmead Sq 9 SL7 . . 183 F3
Willow Parade SL3 . . . . 207 A3
Willow Pk SL2 . . . . 199 A5
Willow Pl SL4 . . . . 210 C8
Willow Rd
Aylesbury HP19 . . . . 101 D1
Brackley NN13 . . . . 38 A6
Chinnor OX39 . . . . 147 C6
Great Horwood MK17 . . . . 55 A3
Poyle SL3 . . . . 212 E5
Thame OX9 . . . . 125 F1
Willow Rise HP17 . . . . 127 A7
Willows Rd SL8 . . . . 185 B4
Willows Riverside Pk The SL4 . . . . 209 C7
Willows Sch The MK6 . . . 35 A2
Willows The
Amersham HP6 . . . . 154 B4
4 Bourne End SL8 . . . . 185 B3
Edlesborough LU6 . . . . 92 F3
High Wycombe HP12 . . . 172 E8
Longwick HP27 . . . . 138 E6
Windsor SL4 . . . . 209 D7
Willow Way
Loudwater HP11 . . . . 174 B2
Milton Keynes MK2 . . . . 58 C7
Princes Risborough HP27 . . . . 139 A3
Wing LU7 . . . . 79 E3
Willow Wlk HP15 . . . . 163 A3
Willow Wood Cl SL1 . . . 197 B3
Willow Wren MK14 . . . . 21 F2
Wilmar Cl UB8 . . . . 201 D5
Wilmin Gr MK5 . . . . 46 B7
Wilmot Rd SL1 . . . . 197 B2
Wilsley Pound MK7 . . . . 48 B8
Wilson Ct MK8 . . . . 45 E7
WILSTONE 104 D1
WILSTONE GREEN 118 D8
Wilstone Resr★ HP22, HP23 . . . . 118 C7
Wilton Ave MK3 . . . . 58 A8
Wilton Cl UB7 . . . . 213 D8
Wilton Cres
Beaconsfield HP9 . . . . 175 E3
Windsor SL4 . . . . 209 D4
Wilton Hollow HP9 . . . . 175 F3
Wilton La HP9 . . . . 176 E4
WILTON PARK 176 B1
Wilton Rd HP9 . . . . 175 E3
Wiltshire Ave SL2 . . . . 198 C1
Wiltshire Lodge 2 SL6 . 202 F6
Wiltshire Rd 2 SL7 . . . . 183 F3
Wiltshire Way MK3 . . . . 46 E1
Wimbledon Pl MK13 . . . . 34 D3
Wimblington Dr MK6 . . . 47 A4
Wimborne Cres MK4 . . . . 45 F2
Wimpole Rd UB7 . . . . 208 D5
Winbury Ct SL6 . . . . 202 E7
Winbury Pl SL6 . . . . 203 B3
Winbury Sch SL6 . . . . 203 B4
Wincanton Hill MK3 . . . . 57 C6
Winchbottom La
High Wycombe HP10 . . . 173 B1
Little Marlow SL7, HP10 . 184 B7
Winchendon Rd HP18 . . 112 B2
Winchester Circ MK10 . . . 36 B1
Winchester Cl
Amersham HP7 . . . . 165 E8
Poyle SL3 . . . . 212 E6
Winchester Ct HP11 . . . 174 B3
Winchester Dr SL6 . . . . 202 B3
Winchester Ho HP21 . . . 115 F6
WINCHMORE HILL 164 D2
Winch Terr SL4 . . . . 209 D5
Windermere Cl
Aylesbury HP21 . . . . 116 B6
Chorleywood WD3 . . . . 167 D4
Windermere Dr MK2 . . . . 58 D5
Windermere Gdns LU7 . . 80 C7
Windermere Way
Slough SL1 . . . . 204 C7
West Drayton UB7 . . . . 208 E5
Windmill Cl
Aylesbury HP19 . . . . 115 B8
Buckingham MK18 . . . . 41 F1
Ivinghoe LU7 . . . . 105 F5
Windsor SL4 . . . . 210 B5
Windmill Dr HP15 . . . . 162 F6
Windmill Hill
Chipperfield WD4 . . . . 156 F7
Coleshill HP7 . . . . 164 F2
Princes Risborough HP27 . . . . 139 B2
Windmill Hill Dr MK3 . . . 57 D7
Windmill Hill Rdbt MK4 . 46 C1
Windmill La HP15 . . . . 162 F7
Windmill Par HP15 . . . . 162 F6
Windmill Rd
Chalfont St Peter SL9 . . . 177 D3
Cookham Rise SL6 . . . . 195 E6
Fulmer SL3 . . . . 199 D7
Haddenham HP17 . . . . 126 F6
Slough SL1 . . . . 205 D5
Thame OX9 . . . . 126 E1
Windmill St HP18 . . . . 96 A1
Windmill Way
Cranfield MK43 . . . . 25 C3
Tring HP23 . . . . 118 F4
Windmill Wood HP6 . . . 154 A2
Windrush Ave SL3 . . . . 207 B3
Windrush Cl
Ickenham UB10 . . . . 201 F8
Milton Keynes MK15 . . . . 35 A6
Windrush Ct
Aylesbury HP21 . . . . 115 D4
High Wycombe HP13 . . . 173 F6
Windrush Dr HP13 . . . . 173 F6
Windrush Ho SL8 . . . . 185 B4
Windrush Way SL6 . . . . 203 A8
WINDSOR 210 E6
Windsor Ave
Leighton Buzzard LU7 . . . 80 F7
Newport Pagnell MK16 . . . 22 C4
Windsor Boys' Sch Performing Arts Coll The SL4 . . . . 210 B6
Windsor Bsns Ctr SL4 . . 210 C6
Windsor Castle★ SL4 . . . 210 E7
Windsor Cl
Bovingdon HP3 . . . . 146 A3
Burnham SL1 . . . . 197 C1
Windsor Cres HP10 . . . . 174 C2
Windsor Ct HP6 . . . . 154 D1
Windsor Dr HP13 . . . . 162 D1
Windsor End HP9 . . . . 186 F8
Windsor & Eton Central Sta SL4 . . . . 210 D6
Windsor & Eton Riverside Sta SL4 . . . . 210 D7
Windsor Girls' Sch SL4 210 A4
Windsor Great Pk★ SL4 . . . . 210 B2
Windsor Hall SL4 . . . . 210 F4
Windsor Hill
Monks Risborough HP27 . . . . 139 C5
Wooburn Green HP10 . . . 185 F5
Windsor Ho 4 SL1 . . . . 205 F3
Windsor La
Burnham SL1 . . . . 197 C1
Little Kingshill HP16 . . . . 152 C3
Windsor Rd
Aylesbury HP21 . . . . 116 A7
Chesham HP5 . . . . 144 B3
Datchet SL3 . . . . 211 A7
Gerrards Cross SL9 . . . . 188 C3
Maidenhead SL6 . . . . 203 C2
Oakley Green SL4 . . . . 209 A7
Pitstone LU7 . . . . 105 C3
Slough SL1 . . . . 205 E4
Wraysbury TW19 . . . . 211 E1
Windsor Royal Sta 1 SL4 . . . . 210 D6
Windsor St
Milton Keynes MK2 . . . . 58 C7
Milton Keynes, Wolverton MK12 . . . . 33 C6
Uxbridge UB8 . . . . 201 C5
Winemar Cl MK19 . . . . 11 A3
Winfold La MK4 . . . . 46 B1
WING 79 F2
Wingate Ave HP13 . . . . 173 E7
Wingate Circ MK7 . . . . 48 A4
Wingate Cl HP13 . . . . 173 E7
Wingate Wlk HP20 . . . . 116 A7
Wingbury Ctyd Bsns Village HP22 . . . . 89 D5
Wing Cl SL7 . . . . 183 C1
Wingfield Gr MK10 . . . . 36 A2
WINGRAVE 89 C3
Wingrave CE Comb Sch HP22 . . . . 89 A3
Wingrave Cross Rds HP22 . . . . 88 F4
Wingrave Rd
Aston Abbotts HP22 . . . . 88 E4
Long Marston HP23 . . . . 104 D1
Tring HP23 . . . . 119 B5
Wing Rd
Cublington LU7 . . . . 78 C1
Leighton Buzzard LU7 . . . . 80 D5

Wing Rd *continued*
Stewkley LU7 .... 78 F6
Winkers Cl SL9 .... 177 F2
Winkers La SL9 .... 177 F3
Winkfield La SL4 ...... 209 A1
Winkfield Rd SL4 ...... 209 E2
Winnock Rd UB7 ...... 208 D5
WINSLOW 66 B4
Winslow CE Comb Sch
MK18 .... 66 A5
Winslow Field HP16 ... 151 F8
Winslow Gdns HP13 ... 174 A7
Winslow Rd
Granborough MK18 ..... 75 F1
Great Horwood MK17 .... 54 F1
Little Horwood MK17 .... 55 D1
Nash MK17 .... 55 C8
Swanbourne MK17 ..... 66 F3
Wingrave HP22 .... 89 B3
Winstanley La MK5 .... 46 C4
Winston Ct SL6 .... 202 A8
Winstone Cl HP6 ...... 154 B5
Winston Gdns HP4 .... 134 F4
Winston Ho HP11 ...... 174 A4
Winterburn MK13 ...... 34 B5
Winter Ct 6 SL7 ...... 183 E2
WINTERHILL 46 D8
Winter Hill SL6 ...... 184 C1
Winter Hill Rd SL6 .... 195 A4
Winters Way HP15 .... 163 D7
Winterton Dr HP21 .... 115 E4
Wintoun Path SL2 .... 197 E1
Winvale SL1 .... 205 E3
Winwood
Slough SL2 .... 206 C7
Windsor SL4 .... 209 F6
Winwood Cl MK19 .... 31 E5
Winwood Dr HP22 .... 85 A5
Wise La UB7 .... 208 D1
Wisewood Rd MK4, MK5 .45 E4
Wishart Gn MK7 ...... 48 E5
Wisley Ave MK13 ...... 34 D3
Wistmans MK4 .... 46 D4
Witan Ct MK9 .... 34 D2
Witan Gate MK9 ...... 34 D1
Witchell HP22 .... 131 B4
Witham Ct MK3 ...... 46 D1
Witham Way HP21 .... 115 C4
Witheridge La HP9,
HP10 .... 175 B7
Withey Cl SL4 .... 209 E4
Withington MK13 ...... 34 A5
Withycombe MK4 ..... 46 E3
Withycroft SL3 ...... 206 E7
Witney Cl UB10 ...... 201 F8
Wittington Cotts SL7 .. 193 E6
Wittmills Oak MK18 .... 41 E1
Witton Ho WD3 ...... 167 D4
Wivelsfield LU6 ...... 92 E4
Wixon Path HP19 .... 115 A8
Woad La MK14 .... 34 E8
WOBURN 60 F7
Woburn Ave MK12 .... 33 C6
Woburn Ct LU7 ...... 80 E6
Woburn La MK4 ...... 49 E4
Woburn Lower Sch
MK17 .... 60 F7
Woburn Rd
Aspley Heath MK17 ..... 49 C2
Little Brickhill MK17 ..... 59 C1
Sheeplane MK17, LU7 .... 60 C1
WOBURN SANDS 49 A5
Woburn Sands Rd MK17 48 D3
Woburn Sands Sta
MK17 .... 49 A5
Wodehouse Wlk MK16 .. 22 A5
Wolf La SL4 .... 209 E4
Wolfscote La MK4 ..... 46 B3
Wolsey Gdns MK13 .... 34 A4
Wolstan Cl UB9 ...... 190 A1
Wolston Mdw MK10 .... 35 F3
WOLVERTON 33 C5
WOLVERTON MILL 33 A6
Wolverton Rd
Castlethorpe MK19 ..... 20 B5
Milton Keynes, Giffard Park
MK16 .... 21 E2
Milton Keynes, Stony Stratford
MK11 .... 32 E6
Milton Keynes, Wolverton MK12,
MK19 .... 33 B8
Newport Pagnell MK16 .. 22 B4
Wolverton Sta MK12 .... 33 E7
WOOBURN 185 D4
Wooburn Common Rd HP10,
SL1 .... 186 A2
Wooburn Grange HP10 185 D3
WOOBURN GREEN 185 F7
Wooburn Green La
HP9 .... 186 A8
Wooburn Manor Pk
HP10 .... 185 E5

Wooburn Mead HP10 ... 185 E6
Wooburn Mews HP10 ... 185 E5
WOOBURN MOOR 174 E1
Wooburn Town HP10 ... 185 D4
Woodall Cl MK10 ...... 35 E3
Woodbank HP27 ...... 149 C5
Woodbank Ave SL9 .... 188 D5
Woodbank Dr HP8 .... 177 D7
Woodbine Cl HP27 .... 138 E5
Woodbine Cotts SL9 .. 188 D8
Woodbridge Ho UB8 .. 201 C5
WOODBURN
COMMON 186 B3
Woodbury Cl SL8 ...... 185 C3
Woodchester Pk HP9 .. 175 C6
Wood Cl SL4 .... 210 C3
Woodcock Ave HP14 .. 161 B8
Woodcote SL6 .... 202 D6
Woodcote Gn HP13 .... 161 D2
Woodcote Lawns HP5 .. 144 A3
Woodcroft Rd HP5 .... 144 D3
WOOD END
Little Horwood 55 E2
Nash 55 C8
Wood End
Little Horwood MK17 .... 55 E2
Nash MK17 .... 55 C8
Wood End Cl SL2 ...... 187 D1
Wood End Fst Sch MK14 34 D8
Wood End La MK16 .... 23 E1
Woodfield HP27 ...... 149 D6
Woodfield Dr SL6 ...... 202 A6
Woodfield Pk HP6 .... 154 B3
Woodfield Rd HP27 .... 139 C4
Woodford Cl HP19 .... 115 B7
Woodford Way SL2 .... 198 A2
Wood Gn MK10 ...... 47 F8
WOOD GREEN 27 F2
Woodhall Cl UB8 ...... 201 D7
WOODHAM 83 E1
Woodhill Ave SL9 .... 189 A5
Woodhill Ct
Amersham HP6 .... 154 D2
Gerrards Cross SL9 .... 188 E4
Woodhouse Ct MK14 .. 34 D6
Woodhurst Dr HP9 .... 189 F6
Woodhurst Rd SL6 .... 196 B1
Woodhurst South SL6 .196 C1
Wood La
Aspley Guise MK17 ..... 49 D4
Iver SL0 .... 207 C4
Milton Keynes MK14 .... 34 E8
Slough SL1 .... 205 A4
South Heath HP16 ..... 152 E8
Tingewick MK18 ...... 51 B6
Weston Underwood MK46 .. 6 A2
Woodland Ave
Leighton Buzzard LU7 .... 70 F2
Slough SL1 .... 205 D6
Windsor SL4 .... 209 F3
Woodland Cl
High Wycombe HP12 .. 172 C6
Marlow SL7 .... 183 E4
Tring HP23 .... 118 F2
Woodland Glade SL2 .. 187 D1
Woodland Grange SL0 .207 E3
Woodland La WD3 .... 167 D6
Woodland Pl WD3 .... 167 F5
Woodland Rd WD3 .... 178 D5
Woodlands SL9 ...... 188 F5
Woodlands Ave MK4 .. 135 D3
Woodlands Bsns Pk
SL6 .... 202 A2
Woodlands Cl
Buckingham MK18 ..... 41 E2
Gerrards Cross SL9 .... 189 A5
Holmer Green HP15 .... 163 C6
Woodlands Cotts 1
SL2 .... 198 C7
Woodlands Cres MK18 .. 41 D2
Woodlands Dr
Beaconsfield HP9 ..... 175 C4
Walter's Ash HP14 ..... 161 C8
Woodlands Farm SL6 .. 195 C6
Woodlands Glade HP9 175 C4
Woodlands Hill HP9 .. 186 E5
Woodlands Park Ave
SL6 .... 202 A2
Woodlands Park Prim Sch
SL6 .... 202 A1
Woodlands Park Rd
SL6 .... 202 A3
Woodlands The
Amersham HP6 .... 154 C4
Tylers Green HP10 .... 162 F3
Woodlands View HP13 .174 A7
Woodland View
Chesham HP5 .... 154 D6
Milton Keynes MK12 .... 33 D5
Woodland Way
Marlow SL7 .... 183 E4
Woburn Sands MK17 .... 49 B4
Woodlane Cl HP10 .... 173 F1

Wood Lane Cl
Flackwell Heath HP10 .. 173 F1
Iver Heath SL0 .... 200 B2
Woodlane Gdns HP10 .174 A1
Woodley Ct HP7 ...... 165 D8
Woodley Headland MK6 .47 C7
Woodley Hill HP5 .... 154 D5
Woodman Cl LU7 ...... 79 F3
Woodmans MK17 ...... 55 C8
Woodmans Croft HP19 .115 A8
Woodmoor End SL6 .. 196 B7
Woodpiece Rd OX25 .... 94 E7
Woodpits La MK46 ...... 6 E5
Wood Pond Cl HP9 .... 176 C4
Wood Rd MK43 .... 3 F7
WOODROW 164 D5
Woodruff Ave MK14 .... 34 E4
Woodrush Cl MK6 ...... 47 B4
Woodside
Aspley Guise MK17 ..... 49 D3
Eaton Bray LU6 .... 92 E6
Flackwell Heath HP10 .. 185 C6
Milton Keynes MK11 .... 32 E6
Woodside Ave
Amersham HP6 .... 154 D3
Beaconsfield HP9 ..... 175 C4
Flackwell Heath HP10 .. 185 C7
Woodside Cl
Amersham HP6 .... 154 D1
Beaconsfield HP9 ..... 175 C3
Chalfont St Peter SL9 .. 177 E1
Loudwater HP11 ...... 174 B2
Woodside Hill SL9 .... 177 E1
Woodside Jun Sch &
Amersham Music Ctr
HP6 .... 154 E1
Woodside Rd
Amersham HP6 .... 154 D1
Beaconsfield HP9 ..... 175 C3
High Wycombe HP13 .. 174 A8
Woodside Way
Leighton Buzzard LU7 .... 80 D6
Tylers Green HP10 .... 174 C8
Woods La NN12 ...... 18 E3
Woods Pl
13 Tring HP23 .... 119 A3
Wendover HP22 ...... 131 B4
Woodspring Ct 2 MK10 . 35 F1
Wood St
Milton Keynes MK13 .... 33 F7
Waddesdon HP18 ...... 99 A7
Woburn Sands MK17 .... 49 B4
Woodstock Ave SL3 .. 206 D2
Woodstock Cl
Aylesbury HP21 ...... 116 B6
Maidenhead SL6 ...... 195 F1
Woodstock Ct MK13 .... 34 B7
Woodstock Dr UB10 .. 201 F8
Woodview Cl HP12 .... 161 B2
Wood View Cotts HP5 .144 B7
Woodview Dr HP16 .. 150 C5
Woodville OX39 ...... 147 C5
Woodville Cres NN12 .. 18 E6
Woodward Ho 4 MK2 .. 58 C8
Woodward Pl MK8 ...... 34 A1
Woodway HP27 ...... 149 D6
Wood Way HP9 ...... 174 D1
Woodway Farm Ind Est
HP18 .... 124 F8
Woodways HP17 ...... 127 A6
Woodwicks WD3 ...... 178 C6
Woollerton Cres HP22 .131 D5
Woollerton Ct HP27 .. 139 B4
Woolmans
Fullers Slade MK11 .... 33 A4
Milton Keynes MK11 .... 33 A4
Woolrich Gdns MK11 .. 32 E5
WOOLSTONE 35 D3
Wooster Rd HP9 ...... 175 D4
Wooton Ct MK13 ...... 33 F8
WOOTTON BOURNE
END 25 F8
Wootton Dr HP10 .... 185 E8
Wootton Gn OX27 ...... 72 E6
Wootton La HP17 .... 113 E1
Wootton Way SL6 .... 202 C6
Worcester Cl
Maidenhead SL6 ...... 202 D3
Newport Pagnell MK16 .. 22 A2
Worcester Gdns SL1 .. 205 D4
Worcester Ho MK3 ...... 46 F2
Worcester Rd UB8 .... 208 D8
Wordsworth Ave MK16 .. 22 A4
Wordsworth Dr MK3 .. 58 A7
Wordsworth Rd
High Wycombe HP11 .. 173 A5
Slough SL2 .... 197 D1
Wordsworth Way UB7 .208 E2
WORLD'S END 130 F7
World's End La HP22 .. 130 F8
Worley Pl HP9 ...... 176 D5
WORMINGHALL 123 E6
Worminghall Rd

Ickford HP18 .... 123 F4
Oakley HP18 .... 109 D4
Wormsley Cres HP14 .. 158 C4
WORMSTONE 99 C5
Wornal Pk HP18 ...... 123 C8
Worple The TW19 .... 211 F1
Worrelle Ave MK10 .... 36 A3
Worster Rd SL6 ...... 195 E6
Worth Ct MK10 ...... 36 B1
Worthies The HP7 .... 165 B7
Worthington Rd LU6 .... 93 F8
Wotton End HP18 ...... 96 C7
Wotton Path HP21 .... 115 E3
Wotton Rd HP18 ...... 97 E1
WOTTON UNDERWOOD .. 97 C4
Woughton L Ctr MK6 .... 46 F7
WOUGHTON ON THE
GREEN 47 D8
WOUGHTON PARK 47 E6
Wraxall Way MK4 ..... 47 D5
Wray Ct MK4 .... 46 A2
WRAYSBURY 211 E1
Wraysbury Prim Sch
TW19 .... 211 E1
Wraysbury Dr UB7 .... 208 D6
Wraysbury Sta TW19 .. 212 A1
Wren Cl MK18 .... 52 F7
Wren Ct SL3 .... 207 A3
Wren Dr UB7 .... 208 D3
Wren Path HP19 ...... 114 F8
Wren Rd HP16 .... 151 C5
Wrensfield SL7 ...... 183 C2
Wrens Pk MK10 ...... 36 B2
Wren Vale HP13 ...... 173 A8
Wren Wlk LU6 .... 92 E4
Wright SL4 .... 209 C4
Wrights Cl HP14 ...... 171 B5
Wright's La HP16 ...... 151 C5
Wright Sq SL4 .... 209 C4
Wrights Yd HP16 ...... 152 A7
Wright Way SL4 ...... 209 C4
Wroxton Ct MK4 ...... 45 F2
Wyatt Cl HP13 .... 172 F8
Wyatt Rd SL4 .... 209 D4
Wyatt's Rd WD3 ...... 167 F5
Wychwood HP16 ...... 152 B4
Wychwood Gdns HP12 172 C6
Wychwood Rise HP16 .152 B4
Wyclands Ho HP12 .... 161 B2
Wycombe Abbey Sch
HP11 .... 173 A6
Wycombe Air Pk SL7 .. 171 F2
Wycombe Cl HP21 .... 116 B4
Wycombe End HP9 .... 175 E1
Wycombe High Sch
HP11 .... 173 A6
Wycombe Hospl HP11 .173 A6
Wycombe Ind Mall
HP11 .... 172 F7
Wycombe La HP10 .... 185 E7
WYCOMBE MARSH ... 173 F4
Wycombe Mus★ HP13 .173 B7
Wycombe Mus & Gdn 18
HP13 .... 173 B7
Wycombe Rd
Beacon's Bottom HP14 .159 D3
Holmer Green HP15 .. 163 B6
Lacey Green HP14 .... 149 B4
Marlow Bottom SL7 .. 183 E6
Marlow SL7 .... 183 E4
Prestwood HP15 ...... 151 C5
Wycombe Ret Pk HP11 173 F4
Wycombe Sp Ctr HP11 .172 F3
Wycombe Swan Theatre
HP11 .... 173 B6
Wycombe View HP10 .174 A2
Wye Cl
Aylesbury HP21 ...... 115 C5
Milton Keynes MK3 .... 46 E1
Wye Ct 2 SL8 ...... 185 A3
Wye Est HP11 .... 173 E5
Wye Gdns HP12 ...... 172 D8
Wye Rd HP10 .... 185 D8
Wye River Bsns Ctr 8
HP11 .... 172 F7
Wye Valley Sch The
SL8 .... 185 B4
Wykeham Gate HP17 .126 F5
Wykeham Rise OX39 .. 147 D6
Wykeham Way HP17 .. 126 F6
Wykeridge Cl HP5 .... 144 B4
Wylands Rd SL3 ...... 207 C3
Wylie End MK13 ...... 34 A7
WYMBUSH 33 F2
Wymering Rd HP21 .. 116 C6
Wymers Cl SL1 ...... 197 B3
Wymers Wood Rd SL1 .197 A3
Wymondham MK10 .... 36 B1
Wynbury Dr HP13 .... 162 E1
Wyndale Cl RG9 ...... 191 E1
Wyndham Ave HP13 .. 161 F2
Wyndham Cres SL1 .. 197 B3
Wyness Ave MK17 ...... 59 E5

Wynford Gn HP21 .... 115 F6
Wyngates LU7 .... 80 E5
Wyngrave Pl HP9 .... 175 C5
Wynne-Jones Ctr HP21 115 F8
Wynn Gr MK15 ...... 163 B3
Wynnstay Gdns SL7 .. 183 E5
Wynnswick Rd HP9 .. 176 C5
Wynyard Ct MK6 ...... 46 E7
Wyre Cl HP17 .... 127 A5
Wyvern Sch MK12 .... 33 C6
Wyvern Way UB8 .... 201 C4

X

Xscape★ MK6 .... 34 F2

Y

Yalts Brow MK4 ...... 46 B2
Yardley Ave LU7 ...... 105 D4
Yardley Gn HP20 .... 101 F2
YARDLEY GOBION 18 E5
Yardley Gobion CE Prim
Sch NN12 .... 18 E5
YARDLEY HASTINGS ... 1 B6
Yardley Hastings Prim Sch
NN7 .... 1 A7
Yardley Rd
Cosgrove MK19 .... 19 D2
Olney MK46 .... 6 E6
Potterspury NN12 ..... 18 F4
Yarmouth Rd SL1 .... 205 C6
Yarrow Pl MK14 ...... 34 E4
Yarrowside HP7 ...... 166 B7
Yeates Cl
Thame OX9 .... 125 F1
Winslow MK18 .... 65 F4
Yeats Cl MK16 ...... 21 F5
Ye Meads SL6 .... 203 E5
Ye Meads Cotts SL6 .. 203 E5
Ye Meads Ho SL6 .... 203 E5
Yeomans Cl NN13 .... 38 A8
Yeomans Dr MK14 .... 22 B1
Yeovil Ent Ctr SL1 .. 204 F8
Yeovil Rd SL1 ...... 204 E8
Yew Ave UB7 .... 208 E6
Yewtree Cl LU7 ...... 105 E5
Yew Tree Cl
Beaconsfield HP9 .... 175 F1
Botley HP5 .... 145 A1
Eaton Bray LU6 .... 92 F5
Maidenhead SL6 ...... 202 E8
Newton Longville MK17 .57 C3
Stoke Mandeville HP22 .116 A1
Yew Tree Dr
Bovingdon HP3 ...... 146 B3
Hazlemere HP15 ...... 162 F6
Yew Tree Rd
Slough SL1 .... 206 A3
Uxbridge UB10 ...... 201 F4
Yew Wlk HP15 ...... 163 A3
Yiewsley Ct UB7 ...... 208 E5
Yolsum Cl HP17 ...... 126 E6
Yonder Slade MK18 .... 52 D6
York Ave
Slough SL1 .... 205 C2
Windsor SL4 .... 210 B5
York Cl HP7 .... 165 F8
York Ct 3 LU7 ...... 80 F7
Yorke Cl HP22 ...... 117 E5
York Ho
High Wycombe HP13 ... 173 F8
Milton Keynes MK3 .... 57 E7
York Pl HP21 .... 115 D7
York Rd
Henley-on-Thames
RG9 .... 191 D2
Maidenhead SL6 ...... 203 A7
Marlow SL7 .... 183 D2
Milton Keynes MK11 .. 32 D5
Uxbridge UB8 .... 201 D5
Windsor SL4 .... 210 B5
Yorkshire Cl MK3 ...... 46 F1
York Way HP12 ...... 172 E4
Youens Rd HP12 ...... 172 C5
Young Cl HP21 ...... 116 A6

Z

Zealand Ave UB7 ...... 213 E7
Zetland Ct SL6 ...... 203 B8
Zodiac Bsns Pk UB8 .208 D7
ZSL Whipsnade Zoo★
HP4 .... 107 E8